Distributed by Littlehampton Book Services, Ltd
Faraday Close, Durrington, Worthing, West Sussex, BN13 3RB
Copyright © Waitrose Ltd, 2016. Waitrose Ltd, Doncastle Road, Bracknell, Berkshire, RG12 8YA

Data management and export by AMA DataSet Ltd, Preston
Printed and bound in Italy by L.E.G.O. S.p.A.

A catalogue record for this book is available from the British Library
Main edition ISBN: 978 0 95379 834 6
(Promotional MyWaitrose ISBN: 978 0 95379 835 3)

Maps designed and produced by Cosmographics Ltd, www.cosmographics.co.uk
Mapping contains Ordnance Survey data © Crown copyright and database right 2016
UK digital database © Cosmographics Ltd, 2016. Greater London map and North and South London
maps © Cosmographics Ltd, 2016. West, Central and East London map data © Cosmographics Ltd,
2016 used with kind permission of VisitBritain. Illustrations for features courtesy of Shutterstock.

Consultant Editor: Elizabeth Carter
Editor: Rochelle Venables
Editorial Assistant: Ria Martin

The Good Food Guide makes every effort to be as accurate and up to date as possible. All inspections are
anonymous, and Main Entries have been contacted separately for details. As we are an annual Guide,
we have strict guidelines for fact-checking information ahead of going to press, so some restaurants
were removed if they failed to provide the information we required. The editors' decision on inclusion
and scores in *The Good Food Guide* is final, and we will not enter into any discussion on the matter with
individual restaurants.

The publisher cannot be held responsible for any errors or omissions or for changes in the details given
in this Guide. Restaurants may close, change chefs or adjust their opening times and prices during the
Guide's lifetime, and readers should always check with the restaurant at the time of booking.

We would like to extend special thanks to the following people: Iain Barker, Jackie Bates, Ruth
Coombs, Tom Fahey, Alan Grimwade, Joanne Murray, Alan Rainford, Emma Sturgess, Mark Taylor,
Steve Trayler, Andy Turvil, Stuart Walton, Jenny White, Lisa Whitehouse and Blanche Williams.
And thanks in particular to all of our hard-working inspectors.

thegoodfoodguide.co.uk

FSC
www.fsc.org
MIX
Paper from
responsible sources
FSC® C023419

The restaurants included in
The Good Food Guide
are the very best in the UK.

Contents

A Decade of Eating for *The Good Food Guide*

Elizabeth Carter, Consultant Editor

The 2017 edition of the UK's best-loved and bestselling restaurant guide represents something of a personal landmark for me – it marks my tenth book as Consultant Editor. It has been, without doubt, a revolutionary decade for food in the UK. Across a wide swathe of the population there has been a tremendous growth of interest in, and knowledge about, food: from quality, provenance and nutrition to good, plain eating. There has been a corresponding growth of understanding among the country's chefs – and not just those running top-scoring restaurants. An active appreciation and zest for good food has extended right across the spectrum; how many pub chefs were growing their own fruit and vegetables, raising pigs, keeping hens and tending bees ten years ago?

A decade when food has become central to British culture

Looking back over the sea changes of the past ten years, it's clear that some have been oceanic. Dining out has become less structured, less formal, with more flexible opening times and menus. This is the way we want to live now. Latterly, creative food startups, supper clubs, pop ups, underground restaurants and dining events have exerted their influence on the restaurant scene, with many successful chefs beginning their careers in the playground of the millennials.

Perhaps more unexpectedly, 'good value' has become a game changer. The 2007 edition of the guide included relatively few entries in the lower-price brackets – quality, outside of top-end dining, was hard to find. In this edition you will find all-day eateries, cafés, pizzerias, seafood shacks and pubs of genuine high quality offering everyday eating at everyday prices. Moreover, there are a number of local restaurants representing a melting pot of world cuisines across the country, not just in London: the Baltic/Russian cooking at Two Cats Kitchen in Birmingham; South Indian cuisine at Tharavadu in Leeds; Lily's Vegetarian Indian Cuisine in Ashton-under-Lyne; Korean cooking at Sky Kong Kong in Bristol; Japanese at Shiki in Norwich, to name but a few.

Passing the baton...

The burgeoning restaurant scene beyond the capital, driven by more affordable start-up costs and increasingly sophisticated audiences, has made our great regional cities viable

'It has been, without doubt, a revolutionary decade for food in the UK'

dining destinations. Partly inspired by the success of the London-based Hawksmoor group's Manchester branch, big operators are looking outside the capital to expand while young chefs, finding themselves priced out of London, are seeking to make their mark in first solo ventures. A decade ago, *The Good Food Guide* listed nine restaurants in Bristol; in the 2017 edition there are twenty-five. Indeed, Adelina Yard and Bulrush, two of Bristol's most in-demand eateries, have both been established by talented ex-London chefs and are typical of the modern, casual dining spots bringing a refreshing new energy to the city. In addition, the newly located Casamia is making an impact way beyond the city limits with its urbane feel, quiet professionalism, and remarkably nuanced, truly memorable dishes.

In Yorkshire, Leeds is also making its mark, with Michael O'Hare's smash hit The Man Behind the Curtain firmly establishing itself as a destination restaurant. Our experts have also been impressed by Ben Davy's cooking at Ox Club ('channelling the cachet of the Clove Club') and Stuart Myers' The Swine that Dines ('most original food of the year'). These are among our chefs to watch.

Food for thought

Over the past decade, *Good Food Guide* readers have had to come to terms with exposed ductwork, battered fixtures and fittings, hard seats, crepuscular lighting, small plates and communal tables – tick-box trends for today's modern, mid-priced restaurants. They've taken no-booking policies in their stride, queued with stoicism in the cold ('we took it in turns to have a wee and a shot of whisky in the pub next door'), and why? Because once inside, the atmosphere buzzes, the food is good, prices kind and service willing. This new generation of diners does not want to book a month in advance.

What *Good Food Guide* readers are increasingly objecting to is no-choice, multi-course and fixed-price tasting menus. A decade ago such menus were nothing more than a high-end anomaly, only seen in restaurants like the Fat Duck. However, in the last few years it looked as if these three- or four-hour marathons were going to be the future of fine dining. In the hands of a great chef, like Heston Blumenthal or Simon Rogan, a tasting menu can offer an experience unlike anything else, but the format can also present a challenge for customers. This is typical:

'The eating of this meal lasted more than three hours and in the end felt rather like the completion of a successful obstacle course. Has this type of dining gone too far, and would not the option of an à la carte menu add to, rather than diminish, the quality of the restaurant?'

When chefs in ordinary country pubs start to offer tasting menus, we need to ask – has the concept had its day?

Some chefs think it has. Claude Bosi, previously of Hibiscus, one of the leading exponents of the tasting-menu only concept is, in moving forward, changing his focus to à la carte in order to give choice back to his guests. Coming to a similar conclusion is Richard Turner, of Turners in Birmingham. He believes his customers are looking for a change and is no longer offering his £90 tasting menu; instead, diners will be presented with a simplified à la carte at

> *'The Good Food Guide's* essence lies in its army of readers who inundate our feedback system with recommendations…In this way *The Good Food Guide* has exerted a powerful influence for more than six decades'

gentler prices. It is a shift that cannot be ignored.

There are chefs, however, for whom à la carte is not the obvious alternative to a tasting menu. By offering a finite number of dishes, chefs have been able to run their kitchens in a more sustainable manner – ticking both green and money-saving boxes. More choice means more kitchen waste. If I were to put my money on an emerging trend this year, it would be the growth of the simplified menu – uncompromisingly short, often changing daily. It has been the smart option for restaurants such as Portland in London and Wilsons in Bristol. With their three choices per course approach, they may be offering fewer dishes, but they do them brilliantly – and to great acclaim.

Be the critic

We may be living in food's golden era, but it must be said that we chart the exceptions. It has always been the case; we eat the bad meals so you don't have to. *The Good Food Guide's* essence lies in its army of readers who inundate our feedback system with recommendations, which we then verify using professional, expert restaurant reviewers who make anonymous inspections on our behalf, and at our expense. In this way *The Good Food Guide* has exerted a powerful influence for more than six decades. Waitrose, which now owns the Guide, has kept intact the principles that have justified the trust of our readers. In the last few years the print-run has risen to more than 70,000 copies and as a result the Guide's intelligence and information network has grown.

Our continued success depends on you, the reader, continuing to support us in this practical way. With a proliferation of choice, and many more decent places to eat, we need your help more than ever in finding those restaurants that rise above the pack. I hope you take great pleasure in the restaurants featured here, and that you will find time to tell us about your experiences at thegoodfoodguide.co.uk.

And even as we become more food-literate, it is worth reminding ourselves that *The Good Food Guide* has been consistently championing improved standards in food and restauraturing for 66 years. When I first took this job, in 2006, I never expected to stay this long, but it has been, in truth, one of the happiest and most professionally satisfying periods in my life. Only the guide's founder, Raymond Postgate, and its distinguished second editor Christopher Driver, have been at the helm longer. Here's to the next ten years.

Elizabeth Carter
Consultant Editor

The Top 50

The UK's best restaurants

1 L'Enclume, Cumbria (10)
2 Restaurant Nathan Outlaw, Cornwall (10)
3 Restaurant Sat Bains, Nottinghamshire (9)
4 Pollen Street Social, London (9)
5 Hibiscus, London (9) *see pg 56*
6 The Fat Duck, Berkshire (9)
7 Restaurant Gordon Ramsay, London (9)
8 Hedone, London (8)
9 Restaurant Andrew Fairlie, Tayside (8)
10 Fraiche, Merseyside (8)
11 The Ledbury, London (8)
12 Midsummer House, Cambridgeshire (8)
13 Le Champignon Sauvage, Gloucestershire (8)
14 Alain Ducasse at the Dorchester, London (8)
15 Fera at Claridges, London (8)
16 Le Gavroche, London (8)
17 Marcus, London (8)
18 The French, Manchester (8)
19 André Garrett at Cliveden, Berkshire (8)
20 The Peat Inn, Fife (8)
21 Whatley Manor, The Dining Room, Wiltshire (8)
22 Castle Terrace, Edinburgh (7) *New*
23 The Kitchin, Edinburgh (7)
24 Bohemia, Jersey (7)

25 The Greenhouse, London (7) *New*
26 The Waterside Inn, Berkshire (7)
27 Casamia, Bristol (7)
28 Paul Ainsworth at No. 6, Cornwall (7)
29 Dinner by Heston Blumenthal, London (7)
30 Artichoke, Buckinghamshire (7)
31 Le Manoir aux Quat'Saisons, Oxfordshire (7)
32 Restaurant Story, London (7)
33 Gidleigh Park, Devon (7)
34 Restaurant James Sommerin, Glamorgan (7)
35 Simpsons, Birmingham (7) *New*
36 Sketch, London (7)
37 Forest Side, Cumbria (7) *New*
38 Murano, London (7)
39 Restaurant Martin Wishart, Edinburgh (7)
40 Ynyshir, Powys (7)
41 Adam's, Birmingham (7)
42 The Raby Hunt, Durham (7)
43 Freemasons at Wiswell, Lancashire (7)
44 Orwells, Oxfordshire (7) *New*
45 Restaurant Marianne, London (7) *New*
46 Hambleton Hall, Rutland (7)
47 The Whitebrook, Gwent (7) *New*
48 Llangoed Hall, Powys (7)
49 Lake Road Kitchen, Cumbria (6)
50 The Dairy, London (6)

Best New Entries

All new to *The Good Food Guide* this year, the following 25 restaurants, which range across the scoring system, represent the very best in an impressively strong field of new entries for 2017.

Aizle, Edinburgh
Birlinn Restaurant, Isle of Skye
Blandford Comptoir, London
Bulrush, Bristol
Cook House, Newcastle
Eusebi Deli, Glasgow
Forest Side, Grasmere
Frenchie, London
Kricket, London
Noble Rot, London
North Port, Perth
Padella, London
Pidgin, London
The Pointer, Brill
Sugo, Altrincham
The Swine that Dines, Leeds
The Cornish Arms, Tavistock
The Little Gloster, Isle of Wight
The Longs Arms, South Wraxall
The Muddlers Club, Belfast
The Woodford, London
TwoCann, Swansea
Upstairs at Baileys, Beccles
Wilsons, Bristol
Wine & Brine, Moira

Editors' Awards

The editors of *The Good Food Guide* are delighted to recognise the following restaurants and chefs for their talent and commitment to excellence.

Chef of the Year
James Close
The Raby Hunt, Durham

Chef to Watch
Ben Murphy
The Woodford, South Woodford, London

Restaurant of the Year
Orwells
Oxfordshire

Best New Entry
Forest Side
Cumbria

Best Front-of-House
Pollen Street Social
London

Best Small Group
Dishoom
London

Local Restaurant of the Year
Wine & Brine
Moira, Armagh

Local Restaurant Awards

The Local Restaurant of the Year Awards celebrate independent neighbourhood restaurants. An asset to their cities, towns and villages, our winners run from pubs with straightforward menus to special occasion restaurants – what they share is a passion for local produce, a commitment to the community and a genuine warm welcome.

LOCAL RESTAURANT OF THE YEAR – OVERALL WINNER

Northern Ireland
Wine & Brine, Moira, Armagh

REGIONAL WINNERS

London
Portobello Ristorante Pizzeria, Notting Hill

East England
The Duck Inn, Stanhoe

Midlands
The Jockey, Baughton, Worcestershire

North East
Peace and Loaf, Newcastle

North West
Mrs Miller's, Culgaith, Cumbria

Scotland
The Whitehouse, Lochaline, Highlands

South East
The Compasses Inn, Crundale, Kent

South West
Wilks, Bristol

Wales
Sosban and the Old Butcher's, Menai Bridge, Anglesey

How to use
The Good Food Guide

In our opinion, the restaurants included in *The Good Food Guide* are the very best in the UK; this means that simply getting an entry is an accomplishment to be proud of, and a Score 1 or above is a significant achievement.

The Good Food Guide is completely rewritten every year and compiled from scratch. Our research list is based on the huge volume of feedback we receive from readers, which, together with anonymous inspections by our experts, ensures that every entry is assessed afresh. Please keep the reports coming in: visit thegoodfoodguide.co.uk for details.

Symbols

We contact restaurants that we're considering for inclusion ahead of publication to check key information about opening times and facilities. They are also invited to participate in the £5 voucher scheme. The symbols against each entry are intended for at-a-glance identification and are based on the information given to us by each restaurant.

Accommodation is available

£30 It is possible to have three courses, excluding wine, at the restaurant for less than £30.

£XX The average price of a three-course dinner, excluding wine.

£5 OFF The restaurant is participating in our £5 voucher scheme. See vouchers for terms and conditions.

The restaurant has a wine list that our experts have considered to be outstanding, either for strong by-the-glass options, an in-depth focus on a particular region, or attractive margins on fine wines.

V We will no longer display the V symbol; we will list 'v menu' in the details to indicate that the restaurant has a separate vegetarian menu.

Scoring

We add and reject many restaurants when we compile each guide. There are always subjective aspects to rating systems, but our inspectors are equipped with extensive scoring guidelines to ensure that restaurant bench-marking around the UK is accurate. As we take into account reader feedback on each restaurant, any given review is based on several meals.

'New chef' in place of a score indicates that the restaurant has had a recent change of chef and we have been unable to score it reliably; we particularly welcome reports on these restaurants.

Readers Recommend

These are direct quotes from our reader feedback and highlight places that have caught the attention of our loyal followers. Reports are particularly welcome on these entries also.

Local Gem

Local Gems highlight a range of brilliant neighbourhood venues, bringing you a wide choice at great value for money. Simple cafés, bistros and pubs, these are the places that sit happily on your doorstep, delivering good, freshly cooked food.

The Good Food Guide scoring system

1 Capable cooking with simple food combinations and clear flavours, but some inconsistencies.

2 Decent cooking, displaying good technical skills and interesting combinations and flavours. Occasional inconsistencies.

3 Good cooking, showing sound technical skills and using quality ingredients.

4 Dedicated, focused approach to cooking; good classical skills and high-quality ingredients.

5 Exact cooking techniques and a degree of ambition; showing balance and depth of flavour in dishes.

6 Exemplary cooking skills, innovative ideas, impeccable ingredients and an element of excitement.

7 High level of ambition and individuality, attention to the smallest detail, accurate and vibrant dishes.

8 A kitchen cooking close to or at the top of its game. Highly individual with impressive artistry. There is little room for disappointment here.

9 Cooking that has reached a pinnacle of achievement, making it a hugely memorable experience for the diner.

10 Just perfect dishes, showing faultless technique at every service; extremely rare, and the highest accolade the Guide can give.

London Explained

London is split into six regions. Restaurants within each region are listed alphabetically. Each main entry and local gem entry has a map reference. Here are the areas covered in each region.

London CENTRAL

Belgravia, Bloomsbury, Covent Garden, Fitzrovia, Green Park, Holborn, Hyde Park, Lancaster Gate, Leicester Square, Marble Arch, Marylebone, Mayfair, Oxford Circus, Piccadilly, Pimlico, Soho, Victoria, Westminster

London NORTH

Archway, Camden, Finsbury Park, Golders Green, Hampstead, Islington, Kensal Green, Kentish Town, King's Cross, Maida Vale, Muswell Hill, Neasden, Primrose Hill, Stoke Newington, Swiss Cottage, Willesden

London EAST

Barbican, Bethnal Green, Canary Wharf, City, Clerkenwell, Dalston, Farringdon, Hackney, Hoxton, St Paul's, Shoreditch, Spitalfields, Tower Hill, Whitechapel

London SOUTH

Balham, Battersea, Bermondsey, Blackheath, Borough, Brixton, Camberwell, Clapham, East Dulwich, Elephant & Castle, Forest Hill, Greenwich, Herne Hill, Peckham, Putney, South Bank, Southwark, Stockwell, Tooting, Wandsworth, Wimbledon

London WEST

Belgravia, Chelsea, Chiswick, Ealing, Earl's Court, Fulham, Gloucester Road, Hammersmith, Kensington, Knightsbridge, Ladbroke Grove, Notting Hill, Olympia, Parsons Green, Shepherd's Bush, South Kensington

London GREATER

Barnes, Croydon, Crystal Palace, East Sheen, Harrow-on-the-Hill, Kew, Richmond, South Woodford, Southall, Surbiton, Teddington, Twickenham, Walthamstow, Wood Green

LONDON

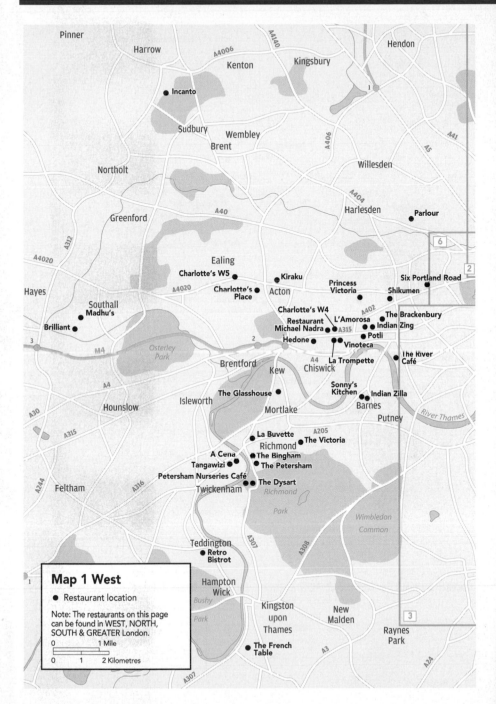

Pinner

Harrow

Kenton

Kingsbury

Hendon

A4006

A4140

1

● Incanto

Sudbury

Wembley

Brent

A406

A41

A5

Northolt

Willesden

A404

Greenford

A40

Harlesden

● Parlour

A312

6

A4020

Ealing

2

Charlotte's W5 ●   ● Kiraku

Six Portland Road ●

Hayes

A4020   Acton

Princess
Victoria

Shikumen

Charlotte's
Place

Southall
Madhu's ●

Charlotte's W4

A402

The Brackenbury ●

Brilliant ●

Restaurant
Michael Nadra ●

L'Amorosa

Indian Zing

3

M4

Osterley
Park

Hedone ●

A315   ● Potli

The River
Café

2

Vinoteca

Brentford

A4

La Trompette

Kew

Chiswick

Hounslow

Isleworth

The Glasshouse ●

Sonny's
Kitchen

Indian Zilla

A30

A315

Mortlake

Barnes

Putney

River Thames

A244

A316

La Buvette   The Victoria ●

A205

Richmond

Feltham

A Cena ●

The Bingham

Tangawizi ●   The Petersham

Petersham Nurseries Café

The Dysart

Richmond

Twickenham

Park

Wimbledon
Common

Teddington

● Retro
Bistrot

A307

A308

Hampton
Wick

Bushy

Kingston
upon
Thames

New
Malden

Raynes
Park

Park

● The French
Table

A3

A24

A307

Map 1 West

● Restaurant location

Note: The restaurants on this page
can be found in WEST, NORTH,
SOUTH & GREATER London.

0   1 Mile

0   1   2 Kilometres

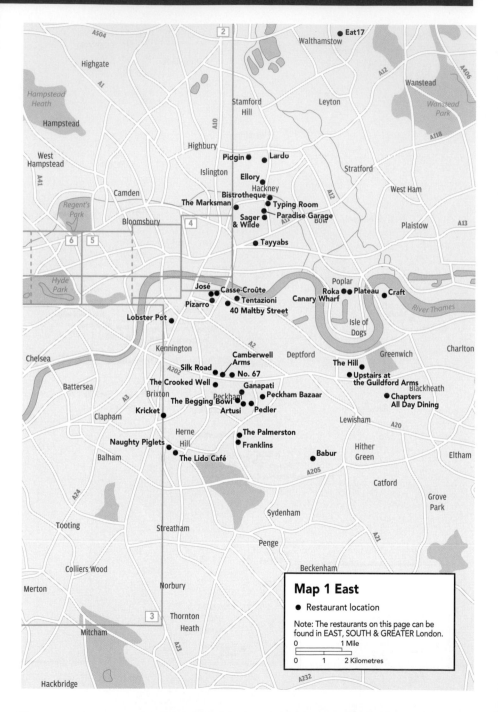

A504

Eat17
Walthamstow

Highgate

Wanstead

A1

Hampstead
Heath

Stamford
Hill

Leyton

Wanstead
Park

A406

A12

Hampstead

A10

A118

West
Hampstead

Highbury

Stratford

West Ham

A41

Islington

Pidgin ● ● Lardo

Camden

Ellory ●

Hackney

Regent's
Park

Bistrotheque ●

The Marksman ● ● ● Typing Room

Plaistow

A13

Bloomsbury

Sager ● ● Paradise Garage
& Wilde

Bow

6 5

● Tayyabs

Poplar

Hyde
Park

José ●
Casse-Croûte

● Roka ● Plateau ● Craft

Pizarro ● ● Tentazioni
40 Maltby Street

Canary Wharf

River Thames

Lobster Pot ●

Isle of
Dogs

Chelsea

Kennington

A2

Deptford

Greenwich

Charlton

Camberwell
Arms

Battersea

Silk Road ●
A202 ● No. 67

The Hill ●

The Crooked Well ●

● Upstairs at
the Guildford Arms

Blackheath

A3

Brixton

Ganapati ●

Peckham

The Begging Bowl ● ● Peckham Bazaar

● Chapters
All Day Dining

Kricket ●

Artusi ● ● Pedler

Clapham

Lewisham

A20

Naughty Piglets ●

Herne
Hill

● The Palmerston

Hither
Green

Eltham

Balham

● Franklins

● Babur

● The Lido Café

A205

Catford

Grove
Park

A24

Tooting

Streatham

Sydenham

A21

Penge

Colliers Wood

Beckenham

Merton

Norbury

Map 1 East

● Restaurant location

Note: The restaurants on this page can be
found in EAST, SOUTH & GREATER London.

0   1 Mile

Thornton
Heath

0   1   2 Kilometres

Mitcham

A23

Hackbridge

A232

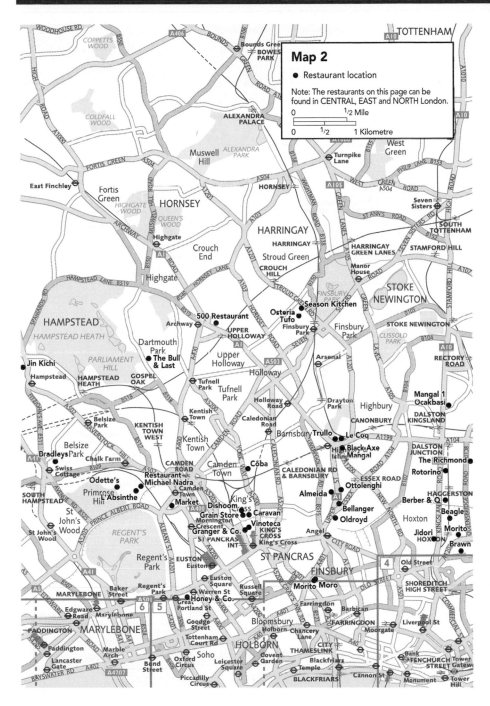

Map 2

● Restaurant location

Note: The restaurants on this page can be found in CENTRAL, EAST and NORTH London.

0   1/2 Mile

0   1/2   1 Kilometre

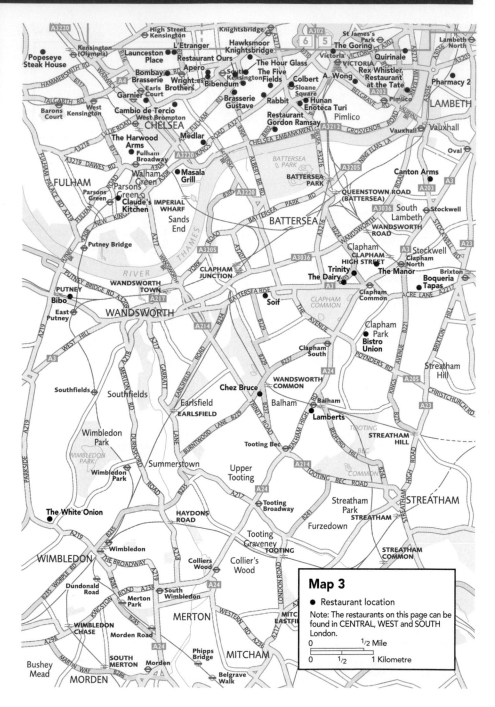

Map 3

● Restaurant location

Note: The restaurants on this page can be found in CENTRAL, WEST and SOUTH London.

| 0 | | ½ Mile |
| 0 | ½ | 1 Kilometre |

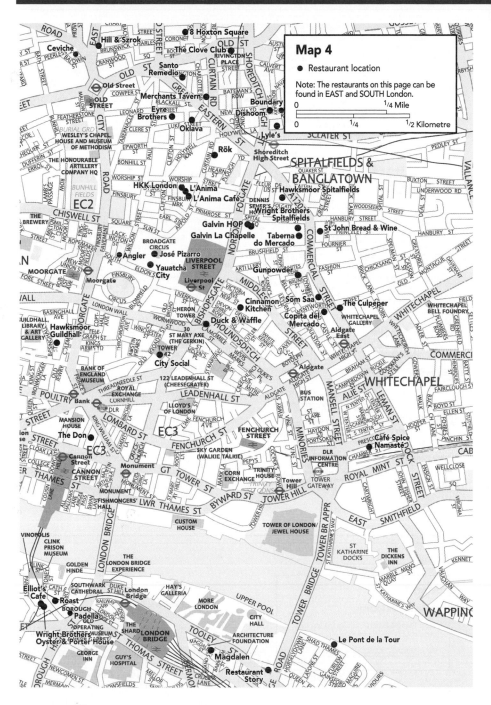

Map 4

● Restaurant location

Note: The restaurants on this page can be found in EAST and SOUTH London.

0   1/4 Mile
0   1/4   1/2 Kilometre

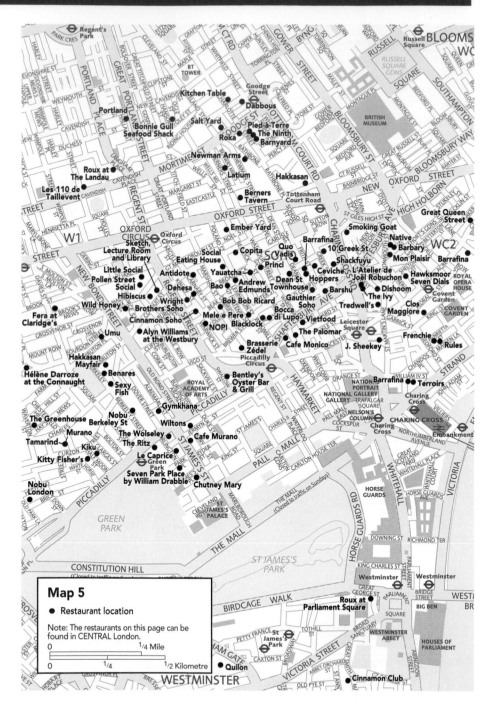

Regent's Park

PARK CRES

BT TOWER

Kitchen Table
Goodge Street
Dabbous

Portland
Bonnie Gull Seafood Shack
Salt Yard
Pied-à-Terre
Roka
The Ninth
Barnyard

Newman Arms

Roux at The Landau
Latium
Hakkasan

Les 110 de Taillevent

OXFORD STREET

Berners Tavern
Tottenham Court Road

BRITISH MUSEUM

OXFORD
W1
CIRCUS

OXFORD STREET

NEW OXFORD STREET

HIGH HOLBORN

Great Queen Street

WC2

Ember Yard

Smoking Goat

Sketch, Lecture Room and Library
Oxford Circus
Social Eating House
Copita
Quo Vadis
Barrafina
10 Greek St
Native
Barbary

Little Social
Antidote
Yauatcha
Princi
Shackfuyu
Mon Plaisir
Barrafina

Pollen Street Social
Dehesa
Andrew Edmunds
Bao
Ceviche
Hoppers
L'Atelier de Joël Robuchon
Hawksmoor Seven Dials

Hibiscus
Wright Brothers Soho
Bob Bob Ricard
Dean St Townhouse
Gauthier Soho
Barshu
Dishoom

Wild Honey
Cinnamon Soho
Mele e Pere
Bocca di Lupo
Vietfood
Tredwell's
The Ivy
Clos Maggiore

Fera at Claridge's
NOPI
Blacklock
The Palomar
Leicester Square

Umu
Alyn Williams at the Westbury
Brasserie Zédel
Cafe Monico
J. Sheekey
Frenchie
Rules

Hakkasan Mayfair
Piccadilly Circus

Hélène Darroze at the Connaught
Benares
Sexy Fish
ROYAL ACADEMY OF ARTS
Bentley's Oyster Bar & Grill
Barrafina
Terroirs

NATIONAL PORTRAIT GALLERY
NATIONAL GALLERY
TRAFALGAR SQUARE
Charing Cross

The Greenhouse
Nobu Berkeley St
Gymkhana
PICCADILLY
Wiltons
NELSON'S COLUMN
CHARING CROSS

Murano
Tamarind
Nobu
The Wolseley
Cafe Murano
Charing Cross
Embankment

Kiku
The Ritz
Kitty Fisher's
Le Caprice
Green Park

Nobu London
Seven Park Place by William Drabble
Chutney Mary

GREEN PARK

ST JAMES'S PALACE

THE MALL (Closed to traffic on Sundays)

HORSE GUARDS

HORSE GUARDS AVE

VICTORIA

CONSTITUTION HILL

ST JAMES'S PARK

THE MALL

DOWNING ST
RICHMOND TER

KING CHARLES ST

Westminster

BIRDCAGE WALK
Roux at Parliament Square

BIG BEN

Quilon

WESTMINSTER

WESTMINSTER ABBEY

HOUSES OF PARLIAMENT

Cinnamon Club

Map 5

● Restaurant location

Note: The restaurants on this page can be found in CENTRAL London.

0   1/4 Mile

0   1/4   1/2 Kilometre

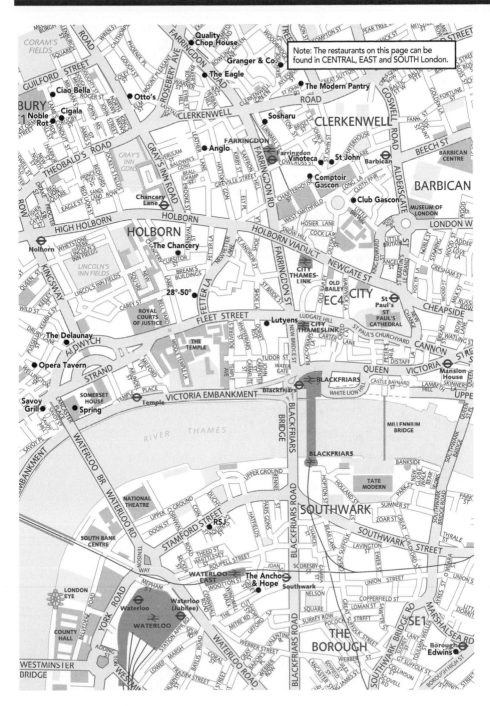

Note: The restaurants on this page can be found in CENTRAL, EAST and SOUTH London.

CORAM'S FIELDS

Quality Chop House

Granger & Co.

The Eagle

Ciao Bella

Otto's

The Modern Pantry

BURY

Noble Rot

Cigala

Sosharu

CLERKENWELL

FARRINGDON

Anglo

Farringdon

Vinoteca

St John

Barbican

BARBICAN CENTRE

BARBICAN

Comptoir Gascon

Chancery Lane

Club Gascon

MUSEUM OF LONDON

LONDON W

HOLBORN

HOLBORN

The Chancery

Holborn

HOLBORN VIADUCT

NEWGATE ST

CITY THAMESLINK

28°-50°

EC4

CITY

St Paul's

ST PAUL'S CATHEDRAL

CHEAPSIDE

Lutyens

THAMESLINK

The Delaunay

Opera Tavern

STRAND

THE TEMPLE

QUEEN VICTORIA

Mansion House

BLACKFRIARS

Savoy Grill

Spring

Temple

VICTORIA EMBANKMENT

Blackfriars

WHITE LION HILL

RIVER THAMES

MILLENNIUM BRIDGE

BLACKFRIARS

NATIONAL THEATRE

TATE MODERN

SOUTHWARK

SOUTH BANK CENTRE

RSJ

LONDON EYE

WATERLOO EAST

The Anchor & Hope

Southwark

COUNTY HALL

Waterloo (Jubilee)

Waterloo

WATERLOO

THE BOROUGH

SE1

Borough

Edwins

WESTMINSTER BRIDGE

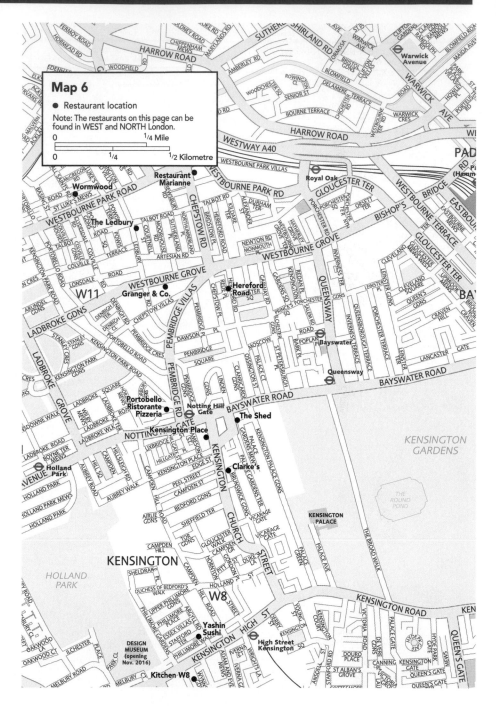

Map 6

● Restaurant location

Note: The restaurants on this page can be found in WEST and NORTH London.

0 ————————— 1/4 Mile

0 ——— 1/4 ——— 1/2 Kilometre

Wormwood

Restaurant Marianne

The Ledbury

Royal Oak

Granger & Co.

Hereford Road

W11

Bayswater

Queensway

Portobello Ristorante Pizzeria

Notting Hill Gate

Kensington Place

The Shed

Clarke's

Holland Park

KENSINGTON GARDENS

THE ROUND POND

KENSINGTON PALACE

HOLLAND PARK

KENSINGTON

W8

DESIGN MUSEUM (opening Nov. 2016)

Yashin Sushi

High Street Kensington

Kitchen W8

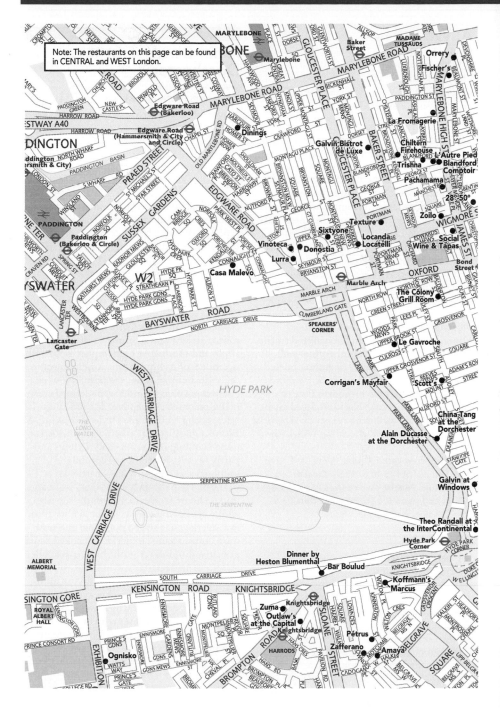

Note: The restaurants on this page can be found in CENTRAL and WEST London.

A. Wong

Cooking score: 4
⊖ Victoria, map 3
Chinese | £35
70-71 Wilton Road, Victoria, SW1V 1DE
Tel no: (020) 7828 8931
awong.co.uk

The cool, Scandi-style interior gives nothing away, it's another contemporary space that suits the mood of our times – casual and egalitarian. As it turns out, Andrew Wong's restaurant is one of the most beguiling Chinese addresses in the capital, where the full range of that nation's cuisine is explored and updated. If you fancy a more overtly oriental mood, head into the new Forbidden City Bar in the basement for a classy small plate and cocktail. Impressive lunchtime dim sum include foie gras in sticky sesame dumplings and rabbit and carrot 'glutinous puff', while the main menu offers up dishes that reference the many and varied regions of China; Yunnan wild mushroom, red date and truffle casserole, Szechuan-style aubergines and, from the Eastern province of Anhui, braised fermented fish belly. Crispy duck is a more familiar staple and the 10-course Taste of China menu showcases the undoubted talent in the kitchen. Finish with tea-smoked banana with nut crumble and chocolate. Wines start at £20.
Chef/s: Andrew Wong. **Open:** Tue to Sat L 12 to 2.30, Mon to Sat D 5.30 to 10.30. **Closed:** Sun, 22 Dec to 4 Jan. **Meals:** main courses £6 to £15. Set L £15. Tasting menu £55 (10 courses). **Details:** 65 seats. 12 seats outside. Bar. Music.

Please send us your feedback

To register your opinion about any restaurant listed in this guide, or a new restaurant that you wish to bring to our attention, please visit the web address at the bottom of the page. Your feedback informs the content of the book and will be used to compile next year's reviews.

★ TOP 50 ★

Alain Ducasse at the Dorchester

Cooking score: 8
⊖ Hyde Park Corner, map 6
Modern French | £95
The Dorchester Hotel, 53 Park Lane, Hyde Park, W1K 1QA
Tel no: (020) 7629 8866
alainducasse-dorchester.com

'A lovely place to revisit,' summed up one reporter on behalf of several. That Jean-Philippe Blondet, who has taken over from Jocelyn Herland, has maintained such an impeccably high standard and made a virtually seamless transition is a remarkable accomplishment. Alain Ducasse's London outpost is a serious restaurant with a high comfort level – plush and discreet, the style is classical, the mood is formal, but the dining room, under the watchful eyes of Daniel Pépin and sommelier Christopher Bothwell, is a model of its kind. Some might object to the style, but that is not the point. Nowhere else is it possible to find a well-defined cuisine being practised in such breadth and range. In interpreting M. Ducasse's style of cooking, M. Blondet gratifies partly because he has a true understanding of flavours and textures and partly because his ability to combine indulgence and lightness is a particular strength. He packs in a lot of flavour: in an intense hit of Dorset crab with the superb addition of caviar and welcome acidity from raw celeriac; in a seared duck foie gras with morel mushrooms; in perfectly cooked 'sauté gourmand' of lobster with chicken quenelles and homemade pasta; and in beautifully flavoured duck from Burgaud (in the midi-Pyrenees) served with chickpeas and more morels. This is food in which elastically deep sauces play off against ingredients of outstanding quality, reflected in the provision of a spoon with each course to ensure that every drop of sauce can be savoured. As for dessert, it really is hard to pass on 'the lightest baba au rhum ever tasted'. And there's no doubt that minor details can be star attractions – in the gougères, the very moreish barbajuans, cheeses as good as you will find, the row of petits fours with coffee. A list of thoroughbred wines teams with quality, from imperious French vintages to a fabulous bunch by the glass (from £10). For bottles, you will need at least £40.

Chef/s: Jean-Philippe Blondet. **Open:** Tue to Fri L 12 to 1.30, Tue to Sat D 6.30 to 9.30. **Closed:** Sun, Mon, 26 to 31 Dec, first week Jan, Easter, 3 weeks Aug. **Meals:** set L £60 (3 courses). Set D £95 (3 courses) to £115. Tasting menu £135 (7 courses) to £180. **Details:** 82 seats. V menu. Wheelchairs. Music. Parking. Children over 10 yrs only.

Alyn Williams at the Westbury

Cooking score: 6
⊖ Oxford Circus, map 5
Modern European | £70
The Westbury Hotel, 37 Conduit Street, Mayfair, W1S 2YF
Tel no: (020) 7078 9579
alynwilliams.com
£5 OFF 🛏

Reports on this civilised restaurant in the Westbury Hotel emphasise the pleasant ambience and sensibly spaced tables. Most also mention the friendly and skilful service, extending to the handling of wines from the extensive list. Alyn Williams' modern European food has 'a lot of work going on in each dish, and plenty of imagination' and wide appeal: in the sweet–umami hit in a dish of poached foie gras with smoked eel, dulse (seaweed) and mushroom broth, for example, or in the deft cooking of a sparkling fresh piece of Cornish turbot with ratatouille, rouille and bouillabaisse. Flavours, textures and timing have been notably good in a lunch that took in celeriac risotto with glazed chicken oyster, hazelnut and celery, and Ring of Kerry lamb with anchovy and onion relish and smoked broccoli. The cheese selection is recommended, along with a range of desserts: rhubarb pavlova with vanilla and rhubarb ice

cream, say, or chocolate tart with crystallised sorrel and lemon sorrel ice cream. Wines start at £27.

Chef/s: Alyn Williams. **Open:** Tue to Sat L 12 to 2.30, D 6 to 10.30. **Closed:** Sun, Mon, first 2 weeks Jan, last 2 weeks Aug. **Meals:** set L £30, Sat L £40. Set D £65. Tasting menu £80 (7 courses). **Details:** 45 seats. Bar. Wheelchairs. Music. Parking.

Andrew Edmunds

Cooking score: 2
⊖ Oxford Circus, Piccadilly Circus, map 5
Modern European | £30
46 Lexington Street, Soho, W1F 0LW
Tel no: (020) 7437 5708
andrewedmunds.com
🍷

Nothing much seems to change in Andrew Edmunds' long-running restaurant – established in 1986, it is considered one of the last bastions of old Soho. Shoehorned into the ground floor (the preferred spot) and basement of a charming 18th-century town house it may be 'too squashed to be romantic' but, with lots of dark wood and candles, scores highly when it comes to atmosphere. The kitchen continues to aim for gutsy, bold dishes on its daily-changing menu and might offer smoked ox tongue with charred January King cabbage and radishes, or a straightforward pork, pigeon and pistachio terrine among starters, while mains take in Swaledale lamb cutlets with chard, white beans and salsa verde or stone bass fillet with spinach, sasify and Seville orange beurre blanc. Finish with treacle tart or a bergamot and pistachio cheesecake. The wine list presents a broad sweep of well-chosen wines with prices from £19.50.

Chef/s: Bob Cairns. **Open:** all week L 12 to 3.30 (12.30 Sat, 1 to 4 Sun), D 5.30 to 10.45 (6 to 10.30 Sun). **Closed:** 24 to 30 Dec, Easter. **Meals:** main courses £14 to £24. **Details:** 61 seats. 4 seats outside.

Antidote

new chef/no score
⊖ Oxford Circus, map 5
Modern European | £42
12A Newburgh Street, Soho, W1F 7RR
Tel no: (020) 7287 8488
antidotewinebar.com

In a city that's now brimming with exciting and unusual wine bars, Antidote may not be the first to fully dissolve the boundaries between wine bar and restaurant, but it has got the right balance between emphasis on food or wine by doing both well. It's a fairly lively, small space on two levels (upstairs is quieter), with cramped tables inside and easy-going service, and follows the formula of an excellent wine list, small sharing plates and low mark-ups. William Dee took over the kitchen too late for us to organise an inspection, but the food here has always been clean-cut, seasonal bistro-style assemblies, and Dee's simple, nose-to-tail approach should suit this understated venue to a T. No-nonsense home-grown classics are his forte, such as Angus bavette with fried potatoes, lettuce and anchovy, crab with Essex samphire and mayonnaise, and mackerel with kohlrabi, wild fennel and lemon. The bookable terrace is a big draw when the weather co-operates. • Desserts hit the Swiss lemon meringue tart/ chocolate mousse with sherry cream comfort zone, but the headline attraction is, of course, the French-centric wine list bursting with natural and biodynamic options. Prices from £22.
Chef/s: William Dee. **Open:** Mon to Sat L 12 to 3, D 6 to 10.30. **Closed:** Sun, bank hols. **Meals:** main courses £16 to £24. Tasting menu £45. **Details:** 45 seats. 20 seats outside. Bar. Music.

L'Atelier de Joël Robuchon

Cooking score: 6
⊖ Leicester Square, map 5
Modern French | £90
13-15 West Street, Covent Garden,
WC2H 9NE
Tel no: (020) 7010 8600
joelrobuchon.co.uk

In the heart of the theatre district, the Atelier makes quite a show of itself, with three floors of razzle-dazzle glamour, from the ground- and first-floor dining rooms to the rooftop terrace bar, where streams of cocktails are flowing. Axel Manes conforms to modern expectations with a mixture of small tasting plates or an eight-course Menu Découverte taster with a sommelier's selection of small glasses to accompany. The food is restlessly creative, full of dynamic contrasts, but rooted appreciably in classical French practice. Pressed foie gras terrine is offset by a jellied coating of mango and passion fruit, while stewed Savoy cabbage adds the earthy note to truffled langoustine ravioli. Cutlets of milk-fed Pyrenean lamb are prettily adorned with thyme flowers, and the aromatic principle is celebrated again in a serving of veal sweetbreads in bay, accompanied by a romaine leaf stuffed with smoked bacon. Delicately constructed desserts take in vanilla-roasted pineapple with crunchy meringue and Tahitian vanilla cream.
Chef/s: Axel Manes. **Open:** all week L 12 to 3, D 5.30 to 11 (10.30 Sun). **Closed:** 25 Dec. **Meals:** main courses £25 to £52. Small plates £14 to £35. Tasting menu £139. **Details:** 88 seats. Bar. Wheelchairs. Music.

L'Autre Pied

Cooking score: 5
⊖ Bond Street, map 6
Modern European | £50
5-7 Blandford Street, Marylebone, W1U 3DB
Tel no: (020) 7486 9696
lautrepied.co.uk
£5 OFF

With its low-key décor, close-packed tables and soft lighting L'Autre Pied is an attractive and relatively intimate space. Andrew McFadden's departure for big brother Pied à Terre (see entry) left big shoes to fill, but with the appointment of Graham Long – who has worked at Pied à Terre in the past – the thrust of the cooking remains the same: expect classic technique and modern flavour combinations on a menu that plays off the seasons. The span of reference takes us from the wilder shores (Cornish crab, bisque pannacotta, butternut, sea buckthorn, purslane) to the beaten track (Goosnargh chicken, ceps, Parmesan gnocchi, black cabbage, truffle), but always with a confident sense of orientation. Elsewhere, there's good bread 'very generously proffered', and desserts such as buttermilk and rhubarb slice with mandarin sorbet. Regulars continue to be impressed with the service and note the lunch menu offers the best value. Wines from £26.
Chef/s: Graham Long. **Open:** all week L 12 to 2.15 (2.30 Sat and Sun), Mon to Sat D 6 to 10.30. **Closed:** 25 and 26 Dec, 1 Jan. **Meals:** main courses £25 to £28. Set L £24 (2 courses) to £29. Set D £39 (2 courses) to £49. Tasting menu £79 (8 courses). **Details:** 48 seats. 6 seats outside. V menu. Bar. Music.

★ NEW ENTRY ★

Bao

Cooking score: 3
⊖ Oxford Circus, map 5
Taiwanese | £28
53 Lexington Street, Soho, W1F 9AS
baolondon.com
£30

'We arrived at 6pm and joined the queue, gazing at the lucky ones already drinking beers and eating pig-blood cake in Bao's window seats,' recalled one intrepid reader, faced with a 30-minute wait. Is it worth it? If you can bear being 'jam-packed, elbow-to-elbow' with fellow diners you'll find excellent bao (steamed buns) and delicious xiao chi (snacks) served apace against a minimalist backdrop of blond wood and bare surfaces. A tick-box order sheet offers half a dozen bao, perhaps with a classic filling of braised pork, peanut powder, fermented greens and coriander, or a toasted sesame version with soy milk-marinated chicken, Szechuan mayonnaise and golden kim-chee. Don't neglect the xiao chi, where meaty slices of eryngii mushrooms are served with tiny cubes of jellified century egg, and a 'fabulous' scallop comes in its shell with a perfectly balanced, sweet, sharp, garlicky sauce. Round things off with the only sweet option: a hot, puffy Horlicks ice cream bao. Wine is £6 a glass, but opt instead for cold-brew oolong tea, or saké. Bao has gained a sibling restaurant in Fitzrovia, 31 Windmill Street, W1T 2JN.
Chef/s: Erchen Chang. **Open:** Mon to Sat L 12 to 3, D 5.30 to 10. **Closed:** Sun, 24 Dec to 2 Jan. **Meals:** bao £4 to £5. Xiao chi £3 to £6. **Details:** 32 seats.

Nieves Barragán Mohacho

Barrafina, London

What food could you not live without?
Olive oil, because it changes everything. If you have vegetables, good olive oil, salt and pepper, you're set.

What is the vital ingredient for a successful kitchen?
Don't mess around, don't put too many things on the plate, and use great quality ingredients.

How do you start developing a new recipe?
I always have a notebook in which I write down ideas, always sparked by ingredients. These notes then inspire recipes for specials that I create daily with the team, depending on what ingredients come in.

Who is the most interesting person you have cooked for?
The counter-dining style at Barrafina means that we are cooking in front of the guests and have direct interaction with them. It would be impossible to single one person out, it's just great to have that engagement with every person, seeing their reaction to the food as they eat it.

★ NEW ENTRY ★

The Barbary

Cooking score: 4
⊖ Covent Garden, map 5
North African | £30
16 Neal's Yard, Covent Garden, WC2H 9DP
thebarbary.co.uk

Bringing some Mediterranean sunshine to an alleyway leading off Neal's Yard, the Barbary is a no-reservations eatery from the folk behind the Palomar (see entry), taking its inspiration from North Africa. A seductive interior – distressed, whitewashed brick, petrol-blue woodwork, moody lighting – is filled by a horseshoe-shaped bar seating 24, in the centre of which the cooking action takes place, and where servers ('cool, laidback, friendly') circulate easily and advise on the menu. Our inspection started well with char-grilled naan with zhug (spicy, herby sauce), harissa, and burnt and pickled chilli, and 'a fresh and crunchy medley' of kohlrabi, rocket, peas, feta and sumac vinaigrette salad. Chicken msachen, possibly the 'tenderest, smokiest chicken I've ever had,' appears in a mini tagine smeared with thick, tangy yoghurt and a heap of sweet, caramelised onions scattered with coriander leaves, while harissa-marinated monkfish chermoula arrives with braised fennel bulbs – silky and falling apart – lemon yoghurt and a harissa sauce 'with just the right amount of heat'. And then there is basbousa ('my perfect dessert'), a warm semolina cake, the colour of golden sunshine, drenched in sweet orange syrup with a dollop of crème fraîche and a scattering of crunchy caramelised almonds. There's a noisy, happy soundtrack and wine starts at £29.
Chef/s: Eyal Jagermann. **Open:** Tue to Sun 12 to 10. **Closed:** Mon. **Meals:** main courses £13 to £14. **Details:** 24 seats. Music.

Barnyard

Cooking score: 1
⊖ Goodge Street, Tottenham Court Road,
map 5
British/American | £24
18 Charlotte Street, Fitzrovia, W1T 2LZ
Tel no: (020) 7580 3842
barnyard-london.com
£30
🔻

An American barn where British food is
purveyed by a French chef might be what
modern eating is all about. Oval mirrors hang
on corrugated metal walls, and a menu of
grazeable items – mushroom and smoked
butter croquettes, say – moves into the big
time with the wildly popular crispy chicken
wings in smoked paprika, garlic and lemon,
like 'especially moreish KFC'. The logistics of
serving everything at once, where many
things come on toast and go soggy as they wait
their turn, needs looking at, but there are
'simple finger-licking pleasures' to be had
from the likes of lobster roll, or roast beef with
garlic buttermilk and pickles. In the drinks
department, the wickedest shandies in town,
served by the half-pint, compete with a few
wines from £20.
Chef/s: Ollie Dabbous. **Open:** all week 12 to 10.30
(11pm Thur and Fri, 11 to 11 Sat, 11 to 9 Sun).
Closed: 25 to 26 Dec. **Meals:** main courses £9 to
£14. Set L £15 (2 courses) to £18. **Details:** 48 seats.
4 seats outside. Music.

Barrafina Adelaide Street

Cooking score: 4
⊖ Charing Cross, map 5
Spanish | £35
10 Adelaide Street, Covent Garden,
WC2N 4HZ
barrafina.co.uk

A minute's stroll from Trafalgar Square will
bring you to the Covent Garden offshoot of
the Soho original (see entry), recognisable by
its rounded frontage on a corner site. The
format is the same, a tapas and sherry bar with
counter seating only, its modest proportions
feeling deceptively spacious, with a menu of

classic small bites and more unusual items to
go at. Frituras are tempting: salt cod fritters,
chillied oysters, pig's ear, lamb's brain,
ortiguillas (sea anemones). They are
supplemented by char-grilled and braised
items – Iberian pork ribs or ox tongue with
crushed potatoes – and nor are the veg options
to be overlooked, not when fennel comes with
Comice pear and radish, or yellow chicory
with anchovies in salmorejo (tomato and
bread soup). Finish with the mysteriously
unspecific 'flan' (aka crème caramel) or, if your
tooth enamel will support it, a selection of
turrón. Sherries in all styles, cavas and Spanish
wines seal the deal, the last from £22.
Chef/s: Nieves Barragán Mohacho. **Open:** all week
L 12 to 3 (1 to 3.30 Sun), D 5 to 11 (5.30 to 10 Sun).
Closed: 25 and 26 Dec, 1 Jan, bank hols.
Meals: tapas £6 to £15. **Details:** 28 seats.

★ NEW ENTRY ★

Barrafina Drury Lane

Cooking score: 4
⊖ Covent Garden, map 5
Spanish | £35
43 Drury Lane, Covent Garden, WC2B 5AJ
barrafina.co.uk

The third of Sam and Eddie Hart's dynamic
Barrafina group is small so you may have to
queue, but when you squeeze in at one of the
high counter-stools you are in for a treat: this
is not your average tapas. It's all about
wonderful ingredients, simply cooked with
precision, and while there's some crossover
with its older siblings (pan con tomate,
chipirones, tortilla), Drury Lane features some
brilliant, unusual (for London) choices. That
Madrileño favourite, bocadillo de calamar
(squid bun) impressed at a March meal, as did
migas con morcilla patatera y papada Ibérica
(cubes of fried bread with blood sausage and
fried egg), and an exceptional salad of baby
gem lettuce with bottarga, walnuts, pancetta
and Manchego. After that, the Lenten
speciality torrijas – bread soaked in milk,
wine, honey and spices – just begged a glass of

Pedro Ximénez. Service is charming and perfectly timed. The short Spanish wine list starts at £22.

Chef/s: Nieves Barragán Mohacho. **Open:** all week L 12 to 3 (1 to 3.30 Sun), D 5 to 11 (5.30 to 10 Sun). **Closed:** 25 and 26 Dec, 1 Jan, bank hols. **Meals:** tapas £6 to £19. **Details:** 23 seats.

Barrafina Frith Street

Cooking score: 5
🚇 Tottenham Court Road, map 5
Spanish | £40
54 Frith Street, Soho, W1D 4SL
Tel no: (020) 7813 8016
barrafina.co.uk

'I got here about half an hour beforehand and by the time it opened, the queue got to the corner.' Proof indeed that ten years on, Sam and Eddie Hart's famously reservation-free Barrafina continues to be a real crowd-puller. But as we went to press we learnt that Barrafina is to move to Dean Street in autumn 2016, to the revamped ground-floor dining room of the Hart brothers restaurant Quo Vadis (see entry). What will be constant, however, is a culinary compass that points firmly to Spain, delivering tapas at its very best – simple, authentic and big on natural flavour. Expect, too, scrupulously sourced ingredients delivering clear, precise flavours in dishes as diverse as prawn and piquillo pepper tortilla, gambas al ajillo, grilled quail with aïoli, and milk-fed lamb served with hand-cut chips, sprinkled with garlic salt and a brava sauce. Cold meat platters, ham croquetas and pan con tomate have their place, too, as does an all-Spanish wine list which opens at £19.

Chef/s: Nieves Barragán Mohacho. **Open:** all week L 12 to 3 (1 to 3.30 Sun), D 5 to 11 (5.30 to 10 Sun). **Closed:** 25 and 26 Dec, 1 Jan, bank hols. **Meals:** tapas £6 to £15. **Details:** 23 seats. 8 seats outside.

Barshu

Cooking score: 4
🚇 Leicester Square, map 5
Chinese | £35
28 Frith Street, Soho, W1D 5LF
Tel no: (020) 7287 8822
barshurestaurant.co.uk

As British diners start to understand more about China's rich and varied regional cuisine, its most forthright dishes – among them the pepper-laced hotpots of Szechuan – have gained a formidable reputation. Now specialist restaurants must prove that Szechuan food can also be complex and delicate, and Barshu is giving it a good go. On a busy corner bordering Chinatown, with straightforward décor and service, it might not stand out, but the food is certainly distinguished. To start, classic appetisers include garlicky smacked cucumbers, slivers of bang-bang chicken and anything 'numbing and hot' – dried beef and fish fillets both get this resonant treatment. There's also a brief selection of noodly Chengdu street snacks, to be followed, perhaps, by scallops in a fish-fragrant sauce, red-braised beef with beancurd, or fragrant and hot crab. Glutinous rice balls filled with black sesame paste provide a sweet finish. Wine is from £23.90.

Chef/s: Bing Fu. **Open:** all week 12 to 11 (11.30pm Fri and Sat). **Closed:** 24 and 25 Dec. **Meals:** main courses £13 to £43. **Details:** 100 seats. Music.

Benares

Cooking score: 5
🚇 Green Park, map 5
Indian | £60
12a Berkeley Square, Mayfair, W1J 6BS
Tel no: (020) 7629 8886
benaresrestaurant.com

Next to the famous Rolls-Royce showroom on Berkeley Square, Atul Kochhar's Indian-British fusion cuisine fits glamorously into its moneyed purlieu. Climb the stairs to the slinky bar and sepulchrally lit monochrome dining room, divided from each other by a pond garlanded with water lilies. Executive

chef Brinder Narula arrived in 2015 and maintains the style of elegantly inventive cooking for which the place is celebrated. Expect to start with crispy soft-shell crab in passion fruit sauce with celeriac and apple slaw, or wood pigeon marinated in Sarawak pepper and fennel, with vanilla beetroot, as preludes to multi-faceted main dishes like sea bream with mustard samphire upma in coconut curry, and venison biryani in peanut and sesame gravy. Purists might appreciate Old Delhi-style tandoori chicken bursting with assertive spice, while desserts include bhapa doi, a traditional milk pudding flavoured here with rhubarb and pomegranate, served with a classic Indian sweet, pistachio burfi. An enterprising wine list opens at £29.
Chef/s: Atul Kochhar and Brinder Narula. **Open:** Mon to Sat L 12 to 2.30, all week D 5 to 11 (6 to 10 Sun). **Closed:** 25 Dec, 1 Jan. **Meals:** main courses £28 to £37. Set L and D £29 (2 courses) to £35. Tasting menu £98 (7 courses). **Details:** 150 seats. Bar. Wheelchairs. Music. No children after 7.30.

Bentley's Oyster Bar & Grill

Cooking score: 5
⊖ Piccadilly Circus, map 5
Seafood | £80
11-15 Swallow Street, Piccadilly, W1B 4DG
Tel no: (020) 7734 4756
bentleys.org

A century since it was founded, and nigh on a dozen years since Richard Corrigan brought renewed vigour, Bentley's is wearing well. The appeal, in a nutshell, is spanking-fresh fish and shellfish served in the convivial, highly polished atmosphere of the ground-floor bar and oyster bar – the Grill restaurant upstairs is a more sedate affair. Whether you perch at the bar or occupy a close-set table, you can look forward to classics such as oysters, shellfish platters, lobster bisque, Dover sole meunière and fish pie, mixed with the likes of salmon and oyster tartare with ginger, soy and mirin or sea bass with artichoke, squid, wild rocket and basil – all showcasing the finest

materials. You'll also find a few meat dishes (say rack of Snowdonia lamb with young feta and ratatouille), while for dessert, few can resist the appeal of Bentley's trifle. On the wine front, it's a superb collection (from £26) with exemplary choice by the glass.
Chef/s: Michael Lynch. **Open:** Oyster bar: all week 11.30 to 11.30 (10.30 Sun). Grill: Mon to Fri L 12 to 3, Mon to Sat D 5.30 to 11. **Closed:** 25 and 26 Dec, 1 Jan. **Meals:** main courses £19 to £80. Set L £25 (2 courses) to £29. Sun L £45. **Details:** 100 seats. 30 seats outside. Bar. Music.

Berners Tavern

Cooking score: 5
⊖ Tottenham Court Rd, Oxford Circus, map 5
Modern British | £50
10 Berners Street, Fitzrovia, W1T 3NP
Tel no: (020) 7908 7979
edition-hotels.marriott.com

As part of Jason Atherton's group of London restaurants, this Edition Hotel venue maintains the glamorous family resemblance – the gorgeously ornate, beautifully lit room has a contemporary gloss and looks every inch the brasserie deluxe. Measured service keeps the mood buoyant and it makes a great rendezvous for power breakfasts, working lunches, afternoon tea, late suppers and more besides. Here, the menu contrives to comfort with familiarity yet excite with novelty – witness prawn cocktail with lobster jelly, avocado and crispy shallot or a traditional British pork pie with piccalilli, alongside mac and cheese with braised oxtail, and stone bass with caramelised cauliflower, fennel and cockle velouté. In addition, there's classic ribeye or Buccleuch Estate côte de boeuf for two to share, and the baked Alaska is, by all accounts, not to be missed. A globetrotting wine list spills over with magnificent bottles (from £30) – the excellent selection by the glass offers best value.
Chef/s: Phil Carmichael. **Open:** all week L 12 to 3 (4 Sun), D 5 to 10.30 (6 Sun). **Meals:** main courses £20 to £35. Set L £25 (2 courses) to £30. **Details:** 145 seats. Bar. Wheelchairs. Music.

★ NEW ENTRY ★

Blacklock

Cooking score: 2
⊖ Piccadilly Circus, map 5
British | £25
24 Great Windmill Street, Soho, W1D 7LG
Tel no: (020) 3441 6996
theblacklock.com
£30

Run by alumni from the Hawksmoor group who know their meat, Blacklock has a singular focus − 'skinny' or 'big' beef, lamb and pork chops, chalked up by weight. In other words, beef short rib, lamb T-bone or pork belly gently charred on flatbread, or an exemplary 50-day aged porterhouse, with a side of courgettes, chicory and Stilton, before the (stand-alone) dessert. Sunday lunch deviates from the formula, offering roast beef fore rib, lamb leg and pork loin, and delivering for one reporter 'possibly the best roast beef − the bone-marrow gravy still haunts me'. Good-value retro cocktails such as a nettle Gimlet or Old Fashioned are wheeled out on a trolley and pack a boozy punch. It's cheaper on 'Butcher Price Mondays', when the slightly 'thrown-together' décor − think bare bulbs, painted brick and wooden benches − might feel more palatable. Reservations taken for lunch only. Wine from £21.
Chef/s: Mirek Dawid. **Open:** all week L 12 to 3 (6 Sun), Mon to Sat D 5 to 11. **Closed:** 24 to 27 Dec, 1 Jan. **Meals:** main courses £8 to £18. **Details:** 70 seats. Music.

Please send us your feedback

To register your opinion about any restaurant listed in this guide, or a new restaurant that you wish to bring to our attention, please visit the web address at the bottom of the page. Your feedback informs the content of the book and will be used to compile next year's reviews.

★ NEW ENTRY ★

Blandford Comptoir

Cooking score: 3
⊖ Baker Street, Bond Street, map 6
Modern European | £30
1 Blandford Street, Marylebone, W1U 3DA
Tel no: (020) 7935 4626
blandford-comptoir.co.uk

Xavier Rousset made his name as one half of the partnership behind Texture and the 28°-50° group of wine bars (see entries). His new venture is a slick, modern wine bar: a fairly small but smartly designed space dominated by a long bar with counter seating, with tables clustered in the plate-glass window and at the back. Thanks to the quality of Mr Rousset's wine list, the place has a real buzz about it as bottle after glorious bottle is sampled and hunger pangs staved off by a menu of delicious small and large plates. At an early test meal we enjoyed slices of raw sea bream with blood orange and just a hint of rosemary, meltingly tender Fassone beef carpaccio with truffle dressing and aged Parmesan, delicate octopus with potato and Kalamata olive, and roast quail served atop a superb truffle boudin. And wise counsel is priceless when it comes to navigating the stupendous, globetrotting list. Selections by the glass (from £4.50) provide a mouthwatering snapshot of the complete cellar, with bottles from £23.
Chef/s: Ben Mellor. **Open:** all week 12 to 10. **Meals:** main courses £14 to £24. **Details:** 40 seats.

★ NEW ENTRY ★

Bob Bob Ricard

Cooking score: 3
⊖ Piccadilly Circus, map 5
British/Russian | £45
1 Upper James Street, Soho, W1F 9DF
Tel no: (020) 3145 1000
bobbobricard.com

If you know what is meant by the Soho vibe, then BBR is the antithesis. This place is lavish, ostentatious, excessive − in other words, 'it's a whole lot of expensive fun'. There's a buzzer on each table declaring 'press for Champagne', for heaven's sake. It has proven to be a stayer, with its British and Russian comfort food executed with assurance, and a laudable fixed mark-up policy on higher-priced wines. The service is old-school smooth, the sumptuous leather-seated booths give privacy, while the overall decorative effect is 'like the luxurious interior of the Tsar's train'. Sea bass ceviche caviar and Waldorf salad defy the Anglo-Russian alliance, but pretty pink pelmeni dumplings filled with lobster, crab and shrimp fly the Russian tricolor. Chicken, mushroom and Champagne pie has a perfect crust, the chicken Kiev outshines many another, and lobster mac and cheese is a modern classic. Sour cherry soufflé makes a light and sophisticated finale. Drink chilled vodka or wines starting at £30.

Chef/s: Anna Haugh. **Open:** all week L 12.30 to 3, D 6 to 11.15 (5.30 to 12 Fri and Sat). **Meals:** main courses £17 to £45. **Details:** 160 seats. V menu. Bar.

Bocca di Lupo

Cooking score: 2
⊖ Piccadilly Circus, map 5
Italian | £38
12 Archer Street, Piccadilly, W1D 7BB
Tel no: (020) 7734 2223
boccadilupo.com

This stylish little corridor of an Italian restaurant comes with statement lighting, granite flooring and a grand marble counter (with bar-stool seating) stretching three-quarters of the length of the room. There's a smallish table area at the back, too, and it's noisy and tightly packed so expect a 'dynamic atmosphere'. The menu is far too long, delivering regional dishes in varying portion sizes – which makes ordering confusing – and consistency is a bugbear. However, homemade salami with 'warm, puffy and golden' crescentine and squacquerone (a tangy cream cheese), home-salted cod in a fabulous crisp batter, grilled mussels with chilli oil, and 'gorgeous' baby courgettes with garlic and chilli are all dishes that garner fulsome praise. Italian wines from £21.50.

Chef/s: Jacob Kenedy and Jake Simpson. **Open:** all week L 12.15 to 3, D 5.15 to 12 (11 Sun). **Closed:** 25 Dec, 1 Jan. **Meals:** main courses £7 to £34. **Details:** 82 seats. Wheelchairs. Music.

Bonnie Gull Seafood Shack

Cooking score: 2
⊖ Oxford Circus, Goodge Street, map 5
Seafood | £40
21A Foley Street, Fitzrovia, W1W 6DS
Tel no: (020) 7436 0921
bonniegull.com

Alex Hunter and Danny Clancy's 28-seater restaurant has settled into a rhythm since it opened in 2012. It's cool, relaxed and decked out in an artfully rustic beach-hut style that's tight and almost always packed. Like the simple décor, there's nothing cluttered or fancy about the menu, which specialises in the freshest fish and seafood. A lot of care and thought have gone into the details and simple classics have a please-all appeal, from native oysters or grilled Scottish langoustines with garlic and herb butter, to bouillabaisse with rouille and croûtons or Schiehallion beer-battered haddock with beef-dripping chunky chips, tartare sauce and mushy peas. The food delivers plenty of flavour without pretension, something as simple as Selsey crab with dressed brown meat and legs to crack is widely praised, while desserts such as Braeburn apple tarte fine with crumble ice cream add a finishing touch. Fish-friendly wines from £22.

Chef/s: Christian Edwardson. **Open:** all week L 12 to 3 (4 Sat and Sun), D 6 to 10 (8.30 Sun). **Closed:** 25 Dec to 3 Jan. **Meals:** main courses £16 to £26. **Details:** 28 seats. 10 seats outside. Music.

Symbols

🛏 Accommodation is available
£30 Three courses for less than £30
£5 OFF £5-off voucher scheme
🍾 Notable wine list

LOCAL GEM

Brasserie Zédel
🚇 Piccadilly Circus, map 5
French | £23
20 Sherwood Street, Soho, W1F 7ED
Tel no: (020) 7734 4888
brasseriezedel.com

£30

This Art Deco beauty – a former hotel ballroom – makes a spectacular setting for Chris Corbin and Jeremy King's take on the grand Parisian brasserie. Expensively renovated in gilt and marble, the high-impact décor draws an appreciative crowd, lured as much by the kind prices as by the pleasing classics of steak tartare, fish soup, beef braised in red wine sauce, and daily specials of, say, rabbit in mustard sauce. Service is remarkably good considering the place seats nearly 300. French wines from £21.

★ NEW ENTRY ★

Cafe Monico
Cooking score: 3
🚇 Piccadilly Circus, Leicester Square, map 5
European | £32
39-45 Shaftesbury Avenue, Soho, W1D 6LA
Tel no: (020) 3727 6161
cafemonico.com

'This is a most welcome addition to a touristy part of London,' thought one reporter, surprised to find such an ambitious brasserie in the unlikely environs of Shaftesbury Avenue. But then this is a collaboration between the Soho House Group and chef Rowley Leigh. The setting is glamorous, with a chandelier hanging from the double-height ceiling, while a marble-topped bar, green leather seats, bare tables, dark-wood panelling and an open kitchen make up the lively ground-floor area. Or you can head to the mezzanine and sit at crisp white-clothed tables 'where you can see the tops of the buses whizzing by'. The all-day menu provides sandwiches alongside familiar choices of shellfish, crustacean and grills. From the outset, the cooking delivers: a well-timed char-grilled octopus paired with a potato salad, lifted by a vibrant spicy romesco sauce, say, followed by lobster spaghetti teamed with a velvety shellfish bisque, and a crêpes soufflé with Grand Marnier and orange peel ensuring a 'decadent end'. Wines from £22.

Chef/s: Rowley Leigh. **Open:** all week 8am to midnight (1am Fri, 11am to 1am Sat, 11am to midnight Sun). **Meals:** main courses £13 to £21. **Details:** 180 seats. Bar.

Café Murano
Cooking score: 4
🚇 Green Park, map 5
Italian | £35
33 St James's Street, St James's, SW1A 1HD
Tel no: (020) 3371 5559
cafemurano.co.uk

Angela Hartnett once worked at this address when it was Gordon Ramsay's original Pétrus, so it seems rather fitting that she should pitch up here with a dressed-down version of her Mayfair big hitter Murano (see entry). As the name suggests, Café Murano is casual and (relatively) affordable, although the location demands some posh trappings – a marble-topped bar, leather banquettes, swanky lighting and so forth. The food is northern Italian by inclination, with Hartnett's gastronomic thumbprints all over the menu – especially when it comes to seasonal flavours. There are cracking cicchetti to nibble with Italian cocktails, before the kitchen delivers some equally spirited antipasti – say cured sea trout with radicchio and caper dressing. Pasta is naturally one of the stars (lamb pappardelle with Pugliese olives, for example), while robust generosity typifies secondi such as pork neck with chicory, pangrattato and mustard fruits. Set deals are a guaranteed crowd-puller, and the all-Italian wine list promises regional bottles from £20.50. There's an offshoot at 34-36 Tavistock Street, Covent Garden.

Chef/s: Sam Williams. **Open:** all week L 12 to 3 (11.30 to 4 Sun), Mon to Sat D 5.30 to 11. **Closed:** 25 and 26 Dec. **Meals:** main courses £16 to £22. Set L and D £19 (2 courses) to £23. **Details:** 86 seats. 4 seats outside. Music.

Le Caprice

Cooking score: 4
⊖ Green Park, map 5
Modern British | £35
Arlington House, Arlington Street, Mayfair,
SW1A 1RJ
Tel no: (020) 7629 2239
le-caprice.co.uk

Part of London restaurant history, or royalty you might say, Le Caprice was originally relaunched back in 1981 (it first opened in 1947) and was one of that decade's most high-profile addresses. It might not garner the same column inches these days, but it has lost remarkably little of its broad appeal and glamour. Part of Richard Caring's Caprice Holdings group since 2005, the black-and-white David Bailey photos remain and it's all very civilised. European ideas vie for your attention with pan-Asian preparations, so you might start with char-grilled squid with romesco sauce and Padrón peppers, move on to Thai-baked sea bass with fragrant rice and finish with Bramley apple pie. The all-day terrace is hidden behind topiary planters with royal blue awnings offering elemental protection, while live music livens up Saturday lunches and Sunday dinners. It's priced for the postcode. Drink classic cocktails or wines from £29.
Chef/s: Will Halsall. **Open:** all week 12 to 12 (11.30 to 11 Sun). **Closed:** 25 and 26 Dec. **Meals:** main courses £17 to £35. Set L £20 (2 courses) to £25. **Details:** 74 seats. 16 seats outside. Bar. Wheelchairs. Music. Parking.

Casa Malevo

Cooking score: 3
⊖ Marble Arch, map 6
Argentinian | £40
23 Connaught Street, Marylebone, W2 2AY
Tel no: (020) 7402 1988
casamalevo.com

This chic, intimate steak joint is just minutes from two of London's busiest thoroughfares. But you'd never know it. Cosy, homely and welcoming, Casa Malevo feels more like a local in-the-know bolt-hole than a coveted central London restaurant. The cooking, however, is a cut above your average neighbourhood eatery. Starters may include the likes of Ibérico ham, figs and buffalo mozzarella, or grilled scallops with celeriac purée, lentils and chorizo. As for the mains, hefty hunks of expertly cooked beef dominate, including sirloin, ribeye, fillet and flank, all served with peppercorn, béarnaise or house-made horseradish sauce. Reassuringly, all the cuts are grass-fed and imported from a select group of Argentine producers. Steak not your thing? Fear not, there's a small but impressive selection of such dishes as half a roasted free-range chicken with lemon, or grilled sea bass, prosciutto, tomato and artichoke purée. All the wines are sourced from Argentina and bottles start at £21.95.
Chef/s: Jan Suchanek. **Open:** all week L 12 to 2.30 (3 Sun), D 5.30 to 10.30 (9 Sun). **Closed:** 25 and 26 Dec, bank hols. **Meals:** main courses £14 to £28. **Details:** 37 seats. 6 seats outside. Music.

LOCAL GEM

Ceviche

⊖ Tottenham Court Road, map 5
Peruvian | £24
17 Frith Street, Soho, W1D 4RG
Tel no: (020) 7292 2040
cevicheuk.com

£30

A raft of pisco sours including Shark Ahoy! and Callao Sling keep this colourful Peruvian hot spot on the radar in an area not short of hip eating and drinking establishments. They come for the likes of baby back pork ribs, too, cooked on the open char-grill and lomo saltado (flame-cooked beef with red onions and tomatoes). The eponymous ceviche run to hand-dived scallop and sea bass versions, best enjoyed at the bar counter with a view of the chefs at work. Wines start at £20.

The Chancery

Cooking score: 6
● Chancery Lane, map 5
Modern European | £47
9 Cursitor Street, Holborn, EC4A 1LL
Tel no: (020) 7831 4000
thechancery.co.uk

On a quiet street in the heart of lawyerland, lesser restaurants might flounder, but the Chancery, a long-time purveyor of ambitious, finely wrought cuisine, hits the mark. Since taking the reins in early 2016, head chef Yuma Hashemi has led a refit that has seen stiffer fine-dining accoutrements abandoned for a more casual feel in the two bijou dining rooms, where softer hues and bare tables host a smart crowd of business-lunchers and make for an intimate dinner spot. Whipped homemade butter with sourdough and delicate amuse-bouche set the bar high, followed, perhaps, by lively oyster ceviche, lime and piment d'Espelette (ceviche proving a popular mainstay). Outstanding French technique and exact execution never waver, and the deep richness of wood pigeon with Soleis figs and Jerusalem artichoke or ethereal skrei cod with borscht vegetables continue the delicate season-led fare. 'Chocolate, caramel, mousse' is a riot of textures and flavours, bringing things to a triumphant close. Global wines (from £17.50) range from keenly priced Old World bottles to a top-end 'treasury' selection.
Chef/s: Yuma Hashemi. **Open:** Mon to Fri L 12 to 3, Mon to Sat D 6 to 11. **Closed:** Sun, 23 Dec to 4 Jan, bank hols. **Meals:** set L and D £40 (2 courses) to £47. Tasting menu £68 (6 courses). **Details:** 55 seats. 14 seats outside. Bar. Music.

Chiltern Firehouse

Cooking score: 5
● Baker Street, Bond Street, map 6
Modern American | £70
1 Chiltern Street, Marylebone, W1U 7PA
Tel no: (020) 7073 7676
chilternfirehouse.com

This transformation of a listed Victorian fire station into a luxury hotel and restaurant comes with enormous swagger. The ultra-cool dining room with its mix of unyielding surfaces, pillars and dangling lights can seem crowded and hard-edged, but it hasn't wanted for custom since it opened in 2014 and 'is still fun and buzzy'. Nuno Mendes' inspired cooking is at its heart, and he delivers good renditions of modern American classics – bacon cornbread with chipotle-maple butter, steak tartare, Caesar salad with crispy chicken skin, key lime pie – alongside more contemporary ideas such as smoked eel with turnip, pickled onion and eel broth, and Ibérico pork with broken rice porridge, wild garlic and cuttlefish. Most dishes work well, although the sheer pace and turnover of the place may occasionally cause mishaps and prices are on the high side for what is offered. On the other hand, the welcome is generally warmer than usual for such a high-profile London destination. The wine list opens at £22.
Chef/s: Nuno Mendes and Patrick Powell. **Open:** all week L 12 to 2.30 (3 Thur and Fri, 11 Sat and Sun), D 5.30 to 10.30 (6 Thur to Sun). **Meals:** main courses £19 to £42. **Details:** 120 seats. 80 seats outside. Bar. Wheelchairs. Music.

China Tang at the Dorchester

Cooking score: 2
⊖ Hyde Park Corner, map 6
Chinese | £80
The Dorchester Hotel, 53 Park Lane, Hyde Park, W1K 1QA
Tel no: (020) 7629 9988
chinatanglondon.co.uk

The appeal of China Tang has always been a little bemusing. Conceived by Hong Kong academic-turned-entrepreneur Sir David Tang, a lacquered and gilded vision of Shanghai between the wars is conjured within the confines of the Dorchester, with contemporary Chinese art and shelves of books to boot. Some criticise what can be a feeling of corporate blandness in the renditions of Cantonese and Szechuanese cuisine – the roaring fire of the latter often feels partly extinguished – but then a reporter claims the kitchen turns out 'surely the finest noodles to be found in central London'. There's a challenge. Look to scallops steamed on the half-shell with shredded garlic and vermicelli, or black bean beef in rice noodles, for the evidence. Congee with pork and century eggs has the ring of authenticity, as does abalone in fried rice. Finish with beautifully presented sago in coconut milk, garnished with fried taro, pomegranate and melon. Wines begin at £29.
Chef/s: Chun Chong Fong. **Open:** all week 12 to 11.30. **Closed:** 24 and 25 Dec. **Meals:** main courses £14 to £68. Set L £30. Set D £75. **Details:** 120 seats. Bar. Wheelchairs. Music. Children over 5 yrs only after 7.30pm.

Chutney Mary

Cooking score: 5
⊖ Green Park, map 5
Indian | £45
73 St James's Street, Mayfair, SW1A 1PH
Tel no: (020) 7629 6688
chutneymary.com

Comfortably embedded within the Mayfair premises that were once home to Wheeler's, Chutney Mary looks positively radiant – a glamorous picture complete with lavish upholstery, flamboyant wallpaper, artefacts and soft, flattering illumination. The kitchen is on song, too, delivering a forward-thinking take on Indian cuisine that makes room for influences from across the gastronomic spectrum. A glance at the fascinating line-up of small plates reveals familiarity as well as startling invention – witness lobster chilli fry with mango salad or tandoori foie gras with fig chutney alongside vegetable samosas and Goan crab cakes. After that, slow-cooked curries and grills (served with papaya pickle) are the mainstays – perhaps kid gosht biryani simmered in a sealed brass pot with fragrant saffron and Himalayan screw-pine flower or duck 'jardaloo' with apricots, chilli, jaggery and ginger. Fastidious extras also elevate the cooking to another level, from aged basmati rice and gluten-free roti to sides of mustard leaves with sorrel and butter, and imaginatively chosen wines (from £28) chime perfectly with the food.
Chef/s: Manav Tulli and Uday Salunkhe. **Open:** Mon to Sat L 12 to 2.15 (12.30 to 2.45 Sat), D 6 to 10.30. **Closed:** Sun. **Meals:** main courses £17 to £39. Set L £26 (2 courses) to £30. **Details:** 110 seats. Bar. Wheelchairs.

Ciao Bella
⊖ **Holborn, Russell Square, map 5**
Italian | £28
86-90 Lamb's Conduit Street, Bloomsbury,
WC1N 3LZ
Tel no: (020) 7242 4119
ciaobellarestaurant.co.uk

£30

That this unassuming Italian joint is an off-duty hangout for so many of London's top chefs might explain why it seldom makes 'best restaurant' lists – they want to keep it to themselves. Rustic food served generously is the score, with pasta the main draw: seafood spaghetti in a bag is a show stopper. Expect it to be heaving and make a reservation (opt for the ground floor; the windowless basement is a touch bleak). Easy on the wallet, you'll have ample change for a digestif in the pub next door. Wines from £14.

Cigala
Cooking score: 1
⊖ **Holborn, Russell Square, map 5**
Spanish | £34
54 Lamb's Conduit Street, Bloomsbury,
WC1N 3LW
Tel no: (020) 7405 1717
cigala.co.uk

This spacious corner-site restaurant is a find if you are a fan of classic Spanish dishes. Not the heavy, unsubtle cooking of the Spanish old school, but light, vervy assemblies of very fresh, first-rate ingredients such as grilled homemade chorizo with fried breadcrumbs, peppers and cumin, and fried chicken livers with softened onions and Pedro Ximénez. Elsewhere, there are old favourites along the lines of charcuterie, Spanish omelette and gambas al ajillo, but it is worth making room for heartier dishes such as seafood or chicken paella, arroz negro and lamb stew with honey, shallots and white wine sauce with a celeriac mash. The Spanish wine list starts at £18.50.

Chef/s: Clayton Felizari. **Open:** all week 12 to 10.45 (12.30 Sat, 12.30 to 9.45 Sun). **Closed:** 25 and 26 Dec, 1 Jan. **Meals:** main courses £14 to £21. Set L £19 (2 courses) to £22. Set D £25 (2 courses) to £28. Sun L £19. **Details:** 65 seats. 32 seats outside.

Cinnamon Club
Cooking score: 5
⊖ **Westminster, map 5**
Indian | £55
30-32 Great Smith Street, Westminster,
SW1P 3BU
Tel no: (020) 7222 2555
cinnamonclub.com

£5
OFF

'It's not obvious, but thanks to my trusty Google Maps buzzing, I looked closer and saw the sign on a stand by the door.' With Westminster Public Library carved above the arched entrance, it's easy to assume that Cinnamon Club is the library of its former life, but once inside, the rather grand, book-lined room is posh, worldly and newly revitalised since Ranjit Singh Boparan acquired the restaurant – think cool colours and expensive trappings. Chef Vivek Singh remains, conjuring up creative ideas and scintillating flavours for a smart crowd. Spiced herring roe on toasted cumin brioche, and tandoori breast of Anjou squab pigeon, tawa mince of legs and black stone flower reduction are typical of his style, and gold-star service helps to justify the high prices – although the set lunch is seriously good value. A subtly flavoured saffron and sandalwood chicken tikka with mango mint sauce and a cucumber and mint raita almost merit the visit alone; similarly a home-style curry of Kentish lamb leg with ghee rice, a warm, hearty Bengali dish: 'I was unexpectedly transported back to India, it reminded me of the home cooking I had enjoyed during my time there.' Wines from £22.
Chef/s: Vivek Singh. **Open:** Mon to Sat L 12 to 2.45, D 6 to 10.45. **Closed:** Sun, 26 Dec, 1 Jan.
Meals: main courses £16 to £34. Set L and D £22 (2 courses) to £24. **Details:** 250 seats. Bar.

Cinnamon Soho

Cooking score: 3
⊖ Oxford Circus, map 5
Indian | £25
5 Kingly Street, Soho, W1B 5PF
Tel no: (020) 7437 1664
cinnamonsoho.com
£30

Vivek Singh's knowing Indian fusion food is translated to Soho and its prevailing small-plates ethos at this casual branch of the three-strong chain (expect more to follow). Dark and minimally attired on both ground floor and basement levels, the place is formal enough for ties-off working lunches, but the staff are equally accommodating to single shoppers. The menu is similarly catch-all. Start, perhaps, with freshly fried crab and curry-leaf balls, then opt for further snacks or go the three-course route with the likes of rich, spicy ox cheek stew with masala mash. Perfectly weighted naans and creamy dhal show the kitchen also excels at the basics. At inspection, only a Chinese-like stir-fried vegetable side dish was a fusion too far. Pudding, in contrast, showed mastery of the genre: intense chocolate tart, its bitter notes coaxed out by cumin. Indian afternoon tea adds another dimension to this useful spot. Wine from £20.
Chef/s: Vivek Singh. **Open:** Sun L 12 to 4, Mon to Sat 11 to 11. **Closed:** 1 and 2 Jan. **Meals:** small plates £5 to £16. **Details:** 75 seats. 22 seats outside. Music.

Clos Maggiore

Cooking score: 3
⊖ Covent Garden, map 5
French | £55
33 King Street, Covent Garden, WC2E 8JD
Tel no: (020) 7379 9696
closmaggiore.com
🍾

The most covetable part of Clos Maggiore is the conservatory room, where climbing foliage envelops the overhead space, a log fire burns and little spotlights gleam, but most of

it is fairly lovely. A winged pig oversees proceedings in another room, while gilded baubles and framed cartoons adorn the walls. In these cocooning surroundings, the classical French food is rich and soothing, and has the patina of long endeavour, Marcellin Marc having been here nigh on 20 years. Expect Burgundy-braised hare to start things off, or perhaps crab in smoked anchovy mayonnaise, before the big guns are wheeled out for mains like whole corn-fed chicken stuffed with a mousseline of morteau sausage and ceps in a sauce dotted with Alsace bacon. Desserts ply a more new-fangled line for goat's milk and tonka pudding, or Pink Lady apple fondant with Granny Smith and yuzu sorbet. A gargantuan wine list is ably and thoughtfully compiled, with quality the watchword, and there is genuine choice at the affordable end, starting at £20.
Chef/s: Marcellin Marc. **Open:** all week L 12 to 2.30, D 5 to 11 (10 Sun). **Closed:** 24 and 25 Dec. **Meals:** main courses £18 to £33. Set L and D £25 (2 courses) to £30. Sun L £30. Tasting menu £55 (5 courses). **Details:** 70 seats. V menu. Music. Children at L only.

The Colony Grill Room

Cooking score: 3
⊖ Bond Street, map 6
North American | £50
The Beaumont, 8 Balderton Street, Brown Hart Gardens, Mayfair, W1K 6TF
Tel no: (020) 7499 9499
colonygrillroom.com
🛏

When it comes to giving people what they want, Chris Corbin and Jeremy King know a thing or two. They certainly nailed all-day dining when they opened The Wolseley (see entry) some 14 years ago, and subsequent riffs on European cafés and Parisian brasseries all play to a packed house. The Colony Grill Room on the ground floor of the Art Deco Beaumont hotel is no exception, offering grown-up glamour all day. The room (dark wood, red leather and soft lighting), is seductive, its American-themed dining

delivering classics such as lobster rolls, New York strip steak tagliata, buttermilk fried chicken and Caesar salad, not forgetting pancakes, French toast and corned beef hash for breakfast. There are British flavours (shepherd's pie, dressed Weymouth crab), a few French interlopers (rognons de veau, pommes purée) and the chance to build your own sundae should pistachio and cherry baked Alaska not appeal. Wines from £24.
Chef/s: Christian Turner. **Open:** all week 7am to 11.30pm (10.30pm Sun). **Meals:** main courses £9 to £40. **Details:** 100 seats. Bar. Wheelchairs. Music.

Copita
Cooking score: 3
⊖ Oxford Circus, Tottenham Court Rd, map 5
Spanish | £23
27 d'Arblay Street, Soho, W1F 8EP
Tel no: (020) 7287 7797
copita.co.uk

Competition is fierce in the bustling streets of Soho, but this 'really sharp' tapas joint more than holds its own. It's a small, cramped space but easy-going staff keep everything chilled and the place is custom-built for grazing. Well-sourced produce and unfussy execution are typical of the Copita style, trademarks include excellent charcuterie and cheeses, and tapas classics are given an update – octopus comes with mashed potato and smoked paprika, sweet potato is teamed with bravas sauce, aïoli and peanuts. Otherwise, there could be duck egg with butter beans, spinach and dried tomato, cured sardines with black olive and quince, empanadillas of sobrasada, peppered beef onglet with piquillo and pepper, and pork jowl with rosemary onion and cane molasses. When it comes to dessert, few can resist the churros with chocolate. Spanish to the end, sherry from peerless producers vies with a taut list of astutely assembled wines (from £24), and there's plenty by the glass, too.

Chef/s: Khowma Ngedhi. **Open:** Mon to Fri L 12 to 4, D 5.30 to 10.30. Sat 1 to 10.30. **Closed:** Sun, 24 Dec to 1 Jan, bank hols. **Meals:** tapas £12 to £28. **Details:** 38 seats. 7 seats outside. Music.

Corrigan's Mayfair
Cooking score: 4
⊖ Marble Arch, map 6
Modern British | £52
28 Upper Grosvenor Street, Mayfair, W1K 7EH
Tel no: (020) 7499 9943
corrigansmayfair.com

The spacious room is understated but striking, with large photographic prints punctuating the window side, light fittings strung on chains and handsome grey leather upholstery ensuring comfort. That last could equally be said of Richard Corrigan's culinary approach, which has always showcased down-to-earth traditional Irish and British ingredients, but presented them with modern panache. Alan Barrins heads a kitchen that turns out confident, robust flavours such as black pudding hash and apple as partners to smoked eel, or mingles sugar snaps and pickled rhubarb into lobster salad. An extensive main-course repertoire looks to sea and land for offerings such as whole Dover sole in brown shrimp meunière, roast rabbit saddle with wild leeks and spinach, or breast and confit leg of duck in soubise. Speculative Asian notes are creeping in here and there, including in desserts such as Alphonso mango with lemongrass and lime, although the farmhouse cheeses uphold the Anglo-Irish guiding principle. Wines arranged largely by style start at £35.
Chef/s: Alan Barrins. **Open:** Sun to Fri L 12 to 3 (4 Sun), Mon to Sat D 6 to 10. **Closed:** 25 to 30 Dec. **Meals:** main courses £16 to £42. Set L £25 (2 courses) to £29. Sunday L £39. **Details:** 85 seats. Wheelchairs. Music.

Dabbous

Cooking score: 6
⊖ Goodge Street, map 5
Modern European | £36
39 Whitfield Street, Fitzrovia, W1T 2SF
Tel no: (020) 7323 1544
dabbous.co.uk

Ollie Dabbous blazed a trail when he opened this stark, brutalist dining room with its naked light bulbs, industrial piping, concrete, mesh-work and metal. The ideology was simple: stripped-bare interiors and stripped-back prices combined with fashionably arty but deceptively simple food – all driven by the seasons and garlanded with meadow-fresh wild pickings. From the home-baked seeded sourdough bread to the tiny servings of iced sorrel and the 'pipe tobacco' chocolates, this is sensational stuff – delicate and invigorating, if occasionally bewildering. Dabbous might present you with a bowl of primitive acorn noodles bathed in fenugreek and honey broth, or grilled langoustines sprinkled with stardust (well, fennel pollen actually) or even a robust plate of barbecued pork jowl seasoned with juniper, caraway and seaweed, before sending you into raptures with his cherry blossom teacake and vanilla cream. If you missed out on a booking, head downstairs to Oskar's bar for a few tasters from the main menu plus a roll call of showbiz-themed cocktails. A substantial wine list helpfully offers plenty by the glass or carafe, with bottles from £25. **Chef/s:** Ollie Dabbous. **Open:** Mon to Sat L 12 to 2.30, D 6 to 9.30. **Closed:** Sun, 23 Dec to 2 Jan, Easter. **Meals:** main courses £16 to £27. Set L £28 to £35 (4 courses). Set D £59 (4 courses). Tasting menu £69 (7 courses). **Details:** 38 seats. V menu. Bar. Music.

Symbols

🛏 Accommodation is available
£30 Three courses for less than £30
£5 OFF £5-off voucher scheme
🍾 Notable wine list

Dean Street Townhouse

Cooking score: 2
⊖ Tottenham Court Road, map 5
Modern British | £40
69-71 Dean Street, Soho, W1D 3SE
Tel no: (020) 7434 1775
deanstreettownhouse.com

🛏

Behind the Georgian façade, this all-day restaurant can, at busy times, feel like a high-decibel gentlemen's club with its clattery wood floor, red leather, long, stool-lined bar and walls covered with artwork. From breakfast at 7am, via the afternoon tea set to the post-theatre crowd still teeming in after 11pm, the day is a long one. Invariably packed (booking is essential), this is where to come for straight-talking British dishes you can eat every day – twice-baked smoked haddock soufflé, Devonshire crab tart, roast Banham chicken with chipolatas and sage stuffing, sea trout with Scottish mussels and samphire – and that bestseller, mince and potatoes. Sunday roasts have been praised, and straightforward desserts run along the lines of Trinity burnt cream and rice pudding with poached rhubarb. While everyone agrees portions are generous, one grumble is that service is sometimes skew-whiff. Wines from £23. **Chef/s:** Jason Loy. **Open:** all week 7am to midnight (1am Fri, 8am to 1am Sat, 8am to 11pm Sun). **Meals:** main courses £7 to £35. Set D £17 (2 courses) to £20 to £23. Sun L £25 (2 courses) to £30. **Details:** 120 seats. 22 seats outside. Bar. Wheelchairs. Music.

Dehesa

Cooking score: 2
⊖ Oxford Circus, map 5
Spanish/Italian | £35
25 Ganton Street, Oxford Circus, W1F 9BP
Tel no: (020) 7494 4170
dehesa.co.uk

Small plates are proliferating like nobody's business, and you can't turn a corner in the capital now without finding yourself outside

another tapas joint. But it's business as usual for Dehesa (part of the Salt Yard group), which continues quietly serving up smart hybrids of Spanish/Italian tapas from its plum Soho spot. The bijou space is well thought out, with plenty of terrace tables and stools at the windows for people-watching. Pig is the main draw here – top-drawer Ibérico ham, carved to order – and heaven forbid the courgette flower stuffed with goats' cheese and drizzled with honey is ever dropped from the menu. The repertoire takes in far more than your typical porcine treats and tapas classics, however, and spinach and basil risotto with Cornish crab and pickled Jerusalem artichokes, or char-grilled Ibérico presa with caramelised kohlrabi sees the kitchen really flexing its muscles. An affogato with Moscatel raisin and Pedro Ximénez ice cream rounds things off nicely. Italian and Spanish wines from £20.
Chef/s: Ben Tish. **Open:** Mon to Fri L 12 to 3, D 5 to 11. Sat and Sun 10am to 11pm (10pm Sun). **Meals:** tapas £4 to £12. **Details:** 54 seats. 42 seats outside. Bar. Music.

The Delaunay
Cooking score: 3
⊖ Temple, map 5
Modern European | £37
55 Aldwych, Covent Garden, WC2B 4BB
Tel no: (020) 7499 8558
thedelaunay.com

Serial restaurateurs Chris Corbin and Jeremy King have perfected the 'grand Euro café' concept in London with a string of high-profile all-day venues named after vintage automobiles (The Wolseley, Brasserie Zédel et al). Following the blueprint to a T, this Covent Garden outlet lures the crowds with its strikingly handsome interiors (marble floors, polished brass, leather banquettes), cosmopolitan buzz, zippy service and eminently satisfying food. Winning breakfasts promise everything from gorgeous home-baked viennoiserie to rösti with fried eggs, but you can also drop in for a mid-morning bagel or arrive later for something more substantial.

The menu is all about nostalgic European cuisine, moving confidently from eggs Benedict and steak tartare to gallantly unreformed renditions of pork goulash with spätzle, chicken Kiev and kedgeree – plus schnitzels, würstchen galore and flamboyant displays of patisserie (perfect for afternoon tea with a glass of bubbly). Creditable European wines start at £22.50.
Chef/s: Malachi O'Gallagher. **Open:** all week 11.30am to midnight (11pm Sun). **Closed:** 25 and 26 Dec. **Meals:** main courses £12 to £33. **Details:** 185 seats. V menu. Bar. Wheelchairs.

Dinings
Cooking score: 3
⊖ Marylebone, map 6
Japanese | £50
22 Harcourt Street, Marylebone, W1H 4HH
Tel no: (020) 7723 0666
dinings.co.uk

Dinings promises contemporary Japanese cuisine in a very modest package – in this case a tiny ground-floor sushi bar and a 16-seater basement dining room where a concrete floor, low ceiling, tight-packed tables and hard bottomed chairs mean you are definitely here for the food. Fortunately, there is much to catch the eye on the menu: the absorption of non-Japanese ingredients being almost seamlessly achieved and presented as hot or cold tapas. A simple collection of vegetables with a spicy citrus dressing that zings with freshness, for example, or sea bass carpaccio with fresh summer truffle and ponzu jelly, or braised Wagyu beef 'char-siu' bun, even the lunchtime donburi (rice bowls) include freshwater eel and foie gras, as well as an excellent Edo-mae-style assorted tempura. Come here, too, for sushi and sashimi, where everything hinges on supreme freshness and scalpel-sharp precision, whether the subject is turbot, sea bass, yellowtail, salmon or one of many cuts of tuna. Wines from £15.60.
Chef/s: Masaki Sugisaki. **Open:** all week L 12 to 4, D 6 to 10.30 (11 Fri and Sat, 10 Sun). **Closed:** 2 weeks Christmas. **Meals:** tapas £7 to £29. Sushi and sashimi £4 to £9. **Details:** 28 seats. Music.

Dishoom

Cooking score: 2
⊖ Leicester Square, Covent Garden, map 5
Indian | £30
12 Upper St Martin's Lane, Covent Garden,
WC2H 9FB
Tel no: (020) 7420 9320
dishoom.com

A slice of old Mumbai street life transported to Upper St Martin's Lane, this all-day café (with siblings in Shoreditch, King's Cross – see entries – and now 22 Kingly Street) has struck such a chord with its many fans that it is best to book when you can to avoid joining the inevitable queue – you're fine before 5.45pm, after that only six or more may book. Every detail has been nailed here, from the paddle fans on the ceiling, via the photos of Bollywood stars and close-packed tables, to the open kitchen, which serves up some of the most authentic Indian food in central London. The day begins with breakfast (bacon naan, with chilli jam and soft cheese, perhaps); after that expect plenty of sharing plates including the signature house black dhal, lamb biryani, chicken ruby curry, the spicy lamb chops, char-grilled prawns and pav bhaji (mashed vegetables with a hot-buttered pav bun). Most customers skip the short wine list (from £19.90) in favour of cocktails or beer.
Chef/s: Naved Nasir. **Open:** all week 12 to 11 (12 to 12 Fri and Sat). **Closed:** 25 and 26 Dec, 1 and 2 Jan. **Meals:** main courses £6 to £17. **Details:** 140 seats. 18 seats outside. Bar. Wheelchairs. Music.

Donostia

Cooking score: 3
⊖ Marble Arch, map 6
Spanish | £30
10 Seymour Place, Marylebone, W1H 7ND
Tel no: (020) 3620 1845
donostia.co.uk

Away from the crowds in nearby Oxford Street, Seymour Place is a calm oasis by comparison. With its chic, minimalist décor of pristine white walls, arty planks of wood and

open kitchen with a marble counter, Donostia offers up impressive plates of Basque tapas and pintxos. Such is its success, a sister restaurant, Lurra, a Basque grill, has opened up opposite (see entry). Here at the original, expect keen service and classy plates with both classic and modern leanings. The mini Wagyu beef burger reflects the exciting goings on in places like San Sebastián, or keep it traditional and go for crispy croquetas or plates of high-quality charcuterie (the stonking Cinco Jotas jamón Ibérico, say). Monkfish with black rice and lamb cutlets with parsnip purée warrant repeat orders, and, among sweet courses, try the traditional torrija with mint ice cream. The wine list includes interesting stuff from northern Spain; bottles from £20.
Chef/s: Damian Surowiec. **Open:** Tue to Sat L 12.30 to 3, all week D 6 to 10.30 (5 to 9 Sun). **Closed:** 24 to 29 Dec. **Meals:** tapas £8 to £15. **Details:** 42 seats. 8 seats outside. Music.

Ember Yard

Cooking score: 4
⊖ Tottenham Court Road, map 5
Modern European | £25
60 Berwick Street, Soho, W1F 8SU
Tel no: (020) 7439 8057
emberyard.co.uk
🍷 £30

All four of Simon Mullins and Ben Tish's enterprising tapas bars (Salt Yard, Dehesa, Opera Tavern – see entries) have a common style – small plates of Spanish and Italian tapas, including the signature courgette flower stuffed with goats' cheese and drizzled with honey – but each has its own identity. At Ember Yard the hustle and bustle and general informality of the place are all part of the appeal – grab a basement kitchen table for a close-up of the action – while cooking over charcoal makes the most of properly sourced ingredients. Charcoal-smoked dishes that have impressed include Ibérico presa with whipped jamón butter, salmon with caramelised cauliflower and agretti, and octopus with peas, smoked tomato and wild garlic, but other hits have included plates of

Spanish charcuterie, grilled flatbread with honey, thyme and smoked butter, and smoked chocolate cake with cherries, star anise and mascarpone. Wines from £22.
Chef/s: Jacques Fourie. **Open:** Mon to Fri L 12 to 3, D 5 to 11 (12 Thur and Fri). Sat and Sun 11am to midnight (10pm Sun). **Meals:** tapas £8 to £30.
Details: 110 seats. Bar. Music.

★ TOP 50 ★

Fera at Claridges
Cooking score: 8
⊖ Bond Street, map 5
Modern British | £68
49 Brook Street, Mayfair, W1K 4HR
Tel no: (020) 7107 8888
feraatclaridges.co.uk

🍷 🛏

A lovely Mayfair hotel, with chequerboard floors and crystal chandeliers that might just be about to whisk you back to the world of Jeeves and Wooster, when here comes Simon Rogan to set the time machine back on fast forward. From sleepy Cartmel to the pulsing heart of London's West End is a stretch that has, if such a thing were possible, invigorated Rogan's culinary practice anew. Half a dozen willing guinea pigs might take the table in Aulis (the private dining room) on any of three nights a week, and be treated to menu dishes in development. Otherwise, settle in the stone- and taupe-hued dining room to a multi-course tasting menu that proceeds in batches of dishes. A raw scallop with ink-simmered salsify in whey and verjus; cured veal in kohlrabi wrap; crabmeat in rhubarb sauce with goat's yoghurt; and Fowey mussels with hispi in pale ale completed the preliminary rounds on a spring evening. Among mains, Cornish lamb is properly tender and well supported by roast chicory, turnip discs and puréed cime di rapa, or there could be roe deer with caramelised cauliflower and smoked beetroot, as well as halibut in pork fat with butternut and spinach. It may be conceded that, amid such energetic heterogeneity, not everything is as good as everything else, but the hits are legion, not

forgetting a dessert of sheep's milk yoghurt mousse, rapeseed cake, honey, juniper and tarragon sorbet. The wine list puts its best foot forward as it strides confidently out into the world, ably shepherded by a friendly sommelier, but at mark-ups that take no prisoners. Start at £34, or £9 a glass.
Chef/s: Simon Rogan. **Open:** all week L 12 to 2, D 6.30 to 10. **Meals:** main courses £25 to £38. Set L £39. Tasting menu £75 (7 courses) to £110.
Details: 97 seats. Bar. Wheelchairs. Parking.

Fischer's
Cooking score: 2
⊖ Baker Street, Regent's Park, map 6
Austrian | £40
50 Marylebone High Street, Marylebone, W1U 5HN
Tel no: (020) 7466 5501
fischers.co.uk

'Hats off to Corbin and King for continuing to maintain high standards despite the expansion of the group,' enthused one recent visitor, adding that 'the restaurant was rammed and yet the service never dropped the ball'. This Marylebone branch reinforces the owners' fondness for the cafés of Vienna. There's a timeless elegance to the room (dark-wood panelling, black leather banquettes, wall-to-wall paintings) and a wonderful atmosphere – it's all about enjoying food and company. The menu offers renditions of Austrian cooking – käsespätzle and würstchen (sausages) are worth a punt – but less calorific options are equal to the task. At inspection, beetroot-cured salmon with horseradish cream arrived with Nordic bread, and was followed by accurately timed sea bass with a delightfully crispy skin, Jerusalem artichoke, mushrooms and a white onion purée. From an irresistible selection of Viennese patisserie, apple and cinnamon strudel is a winning finale. The largely mittel-European wine list opens at £22.50.
Chef/s: Luis Gonzalez. **Open:** all week 11.30 to 11 (10.30pm Sunday). **Meals:** main courses £13 to £35.
Details: 94 seats. 4 seats outside. V menu. Wheelchairs. Music.

Frenchie

Cooking score: 6
⊖ Leicester Square, Covent Garden, map 5
French | £38
16 Henrietta Steet, Covent Garden,
WC2E 8QH
Tel no: (020) 7836 4422
frenchiecoventgarden.com
£5
OFF

Such is the strength and individuality of the
London restaurant scene that it's becoming a
hard nut to crack for those not completely
switched on to its way of thinking – the short-
lived Parisian import Le Chabanais is a case in
point. But Frenchie is different. This Parisian
spin-off has proved a big hit partly because
chef-proprietor Gregory Marchand
understands London – he has worked at the
Savoy, Mandarin Oriental and Fifteen for
Jamie Oliver (where he got the Frenchie
moniker). Everything feels right: from the
bold, ultra-modern yet rustic cooking to the
light, contemporary décor, informal
atmosphere and well-timed service. The
simple, uncluttered presentation of dishes
highlights that the sourcing of materials and
seasonality are all: a soft, creamy burrata, for
example, strewn with fresh pea pesto and
pecorino cheese or a rich lamb ragù
pappardelle offset by lemon and Kalamata
olives and espelette pepper. These dishes and
others like them are extraordinarily good
because the ingredients are allowed to speak
quietly. The kitchen seems to be trying to strip
food down to the bare elements of flavour, a
'fabulous chunk of Lincolnshire chicken
breast' is brightened by the sweetness of coffee
sabayon, which is in turn offset by the umami
hit of mushroom purée. Desserts are clever
and innovative, especially the lightest
reworking of that Brit classic, banoffee (pie).
Wines from £28.
Chef/s: Gregory Marchand. **Open:** all week L 12 to
2.15, D 6 to 10.30. **Meals:** main courses £22 to £29.
Set L £22 (2 courses) to £29. Set D £30 (2 courses) to
£45. **Details:** 64 seats. V menu. Wheelchairs. Music.

La Fromagerie

⊖ Baker Street, Bond Street, map 6
Modern European | £32
2-6 Moxon Street, Marylebone, W1U 4EW
Tel no: (020) 7935 0341
lafromagerie.co.uk

Patricia Michelson's deli/café has a display of
European cheeses that is second to none in the
capital (plus some from further afield), and if
you're a fan, the chilly cheeseroom is
intoxicating. Grab a place at the communal
table in the shop or settle into a banquette in
the café (which occupies No.6) and expect a
daily-changing menu of cheese and
charcuterie plates, and hot stuff like sea bass
with calico artichokes and braised fennel.
Wines start at £22.30.

Galvin at Windows

Cooking score: 6
⊖ Hyde Park Corner, Green Park, map 6
French | £75
Hilton Hotel, 22 Park Lane, Mayfair, W1K 1BE
Tel no: (020) 7208 4021
galvinatwindows.com

London in its many moods – now laid out in
high-definition focus all the way to Wembley
Stadium arch, now dissolved into skyscraping
hulks softened in Monet mist – is rarely more
invigoratingly enjoyed than from a great
height, as from the 28th-floor wraparound
views in Chris Galvin's dining room at the
Park Lane Hilton. The Galvin menus,
elaborated with technical dazzle by Joo Won,
fully live up to the surroundings in a context
where culinary kitsch could so easily prevail.
Modernist French accents furnish seared
yellowfin tuna and Aquitaine caviar in
grapefruit and soy, or confit duck leg with
gratinated gesiers (gizzards), mushroom
ragoût and pancetta in prune jus with their
glossy cachet, but the more traditional dishes
impress, too. A serving of brandade in lemon
and paprika vinaigrette, or hake in shellfish
broth, are equally carefully considered. Throw

tradition to the winds for desserts such as nougat parfait with banana, muscovado meringues and black pepper ice cream. A superfine wine list for high-rollers, rich in French classics, opens at £28.

Chef/s: Joo Won. **Open:** Sun to Fri L 12 to 2.30 (3 Sun), Mon to Sat D 6 to 10 (10.30 Thur to Sat). **Meals:** set L £28 (2 courses) to £33. Set D £60 (2 courses) to £75. Sun L £50. Tasting menu £110. **Details:** 109 seats. Bar. Wheelchairs. Parking.

Galvin Bistrot de Luxe

Cooking score: 4
θ Baker Street, map 6
French | £39
66 Baker Street, Marylebone, W1U 7DJ
Tel no: (020) 7935 4007
galvinrestaurants.com

Ten years on, standards remain high at the original operation from the Galvin brothers, long-time purveyors of accomplished Gallic fare across the capital and beyond. Its dark wood and leather furnishings, with copper pans glistening from the kitchen at the back, render you gratefully oblivious – as you sip from a bowl of lobster bisque – to the distinctly non-Parisian thoroughfare outside. Familiar bistro classics (steak tartare, escargots, cassoulet) are their calling card, with meticulous sourcing setting them apart from the competition: a plat du jour of soft, rich Denham venison ragù with gnocchi being a fine example, though roast leg of Herdwick lamb with kashke bademjan (a Persian aubergine dip) adds a welcome progressive note. Be persuaded, with a wink and a nudge, to opt for their signature (and faultless) tarte Tatin to finish, and don't keep the remarkably good-value prix fixe to yourself. The Francophile wine list, starting at £21.50 for a robust yet refreshing Gascony white, offers helpful tasting notes and a generous range by the glass.

Chef/s: Chris Galvin and Tom Duffill. **Open:** all week L 12 to 2.30 (3 Sun), D 6 to 10.30 (11 Thur to Sat, 9.30 Sun). **Closed:** 25 and 26 Dec, 1 Jan. **Meals:** main courses £17 to £32. Set L £22. Set D £24. **Details:** 128 seats. 12 seats outside. Bar. Music.

Gauthier Soho

Cooking score: 6
θ Leicester Square, map 5
Modern French | £45
21 Romilly Street, Soho, W1D 5AF
Tel no: (020) 7494 3111
gauthiersoho.co.uk
£5 OFF

'Always a reliable haven of first-class French cooking,' was the verdict of one regular to this well-appointed restaurant in a modest early Georgian terraced house. A solid black front door bars entry until one rings the bell – an action that can induce a feeling of well-being, for this is 'like dining in a friend's house, except the tables are well spaced'. Alexis Gauthier's finely honed contemporary French cuisine, evidenced by an 'extraordinarily good' chanterelle and morel concoction in the 'thinnest, buttery crisp puff pastry' with almond and mushroom purée and Parmesan velouté, is rich with classic combinations. Dishes are built from strong seasonal, often unexpected, flavours – autumn producing a fine, meaty breast of red-legged partridge, stuffed Savoy cabbage, roast celeriac and Bramley apple, and an excellent jus reduction, and late winter bringing Anjou pigeon, again with its 'glorious sticky jus', and chopped heart and liver on crisp, buttery croûton, or halibut baked with sweet lemon and olive oil served with fondant fennel and confit tomato. Among desserts, the signature Golden Louis XV (dark chocolate mousse and crunchy praline) continues to impress reporters. A superb exploration of France has always been one of the glories of the wine list, but there's room for a few tasty interlopers from wine-growing regions elsewhere. Bottles from £28.

Chef/s: Alexis Gauthier and Gerard Virolle. **Open:** Tue to Sat L 12 to 2.30, D 6.30 to 10 (9.30 Tue to Thur, 10.30 Fri and Sat). **Closed:** Sun, Mon, 25 and 26 Dec, bank hols. **Meals:** set L £18 (2 courses) to £25. Set D £45 to £65 (5 courses). Tasting menu £75 (8 courses). **Details:** 45 seats. Children over 8 yrs only.

★ TOP 50 ★

Le Gavroche

Cooking score: 8
θ Marble Arch, map 6
French | £120
43 Upper Brook Street, Mayfair, W1K 7QR
Tel no: (020) 7408 0881
le-gavroche.co.uk
🍾

In a rare sop to modernity, Le Gavroche recently introduced a five-day week, so that staff could get a proper break. Otherwise, this dynastic bastion of French finesse continues to glide along regally in all its *ancien régime* finery – the restaurant will celebrate its 50th birthday in 2017. Readers come here to be 'seduced into an evening of out-and-out hedonism' and to soak up the dark exclusivity of the cocooned basement dining room while dutifully professional staff 'induce just the right feeling of proper enjoyment'. From the 'super-light' soufflé suissesse with its 'cheesy double-cream background' to the last spoonful of spiced pistachio and chocolate cake with rum-soaked dried fruits, Michel Roux and his team pay homage to the glories of haute cuisine. Bewitching displays of gastronomic artistry have delivered: venison carpaccio with horseradish cream, pickled beetroot and 'venison-impregnated' toasted rye bread; 'overwhelmingly pure-tasting' scallops with velvety Chartreuse velouté and a scattering of coral crumbs; 'utterly flavoursome' boudin noir in company with a poached quail's egg, crispy mushroom ravioli and red cabbage relish. Even something as simple as beef cheek braised in red wine is raised to unexpected heights, while the abundant cheese trolley yields many extraordinary items (note the exceedingly rare five-year-old Davidstow Cheddar). Speaking of vintages, the wine list is a veritable encyclopaedia dedicated to the triumphs of viticulture, with a huge contingent of French masters but sufficient breadth and depth to suit those with different palates. Prices soar skywards from £30.

Chef/s: Rachel Humphrey and Michel Roux Jr. **Open:** Tue to Fri L 12 to 2, Tue to Sat D 6 to 10. **Closed:** Sun, Mon, 2 weeks Christmas and New Year, Easter, bank hols. **Meals:** main courses £27 to £61. Set L £56. Tasting menu £126. **Details:** 70 seats. V menu. Bar. Wheelchairs.

Great Queen Street

Cooking score: 3
θ Covent Garden, map 5
Modern British | £28
32 Great Queen Street, Covent Garden, WC2B 5AA
Tel no: (020) 7242 0622
greatqueenstreetrestaurant.co.uk
£30

Opposite the grand Masonic lodge, which played MI5 headquarters in *Spooks*, Great Queen Street is rather less grandiose, but fits the bill for lively, get-stuck-in superior pub dining, like its older sibling the Anchor & Hope (see entry). The range of menus includes a top-value 'Worker's Lunch' that even non-proletarians should enjoy, and the bulk of Sam Hutchins' production is gutsy, often heftily proportioned urban sustenance. A chunky terrine of pork and veal, or cured trout in fennel and orange, could set the scene for a substantial main along the lines of suet-crusted chicken pie with a corncob, or bass for two with cocoa beans, San Marzano tomatoes and aïoli. If your crowd comprises three, consider lamb shoulder braised for seven hours. Tarts of apple or mirabelle plums, or cheesecake topped with damson jam, demand you leave some finishing room. An enterprising wine list starts at £17.

Chef/s: Sam Hutchins. **Open:** all week L 12 to 2.30 (12.30 to 3.30 Sun), Mon to Sat D 6 to 10.30. **Closed:** 25 and 26 Dec, bank hols. **Meals:** main courses £15 to £25. Set L £18 (2 courses) to £20. **Details:** 50 seats. 8 seats outside. Bar. Wheelchairs.

★ TOP 50 ★

The Greenhouse
Cooking score: 7
⊖ Green Park, map 5
Modern European | £95
27a Hay's Mews, Green Park, W1J 5NY
Tel no: (020) 7499 3331
greenhouserestaurant.co.uk

Tucked away at the foot of a tower block in a quiet Mayfair street, this is a destination restaurant where Arnaud Bignon's superb, imaginative cooking, coupled with high levels of thoughtful service, easily compensates for the dull location. A new clientele has usurped the business crowd of previous years – today's high-flyers are often strangers to suits and ties but this is a restaurant worth dressing up for. A small garden with exotic plants, modern sculpture and decking path leads to the front door and inside is airy and spacious with windows on both sides and a sheltered outdoor terrace. Modern European cooking with a touch of the orient, rather than classic French cuisine, includes crab with cauliflower, apple and a hint of curry served in a rich green emulsion or succulent raw scallops marinated ceviche-style in citrus juice with a dusting of crunchy sea urchin. Native lobster arrives warm with featherlight pumpkin ravioli (the 'pasta' made with paper-thin potato slices), and chunks of meaty monkfish use the Egyptian mix of nuts and spices, dukkah, for added flavour and texture. Then there's tender piglet cooked in the tandoor with bitter puntarelle to offset sweet maple syrup. A vast cheeseboard is wheeled ceremoniously through the room, but you may prefer playful desserts such as coconut mousse with coconut sorbet, lime jus and a candied pink bow. The exceptional wine list is in excess of 3,000 bins but staff will guide you, whether you want a single glass, a modest bottle (from £28) or a plutocrat's magnum. **Chef/s:** Arnaud Bignon. **Open:** Mon to Fri L 12 to 2.15, Mon to Sat D 6.30 to 10.15. **Closed:** Sun, 2 weeks Christmas, bank hols. **Meals:** main courses

£35 to £50. Set L £35 (2 courses) to £40. Set D £85 (2 courses) to £95. Tasting menu £110 (6 courses). **Details:** 65 seats. Bar. Wheelchairs.

Gymkhana
Cooking score: 5
⊖ Piccadilly Circus, Green Park, map 5
Indian | £65
42 Albermarle Street, Mayfair, W1S 4JH
Tel no: (020) 3011 5900
gymkhanalondon.com

The Mayfair restaurant of the Sethi family trio (Trishna and Hoppers, see entries) conjures up colonial Indian gymkhana clubs with its rag-rolled walls, languid ceiling fans and mix of dark wood and green leather. Comfortably in tune with its upper-crust W1 postcode, this is not your run-of-the-mill British Indian and you won't find many regular curry-house dishes on the menu. Duck egg bhurjis with lobster and Malabar paratha shows the ambition among first courses. What follows is an intriguing blend of the modern and the classic. Black pepper fish tikka with lasooni tomato chutney, and lamb chops with pickled onion and ginger are served alongside very good renditions of wild boar vindaloo or lamb shank rogan josh. There's sweetness, too, in the shape of blackberry and apple falooda with berry ripple kulfi. In addition, the set lunch is considered very good value, and the wine list has been savvily chosen to match the spicy food. Bottles from £26. **Chef/s:** Rohit Ghai. **Open:** Mon to Sat L 12 to 2.30, D 5.30 to 10.30. **Closed:** Sun, 25 and 26 Dec, 1 Jan. **Meals:** main courses £15 to £38. Set L £25 (2 courses) to £30. Set D £35 (4 courses). **Details:** 90 seats. V menu. Bar. Music. No children after 7pm.

Visit us online

To find out more about
The Good Food Guide, please
visit thegoodfoodguide.co.uk

Hakkasan

Cooking score: 5
⊖ Tottenham Court Road, map 5
Chinese | £65
8 Hanway Place, Fitzrovia, W1T 1HD
Tel no: (020) 7927 7000
hakkasan.com

Tricky to find it may be, but 'when you enter the beautiful labyrinthine underworld that is Hakkasan' you'll find it is a striking oasis amid the drab confines of a small alley linking Oxford Street with Tottenham Court Road. Indeed, with its cosseting womb-like feel and sultry lighting, many prefer this Fitzrovia venue to its brasher Mayfair sibling (see entry). Dim sum continues to generate excited reports from regulars and newcomers alike, with many singling out the good-value dim sum Sunday deal for special praise: 'presentation was beautiful, service was remarkable and the food delicious'. Treats in store from a confident kitchen include steamed scallop shumai dumplings and delicate har gau, as well as salt-and-pepper squid, crispy duck salad with pomelo, pine nut and shallot, stir-fry black pepper ribeye beef with Merlot and the famous grilled Chilean sea bass in honey. Desserts take a European view of things, perhaps a rich jivara hazelnut bomb. There's also plenty of interest in the drinks department from seductive cocktails to a well chosen, if priccy, winc list – though bottles start at £25.
Chef/s: Goh Wee Boon. **Open:** Mon to Sat L 12 to 3.30 (4.30 Sat), D 5.30 to 11.30 (12.30 Thur to Sat). Sun 12 to 11.30. **Closed:** 24 and 25 Dec. **Meals:** main courses £20 to £60. Set L £38. Set D £38 to £128. Sun L £58. **Details:** 200 seats. V menu. Bar. Wheelchairs. Music.

Average price

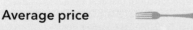

The average price denotes the price of a three-course meal without wine.

Hakkasan Mayfair

Cooking score: 4
⊖ Green Park, Bond Street, map 5
Chinese | £80
17 Bruton Street, Mayfair, W1J 6QB
Tel no: (020) 7907 1888
hakkasan.com

The Hakkasan brand – slinky, sepulchrally lit nightspots with cocktails and premier league Chinese gastronomy – extends across the First World's pleasure grounds, from Vegas to the Emirates to Shanghai. Of its London venues, the Bruton Street branch has the glitzier address. A lightly applied dress code means you will be required to remove your baseball cap once inside. Tong Chee Hwee's Cantonese-based menus bring a high-definition approach to the familiar and the less familiar alike, lighting up salt-and-pepper squid, royal sweetcorn soup and Peking duck with pyrotechnical seasonings, and introducing adventurous palates to stir-fried venison with eryngii mushrooms, baby leeks and dried chilli, or golden-fried silver cod with edamame and pomelo. The vegetarian menus show genuine willingness to please, and are not just all tofu, while the broad range of signature menus caters for all wallets, from pretty well stocked to bulging. Wines are of impeccable pedigree and pneumatic mark-ups, starting at £34.40 for a dry Mosel Riesling that perfectly suits the food.
Chef/s: Tong Chee Hwee. **Open:** all week 12 to 11.15 (12.15am Thur to Sun). **Meals:** main courses £25 to £61. Set D £68 to £128. **Details:** 220 seats. V menu. Bar. Music.

Hawksmoor Seven Dials

Cooking score: 4
⊖ Covent Garden, map 5
British | £55
11 Langley Street, Covent Garden, WC2H 9JG
Tel no: (020) 7420 9390
thehawksmoor.com

Hawksmoor's founders celebrated the chain's 10th anniversary in 2016, and there's no stopping their beefy bandwagon at the moment. This Seven Dials outpost was one of Will Beckett and Huw Gott's earlier forays into the steakhouse scene – a vintage barrel-vaulted basement that fuses girders, ducts and piping with the clubbiness of leather chairs and dark-wood surfaces. Hawksmoor has never been cheap, but it's worth paying top dollar for trencherman hunks of British-reared beef, aged and charred to perfection. Depending on your budget and appetite, you might pick a relatively modest sirloin or fillet; otherwise, share the spoils from a massive T-bone, porterhouse or chateaubriand – perhaps with some beef-dripping fries, grilled bone marrow or a couple of fried eggs. Alternatively, start with Brixham crab on toast, proceed to a brilliant burger or grilled lobster doused in garlic butter, and conclude with lemon and yoghurt cheesecake. Splendid cocktails and spot-on wines from £23.

Chef/s: Karol Poniewaz. **Open:** Mon to Sat L 12 to 3, D 5 to 10.30 (11 Fri and Sat). Sun 12 to 9.30. **Closed:** 24 to 26 Dec. **Meals:** main courses £12 to £50. Set L and D £25 (2 courses) to £28. **Details:** 140 seats. Bar. Wheelchairs. Music.

Hélène Darroze at the Connaught

Cooking score: 5
⊖ Bond Street, Green Park, map 5
Modern French | £92
16 Carlos Place, Mayfair, W1K 2AL
Tel no: (020) 3147 7200
the-connaught.co.uk

For nine years now, Hélène Darroze has split her time between Paris and London, making her mark at the Connaught with her distinctive brand of refined, modern French cooking. Creature comforts are well catered for in the spacious panelled dining room and there is ample elbow room, but the menu is not so easy to come to terms with. Various fixed-price menus (with supplements) are offered and everyone seems to comment on the 'bizarre way of ordering your meal using a solitaire board on the table.' However, the kitchen continues to deliver well-rehearsed

dishes in which prime ingredients and smooth, caressing textures produce seductive results. Darroze is often best at understated finesse: pigeon with roasted foie gras is cited, so too is a fresh-tasting crab over jellied cucumber with yoghurt and mint and a 'wonderfully sauced' John Dory. Popular with reporters this year has been the weekend 'le poulet du dimanche' – a five-course lunch that commences with confit egg yolk and smoked bacon from Alsace, goes on to four different ways with chicken, and concludes with a trio of desserts including an excellent iles flottante and crème caramel. The wine list suits the grand hotel setting: majestic and pricey, with bottles starting at £40.

Chef/s: Hélène Darroze. **Open:** all week L 12 to 2 (3 Sun), D 6.30 to 9.30 (9 Sun). **Meals:** set L £30 (2 courses) to £38. Tasting menus £52 (3 courses) to £125. **Details:** 65 seats. V menu. Bar. Wheelchairs.

★ TOP 10 ★

Hibiscus

Cooking score: 9
⊖ Oxford Circus, map 5
Modern French | £100
29 Maddox Street, Mayfair, W1S 2PA
Tel no: (020) 7629 2999
hibiscusrestaurant.co.uk

Could any change to a restaurant be more dramatic? As the Guide went to press, Claude Bosi told us he had sold Hibiscus – the restaurant will close sometime in the autumn of 2016 – and he will be moving to another London location in early 2017, where his focus will be on à la carte. Eating food cooked by Claude Bosi is memorable, as our last meal at Hibiscus showed. High on flavour, high on thought and inspiration, witty, wide-ranging in technique, it leans on a new generation's interpretation of classical French cuisine. Luxury items are not scattered through to aimlessly lend class; rather, they are used for themselves: a palpably fresh carpaccio of scallop with an unusual strawberry sauce vierge giving roundness to the dish, served at a June lunch, or 'the dish of the evening' from a

January dinner, Devonshire crab, the white meat on top, the brown underneath, with a touch of smoked haddock, an apple crush and sea purslane. Canapés and amuse-bouches have a legendary reputation (the eggshell filled with pea mousse, coconut foam and curry powder has been a recurrent offering for some years) and all the ancillary details – from terrific bread to the daintiest petits fours – are just about as good as it gets. Two hits from the recent past give some idea of the style: sea bream, the cooking judged to a second, accompanying girolles, slivers of green almonds and loquat providing a depth of flavour that complemented the fish perfectly; roasted Anjou pigeon served atop finely diced smoked eel, carrots and peas, a hint of ginger and smokiness to the cooking juices, an orange foam reducing down to a wonderful sauce that was sufficiently rich but had the degree of edge to allow the next mouthful to be approached with glee. Desserts are handled with supreme dexterity – witness a flamboyant exploration of strawberries in a 'Vacherin' consisting of a crisp meringue ball filled with wild strawberries and strawberry ice cream, the sweetness tempered by hundred-year old-balsamic vinegar. The evident brilliance shown in the food is reflected in the wine list, full of French classics and artisan gems.
Chef/s: Claude Bosi. **Open:** Thur to Sat L 12 to 2.30, Tue to Sat D 6.30 to 10.30. **Closed:** Sun, Mon, 24 to 26 Dec, 1 Jan, bank hols. **Meals:** main courses L £19 to £38. Set L £50. Set D £100 to £135 (7 courses). **Details:** 48 seats. Wheelchairs.

Honey & Co.

Cooking score: 3
⊖ Warren Street, map 2
Middle Eastern | £29
25a Warren Street, Fitzrovia, W1T 5LZ
Tel no: (020) 7388 6175
honeyandco.co.uk
£30

Though snug (OK, minuscule), there's nothing diminutive about the lively Middle Eastern food at this all-day operation. The simple interior, softened by shelves heaving with jars of preserves, forms the backdrop for some seriously big-hitting dishes. Sarit Packer and Itamar Srulovich's affection for their native Israel, their culinary nous and desire to make their restaurant a home-from-home has secured them a loyal following. Embrace the expansive take on the flavours and heritage of Middle Eastern cuisine and opt for luxury meze to share so you get to try a bit of everything – spiced falafel with tahini, quince and hazelnut salad, aubergine boureka and more. An Essaouira fish tagine or roasted beef kofta might follow, depending on the season, and they are passionate about their baked goods (check the enticing display on the counter at the back), so let resistance prove futile: cold cheesecake, kadaif pastry and Greek thyme honey is a winner. Breakfast offerings include shakshuka (eggs baked in tomato sauce). Wine from the short list starts at £19.50.
Chef/s: Sarit Packer and Itamar Srulovich. **Open:** Mon to Sat 8am to 10.30pm (9.30am Sat). **Closed:** Sun, 25 and 26 Dec, 1 Jan. **Meals:** main courses £15. Set L and D £27 (2 courses) to £30. **Details:** 33 seats. 6 seats outside. Music.

★ NEW ENTRY ★

Hoppers

Cooking score: 3
⊖ Tottenham Court Road, map 5
Sri Lankan | £25
49 Frith Street, Soho, W1D 4SG
hopperslondon.com
£30

The Sethi family, the people behind Trishna and Gymkhana (see entries), have opened this casual no-reservation eatery devoted to Sri Lankan cooking and majoring on hoppers (lacy, brittle pancake bowls made from fermented rice and coconut milk) and dosas (folded pancakes made from fermented lentils and rice). It's small, cramped and fun – rattan on the ceiling, walls lined with old posters, tiled tables – and value for money is a big plus, especially as it's easy to order too much. Queueing for the food is part of the experience – it certainly doesn't deter regulars who have their favourite dishes. For some it's the hot butter devilled shrimps, for others the Ceylonese spit chicken served with a sambol and grilled coconut rotis. Most, however, seem united in their addiction to the keenly priced, small-plate karis (curries), especially the black pork. Drink beer or inventive cocktails; wine (at £14) is red or white.

Chef/s: Rohit Ghai. **Open:** Mon to Fri L 12 to 2.45, D 5.30 to 10.30. Sat 12 to 10. **Closed:** Sun, 25 and 26 Dec, 31 Dec to 2 Jan. **Meals:** main courses £10 to £19. **Details:** 36 seats. Music.

The Ivy

Cooking score: 2
Θ Leicester Square, map 5
Modern European | £39
1-5 West Street, Covent Garden, WC2H 9NQ
Tel no: (020) 7836 4751
the-ivy.co.uk

Celebrating its first century in 2017, theatreland's most famous restaurant may be eclipsed by others in the celebrity stakes these days but it continues to play to a packed house. The décor is stylish, the cooking confident, though not attention grabbing. There's the option to perch at the circular bar that dominates the oak-pannelled dining room, but most visitors are content with the green leather banquettes around the outside. On the whole, results are good. Dressed Cornish crab 'brought back childhood memories of 'proper' crab', and the same praise extends to 'perfectly pink' calves' liver with 'first-class' crispy bacon. If the menu changes infrequently, it's because many of the dishes are so popular: bang-bang chicken is a mainstay starter, and shepherd's pie a perennial main. Sloe gin fizz jelly with a 'wonderfully tart' lemon sherbet makes a great finish. Service is 'beyond reproach' and wines start at £22.

Chef/s: Gary Lee. **Open:** all week 12 to 11.30 (10.30 Sun). **Closed:** 25 Dec. **Meals:** main courses £15 to £40. Set L and pre/post-theatre D £23 (2 courses) to £28. **Details:** 120 seats. V menu. Wheelchairs. Music.

J. Sheekey

Cooking score: 4
Θ Leicester Square, map 5
Seafood | £37
28-35 St Martin's Court, Covent Garden, WC2N 4AL
Tel no: (020) 7240 2565
j-sheekey.co.uk

There's a lot to like about this Covent Garden institution. It is beautiful and old-fashioned, a long row of small, adjoining dining rooms all with proper linen and heavy silverware, and as a refuge from hard-edged, hip new restaurants with no-booking policies it could hardly be bettered. Just like the surroundings, the menu is steeped in tradition, specialising in fish with just a few nods to current fashion. This is the place to come for 'very well-executed' crab bisque, potted shrimps, and a plate of oysters for starters. Equally time-honoured main courses include 'wonderful' roasted mixed shellfish (a platter of scallops, razor clams in the shell, king prawns and a 'sweet and soft' half lobster with sea vegetables and garlic butter), grilled Dover sole with béarnaise sauce, and shrimp and scallop burger with spiced mayonnaise. It also takes savouries seriously, serving Welsh rarebit as an alternative to hazelnut praline and popcorn parfait. Wines from £19.50. For similar seafood in a more casual setting, head next door to J. Sheekey's all-day Atlantic Bar; tel: (020) 7240 2565.

Chef/s: Andy McLay. **Open:** all week L 12 to 3 (3.30 Sat and Sun), D 5 to 12 (5.30 Sat, 5.30 to 10.30 Sun). **Closed:** 25 and 26 Dec. **Meals:** main courses £16 to £42. Set L £24 (2 courses) to £29. **Details:** 114 seats. 26 seats outside. V menu. Bar. Wheelchairs.

Symbols

🛏 Accommodation is available
£30 Three courses for less than £30
£5 OFF £5-off voucher scheme
🍾 Notable wine list

Kiku

Cooking score: 3
⊖ Green Park, map 5
Japanese | £30
17 Half Moon Street, Mayfair, W1J 7BE
Tel no: (020) 7499 4208
kikurestaurant.co.uk

Little changes at Kiku (chrysanthemum). Located not far from the Japanese embassy, it's a long-standing family business, established in 1978, and is considered a bastion of traditional Japanese cooking. Dining takes place over two levels and there's a choice of à la carte or various kaiseki (set meals). There's a wide range of nigiri, such as saké toro (salmon belly), kazunoka (herring roe) and chutoro (medium fatty tuna), as well as rolled sushi, sashimi and assortments. Zingy small plates such as hakusai zuke (pickled Chinese cabbage), nasu dengaku (deep-fried aubergine served with a warm coating of sweet miso paste) or yakitori (grilled chicken skewers) stimulate the appetite before moving on to sukiyaki or its poached version, shabu-shabu (for two or more). Otherwise, there's gyuteriyaki (grilled beef with teriyaki sauce), assorted tempura and agedashi tofu (deep-fried beancurd with a light soy sauce). Drink beer, saké or wine from £16.50.

Chef/s: F Shiraishi and Y Hattori. **Open:** Mon to Sat L 12 to 2.30, all week D 6 to 10.15 (5.30 to 9.45 Sun). **Closed:** 24 to 27 Dec, 1 Jan. **Meals:** main courses £15 to £45. Set L £24 (4 courses) to £34 (5 courses). Set D £59 (8 courses) to £82 (10 courses). **Details:** 99 seats. Wheelchairs.

Kitchen Table

Cooking score: 6
⊖ Goodge Street, map 5
Modern British | £88
70 Charlotte Street, Fitzrovia, W1T 4QG
Tel no: (020) 7637 7770
kitchentablelondon.co.uk

Once you have pushed through Bubbledogs (the hot dog and Champagne eatery) and slipped through the leather curtain at the back, what to expect? A stark commercial kitchen with 19 counter-stools – not ideal for those looking for an intimate date – and chefs on full display, delivering food that is bold and ultra-modern. There are flashes of brilliance in James Knappett's cooking, his series of small tasting plates built around rigorous seasonal sourcing and an understanding of wild plants and their place in the scheme of things. The result is a daily-changing 12-course menu with extras built around it; a bald version is scrawled on a blackboard. The skill is in packing intriguing ingredients into one composition and coaxing all into harmony, as in the subtle hits of sweet-and-sour in an opener of hand-dived raw scallop, lightly pickled cucumber, elderflowers and lightly effervescent elderflower kombucha. There's delight, too, in a fat spear of sweet, white asparagus paired with monkfish liver, and in the richness of lamb sweetbreads with mint jus and oxalis leaf. Equally deft is the sweet, smoky crunch of deep-fried potato starch dotted with smoked salmon and crème fraîche, the delicacy of steamed plaice invigorated by lemon verbena, shaved summer truffle and elderflower vinegar, and the instantly moreish Parker House rolls – warm, soft-textured milk bread – served with brown butter flavoured with fish roe. And in a closing salvo, beetroot marmalade is teamed with a tangy woodrow ice and sour cream ice cream, while the acidity of new-season gooseberries combines with the resiny tang of spruce tips to give depth to a dish of yoghurt and green almonds. The vibe is casual, the wine list pricey, with bottles from £39.

Chef/s: James Knappett. **Open:** Tue to Sat D only 6 and 7.30 (2 sittings). **Closed:** Sun, Mon, 24 to 28 Dec, 2 weeks Jan, 2 weeks Sept. **Meals:** tasting menu £88. **Details:** 19 seats.

Visit us online

To find out more about The Good Food Guide, please visit thegoodfoodguide.co.uk

Kitty Fisher's

Cooking score: 5
⊖ Green Park, map 5
Modern British | £40
10 Shepherd Market, Mayfair, W1J 7QF
Tel no: (020) 3302 1661
kittyfishers.com

Found in the very heart of Shepherd Market, this intimate restaurant is proving to be a welcoming beacon of hospitality in an area not generally noted for its restaurants. It is on two simply decorated levels, including a cramped ground floor and slightly bigger basement where you can catch a glimpse into the kitchen. With its mix of counter seating and close-packed tables, Kitty Fisher's may lack comfort but it makes up for it with warm, welcoming service and a short, gloriously seasonal menu of food you really want to eat. There are nibbles to have with a drink, say the excellent whipped cod's roe on bread with fennel butter, before going on to grilled Scottish langoustine with lardo and rosemary or the lamb cutlets with anchovy, mint and parsley so loved by readers. It's all such 'damn good quality', with mains producing Cornish monkfish with black cabbage, cider, mussels and bottarga, while Cambridge burnt cream, lemon tart or British cheeses bring up the rear. A short wine list starts at £18.
Chef/s: Tomos Parry. **Open:** all week L 12 to 2.30, D 6.30 to 9.30. **Closed:** 24 Dec to 3 Jan, Easter, bank hols. **Meals:** main courses £20 to £40. **Details:** 36 seats. 6 seats outside. Music.

Latium

Cooking score: 2
⊖ Goodge Street, Oxford Circus, map 5
Italian | £36
21 Berners Street, Fitzrovia, W1T 3LP
Tel no: (020) 7323 9123
latiumrestaurant.com
£5
OFF

It's all change at Latium (which opened in 2003) with the departure of chef-patron Maurizio Morelli. Stefano Motta is now manning the stoves and the plain, modern dining room has been updated with a more informal look of wooden tables, contrasting reddish-brown and olive green seating, black slate flooring and colourful photographs. The cooking continues to please, with dishes built around good-quality ingredients. A June lunch ('very good value') delivered a well-balanced Apulian burrata with Devodier ham, asparagus and pearl barley, veal ravioli ('packed with flavour') with pea cream, chanterelles and pecorino, and char-grilled squid paired with fennel and baby gem and neatly rounded off by a potato cream infused with tarragon. End on a refreshing note with flaky mille-feuille filled with limoncello cream, wild berries and raspberry sorbet. Service is friendly and the interesting regional wines on the all-Italian list start at £16.
Chef/s: Stefano Motta. **Open:** Mon to Fri L 12 to 3, D 5.30 to 10 (11 Sat). Sun 12.30 to 9. **Closed:** 25 and 26 Dec, 1 Jan. **Meals:** main courses £18 to £25. Set L and D £16 (2 courses) to £21. **Details:** 50 seats. Wheelchairs. Music.

Little Social

Cooking score: 6
⊖ Oxford Circus, map 5
Modern European | £50
5 Pollen Street, Mayfair, W1S 1NE
Tel no: (020) 7870 3730
littlesocial.co.uk
🍾

It may not engender the PR bluster or column inches associated with Jason Atherton's restaurants, but this petit bistro has a magic all its own. Situated directly opposite the cool, upmarket Pollen Street Social (see entry), Little Social transports visitors to a humming, noisy Parisian fantasy world complete with posters, red leather banquettes and a big Michelin road map on one wall. However, there's nothing kitsch or pastiche about the menu, or indeed head chef Cary Docherty's mastery of the Atherton house style. As always, fine seasonal ingredients are the building blocks, whether your penchant is for a well-aged ribeye steak or something more intricately *du jour* – perhaps roasted girolles

with smoked almond butter and wild garlic on toasted brioche, grilled côte de porc with courgette, mint, chilli, apple and toasted pine nuts or line-caught turbot with peas, broad beans and 'concentrated' romesco. After that, few can resist the Eton mess or the 'wonderful, glorious and extremely rich' tarte Tatin. Vivacious staff know exactly how to charm, and the Eurocentric wine list is a concise modern slate full of quirky sips and regional discoveries, with bottles from £25.
Chef/s: Cary Docherty. **Open:** Mon to Sat L 12 to 2.30, D 6 to 10.30. **Closed:** Sun, bank hols. **Meals:** main courses £15 to £38. Set L £21 (2 courses) to £25. **Details:** 55 seats.

Locanda Locatelli

Cooking score: 4
⊖ Marble Arch, map 6
Italian | £70
8 Seymour Street, Marylebone, W1H 7JZ
Tel no: (020) 7935 8390
locandalocatelli.com

Buff banquettes, a distorting mirror in the dining room and a snazzily refurbished bar area look chic enough for an Italian interiors' glossy, which is only to be expected from the highly media-visible Giorgio Locatelli. It's been a meteoric trajectory from the northern shores of Lake Comabbio to the environs of Marble Arch, but ancestral traditions came with him in the baggage, as is attested by the hand-cranked pasta, the pounded herbs and oil, and the diamond-fresh, sunny flavours with which the lengthy menus are replete. Squid-ink risottos and oxtail ravioli are flawlessly timed, magisterially intense, and the salt- and herb-crusted baked sea bass is an object lesson. Meat dishes are simplicity itself, perhaps char-grilled spring lamb with morels and minted pea purée, while the fashion for mixing cheese and dessert to obviate choice is celebrated in a Gorgonzola pannacotta that comes with chocolate crumble, pear foam and honey ice cream. From the Pugliese house wines at £6 a glass to the glory that is aged Barbaresco, the capacious Italian list is full of opulent allure, a few foreigners gaining an entrée for measuring up to the Italian mark. Prices are not, of course, low, although the reds start at £17.50.
Chef/s: Giorgio Locatelli. **Open:** all week L 12 to 3, D 6 to 11 (11.30 Fri and Sat, 10.15 Sun). **Closed:** 24 to 26 Dec. **Meals:** main courses £25 to £33. **Details:** 80 seats. Wheelchairs.

★ NEW ENTRY ★

Lurra

Cooking score: 2
⊖ Marble Arch, map 6
Spanish | £45
9 Seymour Place, Marylebone, W1H 5BA
Tel no: (020) 7724 4545
lurra.co.uk

Directly opposite big brother Donostia (see entry), on a stretch that's becoming 'Connaught Village's' destination dining spot, Lurra is a lovely smart, modern restaurant, all clean lines, lots of marble and blond wood. The limited menu has big protein fixes at its heart – on our visit 'almost everyone was tucking into Rubia Gallega ribeye and generous bowls of chips', but there's also slow-cooked milk lamb shoulder ('very young, tender and delicate') and a tranche of grilled turbot. Start by grazing on tapas, perhaps pimentos de Padrón and top-quality jamón Ibérico, tender grilled squid 'rammed with diced prawns and chorizo with bags of salty flavour', or 'stunningly overblown' salt-cod-filled courgette flower fritters – more unusual dishes such as hake kokotxas pil-pil are strictly for hard-core Basque devotees. The wine list, full of northern Spanish and Basque-grown wines, is thankfully full of helpful annotations and starts at £22.
Chef/s: Damian Surowiec. **Open:** Tue to Sun L 12 to 2.30 (11 to 3.30 Sun), Mon to Sat D 6 to 10.30. **Closed:** 24 Dec to 2 Jan. **Meals:** main courses £9 to £16. **Details:** 80 seats. 24 seats outside. Music.

Mele e Pere
⊖ Piccadilly Circus, map 5
Italian | £30
46 Brewer Street, Soho, W1F 9TF
Tel no: (020) 7096 2096
meleepere.co.uk

£5
OFF

A spirited trattoria and 'vermouth bar' for the Soho crowd, spread over two floors (most dining takes place in the basement), Mele e Pere serves feel-good Italian stuff such as deep-fried squid with smoked aïoli, tagliatelle enriched with beef ragù, 28-day aged ribeye steak with Barolo sauce, and gnocchi with Umbrian black truffle. When it comes to libations, they make their own vermouth – so it would be rude not to partake. Italian wines start at £19. A sister restaurant, Gotto, has opened at Canalside, Here East, Hackney.

Mon Plaisir
⊖ Covent Garden, map 5
French | £36
21 Monmouth Street, Covent Garden, WC2H 9DD
Tel no: (020) 7836 7243
monplaisir.co.uk

The number of fans of this long-established and family-run restaurant shows that there is a need for such a simple, no-nonsense French bistro in London. This is the place to come for cassolette d'escargots, coq au vin and carré d'agneau rôti, and as far as value for money goes before and after a show it takes some beating – there's an 'impressive focus on getting one out in time for the theatre'. Elsewhere, île flottante has been praised and there are some good French cheeses. The Gallic wine list starts at £19.

Murano
Cooking score: 7
⊖ Green Park, map 5
Italian | £65
20-22 Queen Street, Mayfair, W1J 5PP
Tel no: (020) 7495 1127
muranolondon.com

'Every penny was worth it,' says a reader of a joyful, wine-matched celebration at Angela Hartnett's mother ship. You'll know you're in Mayfair – big floristry, tasteful murals and luxe finishes – but the room is light and easy, and service responds smoothly to the mood at the table. Hartnett's style is Italia finessed, with its generosity and freshness kept intact, and chef Pip Lacey ensures that continuing quality 'could not be better'. From five courses (the set lunch is three), pick and choose delicate first courses, perhaps scallop ceviche with pink grapefruit, mooli and a touch of dark chocolate, and exemplary pasta; little parcels are a speciality, so try crab tortellini and bisque with cucumber, turnip and spring onion. Readers rate 'light, delicate and flavoursome' duck confit cannelloni, and 'very fresh' pollack with trompette mushrooms, black truffle and hazelnuts. At the meatier end, rack of lamb is served for two with artichoke, rhubarb and red onion. Desserts play on established partnerships, as in pistachio soufflé with hot chocolate sauce, as well as introducing star anise and fennel to a caramelised blood-orange tart (a seasonal variation on Hartnett's Amalfi lemon number) or tarragon to chocolate mousse. A deftly handled wine list is opening up to the New World but offers more choice closer to home, from £28.
Chef/s: Angela Hartnett and Pip Lacey. **Open:** Mon to Sat L 12 to 3, D 6.30 to 11. **Closed:** Sun, 5 days Christmas. **Meals:** set L £28 (2 courses) to £33. Set D £50 (2 courses) to £95. **Details:** 56 seats. Wheelchairs.

★ NEW ENTRY ★

Native

Cooking score: 3
⊖ Covent Garden, map 5
Modern British | £30
3 Neal's Yard, Covent Garden, WC2H 9DP
Tel no: (020) 3638 8214
eatnative.co.uk

Through the Covent Garden throng, in the corner of Neal's Yard, Ivan Tisdall-Downes and Imogen Davis run their bijou restaurant in hands-on fashion. Tisdall-Downes is ex-River Cottage, and Davis used to be a falconer. Their combined experience has kindled great enthusiasm for wild places and home-grown things, with fresh, satisfying dishes served in spartan accommodation over two floors. 'It is all,' says one delighted visitor, 'about feeding you a dinner.' That might start with focaccia with fennel fronds and seed and, for one lucky diner, 'a pot of piping hot butter, straight from the pan in which a pigeon breast has been frying' offered alongside. Rabbit dumplings with smoked bacon dashi and pickled walnuts are juicy and flushed pink, served in an earthy, umami-rich broth, while a main course of hake with dhal and cauliflower leaf pakora is 'intensely enjoyable', the pakora billowy and crisp. Afters are limited and, like everything else about Native, the wine list is teeny, from £19.
Chef/s: Ivan Tisdall-Downes. **Open:** Tue to Sun L 12.30 to 2.30, all week D 7.30 to 10. **Meals:** main courses £13 to £17. **Details:** 32 seats. Music.

★ NEW ENTRY ★

Newman Arms

Cooking score: 3
⊖ Tottenham Court Road, Goodge Street, map 5
British | £30
23 Rathbone Street, Fitzrovia, W1T 1NG
Tel no: (020) 3643 6285
newmanarmspub.com

A Fitzrovia pub that has no truck with contemporary design, the tiny, timeworn Newman Arms is unreconstructed and all the

better for it. You can eat very well here and at remarkable prices – which in London is never to be taken for granted – so clamber up the narrow, semi-spiral staircase to the cramped, bare-bones wood-panelled dining room above. Here the short, modern menu is absolutely correct for the pub setting, offering simple treatments of prime materials sourced by Matt Chatfield in Cornwall (hence the secondary name, Cornwall Project). Seasonal hits include baked beetroot with smoked ricotta, hazelnuts and horseradish, a generous plate of tender, pink-roasted lamb rump with collard greens dressed in their own juices and shallots, and a very good piece of hake served with monk's beard and pepper dulse. At lunch, when pie, mash and parsley green sauce (we tried a superb lamb and rosemary) draws a highly appreciative, mostly male crowd, noise levels can be deafening: but that's part of the experience. Wines from £18.
Chef/s: Eryk Bautista. **Open:** Mon 12 to 10 (pies only). Tue to Fri L 12 to 2.30, D 5.30 to 10. Sun 12 to 6 (roasts only). **Closed:** Sat. **Meals:** main courses £13 to £19. Set L £19 (3 courses). **Details:** 30 seats. Bar.

★ NEW ENTRY ★

The Ninth

Cooking score: 4
⊖ Goodge Street, Tottenham Court Road, map 5
French-Mediterranean | £37
22 Charlotte Street, Fitzrovia, W1T 2NB
Tel no: (020) 3019 0880
theninthlondon.com

The casual interior – bentwood chairs, rough brick and plaster walls, a dominant dark-wood bar – and the insistence that dishes, though full sized, are designed to be shared, gives this eatery a relaxed, chatty atmosphere that's more Shoreditch than Charlotte Street. Jun Tanaka's style of cooking – deceptively simple, relying on classical training and great ingredients – copes well with the concept. A fragrant salad of fennel and blood orange with pomegranate vinaigrette might be too light on its own as a starter, but when paired with a gutsy dish of pickled mussels with chorizo and smoked paprika it makes a perfect contrast. Similarly, the tenderest slow-cooked salted beef cheeks, served in a delicate consommé, makes a great foil for a robust roasted sea bream flavoured with miso, aubergine and lemon. The wine list that, in keeping with the menu, is mostly Old World includes a decent number by the glass, starting at a reasonable £6.50. Even better is no-corkage BYO every Monday.

Chef/s: Jun Tanaka. **Open:** Mon to Sat L 12 to 2.30, D 5.30 to 10.30. **Closed:** Sun, bank hols. **Meals:** main courses £14 to £23. Set L £17 (2 courses) to £21. **Details:** 88 seats. 8 seats outside. Wheelchairs. Music.

★ NEW ENTRY ★

Noble Rot
Cooking score: 4
⊖ Holborn, Russell Square, map 5
British | £35
51 Lamb's Conduit Street, Bloomsbury, WC1N 3NB
Tel no: (020) 7242 8963
noblerot.co.uk

Launched by Mark Andrew and Dan Keeling, co-editors of *Noble Rot* magazine, this Holborn hot ticket 'is a simple place, relaxed – very much the wine bar'. Basic brown-on-brown décor – wood floor, panelled walls, bare, close-packed tables – reflects an aim to provide great food and wine without breaking the bank. Chef Paul Weaver shows his six or so years cooking at the Sportsman in Kent and his time at St John Bread and Wine (see entries) with simple, ingredient-led dishes and the odd smattering of offal (excellent duck hearts, fennel and tarragon, for example). Sourcing is on the money, and flavour, not fashion, is the driving force, as can be seen in a very fresh and simply grilled mackerel on the bone teamed with pink grapefruit and wild rocket, and a triumphant standout halibut braised in oxidised 1998 Bâtard-Montrachet Grand Cru. Impressive, too, is whole roast quail served on a heap of Puy lentils with a dollop of rich aïoli.

For dessert, there's very good pistachio cake with blood orange and mascarpone. As for wine, the list punches above its weight for quality and value and there's a good by-the-glass selection. Bottles from £20.

Chef/s: Paul Weaver. **Open:** Mon to Sat L 12 to 2.30, D 6 to 9.30. **Closed:** Sun. **Meals:** main courses £14 to £23. **Details:** 75 seats. 8 seats outside. Bar.

Nobu Berkeley St
Cooking score: 4
⊖ Green Park, map 5
Japanese | £90
15 Berkeley Street, Mayfair, W1J 8DY
Tel no: (020) 7290 9222
noburestaurants.com

Behind an etched glass frontage is a restaurant of two halves and dramatic volume: the ground floor taken up by a bar and lounge (which can get very lively), with the hard-edged dining room above (high decibels here, too). Over the last few years the high-gloss image has faded, and like big brother Nobu on Park Lane (see entry), it is easier to get a table these days. The house formula is of cutting-edge modern Japanese cuisine, spiked with South American spicing and technique continues, but what powers the food and gives it vitality are the impeccable raw materials and seductive presentation. Old favourites such as yellowtail sashimi with jalapeño and the famous black cod with miso continue to impress, but there's also pork belly with miso, a fresh and zesty lobster salad with spicy lemon dressing, tempura (pumpkin or sweet potato, perhaps) and exemplary sushi and sashimi. However, not all visitors are happy with results, suggesting a degree of variation that a single cooking mark is unable to reflect. Wines from £38 or there's saké, of course.

Chef/s: Mark Edwards. **Open:** Mon to Sat L 12 to 2.30 (3 Sat), all week D 6 to 11 (12 Thur to Sat, 9.45 Sun). **Meals:** main courses £12 to £46. **Details:** 180 seats. Bar. Wheelchairs. Music.

Nobu London

Cooking score: 4
⊖ Hyde Park Corner, map 5
Japanese | £75
Metropolitan Hotel, 19 Old Park Lane, Mayfair,
W1K 1LB
Tel no: (020) 7447 4747
noburestaurants.com

Time may have lent a patina of familiarity to what Nobu does, and yet the appeal endures – precise renditions of Japanese food overlaid with South American sizzle, all served in a long, white first-floor room with the character of an unadorned art gallery, overlooking Hyde Park. Hollywood's glitterati regularly gravitate here, Nick Nolte and Nicole Kidman showing up (separately) in the Christmas run-up. Chef's tasting menus are abidingly popular for those who don't feel emboldened to pick their own way through the processions of sushi and sashimi, tempura variations and crispy rice dishes. It's still worth straying into the less familiar territory of langoustine with red chilli shiso salsa, snow crab in creamy sauce or tea-smoked lamb anticucho, if you're already on more than nodding terms with the perennial black cod miso. Imaginative desserts include Fuji apple crumble with sesame oil, miso salt and peanut ice cream. Exclusive sakés and classy cocktails supplement a plutocrat's wine list, from £35.
Chef/s: Hideki Maeda. **Open:** all week L 12 to 2.15 (12.30 to 2.30 Sat and Sun), D 6 to 10.30 (11 Fri and Sat, 10 Sun). **Closed:** 25 Dec, 1 Jan. **Meals:** main courses £30 to £36. **Details:** 150 seats. Bar. Wheelchairs. Music.

Symbols

🛏 Accommodation is available
🟤 Three courses for less than £30
🔸 £5-off voucher scheme
🍾 Notable wine list

NOPI

Cooking score: 3
⊖ Piccadilly Circus, map 5
Middle Eastern/Mediterranean | £50
21-22 Warwick Street, Soho, W1B 5NE
Tel no: (020) 7494 9584
nopi-restaurant.com

Yotam Ottolenghi has been a breakout star of the small screen and colour supplement pages, his meteoric career now supporting a network of delis and this mother ship Soho venue on two levels: an informal ground-floor dining room of whitewashed brick and an even more informal basement space furnished with refectory tables and an open kitchen. As befits a celeb, there are signed cookbooks on offer. There's also some lively fusion cooking, fusing the Mediterranean shores of Europe and North Africa and the Near East. Vegetables play a big part, as in courgettes with samphire, kefalotyri sheep's cheese and lemon, roast aubergine with sorrel yoghurt, turmeric radish and almonds, and roast butternut and red onion with dressings of tahini and za'atar. Omnivores are not sent away empty, when sea bream comes in rose harissa, or pork belly with winter greens and pineapple chutney. Finish with apple and gingerbread trifle and celery sorbet. House French is £24, or £5.50 a small glass.
Chef/s: Angelo Kremmydas. **Open:** Mon to Thur and Sun L 12 to 2.45 (4 Sun), Mon to Thur D 5.30 to 10.30. Fri and Sat 12 to 10.30. **Closed:** 25 and 27 Dec, 1 Jan. **Meals:** main courses £20 to £24. Early D £25. **Details:** 108 seats. Bar. Music.

★ NEW ENTRY ★

Les 110 de Taillevent

Cooking score: 4
⊖ Oxford Circus, map 5
French | £45
16 Cavendish Square, Marylebone, W1G 9DD
Tel no: (020) 3141 6016
les-110-taillevent-london.com

The team behind the multi-gonged Parisian restaurant Taillevent has come to town with a spin-off of their less formal wine bar and brasserie – 110 refers to the number of wines offered by the glass. It looks discreetly expensive, a pair of grand, high-ceilinged dining rooms with gentle lighting and rich wood panelling, the backdrop for a menu that follows comforting, classic French lines. Here you can eat pâté en croûte, duck foie gras, vol au vent stuffed with lamb sweetbreads and crayfish, and medallions of beef tenderloin with bone marrow, red wine sauce and mustard de Brive, although some concessions to new ideas are allowed, producing squid à la plancha with sweet peppers, Ibérico chorizo and squid ink, and roasted duck fillet with caramelised endive and honey Xerez. With wine and food on an equal footing – each dish comes with four by-the-glass recommendations from £7 to £20+ – this is much more than your average wine bar. There's a knowledgeable sommelier on hand to give advice, too. Bottles from £25.

Chef/s: Raphael Grima. **Open:** all week L 11.30 to 2.30, D 6 to 10.30 (9.30 Sun). **Closed:** 26 Dec, 3 weeks Aug. **Meals:** main courses £19 to £35. Set L and D £30 (2 courses) to £35. **Details:** 70 seats. 16 seats outside. Bar. Wheelchairs. Music.

Opera Tavern

Cooking score: 3
⊖ Covent Garden, map 5
Tapas | £35
23 Catherine Street, Covent Garden,
WC2B 5JS
Tel no: (020) 7836 3680
operatavern.co.uk

Given it's right in the heart of theatreland, just around the corner from the Royal Opera House, Opera Tavern's small-plate concept is ideal for pre- or post-theatre grazing. Don't rush if you don't have to, however, for this part of the high-octane group that brought us Salt Yard, Ember Yard and Dehesa (see entries) delivers impressive plates of Italian- and Spanish-inspired tapas. The old tavern has a lively bar on the ground floor and a more chilled dining room upstairs. A set-menu share-fest is one way to go, or go your own way with a pintxo such as swordfish and

Amalfi lemon to get you going before deep-fried confit rabbit with jamón and wild garlic aïoli, citrus-cured sea trout with samphire and pink peppercorn dressing, and charcoal-grilled asparagus with confit duck egg yolk, polenta and black garlic aïoli. Don't miss the Spanish and Italian charcuterie, and finish with rhubarb and pistachio cheesecake. Wines start at £20.

Chef/s: Michelle Fourie. **Open:** Mon to Fri L 12 to 3, D 5 to 11.30. Sat and Sun 12 to 11.30 (10 Sun). **Meals:** tapas £5 to £11. **Details:** 59 seats. 4 seats outside. Bar. Music.

Orrery

Cooking score: 4
⊖ Baker Street, Regent's Park, map 6
French | £55
55 Marylebone High Street, Marylebone,
W1U 5RB
Tel no: (020) 7616 8000
orrery-restaurant.co.uk

'Stylish, modern – very airy and light,' proclaimed one visitor to this first-floor restaurant above the Conran Shop, who enjoyed 'atmosphere and service, and excellent food (of commendable good value)'. Igor Tymchyshyn's modern-classical French dishes are clearly conceived and lucidly presented, taking in a 'perfect large raviolo, packed with seafood with a strongly flavoured lobster bisque', and roasted cod with pork belly, white asparagus, morels and velouté, and chicken liver parfait with apple chutney and tornedos Rossini with sauce périgourdine. Such combinations are hardly groundbreaking, but timing, materials, judgement and the welcome absence of gimmicks lift them above the norm. A chocolate délice with passion fruit and coconut sorbet made a lasting impression on one diner; the excellent choice of cheeses from the trolley and the good selection of breads are also singled out for praise. Stick with the fixed-price deals and your bills will be predictable, just as long as you don't get lost in the excellent wine list; bottles from £27.

Chef/s: Igor Tymchyshyn. **Open:** all week L 12 to 2.30 (3 Sun), D 6.30 to 10.30 (10 Sun). **Closed:** bank hols. **Meals:** main courses £15 to £39 (L only). Set L £27 (3 courses) to £29. Set D £55 (3 courses). Sun L £33. Tasting menu £75 (6 courses). **Details:** 80 seats. 20 seats outside. Bar. Wheelchairs. Music.

Otto's

Cooking score: 3
⊖ Chancery Lane, map 5
French | £45
182 Gray's Inn Road, Bloomsbury, WC1X 8EW
Tel no: (020) 7713 0107
ottos-restaurant.com

You are truly looked after at idiosyncratic Otto's, an eccentrically garbed Bloomsbury room full of knick-knacks and red plush. It does the almost forgotten ancestral things, pressing ducks and lobsters, mixing tartares, carving Bresse chickens at the table, all via discreet but interested service. After a wildly rich lobster soufflé with bisque, or enthusiastically seared foie gras with sweet potato purée, glazed beetroot and almond foam, that chicken demi-deuil arrives on a glistening silver tray, its skin threaded with truffle shards, the breasts plated with turned veg, the oyster cuts to follow, doused in even trufflier morel cream, with the thigh as a curtain-caller, anointed with – you're ahead of us – a translucent truffle sauce. You'll need to pre-order it; it's £140 for two. Otherwise, go for breaded monkfish tail with vegetable bouillabaisse. The signature dessert is gleaming dark chocolate mousse with salt caramel ice cream and a choux pastry filled with praline cream. Wines from £20 a bottle. **Chef/s:** Thierry Lakermance. **Open:** Tue to Fri L 12 to 2.15, Tue to Sat D 6 to 9.45. **Closed:** Sun, Mon, 24 Dec to 10 Jan, bank hols. **Meals:** main courses £20 to £35. Set L £24 (2 courses) to £28. **Details:** 40 seats.

Pachamama

Cooking score: 2
⊖ Bond Street, map 6
Peruvian | £45
18 Thayer Street, Marylebone, W1U 3JY
Tel no: (020) 7935 9393
pachamamalondon.com

This subterranean 'Peruvian-inspired' restaurant is named after Pachamama, the Incan goddess of fertility. Descending into the dining room, the décor says less Machu Picchu and more mid-century chic, with mismatched furniture, artfully distressed walls and dangling ducts that rattle during the occasional DJ sets. A kitchen shuttling out small plates completes the hipster bingo card but luckily there's substance to go with the style. Triumphant brown crab and cassava churros are 'delicately textured parcels of crustacean deliciousness', though other offerings are less conceptual, like simple and satisfying fried aubergine with smoked yoghurt. Peruvian crowd-pleasers are in attendance – sea bream ceviche with samphire, radish and tiger's milk marinade, for instance, or fried chicken arriving with a dollop of incendiary hot 'Atacama' sauce. A pudding might be Peruvian chocolate with toasted quinoa – though you may instead prefer to adjourn to the bar, where a cocktail list runs through many species of pisco sours. Wines from £24.
Chef/s: Tiago Duerte. **Open:** Tue to Sun L 12 to 3 (4 Sat and Sun), all week D 6 to 12 (11 Sun). **Closed:** 25 and 26 Dec, 1 Jan. **Meals:** main courses £8 to £25. **Details:** 120 seats. Bar. Music.

The Palomar

Cooking score: 5
⊖ Piccadilly Circus, map 5
Middle Eastern | £40
34 Rupert Street, Soho, W1D 6DN
Tel no: (020) 7439 8777
thepalomar.co.uk

There are no airs and graces at this intimate, pared-back haunt – the place is alive with chat and service is charm personified. The long,

narrow space is a mix of non-bookable kitchen-counter stools and tightly squeezed (and bookable) tables at the back, and forms the roughest and readiest setting for some lively, non-kosher Israeli cooking. Ingredients are impeccable and Tomer Amedi's menu encourages experimentation. Nishnushim (snacks) include the not-to-be-missed Yemeni pot-baked bread with tahini and tomato dips, there are punchy raw-bar treats of beef tartare (with yoghurt, pomegranate and harissa) or Morrocan-style oysters, zingy with coriander, lemon zest and harissa oil, while seductively flavoured small plates include a rich pork belly tagine with ras-el-hanout, dried apricots and Israeli couscous, and the famed polenta Jerusalem style, livened by asparagus, mushroom ragoût, Parmesan and truffle oil. There's Jerusalem mess – labneh mousse, almond crumble, strawberries, lemon cream, apple jelly and fresh sorrel – for dessert, and the short, global wine list starts at £25.
Chef/s: Tomer Amedi. **Open:** all week L 12 to 2.30 (3.30 Sun), D 5.30 to 11 (6 to 9 Sun). **Closed:** 25 and 26 Dec. **Meals:** main courses £15 to £25. **Details:** 50 seats. Music.

Pied à Terre
Cooking score: 5
⊖ Goodge Street, map 5
Modern French | £80
34 Charlotte Street, Fitzrovia, W1T 2NH
Tel no: (020) 7636 1178
pied-a-terre.co.uk
£5 OFF 🍾

As far as interior design is concerned, Pied à Terre forgoes edgy statements in favour of an intimate, womb-like dining room of muted hues edged with dressed tables and run with supreme professionalism by a bevy of wonderful staff, a good sommelier and even pace throughout. Chef Andrew McFadden endeavours to maintain the culinary excitement of his predecessor, Marcus Eaves, in a continuation of the modern style he forged at sibling L'Autre Pied (see entry). One couple, returning to taste the 'newish' chef's set lunch, was bowled over by 'fabulous quality

cooking', including an 'extraordinarily tender and tasty' smoked duck breast with globe artichokes, chicory and salad leaves 'with a lovely dressing', and 'superbly cooked' roast chicken with a tarragon flavour, a smear of liquorice and greens. Indeed, ingredients are seldom less than exceptional, such as the Wye Valley asparagus that arrives with a jam-like egg yolk, toasted hazelnuts and Parmesan, and rosy fallow deer with fregola sarda (Sardinian couscous), slow-cooked leg, black pearl curry, smoked bacon, beetroot and red chicory. But the cooking needs sharper focus to keep pace with the wine treasures on a knowledgeably chosen list that pulls together fine drinking from reputable names and forward-looking producers worldwide. Bottles from £25.
Chef/s: Andrew McFadden. **Open:** Mon to Fri L 12 to 2.30, Mon to Sat D 6 to 11. **Closed:** Sun, Mon (Aug), last week Dec, first week Jan. **Meals:** set L £30 (2 courses) to £38. Set D £65 (2 courses) to £80. Tasting menu £105. **Details:** 40 seats. V menu. Bar. Music.

★ TOP 10 ★
★ BEST FRONT-OF-HOUSE ★

Pollen Street Social
Cooking score: 9
⊖ Oxford Circus, map 5
Modern British | £70
8-10 Pollen Street, Mayfair, W1S 1NQ
Tel no: (020) 7290 7600
pollenstreetsocial.com
🍾

Is it really just five years since Jason Atherton roared onto the London dining scene with his first solo venture? Since then he's opened six other London restaurants, but his talent remains firmly rooted in the kitchen at Pollen Street. Mr Atherton's cooking retains an edge, continues to surprise (teaming raw scallop with pickled kohlrabi, nasi pear, black olive and jalapeño granita), has real flavour (chilled pea garden broth with Scottish langoustine, crème fraîche and pickled onions), and is quite simply better than that of most places that produce food in this style. To begin, diners get palate-teasing portions, canapés that are little masterpieces of the genre, followed by a standout umami-laden mushroom tea. A high degree of technical competence suffuses everything, with highlights pouring forth thick and fast: roast squab pigeon served with Alsace bacon jam, peas, broad beans, and a superb leg cottage pie; saddle of rabbit, beautifully rolled, and served with salt-baked turnips and a fabulous tarragon jus; an exceptional blackcurrant Eton mess; marmalade cake with pain d'épices and sea buckthorn sorbet; and a fine Bakewell tart as part of a cavalcade of petits fours. Elsewhere, the set lunch ('bargain for food at this level'), has produced 'absolutely perfect' grouse with a vivid contrast between the breast and richer leg meat and accompanying game cottage pie 'adding yet another level of gaminess'. The restaurant itself is stripped back, with wood floors, good art and formal, white-clad tables. Invariably packed, it can be noisy, but service pleases everyone for its naturalness and essential sense of hospitality – 'how they get this effortlessly relaxed atmosphere into the restaurant I don't know'. Truly wonderful wines are handled with great insight by the 'enthusiastic sommelier', whether by the wine flight, glass or bottle (from £26).

Chef/s: Jason Atherton and Dale Bainbridge. **Open:** Mon to Sat L 12 to 2.30, D 6 to 10.30. **Closed:** Sun, 25 to 26 Dec, 1 Jan, bank hols. **Meals:** main courses £34 to £40. Set L £32 (2 courses) to £37. **Details:** 75 seats. V menu. Bar. Wheelchairs. Music.

Portland

Cooking score: 6
⊖ Great Portland St, Oxford Circus, map 5
Modern British | £47
113 Great Portland Street, Fitzrovia,
W1W 6QQ
Tel no: (020) 7436 3261
portlandrestaurant.co.uk
🍶

Impeccably modern with its house-pickled plum kernels and unconventional wines, Portland also shows an appreciation for the

more traditional pleasures of the table. For every green apple and sorrel juice, there's a game-packed pithiviers to share; it's a seductive combination, despite schoolroom chairs that limit comfortable lingering. 'Excellent' snacks – canapés you order – might be wafer-thin chicken skin with a cargo of floaty-light liver parfait and Muscat grapes, or shallot boats full of cool cod's roe cream. To start, there's delicate white polenta and a chicken wing with sweet langoustine and an intense jus laced with ginger. Bigger plates include pollack with fat Fowey mussels. The much-maligned foam is rightly revived here, carrying the flavours of cider and brown butter over a handsome piece of fish and reverently folded cabbage leaves. Yorkshire woodcock is a generous, seasonal carve-up on dripping toast, piled with chanterelles and foie gras. For pudding, a crisp éclair has a luxurious hazelnut filling and crunchy sugared nuts. Service is warm and gently earnest in the American style, and in the open kitchen at the back, the size of the brigade shows how labour-intensive brilliant simplicity can be, even with a short menu. The wine list is equally neat, but with 'textbook', 'leftfield' and 'special' sections from £21, it's bursting with possibilities.

Chef/s: Merlin Labron-Johnson. **Open:** Mon to Sat L 12 to 2.30, D 6 to 10. **Closed:** Sun. **Meals:** main courses £14 to £27. **Details:** 36 seats. Wheelchairs. Music.

Princi

Cooking score: 2
⊖ Tottenham Court Road, Piccadilly Circus, map 5
Italian | £20
135 Wardour Street, Soho, W1F 0UT
Tel no: (020) 7478 8888
princi.com
£30

In the heart of Soho, Princi plays its role as an Italian bakery and pizzeria well. That is to say, it serves very good coffee, pastries and an appealing range of dishes (good basic pasta, pizza slices, roasted vegetables, salads and the like) in its stylish, all-day self-service café. But head to the adjoining pizzeria for traditional and often authentic Italian cooking, where excellent wood-fired pizzas share the menu with antipasti – say roasted peppers, burrata and bottarga or fritto misto of prawns, soft-shell crab, squid and courgettes – alongside the traditional option of pasta (spaghetti carbonara, linguine vongole) or risotto. There's also chicken cacciatore with polenta, and cuttlefish and pea stew, while desserts include affogato or cakes from the café counter. Weekday breakfasts and weekend brunches are a major draw, too, but be prepared to queue – no bookings are taken. Wines from £22.

Open: all week 8am to 11.30pm (8.30am to 10pm Sun). **Meals:** main courses £8 to £13. **Details:** 56 seats. Wheelchairs. Music.

Quilon

Cooking score: 4
⊖ St James's Park, Victoria, map 5
Indian | £50
41 Buckingham Gate, Westminster, SW1E 6AF
Tel no: (020) 7821 1899
quilon.co.uk
£5
OFF

Elegant lattice screens, contemporary Indian artwork and an undulating wooden ceiling help to dispel any thoughts of corporate anonymity at this glamorous dining room within the St James' Court Hotel. Chef Sriram Aylur's refined take on South Indian coastal cuisine also fires up the senses, as his kitchen delivers a cavalcade of thoughtful dishes full of complex nuances and innovative touches. Aylur is a master of the spice box, blending pinpoint flavours with suave cosmopolitan detailing – especially when seafood is involved. Regional influences from Goa, Kerala and Karnataka abound, as in a gently poached fish moilee, herb-crusted tilapia with mustard sauce or crispy squid with baby spinach, pomegranate and coriander. There's plenty for both veggies and meat eaters, from mini masala dosas or mango and yoghurt curry to a stir-fry of venison and coconut or

Malabar lamb biryani. Saké and sherry are unexpected additions to the spice-friendly wine list, which opens at £30.

Chef/s: Sriram Aylur. **Open:** all week L 12 to 2 (12.30 to 3 Sat and Sun), D 6 to 10 (9.30 Sun). **Closed:** 25 Dec. **Meals:** main courses £20 to £41. Set L £27 (2 courses) to £31. Set D £60 (4 courses). **Details:** 82 seats. Bar. Music.

Quirinale

Cooking score: 3
⊖ Westminster, map 3
Italian | £35
North Court, 1 Great Peter Street,
Westminster, SW1P 3LL
Tel no: (020) 7222 7080
quirinale.co.uk

Just an amble from the corridors of Westminster, Quirinale is justly renowned as an expenses-fuelled lunchtime bolt-hole for lobbyists and pundits, who congregate round well-spaced tables in the light-filled basement dining room. Needless to say, it is unashamedly suited-and-booted, right down to the full-skirted tablecloths and dutiful, smartly uniformed staff. Over the years, the kitchen has learned how to put on the style, delivering handsome, fortifying dishes that are easy on the eye and the palate while pleasing the old and young alike. A conservative choice might be a plate of San Daniele ham and Andria burrata followed by veal milanese, while progressives could vote for warm pearl barley with root vegetables and smoked ricotta ahead of orecchiette with pumpkin, scallops and sambuca or shallot-crusted venison with chestnuts and cavolo nero. To finish, keep things revisionist with a liquorice tiramisu and honey-glazed nuts. Regional Italian wines from £21.

Chef/s: Stefano Savio. **Open:** Mon to Fri L 12 to 2.30, D 6 to 10.30. **Closed:** Sat, Sun, 24 Dec to 2 Jan, Aug, bank hols. **Meals:** main courses £19 to £28. Set L and D £19 (2 courses) to £23. **Details:** 50 seats. Music.

Quo Vadis

Cooking score: 4
⊖ Tottenham Court Road, map 5
Modern British | £38
26-29 Dean Street, Soho, W1D 3LL
Tel no: (020) 7437 9585
quovadissoho.co.uk

Part of this sizeable chunk of Soho real estate was home to Karl Marx in the 1850s, has been a restaurant since 1926, and been called Quo Vadis since the 1950s. This iconic venue has been under the custodianship of the Hart brothers since 2008 and it's in fine fettle. The redevelopment of the ground-floor restaurant to house the Frith Street branch of Barrafina in autumn 2016, with Jeremy Lee's restaurant moving into the bar area, is bound to ring some changes, although the enduring presence of Sam and Eddie Hart and the continuation of the tried-and-tested formula of Jeremy Lee's feisty modern British food are reassuring. The handsome menu serves up the likes of smoked cod's roe with anchovy and a runny boiled egg, followed by pork shoulder with pickles, or a wild duck casserole that gets rave reviews. When it comes to dessert, make it sticky toffee pudding. The impeccable wine list kicks off at £25.
Chef/s: Jeremy Lee. **Open:** Mon to Sat L 12 to 3, D 5.30 to 11. **Closed:** Sun, 25 and 26 Dec, bank hols. **Meals:** main courses £15 to £25. Set L and D £20 (2 courses) to £23. **Details:** 72 seats. 20 seats outside. Bar.

Rex Whistler at the Tate

Cooking score: 2
⊖ Pimlico, map 3
British | £35
Millbank, Pimlico, SW1P 4RG
Tel no: (020) 7887 8825
tate.org.uk

The restaurant at Tate Britain is a beautiful room with plenty of space and lots of white linen. Under Rex Whistler's wraparound mural (a pastorally themed hunting scene) diners can set about a comforting menu that

reads as a celebration of great British ingredients, carefully assembled and cooked simply, with plenty of old favourites such as twice-baked Cornish Blue cheese soufflé with pear-pomegranate salad and walnuts, and Saddleback pork terrine with piccalilli and grilled rye bread. The cooking may play it safe but is rigorously seasonal – a June lunch delivering asparagus and poached duck egg with a hint of truffle, a beautifully cooked Swaledale lamb rump, which added up to 'pretty good value considering the execution, which was excellent in every regard'. The Tate's justly famed wine cellar, sourced by Hamish Anderson with an eye for little-known gems and quality drinking, is a fascinating, insightful triumph with plenty by the glass, half-bottle and with house wine at £27.50.
Chef/s: Anthony Martin. **Open:** all week L only 12 to 3 (11.30 Sat). **Meals:** set L £31 (2 courses) to £37. **Details:** 80 seats. 20 seats outside. Wheelchairs.

The Ritz

Cooking score: 6
⊖ Green Park, map 5
French | £75
150 Piccadilly, Mayfair, W1J 9BR
Tel no: (020) 7300 2370
theritzlondon.com

When the lure of beige minimalism begins to pall, get yourself to The Ritz, which still has a dining room whose magnificence was newly minted in the Escoffier era, where garland chandeliers depend from the celestial ceiling fresco, a gilded Poseidon reclines in state and luxuriant drapes frame oblique views over Green Park. Then order a partridge, served in the Souvaroff manner (with foie gras and truffles in Madeira, obviously). John Williams MBE does the place proud, gilding the lily where it will bear gilding – Norfolk crab with cucumber, egg yolk and Sevruga caviar – and leaving well alone where the strongest message might be simplicity, as when lamb loin comes with couscous and aubergine and a scenting of black garlic. The fixed-price lunch is sensational value in the circumstances, as reported the diner who progressed from goose liver terrine and pineapple to slow-cooked veal fillet with morels, and the ambrosial banana soufflé with rum ice cream. Wines in three and four figures abound, the starting line set at £45.

Chef/s: John Williams. **Open:** all week L 12.30 to 2, D 5.30 to 10. **Meals:** main courses £40 to £49. Set L £49 (3 courses). Set D £95 (3 courses). Sun L £59. Menu Surprise £95 (6 courses). **Details:** 80 seats. 15 seats outside. Bar. Wheelchairs. Music. Parking.

Roka

Cooking score: 4
⊖ Goodge Street, map 5
Japanese | £50
37 Charlotte Street, Fitzrovia, W1T 1RR
Tel no: (020) 7580 6464
rokarestaurant.com

The Roka chain is all about demystifying Japanese eating for a city crowd that isn't especially given to dining in reverential hush to the twanging of a distant zither. This is Charlotte Street and the beat goes on, from the downstairs shochu lounge where fermented rice drinks and cocktails wet the whistle, before you gather around the robata counter for some expertly prepared, demonstrably fresh grill cooking. Sea bream fillet with miso and red onion, scallop skewers in wasabi and shiso, Korean-spiced lamb cutlets – all are strikingly replete with umami, and the less familiar dishes, such as rice hotpot with king crab and wasabi-fired tobiko roe, are convincing demonstrations that Japanese food isn't all ethereal delicacy. A multi-course tasting menu should put paid to that idea. Desserts do Asian things to Western originals, adding sesame pocky sticks to chocolate and peanut sundae, caramelised miso ice cream to almond and yoghurt cake.

Chef/s: Damon Griffith. **Open:** all week L 12 to 3.30 (4 Sat and Sun), D 5.30 to 11.30 (10.30 Sun). **Closed:** 25 Dec. **Meals:** dishes £13 to £36. Tasting menu £83. **Details:** 88 seats. 24 seats outside. Bar. Music.

Roux at Parliament Square

Cooking score: 4
⊖ Westminster, St James's Park, map 5
Modern European | £59
11 Great George Street, Parliament Square, Westminster, SW1P 3AD
Tel no: (020) 7334 3737
rouxatparliamentsquare.co.uk

The Georgian town house is just yards from Horse Guards Parade and the Palace of Westminster, so clusters of policy advisors and ministers of state can be expected at certain sessions. Elegant, well-spaced tables in a lushly carpeted pair of rooms are patrolled by staff who will spread your napkin over your lap. The cooking takes its cue from what might be seen as the Roux house style, a modernish amalgam of French, British and other European modes, where a main course might offer a slender fillet of stone bass on a tasty tarte fine of Datterini tomatoes and Kalamata olives, or perhaps heftier Herdwick hogget with parsnips, pear and red cabbage. Freshness and lightness are the watchwords, from a starter of marinated mackerel with gazpacho ketchup and peas to a dessert of gariguette strawberries seasoned with lemon thyme and served with rich whipped mascarpone. Wines will suit the ministers of state for unabashed opulence, from £28.

Chef/s: Steve Groves. **Open:** Mon to Fri L 12 to 2, D 6.30 to 10. **Closed:** Sat, Sun, bank hols. **Meals:** set L £35 (3 courses). Set D £59 (3 courses). Tasting menu £79. **Details:** 60 seats. Bar. Wheelchairs.

Roux at the Landau

Cooking score: 4
⊖ Oxford Circus, map 5
Modern European | £55
The Langham, 1c Portland Place, Oxford Circus, W1B 1JA
Tel no: (020) 7965 0165
rouxatthelandau.com
🛏

The position of head chef here has been the subject of some mobility in the last couple of years, but the unifying element of Roux *père et fils* – Albert and Michel Jnr – is what keeps the Landau dining room purring along. In a panelled circular room adorned with modern arboreal pictures, the style is a mixture of French tradition and more modern European touches. Lunch feels like a steal: gazpacho poured at table over a bowl of heritage tomatoes and cucumber granita, the latter element forming an icy ripple through the creamy-textured soup; stuffed rabbit leg en crépinette with peas and a well-seasoned jus; mango parfait with caramelised pineapple. At dinner, it all gets ritzier, with mains such as skrei cod and squid with barley, quinoa and purple broccoli, or venison loin with red cabbage, celeriac and sauce poivrade. Pear Tatin with walnut crumble and brandy ice cream makes a regal finale. Wines are French first and foremost, starting at £34.

Chef/s: Chris King. **Open:** Mon to Fri L 12 to 2.30, Mon to Sat D 5.30 to 10.30. **Closed:** Sun, first week Jan. **Meals:** main courses £20 to £48. Set L and D £39. Tasting menu £70. **Details:** 90 seats. Bar. Wheelchairs. Music.

Rules

Cooking score: 3
⊖ Covent Garden, Leicester Square, map 5
British | £49
35 Maiden Lane, Covent Garden, WC2E 7LB
Tel no: (020) 7836 5314
rules.co.uk

London's oldest restaurant has sailed on undaunted through Trafalgar and Waterloo, abdications and financial crashes, weathering the storms with stiff upper lip intact. Amid an ambience pitched somewhere between palace of varieties and gentlemen's club, its specialities of seasonal game make it a favourite autumn draw. However, some feel the sense of tradition outweighs the evidence on the plate, and recent reports on the food have been mixed ('gloopy' crops up in descriptions of mash), with 'some slackness' noted in the service, too. Yet when on form Rules can be an 'amusing and congenial restaurant' where a whole wild duck can be 'safely stowed away and thoroughly enjoyed',

steak, kidney and oyster pudding comes with 'splendid pastry and superlative gravy', and those new to hare receive a comprehensive grounding, in the form of the sliced medium-rare fillet and long-cooked shoulder rolled into a cabbage-leaf cigar, with celeriac and spinach in red wine sauce. House French is £26.

Chef/s: David Stafford. **Open:** all week 12 to 11.45 (10.45 Sun). **Closed:** 25 and 26 Dec. **Meals:** main courses £19 to £38. **Details:** 95 seats. Bar.

Salt Yard

Cooking score: 2
⊖ Goodge Street, map 5
Tapas | £30
54 Goodge Street, Fitzrovia, W11 4NA
Tel no: (020) 7637 0657
saltyard.co.uk

For an informal tapas venue, Salt Yard looks considerably smarter than you may be expecting, with teak-brown banquettes, a mirrored wall and framed pictures of river scenes in the main basement room. Nonetheless, if you just want to pop in for a Martini and a dish of Marcona almonds, or a glass or three of something to accompany some Iberian charcuterie, the Yard is your oyster. Italy as well as Spain provides the culinary inspiration, so expect pea and mint arancini and aged Parmesan, or truffled macaroni cheese, among the more obvious likes of patatas bravas, roast hake with ajo blanco and baby artichokes, and croquetas of jamón, leek and Manchego in salsa rosa. The signature dish is a vegetable side of courgette flowers stuffed with goats' cheese and trickled with honey. Beguile your sweet tooth with Valrhona hazelnut chocolate mousse served with mini-churros and an oloroso-poached plum. Wines from £20 supplement the sherries, cavas and Proseccos.

Chef/s: Ben Tish and Dan Sherlock. **Open:** all week 12 to 11 (10 Sun). **Meals:** tapas £5 to £11. **Details:** 72 seats. 8 seats outside. Music.

Savoy Grill

Cooking score: 2
θ Charing Cross, map 5
Anglo-French | £42
The Savoy, Strand, Covent Garden, WC2R 0EU
Tel no: (020) 7592 1600
gordonramsay.com

Few restaurants have such rich history, and at its prime the Savoy Grill was a byword for power dining. The Art Deco-inspired room has four large and impressive chandeliers hanging from the ceiling, antique mirrors and claret walls and columns, while tables covered with very well-starched white linen and trolley service 'with lots of carving at table' give notice that service is formal. The food has a convincing pedigree too, showcasing comfort food (roasts, braises and pies) with a touch of luxury, as well as a number of tasting menus – including one with Escoffier's signature dishes. Individual elements are noteworthy: asparagus with a thin layer of lardo and a watercress and walnut salad; roasted Lancashire duck breast served with some of its leg meat between layers of pommes Anna; a sublime apple crumble soufflé with a sour apple sorbet; and classy petits fours. The serious and expensive wine list starts from £29.
Chef/s: Kim Woodward. **Open:** all week L 12 to 3 (4 Sun), D 5 to 11 (6 to 10.30 Sun). **Meals:** main courses £20 to £42. Set L and early D £26 (2 courses) to £30. Tasting menus £35 (4 courses) to £95. **Details:** 100 seats. V menu. Bar. Wheelchairs.

Scott's

Cooking score: 4
θ Green Park, map 6
Seafood | £45
20 Mount Street, Mayfair, W1K 2HE
Tel no: (020) 7495 7309
scotts-restaurant.com

It may have flaunted its Mayfair glitz back in the 60s, but nowadays Scott's puts on a more grown-up, mature face – even if it still attracts a clutch of A-listers and minor celebs eager to pose for (or determinedly avoid) the paparazzi

hovering outside. Those seeking delights of a different sort can focus on the oyster bar shimmering with displays of icy crustacea, the multitude of mirrors, the polished oak panelling hung with large modern canvases or the smart green leather banquettes and their rather too-close-together white-clad tables. Top-drawer seafood is the main attraction, and you can play it simple or fancy: traditionalists might fancy a Cognac-laced shellfish bisque followed by Dover sole meunière, while those of a more adventurous bent could veer towards octopus carpaccio, miso-blackened salmon or roast cod with chorizo, beans and Padrón peppers. Meat eaters are helpfully accommodated, while desserts could offer vanilla pannacotta with blood orange. Wines start at £27.
Chef/s: David McCarthy. **Open:** all week 12 to 10.30 (10 Sun). **Closed:** 25 and 26 Dec. **Meals:** main courses £20 to £34. **Details:** 120 seats. 20 seats outside. Bar. Wheelchairs.

Seven Park Place by William Drabble

Cooking score: 6
θ Green Park, map 5
Modern French | £63
St James's Hotel and Club, 7-8 Park Place, Mayfair, SW1A 1LS
Tel no: (020) 7316 1600
stjameshotelandclub.com

The crimson façade and red-carpeted front steps of the St James's look like London clubland incarnate, but you'll need your Art Nouveau goggles on for William Drabble's dining room, where a chocolate and gold colour scheme prevails, with unapologetic geometric patterning everywhere you look. In the circumstances, the cooking does well to compete for attention, but compete it does with finely honed renditions of modern French cuisine that are memorable for their precisely achieved balance. Red mullet is griddled with goats' cheese and rosemary, then deepened with puréed garlic and red wine, ahead of perfectly rendered duck breast with a

truffled potato pithiviers and braised celery in Madeira jus. The seven-course Menu Gourmand is a treat from start to finish, but the fixed-price lunch deal is not to be sniffed at either – perhaps braised snails and parsley purée, roast cod with clams and fregola, and apple and raisin croustade with toffee sauce. A wine list of surpassing finesse accords France its due, but is diligent elsewhere, too, with fine German and Austrian listings, English sparklers and fortified wines to conjure with. Prices open at £30, or £8.50 a glass.
Chef/s: William Drabble. **Open:** Tue to Sat L 12 to 2, D 6.30 to 10. **Closed:** Sun, Mon, Christmas, bank hols. **Meals:** set L £27 (2 courses) to £32. Set D £57 (2 courses) to £63. Menu Gourmand £75. **Details:** 28 seats. Bar. Wheelchairs.

★ NEW ENTRY ★

Sexy Fish

Cooking score: 4
⊖ Green Park, map 5
Seafood | £95
Berkeley Square House, Berkeley Square, Mayfair, W1J 6BR
Tel no: (020) 3764 2000
sexyfish.com

'Fabulous room, beautifully divided and lit so you don't feel overwhelmed by the fact that it can seat 190 people – it felt solid, rather like one of the great brasseries of Paris, but then owner Richard Caring is behind The Ivy, Le Caprice, J. Sheekey – he understands the value of longevity in a restaurant.' There is no doubt that achingly cool Sexy Fish is packing a major punch in Berkeley Square, its lively cross-cultural cooking taking in caviar for the minted, varieties of sashimi, steaks from the robata grill, sticky pork ribs and gochujang (Korean fermented chilli and bean paste) and miso lamb cutlets – so it is much more than the straightforward seafood restaurant the name (and fish-themed art installations) implies. Standout dishes at inspection were silky, beautifully made prawn gyoza, seared salmon with black bean, pickled daikon and sea purslane, and an outstanding crispy duck

salad in a tangle of pomegranate, sesame, pomelo and sakura herbs. Wines, in tune with the food, start at £25.
Chef/s: Tim Hughes. **Open:** all week 12 to 11.30 (11 Sun). **Closed:** 25 and 26 Dec. **Meals:** main courses £19 to £110. **Details:** 190 seats. Bar. Wheelchairs. Music.

★ NEW ENTRY ★

Shackfuyu

Cooking score: 1
⊖ Tottenham Court Road, map 5
Japanese | £30
14a Old Compton Street, Soho, W1D 4TJ
Tel no: (020) 7734 7492
bonedaddies.com

What started as an experimental pop-up from the Bone Daddies ramen bars has turned into the fixed star of this small, no-bookings London chain. At lunch the place is calm, giving you a chance to appreciate the inventive cooking. An innovative menu successfully mixes up Japanese izakaya and western-influenced approaches with bolder Korean and international flavours. The prawn toast 'masquerading as okonomiyaki' is topped with curling, waving bonito flakes; Korean-style rice is served sizzling in a hot stone bowl. French toast dessert is sprinkled with kinako, the toasted soya bean flour complemented by soft-serve green-tea ice cream. In the evenings the noise really ramps up, but this doesn't deter the hipsterish crowd who don't mind queuing. The cocktails, craft beers and saké list are as popular as the wines (from £18.50).
Chef/s: Ross Shonhan. **Open:** Mon to Fri L 12 to 3, D 5.30 to 11 (10 Mon). Sat and Sun 12 to 11 (9 Sun). **Closed:** 25 and 26 Dec. **Meals:** main courses £15 to £22. Set L and D £30 (2 courses) to £35. **Details:** 80 seats. Bar. Music.

Average price

The average price denotes the price of a three-course meal without wine.

Sixtyone

Cooking score: 4
⊖ Marble Arch, map 6
Modern British | £40
61 Upper Berkeley Street, Marylebone,
W1H 7PP
Tel no: (020) 7958 3222
sixtyonerestaurant.co.uk
£5 OFF 🚗

Part of the luxe Montcalm hotel, Sixtyone has its own entrance and is beginning to forge its own identity as a dining destination. In a road without much in the way of passing trade compared to its prestigious near neighbours, Arnaud Stevens and his team deliver pin-sharp modern food with an Anglo-French mindset. The dining room, with its shades of copper and cream, makes for a refined spot, while the service team do their bit with professionalism and gusto. There's both creativity and respect for the classical craft in a repertoire that might see you go from octopus carpaccio, via haunch of Lake District venison with smoked celeriac and blueberries, to apple mille-feuille matched with the flavours of lavender and lime. The suppliers of the first-rate ingredients get a name-check on the menu. A passion for all things Sixtyone includes a stonking range of Bordeaux from the 1961 vintage; prices for mere mortals start at £25.
Chef/s: Arnaud Stevens. **Open:** Mon to Sun L 12 to 3 (5 Sun), D 5.30 to 10.30. **Closed:** 25 to 27 Dec. **Meals:** main courses £18 to £32. Set L and D £26 (2 courses) to £30. **Details:** 70 seats. Bar. Wheelchairs. Music.

Please send us your feedback

To register your opinion about any restaurant listed in this guide, or a new restaurant that you wish to bring to our attention, please visit the web address at the bottom of the page. Your feedback informs the content of the book and will be used to compile next year's reviews.

Sketch, Lecture Room & Library

Cooking score: 7
⊖ Oxford Circus, map 5
Modern European | £108
9 Conduit Street, Mayfair, W1S 2XG
Tel no: (020) 7659 4500
sketch.london

'I liked Sketch,' confessed a reporter, much taken by the private-club feel of the highly glamorised 18th-century town house. However, with several bars and restaurants (one noted for its afternoon tea), Sketch is also very accessible. In the richly designed first-floor Lecture Room the cooking is absolutely correct, totally impressive in execution and difficult to fault for quality. Head chef Johannes Nuding, under the guidance of Pierre Gagnaire, has a commendably modest appreciation of simplicity as well as sophistication, with an intuitive understanding of flavours: note 'very good canapés' of tarragon croquettes, squid-ink wafers with goats' cheese, and chorizo with crunchy beetroot, as well as hare terrine studded with foie gras and truffle, the richness offset by red cabbage, redcurrant and cubes of quince jelly. Others have reported glowingly on wild turbot roasted on the bone and accompanied by a cocotte of mussels flavoured with lemongrass, crunchy winter leaves, Horn of Plenty mushrooms, and lemon, kalamansi lime and Regent's Park honey, and tender, whole roasted pigeon, marinated in lemon and cumin, served with Puy lentils, a physalis and daikon mix and sauerkraut. An assemblage of six small desserts makes up the signature finale: among them a traditional Opéra cake with raspberry coulis, mascarpone and praline, a chestnut cream with tuile, green apple granita and gel, and pistachio pannacotta with coffee meringue and poached pear with bourbon vanilla. There's a good-value set lunch, service is professional yet relaxed, and the wine list is an expensive thoroughbred, although there's an extensive selection by the glass and a few bottles at £25.

Chef/s: Pierre Gagnaire and Johannes Nuding.
Open: Tue to Fri L 12 to 2.30, Tue to Sat D 6.30 to
10.30. **Closed:** Sun, Mon, 25 Dec, 2 weeks Aug.
Meals: main courses £49 to £80. Set L £35 (2
courses) to £40. **Details:** 48 seats. Music. Children
over 6 yrs only.

Smoking Goat

Cooking score: 3
⊖ Tottenham Court Road, map 5
Thai | £30
7 Denmark Street, Soho, WC2H 8LZ
Tel no: (020) 7999 9999
smokinggoatsoho.com

A self-proclaimed 'Soho dive bar & dining
room', if you're trying to get a handle on the
London dining scene, check out Smoking
Goat. This place is so hot, it's smokin'. Thai
street food is hardly a new concept, but it's
done with such swagger here it almost seems
like they invented it, and it all takes place in a
room that stays just the right side of rough-
and-ready. Lamb ribs are cooked over wood
smoke, as is pork belly fired up with five-spice
and sour chilli, while two people can share
whole smoked shoulder of goat flavoured with
Thai herbs. Add spicy green papaya salad on
the side, some sticky rice and you're sorted. It's
hard to stop, though, when small plates such as
crispy pork belly with pickled watermelon
catch the eye. Drink draught beer or
something from the concise wine list (bottles
start at £16 and head north at speed).
Chef/s: Aaron Daulton and Scott Roberts. **Open:**
Mon to Fri L 12 to 3, D 5 to 11. Sat and Sun 12 to 11
(9 Sun). **Closed:** 25 and 26 Dec, 1 Jan. **Meals:** main
courses £11 to £18. **Details:** 60 seats. Bar. Music.

Social Eating House

Cooking score: 6
⊖ Oxford Circus, map 5
Modern British | £47
58 Poland Street, Soho, W1F 7NR
Tel no: (020) 7993 3251
socialeatinghouse.com
🍾

With the Blind Pig cocktail bar upstairs, this
outpost of Jason Atherton's 'Social' empire is
distilled 21st-century Soho – right down to
the deliberately distressed interiors, curios,
gilded mirrors and lurid blue neon signs. It's
fast, furious and deafening, although some feel
that service falls short of Atherton's sky-high
standards elsewhere. By contrast, the food is
always intelligent, creative, jokey and
'beautifully presented' – no surprise given that
head chef Paul Hood honed his skills at
Atherton's mighty Mayfair flagship, Pollen
Street Social (see entry). Top contenders from
the seasonally accented menu could range
from confit and house-smoked salmon with
miso crème fraîche, BBQ cucumber and
autumn truffle to slow-cooked haunch of
venison with wild garlic porridge, white
asparagus and cavolo nero or Cornish brill
with celeriac, watercress, mussel emulsion and
sea vegetables. Trendy sharing 'jars' will set
things rolling, while brilliantly inventive
desserts such as chocolate crémeux with salted
caramel, mascarpone, espresso and almond
biscotti deliver the final hit. The wine list is a
trademark 'Social' compendium full of offbeat
labels, new discoveries and thrilling tipples,
particularly from Europe. Prices start at £22
(£5.50 a glass).
Chef/s: Paul Hood. **Open:** Mon to Sat L 12 to 2.30,
D 6 to 10.30. **Closed:** Sun, 25 and 26 Dec, bank hols
(exc Good Fri). **Meals:** main courses £18 to £32. Set
L £21 (2 courses) to £25. Tasting menu £62 (6
courses). **Details:** 83 seats. V menu. Bar.
Wheelchairs. Music.

Social Wine & Tapas

Cooking score: 4
⊖ Bond Street, map 6
Modern British | £28
39 James Street, Marylebone, W1U 1DL
Tel no: (020) 7993 3257
socialwineandtapas.com
🍾 £30

At the top of a street well known for a series of fairly average European café-culture-style restaurants with deep awnings and tables spilling out over the pavement, Jason Atherton's Social Wine & Tapas is a welcome oasis. Set over several levels, it's like a dark chocolate box with copper panels and detailing, moody lighting and bottles and wine casks galore. Tapas are 'a treat and a delight from start to finish'. Crispy duck egg served with silky-smooth roasted artichoke, truffle adding a gentle muskiness and with welcome saltiness from cured pork, is a 'must order dish', but there's also ham croquetas 'wonderfully light and gone in an instant', raw Orkney scallops served super-chilled on ice with yuzu, radish and a cucumber granita, and generous boards piled with brilliant hams. There are raciones, too, if you fancy a larger dish, say steak, whole lemon sole or roast quail. Not surprisingly, wine plays a key part, with chief sommelier Laure Patry's fabulous, extensive list highlighting small interesting producers. Bottles start at £25, and there are 20 offered by the glass (from £5 to £15).
Chef/s: Frankie Van Loo. **Open:** Mon to Sat L 12 to 2.30, D 5.30 to 10.30. **Closed:** Sun, bank hols. **Meals:** tapas £6 to £20. **Details:** 64 seats. Wheelchairs. Music.

Symbols

🛏 Accommodation is available
£30 Three courses for less than £30
£5 OFF £5-off voucher scheme
🍾 Notable wine list

Spring

Cooking score: 5
⊖ Temple, Waterloo, map 5
Modern European | £55
Somerset House, Lancaster Place, Strand, WC2R 1LA
Tel no: (020) 3011 0115
springrestaurant.co.uk

The gastronomisation of Somerset House over the past generation has been enchanting. Where once public records and tax affairs were logged, there is now, as one reader says of Skye Gyngell's bright-white spacious Spring, 'a very pleasant experience with interesting combinations and creative use of vegetables'. That last note was Gyngell's hallmark at Petersham Nurseries (see entry, Richmond) and even in central London, convincing freshness and seasonality illuminate dishes such as ravioli with Swiss chard, porcini, ricotta and sage butter, halibut with flower sprouts and macadamias, or rabbit with creamed kale and lentils. A defiant boldness at the hot end of the spectrum chases off any lingering delicacy, adding chilli jam to the scallops, and chilli oil and horseradish to grilled lamb with agretti and borlotti beans, while desserts aim to seduce by means of bitter chocolate tart with honeycomb and espresso. Fragrant cocktails frothed with egg white are worth a flutter before you start on the wines at £25.
Chef/s: Skye Gyngell. **Open:** all week 12 to 11 (5 Sun). **Closed:** 25 to 29 Dec. **Meals:** main courses £18 to £31. Set L and D £28 (2 courses) to £32. **Details:** 90 seats. Bar. Wheelchairs.

Tamarind

Cooking score: 4
⊖ Green Park, map 5
Indian | £50
20 Queen Street, Mayfair, W1J 5PR
Tel no: (020) 7629 3561
tamarindrestaurant.com

An early trailblazer in terms of elevating Indian food beyond its end-of-night curry image, Tamarind has built its reputation on

high-end renditions of northern Indian dishes with a dash of innovation, served against a classy backdrop of burnished pillars, crisp linen and polished wood floors. The kitchen, visible through a window, has been in Peter Joseph's hands since 2012 and things are going swimmingly, with diners praising everything from the authenticity of the food to the clarity of flavour. Delicate scallops, perfectly balanced with a smashed tomato and onion seed sauce, are a great introduction to the style, while standout mains have included the signature slow-cooked lamb shank with turmeric, yoghurt and 'a delicious gamut of spices', and the tandoor-grilled chicken breast with a vegetable tikki with a crispy gram-flour coating and a fenugreek-rich tomato sauce. 'The portions were more than sufficient, even when shared, but the quality of both dishes made it extremely difficult to leave anything,' summed up one regular. If you can squeeze in dessert, the house special of pistachio kulfi comes highly recommended, 'representing the very essence of pistachio'. The 'bright, intelligent service' includes a helpful sommelier overseeing a lengthy list that kicks off at £29 and reaches for the sky, offering plenty of special treats for big spenders.
Chef/s: Peter Joseph. **Open:** all week L 12 to 2.45, D 5.30 to 10.45 (6 to 10.15 Sun). **Closed:** 1 Jan. **Meals:** main courses £20 to £40. Set L £22 (2 courses) to £25. Sun L £32. Tasting menu £75. **Details:** 89 seats. Music. No children under 5 yrs after 7pm.

10 Greek Street
Cooking score: 4
⊖ Tottenham Court Road, map 5
Modern European | £35
10 Greek Street, Soho, W1D 4DH
Tel no: (020) 7734 4677
10greekstreet.com

Remember the drill: you can book at lunch, but take your chances in the evening. If the place is rammed by the time you get there, leave your mobile number, go and have a drink and await the call. The no-standing-on-ceremony approach is reflected in the pared-back café ambience, with crammed-in tables on a parquet floor, a chalked-up menu, open kitchen and dining counter. The food is robust rustic European gear with no frills, from Spanish (cuttlefish with chickpeas and chorizo) to Italian (San Daniele prosciutto with goats' curd and fried polenta), to the traditional satisfaction of main dishes like whole lemon sole with fennel, monk's beard and olives, or Brecon lamb with mash, cavolo nero and morels. Finish with a chocolate pot zhuzhed up with blood orange and pomegranate, or pistachio cake with ginger ice cream. Small plates of snacky stuff are served all day. A concise wine list comes in small glasses (from £3), half-bottle carafes (£9) and bottles (£18).
Chef/s: Cameron Emirali. **Open:** Mon to Sat L 12 to 2.30, D 5.30 to 10.45. **Closed:** Sun, 24 to 31 Dec. **Meals:** main courses £16 to £42. **Details:** 35 seats. 2 seats outside. Bar. Music.

Terroirs
Cooking score: 2
⊖ Charing Cross, map 5
Modern European | £25
5 William IV Street, Covent Garden, WC2N 4DW
Tel no: (020) 7036 0660
terroirswinebar.com
£30

With wine-fuelled hubbub at street level and a more serene cellar below stairs, Terroirs is no slouch when it comes to atmosphere – though on busy nights, readers report that service can slacken a little. The wine is, of course, the thing, and it's easy to spend more time studying the list, full of interesting small-scale producers, than the short, easy-to-like menu. Hits on a recent visit included Scottish langoustines, anointed with olive oil, that hadn't spent a second too long in the pan, and well-seasoned pork and pistachio terrine done in true, coarse, country style. Clams with garlic, parsley and lemon are expertly done, but don't take kindly to hanging around when dishes are sent out 'without a considered order'. To finish, chocolate pots with salted caramel are textbook examples. It's all 'good value for money', the more so when the excellent house wine is just £19.50 and a world of minimal-intervention possibility opens up beyond that.

Chef/s: Michal Chacinski. **Open:** Mon to Sat L 12 to 3, D 5.30 to 11. **Closed:** Sun, 25 and 26 Dec, 1 Jan, 1 May, 28 Aug. **Meals:** main courses £17 to £20. **Details:** 65 seats. 6 seats outside. Bar. Music.

Texture

Cooking score: 5
⊖ Marble Arch, map 6
Modern French/Nordic | £74
34 Portman Street, Marylebone, W1H 7BY
Tel no: (020) 7224 0028
texture-restaurant.co.uk

When Texture opened in 2007 it rode the wave of fashionable New Nordic cuisine and chef Aggi Sverrisson showcased ingredients from his native Iceland. But his classical training is evident in today's menus where original recipes have evolved into food of great imagination and technique. A garden-fresh appetiser assembles broad beans, peas and pea shoots, while on a plate the colour of blood oranges, asparagus is joined by herbs, goats' milk snow and a trace of Kalamata olives. A standout dish is smoked eel with textures of turnip and quinoa soaked into the most luxurious bonito broth – umami heaven – but suckling pig studded with cloves is a masterpiece of crisp skin and melting flesh, served with pig's cheek and chopped cabbage with the faintest trace of pickling vinegar. Dessert of Icelandic skyr yoghurt, rhubarb and ice cream is more enjoyable than it sounds. The room is bright and airy with Scandi influences, including birch trees, mossy stones, blond-wood floors and dramatic bare branches. Tables have a rather uncomfortable metal crinoline instead of legs, but the tailored cushions for smaller diners are a considerate touch. Wines from £39.

Chef/s: Agnar Sverrisson. **Open:** Wed to Sat L 12 to 2.30, Tue to Sat D 6 to 11. **Closed:** Sun, Mon. **Meals:** main courses £29 to £42. Set L £29 (2 courses) to £34. Tasting menu £85. **Details:** 50 seats. Bar. Wheelchairs. Music.

Theo Randall at the InterContinental

Cooking score: 6
⊖ Hyde Park Corner, map 6
Italian | £70
InterContinental London Hotel, 1 Hamilton Place, Mayfair, W1J 7QY
Tel no: (020) 7318 8747
theorandall.com

£5 OFF 🚗

Almost ten years on, anyone who feared Theo Randall's union with the InterContinental Hotel would prove an uneasy fit has long ago eaten their words. And with gusto, for that's what Randall's food excels at: punchy, bold flavours, unfussy plates of fiercely seasonal Italian food, conceived with an enthusiasm, technical excellence and confidence that's palpable on the plate. Celebrating his decade's tenure with a refit, the linen and mirrors have been given the heave-ho for an altogether fresher, muted, casual look, albeit in a still windowless room – blond wood, seating every-which-way, olive and grey tones and a touch of marble (this is Park Lane after all). The rejigged daily-changing menu retains signature hits but bumps up the seafood quota and offers more choice for lunchtime diners. So, alongside pan-fried squid with Lamon borlotti beans and some zucchini fritti, you might find baked Fontina cheese soufflé or a primi of ravioli (the pasta is seriously good) followed by tender wood-roasted guinea fowl or monkfish with Roseval potatoes and violet artichokes. Randall's signature Amalfi lemon tart makes for a lip-smacking close. Organising the predominantly Italian wines (from £37) by season is an intriguing idea, but time will tell whether it befuddles or inspires.

Chef/s: Theo Randall. **Open:** Mon to Fri L 12 to 3, Mon to Sat D 6 to 11. **Closed:** Sun, 25 and 26 Dec. **Meals:** main courses £20 to £36. Set L and D £29 (2 courses) to £35. **Details:** 160 seats. Bar. Wheelchairs. Music. Parking.

Tredwell's

Cooking score: 2
⊖ Leicester Square, map 5
Modern British | £40
4A Upper St Martin's Lane, Covent Garden, WC2H 9NY
Tel no: (020) 3764 0840
tredwells.com

Entering Marcus Wareing's Covent Garden gaff is like passing through a time vortex as the modern, boxy building gives way to a stylish split-level space with an Art Deco-esque finish – green leather seats and banquettes, lots of mirrors and retro light fittings. There's a cocktail bar – 'the mixologist certainly knows his onions' – and a menu that covers a lot of ground to deliver feel-good flavours and considers the world to be its oyster. Kick off with fashionable numbers such as harissa-glazed aubergine with peanut, coriander and chilli, or crispy buttermilk chicken with pickled cucumber, and move on to Lake District lamb chop cooked over charcoal, miso-baked cod or a 'very, very juicy' burger. The prix-fixe menu is an essential item in theatreland (the place is even named after an Agatha Christie character), and any dish you fancy can be jazzed up with Bianchetto truffle for twelve quid a pop. Wines start at £26. **Chef/s:** Chantelle Nicholson. **Open:** all week L 12 to 2 (3 Fri, 4.45 Sat, 4 Sun), Mon to Sat D 5 to 10 (11 Fri and Sat). **Closed:** 25 and 26 Dec, 1 Jan. **Meals:** main courses £14 to £29. Set L, early and late D £21 (2 courses) to £25. Sun L £27. **Details:** 120 seats. Wheelchairs. Music.

Trishna

Cooking score: 4
⊖ Baker Street, Bond Street, map 6
Indian | £50
15-17 Blandford Street, Marylebone, W1U 3DG
Tel no: (020) 7935 5624
trishnalondon.com
🍾★

Karam Sethi's well-established Marylebone restaurant is considered a consistent address for first-class Indian cooking. What is on offer is a sophisticated, updated version of Indian coastal cooking vitalised by its subtle yet assertive spicing. The menu's old favourites are justly acclaimed – aloo chaat, madras lamb shank curry and excellent biryanis – while less familiar dishes garner similar praise: a wild rabbit xacuti (keema naan, a complex spiced xacuti masala, rabbit samosa), for example. Seafood is a high point, with praise for Dorset brown crab (with butter, pepper, chilli and garlic), jheenga moilee (king prawns in a lightly spiced, creamy coconut sauce) and machher jhol (cod fillet with mustard oil and potato). Side dishes, vegetables and bread are exemplary and the rich pleasure of cardamom kheer is not to be missed. The wine list is no less delightful, packed with spice-friendly bottles with excellent recommendations by the glass for each dish. **Chef/s:** Rohit Ghai. **Open:** all week L 12 to 2.30 (3 Sun), D 6 to 10.30 (5.30 Sat, 5.30 to 9.45 Sun). **Closed:** 25 and 26 Dec, 1 Jan. **Meals:** main courses £15 to £24. Set L £20 (2 courses) to £26. Set D £28. Tasting menu £60 (5 courses) to £70 (7 courses). **Details:** 60 seats. 6 seats outside. Music. No children after 8pm.

28°-50°

Cooking score: 4
⊖ Bond Street, map 6
French | £32
15-17 Marylebone Lane, Marylebone,
W1U 2NE
Tel no: (020) 7486 7922
2850.co.uk
🍷

'It was a treat to come here and sample some above-average offerings at reasonable prices,' remarked one visitor to the Marylebone branch of Agnar Sverrisson's big-statement wine bars that are dedicated to demotic food and heavenly wines. It makes a confident destination, with a lively central bar surrounded by dining tables, and everyone has a good time. A small but carefully crafted menu gives the impression of all bases being covered as it ranges from oysters, prawn cocktail or goose and mustard terrine to a BBQ pulled pork burger, Aberdeen Angus grass-fed flat-iron steak with skinny fries, and Cornish cod with black rice, Nocellara olives, lemon and radish – winning combinations all. Finish with chocolate madeleines with vanilla crème anglaise or cheeses from La Fromagerie. Reporters continue to applaud the good, engaged service and a wine list that offers some 30 different wines in 75ml, 125 ml, or 250ml glasses. Bottles from £21. The Mayfair branch houses the group's first Champagne bar: 17-19 Maddox Street, W1S 2QH; tel: (020) 7495 1505.
Chef/s: Alex Drayton. **Open:** Mon to Sat L 12 to 3, D 6 to 10 (10.30 Thur to Sat). **Closed:** Sun, 25 Dec, 1 Jan. **Meals:** main courses £15 to £20. Set L and D £17 (2 courses) to £20. **Details:** 59 seats. 16 seats outside. Wheelchairs. Music.

Visit us online

To find out more about
The Good Food Guide, please
visit thegoodfoodguide.co.uk

Umu

Cooking score: 6
⊖ Green Park, Bond Street, map 5
Japanese | £145
14-16 Bruton Place, Mayfair, W1J 6LX
Tel no: (020) 7499 8881
umurestaurant.com

A Mayfair back street leads to a discreet sliding door signposted by a single Japanese character. When you work out how to enter this Bond villain lair, you'll find that Umu successfully emulates the kaiseki (Japanese haute cuisine) restaurants of Kyoto. Umu is correct in every detail from the attentive and well-informed service to the meticulous dish preparation. The slivers of sashimi here are sublime, as chef Yoshinori Ishii is obsessive about fish quality. Dainty morsels of grilled tuna or eel are seared to just the right point and beautifully presented with tiny garnishes such as enoki mushrooms, flowers or herb sprouts. The feast is as much visual as gustatory, but if you prefer something more substantial, there's Japanese Wagyu beef grilled inside a hoba leaf with a nutty miso sauce. The saké list is exemplary and prices reflect this; wine percentage mark-ups are huge, too, but the sommelier can suggest good matches with bottles starting at £35.
Chef/s: Yoshinori Ishii. **Open:** Mon to Fri L 12 to 2.30, Mon to Sat D 6 to 10.30. **Closed:** Sun, 25 Dec to 5 Jan, bank hols. **Meals:** main courses £28 to £95. Set L £25 to £45. Kaiseki menu £145 (8 courses). **Details:** 55 seats.

★ NEW ENTRY ★

Vietfood

Cooking score: 2
⊖ Piccadilly Circus, map 5
Vietnamese | £20
34-36 Wardour Street, Soho, W1D 6QT
Tel no: (020) 7494 4555
vietnamfood.co.uk
£5 OFF £30

The usual suspects – low-hanging lights, bare brick, stripped floors, exposed ventilation system, wooden tables for sharing – mixed

Join us at thegoodfoodguide.co.uk

with bamboo, rope and vintage memorabilia create a 'kind of bright, breezy cabana effect' at this thoroughly modern, unpretentious Chinatown venue. Always busy, all efforts are focused on the simple aim of serving food rapidly – you may not be actively encouraged to hurry your meal but don't expect 'long, gourmet indulgences'. What makes Vietfood so popular is chef-proprietor Jeff Tan's take on Vietnam's vibrant food culture – most of the staples of the cuisine appear on the lengthy menu, including pho (traditional soups) and bun (vermicelli noodles) at very gentle prices. Delicate vegetarian rice-paper summer rolls, four grilled freshwater prawns dressed with semi-caramelised garlic and a lemongrass dressing, stir-fried duck with green papaya in a rich, sweet, soy glaze – the dishes come thick and fast. Don't pass on dessert – lemongrass jelly is hard to skip. Wines from £17.
Chef/s: Jeff Tan. **Open:** all week 12 to 10.30 (11 Fri and Sat). **Closed:** 25 Dec. **Meals:** main courses £7 to £9. **Details:** 90 seats. Bar. Music.

Vinoteca
Cooking score: 2
⊖ Marble Arch, map 6
Modern European | £29
15 Seymour Place, Marylebone, W1H 5BD
Tel no: (020) 7724 7288
vinoteca.co.uk

🍴 🍾 £30

The team behind the Vinoteca group are dab hands at opening down-to-earth wine bars that only make a show of themselves where it matters: on the plate. The décor sports a simple palette – pale walls and closely packed polished wood tables – that matches the straight-to-the-point modern European cooking perfectly. The menu is a tribute to great British produce and plays off the seasons with the likes of smoked mackerel with green tomatoes and horseradish, whole Rye harbour lemon sole with monk's beard, capers and brown butter or baked rabbit leg with Pink Fir potatoes, radishes and baby gem lettuce, with vanilla pannacotta and blueberry compote a good way to finish. Vinoteca also scores with

its reasonable prices, a policy extending to the stash of wines. There are by-the-glass wine suggestions for most dishes; the full list is an impressive compendium stuffed with insightful selections from around the world with bottles from £18.50.
Chef/s: William Lauder. **Open:** all week 12 to 11 (11am Sat, 4 Sun). **Meals:** main courses £13 to £18. Set L £13 (2 courses) to £16. **Details:** 55 seats. Bar. Music.

Wild Honey
Cooking score: 4
⊖ Oxford Circus, Bond Street, map 5
Modern European | £50
12 St George Street, Mayfair, W1S 2FB
Tel no: (020) 7758 9160
wildhoneyrestaurant.co.uk

Located in well-upholstered Mayfair, Wild Honey was a mould breaker when it opened in 2007. Reports indicate that the place now seems designed for fast eating – and service has been known to reinforce this impression – but Anthony Demetre's cooking is serious. Much to his credit, dishes don't get too complicated, opting for simple ideas and finding room for seasonal items such as Wye Valley asparagus with brown shrimps, seaweed butter and preserved lemon peel, and roast veal sweetbreads with roast carrots, peas and broad beans. One winter visitor was delighted with a meal that produced 'Jerusalem artichokes with truffles, and a main course of tender venison', while desserts such as bitter chocolate sorbet with coffee, orange and warm madeleine feel like a lovely treat. If prices seem high, don't forget the classic example of a lunchtime bargain (for Mayfair), where three courses can cost the same as main courses on the carte. More effort could be made, however, to accommodate ordinary drinkers on the prestige-hungry list, which features more bottles over £200 than under £50.
Chef/s: Anthony Demetre and Jamie McCallum. **Open:** Mon to Sat L 12 to 2.30, D 6 to 10.30. **Closed:** Sun, bank hols. **Meals:** main courses £22 to £35. Set L £30. Set D £35. **Details:** 55 seats. Bar.

Wiltons

Cooking score: 4
⊖ Green Park, map 5
British | £67
55 Jermyn Street, Mayfair, SW1Y 6LX
Tel no: (020) 7629 9955
wiltons.co.uk

Savile Row suits aren't obligatory, but jacket and tie please gentlemen if planning a visit to Wiltons. Like a barrow boy made good on the blue-blooded streets of Mayfair, this 18th-century shellfish pedlar is now one of the illustrious old boys – a velvety, phone-free sanctum full of hushed voices and high decorum. History dictates that seafood rules here, and the kitchen prepares its wares with total respect for the time-honoured ways – that means freshly shucked oysters, a proper lobster thermidor without deconstructions, poached turbot on the bone and voluptuously fleshy grilled Dover sole. Game is a natural bedfellow in such hallowed surroundings, roasts sizzle on the trolley and proper puddings come straight out of Mrs Beeton. Money is no object here, but if you must be cautious, go for the set menu and approach the wine list with trepidation; bottles from £35.
Chef/s: Daniel Kent. **Open:** Mon to Fri L 12 to 2.30, Mon to Sat D 5.30 to 10.30. **Closed:** Sun, 10 days Christmas and New Year, bank hols. **Meals:** main courses £16 to £60. Set L and D £30 (2 courses) to £38. **Details:** 100 seats. Bar. Wheelchairs.

The Wolseley

Cooking score: 2
⊖ Green Park, map 5
Modern European | £40
160 Piccadilly, Mayfair, W1J 9EB
Tel no: (020) 7499 6996
thewolseley.com

When Piccadilly's pavements are trodden only by straggling up-all-nighters, The Wolseley is just opening for breakfast. Wouldn't a carb rush of banana granola and a plate of scrambled eggs and smoked salmon on toast go down well? Later in the day, hors d'oeuvres make their appearance, a crottin, spinach and honey tart announcing a hearty lunch follow-up of Holstein schnitzel. Afternoon tea has its devotees among impoverished writers and semi-retired pop stars, the fruit scones slathered in clotted cream to offset the daintiness of the finger sandwiches. If you still haven't moved, dinner might be moules marinière, a doorstop of grilled ribeye in béarnaise, and lemon meringue tart to close. It's all made to happen with unfailing efficiency and courtesy, the kind of full-package experience that the West End of London was deficient in for so long. There is a compact but resourceful wine list, too, starting at £24 for white Bordeaux or Languedoc Cabernet.
Chef/s: Maarten Geschwindt. **Open:** all week 7am to midnight (8am Sat, 8am to 11pm Sun). **Meals:** main courses £13 to £38. **Details:** 140 seats. Bar. Wheelchairs.

Wright Brothers Soho

Cooking score: 2
⊖ Oxford Circus, map 5
Seafood | £35
13 Kingly Street, Soho, W1B 5PW
Tel no: (020) 7434 3611
thewrightbrothers.co.uk

Branches of Wright Brothers are typically busy and noisy, serving a varied menu of fish and shellfish – this tucked away Soho branch, with dining areas on several levels, is no exception. It does a highly professional job offering a mix of home-grown and global flavours including half a dozen kinds of impeccably fresh oyster (raw, dressed or cooked), winkles and whelks, Scottish langoustine, seafood platters (the beating heart of the operation), and anything from tempura soft-shell crab to roast Dorset cod fillet with samphire, leeks, wild mushroom and truffle oil and whole barbecued gilthead bream with boquerones, fennel, basil and chilli. High-quality supplies – perhaps a perfectly timed whole Cornish lemon sole, served with chilli, herb and crabmeat butter – are augmented by the kitchen's confident timing. Prices are high, but the ingredients are top-drawer. Wines do a good job, too, strong on white of course, with bottles from £21.

Chef/s: Sasha Ziverts. **Open:** all week L 12 to 11 (10 Sun). **Closed:** 25 and 26 Dec. **Meals:** main courses £17 to £27. **Details:** 86 seats. 50 seats outside. Wheelchairs. Music.

Yauatcha

Cooking score: 4
⊖ Tottenham Court Road, map 5
Chinese | £40
15-17 Broadwick Street, Soho, W1F 0DL
Tel no: (020) 7494 8888
yauatcha.com

Yauatcha fills that gap in the market that combines French pâtisserie and Chinese dim sum in one handy, voguishly svelte package. Layered petits gâteaux, macarons and tea are just one part of the ground-floor drill, while downstairs is a basement room designed for elegant trysting. All in all, there could be no finer backdrop for the exquisite dim sum menus, where poached chicken dumplings, oatmealed chilli squid, blue swimmer crab in peanut and sesame dressing, and curried taro croquettes push the envelope. Steampot dishes such as chicken and chestnut with dried shrimp and shiitakes, or the luxy lobster vermicelli, offer more robust fare, and the long list of creatively constructed east-west desserts runs to Anxi tieguanyin (Chinese blue tea) pannacotta with dulce de leche crème, Breton shortbread and Papua New Guinea mousse. Drinks do their best to keep up, with sakés, cocktails, and pedigree wines from £29 for a Languedoc Syrah.

Chef/s: Tong Chee Hwee. **Open:** all week 12 to 10. **Meals:** main courses £13 to £38. Set menu £45 to £55. **Details:** 190 seats. Bar. Music.

Zoilo

Cooking score: 3
⊖ Bond Street, map 6
Argentinian | £30
9 Duke Street, Marylebone, W1U 3EG
Tel no: (020) 7486 9699
zoilo.co.uk

'Just so damn appealing,' summed up one reader about this Argentinian cocina away from the crowds that fill the major shopping thoroughfares nearby. It's no tranquil oasis, mind, for Diego Jacquet's restaurant is full of life. The simple and vibrant décor sets the mood, as does the sharing nature of the menu, while a seat at the counter in the basement provides a ringside seat for the fiery kitchen action. The menu focuses on the nation's food from north to south, and offers up empanadas such as a stunner filled with cuttlefish, fennel and chorizo. Ceviche gets a look-in (sea bass with radishes and preserved lemons), but there's also crab on toast and grilled turbot with white polenta. Grilled flank 'asado' shows the way with BBQ meats – served with bone marrow and fresh horseradish – and even the burger is a cut above. The wine list sticks to the home country, starting at £21.95.

Chef/s: Diego Jacquet. **Open:** Mon to Sat L 12 to 2.30, D 5.30 to 10. **Closed:** Sun, bank hols. **Meals:** sharing plates £7 to £23. Set L £10 (2 courses). **Details:** 49 seats. Bar. Wheelchairs. Music.

L'Absinthe
⊖ Chalk Farm, map 2
French | £27
40 Chalcot Road, Primrose Hill, NW1 8LS
Tel no: (020) 7483 4848
labsinthe.co.uk

£30

Jean-Christophe Slowik's volubly *sympathique* French bistro in affluent Primrose Hill has a nicely dressed-down feel, with bubbly informality the keynote. Among dishes honed to a deep allure by tradition are soupe à l'oignon, marinated herrings with potato salad, beef bourguignon with mash, and fillet of sea bass with spinach in sauce vierge. Finish with – what else? – absinthed crème brûlée. Order from the short wine list, from £19.95, or pick up a bottle in the deli next door and pay the £10 corkage if you prefer.

Almeida
Cooking score: 2
⊖ Angel, Highbury & Islington, map 2
French | £40
30 Almeida Street, Islington, N1 1AD
Tel no: (020) 7354 4777
almeida-restaurant.co.uk

The dear old Almeida has never looked quite as bubbly as it does today, with abstract paintings of concentric circles in bold colours on bright white walls, the room filled with daylight from big windows and a partly open kitchen where you are invited to peek. Tommy Boland brings plenty of culinary kudos to the contemporary brasserie dining, combining ingredients and techniques with appreciable panache. An Indian approach to salmon brings in cauliflower, pomegranate, raisins and a bhaji, to be succeeded by seasonally garnished mains such as lamb rump with crushed Jerseys, asparagus and peas, or steamed halibut with mussels, mousserons and onion purée in parsley butter. If you're not in a pre-theatre hurry, try out the six-stage taster, but don't miss the creatively crafted desserts, such as rhubarb and ginger fool with brioche beignets

and rhubarb and ginger-beer sorbet. Miscellaneously listed wines open at £22.50 a bottle, £15.75 a half-litre pot or £6 a glass for house French.
Chef/s: Tommy Boland. **Open:** Tue to Sun L 12 to 2.30 (3.30 Sun), Mon to Sat D 5.30 to 10.30. **Meals:** main meals £18 to £26. Set L and D £19 (2 courses) to £23. Tasting menu £48 (6 courses). Sun L £20 (2 courses) to £25. **Details:** 120 seats. 15 seats outside. Bar. Wheelchairs.

Bellanger
Cooking score: 2
⊖ Angel, map 2
French | £45
9 Islington Green, Islington, N1 2XH
Tel no: (020) 7226 2555
bellanger.co.uk

'It's like the love child of the Colony Grill Room and Fischers,' commented one seasoned sampler of Messrs Corbin and King's various restaurants. As a dining experience, Bellanger rates highly: 'I think it helps that it's not in central London; it feels like a neighbourhood asset, and the crowd is clearly local.' Expect Alsatian-influenced brasserie fare in a Parisian bistro setting – the rather sedate but extremely comfortable, grown-up, double-fronted dining room comes with lots of dark-wood panelling, brass and aged mirrors. Dishes range from salades râpées to coq au vin (coq au Riesling, in this instance); Strasbourg hot-smoked pork and garlic sausage ('full of sweet, smoky, garlicky goodness') with Puy lentils and celeriac rémoulade to a generous plate of veal schnitzel served Holstein-style with fried egg, anchovies and capers. A gloriously boozy baba au rhum, accompanied by a tart passion fruit coulis and whipped cream, makes an impressive finale. Wines from £22.50.
Chef/s: Lee Ward. **Open:** all week 11.30 to 11 (10pm Sun). **Meals:** main courses £11 to £25. Set L £18 to £21. **Details:** 200 seats. Bar. Wheelchairs. Music.

Black Axe Mangal

Cooking score: 1
⊖ Highbury & Islington, map 2
Turkish | £25
156 Canonbury Road, Highbury, N1 2UP
blackaxemangal.com
£30

The queue starts as soon as the door opens at this hipster kebab house, but waiting at the tiny bar-counter is a fun option: you can watch the chefs manning the wood-fired oven or mangal (Turkish open grill). The 'flatbreads' section of the menu includes 'lamb offal', which resembles lahmacun, the Turkish pizza found in the Turkish places along Green Lanes. Squid-ink bread was a round loaf shape, but charcoal black, topped with a dollop of taramasalata and a slow-cooked egg yolk. The meat dishes tend towards robust flavours and gutsy style; the grilled quail is boldly spiced with Szechuan pepper. No desserts, but drinks start with wine by the glass from £4.
Chef/s: Lee Tiernan. **Open:** Sat and Sun L 11 to 3. Tue to Sat D 6 to 10.30. **Closed:** Mon. **Meals:** main courses £10 to £16. **Details:** 20 seats. V menu. Bar. Music.

Bradleys

Cooking score: 3
⊖ Swiss Cottage, map 2
French | £40
25 Winchester Road, Swiss Cottage, NW3 3NR
Tel no: (020) 7722 3457
bradleysnw3.co.uk

The Bradleys' 25-year-old enterprise is truly a local diamond, its broad appeal carefully nurtured over the years. Inside it looks and feels contemporary, and in the kitchen the appeal of Simon Bradley's predominantly French approach lies in materials that are well sourced, intelligently handled and sometimes simply presented – say pine-smoked haunch of venison with cavolo nero, beetroot confit and pickled pear or a commendable fillet of sea bass with kale, ceps and butternut squash. Start with something like hot and cold foie gras with potato galette, butter-poached pear and brioche and finish with Seville orange and chocolate soufflé with Grand Marnier ice cream. With Hampstead Theatre nearby, the various set-meal deals remain astonishingly good value if planning to eat before a visit. Typical of the output has been ham hock terrine 'en gelée' with pickled vegetables, hake with chard, lentils and roasted cauliflower, and raspberry crème brûlée. Wines from £19.50.
Chef/s: Simon Bradley. **Open:** all week L 12 to 2 (2.30 Sat and Sun), Mon to Sat D 5.15 to 10.30. **Meals:** main courses £17 to £21. Set L £19 (2 courses) to £23. Set D £28. Sun L £30. **Details:** 63 seats. V menu.

The Bull & Last

Cooking score: 3
⊖ Tufnell Park, Kentish Town, map 2
Modern British | £42
168 Highgate Road, Hampstead, NW5 1QS
Tel no: (020) 7267 3641
thebullandlast.co.uk

'They are very consistent and a combination of the food, drink, ambience and service always makes for an enjoyable evening,' was the verdict of one regular on this solidly built Victorian pub close to Hampstead Heath. There's no doubt that the Bull & Last is a real crowd-puller, the kind of place where a pint at the bar is just fine – there's a great selection of real ales – but with some good cooking on the menu, the food steals the show. A tried-and-trusted repertoire mixes influences in true modern British style: say smoked haddock with giant macaroni, young leek, egg yolk and sheep's cheese; then English lamb rump with a braised neck fillet, punchy aubergine, wild garlic and pomegranate, or excellent char-grilled onglet; with buttermilk pannacotta with poached rhubarb and almond shortbread or that modern classic – Ferrero Rocher ice cream – to finish. Wines from £19.
Chef/s: Oliver Pudney. **Open:** all week L 12 to 3 (12.30 to 4 Sat and Sun), D 6.30 to 10 (9 Sun). **Closed:** 23 to 25 Dec. **Meals:** main courses £15 to £25. **Details:** 45 seats. Music.

Caravan

Cooking score: 2
⊖ King's Cross, map 2
Global | £30
Granary Building, 1 Granary Square, King's
Cross, N1C 4AA
Tel no: (020) 7101 7661
caravanrestaurants.co.uk

This cannily converted warehouse packs an
earthy punch, delivering a whole lot of flavour
in rough-edged canteen-style surroundings,
although the noise generated when it's full is
not for everyone. With a strong following,
including fashion students from next-door
Central St Martins, Caravan specialises in all-
day, kick-back relaxation with pretty much
any level and style of appetite catered for.
Weekday breakfasts run until 11.30am, but
later the menu kicks into gear with small
plates such as fried soft-shell crab with kim-
chee slaw and chilli tamarind dressing or
spiced Elwy Valley lamb shoulder with
tomato bulgur wheat and cumin sea salt, and
bigger plates bearing baked pollack with ajo
blanco, artichokes and crispy prosciutto or
Shorthorn ribeye with girolles, parsley and
garlic. In addition, there are pizzas, an on-site
coffee roastery and lengthy queues for
weekend brunch (when it's first come, first
served). Wines from £18.
Chef/s: Miles Kirby. **Open:** Mon to Fri 8am to 11pm.
Sat 10 to close, Sun 10 to 4. **Closed:** 25 and 26 Dec,
1 and 2 Jan. **Meals:** main courses £15 to £24.
Details: 120 seats. 70 seats outside. Wheelchairs.
Music.

★ NEW ENTRY ★

CôBa

Cooking score: 1
⊖ Caledonian Road, map 2
Vietnamese | £25
244 York Way, Camden, N7 9AG
cobarestaurant.co.uk
£30
▼

Kingsland Road may be London's destination
for budget Vietnamese dining, but if you don't
mind paying a little extra for a chic setting, cab
it to CôBa – and you'll need to hail a taxi,
unless you're prepared for a dreary 15-minute
walk from King's Cross station. The short
menu is divided into small plates or big bowls.
Both summer rolls and papaya salad are
creditable versions of the Vietnamese classic
dishes, while duck ramen in a notably rich
sauce pushes out the boat from the South
China Sea with its Sino-Viet take on soup-
noodle. The cocktail bar and cool vibe set this
Aussie-run joint an ocean apart from the
Shoreditch crowd. Wines by the bottle start
at £20.
Chef/s: Damon Bui. **Open:** Mon to Fri L 12 to 3,
Mon to Sat D 6 to 10. **Closed:** Sun, 2 weeks Dec.
Meals: main courses £10 to £15. **Details:** 54 seats.
Bar. Wheelchairs. Music.

★ BEST SMALL GROUP ★

Dishoom

Cooking score: 2
⊖ King's Cross, map 2
Indian | £30
5 Stable Street, King's Cross, N1C 4AB
Tel no: (020) 7420 9321
dishoom.com

Dishoom's many fans all agree that this King's
Cross branch 'has a real buzz, with great food
and reasonable prices'. In a reinvented
Victorian railway transit shed (massively
spread over four levels) with an atmosphere
that positively throbs with activity, a
conceptual approach is taken to Indian food.
Bombay street food, more familiar curry-
house dishes and a few Anglo-Indian ideas are
mixed in with a casual approach to eating –
the selection of sharing plates ordered across
the table arriving in a seemingly haphazard
way. Somehow, amid the crazy bustle, it
works. Everyone loves the rich, slow-cooked
house black dhal, the masala prawns and the
spicy lamb chops, but there's also a zesty
assortment of biryanis, chicken tikka laced
with ginger, turmeric, garlic and green chilli,
and nalli nihari (a robust lamb-on-the-bone
stew), alongside various naan, pickles and

chutneys. Bacon naan rolls laced with chilli jam are just the ticket for breakfast. Drink lassi, beer or wine (from £19.90).
Chef/s: Naved Nasir. **Open:** all week 12 to 11 (12 to 12 Fri and Sat). **Closed:** 25 and 26 Dec, 1 and 2 Jan. **Meals:** main courses from £6 to £22. **Details:** 250 seats. 20 seats outside. Bar. Wheelchairs. Music.

LOCAL GEM

500 Restaurant
⊖ Archway, map 2
Italian | £25
782 Holloway Road, Archway, N19 3JH
Tel no: (020) 7272 3406
500restaurant.co.uk

£5 £30
OFF

'A little shabby, and not much chic, but genuine Italian cooking,' thought one visitor to this small restaurant just a stone's throw from Archway tube station. It's clearly popular with a local crowd, who come for generous plates of crab 'lasagnette', a cold lasagne of Sardinian crispbread layered with white crabmeat and diced tomatoes with a light dressing of brown crabmeat, excellent ravioli filled with ricotta, lemon zest and saffron in a herb and butter sauce, and char-grilled veal chop or a pan-fried lemon sole. There's a rich, creamy tiramisu for dessert and the all-Italian wine list starts at £15.50.

Grain Store
Cooking score: 3
⊖ King's Cross, map 2
Global | £30
Granary Square, 1-3 Stable Street, King's Cross, N1C 4AB
Tel no: (020) 7324 4466
grainstore.com

The message that a sustainable food culture depends on us eating less meat and more veg is looking ever more prescient, so Bruno Loubet's vibrant offerings at the vast, bright Grain Store, with its imposing open kitchen, couldn't be more timely. Though meat and fish still get a fair look-in, the all-day restaurant's affection for plants, and the innovative menu

on which they take pole position, has won it plaudits aplenty since it opened in 2013. The cooking is rooted in classic French technique, with shoots reaching far and wide, picking up global inflections en route for the likes of moreish mushroom and celeriac Scotch egg with fermented chilli and miso paste, Asian greens and master stock quail, or the velvety yet punchy beetroot, ricotta and Parmesan ravioli. Desserts prove on occasion to be the only weak note in a roll call of high-voltage, well-composed dishes. Gourmet veg-laced cocktails whet the appetite, while keenly priced wines start at £24.
Chef/s: Bruno Loubet. **Open:** Mon to Sat 10am to 11.30pm (midnight Thur to Sat). Sun 10 to 3. **Meals:** main courses £13 to £22. **Details:** 140 seats. 75 seats outside. Bar. Wheelchairs. Music.

★ NEW ENTRY ★

Granger & Co.
Cooking score: 2
⊖ King's Cross, map 2
Antipodean | £25
7 Pancras Square, King's Cross, N1C 4AG
Tel no: (020) 3058 2567
grangerandco.com

£30

This new opening from Bill Granger is a slick operation, a lively chip off the old Aussie block (in Clerkenwell and Notting Hill, see entries). While competition is beginning to be fierce in this increasingly bustling area behind King's Cross and St Pancras railway stations, this casual all-day eatery more than holds its own. The kitchen stays close to the group's popular cross-cultural style; from breakfast onwards expect the famous scrambled eggs, ricotta hot cakes and sweetcorn fritters, as well as 'delicious' yellow fish curry, 'faultless' sticky chilli belly pork, and shrimp burger with jalapeño mayo, shaved radish salad and sesame gochujang (spicy Korean paste). The casual look has been nailed, too – big, bright and buzzy with close-packed tables, bar-counter seating and spot-on service. Heavy footfall in

the area means that you can book for breakfast and lunch during the week, otherwise join the famous queue. Wines from £20.
Chef/s: Mark Welch. **Open:** Mon to Sat 7am to 11pm. Sun 8am to 10.30pm. **Closed:** 25 Dec. **Meals:** main courses £13 to £21. **Details:** 100 seats. 20 seats outside. Wheelchairs. Music.

Jin Kichi

Cooking score: 2
⊖ Hampstead, map 2
Japanese | £35
73 Heath Street, Hampstead, NW3 6UG
Tel no: (020) 7794 6158
jinkichi.com

Those who share a reporter's nostalgia for 'mom and pop' joints in Tokyo will appreciate this cramped little place that's 'well worth the trek up to Hampstead'. There may be 'little personal space' but it is easy to enjoy this authentic Japanese food, which is not necessarily expensive and attracts hordes of ravenous fans – booking is essential. The menu opens with 'delicious' small dishes such as ohitashi (crunchy cooked spinach dressed with soy and sesame) and maguro natto (strong-tasting fermented soya bean with raw tuna marinated in wasabi). There's also excellent sashimi and various sushi, and 'melt-in-the-mouth' gindara (grilled black cod), and the range is completed with a good choice of grilled skewers (the yakitori is a 'standout'), tempura and variously garnished hot or cold udon or soba noodles. Wine opens at a pricey £28 a bottle, so it may be preferable to drink saké.
Chef/s: Atsushi Matsumoto. **Open:** Tue to Sun L 12.30 to 2, D 6 to 11 (10 Sun). **Closed:** Mon, Tue after bank hols. **Meals:** main courses £8 to £17. **Details:** 42 seats.

Average price

The average price denotes the price of a three-course meal without wine.

LeCoq

Cooking score: 2
⊖ Highbury & Islington, map 2
Modern European | £25
292-294 St Paul's Road, Islington, N1 2LH
Tel no: (020) 7359 5055
le-coq.co.uk
£30

'Every time I've walked past it is super busy,' pronounced one reader, who loves the way this simple place strikes just the right note for a neighbourhood eatery. The close-packed, no-frills décor matters not a jot (plain wooden tables, distressed plaster and brick walls) and the cost is fair. Much is made of the spit-roasted chicken (organic ones from Sutton Hoo), the only main course, except on Sunday when beef topside and a fish (possibly roast cod) expand the menu, but the chicken is full of flavour, juicy and falling off the bone and served with sides that could include rainbow chard, crispy shallots and confit garlic. Weekly changing starters take in shredded lamb shoulder and cabbage or salmon tartare with crème fraîche and coriander, and there are the likes of tarte Tatin, cheeses (say Hereford Hop and Stichelton) or fresh mint ice cream and watermelon for dessert. Wines from £22.
Chef/s: Adam Middleton. **Open:** Thur to Sat L 12 to 3, Mon to Sat D 5 to 10.30. Sun 12 to 9. **Closed:** 24 Dec to 2 Jan. **Meals:** set L and D £17 (2 courses) to £22. Sun L £21 (2 courses) to £26. **Details:** 40 seats. Music.

LOCAL GEM

Mangal 1 Ocakbasi
⊖ Dalston Kingsland, map 2
Turkish | £18
10 Arcola Street, Stoke Newington, E8 2DJ
Tel no: (020) 7275 8981
mangal1.com
£30

'Incredible freshness of ingredients' and well-established grill skills keep Mangal 1 a Hackney institution, despite some reports that its popularity, and accompanying expansion, has diluted some of the original charm. The skewers are at the heart of the menu, offering various ways to experience the powerful allure of meat, salt and fire, and salads are vibrant. Try the adana kebab, grilled quail or fillet of lamb, preceded by lahmacun and cacik. Note: cash only, and it's best to BYO.

Market

Cooking score: 2
⊖ Camden Town, map 2
Modern British | £32
43 Parkway, Camden, NW1 7PN
Tel no: (020) 7267 9700
marketrestaurant.co.uk

Exposed bricks walls, wooden floor, zinc-topped tables, school chairs, a tantalising glimpse into the kitchen at the rear – Market has the look of many a contemporary eatery. But there's an authenticity here, a passion for simple things done well. It's the sort of no-nonsense place you'd love on a corner in your neighbourhood. Dorset brown and white crabmeat on crispbread is something of a signature – fresh and simple – or you might start with devilled chicken livers, or scallops with cured ham, kohlrabi and pear. Onglet, fries, béarnaise says it all when it comes to bistro classics, likewise lemon sole with brown shrimp butter, with weekend brunches offering up duck Scotch egg with salad cream. To finish, Yorkshire forced rhubarb with a custard pavlova and pistachios hits the mark, or go for a selection of Neal's Yard Dairy cheeses. Wines start at £18.35.

Chef/s: Richard Teague. **Open:** all week L 12 to 2.30 (11 to 3 Sat and Sun), D 6 to 10.30. **Closed:** 25 Dec to 2 Jan, bank hols. **Meals:** main courses £15 to £26. Set L £12 (2 courses). Set D £18 (2 courses) to £20. **Details:** 50 seats. 4 seats outside. Music.

Odette's

Cooking score: 5
⊖ Chalk Farm, map 2
Modern British | £36
130 Regent's Park Road, Primrose Hill, NW1 8XL
Tel no: (020) 7586 8569
odettesprimrosehill.com
£5
OFF

A 'secret garden' is just one reason why the sophisticated cognoscenti of NW1 rate Odette's as the undisputed queen of Primrose Hill. Since taking over in 2008, Welsh chef Bryn Williams has quietly made this long-standing neighbourhood favourite his own, and the dining room looks suitably plush in its current garb – soothing brown tones, painted brickwork, dangling globe lights, polished tables and so on. Head chef William Gordon now mans the stoves alongside the proprietor, but the food has lost none of its vigour, verve or seasonal oomph. Fish has always been a sure-fire hit here, whether you go for the now-famous roast turbot with braised oxtail, salsify and cockles (a sensation from the *Great British Menu* back in 2006) or a dainty plate of grilled red mullet with minestrone and crayfish. Given Bryn's roots, it's no surprise that Welsh lamb is a meaty fixture on the succinct menu (perhaps served with swede, onions, capers and mint), while desserts could include Odette's legendary Jaffa cake with marmalade and yoghurt. A well-rounded serviceable wine list starts at £19.95.

Chef/s: Bryn Williams and William Gordon. **Open:** Wed to Sun L 12 to 2.30 (3 Sat and Sun), Tue to Sun D 6 to 10 (10.30 Sat, 9.30 Sun). **Closed:** Mon, 1 week Christmas. **Meals:** main courses £16 to £26. Set L and D £16 (2 courses) to £22. Sun L £22. Tasting menu L £30 (5 courses), D £47 (6 courses). **Details:** 62 seats. 26 seats outside. V menu. Music.

Oldroyd

Cooking score: 3
⊖ Angel, map 2
Modern European | £24
344 Upper Street, Islington, N1 0PD
Tel no: (020) 8617 9010
oldroydlondon.com
£30

It is so cramped it's a miracle so many people can work and eat in such a tiny space, but Oldroyd goes about its business with gusto, a welcome independent restaurant in an area dominated by chains. From a sliver of a kitchen, Tom Oldroyd (former chef director of the Polpo Group) proffers a shared-plates menu with a strong Mediterranean flavour. Dishes vary: some are simple assemblies (a generous heaped salad of artichoke, spring pea, broad bean and goats' curd panzanetta), while others are more worked (grilled octopus with squid-ink risotto, wild garlic aïoli and monk's beard), but value for money is palpable, the quality of the ingredients spot-on. Young urbanites pile up the narrow spiral staircase to the cramped first-floor dining room (ground-floor tables are reserved for walk-ins) and get stuck into plump smoked haddock croquetas served atop tartare sauce, rabbit and Dijon rillettes with pickled carrots, or a pile of delicious, salty, crunchy fritto misto mare with brown shrimps. Clever stuff. Wines from £24.
Chef/s: Louis Lingwood. **Open:** all week 12 to 10.30 (11pm Fri and Sat, 11 to 9.30 Sun). **Closed:** 25 and 26 Dec. **Meals:** main courses £11 to £15. Set L £15 (2 courses) to £18. **Details:** 40 seats. Music.

Osteria Tufo

⊖ Finsbury Park, map 2
Italian | £30
67 Fonthill Road, Finsbury Park, N4 3HZ
Tel no: (020) 7272 2911
osteriatufo.co.uk
£5 OFF

Honest-to-goodness home cooking, a low-key local vibe and bags of good cheer all contribute to Osteria Tufo's neighbourhood appeal. Diners are crammed in, but no one minds when the kitchen can deliver plates of homemade pasta (pappardelle with Luganica sausage and truffle oil, say) as well as stewed baby octopus, grilled veal chops with Sicilian aubergine mousse or the signature polpettone (a large burger-shaped 'meatball' served with roast potatoes and smoked Scamorza cheese). Italian wines from £15.90 (£4.90 a glass).

Ottolenghi

⊖ Highbury & Islington, Angel, map 2
Middle Eastern | £30
287 Upper Street, Islington, N1 2TZ
Tel no: (020) 7288 1454
ottolenghi.co.uk

The source of culinary ideas that have influenced a generation *and* a high street deli, all-day Ottolenghi is also extremely handy to have around. White communal tables and moulded chairs express its noughties origins. Signature salads, served with char-grilled salmon with red peppers or seared beef fillet with coriander and mustard sauce, are big on texture and little flavourbombs, as in slices of roast aubergines layered with spicy seeds and pickled lemon. Cakes and tarts look fabulous and are exemplary; try the baked chocolate tart, cupping a layer of caramel and airy cocoa-dusted filling. Wine is from £23.

Parlour

Cooking score: 2
⊖ Kensal Green, map 1
Modern British | £32
5 Regent Street, Kensal Green, NW10 5LG
Tel no: (020) 8969 2184
parlourkensal.com
£5
OFF

Formerly a backstreet Kensal Green local, a thoughtful renovation has created a wonderful contemporary space, an all-day restaurant-bar-café that still retains plenty of the old pub's original character. It's considered 'a good place to have on your doorstep'. Chef Jesse Dunford-Wood's innovative, free-ranging take on modern British cooking is certainly proving a success. A hit at inspection was duck liver profiteroles (with blood oranges and pistachio) – pronounced 'unusual but incredibly moreish' – and the comfort element of 'very good' cow pie and chicken 'Kyiv' has proved especially popular with the local crowd. Do leave room for pudding, though, as the innovative selection could include a 'delicious' rhubarb and custard éclair, a toasted marshmallow wagon wheel or even old-school Arctic roll. The package also runs to well-reported breakfasts. The reasonably priced wine list, which starts at £17 a bottle, also has plenty available by the glass or carafe.
Chef/s: Jesse Dunford-Wood and Ryan Lowery
Open: Tue to Sun 12 to 10. **Closed:** Mon, 10 days Christmas, last week Aug. **Meals:** main courses £10 to £18. Set L £15 (2 courses) to £18. Set D £18 (2 courses) to £21. **Details:** 100 seats. 50 seats outside. Bar. Wheelchairs. Music.

Restaurant Michael Nadra

Cooking score: 3
⊖ Chalk Farm, map 2
Modern European | £38
42 Gloucester Avenue, Primrose Hill,
NW1 8JD
Tel no: (020) 7722 2800
restaurant-michaelnadra.co.uk
£5
OFF

The canalside area of Primrose Hill is one of its unsuspected charms, and Michael Nadra's idiosyncratic venue fits right in. A modern glass frontage does nothing to prepare you for dining in a brick-vaulted, cobblestoned horse-tunnel, even if a Martini bar and garden terrace are available to fortify you beforehand. The cooking constructs diverting dishes from modern European ideas, with the odd Asian note interposing, as in the starter of salmon ceviche that comes with soft-shell crab tempura, pickled cucumber and sweet potato. Main courses are multi-layered and often complex, the various elements combining in productive synthesis, perhaps for suckling pork belly with king cabbage, Roscoff onion, Alsace bacon and heritage carrots in a dulse and apple broth, or for steamed sea bass with prawn and chive dumplings, Chinese greens and gingered carrot purée in lobster bisque. Finish elementally with treacle tart and clotted cream, cut with raspberry sorbet. A varietally classified wine list offers interest and imagination all through, with small glasses from £4, half-bottle carafes £11 and bottles £20.
Chef/s: Michael Nadra. **Open:** Tue to Sun L 12 to 2.30 (4 Sat and Sun), D 6 to 10 (10.30 Fri and Sat, 9 Sun). **Closed:** Mon, 24 to 28 Dec. **Meals:** set L £22 (2 courses) to £32. Set D £ 32 (2 courses) to £38. Sun L £22. **Details:** 85 seats. 35 seats outside. Bar. Wheelchairs. Music.

Season Kitchen

Cooking score: 3
⊖ Finsbury Park, map 2
Modern British | £28
53 Stroud Green Road, Finsbury Park, N4 3EF
Tel no: (020) 7263 5500
seasonkitchen.co.uk
£5 OFF £30

With its promise of 'honestly sourced produce', plus an urban vegetable patch out back and a buzzword name that needs no explanation, Neil Gill's Finsbury Park eatery fits the prevailing 'country-meets-city' gastro ethos like a pair of baggy corduroy trousers. But there's nothing folksy about this enthusiastically run lilac-hued bistro, with its open-minded approach and menu of feisty globetrotting dishes – lardo on toast with beef consommé and pickles, anyone? Clever ideas abound, from 'rabbit food' (potted rabbit with baby gem lettuce) or devilled whitebait with smoked mayonnaise to smoked salmon with blood orange and seaweed, oxtail lasagne or a creative vegetarian dish of celeriac three ways with pickled apple, raisins and cavolo nero. Chips are the 'crinkle-cut' variety, cheeses are sourced from Tottenham (yes!) and there are sinful rhubarb and custard doughnuts to finish. Around 20 hip wines are also spot-on, with prices from £15.50.
Chef/s: Ben Wooles. **Open:** Tue to Sat D 5.30 to 10.30. Sun 12 to 8. **Closed:** Mon, 25 to 30 Dec. **Meals:** main courses £13 to £18. Set D £16 (2 courses). Sun L £13. **Details:** 35 seats. Music.

Trullo

Cooking score: 3
⊖ Highbury & Islington, map 2
Italian | £32
300-302 St Paul's Road, Islington, N1 2LH
Tel no: (020) 7226 2733
trullorestaurant.com

Judging by the success of this neighbourhood Italian, owner Jordan Frieda clearly learned a thing or two about running a restaurant during his time as front-of-house at the esteemed River Café (see entry). Since arriving in 2010, he has turned Trullo into an Islington cracker – a cool oasis on gritty Highbury Corner. Whether you plump for the street-level space or the brick-walled basement, you can expect spare urban interiors and a menu that gains kudos from its hand-rolled pasta and choice ingredients sizzled over hot coals. Bold, punchy flavours are the norm, from small plates of rabbit arancini or grilled aubergines with golden garlic and mint to tagliarini with bottarga and Amalfi lemon, slow-cooked duck leg with baked cannellini beans or char-grilled monkfish with pancetta, baby gem and sorrel. After that, artisan cheeses or a slice of almond tart should fit the bill. Spot-on Italian wines from £10.50 a carafe.
Chef/s: Conor J Gadd. **Open:** all week L 12.30 to 2.45 (3 Sun), Mon to Sat D 6 to 10.15. **Closed:** 23 Dec to 9 Jan, Easter. **Meals:** main courses £14 to £25. **Details:** 93 seats. Music.

Vinoteca

Cooking score: 1
⊖ King's Cross, map 2
Modern British | £30
One Pancras Square, King's Cross, N1C 4BU
Tel no: (020) 3793 7210
vinoteca.co.uk

Charlie Young and Brett Woonton reinvented the wine bar when they opened their first Vinoteca in Farringdon in 2005 (see entry). Four branches later, the successful drill remains the same: incorporating a wine shop, an exciting, extensive modern wine list (from £17), prompt friendly service and interesting food. This King's Cross offshoot is a sprawling, confident destination on the ground floor of David Chipperfield's Gridiron building. On the food front it delivers seasonal treats such as fillet of Cornish mackerel with Yorkshire rhubarb, chilli and mint, and best end of Somerset lamb with salsa verde.
Chef/s: Kish Raheja. **Open:** all week 7.30am to 11pm (10am Sat and Sun). **Meals:** main courses £6 to £19. **Details:** 90 seats. 50 seats outside. Bar. Wheelchairs. Music.

Angler

Cooking score: 6

⊖ Moorgate, map 4

Seafood | £50

South Place Hotel, 3 South Place, Moorgate, EC2M 2AF

Tel no: (020) 3215 1260

anglerrestaurant.com

Angler sits on the seventh and top floor of South Place Hotel, a 'light-washed place' (lots of glass) smartly furnished with white-clad tables, striped chairs and tan leather banquettes. Gary Foulkes (formerly head chef at the Square) brings modern European dynamics to the City with a menu that embraces sustainable seafood. His style is appealing without being flamboyant and results are rewarding: an amuse-bouche of 'excellent' prawn and squid-ink wafer with cod roe opened a test meal, while steaming brought out the best of a delicate courgette blossom packed with a Dorset crab mouseline, its gentle flavours given depth by an emulsion of white tea scented with lemon verbena. Next up, a meaty piece of Cornish turbot arrived with line-caught squid and oriental mushrooms, and was finished with a bonito dashi bouillon. For dessert, an accomplished plate of contrasting textures of strawberries (ice cream, jelly, gariguette and wild) and a sprinkling of black-olive biscuit crumb proved to be a perfect finish. Service is 'silky-smooth', and the well-thought-out wine list (from £25.50) is a good match for the food.

Chef/s: Gary Foulkes. **Open:** Mon to Fri L 12 to 2.30, Mon to Sat D 6 to 10. **Closed:** Sun, 24 to 26 Dec, 1 week Jan. **Meals:** main courses £28 to £35. Set L £35 (3 courses) to £49. Tasting menu £85 (10 courses). **Details:** 80 seats. 40 seats outside. Bar. Wheelchairs. Music.

★ NEW ENTRY ★

Anglo

Cooking score: 6

⊖ Farringdon, map 5

Modern British | £35

30 St Cross Street, Farringdon, EC1N 8UH

Tel no: (020) 7430 1503

anglorestaurant.com

An unassuming little place done out in sparse contemporary style, Anglo is packing a major punch in Farringdon. Found just off Hatton Garden, it's run by Mark Jarvis (ex Bingham) and Jack Cashmore (ex Sat Bains, Nottingham, In De Wulf, Belgium) who appear to be dab hands at making a show of themselves where it matters: on the plate. Whether you are there for lunch (when a short à la carte is offered) or dinner (a seven-course taster), the cooking is a tribute to great British produce. Intensely seasonal dishes are fashionably straightforward and involve simple assemblies and inspired finishing touches in, say, a big-flavoured dish of red mullet with carrot, sea beet and seaweed butter or a more delicate assembly of English asparagus, spring leaves and a delicious smoked mousseline. There's delight, too, in superbly timed cod, served with roast fennel and sea vegetables, and full-flavoured aged Hereford beef with a dollop of wild garlic purée and sweet glazed shallot. English strawberries with lemon thyme and burnt meringue make a perfect finale. Most of the short list of European wines is under £40, but check out the beer selection, too.

Chef/s: Mark Jarvis and Jack Cashmore. **Open:** Tue to Fri L 12.30 to 2.30, Tue to Sat D 6.30 to 9.30. **Closed:** Sun. **Meals:** main courses £17 to £19 (L only). Tasting menu £45 (7 courses, D only)

L'Anima

Cooking score: 4
⊖ Liverpool Street, map 4
Italian | £55
1 Snowden Street, City, EC2A 2DQ
Tel no: (020) 7422 7000
lanima.co.uk

Italian design, all chrome, white leather and marble, gives L'Anima the wow factor you'd more usually find 'up West'. You could say the same about the staff-to-guest ratio – and the prices. Co-founder Francesco Mazzei has moved on but L'Anima's regulars have not; we found the see-and-be-seen ristorante as buzzy as ever. Now with Mazzei's deputy Antonio Favuzzi at the stove, one can expect refined, modern Italian dishes including bestsellers of tuna crudo, shellfish ravioli and lobster broth and moreish fried zucchini. Favuzzi's style is complex, verging on overcomplicated sometimes, as in the case of beetroot and smoked burrata tortelli with capers, beetroot, sage and aged balsamic. Crisp-skinned brill to follow, however, held its own against purple potato crisps, crosnes, fennel fronds and sausage. To finish, the famous 'chocolate dome' was exquisitely tempered, but thrown off balance by a too-sweet caramel sauce. The all-Italian wine list boasts some wonderful finds (from £26.50).

Chef/s: Antonio Favuzzi. **Open:** Mon to Fri L 11.45 to 3, Mon to Sat D 5.30 to 11 (11.30 Sat). **Closed:** Sun, bank hols. **Meals:** main courses £18 to £37. **Details:** 120 seats. Bar. Wheelchairs. Music.

L'Anima Café

Cooking score: 2
⊖ Shoreditch High Street, map 4
Italian | £35
10 Appold Street, Shoreditch, EC2A 2AP
Tel no: (020) 7422 7080
lanimacafe.co.uk

There's a friendly '*buongiorno*' for everybody from the Italian staff – natty in jeans and waistcoats – at L'Anima's dressed-down sibling. Much more than a café, it's a buzzing bar, pizzeria, deli and vast, glass-walled

restaurant, well suited to the City's social life, from office outings to payday splurges. Standards appear not to have slipped since Francesco Mazzei's departure, although the menu at inspection wasn't as seasonally inspired as it has been. Salmon tartare with purple potatoes to start looked pretty but its black olive tapenade couldn't help the fatty, rather under-seasoned salmon. Much better was truffle-flecked wild boar and Tuscan sausage lasagne to follow, featuring yielding egg pasta, crunchy edges and wobbly bechamel – terrific. Classic Italian desserts include a nicely made 'pasticcini' selection. Drinks are, fittingly, (almost) all-Italian, including draught Menabrea, sodas, aperitivi and regional wines. House vino is £21.

Chef/s: Luca Terraneo. **Open:** Mon to Fri 11.30 to late. **Closed:** Sat, Sun. **Meals:** main courses £14 to £20. **Details:** 120 seats. Wheelchairs. Music.

Beagle

Cooking score: 3
⊖ Hoxton, map 2
British | £35
397-399 Geffrye Street, Hoxton, E2 8HZ
Tel no: (020) 7613 2967
beaglelondon.co.uk

Seemingly evoking the grand steam trains that once trundled above, this stylish industrial-chic railway arch turned restaurant indulges in earthy, back-to-basics dishes wrought from seasonal British ingredients. At the helm is ex St John Bread & Wine chef, Tom Ryalls – and it shows. Hearty, uncomplicated starters, such as pork and pigeon terrine, or smoked cod's roe on toast, are outstanding. This does-what-it-says-on-the-tin approach continues to shine with mains like wood-grilled bavette, served with wild garlic and new potatoes, and succulent hake, with pistachio, preserved lemon and sea beet. But Beagle's commitment to 'local' provenance doesn't end here. Puddings include a standout English cheeseboard of Isle of Mull Cheddar, Edmund Tew and Harbourne Blue. And ultra-pale, lightly sour coffee beans are sourced from local roastery, Workshop – 'is this the best

restaurant coffee in London?' For a digestif, consult the restaurant's impressive list of cocktails and craft beers. Wines start at £25.
Chef/s: Tom Ryalls. **Open:** Fri to Sun L 12 to 3 (11 Sat, 11 to 4 Sun), Mon to Sat D 6 to 10.30. **Closed:** 24 to 30 Dec. **Meals:** main courses £15 to £19. Set D £19 (2 courses) to £23. **Details:** 54 seats. 36 seats outside. Bar. Wheelchairs. Music.

LOCAL GEM

Berber & Q
⊖ Haggerston, map 2
Middle Eastern | £25
338 Acton Mews, Haggerston, E8 4EA
berberandq.com

£30

Housed in a railway arch ('with no reservations, thanks very much'), this east London grill-spot is 'fun and unique' with its low-fi décor, communal seating and a really inventive cocktail list that ensures the entire room is 'packed beard-to-beard'. Expect a menu of grilled meats and vegetables, with the emphasis on the eastern end of the Med. Locals make a beeline for the likes of hand-pulled lamb shawarma or smoked short rib with a date-syrup glaze, both served with cumin salt, harissa and grilled pitta. Butternut squash tahini, beets with whipped feta and saffron candied orange, and hispi cabbage with harissa crème fraîche and preserved lemon make good openers. Wines from £19.

Bistrotheque
Cooking score: 2
⊖ Bethnal Green, map 1
Modern British | £45
23-27 Wadeson Street, Bethnal Green, E2 9DR
Tel no: (020) 8983 7900
bistrotheque.com

No slave to the conventions of exterior signage, this Bethnal Green stalwart must accept that newcomers 'venture into the former warehouse with some apprehension'. But a 'cheerful welcome and very competent service' soften the edges of this big, white

industrial space, established in 2003. The menu is built for comfort, too, especially once you're past 'admirable' starters such as brown crab with fennel and crème frâiche or roast leeks with yoghurt, chickpeas and coriander and on to half a roast chicken with rocket and aïoli, cod and chips, or steak tartare. More evolved mains appear alongside, though, in the form of whole bream with potato and celeriac and smoked anchovy, or smoked lamb shoulder broth with pickled chicory. 'Lively' diners can move on to chocolate mint ice cream pie with ale cream, or banana and peanut sponge with dulce sauce, and a dessert cocktail – the espresso Martini lives on. Wine starts at £22.50.
Chef/s: Blaine Duffy. **Open:** Sat and Sun L 11 to 4, all week D 6 to 10.30 (11 Fri and Sat). **Closed:** 24 to 26 Dec. **Meals:** main courses £10 to £33. Set D £23 (3 courses). **Details:** 116 seats. Bar. Music.

Boundary
Cooking score: 3
⊖ Shoreditch, Old Street, map 4
Modern French | £45
2-4 Boundary Street (entrance in Redchurch Street), Shoreditch, E2 7DD
Tel no: (020) 7729 1051
theboundary.co.uk

You have to descend several flights of stairs to reach the basement restaurant of Sir Terence Conran's boutique hotel. It's an elegant space, the exposed brickwork, marble flooring and open-to-view kitchen softened by curved claret-leather banquettes, white-clad tables, comfortable chairs, and illuminated murals of constellations of the zodiac overhead. The cooking is French, from the chariot of charcuterie, via the soufflé suissesse, to gigot d'agneau and the cheese trolley. At inspection, very fresh brown and white Devon crab with an apple and fennel salad showed skill, while a well-timed, crisp-skinned gilthead bream with courgette, fennel and segments of orange and pink grapefruit had lovely flavours. Desserts are a high point: banana soufflé, which arrived with bitter chocolate sorbet and hazelnut praline, was well worth the 20-minute wait. Service is 'really friendly and professional', and there are some interesting bottles from regional France on the heavyweight wine list (from £24). **Chef/s:** Harry Faddy. **Open:** Tue to Sat D only 6.30 to 10.30. **Closed:** Sun, Mon, bank hols. **Meals:** main courses £17 to £35. Set D £26 to £35. **Details:** 100 seats. Bar. Wheelchairs.

Brawn
Cooking score: 4
⊖ Shoreditch, map 2
Modern European | £28
49 Columbia Road, Shoreditch, E2 7RG
Tel no: (020) 7729 5692
brawn.co

🍴 £30

Ed Wilson's Columbia Road indie bistro is one for east London's hipsters and their in-laws, it being both seriously cool and seriously good. We found the kitchen firing on all cylinders at inspection, cooking from a daily A4 menu of rustic Italian and French classics that go hand in hand with the astutely chosen list of boutique and natural wines from the same countries. As the piggy logo suggests, pork is a strong suit, be it terrine, saucisson or our thyme-scented pork belly and textbook endive salad dressed with good strong mustard. Even the simplest of ingredients deliver impressive clarity of flavour; we found orecchiette pasta with turnip tops and a humble leek, chard and bean broth every bit as strong as red mullet with mussels and monk's beard (the priciest dish that day at just £19). Puds such as pannacotta or tiramisu are simple but effective. Wines from £18.
Chef/s: Ed Wilson. **Open:** Tue to Sun L 12 to 3 (4 Sun), Mon to Sat D 6 to 10.30 (11 Fri and Sat). **Closed:** 24 Dec to 2 Jan, bank hols. **Meals:** main courses £11 to £22. Sun L £28. **Details:** 60 seats. Bar. Wheelchairs. Music.

Café Spice Namasté
Cooking score: 2
⊖ Tower Hill, map 4
Indian | £35
16 Prescot Street, Tower Hill, E1 8AZ
Tel no: (020) 7488 9242
cafespice.co.uk

£5 OFF

With its lengthy laminated menus, playful, multi-coloured interior and suited-city-working clientele, entering this 20-odd-year-old restaurant can sometimes feel like stepping back to the mid 1990s. But first impressions aren't everything. Owners Cyrus and Pervin Todiwala excel at creating Goan, Hyderabadi and Kashmiri-fusion dishes, which represent a truly fresh approach to Indian cooking. Locals rave about the restaurant's classics, including a starter of ultra-hot piri-piri squid, a Goan-style coconut prawn curry and a dhansak made with tender lamb shank, brown rice and lentils. Off-piste, a deliciously vibrant bhuna is prepared with pan-grilled ostrich. And pungent smoked aubergine bharta is beautifully paired with green chilli, cumin and beaten yoghurt. Be warned; at almost £20 a dish, the food isn't cheap. But quality, provenance-driven ingredients abound, from Northumberland English heritage potatoes to Lancastrian Goosnargh duck and Suffolk Denham Estate Venison. Fruity upfront reds and minerally, dry whites have been handpicked to handle spice. Bottles start at £23.75.
Chef/s: Cyrus Todiwala. **Open:** Mon to Fri L 12 to 3, Mon to Sat D 6.15 to 10.30 (6.30 Sat). **Closed:** Sun, 25 Dec to 1 Jan, bank hols. **Meals:** main courses £15 to £20. Set L and D £35 (3 courses). Tasting menu £75. **Details:** 130 seats. Wheelchairs. Music.

LOCAL GEM

Ceviche

⊖ Old Street, map 4
Peruvian | £24
2 Baldwin Street, Old Street, EC1V 9NU
Tel no: (020) 3327 9463
cevicheuk.com

£30

The substantial Victorian premises used to house the Alexandra Trust Dining Room, which fed the needy back in the day, while today's incarnation satisfies the hip local crowd's craving for pisco, ceviche and Peruvian art. There's a happy hum in the pub-like room where a feisty take on South American cuisine sees sustainable black cobia ceviche dressed with homemade plantain vinegar, and panca-marinated beef heart cooked on the grill. Drink cocktails or their own beer, made in conjunction with the Hammerton Brewery. House wine is £20.

Cinnamon Kitchen

Cooking score: 3
⊖ Liverpool Street, map 4
Indian | £40
9 Devonshire Square, City, EC2M 4YL
Tel no: (020) 7626 5000
cinnamon-kitchen.com

£5
OFF

This sleek, industrial-chic offshoot of Westminster's patrician Cinnamon Club (see entry) dances to a different tune with its flashy cocktails and modish designer trappings – grey leather banquettes, exposed piping, mosaic-tiled floors and counter seating by the open kitchen. It's a brash, high-energy proposition for the suited crowds that circulate around Devonshire Square. To match the mood, executive chef Vivek Singh has designed a bullish menu that deploys carefully sourced British produce for a roster of smart-looking contemporary dishes: tandoori fruits with passion fruit raita; grilled squid with chilli and apricot glaze; sandalwood chicken with rich onion sauce and curry-leaf quinoa. Those looking for fail-safe options might veer towards the garlicky lamb chops or the Peshawari-style beef curry with pilau rice, although desserts throw down more crossover curve balls in the shape of, say, spiced pistachio cake with lime sorbet. Well-matched wines start at £20.

Chef/s: Vivek Singh. **Open:** Mon to Fri L 12 to 2.45, Mon to Sat D 6 to 10.45. **Closed:** 26 Dec, 1 Jan, bank hols. **Meals:** main courses £13 to £32. Set L £15 (2 courses) to £18. Set D £19 (2 courses) to £21. Tasting menu £55 (6 courses). **Details:** 130 seats. 45 seats outside. Bar. Wheelchairs. Music.

City Social

Cooking score: 6
⊖ Liverpool Street, map 4
Modern British | £54
Tower 42, 25 Old Broad Street, City, EC2N 1HQ
Tel no: (020) 7877 7703
citysociallondon.com

🍾

The view from the 24th floor is impressive – you peer down on people, cars, get a close look at buildings. The design is stylish, too (what else from Jason Atherton?), though nobody could accuse the glass-fronted dining room of being colourful, given its two tones of buff and boardroom brown, but a lively, happy bustle and noise comes with the territory, especially in the adjacent bar. Paul Walsh has settled into his stride, his cooking a brilliant amalgam of flavours, textures and combinations, as seen in openers such as raw scallops with soy, green apple, pickled ginger, puffed black rice and wasabi, or pig's trotter and ham hock with crisp Lancashire black pudding, tangy apple gel and Madeira. Unabashed simplicity is the key to a staggeringly fine plate involving tender Romney Marsh lamb fillet, an intense mint-flavoured sauce and a side dish of navarin of shoulder topped with a bacon crumb. As for dessert, it is well worth the 20-minute wait for the raspberry soufflé with white chocolate raspberry ripple ice cream. The wine list is

another Social group winner, with intelligent choosing written all over it and real choice by the glass. Bottles from £29.
Chef/s: Paul Walsh. **Open:** Mon to Fri L 12 to 2.30, Mon to Sat D 6 to 11. **Closed:** Sun, 25 and 26 Dec, Jan 1, bank hols. **Meals:** main courses £25 to £42. **Details:** 110 seats. Bar. Wheelchairs. Music.

The Clove Club

Cooking score: 6
⊖ **Old Street, Shoreditch High Street, map 4**
Modern European | £65
Shoreditch Town Hall, 380 Old Street, Shoreditch, EC1V 9LT
Tel no: (020) 7729 6496
thecloveclub.com

As Shoreditch transforms daily outside, the Clove Club provides a welcome haven away from cars, Crossrail and high-speed cyclists. Housed in the old Shoreditch Town Hall, the bar and dining room have a fabulous character and patina into which furnishings and the simple, stylish open kitchen slot sympathetically. Isaac McHale's style and ethos have been a great influence on many young chefs, his flawlessly executed dishes, characterised by powerful British produce, are known for balance, bold flavour combinations and crystal-clear innovation. Seasonal ingredients are an integral part of the plan, so a June à la carte lunch may feature 'supremely fresh' flamed Cornish mackerel sashimi with cucumber and English mustard, roast suckling pig served with white asparagus and turnip tops – 'possibly the nicest dish I have eaten all year' – served with two crisp pillows of puffed potato and dressed with a 'wonderful sucre-salé sauce of honey and vinegar', and warm blood orange with sheep's milk yoghurt mousse and fennel pollen granita, 'a wonderful balance of temperatures, textures, sweet and sour'. Opt for the five-course tasting menu or the full-on nine-course taster that fires up in the evening, and both will open with an explosion of flavours from a succession of little 'snacks'. Finally with coffee, more delights – 'dark and bitter truffles well dusted with cocoa'. The extensive wine list opens at £30.

Chef/s: Isaac McHale. **Open:** Tue to Sat L 12 to 2.30, Mon to Sat D 6 to 10. **Closed:** Sun, 2 weeks Christmas. **Meals:** main courses L only £19 to £26. Tasting menu £65 (5 courses) to £95 (9 courses). **Details:** 50 seats. V menu. Bar. Music.

Club Gascon

Cooking score: 5
⊖ **Barbican, Farringdon, map 5**
Modern French | £60
57 West Smithfield, City, EC1A 9DS
Tel no: (020) 7600 6144
clubgascon.com
🍾

It's not far off 20 years since Pascal Aussignac opened in this marble-façaded former Lyons tea house near St Bart's. The twin prongs of what was then a brand-new strategy were small plates for mixing and matching, most of which involved a creative reinterpretation of the food of Aussignac's native south-west France. There have been occasional worries latterly that the place may be treading water, but when the kitchen is on song, the novelties can still inspire. A pressing of foie gras and crab in a pastis-laced spiced tomato coulis should awaken the tastebuds, and there are artful combinations such as lamb with its sweetbread and mussels in vermouth, or duck tartare with winkles, salt cod and aromatic artichokes. Textures are usually fascinating, as when black figs and pickled gooseberries arrive with frosted geraniums and crumble, while 72 per cent Colombian black (chocolate) comes with black olive and lemon gel. The wine list is a golden treasury of France's finest, leading with the lesser-known byways of Gascony, but equally good in Languedoc-Roussillon and even Corsica. It starts at £22, or go little for wines by the glass from £7.50.

Chef/s: Pascal Aussignac. **Open:** Tue to Fri L 12 to 2, Mon to Sat D 6.30 to 10 (10.30 Fri, 6 Sat). **Closed:** Sun, 23 Dec to 5 Jan, bank hols. **Meals:** main courses £14 to £27. Set L £29 (2 courses) to £35. Set D £35. Tasting menu £68. **Details:** 42 seats. V menu. Bar. Wheelchairs. Music.

Comptoir Gascon

Cooking score: 4
⊖ Farringdon, Barbican, map 5
French | £28
61-63 Charterhouse Street, Clerkenwell,
EC1M 6HJ
Tel no: (020) 7608 0851
comptoirgascon.com
£30

Popular as ever, and with its duck burger with double-cooked duck fat chips close to achieving cult status, this bistro-deli remains one of the best restaurants of its kind in London. Related to nearby Club Gascon (see entry) and dealing in the produce and cooking of south-west France, regulars list a friendly welcome, excellent food at reasonable prices and good service among its attributes. Virtually every item on the menu is designed to reassure and comfort, from duck rillettes with sourdough toast to barbecue lamb with confit garlic, black trompettes and croquettes, and from cured salmon with juniper-glazed beetroot and verjus to cassoulet Toulousain, and everything is underpinned by quality ingredients. Desserts stick to a small repertoire, taking in chocolate mousse with crème Chantilly, meringue and cobnuts and a classic crème brûlée, while growers from south-west France make up the short, good-value wine list. Bottles from £18.
Chef/s: Pascal Aussignac. **Open:** Tue to Sat L 12 to 2, D 6.30 to 10. **Closed:** Sun, Mon, 24 Dec to 6 Jan, bank hols. **Meals:** main courses £10 to £19. Set L £15 (2 courses) to £20. **Details:** 35 seats. 6 seats outside. Wheelchairs. Music.

Copita del Mercado

Cooking score: 3
⊖ Aldgate East, map 4
Spanish | £25
60 Wentworth Street, Whitechapel, E1 7AL
Tel no: (020) 7426 0218
copitadelmercado.com
£30

'A lovely space,' enthused one visitor to this off-the-beaten-track tapas bar, the much larger sibling of Copita in Soho (see entry). A lively atmosphere, efficient service, unfussy cooking and an excellent drinks list (with great gin and sherry selections) make an appealing package. From the powerful punch of black rice and the full-on flavours of neck of lamb with pistachio and apricots or kid with chickpea stew, there's a real taste of the Mediterranean about the food. Roasted aubergine with hazelnut, tomato, honey and coriander has been praised, and you can expect boquerones with cider vinegar and extra virgin olive oil, some good jamón Ibérico de Bellota, grilled octopus with crushed parsnip and sobrasada, and an unusual version of patatas bravas made with sweet potatoes. Everyone orders the churros with chocolate but there's also peanut mantecada with Maldon salt and extra-virgin olive oil. The all-Spanish wine list starts at £23.
Chef/s: Ignacio Pinilla. **Open:** all week L 12 to 3.30, Mon to Sat D 5.30 to 10.30. **Closed:** 24 Dec to 1 Jan, Easter bank hol. **Meals:** tapas £6 to £14. **Details:** 80 seats. 40 seats outside. Bar. Wheelchairs. Music.

The Culpeper

Cooking score: 2
⊖ Aldgate East, map 4
Modern European | £30
40 Commercial Street, Whitechapel, E1 6LP
Tel no: (020) 7247 5371
theculpeper.com

Taking its name from polymath Nicholas Culpeper – a local 17th-century astrologer, physician and botanist – the Culpeper pub also likes a spot of multi-tasking. There's a busy bar on the ground floor where city types sink pints, a serene greenhouse atop the roof where vegetables grow, and, sandwiched in between, a dining room serving its own distinct menu. And a very dapper dining room at that: a mix of high Victoriana and post-industrial chic, reached by a swooping staircase. Our inspection opened promisingly with refreshing mackerel tartare, skilfully paired with pickled ginger and cucumber. A main-course pork chop was vigorously flavoursome, with garlic, crispy-skinned courgettes and a dollop of romesco sauce – but a dish of wild red rice with Jerusalem artichokes and caramelised shallots felt rather muddled. Populist puddings pull no punches: treacle tart, or walnut brownie with caramel and vanilla ice cream for instance. Wines start at £24, and there's a commendable line-up of local beers noting their London postcodes.
Chef/s: Sandy Jarvis. **Open:** Tue to Sun L 12 to 3, D 6 to 10.30. **Closed:** Mon, 24 to 30 Dec. **Meals:** main courses £12 to £18. **Details:** 38 seats. Bar. Music.

Please send us your feedback

To register your opinion about any restaurant listed in this guide, or a new restaurant that you wish to bring to our attention, please visit the web address at the bottom of the page. Your feedback informs the content of the book and will be used to compile next year's reviews.

Dishoom

Cooking score: 2
⊖ Old Street, Liverpool Street, map 4
Indian | £30
7 Boundary Street, Shoreditch, E2 7JE
Tel no: (020) 7420 9324
dishoom.com

Inspired by a specific style of almost defunct cafés found in Mumbai, opened by Zoroastrian immigrants from Iran, Dishoom has the sort of shabby-chic décor that fits right in around this part of town, with a touch of 'days of the Raj' for good measure. Now one of four across the capital, expect 'exemplary lamb samosas', open-ended naan rolls (stuffed with chicken tikka among other things) and curries like a cracking veggie paneer. Lamb raan is a leg marinated overnight and cooked over flame, while the same sort of attention is lavished on the biryanis; chicken, maybe, with cranberries bringing a fruity hit to the party. The spicing is spot-on throughout, not least in a dessert of pineapple and black pepper crumble. Cocktails such as the chaijito (with rum and sweet, spicy tea) get the thumbs up, or drink lager, pale ale and wines from £19.90.
Chef/s: Naved Nasir. **Open:** all week 12 to 11 (12 to 12 Fri and Sat). **Closed:** 25 and 26 Dec, 1 and 2 Jan. **Meals:** main courses £6 to £23. **Details:** 235 seats. Bar. Music.

The Don

Cooking score: 2
⊖ Bank, Cannon Street, map 4
Modern European | £45
The Courtyard, 20 St Swithin's Lane, City, EC4N 8AD
Tel no: (020) 7626 2606
thedonrestaurant.co.uk

£5 OFF

The tradition of preparing dishes at the table is none too common these days, but you'll find some carving action going on here if you go for the smoked salmon or Black Angus beef. There's a cracking cheese trolley, too. The fine-dining part of the Don enterprise, which

includes bistro, bar and private dining, is accessed via a little cobbled courtyard. The 18th-century property was once cellarage for Sandeman – hence the Don connection – and the building's antiquity is best appreciated in the basement bistro. The restaurant has a contemporary feel thanks in part to vast John Hoyland abstracts, and the kitchen sets a pan-European course from terrine of foie gras with mango relish, via lobster risotto or veal entrecôte with béarnaise sauce to pineapple tarte Tatin. The feature wine tower in the restaurant is a clue that wine is a key part of the operation, with some 400 bins up for grabs; bottle prices start at £22.
Chef/s: Matthew Burns. **Open:** Mon to Fri L 12 to 3, D 6 to 10. **Closed:** Sat, Sun, 24 Dec to 3 Jan. **Meals:** main courses £17 to £33. **Details:** 130 seats. Bar. Wheelchairs.

Duck & Waffle
Cooking score: 3
⊖ Liverpool Street, map 4
International | £35
Heron Tower, 40th floor, 110 Bishopsgate, City, EC2N 4AY
Tel no: (020) 3640 7310
duckandwaffle.com

A restaurant that never sleeps, Duck & Waffle matches its rare 24/7 offer with some truly jaw-dropping cityscapes – thanks to a prime perch on the 40th floor of the Heron Tower. Whatever the hour, take a fast ride in the glass lift that scales the heights before being decanted into a corridor that leads to a spectacular room defined by floor-to-ceiling windows. The menu is an international mash-up, with a strong US accent and a raw bar catering to the clean-living trend. Nevertheless, calorie counts and indulgence levels are routinely off the scale, from foie gras crème brûlée or kid, pork belly and offal meatballs with anise-flavoured cranberries to the signature 'duck and waffle' combo lathered in maple mustard syrup. Sharers might plump for a whole sea bass with trompettes and oyster

emulsion, while sweet-toothed types spoon their way through the baked Alaska with lemon curd. Wines from £30.
Chef/s: Tom Cenci. **Open:** all week 24-hour opening. **Meals:** main courses £10 to £40. **Details:** 120 seats. Bar. Wheelchairs. Music.

The Eagle
Cooking score: 2
⊖ Farringdon, map 5
Modern European | £20
159 Farringdon Road, Clerkenwell, EC1R 3AL
Tel no: (020) 7837 1353
theeaglefarringdon.co.uk
£30

Over the course of 25 years the Eagle has steadfastly remained true to itself and proudly remains a pub. It helps that Michael Belben and his early collaborators got it right from the off – the no-frills décor, the no-bookings policy, the ever-changing blackboard menus and drinkers more than welcome (if they can find some space at peak dining times) The robust Mediterranean- and British-inspired menus add to the feel-good vibe; a veggie lasagne, say, with squash, fennel and sage, or some chunky Swaledale lamb chops fired up with sumac and pomegranate molasses. There are little tapas plates, too (maybe pork belly with piccalilli), but it's really aimed at one-plate action – roast monkfish with focaccia and aubergine caponata, or osso buco with its classic saffron risotto and gremolata accompaniments. Finish with a cake flavoured with lemon, almonds and rosemary, or pasteis de nata. Drink craft beer or wines from £14.70.
Chef/s: Ed Mottershaw. **Open:** all week L 12 to 3 (12.30 to 3.30 Sat, 12.30 to 4 Sun), Mon to Sat D 6.30 to 10.30. **Closed:** 10 days Christmas, bank hols. **Meals:** main courses £8 to £18. **Details:** 65 seats. 16 seats outside. Bar. Music.

8 Hoxton Square

Cooking score: 4
Ⓔ Old Street, map 4
Modern European | £35
8-9 Hoxton Square, Hoxton, N1 6NU
Tel no: (020) 7729 4232
8hoxtonsquare.com

Said to be one of the oldest squares in London, this is the epicentre of the media/arts community that has grown up hereabouts. A relative newcomer, 8 Hoxton Square has continued the naming style of its sister Soho gaff, 10 Greek Street, and serves up a similar mode of punchy, rustic, Med-inspired grub. The dressed-down room suits the location with its pared-back look of exposed brickwork, wooden tables and banquette seats, and there are some outside tables, too. Check out the blackboard and tuck into a colourful spring opener of Monte Enebro (a Spanish goats' cheese) with broad beans, peas and mint or how about crumbed lamb's sweetbreads with cauliflower and pomegranate? Brecon lamb pie is a joyously flavour-packed plateful, or keep it lighter with small plates to share (fried baby squid, say). Finish with lemon curd tart. Brunch gets hipsters going at the weekends, and Sunday lunch is a full-on roast. Wines start at £18.
Chef/s: Cameron Emirali. **Open:** Tue to Sun L 12 to 3 (10 Sat, 10 to 5 Sun), Mon to Sat D 6 to 10.30. **Closed:** 24 to 31 Dec. **Meals:** main courses £16 to £42. Sun L £20 to £44. **Details:** 45 seats. 24 seats outside. Bar. Wheelchairs. Music.

Symbols

🥄

🛏 Accommodation is available
£30 Three courses for less than £30
£5 OFF £5-off voucher scheme
🍾 Notable wine list

Ellory

Cooking score: 3
Ⓔ London Fields, map 1
Modern British | £53
Netil House, 1 Westgate Street, Hackney, E8 3RL
Tel no: (020) 3095 9455
ellorylondon.com
£5 OFF

Chef Matthew Young has found a new home in Hackney's Netil House, a business 'incubator' to fledgling east London creatives. Having established himself at the sadly missed Wapping Food and Mayfields, Young has cranked up the front-of-house and décor in this new venture, and the result 'feels like a serious restaurant, bedding in for the duration'. The marble bar, neat table settings and comfy chairs are a refreshing antidote to the hard-edged, tick-box industrial tropes that typify the area's restaurants, and Young keeps things classy in the kitchen, too, where he applies the sparsest of preparation to pristine ingredients, as in 'simple, but perfectly balanced' flash-fried squid with a tinge of orange char, a single grilled calçot onion, sorrel purée and apple. Elsewhere, slices of scallop with chunks of raw turnip are 'great ingredients' but are overwhelmed by their blood-orange accompaniment. Desserts of rhubarb and ricotta ice cream or chocolate mousse with fennel sorbet make a straight-forward conclusion. A Sicilian white is yours for £20, and an interesting selection of 12 wines by the glass is drawn from across the list.
Chef/s: Matthew Young. **Open:** Fri to Sun L 12 to 2.30 (5 Sun), Tue to Sat D 6 to 10.30. **Closed:** Mon, 25 Dec. **Meals:** set L £20 (2 courses) to £23. Set D £38 (5 courses). Sun L £23. **Details:** 48 seats. 10 seats outside. V menu. Bar. Wheelchairs. Music.

Eyre Brothers

Cooking score: 3

⊖ Old Street, map 4

Spanish-Portuguese | £35

68-70 Leonard Street, Shoreditch, EC2A 4QX

Tel no: (020) 7613 5346

eyrebrothers.co.uk

£5
OFF

A large menu isn't always a good sign; Eyre Bros' is the exception that proves the rule. It's restaurateur David Eyre's love letter to the Iberian Peninsula, offering no end of delicious things to eat, drink and discover. Tapas is a good starting point with mussels 'en vinegreta' or Portuguese salt cod cakes, served at the counter, in the attractive lounge or as an 'opener' to a feast in the wood-floored, white-clothed restaurant proper. Ingredients are tip-top; presentation rustic rather than refined. Monte Enebro cheese with artichokes, peppers and char-grilled green onions was a lively assembly, typical of the kitchen's generous approach, while a main of wild tiger prawns with rice pilaf and simple cucumber salad seemed a mark of the kitchen's confidence, won over 16 years. Tradition rules come dessert – choose tarta de Santiago or pasteis de nata. The wine list blends modern and traditional styles, with house at £19.

Chef/s: David Eyre. **Open:** all week L 12 to 2.30 (4 Sat and Sun), Mon to Sat D 6.30 to 10.30. **Closed:** 24 Dec to 4 Jan, bank hols. **Meals:** main courses £12 to £25. **Details:** 84 seats. Bar. Wheelchairs. Music.

★ NEW ENTRY ★

Galvin HOP

Cooking score: 2

⊖ Liverpool Street, map 4

Modern British | £29

35 Spital Square, Spitalfields, E1 6DY

Tel no: (020) 7299 0404

galvinrestaurants.com

£30

Keen observers on Spital Square will notice Gavin Café à Vin has morphed into Galvin HOP, forsaking its focus on wine and instead announcing itself as a 'pub deluxe'. Inside, giant copper tanks of Pilsner Urquell teeter over the bar: their hoppy contents imported weekly from the Czech Republic. Down below, the food also has City types hopping with excitement: the deluxe hot dogs have quickly become the signature dish, served submerged in melted Comté cheese and with a dollop of Maille mustard. In fact, the whole menu shows a Falstaffian inclination: from nostalgic gala pie and crab on toast among the starters, to brasserie-esque mains of Dorset snails and garlic butter, or spiced yoghurt-marinated chicken – which, like all grill dishes, arrives with a phalanx of chunky homemade crisps. Portions are generous: it's questionable whether you'll find space for Yorkshire rhubarb doughnut or Bakewell tart and clotted cream. House wines from £18.50.

Chef/s: Jack Boast. **Open:** Mon to Sat L 11.30 to 3, D 6 to 10.30. Sun 11.30 to 9.30. **Closed:** 25 and 26 Dec, 1 Jan. **Meals:** main courses £13 to £19. Set L and D £17 (2 courses) to £20. Sun L £17 (2 courses) to £23. **Details:** 48 seats. 100 seats outside. Bar. Wheelchairs. Music.

Laurie Fletcher

Nirmal Save
Gunpowder, London

What inspired you to become a chef?
I started cooking at 12, inspired by my grandmother and mother's passion for regional delicacies. They introduced me to a world of flavours and I was constantly testing new recipes, trying to unearth their secrets. I grew up on my family's farm, which meant I was surrounded by fresh produce that I could experiment with.

What food could you not live without?
My mother's dry masala crabs. I grew up close to the coast and crabs were our biggest treat, they were only cooked for celebrations. The sweet meat with the hot spices tastes fantastic. It brings back beautiful memories of home.

How do you start developing a new recipe?
All our recipes are inspired by dishes that our families and friends have been cooking for years, whether it's maa's Kashmiri lamb chops or aunty Sulu's rabbit pulao, so quite often developing new recipes requires lots of phone calls begging for secret ingredients! We'll then take those treasured recipes, update them with local produce and add our own interpretation.

Galvin La Chapelle
Cooking score: 5
Ⓔ Liverpool Street, map 4
French | £58
35 Spital Square, Spitalfields, E1 6DY
Tel no: (020) 7299 0400
galvinrestaurants.com

An imaginative conversion of a former girls' school sees the bare brick of the original building juxtaposed with sheer glass banisters, the vaulted roof open to the rafters sitting above neoclassical marble pillars. For the diner, it lends an airy space filled with a happy hubbub from salarymen during the week, while at the weekend, thanks to a kind children's menu and a live jazz band, smart urban families find their way through the doors. Cooking is classically French, not groundbreaking, but very well done. A char-grilled fillet of mackerel in the cleanest of fish broths is given texture with delicate slivers of radish and daikon; an elegant salad of heritage beetroot, aromatic pear and candied walnut is given depth with the addition of whipped goats' curd; a fillet of sea bream to follow arrives crisp but astutely cooked, accompanied by fat, juicy mussels and spiced orzo. Amalfi lemon curd tartlet with Speculoos biscuit to finish is a work of art. The French-leaning wine list is a first-class collection, yet with plenty by the glass below £10.
Chef/s: Jeff Galvin and Eric Jolibois. **Open:** all week L 12 to 2.30 (3 Sun), D 6 to 10.30 (9.30 Sun). **Closed:** 24 to 26 Dec, 1 Jan. **Meals:** main courses £26 to £36. Set L and D £35. **Details:** 110 seats. 30 seats outside. Bar. Wheelchairs. Music.

Granger & Co.

Cooking score: 2
⊖ Farringdon, map 5
Australian | £35
50 Sekforde Street, Clerkenwell, EC1R 0HA
Tel no: (020) 7251 9032
grangerandco.com

Australian chef Bill Granger hit the ground running when he opened his casual eatery in Westbourne Grove in 2012 (see entry). His Clerkenwell offshoot has the same laid back, bright city feel and friendly, jovial, knowledgeable staff do their bit, too. What they will bring you is cool, mix-and-match cooking of the modern global stamp, from a zingy sambal chicken salad with green papaya, coriander, peanuts, Thai basil and char-grilled spring onion to soft-shell crab with chorizo and kim-chee fried rice and a poached egg, or za'atar-roasted lamb rump with cannellini beans, tahini yoghurt, preserved lemon and parsley salad. It all pleases and satiates in equal measure, although desserts are worth a punt if you've room: white chocolate and pistachio pavlova with rhubarb and yoghurt cream is but one possibility. Good for breakfast, too (try the ricotta hot cakes). The short, global wine list starts at £19.50.
Chef/s: Tom Cajone. **Open:** Mon to Sat 8am to 11pm (9am Sat). Sun 10 to 6. **Closed:** 25 and 26 Dec. **Meals:** main courses £12 to £21. **Details:** 90 seats. Bar. Wheelchairs. Music.

★ NEW ENTRY ★

Gunpowder

Cooking score: 2
⊖ Liverpool Street, Aldgate East, map 4
Indian | £25
11 White's Row, Spitalfields, E1 7NF
Tel no: (020) 7426 0542
gunpowderlondon.com
£30

'Elbows at the ready – this is a restaurant in miniature,' warned a reporter of this cramped husband-and-wife-run restaurant serving food inspired by family recipes from Kolkata (formerly Calcutta). Just off Commercial Road, around the corner from the glitz of newly sanitised Spitalfields ('in a road that still has a refreshing degree of grot about it'), it's young and fun and no-nonsense – exposed brickwork, sensible white crockery – with a stripped-down menu of some 16 dishes, all designed to be shared. Frying is spot-on, especially a comforting fried chutney cheese sandwich with coriander and mint raita or the sensational porzhi okra fries that are 'subtly spiced, salty, perfectly crisp'. Saffron 'pulau' is fragrant and delicate, whole baby chicken char-grilled in tandoori spices is well executed, while word on the street is that maa's Kashmiri lamb chops 'are a match for Tayyabs' – fall-apart tender and drizzled with salty juices. Expect gracious service, too, and wines from £19.
Chef/s: Nirmal Save. **Open:** Mon to Sat L 12 to 3, D 5.30 to 10.30. **Closed:** Sun, 25 and 26 Dec. **Meals:** main courses £8 to £15. **Details:** 28 seats. Wheelchairs. Music. Children over 12 yrs only.

Hawksmoor Guildhall

Cooking score: 4
⊖ Bank, map 4
British | £50
10-12 Basinghall Street, City, EC2V 5BQ
Tel no: (020) 7397 8120
thehawksmoor.com

Appropriately, this branch of Will Beckett and Huw Gott's barnstorming chain is situated just a stone's throw from what was (reputedly) London's first steakhouse – an 18th-century tavern called Dolly's. Located deep in the Square Mile, Hawksmoor continues the tradition in a sprawling, masculine setting of dark-wood panelling, mirrors and plump leather upholstery (ideal for power breakfasts). Although the menu now touts seafood (think lobster mac 'n' cheese, grilled monkfish or hake with green harissa), at heart it's still a sizzling advert for slabs of well-aged, British-reared beef: eight classic cuts ranging from porterhouse and sirloin to bone-in prime ribs and 55-day D-rumps – all accompanied by triple-cooked chips, buttered greens or grilled bone marrow. A starter of crunchy fried

oysters with jalapeño tartare should pique the palate, while sticky toffee pud is a typically indulgent dessert. Hawksmoor is famed for its brilliant cocktails, but there's a tantalising wine list, too, with prices from £23.
Chef/s: Phillip Branch. **Open:** Mon to Fri L 12 to 3, D 5 to 10.30. **Closed:** Sat, Sun. **Meals:** main courses £13 to £36. Set L and early D £25 (2 courses) to £28. **Details:** 160 seats. Bar. Wheelchairs. Music.

Hawksmoor Spitalfields

Cooking score: 3
⊖ Liverpool Street, Aldgate East, map 4
British | £55
157a Commercial Street, City, E1 6BJ
Tel no: (020) 7426 4850
thehawksmoor.co.uk

Spitalfields is where Huw Gott and Will Beckett established the British steakhouse concept that has gone on to seduce customers in select London locations and beyond. It has just passed its 10th birthday, and the central tenets – magnificent steak, best-in-class service, desserts that flirt with confectionery copyright – are still hard to argue with, especially in a sexily darkened city location. Starters of potted beef and bacon with Yorkshires or Brixham crab on toast set the tone for a proudly British experience with an emphasis on provenance. The beef, sold by weight with potential add-ons of triple-cooked chips, bone-marrow gravy or the celebrated Stilton hollandaise, is pretty special, and desserts include the 'crunchy bar' and peanut-butter shortbread with salted caramel ice cream. The basement bar offers more meat, on a snackier scale. A well thought-out wine list starts at £23 and, understandably in this spot, heads skywards.
Chef/s: Pavlos Costa. **Open:** Mon to Sat L 12 to 2.30, D 5 to 10.30. Sun 12 to 8. **Closed:** 24 to 26 Dec, 1 Jan. **Meals:** main courses £13 to £50. Set L and D £25 (2 courses) to £28. **Details:** 116 seats. Bar. Wheelchairs. Music.

Hill & Szrok

Cooking score: 1
⊖ Old Street, map 4
Modern British | £25
8 East Road, Old Street, N1 6AD
Tel no: (020) 7324 7799
hillandszrok.co.uk
£30

Sparkly new-builds on Old Street are soaring ever skywards, but back on street level, just a stone's throw from the roundabout, there's still Victorian charm to be found in the form of Hill & Szrok, a handsome pub that's been given a fashionable refit. The menu changes daily and might offer celeriac with garlicky curds and whey to start, but the best-reported dishes are the simpler spit roasts and quality cuts of meat, as in a 'beautiful big pork chop with a decent layer of fat and good crunchy skin' – no surprise given the pub is owned by the celebrated Hackney butcher of the same name and carcasses are butchered in-house. And where else would chipolatas come as a side dish? Port-and-tonic cocktails might begin proceedings, while 'Nige's vanilla cheesecake' is a fuss-free finish. Carafes of wine from £16.50.
Chef/s: Alex Szrok. **Open:** Tue to Fri L 12 to 3, Mon to Sat D 6.30 to 10.30. **Closed:** Sun. **Meals:** main courses £9 to £11. **Details:** 40 seats. Bar.

HKK London

Cooking score: 6
⊖ Liverpool Street, map 4
Chinese | £88
Broadgate West, Worship Street, City, EC2A 2BE
Tel no: (020) 3535 1888
hkklondon.com

In the confines of the Broadgate Quarter behind Liverpool Street station, HKK represents one of the further-flung outposts of the Hakkasan global empire. In a silkily high-tech environment, an energetically forward-

looking Chinese cuisine under the resourceful aegis of Tong Chee Hwee represents an important development in the encounter between the efflorescence of traditional Chinese gastronomy and Western modernism. The tasting menu of around a dozen picks is a matchless journey through the repertoire but, however you roll, individual dishes that should not be missed include an exemplary seafood soup with langoustines, the richness of which is offset by bitter gai lan leaves and sweet goji berries; salt-baked chicken in coriander and porcini jus, which comes to table on fire; and the signature Peking duck, washed in sugar and spice for two days, then roasted over cherrywood and served with umami-sodden hoisin. Desserts maintain the dazzle: try green apple parfait with cardamom cake and crispy apple noodles. A stunning wine list does justice, from its glass selections, which begin with a chilled Turkish red at £7.10, to its roll call of offbeat grape varieties (Albillo, Arneis, Agiorgitiko, etc). Bottles start at £28.
Chef/s: Tong Chee Hwee. **Open:** Mon to Sat L 12 to 2.30 (4 Sat), D 6 to 10. **Closed:** Sun, 25 and 26 Dec, bank hols. **Meals:** main courses £12 to £88. Set L £29. Tasting menu £88. **Details:** 72 seats. V menu. Wheelchairs. Music.

★ NEW ENTRY ★

Jidori

Cooking score: 2
⊖ Dalston Kingsland, map 2
Japanese | £20
89 Kingsland Road, Hackney, E8 2PB
Tel no: (020) 7686 5634
jidori.co.uk
£30

Blink and you might miss this utilitarian-chic Dalston gem. Stealthily housed in a former bridalwear shop (its old sign still intact), Jidori takes its name from a breed of outdoor-reared Japanese chicken renowned for incredible freshness and full-bodied flavour. True to its name, the restaurant specialises in succulent, free-range Leicestershire chicken served yakitori style: skewered and cooked to order

on a custom-made grill imported from Tokyo. Standout plates may include tsukune-style minced chicken and egg yolk balls, and wings with shiso and grilled lemon. But it isn't all poultry. Diners are encouraged to punctuate their skewers with lighter, zingier sides, ranging from Japanese-style pickled vegetables to a mizuna and tofu salad with wild rocket, radish and sesame dressing. The single dessert offering – ginger ice cream with miso caramel, sweet potato crisps and black sesame – is genuinely unmissable. Specialist Japanese whiskies and saké start at £6.50. No bookings.
Chef/s: Shunta Matsubara. **Open:** Tue to Sun L 12 to 3 (11 to 4 Sat and Sun), Mon to Sat D 6 to 10 (11 Fri and Sat). **Closed:** 25, 26 and 31 Dec, 1 Jan. **Meals:** small plates £3 to £6. **Details:** 44 seats. Wheelchairs. Music.

José Pizarro

Cooking score: 2
⊖ Liverpool Street, map 4
Spanish | £28
36 Broadgate Circle, City, EC2M 1QS
Tel no: (020) 7256 5333
josepizarro.com
£30

'A fun place, buzzing with life,' enthuses a reader who found this City venue 'friendly and very Spanish'. José Pizarro's third opening has rather higher ambitions than most nearby eating places and is certainly good news for Broadgate Circus. It has a modern, hard-edged look – tiles, ducting, concrete, long bar – with outside tables that beckon on fine days and a simple, to-the-point menu that attracts a wide range of customers. Pizarro trademarks, including top-drawer Ibérico charcuterie, tortilla and croquetas, share the billing with the likes of quail in escabèche with dried fruit, pork cheeks in red wine sauce or butter beans with chorizo and morcilla. Pan con tomate or spicy prawn fritters are a good lead-off, and you can close with Spanish cheeses and membrillo or chocolate pot with salt and olive oil. Drinkers can pick from a fine choice of sherries and native wines, from £22.

Chef/s: Zoltan Polgar. **Open:** Mon to Sat 11.30 to 10.45 (9.45pm Sat). **Closed:** Sun, 22 Dec to 4 Jan, bank hols. **Meals:** main courses £12 to £17. **Details:** 40 seats. 20 seats outside. Bar. Wheelchairs. Music.

Lardo

Cooking score: 2
⊖ Hackney Central, map 1
Italian | £26
205 Richmond Road, Hackney, E8 3NJ
Tel no: (020) 8985 2683
lardo.co.uk
£30

So many restaurants seem interchangeable these days. Nobody would notice if they traded menu items, filament light fixtures or (reclaimed) furniture. But Lardo has its own way of looking at things. 'I have to say that of all the cool restaurants in Hackney, this is the one locals still love,' is one endorsement of Eliza Flanagan and Hugh Thorn's Italian eatery in the striking Arthaus building not far from London Fields. It's busy every day, even lunchtimes – which can be quiet in this neighbourhood – and offers a lovely, relaxed and homely atmosphere. Named after the cured back fat of a pig, homemade charcuterie is a staple of a menu that feels personal, too, what with its pillowy, creamy burrata, seasonal dishes of pheasant ravioli, pork ragù, and guinea fowl with Jersey Royals, carrots and tarragon, all served alongside crisp pizzas from a spangly wood-fired oven. The contemporary European wine list has plenty of smart choices by the glass.
Chef/s: Matthew Cranston. **Open:** all week 11 to 11. **Meals:** main courses £11 to £18. **Details:** 60 seats. 50 seats outside. Bar. Wheelchairs. Music.

Visit us online

To find out more about The Good Food Guide, please visit thegoodfoodguide.co.uk

Lutyens

Cooking score: 4
⊖ Chancery Lane, St Paul's, Temple, map 5
Anglo-European | £60
85 Fleet Street, City, EC4Y 1AE
Tel no: (020) 7583 8385
lutyens-restaurant.com

Designed by Sir Edwin Lutyens, converted by Sir Terence Conran, the grand old Reuters building is exactly what you expect: a smooth, slick, professional operation. It may all seem sober and restrained but this is a posh address and customers are unlikely to flinch at the prices (at the more affordable end of the scale, consider the set lunch and evening deals). Simple techniques are responsible for much of the output and the cooking is competent if understandably rather conservative, ranging from brown crab velouté with crab toast to demonstrably fresh grilled Dover sole with herb butter, from beetroot, goats' curd and hazelnut vinaigrette to rack of Dingley Dell pork with apple purée, Agen prunes, pine nuts and sage. Desserts are equally reassuring: perhaps a clementine tart with crème fraîche sorbet. The pedigree international wine list encourages big spending but there is a section listing 35 wines for under £35.
Chef/s: Henrik Ritzen. **Open:** Mon to Fri L 12 to 2.45, D 6 to 9.45. **Closed:** Sat, Sun, 2 weeks Christmas and New Year. **Meals:** main courses £18 to £39. Set L £25 (2 courses) to £29. Set D £33. **Details:** 120 seats. Bar. Wheelchairs. Music.

Lyle's

Cooking score: 5
⊖ Shoreditch High Street, map 4
Modern British | £35
Tea Building, 56 Shoreditch High Street, Shoreditch, E1 6JJ
Tel no: (020) 3011 5911
lyleslondon.com

Simplicity is, of course, rarely simple. The deliberate restraint at Lyle's is of a very specific kind, with the white anti-décor and plain plating that draws inevitable comparisons to St John, one of chef James Lowe's former

habitats. But Lowe's food is more delicate and less muscular than might be expected, whether at lunch (when there are à la carte options) or dinner (a set four courses). Intensely seasonal dishes are bathed in light from the converted Tea Building's generous windows, and might involve simple assemblies of artisan cheeses and bitter leaves, vivid smoked eel with beetroot and horseradish, or Dexter flank with radicchio and anchovy. To finish, treacle tart with goats' milk ice cream has been a winner since the early days, though at dinner you might find a pudding of blood orange, cow's curd and fennel. Service is laid-back, with staff willing and able to fill in the gaps left on the sparingly-written menu. Prices are almost as pared back as the décor; you'll get a glass of Hungarian white for £4, or £23 the bottle.
Chef/s: James Lowe. **Open:** Mon to Sat L 12 to 2.30, D 6 to 10. **Closed:** Sun, 2 weeks Christmas, bank hols. **Meals:** main courses £14 to £19. Set D £44 (4 courses). **Details:** 48 seats. Bar.

★ NEW ENTRY ★

The Marksman
Cooking score: 3
⊖ Cambridge Heath, Hoxton, map 1
Modern British | £34
254 Hackney Road, Hackney, E2 7SJ
Tel no: (020) 7739 7393
marksmanpublichouse.com

Amid the creeping gentrification of Hackney Road, the Marksman still looks like a veteran East End boozer – all dusky wood panelling, mirrors and jukeboxes, locals sipping silently at a grand timber bar crowned by a model ship. What has changed of late is the menu: a spirited and generous take on modern British cooking by alumni of Fifteen and the former St John Hotel. Start by setting your sights on the signature dish: beef and barley bun with horseradish cream, or take aim at simple, satisfying starters like cured sea trout with fennel and dill. There's more than a pinch of nostalgia to mains like mutton neck curry with roti and piquant chutney – a star on our visit – meat slipping off the bone with the

slightest nudge, or else pot roast ham – arriving as a hefty slab – best savoured with a side of fried potatoes and burnt onion mayo. A chocolate ice cream and caramel sandwich is a appropriately retro way to sign off. House wines from £19.
Chef/s: Tom Harris and Jon Rotheram. **Open:** Fri to Sat L 12 to 3, Mon to Sat D 6 to 10. Sun 12 to 8. **Closed:** 25 to 30 Dec. **Meals:** main courses £14 to £21. Sun L £24. **Details:** 95 seats. Music.

Merchants Tavern
Cooking score: 5
⊖ Old Street, map 4
Modern European | £40
36 Charlotte Road, Shoreditch, EC2A 3PG
Tel no: (020) 7060 5335
merchantstavern.co.uk

Housed in a vast industrial warehouse with exposed brick walls and plump, circular leather seating, this Shoreditch restaurant by Angela Hartnett and Neil Borthwick feels more New York than London. The menu, however, is a distinctly British affair with some deft European inflections. Starters, for example, may include Dorset crab salad with baby gem and basil, or English asparagus paired with a fried duck egg, prosciutto and Parmesan. At almost £20 per dish, the mains aren't cheap but they are certainly good value. A sublime (and very memorable) serving of Saddleback pork belly is crunchy and melt-in-your-mouth in all the right places. And braised cuttlefish, served with 'nduja and borlotti beans, is as good as anything you'd find in a Venetian trattoria. In keeping with the restaurant's convivial atmosphere, there is also a small selection of hearty, seasonal sharing plates, such as Herdwick lamb with devilled kidneys, creamed potato and greens. And exquisite desserts include baked peach, vanilla and lemon thyme ice cream and Honduras chocolate tart with crème fraîche and hazelnuts. European wines from £20.
Chef/s: Neil Borthwick. **Open:** all week L 12 to 3 (4 Sun), D 6 to 11 (9 Sun). **Meals:** main courses £15 to £24. Set L £18 (2 courses) to £23. Sun L £20 (2 courses) to £25. **Details:** 85 seats. Wheelchairs.

The Modern Pantry

Cooking score: 3
⊖ Farringdon, map 5
Fusion | £36
47-48 St John's Square, Clerkenwell, EC1V 4JJ
Tel no: (020) 7553 9210
themodernpantry.co.uk
🍾

'About halfway between a smart restaurant and a pop-in-pop-out café,' thought one visitor to Anna Hansen's smart, relaxed and modern eatery set in a striking Georgian town house. Nowadays Ms Hansen's style of fusion cooking feels 'very brunchy', hinting at the superfood trend with its love of exotic ingredients, but there's plenty to applaud. Smoked mozzarella, wild garlic and nigella seed roast sweet potato fritters, served with preserved lemon yoghurt, were 'lovely, like slightly sweet, gooey pakoras with added cheese'. Larger plates are similarly spirited: 'superb' onglet brushed with miso and tamarind, and a pork chop marinated in garlic and Aleppo chilli – 'a lovely piece of meat, cooked just right with crisp fat, a juicy centre'. To finish, it's hard to ignore the chocolate cherry brownie ice cream: 'a perkier brown bread ice cream and a hundred times better'. Drinks run from cocktails and craft beers to an interesting global selection of wines starting with an easy-drinking Sicilian white for £22.50.
Chef/s: Lizzy Stables. **Open:** Mon to Fri 12 to 10.30 (10 Mon). Sat and Sun 9 to 4 (10am Sun), D 6 to 10.30 (6.30 to 10 Sun). **Closed:** 25 and 26 Dec, Aug bank hol. **Meals:** main courses £17 to £22. **Details:** 100 seats. 36 seats outside. Music.

Symbols

🛏 Accommodation is available
£30 Three courses for less than £30
£5 OFF £5-off voucher scheme
🍾 Notable wine list

★ NEW ENTRY ★

Morito

Cooking score: 4
⊖ Hoxton, map 2
Spanish/North African | £30
195 Hackney Road, Hackney, E2 8JL
Tel no: (020) 7613 0754
moritohackneyroad.co.uk

First came Moro, then its pint-size Clerkenwell neighbour Morito (see below). Now Sam and Samantha Clark have taken Morito eastwards to Hackney for its second, larger iteration. An early days inspection revealed an open kitchen in full control but a restaurant still adjusting to the hype around it. Expect that to calm down, eventually. Waiting staff, cool in all black, seemed distracted (by guests more important than this anonymous inspector) and the place was fully booked except for seats in the window and at the beautiful blue marble bar. Greek head chef Marianna Leivaditaki has created a free-roaming tapas or meze menu of evocative summer holiday flavours. Witness a chopped salad of cooling avocado and Lebanese cucumber enlivened by the warmth and heat of chilli butter; tender, spicy Moroccan goat méchoui, garnished with golden chips; and ethereal filo sheets layered with rhubarb and subtly resinous gum mastic labneh. Prices are sensible (though bread at £2.50 sends the wrong message). Spanish wines and sherries from £15 a bottle, £4 a glass.
Chef/s: Marianna Leivaditaki. **Open:** Tue to Sun L 12 to 3, all week D 6 to 10.30 (9 Sun). **Meals:** tapas £4 to £12. **Details:** 72 seats.

Morito

Cooking score: 3
⊖ Farringdon, map 2
Spanish/North African | £30
32 Exmouth Market, Clerkenwell, EC1R 4QE
Tel no: (020) 7278 7007
morito.co.uk

'I really enjoyed the atmosphere, the chatty service and the food,' noted a visitor to this tiny tapas bar, an offshoot of Moro next door.

Small and long, dominated by an orange Formica counter (with stool seating) and small wood tables filling all the other available space, it's best to get there early in the evening or be prepared to queue (bookings are taken for lunch). Come here for salt cod croquettes, wild garlic and watercress tortilla, crunchy puntillitas 'coated heavily in sumac to give a zingy citrus flavour', a 'standout' dish of octopus, tomatoes and garlic rusks ('very simple but perfect'), sweet char-grilled lamb chops with cumin and paprika, chicharrones ('lovely fatty pieces of belly pork') served with a pungent mojo verde, and crisp, golden aubergine chips, tossed in a crunchy semolina flour, beautifully matched with whipped feta, sweet and tangy date molasses and a sprinkle of shredded mint. Wine from £18.

Chef/s: Samantha Clark. **Open:** all week L 12 to 4, Mon to Sat D 5 to 11. **Meals:** tapas £3 to £10. **Details:** 36 seats. 6 seats outside. Wheelchairs. Music.

Moro

Cooking score: 5
⊖ Farringdon, map 2
Spanish/North African | £40
34-36 Exmouth Market, Clerkenwell, EC1R 4QE
Tel no: (020) 7833 8336
moro.co.uk

Once pioneering, now definitive, Moro has anchored a bustling foodie area, schooled a generation of new chefs and served a lot of labneh since it opened in 1997. And it goes on, with the house enthusiasm for the food of Spain and North Africa matched by that of its legions of customers – bookings are taken, and you're well advised to make one. Tapas at the bar is the simplest expression of the kitchen's capabilities in dishes like sardines with tomato toast, Syrian lentils or baba ganoush. The menu proper relies on the wood oven and charcoal grill for main courses such as lemon sole with grilled Turkish peppers, potatoes, anchovies and arak or lamb with slow-cooked artichokes, chickpeas, baby gem, dill and lemon sauce. Layered flavours are

combined deftly, too, in starters including octopus with red wine, purple potatoes and fennel salad. To finish, yoghurt cake with pistachios and pomegranate is the classic, but there's room for Malaga raisin ice cream. Other grape-led adventures come via a user-friendly sherry list and Iberian wines from £21.50.

Chef/s: Sam and Samantha Clark. **Open:** all week L 12 to 2.30 (12.30 to 3.30 Sun), Mon to Sat D 6 to 10.30. **Closed:** 28 Dec to 1 Jan, bank hols. **Meals:** main courses £17 to £24. **Details:** 90 seats. 20 seats outside. Bar. Wheelchairs.

★ NEW ENTRY ★

Oklava

Cooking score: 3
⊖ Shoreditch High Street, map 4
Turkish-Cypriot | £35
74 Luke Street, Shoreditch, EC2A 4PY
Tel no: (020) 7729 3032
oklava.co.uk

Young Londoner Selin Kiazim has emerged from the supper club circuit where her colourful cooking, drawing on her Turkish-Cypriot heritage, was a runaway success. Judging by an inspection lunch at her pleasant corner eatery, Oklava, the raves are justified. Kiazim advances a case for the 'more is more' camp with flavour-packed plates (salads, flatbreads, kebabs) that fuse the traditional with the fashionable or seasonal. Carrot borani and muhammara pepper dip with filo and tulum cheese shards kept us interested to the last mouthful; Cypriot beef kebab wrapped in lamb caul fat had a harder job, with only a wee red onion salad to help it, but as a sharing dish (sharing is encouraged), it worked. To finish, medjool date ice cream and rosemary filo enlivened a sweet milk cake nicely. Oklava has perhaps not quite hit its stride – waiting staff needed a few prompts – but the signs are promising. Wines, from £24, are modern Turkish finds.

Chef/s: Selin Kiazim. **Open:** Tue to Sun L 12 to 3 (11 to 4 Sat and Sun), Tue to Sat D 5.30 to 11.30. **Closed:** Mon. **Meals:** Small plates £2 to £12. **Details:** 46 seats. Wheelchairs. Music.

Robin Gill

The Dairy, The Manor
& Paradise Garage, London

What inspired you to become a chef?
Summers spent on my auntie's farm in
Cork where they cured ham and grew
organic vegetables. Then I followed two
of my best mates into the cooking world
with huge aspirations to travel and learn
different cooking cultures.

What food could you not live without?
A good sourdough and cultured butter.
The breaking of bread is such a wonderful
ritual; the comfort of a warm crusty loaf is
hard to beat.

**What's your favourite dish on your
menu?**
Our bread course with our house-cured
meats, chicken liver mousse and smoked
bone-marrow butter. It is a plate of
traditional artisan skills that can take
months to mature, which represents the
way our kitchen is moving.

Do you have a favourite restaurant?
Barrafina on Adelaide Street. I've eaten
there more than 60 times!

**And finally...tell us something about
yourself that will surprise your diners.**
My mum is a famous choreographer
who was a driving force in the success of
Riverdance.

★ NEW ENTRY ★

Paradise Garage
Cooking score: 4
⊖ Bethnal Green, map 1
Modern British | £27
254 Paradise Row, Bethnal Green, E2 9LE
Tel no: (020) 7613 1502
paradise254.com
£30

Robin Gill, the chef behind Clapham's The
Dairy and The Manor (see entries), does seem
to have that magic touch. His latest venture
occupies a converted railway arch in Bethnal
Green, a relaxed, noisy affair where the casual
mood, refreshing prices and unfussy manner
perfectly echo the functional surroundings of
white tiles, bare tables and dangling filament
lights. In the open-to-view kitchen there's the
same studied craft that has earned its Clapham
sisters legions of fans – with fermentation
(fennel kim-chee), preserving (artichoke
piccalilli), house-cured salami (beer, beef and
horseradish) and a very winning way with
vegetables enlivening a simple, small plates
menu of ferociously seasonal food. Sourdough
bread and whisky-churned butter is a crowd
pleaser, while salt cod brandade with squid
ink, olives and shell fish crisp, as well as Tilley's
farm egg with Roscoff onions, spinach and
lardo, and Welsh lamb with artichoke,
aubergine, winter tomato and monk's beard
have been winter hits. A modern, European
wine list opens at £24.
Chef/s: Simon Woodrow. **Open:** Wed to Sun L 12 to
3, Tue to Sat D 6 to 10. **Closed:** Mon, Christmas
week. **Meals:** main courses £11 to £12.50. Set L £25
(4 courses). Tasting menu £45 (8 courses).
Details: 60 seats. V menu. Bar. Music.

★ NEW ENTRY ★

Pidgin

Cooking score: 4
⊖ Hackney Central, map 1
Modern British | £37
52 Wilton Way, Hackney, E8 1BG
Tel no: (020) 7254 8311
pidginlondon.com

Pidgin was born out of a supper club, the Secret Larder, and if that isn't fashionable enough a beginning, its Hackney location, gripping weekly changing four-course set menu and a mellow prevailing mood confirm this is latter-day dining undiluted. The dinky premises has not much more than a few shapely branches by way of decoration, and its none the worse for that, with the neutral urban space watched over by an engaged and engaging crew. An opening snack might be a crisp chicharrón (pork fat) with beetroot powder and vivid dill emulsion, before the first course proper, a chubby char-grilled prawn with crispy tofu wafer sandwich filled with hits of avocado, soy and coriander, and an emulsion made from the prawn heads. An evocative smokiness hangs over a plate of steak tartare, roasted pistachios, grated cured egg yolk and toast emulsion (they've more emulsion than Farrow & Ball), and a ravishing fermented shrimp beurre blanc enriches a beautiful piece of jet-black pollack (the colour from its nori coating). Start with a house G&T or look to the very short wine list; bottles start at £24.
Chef/s: Elizabeth Allen. **Open:** Sat and Sun L 1 to 3, Tue to Sun D 6 to 9.45 (8 Sun). **Closed:** 2 weeks Christmas. **Meals:** set L and D £37 (4 courses). **Details:** 28 seats. 4 seats outside. Wheelchairs. Music.

Plateau

Cooking score: 4
⊖ Canary Wharf, map 1
Modern European | £45
4th Floor, Canada Place, Canary Wharf,
E14 5ER
Tel no: (020) 7715 7100
plateau-restaurant.co.uk
🍷

With the gleaming towers of Canary Wharf all around, this is a proper big-city venue, matching stunning views with sophisticated modern food from its perch above Canada Square. Take the lift to the fourth floor and you'll discover a glass-framed dining room complete with clean-lined contemporary furnishings, a sought-after covered terrace and a semi-open kitchen dividing the main restaurant from the more casual bar/grill. Choose the former if you're looking for finely honed, calendar-driven cooking defined by freshness and impressive culinary technique – think roasted salt marsh lamb with asparagus and Jersey Royals or steamed lemon sole with parsley gnocchi, brown shrimps and confit lemon sauce. Start with a spring vegetable tart or a plate of Orkney scallop, oyster and lettuce velouté, lovage and almonds; round off with pear mousse, chocolate fondant or strawberry cheesecake with Champagne granita – depending on the season. An impressive selection of half-bottles and wines by the glass kicks off the authoritative globetrotting list; prices from £21.50.
Chef/s: Daniel McGarey. **Open:** Mon to Fri L 11.30 to 3, Mon to Sat D 6 to 10.30. **Closed:** Sun, 25 Dec, 1 Jan. **Meals:** main courses £20 to £31. Set L £25 (2 courses) to £28. Set menu £45 (4 courses). Tasting menu £60 (6 courses). **Details:** 190 seats. 46 seats outside. V menu. Bar. Wheelchairs. Music.

Quality Chop House

Cooking score: 3
⊖ Farringdon, map 5
Modern British | £35
94 Farringdon Road, Clerkenwell, EC1R 3EA
Tel no: (020) 7278 1452
thequalitychophouse.com

£5
OFF

On this site since 1869, the self-styled
'progressive working-class caterer' has
expanded into adjoining properties over the
years and is now a dining room, wine bar,
butcher and foodshop. The black-and-white
tiled floor, Anaglypta walls and mahogany
booths with the famously narrow bench
seating remain in the original (listed) dining
room – the adjoining room is considered
more comfortable but less atmospheric – and
under the ownership of Will Lander and Josie
Stead the cooking has regained its strong
British focus. However, a range of humble
dishes, from leeks, chopped egg and anchovy
to Galloway mince on dripping toast and
exemplary Sunday roasts, doesn't preclude the
incorporation of lardo di colonnata, Middle
White pork with bagna cauda and a well-
handled cod with langoustine butter, egg yolk
and monk's beard. Mast Brothers chocolate
délice with milk ice cream has been pretty
good, too. Wines start at £21.
Chef/s: Shaun Searley. **Open:** all week L 12 to 3 (4
Sun), Mon to Sat D 6 to 11. **Closed:** 24 Dec to 1 Jan,
Easter Sun and Mon. **Meals:** main courses £14 to
£25. Set L and early D £15 (2 courses) to £20.
Details: 64 seats. 6 seats outside. Music.

The Richmond

Cooking score: 2
⊖ Dalston Junction, map 2
Modern European | £30
316 Queensbridge Road, Hackney, E8 3NH
Tel no: (020) 7241 1638
therichmondhackney.com

Glowing in electric blue on a Dalston corner,
the Richmond outperforms its ancestral duty
as an urban watering hole and incorporates
what claims to be east London's first raw

seafood bar, as well as a menu of energetic
modern European cooking and all-day
servings of Negroni, aperitif cocktail of the
gods. The come-as-you-are ambience of
shimmering vermilion walls, bentwood
chairs and bare floor painted with octagons
seems perfect for experimenting your way
through a menu that tickles the taste-buds
with Doddington cheese puffs, before coming
on strong with devilled mussels on wild garlic
toast, or merguez meatballs with semolina and
pistachio gremolata. Shorthorn beef ribeyes,
sirloins and T-bones are aged 35 days, then
sizzled on the oak-fired grill, as the pub classic
alternative to cod with cured pork cheek,
crushed potatoes and peas. The latterly
indispensable salt caramel then turns up on cue
with chocolate ganache and coffee ice cream.
When you've finished with the cocktails,
wines start at £19.
Chef/s: Brett Redman. **Open:** Sat and Sun L 1 to 3 (4
Sun), Mon to Sat D 6 to 10 (5 to 10.30 Sat). **Closed:**
24 and 25 Dec. **Meals:** main courses £14 to £25.
Details: 40 seats. 30 seats outside. Bar. Music.

Roka Canary Wharf

Cooking score: 2
⊖ Canary Wharf, map 1
Japanese | £50
4 Park Pavilion, Canary Wharf, E14 5FW
Tel no: (020) 7636 5228
rokarestaurant.com

With branches in Mayfair, Aldwych, Fitzrovia
(see entry) and Canary Wharf, Roka now has
its tentacles entwined around some of
London's more moneyed enclaves. Occupying
the first floor of a gleaming glass-and-steel
building in Docklands' financial quarter, this
eastern outpost looks and feels less
sophisticated than its siblings: expect acres of
polished grainy wood and shimmering
filigree, plus a rambunctious bar and a red-hot
robata grill at the centre of things. The
cooking is nominally Japanese, although pan-
Asian fusion is never far away – as in tuna
tataki with apple and mustard dressing. Sushi,
sashimi and maki rolls are given a
contemporary lift, tempura might include

Padrón peppers and the aforementioned grill delivers everything from sweet potato baked in bamboo husk to glazed baby back ribs with 'master sauce' and cashews. Multi-course tasting menus are designed for sharing, and brunch is a weekend crowd-puller. Drink exotic saké cocktails or spice-friendly wines from £26. **Chef/s:** Hamish Brown. **Open:** Mon to Sat L 11.45 to 3, D 5.30 to 11. Sun 11.30 to 8.30. **Closed:** 25 Dec. **Meals:** dishes from £13 to £36. Tasting menu £55. **Details:** 89 seats. 40 seats outside. Bar. Wheelchairs. Music.

Rotorino

Cooking score: 3
⊖ Haggerston, Dalston Junction, map 2
Italian | £30
134 Kingsland Road, Hackney, E8 4AA
Tel no: (020) 7249 9081
rotorino.com

Stevie Parle's Italianate Dalston diner has reservable booth seating in the main room, with a separate bar area for walk-ins and drinkers. Distorting mirrors and a skylight throw different kinds of light on the proceedings, while the culinary doings are essentially modernish but traditionally rooted; variations on an Italian theme. Start with cured coppa and pickled beetroot, rock on with a pasta second such as crab reginette (pasta frills) in tomato and chilli, and then turn to the wood-grill for big hearty mains like Galloway T-bone revealingly dressed in nothing but new season's olive oil and black pepper, or whole sea bream in tomato, almonds and mint. Sides include chard wilted in garlic and chilli, and there are pedigree English cheeses where you might be expecting Gorgonzola. A constantly rotating Producer of the Month introduces new showcase wines by the glass, while the Italian-led list offers interest and imagination, from £20. **Chef/s:** Stevie Parle. **Open:** Mon to Sat D only 6 to 10 (5 Sat). Sun 12 to 10. **Meals:** main courses £9 to £19. **Details:** 60 seats. Bar. Music.

Rök

Cooking score: 2
⊖ Shoreditch High Street, map 4
Scandinavian | £26
26 Curtain Road, Shoreditch, EC2A 3NZ
Tel no: (020) 7377 2152
roklondon.com
£30

Smoked and Nordic are two food trends that have become widespread enough to seem drastically uncool in the tangle of trends that is east London. So, being a Nordic smokehouse, Rök seems a little late to the party; this goes for the ode-to-salvage décor, too. But for those who like pretty much anything that involves a grill and don't mind the lack of proper smoke-extraction facilities, the kitchen pulls off some neat tricks. Flavour is everything. At a test meal, a giant lamb chop ('I think mutton'), cut long across the ribs and 'blackened into oblivion', proved to be 'seriously fatty, seriously pink inside', while a side of blackened cabbage stuffed with nori rice and buried in nuts and Västerbotten cheese was 'the best thing I ate'. Don't leave without trying dessert, especially the birch syrup chocolate pudding with smoked beetroot ice cream. Wines from £22. **Chef/s:** Matt Young. **Open:** Mon to Fri 12 to 11 (1am Fri). Sat 5 to 1am. **Closed:** Sun. **Meals:** main courses £12 to £16. **Details:** 40 seats. Bar.

Sager and Wilde

Cooking score: 3
⊖ Bethnal Green, map 1
Modern British | £42
250 Paradise Row, Bethnal Green, E2 9LE
Tel no: (020) 7613 0478
sagerandwilde.com
£5 OFF

Housed in a cavernous Victorian railway arch and staffed by a requisite team of (largely) bearded, inked and impeccably dressed thirty-somethings, Sager and Wilde certainly ticks all the boxes of a hip east London eatery. But this wine-bar-cum-restaurant has more to offer than just good looks. Australian chef Sebastian Myers, previously head chef at Chiltern Firehouse and Viajante, offers up a reassuringly terse set menu focused on seasonal British ingredients, as well as genuinely attention-grabbing flavour combinations. Ginger curd is served with delicately sweet crab and lightly tart rhubarb; an exquisitely juicy langoustine tail arrives in an earthenware pot of millet and rice porridge; and pudding takes the form of saké-infused ice cream with strawberries and wild violet petals. At over ten pages long, the wine list takes in an impressive number of Old and New World varieties, including an ample selection from the States. Sicilian bottles start at £25.

Chef/s: Sebastian Myers. **Open:** Fri to Sat L 12 to 3, Wed to Sun D 6 to 12. **Closed:** Mon, Tue, 23 Dec to 2 Jan. **Meals:** small plates £3 to £18. Set L and D £42 (4 courses). **Details:** 90 seats. 50 seats outside. Bar. Wheelchairs. Music.

St John

Cooking score: 5
⊖ Farringdon, map 5
British | £40
26 St John Street, Clerkenwell, EC1M 4AY
Tel no: (020) 7251 0848
stjohngroup.uk.com/smithfield

Not much seems to have changed since Fergus Henderson and Trevor Gulliver first opened St John in 1994, though the menu may not always be as 'nose to tail' as some would think: 'Were I anywhere else I would have started my meal with a classic cured sea trout with cucumber and dill, but when in Rome etc – so lamb tongues and bone marrow it was.' The restaurant has always celebrated British earthiness, and that continues to form the basis of its menu today, with basic seating, a no-nonsense approach and reasonable pricing remaining at the heart of the enterprise. After a meal of bone marrow, toast, a parsley leaf salad and a little pile of sel gris, a dish of 'very simple and beautifully cooked' rabbit saddle with braised radishes, and a classic hot chocolate pudding with a melting middle and

a scoop of vanilla ice cream, one reporter felt she had received 'full value for money'. The gamut of dishes runs from mussels and white cabbage, via skate, salsify and capers, to kid's liver, lentils and kale, all straightforward ideas that don't go in for frills. It is likewise with puddings of rhubarb and custard pie or blackberry ripple ice cream, and a compact, all-French wine list with bottles from £25.

Chef/s: Jonathan Woolway. **Open:** Sun to Fri L 12 to 3 (12.30 to 4 Sun), Mon to Sat D 6 to 11. **Closed:** 25 Dec to 1 Jan, bank hols. **Meals:** main courses £15 to £28. **Details:** 90 seats. Bar.

St John Bread & Wine

Cooking score: 3
⊖ Liverpool Street, map 4
British | £35
94-96 Commercial Street, Spitalfields, E1 6LZ
Tel no: (020) 7251 0848
stjohngroup.uk.com

There's been a market in Spitalfields for 350 years or so. Just across the road, St John Bread & Wine's nose-to-tail ethos, born in its pioneering older sister St John, delivers big-hitting flavours and food that owes as much to the past as to the present. The on-site bakery turns out fabulous breads and cakes, and it's open for breakfast (rare-breed bacon sandwich). The starkly minimalist, canteen-like décor is a St John signature, and if it gets a little noisy with all those hard surfaces, the food keeps one 'simply enraptured', according to one reader. Braised squid with red onion and aïoli is a rustic opener, before lamb's sweetbreads with peas, bacon and mint, or a whole quail presented with a sharp knife so you can get stuck in. Finish with pear and sherry trifle if you can resist the Eccles cake with Lancashire cheese. Wines start at £25.

Chef/s: Arnold Hoeksma. **Open:** all week 8am to 11pm (9pm Mon). **Closed:** 25 and 26 Dec, 1 Jan. **Meals:** small plates £4 to £10. Large plates £15 to £19. **Details:** 64 seats.

Santo Remedio

Cooking score: 1
⊖ Old Street, map 4
Mexican | £25
22 Rivington Street, Shoreditch, EC2A 3DY
santoremedio.co.uk
£30

Santo Remedio (holy remedy), a diminutive Mexican taqueria at the grittier end of Rivington Street, aims to restore our souls with its lively interpretation of traditional street food. Squeeze on to a communal table for guacamole (a sprinkle of grasshoppers optional), and homemade corn tortillas. Tacos take in chicken pibil from from the Yucátan Peninsula – pulled chicken marinated in orange juice and achiote, and scattered with a tangle of rosy pink, pickled onion slices – six-hour braised beef, grilled cactus or potato flautas – crisp, rolled tacos filled with a comforting mash of baby potatoes, jalapeños and coriander, served with Chihuahua, an artisanal cheese from the Gringa Dairy in Peckham. The margarita Santa with tajin chilli powder is deservedly popular, otherwise wines are from £22. No bookings.
Chef/s: Edson Diaz-Fuentes. **Open:** Mon to Fri L 12 to 3, D 6 to 10.30. Sat 12 to 11.30. **Closed:** Sun. **Meals:** small plates £7 to £12. **Details:** 22 seats.

Som Saa

Cooking score: 2
⊖ Aldgate East, map 4
Thai | £30
43a Commercial Street, Spitalfields, E1 6BD
Tel no: (020) 7324 7790
somsaa.com

'All in all it feels like really authentic food that keeps away from the clichéd pad Thais of usual Thai restaurants, is not reliant on curries, has clearly defined flavours without too much heat,' is praise indeed for this Spitalfields newcomer. Previously a pop-up, Som Saa's permanent site feels like 'a proper restaurant' –

albeit one with a limited reservation policy – successfully pulling off a mix of traditional Thai and modern restaurant trends (reclaimed wood, scuffed wooden shutters fronting the bar, exposed whitewashed brickwork, wicker-caged, naked and vintage lights). Fragrant flavour-packed dishes (designed for sharing) have diners hooked, whether a 'really tender' grilled rosy pork neck in a fragrant, sweet and sour dipping sauce, or a glossy panang curry of braised, salted beef cheeks and Thai basil. Uncommonly good, too, are stir-fried morning glory and silky, woody chanterelle mushrooms in an oyster and soy sauce, and a soft, crunchy Bangkok-style green papaya salad with snake beans, dried shrimp, peanuts and cherry tomatoes. Wines from £20. As we went to press, Som Saa was still dinner only, but the website indicates that lunch is 'coming soon'.
Chef/s: Andy Oliver and Mark Dobbie. **Open:** all week D 6 to 10.30 (10 Sun). **Meals:** small plates £7 to £16. **Details:** Bar. Music.

Sosharu

Cooking score: 4
⊖ Farringdon, map 5
Japanese | £40
64 Turnmill Street, Clerkenwell, EC1M 5RR
Tel no: (020) 3805 2304
sosharulondon.com

Sosharu is the Japanese loan word for 'social', the main clue that this is yet another from the stable of serial restaurateur Jason Atherton's Social group. The menu is modern Japanese and aimed at the mid- to upper-market; the basement cocktail bar does busy trade with homeward-bound City suits, while expense accounts keep the private dining room busy. In the large main dining room, a Korean-style rice pot flavoured with mushroom stock, topped with pickled mushrooms and garnished with mitsuba leaves was earthy and filling, especially when paired with tiny skewers of yakitori-style chicken skin and tsukune (minced chicken meatballs). Highlights included a day's special of

mushroom salad with buckwheat, and a roasted aubergine dish inspired by the Japanese classic nasu dengaku. The Instagram generation will be delighted by the tapas-sized portions and numerous pretty side dishes. Wines start at £4.80 per glass/£26 per bottle, but prices ramp up quickly thereafter.
Chef/s: Alex Craciun. **Open:** Mon to Sat L 12.30 to 2.15, D 5.30 to 10 (10.30 Fri and Sat). **Closed:** Sun. **Meals:** small plates £9 to £25. **Details:** 75 seats. Bar. Wheelchairs. Music.

Taberna do Mercado
Cooking score: 4
⊖ Liverpool Street, Aldgate East, map 4
Portuguese | £30
Old Spitalfields Market, 107b Commercial Street, Spitalfields, E1 6BG
Tel no: (020) 7375 0649
tabernamercado.co.uk

Based on the vibrant joints that abound in Lisbon, Taberna is open in the morning for takeaway coffee and pastries, and from noon fills up with eager devotees seeking Nuno Mendes' take on Portuguese traditional pesticos (small plates). An effusive welcome from the team and minimalist, urban-rustic décor sets the mood, while Mendes' invigorating interpretation of his home nation's cuisine brings in the crowds. Kick off with a 'fantastic cocktail' of cava with white port and Angostura bitters, before tucking into fabulous cured meats (rolled belly of black pig, say) or cod with confit tomatoes and capers. Cuttlefish with pig's trotter coentrada is a star among the small plates, or keep whole brill (a daily special) all to yourself. There are modern versions of the traditional bifana sandwich, too, and among desserts abade de Priscos is a deeply satisfying egg yolk and pork fat pudding. The wine list is exclusively Portuguese; bottles start at £24.
Chef/s: Nuno Mendes. **Open:** all week L 12 to 3, D 6 to 10 (8.30 Sun). **Meals:** tapas £8 to £12. Set L £15. **Details:** 37 seats. 40 seats outside.

Tayyabs
Cooking score: 2
⊖ Whitechapel, Aldgate East, map 1
Pakistani | £20
83-89 Fieldgate Street, Whitechapel, E1 1JU
Tel no: (020) 7247 6400/9543
tayyabs.co.uk
£30 ▼

Pretty much taking up an entire block, Tayyabs holds up to 350 souls at any given time yet manages to maintain a consistently high standard. Mind you, they've been going since 1972 and in the same family the entire time, so they've had plenty of practice. It hums, it buzzes and it's usually busy. The illustrated menu covers a lot of ground with classic Punjabi grill dishes and curries and daily specials that include lamb biryani (Fridays). Start with tender chicken cooked in the tandoor, lamb chops or masala fish, before a silky chicken karahi curry or a king prawn version. Spicing is clean, clear and punchy, and incidentals such as the breads and rice are no slackers. Vegetarians fare very well – baby pumpkin masala, say, or a lentil dhal with baby aubergines. They don't have a licence, so BYO.
Chef/s: Wasim Tayyab. **Open:** all week 12 to 11.30. **Meals:** main courses £6 to £12. **Details:** 350 seats. Wheelchairs. Music.

28°-50°
Cooking score: 4
⊖ Chancery Lane, map 5
French | £33
140 Fetter Lane, City, EC4A 1BT
Tel no: (020) 7242 8877
2850.co.uk
🍾

The founding branch of the 28°-50° group is in the heart of the City of London, historically the hub of the world wine trade. So it feels right that the celebration of all things vinous is the principal focus, in a comfortable basement bar with bare-boarded floor and what looks like an outsized dresser laden with bottles. Before you get stuck into the list, though, have a nibble. They've some satisfying bistro

Join us at thegoodfoodguide.co.uk

cooking of the *ancien école*, starting with charcuterie platters and proper gravadlax, and powering ahead with hefty ribeyes in liberal dollopings of béarnaise, corn-fed chicken breast with lardons in Madeira, and whole plaice on the bone. For something a little more *au courant*, look for sea bream with pak choi and enokis in Asian-spiced broth. Dessert could be chocolate délice with pear sorbet and a ginger biscuit, by which time you could be piling into the stickies. Drink something, for heaven's sake. The list is teeming with invigorating choice, with Collector's Lists of the crown jewels for the extravagant, but many listings coming in subdivisions of bottles (which start with house Spanish at £21) – large glasses, small glasses, and glasses so tiny you'll barely notice them.
Chef/s: Julien Baris. **Open:** Mon to Fri L 12 to 3, D 6 to 9.30. **Closed:** Sat, Sun. **Meals:** main courses £14 to £32. Set L £17 (2 courses) to £20. **Details:** 70 seats. Music.

Typing Room
Cooking score: 6
⊖ Bethnal Green, map 1
Modern European | £60
Town Hall Hotel, Patriot Square, Bethnal Green, E2 9NF
Tel no: (020) 7871 0461
typingroom.com

Consider the Typing Room the template for the modern urban restaurant: marble-topped tables, open kitchen, staff in (pressed) jeans, edible flowers served in hand-thrown ceramics. Plenty of London's restaurants aspire to this Scandi-inspired look but few achieve it with even half the dash of Lee Westcott's smart-casual venue in Bethnal Green's Town Hall Hotel. Sneaker-clad twentysomethings and dressy couples are met with the same welcome, whether they're in for the £29 lunch (excellent value) or the five- or seven-course tasting menu. 'Snacks' to start are typically modern, exact and pretty and everything else is on-point: from glorious ale bread with Marmite butter to the savoury-

sweet desserts such as barbecued orange with chocolate, milk and salt. Westcott's signature cauliflower dish is not to be missed; more seasonal offerings might include Herdwick lamb with St George's mushrooms and nettles, or crab and white asparagus. The wine list opens with a better-than-the-average house Beaujolais at £25, and embraces saké, sherry and quality natural wines.
Chef/s: Lee Westcott. **Open:** Wed to Sat L 12 to 2, Tue to Sat D 6 to 10. **Closed:** Sun, Mon, 24 to 27 Dec. **Meals:** set L £24 (2 courses) to £29. Tasting menu £60 (5 courses) to £75. **Details:** 37 seats. Bar. Wheelchairs. Music.

Vinoteca
Cooking score: 2
⊖ Farringdon, Barbican, map 5
Modern British | £32
7 St John Street, Farringdon, EC1M 4AA
Tel no: (020) 7253 8786
vinoteca.co.uk

Taking inspiration from the wine bars found in Spain and Italy rather than those in the city of London, Vinoteca opened up in Farringdon in 2005 and now there are five across the capital (see entries in Marylebone, Chiswick and King's Cross). It's a simple formula, 'honest, true and seriously appealing', with a lively bar and wine shop. Check out the blackboards listing wines by the glass, and tuck into rollicking stuff like braised Cornish cuttlefish with chorizo ragù and smoked paprika mayo. Plates of cured European meats and British cheeses suit snacking with a glass of something, or go the whole hog with Yorkshire venison ragù with gnocchi and truffled hazelnuts, or whole lemon sole with chilli and caper crumb. The wine list is a terrific document arranged by style and packed full of useful info. Bottle prices start at £17.
Chef/s: Klaudiusz Wiatrak. **Open:** Mon to Sat 12 to 10.30. **Closed:** Sun, 25 Dec to 2 Jan. **Meals:** main courses £13 to £19. Set L £13 (2 courses) to £16. **Details:** 35 seats. 8 seats outside. Music.

Wright Brothers Spitalfields

Cooking score: 3
⊖ Liverpool Street, map 4
Seafood | £40
8-9 Lamb Street, Old Spitalfields Market,
Spitalfields, E1 6EA
Tel no: (020) 7377 8706
thewrightbrothers.co.uk

With its spacious brick interior voguishly
fitted out with a marble oyster bar, hard-
edged vibes, clamorous buzz and all-day
opening, this Old Spitalfields Market chip off
the Wright Brothers block (in Soho, Borough
Market and Kensington, see entries) continues
to delight. Caviar and crustacea are a given,
but the menu also wends its way from dressed
Devon crab with mayonnaise and crumbled
egg via fillet of Bideford hake with braised
arrocina beans, chorizo and spinach to a
shrimp burger with chipotle mayonnaise,
chips and dill pickle. The kitchen deserves
credit for its lack of ostentation, there are no
pretensions or unnecessary garnishes –
flavours are direct and enjoyable, whether a
classic haddock, mushy peas and chips, salt-
baked sea bream, char-grilled hanger steak for
those not in the mood for fish, or a perfect
crème brûlée for dessert. The express lunch
menu is popular, and the short, global wine
list starts at £21.
Chef/s: Richard Kirkwood. **Open:** all week L 12 to
10.30 (9 Sun). **Closed:** 25 and 26 Dec. **Meals:** main
courses £17 to £26. Set L £25 (2 courses) to £30.
Details: 64 seats. 37 seats outside. Wheelchairs.
Music.

Yauatcha City

Cooking score: 1
⊖ Liverpool Street, map 4
Chinese | £40
Broadgate Circle, City, EC2M 2QS
Tel no: (020) 3817 9888
yauatcha.com

Tailored precisely to the needs of hungry
time-pressed City workers, this eastern
offshoot of Yauatcha Soho (see entry) sweeps
impressively around the upper tier of the
Broadgate Circle development. Inside, the
pace is fast as on-the-ball staff whizz around
with small plates of dim sum for customers
with big appetites. All the usual Yauatcha
suspects are here, from the oatmeal-dusted
chilli squid and Wagyu beef buns to crispy
duck salad, jasmine tea-smoked ribs and
steamed halibut with chilli and salted radish.
There's also a little shop selling cakes and
sweet things for those with one eye on the
clock. Wines from £29.
Chef/s: Tong Chee Hwee. **Open:** Mon to Sat 12 to
11.30. **Closed:** Sun. **Meals:** main courses £13 to
£21. Set menu £45 to £55. **Details:** 110 seats. Bar.
Music.

Please send us your feedback

To register your opinion about any
restaurant listed in this guide, or a new
restaurant that you wish to bring to our
attention, please visit the web address at
the bottom of the page. Your feedback
informs the content of the book and will
be used to compile next year's reviews.

The Anchor & Hope

Cooking score: 3
⊖ Waterloo, Southwark, map 5
Modern European | £30
36 The Cut, South Bank, SE1 8LP
Tel no: (020) 7928 9898
anchorandhopepub.co.uk

This working pub turned gastronomic mecca might have an endearingly dishevelled countenance, battered old furnishings and as-you-please service, yet it still manages to lift the spirits. That's mainly down to its deliberately unreformed food – particularly as the kitchen takes an accommodating approach, changing its menus each session and happily garnering influences from near and far. As expected, there are British champions such as Orkney kippers and suet-crusted steak pie, but there's also room for cassoulet, cuttlefish and ink risotto, a 'brilliant' monkfish with pear couscous and baked Vacherin on garlic toast with salsify, celeriac, chestnuts and kale. Flavours are as big as can be and ingredients are seasonally spot-on, right down to the Yorkshire rhubarb served with buttermilk pudding for dessert and a crème caramel that was recently reported as 'the best I've eaten in twenty-five years'. As for refreshment, British ales, cocktails and gutsy wines from European vineyards (£17 upwards) suit the food admirably. Note: no bookings, apart from Sunday lunch.
Chef/s: Alex Crofts. **Open:** Tue to Sun L 12 to 2.30 (3.15 Sun), Mon to Sat D 6 to 10.30. **Closed:** 2 weeks Christmas and New Year, bank hols. **Meals:** main courses £11 to £25. Set L £15 (2 courses) to £17. **Details:** 85 seats. 30 seats outside. Bar. Wheelchairs. Music.

Symbols

- Accommodation is available
- Three courses for less than £30
- £5-off voucher scheme
- Notable wine list

Artusi

Cooking score: 3
⊖ Peckham Rye, map 1
Italian | £25
161 Bellenden Road, Peckham, SE15 4DH
Tel no: (020) 3302 8200
artusi.co.uk

Formerly of the Clove Club and Peckham Bazaar, Jack Beer opened his own Italian restaurant in 2014. The 'lovely, minimalist, grown-up' Artusi has been warmly embraced by 'posh Peckham' and beyond; clientele are a mixed and appreciative bunch. They might be eating various preparations of ox heart (a cut that's been on the menu since the early days), perhaps smoked and served with romesco sauce or chanterelles. 'Memorable' grilled Savoy cabbage with bagna cauda and olives may also come before a pasta course of casarecce with sausage and saffron or pappardelle with girolles in butter and Parmesan. Mains employ traditional techniques, such as baking Old Spot pork loin with milk and lemon, or pair meat with roots: duck with beetroot, pork belly with swede. Pudding could be ice cream (buttermilk and lemon, perhaps), or a simple bake such as milk cake with figs. Wines are all Italian, from £20.
Chef/s: Jack Beer. **Open:** Tue to Sat L 12 to 2.30, Mon to Sat D 6 to 10 (10.30 Fri and Sat), Sun 12.30 to 8. **Closed:** 2 weeks Christmas. **Meals:** main courses £11 to £24. Sun L £20 (3 courses). **Details:** 40 seats. Wheelchairs. Music.

Babur

Cooking score: 2
map 1
Indian | £26
119 Brockley Rise, Forest Hill, SE23 1JP
Tel no: (020) 8291 2400
babur.info

The good folk at Babur marked their recent 30th anniversary by commissioning a huge mural on a wall adjacent to the restaurant, which goes some way to demonstrate that this is a singular kind of place. Its 'modern Indian' tag extends to the contemporary look of exposed brick and bespoke artworks, and a menu that eschews cliché in favour of a more creative output. Cod cheeks, say, to get you off the mark, sautéed in ginger and garlic, or venison cooked in the tandoor and flavoured with black spices. Follow on with spice-crusted lamb shoulder marinated for 100 hours in rich Punjabi masala sauce, or pot-roasted rabbit cooked in a broth flavoured with mustard and ginger (and served with garlic roti). There's meat and veggie versions of the tasting menu, and, to drink, cocktails and wines from a highly informative list. Wines start at £21.50

Chef/s: Jiwan Lal. **Open:** all week L 12 to 2.30 (4 Sun), D 6 to 11.30. **Meals:** main courses £14 to £18. Sun L £14 (buffet). **Details:** 72 seats. V menu. Music.

The Begging Bowl

Cooking score: 2
⊖ Peckham Rye, map 1
Thai | £25
168 Bellenden Road, Peckham, SE15 4BW
Tel no: (020) 7635 2627
thebeggingbowl.co.uk
£30

While some dishes at this buzzing, no-reservations Thai won't get full marks for authenticity – yes, we're talking about you, ash-baked celeriac – there's much to like about a place that takes seasonal British ingredients and gives them a decidedly South-East Asian spin. Flakes of sweet Dorset crab are pepped up by citrusy strands of pomelo and aromatic coriander, while pea aubergines bring a welcome bitter note to a warming curry of monkfish. Like the restaurant itself, the specials can be wildly popular (we were beaten to the last char-grilled coquelet jaune before 8pm) so get there early to give the menu a decent workout. Uncommonly good desserts, including a palate-cleansing lime granita in a lemongrass syrup, are more than just an afterthought. Service is more hip than slick,

but stellar cocktails (don't miss the kaffir sour), spice-friendly wines (from £19.75) and beers keep things on track.

Chef/s: Jane Alty. **Open:** all week L 12 to 2.30 (3 Sat), D 6 to 10 (9.30 Sun). **Closed:** 24 to 27 Dec, 1 Jan. **Meals:** sharing plates £5 to £20. **Details:** 50 seats. 30 seats outside. Wheelchairs. Music.

Bibo

Cooking score: 3
⊖ East Putney, map 3
Italian | £32
146 Upper Richmond Road, Putney, SW15 2SW
Tel no: (020) 8780 0592
biborestaurant.com
🍾

Part of Rebecca Mascarenhas' mini food empire (Kitchen W8, Sonny's Kitchen, see entries), Bibo reflects a love affair with Italian flavours. The décor is agreeably understated, with a spacious bar-cum-eatery at the front overlooked by a mezzanine dining room. Nibbles of 'nduja crocchette, truffled arancini and antipasti of scallops with celeriac purée and pancetta crumbs are capably done. Pasta is a decent shout, too, perhaps pappardelle with slow-cooked pork ragù, and it might be hard to choose between calf's liver with rainbow erbette (chard), caramelised onions, pine nuts, raisins and balsamic, and roast guinea fowl with farro (nutty-flavoured grain), cabbage and pancetta, both well reported this year. Round off with lemon polenta cake with crème fraîche or Italian cheeses from La Fromagerie. The all-Italian wine list is no less delightful, well chosen and keenly priced, with a good selection of wines by the glass from £5.50, bottles from £18.50.

Chef/s: Tomasz Zadlo. **Open:** all week L 12 to 2.30 (11 to 3.30 Sat and Sun), D 6 to 10 (11 Fri and Sat, 9 Sun). **Closed:** 24 to 28 Dec, bank hols. **Meals:** main courses £13 to £18. Set L £17 (2 courses) to £20. Set D £23. Sun L £23. **Details:** 70 seats. 12 seats outside. Bar. Wheelchairs.

Bistro Union

Cooking score: 3
⊖ Clapham South, map 3
British | £27
40 Abbeville Road, Clapham, SW4 9NG
Tel no: (020) 7042 6400
bistrounion.co.uk
£30

'I'd be very pleased if I was local and had this nearby,' noted a reporter who thought the residents of Abbeville Road must be delighted by their street's foodie reinvigoration. A stripy awning marks out this low-key spot, while inside the tiles are bright, the metal polished and the banquette seating buttoned-up. Flexibility is key – it's smart enough for an evening date, while families can enjoy a casual lunch. There's beer on tap, plenty of wine by the glass, and dishes from the daily menu roll out of the kitchen and on to the enamelware, ranging from the beefiness of braised oxtail and snails with parsley and garlic butter to mussel 'chimneys' on a piping hot fish pie with crushed peas and dill, or even slow-braised haunch of venison with hibiscus and boulangère potatoes. It's all finely turned out and good value, too. Service is friendly and assured, and wine is from £20.
Chef/s: Adam Byatt. **Open:** all week L 12 to 3, Mon to Sat D 5 to 10. **Closed:** 23 Dec to 1 Jan. **Meals:** main courses £11 to £22. Sun L £16. Sunday supper £26. **Details:** 48 seats. 12 seats outside. Wheelchairs. Music.

Boqueria Tapas

Cooking score: 3
⊖ Clapham North, Brixton, map 3
Spanish | £25
192 Acre Lane, Brixton, SW2 5UL
Tel no: (020) 7733 4408
boqueriatapas.com
£30

The location is unassuming but the wood-floored interior is bright and cheerful with a bar at the front, a dining space with natural light coming from the glass ceiling at the rear and more seats in the basement. The

atmosphere is laid-back, buzzy and sociable, there's Spanish music, specials chalked up on a blackboard, and enthusiastic staff. The food 'is terrific': tender octopus, lightly dusted with paprika, followed by sweet king prawns cooked on the plancha with garlic and parsley were hits at a test meal, as was a single fried egg served with Mallorcan chorizo and crispy potatoes topped off with Iberian ham, and slices of Iberian pork shoulder that sat over a couple of Pont Neuf chips and was finished off with roasted peppers marinated in garlic and cumin and a goats' cheese sauce. End with passion fruit cheesecake with a mango mousse. A short wine list starts at £18.
Chef/s: Julian Gil. **Open:** Mon to Fri D 5 to 11.30. Sat and Sun 12.30 to 12 (10.30pm Sun). **Closed:** 25 Dec. **Meals:** tapas £5 to £9. **Details:** 120 seats. Bar. Wheelchairs. Music.

Camberwell Arms

Cooking score: 3
map 1
Modern British | £30
65 Camberwell Church Street, Camberwell, SE5 8TR
Tel no: (020) 7358 4364
thecamberwellarms.co.uk

It may seem like any other high street pub with its stripped-back, knocked around the edges look and rotating selection of real ales in the front bar, but the sight of loaves of bread cooling on racks gives notice that the Camberwell Arms is a trusted neighbourhood eatery – a brilliant local with a great welcome and consistently delicious food. Michael Davies has made a success of providing sensible rustic dishes in the modern no-frills British style, as befits a pub in the Anchor & Hope, Great Queen Street family (see entries). A scan through the starters might yield spiced pumpkin croquettes with pickled ginger and lime or else something as simple and satisfying as game liver parfait with brioche. Slow-cooked ox cheek with smoked sausage, red wine and mash delivers gutsy flavours, and spit-roast chicken with potatoes, wholegrain mayonnaise and salad (for two or four) consistently gets the thumbs-up, as does a delicate pannacotta with poached Yorkshire rhubarb and pistachio praline. Wines from £17.50. **Chef/s:** Michael Davies. **Open:** Tue to Sun L 12 to 2.30 (4 Sun), Mon to Sat D 6 to 10. **Closed:** 25 and 26 Dec, 1 Jan, bank hols. **Meals:** main courses £14 to £25. **Details:** 103 seats. 3 seats outside. Bar. Music.

Canton Arms

Cooking score: 1
⊖ Stockwell, map 3
Modern British | £29
177 South Lambeth Road, Stockwell, SW8 1XP
Tel no: (020) 7582 8710
cantonarms.com
£30

An old-fashioned city pub on the stretch of main road between Vauxhall and Stockwell, the Canton is all dignified dark wood, distressed floor and maroon walls inside. Banish all thought of pastry-lidded pot pies, though, for there are more inspired culinary doings afoot. Smoked herring served warm and dressed in lentils and chopped herbs might be the prelude to slow-cooked leg of hare with porcini and soft polenta in red wine, or gurnard poached in fish broth, garnished with shaved fennel and aïoli. Bring the curtain down with buttermilk pudding and blood orange, or a little chocolate pot. House French is £17.50 (£4.20 a glass). **Chef/s:** Trish Hilferty. **Open:** Tue to Sun L 12 to 2.30 (4 Sun), Mon to Sat D 6 to 10. **Closed:** 24 Dec to 2 Jan. **Meals:** main courses £10 to £25. **Details:** 70 seats. 30 seats outside. Bar. Wheelchairs. Music.

Symbols

🛏 Accommodation is available
£30 Three courses for less than £30
£5 £5-off voucher scheme
OFF
🍶 Notable wine list

Casse-Croûte

Cooking score: 4
⊖ London Bridge, Borough, map 1
French | £30
109 Bermondsey Street, Bermondsey, SE1 3XB
Tel no: (020) 7407 2140
cassecroute.co.uk

A convincing slice of France with cramped tables and an ambience of deeply endearing charm, tiny Casse-Croûte looks like many people's idea of a typical French bistro with French posters, gingham tablecloths topped with paper covers and a black-and-white tiled floor. Classic bistro dishes form the nerve centre, the scrawled daily blackboard menu offering cooking that delivers punchy, immediate flavours and exemplary renditions of the classics – don't be surprised to see plenty of dishes straight out of *Larousse Gastronomique*. Just three choices per course are offered, perhaps terrine de foie et volaille or cuisses de grenouilles au cerfeuil, then lapin à la moutarde or carré d'agneau, artichaut, beurre anchois, then Paris-Brest, fondant au chocolat or tarte citron to finish. The cooking may not be the most adventurous, but the quality consciousness and precision is spot on and laid back, hard-working staff and happy customers fill the place with joy. A likeable French wine list opens at £22. **Chef/s:** Sylvain Soulard. **Open:** Sun L 12 to 4. Mon to Sat 12 to 10. **Closed:** 24 to 28 Dec. **Meals:** main courses £17 to £20. **Details:** 25 seats. 2 seats outside. Music.

Chapters All Day Dining

Cooking score: 3
map 1
Modern British | £27
43-45 Montpelier Vale, Blackheath, SE3 0TJ
Tel no: (020) 8333 2666
chaptersblackheath.com
£30

Putting on the style comes naturally to the team at this flexible, user-friendly brasserie, which goes about business against a glossy contemporary backdrop of polished surfaces, Art Deco mirrors and exposed brickwork – with floor-to-ceiling views of the heath for good measure. From lingering breakfasts and brunch to convivial family suppers and late cocktails, Chapters lives up to its 'all-day' promise, pleasing the early birds with kippers and croques, assuaging daytime hunger pangs with plates of charcuterie or deep-fried cod brandade and knocking out more substantial offerings for those who want to splurge. The Josper oven has its way with Kentish lamb chops, burgers and Aberdeen Angus ribeyes, although Chapters' broad-minded approach also allows room for Caesar salad, beer-battered fish and confit duck with plum compote, cavolo nero and Pommery mustard mash. After that, generous helpings of Valrhona chocolate pudding or caramelised banana pannacotta promise sweet satisfaction. Wines start at £16.95.

Chef/s: Nick Simmons. **Open:** all week 8am to 10.45pm (12 to 8.45 Sun). **Closed:** 2 to 4 Jan. **Meals:** main courses £12 to £25. Set L £13 (2 courses) to £15. Set D £15 (2 courses) to £18. **Details:** 100 seats. 20 seats outside. Bar. Wheelchairs. Music.

Chez Bruce

Cooking score: 6
⊖ Balham, map 3
Modern British | £50
2 Bellevue Road, Wandsworth, SW17 7EG
Tel no: (020) 8672 0114
chezbruce.co.uk
🍾⭐

The very model of a high-achieving neighbourhood restaurant, Bruce Poole's understated but immensely likeable bolthole overlooking Wandsworth Common promises fine food in a setting that is perfectly suited to socialising – think wood floors, neatly laid tables and striking modern art on gleaming white walls. The cooking builds on a bedrock of rustic European cuisine, adding some contemporary notes and lightening the textures while retaining its reputation for emphatic, no-nonsense flavours. The result is

pleasurable, thrilling and comforting in equal measure – as in devilled lamb's kidneys with semolina gnocchi, crisp shallots and red wine or scallop sashimi emblazoned with pickled rhubarb, pink peppercorns, shiso and ginger. Meanwhile, prime cuts and earthy platefuls share the limelight when it comes to mains of côte de boeuf with béarnaise, glazed pig's cheeks with Parmesan polenta or a triumphant duck cassoulet packed with garlic sausage and more besides. It's a mightily impressive package, topped off by fabulously ripe cheeses, a near-legendary crème brûlée and a trans-global wine list promising class and pedigree at every turn. Expect tantalising diversity across the range, with house selections starting at £11.50 a carafe.

Chef/s: Matt Christmas. **Open:** all week L 12 to 2.30 (3 Sat and Sun), D 6.30 to 10 (10.30 Fri and Sat, 9.30 Sun). **Closed:** 24 to 26 Dec, 1 Jan. **Meals:** set L £25 (2 courses) to £30. Set D £42 (2 courses) to £50. Sun L £30 (2 courses) to £35. **Details:** 80 seats. Wheelchairs.

Craft

Cooking score: 3
⊖ North Greenwich, map 1
Modern British | £50
Peninsula Square, Greenwich, SE10 0SQ
Tel no: (020) 8465 5910
craft-london.co.uk

Opposite the O2 Arena, with commanding views of the Greenwich Peninsula, Craft is a restaurant for our times. It features the produce of artisanal producers from all over, beekeepers, cheesemakers and vegetable-picklers galore, and then presents them on three floors of hot contemporary design by Tom Dixon. Gold lighting pods hover over proceedings in the ground-floor eatery, with exhilarating aerial views from elevated violet seats in the top-floor bar. Multi-course tasting menus drive the kitchen business, which takes in smoked and grilled eel in treacle and malt vinegar with brined leek; brill and celeriac with sea purslane and egg yolk; and the signature clay-baked duck in honey, with broad bean and barley miso, and pickled veg.

If you're still dithering, snack on an einkorn wheat scone with duck liver and last summer's thriftily preserved damsons, and finish with salted plum caramel and yoghurt. Wines take the same tack, from English fizz to micro-estate Burgundies, at prices from £22.
Chef/s: Stevie Parle and Oliver Laumay. **Open:** Sat L 1 to 4, Tue to Sat D 5.30 to 10.30. **Closed:** Sun, Mon. **Meals:** main courses £18 to £29. Tasting menus £35 (4 courses) to £55 (6 courses). **Details:** 87 seats. Bar. Wheelchairs. Music.

LOCAL GEM

The Crooked Well
θ Oval, map 1
Modern British | £30
16 Grove Lane, Camberwell, SE5 8SY
Tel no: (020) 7252 7798
thecrookedwell.com

With décor that blends character with modern vogue and various meal deals pitched just right for the locale, this solid Victorian pub hits all the right notes. The crowd-pleasing menus offer plenty of interest at reasonable prices, from simple classics like salt-and-pepper squid with spiced mayonnaise, and char-grilled ribeye with pommes frites to goats' cheese in brik pastry with black olive mousse and rocket salad, and sea bass fillet with carrot, cumin, samphire and anchovy Chantilly. Come here, too, for sharing dishes – steak and ale, fish pie or Sunday roasts for two – an impressive cocktail list and a short but interesting list of wines (from £16.50).

★ TOP 50 ★

The Dairy
Cooking score: 6
θ Clapham Common, map 3
Modern British | £40
15 The Pavement, Clapham, SW4 0HY
Tel no: (020) 7622 4165
the-dairy.co.uk

'Who would have thought that behind such an inauspicious and ordinary front door there could be such quality,' expresses a feeling

shared by many who have eaten at Robin Gill's 'seriously good venue', a big sister to the nearby Manor, and Paradise Garage in Bethnal Green (see entries). Diversion from 'basic comfort levels' comes in the form of views into the busy kitchen and Gill's absolutely untiring devotion, enthusiasm, skill and innate sense of hospitality. Ingredients are all – herbs and vegetables are grown on the roof, the industrious kitchen bakes, pickles, ferments, cures and bottles – and the tone is set immediately with snacks of 'absolutely delightful' chicken liver mousse with quince and apple, and Cornish crab with crisp potato (two huge crisps) and sea lettuce. Punchy small plates follow, to share or not, perhaps toasted grains and wild mushrooms, then medium-rare Chart Farm venison with Brogdale pear and crisp Jerusalem artichoke, and Lady Hamilton cod with English radish and soft yolk ('terrific yolk'). Highly recommended is roast quince with burnt meringue and buttermilk, followed by 'two small warm doughnuts resting in cream – simple and superb' served with coffee. Good bread and attentive service, too. Reasonable prices extend to a stash of fascinating modern wines, with bottles from £23. Note: next door, Robin Gill has opened Counter Culture, a 15-seat pintxos bar offering the likes of beef tartare, bone-marrow salad cream and caviar, and lamb kebab with fermented cabbage and focaccia. Best of all, it's BYOB, which should keep all-comers smiling in the face of the no reservations policy.
Chef/s: Robin Gill. **Open:** Wed to Sun L 12 to 3, Tue to Sat D 6 to 10. **Closed:** Mon, 1 week Christmas. **Meals:** small plates £9 to £13. Set L £25 (4 courses). Tasting menu £45 (7 courses). **Details:** 60 seats. Bar. Music.

Visit us online

To find out more about The Good Food Guide, please visit thegoodfoodguide.co.uk

Edwins

Cooking score: 1
⊖ Borough, map 5
Modern European | £30
202-206 Borough High Street, Borough,
SE1 1JX
Tel no: (020) 7403 9913
edwinsborough.co.uk

The entrance to this bijou, first-floor dining room may be easy to miss – look for a door by the side of the Trinity pub – but Edwins has become a badly kept secret among local food lovers. The kitchen is a champion of seasonal produce, offering a menu bristling with down-to-earth ingredients, so expect small plates of purple sprouting broccoli with duck egg, cobnut and beurre noisette or wood pigeon with Jerusalem artichoke, mushrooms and port. Alternatively, opt for larger plates of braised short rib with leek and potato gratin and roasted root vegetables or roast plaice with fennel, salsify and Pernod and mussel sauce. Wines from £20.
Chef/s: Salim Massouf. **Open:** all week L 12 to 2.30 (10am Sat and Sun), Mon to Sat D 6 to 10. **Closed:** 24 to 26 Dec, 1 to 3 Jan. **Meals:** main courses £14 to £19. Sun L £17. **Details:** 35 seats. Music.

Elliot's Café

Cooking score: 3
⊖ London Bridge, map 4
Modern European | £26
12 Stoney Street, Borough, SE1 9AD
Tel no: (020) 7403 7436
elliotscafe.com
£30

Brett Redman's eatery opposite Borough Market is a simple enough room, unpretentious, informal and welcoming, with a kitchen that celebrates the pick of seasonal produce. It makes a great bolt-hole with plenty of buzz and easily priced food. The short, regularly changing menu is a zesty assortment of dishes with influences from all over – don't be surprised to see chicken hearts and lardo, and charred January King cabbage with aïoli. A platter of Cobble Lane

charcuterie is a tasty, tapas-y way to begin and there might be quail with calçots, pomegranate and coriander, 40-day dry-aged Dexter beef steaks or braised Herdwick lamb for two or more to share. There is fish, too, perhaps hake served with salsify, monk's beard and a crab bisque. Warm rice pudding with spiced clementines is just one of the comfort-zone desserts. Organic and biodynamic wines start at a pricey £32.
Chef/s: Matt Goddard. **Open:** Mon to Sat L 12 to 3 (4 Sat), D 6 to 10. **Closed:** Sun, bank hols. **Meals:** large plates £11 to £15. **Details:** 50 seats. 12 seats outside.

40 Maltby Street

Cooking score: 2
⊖ Bermondsey, map 1
Modern British | £28
40 Maltby Street, Bermondsey, SE1 3PA
Tel no: (020) 7237 9247
40maltbystreet.com
£30

Amid an interesting mix of south London grit and jolly Cath Kidston-style bunting, a growing number of eateries and food shops can be found underneath the railway arches in Bermondsey, including 40 Maltby Street – 'a wine bar with a tiny kitchen levered in'. Although mainly cherished for owner Gergovie Wines' splendid list of organic wines from small-scale European producers, the food is by no means an afterthought. The execution tends towards the simple, with raw scallops, radishes and horseradish, duck hearts with bacon, nettle and bread sauce, and crumbed cod with Jersey Royals, anchovy and lettuce showcasing seasonal and British ingredients on the daily-changing blackboard menu. Comforting desserts could include steamed marmalade sponge with Jersey cream. The mood in the no-frills, hard-edged industrial space is youthful and casual, it is a reservation-free zone and wines start at £25.
Chef/s: Steve Williams. **Open:** Fri and Sat L 12.30 to 2.30 (11 to 3.30 Sat), Wed to Sat D 6 to 9.30. **Closed:** Sun, Mon, Tue. **Meals:** main courses £6 to £15. **Details:** 40 seats. Bar.

Franklins

Cooking score: 2
map 1
Modern British | £28
157 Lordship Lane, East Dulwich, SE22 8HX
Tel no: (020) 8299 9598
franklinsrestaurant.com
£30

A corner pub with its sister 'farm shop' opposite, Franklins has a small bar at the front that still operates as a boozer – a couple of hand-pumped real ales, locals reading the paper – but it's in the restaurant area that its true colours are revealed: a passion for seasonal British ingredients is the foundation on which this place was built. Tablecloths bring just a touch of class to the simple setting. The daily changing menu is modern British inasmuch as it takes British ingredients and applies techniques from both these shores and a broader European repertoire. Thus salt cod brandade stands alongside cured duck breast with rémoulade among first courses, and main courses might be a choice between ox tongue with black pudding, ham hock hash with a fried egg on top, or whole plaice with Jerusalem artichokes and hollandaise sauce. Finish with bread-and-butter pudding. Wines start at £17.
Chef/s: Ralf Wittig. **Open:** all week 12 to 10.30. **Closed:** 25 and 26 Dec. **Meals:** main courses £15 to £23. Set L £14 (2 courses) to £17. **Details:** 70 seats. 12 seats outside. Bar. Wheelchairs. Music.

Ganapati

Cooking score: 3
⊖ Peckham Rye, map 1
Indian | £30
38 Holly Grove, Peckham, SE15 5DF
Tel no: (020) 7277 2928
ganapatirestaurant.com

'Authentic' is a word bandied around willy-nilly these days, but some places really do deliver an experience that can take you to another place. Such is Ganapati. Sitting at rustic wooden tables (most likely shared with somebody else) and drinking water from stainless steel cups, tuck into food that resonates with the aromas and flavours of the southern Indian streets. Pop in for a lunchtime masala dosa or kingfish curry and rice, or go the whole hog with a starter such as prawn peera, before a main course such as Andhra chicken curry, made with a free-range bird simmered in a fragrant masala sauce, or a lamb curry flavoured with gongura leaves (similar to sorrel). Vegetarians fare very well indeed, and, to finish, classics like gulab jamun sit alongside dark chocolate, chilli and cardamom cake. Wines start at £22.
Chef/s: Aboobacker Koya. **Open:** Tue to Fri L 12 to 2.45, D 6 to 10.30. Sat and Sun 12 to 10.30 (10pm Sun). **Closed:** Mon, 1 week Christmas. **Meals:** main courses £11 to £15. **Details:** 38 seats. 10 seats outside. Wheelchairs. Music.

LOCAL GEM

The Hill

⊖ Greenwich, map 1
Mediterranean | £27
89 Royal Hill, Greenwich, SE10 8SE
Tel no: (020) 8691 3626
thehillgreenwich.com
£30

Locals are vociferous in their support of this relaxed neighbourhood eatery/bar, admiring its consistency, casual outlook and 'reliable' Mediterranean food. A few South American ideas reflect the owners' roots, but Spain and Italy are the main contributors to a menu that has yielded plenty of top stuff: 'notably fresh' tricolore salad; 'meaty' ham croquetas (a favourite); well-seasoned linguine with scallops, clams and mussels; 'succulent' braised duck; juicy bife ancho (Argentinian ribeye with chips). Pizzas and paellas also feature, along with desserts such as tiramisu. Wines from £17.50.

Average price

The average price denotes the price of a three-course meal without wine.

José

Cooking score: 3
⊖ London Bridge, Borough, map 1
Spanish | £27
104 Bermondsey Street, Bermondsey,
SE1 3UB
Tel no: (020) 7403 4902
josepizarro.com
£30

Not many tapas joints in London feel quite as authentically rootsy as this. Crowded around the tiny counter, either perched on high stools or standing in the convivial press, you could almost fancy yourself somewhere arid and dusty in the deep Andalusian south. 'It's a good place to spend time with friends and feel the Spanish vibe,' writes a Spanish reader, 'plus the staff are great.' Expect to graze on tuna confit with guindilla, anchovy and onion, asparagus in two colours with smoked Idiazabal sheep's cheese, grilled octopus with peppers and aubergine, cod tongues (the lower part of the fish head) in cider vinegar, sukalki (Basque beef stew), and fried chorizo and peas, and still be on your feet for another round of sherries. The grown-up sibling, Pizarro, is further up Bermondsey Street (see entry). Hidalgo and Lustau sherries in all styles supplement a whistle-stop tour of the Spanish regions, from fragrant delicate whites to turbo-charged reds, from £20.
Chef/s: José Pizarro and Zoltan Polgar. **Open:** all week 12 to 10.30 (5.30 Sun). **Closed:** 24 to 26 Dec, 1 Jan. **Meals:** tapas £3 to £16. **Details:** 17 seats. Wheelchairs. Music.

Please send us your feedback

To register your opinion about any restaurant listed in this guide, or a new restaurant that you wish to bring to our attention, please visit the web address at the bottom of the page. Your feedback informs the content of the book and will be used to compile next year's reviews.

Best of... South London

Our undercover inspectors open their Little Black Books

For coffee, try **Peckham Refreshment Rooms**. They have great cappuccino (from Coleman Coffee Roasters) and are in a handy location for the station.

For vintage vibes, local art, and most importantly home-made cakes, **St David Coffee House** is a Forest Hill fave.

Try the 'full Spanglish': chargrilled chorizo and morcilla with eggs, house-baked beans and toast for brunch at **No. 67** at the South London Gallery.

Grab a pint at **Watson's General Telegraph**, East Dulwich, they have 12 craft beers on tap, including eight on rotation at this recently refurbished pub.

For a wine bar and shop with knowledgeable staff and simple food, look no further than **Humble Grape**, Battersea.

Stop off at **Olley's Fish Experience**, Norwood Road, for quirky decor and sustainable fish. They even have gluten-free Mondays and Tuesdays.

The **Gowlett Arms** in Peckham offers fabulous, thin-crust pizzas from a wood-panelled boozer. Love the Fiorentina, but the Gowlettini is the house speciality. They offer takeaway if you can't stop in.

Ganapati (in Peckham), a south-Indian restaurant, now has a separate takeaway. Whatever you do, order the paratha.

One foodie thing you must do is head to **Brixton Village** and **Pop Brixton**.

Kricket

Cooking score: 3
⊖ Brixton, map 1
Indian | £18
Pop Brixton, 49 Brixton Station Road, Brixton,
SW9 8PQ
kricket.co.uk
£5 OFF £30

Much is made of Brixton's gentrification, but wander down Electric Avenue and through the market looking for new foodie destination Pop Brixton (the village of shipping containers and home to Kricket), and it's still pleasingly urban and gritty. The 16-seater restaurant is perched on the upper level, reached by scaffolding steps, décor is simple – they've done a good job of making you feel you are not in a metal box – and it takes no reservations. From a short menu ('the sort from which you want to order everything'), fragrant, spicy interpretations of Indian cooking include bhel puri ('a joy to dig my spoon right in'), 'moreish' samphire pakora, 'salty, crunchy and utterly delicious' grilled sweet potato with gunpowder, black garlic and labneh, and a delicate dish of grilled lamb rump with black stone flower, burnt onion raita and glossy green wild garlic chutney. Wine from £19. Look out for a second, larger Kricket in Soho, offering the same menu, coming late 2016.

Chef/s: Will Bowlby. **Open:** all week L 12 to 3 (11 to 4 Sun), Mon to Sat D 5.30 to 10 (10.30 Fri and Sat). **Meals:** small plates £4 to £10. **Details:** 16 seats. 8 seats outside. Music.

Lamberts

Cooking score: 2
⊖ Balham, map 3
Modern British | £30
2 Station Parade, Balham High Road, Balham,
SW12 9AZ
Tel no: (020) 8675 2233
lambertsrestaurant.com
£5 OFF

Since opening its doors back in 2002, Lamberts has put the ingredients centre stage, with 'seasonal British food' the defining mantra. Joe Lambert has long championed small independent producers and growers, which given the vagaries of the supply chain isn't always easy – 'three cheers for showing a commitment to the small guys'. Settle into the simply smart dining room with its understated contemporary sheen and expect menus headed 'field', 'sea' and 'farm' (and 'puddings' of course). An appealing opener might be a fashionable partnership of heritage beetroot with goats' curd and buckwheat, and, from the sea, charred mackerel with fermented carrot and horseradish cream. Smoked chestnut brings an earthy aroma to a haunch of venison, while charred sea bream is matched with fennel and pickled cucumber. It's a thoroughly contemporary output, right down to a dessert of burnt honey tart with brown-bread ice cream. Drink cool cocktails or wines from £20.

Chef/s: Leon Bugler. **Open:** Tue to Sun L 12.30 to 2.30 (12 to 5 Sun), Tue to Sat D 6 to 10. **Closed:** Mon, 25 and 26 Dec. **Meals:** main courses £13 to £18. Set D Tue to Thur £17 (2 courses) to £20. **Details:** 53 seats. 8 seats outside. Music.

LOCAL GEM
The Lido Cafe
⊖ Brixton, map 1
Modern British | £30
Brockwell Park, Dulwich Road, Herne Hill,
SE24 0PA
Tel no: (020) 7737 8183
thelidocafe.co.uk

Whether or not you fancy dipping your toes into the clear blue waters of Brockwell Lido, the café is not to be missed. It's a spirited, easy-going place, open for breakfast, lunch and dinner, with a no-frills interior that scrubs up quite well in the evening when candles increase the intimacy. The kitchen's rustic output is the comfort food of the 21st century – Cornish clams with chorizo and cider (served with sourdough bread of course), aged ribeye steak, wild sea trout with spicy pickled fennel, and a burger in a brioche bun. Good stuff. Wines start at £17.

LOCAL GEM
Lobster Pot
⊖ Kennington, map 1
Seafood | £44
3 Kennington Lane, Elephant and Castle,
SE11 4RG
Tel no: (020) 7582 5556
lobsterpotrestaurant.co.uk

A six-metre-long aquarium ensures the seafood is as fresh as possible before passing through the kitchen and out into the charmingly kitsch dining room where porthole fish tanks, hanging nets and seafaring knick-knacks are all part of Hervé Régent's homage to Brittany. It's a lot of fun. Le plateau de fruits de mer, grilled lobster, smoked trout with caper mayonnaise, whole grilled Dover sole – what's not to like about fresh seafood done right? Wines start at £19.50.

Magdalen
Cooking score: 4
⊖ London Bridge, map 4
Modern British | £36
152 Tooley Street, Southwark, SE1 2TU
Tel no: (020) 7403 1342
magdalenrestaurant.co.uk

The corner site near London Bridge offers an eye-catching mix of messages inside, with its austere burgundy walls, dark-wood floor, crisp linens and crystal chandeliers. Who knew there were chandeliers on Tooley Street? James Faulks contributes to the characterful nature of the place, with menus that meld European classic techniques with modern presentations, as in warm salt cod with a boiled egg and olives, or hot-smoked salmon with a potato pancake and crème fraîche, followed by softly braised lamb shoulder with butter beans and rosemary. The emphasis is on meat more than fish, although that doesn't preclude a signature fish stew of hake, bream and clams with aïoli, which – remarkably enough – is a fixture of the sub-£20 lunchtime prix fixe. Finish with rhubarb ripple ice cream, or pear frangipane tart. A wine list of considered discernment rises from £22 for grassy south-western Gaillac to a perfectly judged upper end of Chavy's Puligny-Montrachet and Vajra's Barolo. Only a mature classed-growth claret and one of the Champagnes nudges into three figures.
Chef/s: James Faulks. **Open:** Mon to Fri L 12 to 2.30, Mon to Sat D 6.30 to 10. **Closed:** Sun, 2 weeks Aug, bank hols. **Meals:** main courses £17 to £20. Set L £17 (2 courses) to £20. **Details:** 82 seats. Wheelchairs.

The Manor

Cooking score: 5

⊖ Clapham Common, Clapham North, map 3

Modern British | £40

148 Clapham Manor Street, Clapham,
SW4 6BX

Tel no: (020) 7720 4662

themanorclapham.co.uk

Totally laid-back, and delivering the same
functional, scuffed style as siblings the Dairy
and Paradise Garage (see entries), it's no
surprise that the Manor is usually buzzy.
Mismatched tables and rickety chairs are part
of the charm and the venue is youthful and
casual like most (though by no means all) of its
customers. It keeps regulars returning with a
monthly-changing menu that plays
obsessively off the seasons and straddles the
Eurozone and beyond. The unfussy,
purposeful cooking is all about small plates
(order four per person), first-class ingredients
and the big, bold flavours seen in such dishes as
charred leeks with caramelised Comté and
wild garlic, or applewood smoked eel with
BBQ kohlrabi, rhubarb and oats, and pine-
smoked pigeon with grains, parsnips, cavolo
nero and sloe berry. Start with snacks such as
crispy chicken skin with kim-chee and BBQ
sauce and finish with a dessert of, say,
gloriously poached rhubarb with cultured
custard and chamomile-kombucha (green tea)
sorbet. A big plus is the 'really engaged' staff,
likewise the modern wine list that opens
at £23.

Chef/s: Dean Parker. **Open:** Wed to Sun L 12 to 3,
Tue to Sat D 6 to 10. **Closed:** Mon, 21 to 28 Dec.
Meals: main courses £10 to £12. Set L £25 (4
courses). **Details:** 48 seats. Bar. Wheelchairs. Music.

Visit us online

To find out more about
The Good Food Guide, please
visit thegoodfoodguide.co.uk

Mr Bao

Taiwanese

293 Rye Lane, Peckham, SE15 4UA

Tel no: (020) 7635 0325

mrbao.co.uk

'As a local café it's great. The bao are of a high
standard and made using meat from local
butcher Flock & Herd. It's worth trying the
lovely Taiwanese barley tea, too.'

Naughty Piglets

Cooking score: 2

⊖ Brixton, map 1

Modern European | £28

28 Brixton Water Lane, Brixton, SW2 1PE

Tel no: (020) 7274 7796

naughtypiglets.co.uk

Joe Sharratt's neighbourhood eatery fits the
south London template to perfection, with its
open kitchen, bar seating and pocket-sized
dining area. It may feel like a sublimated caff,
but the unwavering commitment to quality
prime materials is what distinguishes it from
any mere pit-stop. The daily-changing
offerings have a tapas-like directness to them,
although the range of reference is wide. Ham
croquettes, or burrata with broad beans and
black olives, might be the appetising openers
to some seriously inspired main dishes full of
surprising juxtapositions, perhaps John Dory
in smoked tomato broth, a wild rabbit faggot
with Earl Grey prunes and lardo, or raw beef
fillet in coffee with sorrel and spring greens. It
all makes sense on the palate, and it's worth
leaving space for a sweet/savoury crossover
finisher like grilled pear with brown butter,
hazelnuts and blue cheese. A tremendous wine
list reflects the avant-garde of today's
oenological world, taking in listings of
oxidative orange natural wines, lightly prickly
pétillants retaining a little of their
fermentation gas, as well as biodynamic,
organic and unfiltered wines by the dozen.
Nor do prices get outrageous, from a base of
£25.50, or £6 a glass.

Chef/s: Joe Sharratt. **Open:** Thur to Sun L 12 to 3 (2.30 Thur), Tue to Sat D 6 to 10. **Closed:** Mon, 10 days Dec, 1 week Aug. **Meals:** small plates £8 to £14. **Details:** 34 seats. Music.

No. 67

Cooking score: 1
⊖ Peckham Rye, map 1
Modern European | £24
South London Gallery, 67 Peckham Road, Peckham, SE5 8UH
Tel no: (020) 7252 7649
number67.co.uk

Linked to the South London Gallery, with Camberwell College of Art adjacent, and with opening times pitched just right for the locale, this casual all-day café is popular for breakfast (from 8am) and weekend brunch (from 10am), lunch, or just coffee and luscious cakes. It is also open Wednesday to Saturday evenings, when a short, fashionable menu offers plenty of interest, say devilled chicken livers on toast, roasted guinea fowl with parsnip purée, blackberry sauce and cobnuts, and rhubarb crumble ice cream. Cheery staff, reasonable prices and outside seating for when the sun shines are a bonus. Wines from £18.
Chef/s: Raul Cruz. **Open:** Tue to Sun L 12 to 3.30 (10am Sat and Sun), Wed to Sat D 6.30 to 10. **Closed:** Mon, 24 Dec to 2 Jan. **Meals:** main courses £12 to £15. **Details:** 44 seats. 30 seats outside. Wheelchairs. Music. Parking.

★ NEW ENTRY ★

Padella

Cooking score: 2
⊖ London Bridge, map 4
Italian | £20
6 Southwark Street, Borough, SE1 1TQ
padella.co
£30

We're in food lovers' territory here, right on top of Borough Market, and this two-tiered pasta bar makes a brilliant addition to an area that's big on produce but relatively low on

restaurant talent. As an operation it's pretty slick with mainly counter seating at ground-floor level – more tables downstairs – and plate glass windows that allow passers-by to watch the pasta being made in the mornings or to check out what diners are eating later. Simple starters are nothing more than radicchio and watercress salad, bruschetta with borlotti beans and salsa rossa or a generous dollop of super-fresh burrata, while half a dozen pasta dishes include fat ribbons of tagliatelle with Italian fennel sausage ragù or elegant, delicate ravioli filled with silky ricotta and finished with sage butter – all representing 'fantastic value for this level of cooking'. There's home-baked sourdough, terrific olive oil, outstanding almond and rhubarb tart, and the genuinely committed staff are much appreciated. 500ml wine carafes are available from £12, while a caffè corretto makes an authentic finish.
Chef/s: Ray O'Connor. **Open:** Mon to Sat 12 to 10, Sun L 12 to 5. **Meals:** main courses £6 to £10. **Details:** 50 seats.

The Palmerston

Cooking score: 1
map 1
Modern British | £35
91 Lordship Lane, East Dulwich, SE22 8EP
Tel no: (020) 8693 1629
thepalmerston.co.uk
£5
OFF

An animated local institution, this solid corner pub has been lighting up the eating scene in East Dulwich for nigh on 13 years – although drinkers are welcomed. Jamie Younger is the driving force behind the menu and delivers contemporary classic food such as confit rabbit tortellini with game broth, sautéed English rose calf's liver served with chorizo, Padrón peppers, pine nuts, oregano, and a sherry sauce, or fillet of skrei cod with Jerusalem artichoke, salsify, chanterelles and a Madeira and roast chicken sauce. Then again, a Sunday lunch of roast beef and Yorkshire with deeply flavoured gravy pushes many buttons, too. Finish with rhubarb baked Alaska. House wines from £18.50.

Chef/s: James Donnelly. **Open:** all week L 12 to 2.30 (3 Sat, 3.30 Sun), D 6 to 10 (10.30 Sat, 9.30 Sun). **Meals:** main courses £15 to £28. Set L £15 (2 courses). **Details:** 56 seats. 20 seats outside. Wheelchairs. Music.

Peckham Bazaar

Cooking score: 2
Ɵ Peckham Rye, map 1
Middle Eastern | £35
119 Consort Road, Peckham, SE15 3RU
Tel no: (020) 7732 2525
peckhambazaar.com

It promises 'all the good stuff' to its legions of fans, and that's what you'll find in this former pub that seems to run on charcoal. It's an immersive experience thanks to the grill and a menu that pairs seasonal UK ingredients with the spices and savour of pan-Balkan cooking. To start, Scottish langoustines come with sprouting broccoli, toasted almonds and garlicky skordalia, while lamb sweetbreads have the melting sweetness of braised pearl onions and a fresh green hit of watercress. For bigger plates, monkfish is protected with a wrapping of vine leaves and served with salt-baked Jersey Royals, green olives and zhug, the Yemeni hot sauce much loved in Israel, while onglet and rabbit leg both get the grill treatment. Daily changes mean that even devotees don't get bored. BYO in a former incarnation, the restaurant now has a wine list dominated by Greek producers, from £20.

Chef/s: John Gionleka. **Open:** Sat and Sun L 12.30 to 4, Tue to Sun D 6 to 10 (8 Sun). **Closed:** Mon, 25 Dec. **Meals:** main courses £13 to £19. **Details:** 33 seats. 22 seats outside. Wheelchairs. Music.

Local Gem

Local Gems are the perfect neighbourhood venues, delivering good, freshly cooked food at great value for money.

Pedler

Ɵ Peckham Rye, map 1
Modern European | £25
58 Peckham Rye, Peckham, SE15 4JR
Tel no: (020) 3030 5015
pedlerpeckhamrye.com

£5 OFF   £30

Charming staff squeeze you in wherever they can at this endearingly unpretentious and cramped café and the place buzzes with a thrum of constant activity. Locals linger over weekend brunch, drawn by homemade baked beans, gin sausages, ricotta pancakes, and toast and maple salted butter. The dinner crowd is enticed, too, with adventurous, broad-shouldered sharing plates, say beetroot tarte Tatin with caramel, Stilton and rocket, grilled quail with chimichurri and chipotle pineapple slaw or whole lemon sole with broccoli, pistachio and balsamic. Inventive cocktails and wines from £18.

★ NEW ENTRY ★

Pharmacy 2

Cooking score: 3
Ɵ Lambeth North, Vauxhall, map 3
Modern British | £35
Newport Street Gallery, Newport Street, Vauxhall, SE11 6AJ
Tel no: (020) 3141 9333
pharmacyrestaurant.com

The artist Damien Hirst has amassed so many artworks that he's converted his former studio in south London into the Newport Street Gallery. As part of this redevelopment he's resurrected a version of his former Pharmacy restaurant, which was the happening place to be seen in Notting Hill for a couple of years in the late 1990s. Pharmacy 2 has a similar pill-popping décor to the original, yet number 2 is no repeat prescription. This time Hirst has collaborated with restaurateur Mark Hix for a seasonal British menu that might include croquettes of cuttlefish with wild garlic mayonnaise, or dessert of poached rhubarb with saffron ice cream. The fish of the day could be Torbay haddock, perfectly cooked, then topped with a poached egg and mustard sauce; or barbecued sugar-pit beef, with its sweetly roasted flesh cut by the acidity of a Bavarian-style potato salad. A succinct wine list starts at £20.50 but the prices increase faster than a former Young British Artist's net worth.

Chef/s: Fabrizio Pusceddu. **Open:** Tue to Sat 12 to 12 (10.30am Sat). Sun 10.30 to 6. **Closed:** Mon. **Meals:** main courses £15 to £45. **Details:** 70 seats. V menu.

Pizarro

Cooking score: 4
● London Bridge, Borough, map 1
Spanish | £30
194 Bermondsey Street, Southwark, SE1 3TQ
Tel no: (020) 7378 9455
pizarrorestaurant.com

Pizarro offers the fuller Spanish dining package to the tapas-and-fino alternative at nearby José (see entry), and the décor does a clever job of creating the impression of old Bilbao with its decorative tiling, bare brickwork and shared refectory and window tables, snugly niched within gastronomically gentrified Bermondsey Street. A little cosmopolitan panache leads to the panko-crumbing of baked crab in velouté, but baby squid in ink, duck egg with black butifarra and pimentón, and main dishes like chorizo and morcilla lentil stew with piparra (Basque pickle), or lamb cutlets with chipped and puréed aubergine, will soon reorientate you. It's all served with brisk dispatch in an atmosphere of properly Iberian conviviality, right up to celebrations of the Spanish sweet tooth such as chocolate buñuelos or the way-out cream cheese ice cream trickled with blackcurrant and chamomile syrup. Sherries and cavas proudly lead off a cavalcade of Spanish wines (from £22.50), sweet Moscatels and brandies.

Chef/s: José Pizarro. **Open:** all week 12 to 10.45 (9.45 Sun). **Closed:** 24 to 26 Dec. **Meals:** main courses £13 to £22. **Details:** 80 seats. Wheelchairs. Music.

Le Pont de la Tour

Cooking score: 3
● London Bridge, Tower Hill, map 4
French | £50
36D Shad Thames, Bermondsey, SE1 2YE
Tel no: (020) 7403 8403
lepontdelatour.co.uk

There can be few finer places to lunch on a summer's day than the Thames-side terrace of Le Pont de la Tour, with its view of Tower Bridge and beyond. It is owned by D&D Restaurants, which means visitors can expect a familiar combination of slick service, well-prepared (if undemanding) cooking and, after 2015's revamp, stylish surroundings. Beyond the bar (dark wood and leather) is a smart, agreeable Art Deco-style dining room offering Frederick Forster's modern French menu. His kitchen doesn't stint on good ingredients, which may go some way towards explaining the prices – though set-price deals are good value – and the mostly classic dishes are generally well rehearsed and delivered: beautifully caramelised foie gras with poached rhubarb and puffed wild rice and tender, high-quality fillet of rose veal with violet artichokes, baby carrots, cauliflower purée and caper dressing. Among desserts, soufflés live up to expectations, for example a raspberry version with white chocolate ice cream. Wines from £25.

Chef/s: Frederick Forster. **Open:** all week L 12 to 2.30 (3 Sat and Sun), D 6 to 10.30 (9.30 Sun). **Meals:** main courses £16 to £39. Set L and D £24 (2 courses) to £29. **Details:** 156 seats. 140 seats outside. Bar. Wheelchairs. Music.

Please send us your feedback

To register your opinion about any restaurant listed in this guide, or a new restaurant that you wish to bring to our attention, please visit the web address at the bottom of the page. Your feedback informs the content of the book and will be used to compile next year's reviews.

★ TOP 50 ★

Restaurant Story

Cooking score: 7
⊖ London Bridge, map 4
Modern British | £100
199 Tooley Street, Bermondsey, SE1 2JX
Tel no: (020) 7183 2117
restaurantstory.co.uk
🍶

Tom Sellers bowled almost everyone over when he opened in this unassuming glass and wood building at the grittier end of Tooley Street in 2013 ('closer to Tower Bridge than I thought'). A few years down the line his cooking continues to be creative, confident, full of twists, turns and surprising technique, with a strong sense of freshness, flavour and balance. It is also bold and ultra modern. One minute you're nibbling on exquisite 'snacks', say a crisp 'Oreo' cookie (smoked eel cream sandwiched by squid-ink biscuits), the next you're spooning up the sweet-tangy juice from a fabulous concoction of onions and gin. It's a highly worked approach, but every detail makes sense, from the subtle hit of heritage potato and asparagus with its vinegary-buttery reduction to the intense, umami flavours in charred squid or the breathtaking richness and clarity of Herdwick lamb served four ways. Equally deft are the beef-dripping candle and the picnic hamper cheese course. Desserts are clever and innovative, scaling the heights with stunningly good textures of lemon or an evocative assemblage of almond and dill. Front-of-house is spot-on, talking everyone through the courses, whether you are in for the good-value set lunch or for the multi-course 'full story', which moves along at a steady pace but takes three hours or so. The drinks list champions cocktails, London-brewed beers and plenty of wines by the glass. Bottles from £25.
Chef/s: Tom Sellers. **Open:** Tue to Sat L 12 to 2, Mon to Sat D 6.30 to 9. **Closed:** Sun, 23 Dec to 4 Jan. **Meals:** set L £39. Tasting menu L £80, D £100. **Details:** 40 seats. V menu. Bar. Wheelchairs.

Roast

Cooking score: 2
⊖ London Bridge, map 4
British | £60
Floral Hall, Stoney Street, Southwark, SE1 1TL
Tel no: (020) 3006 6111
roast-restaurant.com

There's a wow factor in the setting, a striking Victorian glass and steel structure (originally part of the old Covent Garden market) perched above Borough Market. It's flooded with natural light, and the views are not just of the traders below but also of teeming streets, railway arches and overhead trains going into London Bridge. Roast is an individual venue, dedicated to the very best of British produce, though prices seem to have moved north since opening in 2005. The smart move is to plan to take the set menu, where the likes of gin-cured salmon with white crabmeat and beetroot dressing or Scotch egg with lorne sausage and piccalilli, followed by pork belly with mashed potato and Bramley apple sauce, then sticky date pudding with toffee sauce and clotted cream, will hit the spot. Surprisingly, service lacks the commanding presence that would do the room justice. Wines start at £25.
Chef/s: Stuart Cauldwell. **Open:** Mon to Sat L 12 to 3.30, D 5.30 to 10.45 (6 Sat). Sun 11.30 to 6.30. **Closed:** 25 and 26 Dec, 1 Jan. **Meals:** main courses £24 to £40. Set L and D £30. Sun L £38. **Details:** 120 seats. Bar. Wheelchairs. Music.

RSJ

Cooking score: 2
⊖ Waterloo, Southwark, map 5
Modern European | £30
33 Coin Street, Southwark, SE1 9NR
Tel no: (020) 7928 4554
rsj.uk.com
🍶

A promotion has put chef Paul Fillis in charge at one of Waterloo's favourite restaurants, a former stable where nosebag was historically provided for the Duchy of Cornwall horses. Nowadays, customers are likely to be en route to the theatre, or in search of the organic

French wines that are a house speciality. Dishes put comfort before complication. Kick off with confit chicken and pigeon terrine with fruit chutney, or potted shrimps with watercress and lemon. To follow, guinea fowl comes with with wild mushrooms, Savoy cabbage and 'good juice', and there's a fillet of sea bass with new potatoes, spinach, braised fennel and saffron broth. For afters, plum and parkin pudding with treacle toffee sauce and liquorice tea ice cream has a breath of autumn, and ices and sorbets are homemade. The wine list has plenty for the obsessive to pore over, including vintage-by-vintage notes on Loire wine harvests, and starts at £19.75.
Chef/s: Paul Fillis. **Open:** Mon to Fri L 12 to 2.30, Mon to Sat D 5 to 11. **Closed:** Sun, 24 to 26 Dec, bank hols. **Meals:** main courses £15 to £23. Set L and D £17 (2 courses) to £21. **Details:** 95 seats. 12 seats outside.

LOCAL GEM
Silk Road
map 1
Chinese | £15
49 Camberwell Church Street, Camberwell, SE5 8TR
Tel no: (020) 7703 4832
£30

You may not be convinced by its dull exterior and rudimentary décor, but the northern Chinese cooking (from Xinjiang) is homely, fresh and authentic and can hit heights with the likes of double-cooked pork, and skewer of lamb's kidneys. Other favourites to look out for are the shredded kelp salad, pork dumplings (all noodles and dumplings are made in-house), big plate chicken and a cold dish of garlic pork belly with chilli and Szechuan pepper oil. Booking essential. Note: cash only.

Average price

The average price denotes the price of a three-course meal without wine.

Soif
Cooking score: 1
⊖ Clapham South, map 3
Modern European | £30
27 Battersea Rise, Battersea, SW11 1HG
Tel no: (020) 7223 1112
soif.co

Did someone say 'rustic chic'? This neighbourhood bistro and wine specialist (the name means 'thirst') near the western extremity of Clapham Common is done in nursery colours with clumping wood furniture, distressed tiles and blackboards galore. Food-wise, expect little and large plates of European bistro fare, from smoked mackerel with horseradish and apple to lamb neck with pearl barley and turnips or onglet and chips in red wine shallot butter. Cram in a tarte vigneronne to capture the atmosphere, but don't miss the seriously exciting wine list, where a Négrette-based Fronton rosé (£5.75) is among the glass options, and there's space for oxidative oddballs from the Jura, sun-splashed island wines from Sardinia and Santorini, orange things, pét-nats (they've still got some of their fermentation spritz in them) and wines made in clay amphorae. Prices open at £19.50 and remain reasonable, however high you go.
Chef/s: Nico Rasile. **Open:** Tue to Sun L 12 to 3 (4 Sun), Mon to Sat D 6 to 10.30. **Closed:** bank hols. **Meals:** main courses £17 to £22. **Details:** 56 seats.

Tentazioni
Cooking score: 3
⊖ Bermondsey, London Bridge, map 1
Italian | £35
Lloyds Wharf, 2 Mill Street, Bermondsey, SE1 2BD
Tel no: (020) 7237 1100
tentazioni.co.uk
£5 OFF

Tempting by name and tempting by nature, Tentazioni has been plying its trade in Bermondsey for nigh on 20 years – look for the neon sign pointing down an alley off Mill

Street. Inside, it's a charming prospect with sparkly lighting, big arched windows and contemporary artworks covering almost every square inch of the rich red walls. The kitchen delivers a dressed-up take on Italian cuisine, adding a few influences and ideas from less familiar quarters – note the onion soup with Gruyère bignè (beignet), quail's egg and crispy black bread or the slow-cooked veal cheek with cinnamon, apples and soft polenta taragna (including buckwheat). Sardinian ingredients also pop up here and there, from bottarga with Apulian burrata to Pecorino Sardo with soft gnocchi and lamb ragù. Meanwhile, expect the unexpected when it comes to dessert: how about a luscious Tentazioni sundae or a flambéed tiramisu Martini? Soundly chosen all-Italian wines start at £15.

Chef/s: Alessandro Cattani. **Open:** Mon to Fri L 12 to 2.45, Mon to Sat D 6 to 10.45. Sun 12 to 9. **Closed:** 24 to 26 Dec, bank hols. **Meals:** main courses £15 to £27. Set L £12 (2 courses) to £15. Sun L £36. Tasting menu £50 (7 courses). **Details:** 50 seats. Wheelchairs. Music.

Trinity

Cooking score: 5
⊖ Clapham Common, map 3
Modern British | £45
4 The Polygon, Clapham, SW4 0JG
Tel no: (020) 7622 1199
trinityrestaurant.co.uk

A face-lift after more than a decade has transformed Adam Byatt's neighbourhood restaurant. The previous monochromatic space now sports a clean-lined contemporary look of contrasting wood finishes, olive green leather banquettes, pale grey chairs, an open-to-view kitchen and, on the first floor, a less formal dining option (Upstairs). What hasn't changed is the constant praise from reporters for 'terrific food' and 'hospitable service'. A mix of seasonality and impeccable sourcing characterises the cooking here, with asparagus from the Wye Valley, served with buttermilk beurre blanc and smoked cod's roe, impressing

from the outset at inspection. A dish of superbly flavoured new-season lamb followed, teamed with a courgette flower fritter, Isle of Wight tomatoes, an avocado purée and smoked goats' cheese helping to provide an extra taste dimension. Among desserts, baked Wigmore cheesecake with pear in the form of compote and sorbet has shone. The substantial wine list (from £19), majors in France but does not ignore equally exciting and good-value wines from elsewhere.

Chef/s: Adam Byatt. **Open:** all week L 12.30 to 2.30, D 6.30 to 10 (7 to 9 Sun). **Closed:** 24 to 26 Dec, 1 Jan. **Meals:** main courses £24 to £35. Set L £25 (2 courses) to £30. **Details:** 50 seats. 24 seats outside. Wheelchairs.

★ NEW ENTRY ★

Upstairs at the Guildford Arms

Cooking score: 3
⊖ Greenwich, map 1
British | £40
55 Guildford Grove, Greenwich, SE10 8JY
Tel no: (020) 8691 6293
theguildfordarms.co.uk
£5
OFF

Ensconced in a quiet residential zone in the hinterland between Blackheath and central Greenwich, the Guildford Arms is an attractive neighbourhood pub on a triangular junction. Its huge garden is put to good use on fine days, including a barbecue. Inside is all stripped pine and friendly staff, with the main dining going on in an upper room adorned with photographic prints of people doing food-related things. Wild and foraged Kentish materials play a big part in Simon Wills' output, which might open with pigeon broth with spring veg and girolles, or crab with charred hispi, pickled seaweed, radishes and bergamot. Perfectly rendered duck for main comes with parsnip crisps and purée, as well as monk's beard and scurvy grass, in cider jus, while the veggie option could be crispy truffled barley with salsify, cabbage and asparagus. Desserts come as a great array of ice

creams, sorbets, brittles, foams and dried fruits, or settle for a piece of cheese with truffle honey, walnuts and raisins. A concise wine list opens with house Sicilians at £19.50.
Chef/s: Simon Wills. **Open:** Wed to Sat D only 6.30 to 10.30. **Closed:** Sun, Mon, Tue, 25 Dec. **Meals:** main courses £18 to £24. **Details:** 35 seats. 60 seats outside. Bar. Music.

The White Onion

Cooking score: 3
⊖ Wimbledon, map 3
Modern French | £40
67 High Street, Wimbledon Village, Wimbledon, SW19 5EE
Tel no: (020) 8947 8278
thewhiteonion.co.uk

This second venture from Eric and Sarah Guignard of the French Table in Surbiton (see entry) is the sort of neighbourhood French restaurant that suits Wimbledon Village to a T. It projects itself as low-key and relaxed with bare-wood tables, deep blue walls and contemporary art and attracts a prosperous local crowd. And the menu? It's short, modern and obviously French-influenced, with a keen eye for the seasons. Poole Bay rock oysters gratin with organic cider emulsion, seaweed and apple salad and herb oil makes a bright, satisfying lead-in to a deeply flavoured assiette of Herdwick lamb served with a Brussels sprout tartlet, hazelnut purée, pickles and Noilly Prat jus, while desserts continue to delight. Both quince tarte Tatin with Amaretto ice cream, and a coconut, white chocolate and lime pavé teamed with a coconut and Malibu sorbet have been praised this year. The set lunch is excellent value, and the wine list opens at £19.
Chef/s: Frederic Duval. **Open:** Fri to Sun L 12 to 2.30, Tue to Sat D 7 to 10.30 (6.30 Fri and Sat). **Closed:** Mon. **Meals:** main courses £13 to £24. Set L £17 (2 courses) to £20. Sun L £26. **Details:** 70 seats. Wheelchairs. Music.

Wright Brothers Oyster & Porter House

Cooking score: 2
⊖ London Bridge, map 4
Seafood | £40
11 Stoney Street, Southwark, SE1 9AD
Tel no: (020) 7403 9554
thewrightbrothers.co.uk

The consensus on Ben Wright and Robin Hancock's super-busy little seafooder on the edge of Borough Market is 'fantastic food, great service, excellent friendly staff'. It's the original of a small group of restaurants (in Soho, Spitalfields, South Kensington – see entries), and décor-wise is a lesson in bare-brick simplicity – furnishings are on the plain side with cramped, bare tables and some bar-counter seating giving unfettered views of chefs belting out gloriously fresh seafood. There are no pretensions or unnecessary garnishes – flavours are direct and enjoyable, whether it's a daily special of Cornish mackerel fillets with harissa and mixed leaves or their classic salmon and smoked haddock fish pie. Oysters, seafood platters, potted shrimps and moules marinière have always been popular, there's even beef, Guinness and oyster pie, and dark chocolate mousse with hazelnut praline for dessert. On the drinks front, there are porters, ales, stouts, house cocktails and a short selection of wines from £20.
Chef/s: Rob Malyon. **Open:** all week 12 to 11 (10 Sat, 9 Sun). **Closed:** 25 to 26 Dec. **Meals:** main courses £9 to £35. **Details:** 56 seats. 8 seats outside.

Amaya

Cooking score: 4
⊖ Knightsbridge, map 6
Indian | £45
15 Halkin Arcade, Motcomb Street,
Knightsbridge, SW1X 8JT
Tel no: (020) 7823 1166
amaya.biz

'Dress up,' advises one reader after a midweek
visit to Amaya, 'and don't forget your credit
card.' The shiny surfaces, sparkly square plates
and dangling crystals might feel a little dated,
but they speak of the special occasions to
which Amaya is eminently suited. At the back
you'll see tandoors, charcoal grills and flat
griddles, from which issue contemporary
Indian dishes from a flexible system of sharing
plates. This year readers loved the textural
contrast of crisp flash-grilled rock oysters with
thick coconut and ginger moilee sauce, and
stick-to-your-teeth-sweet griddled Indian
white sweet potato with tamarind and
yoghurt. Griddled flaked crab kebab is a
delicately textured crab cake served with
gently spiced yoghurt sauce, while char-
grilled aubergine with tamarind and crusty,
heavily spiced smoked chilli lamb chops both
got top marks. Curries can be ordinary, but
puddings such as a chocolate rasmalai-filled
sphere have tableside theatre. The wine list
opens at £33.
Chef/s: Karunesh Khanna. **Open:** all week L 12.30
to 2.15 (12.45 to 2.45 Sun), D 6.30 to 11.30 (10.30
Sun). **Meals:** main courses £23 to £43. Tasting menu
£65. **Details:** 100 seats. Bar. Wheelchairs. Music. No
children after 8pm.

Please send us your feedback

To register your opinion about any
restaurant listed in this guide, or a new
restaurant that you wish to bring to our
attention, please visit the web address at
the bottom of the page. Your feedback
informs the content of the book and will
be used to compile next year's reviews.

L'Amorosa

⊖ Ravenscourt Park, Stamford Brook, map 1
Italian | £37
278 King Street, Ravenscourt Park, W6 0SP
Tel no: (020) 8563 0300
lamorosa.co.uk
£5 OFF

A proper neighbourhood Italian joint that
happens to have as its chef-patron a certain
Andy Needham, who was head chef at high-
flying Zafferano (see entry) for more than a
dozen years. L'Amorosa is a restaurant devoid
of cynicism, with Andy hands-on in the
kitchen and the menu more fairly priced than
most. Start with burrata with caponata or
sweet-and-sour sardines, or dive straight into
a plate of homemade pasta (pappardelle, say,
with tender beef cheeks and guanciale). The
osso buco is hard to ignore. Italian wines start
at £19.

Apero

Cooking score: 2
⊖ South Kensington, map 3
Mediterranean | £28
The Ampersand Hotel, 2-10 Harrington Road,
South Kensington, SW7 3ER
Tel no: (020) 7591 4410
aperorestaurantandbar.com

This basement restaurant of the Ampersand
Hotel is 'a relaxing and informal spot', a good
place to escape the hustle and bustle around
the museums of South Kensington. The
wood-floored interior is decked out with
Edison-style lighting, bare-bricked walls,
brown and turquoise leather chairs and a long
marble-top bar, and there are cosy spots
dotted around the room. The menu is based on
sharing dishes, which draw inspiration from
the Mediterranean, perhaps well-made
gnocchi simply teamed with wild
mushrooms, truffle oil and Parmesan or the
winning combination of monkfish cheeks and
cocoa beans rounded off with roasted peppers
and chorizo. Cheese is a strength (we enjoyed

the Vacherin Mont d'or), whereas desserts can sometimes go off-piste. There's a good-value lunch and service is low-key and courteous. A short wine list focusing on France and Italy starts from £19.50.
Chef/s: Mark Woolgar. **Open:** all week L 12 to 2.30, D 6 to 10.30. **Meals:** main courses £11 to £18. Set L £12 (2 courses) to £15. **Details:** 40 seats. Wheelchairs. Music.

Bar Boulud
Cooking score: 4
⊖ Knightsbridge, map 6
French/American | £39
Mandarin Oriental Hyde Park, 66 Knightsbridge, Knightsbridge, SW1X 7LA
Tel no: (020) 7201 3899
barboulud.com

£5
OFF

Neatly billeted underneath the Mandarin Oriental hotel, Daniel Boulud's London outpost is a 'rewarding place to visit'. The mood is lively, the room a neat mix of comfort (wood panelling, red leather) and informality (open-plan kitchen, spacious bar, counter seating), while the menu is broad and appealing, based on French bistro classics infused with Boulud's New York style. Signature burgers are the main draw, but the kitchen can deliver sophistication, too: in a brioche roll packed with crabmeat and paired with yuzu mayonnaise, pickled cucumber and topped with tobiko roe; and in a dish of herb-crusted cod, cauliflower pavé and sultana purée, expertly rounded off by a lemon sauce and toasted almonds. Desserts can be adventurous – an exploration of lemon (curd, crispy meringue, crumble, marshmallow, sorbet) finished off with brown-butter snow proved a complete winner at inspection. Prices generally reflect the Knightsbridge location; the less wallet-pounding option would be the good-value set menu. The vast wine list is strong on Burgundy, Bordeaux and the USA, but 'marred by ungenerous premiums'. Bottles from £24.50.

Chef/s: Thomas Piat. **Open:** all week 12 to 12 (11 to 11 Sun). **Meals:** main courses £15 to £35. Set L £18 (2 courses) to £21. Sun L £39 (3 courses). **Details:** 140 seats. Bar. Wheelchairs. Music.

Bibendum
new chef/no score
⊖ South Kensington, map 3
French | £59
Michelin House, 81 Fulham Road, South Kensington, SW3 6RD
Tel no: (020) 7581 5817
bibendum.co.uk

🍷

What was, in the early part of the 20th century, the Michelin Tyre Company's first permanent British headquarters, rescued and refurbished by Sir Terence Conran 30 years ago, is a compelling and gratifying space, a fixture in this Guide for 27 years. However, as we went to press, we learnt that Bibendum was seeking a new chef. This has always been an accomplished operation, serving up some fine (and sometimes luxury) materials in satisfying ways – we are sure it will continue. What will definitely continue is Bibendum's glorious wine list, a formidable treasury taking in the great and the good from all corners of the globe. Grand French vintages dominate, but there are real everyday treasures to be found among the house selections, which offer fine drinking from £24.50.
Open: all week L 12 to 2.30 (3 Sat and Sun), D 7 to 10.30 (10 Sun). **Closed:** 25 and 26 Dec, 1 Jan. **Meals:** main courses £18 to £38. Sun L and D £36. **Details:** 90 seats. Bar.

Bombay Brasserie
Cooking score: 3
⊖ Gloucester Road, map 3
Indian | £50
Courtfield Road, South Kensington, SW7 4QH
Tel no: (020) 7370 4040
bombayb.co.uk

Hanging baskets under the conservatory roof make the place feel rather removed from its South Kensington home, in which the

Bombay has in fact been rooted since the heady days of 1982. Although modern Indian cooking is going on all over the capital now, it's still worth a visit for the stylish look of the place, with what feels like acres of floor space and pictures from the days of the Raj the backdrop for traditionally based but invigorating cooking. Start with the likes of crisp-fried spinach in yoghurt with date and tamarind chutney, or prawns griddled in three shades of peppercorns, before braised lamb shank emerges from the tandoor singing with cinnamon, black cumin and vinegar, or a seafood platter takes in a generous array of grilled scallops, soft-shell crab, monkfish in Kolkata mustard, and king prawns in yoghurt and thymol (think particularly aromatic caraway seeds). Finish with almond and date pudding and rose ice cream. Wines start at £27.

Chef/s: Prahlad Hegde. **Open:** Tue to Sun L 12 to 2.30 (3.30 Sat and Sun), all week D 6 to 11.30 (10.30 Sun). **Closed:** 25 Dec. **Meals:** main courses £9 to £25. Set L £25 (3 courses). Set D £46 (3 courses). **Details:** 80 seats. 100 seats outside. Bar. Wheelchairs. Music.

LOCAL GEM
The Brackenbury
⊖ Hammersmith, map 1
Mediterranean | £30
129-131 Brackenbury Road, Hammersmith, W6 0BQ
Tel no: (020) 8741 4928
brackenburyrestaurant.co.uk

There have been changes at this neighbourhood restaurant in the heart of pretty 'Brackenbury Village'. In the unusual, higgledy-piggledy space there's now a choice of style and ambience in the trio of little dining rooms: a casual jazz-café, a light, elegant garden room or a formal dark-wood dining room. The menu is available throughout, however, ranging from snacks of golden, crisp pig's head croquettes with caper and tarragon mayonnaise, via mackerel fillets

with Pink Fir potatoes, mustard and watercress, to ricotta doughnuts and coffee semifreddo. Wines from £18.50.

Brasserie Gustave
Cooking score: 2
⊖ South Kensington, map 3
French | £39
4 Sydney Street, Chelsea, SW3 6PP
Tel no: (020) 7352 1712
brasserie-gustave.com
£5 OFF

A relaxed place, somewhere to enjoy rather than worship food, Brasserie Gustave aims to be a *restaurant du quartier* and has a strong following for its no-nonsense French cooking. The confident menu keeps to the expected classics of moules marinière, onion soup, roasted bone marrow with parsley and gherkin salad and red wine sauce, and boeuf à la bourguignonne, and while the cooking may not be the most adventurous around, it does show great attention to detail and uses good ingredients. Recent hits have included steak tartare (something of a signature here), tournedos Rossini, superb Dover sole (de-boned at table) and sharply executed desserts such as crêpes suzette and crème brûlée. Applause, too, for the warm and welcoming atmosphere, the amiable Gallic service ('special and informative') and the extensive wine list that doesn't stray much beyond French borders and starts at a reasonable £18.

Chef/s: Laurence Glayzer. **Open:** Sat to Sun L 12 to 3, all week D 6 to 10.30. **Closed:** 24 to 30 Dec, 2 weeks Aug. **Meals:** main courses £17 to £39. Set L and D £20 (2 courses) to £23. Sun L £24. **Details:** 50 seats. Bar. Music.

Local Gem

Local Gems are the perfect neighbourhood venues, delivering good, freshly cooked food at great value for money.

Bush Hall Dining Rooms
International
304 Uxbridge Road, Shepherd's Bush,
W12 7LJ
Tel no: (020) 8749 0731
bushhalldining.co.uk
'Most welcoming, relaxed and family-friendly local eatery, comfortable enough to eat in alone or with friends. Friendly staff frequently seen in local stores buying fresh produce. A little gem of a place and reasonably priced.'

Cambio de Tercio
Cooking score: 5
⊖ Gloucester Road, map 3
Spanish | £45
163 Old Brompton Road, Earl's Court,
SW5 0LJ
Tel no: (020) 7244 8970
cambiodetercio.co.uk

Behind the dark façade with its vivid yellow signage, dynamic Spanish culinary wizardry is afoot. The place may look like an ordinary tapas joint, but a sight of the menu indicates that Alberto Criado is driven by the restless creative urge. The format is flexible enough to permit choosing a range of tapas, or a couple each and then a main course, and the extensive choice will produce much exquisite indecision. Tomatoes roasted for eight hours in oloroso with basil caviar and goats' cheese are an intriguing application for slow cooking, while foie gras cappuccino with roasted corn and Manchego air mobilises the latest technology. There's enough to placate traditionalists, too, but mains such as crispy Salamanca suckling pig with pickled kumquat, caramelised shallots and roast parsnip offer more in the way of food for thought. Add a side of Peruvian grilled asparagus and you're away, but don't overlook the vanilla-roasted blood peaches with peach ice cream to finish. A treasure-chest wine list runs from pages of sherries (have a tot of

Alegría manzanilla at least) to a properly attentive listing of the reference producers in Spain's numerous regions, starting at £25.
Chef/s: Alberto Criado. **Open:** all week L 12 to 2.30 (3 Sat and Sun), D 6.30 to 11.30 (10.30 Sun). **Closed:** 23 Dec to 3 Jan, 2 weeks Aug. **Meals:** main courses £16 to £28. Set L £26 (2 courses) to £29. Set D £35 (2 courses) to £45. Sun L £28. **Details:** 80 seats. 6 seats outside. Bar. Music.

Charlotte's Place
Cooking score: 4
⊖ Ealing Broadway, Ealing Common, map 1
Modern European | £30
16 St Matthew's Road, Ealing, W5 3JT
Tel no: (020) 8567 7541
charlottes.co.uk

Set in what was once a Victorian corner shop opposite Ealing Common, Alex Wrethman's neighbourhood restaurant has been the precursor for postcode-named spin-off branches in W4 and W5. In a breezy, pleasantly informal atmosphere, Lee Cadden oversees menus of contemporary British style, with today's favoured techniques of pickling, curing and braising very much to the fore. Roasted butternut squash with truffled curd and pickled ceps is a stimulating vegetarian opener, or there may be cuttlefish with onions in brine and oyster emulsion, as preludes to the slow cooking of lamb rump and shoulder, alongside salsify, roast garlic and anchovies, or perhaps confit salmon and razor clams with celeriac purée and a beguiling note of vanilla. Imaginative desserts have included a tempting array of bitter chocolate délice with White Russian ice cream and orange sherbet, or simple whipped crème fraîche adorned with raspberries and pistachios. Wines chosen to go with the menu dishes head up an authoritative list, from £18.
Chef/s: Lee Cadden. **Open:** Mon to Sat L 12 to 2.30, D 6 to 10. Sun 12 to 9. **Meals:** set L £20 (2 courses) to £35. Set D £30 (2 courses) to £42. **Details:** 50 seats. 16 seats outside. Music.

Charlotte's W4

Cooking score: 3
⊖ Turnham Green, map 1
Modern European | £30
6 Turnham Green Terrace, Chiswick, W4 1QP
Tel no: (020) 8742 3590
charlottes.co.uk

Chiswick has always been fortunate in its restaurants, and in 2010 Charlotte's added another element to the dynamic mix. It's an appealing neighbourhood venue that covers all fronts from breakfast baps to gin tastings, and a principal menu of modern brasserie food. In the restaurant at the back, brown leather banquettes are teamed with wall-mounted cherrywood box lighting and paraffin lamps on the tables to set the scene for a springtime production of forest-green wild garlic velouté with tarragon gnocchi and a poached egg, followed by a juicy hunk of hake in seaweed emulsion with pickled mussels, samphire and white beans. Crunchy panko crumbs and silky mash add contrasting textures; more forthright seasoning would seal the deal. Meat might be roast breast and confit leg of partridge with celeriac rémoulade and chestnuts, and the finisher perhaps hazelnut tart with burnt white chocolate ice cream. House Languedoc is £19 on a conscientiously chosen and written wine list.
Chef/s: Alex Brown. **Open:** all week 12 to 10.
Meals: main courses £17 to £18. Set L £17 (2 courses) to £20. Sun L £17. **Details:** 65 seats. Bar. Music.

Please send us your feedback

To register your opinion about any restaurant listed in this guide, or a new restaurant that you wish to bring to our attention, please visit the web address at the bottom of the page. Your feedback informs the content of the book and will be used to compile next year's reviews.

Charlotte's W5

Cooking score: 1
⊖ Ealing Broadway, map 1
Modern European | £24
The Old Stable Block, Dickens Yard, Longfield Avenue, Ealing, W5 2UQ
Tel no: (020) 3771 8722
charlottes.co.uk
£30

The third venue in the Charlotte's stable, and by far the most modern and laid-back, is a vast space, carved up into a bright bar area up front, and a moodier, double-height back restaurant. Décor is 'all à la mode', and the place feels relaxed and lively – it's set up for a good time. The menu offers a dozen or so savoury dishes, which you can have in one of three sizes – taster, small or large – perhaps cured salmon with garden peas, avocado and lemon oil, lamb breast with hispi cabbage and salsa verde, and duck breast with confit potato and tomato and shallot relish. Wines from £20.
Chef/s: Lee Cadden. **Open:** all week 12 to 10.
Meals: main courses £10 to £17. **Details:** 120 seats. 75 seats outside. Bar. Wheelchairs. Music.

Clarke's

Cooking score: 3
⊖ Notting Hill Gate, map 6
Modern British | £40
124 Kensington Church Street, Notting Hill, W8 4BH
Tel no: (020) 7221 9225
sallyclarke.com

A light-washed space, an outsized fork and spoon hanging on the wall, drawings by Lucian Freud and well-spaced white-clothed tables make dining here 'an intimate and sophisticated experience'. Chez Panisse etched on to the glassware shows the link to one of the founders (Alice Waters) of Californian cuisine. Indeed, after more than 30 years, Sally Clarke's commitment to fresh seasonal produce remains undiminished – fine materials underpin the set-lunch or no-choice menus and the kitchen continues to demonstrate that food needn't be elaborate to succeed. At inspection, fantastic breads kicked off 'a darn good lunch' of burrata with winter tomatoes, Castelfranco, land cress, and balsamic dressing ('a well-balanced assemblage'), an accurately timed Cornish sea bass fillet with agretti, cime di rapa (broccoli), Jerusalem artichoke and a black olive-lemon tapenade, while caramelised lemon tart with poached rhubarb made for a memorable finish. Service is willing. Sensibly priced wines (from £25) are put together with care. **Chef/s:** Sally Clarke and Michele Lombardi. **Open:** Mon to Sat L 12.30 to 2, D 6.30 to 10. **Closed:** Sun, 1 week Christmas, 2 weeks Aug. **Meals:** main courses £24 to £32. Set L £27 (2 courses) to £33. Set D £49 (3 courses). **Details:** 90 seats. Bar. Wheelchairs.

Claude's Kitchen

Cooking score: 4
♁ Parsons Green, map 3
Modern British | £36
51 Parsons Green Lane, Parsons Green, SW6 4JA
Tel no: (020) 7371 8517
claudeskitchen.co.uk
£5
OFF

It is easy to miss this modest restaurant on the first floor of a Victorian building (it's above the Amuse Bouche wine bar). It's a bare-bones space – floorboards, metal-framed chairs, black banquettes, Edison lights dangling from the ceiling – with a kitchen so tiny it's hard to imagine 'how it manages to deliver such good cooking'. Pine smoke enlivens a dish of crayfish, served alongside a tapenade made with chervil, black olive and red pepper – its delicate flavours stirred into life by fresh coriander. Even better, three pieces of juicy lamb rump share the plate with ewes' milk yoghurt, burnt pickled cucumber and brown shrimps. Elsewhere, carefully kept British cheeses could precede 'ravishing' Yorkshire rhubarb infused with ginger and rosemary and accompanied with a featherlight basil and vanilla custard. Engaging service and fairly priced wines from £21.50 round things off nicely.

Chef/s: Claude Compton. **Open:** Mon to Sat D only 6 to 10.30. **Closed:** Sun. **Meals:** main courses £16 to £20. **Details:** 40 seats. Bar. Music. No children.

Colbert

Cooking score: 2
♁ Sloane Square, map 3
French | £38
50-52 Sloane Square, Chelsea, SW1W 8AX
Tel no: (020) 7730 2804
colbertchelsea.com

Giving a pitch-perfect impression of a grand Parisian café, the postcode is definitely SW1 and the pavement tables are on Sloane Square. Part of the Corbin & King portfolio, and stablemate of The Wolseley and The Delauney (see entries), Colbert takes inspiration from the all-day cafés that other great city to serve up breakfast (full English to omelette au choix), croque-monsieur to fill a gap or the full works, starting with soupe de poissons and finishing with mille-feuille à la vanille. Among main courses, cassoulet de Toulouse stands alongside herb-crusted hake with a classic béarnaise, while Puy lentil and superfood salad is a nod to our times. Caviar and oysters help to lure in local big spenders. It all takes place in a room with red leather banquettes, and posters and black-and-white photos recalling the interwar years. The all-French wine list kicks off at £22.50.

Chef/s: Stuart Conibear. **Open:** all week L 12 to 5, D 5 to 11 (11.30 Fri and Sat, 10.30 Sun). **Closed:** 25 Dec. **Meals:** main courses £10 to £27. **Details:** 118 seats. 22 seats outside. Bar. Wheelchairs. Music.

Symbols

⊨ Accommodation is available
£30 Three courses for less than £30
£5 £5-off voucher scheme
OFF
♦ Notable wine list

Dinner by Heston Blumenthal

Cooking score: 7
⊖ Knightsbridge, map 6
British | £80
Mandarin Oriental Hyde Park, 66 Knightsbridge, Knightsbridge, SW1X 7LA
Tel no: (020) 7201 3833
dinnerbyheston.com

Despite the pace of change in London restaurants, Dinner keeps the concept of retrieving and modernising historic recipes with the wizardry that made Heston Blumenthal a household name. Six years on, the menu still offers many of the original dishes such as meat fruit (c.1500) which cleverly mimics a tangerine while delivering a rich filling of liver parfait. Rice and flesh (c.1390) marries calf tail, saffron and red wine, while salamagundy (c.1720) serves savoury chicken oysters with marrow bone and pickled walnuts. A trio of fine beef dishes from the early 1800s shows why the French admiringly termed the English *les rosbifs*. Indeed, there's a sturdy Britishness about the food: no prettified amuses to whet the appetite, instead, a rough wooden tray with good, simple soda bread and a pat of butter. The large glass-fronted kitchen delivers rich flavours based on technique and imagination as in frumenty (c.1390) with succulent grilled octopus on a bed of spelt, bathed in a smoked seafood broth and garnished with pickled dulse (seaweed) and luscious beads of lovage emulsion. A whole chicken breast cooked with softened lettuces (c.1670) comes with crisp grilled skin, onion emulsion and a subtly spiced celeriac sauce. Desserts include sambocade (c.1390), goats' milk cheesecake with a dusting of coconut ash on the surface along with poached pear and candied walnuts. The handsome dining room has views over leafy Hyde Park and top-notch staff, especially sommeliers who guide diners through a daunting wine list, from £35 a bottle, which offers many treats by the glass.

Chef/s: Ashley Palmer-Watts. **Open:** all week L 12 to 2.30, D 6.30 to 10.30. **Meals:** main courses £28 to £42. Set L £40. **Details:** 127 seats. Bar. Wheelchairs. Parking. Children over 4 yrs only.

Enoteca Turi

Cooking score: 4
⊖ Sloane Square, map 3
Italian | £40
87 Pimlico Road, Chelsea, SW1W 8PH
Tel no: (020) 7730 3663
enotecaturi.com

After 25 years in Putney, the Turi family has moved to Chelsea – and according to reporters, 'upped their game'. The new home is modern with gold-painted brick walls, lots of dark wood, brown leather banquettes and sensibly spaced, white-clad tables, and the cooking continues to showcase Italy's regional dishes. That the kitchen conjures up vibrancy and striking flavours was apparent at a test meal, opening with a comforting plate of agnolotti filled with organic beef, pork and chicken and served with a veal reduction before going on to a fillet of John Dory, cooked with pinpoint accuracy, simply teamed with Taggiasche olives, pine nuts, roasted potatoes and barba di frate. Desserts embrace the classic – maybe a 'straightforward but delectable' pannacotta with Amalfi lemon served with a caramel mousse. Homemade bread and attentive, personal service get the thumbs-up, too, while the wine list is outstanding in breadth and depth, filled with gems to match the food. It covers all the wine regions of Italy and there are some majestic labels from Piedmont and Tuscany, although the budget-conscious can still find comfort in the selection by the glass or carafe, and bottles from £21.

Chef/s: Gonzalo Luzarraga. **Open:** Mon to Sat L 12 to 2.30, D 6 to 10.30 (11 Fri and Sat). **Closed:** Sun, 25 and 26 Dec, 1 Jan. **Meals:** main courses £12 to £28. Set L £23 (2 courses) to £28. **Details:** 70 seats. Music.

L'Etranger

Cooking score: 5
☉ Gloucester Road, South Kensington, map 3
Modern French | £50
36 Gloucester Road, South Kensington,
SW7 4QT
Tel no: (020) 7584 1118
etranger.co.uk

For many years L'Etranger has charmed diners with stylish Franco/Japanese cooking. Now there's a new chef in the kitchen but the restaurant's many regulars need not worry. Peter Tonge is a British chef with experience in top kitchens in North America and Australia, as well as London, and he's comfortable with the kind of cross-cultural cooking that works so well here. Indeed, his imaginative new menu includes 'the porridge', a 'light-as-air dish' of slices of lightly cooked scallop on a bed of granular deconstructed cauliflower, moistened with a sea foam and dressed with togarashi (a fragrant mix of orange zest, pepper, chilli and parsley) and garnished with samphire, sorrel and violets. Elsewhere, cured mackerel is served with pickled daikon, charred leaves and liquid bubbles of lime, while Wagyu flat-iron steak from northern Spain is prepared in the chef's signature marinade and served in juicy strips with seaweed and courgette. The menu also lists oysters and a plutocrat's collection of caviars as well as desserts such as sweet corn ice cream with honey and honeycomb. The restaurant interior is unchanged with chic lacquered tables, leather banquettes and slim metal chains as curtains. Unchanged, too, is the world-class wine list, a magnificent collection of serious wines from vintage French to classy New World, from £28.
Chef/s: Peter Tonge. **Open:** Tue to Sat L 12 to 3, D 5.30 to 10.45. **Closed:** Sun, Mon. **Meals:** main courses £18 to £28. Set L £20 (2 courses) to £32. Set D £32. Tasting menu £75. **Details:** 65 seats. Bar. Music.

The Five Fields

Cooking score: 6
☉ Sloane Square, map 3
Modern British | £60
8-9 Blacklands Terrace, Chelsea, SW3 2SP
Tel no: (020) 7838 1082
fivefieldsrestaurant.com

Behind an unassuming door in a residential street not far from Peter Jones, this pretty, understated restaurant is a revelation – 'it's small, busy, but there's no business going on – it's all personal and everyone is having a good time'. Open for dinner only, time constraints on the kitchen are less important, so whether choosing à la carte or opting for the eight-course tasting menu, expect plenty of 'clever and interesting extra little courses', from delicate cheese tartlets to soft-as-butter morsels of tandoori chicken and squid-ink crackers – an indication of the delicacy and precision of Taylor Bonnyman's cooking. Enthusiastic packed houses testify to the kitchen's prowess when it comes to signature show-stealers such as the glossy beetroot-covered ball of foie gras ('totally flavour-led') presented in 'a glade' of mushrooms and beetroot or a seasonal, summery dish of 'green pea' which arrives with smoked eel and scallop tartare. There are hits in other departments, too: John Dory, taken to another level with its accompanying jamón broth and sweet corn, ribbons of courgette giving a contrasting lightness and freshness; the flavour of the Herdwick mutton (served with green olive, anchovy and baby gem); a ball of lavender meringue encasing an intensely lemony custard on a bed of crunchy, salty almond flakes. Expect pre-desserts, petits fours and something to take home to remind you of the excellence the next day. Service is superb. The magnificent wine list favours the Old World and starts at a very reasonable £8 a glass, £25 a bottle.
Chef/s: Taylor Bonnyman. **Open:** Mon to Fri D only 6.30 to 10. **Closed:** Sun, Sat, 2 weeks Aug. **Meals:** set D £50 (2 courses) to £60. Tasting menu £80 (8 courses). **Details:** 40 seats. Bar. Wheelchairs. Music.

Garnier

Cooking score: 2
⊖ Earl's Court, map 3
French | £40
314 Earl's Court Road, Earl's Court, SW5 9BQ
Tel no: (020) 7370 4536
garnier-restaurant-london.co.uk

Earl's Court needs more places like Didier Garnier's traditional French brasserie. The light decorative theme – two rows of austere tables, red banquettes, cream walls, large mirrors, wood floors – gives no offence at all, no one could fault the quality of the welcome, or its enthusiasm, and it serves up generous food to match. The menu is a classic run through fish soup, foie gras terrine, steak tartare with chips and green salad, and lamb cutlets with béarnaise sauce. Elsewhere, reporters have particularly liked the grilled Dover sole with parsley butter sauce, and a dish of crisp confit duck leg with onion sauce, sautéed potatoes and spinach. Desserts take a steady line as well: crêpes suzette, vanilla crème brûlée and chocolate and orange terrine have all been recommended this year. The all-French wine list is a thoroughly sound collection with bottles from £18.50.
Chef/s: Lucasz Pribilsky. **Open:** Wed to Sun L 12 to 3, D 6 to 10.30 (10 Sun). **Closed:** Mon, Tue. **Meals:** main courses £19 to £34. Set L £18 (2 courses). Set D £22 (2 courses). Sun L £18. **Details:** 48 seats.

The Goring

Cooking score: 5
⊖ Victoria, map 3
Modern British | £57
15 Beeston Place, Belgravia, SW1W 0JW
Tel no: (020) 7396 9000
thegoring.com
🛏

It's one of those gracious London hotels that strikes a luxurious and nostalgic note, but the Goring – family owned for 105 years – is certainly not stuck in the past. There's a decisively modern feel to Shay Cooper's cooking, which draws on classical and traditional British influences but also gently pushes the boundaries here and there. That said, a nostalgic feel prevails in the plush and immaculate dining room, which is swathed in creams and yellows, with ornate plasterwork and a thick, pale carpet that makes you feel you should have left your shoes at the door. Service is about as attentive as it gets, but despite the formality, it's a relaxing experience. Eggs Drumkilbo is a typical starter, while salt marsh lamb with fried sweetbreads, courgette, cauliflower and Stichelton purée typifies Cooper's use of the very best British ingredients. To finish in equally patriotic style, try clotted Cornish cream mousse with apple sorbet, caramelised hazelnuts and crumble. Take time over the 'book-sized' wine list – it has a truly global reach and something for all pockets (from £29).
Chef/s: Shay Cooper. **Open:** Sun to Fri L 12 to 2.30, all week D 6 to 10. **Meals:** set L £45. Set D £57. Sun L £50. **Details:** 70 seats. 50 seats outside. V menu. Bar. Wheelchairs. Parking.

Granger & Co.

Cooking score: 2
⊖ Notting Hill Gate, map 6
Australian | £25
175 Westbourne Grove, Notting Hill, W11 2SB
Tel no: (020) 7229 9111
grangerandco.com
£30

As seen on TV, Bill Granger is an Aussie foodie phenomenon with a host of restaurants in his native country and Japan, plus addresses in Honolulu and Seoul, and now three restaurants in London, of which this is the original. It has that chilled-out Australian vibe and sunny demeanour, with lots of natural wood, white paint and an egalitarian approach to service. Chilli fried egg and bacon brioche roll is a breakfast true to Granger's style, before a lunch offering such as a punchy salmon salad with coconut caramel dressing. The mood remains relaxed in the evening, too, where twice-cooked beef short rib arrives hot from the barbie, and crispy duck is flavoured with mandarin and star anise. Burrata with salsa verde and char-grilled sourdough is a starter born in Europe, and, to finish, jasmine pannacotta with black sesame crumb is the best of fusion. Drink cool cocktails, proper beers or check out the Australians on the wine list; house French is £19.50.

Chef/s: Nick Grundy. **Open:** all week L 12 to 5, D 5 to 11 (10.30 Sun). **Closed:** 25 Dec, 28 Aug. **Meals:** main courses £13 to £21. **Details:** 80 seats. 10 seats outside. Wheelchairs. Music.

The Harwood Arms

Cooking score: 5
⊖ Fulham Broadway, map 3
British | £40
Walham Grove, Fulham, SW6 1QP
Tel no: (020) 7386 1847
harwoodarms.com

Often emulated but seldom bettered, the trail-blazing Harwood Arms stakes its claim with handsome *Country Living* interiors (bare-boarded floors, green-panelled walls), sophisticated provenance-led cooking and a starry pedigree (it's co-owned by Brett Graham from the Ledbury – see entry). As a proper foodie pub it also gets the balance just right, serving pints of real ale and stupendous Scotch eggs to local drinkers, while satisfying everyone else with remarkably seasonal British victuals – witness an old-fashioned dish of buttered crab on muffins invigorated with coastal herbs and pickled lemon or roast haunch of Berkshire fallow deer with celeriac, Brussels tops and smoked bone-marrow tart. Elsewhere, pistachio and blackberry add some pep to the well-worn 'beetroot and goats' cheese' combo, while top-notch desserts receive unanimous praise – think apricot sponge with honey and chamomile or millionaire's shortbread with bay leaf ice cream. Last but not least, the Harwood boasts a thoughtfully chosen 200-bin wine list with the prospect of serious drinking at very keen prices (from £24 a bottle, £6 a glass).

Chef/s: Alex Harper. **Open:** Tue to Sun L 12 to 3, all week D 6.30 to 9.30. **Closed:** 25 and 26 Dec, 1 Jan. **Meals:** set L £20 (2 courses) to £25. Set D £34 (2 courses) to £40. Sun L £40. **Details:** 52 seats. V menu. Music.

Hawksmoor Knightsbridge

Cooking score: 4
⊖ Knightsbridge, South Kensington, map 3
British | £50
3 Yeoman's Row, Knightsbridge, SW3 2AL
Tel no: (020) 7590 9290
thehawksmoor.com

Hawksmoor Knightsbridge sells caviar (ethically farmed in Finland) and lobsters shipped up from Brixham – know your market, they say. The branch with the most exclusive postcode in the group still serves up the prime red meats that have made Hawksmoor a roaring success for 10 straight years. The moodily lit basement (a bit dark for some) has an Art Deco, dark-wood thing going on, and the bar positively rocks at peak times. A light touch is in evidence in a first course of charcoal-roasted scallops, flavoured with white port and garlic, or go for the more hearty Tamworth belly ribs with vinegar slaw. The steaks are hard to ignore; cooked just right, they know what they're doing – bone-in prime rib, porterhouse, ribeye, sirloin and more. Choose a weight and a sauce (bone marrow gravy, say), and note the triple-cooked chips are an extra few quid. Drink cracking cocktails in the buzzy bar, with wines starting at £23.

Chef/s: Flamur Zeka. **Open:** Mon to Sat L 12 to 3, D 5 to 10.30. Sun 12 to 9.30. **Closed:** 24 to 26 Dec, 1 Jan. **Meals:** main courses £12 to £40. Set L and D £25 (2 courses) to £28. **Details:** 130 seats. Bar. Music.

★ TOP 10 ★

Hedone

Cooking score: 8
⊖ Chiswick Park, map 1
Modern European | £85
301-303 Chiswick High Road, Chiswick,
W4 4HH
Tel no: (020) 8747 0377
hedonerestaurant.com

Hedone underwent a structural
transformation in late 2015, when its much-
in-demand table capacity was halved, its
services reduced to six a week. The effect of
such a bold move has been, if anything, to
distil Mikael Jonsson's production to an even
more rarefied level of potency, with the result
that Hedone is undoubtedly in the first rank of
British dining. Every visit seems to raise the
bar, as the fluid menus, which are no longer
written down, expand the horizons of food's
capabilities. Yes, this is highly technical
craftsmanship, but it continues to respect
every ingredient on the plate. The gel-soft
crab, its flavour 'bafflingly both sweet and
saline', dressed with dense hazelnut
mayonnaise, apple and dill oil, is a majestic
dish. An oyster seems less poached than
miraculously inflated, reposing in its shell
with strawberry and sorrel foam, alongside a
soft Parmesan custard the texture of chawan
mushi. A single chop of Basque suckling pig is
'other-worldly', uniformly pink from edge to
centre, teamed with steamed aubergine and
herb salad, sauced with a concentrated pork
essence, a surely unimprovable performance
until the lamb saddle arrives, the flesh again
unblemished pink, the huge fat layer crisp and
delightful, with a single fried artichoke on
emulsified basil dressing, the best dish our
inspector ate all year. The speculation, 'how
does he do this?', is provoked by dish after
dish, scarcely more so than with the vanilla
mille-feuille, every internal leaf of which is
delicately brittle, filled with deliquescent
crème pâtissière, the accompanying ice cream
explosive with vanilla intensity, the coup de
grâce a dressing of aged balsamic poured on at
the table. A stunning wine list contains
sensational drinking, and is best experienced
via one of the selected wine flights.
Chef/s: Mikael Jonsson. **Open:** Fri and Sat L 12 to
2.30, Tue to Sat D 6.30 to 9.30. **Closed:** Sun, Mon.
Meals: set L £45. Tasting menus £85 to £125.
Details: 20 seats.

Hereford Road

Cooking score: 2
⊖ Bayswater, map 6
British | £28
3 Hereford Road, Notting Hill, W2 4AB
Tel no: (020) 7727 1144
herefordroad.org

Tom Pemberton's 'trusted neighbourhood
restaurant' is the home of good sense and
hospitality in Notting Hill. White tiles and
shiny red booths may look stern, and as befits
any alumnus of St John, Pemberton's menu
isn't exactly chatty. But there's a warmth in the
seasonal cooking and the embrace of dishes
that demand a bit of at-table commitment
from patrons: artichoke with vinaigrette, roast
quails or snipe, braised legs of rabbit or duck,
or a steak and kidney pie for two. Cold meat
with pickles (perhaps cold roast lamb with
pickled chicory) is also a nostalgic feature. To
start, beetroot comes with sorrel and a boiled
egg, while main courses might be skate with
cucumber and kohlrabi or pearl barley cooked
with red wine, squash and mushrooms.
Puddings, inevitably, include crumble and
custard and warm rice pudding with jam. The
wine list starts at £23.50 and features a couple
of chilled reds.
Chef/s: Tom Pemberton. **Open:** all week L 12 to 3 (4
Sun), D 6 to 10.30 (10 Sun). **Closed:** 23 Dec to 4 Jan.
Meals: main courses £12 to £17. Set L £14 (2
courses) to £16. **Details:** 55 seats. 8 seats outside.
Wheelchairs. Parking.

The Hour Glass

Cooking score: 3
⊖ South Kensington, map 3
British | £27
279-283 Brompton Road, Kensington,
SW3 2DY
Tel no: (020) 7581 2497
hourglasspub.co.uk
£5 £30
OFF

'It used to be a slightly grotty pub,' noted one visitor to Dave Turcan and Luke Mackay's intimate, narrow dining room on the first floor of the Hour Glass. It may be 'still much the same downstairs' but it's all comfortable above with dark-wood panelling and an 'arm's reach-kitchen' turning out everything from pubby bar snacks such as pork scratchings with wild crab apple sauce, to starters of generous crab parfait with plenty of sweet brown meat, fresh kohlrabi, apple and watercress. As you would expect from the owners of Brompton Food Market, the quality and freshness of ingredients is clearly evident. A rabbit ham and cider pie with Brussels sprouts and mash, gently enveloped by light fluffy pastry, proved a hit at inspection – 'as perfect as I've had in recent memory' – while homemade ginger cookies gave the requisite crunch to a neat posset of rhubarb and meringue. Reporters praise the 'keen cooking at reasonable cost', which extends to a wine list that opens at £17.
Chef/s: Robert Homer. **Open:** all week L 12 to 3 (5 Sun). Mon to Sat D 6 to 10. **Closed:** Christmas and New Year. **Meals:** main courses £13 to £19.
Details: 28 seats. Bar. Music.

Hunan

Cooking score: 3
⊖ Sloane Square, map 3
Chinese | £61
51 Pimlico Road, Chelsea, SW1W 8NE
Tel no: (020) 7730 5712
hunanlondon.com

The trim single frontage behind its row of conifers in tubs eschews traditional Chinese styling, but then so does the place itself. Michael Peng has been at the helm of Hunan since the early 1980s, and still works to the idiosyncratic formula of inviting diners to name their main ingredients and spices of choice as his cue to rustle up a banquet of small plates of well-honed, creatively tooled food. There are some from Peng's eponymous home region – air-dried meats, double-cooked pork, stir-fried spicy aubergine alight with chilli – but the range of reference extends wider. Spring onion pancakes with daikon and beancurd skin, or braised ox tongue salad, are unusual finds, and Peng can also turn out classic sea bass steamed with spring onions, ginger and soy, and crispy duck with pancakes. It's all packed with upstanding flavour, through to the sticky toffee bananas and apples to finish. The cherry on the cake is a true expert's wine list, sorted by style and authoritative in all departments, including dessert wines, Chinese Shaoxing and Japanese saké. Prices open at £24.
Chef/s: Michael Peng. **Open:** Mon to Sat L 12.30 to 2, D 6.30 to 11. **Closed:** Sun, 2 weeks Christmas, bank hols. **Meals:** set L £41. Set D £61. **Details:** 50 seats. V menu.

Indian Zing

Cooking score: 2
⊖ Ravenscourt Park, map 1
Indian | £30
236 King Street, Hammersmith, W6 0RF
Tel no: (020) 8748 5959
indianzing.co.uk

£5
OFF

A local stalwart, Indian Zing continues to provide fresh and interesting Indian food that reaches well beyond the expected Subcontinental favourites. The interior blends simple modern furniture, pale colours and Indian artwork; in warmer weather there is additional seating in the covered patio to the rear. Chef-owner Manoj Vasaikar is a creative cook with a true flair for flavour: typical dishes include prawn lonche (a warm medley of jumbo prawns, aubergine, lemon, caramelised soft onion and pickle masala); chicken shatkora, incorporating fresh herbs and the zesty, citrusy flavour of shatkora lemons from north-east India; and a dessert of tandoori figs with organic apple muesli crumble and vanilla ice cream. There are also regional favourites such as kawari fish curry from the west coast of India, Keralan fish stew, and Goan-style pork vindaloo made with Hampshire outdoor-reared pork leg. A substantial, helpfully annotated list of wines, all chosen to suit the food, opens at £16.

Chef/s: Manoj Vasaikar. **Open:** all week L 12 to 3 (1 to 4 Sun), D 6 to 11 (10 Sun). **Meals:** main courses £9 to £22. Set L £12 (2 courses) to £15. Sun L £12 (2 courses) to £15. **Details:** 51 seats. 32 seats outside. Wheelchairs. Music.

Kensington Place

Cooking score: 2
⊖ Notting Hill Gate, map 6
Modern British | £35
201-209 Kensington Church Street, Notting Hill, W8 7LX
Tel no: (020) 7727 3184
kensingtonplace-restaurant.co.uk

One of the landmarks of the late 1980s food scene, this massive, glass-fronted dining room pits unadorned tables against a chequerboard floor and it can be noisy when busy. On the food front, ideas are up to date but are not designed to impress merely by being fashionable. Fish is to the fore, and grilling, roasting or steaming favoured techniques: roasted skate wing, for example, or whole grilled lemon sole and whole steamed sea bass, served with a choice of herb butter, sauce vierge or hollandaise and a side dish of, say triple-cooked chips or tenderstem broccoli. Elsewhere, the straightforward, no-nonsense modern British cooking is polished and confident – Nutbourne tomato salad with roast tomato vinaigrette and young basil, roast free-range chicken with boulangère potatos, wild garlic and roasting juices, and hazelnut cheesecake with mulled port and praline ice cream – while the kitchen's performance is relaxed and generally successful. Wines from £24.

Chef/s: Tim Peirson. **Open:** Tue to Sun L 12 to 2.30 (3 Sat and Sun), Mon to Sat D 6.30 to 10.30. **Closed:** 25 Dec, 1 Jan, bank hols. **Meals:** main courses £15 to £26. Set L and D £20 (2 courses) to £25. **Details:** 120 seats. Bar. Wheelchairs. Music.

James Knappett

Kitchen Table, London

What inspired you to become a chef?
The love of eating good food.

What food could you not live without?
Seafood. It is such a precious and natural ingredient that it never needs much doing to it in order to taste good, the natural taste is unbeatable.

What's your favourite dish on your menu?
This year's sloe-blossom flavoured set cream served with last year's sloe-gin. I love it because it is so seasonal and it makes me feel very proud to be British.

How do you start developing a new recipe?
We always start with the most in-season ingredient that we want to highlight. Then we set to work developing it and introducing other seasonal ingredients.

What is the most unusual cooking technique you use?
Using high-acid vinegar to cook vegetables.

Do you have anything exciting coming up that you would like to share?
I have couple of new concepts in the works that can seat more than 19 guests.

LOCAL GEM

Kiraku
⊖ Ealing Common, map 1
Japanese | £25
8 Station Parade, Ealing, W5 3LD
Tel no: (020) 8992 2848
kiraku.co.uk

£5 £30
OFF

In a parade of shops opposite Ealing Common tube station, Kiraku is a simple enough proposition: vibrant Japanese food in a no-frills, contemporary setting. Sit at the counter and watch the prep, or grab a table and check out the pictures on the menu. Get going with mackerel marinated in ginger and miso, and don't miss out on the maki rolls, such as a creative version with deep-fried pork, Camembert and miso. Otherwise, go for straight-up sashimi or steaming bowls of noodles. Drink beer, saké or wines from £16.

Kitchen W8
Cooking score: 6
⊖ High Street Kensington, map 6
Modern European | £45
11-13 Abingdon Road, Kensington, W8 6AH
Tel no: (020) 7937 0120
kitchenw8.com

The Kitchen is a relaxing neighbourhood restaurant with a big-city attitude, as befits the dual ownership of movers and shakers Philip Howard and Rebecca Mascarenhas. It looks suave and calming, the bare floors and white linen offsetting a beige decorative job enlivened with framed artworks. The contemporary European stylings of Mark Kempson have quite a lot to do with it, too, as he turns out dishes of rare vigour and smoothly crafted style. A pairing of thinly sliced smoked eel with grilled mackerel, matched with golden beets and sweet mustard, is right on trend to begin, following which roast veal rump with bulgur wheat, Jerusalem artichoke and hazelnuts produces plenty of earthy satisfaction. Sticking with fish might be rewarded by Cornish brill and mussels, in a stimulating array of monk's beard, nori, peanut and blood orange. The populist touch is assured by chocolate pavé with peanut ice cream, praline and lime. Wines start at £22, £13.50 the half-bottle carafe or £6.75 a glass.

Chef/s: Mark Kempson. **Open:** all week L 12 to 2.30 (12.30 to 3 Sun), D 6 to 10.30 (6.30 to 9.30 Sun). **Closed:** 24 to 27 Dec, bank hols. **Meals:** main courses £20 to £32. Set L £22 (2 courses) to £25. Set D £25 (2 courses) to £28. Sun L £35. **Details:** 70 seats. Wheelchairs.

Koffmann's
Cooking score: 6
⊖ Knightsbridge, Hyde Park Corner, map 6
French | £60
The Berkeley, Wilton Place, Belgravia,
SW1X 7RL
Tel no: (020) 7107 8844
the-berkeley.co.uk

As we went to press, we learnt that Pierre Koffmann will close his restaurant at the Berkeley at the end of December 2016. His reputation has always ensured a room full of sophisticated tourists from all over the world, as well as locals, all eager to try signature dishes such as pig's trotter, snail ravioli, a homely braise of beef cheek and utterly moreish gratin dauphinois – 'God's own way of eating potatoes' – so this may well be your last chance to experience the great chef's cooking. There's luxurious technique and ingredients in tournedos Rossini fluently done with beef fillet, foie gras and truffles, or a fine Dover sole with caper and parsley noisette butter. In a playful squid bolognaise, ribbons of shellfish take the place of pasta with lobster roe crumbled over the top. Warm foie gras with sautéed endive and luscious sweet grapes bathed in a Sauternes sauce is the perfect combination of elegance and flavour, while roast cod is given heft with cocoa beans and grilled chorizo. Among desserts, don't miss oeuf à la neige, light-as-air meringue studded with rose-pink praline, lapped by a moat of crème anglaise and topped with a golden coronet of spun sugar. The dining room uses

masses of flowers, an open kitchen and friendly, thoughtful service to make a cheerful neighbourhood restaurant in brittle Knightsbridge. Wines from £25.

Chef/s: Pierre Koffmann. **Open:** all week L 12 to 2.30 (3 Sat and Sun), D 6 to 10.30. **Meals:** main courses £25 to £42. Set L £23 (2 courses) to £26. Early D £24 (2 courses) to £28. Tasting menu £100. **Details:** 120 seats. Bar. Music.

Launceston Place
Cooking score: 5
⊖ Gloucester Road, map 3
Modern European | £55
1a Launceston Place, South Kensington,
W8 5RL
Tel no: (020) 7937 6912
launcestonplace-restaurant.co.uk

The airy dining room retains the cosy interconnecting rooms of the original town house with large windows and lively modern art, but there's a new chef-patron at the helm. Raphael Francois used to be Hélène Darroze's right-hand man, both at the Connaught in London (see entry) and in Paris, but most recently he was executive chef of Le Cirque in New York and his cooking blends classic French techniques with a modern taste for light, fresh flavours. A witty and delicious take on bacon and egg with hay-baked celeriac, lardo and crunchy hazlenuts is praised for its gentle potency, while fish dishes are subtly worked rather than defiantly robust, witness one reporter's cod 'cooked to translucent perfection' and served with clam pesto, a scattering of cod roe and silky cabbage. However, meats are allowed to shine, as in a gutsy portion of pork belly with a hint of green curry. A pre-dessert of pear and gin with cucumber foam garners extravagant plaudits, and there's a beautifully rendered crema catalana perked up with lime and banana sorbet and burnt lime. Service is formal but friendly. An exceptional wine list includes the better labels of the Old World with bottles from £28.

Chef/s: Raphael Francois. **Open:** Tue to Sun L 12 to 2.30 (3.30 Sun), all week D 6 to 10 (6.30 to 9 Sun). **Closed:** 25 to 30 Dec, 1 Jan. **Meals:** set L £29 (2 courses) to £34. Set D £30 (2 courses) to £35. Sun L £40. Tasting menu £70. **Details:** 50 seats. Bar. Wheelchairs. Music.

★ TOP 50 ★

The Ledbury
Cooking score: 8
⊖ Notting Hill Gate, Westbourne Park, map 6
Modern British | £95
127 Ledbury Road, Notting Hill, W11 2AQ
Tel no: (020) 7792 9090
theledbury.com

🍾

The hottest restaurant in West London by quite a long street, Brett Graham's 12-year-old restaurant (in 2017) is a classy mix of creams and browns, mirrors and a certain amount of happy babble when the place fills, ensuring that the atmosphere is anything but staidly reverential. Staff are young, enthusiastic yet professional and add to the impression that this is very much a restaurant in the round. Indeed, from the moment the amuse-bouches arrive – delicate foie gras puffs, laverbread crisp and smoked roe, and superb braised deer dumplings – it is clear that this is a serious operation. Mr Graham's cooking is modern, with striking combinations of ingredients and lots of visual artistry, and his menus, a set lunch and four-course dinner, plus a tasting menu, deal comfortably with fashionable luxuries. The precision can be remarkable: the freshest hand-dived scallops served ceviche-style with seaweed and herb oil and frozen English wasabi of sufficient intensity to balance the sweetness of the mollusc; a stunning spring salad consisting of a tangle of green beans, slivers of apricot and young almonds, given richness by a heap of finely grated foie gras; or soft, flavoursome grilled cuttlefish with a purée of new season's garlic and cracked wheat. Main courses deliver pink, tender Pyrenean milk-fed lamb deliciously accompanied by a heap of braised meat, with ewes' milk yoghurt, peas and spring savory

completing an artist's palette of a dish, while fish comes in the form of soft, crisp-skinned John Dory, its sweetness modified by a tart lemon butter and fragrant basil leaves. To finish, brown-sugar tart is the rich classic (the extensive cheese trolley is another). The wine list deals in classic names from France and around the globe, but there are plenty of surprises, too, from £28, and the sommelier's advice is worth taking.
Chef/s: Brett Graham. **Open:** Wed to Sun L 12 to 2, all week D 6.30 to 9.45. **Closed:** Christmas, Aug bank hol. **Meals:** set L £50. Set D £95 (4 courses). Tasting menu £115. **Details:** 56 seats. V menu. Wheelchairs.

★ TOP 50 ★

Marcus
Cooking score: 8
⊖ Hyde Park Corner, Knightsbridge, map 6
Modern European | £85
The Berkeley, Wilton Place, Belgravia, SW1X 7RL
Tel no: (020) 7235 1200
marcus-wareing.com

🍾 🚗

Marcus Wareing's spiritual home within the confines of Knightsbridge's Berkeley Hotel still wears a classical look, which it has retained through recent refurbishment. It all looks much lighter now, with silver and grey the prevailing tones, and even though there are windows on to the world, the feeling amid burnished pillars, ecclesiastical linens and the hushed benevolence of the service is still one of hermetic retreat from racketing London. Wareing himself is to be found overseeing *MasterChef: The Professionals* on the BBC these days, but has in Mark Froydenlund an authoritative ambassador for his supremely elegant modern European cuisine. Choose from either a three- or four-course carte, or the eight-course Taste menu, and expect either way a succession of dishes that brings diverse ingredients together in novel and surprising ways, with textural considerations to the fore. An appealing feeling of lightness characterises even the more obviously robust dishes, such as veal sweetbreads with artichoke and Lautrec garlic, while a starter theoretically composed of nothing more complex than calçot onions with a duck egg and the beguiling aroma of truffle has much more to say for itself than you'd think. At the fish stage, beef essence deepens the impact of pearly cod with an oyster and turnips, while main brings on venison with parsnip, pear and hazelnuts. A dessert of pumpkin custard is more treat than trick, its dressings of maple syrup and passion fruit providing clever counterpoint. The wine list is full of the treasures of both hemispheres, too many to provide notes for, but the sommelier is a trustworthy oracle of advice. Prices open at £35, so you'll need to dig deep.

Chef/s: Mark Froydenlund. **Open:** Mon to Sat L 12 to 2.30, D 6 to 10.30. **Closed:** Sun. **Meals:** set L £49 (3 courses). Set D £85 (3 courses) to £105 (4 courses). Tasting menu £120 (8 courses). **Details:** 75 seats. V menu. Bar. Wheelchairs. Children over 12 yrs only at D.

Masala Grill

Cooking score: 2
⊖ Fulham Broadway, map 3
Indian | £32
535 King's Road, Chelsea, SW10 0SZ
Tel no: (020) 7351 7788
masalagrill.com

Now firmly bedded into the premises that were once home to its stablemate Chutney Mary (see entry), Masala Grill offers a sophisticated take on the big-city curry-house experience, complete with a domed conservatory as the focal point of proceedings. Warm Rajasthan colours, ethnic tapestries, sculptures, family artefacts and luxuriant greenery set the scene for an accessible and moderately priced menu that samples many of the Subcontinent's culinary traditions, from street-food snacks to tandoori grills and richly spiced regional curries. Warm up with a plate of pani puri, crispy fried squid or a chicken 'sixer' (a cricket-inspired dish with a 'measure of chilli'), before progressing to a pot of biryani, kasundi salmon with a mustardy marinade or classic Amritsar-style sag gosht

(lamb with spinach). Earthy dhals, vegetables, rice and breads are on the money, too. All-in thalis are worth a punt, and Sunday lunch is an extravagant family buffet. Wines from £23.

Chef/s: Anil Dhar. **Open:** Sun L 12.30 to 3, all week D 6.30 to 11.15 (10.30 Sun). **Closed:** 25 Dec. **Meals:** main courses £15 to £25. Sun L £26. **Details:** 108 seats. Bar.

Medlar

Cooking score: 5
⊖ Sloane Square, Fulham Broadway, map 3
Modern French | £46
438 King's Road, Chelsea, SW10 0LJ
Tel no: (020) 7349 1900
medlarrestaurant.co.uk

'Gimmick-free French cooking is hardly a USP in London, but when it's as good as this, cooked by people who know what they're about and served politely, cheerfully and professionally, it's something special.' So ran the notes of one visitor to this World's End restaurant. The daily-printed menu follows both the classic school (an oversized crab raviolo with a silky-smooth cream bisque sauce, given texture and bite with the addition of samphire and brown shrimp) and the more up to date (a beautifully presented salad of baby artichokes, wild asparagus and coppa, held together with goats' curd and chicory and topped with a crisp-fried pheasant's egg). Follow with sweetbreads cooked with morels and fresh peas on a shallot velouté or the likes of turbot with baby salsify and wet garlic. Puddings follow the same path – a perfect crème brûlée shares menu space with lime and Prosecco jelly adorned with an upmarket Macedonian fruit cocktail. The weighty wine list is not easy to navigate, but there's plenty of help on hand and a fair choice under £30 a bottle.

Chef/s: Joe Mercer Nairne. **Open:** all week L 12 to 3, D 6.30 to 10.30 (6 to 10 Sat, 6 to 9.30 Sun). **Closed:** 25 and 26 Dec, 1 Jan. **Meals:** set L £23 (2 courses) to £28 (Mon to Fri), £30 (Sat). Set D £38 (2 courses) to £46. Sun L and D £35. **Details:** 92 seats. 8 seats outside.

★ NEW ENTRY ★

Ognisko

Cooking score: 3
⊖ South Kensington, map 6
Polish | £30
55 Exhibition Road, South Kensington,
SW7 2PG
Tel no: (020) 7589 0101
ogniskorestaurant.co.uk
£5
OFF

Ognisko (fireplace) is the restaurant of the
Polish Hearth Club, which opened in 1940 for
Polish immigrants. Recently revamped, it sits
on the ground floor of an elegant stuccoed
building, all high ceilings, tall stone columns,
braided cornices and chandeliers. It's 'a
convivial space', the place to enjoy Polish and
eastern European dishes such as barszcz
(beetroot soup), blinis and placki (potato
pancakes), although the menu stretches to
modern European such as roast hake with
spelt and artichoke broth. Moreish pelmeni
dumplings filled with veal and pork opened a
test meal that went on to crisp-skinned confit
of goose leg, its richness neatly offset by
braised red cabbage and an apple and fig
compote, and finished with golden-brown
racuchy (apple fritters) served with an apple
and cinnamon compote and Chantilly cream.
The wine list (from £19.50) has limited
options by the glass, but includes rarely seen
bottles from Macedonia. This is, however, the
place to sample vodka.
Chef/s: Jarek Meynarczyk. **Open:** all week L 12 to 3
(3.30 Sun), D 5.30 to 11 (12 Fri and Sat, 10.30 Sun).
Closed: 25 and 26 Dec. **Meals:** main courses £13 to
£20. Set L and early D £19 (2 courses) to £22. Sun L
£22. **Details:** 85 seats. 50 seats outside. Bar.

Outlaw's at the Capital

Cooking score: 6
⊖ Knightsbridge, map 6
Seafood | £55
Capital Hotel, 22-24 Basil Street,
Knightsbridge, SW3 1AT
Tel no: (020) 7591 1255
capitalhotel.co.uk
🛏

Any restaurant located behind Harrods must
bring expectations of high prices and a certain
well-groomed charm and Nathan Outlaw's
restaurant in the Capital Hotel doesn't
disappoint on either count; the set lunch, on
the other hand, is a bargain. Its small scale,
relative intimacy and superb seafood cookery
attracts people – 'you wouldn't accidentally
discover this place, you have to know it's there'
– but while the hotel may seem like a
venerable institution, the kitchen, now
headed by Tom Brown, has plenty of
contemporary aces up its sleeve. Presentation
is kept simple, as is only fitting with daily
arrivals of ozone-fresh fish from Cornwall,
and the cooking displays an enviable grasp of
technique and a sensitive approach to flavours
– as in a bravura starter of crab Scotch egg
served with crab sauce, fennel and dill, and in a
dish of cod teamed with cauliflower, Cheddar
crumb and chicken and mushroom dressing.
There's a tasting menu, a meat option, lovely
'fish cake' nibbles, delectable homemade bread
and indulgent desserts, say a dark chocolate
tart with malted ice cream and orange syrup.
Service has been courteous, attentive and
professional, and the wine list opens at £29.
Chef/s: Nathan Outlaw and Tom Brown. **Open:** Mon
to Sat L 12 to 2, D 6.30 to 10. **Closed:** Sun.
Meals: set L £24 (2 courses) to £29. Set D £45 (2
courses) to £55. Tasting menu £75 (5 courses).
Details: 33 seats. Bar. Wheelchairs. Music. Parking.

Pétrus

Cooking score: 6
⊖ Knightsbridge, map 6
Modern French | £75
1 Kinnerton Street, Knightsbridge, SW1X 8EA
Tel no: (020) 7592 1609
gordonramsay.com

While Gordon Ramsay's restaurant group
widens its reach and remit, Pétrus, one of its
original outposts, holds fast to napery and
formality. Lahiru 'Larry' Jayasekara has taken
the reins from Neil Snowball, yet the change
of guard hasn't rocked the boat: precise,
modern food with roots firmly planted in
flawless French technique (and a fondness for
sous-vide), remains Pétrus's calling card.
Housed behind a discreet glass façade on the
ground floor of a Belgravia apartment block,
with shutters shielding clientele from the hoi
polloi, it's all very tasteful: soft edges, carpet,
multiple shades of fawn and recessed lighting,
leaving the circular wine store feature to do all
the eye-catching – it's literally at the heart of
the operation, keeping namesake Pétrus
vintages in tiptop condition. Expect luxury
ingredients (even on the good-value lunch
menu) and classic flavours at their best,
starting perhaps with sweet and buttery
poached native lobster with girolles, truffle
cannelloni and wood sorrel followed by soft
Herefordshire beef fillet, Dorset snails,
broccoli and black garlic. Picture-perfect
gariguette strawberries, pistachio, basil,
strawberry ice cream or lemon tart epitomise
the polished puds. Wines start at a steep £36.
Chef/s: Larry Jayasekara. **Open:** Mon to Sat L 12 to
2.30, D 6.30 to 10.30. **Closed:** Sun. **Meals:** set L
£38. Set D £75. Tasting menu £95. **Details:** 50 seats.
Wheelchairs.

Visit us online

To find out more about
The Good Food Guide, please
visit thegoodfoodguide.co.uk

Popeseye Steak House

Cooking score: 1
⊖ Olympia, map 3
Steaks | £40
108 Blythe Road, Olympia, W14 0HD
Tel no: (020) 7610 4578
popeseye.com

Scotsman Ian Hutchinson named his singular
steakhouse after the native word for 'rump'
and, more than 20 years down the line, his
credo remains the same: slabs of properly aged
grass-fed Aberdeen Angus beef (of varying
weights) cooked to order on an open grill and
served with hand-cut chips – plus an optional
salad. It couldn't be simpler. Just add some
farmhouse cheeses, a few homemade puds and
a clutch of beef-friendly wines (from £15.50)
for a genuine, unadulterated 'meat fest'
without a whiff of pomp or hipster posing.
There are branches at 277 Upper Richmond
Road, Putney and 36 Highgate Hill, Archway.
Chef/s: Ian Hutchinson. **Open:** Mon to Sat D only
6.45 to 10. **Closed:** Sun, bank hols. **Meals:** steaks
£13 to £70. **Details:** 36 seats. Wheelchairs.

★ LOCAL RESTAURANT AWARD ★ REGIONAL WINNER

Portobello Ristorante Pizzeria

Cooking score: 2
⊖ Notting Hill Gate, map 6
Italian | £28
7 Ladbroke Road, Notting Hill, W11 3PA
Tel no: (020) 7221 1373
portobellolondon.co.uk

'Fantastic, beautiful-tasting Italian food' is the
beating heart of this 'excellent' restaurant
where you can easily slip into holiday mode.
An outdoor terrace – sensibly covered with
canopies – adds to the cheerful vibe, and
there's always a warm welcome from the staff
who deliver 'quick service with a smile'. Inside
is an open kitchen turning out proper Italian
food that 'is clearly made with love'. Everyone
praises the relatively low cost, as well as the

quality of dishes such as steamed mussels with lemon juice and black pepper, salmon alla vesuviana – slow baked with potatoes, cherry tomatoes, onion, black olives and garlic – and classic tiramisu. Other options include traditional pasta dishes, maybe spaghetti alla vongole or penne alla Siciliana, and the very impressive, traditional sourdough pizzas, all served by the metre. As you'd expect, there is an all-Italian wine list with detailed notes and impressive regional coverage, lots by the glass, carafes from £14.50 and bottles from £21. **Chef/s:** Andrea Ippolito. **Open:** all week 12 to 11.30. **Closed:** 25 Dec, 1 Jan, Easter. **Meals:** main courses £9 to £25. **Details:** 60 seats. 38 seats outside. Music.

Potli

Cooking score: 2

⊖ Ravenscourt Park, Stamford Brook, map 1

Indian | £28

319-321 King Street, Ravenscourt Park, W6 9NH

Tel no: (020) 8741 4328

potli.co.uk

£5 OFF £30

In the bustling interstices of Hammersmith and Chiswick, Potli brings the vibrant cooking of Indian street markets to London's western reaches. Fried, griddled and tandoori-roasted dishes are overlaid with layers of authentic spicing, with pedigree British prime materials as the foundation. Main items include Berkshire venison simmered in a Rajasthani masala, while railway mutton curry, the meat cooked on the bone in a one-pot dish with potatoes, garam masala and black pepper, is from the Anglo-Indian cookbook. Prior to those, there are patrani prawns in fragrant green marinade wrapped in banana leaf, crisp-fried soft-shell crab in 'dynamite sauce' (a furious mix of chilli and coriander), or tandoori variations of chicken tikka. Finish with betel-leaf paan ice cream and gulkand rose-petal preserve, cardamom crème brûlée, or kulfi sticks. It all happens in a plain white room equipped with green

banquettes and charming, willing staff. Indian-spiced vodka Martinis might kick things off; wines, from £18, are less inspired. **Chef/s:** Babul Dey. **Open:** Mon to Sat L 12 to 2.30, D 6 to 10.30 (11 Fri and Sat). Sun 12 to 10.30. **Meals:** main courses £7 to £14. Set L £11 (2 courses) to £15. Sun L £15. **Details:** 70 seats. 24 seats outside. Bar. Wheelchairs. Music.

Princess Victoria

Cooking score: 2

⊖ Shepherd's Bush Market, map 1

Modern British | £28

217 Uxbridge Road, Shepherd's Bush, W12 9DH

Tel no: (020) 8749 5886

princessvictoria.co.uk

£30

Expansion is in the air at this impressively restored Victorian gin palace, with a new terrace out front and more space indoors for those who want to admire the gently curving bar, intricate cornicing and dome-shaped skylights that typify this fine building. There's also plenty to applaud on a menu that promotes mature Cumbrian beef from the pub's own ageing room, boards of home-cured fish with Guinness bread, pies fresh from the oven and a roster of eclectic plates ranging from lemon arancini with Gorgonzola and beetroot salad or rare tuna with pickled mooli and wasabi to spicy homemade sausages with mash or pan-fried hake with char-grilled squid, spinach and romesco sauce. A prodigious list of artisan gins (and infusions) references the pub's past, but top billing goes to the extraordinarily comprehensive wine list – a fascinating tome strewn with quotes, cartoons and trivia. Twenty cracking house selections (from £16.90) lead the charge, but also note the strong organic/biodynamic contingent and obscure 'indigenous varietals'. **Chef/s:** Matt Reuther. **Open:** all week L 12 to 3 (4.30 Sun), D 6.30 to 10.30 (9.30 Sun). **Meals:** main courses £11 to £18. Set L £13 (2 courses). **Details:** 120 seats. 54 seats outside. Bar. Wheelchairs. Music. Parking.

Rabbit

Cooking score: 1
⊖ Sloane Square, map 3
Modern British | £30
172 King's Road, Chelsea, SW3 4UP
Tel no: (020) 3750 0172
rabbit-restaurant.com

First pick your dinner. Conducted foraging trips in the parks are one of the attractions for intrepid Rabbiters. Others may simply be content to bag a table near the pass and watch the prettily presented dishes being plated up. The bar frontage is the bonnet end of a tractor, reinforcing the theme of King's Road rustic, which is further emphasised by dishes like black pudding with brassica flowers, redcurrants and crispy pig's skin, or spring greens with smoked shallots and mushrooms in sherry. Top and tail that with juniper-cured trout and sea bass roe taramasalata, and a honeycomb crunchie, and the job's a good'un. House Languedoc is £22.

Chef/s: Oliver Gladwin. **Open:** Mon D 6 to 11, Tue to Sat 12 to 12. Sun 12 to 6. **Closed:** 25 Dec, 1 Jan. **Meals:** small plates £7 to £16. **Details:** 47 seats. Bar. Wheelchairs. Music.

★ TOP 10 ★

Restaurant Gordon Ramsay

Cooking score: 9
⊖ Sloane Square, map 3
French | £110
68 Royal Hospital Road, Chelsea, SW3 4HP
Tel no: (020) 7352 4441
gordonramsay.com
🍷

Restaurant Gordon Ramsay is as much a fixture on the London dining scene as it was when it opened in Royal Hospital Road in 1998. Tradition is upheld, service is exemplary and the cooking is more or less consistent from year to year. This is not a kitchen that takes risks, and dishes tend not to change greatly, so it is no surprise to learn that since head chef Matt Abé took over from Clare Smyth (who remains for the time being as a consultant), changes have been slight, with

regulars reporting that 'the food coming from Matt is as good as ever'. What appeals about the cooking is that there is no needless experimentation, no attempt at shock effects, just a succession of fine ingredients that work together harmoniously. That's why a signature starter of sautéed foie gras (crisp outside, wobbly and melting within) and roasted veal sweetbreads, with carrots and green almonds, Cabernet Sauvignon vinegar adding a sweetly acidic note, the whole bathed in an ethereal foamed almond velouté, continues to impress. As does a dazzling fresh poached Isle of Gigha halibut of fine flavour and exact cooking, layered with Atlantic king crab, finger lime and cauliflower couscous in a precisely measured and gorgeous ras-el-hanout-flavoured broth vibrant with herbs and spices. Even better, perhaps, is a sublime gariguette strawberry bavarois, the plate strewn with gariguette and wild strawberries, dots of elderflower (jelly and tiny flowers), mini meringues and powdered Marco Polo tea. Soufflés are a strength; one reporter enjoyed a memorable, light-as-air apricot one, served with a 'wonderful' roasted almond ice cream. And then there are the top-drawer accessories – the bread selection, a mighty cheese trolley and a cornucopia of petits fours. The service, under the brilliant supervision of Jean-Claude Breton, is pitch-perfect – food is never handed to you here, it makes an entrance. There has been praise, too, for the sommelier, whose knowledge of his cellar is impressive and whose advice should be followed. Prices start at £28.

Chef/s: Matt Abé. **Open:** Mon to Fri L 12 to 2.30, D 6 to 10.30. **Closed:** Sat, Sun, 1 week Dec. **Meals:** set L £65 to £110. Set D £110. Tasting menu £145 to £195. **Details:** 45 seats. V menu. Music.

Symbols

🛏 Accommodation is available
£30 Three courses for less than £30
£5 OFF £5-off voucher scheme
🍷 Notable wine list

★ TOP 50 ★

Restaurant Marianne

Cooking score: 7
⊖ Royal Oak, map 6
Modern European | £85
104 Chepstow Road, Notting Hill, W2 5QS
Tel no: (020) 3675 7750
mariannerestaurant.com

Restaurant Marianne is proof positive that small is not only beautiful but highly effective, too. The smart, understated six-table dining room exudes quiet confidence, the muted tones and white napery adding up to a pleasing place to linger. And linger you must, for Marianne Lumb's flawless, elegant cooking is a delight in conception and delivery. A six-course tasting menu (five at lunch) opens with titillating canapés and amuse-bouches and segues into a virtuoso performance. The workmanship is undeniably first class whether in a dish of roast English green asparagus teamed with petit violet artichokes (whole and purée), a sprinkling of crumbed Noir de Bigorre ham adding a welcome saltiness, a raviolo of Windsor Park roe deer with aubergines and white miso, or perfectly timed wild sea bass served with yellow courgette purée, intensely sweet Datterini tomatoes augmented by fresh basil, and sweet Roscoff onions cut by the sharpness of baby capers (accoutrements are no afterthought). Though breaking new ground is not Ms Lumb's game, her cooking shows off superlative produce and everything is produced with great assurance. Her signature soufflés – at a test meal a light, sensuous soufflé of carrot cake with Brillat-Savarin ice cream, spiced pecans and butterscotch – make a winning finale. In addition, the three-course set lunch promises commendable value, service is polished to a high shine, formal but nice with it, and the tiny wine list opens at £39. **Chef/s:** Marianne Lumb. **Open:** Fri to Sun L 12 to 2.30, Tue to Sun D 6 to 9.30. **Closed:** Mon, 22 Dec to 5 Jan, Aug bank hol weekend. **Meals:** set L £35. Tasting menu L £65 (5 courses), D £85 (6 courses). **Details:** 14 seats. Music. Children over 12 yrs only.

Restaurant Michael Nadra

Cooking score: 3
⊖ Turnham Green, map 1
Modern European | £38
6-8 Elliott Road, Chiswick, W4 1PE
Tel no: (020) 8742 0766
restaurant-michaelnadra.co.uk
£5 OFF 🍾

Monochrome photos, black slate and leather and dark wooden tabletops give Michael Nadra's restaurant in Chiswick an informal feel. When it comes to the food, the cooking is a mix of classical and modern techniques. Sound materials are carefully handled, for example in a flavoursome quail stuffed with wild mushrooms, 'its legs crispy and spot-on', accompanied by pickled beetroot, blood orange and Bulls Blood leaf. Influences from Asia are never too far away: a grilled sea bass came with delicate prawn and chive dumplings, pak choi and a carrot-ginger purée, the dish rounded off by a crab bisque infused with lemongrass. For the final act, a delightful feuilleté of rhubarb with custard hit all the right notes. The good-natured and 'very attentive' staff contribute to the relaxed atmosphere and knowledgeable dabbling around the globe satisfies most palates and budgets on a wine list that opens at £20. **Chef/s:** Lukasz Kielbasinski. **Open:** all week L 12 to 2.30 (3.30 Sat and Sun), Mon to Sat D 6 to 10 (10.30 Fri and Sat). **Meals:** main courses £17 to £27. Set L £22 (2 courses) to £27. Set D £32 (2 courses) to £38. Sun L £24. Tasting menu L £49, D £59 (6 courses). **Details:** 44 seats. Music.

★ NEW ENTRY ★

Restaurant Ours

Cooking score: 2
⊖ South Kensington, map 3
Modern European | £50
264 Brompton Road, Kensington, SW3 2AS
Tel no: (020) 7100 2200
restaurant-ours.com

The latest venture from chef Tom Sellers (of Restaurant Story, see entry) is accessed along a glamorous walkway under a clever canopy of full-sized twinkling trees. On the night of our visit, diners were 'well-dressed, young and there to be seen' and this *Made in Chelsea* hotspot suits them fine. Highlights of the menu are the starters and salads, which are designed to be shared, so order plenty of them: salmon and cucumber, cut wafer-thin and dressed with citrus and chilli, and topped with salmon tartare, is as beautiful as it is clever; a simple salad of kale and shallot with smoked pecorino and hazelnuts makes a great contrast; 'crab, avocado, apple' has plenty of zing. Monkfish with squid ink and a side of roast courgette that follows is less exciting; however, perfectly pink lamb with a generous scattering of morels and broad beans has plenty going for it. Though portions aren't big, most diners don't make it to dessert, thereby missing a slice of very grown-up chocolate torte with smoked black tea ice cream. Champagne and cocktails are the drinks of choice and there's a shortish wine list starting at £32.

Chef/s: Tom Sellers and Daniel Phippard. **Open:** Mon to Fri L 12 to 2.30, Mon to Sat D 6 to 10 (11 Fri and Sat). **Closed:** Sun, 23 to 29 Dec, 1 to 5 Jan. **Meals:** main courses £18 to £36. **Details:** 120 seats. Bar. Wheelchairs. Music.

The River Café

Cooking score: 5
⊖ Hammersmith, map 1
Italian | £70
Thames Wharf, Rainville Road, Hammersmith, W6 9HA
Tel no: (020) 7386 4200
rivercafe.co.uk

Culinary pleasure at this legendary spot comes at a price that some readers find hard to swallow, but when it offers 'all you would want from a restaurant', most are willing to shell out. A paragon of simple, fresh Italian food since its inception, the River Café's family-orientated ethos and insistence on using outstanding raw materials wins it a place on many a food lover's bucket list. The minimalist dining room, with floor-to-ceiling windows looking out over a landscaped Thames-side courtyard, houses an open kitchen where Ruth Rogers remains on the pass and at the stove. From the menu, which changes twice daily, wild turbot tranche wood-roasted with capers, oregano and lemon zest with agretti might be a typical secondi, following a primi of peerless handmade pasta, perhaps tortelloni stuffed with peas, buffalo ricotta and River Café garden herbs, or char-grilled squid. Alternatively, the popular set lunch menu is a cheaper way in. Chocolate nemesis remains a signature pud. The extensive all-Italian wine list starts at a steep £30 and some might argue it escalates beyond the £50 mark rather too rapidly.

Chef/s: Ruth Rogers, Sian Wyn Owen and Joseph Trivelli. **Open:** all week L 12.30 to 5 (12 Sun), Mon to Sat D 7 to 11 (11.20 Fri and Sat). **Closed:** 24 Dec to 1 Jan, bank hols. **Meals:** main courses £37 to £45. **Details:** 120 seats. 80 seats outside. Bar. Wheelchairs. Parking.

The Shed

Cooking score: 3
⊖ Notting Hill Gate, map 6
Modern British | £30
122 Palace Gardens Terrace, Notting Hill, W8 4RT
Tel no: (020) 7229 4024
theshed-restaurant.com

'The Shed outshines the chains and uber-trendies of Westbourne Grove and gives grubby old Notting Hill Gate a touch of class,' says one fan of this 'cosy and warm' restaurant with strong farming roots. True to its name, the interior has a rustic, thrown-together look, with lots of rough wood and improvised furniture. The first of two restaurants by the brothers Gladwin – one a chef, another a farmer and the third versed in hospitality – the Shed exemplifies their field-to-fork philosophy, with foraged elements thrown in for good measure. Tapas-style choices include opening 'mouthfuls' (mushroom marmite with egg confit; sea bass taramasalata) and sections of slow-cooked and 'fast-cooked' dishes. From the former, choices range from

carrot hummus with cinnamon dukkah and crispbread to black pudding with raisin, pickled onion and wood blewit. Red gurnard with mussel curry, cauliflower and three-cornered garlic is a typical 'fast-cooked' option. To finish, maybe honeycomb crunchie with mascarpone and tarragon sauce. The wine list (from £22) includes a selection from the family vineyard by the glass, carafe or bottle.
Chef/s: Oliver Gladwin. **Open:** Tue to Sat L 12 to 3 (4.30 Sat), Mon to Sat D 6 to 11. **Closed:** Sun, 25 Dec to 1 Jan, Easter Sun and Mon, 1 week Aug. **Meals:** small plates £9 to £13. **Details:** 48 seats. 12 seats outside. Bar. Music.

Shikumen
Cooking score: 3
⊖ Shepherd's Bush Market, map 1
Chinese | £35
Dorsett Hotel, 58 Shepherd's Bush Green, Shepherd's Bush, W12 8QE
Tel no: (020) 8749 9978
shikumen.co.uk
£5
OFF

Named for a particular style of Shanghai arch, Shikumen is softer than a slab of stone – just. With its expanses of polished wood and stiffly linear screens, this sleek adjunct to the Dorsett Hotel (there's another branch at the Xanadu in Ealing) puts an abundance of Cantonese character on the plate. It's to be found in delicate dim sum such as scallop siu mai topped with tobiko, Shanghai dumplings or slippery mushroom cheung fun. Call ahead – or chance your arm there and then – for classic Peking duck carved at the table and presented in two services, or try braised pork belly with Chinese buns, sanpei chicken clay pot (shades of Hakkasan) or fried tofu with steamed egg white and minced meat. Vegetable dishes are simple and vivid. Saké and strong Chinese liquor are joined on the drinks list by a handful of blowout wines, along with more everyday bottles from £21.90.

Chef/s: Mr Kam Choon Lai. **Open:** all week 12 to 10 (11.30 to 9.30 Sun). **Closed:** 25 Dec. **Meals:** main courses £9 to £39. Set L £20 (2 courses) to £25. Set D £30 (2 courses) to £40. Sun L £20. **Details:** 140 seats. Bar. Wheelchairs. Music.

★ NEW ENTRY ★

Six Portland Road
Cooking score: 2
⊖ Holland Park, map 1
French | £32
6 Portland Road, Holland Park, W11 4LA
Tel no: (0207) 229 3130
sixportlandroad.com

'It feels like a restaurant for our times – and one that's here to stay,' was how one visitor summed up this small neighbourhood bistro in a smart little Georgian parade of shops just off Holland Park Avenue. The interior is simply done, a narrow dining room on several levels, with white walls, dark-wood floor, bentwood chairs and white paper tablecloths, leading to a semi-open kitchen at the rear. 'It looks like it could have been here for years, and that's a compliment.' It's owned and run by alumni of Terroirs (see entry), so expect simple, honest cooking of French classics along the lines of brandade de morue with soft boiled egg, sea beets and thick-cut toast, moules mouclade, a curried mussel dish of La Rochelle provenance, and a succulent and well-caramelised pork collar of generous proportions, served with white sprouting broccoli, chickpeas, anchovy and rosemary. The only downside is the high decibel levels when full. The carefully curated wine list is full of irresistible opportunities, from £20.50.
Chef/s: Pascal Wiedemann. **Open:** Sun L 12 to 5. Tue to Sat 12 to 11. **Closed:** Mon. **Meals:** main courses £14 to £20. **Details:** 40 seats.

La Trompette

Cooking score: 5
⊖ Turnham Green, map 1
Modern European | £50
3-7 Devonshire Road, Chiswick, W4 2EU
Tel no: (020) 8747 1836
latrompette.co.uk

In this gastronomic enclave of west London, La Trompette has always been leader of the pack, having plied its trade under the ownership of Nigel Platts-Martin and Bruce Poole since 2001. Beneath the formal trappings of crisp white linen and gleaming glasses beats the heart of a neighbourhood restaurant, where Rob Weston's bold, assured cooking draws locals back again and again for the likes of 'rich and well-flavoured' navarin of Welsh hogget or a 'simple, but very well-executed' Jacob's ladder and rump of Ayrshire beef. The seasonal menu is full of promise – a meal in March bringing 'intricate' wild ransom velouté, served with pickled nameko (mushroom), warm gougères and smoked ricotta, before going on to guinea fowl with Jerusalem artichoke, grilled calçots and hazelnut pesto (pronounced a 'stunning assembly of flavours'), and finishing with rhubarb crumble soufflé with rhubarb ripple ice cream. The fixed-price format means that bills are predictable – even the mark-ups on the superb wine list of some 600 bins of Old and New World wines are gentle. Bottles from £22.
Chef/s: Rob Weston. **Open:** all week L 12 to 2.30 (12.30 to 3 Sun), D 6.30 to 10.30 (7 to 9.30 Sun). **Closed:** 24 to 26 Dec, 1 Jan. **Meals:** set L £25 (2 courses) to £30. Set D £42 (2 courses) to £50. Sun L £33 (2 courses). **Details:** 88 seats. 14 seats outside. Wheelchairs.

Visit us online

To find out more about
The Good Food Guide, please
visit thegoodfoodguide.co.uk

Vinoteca

Cooking score: 2
⊖ Turnham Green, map 1
Modern European | £28
18 Devonshire Road, Chiswick, W4 2HD
Tel no: (020) 3701 8822
vinoteca.co.uk

Taking inspiration from the kind of drinking dens that can be found in the narrow streets of cities in Spain and Italy, Vinoteca is an invigorating spot with wine bottles filling the shelves, an open kitchen, an easy charm and a serious approach to matters of food and drink. One of five across the capital, in a group that runs from Farringdon in the east to here in W4, expect an interesting slate of wines by the glass and a culinary output that's full of inspiring combinations. Slow-braised Mersea cuttlefish come with brown shrimps and black rice, Middle White pork terrine gets Sicilian kumquats to cut through its richness, and steamed mussels get fired up with 'ndjua and wild garlic. And that's just for starters. Main-course grilled leg of Elwy Valley lamb keeps Italian company with caponata and salsa verde, and, to finish, apple and almond tart is a French classic. Wines start at £16.50.
Chef/s: James Robson. **Open:** all week L 12 to 2.45 (11am Sat), Mon to Sat D 6 to 10. **Closed:** 31 Dec to 1 Jan. **Meals:** main courses £13 to £20. Set L £13 (2 courses) to £16. **Details:** 50 seats. Bar. Wheelchairs. Music.

Wormwood

Cooking score: 4
⊖ Ladbroke Grove, Westbourne Park, map 6
Mediterranean | £35
16 All Saints Road, Notting Hill, W11 1HH
Tel no: (020) 7854 1808
wormwoodrestaurant.com

By day an unpromising space, looking more like a tea room than a proper restaurant, with its white chairs and tables and precious little in the way of luxury finishes, but come evening, the room is abuzz with a well-to-do multicultural crowd drawn by the chef's

original Moorish-North African cooking. The short menu is designed for sharing (five or so dishes are recommended between two people): crunchy squid-ink croquetas with a 'sensuously soft, disorientatingly black interior', dotted with pieces of squid, and served with an equally black squid-ink mayonnaise; an absolutely fresh, just-seared thick pink tuna steak; and an aubergine theme and variations, which includes a smoked baba ganoush, an aubergine caviar and a confit, have been praised. But it's the Andalusian lamb tartare, which delivers a spiced-up pile of seared and raw lamb, buzzy with cumin and touched with chilli, that was the star at a test meal. The short, well-priced but truly international wine list roams the wilds of Syria and Lebanon but kicks off at around £5 a glass.
Chef/s: Rabah Ourrad. **Open:** Tue to Sun D only 6 to 10. **Closed:** Mon. **Meals:** small plates £9 to £16. **Details:** 44 seats. Music.

Wright Brothers

Cooking score: 2
⊖ South Kensington, map 3
Seafood | £35
56 Old Brompton Road, South Kensington, SW7 3DY
Tel no: (020) 7581 0131
thewrightbrothers.co.uk

A name anchored on sea-to-plate freshness means that while this South Kensington branch is smaller and more intimate than sister restaurants in Soho, Borough and Spitalfields, it is still a fine place for a seafood surfeit. The décor is French-accented bistro style, all tight-packed tables, Toulouse-Lautrec and brass, lace-covered doors on to the street and copious seafood platters – the 'petit' plenty for two. It's best to order simply and let the quality shine through, say half a dozen oysters, moules marinière or whole cracked South Coast crab, although specials like panzanella with grilled anchovies or roast Eastbourne brill with sweetcorn and ginger are delivered capably. If you're not in the mood for fish there's always a

meat dish, perhaps pork belly with miso and chilli. For dessert, crème brûlée and chocolate mousse have been praised. The bar downstairs serves good cocktails and wines starts at £21.
Chef/s: Phil Coulter. **Open:** all week 12 to 10.30 (9.30 Sun). **Closed:** 25 and 26 Dec. **Meals:** main courses £17 to £21. Set L £17 (2 courses) to £20. **Details:** 28 seats. 4 seats outside.

Yashin Sushi

Cooking score: 4
⊖ High Street Kensington, map 6
Japanese | £50
1a Argyll Road, Kensington, W8 7DB
Tel no: (020) 7938 1536
yashinsushi.com

Tucked away off Kensington High Street, this small Japanese restaurant has a discreet entrance but the interior is stylish and sophisticated with dining taking place over two floors – counter seating on the ground floor is the preferred spot. 'It's a real treat to dine here,' thought one regular, who was impressed by the quality and creativity of the sushi, though there is innovation throughout the menu. Barely cooked Paradise prawns arrive on top of a Himalayan salt mound served with sesame (seeds and popcorn), edible flowers and crystallised chilli, or there could be sliced beetroot, black radish, carrots and potato crisps stirred into life by a delightful ginger and yuzu dressing, while faultless deep-fried soft-shell crab rolls with avocado and tobiko roe are finished off with a sweet soy dip. The set menus (omakase and bento boxes) are justifiably popular. Service is well drilled and friendly. An expensive wine list, augmented by classy sakés, starts at £28.
Chef/s: Yasuhiro Mineno and Shinya Ikeda. **Open:** all week L 12 to 2, D 6 to 10. **Meals:** sashimi £11 to £25. Tapas £6 to £28. Omakase £30 (8 pieces) to £60. **Details:** 37 seats. Music.

Average price

The average price denotes the price of a three-course meal without wine.

Zafferano

Cooking score: 4
⊖ Knightsbridge, map 6
Italian | £65
15 Lowndes Street, Belgravia, SW1X 9EY
Tel no: (020) 7235 5800
zafferanorestaurant.com

A distinguished ambassador and champion of high-end Italian cuisine since the mid-90s, Zafferano has enduring appeal for the Knightsbridge crowd. Inside, it knows how to put on the style, with exposed brick walls, stone floors and extravagant floral displays, while the kitchen specialises in seasonal, ingredients-led cookery. Freshly made pasta remains one of the highlights, with the likes of orecchiette with Sicilian tomatoes, anchovies and breadcrumbs or veal osso buco ravioli with gremolata on offer. Otherwise, daisy-fresh salads are a favourite way to start (orange and fennel with almonds and black olives, say), while mains show off the quality of meticulously sourced raw materials – from pan-seared sea bream with spinach and Modena balsamic dressing to duck breast with caramelised butternut squash and apple gel. To finish, investigate the dark chocolate sphere with raspberries. The voluminous all-Italian wine list is stuffed with regional treasures, but prices take no prisoners – bottles start at £39.

Chef/s: Daniele Camera. **Open:** all week 12 to 11 (10.30 Sun). **Closed:** 25 Dec. **Meals:** main courses £24 to £32. Set L £27 (2 courses) to £32. **Details:** 150 seats. 20 seats outside. Bar. Music.

Zuma

Cooking score: 5
⊖ Knightsbridge, map 6
Japanese | £50
5 Raphael Street, Knightsbridge, SW7 1DL
Tel no: (020) 7584 1010
zumarestaurant.com

Zuma landed in London in 2002 and as we speak there are siblings across the world from Bangkok to Miami. Rainer Becker got it right from the get-go with the cool, seductive mood, like something we'd only seen in James Bond movies, and the modern take on Japanese food, a glammed-up version of the humble stuff found in izakaya joints across Japan. There's nothing humble about Zuma. Grab a tosho table if you want some privacy; go for a stool at the sushi counter or robata grill if you want to see the cheffy action up close. Spicy yellowtail tuna maki roll with sansho pepper, avocado and wasabi mayo reflects the new world order, while brilliant sashimi and nigiri are classically done. Crispy fried sole with spicy ponzu sauce, marinated black cod wrapped in hoba leaf, Ibérico pork cooked on the robata grill – it's hard to stop (probably best to let the bank manager decide). Drink fabulous sakés or wines from £26.

Chef/s: Rainer Becker. **Open:** all week L 12 to 3 (3.30 Sat and Sun), D 6 to 11 (10.30 Sun). **Closed:** bank hols. **Meals:** sharing plates £5 to £79. Tasting menu £71. **Details:** 150 seats. Bar. Wheelchairs. Music.

A Cena

Cooking score: 2
⊖ Richmond, map 1
Italian | £35
418 Richmond Road, Twickenham, TW1 2EB
Tel no: (020) 8288 0108
acena.co.uk

£5
OFF

A trim, simple but smart monochrome look is the drill for Justine Kemsley's neighbourhood Italian, bang on the invisible border between Twickenham and Richmond. The candlelit bar is a picture of cheer with its gleaming Galliano bottles, and Nicola Parsons does her bit in the kitchen, producing capable renditions of north Italian food, served in the traditional menu format. Brush up your vocabulary with a starter of sgombro – grilled mackerel with wild garlic leaves and lemon – before a primo of saffron risotto and bone marrow, or spaghetti in an appealing mélange of ricotta, lemon, pine nuts and Parmesan. Quality proteins are the mainstay of principals like marinated hake in capers, kale and lemon butter, or rump of salt marsh lamb with smashed white beans and salsa verde. Sweeten your tooth for dolci: salted caramel ripple ice cream or baked mascarpone with blueberries and roast sugared almonds. The all-Italian wine list opens with house Sicilians at £19.50 (£5 a glass).
Chef/s: Nicola Parsons. **Open:** Tue to Sun L 12 to 2, Mon to Sat D 6 to 10. **Closed:** 2 weeks Aug, bank hols. **Meals:** main courses £7 to £24. Sun L £21 (2 courses). **Details:** 55 seats. Bar. Music.

Albert's Table

Cooking score: 3
Modern British | £35
49b/c Southend, Croydon, CR0 1BF
Tel no: (020) 8680 2010
albertstable.co.uk

£5
OFF

The relaxing long room done in light neutrals, furnished with linened-up tables, brings a touch of class to the dining environs of South Croydon. Joby Wells enthusiastically draws on the produce of the southern counties for carefully crafted constructions of modern British food driven by reliable culinary logic rather than the urge to grandstand. A shortcrust tart of Dorset crab with rouille and saladings is what's on the bistro menu, alongside salmon ballotine with beetroot vinaigrette and horseradish crème fraîche. The same confident straightforwardness characterises mains such as venison two ways – roast haunch and a little pie – with parsnips and carrots, or the painstakingly jointed poussin that arrives as the roast breast, glazed thigh and breaded drumstick, with salsify and crushed swede in meat juices. A taste of everything Britain once treasured is offered in a pudding of spotted dick and custard with rhubarb and vanilla ice cream and baked apple. An adequate wine list opens at £20.
Chef/s: Joby Wells and Josse Anderton. **Open:** Tue to Sun L 12 to 2.30 (3.30 Sun), Tue to Sat D 6.30 to 10.30. **Closed:** Mon. **Meals:** set L £21 (2 courses) to £24. Set D £28 (2 courses) to £35. Sun L £24. **Details:** 60 seats. Wheelchairs. Music. Parking.

The Bingham

Cooking score: 4
⊖ Richmond, map 1
Modern British | £37
61-63 Petersham Road, Richmond, TW10 6UT
Tel no: (020) 8940 0902
thebingham.co.uk

£5
OFF

'The view from the restaurant on to the Thames is gorgeous. I love watching the boats going past. The service is attentive and generous, and when I dine with my young children, staff are helpful in giving paper and pens to keep them occupied.' So writes a reporter of this early Georgian riverside townhouse, where inspired modern British cooking adds to the allure. Andrew Cole stepped up to head the kitchens at the beginning of 2016, and works in vivid outlines and contrasting flavours to produce dishes that excite. Sea bream tartare with compressed cucumber and orange granita may be the prelude to cornfed chicken breast with confit leg, yeast purée and kale, or salmon and leeks with puréed prunes in clam butter. Desserts come in scented array, all apple blossom, bergamot and rosemary, the last fragrancing the orange ice cream that comes with hot chocolate fondant. An encyclopaedic wine list is replete with classics from Old World and New, from £25 (glasses £6).

Chef/s: Andrew Cole. **Open:** Mon to Sat L 12 to 2.30, D 6.30 to 10 (10.30 Fri and Sat). Sun 12 to 8. **Meals:** main courses £12 to £28. Set L and D £17 (2 courses) to £20. Sun L £38 (3 courses). **Details:** 40 seats. 14 seats outside. Bar. Wheelchairs. Music. Parking.

Brilliant

Cooking score: 4
⊖ Hounslow West, map 1
Indian | £25
72-76 Western Road, Southall, UB2 5DZ
Tel no: (020) 8574 1928
brilliantrestaurant.com
£5 OFF £30

A family business since 1975, constant evolution has kept Brilliant at the vanguard of Indian dining in the UK. It's grown into a 220-seater behemoth with a private function room upstairs, but miraculously not lost any of its culinary edge. It's the North Indian region of Punjab that is the inspiration for a menu that may look familiar to curry-house regulars, but delivers distinct spicing and a whole heap of satisfaction. There's a weekend cookery school if you fancy learning how it's done. The vibrant dining room with splashes of burnt orange and flickering TVs fills up fast and generates quite a cacophony. Tandoori lamb chops, tandoori salmon, aloo tikki – whichever way you start, it's quality all the way. Follow on with a classic curry – lamb, say, in a rich masala gravy – or as good a chicken tikka masala as you'll find anywhere in the country. Wines start at £11.

Chef/s: Jasvindersit Singh. **Open:** Tue to Fri L 12 to 2.30, Tue to Sun D 6 to 11.30. **Closed:** Mon, 25 Dec, bank hols. **Meals:** main courses £7 to £32. **Details:** 220 seats. Music. Parking.

La Buvette

Cooking score: 3
⊖ Richmond, map 1
French | £29
6 Church Walk, Richmond, TW9 1SN
Tel no: (020) 8940 6264
labuvette.co.uk
£30

'The money is obviously spent in the kitchen,' thought one reporter of this frill-free restaurant. The loos are outside and 'it feels like a fifties tea room', with paper tablecloths (and a supply of pencils just in case you need to write a business plan) and 'cheap as chips' glasses and cutlery, 'but the cooking is remarkably good'. The menu is the antithesis of modern French: onglet steak, served properly rare, with herb butter and chips, and choucroute with all its classic accompanying meats, the flavours melding together to create something so much better than the sum of its parts. Pissaladière delivers the richness of long-cooked onions, a perfect foil for the brininess of the anchovy and olive garnish. Puds – ice creams, and the likes of rhubarb with crème fraîche – are for those who aren't beguiled by the perfectly ripe Brie. The all-French wine list, with plenty by the glass and carafe, starts at £13.50 per 50cl.

Chef/s: Buck Carter. **Open:** all week L 12 to 3, D 5.45 to 10. **Closed:** 25 and 26 Dec, Good Fri, Easter Sun. **Meals:** main courses £14 to £19. Set L and D £18. Sun L £18. **Details:** 48 seats. 34 seats outside.

The Dysart

Cooking score: 5
⊖ Richmond, map 1
Modern British | £43
135 Petersham Road, Richmond, TW10 7AA
Tel no: (020) 8940 8005
thedysartpetersham.co.uk
£5 OFF

With a big, well-stocked bar welcoming customers as they walk in and a room full of scrubbed wooden tables and chairs, the Dysart looks for all the world like a classic dining pub. Don't let appearances fool you – its pub

origins have been left to the annals of history. Kenneth Culhane, a former Roux scholar, is the man in charge and he combines his classical training with local, home-grown and foraged ingredients and global flavours to produce a unique combination. 'There's no doubt the guy can cook, and really well at that,' but sometimes enthusiasm gets the better of him. A perfectly smooth, rich crème brûlée, for example, would be better without the tonka bean addition, but there's no gainsaying a simple charred mackerel enlivened with kobu-braised daikon and ginger, or a plate of Middle White pork, which delivered many different cuts, each cooked to its best advantage. A strong, clever wine list kicks off at £20.
Chef/s: Kenneth Culhane. **Open:** Tue to Sun L 11.30 to 2.45 (3.15 Sat, 3.45 Sun), Tue to Sat D 5.30 to 9.15 (6 Sat). **Closed:** Mon (exc bank hols), 25 Dec. **Meals:** main courses £19 to £30. Set L £25 (2 courses) to £30 (Tue to Fri), Set D £25 (2 courses) to £30 (Tue to Thur). Sun L £35. Tasting menu £73. **Details:** 50 seats. 25 seats outside. V menu. Wheelchairs. Music. Parking.

Eat17

Cooking score: 2
⊖ Walthamstow Central, map 1
British | £26
28-30 Orford Road, Walthamstow, E17 9NJ
Tel no: (020) 8521 5279
eat17.co.uk
£30

Walthamstow restaurant Eat17 will soon celebrate a decade in business, during which time it's spawned a satellite branch in Hackney and a nationwide fanbase for the 'bacon jam' invented here. The headquarters, however, is still here, where it all began, looking smart as ever after a recent refurb with whitewashed walls, long mirrors and comfy Chesterfield sofas. The menu, too, sits in comfort-food space, though not without clever touches: a starter of tandoori scallops, Puy lentils and yoghurt showed good ideas in the kitchen. Bistro philosophy defines the mains: posh burgers, steaks and dishes such as duck breast,

sweet potato and tahini mash and caramelised endive — the bird subtle and succulent on our visit. Crumbles, crème brûlées and chocolate puddings appease those who want to linger in the dining room; a cocktail menu and a line up of local ales bring punters to the handsome copper bar. House wines from £19.50.
Chef/s: Chris O'Connor. **Open:** all week L 12 to 3 (12.30 Sat, 12.30 to 3.30 Sun), D 6 to 10 (5 Sat, 5.30 to 9 Sun). **Meals:** main courses £12 to £20. Set L and D £15 (2 courses) to £18. **Details:** 66 seats. Bar. Wheelchairs. Music.

The French Table

Cooking score: 4
map 1
French | £42
85 Maple Road, Surbiton, KT6 4AW
Tel no: (020) 8399 2365
thefrenchtable.co.uk

Surbiton locals are full of praise for Eric and Sarah Guignard's suburban treasure — not least because they don't have to haul up to London when serious eating is required. Since launching in 2001, Eric has honed his cooking, injecting some engaging contemporary ideas into his beloved bourgeois repertoire: the result is an approachable but tantalising menu that might tout a salad of lobster with cauliflower couscous and orange miso sauce ahead of, say, monkfish wrapped in Bayonne ham with creamy truffle risotto. By contrast, find solace in comforting plates of venison Wellington or an assiette of Herdwick lamb accompanied by parsnip purée, Jerusalem artichokes and mustard spätzle. To finish, the chef's love of patisserie is given full rein in desserts such as chocolate linzer slice with spiced plum compote and vanilla pannacotta. A predominantly European wine list starts at £18.95. Time-pressed folk, meanwhile, might fancy the French Tarte — Guignard's café/ boulangerie next door.
Chef/s: Eric Guignard. **Open:** Tue to Sat L 12 to 2.30, D 7 to 10.30 (6.30 Fri and Sat). **Closed:** Sun, Mon, 2 weeks Christmas, last 2 weeks Aug.

Meals: set L £20 (2 courses) to £25. Set D £38 (2 courses) to £42. Tasting menu L £28, D £48.
Details: 45 seats. Music.

The Glasshouse

Cooking score: 5
⊖ Kew Gardens, map 1
Modern European | £50
14 Station Parade, Kew, TW9 3PZ
Tel no: (020) 8940 6777
glasshouserestaurant.co.uk

A stalwart of the Kew dining scene, the Glasshouse has long been a beacon of quality and still knows how to please its customers. Behind a discreet frontage lies a neutral-toned but pleasant enough dining room with a polished-wood floor and white-clad tables, and it comes across as a well-regarded local asset. The appeal is chef Berwyn Davies' smart, confident cooking that fully exploits the contemporary Anglo-French style. His menu is a glorious roll call of top-notch seasonal ingredients: a splendid winter dish of red-legged partridge with boudin blanc, Puy lentils and roasted baby beetroot for example, or, in spring, a loin of Welsh lamb with braised shoulder, boulangère potatoes, pea and wild garlic emulsion. Elsewhere, there's spiced duck breast with caramelised endive, quince purée and chestnut raviolo to start, and an ethereal warm custard brioche with roasted apples and tarte Tatin ice cream to finish. To cap it all the wine list is a knowledgeable, worldwide compendium (from £22) made more accessible by a good by-the-glass selection.
Chef/s: Berwyn Davies. **Open:** all week L 12 to 2.30 (12.30 to 3 Sun), D 6.30 to 10.30 (7 to 10 Sun). **Closed:** 24 to 26 Dec, 1 Jan. **Meals:** set L £25 (2 courses) to £30. Set D £45 (2 courses) to £50. Sun L £35. **Details:** 67 seats.

Incanto

Cooking score: 3
⊖ Harrow-on-the-Hill, map 1
Italian | £35
41 High Street, Harrow-on-the-Hill, HA1 3HT
Tel no: (020) 8426 6767
incanto.co.uk

This former Post Office in the centre of villagey Harrow-on-the-Hill might at first sight resemble a contemporary tea room, but behind the deli lies something of serious gastronomic intent. Incanto's smart dining area – polished wooden flooring, white walls, large skylight and compact mezzanine – matches a menu where excellent British ingredients form the mainstay of expertly presented modern Italian dishes. At inspection, lobster tagliatelle showcased fine pasta-making skills, tender crustacea and a flavourful basil and tomato sauce, while lamb arrived as juicy pink rack and tender slow-cooked shoulder, with pea purée and broad beans: a vernal delight. Only a chicken dish (roundels of breast stuffed with peppers and courgette) lacked flavour, being outmatched by the accompanying tarragon gnocchi. Puddings are a highlight, especially the indulgent chocolate fondant with caramelised pistachios and raspberry sorbet. The set lunch is a bargain for food of this quality, and the mostly Italian wine list is a forte, too: well-annotated, well-chosen, and starting at £19.
Open: Tue to Sun L 12 to 2.30 (12.30 to 4 Sun), Tue to Sat D 6.30 to 10.30. **Closed:** Mon. **Meals:** main courses £11 to £22. Set L and D £19 (2 courses) to £24. **Details:** 64 seats. Wheelchairs. Music.

Indian Zilla

Cooking score: 3
map 1
Indian | £27
2-3 Rocks Lane, Barnes, SW13 0DB
Tel no: (020) 8878 3989
indianzilla.co.uk

£5 OFF £30

With Indian Zing in Hammersmith (see entry) and Indian Zest in Sunbury-on-Thames complementing this Barnes outlet, chef Manoj Vasaikar now has much of suburban west London covered. A 'zilla' is a district or neighbourhood, and there's a local feel to proceedings here – although Manoj has imbued the restaurant with his trademark artefacts, gentle colours and clean lines. On the food front, he absorbs influences and ideas, taking inspiration from the Subcontinent's multifarious traditions and regional styles while keeping an eye on the provenance of his raw materials. Outdoor-reared Hampshire pork appears in an authentic Goan vindaloo, Irish mussels are poached in a soothing coconut broth with green herbs, while venison meatballs are the basis of a rich kofta curry. Vibrant meat-free dishes are also a cut above – from griddled vegetable 'bhanola' drizzled with tamarind relish to the signature banana flower and colocasia dumplings simmered in delicate pumpkin gravy. Well-chosen aromatic wines from £16.
Chef/s: Manoj Vasaikar. **Open:** Sun L 12 to 3, all week D 6 to 11 (10 Sun). **Closed:** 25 Dec. **Meals:** main courses £9 to £22. Sun L £12 (2 courses) to £15. **Details:** 75 seats. 4 seats outside. Music.

Readers recommend

A 'readers recommend' review is a genuine quote from a report sent in by one of our readers. We intend to follow up these suggestions throughout the year to come.

Madhu's

Cooking score: 3
map 1
Indian | £25
39 South Road, Southall, UB1 1SW
Tel no: (020) 8574 1897
madhus.co.uk

£30

Madhu's was established at the outset of the 1980s, when the revolution in Indian dining was barely a twinkle in the eye. Founder Sanjay Anand was awarded an MBE for his services to the restaurant industry, and even in its early middle age, the place still feels glamorously youthful, its high-gloss chic a beacon of Southall style. The kitchen has never seen fit to go down the experimental road, but offers dependable Punjabi cooking with one or two Kenyan touches, such as the Masai Mara-style lamb ribs marinated in lemon and chilli, or tilapia curry in cumin-spiked masala. Otherwise, you'll find a whole new oomph given to the familiar likes of mattar paneer, king prawns achari, butter chicken and rogan gosht. Masses of vegetarian choice, and a range of rotis and naans to accompany, ensure the package is complete, and if you can forgo the Häagen-Dazs, there are proper gulab jamun to finish. Wines start at £16.
Chef/s: Rakesh Verma. **Open:** Mon and Wed to Fri L 12.30 to 3, Wed to Mon D 6 to 11.30. **Closed:** Tue. **Meals:** main courses £6 to £14. Set L and D £25. **Details:** 104 seats. Wheelchairs. Music. Parking.

READERS RECOMMEND

Olympic Studios Café and Dining Room

Modern British
Olympic Studios, 117-123 Church Road, Barnes, SW13 9HL
Tel no: (020) 8912 5170
olympiccinema.co.uk
'Pan-fried scallops with Alejandro chorizo, crushed peas, celeriac and rosemary were excellent: really fresh scallops and perfectly

balanced accompaniments. Exceptionally thoughtful and intelligent service. All in all a memorable meal.'

Petersham Nurseries Café
Cooking score: 3
⊖ Richmond, map 1
Modern European | £40
Church Lane, off Petersham Road, Richmond, TW10 7AG
Tel no: (020) 8940 5230
petershamnurseries.com

Richmond's greenhouse of earthly delights – aka the Petersham Nurseries Café – is manna for those who relish the prospect of dining amid a veritable Arcadia of luxuriant plants, flowerpots, sculptures and gardening bric-à-brac. On offer is a cornucopia of heritage vegetables, salad leaves and herbs from the nearby walled garden, transformed into sunny seasonal dishes rooted in the Mediterranean region. The day's menu also accommodates sustainable fish, rare-breed meats and game for a sprightly line-up that might run from marinated scallops with chilli, nasturtium leaves, flowers and Zisola olive oil to spatchcock poussin with autumn leaves, kohlrabi, pomegranate and hazelnuts or bulgur wheat with carrots, harissa, labneh and date flatbread. Although the café is normally only open for lunch, it's worth keeping an eye out for occasional supper clubs throughout the year. The food is matched by a savvy list of Italian regional wines from £24.
Chef/s: Damian Clisby. **Open:** Tue to Sun L only 12 to 3. **Closed:** Mon, 24 to 27 Dec. **Meals:** main courses £19 to £37. **Details:** 120 seats. 120 seats outside. Wheelchairs.

The Petersham
Cooking score: 3
⊖ Richmond, map 1
Modern European | £41
Nightingale Lane, Richmond, TW10 6UZ
Tel no: (020) 8939 1084
petershamhotel.co.uk

John Giles, he of the Langham in central London (see entry), built the Petersham in the 1860s on top of Richmond Hill, overlooking the park and the river. It's a work of fantastical Italian Gothic, with its many-balconied exterior and majestic unsupported staircase of Portland stone within. Adebola Adeshina arrived here from a trail of smart London addresses, and brings energetic contemporary cuisine to the august surroundings. Steamed crab lasagne in tomato and coconut sauce gets things off to a stimulating start, and today's vogue for pickling is acknowledged in another opener of grilled pears with pomegranate and Jersey milk curd. Black quinoa is among the fashionable partners to a tranche of stone bass, alongside shrimp curry and raisin vinaigrette, while short rib and fillet of Scottish beef is classically served with pommes Anna in bordelaise. Eton Mess appears in the cold months with winter berries and cheese and vanilla mousse. Wines on a French-orientated list open at £24.
Chef/s: Adebola Adeshina. **Open:** all week L 12.15 to 2.15 (12.30 to 3.30 Sun), D 7 to 9.45. **Closed:** 25 and 26 Dec. **Meals:** main courses £16 to £34. Set L and D £23 (2 courses) to £27. Sun L £35. **Details:** 70 seats. Bar. Wheelchairs. Parking.

Retro Bistrot

Cooking score: 3
map 1
French | £35
114-116 High Street, Teddington, TW11 8JB
Tel no: (020) 8977 2239
retrobistrot.co.uk
£5
OFF

Fun-loving Retro Bistrot rocks to an ebullient tune, enveloping everyone with its genuine love of feeding customers. Owner Vincent Gerbeau has created an authentic-feeling venue that somehow combines old-school propriety with contemporary swagger, giving a fine impression of an upmarket Parisian eatery. The menu sticks to the programme with a rendition of classy bistro classics. Fish soup with almond and saffron rouille and seared foie gras with spiced bread, mango chutney and balsamic reduction set the pace, chateaubriand with frites and béarnaise sauce is a fixture, while roast cauliflower with sweet potato gnocchi, Comté cheese and truffle cream, pickled mushroom and curried walnut shows that even vegetarians get a look-in. Among desserts, citrus cheesecake with pink grapefruit and basil sorbet is hard to skip. Unsurprisingly, wines are strongest in France, but there are global forays and a decent by-the-glass selection. Bottles from £18.50.
Chef/s: François Fayd'Herbe de Maudave. **Open:** Tue to Sun L 12 to 3.30, Tue to Sat D 6.30 to 11. **Closed:** Mon, 25 and 26 Dec, 1 week Jan. **Meals:** main courses £8 to £18. Set L £11 (2 courses) to £16. Set D £20 (2 courses) to £26. Sun L £26. **Details:** 90 seats. Bar. Music.

Sonny's Kitchen

Cooking score: 2
map 1
Modern European | £33
94 Church Road, Barnes, SW13 0DQ
Tel no: (020) 8748 0393
sonnyskitchen.co.uk

The inhabitants of Barnes look kindly on Phil Howard and Rebecca Mascarenhas' gregarious, good-natured bar and restaurant

(with a food shop next door) and it's easy to see why. Sonny's Kitchen strikes just the right note for a neighbourhood restaurant: an unfussy atmosphere, nicely spaced tables, simple, seasonal dishes and a good choice of wines by the glass. The changing menu plays off the seasons and straddles the Eurozone with dishes such as foie gras and chicken liver parfait or grilled salmon salad with Jersey Royals, pickled cucumber and herb mayonnaise. Mains might include roast Cornish pollack with leeks, samphire and mussels or sirloin of White Park beef with very good French fries and wild garlic pesto, while chocolate fondant with vanilla ice cream and hot chocolate sauce or salted caramel tart should provide the right sweet hit. There are popular Sunday roasts, too. Wines start at £17.25.
Chef/s: Elliot Luscombe. **Open:** all week L 12 to 2.30 (3 Sat and Sun), D 6.30 to 10.30 (9.30 Sun). **Closed:** 25 Dec to 1 Jan, bank hols. **Meals:** main courses £15 to £30. Set L and D £20 (2 courses) to £23. **Details:** 90 seats. Music.

Tangawizi

Cooking score: 2
⊖ Richmond, map 1
Indian | £28
406 Richmond Road, Twickenham, TW1 2EB
Tel no: (020) 8891 3737
tangawizi.co.uk
£5   £30
OFF

'This was a real treat in an area I only visit occasionally,' enthused one visitor, who loved everything from the stylish contemporary décor to the 'competent cooking served by very efficient friendly staff'. Just across the bridge from Richmond, Tangawizi has been impressing locals for some 14 years, its positive spin on hardcore curry-house favourites interspersed with more ambitious specials of soft-shell crab coated in a light rice flour batter or cod cooked in a sauce with coconut and mustard seeds. Tangawizi's many regulars all have their favourite dishes: for some it's the chilli lamb kadhai and chicken chettinad, for others it's the vegetable curries. Most,

however, seem united in their addiction to the onion patties, the lamb chops marinated in traditional tandoori spices, the homemade chutneys and pickles, the wonderful naan bread – 'the best in London' – and the chocolate samosa for dessert. Wines from £15.95.
Chef/s: Surat Singh Rana. **Open:** all week D only 6 to 11 (10.30 Sun). **Closed:** 25 and 26 Dec, 1 Jan. **Meals:** main courses £7 to £16. Set D £28 to £33. **Details:** 60 seats. V menu. Music.

The Victoria
Cooking score: 4
⊖ Richmond, map 1
Modern British | £35
10 West Temple Sheen, East Sheen, SW14 7RT
Tel no: (020) 8876 4238
thevictoria.net

£5 OFF

'I really like this place – I've been for breakfast after dog walks, for drinks and for dinner. It's always reliable.' Readers rate this 'proper' neighbourhood pub with a 'chap pulling pints at the front'. Make your way to the conservatory at the back if you're after something more substantial than (very acceptable) bar snacks – there's something for everyone on the menu. Start with a hearty stout and onion soup with cheesy beer bread or seared mackerel with pickled cucumber and mustard seeds on a pool of horseradish buttermilk, and follow with excellent, well-aged steaks with thrice-cooked chips or roast hake with skordalia potato, monk's beard and smoked tomato. Ability in the kitchen, and presentation, will be great either way, and the only reminder that this is a pub at heart will be the slightly feisty service and a surprisingly affordable price/quality ratio. Though the management takes its wine list very seriously, house wine kicks off at a quaffable £5 a glass.
Chef/s: Charles Boyce. **Open:** Mon to Sat L 12 to 2.30 (11 to 3 Sat), D 6 to 10. 12 to 8 Sun. **Meals:** main courses £13 to £22. **Details:** 80 seats. 80 seats outside. Bar. Wheelchairs. Music. Parking.

★ CHEF TO WATCH ★
★ NEW ENTRY ★

The Woodford
Cooking score: 4
⊖ South Woodford
Modern European | £50
159 High Road, South Woodford, E18 2PA
Tel no: (020) 8504 5952
thewoodford-e18.com

'Having expected an undercurrent of Essex bling – I feel I can say this as an Essex girl – I was genuinely thrilled by the understated elegance and luxury of the Woodford.' So ran one reporter's notes of this handsomely renovated former nightclub, where the colour scheme is 'sleek greys and dark woods', there's 'carpet, real carpet', a glossy bar, upstairs Champagne bar, open kitchen, and a spacious dining room where curved banquettes carve out intimate spaces. It all plays host to Ben Murphy's innovative contemporary cooking. Everything points to impressive cooking skills, from warm breads via dainty canapés to petits fours. Excellent raw materials are cooked with precision timing, and the seasonal menus offer an intriguing array of dishes: a pretty assembly of white asparagus, pea sorbet, lime and shiso ('a perfect, light opening, refined and elegant'), ahead of monkfish served with a spoonful of banana purée, roasted shallots, miniature pickled onions adding a sharp acidic zing 'that worked wonderfully with the fish,' and red wine jus. Textures of chocolate, chocolate aero, milk sorbet and lavender is an indulgent finale. The set lunch is terrific value, delivering the likes of silky chicken liver parfait dusted with pain d'épices powder, pork with horseradish, lime and hazelnut, and lemon meringue pie with thyme and rosemary. Service is 'exceptional'. Wines from £28.
Chef/s: Ben Murphy. **Open:** Wed to Sun L 12 to 2.30 (4 Sun), Wed to Sat D 6 to 9.30. **Closed:** Mon, Tue. **Meals:** main courses £19 to £29. Set L £24 (2 courses) to £29. **Details:** 100 seats. Bar. Parking. Children over 12 yrs only (exc Sun).

ENGLAND

Bedfordshire, Berkshire, Buckinghamshire,
Cambridgeshire, Cheshire, Cornwall,
Cumbria, Derbyshire, Devon, Dorset,
Durham, Essex, Gloucestershire & Bristol,
Greater Manchester,
Hampshire (inc. Isle of Wight),
Herefordshire, Hertfordshire, Kent,
Lancashire, Leicestershire and Rutland,
Lincolnshire, Merseyside, Norfolk,
Northamptonshire, Northumberland,
Nottinghamshire, Oxfordshire, Shropshire,
Somerset, Staffordshire, Suffolk, Surrey,
Sussex – East, Sussex – West, Tyne & Wear,
Warwickshire, West Midlands, Wiltshire,
Worcestershire, Yorkshire

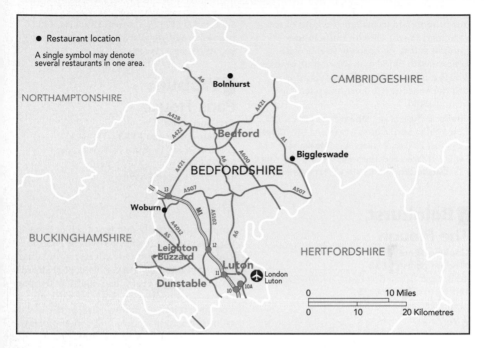

- Restaurant location

A single symbol may denote several restaurants in one area.

NORTHAMPTONSHIRE

CAMBRIDGESHIRE

Bolnhurst

Bedford

Biggleswade

BEDFORDSHIRE

Woburn

BUCKINGHAMSHIRE

Leighton Buzzard

HERTFORDSHIRE

Dunstable

Luton

London Luton

0   10 Miles

0   10   20 Kilometres

▌Bedford

Pavilion

British
Bedford Park, Park Avenue, Bedford,
MK41 7SS
Tel no: (01234) 351104
pavilion.attheparkbedford.co.uk
'Bedford Park has come alive! What was a sad,
unloved pavilion building is now a thriving
community hub serving delicious home-
cooked meals using ingredients sourced
locally and combined imaginatively.'

Readers recommend

A 'readers recommend' review is a
genuine quote from a report sent in by
one of our readers. We intend to follow
up these suggestions throughout the year
to come.

▌Biggleswade
The Croft Kitchen

Cooking score: 5
Modern British | £45
28 Palace Street, Biggleswade, SG18 8DP
Tel no: (01767) 601502
thecroftbiggleswade.com

Biggleswade was once a conurbation with zero
foodie clout – until Kieron and Michael
Singh opened the Croft Kitchen. Occupying a
pair of low-ceilinged cottages, this modest
enterprise is all laminate floors, black lanterns
and posters on white walls, swathes of white
linen and a central brick fireplace. It's
'unpretentious and intimate' and the cooking is
a blast – fiercely contemporary, full of
invention and seriously refined. Chef Michael
knows all about provenance and seasonal
sourcing, too – witness a plate of
Bedfordshire duck salami with heritage
beetroot, port and shallot dressing. Detailing
is sharp and the flavours sing, from a dressed-
up game pie with smoked mash, wild

mushrooms and Jerusalem artichoke or sous-vide charred salmon with fluffy lobster gnocchi and soused parsnip to chocolate nemesis with blood orange and pink praline. The bread is terrific, staff are well informed and the wine list is a short, sharp selection from £18.50.

Chef/s: Michael Singh. **Open:** Fri to Sun L 12 to 1.30, Wed to Sat D 6.30 to 8 (9 Fri and Sat). **Closed:** Mon, Tue, 26 Dec, 2 weeks Aug. **Meals:** set L £31. Set D £31 (Wed and Thur), £45 (Fri and Sat). Sun L £35. **Details:** 25 seats. Bar. Music. No children Sat D.

Bolnhurst
The Plough

Cooking score: 5
Modern British | £38
Kimbolton Road, Bolnhurst, MK44 2EX
Tel no: (01234) 376274
bolnhurst.com

🍾

The sort of place for which one should, as one reader put it, 'go somewhat further afield than usual', The Plough, situated in splendid rural isolation, is much more of a dining destination than country pub these days. There's plenty of charm in its 15th-century bones, with an abundance of beams, exposed stone and real fires, but there are brighter, more modern areas, too, and it feels firmly placed in the 21st century with its 'youthful' service and Martin Lee's robust and cultivated cooking. The menu is packed with British and broader European ideas, where flavour, seasonality and quality point the way. White onion soup keeps company with crispy hen's egg and a splash of truffle oil, and scallops get the ceviche treatment. Main-course roast monkfish has an Asian spin, or go for Aberdeenshire steaks cooked on the Josper grill, or fresh fish shipped up from Cornwall. Finish with pistachio soufflé or superb artisan cheeses. The wine list covers a lot of bases without overwhelming; bottles start at £16.95.

Chef/s: Martin Lee. **Open:** Tue to Sun L 12 to 2, Tue to Sat D 6.30 to 9 (9.30 Sat). **Closed:** Mon, 31 Dec, first 2 weeks Jan. **Meals:** main courses £16 to £25.

Set L and D £19 (2 courses) to £23. Sun L £22 (2 courses) to £28. **Details:** 30 seats. 80 seats outside. Bar. Wheelchairs. Parking.

Woburn
Paris House

Cooking score: 6
Modern European | £83
London Road, Woburn Park, Woburn, MK17 9QP
Tel no: (01525) 290692
parishouse.co.uk

£5
OFF

Shipped in carefully numbered pieces from a Paris Exposition in the Victorian era, the faux-Tudor timbered house was always more suited to the spreading acres of the Duke of Bedford's estate than it was to absinthe-marinated urban France. That's not to say that it hasn't acquired a certain raciness in our own day, with asymmetric light fixtures and contemporary sculptures adding style. Phil Fanning's cooking fires on all cylinders, with a choice of tasting menus from six to ten courses, all exquisitely presented and truly innovative. Tom yum with pork gyoza is one of many dishes sizzling with South-East Asian spice. Malt-baked crab and avocado comes in a bread roll, ahead of a fruity treatment of goose liver, with blood orange and grilled plum. Muscovy duck in red miso swings eastwards again, and mandarin saké trifle with black beans and coriander maintains momentum to the end. Wine flights suit the menus, starting at £16 for three small glasses, bottles from £28.

Chef/s: Phil Fanning. **Open:** Wed to Sun L 12 to 1.30 (2 Sun), Wed to Sat D 7 to 8.30. **Closed:** Mon, Tue, 23 Dec to 4 Jan. **Meals:** Tasting menu L £43 (6 courses), D £83 (6 courses) to £109 (10 courses). Sun L £63 (5 courses). **Details:** 32 seats. V menu. Bar. Music. Parking.

Average price

The average price denotes the price of a three-course meal without wine.

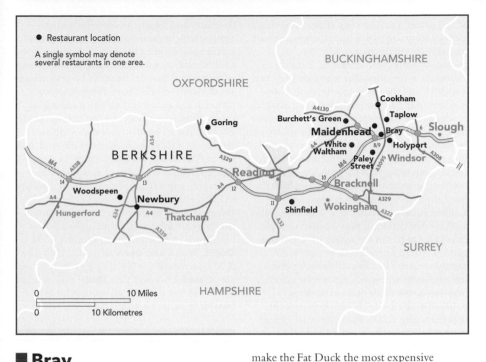

- Restaurant location

A single symbol may denote
several restaurants in one area.

BUCKINGHAMSHIRE

OXFORDSHIRE

Cookham

A4130

Taplow

Goring

Burchett's Green

Maidenhead

Bray

Slough

BERKSHIRE

A329

White
Waltham

8/9

Holyport

Paley
Street

Windsor

Reading

10

Bracknell

14

13

A4

12

Woodspeen

Newbury

11

Shinfield

Wokingham

A329

A322

A4

Hungerford

Thatcham

SURREY

0   10 Miles

0   10 Kilometres

HAMPSHIRE

▌Bray

★ TOP 10 ★

The Fat Duck

Cooking score: 9
Modern British | £255
1 High Street, Bray, SL6 2AQ
Tel no: (01628) 580333
thefatduck.co.uk

After a £2.5 million renovation (creating 'a completely blank canvas' or a 'shock in its ordinariness' according to your point of view) and a conceptual reboot, one of the world's most renowned restaurants is back with a new USP for the 21st century. Even at his most idiosyncratic and inventive, Heston Blumenthal has always been rooted in nostalgia and history, and he's now fiercely focused on how to enhance the dining experience by evoking emotions. The concept – this is not a restaurant but a day-trip to the seaside – is theatrical experimentation for which you buy a ticket on booking. At £255 a head, excluding drinks and service, this does

make the Fat Duck the most expensive restaurant in the UK, but puts it in line with other restaurants operating on a world stage: Eleven Madison Park, New York, $295; l'Arpège, Paris, €380; Fäviken, Sweden SEK 3,000. Crucially, the menu (or 'The Journey') has not ditched too many old favourites ('sounds of the sea' is as ravishing as ever), but is boosted by some stunning new dishes. 'Then we went rockpooling' is an incredible, multi-layered sensation served in a chunky model of a rock pool ('like a plastic volcano out of a children's board game') containing seaweed and an edible crab shell. When a herb, seaweed and bacon-infused mussel velouté is poured over, it causes the shell to melt and release crabmeat, smoked caviar and trout roe. Other revelations have been the 'extraordinary' 'variety pack' breakfast cereal, 'damping through the borough groves', a 'textually brilliant' truffle log layering mushroom, consommé jelly, truffle butter and shavings, beetroot, blackcurrant jelly and lovage purée (with dry ice pouring out of a glass vase containing a mystical little tree), and croquette of coq au vin, a perfect crisp cube containing a glossy, runny coq au vin (the chicken minced), served with a little chicken foot the consistency of a pork scratching. Botrytis chimera is as sensational as when we first tried it in 2014, and the sweeties still come at the end, now popping out of drawers in a magical, mechanical doll's house that is wheeled to your table. The mark of a great chef is his ability to assert his individuality both in each dish and throughout a menu. Mr Blumenthal's skill has always been to work at the frontiers of taste, innovating, experimenting, pushing back the horizons of our gastronomic experiences – and here he succeeds: his food is thrilling. But with modest drinking plus service, a couple can expect to pay in the region of £750 and cost is a crucial factor. At these prices, the experience must be extraordinary for every serious foodie who goes, and it seems that front-of-house is not quite as dazzlingly polished as the food. The day-trip concept requires acting ability but many staff appear uncomfortable with the script and can leave you dangling between courses, wondering what is going to happen next. A flamboyant master of ceremonies might help, as would a little kindness in prices on the otherwise treasure-filled wine list – there are more bottles over £1,000 than under £60.

Chef/s: Heston Blumenthal and Jonny Lake. **Open:** Tue to Sat L 12 to 1.45, D 7 to 8.45. **Closed:** Sun, Mon, 2 weeks Christmas. **Meals:** Tasting menu L and D £255. **Details:** 42 seats. Parking.

The Hinds Head
Cooking score: 5
British | £35
High Street, Bray, SL6 2AB
Tel no: (01628) 626151
hindsheadbray.com

Generous of spirit and appetite, this oak-panelled 15th-century hostelry plays Falstaff to the nearby Fat Duck's renegade Prince Hal, with Heston Blumenthal rather than the Bard of Avon calling the tune in both venues. The Hinds Head also keeps up appearances with its creaking floors, ancient timbers, brick

fireplaces and locally brewed ales on tap, although the aspirational menu and equally aspirational foodie crowd tell a different story. Old Albion's finest victuals and an assortment of reinvented flavours from cookbooks of yore are the scene-stealers here, from devils on horseback or oxtail and kidney pudding to more madcap experimental conceits out of the Blumenthal archives – say a crab 'soup and sandwich', a fish pie advertised with 'sand and sea' or fillet of duck with beetroot, barley and turnips. And if you want to sample HB's legendary triple-cooked chips, this is the place to do it. For pudding, consider a cherry Bakewell with yoghurt ice cream or channel that 'wassail' vibe with a caramelised butter loaf, apple and mead. Wines start at £17.50.

Chef/s: János Veres. **Open:** all week L 12 to 2.30 (3.30 Sun), Mon to Sat D 6.15 to 9.15 (9.30 Fri and Sat). **Closed:** 25 and 26 Dec. **Meals:** main courses £18 to £35. Set L £48 (4 courses). Sun L £26. **Details:** 90 seats. Bar. Music. Parking.

★ TOP 50 ★

The Waterside Inn
Cooking score: 7
French | £150
Ferry Road, Bray, SL6 2AT
Tel no: (01628) 620691
waterside-inn.co.uk

Bray is scarcely light on attraction these days, but perhaps has no finer sight than the Waterside jetty at dusk, when strategically placed lamps illumine the Thames, the boats chafe at their moorings and a pendulous willow shrouds the terrace tables. It's been in the charm game since 1972, when the upper echelon of French gastronomy was still a thing of rarity and wonder, and has lived long enough to see it, in the era of ubiquitous modern British, regain that status. Battalions of staff see to it that everybody is treated with solicitous respect, and Alain Roux continues papa Michel's decades-long mission to expound the glory of haute cuisine. Evolution brings new ideas through from time to time, not every five minutes, and certain long-serving dishes are still very much in the race. The quenelles of pike mousse with langoustines had one pair of veterans 'smiling with pleasure', as had the escalope of sauté foie gras on pain d'épices, served with quince compote, sauced in mulled wine. Occasional queries arise as to the overall balance of a dish, as when passion fruit marinade seems too shrill in an octopus and sea bass ceviche. A game duo might sign up for a game-duo main of partridge and venison in poivrade, and classic skills are on display in orange soufflé garnished with candied peel and wild lingonberries. Exploration of the flawlessly connoisseurial wine list, from £29, will rapidly lighten the bank balance.

Chef/s: Alain Roux. **Open:** Wed to Sun L 12 to 2 (2.30 Sun), D 7 to 10. **Closed:** Mon, Tue, 26 Dec to 1 Feb. **Meals:** main courses £52 to £60. Set L £50 (2 courses) to £62 (Mon to Fri) £70 (Sat). Sun L £80 (3 courses). Tasting menu £160 (6 courses). **Details:** 70 seats. Bar. Parking. Children over 9 yrs only.

LOCAL GEM
The Crown at Bray
British | £30
High Street, Bray, SL6 2AH
Tel no: (01628) 621936
thecrownatbray.com

The Crown may well be part of Heston Blumenthal's portfolio, but it is still very much a pub, with gnarled beams, real fires, well-kept ales at the pumps and a beer garden for when the weather is fine. The food is proper pub stuff, too, though the lunchtime egg mayo sandwich will be a duck version with truffle mayonnaise. Elsewhere, fish and chips stands alongside confit duck leg on a menu that aims to satisfy. Wines start at £20.

■ Burchett's Green
The Crown
Cooking score: 5
French | £28
Burchett's Green, SL6 6QZ
Tel no: (01628) 824079
thecrownburchettsgreen.com
£30

In a world where so many restaurants try to mix exotic ingredients and follow the latest fads, it is comforting to find one with an enduringly common-sense approach. This early 19th-century country pub is a tiny, no-frills operation with much of the appeal lying in Simon Bonwick's simple and straightforward cooking. His orientation is classic French, his food based on unimpeachable standards and high-quality ingredients: perhaps an earthenware dish of 'pink beyond pink' pork liver pâté with a wobbly jelly of dark stock dotted with Puy lentils, or a bowl of gigante beans on a luxuriously earthy sauce of truffle and butter, topped with two lightly poached slabs of foie gras and a ball of spinach. Mr Bonwick has also turned out a spanking-fresh sea bass fillet on a tomatoey cassoulet of just-tender haricots, containing chunks of morteau sausage and bacon, and delivered 'a very special rum baba' topped with autumn berries and accompanied by a giant jar of Rumtopf to be spooned over the top ('as if the whole thing wasn't boozy enough already'). His son Dean (ex Waterside Inn, see entry) runs front-of-house, and has made 'the wine, style and service very much his own'. Bottles from £18.50.

Chef/s: Simon Bonwick. **Open:** Sun L from 12.30, Tue to Sat D from 6.30. **Closed:** Mon, Tue, 25 Dec to 2 Jan, first 2 weeks Aug. **Meals:** main courses £13 to £19. **Details:** 28 seats. 32 seats outside. Bar. Wheelchairs. Parking. No children.

█ Cookham
The White Oak

Cooking score: 3
British | £35
The Pound, Cookham, SL6 9QE
Tel no: (01628) 523043
thewhiteoak.co.uk
£5 OFF

'They've achieved that balance of creating a restaurant but retaining a pubby vibe,' noted a visitor to this handsome pub on the outskirts of Cookham. Lots of thought (and money) has gone into the décor, a clever mix of light wood and brown leather, natural colours and comforting simplicity. Adam Hague is responsible for the day-to-day running of the kitchen, and he goes about his work with flair and dexterity, whether serving an 'elegantly presented' and 'really fresh' Cornish crab salad with radish, pickled cucumber, sorrel and caper berries, or a 'textural treat' of charred cauliflower cheese with Granny Smith apple, Parmesan sauce ('really good depth') and garlic crumb. You might also choose roast Hampshire lamb with wild garlic, Jerusalem artichoke purée and salsify, or sirloin on the bone with triple-cooked chips. The bar menu flies the flag for updated pub classics (cider-battered fish goujons with curry mayonnaise), the set lunch is very good value and wines start at £17.

Chef/s: Adam Hague. **Open:** all week L 12 to 2.30 (5 Sun), Mon to Sat D 6 to 9.30. **Meals:** main courses £14 to £26. Set L £12 (2 courses) to £15. Set D £15 (2 courses) to £19. **Details:** 72 seats. 30 seats outside. Bar. Wheelchairs. Music. Parking.

█ Goring
The Miller of Mansfield

Cooking score: 4
British | £35
High Street, Goring, RG8 9AW
Tel no: (01491) 872829
millerofmansfield.com
£5 OFF 🛏

A recent recruit to the Miller's fan club sees the place 'as more of a modern inn than a straight-up pub or dining pub', while another concluded 'it felt like home'. Mary and Nick Galer's lovingly run 18th-century coaching inn has quickly established a loyal local following since they took over in 2014. Don't be put off by the stripped-back décor (it's a work in progress), because there's serious business going on in the kitchen. Nick excels at no-holds-barred seasonal cooking; indeed, his dishes can change daily depending on available produce and his menu is ambitious yet deceptively simple. An ingenious starter of whipped Baron Bigod cheese with quince jam, tomato relish, candied hazelnuts and treacle toast delighted one reporter, while others have praised whole roasted local partridge served with bacon and shallot potato cake, Brussels tops, Jerusalem artichoke and partridge sauce. Roasted pineapple with rum sponge, coconut sorbet and lime is typical of the noteworthy desserts. Wines from £15.

Chef/s: Nick Galer. **Open:** all week L 12.30 to 2.30 (3.30 Sun), D 6.30 to 9 (8 Sun). **Meals:** main courses £14 to £30. Set L £16 (2 courses) to £20. Set D £21 (2 courses) to £35. Sun L £26 (2 courses) to £31. **Details:** 80 seats. 60 seats outside. Bar. Music.

Nick Galer

The Miller of Mansfield, Goring

What inspired you to become a chef?
A desire to work ski seasons; it was either bar work or kitchens.

What food could you not live without?
I really love cheese, all types. My absolute favourites are Époisses and good old strong Cheddar.

At the end of a long day, what do you like to cook?
If I'm at home for an evening we will eat fairly healthily, some kind of salad, with a little cheese.

Who is the most interesting person you have cooked for?
Prince William and the Duchess of Cambridge, just before they were engaged to be married.

And finally...tell us something about yourself that will surprise your diners.
Up until the age of 20, I spent 16-20 hours a week training for swimming. It shaped me and I still maintain the friendships I made during those times.

What is the vital ingredient for a successful kitchen?
Leadership, team work and togetherness.

Holyport
The Belgian Arms

Cooking score: 3
Modern British | £30
Holyport, SL6 2JR
Tel no: (01628) 634468
thebelgianarms.com
£5 OFF

Nick Parkinson has already proved his worth as an innkeeper with the Royal Oak, Paley Street (see entry) and he's applying the same sure touch to this sibling venue – a 200-year-old Berkshire pub in a dreamy spot complete with a beer garden backing on to the village green and duck pond. Inside, the Belgian Arms has been smartly revamped, although the mood is still comfortably relaxed and the menu is full of little surprises – salt cod and crab cakes with rhubarb chutney, for example. Elsewhere, a dish of cider-cured gammon with peppered pineapple, celeriac chips and pea and honey purée is a savvy reimagining of a 1970s pub classic, while spiced beef pie with caramelised Brussels sprouts is hearty sustenance of the best sort. For afters, consider the treacle and rhubarb tart with stem ginger ice cream. Ales are from Brakspear and there are some very decent wines from £19.
Chef/s: Graham Kirk. **Open:** Tue to Sun L 12 to 2.30 (4 Sun), Tue to Sat D 6.30 to 9.30 (6 to 10 Fri and Sat). **Closed:** Mon. **Meals:** main courses £15 to £24. **Details:** 60 seats. 40 seats outside. Bar. Music. Parking.

Maidenhead
Boulters Riverside Brasserie

Cooking score: 2
Modern British | £35
Boulters Lock Island, Maidenhead, SL6 8PE
Tel no: (01628) 621291
boultersrestaurant.co.uk
£5 OFF

Whether you're out on the expansive terrace, loafing on a sofa in the bar or enjoying some capably rendered food in the Riverside Brasserie, you can watch the world cruise by from this superbly appointed venue. Marooned on its island perch, with terrific views of the rolling Thames from fully glazed floor-to-ceiling windows, Boulters is naturally at its best in high summer – although the kitchen delivers whatever the time of year. Fresh seasonal ingredients are deployed in imaginative ways, from ballotine of English lamb shoulder with pistachio-coated quince and cumin tuile to liquorice-glazed pork tenderloin or hazelnut-crusted hake fillet with creamed leeks and oxtail croustade. There are steaks and burgers for the diehards, while desserts could feature raspberry crumble soufflé with lemon curd ice cream. Prompt yet relaxed service suits the buzzy vibe, and there are some decent wines by the glass on the affordable list; bottles start at £15.95.

Chef/s: Daniel Woodhouse. **Open:** Sun L 12 to 3.30, Mon to Sat 12 to 9.30. **Closed:** 27 to 30 Dec. **Meals:** main courses £13 to £24. Set L £16 (2 courses) to £20. Sun L £22 (2 courses) to £27. **Details:** 80 seats. Bar. Music. Parking.

▌Newbury

Brebis

Cooking score: 2
French | £32
16 Bartholomew Street, Newbury, RG14 5LL
Tel no: (01635) 40527
brebis.co.uk

£5
OFF

'Brebis' is French for 'ewe' – a reminder of this restaurant's Gallic outlook, but also (perhaps) a nod to the owners' Oxfordshire farm, where they rear lamb and hogget for the table. If that conjures up a picture of clod-hopping rusticity, think again: the dining room is a spare, modern space with wooden floors, dangling metal lampshades, big windows and various chalked-up blackboards, while the kitchen gives bistro cooking a distinctive contemporary spin. Chef-proprietor Samuel Mansfield has a sure touch and an eye for the trends, serving aigo boulido (Provençal garlic soup) with a 63°C poached Cacklebean egg, offsetting rabbit terrine with black radish, and

partnering home-cured salmon with salt-baked beetroot. The aforementioned lamb (from Malherbe Farm) might appear with cauliflower couscous, fennel and pistachio, while desserts could feature crème caramel with grapefruit sorbet. Matching French wines are served by the glass, with bottles from £18.50; regular 'wine dinners' are worth noting, too.

Chef/s: Samuel Mansfield. **Open:** Wed to Sat L 12.30 to 2.30, D 6.30 to 9. **Closed:** Sun, Mon, Tue, 25 Dec to 1 Jan, last 2 weeks Aug. **Meals:** main courses £17 to £20. Set L £20 (2 courses) to £23. **Details:** 30 seats. Wheelchairs. Music.

The Vineyard

Cooking score: 4
Modern French | £65
Stockcross, Newbury, RG20 8JU
Tel no: (01635) 528770
the-vineyard.co.uk

🍷 🛏

The almost concealed entrance off the road to Stockcross, just outside Newbury, leads to Sir Peter Michael's California-style ranch hotel, a Berkshire Shangri-La of contemporary artworks, aspirational dining and gargantuan wine cellar. Heading up the kitchen since the start of 2016 is Robby Jenks, who has set out to maintain the restaurant's reputation for cutting-edge avant-garderie. Breads are excellent and plentiful, a huge range that keeps on coming, and certain dishes hit the mark. A piece of seared foie gras with hazelnut biscuit crumb, semi-dried grapes and raisin purée is a clever combination, and the floret of butter-braised cauliflower sopping in brown juices, together with rainbow-striped cauliflower couscous, were the perfectly judged accompaniments to a tranche of over-salted cod. The spirits sink when a small cut of over-brined pork fillet appears with star billing on the tasting menu, but rise again to greet a square of dense chocolate mousse cake with gooey caramel and fromage-blanc sorbet. It's to be hoped that Jenks hits his stride because the wines, from around £29, are worth the journey alone. A pricey but brilliant

sommelier's selection comes with the option of a blind serving so you can try out your tasting abilities, and the legions of mature California wines, many of them from Sir Peter's own vineyard, are unrivalled in the UK. There are no fewer than 100 by the glass, starting at £5 for an Essex Pinot Gris.
Chef/s: Robby Jenks. **Open:** all week L 12 to 2, D 7 to 9. **Meals:** set L £29. Set D £65 (3 courses). Tasting menus £75 (5 courses) to £99. Sun L £39. **Details:** 90 seats. 60 seats outside. Bar. Wheelchairs. Music. Parking.

Paley Street
The Royal Oak
Cooking score: 4
Modern British | £35
Littlefield Green, Paley Street, SL6 3JN
Tel no: (01628) 620541
theroyaloakpaleystreet.com
£5 OFF 🍾

Nick Parkinson's smart whitewashed village pub not far from Maidenhead is very much in the modern idiom, with an interior mix of contemporary furnishings against exposed beams and brickwork, its walls hung with a heterogeneous collection of British and Australian artworks. A further changing of the kitchen guard saw former sous-chef James Bennett step up to the plate at the end of 2015, but the menus retain their stylishly rustic appeal. Roast quail with braised endive and toasted hazelnut and pear salad is a generous, refreshingly straightforward opener, the prelude perhaps to rump and shoulder of lamb with boulangère potato and kale, or a small fillet of turbot on broad beans and peas in a boilerplate cream sauce. At inspection, Ibérico pork chop was mistimed and overloaded by its herb blanket, but the signature Snickers dessert – chocolate mousse, peanut ice cream and salt caramel on a brownie base – still rocked our world. The wine list is full of intelligent choices, confident in both hemispheres, and with a broad selection in three glass measures and the half-litre carafe. Bottles start at £19.50 for Languedoc Chardonnay and Merlot.

Chef/s: James Bennett. **Open:** all week L 12 to 3 (4 Sun), Mon to Sat D 6 to 10 (12 Fri and Sat). **Closed:** 26 Dec. **Meals:** main courses £18 to £29. Set L £25 (2 courses) to £30. **Details:** 80 seats. Bar. Music. Parking.

Shinfield
L'Ortolan
Cooking score: 5
Modern French | £65
Church Lane, Shinfield, RG2 9BY
Tel no: (0118) 9888500
lortolan.com
£5 OFF 🍾

Set in pastoral surroundings a little outside Reading, the Ortolan has been fortunate in the cavalcade of frontline chefs it has played host to over the years, Tom Clarke stepping up in 2014 to maintain the heritage. Highly polished modern French cuisine is what to expect, with all the little extras fitted in, served throughout a trio of refined dining rooms. A top-value *menu du jour* leads the charge, while the carte and taster deal in the likes of celeriac textures with truffled trompettes in ravioli, stone bass with braised chicory and monk's beard in red wine jus, or the lamb study that offers the loin and sweetbreads in a richly meaty jus with Jerusalem artichoke and fermented barley. Cheeses from the trolley come with raisin bread, or look to buttermilk pannacotta with poached rhubarb, gingerbread purée and rosemary ice cream. A procession of wonderful wines by the glass, from £7, opens a thrilling French-led list that also includes Cornelissen's Mount Etna Sicilians and pedigree South Americans. Bottles start at £29.

Chef/s: Tom Clarke. **Open:** Tue to Sat L 12 to 2, D 7 to 9 (9.30 Fri and Sat). **Closed:** Sun, Mon, 24 Dec to 3 Jan. **Meals:** set L £28 (2 courses) to £32. Set D £58 (2 courses) to £65. Tasting menu £75 (7 courses). **Details:** 58 seats. V menu. Bar. Wheelchairs. Music. Parking. Children over 3 yrs only.

Taplow

★ TOP 50 ★

André Garrett at Cliveden

Cooking score: 8
Modern European | £73
Cliveden House, Taplow, SL6 0JF
Tel no: (01628) 607100
clivedenhouse.co.uk

£5 OFF ♦ 🍴 🛏

Just to resolve the odd outbreak of dissension among readers, although Taplow is in Bucks, nearby Cliveden itself is just over the border in Berkshire. Whatever, it's an indubitably grand 17th-century pile, built by the second Duke of Buckingham in the year London went up in flames, surrounded by a galumphing 376 acres of National Trust gardens, and famous over the past century for hosting some of the more salacious society goings-on and some absolutely cracking cooking. The last, overseen by the titular presence since 2013, represents an extension of high-class French tradition into the era of British modernism. Ingredients are combined in stimulating and adventurous ways in an opening crab salad that offers shredded white and moussed brown meat with avocado, espelette pepper, chickweed and delicate lemon purée. At main, the fallow deer will have been locally stalked for you, offset with pear and sauced with bitter chocolate. At a meal in June, grilled Wye Valley asparagus was served with a soft-boiled pheasant's egg, seaweed butter and some grains for texture, while roast fillet of hake, 'with a delicious savoury jus', was accompanied by a 'salad' of Jersey Royals, octopus and piquillo pepper. Manjari chocolate tart 'was a perfect example of its kind with a very surprising and successful sweet pea-and-mint ice cream'. A five-strong wine team oversees a list of huge reach, the authoritative choices extending all the way to lush Pinots from New Zealand's South Island, via super-Tuscans, a phalanx of ten Chablis and the pick of the English Home Counties. Be prepared though: prices only get going from £35.

Chef/s: André Garrett. **Open:** all week L 12.15 to 2.30, D 6.30 to 9.45. **Meals:** set L £33 (3 courses). Set D £73 (3 courses). Sun L £60. Tasting menu £98. **Details:** 64 seats. V menu. Bar. Wheelchairs. Parking.

★ NEW ENTRY ★

The Astor Grill

Cooking score: 4
British/American | £40
Cliveden House, Taplow, SL6 0JF
Tel no: (01628) 668561
clivedenhouse.co.uk

🛏

André Garrett's 'second' restaurant at Cliveden neatly fills the gap between the estate's National Trust café and a jacket-and-tie dinner at Garrett's celebrated fine-dining restaurant. The Astor Grill takes its name from the American Waldorf-Astor family who lived at Cliveden from the end of the 19th to the middle of the 20th century, and early indications suggest that this snug, smart-casual, all-day eatery with its fun equestrian theme (it's housed in the old stables) and well-appointed, sheltered terrace will work both as a local favourite and a tourist treat. The menu is broad and appealing, encompassing American classics of Maryland crab-cakes, a giant burger, and an excellent, 'crisp and well-balanced' Waldorf salad. More current fashions are reflected by sea-bass ceviche with fennel, melon and coriander, and burrata with a variety of 'superb' tomatoes and fennel pollen. Elsewhere, roast poussin is given heft by an intense jus and punchy cauliflower cheese, while lemon thyme enlivens the custard that accompanies a raspberry jam soufflé. The wine list, from £30, includes many options by the glass.
Chef/s: André Garrett. **Open:** all week 12 to 10. **Meals:** main courses £12 to £33. **Details:** 45 seats. 36 seats outside. Wheelchairs. Music. Parking.

▌White Waltham
The Beehive

Cooking score: 5
British | £28
Waltham Road, White Waltham, SL6 3SH
Tel no: (01628) 822877
thebeehivewhitewaltham.com
£5 OFF £30 OFF

This village hostelry overlooking the cricket pitch has strong pubby virtues, real ales and a feel for good food. That it seems to be everyone's vision of the perfect pub is a tribute to the dedication and professionalism of chef-proprietor Dominic Chapman, who cooks with a big heart and big flavours. His menu is peppered with ideas that attempt to please all palates – a policy that seems to work well as crowds of regulars keep the mood buoyant. But alongside the ribeye steak and chips, the fried Cornish haddock with mushy peas and tartare sauce, and irresistible pies (perhaps chicken, ham and mushroom with exemplary mashed potato), you'll find a superb lasagne of wild rabbit with wood blewits and chervil, lemon sole with brown shrimps, cucumber, dill and lemon butter and seasonal treats such as pot-roast Berkshire pheasant or a 'truly memorable' peppered haunch of Denham Estate venison with creamed spinach and a 'magnificent' sauce poivrade. Desserts play with a straight bat, perhaps treacle tart or a well-made sticky toffee pudding. Wines from £16.95.

Chef/s: Dominic Chapman. **Open:** all week L 12 to 2.30 (3 Sat), Mon to Sat D 6 to 9.30 (10 Sat). **Closed:** 25 and 26 Dec. **Meals:** main courses £15 to £24. **Details:** 70 seats. 40 seats outside. Bar. Wheelchairs. Music. Parking.

▌Woodspeen
The Woodspeen

Cooking score: 6
British | £42
Lambourn Road, Woodspeen, RG20 8BN
Tel no: (01635) 265070
thewoodspeen.com
£5 OFF

Clearly the Woodspeen is the kind of approachable eatery you can make friends with. It's a bright, impressive space with an open kitchen and big windows offering views of the Berkshire countryside, but it all plays second fiddle to John Campbell's highly assured, 21st-century food. Knowledgeably sourced produce is the jumping-off point for forthright seasonal dishes and reporters are voluble in their praise, the details of dishes lingering passionately in the memory. For one couple, it was a raviolo tightly packed with crab and served atop a silky-smooth crab mayonnaise with charred leeks and beetroot tartare, hand-dived scallops and deliciously crispy chicken, which arrived with pickled onion, bacon and a 'deeply flavoured and sticky' red wine sauce, and a sharing plate of lobster 'fish and chips' (lobster and cod raviolo, pieces of lobster in a tempura batter, mushy peas 'bursting with flavour' and a cup of lobster bisque – 'a really fun main'). The 'cooked to absolute perfection' beef fillet and fritter served with rosemary and garlic potato terrine, roasted shallot and cavolo nero also receives rave reviews, as does the warm cinnamon brioche with pear and Muscatel ice cream; there are thoroughbred British cheeses, too. Just add a classy, modern and democratic wine list, with prices from £19.

Chef/s: John Campbell. **Open:** Tue to Sun L 12 to 2.30 (3 Sat, 4 Sun), Tue to Sat D 6.30 to 9.30. **Closed:** Mon, 26 Dec. **Meals:** main courses £17 to £34. Set L £19 (2 courses) to £25. **Details:** 66 seats. 32 seats outside. Bar. Wheelchairs. Music. Parking.

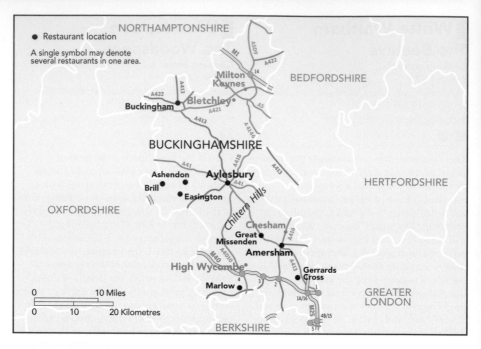

Amersham

Artichoke

Cooking score: 7
Modern British | £48
9 Market Square, Amersham, HP7 0DF
Tel no: (01494) 726611
artichokerestaurant.co.uk

A beamed Tudor building that has been
shoehorned into the modern age (and is to be
given another decorative upgrade before too
long, we learn), the Gears' characterful
neighbourhood restaurant has been amazing
Amersham since 2002. Laurie Gear's *stage* in
vanguard Scandinavian cuisine reinspired his
and Ben Jenkins' approach here, which mixes
forthright innovation and deceptive simplicity to constructive effect. Lunch dishes have
an almost traditional air, when proceedings
might open with parsley root risotto outlined
in oxtail and red wine jus, or foie gras – roast

and pâté – in a dressing of curried raisins.
Things take wing for the evening carte, where
stone bass with flawless crab gnocchi, fennel
and courgette in basil sauce might be followed
by Chilterns partridge with charred pear on a
bed of kale, alongside puréed parsnip and
chestnuts. A pre-dessert of goats' milk mousse
and sorrel fragrantly heralds sweet treats such
as raspberry bavarois with lemon jelly,
yoghurt curd, whey meringue and basil
sorbet, or count the 15 minutes to the arrival of
a mandarin and rice pudding soufflé with
Brazil nut crumble and chocolate sorbet.
Wines by the glass (from £7) head up a
capacious list that displays obvious brio in the
classic French and Italian regions, but also
finds inspiring shorter choices in the southern
hemisphere. Bottles start at £29.

Chef/s: Laurie Gear and Ben Jenkins. **Open:** Tue to
Sat L 12 to 2 (1.45 Sat), D 6.30 to 10 (6 Fri and Sat).
Closed: Sun, Mon, 2 weeks Christmas, 1 week
Easter, 2 weeks Aug/Sept. **Meals:** main courses £23
to £25. Set L £28 (3 courses). Set D £43 (2 courses)
to £48. Tasting menu L £38 (5 courses), D £68 (7
courses). **Details:** 48 seats. 2 seats outside. Music.

Gilbey's

Modern British | £38
1 Market Square, Amersham, HP7 0DF
Tel no: (01494) 727242
gilbeygroup.com

'Lots of birthdays, locals and sets of couples dining out,' enthused one reporter, who enjoyed eating at this former 17th-century schoolhouse on the high street. Indeed, regulars hail Gilbey's as a local 'standout' that 'delivers every time'. Colourful artwork fills the beamed interior, tables are crammed in, and the kitchen deals in 'inventive' modern British cooking, say gin-cured salmon with tonic gel, pickled lemon and dill emulsion, and chicken with shiitake mushrooms, fennel and bacon croquette. Service is friendly and assured. A 'fantastic' wine list opens at £13.50.

Ashendon

★ NEW ENTRY ★

The Hundred

Cooking score: 4
British | £27
Lower End, Ashendon, HP18 0HE
Tel no: (01296) 651296
thehundred.co.uk
£5
OFF £30

A distinctly cool, contemporary feel, (think artfully distressed interior, mismatched furniture and artwork) gives a sense that something special is in store at this ancient village boozer. Matthew Gill (ex St John, Hand & Flowers – see entries) has a passion for local, seasonal food and his brief, understated menu reveals great attention to detail with 'everything so beautifully thought through'. Take a dish such as a 'salad' of salt skate, chunks of bouncy bread and green sauce – a superlative mix of ingredients and flavour. Or a slightly sweet, smoky, glossy skirt steak served with a pile of peerless matchstick fries and accompanied by a tangle of watercress with capers, a handful of charred shallots and a mustardy vinaigrette. Hits, too, at a test meal

were a slice of pressed potato, onion and Berkswell cheese, and an accomplished apple crumble and custard. A selection of wines by the glass are from £6; by the bottle from £20.
Chef/s: Matthew Gill. **Open:** Tue to Sun L 12 to 2.45 (3 Sun), Tue to Sat D 6.45 to 9. **Closed:** Mon, 1 week Jan. **Meals:** main courses £13 to £18. **Details:** 40 seats. 20 seats outside. Bar. Music. Parking.

Aylesbury

Hartwell House

Cooking score: 2
Modern British | £36
Oxford Road, Aylesbury, HP17 8NR
Tel no: (01296) 747444
hartwell-house.com
£5
OFF

This historic home (now a hotel/spa) was built in the 17th century and has its own intrinsic splendour – 'one of our favourite venues for its stately country-house setting and interior' – and is approached via 90 acres of parkland. Traditional country-house elegance is the prevailing style, from canapés and cocktails in one of the drawing rooms to a meal in the light, attractive dining room. Daniel Richardson still heads the kitchen, relying on first-class materials to underpin the operation. He offers an attractive range of dishes from set-price menus, and his approach is uniformly straightforward. A well-reported winter lunch took in terrine of poached ham hock with piccalilli and grilled sourdough bread, then braised ox cheek with cauliflower croquettes, glazed carrots and braising juices, with caramelised puff pastry filled with Hartwell Orchard five apple flavours to finish. Service may be old-fashioned but it is done well. Wines from £29.75.
Chef/s: Daniel Richardson. **Open:** all week L 12.30 to 1.45, D 7.30 to 9.30. **Meals:** Set L £25 (2 courses) to £32. Set D £29 (2 courses) to £62. Sun L £36 (3 courses). **Details:** 90 seats. Bar. Wheelchairs. Parking. Children over 6 yrs only.

Brill

The Pointer

Cooking score: 4
Modern British | £35
27 Church Street, Brill, HP18 9RT
Tel no: (01844) 238339
thepointerbrill.co.uk
£5
OFF

Readers are effusive in their praise for a local farming family's sympathetic revival of this heart-of-the-village pub, including a 'brick-by-brick' rebuild of the neighbouring butcher's shop, and a nascent Saturday farmer's market. Inside, it's simply but tastefully done, with furs slung over chairs 'ready for winters curled up by the fire', contemporary paintings of animals and a tranquil garden out back. A modern British menu with the emphasis very firmly on local and homegrown means serious quality and freshness throughout, from the 'amazing' rosemary and herb bread spread with Marmitey homemade beef dripping to starters such as a salad of soft roe-deer tartare with Douglas fir oil, kohlrabi, pumpkin seeds and pickled mushroom demonstrating mastery of both texture and taste. Elsewhere, loch-reared sea trout with brown shrimps arrives with bright heritage tomatoes and the freshest leaves, with samphire a welcome addition, while a splendid dessert of über-rich dark chocolate bar is cut with sharp passion fruit sauce. Wines from £17.
Chef/s: Mini Patel. **Open:** Tue to Sun L 12 to 2.30 (3 Sun), D 6.30 to 9 (10 Fri and Sat). **Closed:** Mon, first week Jan. **Meals:** main courses £16 to £30. Set L £18 (2 courses) to £23. **Details:** 60 seats. 40 seats outside. Bar. Music. Parking.

Symbols

- 🛏 Accommodation is available
- £30 Three courses for less than £30
- £5 OFF £5-off voucher scheme
- 🍷 Notable wine list

Buckingham

LOCAL GEM

Nelson Street Restaurant

Modern British | £29
53-54 Nelson Street, Buckingham, MK18 1BT
Tel no: (01280) 815556
nelsonstreetrestaurant.co.uk
£5 OFF £30

This affable neighbourhood eatery has earned itself a solid local reputation, its easy-going flexibility a godsend for the area. Bespoke burgers and 'different' fish and chips are fixtures, but the kitchen's lively global repertoire runs all the way from warm squid and chorizo salad or smoked haddock omelette to devilled calf's liver and bacon, jerk chicken or Moroccan lamb with Puy lentil salsa. 'Tidbits' kick things off, while puds might include salted-caramel and chocolate brownie. House wine is £16.

Easington

The Mole & Chicken

Cooking score: 2
Modern British | £35
Easington Terrace, Easington, HP18 9EY
Tel no: (01844) 208387
themoleandchicken.co.uk
🛏

This attractive ivy-and-wood-clad country pub-cum-restaurant-with-rooms offers an idyllic view from the terrace, while inside it's a classic 'mind your head' wooden-beamed affair, with winter wood-burners and warm colours. Reporters have praised a menu of more inherent complexity than the classic pub appearance suggests, from the delicate sweet-spicy balance of deep-fried squid with butternut, aïoli, rocket, lime and chilli, to the simple crunch of Wye Valley asparagus served with a perfectly poached Arlington White egg. Elsewhere, onion pickled in red wine adds piquancy to just yielding braised beef short rib (served with crispy batons of truffle Parmesan chips, celeriac purée and watercress) while thinly sliced fennel adds a welcome

Join us at thegoodfoodguide.co.uk

texture to luxurious fresh asparagus ravioli with Berkswell cheese and dill cream. For dessert, there could be blood-red gariguette strawberries with 'just gooey' meringue. Wines from £18.

Chef/s: Steve Bush. **Open:** all week L 12 to 2.30 (4 Sun), D 6.30 to 9.30 (6 to 9 Sun). **Closed:** 25 Dec. **Meals:** main courses £14 to £28. **Details:** 62 seats. 60 seats outside. Bar. Wheelchairs. Music. Parking.

▌ Gerrards Cross

★ NEW ENTRY ★

The Three Oaks

Cooking score: 4
Modern British | £28
Austenwood Lane, Gerrards Cross, SL9 8NL
Tel no: (01753) 899016
thethreeoaksgx.co.uk

£30

Chef Mikey Seferynski's CV takes in the Fat Duck, the Grove and the Hand & Flowers, and after a near-miss on winning the Polish equivalent of MasterChef, he's back – to Gerrards Cross's gain. His dedicated, focused approach to food sits well in the updated pub surroundings – 'comfortable not stuffy', with tasteful tartan décor, an original brick fireplace and a pub garden that's perfect for when the sun shines. At a test meal, Cornish crab on toast came canapé-style on crostini, with a quiver of English asparagus arrows and the richness of lemon salad cream offset by the tang of pickled cucumber. Suckling pig belly was crunchy on the outside with the softest of meat and accompanied by heritage carrot, a loose-leaf assembly of wafer potato and crisp-fried morsels of black pudding, the whole dish sweetened by chorizo and apple jam. A dessert of milk chocolate crémeux, with peanut caramel and salted-caramel ice cream was pure candy shop meltdown – a sweet tooth's dream. Wines from £17.

Chef/s: Mikey Seferynski. **Open:** all week L 12 to 2.30 (5.30 Sun), Mon to Sat D 6.30 to 9.30. **Meals:** main courses £13 to £25. Set L 12 (2 courses) to £15. Set D £15 (2 courses) to £19. **Details:** 80 seats. 50 seats outside. Bar. Wheelchairs. Music. Parking.

▌ Great Missenden

La Petite Auberge

Cooking score: 2
French | £38
107 High Street, Great Missenden, HP16 0BB
Tel no: (01494) 865370
lapetiteauberge.co.uk

£5 OFF

A little corner of Buckinghamshire that is for ever France, the Martels' paragon of Gallic virtues has been conversing amicably in its native tongue for almost three decades, pleasing the burghers of Great Missenden and beyond with its unabashed take on *cuisine domestique*. This 'petite auberge' lives up to its billing, matching a warm, chatty conversational mood with precise, generous cooking that hits all the right accents. Here you can revel in a bowl of soupe de poissons or nibble on a salad of smoked duck breast with French dressing, before tackling medallions of monkfish with vibrant saffron sauce, rack of lamb with rosemary, or breast of guinea fowl and mushrooms sauced with Madeira. Main dishes generally arrive with 'légumes du marché', while desserts are a classic run from mousse au chocolat to chaud-froid de pomme glacé cannelle (hot apple with cinnamon ice cream). Wines (French, of course) start at £24.80.

Chef/s: Hubert Martel. **Open:** Mon to Sat D only 7 to 10. **Closed:** Sun (exc Mothering Sun), 2 weeks Christmas, 2 weeks Easter, bank hols. **Meals:** main courses £18 to £23. **Details:** 30 seats. Wheelchairs.

▌Marlow
The Coach

Cooking score: 5
Modern British | £30
3 West Street, Marlow, SL7 2LS
thecoachmarlow.co.uk

If you've had no luck bagging a table at the Hand & Flowers (see entry, opposite), head to this gleaming, modernised black-and-white pub nearby to taste Tom Kerridge's delicious, refined but simple cooking. Mind you, it's popular and they don't take bookings. Here's a tip from one who went for lunch: 'to eat at a table, get there 20 minutes before they start taking food orders on the dot of midday. Otherwise you're eating at the bar, and from about 12.15 onwards you'll have to come back later.' The menu offers up small plates – like a DIY tasting menu – and the bill can escalate, but this is 'as good as casual eating gets': classic pub-bistro food along the lines of a very good fish fritter – whiting in a flavoursome crisp batter with smooth yellow pea purée and tartare sauce – a little lamb shank and goats' cheese 'demi pie' with a separate jug of sauce on the side, and a burger topped with smoky, pulled brisket and mozzarella, served with 'fantastic, thick, very crunchy' chips, béarnaise on the side, and as far from a standard pub offering as you can get. Hot chocolate tart with hazelnut ice cream, and banana custard with date and honeycomb have been standout desserts. Staff really make you feel valued and engaged. Drink real ales, bottled beers or well-chosen wines starting at £22.
Chef/s: Nick Beardshaw. **Open:** all week L 12 to 2.30 (3 Sat and Sun), D 6 to 10.30 (9 Sun). **Closed:** 25 Dec. **Meals:** main courses £5 to £15. **Details:** 45 seats. Music.

The Hand & Flowers

Cooking score: 5
Modern British | £56
126 West Street, Marlow, SL7 2BP
Tel no: (01628) 482277
thehandandflowers.co.uk

🛏

It may have come to readers' attention that Tom Kerridge has spent a fair bit of time on the telly over the past year or so, so it's no surprise that it's not easy to secure a booking at the Hand & Flowers. Those who make it will find a pretty roadside pub with a modern bar extension, pitched roof, ceiling-beams, leather chairs and banquettes, alcoves, bare brick and open fires. The atmosphere is lively, pleasingly informal even, and as long as you understand upfront that there is a time constraint on your table – which you may find cramped – the experience is an enjoyable one. 'Delicious, coarsely textured' pork and mushroom terrine with dill, little pickled onions and toasted sourdough with black truffle butter, a gala pork pie with 'Matson' spiced sauce – 'rather like chip shop curry with a tang' – and herb-crusted stone bass with crab pancake, brown crab taramasalata, green apple and garden garnish, have been reporters' highlights this year. As may be seen, there is no shyness in going for it, but the overall balance remains stable, though a dull dessert of sweet malt gateau with malted milk ice cream, yeast tuile and crème fraîche was a let down at inspection – white peach soufflé with tea sorbet and rosemary custard has been a better bet. Wines from £44.
Chef/s: Tom Kerridge. **Open:** all week L 12 to 2.45 (3.15 Sun), Mon to Sat D 6.30 to 9.45. **Closed:** 24 to 26 Dec. **Meals:** main courses £27 to £39. Set L £15 (2 courses) to £20. **Details:** 52 seats. Bar. Wheelchairs. Music. Parking.

Sindhu

Cooking score: 6
Indian | £40
Compleat Angler, Bisham Road, Marlow,
SL7 1RG
Tel no: (01628) 405405
sindhurestaurant.co.uk

The views are of Marlow weir and the racing
Thames, not the namesake Indus river
('Sindhu' in Sanskrit), but this remarkable
out-of-town opening from chef Atul Kochhar
promises a bonanza of thrilling flavours,
telling textures and riotous colours – in other
words, Indian regional food garlanded for the
21st century. Those who know Kochhar's
Mayfair flagship Benares (see entry) will
recognise many familiar themes here – the
cross-pollination of east and west, the intricate
detailing and the dutiful sourcing of British
ingredients, for example. But the results on the
plate are even more dramatic and dazzling:
consider delicate hand-dived scallops with
three textures of parsnip (purée, pickles and
crisps), crispy soft-shell crab with squid rings,
chilli and coconut drizzle, or a rack of
Chettinad-style Romney Marsh lamb with
vegetable polenta and turnips – plus perfect
breads and top-drawer rice. Clever desserts
also pick up on the crossover theme. The food
looks absolutely perfect against a classy
backdrop of vibrant canvases, muted tones and
plush, saffron-hued furniture, while the
drinks list accommodates exotic cocktails as
well as wide-ranging cosmopolitan wines,
with prices from £24.
Chef/s: Gopal Krishnan. **Open:** all week L 12 to
2.30, D 6 to 10 (10.30 Fri and Sat, 9 Sun).
Meals: main courses £17 to £25. Set L £19 (2
courses) to £22. Sun L £25. **Details:** 60 seats. V
menu. Bar. Wheelchairs. Music. Parking.

The Vanilla Pod

Cooking score: 5
Modern European | £45
31 West Street, Marlow, SL7 2LS
Tel no: (01628) 898101
thevanillapod.co.uk
£5
OFF

There are restaurants in Marlow with a higher
profile, but few can match the Vanilla Pod for
neighbourly good humour, value or
consistency. Set in a narrow two-storey
townhouse that was once home to poet TS
Eliot, this is a smart but thoroughly relaxed
bolt-hole noted for Michael Macdonald's deft,
precisely executed cooking. There's nothing
flighty here, but the food has other virtues –
not least the emphasis on fine ingredients and
the attention to detail that goes into all those
pretty plates. Deceptively simple dish
descriptions don't give much away, but
enjoyment is guaranteed, whether you open
with a taster of smoked quail and celeriac
purée or a full-bodied butternut squash
risotto. After that, quality is the watchword
when it comes to, say, roast skate with fennel
pollen and lentils or rump of lamb with
creamed Savoy cabbage and bacon. To
conclude, the candied pear with salted-
caramel and croissant ice cream stands out, or
you could try some Swiss Tête de Moine
cheese with 'jams'. A comprehensive wine list
promises choice pickings from £24.
Chef/s: Michael Macdonald. **Open:** Tue to Sat L 12
to 3, D 7 to 10. **Closed:** Sun, Mon, 2 weeks
Christmas, 1 week Aug. **Meals:** set L £16 (2 courses)
to £20. Set D £45. Tasting menu £60 (7 courses).
Details: 28 seats. 15 seats outside. V menu. Bar.

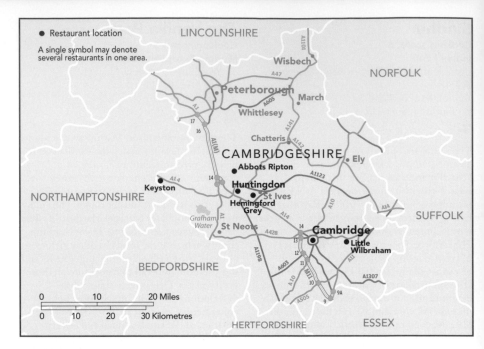

LINCOLNSHIRE

NORFOLK

Wisbech

Peterborough

March

Whittlesey

Chatteris

CAMBRIDGESHIRE   Ely

Abbots Ripton

Huntingdon

Keyston

St Ives

Hemingford
Grey

NORTHAMPTONSHIRE

Grafham
Water

St Neots

SUFFOLK

Cambridge

Little
Wilbraham

BEDFORDSHIRE

| 0 | 10 | 20 Miles |
| 0 | 10 | 20 | 30 Kilometres |

HERTFORDSHIRE   ESSEX

■ Abbots Ripton
The Abbot's Elm
Cooking score: 2
British | £26
Abbots Ripton, PE28 2PA
Tel no: (01487) 773773
theabbotselm.co.uk
£5 OFF

Sometimes, pubs hit that 'something for
everyone' note pitch-perfect. Drop into this
delightful village pub for a light bite in the bar
or garden – omelette with lamb's kidneys,
chips and salad maybe – or linger over heartier
fare in the spacious vaulted dining room with
its centrepiece inglenook. Portions are as
generous as the flavours are meaningful: a
game terrine 'packed with well-cooked game
and served with a crisply pickle' gets the
thumbs-up from one diner, as does a
Guinness-braised ox cheek with mash and
winter vegetables, while it seems few can resist
chef-patron Julia Abbey's fish pie. End with a
'perfect wobble' cassis pannacotta with fig

sorbet and ginger snap, or a sticky toffee
pudding that 'hits the spot'. House wines
(from £18.50) are produced in Chablis
exclusively for the pub, and a generous
selection by the glass and carafe is the prelude
to a carefully chosen line-up of fine bottles.
Chef/s: Julia Abbey. **Open:** all week L 12 to 2 (2.30
Sun), Mon to Sat D 6 to 9. **Closed:** 2 weeks Jan.
Meals: main courses £9 to £26. Sun L £25 (3
courses). **Details:** 80 seats. 30 seats outside. Bar.
Wheelchairs. Music. Parking.

■ Cambridge
Alimentum
Cooking score: 6
Modern British | £65
152-154 Hills Road, Cambridge, CB2 8PB
Tel no: (01223) 413000
restaurantalimentum.co.uk
£5 OFF

There's no doubting Alimentum's standing as
a purveyor of 'skilful, refined food', but the
look and feel of this Cambridge high-roller

still divides opinion: some find the interior slick and smart; others think it resembles 'a 90s nightclub', with garish red walls and bare black-painted tables. Behind the kitchen window, however, Mark Poynton's team delivers some seriously creative, big-impact dishes, from a taster of truffled pea salsa with pea sorbet and shreds of jamón to moist, chewy pistachio and chocolate cakes – elaborately embellished and arranged as a 'chequerboard take on Battenberg'. In between, there's much to cheer: a terrine of purple, yellow and orange carrot strips plus carrot purée, yoghurt and tarragon sorbet ('really clear flavours here'); a nugget of duck liver cooked yakitori style alongside a 'mystifyingly light' turnip purée, roasted peanuts and pickled turnip; half a roasted lobster with 'butter-loaded' pomme purée, daisy-fresh spring vegetables and a deep brown sauce. On the downside, misfires are not unknown (witness an 'uninspired and incompetently executed' set lunch) and front-of-house would benefit from tighter management. The intelligent, broadly based wine list starts with house selections from £27.

Chef/s: Mark Poynton. **Open:** all week L 12 to 2.30 (2 Sun), D 6 to 10 (9 Sun). **Closed:** 24 to 31 Dec, bank hols. **Meals:** alc £65 (3 courses). Set L (all week) and early D (Sun to Thur only) £21 (2 courses) to £29. Tasting menu £75 (7 courses) to £95. **Details:** 62 seats. V menu. Bar. Wheelchairs. Music.

★ TOP 50 ★

Midsummer House
Cooking score: 8
Modern British | £83
Midsummer Common, Cambridge, CB4 1HA
Tel no: (01223) 369299
midsummerhouse.co.uk

This solid Victorian villa, fronted by Midsummer Common and backed by the river Cam, has an interior that is entirely agreeable and happily relaxed. While the neat exterior gives nothing away, the consensus – that this is one of the country's finest restaurants – is amply testified by a succession of recommendations. Daniel Clifford's cooking stands out from the crowd not least because he starts with high quality raw materials, takes seasonality seriously and his dishes aim to entice rather than baffle. The ten-course tasting menu is no more, replaced by a more manageable eight-course version (five for a weekday lunch) where a mixing and melding of culinary styles produces a triumphant dish of English asparagus and beurre noisette, wrapped in foil and cooked on a heated stone at table, then served with burnt onions and a fresh green asparagus with a deep-fried potato stem and truffled filling, alongside dabs of mousse-like aerated sauce hollandaise. Another winner is a perfect balancing act of Granny Smith jelly, celeriac cooked with truffle and sautéed scallop, the sweetness of the latter beautifully contrasted against a love apple caramel blob and apple batons. There's memorable alchemy, too, in a dish of sautéed duck liver with tangerine jelly and gingerbread crumbs, served with a salad of red chicory and little pear discs. Reporters have singled out a 'standout' celeriac baked for hours in the Green Egg barbecue (a signature piece of kit in the kitchen) and served with a frozen hollandaise sauce, the superb quality of the roasted rack of Cumbrian lamb teamed with its confit shoulder, and an 'intriguing' pre-dessert, a refreshing concoction of aerated pear and blueberry under a white chocolate dome, 'which managed to be intensely flavoured and not too sweet'. At the same time, some reporters have not been convinced by each and every flavour combination, and service can be un-coordinated at times – as we have said before, as though staff are unaware of the calibre of the place. The wine list is exemplary, if pricey (from £30).

Chef/s: Daniel Clifford. **Open:** Wed to Sat L 12 to 1.30, Tue to Sat D 7 to 9.30 (6.30 Sat). **Closed:** Sun, Mon, 2 weeks Christmas. **Meals:** tasting menus £48 (5 courses) to £105 (8 courses). **Details:** 53 seats. V menu. Bar.

Top Puds

It's a tough job, but someone's got to do it. We asked our undercover inspectors to name their best desserts of the year.

'**The Exmoor Beastro** in Devon served a ginger panna cotta with own-grown rhubarb compote and crumbled shortbread. Perfect trembling texture, gorgeously creamy, strewn with crystallised ginger and a slew of stewed rhubarb. Simple perfection.'

'North of the Border Tart at the **Whitehouse, Lochaline** – a pastry case filled with dried fruits, cherries, nuts and whisky and a mixture of eggs, butter and ground almonds – a bit like a light Christmas pud. Nothing fancy, no towers, or twirls or crisps, just a really comforting pud.'

'Warm blood-orange, sheep's milk yoghurt and wild fennel granita at the **Clove Club, London**. It came with shards of dehydrated milk-froth – like eating a crisp, malty cloud. The blood orange was in the form of a warm curd. The whole thing was seriously delicious.'

'At the **Village Pub** in Barnsley I had one of the finest sticky toffee puddings I have every tasted: a dark, moist, treacly sponge swimming in a runny toffee sauce, dark and rich as muscovado, with a scoop of home made vanilla ice cream.'

LOCAL GEM
The Dumpling Tree
Chinese | £20
8 Homerton Street, Cambridge, CB2 8NX
Tel no: (01223) 247715
thedumplingtree.com

£30

This unpretentious and low-key Chinese eatery, at the base of a modern block not far from the arts venue Cambridge Junction, fills with regulars who appreciate the relaxed style and the food. Successful dishes from the usual repertoire have included the great selection of dumplings and 'the best traditional' rice noodle soups, but there's also zesty seaweed salad, BBQ pork buns, slow-braised beef, chicken in Thai sauce and sweet steamed buns. It is all very good value. Wines from £17.

LOCAL GEM
Fitzbillies
Modern British | £26
51-52 Trumpington Street, Cambridge, CB2 1RG
Tel no: (01223) 352500
fitzbillies.com

£30

A Cambridge institution, famous for its Chelsea buns, this attractive bakery and café is a real crowd-puller. Noted for casual dining, Fitzbillies is popular not only with early birds arriving for breakfast, but also for a lunchtime menu that delivers the likes of Porter's pie (packed with chunks of prime pork and rich gravy), and roast cod with lentils, green sauce and purple sprouting broccoli. The wide selection of cakes always catches the eye, while hefty sausage rolls and grilled cheese sandwiches are tried-and-trusted favourites. No reservations. Wines from £21.

Pint Shop

British | £25
10 Peas Hill, Cambridge, CB2 3PN
Tel no: (01223) 352293
pintshop.co.uk

£30

Readers consider Cambridge 'lucky to have this place – it is well pitched, priced and delivered'. The clattery wood-floored bar and old-school dining rooms showcase an ever-changing beer menu ('one of the best in the city') from small, mostly British brewers, while the menu resounds with plucky flavours, whether potted rabbit, smoked haddock pasty or beer-brined chicken and chips. Devilled lamb shoulder kebab with flatbread and chilli sauce has been a recent hit, service is friendly and wines start at £20.

■ Hemingford Grey

The Cock

Modern British | £30
47 High Street, Hemingford Grey, PE28 9BJ
Tel no: (01480) 463609
cambscuisine.com

A village pub by the river Ouse, where a clear distinction between drinking and dining sees the Cock's two personalities coexisting harmoniously. Head into the rustic-chic restaurant to tuck into feel-good British stuff such as potted rabbit with beetroot chutney, leg of lamb with pea and spinach fricassee, a couple of steaks with hand-cut chips, and their own sausages with a choice of mash and sauces. Aubergine and onion fritters with lentil and spinach dhal is a winning veggie option. Wines start at £19.

■ Huntingdon

The Old Bridge Hotel

Cooking score: 2
Modern British | £32
1 High Street, Huntingdon, PE29 3TQ
Tel no: (01480) 424300
huntsbridge.com

It may have started life as an 18th-century bank, but this solid-looking ivy-clad hotel by a bridge over the Ouse is now built for pleasure. Smart-casual hospitality is the name of the game, with gardens running down to the water, an all-day foodie offer for casual passers-by and a summery conservatory dining room emblazoned with classical trompe l'oeil murals. Monthly menus add a vibrant Mediterranean sheen to carefully sourced British ingredients, as in girolles on toast with artichoke and tarragon sauce or turbot fillet with prawn ravioli, samphire and lobster bisque. Fishcakes, lobster burgers and char-grilled steaks provide some extra heft, before Neal's Yard Dairy cheeses and desserts such as baked custard tart with prunes in brandy bring the curtain down. With John Hoskins MW at the helm, it's no surprise that the wine list is a global show stopper, noted for its flat mark-ups and brilliant house selections; prices start at £17.95 (£5.50 a glass). There's even a wine shop for browsing and sipping.
Chef/s: Jack Woolner. **Open:** all week L 12 to 2 (2.30 Sun), D 6.30 to 10 (9.30 Sun). **Meals:** main courses £15 to £29. Set L £19 (2 courses) to £24.
Details: 80 seats. 40 seats outside. Bar. Wheelchairs. Music. Parking.

Keyston
The Pheasant

Cooking score: 2
Modern British | £30
Loop Road, Keyston, PE28 0RE
Tel no: (01832) 710241
thepheasant-keyston.co.uk
£5 OFF

Neat thatch, pretty hanging boxes, charming village setting – the Pheasant is straight out of central casting. It's been associated with good food for some 50 years and continues to impress with chef-patron Simon Cadge at the stoves. Oak beams and real fires keep up the good work in the main bar area, with a dining area at the back giving a view of the patio garden. Making use of the pub's kitchen garden, Simon and his team follow the seasons and deliver a modern output that also covers traditional bases. Duck ragoût enriches pan-fried gnocchi in a starter with European sensibilities, or go for a trendy salad with cow's curd and pears. Main course glazed Barbary duck is a riff on a classic with its orange and thyme sauce, while fishcakes come with samphire, cockles and dill cream. The wine list is a treasure trove by the glass, carafe and bottle, the latter starting at £17.
Chef/s: Simon Cadge. **Open:** Tue to Sun L 12 to 2 (2.30 Fri and Sat, 3.30 Sun), Tue to Sat D 6.30 to 9.30. **Closed:** Mon, 2 to 16 Jan. **Meals:** main courses £12 to £22. Set L and D £15 (2 courses) to £20. Sun L £25. **Details:** 80 seats. 40 seats outside. Bar. Parking.

Little Wilbraham
The Hole in the Wall

Cooking score: 3
Modern British | £35
2 High Street, Little Wilbraham, CB21 5JY
Tel no: (01223) 812282
holeinthewallcambridge.com
£5 OFF

Locals show loyalty to the Hole in the Wall for good reason – it's worth knowing about if you're in the area. Alex Rushmer has been carefully nurturing this pretty, well-kept and sociable village pub since 2010, gradually refining his version of modern British cooking. The result is a pared-back seasonal menu where the likes of mackerel two ways – grilled fillet and smoked pâté – with lime gel, crispy kale leaves and a crunchy onion seed wafer have shone. Likewise 'a real knockout dish' consisting of two fat chunks of juicy pork loin with a generous layer of fat, a cube of braised shoulder atop a swipe of apple gel, some soft-roasted cauliflower with pickled shavings, cauliflower purée, raisins and a lightly spiced granola of seeds and nuts. Praise, too, for a scoop of glossy chocolate crémeux with salted caramel, honeycomb pieces, chocolate biscuit crumbs and 'a fine rubble of pistachio' – lovely stuff. A list of wines, chosen because 'they taste great', opens at £24.
Chef/s: Alex Rushmer. **Open:** Wed to Sun L 12 to 1.45, Tue to Sat D 6.30 to 8.30. **Closed:** Mon, 2 weeks Christmas. **Meals:** set L £20 (2 courses) to £24. Set D £30 (2 courses) to £35. Tasting menu £60. Sun L £26 (2 courses) to £30. **Details:** 50 seats. 25 seats outside. Bar. Music. Parking.

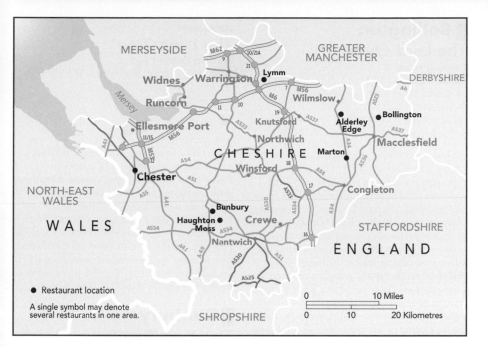

Restaurant location

A single symbol may denote several restaurants in one area.

| 0 | | 10 Miles |
| 0 | 10 | 20 Kilometres |

▮ Alderley Edge
Alderley Edge Hotel
Cooking score: 3
Modern British | £50
Macclesfield Road, Alderley Edge, SK9 7BJ
Tel no: (01625) 583033
alderleyedgehotel.com

Long established at the corner of Cheshire's golden triangle, the Alderley Edge Hotel is a grand presence on the road through mansionville. Its formal conservatory restaurant (there's also a brasserie option) boasts good bread and 'proper plates of food', albeit punctuated by mini-courses and with prices pitched at 'sharp intake of breath'. To start, 'perfectly made' crab omelette comes with a sauce zinging with basil, and main courses are straightforward preparations of good meat 'n' veg; cannon of Herdwick lamb with crushed Jersey Royals, cherry tomatoes and baby carrots, or pork loin with belly, crackling, black pudding and sage-scented

potato croquettes. When it comes to dessert, flavour combinations are tried and true, as in chocolate mousse encased in chocolate and served with raspberries, or rhubarb mousse on a gingerbread base. Service is entirely professional, and can be 'delightful'. A hefty wine list, big on traditional French players, starts at £24.50

Chef/s: Sean Sutton. **Open:** all week L 12 to 2 (4 Sun), Mon to Sat D 7 to 10. **Meals:** main courses £23 to £27. Sun L £28. **Details:** 64 seats. Wheelchairs. Music. Parking.

Please send us your feedback

To register your opinion about any restaurant listed in this guide, or a new restaurant that you wish to bring to our attention, please visit the web address at the bottom of the page. Your feedback informs the content of the book and will be used to compile next year's reviews.

◼ Bollington
The Lord Clyde
Cooking score: 3
Modern British | £37
36 Clarke Lane, Kerridge, Bollington,
SK10 5AH
Tel no: (01625) 562123
thelordclyde.co.uk

A pleasing flexibility distinguishes this stone-built country inn (fashioned from a pair of 19th-century weavers' cottages), providing a welcome for drinkers, lunchtime sandwiches and traditional Sunday lunches. But for real culinary action look to Ernst Van Zyl's intricate contemporary cooking showcased on seasonally inspired à la carte and seven- and ten-course tasting menus. Although dishes can verge on the overly complicated, there is unquestionable talent on show. Expect the unexpected, as a meal might take you from cured cod cheek with shallot, pancetta, wild garlic, roasted onion and smoked bacon dashi to lamb rump served with a spiced lamb sausage, beets, toasted spelt and spring onion – ask the well-drilled staff for details, as menu descriptions don't always tell the whole story – and it all comes to a suitably innovative conclusion with an intense bitter chocolate riff on tiramisu. Elsewhere there is excellent bread and tempting British cheeses, and the carefully sourced wine list (from £17.50) is a balanced affair with good tasting notes.
Chef/s: Ernst Van Zyl. **Open:** Tue to Fri and Sun L 12 to 2 (5 Sun), Mon to Sat D 6.30 to 9. **Meals:** main courses £16 to £25. Set L £35. Sun L £18 to £23. Tasting menu £53 (7 courses) to £79. **Details:** 45 seats. 12 seats outside. Wheelchairs. Music. Parking. No children Fri and Sat D.

Average price

The average price denotes the price of a three-course meal without wine.

LOCAL GEM
The Lime Tree
Modern British | £29
18-20 High Street, Bollington, SK10 5PH
Tel no: (01625) 578182
limetreebollington.co.uk
£30

The conversion of a pair of Victorian shops gives Didsbury's long-standing Lime Tree a handsome double-fronted presence in Bollington. The rambling, tasteful restaurant now has more space in its conservatory for customers to try dishes that, like the seafood lasagne with sauce nantais, can strongly reflect the kitchen team's time spent with the Galvin brothers. Produce, some of which comes from the owner's smallholding, is treated simply in crowd-pleasing dishes like piri-piri poussin or rhubarb crumble. Wines are from £16.

◼ Bunbury
The Yew Tree Inn
Cooking score: 1
Modern British | £25
Long Lane, Spurstow, Bunbury, CW6 9RD
Tel no: (01829) 260274
theyewtreebunbury.com
£5 OFF £30

The Earl of Crewe built this country pub in the 19th century and Jon and Lindsay Cox saved it from dereliction in the 21st. Still very much a traditional hostelry dispensing a rotating choice of real ales, the bar shows its more contemporary side with around 20 wines by the glass. Fish pie and bangers and mash provide the pubbier staples, with more involved dishes including gin-cured salmon and blood-orange salad, rack of lamb with hot-pot potatoes, pearl barley and tomato jus, then iced coffee parfait with cinnamon doughnut. Wines from £16.50.
Chef/s: Rob McDiarmid. **Open:** all week 12 to 9.30 (10 Fri and Sat, 9 Sun). **Closed:** 25 Dec. **Meals:** main courses £11 to £18. **Details:** 65 seats. 65 seats outside. Bar. Music. Parking.

▌Chester
Joseph Benjamin

Cooking score: 3
Modern European | £27
134-140 Northgate Street, Chester, CH1 2HT
Tel no: (01244) 344295
josephbenjamin.co.uk
🍷 £30

An easy-going but stylish restaurant right by
the city gate, Joseph Benjamin takes its name
from the two Wright brothers: Joe (heading up
the kitchen) and Ben (front-of-house). Inside
it's all pale blue walls and simple modern
furniture, but there's plenty of colour on the
plate, with top-quality ingredients treated
with gusto and originality – an oversized,
unctuous sourdough cheesy garlic bread
(described as 'the best I've ever tasted'),
pointing the way for a generous,
unpretentious style of cooking. A 'velveteen'
beetroot and orange soup with 'springy-crusty
sourdough' is a typical opener while a main
course of Galician octopus with sea bass,
caramelised fennel, cannellini beans and
blood orange typifies the European bent of the
menu. Dishes are 'deeply satisfying,' not least a
buttery-sweet and warmly spiced muscovado
rice pudding with apple and blackberry
compote and cinnamon crumble. A relatively
short but appealing international wine list
offers much by the glass or carafe, with bottles
starting at £18.50.
Chef/s: Joe Wright. **Open:** Tue to Sun L 12 to 3 (4
Sun), Thur to Sat D 6 to 9.30. **Closed:** Mon.
Meals: main courses £11 to £19. **Details:** 38 seats.
Bar. Wheelchairs. Music.

Simon Radley at the Chester Grosvenor

Cooking score: 6
Modern European | £75
Eastgate, Chester, CH1 1LT
Tel no: (01244) 324024
chestergrosvenor.com
🍷 🛏

The old lady of Eastgate has never been
outdone in the luxury stakes, and the jewel in
her crown, Simon Radley's eponymous
restaurant, has no shortage of tasteful gleam.
'Formal and attentive' service carries the
experience through 'excellent' canapés and a
thrillingly loaded bread trolley (of which the
baguette is the star) to contemporary dishes
based on confident understanding of effective
combinations and how far to push them.
Granny Smith is the freshening agent on a
plateful of haslet, brawn fritter, pork belly,
octopus and squid, while a main of heritage
carrot tandoori adds grilled veal fillet, spiced
and seared kidneys, crisp sweetbreads and
scampi tails to the root. If portions can be
'restrained' at times, staff are intuitive,
recommending the right sort of pudding (in
this case shaved Tête de Moine cheese with
charred pears, walnuts and candied celery) for
the right sort of person. The wine list is vast
and potentially ruinous, but starts at £31.
Chef/s: Simon Radley and Raymond Booker. **Open:**
Tue to Sat D only 6.30 to 9. **Closed:** Sun, Mon, 24
and 25 Dec, first week Jan. **Meals:** set D £75 (3
courses). Tasting menu £99 (8 courses). **Details:** 40
seats. Bar. Wheelchairs. Parking. Children over 12
yrs only.

Sticky Walnut

Cooking score: 4
Modern European | £30
11 Charles Street, Chester, CH2 3AZ
Tel no: (01244) 400400
stickywalnut.com

Social media might bring people to Sticky
Walnut, but good cooking keeps them
coming back. Chef-owner Gary Usher's voice
in the Twitterverse helped him to popularise

Symbols

🛏   Accommodation is available
£30 Three courses for less than £30
£5   £5-off voucher scheme
OFF
🍷   Notable wine list

this first bistro and crowdfund its sister, Burnt Truffle, in Heswall (see entry). But he hasn't taken his eye off the ball here; the food remains well thought out and carefully cooked, though occasionally served in less-than-jovial style. Set over two convivial, clattering floors, the dining room is 'basic but homely' and the food big on well-worn but effective combinations with a contemporary spin. Try the gorgeously light white wine risotto with clams and lardo to start, followed by big-hitting glazed ox cheek with buttered kale, onion purée and the signature truffle and Parmesan chips. Puddings are a lesson in perfectly executed simplicity, though you can go fancier with toasted porter ice cream with baked treacle, caramel, peanuts and Armagnac prunes. Wine is from £17.50, with nothing to bankrupt the bill-payer.

Chef/s: Gary Usher. **Open:** all week L 12 to 2.30, D 6 to 9 (10 Fri and Sat). **Closed:** 25 and 26 Dec. **Meals:** main courses £15 to £20. Sun L £18 (2 courses) to £22. **Details:** 48 seats. Music.

▌ Haughton Moss

LOCAL GEM
The Nag's Head
British | £29
Long Lane, Haughton Moss, CW6 9RN
Tel no: (01829) 260265
nagsheadhaughton.co.uk
£30

This pretty 17th-century timbered pub presents the kind of rural picture townies dream about – reinforcing the image with blazing winter fires, beams galore and alfresco summer tables. A strongly rooted policy in first-class produce gives notice that this is part of Ribble Valley Inns, and house classics of cheese and onion pie and the exemplary Lancashire hotpot appear alongside clear-flavoured, no-nonsense dishes such as fish and chips, British rump steak burger, rose veal chop and grilled lobster with garlic butter. Wines from £16.

▌ Kettleshulme

READERS RECOMMEND
The Swan Inn
Seafood
Macclesfield Road, Kettleshulme, SK23 7QU
Tel no: (01663) 732943
'We were bowled over by the quality achieved at this small pub on the edge of the Peak District; an outstanding selection of fish dishes marked it out as very special.'

▌ Lymm

The Church Green
Cooking score: 2
Modern British | £28
Higher Lane, Lymm, WA13 0AP
Tel no: (01925) 752068
aidenbyrne.co.uk
£30

In lovely Lymm, Aiden Byrne's food pub is the best place to start or end a walk around the dam. Byrne's own circumnavigation of the modern canon finds a relaxed outlet in his small plates menu, which includes some dishes also found on the carte. It can be elegant; cured salmon salad is scattered with samphire, cucumber and citrus wedges, and smoked haddock arancini are served with tartare sauce and mined with peas, bringing the Italian snack closer to these shores. Pork lyonnaise, a slice of fat belly with boozy caramelised onions and a fried egg, might work better as a main course, though there are plenty of other,

Join us at thegoodfoodguide.co.uk

larger offerings, including Hereford beef and market fish from the grill. Desserts aren't always consistent, but praline-topped coffee pannacotta certainly works. As befits the pub setting, eat in the bar, restaurant or garden; service is willing throughout. Wines are from £18.

Chef/s: Aiden Byrne. **Open:** all week 12 to 9 (10 Fri and Sat, 12.30 to 7 Sun). **Closed:** 25 Dec. **Meals:** main courses £18 to £40. Set L and D £23 (2 courses) to £28 (3 courses). Sun L £18. **Details:** 86 seats. 94 seats outside. Bar. Wheelchairs. Music. Parking. Children before 8pm only.

▊ Marton
La Popote
Cooking score: 1
French | £40
Manchester Road (A34), Marton, SK11 9HF
Tel no: (01260) 224785
la-popote.co.uk
£5
OFF

'This was like stepping back into the late 1980s – lots of fuss and frills and rich sauces, even a flambé trolley,' observed a visitor, happily adding that the Janssens' converted coach-house restaurant is clearly popular, offers a 'personal, warm welcome' and the 'food was good'. The menu reads like a Francophile's dream, liberally sprinkled with hearty portions of moules marinière, French onion soup, duck rillette pâté, entrecôte café de Paris and lobster thermidor. Notable hits with readers have been boeuf bourguignon and crêpe suzette (prepared at table) and it's all brought off with reliable verve. Good value, predominantly French wines from £18.50.
Chef/s: Victor Janssen and Chris Rooney. **Open:** Wed to Sun L 12 to 3 (6 Sun), Wed to Sat D 6 to 12. **Closed:** Mon, Tue, 1 week Jan, 1 week Aug. **Meals:** main courses £17 to £25. Set L £16 (2 courses) to £20. Sun L £19. **Details:** 40 seats. 25 seats outside. Bar. Wheelchairs. Music. Parking. No small children at D.

Scoring – Explained

Local Gems, Scores 1 and 2
Scoring a 1 or a 2 in *The Good Food Guide*, or being awarded Local Gem status, is a huge achievement. We list the very best restaurants in the UK; for the reader, this means that these restaurants are well worth visiting if in the area – and you're extremely lucky if they are on your doorstep.

Scores 3 to 6
Further up the scale, scores 3 to 6 range from up-and-coming restaurants to places to watch; there will be real talent in the kitchen. These are the places that are well worth seeking out.

Scores 7 to 9
A score of 7 and above means entering the big league, with high expectations of the chef. In other words, these are destination restaurants, the places you'll long to talk about – if you're lucky enough to get a booking.

Score 10
This score is extremely rare, with chefs expected to achieve faultless technique at every service. In total, only eight restaurants have achieved 10 out of 10 for cooking since the scoring system was introduced in 1998.

See page 16 for an in-depth breakdown of *The Good Food Guide*'s scoring system.

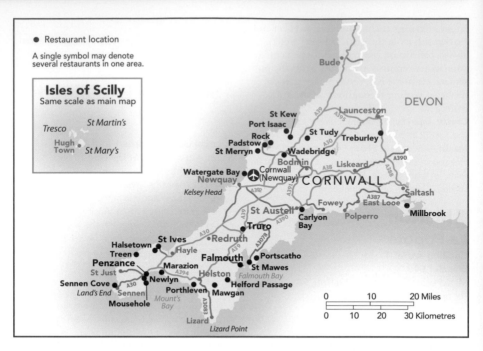

▊ Carlyon Bay
Austell's

Cooking score: 3
Modern British | £28
10 Beach Road, Carlyon Bay, PL25 3PH
Tel no: (01726) 813888
austells.co.uk
£5 OFF £30 ♨

Don't be deterred by the unpromising location
in a parade of suburban shops, because
Austell's open-plan interior paints a much
brighter picture with its cool colour schemes,
shiny surfaces, prints and bustling open
kitchen. Chef-proprietor Brett Camborne-
Paynter looks to the West Country larder for
inspiration, delivering a menu stuffed with
inspired contemporary ideas, from a Terras
Farm duck broth involving smoked breast,
confit leg tortellini, liver parfait, quince,
celeriac and truffled mushrooms to regional
cheeses embellished with crab apple jelly, fruit
cake purée and frosted walnuts. His cooking is
thoughtful and creative in equal measure,
moving confidently from confit local pork
belly with spiced red cabbage and chutney jus
to pan-fried sea bass and seared scallops with
carrot purée, crushed peas and green beans in
pancetta. Brett's home-baked breads deserve a
special mention, while desserts such as crispy
rice pudding croquettes with spiced apple
compote are an intriguing prospect. Wines
from £16.95.
Chef/s: Brett Camborne-Paynter. **Open:** Tue to Sun
L 10 to 4 (12 to 2 Sun), D 6 to 9. **Closed:** Mon.
Meals: main courses £17 to £22. Set L £18 (2
courses) to £24. Set D £23 (2 courses) to £28. Sun L
£24. **Details:** 46 seats. 2 seats outside. Music.
Parking.

Symbols

- ⊨ Accommodation is available
- £30 Three courses for less than £30
- £5 OFF £5-off voucher scheme
- ♨ Notable wine list

Falmouth

Oliver's

Cooking score: 3
Modern British | £30
33 High Street, Falmouth, TR11 2AD
Tel no: (01326) 218138
oliversfalmouth.com

Subtitled 'the eatery', Ken and Wendy Symons' cheerfully run bistro is everything you might hope for – 'small, exclusive and welcoming', with seasonal raw materials shining brightly on an idiosyncratic daily menu. Snuggled away among Falmouth's boho shops and surfing hangouts, it attracts locals and holidaymakers alike with its deft ideas and 'fabulous' flavours. Dishes are listed on an orange plastic board and there's plenty of enterprise, skill and industry at work – from handmade garlic-smoked ewes' cheese with pickled vegetables and a foraged salad to turbot with dill-spiked lobster gnocchi, sea vegetables and salsa verde. The 'finest local produce' from named suppliers also gets a good showing, as in Terras Farm duck with asparagus, spiced peach, land cress, blackberry and vanilla, while creative puds could include salt-baked pineapple with mulled cider sorbet. Meanwhile, Wendy is a 'treasure' out front, delivering spot-on service 'with a wicked sense of humour'. Easily priced wines start at £16.50.
Chef/s: Ken Symons. **Open:** Tue to Sat L 12 to 2, D 7 to 9. **Closed:** Sun, Mon, 25, 26 and 31 Dec, first 3 weeks Nov. **Meals:** main courses £16 to £24. Set L £15 (2 courses) to £22. Tasting menu £40 (6 courses). **Details:** 28 seats. V menu. Music.

Local Gem

Local Gems are the perfect neighbourhood venues, delivering good, freshly cooked food at great value for money.

★ NEW ENTRY ★

Star and Garter

Cooking score: 2
British | £27
52 High Street, Falmouth, TR11 2AF
Tel no: (01326) 316663
starandgarterfalmouth.co.uk
£5 OFF   £30

Opposite Falmouth's old town hall, this smart dining pub is sandwiched among the shops and splendid Georgian houses lining the old high street – the rear dining area offers fabulous views across the harbour. Still very much a pub where regulars can enjoy pints of local ale in the front bar, the restaurant is a relaxed affair with unclothed tables and pictures of 'salty old sea dogs and noble 19th-century gents'. Although there is plenty of fish (from local day boats), the main thrust is a butch, meaty 'nose-to-tail' approach – with much smoking and slow-cooking in the searing heat of the kitchen's charcoal-fuelled Green Egg. At a test meal, a salad of warm, smoky, tender, char-grilled octopus with Pink Fir Apple potatoes, celery, capers and 'nduja had 'punchy, assertive flavours', while smoked ox cheek, roasted beets, oregano and horseradish gremolata was a generous if undersauced dish. Sweet-sharp roast Yorkshire rhubarb, rhubarb and buttermilk ice cream and ginger biscuits made a great finish. Wines from £16.
Chef/s: Andi Richardson. **Open:** all week L 12 to 3, Mon to Sat D 6 to 9. **Meals:** main courses £13 to £18. **Details:** 52 seats. Music.

LOCAL GEM

Rick Stein's Fish

Seafood | £29
Discovery Quay, Falmouth, TR11 3XA
Tel no: (01326) 330050
rickstein.com
£30

Be prepared to queue at this no-bookings Falmouth outpost of TV seafood chef Rick Stein's empire, but it's worth the effort. Inside it's casual, bright and contemporary with white tiles and slate floors. Fish and chips from the takeaway counter might be the bestseller here but the globetrotting menu could start with grilled sardines with herbs, garlic, olives and capers, followed by whole steamed sea bass with garlic, ginger, spring onion, sesame and soy. Wines from £17.95.

■ Halsetown
Halsetown Inn
Cooking score: 2
Modern British | £28
Halsetown, TR26 3NA
Tel no: (01736) 795583
halsetowninn.co.uk
£30

The second venture from the team behind Blas Burgerworks in St Ives (see entry), this welcoming granite stone-built pub has gained a loyal following since opening four years ago. With its real fire, the small snug bar 'must be a wonderful bolthole in the winter'. Expect to find locals downing pints of Betty Stogs ale in the bar, while those in for food grab tables in the three higgledy-piggledy dining areas. This is not a place for culinary fireworks, but the kitchen shows a passionate commitment to local produce and sustainability. Dishes are unpretentious, portions are generous and flavours pronounced: in a starter of crisp-fried chilli-battered cauliflower with peanut satay, carrot, mint and lime – 'a riot of Asian flavours' – and in grilled line-caught St Ives Bay mackerel with crushed new potatoes, salsa verde, celeriac rémoulade and lemon. Finish with apple and berry crumble tart, custard and raspberry and orange sorbet. Wines from £16.
Chef/s: Angela Baxter. **Open:** all week L 12 to 2 (3 Sun), Mon to Sat D 6 to 9. **Closed:** Jan. **Meals:** main courses £13 to £23. Set L £13 (2 courses) to £16. **Details:** 70 seats. 30 seats outside. Bar. Wheelchairs. Music. Parking.

■ Helford Passage
Ferryboat Inn
Cooking score: 2
Seafood | £28
Helford Passage, TR11 5LB
Tel no: (01326) 250625
thewrightbrothers.co.uk
£5 OFF £30

Those enterprising Wright brothers have venues in Soho, Southwark, Spitalfields and Kensington (see entries, London), but none may boast quite as seductive a setting as their Cornish outpost, which stands at Frenchman's Creek, looking over its own oyster beds to the river Helford. The place itself is a handsome Tudor inn with age-gnarled beams and winter fires within, and an outdoor terrace for the Cornish sun. Sandwiches and Sunday roasts keep up the pub end of things, but the core is sparkling-fresh seafood from the Newlyn day boats, perhaps a whole grilled plaice with burnt lemon, broccoli, almonds and capers, or classic beer-battered haddock with chips and mushy peas. Light bites to get you started take in beetroot-cured salmon with crème fraîche and soda bread, or ham hock terrine with celeriac coleslaw and cidery raisins. Finish with dark chocolate mousse, trendily accompanied by pickled cherries and honeycomb. House wines are £17.50, or £4.10 a glass.
Chef/s: Robert Bunny. **Open:** all week L 12 to 3, D 6 to 10. **Meals:** main courses £11 to £15. **Details:** 88 seats. 80 seats outside. Music. Parking.

■ Marazion
Ben's Cornish Kitchen
Cooking score: 5
Modern British | £30
West End, Marazion, TR17 0EL
Tel no: (01736) 719200
benscornishkitchen.com
£5 OFF

Chef-proprietor Ben Prior has scored a resounding hit since taking over this pint-sized restaurant in 2009. With refreshingly unfussy décor, no posh table settings and an absence of pomp and ceremony, there's certainly much to like about the down-to-earth style, while on the food front it's all about the kitchen delving into the West Country larder to produce creative modern bistro cooking at attractive prices. There's some seriously good stuff, with the menu moving confidently from scallops with cauliflower, spiced caramel and golden raisin, and smoked haddock chowder, to hake with artichoke, pine nuts, gnocchi and greens. And there are thoroughbred meats, too, as in meltingly tender roe deer or a 'beautiful piece of lamb' with couscous, aubergine, harissa hummus and feta fritter. A must-taste is the sweet curry plate with its cardamom ice cream, spiced rice pudding and sweet poppadom, which continues to intrigue and delight reporters. Well-chosen wines (from £17) should keep everyone happy. without any doubt the dining highlight of our trip') . With refreshingly unfussy décor, no posh table settings and an absence of pomp and ceremony, there's certainly much to like about the down-to-earth style, while on the food front it's all about the kitchen delving into the West Country larder to produce creative modern bistro cooking at attractive prices. There's some seriously good stuff, with the menu moving confidently from scallops with cauliflower, spiced caramel and golden raisin, and smoked haddock chowder, to hake with artichoke, pine nuts, gnocchi and greens. And there are thoroughbred meats, too, as in meltingly tender roe deer or a 'beautiful piece of lamb' with couscous, aubergine, harissa hummus and feta fritter. A must-taste is the sweet curry plate with its cardamom ice cream, spiced rice pudding and sweet poppadom, which continues to intrigue and delight reporters, but a deconstructed vanilla cheese cake with poached peaches and blueberries has garnered praise, too. Well-chosen wines (from £17) should keep everyone happy. →

Chef/s: Ben Prior. **Open:** Tue to Sat L 12 to 1.30, D 7 to 8.30. **Closed:** Sun, Mon. **Meals:** main courses £15 to £18. Set L £17 (2 courses) to £20. Set D £24 (2 courses) to £29. **Details:** 35 seats. Wheelchairs. Music.

▮ Mawgan
New Yard Restaurant
Cooking score: 3
Modern British | £28
Trelowarren Estate, Mawgan, TR12 6AF
Tel no: (01326) 221595
newyardrestaurant.co.uk

Part of Sir Ferrers Vyvyan's historic Trelowarren Estate, New Yard occupies part of what was a coach house in the old cobbled stableyard, and if you're new to the narrow lanes around here, note some have found it tricky to find the place at the first time of asking. Seasonal, home-grown and regional ingredients form the backbone of a menu that deals in straightforward, clear-headed combinations such as an opening salvo of Cornish crab on toasted sourdough with smoked paprika mayonnaise. Homemade goats' curd turns up in a fashionable salad with pickled beetroots and blood orange, and, among main courses, fish of the day comes with lemon butter sauce, soft-shell crab makes an impressive burger (with Singapore slaw and lemongrass and ginger aïoli), and a meat-free option might be sweet potato pancakes with labneh. Finish with vanilla rice pudding with orange and pomegranate. Wines start at £15.
Chef/s: Chris Philliskirk. **Open:** all week L 12 to 2.15, Mon to Sat D 6.30 to 9. **Closed:** Jan. **Meals:** main courses £14 to £20. Set L and D £19 (2 courses) to £20. **Details:** 40 seats. 20 seats outside. Bar. Wheelchairs. Music. Parking.

▋Millbrook
The View
Cooking score: 3
Modern British | £35
Treninnow Cliff, Millbrook, PL10 1JY
Tel no: (01752) 822345
theview-restaurant.co.uk
£5
OFF

Perched above the cliffs at Whitsand Bay, up where the paragliders soar, the View fully lives up to its name and window tables are highly prized. The décor may be basic but Matt and Rachel Corner's restaurant makes a stunning setting on a summer's day, and is cosy in the more challenging winter months, with food as big a lure as the panoramic views. Very fresh seafood, mostly from Looe Harbour, is treated with simplicity and respect, along the lines of carpaccio of tuna with Cornish crab and fennel salsa, or roast turbot with tiger prawns, razor clams with parsley and lime, and grilled monkfish, salsify, lemon and garlic. Devon beef fillet with caramelised shallots, celeriac and horseradish should satisfy anyone not in the mood for fish, or there are savoury tarts such as caramelised tomato and basil. Those with a sweet tooth will be tempted by dark chocolate marquise, pistachio praline and apricot. Wines from £18.50.
Chef/s: Matt Corner. **Open:** Wed to Sun L 12 to 2, D 7 to 8.45. **Closed:** Mon, Tue, 1 week Christmas, 2 weeks Feb. **Meals:** main courses £18 to £23. Set L £15 (2 courses) to £18. **Details:** 40 seats. 20 seats outside. Music. Parking.

▋Mousehole
The Old Coastguard
Cooking score: 3
Modern British | £25
The Parade, Mousehole, TR19 6PR
Tel no: (01736) 731222
oldcoastguardhotel.co.uk
£5 ⊨ £30
OFF

Run for the past five years by the Inkin brothers, owners of the Gurnard's Head at nearby Treen and the Felin Fach Griffin in Wales (see entries), this hotel in the tiny fishing village of Mousehole has a 'real buzz'. The ambience is simple and appropriate to the setting, in other words 'relaxing and unstuffy', and service is 'outstanding, informed, enthusiastic, energetic'. The sweeping views across Mount's Bay are spectacular and, weather permitting, a meal taken on the terrace of the enclosed subtropical garden makes for a memorable experience. Inside, the relaxed farmhouse feel adds to the informality and the kitchen sticks to the locality for raw materials on the modern British menu. Local crab 'of generous size' is ever popular, or there could be Porthilly oysters and pickled vegetables, followed by cod with cavolo nero, salsify, mussels and red wine dressing or guinea fowl and morteau sausage cassoulet. Elderflower jelly has been a standout dessert. Wines from £18.50.
Chef/s: Matthew Smith. **Open:** all week L 12.30 to 2.30 (2.15 Sun), D 6.30 to 9 (9.30 Fri and Sat). **Closed:** second week Jan. **Meals:** main courses £14 to £19. Set L £17 (2 courses) to £20. Set D £19 (2 courses) to £24. Sun L £25 (3 courses). **Details:** 80 seats. 40 seats outside. Bar. Wheelchairs. Music. Parking.

2 Fore Street
Cooking score: 3
Modern British | £29
2 Fore Street, Mousehole, TR19 6PF
Tel no: (01736) 731164
2forestreet.co.uk
£30

Opposite the harbourmaster's office overlooking the medieval harbour in a picturesque fishing village, Joe Wardell's little double-fronted restaurant is all distressed wooden tables and nautical artwork on the white walls. Top-drawer, largely local ingredients underpin his simple, no-frills menu, which given the location is a predictably – though not exclusively – fishy affair. Think Cornish crab soup with rouille and Parmesan croûtons, which could be followed by a precisely cooked pan-roasted hake fillet with wilted spinach, basil mayo and skinny fries. If fish isn't your thing, try the organic beef burger with toasted brioche, smoked bacon, Cheddar, relish and rosemary skinny fries. Follow it with rhubarb and ginger baked cheesecake, one of the straightforward desserts. A secluded garden at the back offers plenty of fine-weather alfresco opportunities among the palm trees. The wine list starts at £15.95 and features bottles from notable Cornish vineyards.

Chef/s: Joe Wardell. **Open:** all week L 12 to 3, D 5 to 9. **Closed:** 4 Jan to 12 Feb. **Meals:** main courses £15 to £20. Sun L £15 (2 courses) to £18. **Details:** 36 seats. 26 seats outside. Music.

▌Newlyn
The Tolcarne Inn

Cooking score: 2
Seafood | £29
Newlyn, TR18 5PR
Tel no: (01736) 363074
tolcarneinn.co.uk
£5 OFF £30

'The humble pub is at the edge of the sea, a sprat's throw from Newlyn fish market,' notes a reporter, adding 'the setting is very low-key but the flair of the cooking and the fresh fish are outstanding'. That seems an apt summation of everything that Ben Tunnicliffe is about, and it's good to know it's sufficiently well supported that booking ahead is a wise move. Menus are determined by the day boats, but you won't go far wrong if you expect the likes of tempura-battered ray wing with piccalilli and anchovy-garlic mayo, or fried mackerel with smoked bacon, beetroot and spinach, to start, and then sturdy main-course offerings such as monkfish tail on crab risotto with sprouting black cabbage, or hake with gnocchi in tarragon sauce, served with asparagus and lemon-glazed salsify. To finish, there could be unapologetically rich white chocolate and hazelnut terrine with wine-poached pear and chocolate sorbet. House wine £16.

Chef/s: Ben Tunnicliffe. **Open:** all week L 12 to 2.15 (3 Sun), D 6.30 to 9. **Meals:** main courses £16 to £20. **Details:** 45 seats. 30 seats outside. Bar. Parking.

▌Padstow
★ TOP 50 ★
Paul Ainsworth at No. 6

Cooking score: 7
Modern British | £57
6 Middle Street, Padstow, PL28 8AP
Tel no: (01841) 532093
number6inpadstow.co.uk
🍾 🛏

From a tiny Georgian town house in the centre of Padstow, Paul Ainsworth has built a mighty reputation. Words like 'perfect', 'wonderful' and 'faultless' flow easily from reporters 'surprised and delighted' by Ainsworth's grasp of flavour and texture, and by his ability to push boundaries without descending into self-congratulatory fuss. The restaurant itself is an engaging set-up: small dining rooms set over two floors, the Georgian good looks sharpened with modern touches from oversized ceiling lampshades to simple tables. On the food front, ingredients are the absolute best. Crisp Porthilly oysters, for instance, come with cured pork, green apple and fennel, while Saddleback pork jowl sports crackling, roast cauliflower and smoked eel as accompaniments. Flavoursome hogget from the Tamar Valley is pointed up with sweetbread, yeast-glazed celery root and red wine garlic, while Caesar salad, pommes Anna and béarnaise sauce accompany a barley-finished rib of beef. The dazzling performance extends to dessert, which taps into childhood memories with 'a trifle Cornish' (with rhubarb and saffron) and 'literally my bread and butter' (with vanilla ice cream and Sharp's 6 Vintage Blend beer). This is pin-sharp, supremely intelligent cooking. The wine list is as wide-ranging and interesting as you would hope, with a good spread of price points, starting at at £35.

Chef/s: Paul Ainsworth. **Open:** Tue to Sat L 12 to 2.30, D 6 to 10. **Closed:** Sun, Mon, 24 to 26 Dec, 3 weeks Jan. **Meals:** main courses £30 to £40. Set L £19 (2 courses) to £26. **Details:** 60 seats. 6 seats outside. V menu. Music. Children over 4 yrs only.

The Seafood Restaurant

Cooking score: 5
Seafood | £61
Riverside, Padstow, PL28 8BY
Tel no: (01841) 532700
rickstein.com

Is it really 36 years since Rick and Jill Stein's Seafood Restaurant first appeared in the Guide? Rick Stein may not sweat over the stoves these days but his flagship operation remains close to his heart – and is still a place of pilgrimage, benefiting from the press of custom that a strong presence on the telly can provide. It's an inviting, contemporary space with an 'instant and warm welcome', where the seasonal notes of exemplary fresh ingredients form the backbone of a menu with a pronounced global reach, and includes some high-end options (at high-end prices) such as lobster thermidor, Dover sole meunière and turbot with hollandaise. At a winter meal there was praise for fish and shellfish soup with rouille, excellent mussels with yellow kroeung (Cambodian curry paste), coconut milk and Kaffir lime leaves, and a superb Indonesian seafood curry with monkfish, pollack, squid and prawns. Elsewhere, desserts get positively avant-garde for peanut-butter cheesecake with lime curd and banana ice cream. Wines from £22.
Chef/s: Stephane Delourme. **Open:** all week L 12 to 2.30, D 6.30 to 10. **Closed:** 25 and 26 Dec. **Meals:** main courses £20 to £50. Set L £31 (winter), £40 (summer). **Details:** 120 seats. Bar. Wheelchairs. Music. Children over 3 yrs only.

LOCAL GEM

Rick Stein's Café

Seafood | £28
10 Middle Street, Padstow, PL28 8AP
Tel no: (01841) 532700
rickstein.com

Handy for visitors to 'Padstein' who want a cheap-and-cheerful taste of the Rick Stein experience, and don't mind the hubbub or elbow-to-elbow seating. Fish is, naturally, the main event at this jolly all-day café, with recipes gleaned from Rick's worldwide travels: salt-and-pepper prawns or Madras-style curried gurnard spiked with tamarind might sit beside whole devilled mackerel or hake with beurre blanc and kale. Char-grilled steaks appease the carnivores, while indulgent puds could include sunken chocolate cake with clotted cream. Busy for breakfast, too.

▌Penzance

Bakehouse and Steakhouse

Cooking score: 2
Modern European | £25
Old Bakehouse Lane, Chapel Street, Penzance, TR18 4AE
Tel no: (01736) 331331
bakehouserestaurant.co.uk

The Carrs' bright, attractive restaurant housed in an old bakery is to be found in a secluded courtyard off the main street. Palms and flowers brighten the scene, while inside the action goes on over two floors, one with sandy-coloured banquettes and lattice-backed chairs, the other in marine blue and white, adorned with changing displays of local artwork. Andy Carr cooks modern bistro food with seafood and prime steaks to the fore, and with North African and Thai influences blended in. Buttermilk-fried squid with saffron aïoli might presage roasted pollack crusted in pine nuts and pistachios, served with puréed peas and broccoli, if you're sailing the seafood route. Or it may be smoked duck salad with celeriac, apple, cucumber and beetroot jelly, ahead of a Cornish Angus steak with your choice of sauce, butter or rub. Finish with nutritious hazelnut and oatmeal meringue, served with red berries and clotted cream. French and Spanish house wines are £16.25.
Chef/s: Andy Carr. **Open:** Mon to Sat D only 6 to 9. **Closed:** Sun, 24 to 27 Dec, first two weeks Jan. **Meals:** main courses £10 to £20. Early D £13 (2 courses). **Details:** 56 seats. Music.

The Bay

Cooking score: 3
Modern British | £32
Hotel Penzance, Britons Hill, Penzance,
TR18 3AE
Tel no: (01736) 366890
thebaypenzance.co.uk

Nothing sustains the soul quite like a sea view, and the restaurant arm of the Hotel Penzance offers just that, with Mount's Bay laid out before you, as well as regular exhibitions of contemporary artworks in the dining room. It's an all-day venue, opening for fortifying breakfasts, cruising serenely through lunch and late afternoon tea, up to the evening brasserie menu. Ben Reeve has done his homework, and knows that the likes of sweet-cured mackerel with caper and raisin purée, and mains such as herb-and-sesame-crusted monkfish with smoked potato and confit fennel, or pork fillet with onion pudding in apple velouté, are what people want to eat. Dishes score highly for depth of flavour and the pedigree of prime south-west ingredients, while the Cornish cheese menu is a chance to fill in any gaps in your knowledge. Otherwise, look to peanut and banana bread-and-butter pudding with buttermilk ice cream for a comforting finale. Wines start at £18.50.
Chef/s: Ben Reeve. **Open:** all week L 12 to 2.30, D 5 to 9. **Closed:** first week Jan. **Meals:** main courses £15 to £24. Set L £15 (2 courses) to £20. Set D £23 (2 courses) to £32. **Details:** 60 seats. 15 seats outside. Music. Parking.

Harris's

Cooking score: 2
Modern European | £34
46 New Street, Penzance, TR18 2LZ
Tel no: (01736) 364408
harrissrestaurant.co.uk

This petite restaurant, tucked down a central Penzance side street, is a local institution – run by Roger and Anne Harris for 44 years – although the building itself has been in the restaurant and pub business since 1865. There's

a tried-and-trusted, classic feel to both the interior and to Roger's cooking, which draws on the best produce the local area can provide. Grilled Falmouth Bay scallops on salad leaves with a fresh herb dressing is a typical opener, while loin of venison on beetroot and caraway seed with glazed pear and red wine sauce epitomises the accessible, satisfying Anglo-French main courses that keep the restaurant's loyal regulars coming back for more. To round it off, maybe iced lemon soufflé in a dark chocolate case with fruit sauce. The wine list offers a satisfying scope, with plenty of half-bottles and much in the £30 bracket – though bottles start at £22.
Chef/s: Roger Harris. **Open:** Tue to Sat 12 to 6.30. **Closed:** Sun, Mon, 25 and 26 Dec, 12 Jan, 3 weeks winter. **Meals:** main courses £20 to £30. **Details:** 30 seats. Bar. Music. Children over 5 yrs only.

★ NEW ENTRY ★

The Shore

Cooking score: 3
Modern British | £33
13-14 Alverton Street, Penzance, TR18 2QP
Tel no: (01736) 362444
theshorerestaurant.uk

You can't spot the sea from this compact restaurant opposite Penzance town hall but there's no doubt where Bruce Rennie gets his inspiration. This welcoming little haven for seafood lovers is a first venture for Mr Rennie, who previously worked at Restaurant Martin Wishart in Edinburgh and has the classic skills set to show for it. Local day boats from nearby Newlyn provide the fish, say whiting goujons and locally grown Tregassow asparagus, a dish based on a classic vichyssoise, but rather than using leeks, potatoes and onions, the trimmings from the asparagus were used for the soup – the contrast of the cold soup and the hot, golden-crumbed goujons 'working particularly well'. A main course of fresh monkfish with a light and herby summer vegetable minestrone was packed with flavour. To finish, poached peach, rosemary cream and raspberry sorbet was a fragrant twist on a classic Melba. The dining room is

contemporary with thick carpet, white walls and a few nautical touches including candles in sea urchin shells. Wines from £18.
Chef/s: Bruce Rennie. **Open:** Tue to Sat L 12 to 2, D 6 to 9. **Closed:** Sun, Mon. **Meals:** main courses £14 to £19. Set L £15 (2 courses) to £20. **Details:** 28 seats. Music.

▌Port Isaac
Outlaw's Fish Kitchen
Cooking score: 4
Seafood | £40
1 Middle Street, Port Isaac, PL29 3RH
Tel no: (01208) 881183
outlaws.co.uk
£5 OFF

'This place is heaven,' enthused a visitor to this 'wonky-shaped' ancient building (the oldest in Port Isaac) splendidly sited right on the harbour. Tiny inside, with tight-packed tables, it's another winner from Nathan Outlaw (Restaurant Nathan Outlaw, the Mariners, Rock – see entries), the kind of approachable eatery you can make friends with. Cornish seafood takes centre stage, delivered as small sharing plates, which provokes a dilemma – the general consensus is that the concept doesn't really work – so the trick is to be selfish and not share. Order the smoked haddock brandade, don't miss the beer-cured salmon with cucumber and seaweed, above all eat the grilled lemon sole with green sauce butter, but do keep it all to yourself. Finish with West Country cheeses or desserts such as rhubarb and almond sponge with poached rhubarb and crème fraîche. There's sunny-natured service, too, and a short, keenly priced wine list (from £20).
Chef/s: Tim Barnes. **Open:** all week L 12 to 3, D 6 to 9. **Closed:** Sun and Mon (Oct to May), 1 week Christmas, Jan. **Meals:** small plates £7 to £20. **Details:** 24 seats. Music.

★ TOP 10 ★

Restaurant Nathan Outlaw
Cooking score: 10
Seafood | £119
6 New Road, Port Isaac, PL29 3SB
Tel no: 01208 880896
nathan-outlaw.com
£5 OFF

Nathan Outlaw comes to these pages at a different angle to most. The chef has a commendably modest appreciation of simplicity as well as sophistication and his strikingly modern, first-floor dining room, with its truly spectacular outlook over the Atlantic, is by far the most relaxed of all the Guide's top-scoring restaurants. That it is matched by an extraordinary procession of creativity, passion, subtlety, indeed genius, emanating from the kitchen makes Restaurant Nathan Outlaw quite unique. All great chefs place excellence of raw materials first on their list of essentials, but here it's not just the unimpeachable quality of the Cornish fish and seafood that marks out the cooking, it's the support from local producers who deliver fruit, vegetables, even cheeses, at their optimal best. And the flavours evoked are strikingly vivid. Each dish on the eight-course tasting menu (four or five at lunch) shows the sheer vitality of the ingredients, whether taking an unadorned approach with raw scallops and just layering gentle flavours of radish, cucumber, a hint of chilli and salt, or pulling carpaccio-style slices of cured monkfish into focus with ginger, fennel, lemon zest and yoghurt. Indeed, every detail makes sense, there is nothing unnecessary on the plate: a winning dish of sweet white crabmeat, delicate asparagus mousse, thinly sliced St Enodoc asparagus – a sliver of apple giving just the right acidic hit – proves to be a perfect evocation of spring, while the rich, fleeting, teasing flavours in Outlaw's signature Porthilly sauce work well with gurnard and its crunchy skin. There's brilliant choreography, too, behind a dish of turbot, the lusciousness of the fish offset by the saltiness of bacon crumbs and a surprisingly delicate mushroom purée flavoured with lime. As a finale, creamy Cornish Jack cheese, layered between thin slices of toasted sourdough and served with candied walnuts and pickled and plain celery, primes the palate for the sweetness of local strawberries strewn over a beautifully realised elderflower pannacotta. The engaging and genuinely committed Stephanie Little and her team serve with grace and good humour, while Damon Little oversees a wine list that has global breadth and excellence of pedigree, with rarities sprinkled throughout. If your budget allows, go for the spot-on wine flight. If it's tight, Damon's advice is exemplary, and there is plenty to enjoy by the glass. Bottles from £20.

Chef/s: Nathan Outlaw and Christopher Simpson. **Open:** Fri and Sat L 12 to 2, Wed to Sat D 7 to 9. **Closed:** Sun, Mon, Tue, Jan. **Meals:** set L £49 (4 courses) to £69 (5 courses). Tasting menu £119 (8 courses). **Details:** 28 seats. Music. No children under 12 yrs.

LOCAL GEM
Fresh from the Sea
Seafood | £17
18 New Road, Port Isaac, PL29 3SB
Tel no: (01208) 880849
freshfromthesea.co.uk

£30

Just a few steps from the main car park, this tiny, no-frills café may lack a sea view but the big draw is the crab and lobster landed daily from the owners' boat *Mary D*. Cooked on the premises, they are served in a sandwich or salad, with Cornish cheese and ham, Porthilly oysters, smoked mackerel pâté and exceedingly good cakes expanding the selection. Take away or eat in the cramped café. Glass of white wine £4.

Local Gem

Local Gems are the perfect neighbourhood venues, delivering good, freshly cooked food at great value for money.

▮ Porthleven
Kota
Cooking score: 4
Fusion-Modern European | £34
Harbour Head, Porthleven, TR13 9JA
Tel no: (01326) 562407
kotarestaurant.co.uk

Right opposite the slipway into the harbour, Kota has a prime position in one of Cornwall's most alluring coastal towns. Ignoring seafood would be tantamount to a capital offence, but New Zealander Jude Kereama, who runs the place with his wife Jane, knows his fruits of the sea very well indeed. They also own the more casual Kota Kai nearby. For a menu showing so many Asian twists and turns, there's a real sense of place. The 300-year-old building is unselfconsciously traditional, with wooden tables and exposed beams, and the mood is relaxed. Regional ingredients from land and sea supply a kitchen from which mussels are fired up with chorizo and chilli, venison is dressed with red-vein sorrel and rosemary soy, and hake wrapped in nori and served in ginger dashi broth with squid-ink and crab ravioli. The six-course tasting menu is a good bet. Wines start at £16.95.

Chef/s: Jude Kereama. **Open:** Tue to Sat D only 6 to 9. **Closed:** Sun, 24 to 26 Dec, Jan and Feb. **Meals:** main courses £14 to £22. Set D £20 (2 courses) to £25. **Details:** 32 seats. Bar. Wheelchairs. Music.

▮ Portscatho
Driftwood
Cooking score: 5
Modern European | £60
Rosevine, Portscatho, TR2 5EW
Tel no: (01872) 580644
driftwoodhotel.co.uk

Boutique coastal hotels are becoming quite the thing, and the far south west is an especially happy hunting ground. Driftwood stands in seven acres above Gerrans Bay, with a

concealed woodland path leading down to the beach and sheltered cove. So far, so idyllic, but Chris Eden's confidently assured modern European cooking, founded on premier local materials treated with technical ingenuity, is the icing on the cake. Start with a scallop and its smoked roe in bianchetti white truffle butter, with fennel, pancetta and wild garlic, and you may just forget cauliflower purée ever existed. Mains bring on 40-day Ruby Red beef smouldered over coals, with smoked bone marrow, garlic and spinach, or seared turbot and braised cuttlefish with peas and gem lettuce in hollandaise. Dishes look the part, colourful and appealing, and proceedings might end with a hard-to-resist collation of toffee apple jam, toasted hazelnuts, vanilla cream and cider sorbet. An informative wine list opens at £20.
Chef/s: Chris Eden. **Open:** all week D only 6.30 to 9.30. **Closed:** 5 Dec to 3 Feb. **Meals:** set D £60 (3 courses). Tasting menu £80 to £100. **Details:** 36 seats. Bar. Wheelchairs. Music. Parking. Children over 7 yrs only at D.

▌Rock
The Mariners
Cooking score: 2
British | £30
Rock, PL27 6LD
Tel no: (01208) 863679
themarinersrock.com
£5
OFF

Right on the road running through this well-heeled coastal village, the Mariners is a Sharp's Brewery pub that is perfectly positioned to capitalise on the views across the Camel Estuary from it ground- and first-floor terraces. Plenty of that luminous seaside glow finds its way into the bar and dining rooms via the floor-to-ceiling windows. Now run as part of Nathan Outlaw's mini Cornish empire, you can expect the menu to be fish focused and straight to the point. Simple treatments bring out the best of top-quality raw materials: Porthilly oysters, mussels, spicy potted Cornish crab with Doom Bar bread, and very fresh, perfectly cooked cod (with seaweed dumplings, purple sprouting broccoli and seaweed and lime butter) are present for those wanting a pure seafood hit. Otherwise expect steaks, Sunday roasts and homemade pork sausage or crispy beef focaccia lunch rolls. The Mariners also scores with its reasonable prices, which extends to the modest wine list (from £14.95).
Chef/s: Zack Hawke. **Open:** all week L 12 to 3 (4.30 Sun), D 6 to 9. **Meals:** main courses £9 to £24. Sun £16 (1 course). **Details:** 120 seats. 40 seats outside. Bar. Music.

▌St Ives
Alba
Cooking score: 2
Modern European | £32
Old Lifeboat House, Wharf Road, St Ives, TR26 1LF
Tel no: (01736) 797222
thealbarestaurant.com
£5
OFF

It's 15 years since the old lifeboat house in St Ives was transformed into the glass-fronted restaurant it is today. The window tables overlooking the harbour are highly prized and 'there is no debate that Alba has one of the best positions in St Ives'. A recent change has seen the introduction of more 'small plates' in the downstairs bar, but it's business as usual upstairs. Impeccable local raw materials are treated with respect and given a vigorous Mediterranean spin. Seafood is a strong suit, although an inspection meal starter of Provençal fish soup was underpowered and under-seasoned. There were no such qualms about a precisely cooked pan-fried fillet of wild line-caught local sea bass teamed with confit chicken, forestière potatoes, kale and a rich, dark chicken jus. Deconstructed millionaire's shortbread is one way to finish. Plenty of wines are served by the glass from a global list that kicks off at £15.50.
Chef/s: Grant Nethercott. **Open:** all week L 12 to 2.30, D 6 to 9 (5.30 to 10 Mar to Nov). **Closed:** 25 and 26 Dec. **Meals:** main courses £13 to £25. Set L and D £19 (2 courses) to £22. **Details:** 38 seats. Bar. Music.

The Black Rock

Cooking score: 2
Modern British | £28
Market Place, St Ives, TR26 1RZ
Tel no: (01736) 791911
theblackrockstives.co.uk
£5 OFF £30

Given St Ives' reputation as a hotbed of artistic endeavour, it's hardly surprising that the interior of this modest family-run restaurant is emblazoned with works by local painters and potters. Occupying a former hardware shop just a pebble's throw from the harbour, Black Rock is also in the business of promoting West Country ingredients: chef-proprietor David Symons recently started serving rare-breed Galloway beef from his own farm in Zennor (char-grilled ribeye with duck-fat chips and kale, for example) alongside fish and seasonal picks from a network of regional producers. The result is a line-up of intelligent well-crafted dishes with bright, clear flavours – from roasted half-shell scallops provençale or a simple plate of local mackerel with heritage tomato salad to confit free-range duck with spiced parsnip purée, braised red cabbage and apple. Meanwhile, desserts such as coconut pannacotta with stewed rhubarb and Kaffir lime crumble add an exotic note to proceedings. Wines from £14.95.
Chef/s: David Symons. **Open:** Mon to Sat D only 6 to 10.30. **Closed:** Sun, Nov to Mar. **Meals:** main courses £13 to £21. Set D £17 (2 courses) to £20. **Details:** 38 seats. Bar. Music.

Porthgwidden Beach Café

Cooking score: 1
Modern British | £25
Porthgwidden Beach, The Island, St Ives, TR26 1PL
Tel no: (01736) 796791
porthgwiddencafe.co.uk
£30

Secluded sibling to Porthminster Beach Café (see entry), this laid-back seaside café overlooks 'the most beautiful little beach, one that's still regarded as the best-kept secret of all of the St Ives beaches' and tables on the sea-facing terrace are highly prized. The whitewashed stone walls and simple décor within reflect the uncomplicated approach of the kitchen, which champions local seafood. A specials-board starter of grilled mackerel fillets with labneh, spiced rhubarb and dukkah might precede seafood bouillabaisse with sea bass, prawns, crab and mussels. Finish with limoncello pannacotta, summer berries and lemon sorbet. Wines from £15.50.
Chef/s: Robert Michael. **Open:** all week L 12 to 3, D 6 to 9. **Closed:** 2 weeks Dec. **Meals:** main courses £11 to £17. **Details:** 40 seats. 36 seats outside. Music.

Porthmeor Beach Café

Cooking score: 1
Tapas | £20
Porthmeor, St Ives, TR26 1JZ
Tel no: (01736) 793366
porthmeor-beach.co.uk
£30

'Is there a better view than from a window table (or the terrace)?' asked one visitor to this Antipodean-styled café within touching distance of the white sand and sea at Porthmeor. The glass-fronted conservatory and sought-after terrace are prime spots to catch memorable St Ives sunsets. With its lime-green chairs and pink plastic buckets of cutlery, it's a bright and cheery place guaranteed to put you in a holiday mood. The vibrant global food offers robust, punchy flavours whether it's smoked tofu, Asian salad and sticky soy or seared local scallops with a zesty topping of lemon gremolata crumb. Wines from £16.50. Sister beach cafes at nearby Porthminster and Porthgwidden (see entries).
Chef/s: Nathan Madden. **Open:** all week 9 to 9. **Closed:** Nov to mid Mar. **Meals:** tapas £3 to £10. Main meals £13 to £17. **Details:** 31 seats. 70 seats outside. Bar.

Porthminster Beach Café

Cooking score: 3
Seafood | £35
Porthminster Beach, St Ives, TR26 2EB
Tel no: (01736) 795352
porthminstercafe.co.uk

It's 25 years since this striking white Art Deco building was transformed into the perennially popular beach café it is today and it still meets the exacting demands of tourists, locals and second-home owners. The must-book terrace has a genuinely Mediterranean feel and the views across the bay can also be enjoyed from the whitewashed restaurant with its splashes of blue and yellow. Australian chef Michael Smith has steered the kitchen since 2002 and the cooking is robust, global and exciting, with local seafood given star billing. Crispy fried squid with miso dressing, Thai salad and black spice might be followed by grilled fillet of stone bass with a spicy ras-el-hanout chickpea cassoulet. Finish with an intense and wobbly banana pannacotta, saffron aero sponge, peanut brittle, bee pollen meringue and honey Chantilly cream. The lively wine list starts at £15.95, with 16 offered by the glass.
Chef/s: Ryan Venning and Michael Smith. **Open:** all week L 12 to 4, D 6 to 10. **Closed:** 25 Dec, Jan. **Meals:** main courses £15 to £29. **Details:** 58 seats. 66 seats outside. V menu. Music.

Blas Burgerworks

Burgers | £15
The Warren, St Ives, TR26 2EA
Tel no: (01736) 797272
blasburgerworks.co.uk
£30

Upmarket burger bars using conscientiously sourced local produce may be *de rigueur* these days but Blas Burgerworks was ahead of the pack when it opened more than a decade ago – 'it's still a bit of a find for a Cornish seaside resort'. This tiny backstreet restaurant and takeaway behind St Ives Arts Club takes great pride in using Cornish free-range beef and chicken, as well as fresh local fish from day boats and plenty of innovative vegetarian options, all of it cooked on the searing heat of the char-grill. Wine from £17.

Rum and Crab Shack

Seafood
Wharf Road, St Ives, TR26 1LG
Tel no: (01736) 796353
rumandcrabshack.com
'The rum in the name and the extensive, separate rum list gave the impression that there would be a West Indian flavour here, but in fact it was a simple, quaint café. I opted for the dressed crab, washed down with a decent Viognier and good coffee.'

■ St Kew
St Kew Inn

Cooking score: 2
Modern British | £27
St Kew, PL30 3HB
Tel no: (01208) 841259
stkewinn.co.uk
£30

From the exposed stone, beams, wood-burning range and flag floors, to the well-kept St Austell ale and please-all menu, there's plenty to entice at this ancient rural pub. Its location, fronted by a large garden with views of the 15th-century church and river, is a prime draw in summer, but the surge of visitors who negotiate the narrow lanes off the A39 come for food that comforts rather than challenges. The kitchen looks to the locality for ingredients but also mixes up influences in a true modern British way: a wild mushroom fricassee on Parmesan bread rubs shoulders with game terrine, say, or there could be classic fish and chips, or a chicken, bacon and mushroom pie, alongside pan-roasted monkfish with sag aloo and red curry sauce. Portions are generous so perhaps share the sticky toffee pudding and Guinness ice cream. Wines from £16.50.

Chef/s: Martin Perkins. **Open:** all week L 12 to 2, D 6 to 9. **Closed:** 25 and 26 Dec. **Meals:** main courses £12 to £18. Sun L £12.50 (1 course). **Details:** 70 seats. 100 seats outside. Bar. Parking.

St Mawes
Hotel Tresanton
Cooking score: 3
Modern European | £45
27 Lower Castle Road, St Mawes, TR2 5DR
Tel no: (01326) 270055
tresanton.com

Formerly a yacht club, this luxurious bolt-hole, just a short stroll from the old fishing harbour and the Falmouth foot ferry, has all the sea views you could wish for – in fine weather the terrace comes into its own as the place to have lunch. Creamy wood-panelled walls, mosaic tiled floors and tables clothed in neat white linen lend a refined Mediterranean vibe to the restaurant, where fish tops the bill on an ever-changing menu. Expect simple, classical cooking with an emphasis on freshness and flavour: roast scallops with balsamic glazed carrots and game crisps point the way, perhaps followed by brill on the bone with clams, potatoes, onion, tomatoes and aïoli. Burnt English custard with poached Champagne rhubarb is typical of the classy but comforting desserts. Drinks include cocktails, plenty of fizz and a wine list weighted towards France and Italy, with bottles starting at £22.
Chef/s: Paul Wadham. **Open:** all week L 12.30 to 2.30, D 7 to 9.30. **Closed:** 2 weeks Jan. **Meals:** main courses £18 to £40. Set L £23 (2 courses) to £27. Sun L £23. **Details:** 55 seats. 70 seats outside. Bar. Wheelchairs. Parking. Children over 6 yrs only at D.

Visit us online

To find out more about
The Good Food Guide, please
visit thegoodfoodguide.co.uk

St Merryn
The Cornish Arms
Cooking score: 2
British | £30
Churchtown, St Merryn, PL28 8ND
Tel no: (01841) 520288
rickstein.com

The whitewashed pub behind its five-bar gate looks entirely old-school, and notwithstanding its TV celeb ownership by a certain Mr Stein, it ploughs a hearteningly traditional furrow when it comes to food. A wood-burner flanked by piles of logs is a welcome sight on a bitter day, and so might be a fish finger sandwich slathered with Cornish ketchup and tartare sauce. Expect also to be regaled with post-ironic pub food from an earlier generation, such as half-pints of prawns with bread and mayonnaise, scampi in a basket with chips, or locally produced pork sausages with mash and onion gravy. Those determined to wander a little off-piste will gravitate to piri-piri sardines and Goan fish curry, but probably return to the fold for afters such as sticky toffee and clotted cream, or rice pudding with a splat of strawberry jam. Wines come in regular and large glasses, half-litre carafes, and bottles from £16.95.
Chef/s: Alex Clark. **Open:** all week L 12 to 2.30, D 6 to 8.30. **Meals:** main courses £10 to £18. **Details:** 140 seats. 130 seats outside. Bar. Wheelchairs. Music. Parking.

Rafferty's
Cooking score: 3
Modern British | £30
St Merryn, PL28 8NF
Tel no: (01841) 521561
raffertyscafewinebar.co.uk
£5 OFF

'Warm and welcoming, efficient and cheerful', everybody seems to have a good word for Ed Rafferty's appealing wine-bar-cum-restaurant. Like the no-frills décor – wood floors, rustic wood tables, high-backed rattan chairs and simple modern lighting – there's

nothing cluttered or fancy about the food, which aims to please with the 'dazzling ingredients, big flavours and beautiful simplicity' seen in a mix of tapas and sharing boards and more elaborately worked main courses. Jump-starting proceedings may be ham croquetas, salt hake fritters and aïoli, tempura courgettes with soy dipping sauce, and monkfish scampi with tartare sauce and minted pea purée, but also typical of the kitchen's output are sea bass with crushed new potatoes, spinach and salsa verde, and slow-roast pork belly with chorizo and cannellini bean cassoulet. The raspberry brûlée has been described as 'sublime', service is 'efficient and friendly', and wines start at £16.50.
Chef/s: Barry Horne. **Open:** Sun L 12 to 3, Wed to Mon D 5.30 to 10 (9.30 Sun and Mon). **Closed:** Tue. **Meals:** main courses £14 to £28. **Details:** 30 seats. 15 seats outside. Bar. Music.

▪ St Tudy

★ NEW ENTRY ★

St Tudy Inn
Cooking score: 2
Modern British | £32
St Tudy, PL30 3NN
Tel no: (01208) 850656
sttudyinn.com
£5 OFF

The picture-pretty village of St Tudy may no longer have a shop or post office, but its pub is enjoying a vigorous new lease of life under chef Emily Scott, who took over in 2015. A charming stone-built inn where locals catch up over pints of Padstow-brewed St Tudy ale in the bar (think slate floors and a wood-burner), there are three further dining areas with subtle nautical touches despite the place being some distance from the sea. A passionate advocate of Cornwall and its produce, Emily's concise seasonal menu lists impeccable local suppliers. The cooking is straightforward with no frills or frippery. A starter of scallops, garlic, thyme, lemon and leaves might be followed by hake, green beans, new potatoes, lemon aïoli and pea shoots. For meat eaters,

there's shoulder of lamb, spices with apricots, yoghurt, coriander and rice. Finish with lemon posset, ginger crumb and raspberries. Wines from £16.50.
Chef/s: Emily Scott. **Open:** Tue to Sun L 12 to 2.30, Tue to Sat D 6.30 to 9. **Closed:** Mon. **Meals:** main courses £12 to £19. Set L £18 (2 courses) to £24. Sun L £13. **Details:** 80 seats. 18 seats outside. Bar. Wheelchairs. Music. Parking.

▪ Sennen Cove
Ben Tunnicliffe Sennen Cove
Cooking score: 1
Modern British | £30
Sennen Cove, TR19 7BT
Tel no: (01736) 871191
benatsennen.com

Sticking out of the sand dunes like driftwood in wild and dramatic Sennen Cove, this timber-framed beachside restaurant boasts one of the most stunning locations in a county blessed with plenty. Chef Ben Tunnicliffe also runs Newlyn's Tolcarne Inn (see entry), but this busy, child- and surfer-friendly tourist destination pleases all-comers with beer-battered haddock and chips, burgers and steaks. There's also fresh Cornish mackerel with bacon, peanuts, hazelnuts and salad or scallops with chorizo, spinach and pine nuts, as well as local gurnard, and vanilla pannacotta for dessert. Pop in, too, for breakfast or coffee and cakes. Wines from £15.50.
Chef/s: Ben Tunnicliffe and Adam Ashbourne. **Open:** all week 11.30 to 9.30. **Closed:** 14 Jan to 10 Feb. **Meals:** main courses £12 to £18. **Details:** 80 seats. 90 seats outside. Bar. Wheelchairs. Music.

Symbols

▬ Accommodation is available
£30 Three courses for less than £30
£5 OFF £5-off voucher scheme
▲ Notable wine list

▌Treburley
The Springer Spaniel
Cooking score: 4
Modern British | £28
Treburley, PL15 9NS
Tel no: (01579) 370424
thespringerspaniel.co.uk
£30

A delightfully remade whitewashed Georgian country inn in a Cornish hamlet, the Spaniel is owned by Anton Piotrowski of *MasterChef* fame (also appearing in Devon at the Treby Arms, Sparkwell and Glazebrook House, South Brent – see entries). The operation here conforms more to the idea of a village pub, with local ales on tap, and some distinctly old-fangled offerings – herb-crusted sirloins, wine-battered fish and chips – among the more speculative doings. Coating king prawns in pork crackling is a labour of love, but one that pays off when they're paired with slow-cooked pork belly as a starter, and then there might be duck breast with vanilla mash, ale-braised carrots and broccoli, or cocoa-marinated venison with colcannon. The ubiquitous salted caramel gets a thorough outing in support of dark chocolate cheesecake, or there could be lemon parfait with fennel meringue, lime and cardamom gel and shortbread. House blends are £16.95 on a short list arranged by style.
Chef/s: Alistair Fraiser. **Open:** all week L 12 to 3, D 6 to 9 (7.30 Sun). **Meals:** main courses £12 to £25. Sun L £15 (2 courses). **Details:** 69 seats. 36 seats outside. Bar. Wheelchairs. Music. Parking.

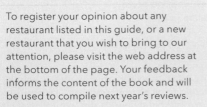

Please send us your feedback

To register your opinion about any restaurant listed in this guide, or a new restaurant that you wish to bring to our attention, please visit the web address at the bottom of the page. Your feedback informs the content of the book and will be used to compile next year's reviews.

▌Treen
The Gurnard's Head
Cooking score: 2
British | £30
Treen, TR26 3DE
Tel no: (01736) 796928
gurnardshead.co.uk

Run along similar lines to the Felin Fach Griffin in Brecon and the Old Coastguard in Mousehole (see entries), this rambling pub on the winding road between St Ives and Penzance overlooks the rocky peninsula of Gurnard's Head itself. The location is stunning – remote, windswept and with no mobile signal for miles – and is a welcome pit-stop for coastal path walkers. Inside, the sunflower yellow and duck egg blue walls, scrubbed pine tables and real fires add a boho farmhouse feel. Food may be the main draw here but ale-quaffing locals still prop up the bar and it all makes for a homely buzz. The kitchen keeps things simple and there is a good selection of local fish, perhaps a starter of grilled mackerel fillet with tenderstem broccoli and lemon and shallot dressing, which might precede pan-fried Newlyn hake teamed with crushed potatoes, chard, dill and shellfish velouté. Cornish strawberry consommé, compressed apple, lime sorbet and basil 'glass' is one of the ambitious desserts. Wines from £23.50.
Chef/s: Max Wilson. **Open:** all week L 12.30 to 2.30 (12 Sun), D 6.30 to 9. **Meals:** main courses £14 to £20. **Details:** 80 seats. 20 seats outside. Bar. Music. Parking.

▌Truro
Tabb's
Cooking score: 5
Modern British | £35
85 Kenwyn Street, Truro, TR1 3BZ
Tel no: (01872) 262110
tabbs.co.uk

After a dozen years in Truro, Nigel Tabb's tiny restaurant is still the go-to place in town, and its many fans are delighted that a recent makeover has given a more modern look and relaxed feel. Mr Tabb does not cut corners, so expect homemade everything (from the delicious bread to the chocolates with coffee), and a wealth of the best local ingredients. Begin with pan-fried scallops with grated cauliflower, bacon and coriander, red pepper reduction or a tasty duck and pork mousse with crisp pancetta, tomato salsa and red onion chutney. Follow with grilled fillet of hake, served with peas and beans, a saffron nage, watercress cream and a little garlic oil or, perhaps, roast breast of duck and shredded leg (served with spring onion), creamed beetroot and a port reduction. Dessert could be 'wonderful' baked lime and Earl Grey cheesecake, that's if West Country cheeses don't tempt. It's all deemed 'excellent value' – including global wines, priced from £16.95.

Chef/s: Nigel Tabb. **Open:** Tue to Sun L 12 to 2, Tue to Sat D 5.30 to 9.30. **Closed:** Mon, 25 and 26 Dec. **Meals:** main courses £16 to £21. Set L and D £20 (2 courses) to £25. **Details:** 28 seats. Bar. Music.

READERS RECOMMEND
Craftworks Street Kitchen
International Street Food
Lemon Quay House, Lemon Quay, Truro, TR1 2LW
Tel no: (07742) 875468
craftworkskitchen.co.uk
'This little restaurant is an absolute gem. The food tastes amazing and is all freshly prepared. There is an emphasis on using local produce and the Cornish beef brisket melts in your mouth. Top of my list of places to eat in Truro!'

Readers recommend

A 'readers recommend' review is a genuine quote from a report sent in by one of our readers. We intend to follow up these suggestions throughout the year to come.

Mannings
International
Lemon Street, Truro, TR1 2QB
Tel no: (01872) 247900
manningshotels.co.uk
'We ordered a lobster special at a very reasonable price. When our plates arrived, a commotion broke out on the surrounding tables because of the size of the lobster, the very generous and well-assorted salad and the more than copious dish of good fries.'

■ Wadebridge

LOCAL GEM
Little Plates
Mediterranean | £20
Polmorla Road, Wadebridge, PL27 7ND
Tel no: (01208) 816377
littleplatesbar.co.uk

£30

Rupert and Sarah Wilson's boho eatery is alive with chat and is charm personified – an eccentric mix of scuffed wood, bright colours and simple furnishings. Matching the mood is a mainly Mediterranean-inspired menu with some global touches. It reads robustly and delivers myriad small plates to a diverse crowd: beef and chorizo meatballs with sticky honey and garlic sauce, courgette, feta and dill fritters, and tempura-battered squid, say, alongside parmigiana di melanzane, hand-fried hake with pak choi, coriander, cashew nuts, sesame oil and soy sauce, and lahmacun (Moorish minted lamb on flatbread). Wines from £16.75.

■ Watergate Bay
Fifteen Cornwall
new chef/no score
Italian | £48
On the beach, Watergate Bay, TR8 4AA
Tel no: (01637) 861000
fifteencornwall.co.uk

You must know the score by now – young people given a break courtesy of Jamie Oliver's Cornwall Food Foundation, with these young apprentice chefs the heartbeat of the place. And it celebrated 10 years in 2016. Right on the beach, the modern wooden structure is white, bright and minimalist within, and the sea view is served up every day, one couple declaring themselves 'well protected inside from the gale raging today'. On the look-out for a new executive chef as we go to press following the departure of top-man Andy Appleton, the Cornish/Italian axis continues on a menu that might take you from rabbit saltimbocca with spicy salami, fontina and Swiss chard, to brill with inzimino di ceci (a stew of chickpeas and chard) and herby salmoriglio. It's open for breakfast and family-friendly lunches (it's not kid-friendly in the evening by the way), and don't go thinking it's cheap. Wines start at £22.50.

Open: all week L 12 to 2.30, D 6.15 to 9.15.
Meals: main courses £21 to £29. Tasting menu £65 (5 courses) to £85. **Details:** 108 seats. Bar. Wheelchairs. Music. Parking. Children over 12 yrs only at D.

LOCAL GEM

The Beach Hut
International | £25
Watergate Bay Hotel, Watergate Bay, TR8 4AA
Tel no: (01637) 860877
watergatebay.co.uk

🛏 £30

Part of the stylish Watergate Bay Hotel development, the Beach Hut is just down the lane and stands on the rocks overlooking the sand. At the 'designer end of the beach hut spectrum', it's a chilled-out space of wood and glass, with a menu that surfs a wave of contemporary fashion. Prawn fritters with Asian slaw, moules marinière or nachos, expect a free-spirited attitude to world flavours, while a host of burgers (a veggie pakora version among them), grilled fish masala and Cornish crab spaghetti confirm its status as a global melting pot. Wines start at £19.

Guilty pleasures

From milkshakes and sweeties to well-known fast food outlets, even our top chefs like to indulge in a guilty pleasure once in a while.

Whilst **Andrew Fairlie** and **Marianne Lumb** are big fans of that British institution fish and chips, the Savoy's **Kim Woodward** gives her fries a Mexican twist with the cheeky addition of guacamole.

James Knappett from **Kitchen Table** occasionally visits the Colonel, but **Dominic Chapman** is more inclined to take his kids to the golden arches for a burger. Talking of burgers, MEATliquor gets a mention from Barrafina's **Nieves Barragán Mohacho** for their meaty offerings while the Dairy's **Robin Gill**, also a fan, plumps for the chicken wings and chilli-cheese fries.

Nathan Outlaw loves penny sweets, but the Grove's **Allister Barsby** is more specific about his poison, citing a love of wine gums, he 'has a thing' for them.

The love for all things sweet doesn't stop there, with **Steve Smith** from the Freemason's tucking into ice cream. Meanwhile **Tyron Ellul** from Glenapp Castle throws caution to the wind and pops the spoon straight into the chocolate-hazelnut spread. Naughty!

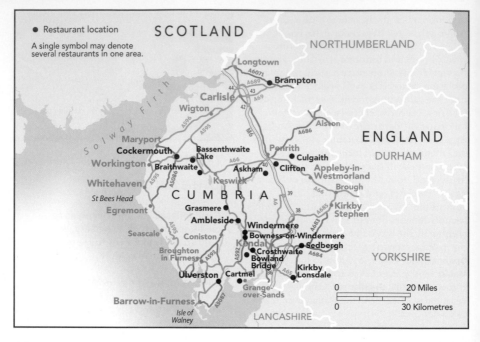

Restaurant location
A single symbol may denote several restaurants in one area.

▌Ambleside

The Drunken Duck Inn

Cooking score: 2
Modern British | £35
Barngates, Ambleside, LA22 0NG
Tel no: (015394) 36347
drunkenduckinn.co.uk

Whatever time of year you visit, this 360-year-old inn can serve up quite a view – snow-topped peaks, lush green hills, this is Lakeland and no mistake. Natty bedrooms, a mollifying bar, an on-site brewery (yes, they brew their own Barngates ales), a culinary output that is a cut above – it's no wonder this compelling package has its fans ('we love the Drunken Duck'). Lunch is a slightly more informal affair ordered at the bar, while the ante is well and truly upped in the evening. A passion for regional ingredients is shown in a Lancashire cheese soufflé, while smoked bacon with a hen's egg, oyster mushrooms and fermented cabbage reveals a finger on the contemporary pulse. Among main courses, shin of beef comes with a stout-rich suet pudding, cod and shrimps flavour gnocchi, and, to finish, chestnut cake is partnered with mulled pear and yoghurt mousse. Wines start at £21.
Chef/s: Jonny Watson. **Open:** all week L 12 to 4, D 6.30 to 9. **Closed:** 25 Dec. **Meals:** main courses £16 to £24. Tasting menu £55. **Details:** 60 seats. 32 seats outside. Bar. Wheelchairs. Parking.

★ TOP 50 ★

Lake Road Kitchen

Cooking score: 6
Modern European | £45
Lake Road, Ambleside, LA22 0AD
Tel no: (015394) 22012
lakeroadkitchen.co.uk

James Cross's restaurant is deeply rooted in Lakeland, but stellar in any context. Offering the 'food of the north' in both the Cumbrian and Nordic senses, it skips culinary asceticism and goes straight to 'interesting and enjoyable'.

Join us at thegoodfoodguide.co.uk

From behind their timbered wall (like a woodsy sauna with a window), Cross and his team send out creative, intelligent dishes shot through with the flavours of the forest. To start, green juniper-cured Norwegian salmon is served with rye, whey gel and nasturtium caper vinaigrette, and cauliflower is roasted with goats' butter and served with pine and viili, a yoghurty fermented milk cultured in-house. Needless to say, foraging, pickling and preserving take up quantities of the kitchen's time, but they set aside enough to mastermind the umami-based pleasures of miso-grilled skrei cod with charred kale, mash and chicken brown butter sauce. There are classical flourishes, too; roast Scottish red deer is served with black truffle purée and leeks vinaigrette, and if hay parfait with lingonberries doesn't sound like a grand enough finale, there's apple tarte fine with Calvados caramel. First-time visitors can't wait to go back for another 'truly memorable' taste of the north. The wine list is short with a handful of surprises, from £24.

Chef/s: James Cross. **Open:** Wed to Sun D only 6 to 9.30. **Closed:** Mon, Tue, 2 weeks Jan. **Meals:** main courses £22 to £29. Tasting Menu £55 (5 courses) to £75. **Details:** 28 seats. Music.

Old Stamp House

Cooking score: 4
Modern British | £40
Church Street, Ambleside, LA22 0BU
Tel no: (015394) 32775
oldstamphouse.com

Pilgrims on the Wordsworth heritage trail ought not to miss this whitewashed building in the town centre, where the poet served a long career in postal administration. If that sounds a little contrarily prosaic, it's at least an excuse for a good lunch or dinner from Ryan Blackburn, whose celebrations of the food traditions, producers and produce of Cumbria are given unpretentious modern treatment. Curry spices and mead are the medium for an opening serving of brown shrimps and roasted baby cauliflower, which might be followed by aged Longhorn beef shin with

dandelions and marrow, wild mushrooms and puréed parsley roots, or an earthy serving of roast turbot with smoked potato and cabbage in a truffle-scented jus. A summer reporter was particularly enamoured by a dish of hogget three ways, served with stem broccoli and goats' cheese gnocchi, while the seasonal dessert was elderflower curd with strawberry sorbet and coulis. An efficiently annotated wine list opens at £19.90.

Chef/s: Ryan Blackburn. **Open:** Wed to Sat L 12.30 to 2, Tue to Sat D 6 to 9. **Closed:** Sun, Mon, 25 and 26 Dec, Jan. **Meals:** main courses £19 to £27. Set L £20 (2 courses) to £25. Tasting Menu £55. **Details:** 28 seats. Music.

■ Askham

★ NEW ENTRY ★

Askham Hall

Cooking score: 5
Modern British | £50
Askham, CA10 2PF
Tel no: (01931) 712350
askhamhall.co.uk
£5 OFF

This handsome manor house a short drive from Penrith is now a small hotel with a fine restaurant. The chef, Richard Swale, is a local chap who trained with John Burton-Race and Anthony Demetre in London and Marc Veyrat in France. His cooking is a light, modern take on classic techniques and he has access to superb kitchen gardens and locally reared meat and poultry. There's dinner in the conservatory restaurant and private dining in the atmospheric old chapel. Swale cleverly combines flavour, texture and visual appeal – a trio of amuses may include venison and beetroot tartare, home-cured duck ham and a squid-ink tuile with the savoury kick of Parmesan cream. Roast scallops are teamed with cod brandade and a rich Madeira sauce while turbot enjoys the salty punch of clams and ras-el-hanout. Desserts are rich but intriguing, say Madagascar chocolate with barley ice cream and a scattering of buckwheat, or a fairy-like assembly of lemon, rhubarb, fennel, hibiscus and meringue. Overnighters can enjoy one of the best-ever British breakfasts with home-reared bacon, sausage, fresh eggs and superb black pudding. **Chef/s:** Richard Swale. **Open:** Tue to Sat D only 7 to 9.30. **Closed:** Sun, Mon, 25 and 26 Dec, 1 Jan to mid Feb. **Meals:** set D £50 (3 courses). Tasting menu £65 (5 courses). **Details:** 54 seats. Bar. Music. Parking. Children over 10 yrs only.

Bassenthwaite Lake

★ NEW ENTRY ★

The Pheasant Inn
Cooking score: 3
British | £30
Bassenthwaite Lake, CA13 9YE
Tel no: (017687) 76234
the-pheasant.co.uk

£5
OFF

'A tad genteel for hairy hikers', but this historic inn has something for everyone: a lively pub bar, the Fell restaurant for special dinners, sedate lounges for afternoon tea and the informal Bistro with remarkably good food and cheerful waiting staff. Malcolm Ennis's menu is fresh and modern, mixing local ingredients, traditional dishes and impressive techniques. A gutsy starter is black pudding served on crumbly brioche with a poached egg and topped with rich, glazed hollandaise sauce. Goats' cheese grilled with fresh figs and caramelised onion has the added crunch of pear and walnut crumble and there's a luscious chicken liver and Madeira parfait with cubes of prune and balsamic jelly. Reassuring mains include steak and chips, roast guinea fowl and duck confit with buttered cabbage as well as ambitious dishes such as a sea bass caught at nearby Ravenglass and served with prawns, noodles, pak choi and Asian broth flavoured with chilli and soy. There's an ironic Arctic roll dessert and unmissable crème brûlée with homemade shortbread. Wines from £18.

Chef/s: Malcolm Ennis. **Open:** all week L 12 to 2.30, D 6 to 9. **Closed:** 25 Dec. **Meals:** main courses £14 to £22. Set L £18 (2 courses) to £21. Set D £19 (2 courses) to £24. Sun L £19 to £25. **Details:** 40 seats. 30 seats outside. Bar. Wheelchairs. Music. Parking.

Bowland Bridge

LOCAL GEM
Hare & Hounds
British | £25
Bowland Bridge, LA11 6NN
Tel no: (015395) 68333
hareandhoundsbowlandbridge.co.uk

🛏 £30

A cosy meal by a log fire is just the ticket after a walk over rugged hills – something the Hare & Hounds excels at, providing all the warmth, welcome and rusticity you could wish for, along with a touch of boutique class. And you really can eat the view here: a local smoked meat platter to start, perhaps, and then a lamb hotpot made with local black pudding, tender local lamb, baby onions and a dauphinois-style topping. The down-to-earth style continues with desserts of the sticky toffee pudding and fruit crumble variety. The 30-strong wine list is 'uncommonly good for this kind of place' and opens at £16.85.

Bowness-on-Windermere
Linthwaite House
Cooking score: 5
Modern British | £58
Crook Road, Bowness-on-Windermere, LA23 3JA
Tel no: (015394) 88600
linthwaite.com

£5
OFF   🍾 🛏

The stretch of hinterland to the east of Lake Windermere is a happy hunting ground for both sedate sightseeing and eating, and here, a little way out of Bowness, is another lovely Lakeland spot. Linthwaite stands in 14 of its own acres overlooking the lake and hills, a beautifully maintained country house hotel of the old school. Within its genteel embrace, Chris O'Callaghan's cooking nudges you gently into the postmodern era though, with dishes that reach hither and thither for inspiration. Beetroot pannacotta with smoked tofu and honeycomb, or dressed crab in tropical livery with mango, passion fruit and lemongrass, could be the opening acts in a show that continues with sea trout in roast chicken consommé with brown shrimps and watercress, while pedigree pork appears as fillet and belly alongside vanilla mash, sauerkraut and apple. A construction of lemon posset with Grasmere gingerbread, elderflower and meringue bids fair to become a modern Cumbrian classic. Wines are carefully sorted by style, whether regional or varietal, intelligently annotated and chosen with impeccable discernment throughout. Prices open at £20.50, or £6.85 a glass.

Chef/s: Chris O'Callaghan. **Open:** all week L 12 to 2, D 7 to 9. **Meals:** set L £17 (2 courses) to £24. Set D £58 (4 courses). Sun L £26. **Details:** 60 seats. 24 seats outside. Bar. Wheelchairs. Music. Parking. Children over 7 yrs only.

■ Braithwaite
The Cottage in the Wood
Cooking score: 4
Modern British | £50
Magic Hill, Whinlatter Forest, Braithwaite, CA12 5TW
Tel no: (01768) 778409
thecottageinthewood.co.uk
£5 OFF

Peeping out from amid the trees on a densely forested mountainside, the black-and-white Cottage is a Georgian house renovated to a high standard as a modern restaurant-with-rooms, with the adjunct of a half-moon dining room with windows all round to provide appetising views of the surroundings. Whether you plan to take your hiking boots or not, it's a glorious setting for Chris Archer's seasonally informed contemporary menus, where six-course tasters come with all the extras and the option of a plate of artisan

cheeses before the dessert duo. Techniques are innovative and exciting, starting with tea-smoked salmon tartare with pickled veg, avocado and grapefruit, and going on to a slow-cooked egg with mushy peas and merguez, before skrei cod and morteau sausage, and then loin and belly of Herdwick lamb with goats' curd and green olives. The closing flourish comes in the form of Amalfi lemon meringue with Kendal mint-cake ice cream. House Italians are £19.95.

Chef/s: Chris Archer. **Open:** Thur to Sat L 12.30 to 2, Tue to Sat D 6 to 9. **Closed:** Sun, Mon, Jan. **Meals:** set L £25 (3 courses). Set D £50 (3 courses). Tasting menu £65. **Details:** 36 seats. Bar. Wheelchairs. Parking. Children over 10 yrs only at D.

■ Brampton
Farlam Hall
Cooking score: 3
Modern British | £48
Hallbankgate, Brampton, CA8 2NG
Tel no: (016977) 46234
farlamhall.co.uk
£5 OFF

The original house is Elizabethan, but its accretions and additions are mainly Victorian, when indoor donkey rides were among the favoured ways of passing the time. The Quinions have owned it, and nurtured it with dedication, since the mid-1970s, ensuring it offers the full rural hotel package, including lovely garden views from the ornate dining room. Here, Barry Quinion cooks a daily-changing dinner menu, served at 8 for 8.30, of soothing country-house food. Start with hot spiced Morecambe Bay shrimps with garlic butter and brioche, before choosing between the likes of halibut in red pepper and saffron sauce, quail stuffed with herb mousse in red wine, or beef medallion in pink peppercorns and brandy. After a board of English cheeses, a longer dessert choice takes in vanilla pannacotta with berries, and crème brûlée with a fruit juice shot. The wine list does the rounds in a whistle-stop tour that starts at £22.50.

Chef/s: Barry Quinion. **Open:** all week D only 8 for 8.30 (1 sitting). **Closed:** 25 to 30 Dec, 8 to 27 Jan. **Meals:** set D £48 (4 courses) to £53. **Details:** 45 seats. Wheelchairs. Parking. Children over 5 yrs only.

▌Cartmel

★ NUMBER ONE RESTAURANT ★

L'Enclume

Cooking score: 10
Modern British | £130
Cavendish Street, Cartmel, LA11 6PZ
Tel no: (015395) 36362
lenclume.co.uk

🍷 ⇌

'The fact that we had eaten at numerous top restaurants didn't really prepare us for the full-on onslaught to the taste-buds provided by L'Enclume,' enthused one diner of Simon Rogan's inimitable style, which 'combines multiple textures and flavours with astonishing results'. The soaring sophistication of Mr Rogan's cooking, interpreted here on a day-to-day basis by Tom Barnes, is matched by the surprising surroundings: the discreet frosted glass door to this modest former blacksmith's opens on to a modern inner space – an abundance of slate and wood, with Scandi retro furniture and views over a cottage garden to a little river. Many diners make this a pilgrimage, staying in L'Enclume's smart bedrooms dotted around Cartmel and taking in a meal at sibling Rogan & Co as part of their stay. Rogan's reach may now extend to The French in Manchester and Fera in London (see entries), but L'Enclume remains the jewel in the crown, with the cooking forever breaking new ground. While some diners itch for a choice of dishes, the set 17-course tasting menu still delights, offering clever elements of technical wizardry to keep the 'oohs' and 'aahs' going: think horseradish snow on a crisp wafer cup of 'deliciously rich' beetroot; pebble-shaped meringues filled with oyster purée; and a smoke-filled glass cloche over crisp-fried onion balls filled with smoked eel and pork belly. Elsewhere, Humphrey's Pool 'smelled gloriously of the sea, containing sea creatures and dainty frozen whelk shapes of béchamel and garlic that melted when a hot, briney broth was poured over them'. After a quick fire succession of openers, the main acts create more space, slowing the pace and satisfying even the most ravenous appetites. Highlights have included a 'beautiful piece' of butter-poached brill with asparagus, watercress, shrimp sauce, watercress oil and ('wonder of wonders') intense, crisp-fried hen-of-the-woods; or a lamb croquette with caper jam and ransom cream, quickly followed by its shoulder with sheep's milk foam, lamb jus, kale, radish and broccoli purée. Ingredients are emphatically local, with much grown on L'Enclume's own 12-acre farm, and other local sources noted – as in a 'fresh and tangy' dessert of aerated Holker sheep milk yoghurt with 'a stunning, light as air yoghurt crisp and poached rhubarb'. While most of the thrills are on the plate rather than in gimmicky flourishes, the team permit themselves a showy final bow: a gold disc bearing L'Enclume's anvil symbol, on to which was poured a hot apple and pine sauce, revealing slow-cooked apple and caramel mousse. Staff 'strike that magical balance of being incredibly slick but also letting their personalities show with touches of humour', while amid much to-ing and fro-ing the sommelier offers sensible but interesting pairings from the weighty wine list. Bottles start at £35, but the wine flight is a good way to go, offering 'less obvious choices that really open up the flavours'.

Chef/s: Simon Rogan, Marcus Noack and Tom Barnes. **Open:** Tue to Sun L 12 to 2, D 6.30 to 9. **Closed:** Mon, 2 to 16 Jan. **Meals:** set L £49 (6 courses). Tasting menu £130. **Details:** 54 seats. V menu. Wheelchairs. Parking. Children L only.

Symbols

⇌ Accommodation is available
£30 Three courses for less than £30
£5 OFF £5-off voucher scheme
🍷 Notable wine list

Rogan & Company

Cooking score: 5
Modern British | £37
Devonshire Square, Cartmel, LA11 6QD
Tel no: (015395) 35917
roganandcompany.co.uk

The relaxed offspring of Simon Rogan's nearby L'Enclume, Rogan & Co tempts plenty of its big brother's customers to stay for a second meal in Cartmel – and they're 'full of praise' for everything from the 'light and interesting' modern interior to the imaginative but accessible cooking. Lee Bird, formerly of Gilpin Hotel & Lake House (see entry), has taken the reins here with convincing confidence and maturity: witness an opening spin on steak tartare with tomato jam, pawpaw brined in vinegar, rye bread and mayonnaise – a 'sensational, melt in the mouth' dish with harmonious breadth of flavour. A main course of sage-crusted pork chop with green beans, creamy tofu, pomme purée and perry gravy impressed with tiptop ingredients and big flavours, while a 'transcendent' dessert of baked rice pudding with wine-poached pear, almond crumble and clotted cream ice cream left one diner feeling she had reached 'nirvana'. Pacey but charming service and a snappy drinks menu complete the picture: look out for beers from the neighbouring brewery, and a short but appealing selection of wines opening at £24.
Chef/s: Lee Bird. **Open:** Tue to Sun L 12 to 2 (12.30 to 5 Sun), Mon to Sat D 6.30 to 9. **Meals:** main courses £16 to £25. Set L £12 (1 course) to £24 (3 courses). **Details:** 40 seats. Wheelchairs. Music.

▌Clifton
George & Dragon

Cooking score: 4
Modern British | £30
Clifton, CA10 2ER
Tel no: (01768) 865381
georgeanddragonclifton.co.uk
£5 OFF 🛏

The feisty sibling of swanky Askham Hall a few miles away (see entry), the George & Dragon is a 200-year-old country inn with a handful of bedrooms. Comfortable seating, an open fire and live music in the winter defines the bar, while the good-value restaurant is the social hub of the area. There's an open kitchen, wooden floors and tables, leather banquettes backed with swirling crewelwork and swags of dried flowers on the walls. The cooking is terrific, with blackboard menus listing the likes of dry home-cured beetroot salmon gravadlax with pickled fennel, rye bread, horseradish crème fraîche and Avruga caviar. Local Saddleback pork is studded with garlic and rosemary, then wrapped in prosciutto and served with caramelised onions, smoked paprika and crushed potatoes. This is food for country appetites with venison from the Lowther Estate, beef from the owner's prime Shorthorn herd and gutsy dishes such as chorizo sausage with smoked pancetta and black pudding, and superior nursery food puddings such as apple crumble, ice cream and red-hot custard. A surprisingly good wine list opens at £18.
Chef/s: Ian Jackson. **Open:** all week L 12 to 2.30, D 6 to 9. **Closed:** 26 Dec. **Meals:** main courses £13 to £18. Set L and D £15 (2 courses) to £19.
Details: 104 seats. 60 seats outside. Bar. Music. Parking.

▌Cockermouth
Quince & Medlar

Cooking score: 2
Vegetarian | £27
11-13 Castlegate, Cockermouth, CA13 9EU
Tel no: (01900) 823579
quinceandmedlar.co.uk
£30

The strikingly colourful interiors of the Le Vois' vegetarian restaurant in a Georgian town house next to the little castle are a reflection of their determination to give the place its own singular identity. Bare tables and Lakeland landscapes are the decorative order in the dining room, and out back two trees, each bearing one of the titular fruits, aim to outdo each other every autumn (the medlar usually wins). Colin's menus are all freshness and imagination, opening perhaps with buckwheat pancakes, kohlrabi rémoulade and plum sauce, or a pâté of char-grilled aubergine and aduki beans served with oaty crackers. At main, there are robust, well-seasoned constructions such as a balsamic-roasted red onion with gingered quinoa, hazelnuts and courgette in smoky red pepper sauce, or slabs of polenta with star anise roast fennel, capers and olives, served with chunky tomato relish. If the quince has fruited abundantly, expect it to load a shortbread-based cheesecake. House Spanish varietals are £16.50.
Chef/s: Colin Le Voi. **Open:** Tue to Sat D only 6.30 to 9.30. **Closed:** Sun, Mon, 24 to 26 Dec.
Meals: main courses £15. **Details:** 26 seats. V menu. Music. Children over 5 yrs only.

▌Crosthwaite
The Punch Bowl Inn

Cooking score: 3
Modern British | £33
Lyth Valley, Crosthwaite, LA8 8HR
Tel no: (015395) 68237
the-punchbowl.co.uk
£5 OFF

St Mary's Church has been around longer than near neighbour the Punch Bowl, but the old stone-built inn is no newbie. The Lyth Valley setting can't have changed much since either of them arrived on the scene – 'a truly peaceful spot'. A smart country-chic finish extends through the building, from the bedrooms to the bar with its slate floor and bar counter. Head into one of the well-dressed dining areas and you'll find some divertingly up-to-date food made from a good dose of regional ingredients. Begin with steak tartare with a Bloody Mary dressing, or a cauliflower soup given oomph from cardamom, raisins and curried croûtons. Follow up with pork belly and cheek cleverly matched with salt-baked pineapple, or loin of cod with mussels and a sauce made from Thatchers cider. Vegetarians fare well with their own menu, while, to finish, damson crumble soufflé with almond ice cream is open to all. Wines start at £22.
Chef/s: Scott Fairweather. **Open:** all week L 12 to 5.30 (4 Sat and Sun), D 5.30 to 9. **Meals:** main courses £14 to £19. **Details:** 85 seats. 44 seats outside. V menu. Bar. Music. Parking.

Culgaith

★ LOCAL RESTAURANT AWARD ★
REGIONAL WINNER

Mrs Miller's

Cooking score: 3
British | £28
Hazel Dene Garden Centre, Culgaith,
CA10 1QF
Tel no: (01768) 882520
mrsmillersculgaith.co.uk

£5 OFF £30

Entering through the garden centre presents opportunities for the purchase of an azalea or two, but the real excitement begins once you enter James Cowin's café-restaurant. The culinary opportunities awaiting are positively stimulating. The interior design is simplicity itself – it's basic, basically – and it's open for traditional breakfasts, hearty lunches (homemade quiche with celeriac slaw) and, two evenings a week, some stonking dinners. This is a kitchen that focuses on local ingredients and knows how to create feel-good flavours. King scallops get a lift from a touch of tandoori spicing among first courses, or go for a pressed terrine of pork, pigeon and pistachio, while grilled Lakeland porterhouse steak is a treat for two. The local landscape also chips in with the lamb that is served with homemade haggis and, to finish, lemon posset with spiced berries shows a lighter touch. The short, well-chosen wine list kicks off at £12.50.

Chef/s: James Cowin. **Open:** all week L 12 to 3, Fri and Sat D 7 to 9. **Closed:** 25 and 26 Dec, 1 Jan, Easter Sun. **Meals:** main courses £10 to £21. **Details:** 54 seats. 20 seats outside. Wheelchairs. Music. Parking.

Visit us online

To find out more about
The Good Food Guide, please
visit thegoodfoodguide.co.uk

Grasmere

★ TOP 50 ★

★ BEST NEW ENTRY ★

Forest Side

Cooking score: 7
Modern British | £50
Keswick Road, Grasmere, LA22 9RN
Tel no: (015394) 35250
theforestside.com

£5 OFF

As if Grasmere didn't have enough to recommend it, Wordsworth's village now boasts a grand hotel restored to the height of nature-inspired tastefulness, and Kevin Tickle to boot. Tickle, former forager and chef for Simon Rogan, is in charge at the Forest Side's ambitious but unstuffy restaurant, a hive of endeavour thanks to the gathering, growing, brewing and preserving that form part of his loving, careful tribute to the flavours of Cumbria. The restaurant, serving as both country-house breakfast room and backdrop to highly evolved culinary doings, is large, pleasant and woody, flush with plank tabletops, sage-green leather and mossy sticks. The food, too, strikes an extremely likeable balance; perhaps, on the tasting menu, between hard-core hedgerow clippings (served with delicate Cumbrian milk-fed lamb, potato purée and the garlicky onslaught of ramsons 'in various stages of flowering') and the fat comfort of a caramelised scallop draped with house-made guanciale. Complete technique is on show in a clear, almost sparkling seaweed broth with sweet dice of kohlrabi, marsh herbs and lightly pickled surf clams, and a keen eye for the possibilities of the natural larder in a salad of tiny beetroots, Ragstone cheese and impossibly crunchy hazelnuts, spiked with the sorrel-like acidity of sunset velvet leaves. Puddings are convincingly puddingy, and in the home of gingerbread a dish of scorched pear with malt cream and damp, nutty cake, paired with complex home-brewed ginger beer, feels absolutely right. Staff are dressed tweedily, as if they're going out for a hack, but attentive (and skilled) nonetheless. The wine list, fittingly dominated by natural and organic choices, starts at £27.

Chef/s: Kevin Tickle. **Open:** Wed to Sun L 12 to 2, all week D 7 to 9.30. **Meals:** set L £35 (4 courses). Set D £50 (3 courses) to £75. **Details:** 50 seats. 22 seats outside. V menu. Bar. Wheelchairs. Music. Parking. Children over 8 yrs only.

The Jumble Room

Cooking score: 1
Global | £40
Langdale Road, Grasmere, LA22 9SU
Tel no: (015394) 35188
thejumbleroom.co.uk
£5 OFF

In a world filled with bland corporate uniformity, the Jumble Room is the polar opposite, run by a dedicated couple for 20 years with friendliness and a personal touch. The mood is chipper, while colourful décor clearly reflects Andy and Chrissy Hill's passion for music and animals. The kitchen's globally inspired output sees first-course Filipino-style spiced beef tapa followed by cod and langoustine thermidor, classic fish and chips, or teppanyaki steak with sticky rice. Wines start at £16.95.

Chef/s: Chrissy Hill. **Open:** Mon, Wed to Sun D only 5.30 to 9.30. **Closed:** Tue, 12 to 26 Dec. **Meals:** main courses £17 to £25. **Details:** 50 seats. Music.

■ Kirkby Lonsdale
Carter at the Sun Inn

Cooking score: 2
Modern British | £34
6 Market Street, Kirkby Lonsdale, LA6 2AU
Tel no: (015242) 71965
sun-inn.info

This is just the kind of cosy, welcoming inn you'd hope to find in the heart of a picturesque Cumbrian town: sunny yellow walls, exposed beams and a wood-burner crank up the traditional charm in the bar, while the

restaurant is slightly dressier with red walls and smart furnishings. You can experience Sam Carter's cooking in either, and while there are plenty of simple pub offerings, the real interest lies in the more complex, modern British dishes. A lunchtime smoked haddock velouté with a poached egg and croûtons was 'perfectly executed' while a corn-fed chicken breast with crispy confit leg, creamed leeks and bacon, fondant potato and thyme jus impressed with 'precise cooking and generous proportions'. Toffee apple brûlée, piled high with apple sauce, crumble, preserved apple and pieces of fudge, was equally generous if 'a little overwhelming'. Drinks include plenty of wines by the glass or carafe, with bottles starting at £19.95.

Chef/s: Sam Carter. **Open:** Tue to Sun L 12 to 3, all week D 6.30 to 9 (9.30 Fri and Sat). **Closed:** 25 Dec. **Meals:** main courses £17 to £21. Set L £21 (2 courses) to £28. Set D £28 (2 courses) to £34. Sun L £23. **Details:** 60 seats. Bar. Wheelchairs. Music.

■ Sedbergh

★ NEW ENTRY ★

Three Hares

Cooking score: 2
Modern European | £30
57 Main Street, Sedbergh, LA10 5AB
Tel no: (015396) 21058
threeharescafe.co.uk

By day, James Ratcliffe and Nina Matsunaga's welcoming patch of lovely Sedbergh is a café and bakery, offering good bread, breakfasts and lunches. On Friday and Saturday evenings they go bistro, showing off a brilliant beer list, cosy interior and the combined food inheritance of James's local roots and Nina's upbringing in Germany with Japanese parents. The menu is captivating, every dish a potential winner whether it's kidney on toast or miso aubergine; cooking is rustic, with huge portions and occasional lack of focus, but the spirit carries through. To start, try rosettes of purple-red 'Sedbergh ham' (it's lamb) with capers and bread, or luxurious Cromer crab thermidor. The miso aubergine is baked to rich creaminess, with an intensely salty miso hit balanced with seaweed and pickled cucumber. For afters, rhubarb and custard jelly evokes the sweet, with a crystal-clear rhubarb jelly punching above its weight. It's all keenly priced, as are wines from £14.95.

Chef/s: Nina Matsunaga. **Open:** Mon to Sat 8.30 to 5 (11pm Fri and Sat). Sun 10.30 to 4. **Meals:** main meals £14 to £17

Ulverston
The Bay Horse

Cooking score: 3
Modern British | £37
Canal Foot, Ulverston, LA12 9EL
Tel no: (01229) 583972
thebayhorsehotel.co.uk

'I just wish I lived nearer,' sighed one reader hankering after the 'beautiful views over the estuary'. The main restaurant at this old coaching inn dating from the 18th century is located in a conservatory that duly serves up the unadulterated watery vista. When darkness falls, candles help to create a romantic mood. Eating in the smart, traditional bar is an option, too. The main menu has old staples such as prawn and avocado cocktail among first courses, or a large field mushroom topped with leeks and a mozzarella and pesto crust. Aberdeen Angus steaks are cooked on the grill, orange-braised Lakeland lamb arrives with ginger syrup and red wine jus, and guinea fowl gets the pot-roasting treatment. Vegetarians get a dedicated section on the menu, while South African bobotie is something of a speciality. Lunch options include sandwiches, light bites and steak and kidney pudding. Wines start at £14.50.

Chef/s: Robert Lyons. **Open:** Tue to Sun L 12 to 3 (4 Sat and Sun), all week D 7.30 for 8. **Meals:** main courses £16 to £27. **Details:** 60 seats. 20 seats outside. Bar. Wheelchairs. Music. Parking. Children over 10 yrs only at D.

Windermere
Gilpin Hotel & Lake House

Cooking score: 5
Modern British | £65
Crook Road, Windermere, LA23 3NE
Tel no: (015394) 88818
thegilpin.co.uk

The Cunliffe family's serene Edwardian retreat by the shores of Lake Windermere has come on in leaps and bounds since its days as plain old 'Gilpin Lodge', with five spanking-new spa suites just one recent addition to its ever-growing portfolio. However, it's business as usual in the hotel's three lavishly appointed lounges and dining rooms, where visitors can admire the views while contemplating a dinner menu imbued with silky-smooth modern ideas. Seasonal ingredients from the North Country and across the border are given a seriously intricate workout, from roast Cartmel venison with a glazed dumpling, spiced aubergine caviar and charred baby gem to fillet of Buccleuch beef with a crispy stuffed shallot, nigella seeds, reduced tomato compote and red wine sauce. Fish is handled with similar dexterity (think turbot fillet, hand-rolled macaroni, brown shrimps, violet artichokes and truffle emulsion), while desserts span everything from a tasting of Yorkshire rhubarb to a sweet-toothed confection involving peanut-butter semifreddo, salted caramel, candied peanuts, hot fudge and banana ice cream. Fine vintages and broad-minded global coverage typify the expansive wine list, with bottles from £29.

Chef/s: Hrishikesh Desai. **Open:** all week L 12 to 2, D 6 to 9. **Meals:** set L £35. Set D £65 (4 courses). Tasting menu £85 (7 courses). Sun L £35. **Details:** 58 seats. 26 seats outside. V menu. Bar. Wheelchairs. Music. Parking. Children over 7 yrs only.

Holbeck Ghyll

Cooking score: 6
Modern British | £68
Holbeck Lane, Windermere, LA23 1LU
Tel no: (015394) 32375
holbeckghyll.com

Darren Comish, previously of Oak Bank
Hotel in Grasmere, now heads up the kitchen
in this gloriously located country house hotel.
Perched high on a hill with spectacular views
– lounge and oak-panelled dining rooms all
have views over Windermere to the rugged
peaks beyond – Lake District produce informs
the menu, from Cartmel Valley smoked
salmon (with textures of beetroot and
horseradish crème fraîche) to best end of
Cumbrian lamb (with Puy lentils, swede
purée and haggis beignets). Mr Comish's style
is modern British cooking with European
influences – as in free-range chicken with
smoked bacon and Jerusalem artichoke risotto
or roasted wild sea bass with aubergine and a
tomato and red pepper sauce. Desserts deliver
the same Anglo-European mix, ranging from
poached rhubarb with vanilla cream, sorbet,
crisps and oat crumble to chocolate soufflé,
délice, tart and orange sorbet. Before all that
you'll be plied with canapés and an amuse-
bouche, and there is a 'small but well-balanced'
cheese selection followed by 'very good' petits
fours. The wine list is 'long and interesting',
with most choices sitting in the £35 to £55
range and plenty available by the glass. Bottles
start at £29.
Chef/s: Darren Comish. **Open:** all week L 12 to
1.30, D 6.30 to 9.30. **Closed:** first 2 weeks Jan.
Meals: main courses L £17 to £25. Set L £30 (2
courses). Set D £68. Gourmet menu £88. **Details:** 46
seats. Bar. Wheelchairs. Music. Parking. Children
over 8 yrs only.

James Cross
Lake Road Kitchen, Ambleside

What inspired you to become a chef?
Greed! I love to eat delicious things.

What would you be doing if you weren't a chef?
I'd probably be a horticulturalist. The two careers are quite closely linked and it was something I had strongly considered before I became a chef.

At the end of a long day, what do you like to cook?
Fish tacos with the tail ends of the skrei cod and turbot.

What's your favourite junk food?
A really good shawarma, which can be hard to find in Cumbria.

Who is the most interesting person you have cooked for?
Definitely Redzepi at Noma project nights. It's an enlightening experience having to explain the minutiae of how and why your dish has come to be. He makes you challenge yourself.

Which chef do you most admire at the moment?
Matt Orlando at Amass, Copenhagen. He's changing the boundaries of what a restaurant can be. His restaurant is much more than kitchen, garden and dining room.

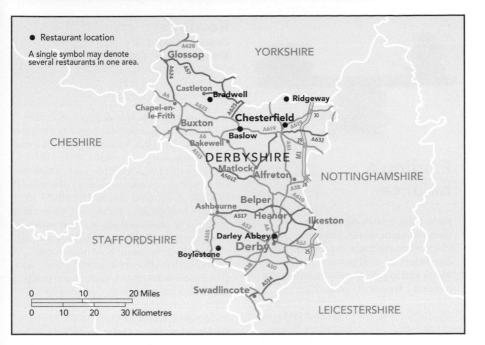

Baslow
Fischer's Baslow Hall
Cooking score: 6
Modern European | £72
Calver Road, Baslow, DE45 1RR
Tel no: (01246) 583259
fischers-baslowhall.co.uk

Built in the Edwardian era to look 300 years older, Baslow lies in the heart of the Peak District, within pottering distance of Chatsworth. High ornate ceilings, big gilt mirrors and vast floral displays set a grandiose tone in the dining room, but there is also a bench to park yourself on in the kitchen if grandiose doesn't cut it. Rupert Rowley draws on local game, Cornish seafood and the provender of the Hall's own kitchen garden for modern European dishes that please many regular reporters. A lunch main dish of pork belly and pak choi in maple syrup and sherry delighted one such, and the starter of scallop with tahini and a black rice cracker is an adventurous combination that succeeds. Worries about the overall balance of the tasting menus are beginning to surface, though; a certain homogeneity of texture let the side down at inspection, the lamb main course unappetisingly bedded on undercooked chickpeas in an oversweet lemon sauce. Over-conceptualised desserts such as the chocolate tree in chocolate soil are less appealing than the fragrant simplicity of an angelica mousse sprinkled with diced melon and chamomile tea crystals. Wines start at £22.

Chef/s: Rupert Rowley. **Open:** all week L 12 to 1.30, D 7 to 8.30. **Closed:** 25 and 26 Dec. **Meals:** main courses £30 (L only). Set L £20 (2 courses) to £27. Set D £55 (2 courses) to £72. Sun L £32 (2 courses) to £38. Tasting menu £60 to £80. **Details:** 60 seats. V menu. Bar. Parking. Children over 5 yrs only at L (exc Sun), over 8 yrs only at D.

Finding a balance

Hospitality has always been a demanding business, but some chef-proprietors are improving staff conditions by cutting back on opening hours and juggling menus – and we're all for it... Here's our pick.

Claude Bosi's Mayfair restaurant **Hibiscus** has dropped two lunch services, giving all that serious gastronomy (and the staff) room to breathe.

Sat Bains in Nottingham is a pioneer in implementing improved working conditions, moving to a four-day week and thereby allowing staff an extra 48 days off a year.

London's best-known urchin-inspired restaurant, **Le Gavroche**, has become a five-day operation, closed on Mondays except for private events and pop-ups.

And following a refurbishment, the **Elephant** in Torquay has combined its more formal first floor dining room with the ground floor operation to ease pressure on staff.

Improved work-life balance makes for a fresher, more focused team, and a better time for diners. It's clearly a win-win.

Rowley's

Cooking score: 1
Modern British | £35
Church Lane, Baslow, DE45 1RY
Tel no: (01246) 583880
rowleysrestaurant.co.uk

A fixture on the Baslow dining scene since 2006, this sturdy, stone-built pub (a sibling of nearby Baslow Hall – see entry) is renowned for its congenial atmosphere and flexible approach that takes you from a quick morning coffee and good-value set lunch right through to a special-occasion dinner. The kitchen looks to local produce for inspiration and aims for a mix of traditional and modern cooking, so expect fish and chips or oxtail and kidney suet pudding for lunch, wild mushroom risotto with truffle and Wigmore cheese, and pork osso buco with pak choi, maple syrup and shallot crust for dinner. For dessert, maybe chocolate rocks with coconut sorbet and peanuts. Wines start at £18.45.
Chef/s: Adam Harper. **Open:** Tue to Sun L 12 to 2.30 (3 Sat and Sun), Tue to Sat D 5.30 to 9 (6 to 9.30 Sat). **Closed:** Mon, 25 Dec. **Meals:** main courses £15 to £25. Set L £17 (2 courses) to £21. Sun L £21. **Details:** 78 seats. 16 seats outside. Bar. Music. Parking.

■ Boylestone
The Lighthouse Restaurant

Cooking score: 4
Modern British | £42
New Road, Boylestone, DE6 5AA
Tel no: (01335) 330658
the-lighthouse-restaurant.co.uk

Set amid the tranquil green acres of the Derbyshire-Staffordshire border country, the Lighthouse is hard pushed to find any shipping to warn, but does nonetheless represent a beacon of quality in its serious commitment to expounding the relations between landscape and produce. The young kitchen and front-of-house teams are full of inspiring enthusiasm, and Jon Hardy has a clear, and excitingly progressive, vision of what he wants to do. A family who ate here

Join us at thegoodfoodguide.co.uk

just before Christmas were delighted with the whole deal, from a duo of scallop and beef cheek on truffled risotto with onion oil to a cheek's most intuitive neighbour, a jowl of pork with orange and damsons. The tasting menus are radiant with ambition – skrei cod and confit chicken wing with smoked eel and sea herbs – and reinvented tradition, in duck à l'orange with citrus gel and carrot pesto. Winter apple crumble with honeyed oats, Earl Grey and vanilla is a revelation. The brief wine list, from £14.95, scarcely does justice to the food.

Chef/s: Jonathan Hardy. **Open:** Sun L 12 to 3, Thur to Sat D 7 to 12. **Closed:** Mon, Tue, Wed, first 2 weeks Jan. **Meals:** main courses £23 to £25. Tasting menu £50. **Details:** 40 seats. Bar. Wheelchairs. Music. Parking.

▌Bradwell
The Samuel Fox Inn

Cooking score: 3
British | £30
Stretfield Road, Bradwell, S33 9JT
Tel no: (01433) 621562
samuelfox.co.uk

£5
OFF

Samuel Fox was a son of Bradwell and inventor of the modern umbrella. James Duckett is a son of Lancashire, and bringer of warm hospitality and immensely likeable cooking to this refurbished village pub in the Hope Valley. Cuisine is British with bells on, so cauliflower soup with shepherd's bread is spiked with chorizo, and Stilton and cider are used to stuff tortelli with roast butternut squash and hazelnut pesto. White radish Tatin with Szechuan pepper, goats' cheese, beetroot and radicchio is an inventive veggie main course, and sea bream is pan-fried and served with stuffed Jerusalem artichokes, Brussels sprouts and crab sauce. Reasonable prices (the seven-course tasting menu is £49) and flexible, friendly staff keep readers coming back, though the same could be said of the chocolate walnut and coffee tart or the rhubarb and almond trifle. The wine list is short, from £19.

Chef/s: James Duckett. **Open:** Fri and Sat L 12 to 3, Wed to Sat D 6 to 11. Sun 1 to 9. **Closed:** Mon, Tue, Jan, last week Jul. **Meals:** main courses £14 to £20. Set L £20 (2 courses) to £26. Sun L £26. Tasting menu £49 (7 courses). **Details:** 40 seats. 16 seats outside. Bar. Wheelchairs. Music. Parking.

▌Chesterfield

LOCAL GEM
Calabria

Italian | £30
30 Glumangate, Chesterfield, S40 1TX
Tel no: (01246) 559944
calabriacucina.co.uk

£5
OFF

Doors open early for cracking Calabrian breakfasts at this independently minded, family-run eatery named after the sun-baked southern Italian province. Alternatively, drop by later for a light lunch (bruschetta, frittata, pasta, salads) or go for the full works in the evening, when a more ambitious modern menu comes into play. Expect lively sounding ideas ranging from leek and Gorgonzola risotto with walnut crumble to seared salmon with smoked salmon cannelloni, wilted spinach and caper mayonnaise. Inviting Calabrian antipasti, too, plus regional Italian wines from £17.50.

▌Darley Abbey
Darleys

Cooking score: 3
Modern British | £39
Darley Abbey Mills, Haslams Lane, Darley Abbey, DE22 1DZ
Tel no: (01332) 364987
darleys.com

The building is a slice of English industrial heritage, an erstwhile mill on a weir by the river Derwent, though if you're expecting a ruggedly grim interior, be prepared for the pleasant surprise of smartly linened tables, swagged drapes and ornate mirrors. A suntrap terrace offers dining right over the river. Voguish ingredients and modern classic presentations bestrew the menus, with Indian-garnished parsnip soup one minute, hoisin-dressed venison, cabbage hearts and plum the next. The technical range is nothing if not ambitious, when you might start with confit Duart salmon with semolina squid, lemon curd, lemon snow and candied fennel, but there's always the traditional back-up of slow-cooked local lamb with layered potato and carrots, or poached rhubarb with vanilla custard and gingerbread ice cream. A seven-course tasting menu takes in everything from seared scallop with caper flowers to a cocktail shaken at the table, and one of Alex James's cheeses. House French Sauvignon and Merlot are £18.45.

Chef/s: Jonathan Hobson. **Open:** all week L 12 to 2 (2.30 Sun), Mon to Sat D 7 to 9 (9.30 Fri and Sat). **Closed:** 25 Dec to 9 Jan. **Meals:** main courses £22 to £25. Set L £20 (2 courses) to £25. Sun L £30. Tasting menu £50 (7 courses). **Details:** 60 seats. V menu. Bar. Music. Parking.

▌Ridgeway
The Old Vicarage
Cooking score: 6
Modern British | £75
Ridgeway Moor, Ridgeway, S12 3XW
Tel no: (0114) 2475814
theoldvicarage.co.uk

Those clergy built themselves nice homes back in the day, and this one-time vicarage is no exception, with its generous Victorian proportions and delicious two-acre garden. It gives the impression of a rural idyll when central Sheffield is only a short drive away. Tessa Bramley has run the show for 30 years and it's fair to say she's 'a bit of a legend', while head chef Nathan Smith has clocked up over 20 years at the stoves himself. The kitchen's output still feels current and fresh (fresh indeed, for much of the produce is grown in the garden). After an opening salvo of canapés comes monkfish poached in seaweed with tempura of its cheek and dashi sauce. Then expect complex constructions with layers of satisfying flavours; salt marsh lamb, say, with

lightly devilled kidneys and crab apple and thyme jelly, or a dessert of poached Wakefield rhubarb with blood-orange curd tart. The impressive wine list is arranged by style; bottles start at £22.

Chef/s: Tessa Bramley and Nathan Smith. **Open:** Tue to Fri L 12.30 to 2, Tue to Sat D 6 to 10. **Closed:** Sun, Mon, 26 Dec to 5 Jan, 1 week Easter, 1 week Aug, bank hols. **Meals:** set L £40 (3 courses). Set D £75 (4 courses). Tasting menu £85. **Details:** 46 seats. 24 seats outside. Parking. Children over 6 yrs only at D.

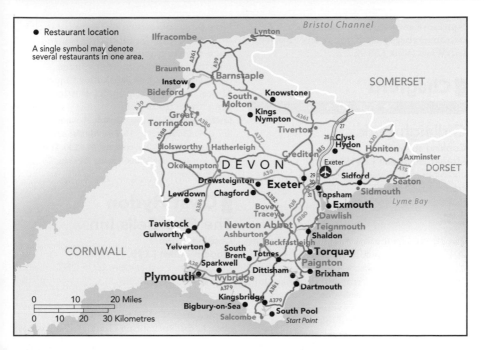

Restaurant location

A single symbol may denote several restaurants in one area.

■ Bigbury-on-Sea

LOCAL GEM

The Oyster Shack

Seafood | £30

Stakes Hill, Bigbury-on-Sea, TQ7 4BE
Tel no: (01548) 810876
oystershack.co.uk

A 'relaxed atmosphere' at this fun oyster shack continues to impress loyal locals and our holidaying readers. Plying its trade on the site of an old Avon Valley oyster farm, spanking-fresh and locally sourced bivalves and creatures of the sea come served every which way: garnished or unadorned on sharing platters, as smarter carte options or 'bargain' fixed-price menus. Don a bib to crack into a whole Devon crab outside, perhaps, under the sprawling sail awning if the weather's fine: mess is mandatory. The 50cl carafe is popular with readers (bottles from £16). Closed Jan.

■ Brixham

LOCAL GEM

Poopdeck

Seafood | £28

14 The Quay, Brixham, TQ5 8AW
Tel no: (01803) 858681
poopdeckrestaurant.com

£5 OFF   £30

Above a souvenir shop, overlooking the quayside, Poopdeck is a fish restaurant straight from central casting, with roughcast walls painted salmon, blackboards offering catches and dishes of the day, and an altogether cheery ambience. Look to plainly dressed market-priced specials, or Neptune's Feast platters of fresh seafood, whole lobsters and the like. There are core dishes too, such as a hefty fishcake of smoked haddock and black pudding with garlic and dill mayo, or mains like grilled monkfish topped with tapenade and pancetta in a creamy tarragon sauce.

Squeeze in a wodge of blueberry and cinnamon cheesecake if you've any capacity left. Wines from £15.95.

Chagford

★ TOP 50 ★

Gidleigh Park

Cooking score: 7
Modern European | £110
Chagford, TQ13 8HH
Tel no: (01647) 432367
gidleigh.co.uk

The seismic change that was announced in late 2015 when the long-resident Michael Caines departed for pastures new, to be replaced by Michael Wignall (ex Pennyhill Park, Bagshot, Surrey, see entry), has been enterprisingly borne by Gidleigh's many venerable regulars. Our inspector was touched to note that it isn't just teenagers who photograph their food. Wignall's cooking, presented in the form of seven- or ten-course tasting menus at dinner, is nothing if not photogenic, not to mention teeming with fresh energetic ingenuity, exuberance and wit. Textural contrasts are not just mixtures of soft and crisp, but embrace little bubbles of gel that burst on the palate, as well as great clods of what look like marine sponge or Chinese prawn cracker, but which dissolve instantly to nothing in ghosts of penetrating flavour when eaten. Ideas come thick and fast: a stick of rabbit loin, white and creamy as milk-fed veal, encased in foam, with chorizo porridge, snail bolognaise, girolles and a bubble of blasting amontillado sherry; a brace of fat St Austell mussels in pungent sardine dressing, one of them nested in a hollowed braised onion; roe deer with barbecued beets, black pudding purée, ox tongue and smoked potato; a glorious dessert of fresh and gelled apricot with a custard of the kernels shoehorned into brik pastry and a scattering of new season's almonds. It all comes with sweeping views of sheltered Dartmoor around the Teign, and battalions of well-rehearsed staff, including a great

Neapolitan sommelier. The wine list itself is a treasure trove of the good, the great and the mind-blowing, and the pre-selected servings with the tasting menu, from vintage Normandy cider to Clare Valley Liqueur Muscat, are full of originality. Bottles from the main list go from £38.
Chef/s: Michael Wignall. **Open:** all week L 12 to 2, D 7 to 9. **Closed:** 3 to 15 Jan. **Meals:** set L £50 (3 courses). Set D £110 (7 courses) to £130. **Details:** 52 seats. V menu. Bar. Wheelchairs. Parking. Children over 8 yrs only.

Clyst Hydon
The Five Bells Inn

Cooking score: 1
Modern British | £35
Main Street, Clyst Hydon, EX15 2NT
Tel no: (01884) 277288
fivebells.uk.com

Named after the five bells of Clyst Hydon church, this enchanting Grade II-listed inn is a flourishing community hub, complete with a pool room and Devon brews on tap. A thatched roof, ancient timbers and slate floors add to its rustic charms, but there's serious foodie intent, too. As expected, West Country ingredients get a robust workout, from Brixham scallops with butternut squash, Dorset-cured guanciale, fennel and smoked paprika to aged Dartmoor hogget accompanied by cavolo nero, clapshot and turnip. Wines (from £15.50) come courtesy of respected Devon merchant Chris Piper.
Chef/s: Ian Webber. **Open:** all week L 12 to 2 (4.30 Sun), D 6 to 9 (9.30 Fri and Sat). **Closed:** 25 and 26 Dec. **Meals:** main courses £17 to £21. Set L £17 (2 courses) to £20. Tasting menu £45 (5 courses). **Details:** 74 seats. 80 seats outside. V menu. Wheelchairs. Music. Parking.

Average price

The average price denotes the price of a three-course meal without wine.

▮ Dartmouth
The Seahorse
Cooking score: 5
Seafood | £45
5 South Embankment, Dartmouth, TQ6 9BH
Tel no: (01803) 835147
seahorserestaurant.co.uk

£5 OFF ▮

Tourists and trippers throng the Dartmouth waterfront on sunny days, and it's no surprise that booking is essential at the Mitch Tonks/ Mat Prowse flagship venue. The views of pleasure boats pottering along the Dart is appetising, and so are the fish and seafood specials that are the elevated stock-in-trade. 'The lobster linguine is a particular favourite,' confides a regular, 'and the mixed fish grill is very attractively presented too, a good selection of what's fresh.' The menu looks in the general direction of Italy for specialities such as cuttlefish puttanesca with fried polenta, or hake with salsa rossa, and the sides take in Castelfranco radicchio dressed with aged vinegar and hazelnuts, but Dover sole simply grilled over charcoal and seasoned with savory is an attractive proposition, too. The sophisticated way to finish is with affogato shot with pruney PX sherry or Frangelico liqueur. Italian wines lead the charge, but Loire house varietals are £19.
Chef/s: Mitch Tonks, Mat Prowse and Jake Bridgewood. **Open:** Tue to Sat L 12 to 2.30, Tue to Sat D 6 to 9.30. **Meals:** main courses £20 to £32. Set L and D £20 (2 courses). **Details:** 40 seats. Wheelchairs. Music.

Local Gem

Local Gems are the perfect neighbourhood venues, delivering good, freshly cooked food at great value for money.

Rockfish
Seafood | £25
8 South Embankment, Dartmouth, TQ6 9BH
Tel no: (01803) 832800
therockfish.co.uk

£30

This Dartmouth link in the small seafood chain owned by Mitch Tonks and Mat Prowse (of the Seahorse fame – see entry) is deservedly popular with everyone who enjoys the local fish. It's considered quite an asset in the town, offering service that is efficient and cheerful and delivering good value for money. Deliciously fresh hake or lemon sole simply grilled with chips and tartare sauce, plus mushy or buttered garden peas are typical offerings, with dressed crab to start and banana split to finish. House Sauvignon Blanc is £17.95.

▮ Dittisham
Anchorstone Café
Cooking score: 3
Seafood | £23
Manor Street, Dittisham, TQ6 0EX
Tel no: (01803) 722365
anchorstonecafe.co.uk

£30

'One of my highlights of the year,' noted one visitor to this 'brilliant spot right by the Dart'. The freshest seafood, purchased from Dartmouth-based day boats or from Brixham and Plymouth fish markets, brings a mix of locals and tourists to this hard-to-reach café. It's quite rustic, with most of the tables outside, but under cover with heaters, and this year reporters have given good account of crab sandwiches, superb scallops, bowls of mussels (with fries) and bouillabaisse, while fresher than fresh whole crabs 'can be huge and need some strength to best enjoy'. Dover sole, hake, whole monkfish tail char-grilled with fresh herbs, haddock and chips, and lemon tart with clotted cream have also been endorsed. Clare

Harvey and her team 'really care that you have a good time and are so enthusiastic'. The modest wine list opens at £18.95.

Chef/s: Clare Harvey. **Open:** Wed to Sun L 12 to 4. **Closed:** Mon, Tue, Nov to Mar. **Meals:** main courses £12 to £15. **Details:** 28 seats. 70 seats outside.

■ Drewsteignton
The Old Inn
Cooking score: 4
Modern European | £52
Drewsteignton, EX6 6QR
Tel no: (01647) 281276
old-inn.co.uk

Sitting on a corner of the village square that's pretty much all there is to Drewsteignton, the Old Inn is a comforting restaurant-with-rooms run with warmth and intelligence. A couple of big dogs greet you in the sitting room, where shelves of books are worth browsing before you go into either of the two small, sparely decorated dining rooms. Duncan Walker's cooking is full of panache, with sharply defined flavours and confident combining. Lunch of scallops with a salad of new potatoes and toasted pine nuts in basil oil, followed by breast and leg croquette of duck with aubergine purée and roast shallots, is a deeply satisfying affair, while evenings bring on the likes of lobster and saffron lasagne with red peppers in shellfish velouté, oxtail with sautéed veal sweetbreads and smoked bacon in hearty port reduction, and a classic prune and Armagnac soufflé with cinnamon ice cream. Wines are an inspired miscellany from £23. A few more by the glass would help.

Chef/s: Duncan Walker. **Open:** Fri and Sat L 12 to 2, Wed to Sat D 6 to 9. **Closed:** Sun, Mon, Tue, 3 weeks Jan, 1 week Jun. **Meals:** set L £32. Set D £46 (2 courses) to £52. **Details:** 17 seats. No children.

■ Exeter
ABode Exeter
Cooking score: 4
Modern European | £35
Cathedral Yard, Exeter, EX1 1HD
Tel no: (01392) 223638
abodeexeter.co.uk

Enclosed within the confines of the old Royal Clarence Hotel, virtually cheek by jowl with the cathedral, whose northern elevation looms in the dining room windows, Exeter's ABode is a bare-floored, bare-tabled, cream room adorned with boldly delineated food paintings. Alex Gibbs, promoted from sous to head chef, survives the change of ownership, and makes a good fist of mostly seasonal modern brasserie cooking with plenty of vivid upstanding seasoning. A piece of crisp-skinned gilthead bream is sauced with puréed tarragon, mustard and cream, while a whole bouquet of spring veg accompanies a serving of minted pink spring lamb and aubergine purée, as an alternative to roasted stone bass with confit fennel and tapenade in shellfish sauce. Seasonality may not always be British seasonality, when raspberries arrive in early May, in mousse and parfait forms encased in dark chocolate, but banana soufflé with its own ice cream and butterscotch sauce transcends all such niceties. Varietally listed wines open at £25.

Chef/s: Alex Gibbs. **Open:** all week L 12 to 2.30, D 6 to 9.30 (10 Fri and Sat, 9 Sun). **Meals:** main courses £19 to £26. Set L £17 (2 courses) to £22. Set D £20 (2 courses) to £25. Tasting menu £65 to £85. **Details:** 70 seats. Bar. Wheelchairs. Music.

Exmouth
Les Saveurs
Cooking score: 2
French | £35
9 Tower Street, Exmouth, EX8 1NT
Tel no: (01395) 269459
lessaveurs.co.uk
£5 OFF

Tucked away on a quiet pedestrianised street behind the Methodist church, Les Saveurs is a French bistro of the old school, run with personable charm and dedicated to doing the traditional things well. The ambience is a mix of smartly dressed tables and undressed brick walls, and the menu deals in unabashed renditions of the kinds of dishes that sustained French gastronomy in the UK back in the post-war day. Real fish soup with shredded Emmental and spicy rouille, or devilled lamb's kidneys, might pave the way into main courses that come with battalions of side veg, alongside perhaps locally caught fish such as sea bass on chive mash in sauce armoricaine. 'The roast marinated duck breast with blackberry sauce was the best I've eaten for a number of years,' thought one reader. Classic desserts take in prune and Armagnac parfait, and pistachio crème brûlée in a fetching shade of eau de nil. A serviceable French wine list opens at £19.
Chef/s: Olivier Guyard-Mulkerrin. **Open:** Tue to Sat D only 7 to 9. **Closed:** Sun, Mon, 1 Jan to 12 Feb. **Meals:** main courses £18 to £25. **Details:** 50 seats. Music. Children over 10 yrs only.

Gulworthy
The Horn of Plenty
Cooking score: 3
Modern British | £50
Gulworthy, PL19 8JD
Tel no: (01822) 832528
thehornofplenty.co.uk

Overlooking the glorious Tamar Valley, this creeper-clad Georgian manor house on the edge of Dartmoor National Park oozes class

and tranquillity. On a warm summer's day, there can few more alluring prospects than a meal on the terrace or in the conservatory overlooking the well-manicured garden, in spring ablaze with azaleas, camellias and rhododendrons. Scott Paton has departed and Ashley Wright now heads the kitchen and an early inspection meal displayed a steady hand on the tiller. The British cooking is driven by local and seasonal raw materials. From the good-value lunch menu, a starter of hand-picked Brixham crab and crayfish salad, apple and garden sorrel was artfully presented if under-seasoned, and was followed by precisely timed pan-roasted Brixham stone bass served with Cornish asparagus, nasturtium and ricotta gnocchi, with a milk chocolate mousse with an intense, refreshing cherry sorbet for dessert. The house wines start at £21.50, with 10 offered by the glass.
Chef/s: Ashley Wright. **Open:** all week L 12 to 2.45, D 7 to 9. **Meals:** set L £20 (2 courses) to £25. Set D £50. Sun L £19 (2 courses) to £25. **Details:** 50 seats. 20 seats outside. Wheelchairs. Music. Parking.

Instow
The Exmoor Beastro
Cooking score: 4
Modern British | £34
Tapeley Park, Instow, EX39 4NT
Tel no: (01271) 861796
theexmoorbeastro.com
£5 OFF

The Beastro moved in January 2016. It now inhabits the tea room of Tapeley Park, an extensive rural estate with landscaped gardens and woodland leading down to a turbid green lake that sits in dignified hush amid tropical trees. Wrought-iron tables on the lawn, or three huge sharing tables inside, are the drill, and you can freely wander into the kitchen, where Alex Nutt is at work single-handed, occasionally haring off to the kitchen garden with his secateurs. The day's dishes are scrawled on a little blackboard. Virtually everything that's served is a tribute to organic and sustainable principles, the natural flavours and exhilarating freshness of it all elbowing

aside any misplaced expectation of culinary wizardry or conceptualised presentations. Three Brixham scallops in a wash of cider vinegar dressing, garnished with pancetta and slender new asparagus; glorious charcuterie (rosy coppa, creamily fatted prosciutto, cured venison); an enormous middle cut of vivid pink sea trout in chive hollandaise, its scorched skin strewn with sea salt and pesto, on a mountain of spring veg, including balsamic onions, slivered beetroot and broad beans; 65-day dry-aged beef fillet. Fiona O'Mahoney does the desserts, which might include gluten-free orange and almond polenta cake, and a triumphant crystallised ginger pannacotta, shivering like an aspen tree, served with gingered rhubarb compote. There's no wine list; take your own and ask for glasses. NB: payment is by cash or cheque only.
Chef/s: Alex Nutt and Fiona O'Mahoney. **Open:** Sun to Fri L 11 to 4. D bookings only. **Closed:** Sat, Nov to Mar. **Meals:** main courses £11 to £17. Set L £12 (2 courses) to £25. Set D £25 (2 courses) to £35. Sun L £18. **Details:** 40 seats. 40 seats outside. Bar. Wheelchairs. Music. Parking.

Kings Nympton

LOCAL GEM
The Grove Inn
British | £22
Kings Nympton, EX37 9ST
Tel no: (01769) 580406
thegroveinn.co.uk

£5 OFF £30

The Grove looms large in the life of Kings Nympton, both socially and physically. It sits on a bend in the tiny road, its frontage the colour of clotted cream, and presents a low-ceilinged picture of old England inside, the walls crowded with antique photographs, the rafters with thousands of bookmarks. The kitchen pulls in fine regional produce for simple and filling dishes: two trout with buttered granary bread and saladings; a chicken breast stuffed with asparagus, cheese and ham, served with lovely dauphinois potato in thick slices; generous ramekins of

burnt cream with a treasure trove of stewed rhubarb beneath. Nearly everything on the wine list comes by the glass, with bottles from £15.

Kingsbridge

LOCAL GEM
Beachhouse
Seafood | £30
South Milton Sands, Kingsbridge, TQ7 3JY
Tel no: (01548) 561144
beachhousedevon.com

£5 OFF

Right next to the beach, it's a hut, plain and simple, and the atmosphere is 'awesome', mainly because everyone is so glad to have a table. Sit outside if you can. Breakfast, lunchtime sandwiches – Salcombe crab, say – and takeaways for the beach are great, but don't miss out on the main menu of locally sourced seafood with an Italian flavour – 'so fresh it has practically hopped from the sea on to your plate'. Arancini enriched with crab, Start Bay scallops with capers and sage, whole bream cooked in a bag, lobster plainly grilled – why can't every beach have one? Wines start at £17.50.

Knowstone
The Masons Arms
Cooking score: 4
Modern British | £48
Knowstone, EX36 4RY
Tel no: (01398) 341231
masonsarmsdevon.co.uk

There's a little of the rustic French auberge to the Masons from the outside, a buff-coloured, rough-hewn country hostelry turned destination dining spot. No extraneous poshing up affects the dining room, where a cod-Rubens ceiling fresco of classical scenes hovers over a roomful of chunky furniture, and the windows look out on the surrounding fields where cattle entertainingly frolic. Mark Dodson's time with Michel Roux brings a high-class gloss to many of the dishes, but modern treatments have the last word, as in the cured salmon that comes with strongly pickled fennel, tapenade and pink grapefruit, while Vulscombe goats' cheese is fashioned into billiard-ball arancini with tomato coulis and pesto. Spring lamb was rather devoid of flavour at inspection, an unaccountable lapse on a menu where guinea fowl in morel cream sauce may be the safer luxury. Finish with glossy dark chocolate and passion fruit délice and raspberry sorbet. House wines are £22, with the exception of a Sicilian white blend at £16.

Chef/s: Mark Dodson. **Open:** Tue to Sun L 12 to 2, Tue to Sat D 7 to 9. **Closed:** Mon, first week Jan, last week Aug. **Meals:** main courses £20 to £27. Set L £20 (2 courses) to £25. Sun L £37. **Details:** 28 seats. 16 seats outside. Bar. Music. Parking. Children over 5 yrs only at D.

◼ Lewdown
Lewtrenchard Manor
Cooking score: 5
Modern British | £50
Lewdown, EX20 4PN
Tel no: (01566) 783222
lewtrenchard.co.uk
£5 OFF ◼

Enter the sometime home of the Revd Baring-Gould, who composed 'Onward Christian Soldiers' amid the weathered dark panelling and creaking floorboards of a reconstructed Tudor manor house. Eating is split between two panelled and mullioned rooms, and the house is as much a treat on a firelit winter night as amid the fluting birdsong of summer. Matthew Peryer cooks to the modern British template, with intuitive culinary logic underpinning the contemporary flourishes. A lunch dish of translucent cod fillet in a slew of shellfish, monk's beard and a velouté of Cornish pastis offers exemplary balance, but there are good things all round, extending from a serving of quail done up in pancetta with maple-glazed foie gras, through cannon of lamb with Puy lentil cassoulet and haggis hash, to the lightest of dessert seductions — perhaps ginger parfait with raspberries and

rhubarb foam. Wines are less opulent than you may be expecting, but hardly extortionate, starting at £22.

Chef/s: Matthew Peryer. **Open:** all week L 12 to 2, D 7 to 9. **Meals:** set L £20 (2 courses) to £24. Set D £50. Sun L £25. **Details:** 40 seats. 30 seats outside. V menu. Bar. Wheelchairs. Parking. Children over 8 yrs only in restaurant.

◼ Plymouth
The Greedy Goose
Cooking score: 4
Modern British | £32
Prysten House, Finewell Street, Plymouth, PL1 2AE
Tel no: (01752) 252001
thegreedygoose.co.uk
£5 OFF

Erected in the year 1500 and lauded as Plymouth's oldest building, the dramatic stone-walled interior of Prysten House has been home to chef Ben Palmer for a couple of years now and he's 'an absolute credit to the profession', according to one reader who appreciated his ability to 'capture the freshest local ingredients around'. Others have cited the thoughtfulness that typifies 'beautifully crafted' dishes such as Cornish crab with grapefruit, cucumber and smoked salmon, or Creedy Carver duck breast with cavolo nero and garlic polenta. Beef from Nick Bibby-Jones' farm in Coryton features heavily (try the tartare toasts as an opener), and there are high levels of creativity in the vegetable department, too — heritage carrots with goats' cheese and pistachios, say. Everything is 'prepared with passion and served with care', right down to desserts such as lemon curd rice pudding. Decently priced wines from £17.

Chef/s: Ben Palmer. **Open:** Tue to Sat L 12 to 2.30, D 6 to 9 (9.30 Fri and Sat). **Closed:** Sun, Mon. **Meals:** main courses £13 to £30. Set L and early D £10 (2 courses) to £12. Tasting menu £50 (7 courses). **Details:** 70 seats. 30 seats outside. Bar. Wheelchairs. Music. No children under 4 yrs.

Rock Salt

Cooking score: 2
Modern British | £26
31 Stonehouse Street, Plymouth, PL1 3PE
Tel no: (01752) 225522
rocksaltcafe.co.uk

£5 OFF £30

With a repertoire that runs from brunch to afternoon tea and cakes, and from snappy lunches to indulgent tasting menus, nobody can accuse Rock Salt of having limited scope. Better still, it does all of this well, with visitors happy to negotiate tricky parking to spend time in this 'gem' of a venue that 'never disappoints'. For some, it's a regular port of call before hopping on the ferry to France (the fish and chips attracts special praise); others favour a lengthier visit and a meal from the tasting menu. The cooking has a modern, global flavour: cured and blowtorched salmon with a soft-shell crab fritter, seaweed and wasabi mayonnaise; confit lamb shoulder with parsley risotto, Jerusalem artichoke and kale pesto; and poached rhubarb with elderflower sago, honeycomb and poached meringue. The international wine list offers something for all tastes, kicking off at just £14.95 a bottle.
Chef/s: David Jenkins and Joe Turner. **Open:** all week L 11.30 to 3, D 5 to 9.30. **Closed:** 25 Dec. **Meals:** main courses £10 to £20. Set L £12 (2 courses) to £16. Set D £22 (2 courses) to £26. Sun L £15. Tasting menu (7 courses) £50. **Details:** 80 seats. Bar. Music.

LOCAL GEM

Lemon Tree Café & Bistro

Modern European | £15
2 Haye Road South, Elburton, Plymouth, PL9 8HJ
Tel no: (01752) 481117
lemontreecafe.co.uk

£30

In the suburb of Elburton, just off the A379, the Lemon Tree is a stylish café-bistro that covers all bases from morning coffee to late lunch. A serviceable menu of paninis, croques, omelettes and sandwiches (including a New York special of pastrami, pickles, mustard, saladings and mayo) is augmented by daily blackboard specials such as split pea soup with spiced butter, Spanish-style chicken with chorizo, chickpeas and peppers, and pineapple grilled in star anise and chilli, served with vanilla ice cream. To accompany, there's a Chilean wine in all three colours at £14.95. NB: cash only.

■ Shaldon

ODE Dining

Cooking score: 6
Modern British | £45
21 Fore Street, Shaldon, TQ14 0DE
Tel no: (01626) 873977
odetruefood.com

The little dining room in a row of cottages in a fishing village across the Teign estuary from Teignmouth doesn't do many sessions each week (it dropped to just two for a while), but is worth the wait to gain access. In a terracotta-tiled front room, with an industrious open kitchen behind, Tim Bouget cooks locally sourced, organically and sustainably produced food in magical combinations of ingredients, seasoned with almost confrontational emphasis and yet retaining impeccable balance. An opener of cured skrei cod is garnished with red-hot harissa labneh, wafer-thin shallot fritters and cuminy dried aubergine for a bravura start, followed perhaps by tenderly pink lamb rump with baby pak choi, parsnip mash and garlic cream, or rolled guinea fowl with ham hock, roasted onions and broad beans. Dessert may be amazingly light chocolate brownie with brown-butter ice cream and raspberries, or sublime white chocolate parfait with chai cream. Breads, which come with local butters (cow and goat) and sensational tapenade, are also superb. A short list of organically and biodynamically grown wines opens at £18.50.
Chef/s: Tim Bouget. **Open:** Wed to Sat D only 7 to 9.30. **Closed:** Sun, Mon, Tue, Oct. **Meals:** set D £35 (2 courses) to £45. **Details:** 24 seats. Music. No children under 7 yrs after 8.

▌Sidford
The Salty Monk
Cooking score: 2
Modern British | £45
Church Street, Sidford, EX10 9QP
Tel no: (01395) 513174
saltymonk.co.uk
£5 OFF

Benedictine monks used this building as a salt store during the 16th century, hence the name-check from current owners Andy and Annette Witheridge. Lunch is a relatively simple affair at their locally focused restaurant-with-rooms, but Andy's sympathetic and creative approach to Devon produce is allowed full rein in the evening. Freshly baked breads and home-smoked fish point to an industrious kitchen, while the day's menu reflects an open-minded approach that can accommodate local gurnard on a lightly curried Thai sauce with Puy lentils as well as roast pigeon breast with warm pear chutney and pecans or a confit duck tartlet with pork belly, champ and smoked onion purée. To finish, look no further than the lemon tart served hot from the oven with a 'candy twist' and clotted cream. The colourful wine list includes plenty of enterprising organic/biodynamic stuff; prices from £19.

Chef/s: Andy Witheridge and Scott Horn. **Open:** Thur to Sun L 12 to 2, all week D 6.30 to 9. **Closed:** Jan. **Meals:** set L £25 (2 courses) to £30. Set D £39 (2 courses) to £45. Sun L £30. Tasting menu £65. **Details:** 35 seats. 20 seats outside. V menu. Bar. Music. Parking.

▌South Brent
Anton Piotrowski at the Glazebrook
Cooking score: 6
Modern British | £38
Wrangaton Road, South Brent, TQ10 9JE
Tel no: (01364) 73322
glazebrookhouse.com
£5 OFF

Sitting amid mature trees and ferny walks a comforting distance from the A38 on the southern fringe of Dartmoor, Glazebrook is a country house with personality. Looming over the lobby on a plinth is an ostrich skeleton, there are wall-mounted displays of snare drums and tea trays, and outsized busts of Churchill and the Queen. There's also Anton Piotrowski, who has given the kitchen here a turbo-charged boost with a menu of exciting British modernism. Attention to detail distinguishes complex assemblages such as beef fillet carpaccio with horseradish ice cream, onion rings, cucumber and nasturtiums, and mains such as a tasting of expressively flavoured, locally farmed chicken, its cinnamon rissole offsetting a beautiful piece of seared breast, as well as shiitakes, baby parsnips and a layer of pomme purée flavoured with burnt hay. A world of ginger lights up a dessert of spiced poached pear, which comes with gingerbread ice cream, honeycomb and gingery pear cider granita. The serviceable wine list, arranged by style, starts at £19.50.

Chef/s: Anton Piotrowski and Daniel Bennetts. **Open:** all week L 12 to 3, D 6.30 to 9. **Closed:** 2.5 weeks Jan. **Meals:** main courses £16 to £32. Set L £15 (2 courses) to £20. Sun L £17. **Details:** 45 seats. 24 seats outside. Bar. Wheelchairs. Music. Parking.

Anton Piotrowski at the Glazebrook

Notes from a happy undercover inspector

The Glazebrook is on a turbo-charged uptick since the arrival of Anton Piotrowski. The food is inspired, exciting, full of confidence, inventive without being technologically gimmicky, and obviously founded on sterling ingredients.

For a main course, a tasting of Pipers Farm chicken, burnt hay pomme purée, carrot, parsnip and shiitake was a triumph. The chicken consisted of a large hunk of breast with well-seasoned crisped skin; a cake of shredded thigh meat mixed with finely diced carrot and cabbage and wrapped in cabbage leaf; and a golfball-sized rissole with pané coating, strongly flavoured with cinnamon. A layer of puréed potato, delicately flavoured with burnt hay, was spread on to the plate.

This was a sensational marriage of flavours, and a riposte to any notion that the chicken option is always likely to be the safe and boring choice. Overall, it's the attention to detail in every last element of a dish that impresses so much.

■ South Pool
The Millbrook Inn
Cooking score: 2
French | £35
South Pool, TQ7 2RW
Tel no: (01548) 531581
millbrookinnsouthpool.co.uk
£5
OFF

With its crooked timbers, roaring fires and local ales – plus entrancing views of the Salcombe estuary outside – this cracking 17th-century hostelry is the sort of idyllic village boozer that holidaymakers dream of discovering. So it's a bit of a culture shock to find dishes such as a warm salad of duck gizzard, smoked duck, black pudding and duck egg on the menu. The pub's owners are Brits, but the kitchen is headed up by Jean-Philippe Bidart, who imbues seasonal Devon ingredients with the culinary traditions of a Gallic auberge – witness Start Bay crab bisque, pot au feu or moules marinière with frites, in addition to the aforementioned duck collation. One holidaying family who dropped in for lunch also enjoyed devilled kidneys on toast, a 'perfectly cooked' hunk of cod on leeks and capably executed plum crumble to finish. Wines from £18.
Chef/s: Jean-Philippe Bidart. **Open:** all week L 12 to 5, D 7 to 9. **Meals:** main courses £14 to £20. Set L £12 (2 courses) to £15. Sun L £18 (2 courses). **Details:** 40 seats. 40 seats outside. Bar. Wheelchairs.

■ Sparkwell
The Treby Arms
Cooking score: 5
Modern British | £40
Sparkwell, PL7 5DD
Tel no: (01752) 837363
thetrebyarms.co.uk

Anton Piotrowksi has put his victory in the *Masterchef Professionals* competition of 2012 to energetic use, now spreading his Devon wings at Glazebrook House (see entry, South Brent) as well as at the original whitewashed country inn. The balancing act seems to be working, and the Treby can boast that 70 per cent of its fresh produce is grown here, while a gamekeeper oversees the estate. Attention to detail is one of Piotrowski's strongest cards, seen in a starter combination of smoked eel with ox heart, ham hock, chorizo jam and confit egg yolk. That could be succeeded by venison roasted in cocoa with colcannon, portobellos, salami and foie gras. Vegetarian dishes are quite as imaginative, perhaps poached egg in leek ash with artichoke purée, wild mushrooms and herbed Brie, before a closer of rhubarb frangipane with matching sorbet and custard. Cheeses are excellent, and 'staff are both attentive and knowledgable of the provenance of the ingredients used'. An enterprising wine list keeps prices restrained, from £18.50.

Chef/s: Anton Piotrowski. **Open:** all week L 12 to 2, D 6 to 9 (8.30 Sun). **Closed:** 25 and 26 Dec, 1 Jan. **Meals:** main courses £17 to £34. Set L £18 (2 courses) to £23. **Details:** 60 seats. 30 seats outside. Bar. Wheelchairs. Music. Parking.

▌Tavistock

★ NEW ENTRY ★

The Cornish Arms

Cooking score: 3
British | £26
15 West Street, Tavistock, PL19 8AN
Tel no: (01822) 612145
thecornisharmstavistock.co.uk
£5 OFF £30

Set in a terrace on the edge of the town centre, the Cornish Arms is indisputably in west Devon, but makes a good fist of not noticing, from its mineral waters and soft drinks to its Newlyn seafood. An extended pub with a strong focus on dining in two split-level areas with monochrome photographs and bare-boarded floors, it pleases a pub clientele up for some ale-battered fish and chips, steak and kidney pudding or duck confit. The specials menu is where much of the imaginative energy is concentrated, though, producing a fine inspection lunch of chunky roast chicken terrine with an egg yolk, a majestic piece of

browned cod fillet on braised lettuce with exquisite crab gratin and a jug of bisque, and a strawberry trifle that comes with high-octane sorbet and a sugared doughnut. The evening might bring on slow-cooked ox cheek with mash and horseradish cream in a rich beefy gravy, and there are fine artisan English cheeses. Wines from £14.95.

Chef/s: John Hooker. **Open:** all week L 12 to 3, D 6 to 9.30 (9 Sun). **Meals:** main courses £11 to £24. **Details:** 80 seats. 97 seats outside. Bar. Wheelchairs. Music. Parking.

▌Topsham

★ NEW ENTRY ★

Salutation Inn

Cooking score: 4
Modern European | £40
68 Fore Street, Topsham, EX3 0HL
Tel no: (01392) 873060
salutationtopsham.co.uk

Styling itself as a restaurant-with-rooms these days, this early 18th-century coaching inn on Fore Street is a popular venue, with a contemporary café in the glazed courtyard and a tidy, evening-only dining room that feels 'calm, respectable and slightly old-fashioned'. The formula at dinner is a series of four-, six- or eight-course tasting menus of modern European cooking. Skill and dedication are part of the package, applied to well-sourced materials that might take in a chef's appetiser consisting of Somerset rainbow trout with fennel, lemon, caper and raisin dressing, and a first course of boudin chicken mousse teamed with baby spinach, wild mushrooms and chicken jus. Main courses deliver some neat spins on intuitive combinations, as in turbot with asparagus, morels and potato purée. Cheeses are prime West Country specimens, extras extend to canapés in the lounge – all in all, this is provincial fine dining of the old school, run with personable charm and dedicated to doing things well. Wines from £19.50.

Chef/s: Tom Williams-Hawkes. **Open:** Mon to Sat 6.30 to 9. **Closed:** Sun. **Meals:** set D £40 (4 courses). Tasting menu £60 (6 courses) to £80 (8 courses). **Details:** 29 seats. Bar. Wheelchairs. Music. Parking.

■ Torquay
The Elephant
Cooking score: 5
Modern British | £45
3-4 Beacon Terrace, Torquay, TQ1 2BH
Tel no: (01803) 200044
elephantrestaurant.co.uk

£5
OFF

The two-tier system that Simon Hulstone ran here for many years has now been seamlessly amalgamated into a single ground-floor operation in a refreshed bare-boarded room that has oblique views of the harbour. Showcasing county produce, some of it from the Elephant's own smallholding, the menus are full of cutting-edge modern brasserie appeal. Paignton crab in both colours appears with little turrets of spring pea pannacotta and dashi-spiked mango sorbet for a refreshing opener, before mains offer a range of pedigree meats and locally landed fish. Exmoor venison comes with haricots, girolles and onion ash, while the little 'croquettes' of delicious Crediton duck leg confit in their crackly skin make up for the not widely preferred blush-pink approach to the breast. Hake appears in its Spanish suit with chorizo in a meaty chicken jus, and simply presented desserts, such as lemon and passion fruit tart with intense banana sorbet, make big closing statements. Wines start at £19.50.
Chef/s: Simon Hulstone. **Open:** Tue to Sat L 12 to 2, D 6.30 to 9.30. **Closed:** Sun, Mon, 2 weeks Jan. **Meals:** main courses £15 to £25. Set L £15 (2 courses) to £17. **Details:** 60 seats. Bar. Wheelchairs.

Visit us online

To find out more about
The Good Food Guide, please
visit thegoodfoodguide.co.uk

The Orange Tree
Cooking score: 2
Modern European | £35
14-16 Parkhill Road, Torquay, TQ1 2AL
Tel no: (01803) 213936
orangetreerestaurant.co.uk

The Orange Tree flourishes in the distinctly sheltered microclimate of a narrow back street, hidden away in the town centre not far from the harbour. It's run with gracious aplomb by Sharon Wolf and her team out front, a candlelit cocoon of an evening venue in which nobody will bump you off your table in accordance with a schedule. Bernd Wolf cooks confidently (take a peek as you pass through the back corridor), using regional materials to positive effect in dishes that make culinary sense. Start with seared bream and marinated beetroot dressed in blood orange, or daringly rich crab bisque dotted with scallops, prior to pancetta-wrapped tenderloin and ale-braised cheek of pork with choucroute in caraway jus. Great aromatic impact distinguishes herb-crusted tournedos with morels in truffle-oiled Madeira jus, and there need be no guilt attached to sticky toffee pudding, butterscotch and clotted cream when it comes with apple and lingonberries for your vitamins. House French is £18.50.
Chef/s: Bernd Wolf. **Open:** Tue to Sat D only 7 to 9. **Closed:** Sun, Mon, 26 Dec, 1 week Jan, 2 weeks Oct. **Meals:** main courses £15 to £26. Tasting menu £48. **Details:** 42 seats. Music.

■ Totnes
Rumour
Cooking score: 1
Modern British | £29
30 High Street, Totnes, TQ9 5RY
Tel no: (01803) 864682
rumourtotnes.com

£30

A fixture of boho Totnes since 2006, this indie wine-bar-cum-restaurant entertains local drinkers and socialisers throughout the day, while mealtimes see a big blackboard menu for those in need of solid sustenance. In true modern British style, the kitchen cherry-picks ideas from far and wide, so don't be surprised to see chicken satay, smoked haddock brandade or breaded sardines with home-preserved lemon relish alongside Teign mussels in cider with celeriac milk or slow-roast pork belly with sweet potato purée and polenta chips. Burgers and 'handmade' pizzas hit the spot, while dessert might bring affogato or rhubarb and custard trifle. Wines from £15.95.

Chef/s: Lee Hegarty. **Open:** Mon to Sat L 12 to 3, all week D 6 to 10 (9 Sun). **Closed:** 25 and 26 Dec. **Meals:** main courses £14 to £18. **Details:** 64 seats. Wheelchairs. Music.

▮ Yelverton
Prince Hall Hotel
Cooking score: 3
British | £48
Yelverton, PL20 6SA
Tel no: (01822) 890403
princehall.co.uk

£5
OFF

A pretty burst of buttercup yellow in a wild green landscape, this modestly proportioned country house hotel is a real one-off, welcoming canines and humans with equal warmth. It has a gently bohemian, home-from-home feel enhanced by original artwork, a real fire, capacious armchairs and country views. The cooking is fuelled by an impressive list of local suppliers, but influences are wider ranging: West Country lamb might feature in a tagine with lemon couscous and wilted spinach, while pork tenderloin could come with crispy pancetta Puy lentils, Savoy cabbage, heritage baby carrots and sage jus. Before that, expect superb homemade breads and starters such as spinach and Parmesan soup with lemon oil and mixed herb croûtons or beetroot tortellini with roasted Mediterranean vegetables, Parmesan crisps and basil oil. Desserts centre on the homely comforts of plum crumble or apple and cinnamon tart. An impressive list of mostly organic wines kicks off at £22.50.

Chef/s: Chris Daly. **Open:** all week L 12 to 3, D 7 to 8.30. **Meals:** set L £26 (2 courses) to £30. Set D £40 (2 courses) to £48. Sun L £25. **Details:** 36 seats. 20 seats outside. Bar. Wheelchairs. Music. Parking.

Please send us your feedback

To register your opinion about any restaurant listed in this guide, or a new restaurant that you wish to bring to our attention, please visit the web address at the bottom of the page. Your feedback informs the content of the book and will be used to compile next year's reviews.

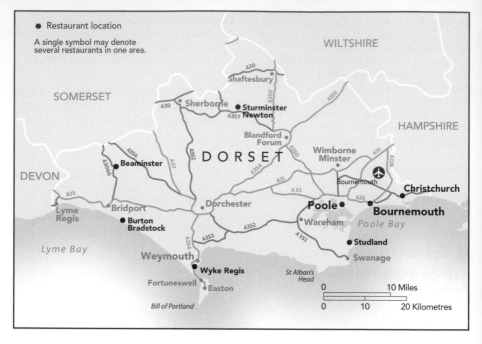

▌ Beaminster
Brassica

Cooking score: 4
Modern British | £30
4 The Square, Beaminster, DT8 3AS
Tel no: (01308) 538100
brassicarestaurant.co.uk

In prime position on the town square, Brassica occupies a building that was the model for the pub at Emminster, Thomas Hardy's fictionalised Wessex version of Beaminster, home of Angel Clare. It was given a light contemporary makeover for its opening in 2014, with pictures of ducks and fish, but retaining the essential brick fireplace with adjacent woodpile. The 'highly accomplished' Cass Titcombe offers an elevenses selection to the early doors crowd, and a fuller menu of lively modern brasserie food for later, taking in grilled crevettes for dunking in aïoli to start, or pheasant rillettes and cornichons, ahead of robust mains such as pork chop with pickled rhubarb and grilled chicory, or hake

with spiced cauliflower and preserved lemon. A hungry pair might sign up for sliced Hereford ribeye adorned with rocket and black garlic, but save a space for molten chocolate pudding served with strained orange yoghurt. Well-chosen wines are informatively presented, starting at £19.
Chef/s: Cass Titcombe. **Open:** Wed to Sun L 12 to 2.30, Tue to Sat D 6.30 to 9.30. **Closed:** Mon, 24 to 26 Dec, first 2 weeks Jan. **Meals:** main courses £10 to £22. Set L £15 (2 courses) to £18. **Details:** 40 seats. 6 seats outside. Music.

Symbols

🛏 Accommodation is available
£30 Three courses for less than £30
£5 OFF £5-off voucher scheme
🍾 Notable wine list

Bournemouth

★ NEW ENTRY ★

Roots

Cooking score: 1
Modern European | £33
141 Belle Vue Road, Bournemouth, BH6 3EN
Tel no: (01202) 430005
restaurantroots.co.uk

This whitewashed, glass-fronted little restaurant is bright and warm, and has been lavished with tactile custom-made accessories. Jan Bretschneider and his wife Stacey, both chefs, have packed professional ambition into every dish. While both tasting menus and à la carte can be hit-and-miss, with culinary homages rather too much in evidence, potential abounds in the best of the dishes. Get lucky with lovely bread and whipped herb butter, cured sea trout with cucumber, and lamb in three servings, including a crisp samosa with foamy pea dip and superb rump with asparagus, 'the essence of great spring ingredients'. The sometimes inflexible service needs work, and wine is from a brief list, opening at £19. It's one to watch.
Chef/s: Jan Bretschneider. **Open:** Thur to Sun L 12 to 2.30 (6 Sun), Wed to Sat D 6 to 9.30. **Closed:** Mon, Tue. **Meals:** set L £17 (2 courses) to £22. Set D £33 (6 courses) to £40. **Details:** 24 seats. V menu. Music.

LOCAL GEM

West Beach

Seafood | £33
Pier Approach, Bournemouth, BH2 5AA
Tel no: (01202) 587785
west-beach.co.uk

Andy Price's long-serving beachside eatery is a bonus for Bournemouth with its sought-after terrace tables, spruce maritime interiors and fish from the boats. Whole crabs, lobsters and seafood platters are bestsellers, although the kitchen also rustles up more fancy global plates such as soy-and-maple-cured tuna with crispy mussels and sesame caramel or grey mullet with aubergine purée, chorizo, peperonata

and saffron oil. Meat eaters aren't ignored, and readers have enjoyed the 'delicious' Christmas turkey, too. Wines from £17.50

READERS RECOMMEND

The Larder House

Modern British
Southbourne Grove, Bournemouth, BH6 3QZ
Tel no: (01202) 424687
thelarderhouse.co.uk
'My "go to" restaurant; you're guaranteed amazing food, with service that is always on the money. Their chefs have an incredible knowledge and the management team truly cares and is passionate about giving its patrons the very best experience.'

Burton Bradstock

LOCAL GEM

Hive Beach Café

Seafood | £30
Beach Road, Burton Bradstock, DT6 4RF
Tel no: (01308) 897070
hivebeachcafe.co.uk

£5 OFF

'We are lucky to have this facility near to where we live but the testament to this café is it stays open all year, and has continued to do so through all the storms.' So concluded one regular to Steve Attrill's sprawling, first-come, first-served café overlooking a shingle beach. Open for breakfasts and lunch (and dinner on summer evenings) the kitchen deals in local fish, from tempura Lyme Bay cod fillet and chips, via char-grilled West Bay mackerel to Cornish coast mussels. Wines from £15.50. Note: head to the beach at nearby West Bay to find sibling Watch House Café.

Local Gem

Local Gems are the perfect neighbourhood venues, delivering good, freshly cooked food at great value for money.

▌Christchurch
The Jetty
Cooking score: 4
Modern British | £40
Christchurch Harbour Hotel & Spa, 95
Mudeford, Christchurch, BH23 3NT
Tel no: (01202) 400950
thejetty.co.uk
£5 OFF

The Jetty is one of an ever-expanding group of similarly named restaurants that overlook some of the most captivating stretches of English coastline. In the present case, it's Mudeford Quay and Christchurch Harbour that provide the wows, in an officially designated Area of Outstanding Natural Beauty. Catch of the day from the quay itself, or from around the South Coast generally, is an obvious punt, with Poole Bay oysters, mussels in tomato and chilli, and skate in caper-shrimp beurre noisette with creamy mash, all here for the taking. If you want to get all *moderne*, Alex Aitken's tasting menu brings on hay-smoked steak tartare with quail's egg; scallop and bacon jam in maple dressing; and a main of lamb blanquette with sweetbreads and cockles to brighten the prospect still more. Isle of Wight Blue with wine-poached pear is a cheese course worth investigating, and the signature passion fruit soufflé is as fluffy as a down-stuffed pillow. Wines start at £18.95.
Chef/s: Alex Aitken. **Open:** Mon to Sat L 12 to 2.30, D 6 to 9.30. Sun 12 to 8. **Meals:** main courses £20 to £29. Set L and D £20 (2 courses) to £24. Sun L £25 (2 courses) to £30. **Details:** 80 seats. 30 seats outside. Bar. Wheelchairs. Music. Parking.

Readers recommend

A 'readers recommend' review is a genuine quote from a report sent in by one of our readers. We intend to follow up these suggestions throughout the year to come.

▌Poole
LOCAL GEM
Guildhall Tavern
French | £35
15 Market Street, Poole, BH15 1NB
Tel no: (01202) 671717
guildhalltavern.co.uk

The setting is a listed building with a covered and heated patio in Poole's Old Town, but this promising restaurant looks tastefully contemporary. The menu has a prominent French accent, offering 'perfectly cooked' herring roes on toast (a 'real treat'), otherwise a meal might begin with double-baked cheese soufflé before going on to fresh scallops with prawns, fresh crab and mushroom mornay or a rich, glossy boeuf bourguignon. Finish in true style with French cheeses and typically Gallic desserts. An almost all-French wine list opens with house Duboeuf at £18.50.

▌Studland
LOCAL GEM
Pig on the Beach
Modern British | £35
Manor House, Manor Road, Studland, BH19 3AU
Tel no: (01929) 450288
thepighotel.com

Keeping the customer and the produce in close proximity, the Pig on the Beach is a delightfully laid-back country house hotel for the 21st century. The kitchen turns out some nifty plates of food that reflect a dedication to localism and sustainability, while its setting, overlooking Studland Bay, means that fish is a strength, from 'really fresh' mackerel and wild fennel to 'utterly delicious' gurnard with Hampshire chorizo. Home-cured salt beef, and pigeon breast and purple sprouting broccoli with pickled rhubarb and artichoke purée are meatier options, all served in a rustic-chic glasshouse-style restaurant. Wines from £17.50.

READERS RECOMMEND

Shell Bay

Seafood
Ferry Road, Studland, BH19 3BA
Tel no: (01929) 450363
shellbay.net

'A fairly short menu, almost all seafood, and to a good standard; not fine dining, but setting a good standard for enjoyable family outings and cheerful groups to enjoy a range of dishes from grilled lobster to simple fish and chips.'

■ Sturminster Newton
Plumber Manor

Cooking score: 2
Anglo-French | £38
Sturminster Newton, DT10 2AF
Tel no: (01258) 472507
plumbermanor.com

£5 OFF

Owned by the Prideaux-Brunes since its inception in the 17th century (and a Guide stalwart for more than 40 years), historic Plumber Manor certainly has formidable staying power. And like some treasured vintage automobile, it benefits from lavish amounts of loving care and attention: this is a family seat *par excellence*, a stronghold of old-school English propriety replete with portraits, swagged curtains and sweeping staircases, where the food promises pleasurable comforts, reassurance and determinedly unfashionable satisfaction. Take a few steps back in time as you consider a menu that begins with chicken liver pâté and grilled goats' cheese salad, before moving on to salmon and sole roulade, slow-roast pork belly with celeriac mash or chicken suprême with lemon and tarragon. True to form, proceedings conclude with a luxuriously calorific sweet trolley loaded with myriad Beeton-esque confections, including cheesecakes, tortes, double chocolate mousse and so forth. House wines start at £18.50.

Chef/s: Brian Prideaux-Brune. **Open:** Sun L 12.30 to 1.30, all week D 7.30 to 9. **Closed:** 25 Jan to 6 Mar. **Meals:** set D £38. Sun L £30. **Details:** 60 seats. Wheelchairs. Parking.

■ Wyke Regis

LOCAL GEM

Crab House Café

Seafood | £30
Ferryman's Way, Portland Road, Wyke Regis, DT4 9YU
Tel no: (01305) 788867
crabhousecafe.co.uk

Follow the road south from Weymouth to find this little wooden shack overlooking the pebbles of Chesil Beach. In return, you'll be rewarded with some terrific views, bracing breezes and heaps of ozone-fresh seafood: standouts include Portland Royal oysters from the owners' beds nearby, whole crabs, home-smoked eel and a rolling selection dictated by the day's catch – perhaps brill fillet with lime and coriander butter or skate wing roasted with chorizo, spring onion and paprika. The quality is never in doubt. Wines from £15.90.

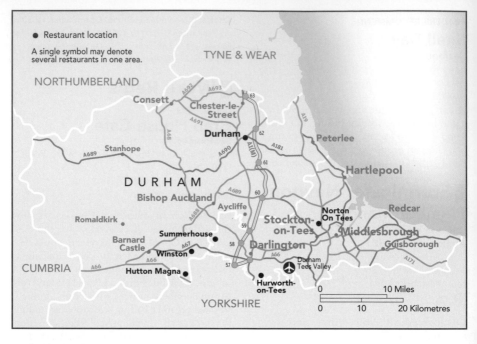

Durham

★ NEW ENTRY ★

The Garden House Inn

Cooking score: 1
International | £23
Framwellgate Peth, Durham, DH1 4NQ
Tel no: (0191) 3863395
gardenhouseinn.com

Chef Ruari MacKay was last seen in the Guide cooking at Bistro 21, just up the road from this roadside pub. A short walk north of the train station, and therefore away from the cathedral and castle, it is off the tourist path and has a villagey feel with its smart, low-beamed country-rustic interior. Drinkers are attracted by the range of regional real ales, although they are increasingly outnumbered by diners enjoying globetrotting dishes such as Thai prawn and mussel broth, which might precede monkfish, 'nduja, wild garlic and roast potatoes or curried lamb shoulder, aromatic

rice and flatbread. Sticky toffee pudding flies the British flag on the dessert menu. Wines from £15.
Chef/s: Ruari MacKay. **Open:** all week L 12 to 3 (5.30 Sun), Mon to Sat D 5 to 9.30. **Meals:** main courses £10 to £15. **Details:** 80 seats.

Restaurant DH1

Cooking score: 3
Modern British | £40
The Avenue, Durham, DH1 4DX
Tel no: (0191) 3846655
restaurantdh1.co.uk

£5
OFF

Shades of purple reign at DH1, Stephen Hardy's restaurant occupying the ground floor of a Victorian building (now Farnley Tower guesthouse), where, with wife Helen leading the line front-of-house, he offers up compellingly contemporary menus. Creative presentation, up-to-the-minute cooking techniques – expect a thoroughly 21st-century experience, which for the most part is pulled off. Things get under way with a slate of amuse-bouches including tartlet of beetroot and smoked eel, 'the pastry so thin it was almost transparent'. A couple of tasting menus take you from 'various organic carrots' with oxtail and béarnaise, via wonderfully tender roast breast of Goosnargh duck flavoured with five-spice, plus salt-baked beetroots, fig and fennel, to a nicely sharp orange curd number with blackberry sorbet, tarragon and caramelised white chocolate. A wine flight is available with the main nine-course tasting menu; bottle prices start at £18. **Chef/s:** Stephen Hardy. **Open:** Tue to Sat D only 6 to 9. **Closed:** Sun, Mon, 25 and 26 Dec, 1 week Jan, 2 weeks Oct. **Meals:** set D £32 (2 courses) to £40. Tasting menu £60 (9 courses). **Details:** 22 seats. V menu. Bar. Wheelchairs. Music. Parking.

■ Hurworth-on-Tees
The Bay Horse
Cooking score: 4
Modern British | £35
45 The Green, Hurworth-on-Tees, DL2 2AA
Tel no: (01325) 720663
thebayhorsehurworth.com

'Looking great' after a tasteful upgrade in early 2016, with special praise for the glass-roofed extension to the rear of the restaurant and for the private dining rooms upstairs, visitors report that this ancient village inn has nevertheless retained its considerable charm as well as a distinct bar for drinkers. And there's substance as well as style, thanks to Marcus Bennett's classy but accessible cooking. Set menus are startlingly good value: braised pork hash cake with carrot roulade and horseradish cream and rabbit ballotine with roast carrot, pommes dauphine and red wine jus are both intricate enough to belie such kind pricing. Trouble is taken over sourcing quality raw materials and the kitchen distinguishes itself with enthusiasm and honest effort, which stretches to first-class bread, excellent pressed duck terrine with grapes, Madeira, hot foie gras and brioche croûtons, and stone bass with

crab and lime gnocchi and roasted sweet potatoes. Among desserts, the caramelised rice pudding has impressed. Wines from £18. **Chef/s:** Marcus Bennett and James Burkhart. **Open:** all week L 12 to 2.30 (4 Sun), D 6 to 9 (9.30 Fri and Sat, 6.30 Sun). **Closed:** 25 and 26 Dec. **Meals:** main courses £18 to £28. Set L £15 (2 courses) to £19. Set D £23 (2 courses) to £27. **Details:** 70 seats. 60 seats outside. Music. Parking.

■ Hutton Magna
The Oak Tree Inn
Cooking score: 2
Modern British | £38
Hutton Magna, DL11 7HH
Tel no: (01833) 627371
theoaktreehutton.co.uk

With its roughcast whitewashed walls, stacks of books and bottle-green dining room, the Oak Tree has undergone some modification from its original function as a local watering hole pure and simple. The Rosses ensure the place exudes a warm welcome, and Alastair's menus are built on a foundation of comforting country-pub ideas. Expect smoked haddock with celeriac, leek and quails' eggs, or a ham hock croquette with yellow peas and pineapple to kick things off, before turning to the likes of turbot and brown shrimps with raisins and capers, or a serving of best end of lamb and sticky red cabbage, its accompanying shepherd's pie given extra richness with black pudding. Desserts tread the populist path of chocolate, salt caramel, peanut butter and gingerbread more than fruity fibre; coffee and almond pannacotta with a brownie and almond milk ice cream is one of the lighter options. An appealing international grab-bag of wines starts at £17. **Chef/s:** Alastair Ross. **Open:** Tue to Sun D only 6 to 9. **Closed:** Mon, 24 to 27 Dec, 31 Dec to 2 Jan. **Meals:** main courses £22 to £25. **Details:** 20 seats. Bar. Music. Parking.

James Close: Chef of the Year

A glimpse into our inspector's report on Chef of the Year, James Close

The last time I visited the Raby Hunt, James Close showed an incredibly mature approach to emphasising and combining flavours, never losing the clarity of ingredients. Now, having closed the Raby Hunt for lunches to give staff better work-life balance, he has used the extra time to invest in experimentation.

There are two really obvious changes: an obsessive focus on buying ingredients to which other restaurants don't have access, then employing unique techniques to make those products the absolute best they can be. There is a shift away from complex, garnish-heavy plates towards investing time in ingredients that carry dishes on their own.

If a single dish illustrates this, it's the Raby Hunt's raw beef. So simple, yet so brilliant, it underlines how the most impactful creativity is rarely the most obvious. Thin slices of extremely lean, ruby-coloured beef, are each folded in on themselves to conceal flecks of dripping. This is incredibly clever. The added fat gives the meat an unmistakable beefiness; the meat itself is incredibly clean, melting into nothing in the mouth - the perfect modern reinvention of steak tartar.

▌Norton On Tees

LOCAL GEM

Café Lilli
Modern British | £29
83 High Street, Norton On Tees, TS20 1AE
Tel no: (01642) 554422
lillicafe.co.uk

£30

The Italian input at this busy, modern-day café owes a lot to owner Roberto Pittalis, although the food is a real mix of ideas ranging from steamed Shetland mussels with pancetta, leeks and garlic cream, and oxtail terrine, to beef burgers in a brioche bun, and venison steak with curly kale, wild mushrooms, honey parsnips and peppercorn sauce. There are blackboard specials of homemade pasta, risotto, and fish of the day (delivered daily from Hartlepool), the bread is delicious and local supporters are unanimous that Café Lilli is an 'exceptional and lovely place to eat'. All-Italian wines from £18 (a litre).

▌Summerhouse

★ TOP 50 ★

★ CHEF OF THE YEAR ★

The Raby Hunt
Cooking score: 7
Modern British | £55
Summerhouse, DL2 3UD
Tel no: (01325) 374237
rabyhuntrestaurant.co.uk

Standing in open ground in a village near Darlington, its stone frontage wholly concealed by trim foliage, the Raby once provided bed and board for drovers en route to Northumbria and the border. Built in the late Georgian era, it's been done over with the contemporary designer's touch inside, where aubergine banquettes, an uncovered floor and white walls sparsely adorned with long mirrors are the look. James Close is cooking at the razor-edge of modern style, acquiring premium ingredients and subjecting them to ingenious techniques and subtle enhancements, all the way to whizzbang novelty presentations. Canapés alone are little masterpieces of the genre, as exemplified by a Jerusalem artichoke cup filled with its pickled flesh and chopped offals, buried in nitro-frozen foie gras parfait. It's gone in a bite. The dinner drill is a complex tasting menu built on outstanding regional produce, with highlights pouring forth thick and fast: diced razor clam in mace-spiked butter, served in its shell with brown shrimps, samphire and girolles; crisped sea bass with dried and puréed smoked cod roe; half a roasted squab cooked in one piece from breast to talon, with anchovy emulsion, radicchio and olive jus. The intermediate dishes of locally grown vegetables are beautiful in every sense, while the main dessert is an endearingly semi-collapsed warm chocolate mousse garnished with dried olives and topped with sheep's yoghurt ice cream. A cavalcade of biodynamic and natural wines is interlarded through an authoritative list that features Philipponnat Champagnes, Marlborough's Little Beauty vineyard, Bernhard Huber's Baden Pinot and Lucien Lardy's cru Beaujolais. A good glass selection starts at £7.50, bottles at £29.

Chef/s: James Close. **Open:** Sat L 12 to 2, Wed to Sat D 6 to 9.30. **Closed:** Sun, Mon, Tue, 1 week Christmas, 2 weeks Aug. **Meals:** set L £45 (5 courses) to £70 (10 courses). Set D £55 (5 courses) to £80 (10 courses). **Details:** 30 seats. 6 seats outside. Bar. Wheelchairs. Parking.

Cheddar and spinach soufflé, seafood pancakes, moules marinière and hefty ribeye steaks in peppery sauce. Not that things don't occasionally get a little more elaborate, as in poached crab-stuffed plaice fillets on chive mousseline. There's a separate vegetarian menu, and to finish, perhaps Turkish Delight ice cream in hot chocolate sauce. Pedigree English cheeses with grapes and chutney are another lure. House Chilean is £15.50.

Chef/s: Paul Grundy. **Open:** Tue to Sat L 12 to 2, D 6 to 9. **Closed:** Sun, Mon, 25 and 26 Dec, 1 Jan. **Meals:** main courses £17 to £32. **Details:** 50 seats. 16 seats outside. Wheelchairs. Music. Parking.

▌Winston
The Bridgewater Arms

Cooking score: 1
British | £38
Winston, DL2 3RN
Tel no: (01325) 730302
thebridgewaterarms.com

Paul Grundy's characterful local pub was once the village school and, in a discreetly smart ambience of white-clothed tables and high-backed chairs, serves homely food based on local supplies, with daily specials maintaining the appeal. Reporters' favourites include

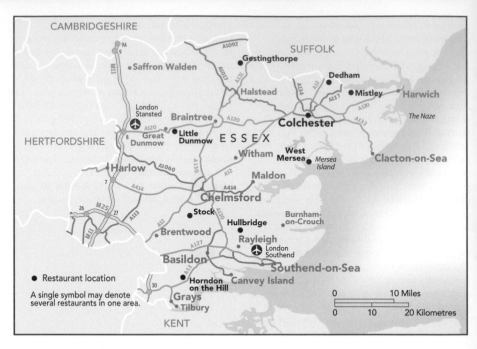

■ Colchester

Church Street Tavern

Cooking score: 2
Modern British | £25
3 Church Street, Colchester, CO1 1NF
Tel no: (01206) 564325
churchstreettavern.co.uk
£30

Wade through Colchester's dismal chainery to this hospitable bar-restaurant, a ray of light from the people behind Dedham's Sun Inn (see entry). It's 'a lovely spot' with 'a very comfy lounge space as well as bar tables and restaurant upstairs,' and the menu has plenty of interest, offering 'really really tasty, simple food'. Perfectly grilled mackerel with smoky 'nduja, vinegary piquillo peppers and peppery rocket is a thoughtful masterclass in balancing flavour, texture and looks; it's not to be outdone by equally tasty hake with clams and wild garlic. Hungrier? Choose salt-marsh-reared lamb chops, a packed seafood stew with rouille or a handsome rare-breed beef burger in a brioche bun. A passion fruit tartlet with zesty, finely cubed pineapple salsa, blood-orange and lime sorbet is the pick of some fine puddings. Wines from a reasonable £16.50.
Chef/s: Ewan Naylon. **Open:** all week L 12 to 2.30 (3 Sat and Sun), Mon to Sat D 6 to 9.30 (10 Fri and Sat). **Closed:** 25 and 26 Dec, first week Jan. **Meals:** main course £10 to £25. Set L and D £15 (2 courses) to £18. Sun L £21. **Details:** 85 seats. 15 seats outside.

■ Dedham
The Sun Inn

Cooking score: 3
Modern British | £27
High Street, Dedham, CO7 6DF
Tel no: (01206) 323351
thesuninndedham.com
£5 OFF 🍷 ▭ £30

Even the church opposite can't beat the Sun Inn for historical credibility – they both date from the 15th century. The old inn at the heart of this pretty-as-a-picture village has been owned by Piers Baker since 2003. The period character looms large within thanks to copious beams, huge fireplaces and oak panels, while some smart bedrooms and an opened-up dining area at the rear help create a more contemporary mood. The kitchen draws on regional ingredients to deliver a modern British repertoire that shows Italian sensibilities; thus you might kick off with antipasti of hake fritti with saffron aïoli or Ardleigh asparagus with a Parmesan crumb. A pasta/risotto section delivers the latter flavoured with brown shrimps and vermouth, or go for a main-course proper such as whole black bream acqua pazza or spring stew of Mersea Island lamb. A custard tart with braised rhubarb brings things to a close. The mightily impressive wine list is arranged by style and is fairly priced; bottles start at £15.50.

Chef/s: Jack Levine. **Open:** all week L 12 to 2.30 (3 Sat and Sun), D 6 to 9.30 (10 Fri and Sat). **Closed:** 25 and 26 Dec. **Meals:** main courses £10 to £19. Sun L £14. **Details:** 82 seats. 40 seats outside. Bar. Music. Parking.

Le Talbooth

Cooking score: 4
Modern British | £54
Gun Hill, Dedham, CO7 6HP
Tel no: (01206) 323150
milsomhotels.com
£5 OFF 🍴

In the days when horses plashed across the Stour with their carriages, this is where the tolls were taken. Since the 1950s, the place has been welcoming visitors with more recreational intent on their minds, and sitting under the canvas awning at an alfresco table with the river rolling by, what other intent could there be? It's run with great conviviality, and the cooking continues to reflect the tidal swell of culinary fashion. Starter may be terrine and crisped leg of squab pigeon with accoutrements of mooli, pickled red onion and blackberries, a palate-priming way into ingeniously composed mains such as pan-

roasted sea bass in truffled linguine with ceps and an egg yolk, or thyme-scented veal sirloin with butternut, nutmegged polenta and Madeira-braised snails. Sunday lunches are a draw, with Dingley Dell pork and local lamb on parade, and exotic afters could be pineapple and coconut soufflé with piña colada ice cream. A broadly based wine list opens at £19.25.

Chef/s: Andrew Hirst. **Open:** all week L 12 to 2.30, Mon to Sat D 7 to 9.30. **Meals:** main courses £20 to £33. Set L £26 (2 courses) to £32. Sun L £38. **Details:** 80 seats. 60 seats outside. Bar. Wheelchairs. Parking.

▉ Epping

READERS RECOMMEND

Haywards

Modern European
111 Bell Common, Epping, CM16 4DZ
Tel no: (01992) 577350
haywardsrestaurant.co.uk
'I never dreamed Essex would have a restaurant of this quality and at such a good price. Their lunchtime offers are a steal. On top of that the owners are a joy to talk to. Why travel to the West End when you can enjoy a nice drive into the countryside?'

Gestingthorpe
The Pheasant
Cooking score: 1
Modern British | £25
Church Street, Gestingthorpe, CO9 3AU
Tel no: (01787) 465010
thepheasant.net

The view over the Stour Valley shows the best of Essex and there's plenty of love for this pub too. Its bedrooms are named after folk with connections to the area – Constable, naturally, but Captain Oates as well – while its rustic charms are enhanced by the fact that 'attention to detail is spot on'. Chef/landlord James Donoghue grows his own veg and keeps chickens in a plot across the way, while his menu is British and broadly appealing. Tuck into pheasant terrine with truffle butter, slow-roasted pork belly with crackling, homemade steak and mushroom pie or Arctic char with clam butter. Wines start at £16.50.
Chef/s: James Donoghue. **Open:** Tue to Sun L 12 to 2, D 6.30 to 9. **Closed:** Mon, 24 to 26 Dec, first 2 weeks Jan. **Meals:** main courses £13 to £20. **Details:** 40 seats. 20 seats outside. Bar. Music. Parking.

Horndon on the Hill
The Bell Inn
Cooking score: 3
Modern European | £32
High Road, Horndon on the Hill, SS17 8LD
Tel no: (01375) 642463
bell-inn.co.uk

The Vereker family took over this medieval pub way back in 1938, and more than 75 years down the line it's still a 'great little find' with some real talent in the kitchen. Inside, it is unashamedly old-fashioned (huge faded rugs, heavy panelling, low beams), but there's a 'spirit of intelligent generosity' on the plate, from an on-trend dish of caramelised cauliflower with toasted brioche and poached duck egg to sea trout with new potatoes,

sautéed peas and spring onions ('economy itself'). Elsewhere, a complex assemblage of veal ballotine and rabbit ravioli followed by a 'cluttered' plate involving pigeon breasts, carrot purée, braised venison and cheese-crusted mash provided satisfaction for one reader, while a big choux bun with white chocolate parfait and fudge sauce completed a 'hat-trick of solid, enjoyable dishes'. Pub grub and real ales keep the bar ticking over, with workaday wines starting at £16.50.
Chef/s: Stuart Fay. **Open:** all week L 12 to 1.45 (2.15 Sun), D 6.30 to 9.45 (6 Sat, 7 Sun). **Closed:** 25 and 26 Dec, bank hols. **Meals:** main courses £12 to £23. **Details:** 80 seats. 36 seats outside. Bar. Wheelchairs. Parking.

Hullbridge
★ NEW ENTRY ★
The Anchor Riverside
Cooking score: 4
Modern British | £30
Ferry Road, Hullbridge, SS5 6ND
Tel no: (01702) 230777
theanchorhullbridge.co.uk

The Anchor is a model for modern pub dining, playing host to a truly talented kitchen. Dishes are frequently show stoppers, but the repertoire is bolstered by the sort of pub grub that keeps customers happy (scampi or fish and chips, cottage pie with Cheddar mash, burgers). It's all offered on a 'chunky menu' that is nonetheless dwarfed by the size of the huge riverside hostelry: a long wraparound bar with circular booths and tables, and a conservatory dining room that leads through to a not-inconsiderable terrace. From the wood-roasted scallops that, with Ibérico pork, apple and mustard, made up one reporter's starter, via two fat pieces of perfectly pink fillet steak, which came with a blob of truffle mayo, grated truffle, sautéed St George's mushrooms, a puddle of buttermilk dressing, a whole pot of rich, creamy mushroom gratin and chips, it's all very appealing. Service, like the food, strikes a great balance. Wines from £18.50.

Chef/s: Daniel Watkins. **Open:** Mon to Sat L 12 to 3, D 6 to 9.30. Sun 12 to 8. **Closed:** 25 Dec. **Meals:** main courses £14 to £23. Sun L £17. **Details:** 110 seats. 120 seats outside. Bar. Wheelchairs. Music. Parking.

Little Dunmow
★ NEW ENTRY ★
The Flitch of Bacon
Cooking score: 3
Modern British | £34
The St, Little Dunmow, CM6 3HT
Tel no: (01371) 821660
flitchofbacon.co.uk

Not everyone favours the pared-back neutrality that is the default setting of today's restaurant designers, so anyone hankering after swirly patterned carpets and country-style furniture should stay away from Daniel Clifford's vision of a country pub. The chef-owner of Cambridge's Midsummer House (see entry) has brought this whitewashed local up to date with more than just a lick of paint and provides a suitably understated but comfortable setting for the contemporary cooking that is his forte – a far cry from what you might expect in the Essex countryside – though don't go expecting Midsummer House. A 'fresh and feisty' salad of beetroot and goats' cheese with rocket and hazelnut shortbread points the way, there are main courses of braised beef cheek with buttered mash, crispy bacon, mushrooms and green beans, or parsley-crusted cod with a tomato butter sauce, and praiseworthy desserts such as tarte Tatin for two. Wines start at £17.

Chef/s: Daniel Clifford and Luke Finegan. **Open:** Wed to Sat L 12 to 2.30, D 6.30 to 9. Sun 12 to 6.30. **Closed:** Mon, Tue. **Meals:** main courses £13 to £29. Set L £18 (2 courses) to £23. **Details:** 54 seats. Bar. Wheelchairs. Music. Parking.

Messing
READERS RECOMMEND
The Old Crown
Modern British
Lodge Road, Messing, CO5 9TU
Tel no: (01621) 815575
oldcrownmessing.com
'It has an ever-changing menu and they have something for everyone: classics such as steak and ale pie, to more refined dishes. It was an absolute treat   from the homemade bread to the brown-bread ice cream to the hazelnut biscotti I got with my coffee.'

Mistley
The Mistley Thorn
Cooking score: 2
Modern European | £25
High Street, Mistley, CO11 1HE
Tel no: (01206) 392821
mistleythorn.co.uk
🛏 £30

A neighbourhood restaurant that 'just keeps on giving' is how one regular describes this former coaching inn by the Stour estuary. Seafood takes centre stage, much of the gleaming-fresh fish on the menu bought from local day boats: a seared fillet of sea bass with a samphire and lemon butter sauce, or grilled Harwich skate wing with seaweed butter, could follow house-smoked mackerel rillettes or smoked haddock arancini. Mersea oysters in varying guises couldn't be fresher: stick with convention and choose a dozen with a shallot and ginger mignonette, or go for the rich, baked, Rockefeller, with spinach, Pernod and a sourdough crumb. Otherwise, go home happy having chosen a handsome Red Poll ribeye steak, or duck breast with port and orange sauce. A vanilla pot de crème with dulce de leche, Marcona almonds and chocolate makes an indulgent finale; blood-orange and cardamom jelly is a lighter choice. A fish-friendly Garganega from the Veneto opens the wine list at £15.95.

Chef/s: Sherri Singleton and Karl Burnside. **Open:** all week L 12 to 2.30 (4 Sat, 5 Sun), D 6.30 to 9.30 (10 Fri, 6 to 10 Sat). **Meals:** main courses £12 to £21. Set L and D £14 (2 courses) to £17. Sun L £17 (2 courses) to £20. **Details:** 80 seats. 12 seats outside. Bar. Music. Parking.

▌Stock
The Oak Room at the Hoop

Cooking score: 1
Modern British | £30
21 High Street, Stock, CM4 9BD
Tel no: (01277) 841137
thehoop.co.uk

Unpretentious – that goes for the décor, menu and food – just about sums up this white-painted clapboard village pub. The bar dispenses real ale and drinkers are made very welcome (one also enjoyed 'the best salt-beef sandwich I have ever had'), but the value-for-money cooking in the upstairs restaurant is the thing, and people come from miles around to eat here. The straightforward menu might see the likes of pig's head sausage roll with homemade brown sauce followed by roast rump of lamb with a mini shepherd's pie or slow-braised beef cheek with creamed potato, with treacle tart and vanilla ice cream to finish. Wines from £15.

Chef/s: Phil Utz. **Open:** Tue to Fri and Sun L 12 to 2.30 (3 Sun), Tue to Sat D 7 to 9. **Closed:** Mon, 1 week Christmas, last week May. **Meals:** main courses £12 to £28. Sun L £25. **Details:** 40 seats. Bar. Music.

▌West Mersea

LOCAL GEM
West Mersea Oyster Bar

Seafood | £20
Coast Road, West Mersea, CO5 8LT
Tel no: (01206) 381600
westmerseaoysterbar.co.uk

£30

'The world is your oyster' proclaims a wall banner, and the Oyster Bar may well become your world if you're a local. In a cheery atmosphere of chunky tables and blackboard menus, with plates lined up on the counter waiting to go, people happily pack the place for hearty bowls of crab chowder, smoked salmon and crayfish salads, whole grilled lobsters, battered skate wings, and of course the indispensable platters, laden with the bounty of the sea from rollmops to chillied-up tiger prawns. The oysters themselves are cultivated in the marshy Mersea creeks around the island, and are in demand worldwide.

Please send us your feedback

To register your opinion about any restaurant listed in this guide, or a new restaurant that you wish to bring to our attention, please visit the web address at the bottom of the page. Your feedback informs the content of the book and will be used to compile next year's reviews.

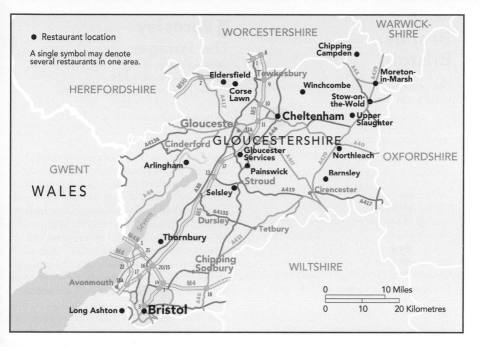

Arlingham
The Old Passage

Cooking score: 4
Seafood | £40
Passage Road, Arlingham, GL2 7JR
Tel no: (01452) 740547
theoldpassage.com

The converted farmhouse marks the site of an ancient ford across the river Severn and offers fine views across the water to the pretty village of Newnham and the Forest of Dean – it's about 'as off the beaten track as it's possible to be', and well worth seeking out. The building itself may not be 'particularly beautiful' but the restaurant deals in beautifully fresh fish and seafood cooked with an impressive lightness of touch. A starter of blowtorched mackerel with an apple, cucumber, mint and horseradish gazpacho, pickled kohlrabi and oyster mayonnaise, and main course of fillet of hake on a warm salad of heritage tomatoes, fennel, asparagus, samphire and brown

shrimps and served with 'melt in the mouth parsley croquettes', were matched at a test meal by excellent little touches, especially the 'exemplary' sourdough with seaweed butter. If you've still got space, round things off with a pudding of roast figs with star anise cream. Service is good and the wine list, understandably concentrating on whites, starts at £19.20.

Chef/s: Mark Redwood. **Open:** Tue to Sun L 12 to 2 (3 Sun), Tue to Sat D 7 to 9. **Closed:** Mon, Tue and Wed D (Jan and Feb), 25 and 26 Dec. **Meals:** main courses £20 to £48. Set L £16 (2 courses) to £22. **Details:** 40 seats. 26 seats outside. Wheelchairs. Music. Parking. Children at L only.

Symbols

🛏 Accommodation is available
£30 Three courses for less than £30
£5 OFF £5-off voucher scheme
🍷 Notable wine list

Best of... Bristol

Our undercover inspectors open their Little Black Books

When it comes to artisanal coffee served with skill, knowledge and passion, **Full Court Press** on Broad Street is second to none.

Tucked away in Boyce's Avenue in Clifton Village, **ANNA** is the go-to place for exquisite cakes washed down with pots of loose-leaf tea.

On the water's edge opposite the SS Great Britain, a lazy brunch at **Spoke & Stringer** is a must for many in-the-know Bristolians.

The King Street area is known locally as 'Beermuda Triangle' due to the number of craft ale pubs and **Small Bar** is one of the best places to grab a pint.

Dream you are in France as you road-test the concise and interesting range of natural wines at **Bar Buvette** on Baldwin Street.

In a converted archway beneath Temple Meads railway station, **Hart's Bakery** serves the finest cheese on sourdough toastie for miles.

Be prepared to queue for the lunchtime kebabs and Kurdish breads at the **Matina** stall in St Nicholas Market, but they are worth the wait.

One foodie thing you must do is try the bacon sandwiches at **Brunel's Buttery**, an alfresco Bristol institution on the harbourside.

Barnsley
The Potager
Cooking score: 3
Modern European | £34
Barnsley House, Barnsley, GL7 5EE
Tel no: (01285) 740000
barnsleyhouse.com

A proper piece of horticultural eye candy, Barnsley House is surrounded by romantic gardens created by the late garden designer Rosemary Verey. These include a potager – an ornate kitchen garden whose produce fuels the menu. The restaurant rambles through adjoining gracious, high-ceilinged rooms whose pale heritage-green wood panels and simple oak-effect furniture create a light, garden vibe befitting the leafy views. Begin in the bar with its 70s-style brown walls and retro prints, then settle at your table for crusty rolls with a garden herb dip and, perhaps, a soft-boiled egg, Ibérico ham and pea purée. Main courses include the signature never-off-the-menu vincisgrassi, and seasonal offerings such as chicken breast with a sweetcorn pancake and asparagus, or gurnard with tomato, avocado and capers. There's a commendable simplicity to the delivery, which extends to classic desserts such as a crisp and caramelised tarte Tatin with homemade vanilla ice cream. Wines from £22.75.
Chef/s: Francesco Volgo. **Open:** all week L 12 to 2 (2.30 Sat and Sun), D 7 to 9.30 (10 Fri and Sat, 9 Sun). **Meals:** main courses £13 to £31. **Details:** 40 seats. 24 seats outside. Bar. Music. Parking.

The Village Pub
Cooking score: 2
Modern British | £27
Barnsley, GL7 5EF
Tel no: (01285) 740421
thevillagepub.co.uk

A charming old-timer in mellow Cotswold stone, the Village Pub is the informal offshoot of Barnsley House, which sits just across the

road. Relaxed it may be, but it's also an upmarket setting sporting heritage paintwork, real fires and comfy armchairs. Food-wise, expect classy modern pub fare, with favourites like homemade Scotch eggs and steak and chips bumping up against diverse international offerings: onion bhaji with homemade chutney and slow-cooked piri-piri pork belly with sweetcorn, red pepper and coriander rice are typical of the scope. A wholesome, perfectly seasoned pea soup impressed at inspection, as did a homemade chicken Kiev with greens and crisp sautéed potatoes, while a dark, treacly sticky toffee pudding is 'one of the best I've ever tasted'. Besides an impressive selection of ales and lagers, there's a respectable wine list, with bottles starting at £19.50.
Chef/s: John Jewell. **Open:** Mon to Sat L 12 to 2.30 (3 Sat), D 6 to 9.30. Sun 12 to 9. **Meals:** main courses £11 to £20. **Details:** 60 seats. 50 seats outside. Bar. Wheelchairs. Parking.

▌Bristol

★ NEW ENTRY ★

Adelina Yard
Cooking score: 3
Modern European | £34
3 Queen Quay, Welsh Back, Bristol, BS1 4SL
Tel no: (0117) 9112112
adelinayardrestaurant.com
£5
OFF

Named after their old flat in London's East End, Adelina Yard is the first project for Jamie Randall and Olivia Barry, who have worked in a number of noteworthy restaurants in the capital including Murano and Odette's (see entries). A narrow, L-shaped room with a partially open-view kitchen, this compact restaurant on Bristol's harbourside is understated ('mushroomy' walls and distressed-paint chairs), while the tersely written menu combines Nordic influences (fermented vegetables, raw venison and preserved egg yolks all make an appearance) with modern British classics (think roast ribeye for two to share or warm rice pudding

with apple compote and boozy prunes). At inspection, fermented kale, hand-rolled cavatelli, slow-cooked egg, goats' cheese and chives proved to be 'an arresting starter', and a pink and smoky barbecued breast of Goosnargh duck worked particularly well with salty-sweet bacon 'jam', char-grilled hispi cabbage and spiced plum. Dessert was a 'sublime' ironbark pumpkin tart with maple syrup ice cream. Wines from £18.
Chef/s: Jamie Randall and Olivia Barry. **Open:** Tue to Sat L 12 to 3, D 6 to 11. **Closed:** Sun, Mon, 2 weeks Christmas. **Meals:** main courses £18 to £23. Set L and D £13 (2 courses) to £15. **Details:** 38 seats. 10 seats outside. Wheelchairs. Music.

Bell's Diner
Cooking score: 5
Mediterranean | £30
1-3 York Road, Montpelier, Bristol, BS6 5QB
Tel no: (0117) 9240357
bellsdiner.com

In an age when even modern restaurants are artfully distressed, it's good to come across an original. The former grocer's shop (now a tiny bar) and three wood-floored dining rooms are not so much distressed as (after more than three decades) comfortably lived in. Set in the narrow, graffiti-strewn streets of Montpelier, Bell's Diner is the perfect neighbourhood restaurant with its warm heart, highly cohesive modern cooking, excellent value and flexible set-up. Dishes are designed for sharing, with the kitchen conjuring up vibrancy, colour and striking flavours from a myriad of fresh, seasonal ingredients: goats' curd, for example, is teamed with raw rhubarb ('a brilliant addition'), cucumber, almond and mint salad or there could be fresh, zingy courgette, feta, mint and dill fritters served with a sweet tomato sauce. There's also seared duck breast with sautéed spinach and Pedro Ximénez and rhubarb sauce, and a light mango and pomegranate cheesecake for dessert. Wines from £18.
Chef/s: Sam Sohn-Rethel. **Open:** Tue to Sat L 12 to 3, Mon to Sat D 6 to 10. **Closed:** Sun. **Meals:** small plates £5 to £16. **Details:** 60 seats. Bar. Music.

Bellita

Cooking score: 3
Mediterranean | £25
34 Cotham Hill, Bristol, BS6 6LA
Tel no: (0117) 923 8755
bellita.co.uk
£30

The latest venture from the team behind Bell's Diner (see entry) is lively and welcoming. On the site of Flinty Red, the décor has been tweaked rather than overhauled, 'but it's amazing what adding some Liberty fabric and removing overhead air-conditioning units can do to change the atmosphere'. Pop in for a bar snack, say a jamón Ibérico croqueta, its crispy exterior yielding an ooze of ham-perfumed bechamel, and a 'shim' or a 'shrub' – homemade cocktails and cordials – and chat to the cheery, attentive staff. Fans of Bell's will feel at home with the 'not dissimilar Mediterranean menu'. Share spiced lentil and piquillo peppers with yoghurt with crispy fried red onions, and clams and wild garlic cooked in Pernod and jamón butter, but order, perhaps, a whole blood-orange posset with honeycomb for yourself. The wine list, sourced exclusively from female winemakers, is largely offered by glass, 500ml carafe and bottle and starts at £20 for a punchy Nero d'Avola.
Chef/s: Joe Harvey. **Open:** Thur to Sat L 12 to 3, Mon to Sat D 6 to 10. **Closed:** Sun, 25 and 26 Dec. **Meals:** small plates £2 to £12. **Details:** 40 seats.

Birch

Cooking score: 4
Modern British | £25
47 Raleigh Road, Bristol, BS3 1QS
Tel no: (0117) 9028326
birchbristol.co
£30

Pared back partly by necessity and partly by aesthetic, Birch is the restaurant that grew out of the supper clubs run by partners Beccy Massey and Sam Leach. And growing is still very much the word; they raise some produce, while the restaurant's reputation keeps getting better. A simple corner premises is the backdrop for Sam's daily-changing menu, which has all the hallmarks of a chef schooled at St John. But plain cooking can be vibrant, and colourful assemblies might include small plates of Little Gem squash with Cheddar and chervil or brown shrimp, leek and egg tart. There are usually just a couple of main courses, such as boiled ham, carrots and mustard, with the choice widening again at dessert with pear and whey caramel tart and house-made ice creams and sorbets. Beccy takes very good care of the wines, with a list dominated by small producers starting at £20.
Chef/s: Sam Leach. **Open:** Wed to Sat D only 6 to 10. **Closed:** Sun, Mon, Tue, 2 weeks Christmas, 2 weeks Aug. **Meals:** main courses £12 to £16. **Details:** 24 seats. Music.

Bravas

Cooking score: 2
Spanish | £15
7 Cotham Hill, Bristol, BS6 6LD
Tel no: (0117) 3296887
bravas.co.uk
£30

This cramped and busy tapas bar started life as an underground supper club, run by Kieran and Imogen Waite from their Bristol home. Since finding a permanent site, Bravas has become one of Bristol's favourite eateries, with the tiny open kitchen operating behind a well-stocked bar. With exposed brick walls and copper piping, shelves of cookbooks and imported ingredients, it's a genuinely lively place with an authentic Spanish atmosphere. Grab a stool at the counter or bag a more intimate table at the back and order from a daily-changing menu that may include fried aubergine with molasses; cabbage, pomegranate and almond; hake with garlic, parsley and lemon; or marinated lamb shoulder pinchos. Finish with Valencian orange and cardamom ice cream or a plate of rosemary Manchego with membrillo. A meticulously sourced all-Spanish wine list starts at £17.95 and there is an interesting sherry selection.

Chef/s: Mark Chapman. **Open:** Mon to Sat 11.30 to 11. **Closed:** Sun, 24 to 26 Dec, 1 Jan. **Meals:** tapas £3 to £7. **Details:** 45 seats. Music.

★ NEW ENTRY ★

The Brigstow

Cooking score: 2
Modern European | £29
Millennium Promenade, Bristol, BS1 5SY
Tel no: (0117) 3250898
brigstowbarandkitchen.co.uk
£30

This contemporary waterfront bar and restaurant, situated in the harbour inlet opposite the SS *Great Britain*, is part of a relatively new concentration of small businesses in this redeveloped part of the old docks. Andrew Clatworthy arrived here in March 2016 after making a name for himself at the Rummer across town (see entry), and his cooking is certainly punching well above its weight. Clatworthy makes everything from scratch, from the excellent breads ('the treacle bread is epic') to three different flavoured butters and accompanying salts, and is proud of his raw materials, many of which are wild and foraged. Highlights at inspection included a light and seasonal starter of spring pea salad, cucumber 'cheese', Wye Valley asparagus and butter breadcrumbs; a signature dish that's an assemblage of various mushrooms, leaves and truffle; followed by hake three ways (fresh fillet, salted, and a croquette of salt cake) with tiny, crunchy carrots cooked with a hint of vanilla, a raw seaweed and herb salad and lumpfish roe adding an extra fishiness. A hit, too, was a delicate assembly of sliced ripe strawberries with lovage, sorrel, a malt custard and shards of brik pastry for texture and crunch. The lunch/brunch menu is more straightforward affair. Wines from £17.

Chef/s: Andrew Clatworthy. **Open:** All week L 11 to 5 (12 to 4 Mon, 9 to 5 Fri to Sun), Tue to Sat D 6 to 10. **Meals:** main courses £14 to £18. Set L £12 (2

courses) to £15. Set D £18 (2 courses) to £21. Tasting Menu £46 (7 courses). Sun L £14. **Details:** 36 seats. 40 seats outside. Bar. Wheelchairs. Music.

★ NEW ENTRY ★

Bulrush

Cooking score: 4
Modern British | £35
21 Cotham Road South, Bristol, BS6 5TZ
Tel no: (0117) 3290990
bulrushrestaurant.co.uk
£5 OFF

This former greengrocer's was once the site of a 1980s Bristol dining institution (and *Good Food Guide* regular), Bistro 21. The new custodians are George Livesy and Katherine Craughwell, who previously ran supper clubs in London, although George has also worked in some notable places including St John (see entry, London). With its whitewashed walls and simple bistro furniture, the restaurant presents a blank canvas for some vividly ambitious dishes combining old and new techniques. A commitment to local suppliers extends to wild herbs and hedgerow gluts from foragers – some of which end up in the fermentation room. A stunning starter of Wye Valley asparagus, served with hollandaise flavoured with homemade elderflower vinegar, was 'bang in season for April', while 'pink, juicy' loin of goat is teamed with seaweed faggot, wild garlic, ricotta and chicory. Finish with a rich chocolate délice paired with refreshing yoghurt sorbet, crunchy honeycomb, parsnip sponge and blobs of the same vegetable. Wines from £15.95.

Chef/s: George Livesey. **Open:** Thur to Sat L 12.30 to 3, Tue to Sat D 6.30 to 10. **Closed:** Sun, Mon, 2 weeks Jan, 1 week May, 2 weeks Aug. **Meals:** main courses £13 to £19. Set L £15. Tasting menu £43. **Details:** 52 seats. V menu. Bar. Music.

★ TOP 50 ★

Casamia

Cooking score: 7
Modern British | £68
The General, Lower Guinea Street, Bristol,
BS1 6SY
Tel no: (0117) 9592884
casamiarestaurant.co.uk

£5
OFF

In 2008, Jonray and Peter Sanchez-Iglesias zipped into the Guide, picking up our 'best up and coming chef(s)' award at the same time. 'Chef(s) of the year' followed in 2015, as we noted their emergence as serious reputation makers. Then, in late 2015, Jonray died at the age of 32. His death could easily have brought the curtain down, but it is a tribute to his younger brother Peter that he has carried on without him, continuing with a planned move from Westbury-on-Trym to the centre of Bristol, where Casamia has bagged itself a prime spot, occupying the ground floor of a former hospital overlooking the Floating Harbour. Fittingly discreet from the outside, warm, understated and spacious within, the centrepiece is a prominent open kitchen where Peter follows the seasonal rhythm of the old Casamia – four quarterly-changing menus that are tweaked as the produce changes. His 14-course tasting menu has a wonderfully light touch and meticulous craftsmanship, as these highlights from the spring menu reveal: a gorgeously fresh scallop tartare given texture by 'scrumps' (crumbs of crisp batter); an intensely flavoured mackerel risotto beneath a tangle of crisp vermicelli straw; the magnificently simple combination of monkfish with springtime creams and a lip-smacking, creamy marinière-style cider sauce; and 'hit of the evening', exquisite lamb finished on the BBQ to give a hint of smokiness, offset by a mini lamb croquette riding high on an intense nasturtium jelly, so bright that it tingles. Equally notable is a crisp, voluptuous little sandwich of Quicke's Cheddar, a lovely composition of fresh, freeze-dried and granita blood orange layered with rosemary custard, and in a grand finale,

who would have thought the flavour of gin would go so well with rhubarb? Service is excellent, dismantling the formalities and making the whole experience more personal. The wine list is compiled with an eye for quality drinking, with bottles from £27.
Chef/s: Peter Sanchez-Iglesias. **Open:** Wed to Sat L 12 to 1.30, D 6 to 9.30. **Closed:** Sun, Mon, Tue, Christmas, 1 Jan, bank hols. **Meals:** tasting menu L £38 (5 courses) to £68 (10 courses). Tasting menu D £68 (Wed and Thur) to £88 (Fri and Sat). **Details:** 35 seats. V menu. Bar. Music.

Flour & Ash

Cooking score: 1
Italian | £20
203b Cheltenham Road, Bristol, BS6 5QX
Tel no: (0117) 9083228
flourandash.co.uk

£30

All pizzas are not created equal and at Flour & Ash there's something about the airy crunch of their sourdough base, seared in a wood-fired oven, that borders on the celestial. The only problem has been getting a table, but now, thanks to a second branch in Westbury-on-Trym (in the old Casamia) your luck might be in. Everything here makes the best of high-quality ingredients: from a fat orb of burrata in a slick of olive oil to start, to the incredibly moreish side dishes of truffled polenta chips and a citrusy shredded courgette, feta and piquillo pepper slaw. The pizzas, topped with anchovies, garlic and buffalo mozzarella or, say, ox cheek and red wine ragù, are sophisticated enough to satisfy parents but simple enough to please the kids. Likewise the homemade ice creams in a range of flavours from comforting (the creamiest strawberry) to Blumenthal-esque (bay and nutmeg). A well-chosen selection of excellent local beers and ciders complements the good-value wine list, which starts at £16.80.
Chef/s: Steve Gale and Joe Wilkin. **Open:** Mon to Fri D 5 to 9.30. Thur to Sun 12 to 10 (9 Sun). **Closed:** 24 to 26 Dec. **Meals:** main courses £8 to £16. **Details:** 41 seats. Music.

Greens

Cooking score: 3
Modern European | £27
25 Zetland Road, Bristol, BS6 7AH
Tel no: (0117) 9246437
greensbristol.co.uk
£30

Martin Laurentowicz and Nick Wallace took over this neighbourhood restaurant in 2012. It's tucked away down a leafy side street in one of Bristol's more desirable locations and is much loved by locals, who are delighted that the long-established reputation of Greens for offering quality cooking and value for money has been retained. Laurentowicz's no-frills style of modern European cooking deals in bold flavours and the minimum of fuss. Grilled sardines with rhubarb and horseradish sauce is an assertive starter and might lead on to a precisely cooked fillet of sea beam with salt-baked celeriac purée and brown shrimp and fennel sauce. For dessert, consider apple tarte Tatin with clotted cream ice cream. A two-course lunch deal and separate vegetarian menu remain popular options. The short but interesting wine list starts at £17.50 and offers plenty of good drinking under £20.
Chef/s: Martin Laurentowicz. **Open:** Tue to Sat L 12 to 2.30, Mon to Sat D 6 to 10. Sun 12 to 10. **Closed:** 24 to 30 Dec. **Meals:** main courses £12 to £22. Set L £12 (2 courses) to £15. Set D £17 (2 courses) to £22. Sun L £17. **Details:** 40 seats. 8 seats outside. V menu. Music.

Lido

Cooking score: 3
Mediterranean | £35
Oakfield Place, Clifton, Bristol, BS8 2BJ
Tel no: (0117) 9339530
lidobristol.com

There's a glass-plated viewing gallery overlooking the stylishly refurbished open-air swimming pool, just one of many reasons why the Lido restaurant and accompanying poolside bar (with separate tapas menu) remains one of Bristol's singular dining experiences. Head chef Freddy Bird trained at

Moro – evident in his skilful use of the wood-fired ovens to wring every last drop of flavour from carefully sourced ingredients. Whether it's a starter of roast asparagus with almond sauce and jamón, wood-roast scallops with garlic butter and sweet herbs or a dish of poussin with braised Baby Gem lettuce, morels and broad beans, peas and spring onions, the results are 'a kind of alchemy'. Round your meal off with one of the Lido's homemade ice creams (salted-butter caramel, say, or Pedro Ximénez and raisin), salted dark chocolate and olive oil mousse with pistachio biscotti, or Spanish cheeses. The wine list, mainly drawn from Spain and Italy, starts at £18.50.
Chef/s: Freddy Bird. **Open:** all week L 12 to 2.45, D 6 to 9.45. **Closed:** 25 and 26 Dec, 1 Jan. **Meals:** main courses £16 to £32. Set L and D £16 (2 courses) to £20. **Details:** 150 seats. 30 seats outside. Bar. Music.

Manna

Cooking score: 2
Modern European | £25
2B North View, Bristol, BS6 7QB
Tel no: (0117) 9706276
mannabar.co.uk
£30

'This is a consistent place and a very popular neighbourhood restaurant,' noted one regular visitor to this sibling to Prego (see entry) across the road. Opened in 2012, the geographical axis of the cooking has slowly shifted away from the Middle East and Spain and now owes more to Italy, but with, as always, an emphasis on seasonal British produce – much of it as local as from the butcher a few doors down. Grab a high table at the front or a cosy booth at the back and order the likes of 'rich and creamy' lamb sweetbreads, wild mushroom ragù, fresh peas and pecorino, and a robust dish of char-grilled Cornish monkfish and scallops with a warm cannellini bean salad or overnight lamb shoulder with braised cauliflower, roast peppers and salsa verde. For desserts, try baked blueberry cheesecake with blueberry sauce and candied almonds. An Italian-leaning wine list starts at £16.50.

Chef/s: Olly Gallery. **Open:** Mon to Sat D only 6 to 10. **Closed:** Sun, 25 to 27 Dec. **Meals:** main courses £12 to £20. Set D £15 (2 courses). **Details:** 40 seats. Bar. Wheelchairs. Music.

★ NEW ENTRY ★

No Man's Grace

Cooking score: 2
Modern European | £30
6 Chandos Road, Bristol, BS6 6PE
Tel no: (0117) 9744077
nomansgrace.com
£5 OFF

In a former life, this tucked-away corner building in Redland was one of the late TV chef Keith Floyd's bistros, but the man behind the stoves these days is John Watson. This is Watson's first solo venture; he cut his teeth at a number of local restaurants including Casamia (see entry) and his modern European approach is underpinned by classic technique – though his biggest influence is US chef Thomas Keller. Every dish on the concise menu is described as a 'small plate': larger than a tapas or traditional starter but smaller than a main course, and three per person would probably be sufficient. Intelligent flavour combinations and confident cooking were the themes running through an inspection meal that included duck breast served with kohlrabi, celeriac and pickled mustard seeds, a 'really standout dish' of hand-dived Orkney scallop with chicken wing and carrot, and a dessert of forced rhubarb cobbler and vanilla ice cream. Wines from £17.

Chef/s: John Watson. **Open:** Fri to Sun L 12 to 3 (5 Sun), Wed to Sat D 6 to 10. **Closed:** Mon, Tue, last 2 weeks Aug. **Meals:** main courses £7 to £13. **Details:** 34 seats. 24 seats outside. Bar. Music.

The Ox

Cooking score: 3
British | £33
The Basement, 43 Corn Street, Bristol, BS1 1HT
Tel no: (0117) 9221001
theoxbristol.com
£5 OFF

A quietish shopping street by day, Corn Street turns into a lively thoroughfare at night, full of bars and restaurants. Those in the know make a beeline for this oak-panelled former bank vault, descending a spiral marble staircase to find a welcoming, unstuffy environment in which to enjoy a proper steak dinner: locally sourced ribeye, sirloin or fillet, expertly cooked over charcoal, with sides of triple-cooked chips and a choice of peppercorn, béarnaise or charred chilli romesco sauce. A good-value set lunch, perhaps hot-smoked salmon, crisp pork belly with red pepper lyonnaise and chanterelles, and peanut-butter parfait with dark chocolate cheesecake and peanut-butter crunch, is a good way to tour the rest of the menu. At dinner look out for small plates of, say, charcoal-roasted monkfish tail, a prime-cuts burger and seasonal game such as breast of pheasant with celeriac, apple, pommes dauphine and fried sprouts. Staff are animated and on the ball, and wines start at £22. A second branch has opened on Whiteladies Road, BS8 2QX; tel: (0117) 973 0005.

Chef/s: Todd Francis. **Open:** Mon to Fri and Sun L 12 to 2.30 (4 Sun), Mon to Sat D 5 to 10.30. **Closed:** 23 to 27 Dec. **Meals:** main courses £15 to £30. Set L £14 (2 courses) to £17. Early D £15. Sun L £18. **Details:** 70 seats. Music.

Prego

Cooking score: 3
Italian | £30
7 North View, Bristol, BS6 7PT
Tel no: (0117) 9730496
pregobar.co.uk

Bustling and noisy (blame the wooden floor and functional furniture), Olly Gallery and Julian Faiello's rustic Italian eatery is a great hit with in-the-know locals. Things are equally upbeat in the kitchen, where big-hearted flavours are stuffed into a lively menu that might jump from charcuterie sharing plates to fritto misto with aïoli, and local pork loin chop with truffled polenta. The rest of the repertoire is a zesty assortment of handmade pizzas (slow-proven sourdough bases) and pasta – wild mushroom ravioli with white wine, cream and truffle oil, crab linguine, rich beef shin ragù with pappardelle, and pork and beef polpette (meatballs) with penne. Monday is pizza night, with drinks, salads and dessert. Vanilla and lemon-baked cheesecake with Yorkshire rhubarb is a sure-fire winner for dessert. Prices are keen (the set lunch, in particular, is good value), and the all-Italian wine list is equally affordable, with bottles from £14.50.
Chef/s: Andrew Griffin. **Open:** Tue to Sun L 12 to 2 (3 Sun), Mon to Sat D 5.30 to 10 (9 Mon). **Meals:** main courses £10 to £20. Set L £12 (2 courses) to £15. Sun L £15. **Details:** 52 seats. 16 seats outside. Wheelchairs. Music.

The Pump House

Cooking score: 3
Modern British | £40
Merchants Road, Hotwells, Bristol, BS8 4PZ
Tel no: (0117) 9272229
the-pumphouse.com

£5
OFF

The historic control centre for Bristol's famous floating harbour, this converted Victorian pumping station now plies its trade as a rustic-chic waterside pub with a mezzanine restaurant for those who want to dine in style. Chef-proprietor Toby Gritten is a forager and disciple of big-boned back-to-the-roots cookery, loading his menu with resolutely seasonal ingredients and homemade provisions (note the jars of pickles and preserves on display). Nibble on sloe-gin-cured salmon with a pint of West Country ale in the bar, or head upstairs for something more substantial – perhaps torched mackerel with forced rhubarb, radish and Granny Smith apple followed by roast venison with juniper, parsnips, Scots pine and chanterelles or Devon trout mi cuit with vanilla, roasted lemon purée, cauliflower and quinoa. Char-grilled dry-aged steaks also make the line-up, along with traditional desserts such as Cambridge burnt cream with blood orange. Wines from £20, and a prodigious array of gins, too.
Chef/s: Toby Gritten. **Open:** all week L 12 to 3 (4 Sun), Mon to Sat D 6.30 to 9.30. **Meals:** main courses £16 to £23. Tasting menu £45 (8 courses). **Details:** 80 seats. 80 seats outside. Bar. Music. Parking.

riverstation

Cooking score: 3
Modern European | £30
The Grove, Bristol, BS1 4RB
Tel no: (0117) 9144434
riverstation.co.uk

£5
OFF

For many years riverstation's airy, modern first-floor restaurant was ahead of the pack with its precisely cooked and carefully sourced dishes such as roast guinea fowl with bubble and squeak, cavolo nero and spiced pear or passion fruit crème brûlée and langue de chat biscuit. These days, however, worthy competitors are legion and although the quality hasn't diminished, riverstation feels like the ideal place for a business lunch rather than a romantic dinner. On the ground floor the Bar + Kitchen is a convivial brasserie with an interesting menu and cheerful service. Offering small, medium and large plates to share (or not), dishes such as falafel with labneh and dukkah or vegetable ribbons with ham hock, ewes' curds, hazelnuts and tangy achiote dressing lack the finesse you'll find upstairs, but are excellent value. An impressively wide range of house wines are available by glass, 500ml carafe or bottle in both eateries, starting at £17 for the latter in the restaurant and £15.50 in the Bar + Kitchen.

Chef/s: Matt Hampshire. **Open:** all week L 12 to 2.30 (3 Sun), Mon to Sat D 6 to 10.30 (11 Fri and Sat). **Closed:** 24 to 26 Dec. **Meals:** main courses £16 to £20. Set L £14 (2 courses) to £17. Set D £15 (2 courses) to £19. Sun L £19 (2 courses) to £24. **Details:** 120 seats. 20 seats outside. Bar.

The Rummer

Cooking score: 3
British | £30
All Saints Lane, Bristol, BS1 1JH
Tel no: (0117) 9294243
therummer.net
£5
OFF

Everyone mentions the wonderfully warm welcome, engagingly friendly service and happy vibes that pervade this former Georgian coaching inn tucked down an ancient alley off Corn Street. It displays its heritage with cream stucco, sash windows, an extremely well-stocked bar and a massive log-burning inglenook in the ground-floor dining room, where a blackboard menu of small plates is served during the day. Dinner is served in the medieval barrel-vaulted stone cellar. That cellar may be slightly 'dingy' for some, but all are agreed that the food is 'stunning, individual, brilliantly cooked'. Typically accomplished dishes might run to rabbit rillettes with apple relish and rye or smoked Cheddar croquette with leek and pickled mustard, and a satisfying combination of sea trout with celeriac, pickled apple and brown shrimp or onglet steak with fried potato and mushroom ketchup. To finish, buttermilk pannacotta with poached rhubarb went down a treat with one reporter. Wines from £18.

Chef/s: Brett Hirt. **Open:** all week L 10 to 5 (11 Sat, 12 Sun), Mon to Sat D 6 to 10. **Closed:** 25 and 26 Dec, 1 Jan. **Meals:** main courses £14 to £17. Sun L £25. **Details:** 28 seats. 16 seats outside. Bar. Music. No children.

James Wilkins

Wilks, Bristol

What food could you not live without?
Mushrooms. They are delicious and inject big flavour on to a plate. I love them, so I use them as much as I can.

What's your favourite dish on your menu?
Turbot, the king of fish. I've had it on the menu since day one. We buy 5kg of fish direct from Brixham fish market. It gives you a nice thick 'steak' which can then be cooked very accurately.

How do you start developing a new recipe?
I go to the wholesale fruit and vegetable market twice a week to buy direct from suppliers. I can pick the exact produce I want in the kitchen, but also chat with the people who know the supply chain and what is at its best. This is where a dish starts for me.

Which chef do you most admire?
I spent a long time working with Michel Bras and his family. The restaurant he created is an honest expression of their way of life and the lands that surround it. He completely transformed the way I think about food and I often think of him when decisions need making at the restaurant.

The Spiny Lobster

Cooking score: 4
Seafood | £35
128-130 Whiteladies Road, Bristol, BS8 2RS
Tel no: (0117) 9737384
rockfishgrill.co.uk

£5
OFF

On a corner site in Clifton, Mitch Tonks' long-running seafood venue has the pleasant feeling of being almost afloat. Surrounded by observation-deck windows and pictures of seashells, with hake, monkfish and Dover sole being roasted over the open fire, it's a haven of all things piscatorial, much of it hauled in from the Brixham catch. Scallops toasted in their shells and glistening with garlic butter, Exe mussels fragrant with bay, garlic and chilli, or crisp-fried squid in aïoli are the opening lures. Fish is treated robustly rather than with undue delicacy, bringing all the sea-fresh flavour out of bass baked in paper with rosemary and chilli, saucing a brill steak with mushrooms and sherry, scattering a whole plaice with tiny savoury brown shrimps. Plenty of garlic is likely to come your way, even in the side dishes, though not in the citrus-sharp crema catalana. A short wine list of fairly priced wines starts at £18.
Chef/s: Neil Roach. **Open:** Tue to Sat L 12 to 2.30, D 6 to 10 (10.30 Fri and Sat). **Closed:** Sun, Mon, 25 Dec to 2 Jan. **Meals:** main courses £14 to £33. Set L and D £15 (2 courses) to £18. **Details:** 45 seats. Music.

Wallfish Bistro

Cooking score: 4
Seafood | £35
112 Princess Victoria Street, Clifton, Bristol, BS8 4DB
Tel no: (0117) 9735435
wallfishbistro.co.uk

Taking its name from the old English word for snails, Wallfish makes good use of bounty from local foragers – although fish from the West Country boats is its prime source of culinary inspiration. Depending on the catch, you might find 'silver darlings' (aka herrings)

with sea buckthorn, celeriac and rhubarb, ahead of gurnard fillet with fennel, crab butter, clams and ramsons or turbot roasted on the bone with mussels, cabbage, bacon and caraway – well-considered seasonal tributes to the British larder. Those who don't fancy fish can order an 'astonishing-value' steak or roast Middle White pork, while desserts dip into the cookbooks of yore for buttermilk pudding or ginger loaf with clotted cream. For some readers, these premises will forever be associated with the late Keith Floyd, although the current incarnation is a pleasing mix of 'colander' lampshades, toffee-coloured leather banquettes, sturdy bare tables and mismatched chairs. As for drinks, sip aperitifs, Bristol-brewed beers or 'reasonably priced' wines from £17.
Chef/s: Seldon Curry. **Open:** Wed to Sun L 12 to 3 (10am Sat and Sun), D 6 to 10 (9 Sun). **Closed:** Mon, Tue, 5 days Christmas, 2 weeks Jan, 2 weeks Sept. **Meals:** main courses £14 to £38. Set L and D £11 (2 courses) to £14. **Details:** 38 seats. Music.

★ **LOCAL RESTAURANT AWARD** ★
REGIONAL WINNER

Wilks

Cooking score: 5
Modern European | £48
1-3 Chandos Road, Bristol, BS6 6PG
Tel no: (0117) 9737999
wilksrestaurant.co.uk

£5
OFF

'I had the most brilliant lunch at Wilks yesterday,' is one regular's verdict, while another insisted 'it goes without saying that the food is unbelievably delicious'. Locals are in complete agreement that this polished contemporary neighbourhood restaurant, concealed down a quiet side street in one of Bristol's leafier suburbs, has made quite an impression on the city's dining scene since it opened in 2012. Slate-grey walls offset by black enamel lamps and handmade Italian armchairs add a stylish edge, with cruet sets made by a local pottery. Chef-owner James Wilkins previously worked under renowned French chef Michel Bras and his innovative

dishes conjured from largely local produce demonstrate a solid understanding of classic techniques. Scottish langoustine and crab dumpling with purple sprouting broccoli and lemon shellfish vinaigrette might precede a boldly flavoured main course of new-season lamb, bulgur, wild garlic, baked onion, roasted ceps and lamb jus. The technical astuteness continues through to a dessert of banana mousse, milk caramel, brown-butter ice cream, cinnamon and walnut crunch. A thoughtfully sourced wine list with an emphasis on France starts at £19.50.
Chef/s: James Wilkins. **Open:** Thur to Sun L 12 to 2, Wed to Sun D 6.30 to 10 (9 Sun). **Closed:** Mon, Tue, 3 weeks Dec and Jan, 3 weeks Aug. **Meals:** main courses £20 to £28. Set L £21 (2 courses) to £25 (Thur and Fri only). Set L and D £55 (4 courses). Tasting menu £75. **Details:** 30 seats. V menu. Wheelchairs. Children over 6 yrs only at D.

★ NEW ENTRY ★

Wilsons
Cooking score: 2
Modern British | £28
22a Chandos Road, Bristol, BS6 6PF
Tel no: (0117) 9734157
wilsonsrestaurant.co.uk
£30

Before arriving in Bristol, Jan Ostle worked in some notable places around the UK, with the Clove Club and L'Enclume (see entries) both on his impressive CV. His first solo venture, in a converted shop a few doors down the road from other rising Bristol stars Wilks and No Man's Grace (see entries), is a modest, pared-back affair with white walls, black floorboards and vintage vases of flowers from the owners' allotment. Not that there's anything low-key about the confidently cooked food, which sticks rigidly to the seasons and is free from unnecessary garnishes and frippery. From the blackboard-only menu, a meal might begin with impeccably cooked, properly seasoned lamb sweetbreads, Little Gem, peas and mint, followed by a bold-flavoured main of juicy, flaked cod cooked sous-vide and teamed with

a creamy Jerusalem artichoke purée and chicken juices. Rhubarb, roses and yoghurt is one of the striking desserts. Wines from £18.
Chef/s: Jan Ostle. **Open:** Wed to Sat L 12 to 2.30, Tue to Sat D 6 to 9.30. **Closed:** Sun, Mon. **Meals:** main courses £14 to £16. **Details:** 24 seats.

LOCAL GEM

Pata Negra
Spanish | £25
30 Clare Street, Bristol, BS1 1YH
Tel no: (0117) 9276762
patanegrabristol.com
£30

In the heart of Bristol's old banking district, this tapas bar is owned by the same team behind the Ox (see entry). Its dark good looks (leather armchairs, bar with its backdrop of whole jamóns) make it more of a post-work and evening hang-out. Service is excellent throughout and knowledgeable about the food and the wine list. The '3 tapas for £10' rapido menu is great value and portions are bigger than the average tapas. Elsewhere, the menu is packed with boldly flavoured dishes, whether pan-fried cod, romesco, calçots and crispy Serrano or lamb ribs with salsa verde. Kicking off at £19, the wine list sticks close to the Iberian peninsula.

LOCAL GEM

Sky Kong Kong
Korean | £15
Unit 2, Haymarket Walk, Bristol, BS1 3LN
Tel no: (0117) 2399528
skykongkong.co.uk
£5 OFF £30

A diamond in the rough – between the bus station and the Bear Pit (a roundabout underpass) – this organic Korean restaurant may be short on frills but is delightfully eccentric. Chef Hwi Shim (Wizzy to her friends) has worked at Nobu and Hakkasan (see entries, London) and this shines through in her fabulously fresh and flavourful cooking. There's no choice for the lunchtime bento box or evening set meal and just one refectory table to sit around, but this is all part of the charm. It's great value, unlicensed (BYO) and booking is essential in the evening.

LOCAL GEM
Spoke & Stringer
Spanish | £20
The Boathouse, Unit 1, Lime Kiln Road, Bristol, BS1 5AD
Tel no: (0117) 9259371
spokeandstringer.com

£30

On the water's edge, offering prized views of Bristol's harbourside, Spoke & Stringer is owned by the cool bike shop next door, a theme that extends to the bar, with fixies on the bare concrete walls. Pintxos is one way to eat here, but the cooked-to-order dishes have generated an equally enthusiastic local following, perhaps the 'irresistible' truffled mushroom Scotch eggs, tender ox cheek slow-cooked in Pedro Ximénez or a special of mackerel with fiery harissa and blood-orange salad, with a 'perfect' crème brûlée to finish. Wines from £19.

▉ Brookthorpe

LOCAL GEM
Gloucester Services
British | £15
M5 (between junc. 12 & 11a), Brookthorpe, GL4 0DN
Tel no: (01452) 813254
gloucesterservices.com

£30

This 'modern marvel' – an independently run motorway pit-stop – is committed to locally sourced food and has taken many a visitor by surprise. You pass a table groaning with artisan bread at the entrance, in front of you is a vast Scandi-chic canteen flanked by two long food counters, and there's a superb farm shop to browse after your meal. Options include rustic sandwiches, quiches with colourful salads, or fish and chips. One reporter enjoyed a hot wrap crammed with roasted mushrooms and punchy goats' cheese, a simple, crunchy salad, and 'perfect' chocolate brownie. Located northbound and southbound between junctions 11a and 12 of the M5, it is 'just the best find ever – a godsend for the journey'.

▉ Cheltenham
★ TOP 50 ★
Le Champignon Sauvage
Cooking score: 8
Modern French | £63
24-26 Suffolk Road, Cheltenham, GL50 2AQ
Tel no: (01242) 573449
lechampignonsauvage.co.uk

No one could accuse David Everitt-Matthias of celebrity grandstanding or kowtowing to the media; no, he's a chef-patron who still puts in the hours at every service – even after three decades as the guiding presence behind this long-serving Cheltenham aristocrat. It helps that he's ably supported by his wife Helen, a perfect hostess who brings all her heartfelt charm and engaging warmth to the sophisticated but approachable dining room. Together, they make eating at Le Champignon Sauvage a rare and inestimable pleasure. David's cooking is tuned into the zeitgeist without ever seeming mannered or effete, and his treatment of the very best seasonal produce is a wonder to behold: consider a revelatory starter of butter-poached native lobster embroidered with pear slices, Jerusalem artichoke crisps, sorrel purée and a sprinkling of malt crumbs, or fillet and braised breast of Cinderford lamb with accompaniments garnered from the great outdoors – perhaps a zesty wild garlic pesto or dandelion and burdock salsa. In fact, foraged ingredients are generously strewn across the menu, from mugwort with Cotswold venison to ceps and chestnuts with a dish of halibut. There's no dumbing down or short-changing when it comes to the brilliant set lunch either: lamb's sweetbreads with broad beans, peas and parsley purée; seared mackerel with mackerel tartare, wasabi and apple; chocolate and sesame cannelloni with poached cherries and pistachio ice cream – 'the highest-quality cooking, and all for £32', cheered one recipient. The serious-minded wine list packs in a host of dependable producers, with plenty for the traditionalists and a smattering of off-piste labels, too; prices start at £22.

Chef/s: David Everitt-Matthias. **Open:** Tue to Sat L 12.30 to 1.15, D 7.30 to 8.30. **Closed:** Sun, Mon, 2 weeks Christmas, 3 weeks Jun. **Meals:** set L £26 (2 courses) to £32. Set D £50 (2 courses) to £63. **Details:** 38 seats. Bar.

Lumière

Cooking score: 5
Modern British | £60
Clarence Parade, Cheltenham, GL50 3PA
Tel no: (01242) 222200
lumiere.cc

£5
OFF

'Blow London, stay in Cheltenham and visit Lumière.' There's no doubt that Jon and Helen Howe's small, elegant restaurant is an asset to the town. The interior of mushroom walls, discreet banquettes and oversized mirrors resembling giant flowers 'exudes class', while the kitchen delivers vibrant contemporary flavours starting with beautifully presented 'snacks' such as a tiny granola-topped cornet filled with duck liver parfait or 'the lightest pork scratchings topped with caramelized apple and fennel pollen'. Ham hock terrine is teamed with gingerbread, pineapple and smoked eel, while a main course of beef fillet comes with wild garlic, morels and tiny broad beans that 'pop pleasingly in the mouth'. A palate-cleansing pre-dessert of coconut water granita with mango pannacotta, passion fruit and Szechuan pepper could be followed by textures of strawberry accompanied by pistachios, droplets of tangy lemon and mint. Vegetarians are unusually well catered for, with their own menu a genuine alternative not an afterthought. The 'friendly knowledgeable' service is spot-on, lunch is particularly good value and the wine list opens at £18.

Chef/s: Jon Howe. **Open:** Fri and Sat L 12 to 1.30, Tue to Sat D 7 to 9. **Closed:** Sun, Mon, 2 weeks winter, 2 weeks summer. **Meals:** set L £24 (2 courses) to £30. Set D £50 (2 courses) to £60. Tasting menu £65 (7 courses) to £80. **Details:** 24 seats. V menu. Music. Children over 8 yrs only.

Purslane

Cooking score: 6
Modern British | £38
16 Rodney Road, Cheltenham, GL50 1JJ
Tel no: (01242) 321639
purslane-restaurant.co.uk

'The most interesting, exciting and unpretentious restaurant we've been to in years,' says one returning fan of this Cheltenham sparkler. Chef and co-owner Gareth Fulford takes an exceptionally skilled and creative approach to Gloucestershire's bounty, and top-notch British seafood is a continuing draw. Dishes are technically precise, but 'robust and tasty'. To start, try hand-dived Oban scallop with fregola, ham hock, sea purslane and parsley pesto or Cacklebean egg with watercress, smoked Mayan Gold potato, winter truffle and sourdough. To follow, it might be red gurnard with sea kale, mussels, salsify sponges and sea spinach, and a coffee macaron with chocolate, caramel cream and macchiato ice cream. Tasting menus and lighter, simpler lunchtime and early evening dishes keep things flexible. In the dining room, co-owner Stephanie Ronssin and her team kindle a 'nice relaxed buzz' and the pleasant suspicion that nothing is too much trouble. A short wine list opens at £20.

Chef/s: Gareth Fulford. **Open:** Tue to Sat L 12 to 2, D 6.30 to 9.30. **Closed:** Sun, Mon, 24 to 27 Dec, 2 weeks Jan, 2 weeks Aug. **Meals:** main courses £20. Set L £20 (2 courses). Set D £38 (3 courses). Tasting menu £55. **Details:** 34 seats. 4 seats outside. Music.

The Tavern

Cooking score: 1
British | £25
5 Royal Well Place, Cheltenham, GL50 3DN
Tel no: (01242) 221212
thetaverncheltenham.com

£30

With its agreeable blend of rusticity and easy-going vibes, this welcoming modern hostelry is everything an urban pub should be. Alongside real ales, there's a mixed bag of straightforward, accessible dishes ranging from mac 'n' cheese, beef and onion sliders and French dip (a sub roll loaded with thinly sliced slow-cooked brisket, Cheddar cheese and onions, served with a pot of cooking juices) to lemon sole with clams, monk's beard and capers, and pork cheek ragù with rigatoni. British classics like steak and ale pie have their say, cheeses are from Neal's Yard Dairy, and there's lemon meringue pie for dessert. Wines from £17.
Chef/s: James de Jong. **Open:** Mon to Fri L 12 to 3, D 6 to 9.30 (10.30 Fri). Sat 9am to 10.30pm. Sun 9am to 4, D 6 to 9. **Closed:** 25 and 26 Dec. **Meals:** main courses £10 to £19. Set L and D £28 (2 courses) to £35. **Details:** 68 seats. Bar. Music.

■ Chipping Campden
The Chef's Dozen

Cooking score: 3
British | £28
Island House, High Street, Chipping Campden, GL55 6AL
Tel no: (01386) 840598
thechefsdozen.co.uk

£30

'What is so delightful about this individual restaurant is that it has real personality,' enthused one returning visitor. Richard and Solanche Craven have certainly created something special in this old stone building in the centre of Chipping Campden. In the first-floor dining room, period features twinned with elegant modern furniture create a welcoming space, while the kitchen's contemporary, ingredient-driven British style 'is clearly created with great care and thought'. Seasonality is everything, from local rabbit raviolo to local red-legged partridge, and the 'most delicious bread served with homemade butter and pork dripping' is a 'real treat'. Elsewhere, lamb's sweetbreads might turn up with a brandy sauce, pastry, capers and baby spinach, and a main course of stone bass with Crown Prince pumpkin, potato dumpling and roasted lemon purée. The bold flavours continue with a dessert of blood orange, which makes a seasonal appearance in its fresh form but also as a soufflé and sorbet. Wines from £20.
Chef/s: Richard Craven. **Open:** Fri and Sat L 12 to 1.20, Tue to Sat D 6.30 to 9. **Closed:** Sun, Mon, 25 and 26 Dec, 23 Jan to 8 Feb. **Meals:** set L and D £28 (3 courses) to £45. **Details:** 26 seats. 20 seats outside. Music.

■ Corse Lawn
Corse Lawn House Hotel

Cooking score: 3
Anglo-French | £38
Corse Lawn, GL19 4LZ
Tel no: (01452) 780771
corselawn.com

The 12 acres of lush grounds have at their heart a majestic Queen Anne house with a large round ornamental pond in front of it. It has been solicitously run by the Hine family as a refined country hotel since the late 1970s. Shell-pink walls and chandeliers set an elegant tone in the main dining room, where an extensive menu of modernised Anglo-French cooking is offered. Start with potted Cornish crab and mango salsa, or Hereford snails with flageolets in garlic butter, and then consider the likes of roast loin and braised belly of wild boar with carrot purée and glazed quince, or perhaps sea bream and spinach in saffron sauce. Dessert might ring changes on a lemon theme with posset, tartlet and ice cream, or offer a traditional queen of puddings with roasted figs. The compendious wine list is sourced from key independent merchants,

with a roll call of opulent French classics succeeded by confident selections from Italy, California and South Africa, not forgetting a ten-strong line-up of German Rieslings. Prices open at £20.50.
Chef/s: Martin Kinahan. **Open:** all week L 12 to 2, D 7 to 9.30. **Closed:** 24 to 26 Dec. **Meals:** main courses £16 to £25. Set L £23 (2 courses) to £26. Set D £34. Sun L £26. **Details:** 80 seats. 50 seats outside. Bar. Wheelchairs. Parking.

■ Eldersfield
The Butchers Arms
Cooking score: 5
Modern British | £50
Lime Street, Eldersfield, GL19 4NX
Tel no: (01452) 840381
thebutchersarms.net

Wood-burners, beams, mismatched tables and chairs, even linoleum flooring, help to maintain the feel of a beguilingly unassuming rural pub – one where drinkers are welcome, service is pleasantly unhurried and the short menu of high-class comfort food is in keeping with the tone. James Winter has seasonality in his blood and proves his worth with dishes that are a real pleasure to eat. A fine Salcombe crab and smoked eel tart with fried chorizo and parsley pesto is a good way to start, following which there might be a broad-shouldered plateful of rare fillet of Hereford beef with a mini oxtail pie, crispy potato and butternut purée or a lovely combo of roasted turbot, lobster tortellini and buttered pak choi. Puddings, too, show flair – both Seville orange marmalade pudding with Drambuie custard, and brown-sugar doughnuts with dark chocolate ice cream provide a luscious finish. In addition, there are well-chosen, affordable wines (from £23.50) or local ales.
Chef/s: James Winter. **Open:** Fri to Sun L 12 to 1, Tue to Sat D 7 to 9. **Closed:** Mon, 2 weeks Jan, 2 weeks Aug, bank hols. **Meals:** main courses £20 to £28. **Details:** 25 seats. Parking. No children under 10 yrs.

■ Long Ashton
The Bird in Hand
Cooking score: 2
British | £27
17 Weston Road, Long Ashton, BS41 9LA
Tel no: (01275) 395222
bird-in-hand.co.uk
£5 OFF £30 ■

Just a short drive out of Bristol, this village pub is part of a brace owned by Toby Gritten, the other being the dockside Pump House in the city (see entry). Food plays a big part in both operations – Toby is a chef after all – and there's evident determination to do things right. The Bird in Hand is still very much a proper pub with real ales, artisan gins and the like. The team in the kitchen make everything in-house, they're not averse to a bit of foraging and the culinary output includes bar snacks, traditional Sunday lunches and a sensibly short carte. Cornish fish stew with rouille and croûtons is a flavour-packed opener, followed by haunch of wild venison, roasted hake with cuttlefish, or a veggie number combining ramson polenta, Colston Bassett Stilton and cabbage. Bitter chocolate délice with honeycomb and banoffee ice cream is a classy finisher. Wines start at £16.50.
Chef/s: Sylvie Platek. **Open:** all week L 12 to 3 (4 Sun), D 6 to 9 (9.30 Fri and Sat). **Meals:** main courses £14 to £17. Set L £16 (2 courses) to £21. Set D £22 (2 courses) to £29. Sun L £16. **Details:** 30 seats. 40 seats outside. Bar. Music.

■ Moreton in Marsh
Horse & Groom
Cooking score: 2
Modern British | £27
Bourton on the Hill, Moreton in Marsh, GL56 9AQ
Tel no: (01386) 700413
horseandgroom.info
£5 OFF ■ £30 ■

'Excellent food in a pub atmosphere' is one reporter's appraisal of Will and Tom Greenstock's classy hilltop coaching inn. Far-reaching views, Georgian good looks and a large garden make for a charming setting, backed up by Will's cooking, which delivers freshness and flavour with minimal fuss. Try home-cured salt cod fritters with rouille, lemon and rocket, and then pan-roasted fillet of halibut with butter-braised leeks, brown shrimps and tarragon or maybe a simple griddled Longhorn sirloin steak with café de Paris butter and crisp homemade chips. Desserts cleave to the same simple, traditional style, with typical options including pear and almond tart, and lemon posset. A homely apple crumble with a flapjack topping served 'as it should be – in a bowl, not deconstructed' with decent homemade custard delighted one diner. Good ales, too, but if you fancy wine, there are plenty, from £15.75.

Chef/s: Will Greenstock. **Open:** all week L 12 to 2 (2.30 Sun), Mon to Sat D 7 to 9 (9.30 Fri and Sat). **Closed:** 25 Dec, 31 Dec, 1 week Jan. **Meals:** main courses £12 to £22. **Details:** 75 seats. 54 seats outside. Bar. Parking.

■ Northleach
The Wheatsheaf Inn
Cooking score: 3
Modern British | £35
West End, Northleach, GL54 3EZ
Tel no: (01451) 860244
cotswoldswheatsheaf.com

The Wheatsheaf is one of those gloriously ancient village inns reinvented for the 21st century – a mix of country house hotel, pub and restaurant. Its chilled-out atmosphere and easy-going service work well with the charm of the interior – open fires, a traditional drinkers bar, dining rooms with leather, wood and auction-house finds – but it's the competent modern British cooking that draws the crowds. The menu takes its cue from seasonal and local ingredients and offers pub classics such as a half-pint of shell-on Atlantic prawns with mayonnaise, and ox cheek, rib and oyster pie with mash and roasted beets, alongside a neatly contrived warm pigeon saltimbocca (with lamb's lettuce, hazelnut and

caper dressing), and Pyrénées wild boar with blood orange, creamed polenta and Parmesan. Finish with a sticky date pudding with salted-caramel sauce and pistachio biscotti. Wines from £16.

Chef/s: Ethan Rogers. **Open:** all week L 12 to 3 (4 Sun), D 6 to 9 (10 Fri and Sat). **Meals:** main courses £12 to £25. Set L £13 (2 courses) to £15. **Details:** 70 seats. 40 seats outside. Bar. Wheelchairs. Music. Parking.

■ Painswick
★ NEW ENTRY ★
The Painswick
Cooking score: 4
Modern European | £35
Kemps Lane, Painswick, GL6 6YB
Tel no: (01452) 813688
thepainswick.co.uk

The Painswick is a stunning Palladian mansion with Italianate gardens and views across the Slad Valley, made famous by Laurie Lee in *Cider With Rosie*. The new owners (who also run the the Potager at Barnsley House – see entry), have refurbished to a very high standard, mixing contemporary and artistic touches, and secured the talents of chef Michael Bedford, last seen in the Guide in 2013 when he ran the Chef's Table in Tetbury. The dining room is two interconnecting rooms lined with sage-wood panels and sash windows, with teal-blue leather chairs and dark-wood tables; it is well appointed, an elegant setting for Bedford's refined rustic French cooking. At a test meal, lobster and black pudding pie with a mini copper pan of lobster gravy ('a sensational starter'), was followed by precisely timed roasted stone bass with a white bean and crab cassoulet, with a large wine glass of 'seasonal, refreshing' wild strawberries macerated in red wine with a light jelly and a sprig of basil making a triumphant finish. Wines from £21.

Chef/s: Michael Bedford. **Open:** all week L 12 to 2.30 (3 Sat and Sun), D 7 to 9.30. **Meals:** main courses £16 to £32. **Details:** 34 seats. Bar. Parking.

Selsley

★ NEW ENTRY ★

The Bell Inn

Cooking score: 1
British | £25
Bell Lane, Selsley, GL5 5JY
Tel no: (01453) 753801
thebellinnselsley.com
£5 OFF £30

'We sat in the garden room, which had a fab view down the steep neighbouring valley,' enthused one visitor to this tastefully refurbished and extended old stone inn. Mark Payne (ex mark@street in Nailsworth) does things properly, making as much as possible in-house – from the bread for the lunchtime sandwiches to the clove-and-molasses baked ham served at dinner (with a fried egg and triple-cooked chips). But it's not all pub classics, check out the quinoa, pine nut and aubergine salad, hake with sprouting broccoli, roasted garlic and toasted almonds, and pistachio soufflé to finish. There's plenty of local produce, too, service is excellent and wines start at £16.
Chef/s: Mark Payne. **Open:** all week L 12 to 2.30 (4 Sun), Mon to Sat D 6.30 to 9.30. **Meals:** main courses £11 to £18. **Details:** 55 seats. 40 seats outside. Bar. Music. Parking.

Stow-on-the-Wold

LOCAL GEM
The Old Butchers

Modern European | £30
7 Park Street, Stow-on-the-Wold, GL54 1AQ
Tel no: (01451) 831700
theoldbutchers.com

'Wonderful welcome, service and atmosphere – and above all the food was very good,' thought one visitor to this stylish Stow-on-the-Wold eatery. Travertine floors, simple modern furniture and grey walls bearing retro prints and posters create a relaxed but pulled-together look, while the lengthy menu seeks to please all, with choices running from charcuterie to an impressive selection of fresh seafood. A meal could take in Cornish fish soup with croûtons and rouille; navarin of lamb with spring vegetables; and crème brûlée. Wines from £17.75.

Thornbury
Ronnies

Cooking score: 3
Modern European | £38
11 St Mary Street, Thornbury, BS35 2AB
Tel no: (01454) 411137
ronnies-restaurant.co.uk
£5 OFF

'We have eaten enjoyably at Ronnie's over several years but the recent return to fine dining seems to have taken it to a whole new level', is just one of many endorsements for Ron Faulkner's rejuvenated restaurant, which has recently reverted to doing what it does best after dabbling with a more casual concept. Faulkner has been running his well-appointed restaurant in this 17th-century converted schoolhouse since 2007 and the bare stone walls and neutral colours make for a smart setting for the meticulous plates of seasonal, produce-driven food, always with a focus on local suppliers. A starter of crab and pistachio cannelloni with charred pineapple, prawns and red pepper might precede Badminton Estate venison, celeriac, salsify and chocolate. If fish is your thing, try the curried monkfish with dhal lentils and shallot bhaji. For dessert, go for pear tarte Tatin with Stilton. The global wine list starts at £19.
Chef/s: Ronnie Faulkner. **Open:** Tue to Sun L 12 to 2.30, Tue to Sat D 6 to 9.30. **Closed:** Mon, 25 and 26 Dec, 2 weeks Jan, bank hols. **Meals:** main courses £17 to £24. Set L £15 (2 courses) to £20. Sun L £21 (2 courses) to £25. **Details:** 58 seats. Wheelchairs. Music.

Average price

The average price denotes the price of a three-course meal without wine.

Romy's Kitchen
Indian | £22
2 Castle Street, Thornbury, BS35 1HB
Tel no: (01454) 416728
romyskitchen.co.uk

£5 OFF £30

From the street, it looks like a typical small-town tea room, but step inside and the enticingly spicy aromas emerging from the open kitchen are more Bengal than Bristol. Chef-proprietor Romy Gill was born near Kolkata but has lived in Thornbury for years and built her reputation hosting local dinner parties before launching this, her first restaurant. It's authentic home cooking, reflected in dishes such as tandoori quail and Rajasthan-style wild boar curry. Wines from £20.

∎ Upper Slaughter
Lords of the Manor
Cooking score: 4
Modern British | £73
Upper Slaughter, GL54 2JD
Tel no: (01451) 820243
lordsofthemanor.com

£5 OFF

This dashing honey-coloured manor (once a rectory) is a vision of English pastoral loveliness that never ages, although the hotel's interiors have benefited from a contemporary makeover in recent years. Massive canvases now dominate the dining room, where staff maintain a 'perfect tempo' amid the 'polite buzz' of contented guests. The kitchen sets high standards, delivering intricate dishes ranging from 'imaginatively presented' lobster linguine with tomato concassé, fish roe and bisque foam ('the kind of dish we cannot have enough of') to a prune soufflé 'elevated to brilliant status' by virtue of the chocolate and bergamot ganache at the bottom of the dish. In between, venison with sloe gin sauce is a perennial favourite, or you could try roast John Dory with smoked sausage, white beans,

cauliflower and poultry jus. Superlative wine matches hit the mark, and the full list is a majestic tome that ventures along lesser-known oenological byways as well as giving full rein to the big hitters; prices from £26. **Chef/s:** Richard Picard-Edwards. **Open:** Sat and Sun L 12 to 2, all week D 6.45 to 8.45. **Meals:** set L £38. Set D £73. Tasting menu £85 (7 courses). **Details:** 45 seats. Bar. Parking.

∎ Winchcombe
5 North Street
Cooking score: 6
Modern European | £48
5 North Street, Winchcombe, GL54 5LH
Tel no: (01242) 604566
restaurant5northstreet.co.uk

'Gus' and Kate Ashenford run a tight ship at this bijou low-key restaurant squeezed into a crooked, half-timbered house on Winchcombe's main thoroughfare. Inside, 5 North Street is a comfy, warm-hearted kind of place, with affable service, a good-value set lunch, and dinner revolving around three fixed-price menus (plus a roster of vegetarian options) that diners are encouraged to mix and match – with prices adjusted accordingly. Those who have taken the plunge have been rewarded with some truly sublime dishes noted for their clarity, balance and sheer technical finesse: roasted scallop accompanied by samphire, confit chicken wing and a near-miraculous potato and pancetta terrine; delectable turbot with fennel, clam and squid tortellini, broad beans, sweet grapes and an epic red pepper coulis; a choice cut of local lamb and classily rendered confit shoulder with sweetbreads, pomme purée and slow-cooked tomatoes. There are also great things to savour when it comes to dessert – perhaps a five-part 'presentation of chocolate' or apple parfait with blackberry sorbet, poached fruits, apple blossom, muesli and apple sauce. Wines with gentle mark-ups start at £24. **Chef/s:** Marcus Ashenford. **Open:** Tue to Sun L 12.30 to 1.30, Tue to Sat D 7 to 9. **Closed:** Mon, 2 weeks Jan, 2 weeks Aug. **Meals:** main courses £25 to £27. Set L £25 (2 courses) to £29. Set D £38 (2 courses) to £49. Sun L £35. **Details:** 26 seats. V menu. Music.

The Lion Inn

Cooking score: 1
Modern British | £30
37 North Street, Winchcombe, GL54 5PS
Tel no: (01242) 603300
thelionwinchcombe.co.uk

A Plantagenet-era country inn in the heart of the Cotswolds will look like heaven to tourers and explorers. Exposed stone walls and a light white backdrop with some strategic distressing move the place into the modern decorative era. The resourceful cooking draws on conscientiously sourced local supplies, but finds plenty of global inspiration for dishes such as lobster in squid-ink tagliatelle with lemongrass and coriander, braised Wagyu brisket with potato skins, wild mushrooms and spring greens, and apple and pear Tatin with cinnamon ice cream and caramel sauce. Wines are articulately noted, and start at £19, or £4.40 a glass.
Chef/s: Alex Dumitrache. **Open:** all week L 12 to 3, D 6 to 9. **Meals:** main courses £14 to £25. **Details:** 52 seats. 64 seats outside. Bar. Wheelchairs. Music.

Wesley House

Cooking score: 2
Modern European | £30
High Street, Winchcombe, GL54 5LJ
Tel no: (01242) 602366
wesleyhouse.co.uk

£5
OFF

Named after Anglican minister and theologian John Wesley, who dropped by in 1755, this wonky-looking medieval merchant's house proudly flaunts its antiquity – right down to its crooked beams, ancient stonework and mighty inglenook fireplace. As a personally run restaurant-with-rooms, however, it also shows a more modern aspect with stylish contemporary touches in the bar

and dining room plus an accessible menu that's firmly in the mainstream Anglo-European mould. On a typical day, you might be offered venison carpaccio with parsnip, pickled pear and sherry dressing or oat-crusted smoked haddock with leek fondue ahead of brill poached in red wine with roast beetroot and forestière sauce or roast rump and braised shoulder of Cotswold lamb with spinach, purple sprouting broccoli and truffle jus. Steaks sizzle on the grill, while desserts play it safe with the likes of sticky toffee pudding, lemon posset or dark chocolate torte with griottine cherries. Wines start at £19.
Chef/s: Cedrik Rullier. **Open:** Tue to Sun L 12 to 2, Tue to Sat D 6 to 9. **Closed:** Mon. **Meals:** main courses £16 to £20. Set L £20 (2 courses) to £25. Set D £22 (2 courses) to £28. Sun L £22 (2 courses). **Details:** 60 seats. Bar.

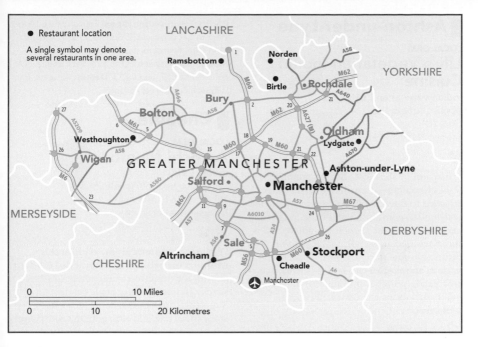

■ Altrincham

★ NEW ENTRY ★

Sugo

Cooking score: 3
Italian | £30
22 Shaw's Road, Altrincham, WA14 1QU
Tel no: (0161) 9297706
sugopastakitchen.co.uk

'Nonna's loss is Altrincham's gain'; the team behind Sugo have drawn on their Pugliese roots to open a pasta restaurant with a rootsy Southern flavour. Even in close and basic quarters, dominated by handsome but inflexible communal tables, it's a flavour-forward, saucy-chinned success. From a brief menu, primi might be bruschetta spread with lemon ricotta and overlaid with char-grilled radicchio and a punchy herb salsa with flakes of salt, slivers of caper and the brightness of chilli. The house special, a slow-cooked beef shin and pork shoulder ragù punched up with cubes of spicy Calabrian sausage, comes on definitively al dente orecchiette. There's always another meat option, one veggie and two fish, such as strozzapreti with mackerel, roasted pumpkin and pangrattato. Puddings, based around excellent Ginger's Comfort Emporium ice cream, could do with a bit more attention, but service is pitched so that no customer feels unloved. Italian wines are from £4.50 a glass.

Chef/s: Jonny Mulyk. **Open:** Tue to Thur D 5 to 10. Fri and Sat 12 to 10. **Closed:** Sun, Mon, 25 to 27 Dec, first 2 weeks Jan, last 2 weeks Aug. **Meals:** main courses £11 to £18. **Details:** 25 seats. Music.

Symbols

- Accommodation is available
- £30 Three courses for less than £30
- £5 OFF £5-off voucher scheme
- Notable wine list

Ashton-under-Lyne

LOCAL GEM

Lily's Vegetarian Indian Cuisine

Indian vegetarian | £10
75-83 Oldham Road, Ashton-under-Lyne,
OL6 7DF
Tel no: (0161) 3394774

£30

It may not be the most alluring premises – 'looks like a greasy spoon' – but this diner attached to the ASM Indian grocery store is a real 'hidden gem'. Inside it is basic, bright and cheerful, while the vegetarian Indian food is full-flavoured and terrific value. Expect distinctive bhel puri, sev puri, dosas, raj kachori and samosa chaat, plus curries such as aloo palak (potatoes and spinach) or paneer makhani. Vegans fair very well indeed. Unlicensed.

Birtle

The Waggon at Birtle

Cooking score: 1
Modern British | £28
131 Bury and Rochdale Old Road, Birtle,
BL9 6UE
Tel no: (01706) 622955
thewaggonatbirtle.co.uk

£5 OFF   £30

The Waggon, an erstwhile pub turned comfortable restaurant, takes great delight in showing off local produce: note the tasty Chadwick's Bury black pudding tempura with apple, bacon, Lancashire cheese and mustard vinaigrette – 'clearly a regular favourite' – and Goosnargh duck with truffle mash. With Fleetwood not that far away, look out for fish such as cod pan-fried with stewed peppers, tomatoes, garlic and basil or a superb piece of halibut with black olives and char-grilled peppers. Finish with rhubarb brûlée and an excellent-tasting rhubarb sorbet. Wines start at £15.95.

Chef/s: David Watson. Open: Thur and Fri L 12 to 2, Wed to Sat D 6 to 9.30. Sun 12.30 to 7. Closed: Mon, Tue, first week Jan, first 2 weeks Jul. Meals: main courses £11 to £24. Set L and D £17 (2 courses) to £19. Sun L £13. Details: 45 seats. Bar. Wheelchairs. Music. Parking.

Cheadle

LOCAL GEM

Aamchi Mumbai

Indian | £20
2A Gatley Road, Cheadle, SK8 1PY
Tel no: (0161) 4283848
aamchimumbai.co.uk

£5 OFF   £30

'We serve happiness', is the claim at this Mumbai specialist, which has added outdoor seating for the alfresco enjoyment of street snacks and masterfully made curries. Vegetables are handled deftly; see a starter of spicy misal pav, and aloo gobi in a satisfyingly clingy sauce. 'The rice is fluffy, the roti is crisp, the meat is juicy – what more do you need?' asks one satisfied customer of the lamb leg special, a boon for regulars given the short menu. Wine is from £14.95.

Lydgate

The White Hart

Cooking score: 4
Modern British | £33
51 Stockport Road, Lydgate, OL4 4JJ
Tel no: (01457) 872566
thewhitehart.co.uk

£5 OFF

Many things to many people, the resourceful White Hart hosts weddings, conferences and events as well as village drinkers consuming draughts of fresh Saddleworth air alongside their pints. Charles Brierley's pub-with-extras was recently refurbished, and although the snug, lounge and bar are all new, the major beneficiary is the restaurant space, now the Dining Room, done out sleekly in shades of chrome and pewter. Food here is ambitious but still aims to please, as in squab pigeon with

Umbrian lentils and smoked garlic sausage, followed perhaps by lemon sole with chard, truffle potato and lobster sauce and hot blackcurrant soufflé with liquorice ice cream. If that doesn't sound very Oldham, head to the more laid-back brasserie for Lancashire cheese and spring onion macaroni, sausage and mash, and parkin with Yorkshire rhubarb — it's not far from here to white rose country. The wine list (which could profitably lose its quips 'n' quotes) starts at £17.50.
Chef/s: Michael Shaw. **Open:** Mon to Sat L 12 to 2.30, D 6 to 9.30. Sun 12 to 8. **Closed:** 26 Dec, 1 Jan. **Meals:** main courses £12 to £26. Set L £14 (2 courses) to £17. Sun L £25. **Details:** 55 seats. 20 seats outside. Bar. Wheelchairs. Music. Parking.

∎ Manchester
Australasia
Cooking score: 2
Pan-Asian | £45
1 The Avenue, Spinningfields, Manchester, M3 3AP
Tel no: (0161) 8310288
australasia.uk.com

The entrance, under a glass pyramid like a mini-Louvre, leads down to a cavernous but airy basement, where a light monochrome look keeps things feeling fresh. One of Manchester's more singular venues is the spot for pan-Asian cooking that embraces Australian, Indonesian and Japanese influences in a creative ferment. Small bites of trad sushi and robata-grilled items mingle with chillied-up tempura of soft-shell crab and courgette flowers, before you get on to the likes of yum yum rice squares with spicy tuna, Thai duck and mango salad, crispy suckling pig curry with pineapple, or a sublime pairing of seared yellowfin and foie gras in sweet miso. Seasonings are anything but shy, from the wasabi and chilli that light up grilled mackerel to the passion fruit and yuzu gel that adds fruity lift to razor-sliced octopus. Sorely tempting desserts take in ginger and green-tea cheesecake, and Kaffir lime brûlée with pineapple sorbet. Drink cocktails, saké or wines from £21.

Chef/s: Phil Whitehead. **Open:** all week 12 to 11. **Meals:** main courses £17 to £21. **Details:** 147 seats. Bar. Wheelchairs. Music.

★ TOP 50 ★
The French
Cooking score: 8
Modern British | £65
The Midland, 16 Peter Street, Manchester, M60 2DS
Tel no: (0161) 2363333
the-french.co.uk

This sibling of the trailblazing L'Enclume (see entry, Cumbria) courts the Mancunian vote in a stand-alone restaurant in the lobby of the Midland Hotel. In truth, fans of The French love everything about the place, from the elegant, intimate room with its high-curved banquettes, ethereal chandeliers and 'very impressive service', to the vivid sense of seasonality about the food. Lunch brings the easy choice of a four-per-course à la carte, but it's the six- or ten-course tasting menus that allow Rogan's frontman Adam Reid to flex his muscles and show his talent for brilliantly executed modern cuisine. It's creative, confident stuff, full of twists, turns and surprising techniques, with a strong sense of freshness, flavour and balance. A talent for injecting thrills into earthy practices might see mushrooms (chopped and generously enriched with a goodly quantity of black truffle) with turnip and beer bread as an opener for a late-winter tasting menu. Ox in coal oil with pumpkin seed, kohlrabi and young shoots is an inimitable signature dish, but reporters have also endorsed Cornish crab, caramelised cabbage, chicken skin ('a clever idea, this') and a horseradish cream, as well as the 'delicious and original flavours' in butter-poached hake with a smoked scallop with a roe butter sauce and carrots cooked in whey, and breast of duck smoked over heather with purple sprouting broccoli, salsify and pickled elderberry. In the season, you might finish with forced Yorkshire rhubarb with yoghurt, oats and Douglas fir. The clued-up sommelier provides astute guidance when it comes to the extensive wine list – not everyone feels they can manage the set pairings. Bottles from £26.

Chef/s: Adam Reid. **Open:** Wed to Sat L 12 to 1.30, Tue to Sat D 6.30 to 9. **Closed:** Sun, Mon, 1 week Aug, 1 week Dec. **Meals:** main courses £18 to £28 (L only, Wed to Fri). Set L and D £65 (6 courses) to £85. **Details:** 56 seats. V menu. Bar. Wheelchairs. Children over 8 yrs only.

★ NEW ENTRY ★

El Gato Negro
Cooking score: 2
Spanish | £30
52 King Street, Manchester, M2 4LY
Tel no: (0161) 6948585
elgatonegrotapas.com

Simon Shaw has come in from the hills, and he's brought his black cat with him. Previously in Ripponden, the restaurant has a new, city-glam location in long, narrow multi-storey premises on King Street – top of the stack is a handsome bar with a retractable roof, with the restaurant in the middle and a more casual bar at street level. At inspection, some of the former focus (both front- and back-of-house) seemed to have been lost en route, but while it's being regained there's heaps of atmosphere, and some effective dishes, to pacify throngs of customers. From a menu that covers charcuterie, small plates and Josper oven-grilled meat, fish and veg, simple Catalan bread with tomato ('just about perfect' for one reader) stood out alongside the oozy Manchego rice served with roast onion and char-grilled artichokes. Jospered lamb skewers, really juicy and tender, almost breathe welcome smoke. Give puds a miss for now. Wines are from £17.

Chef/s: Simon Shaw. **Open:** Tue to Sun L 12 to 3, all week D 5 to 10 (11 Fri and Sat, 9.30 Sun). **Meals:** tapas £3 to £15. **Details:** 40 seats. Bar.

Greens
Cooking score: 2
Vegetarian | £23
43 Lapwing Lane, West Didsbury, Manchester, M20 2NT
Tel no: (0161) 4344259
greensdidsbury.co.uk
£30

As late as 1990, when Greens was established, a vegetarian restaurant was something of a business risk, a worry that its quarter-century (and counting) of feeding Didsbury on healthy meat-free cooking has put to flight. What vegetarian cooking sorely needed at the time was vigorous inventiveness, and in Simon Rimmer's hands the picture was duly transformed. In a convivial space decorated with vivid paintings, modern British modes are brought to bear on roasted cauliflower with pickled mushrooms and truffled cauliflower purée, and salads of beetroot and whipped goats' cheese in walnut vinaigrette with cucumber jelly, ahead of sturdy mains like Tuscan bean stew with red onion and rosemary polenta cake, or spinach, pistachio and feta filo pie with tomato and cinnamon sauce. The global cookbook is mined for influences from Greece, India and the Caribbean, and veggie nostalgiaphiles can celebrate Sunday with hazelnut and pecan nut roast and Yorkshire pud. Finish with sticky toffee pudding. House Spanish is £16.

Chef/s: Simon Rimmer and Tom Pattinson. **Open:** Tue to Sun L 12 to 2 (4 Sun), all week D 5.30 to 10.30 (9.30 Sun). **Closed:** 25 and 26 Dec, 1 Jan. **Meals:** main courses £13 to £14. Set L £12 (2 courses). Set D £15 (2 courses). **Details:** 85 seats. 8 seats outside. V menu. Music.

Hawksmoor

Cooking score: 4
British | £45
184-186 Deansgate, Manchester, M3 3WB
Tel no: (0161) 8366980
thehawksmoor.com

There's no mistaking the family likeness at this Manchester offshoot of Will Beckett and Huw Gott's revivalist steakhouse group. Like its five London siblings, dark-wood clubbiness is mixed with a tub-thumping approach to British beef and the legions of fans love the 'high-quality everything, staff, food'. This is the sort of place where you can just settle in the bar with a glass of wine and 'the best burger ever' or dive into a big-hearted menu for 'bone marrow and onions for starters, followed by a ribeye steak, cooked rare, with a combo of triple-cooked and dripping chips, two sauces – bone-marrow gravy for the chips and peppercorn for the steak – with buttered greens', the unvarying order of one regular. There's fish, too, perhaps hake with romesco sauce or a whole native lobster, and sturdy old English puddings such as sticky toffee or rhubarb and custard. This place is the real deal, especially when you factor in brilliant cocktails and a wine list that offers serious drinking from £22. **Chef/s:** Modesta Latockaite. **Open:** Mon to Sat L 12 to 3, D 5 to 10 (10.30 Fri and Sat). Sun 12 to 9.30. **Closed:** 25 and 26 Dec, 1 Jan. **Meals:** main courses £13 to £35. Express menu £25 (2 courses) to £28. **Details:** 139 seats. Bar. Wheelchairs. Music.

Indian Tiffin Room

Cooking score: 3
Indian | £23
2 Isabella Banks Street, Manchester, M15 4RL
Tel no: (0161) 2281000
indiantiffinroom.com
£30

The Indian Tiffin Room's big city adventure involves a contemporary space less intimate than the atmospheric Cheadle orginal, but which boasts the same 'spot-on' cooking in small plates, thalis and street-inspired snacks.

Paani puri, into which diners pour spiky minted water, repay the modest hike from the shopping district in moments, while bhel puri is 'an absolute belter'. Carbs are a speciality; huge puffy breads served with intense, almost creamy chickpea masala, elegantly slender dosas with excellent sambar, chutneys and chilli oil, and goat keema pav with a perfectly soft bun. At lunch, thalis are a happy tour around the menu, perhaps butter chicken with dhal, tender, coconutty green beans, salad, rice and more bread. At dinner, don't leave without a tandoori lamb chop under your belt. The bar is a luxury not possible in the Cheadle branch – at Chapel St, Cheadle, Cheshire, SK8 1BR; tel: (0161) 4912020 – and dispenses cocktails alongside wine from £16.50. **Chef/s:** Selvan Arul. **Open:** all week L 12 to 2.30, D 5 to 9.30. **Meals:** main courses £7 to £12. **Details:** 100 seats. Bar.

The Lime Tree

Cooking score: 3
Modern British | £30
8 Lapwing Lane, West Didsbury, Manchester, M20 2WS
Tel no: (0161) 4451217
thelimetree.co.uk

To celebrate its 30th birthday, Paddy Hannity's West Didsbury stalwart is undergoing some sprucing. The refurbishment is unlikely to alter the spirit of the place, though; its modern Brit bistro drill has become part of the culinary character of a fast-evolving suburb. Starters of twice-baked Lancashire cheese and hazelnut soufflé with poached pear salad, or seared scallops with sweet chilli, rocket and crème frâiche, may be predictable, but, say readers gratefully, they also work. Mains could be monkfish tail wrapped in Parma ham with creamed cabbage, potato, leek and carrot velouté or roast loin of Cheshire lamb with stuffed lamb breast and squash purée, and the Cheshire origin might easily be the restaurant's own smallholding, not far away. To finish, summer pudding, rhubarb and apple crumble and cheese plates take customers straight to the comfort zone. Wine is taken seriously, with new monthly wine dinners and bottles from £16.

Chef/s: Jason Parker and Gary Hinchcliffe. **Open:** Tue to Sat L 12 to 2.30, Mon to Sat D 5.30 to 10. Sun 12 to 9. **Closed:** 25 and 26 Dec. **Meals:** main courses £13 to £25. Set L £11 (2 courses). Set D £15 (2 courses) to £18. **Details:** 75 seats. 20 seats outside. Music.

★ NEW ENTRY ★

Lunya

Cooking score: 1
Spanish | £26
Barton Arcade, Deansgate, Manchester, M3 2BB
Tel no: (0161) 4133317
lunya.co.uk

 £5 OFF £30

Liverpool, by way of Catalonia, has landed. Peter and Elaine Kinsella's Spanish shop, bar and restaurant follows their much-loved Scouse enterprise with a great spot in Barton Arcade. Their sourcing is faithful and enthusiastic, making the extensive selection of cheese and jamón a shoo-in alongside bread served with a rabbit-from-the-hat selection of oils and vinegars. If the kitchen lacks delicacy at times, it's not to the detriment of a Catalan potato and chorizo hotpot rich with herb flavours, or the masterful frying of broccoli and cauliflower buñuelos with a coolly sweet romesco sauce. Wine from a fairly priced Spanish list starts at £17.95.

Chef/s: Darek Chmielnicki. **Open:** all week 12 to 10 (11 Fri and Sat, 9.30 Sun). **Closed:** 25 Dec, 1 Jan. **Meals:** tapas £5 to £12. Set L £15. **Details:** 174 seats. 60 seats outside. Bar. Wheelchairs. Music.

Manchester House

Cooking score: 5
Modern British | £60
Tower 12, 18-22 Bridge Street, Manchester, M3 3BZ
Tel no: (0161) 8352557
manchesterhouse.uk.com

It takes a Liverpudlian and a Tasmanian to create a Mancunian one-off. Manchester House is the joint endeavour of chef Aiden Byrne and much-missed hospitality pioneer Tim Bacon, who died in 2016. A tribute to his confidence, ambition and expertise, it has mellowed since it opened. The big, loft-style dining room, with its capacious tables and low-hanging lighting, feels pleasantly lived-in, and the cooking, while still complex, has shrugged off excessive gimmickry. Tasting menus are the bread and butter of the open kitchen – at lunch, you can select two or three dishes from the 10-courser at a keen price – and many plates are intricately detailed. To start, baked beetroot with yoghurt and cod gravadlax pairs dilled cucumber and silky beetroot, some powerfully acidulated for contrast, with a pale sheet of crème fraîche jelly; it barely needs the cod. Poached brill, served just-warm in a shallow sea of asparagus gazpacho, is an experiment in cool spring cooking, completed effectively with coins of sliced langoustine, asparagus and an intense lemon pureé. Pudding might be beurre noisette parfait with buttery sweet potato toast crumbs and an orange pureé with a breath of anise. It's all delivered in the self-consciously casual style that, despite the advice about which cutlery to use, readers maintain is 'spot on'. Wine starts at £28, with plenty above.

Chef/s: Aiden Byrne. **Open:** Tue to Sat L 12 to 2.30, D 7 to 9.30 (6 to 10 Fri and Sat). **Closed:** Sun, Mon. **Meals:** main courses £37. Set L £23 (2 courses) to £28. Tasting menu £65 (10 courses) to £95 (14 courses). **Details:** 78 seats. Bar. Wheelchairs. Music.

Mr Cooper's

Cooking score: 2
Modern European | £38
The Midland Hotel, Peter Street, Manchester,
M60 2DS
Tel no: (0161) 9324198
mrcoopershouseandgarden.co.uk

Two restaurants occupy the ground floor of
the Midland Hotel, both run by Simon
Rogan. Mr Cooper's House and Garden (to
give it its full name) is the chef's more down-
to-earth brasserie option, a sizeable space
whose brown-toned, garden-centre-themed
décor may not be to everyone's taste. Yet there's
a sense of relaxed enjoyment, for here is a
kitchen that seems quite at home with a range
of modern European ideas but is unafraid to
lob a bit of Asia and the Far East into the mix.
Among an 'exciting choice of dishes' you
might find buttermilk-fried prawns with
kim-chee purée, pear and pickled fennel
alongside 'light and well-executed' mains such
as mussel, monkfish and potato romesco with
spinach and olive oil or Herdwick lamb rumps
with Swiss chard gratin and spiced lentils.
Desserts take in an impressive hot white
chocolate mousse cake with a pineapple-
cardamom compote as well as British cheeses.
Wines from £19.
Chef/s: Sean McGinlay. **Open:** Mon to Sat L 12 to 2
(2.30 Fri and Sat), D 5 to 10. Sun 1 to 8. **Closed:** 25
and 26 Dec, 1 Jan. **Meals:** main courses £14 to £24.
Set L £16 (2 courses) to £20. Set D £20 (2 courses) to
£24. **Details:** 120 seats. Bar. Wheelchairs. Music.

TNQ

Cooking score: 2
Modern British | £29
108 High Street, Manchester, M4 1HQ
Tel no: (0161) 8327115
tnq.co.uk
£5 £30
OFF

A stalwart of the city scene for many a year –
'can't say how happy we are to have somewhere
like this in Manchester' – this animated all-
day brasserie is a 'lovely place to eat'. It's not

hard to see why it's a local favourite – who
could resist friendly, unpretentious service, a
short menu of modern British dishes that play
to regional ingredients and spot-on
seasonality, and such kind pricing. Indeed, set
menus are startlingly good value, offering the
likes of ham hock and Shorrocks Lancashire
Bomb terrine with apple relish, and Brixham
crab linguine with courgette, chilli and garlic.
Elsewhere, steaks showcase Cheshire beef and
come with roasted bone marrow and a choice
of sauces, there's confit Goosnargh duck legs
with chorizo, bean and tomatoes, and slow-
cooked lamb shoulder with kale, roasted and
puréed squash and lamb jus. Sticky toffee
pudding is a popular dessert. Wines from £18.
Chef/s: Anthony Fielden. **Open:** all week 12 to
10.30 (7 Sun). **Closed:** 25 and 26 Dec, 1 Jan.
Meals: main courses £12 to £21. Set L £14 (2
courses) to £17. Set D £30 (3 courses). Sun L £14.
Details: 54 seats. 70 seats outside. Wheelchairs.
Music.

Volta

Cooking score: 2
Modern European | £25
167 Burton Road, West Didsbury, Manchester,
M20 2LN
Tel no: (0161) 4488887
voltafoodanddrink.co.uk
£5 £30
OFF

Only a third of the covers are reservable each
evening. Walk-ins are invited to grab a drink at
the bar, and make their way to a table with the
obliging staff. The outlying district of West
Didsbury is Manchester at its leafiest, and
Volta aims for an intimate feel in converted
shop premises that feature a small outdoor
terrace and a room adorned with café tables,
bar seating and mustard walls. Modern
European bistro food is the mood du jour,
with small plates offering expansive variety as
they crowd the little tabletops. Figs and
haloumi splashed in balsamic and mustard
seeds, blue crab linguine, roast duck in gin and
juniper, crispy artichokes in seaweed and
anchovy butter: it's all high on potent flavour.
Platters of traditional Spanish cured meats or

European cheeses might top or tail a session, and the crème brûlée is ritzed up with white chocolate and cardamom. A few wines start at £15.50.

Chef/s: Alex Shaw. **Open:** Tue to Sat L 12 to 4 (3 Sat), D 5 to 9.30. Sun 12.30 to 7.30. **Closed:** Mon, 25 and 26 Dec. **Meals:** small plates £5 to £11. **Details:** 60 seats. 25 seats outside. Music.

Wing's

Cooking score: 3
Chinese | £45
Heron House, 1 Lincoln Square, Manchester, M2 5LN
Tel no: (0161) 8349000
wingsrestaurant.co.uk

It's easy to see the attraction of the banquet menus and dim sum platters – it saves wading through a very long menu. Take the time, though, and you will be rewarded with a clay pot filled with tender pork belly and yam, or abalone with Chinese greens. Wing's occupies a modern block in Lincoln Square and its contemporary interior serves up cosy booths and those big round tables beloved of Chinese restaurants. Dim sum is a star attraction, with classic steamed favourites like har-gau, char siu bao and siu mai alongside Vietnamese spring rolls and Thai fishcakes. The sharing starter plate is a good bet, with Peking hot-and-sour soup or aromatic crispy duck to follow. Among main courses, king prawns and asparagus arrive in a piquant XO sauce, pork chops are spiced up Shanghai style, and 'sizzling' fillet steak comes with satay sauce. Wines start at £23.90.

Chef/s: Mr Chi Wing Lam. **Open:** all week 12 to 12 (4 to 12 Sat, 1 to 11 Sun). **Meals:** main courses £14 to £40. Set L and D £26 (2 courses) to £45. **Details:** 85 seats. V menu. Bar. Wheelchairs. Music.

Local Gem

Local Gems are the perfect neighbourhood venues, delivering good, freshly cooked food at great value for money.

Yuzu

Cooking score: 3
Japanese | £20
39 Faulkner Street, Manchester, M1 4EE
Tel no: (0161) 2364159
yuzumanchester.co.uk
£30

Sushi excepted, Yuzu deals in Japan's greatest culinary exports from teriyaki to tempura. The house versions of each, made with precision and care, don't risk any dish's international reputation; in the best possible sense, this is safe Japanese cooking. Well loved for its attractive lunchtime deals, Yuzu also runs an accessibly priced à la carte brimming with good things. Agedashi tofu has a delicate moth-wing coating, potent topping of grated ginger and its own deep bath of broth, and gyoza are generously filled with pearly chunks of prawn. Chicken karaage, now powerfully associated with this restaurant on the edge of Chinatown, is a masterful piece of frying. Donburi bowls, served with miso and a little salad of sesame-dressed cucumber, are a sure-fire main course; try kaisen don, topped with immaculate scallop, tuna, salmon, prawn and Day-Glo roe. Rather than wine there's beer and a selection of saké, from £6.50 a cup.

Chef/s: David Leong. **Open:** Tue to Sat L 12 to 2 (2.30 Sat), D 5.30 to 10. **Closed:** Sun, Mon, 2 weeks Christmas. **Meals:** main courses £8 to £17. Set L and D £9 (2 courses). **Details:** 26 seats. Music.

LOCAL GEM

Albert Square Chop House

British | £29
The Memorial Hall, Albert Square, Manchester, M2 5PF
Tel no: (0161) 8341866
albertsquarechophouse.com
£30

'Proper food, done properly,' says one correspondent of this clubby, semi-subterranean restaurant. Hung, like the bar upstairs, with portraits of northerners at work, it's all bare bricks, burnished leather and booths. A characterful menu goes big on

Lancashire butter pie, bacon chops and Eccles cakes, with comfort writ large in a fritter of pillowy corned beef hash with fruity house brown sauce and Bakewell tart with raspberry ripple ice cream. If the kitchen occasionally loses focus, the wine list is sharp, from £18.

LOCAL GEM

The Pasta Factory
Italian | £25
77 Shudehill Street, Manchester, M4 4AN
Tel no: (0161) 2229250
pastafactory.co.uk

£30

The pasta is considerably better than the name at this simple, friendly specialist in the grittier bit of the Northern Quarter. Freshly made in-house, it includes trottole with ragù, prosciutto-stuffed ravioli, and squid-ink ribbons with green olive and mackerel, but just as satisfying are the kinked lengths of bucatini, looking like unravelled wool coated with rich, silky tomato sauce or fresh pesto. Starters and desserts do the job, but loyal followers are here for the main event. Wine is from £12.

LOCAL GEM

Teacup Kitchen
Modern British | £20
55 Thomas Street, Manchester, M4 1NA
Tel no: (0161) 8323233
teacupandcakes.com

£30

A Northern Quarter stalwart, Teacup Kitchen trades on its lively location, stark functionality and honest food, a formula that attracts a full house. It's a versatile space, serving breakfasts and cream teas as well as simple, well-prepared dishes such as ham hock with mature Cheddar and curried piccalilli or confit chicken in puff pastry with a mushroom cream. Other pluses include the extensive menu of proper leaf teas, the dressed-down service and the sheer good value of it all. Wines from £16.

Best of... Manchester

Our undercover inspectors open their Little Black Books

For coffee, have the house roast (or your favourite brew) at **Grindsmith**, Deansgate, or if you're on the go, pop along to their 'pod' on Greengate Square.

At Manchester Cathedral, **Propertea** (brought to us by broadcaster Yvette Fielding), is much more than an excuse for 'more tea, vicar?' jokes. Try one of their many Earl Greys.

From keg or cask, whatever's pouring at **Café Beermoth** (Brown Street) is chosen with extreme - some might say obsessive - care. If you can't stop, pop along to their shop on Tib Street.

At the sister shop to their pasta-kitchen restaurant, be sure to try a panino stuffed with prosciutto and aubergine from **Sugo**, Shaw's Road, Altrincham.

For the best fish and chips head to **Hip Hop Chip Shop**, at The Kitchens in Spinningfields, or at MediaCity. Try an unconventional 'Feastie boys box' or 'Shell L Cool J'.

There may be a queue, but the Neapolitan-style buffalo mozzarella pizza at **Rudy's** in Ancoats is worth the wait.

Take away a savoury Danish from **Companio Bakery**, to be found twice weekly at Victoria station.

One foodie thing you must do is take the tram to Altrincham's **Market House** for a brilliant lunch from one of its refectory counters.

Norden

Nutters
Cooking score: 2
Modern British | £34
Edenfield Road, Norden, OL12 7TT
Tel no: (01706) 650167
nuttersrestaurant.co.uk

Fully embracing what might be considered a loaded surname, Nutter branding looms large at this rather grand 18th-century manor. The man himself, Mr Andrew Nutter, has written cookbooks called *Utter Nutter* and *Nuts About Food*. A family affair, he runs the place with his mum and dad, and there's no denying they are doing it their way. Andrew is definitely serious when it comes to ingredients, sourcing locally and picking herbs from his new herb garden. Expect some sharply modern food with British and French influences. An ambitious first course sees roast turbot dressed in the chef's version of gremolata, served with a fricassee of braised chervil root and girolles, while caramelised duck breast stars in a main course with ravioli filled with its leg meat, and a ginger-infused consommé. A dessert of cherry délice looks the business with its shards of praline and molten chocolate and cinnamon doughnuts. Wines start at £17.20.
Chef/s: Andrew Nutter. **Open:** Tue to Sun L 12 to 2 (4 Sun), D 6.30 to 9.30 (8 Sun). **Closed:** Mon, 2 days after Christmas and New Year, bank hols. **Meals:** main courses £18 to £25. Set L £17 (2 courses) to £20. Set D £44 (6 courses). Sun L £25. **Details:** 146 seats. V menu. Bar. Wheelchairs. Music. Parking.

Please send us your feedback

To register your opinion about any restaurant listed in this guide, or a new restaurant that you wish to bring to our attention, please visit the web address at the bottom of the page. Your feedback informs the content of the book and will be used to compile next year's reviews.

Ramsbottom

★ NEW ENTRY ★

Baratxuri
Cooking score: 1
Spanish | £25
1 Smithy Street, Ramsbottom, BL0 9AT
Tel no: (01706) 559090
levanterfinefoods.co.uk
£30

Baratxuri, pronounced 'Barra-churri' – garlic in Basque – is partner to Levanter round the corner (see entry) and is smart and authentic-looking with 'beautiful modern versions of ornate and colourful Spanish tiles'. This is pintxo territory: 'fresh tasting and delicious' toasted bread with various toppings, say sheep's cheese and fresh anchovy, cured ham or prawns, while hot versions include morcilla with a fried quail's egg, scallop set 'on a sweetish, rich tomato base' or ('best of all') tender fat discs of octopus marinated in onions and peppers with a light oil and vinegar dressing. The wine list is faithfully Spanish, from £3.25 a glass.
Chef/s: Rachel Stockley. **Open:** Wed to Sun 12 to 10 (6 to 10 Wed, 10.30 Fri and Sat, 12 to 6 Sun). **Closed:** Mon, Tue, first week Jan. **Meals:** pintxos from £2. Sharing platter £35. **Details:** 24 seats. Bar. Music. No children after 7pm.

★ NEW ENTRY ★

Levanter Fine Foods
Cooking score: 1
Spanish | £22
10 Square Street, Ramsbottom, BL0 9BE
Tel no: (01706) 551530
levanterfinefoods.co.uk
£30

'Ramsbottom really remains a bit of a foodie destination,' commented one visitor, noting that no-booking Levanter is the go-to place for tapas, with its nearby sibling, the Basque-orientated Baratxuri (see entry) offering stiff competition. In a relaxed and distinctly Spanish setting – scrubbed wooden floors and tables on two levels with a busy, visible little kitchen – there's plenty to applaud, from sharing platters of cured meats to razor clams with garlic or salt cod and chickpeas. For something more gutsy there's white sausage, morcilla and sweet chorizo stew with plump Spanish butter beans and a thick, rich tomato sauce. An all-Spanish wine list starts at £3.25 a glass.

Chef/s: Joe Botham. **Open:** Wed D 5 to 10. Thur to Sun 12 to 10 (7.30 Sun). **Closed:** Mon, Tue, first week Jan. **Meals:** tapas £4 to £9. **Details:** 36 seats. Music.

Sanmini's

Cooking score: 3
Indian | £27
Ramsbottom Lane, Ramsbottom, BL0 9DJ
Tel no: (01706) 821831
sanminis.com

£5 OFF   £30

A doctor whose passion for the cooking of South India drove her to set up a business, Padmini Sankar opened her restaurant with her husband (an anaesthetist) in a rather quaint 19th-century gatehouse in 2008. It's very much a family affair. The unassuming interior is neutral and contemporary, while the menu is sensibly short and focused. Vegetarians fare very well indeed with classic tiffin options such as masala dosa and onion uthappam up for grabs, plus starters like cashew and spinach pakora. Sautéed Madras prawns is a winning seafood opener, which might be followed by Mini's mutton kozambhu (shoulder or leg of lamb in a 'special' gravy), chicken biryani or a veggie main course such as ennai kathirikkai (aubergines and tomatoes flavoured with mustard seeds and fenugreek). Accompaniments such as rice of the day and chapatis are equally on the money. Drink mango lassi or wines from £14.95.

Chef/s: Dr Padmini Sankar and Sathyanand Nagarupillai. **Open:** Tue, Wed, Fri and Sat D 6.30 to 10.30. **Closed:** Sun, Mon, Thur, 2 weeks Jan. **Meals:** main courses £9 to £17. **Details:** 40 seats. V menu. Bar. Wheelchairs. Music.

▌ Stockport

Damson

Cooking score: 3
Modern British | £40
113-115 Heaton Moor Road, Stockport, SK4 4HY
Tel no: (0161) 4324666
damsonrestaurant.co.uk

Damson continues to win local approval with its innovative cooking and genuinely warm welcome. The smart, comfortable dining room, with 'a lot of purple going on', showcases regularly changing, keenly priced menus of familiar favourites punctuated by top-notch ingredients: tagliatelle of squid, lobster, scallop and crab vierge, and slow-cooked duck egg with smoked haddock brandade, capers, grain-mustard butter, tomato and sourdough crisps were the triumphant openers of one meal in March, but glowing recommendations span the entire repertoire. Roasted rump of lamb, which arrived with fluffy Parmesan gnocchi, buttered spinach, smoked anchovy and lamb gras, was 'very good indeed', while grilled halibut with glazed turnips, sprouting broccoli, parsley creamed potato and grapes, pickled cucumber and smoked oyster butter was pronounced the 'best dish of the evening'. Desserts include a glossy, not oversweet Valrhona Caramelia chocolate and peanut délice, with banana ice cream and salted-caramel ganache. Wines organised by grape variety start at £18.95.

Chef/s: Jake Buchan. **Open:** Tue to Fri L 12 to 2.30, Mon to Sat D 5.30 to 9.30 (5 to 9 Sat). Sun 12 to 7.30. **Closed:** 26 Dec, 1 Jan. **Meals:** main courses £20 to £29. Set L and early D £20 (2 courses) to £25. **Details:** 75 seats. 25 seats outside. V menu. Bar. Wheelchairs. Music.

★ NEW ENTRY ★

Easy Fish Company

Cooking score: 1
Seafood | £30
117 Heaton Moor Road, Stockport, SK4 4HY
Tel no: (0161) 4420823
theeasyfishco.com

Heaton Moor's indie fishmonger caters for both cooks and eaters. Pass the well-stocked counter to find the large, plain-but-pleasant restaurant, where staff are 'genuinely nice' and freshness and variety come as standard. The catch is turned into a multiplicity of dishes, but the simplest are the most appealing: fish and chips, a 'shells' section crammed with lobster, clams and oysters, sharing platters and tasting boards. To start, fish roe croûtes with horseradish and crème fraîche are crisper than they look. A perfect fishcake with the sweetness of allium is topped with ribbons of lightly acid fennel and cucumber, working better than the slight blandness of the traditional parsley sauce. Poached trout with a garnish too many (pea mousse, a potato and leek terrine *and* an anchovy roll) might be confused, but the fish is perfect; readers also rate the monkfish curry. Service is warm and solicitous, with wines from £16.
Chef/s: Steven Green. **Open:** Tue to Sat 12 to 11.30. **Closed:** Sun, Mon. **Meals:** main courses £13 to £22

▌Westhoughton

★ NEW ENTRY ★

Provenance

Cooking score: 1
Modern British | £28
46-48 Market Street, Westhoughton, BL5 3AZ
Tel no: (01942) 812398
provenancerestaurant.co.uk
£30

'Smart and relaxed, feels very now', thought one visitor of this bright downstairs deli and upstairs eatery. As the name suggests, the emphasis is on quality ingredients, locally sourced, with various menus offering perhaps a too wide choice but covering everything

from breakfast via afternoon tea to dinner. The à la carte shows ambition, delivering, in late winter, first rate frogs' legs with cheese and onion tortellini and 'sweet, nutty' confit of roast garlic, 'a very earthy plateful' of chicory Tatin with orange reduction and candied walnuts, and excellent-quality battered haddock with crushed peas and tartare sauce. All in all, this addition to Market Street is 'the best thing for Westhoughton'. Wines start at £3.85 a glass.
Chef/s: Lewis Gallagher. **Open:** Tue to Sun L 12 to 2.30 (5.30 Sun), Tue to Sat D 5.30 to 8.30 (9.30 Thur to Sat). **Closed:** Mon, 26 Dec. **Meals:** main courses £8 to £22. Set L £12 (2 courses) to £15. Sun L £13. **Details:** 46 seats. Music.

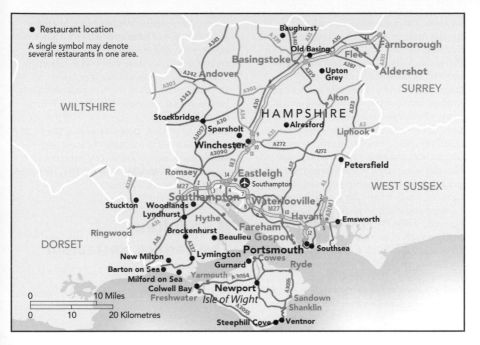

- Restaurant location

A single symbol may denote
several restaurants in one area.

Alresford
Pulpo Negro
Cooking score: 3
Spanish | £25
28 Broad Street, Alresford, SO24 9AQ
Tel no: (01962) 732262
pulponegro.co.uk
£30

Andres Alemany and his wife left the Purefoy
Arms in mid-2016 to focus on their tapas
restaurant. It's a simple enough set-up, with an
open kitchen, windows looking out on to
Broad Street and a menu built around dozens
of sharing dishes ranging from charcuterie to
seafood, tortillas and cheeses. The spider-crab
croquetas are very popular, as is the pulpo
negro ('very tender octopus served in an ink
sauce – very moreish'). Also singled out for
praise are the Ibérico pork sliders, the
'generous' cured meat board and the gambas al
ajillo, which come 'shelled and easy to eat'.
There's an interesting selection of meat-free
options, including Gypsy potatoes with ceps

and yolk, and salt-roasted beetroot with mojo
verde. Desserts include tarta de whiskey and a
'light and tasty' crema catalana. The wine list
favours Spain and Portugal, with lots available
by the glass. Bottles start at £19.50.
Chef/s: Andres Alemany. **Open:** Tue to Sat L 12 to
3, D 6 to 10. **Closed:** Sun, Mon, 25 and 26 Dec.
Meals: tapas £2 to £13. **Details:** 40 seats. 12 seats
outside. Wheelchairs. Music. Children over 5 yrs
only.

Barton on Sea
Pebble Beach
Cooking score: 3
Modern European | £35
Marine Drive, Barton on Sea, BH25 7DZ
Tel no: (01425) 627777
pebblebeach-uk.com

Named after Barton on Sea's pebble beach and
famed for its gasp-inducing clifftop location
(gorgeous views of the Needles and the Isle of
Wight included), this upbeat restaurant-with-

rooms is a summertime hit with holidaymakers who take full advantage of its open-air terrace. As befits the setting, chef Pierre Chevillard's focus is on briny-fresh seafood, from whole local lobsters, langoustines and 'plateaux de fruits de mer' to scallops with parsnip purée, chicken and orange butter jus or a mighty 'choucroute of the sea', complete with Riesling-braised sauerkraut and a smoked haddock sausage. There's also plenty for those who prefer red-blooded sustenance in the form of juicy char-grilled steaks, veal rump with sautéed mushrooms or confit duck with braised red cabbage and blueberries. Vegetarians aren't ignored, while the sweet-toothed yearn for desserts such as coconut pannacotta or Calvados baba. Look for inviting seasonal specials on the well-spread wine list; bottles from £19.60.

Chef/s: Pierre Chevillard. **Open:** all week L 12 to 2 (2.30 Sat and Sun), D 6.30 to 9.30 (10 Fri and Sat). **Meals:** main courses £12 to £38. **Details:** 80 seats. 50 seats outside. Bar. Wheelchairs. Music. Parking.

▌Baughurst
The Wellington Arms

Cooking score: 4
British | £37
Baughurst Road, Baughurst, RG26 5LP
Tel no: (0118) 9820110
thewellingtonarms.com

Looking for an antidote to the big-city rat race? Jason King and Simon Page's enterprising venture might just be the answer. Their beautifully extended 18th-century pub-with-rooms is a great advert for self-reliance, with eggs from their free-range hens and home-grown produce from the garden and polytunnels, in addition to rearing the odd sheep or pig and selling jams and chutneys in the bar. Food miles matter here, and Jason King's fiercely seasonal cooking makes a virtue out of simplicity and economy and seems to please the great majority. A straightforward dish of home-cured ham hock, fennel and parsley terrine with English

mustard mayonnaise could precede a flaky pastry pot pie of home-reared Jacob lamb with white wine and rosemary, served with a creamy mash, or skate wing with brown butter, fried capers and Anya potatoes. Desserts such as Eton mess or pancakes with lemon curd make a big impact, too. Wines from £18.

Chef/s: Jason King. **Open:** all week L 12 to 1.30 (3 Sun), Mon to Sat D 6 to 8.30 (9 Fri and Sat). **Meals:** main courses £12 to £25. Set L £16 (2 courses) to £19. **Details:** 40 seats. 30 seats outside. Wheelchairs. Music. Parking.

▌Beaulieu
The Terrace Restaurant

Cooking score: 5
Modern European | £75
Montagu Arms Hotel, Palace Lane, Beaulieu, SO42 7ZL
Tel no: (01590) 612324
montaguarmshotel.co.uk

The Montagu Arms, in its various precursor incarnations, served the village of Beaulieu in the way of timber auctions and cattle markets through the centuries, before it was eventually subjected to an Arts and Crafts transformation in the 1880s. It's a perfect New Forest bolt-hole for visitors to the Beaulieu Motor Museum, and its supremely elegant Terrace dining room was itself extensively refurbished in April 2016. Matthew Tomkinson rules the luxurious roost here, with cooking that draws on the surrounding forest, the South Coast and the kitchen garden for high-impact dishes such as pumpkin velouté with black pudding, caramelised scallop and toasted seeds, prior to turbot with wild mushrooms and braised pearl barley, or saddle of Alresford roe deer with glazed red cabbage, pickled grapes and a little pie of the braised shoulder. The comprehensive menus might conclude with classic custard tart, poached rhubarb and matching yoghurt-based sorbet. True enthusiasm and a knowledge of the latest oenological thinking radiates from a wine list on which every bottle is chosen to be eloquently representative of its style. Prices open at £28, or £6.50 a glass.

Chef/s: Matthew Tomkinson. **Open:** Wed to Sun L 12 to 2.30, Tue to Sun D 7 to 9.30. **Closed:** Mon. **Meals:** set L £25 (2 courses) to £30. Set D £55 (2 courses) to £75. Sun L £38. Tasting menu £90. **Details:** 50 seats. Bar. Music. Parking. Children over 12 yrs only at D.

▮ Brockenhurst

LOCAL GEM

The Pig
Modern British | £35
Beaulieu Road, Brockenhurst, SO42 7QL
Tel no: (01590) 622354
thepighotel.com

🛏

Part of a small herd of Pigs across the south and south west, the restaurant in the Brockenhurst outpost is situated in a Victorian glasshouse. The boutique hotel's garden provides its bounty for a kitchen that focuses on British-influenced stuff such as Portland Bay scallops with baby gem lettuce, Greenford Farm pork chop with creamed cabbage, or a risotto flavoured with garlic, English bresaola and New Forest Blue cheese. Finish with chocolate and rhubarb tart. Wines start at £18.

▮ Emsworth
36 On The Quay
Cooking score: 5
Modern European | £58
47 South Street, Emsworth, PO10 7EG
Tel no: (01243) 375592
36onthequay.co.uk

£5 OFF 🛏

The cream-fronted house with its shallow bay windows overlooking the harbour is older than it looks – 17th century – but has been given a light, refreshing modern look inside, with smartly clothed tables. Ramon Farthing relinquished the stoves to Gary Pearce in 2013, but maintains a guiding role, and the cooking achieves memorable impact through dishes

that are undaunted by complexity. The crab encased in apple jelly with roasted and creamed artichokes and foraged leaves is a signature starter, and seafood is thoroughly reliable throughout, as witness a main course of pan-roasted turbot with snail and onion confit and wild mushrooms in chicken jus. Scallops don't often crop up as a main these days, but are regally served here with salt-baked celeriac, sweet walnuts, celery and cockles. To maintain the maritime theme, there's a filling of sea buckthorn in the chocolate délice, which comes with burnt butter ice cream and citrus crisps. Stylistically listed wines open at £21.95.

Chef/s: Gary Pearce. **Open:** Tue to Sat L 12 to 1.45, D 6.45 to 9.30 (6.30 Sat). **Closed:** Sun, Mon, 2 weeks May, 2 weeks Oct. **Meals:** set L £24 (2 courses) to £29. Set D £48 (2 courses) to £58. **Details:** 50 seats. 8 seats outside. Bar. Wheelchairs.

▮ Isle of Wight

★ NEW ENTRY ★

The Little Gloster
Cooking score: 4
Modern European | £40
31 Marsh Road, Gurnard, Isle of Wight, PO31 8JQ
Tel no: (01983) 298776
thelittlegloster.com

🛏

A homage to Scandi style in the English Channel, the Little Gloster is a single-storey building behind a white picket fence, all stripped wood inside, with comfortable black sofas, nautical ornamentation and panoramic wraparound windows in the dining room, the better to enjoy the sea views. Bargain set lunches are worth clearing Thursday or Friday diary space for, and there are hearty, healthy breakfasts from 9am. Otherwise, the cooking combines modern European ideas with obvious panache: confit duck leg is precisely rendered, bedded on white bean purée and scattered with diced veg and chunks of merguez, or a whopping gurnard fillet with crisped but gooey-centred polenta, charred fennel and carrot velouté. Prior to those might come a signature gravadlax with sprouted rye-bread and horseradish dressing, or crab arancini with rhubarb on light garlic mayo. Finish with one of the seasonally flavoured aquavits, infused in-house, with various sorbets. Wine from £21.

Chef/s: Ben Cooke and Jay Amado Santiago. **Open:** Tue to Sun 9am to 11pm (6pm Sun). **Closed:** Mon, Sun to Wed (Oct to Apr). **Meals:** main courses £15 to £27. Tasting menu £55. **Details:** 75 seats. Bar.

★ NEW ENTRY ★

Thompson's

Cooking score: 5
Modern European | £45
11 Town Lane, Newport, Isle of Wight, PO30 1JU
Tel no: (01983) 526118
robertthompson.co.uk

£5
OFF

It's fair to say Robert Thompson has been the prime mover and shaker on the Isle of Wight food scene in recent years, and his opening in converted shop premises amid the bustle of Newport in 2015 represented a bold new departure. Some of the building's old looks have been retained, but the feel is clean and fresh, white and bright, its kitchen open to view. Don't miss the focaccia rolls with seaweed butter, while you ponder a menu built from thoroughbred island produce refracted through Thompson's elevated technical vision. An array of tomato varieties with goats' cheese mousse is a simple but stunning way in, and could be followed by an astonishing terrine of smoked eel, foie gras, ham hock and apple with celeriac rémoulade. Meats benefit from a straightforward approach, perhaps lamb rump and shoulder with richly stewed morels, spring veg and a dot of glossy mushroom ketchup. Rhubarb parfait was oddly tough at inspection; perhaps go for the espresso crème brûlée made with dulce de leche. Wines feature some interesting growers, but the list is very much in development, starting at £17.

Chef/s: Robert Thompson. **Open:** Tue to Sat L 12 to 3, D 6 to 9.30. **Closed:** Sun, Mon. **Meals:** main courses £16 to £28. Set L £17 (2 courses) to £22. **Details:** 48 seats. Bar. Music.

LOCAL GEM

The Bistro

Modern European | £35
30 Pier Street, Ventnor, Isle of Wight, PO38 1SX
Tel no: (01983) 852271
thebistroventnor.co.uk

£5
OFF

Last year's Hillside Bistro is now just the Bistro, reflecting its separation from the Hillside Hotel. The chef is now the owner, the dining room remains a simply stylish, gently contemporary space with a glass-frontage and open kitchen to the rear, and it's popular as a light-lunch pop-in – Ventnor Bay crab and mayo on toast, say, or salads. If you're after something more substantial look to the short à la carte for island-smoked trout on a curried cauliflower purée with dabs of riata, flatbread crisps and a swipe of mango chutney, 'tender, nicely cooked' chicken leg in a (rather too sweet) tagine-inspired tomato sauce full of olives and aubergine, and 'one of the best îles flottantes I've ever had'. Wines from £17.

LOCAL GEM

The Crab Shed

Seafood | £15
Tamarisk, Love Lane, Steephill Cove, Isle of Wight, PO38 1AF
Tel no: (01983) 855819
steephillcove-isleofwight.co.uk

🛏 £30

Overlooking the beach at ravishing Steephill Cove, the Shed catches its own crabs, lobsters and mackerel in the waters you can see, and does very little to them other than dress them in traditional ways, the better for everyone to enjoy. Expect warm crab pasties, mackerel piled into ciabatta for heavenly sandwiches, and signature lunches of lobster in citrus butter, served with Parmesan-garnished saladings. Other freshly caught fish that don't appear on the core menu are worth enquiring about, and there are wodges of homemade Victoria sponge to ensure the job's a good 'un. Wine is £16.

LOCAL GEM
The Hut
Modern British | £30
Colwell Bay, Colwell Chine Road, Isle of Wight, PO40 9NP
Tel no: (01983) 898637
thehutcolwell.co.uk

Here's a novelty: you can arrive at the Hut by boat. Even if you don't sail, its Colwell Bay location and stylish looks give this seasonal restaurant a charm that's particularly special in touristy west Wight. Seafood purists might balk at the tuna tartare and Norwegian king crab, but there is locally landed stuff to be found (try the specials board) and sunny brasserie influences pervade the rest of the menu in seafood linguine with bouillabaisse or prawn salad with fennel, orange and radicchio. Wine is from £16.50.

■ Lymington
The Elderflower
Cooking score: 4
Modern British | £40
4-5 Quay Street, Lymington, SO41 3AS
Tel no: (01590) 676908
elderflowerrestaurant.co.uk
£5 OFF 🛏

Pitched centre stage on a cobbled street in the heart of the old town, Andrew and Marjolaine du Bourg's small restaurant-with-rooms is decorated in a distinctly stripped back fashion. Yet if it all looks unassuming, think again. Andrew works extremely hard to put good food on the plates of his customers with dishes such as smoked foie gras, popcorn, orange, salt caramel and toasted brioche or stuffed English tulip with home-smoked haddock, watercress, mussel broth and tarragon oil

nodding to time spent as a head chef at Club Gascon, London and Chewton Glen, Hampshire (see entries). Elsewhere, New Forest wild boar served with Jerusalem artichoke, dried figs and prunes, apple and quince, confit beetroot and aromatic jus shows an understanding of how to flatter good meat, while dessert includes the hugely popular 'close but no cigar' (coffee cup and chocolate cigar). At lunch, Les Petites Assiettes brings a selection of small plates including 72-hour slow-cooked beef rib, and chicken, bacon and mushroom pie. Wines from £17.
Chef/s: Andrew du Bourg. **Open:** Tue to Sun L 12 to 2.30, Tue to Sat D 6.30 to 9.30 (10 Fri and Sat). **Closed:** Mon. **Meals:** main courses £20 to £26. Tasting menu £60 (9 courses). **Details:** 40 seats. Music.

■ Lyndhurst
Hartnett Holder & Co.
Cooking score: 3
Italian | £55
Lime Wood Hotel, Beaulieu Road, Lyndhurst, SO43 7FZ
Tel no: (02380) 287167
limewoodhotel.co.uk
🛏

Hotels really don't come any more laid-back than this dazzling country pile with acreage and annexes ('and lots of 4x4s in the large car park'). Of course, the sense of occasion is there – in the formality of the drawing room and library, the generous sofas and armchairs – but the light fittings are funky, the artwork modern, the bar holds centre court and service is young and enthusiastic. Radiating off the bar are a series of dining rooms under the supervision of consultant chef Angela Hartnett (see entry Murano, London) and resident chef Luke Holder – so expect classy plates of Italian food. Reporters have praised the vitello tonnato, wild rabbit bolognaise with Parmesan gnocchi, tortellini with buttered crab and 'nduja, and bream baked in a pastry-topped dish filled with a rich truffled bisque and served with a simple fennel, hazelnut and date salad. The extensive wine list opens at £25.

Chef/s: Angela Hartnett and Luke Holder. **Open:** all week 12 to 11. **Meals:** main courses £18 to £53. Set L £20 (2 courses) to £25. Sun L £38. **Details:** 62 seats. 40 seats outside. Bar. Wheelchairs. Music. Parking.

Milford on Sea

★ NEW ENTRY ★

La Perle

Cooking score: 2
British | £35
60 High Street, Milford on Sea, SO41 0QD
Tel no: (01590) 643557
laperle.co.uk

In this tranquil Hampshire seaside village, bordered on one side by the New Forset, on the other by Chichester Harbour, Sam Hughes' debut restaurant has quickly gained a local following. Prior to taking over La Perle in June 2015, Hughes worked in notable establishments in London, but he's a local boy returning to his roots and raw materials are sourced from small producers in Hampshire and Dorset. Generosity and big flavours are the kitchen's touchstones, from a twice-baked smoked haddock and Old Winchester cheese soufflé (a trusted favourite), via a beautifully presented spring salad of asparagus, Jersey Royals, golden beetroot, and Dorset Blue Vinney cheese, to Huntsham Farm pork cutlet with potato and bacon dauphinois, hispi cabbage, Chantenay carrots and red wine sauce, and a 'beautifully cooked' steak from a small herd in nearby Romsey. Homemade bread and butter are irresistible, and you can indulge a sweet tooth with chocolate and pistachio fondant with pistachio ice cream. Wines from £18.95.

Chef/s: Sam Hughes. **Open:** Wed to Sun L 12 to 2.30. Tue to Sat D 6 to 9.30. **Closed:** Mon. **Meals:** main meals £19 to £29. Set L £15 (2 courses) to £19. Tasting menu £55. **Details:** 28 seats. Wheelchairs.

New Milton

The Dining Room

Cooking score: 4
Modern British | £60
Chewton Glen Hotel, Christchurch Road, New Milton, BH25 6QS
Tel no: (01425) 275341
chewtonglen.com
£5 OFF

Chewton Glen celebrated its 50th anniversary early in 2016, and it continues to evolve as a dream ticket for pleasurable pursuits, with the hotel's capacious restaurant simmering nicely in its current incarnation. Bold contemporary furnishings add some pizazz to proceedings, while the kitchen pulls together influences from faraway lands in its search for flavour and variety: a signature twice-baked Emmental soufflé rubs shoulders with tuna tataki and avocado purée, while mains span everything from Quantock duck breast with sweet potato, ruby chard and heritage carrots to Thai lobster curry with coconut rice. Grills and roasts from the trolley strike a more traditional note, ahead of imaginative desserts such as pineapple and black pepper tarte Tatin. Chewton Glen's encyclopaedic wine list is loaded with treasures for those with money to spare; prices rise steeply from £30.

Chef/s: Luke Matthews. **Open:** all week L 12 to 2 (2.30 Sun), D 6 to 9.30 (10 Fri and Sat). **Meals:** main courses £19 to £42. Set L £22 (2 courses) to £27. Tasting menu £70. **Details:** 158 seats. 100 seats outside. Bar. Wheelchairs. Music. Parking.

Old Basing

The Crown

Cooking score: 3
British | £30
The Street, Old Basing, RG24 7BW
Tel no: (01256) 321424
thecrownoldbasing.com

Thoroughly rooted in the village of Old Basing, this 'proper country pub' is a 'great addition to the Basingstoke area'. The listed building is a cosy, rustic kind of place with an air of no-nonsense simplicity and knows how to win friends with its selection of real ales and appealing cooking. Much of the menu runs along familiar lines, taking in excellent crisp-breaded creamy Tunworth cheese with local ale chutney or a thick slice of chicken and ham hock terrine with pickled vegetables, quince and watercress, then a main course of slow-cooked pork belly with shallots (caramelised and puréed), fondant potatoes and wilted greens. Elsewhere, reporters have praised the twice-baked cheese soufflé and the burger in a brioche bun. There's homemade bread, too, and desserts such as cinnamon doughnuts with chocolate sauce. Wines from £18. Note: Tom Wilson, previously head chef here, has moved to sister establishment, the Hoddington Arms, Upton Grey.

Chef/s: Dale Chamberlain. **Open:** all week L 12 to 2 (2.30 Fri to Sun), Mon to Sat D 6 to 9 (9.30 Fri and Sat). **Closed:** 26 Dec, 1 Jan. **Meals:** main courses £10 to £23. **Details:** 60 seats. 56 seats outside. Bar. Music. Parking.

∎ Petersfield
Annie Jones
Cooking score: 3
Modern British | £40
10 Lavant Street, Petersfield, GU32 3EW
Tel no: (01730) 262728
anniejones.co.uk
£5
OFF

'I was very pleasantly surprised by Annie Jones – and had no hint of just how big the place is,' was the verdict of one visitor who discovered not only a little restaurant smartly and cutely decked out with panelled walls, lovely big table lamps, a polished wood floor and comfy, high-backed chairs, but also an outside terrace and bar offering a large tapas menu, and a café. Back in the restaurant, a simple but apparently ambitious and good-value menu features dishes such as watercress and potato soup with buttered haddock, and 'a deftly done' steak tartare topped with delicately pickled vegetables and served with mellow wild garlic mayonnaise, alongside mains of a 'whacking great piece' of silky turbot matched with a few

slices of new potato tossed in seaweed butter, a medley of peas (a few still in-pod), broad beans and green beans and a subtle bisque, or a ham hock-stuffed rabbit saddle with carrot purée, wild garlic and goats' cheese risotto. A precisely layered trifle of rhubarb, orange, ginger and honeycomb is a good way to finish. Wines from £19.50.

Chef/s: A Parker. **Open:** Wed to Sun L 12 to 2, Wed to Sat D 6 to 10. **Closed:** Mon, Tue, 25 and 26 Dec, first week Jan. **Meals:** set L £28 (2 courses) to £35. Set D £30 (2 courses) to £40. Sun L £16 (1 course). **Details:** 22 seats. 60 seats outside. Bar. Parking.

JSW
Cooking score: 6
Modern British | £50
20 Dragon Street, Petersfield, GU31 4JJ
Tel no: (01730) 262030
jswrestaurant.com

A former coaching inn dating back to the Stuart era, Jake Watkins' place offers a beguiling mix of the age-gnarled and the contemporary with its old beams and glass-covered well, and the sleek contemporary finish of the main dining room. There are tables under cream sunshades out back. Mr Watkins sources conscientiously, mixing local produce with Cumbrian meats and poultry from across the Channel in a style that combines up-to-date freshness with a sparkling vein of wit. 'A cheeky bit of belly' (which is it?) in a distinctly demotic dressing of onions and malt vinegar might open the bidding, prior to a sea-fresh serving of turbot with spiced mussels and lettuce, or there may be duck, its traditional orange in the form of a salted purée, as well as hay-baked parsnips and sea asters. At dessert, two good things are smooshed together in the shape of rice pudding cheesecake, adorned with tropical fruits. The wine list is a triumph of the compiler's art, presented traditionally in its regions, but crammed with important growers and incorporating little flights of this and that, rather than single representatives. Prices open at £19.50.

Chef/s: Jake Saul Watkins. **Open:** Thur to Sun L 12 to 1.30, Wed to Sat D 7 to 9. **Closed:** Mon, Tue, 2 weeks from 25 Dec, 2 weeks spring, 2 weeks Sep. **Meals:** set L £30 (2 courses) to £40. Set D £40 (2 courses) to £50. Tasting menu £60 (6 courses) to £80. **Details:** 50 seats. 28 seats outside. Wheelchairs. Parking.

▌Portsmouth
Abarbistro
Cooking score: 2
Modern British | £26
58 White Hart Road, Portsmouth, PO1 2JA
Tel no: (023) 9281 1585
abarbistro.co.uk
£30

The old hotel on this site was once a holding pen for transportees to the North American penal colonies, and its location still packs them in, on their way these days to nothing more punitive than the Isle of Wight ferry. It's now a jolly, amiably run bistro with bags of personality, bare-wood tables and a glazed ceiling. The kitchen does the traditional things well, offering fat juicy mussels in a creamless wine liquor, good crisply fried squid with pungent aïoli and an unimpeachable take on crab and chips with decent mayo. Roasts are naturally popular on Sundays, while the specials board might run to red mullet with mango and avocado salsa, and sea trout on lemon thyme risotto. Coffee and white chocolate crème brûlée offers 'silky-smooth texture, wizard flavour balance and uniform, properly crackable caramel' – heaven in a ramekin. The brief wine list has some cracking bargains, starting with Campo de Borja varietals at £14.50.
Chef/s: Mark Andrew. **Open:** all week 12 to 10.30 (11 Fri and Sat, 10 Sun). **Closed:** 25 and 26 Dec. **Meals:** main courses £12 to £20. **Details:** 100 seats. 80 seats outside. Bar. Wheelchairs. Music.

▌Southsea
Restaurant 27
Cooking score: 4
Modern European | £45
27a South Parade, Southsea, PO5 2JF
Tel no: (023) 9287 6272
restaurant27.com

Once a gymnasium, Restaurant 27's barn-like dimensions, formality and Spartan décor might seem an odd fit for food that bristles with bold gestures. Kevin Bingham specialises in a kind of free-spirited cooking and his terse menus conceal a huge amount of hard work, intricate detailing and techno-wizardry: roasted chicken terrine, miso and mustard; BBQ glazed beef with caramelised onion; butter-poached king prawns, wild garlic and toasted Parmesan. Seasonal heritage flavours are also given full rein, be it a heritage tomato salad with avocado, goats' curd and gazpacho or umami duck with truffled peas and roasted purple carrot. There's no let-up when it comes to elaborately worked desserts, either – think blueberry-poached pineapple with fennel ice cream and toasted nougat. On Sundays, there is the pleasure of a traditional roast, aided by smiling, unhurried service. A well-balanced wine list starts at £19.50.
Chef/s: Kevin Bingham. **Open:** Sun L 12 to 2.30, Wed to Sat D 6.30 to 9.30. **Closed:** Mon, Tue, 25 and 26 Dec, 1 Jan. **Meals:** set L £29. Set D £45. Sun L £29. Tasting menu £42 (6 courses) to £50 (8 courses). **Details:** 36 seats. V menu. Music.

▌Sparsholt
The Avenue
Cooking score: 5
Modern British | £58
Lainston House Hotel, Woodman Lane,
Sparsholt, SO21 2LT
Tel no: (01962) 776088
lainstonhouse.com
£5 OFF

Named after the mile-long avenue of lime trees that leads up to this red-brick William and Mary mansion, Lainston's showpiece restaurant puts on an impressive show. All the usual country-house rules and axioms apply here, from the starched linen and equally starched service (in a good way) to the vintage portraits, leather upholstery and mahogany-panelled walls in the dining room. Olly Rouse's cooking offers something more contemporary and open-minded, but with an undercurrent of silky sophistication – as in a duo of crab and herring fashionably dressed with green tea, yuzu, black olive and apple or turbot partnered by chicken wing, miso, turnip and grape. By contrast, meat and game often receive more robust treatment, from duck with celeriac, plum and almond to a plate of glazed pork fillet with smoked bacon, black pudding, pickled onion and cracked wheat. Meanwhile, desserts explore more exotic realms for the likes of macadamia with passion fruit, mango and milk ice cream. The wine list promises comprehensive global coverage, with house recommendations from £26.

Chef/s: Olly Rouse. **Open:** Wed to Fri and Sun L 12 to 2, all week D 7 to 9.30. **Meals:** set L £26 (2 courses) to £33. Set D £48 (2 courses) to £58. Sun L £39. Tasting menu £75 (8 courses). **Details:** 60 seats. 50 seats outside. V menu. Bar. Wheelchairs. Music. Parking.

▮ Stockbridge
The Greyhound on the Test
Cooking score: 2
Modern British | £35
31 High Street, Stockbridge, SO20 6EY
Tel no: (01264) 810833
thegreyhoundonthetest.co.uk

This lovingly restored village inn is popular for its delightful location (the garden backs on to the river Test) and décor pitched agreeably somewhere between rustic watering hole and upper-crust inn-with-rooms. Scrubbed tables and candles set an unfussy tone in the dining room and the menu combines classy renditions of pub classics with a bit of brasserie-style razzle-dazzle. Smoked haddock kedgeree, chicken liver parfait or small plates of, say, scallop ceviche with

fennel, pickled mouli, pea and wasabi might precede mains such as herb-crusted cannon of lamb with braised shoulder and crispy sweetbreads. To finish, there might be salted-caramel and peanut parfait with chocolate and olive oil ganache, or a selection of Hampshire cheeses. The set lunch menu is good value and house French is £21.

Chef/s: Chris Heather. **Open:** all week L 12 to 3 (4 Sat and Sun), D 6 to 9.30. **Closed:** 25 and 26 Dec. **Meals:** main courses £13 to £25. Set L £15 (2 courses) to £20. **Details:** 58 seats. 24 seats outside. Bar. Music. Parking.

LOCAL GEM
Woodfire
Mediterranean | £20
High Street, Stockbridge, SO20 6EX
Tel no: (01264) 810248
woodfirestockbridge.co.uk

£30

A colourful café with outdoor tables is the setting for sunny Mediterranean flavours on Stockbridge's main drag. Woodfire is the medium over which the pizzas are baked, toppings including potato, fontina, onion, pancetta and rosemary, and there are classic meze for sharing, such as baba ganoush and grilled haloumi sprinkled with lemon and oregano. Big salad platters are laden with good things, while robust appetites might look to monkfish and chorizo skewers with cannellini and piquillos. Add some crema catalana, and happiness can't be far away.

▮ Stuckton
The Three Lions
Cooking score: 3
Anglo-French | £42
Stuckton, SP6 2HF
Tel no: (01425) 652489
thethreelionsrestaurant.co.uk

£5 OFF

A welcoming country inn with rooms and a conservatory extension, the Three Lions has been Mike and Jayne Womersley's labour of

love for over 20 years now. Buried deep in the New Forest, it's in the kind of setting that lends meaning to the principle of seasonality, and has a visitors' book that includes political VIPs and grand old men of rock. Mike emphatically doesn't favour tricksy modern presentation, so you won't find him smearing or squiggling anything, but his simply based French and English dishes continue to offer genuine satisfaction. Artichoke and cep ravioli remains a favoured way of starting, or there could be smoked haddock galette, prior to truffled venison loin and endive, or the vividly scented delight that is sea bass in saffron and tarragon sauce. Proceedings conclude with hazelnut parfait, decorated with a pistachio tuile and cherries. Wines start at £15.75, or £3.75 a glass, for Italian blends.
Chef/s: Mike Womersley. **Open:** Tue to Sun L 12 to 2, Tue to Sat D 7 to 9. **Closed:** Mon, last 2 weeks Feb. **Meals:** main courses £19 to £27. Set L £24 (3 courses). Set D £30 (3 courses). **Details:** 60 seats. 10 seats outside. Bar. Wheelchairs. Music. Parking.

▌Upton Grey

★ NEW ENTRY ★

The Hoddington Arms
Cooking score: 2
British | £30
Bidden Road, Upton Grey, RG25 2RL
Tel no: (01256) 862371
hoddingtonarms.co.uk
£5 OFF

The small village of Upton Grey has a pretty church, a duck pond and, thanks to Chris and Fallon Barnes, a thriving public house. The Barnes (who also own the Crown at Old Basing, see entry) took over in spring 2015 and have retained the splashes of heritage paint, tweedy cushions and classy country finish. Kick off with a warm Tunworth cheese (a local fave) and caramelised onion tart or a cracking pork and chorizo Scotch egg, before moving on to a Westcombe Cheddar twice-baked soufflé (which didn't quite rise to the occasion for one reader) or dry-aged English steaks with triple-cooked chips. In the summer the

pizza oven and cabana BBQ come into their own. Among desserts, dark chocolate and hazelnut délice with salted-caramel ice cream is an indulgent little number. Wines start at £18.
Chef/s: Chris Barnes. **Open:** all week L 12 to 2 (2.30 Fri and Sat, 3 Sun), Mon to Sat D 6 to 9 (9.30 Fri and Sat). **Meals:** main courses £12 to £25. Set L £18 (2 courses) to £25. **Details:** 60 seats. 60 seats outside. Bar. Wheelchairs. Music. Parking.

▌Winchester
The Black Rat
new chef/no score
Modern British | £45
88 Chesil Street, Winchester, SO23 0HX
Tel no: (01962) 844465
theblackrat.co.uk
£5 OFF

It's a five-minute walk from the city centre, yet it's easy to pass the Black Rat by as it looks like any other ancient town boozer. Now a restaurant, the boho chic of the dining room – itself divided into a number of small rooms – with beams and rug-strewn creaky floorboards and oddball ornaments 'looks less like a converted pub than the house of an eccentric, ageing millionaire'. It made the perfect setting for Ollie Moore's contemporary cooking. However, as we went to press we learned of Ollie Moore's imminent departure with his replacement, John Marsden, yet to take up the position of head chef. Elsewhere, popular set weekend lunches should continue, service is low-key and friendly, and wines start at £22.
Chef/s: John Marsden. **Open:** Sat and Sun L 12 to 2, all week D 7 to 9. **Closed:** 2 weeks Christmas and New Year, 10 days Easter, 10 days end of summer. **Meals:** main courses £20 to £25. Set L £26 (2 courses). Set D £29 (2 courses). **Details:** 40 seats. 16 seats outside. Bar. Music. Children over 12 yrs only at D.

The Chesil Rectory

Cooking score: 4
Modern British | £34
1 Chesil Street, Winchester, SO23 0HU
Tel no: (01962) 851555
chesilrectory.co.uk

The Rectory lays claim to being the oldest house in Winchester, built in 1450 and looking all of its nearly six hundred years, with a top-heavy half-timbered façade and ancient beams and floorboards within. Lighting levels are dim, but there's nothing dim about Damian Brown's star-bright modern bistro cooking, which is full of nice surprises, from the oil and dukkah served with breads to a heavenly starter of cured sea bass, the strips of fish flash-macerated in lime and lemon and garnished with coriander, 'one of the best dishes I've eaten all year,' a reader declared. Otherwise, there might be duck and lentil ballotine with piccalilli and buttered shallots, and robust main dishes like 12-hour braised featherblade with horseradish mash and fine beans, or peppered venison in blackcurrant syrup. Set muscovado cream with sour plums and gingerbread suggests a willingness to think outside the dessert box. House wine £23.
Chef/s: Damian Brown. **Open:** all week L 12 to 2.20 (3 Sat, 4 Sun), D 6 to 9 (10 Fri and Sat). **Closed:** 25 and 26 Dec, 1 Jan. **Meals:** main courses £14 to £21. Set L and D £17 (2 courses) to £20. Sun L £22 (2 courses) to £27. **Details:** 75 seats. Bar. Music. Children at L only.

oven reflecting a penchant for roasting: quail with carrot, smoked egg, yoghurt and charred gem, and poussin with pommes Anna, carrot and girolles are typical of the menu. At a test meal, brill had spent a little too long in the oven, but accompaniments of caviar sauce, crushed peas and pak choi did the fish justice, and a dessert of chocolate crémeux with Amaretto jelly and coffee ice cream was an enjoyable spin on tiramisu flavours. In addition, a lunchtime set menu is popular with locals and represents excellent value. A glass-fronted wine cave is a feature of the dining room, displaying bottles from a singularly impressive list grouped, conveniently, by style and featuring superb value, courtesy of owner Gerard Basset's innumerable contacts. Bottles start at £18.75, but it's the range around the £50 mark that is superb.
Chef/s: Gavin Barnes. **Open:** all week L 12 to 2 (3.15 Sun), D 7 to 9.15 (9.30 Fri and Sat). **Meals:** main courses £19 to £29. Set L £22 (2 courses) to £27. Sun L £24. Tasting menu £65. **Details:** 56 seats. 26 seats outside. V menu. Bar. Wheelchairs. Parking.

▮ Woodlands
Hotel TerraVina

Cooking score: 3
Modern European | £45
174 Woodlands Road, Woodlands, SO40 7GL
Tel no: (023) 8029 3784
hotelterravina.co.uk
£5 OFF 🍾 🛏

TerraVina is a smart – if slightly dated – hotel on the edge of the New Forest. The pretty dining room has 'a lovely view out over a raised wooden patio and immaculate gardens' and features an open kitchen, its huge wood

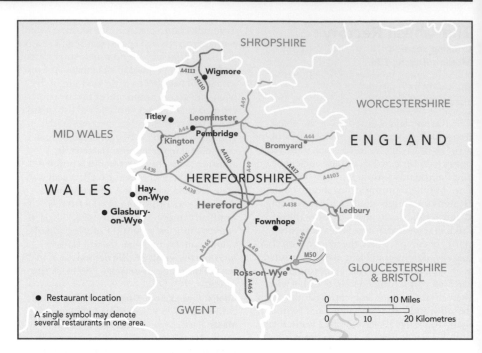

Restaurant location

A single symbol may denote several restaurants in one area.

Fownhope

The Greenman

Cooking score: 1
Modern British | £32
Fownhope, HR1 4PE
Tel no: (01432) 860243
thegreenman.co

A lovely oak-beamed old inn that makes the most of its position in a pretty village within striking distance of Hereford, it's ideally placed for friendly get-togethers and special occasions, though plenty of locals use it on a regular basis. The pub is busy with pint drinkers discussing the day's events, occasionally over a bite to eat, but there's a dedicated dining room for those who want to do it properly. The menu celebrates local produce in season: expect plenty of strawberries, asparagus, apples and pears etc to slip into the dishes, both sweet and savoury.

The kitchen has ambition and drive, but occasionally tries to be a little too clever – diners who stick to the classics get the best results. Locally bred steaks are likely to be more successful than brill with a chorizo dauphinois and sautéed mussels. There's local beer and cider on offer, and an OK wine list, kicking off at around £5 a glass.
Chef/s: Joe Dowling. **Open:** all week 12 to 9.30 (9 Sun). **Meals:** main courses £12 to £19. **Details:** 54 seats. Bar. Parking.

Glasbury-on-Wye

LOCAL GEM
The River Café

International | £23
Glasbury-on-Wye, HR3 5NP
Tel no: (01497) 847007
wyevalleycanoes.co.uk

Not to be confused with its celebrity namesake in Hammersmith (see entry), this River Café is housed within the Wye Valley

Canoe Centre, overlooking the water – an unlikely setting for vivacious food inspired by the global larder. 'Light bites' of spiced chickpea fritters with quinoa salad or hoisin pork belly with Asian slaw might give way to mushroom and spinach pappardelle or Indian-style braised shoulder of lamb, with venison faggots and battered cod flying the Union flag. Handy for breakfast, too. Wines from £15.95.

▌Hay-on-Wye

★ NEW ENTRY ★

St John's Place

Cooking score: 1
Modern British | £32
Lion Street, Hay-on-Wye, HR3 5AA
Tel no: (07855) 783799
stjohnsplacehay.tumblr.com
£5
OFF

In the old hall of a Methodist church in the middle of town, this small, occasional restaurant (it's only open at weekends) has a worthy earnestness that suits its pared down, simple setting – 'there's not much competition for good food in the area, and the kitchen here is head and shoulders above the rest'. The short menu offers three choices per course, shows great inventiveness and gives a real nod to local, seasonal ingredients: a crisp-fried aubergine caponata served with goats' curd might sit alongside a bowl of crab and shrimp on a bed of white polenta or a quick-cooked skirt steak paired with green nectarine and kim-chee. Most stick to the house wines on tap at £18 per bottle. Note: cash only.
Chef/s: Julia Robson. **Open:** Fri and Sat D 6 to 11.
Closed: Sun to Thur, 24 to 26 Dec, 2 weeks May/Jun. **Meals:** main courses £15 to £19. **Details:** 25 seats.

Richard Booth's Bookshop Café

Modern British | £18
44 Lion Street, Hay-on-Wye, HR3 5AA
Tel no: (01497) 820322
boothbooks.co.uk
£30

It may be 'more of a snack place than a proper restaurant', but it is worth paying homage to Richard Booth's splendidly overstocked bookshop and rustic café. A dangerous place for book lovers – so easy to lose track of time – the café serves light dishes all day. Pancakes with vanilla whipped yoghurt and maple syrup, 'some interesting soups' and 'delicious cakes with coffee' have all been praised, but look out for lunch dishes of chicken liver and bacon on ciabatta with chips and herbed aïoli or Caesar salad with crayfish. Dinner is served Friday and Saturday only.

▌Pembridge

The Cider Barn

British | £30
Dunkertons Cider Mill, Pembridge, HR6 9ED
Tel no: (01544) 388161
the-cider-barn.co.uk

Marry an atmospheric old barn – part of an organic cider mill – with a warm welcome and food to nourish belly and soul and you have the Cider Barn. Chef Sophie Griffiths-Goddard's compact menu of 'superb', honest and creative dishes celebrates seasons and unashamedly supports local suppliers. Follow a starter of smoked ham, crispy poached egg and parsnip crisps with a generous haunch of venison with persillade, or tender fillet and braised short ribs of Hereford beef. If you can make room for rapeseed cake with blood-orange and lavender ice cream, you'll leave all the happier.

■ Titley
The Stagg Inn

Cooking score: 4
Modern British | £35
Titley, HR5 3RL
Tel no: (01544) 230221
thestagg.co.uk
£5 OFF ▲ 🛏

The Reynolds' characterful country bolt-hole blazed the trail for local produce-led pub dining in the 1990s and continues to fly the flag today, with Nicola leading a top-notch front-of-house team and Steve in charge of the kitchen. Begin amid the warm glow of the traditional bar – all bare beams and hanging beer jugs – then move to one of the more refined restaurant areas for your meal. Little extras such as homemade potato crisps with balsamic foam and pulled pork bonbons with barbecue dip hit the spot, and a main course of vegetable Wellington with caramelised shallots and a red wine sauce is right on the money, with 'crisp, buttery pastry and clear, interesting flavours'. At the meaty end of the spectrum, the juicy steak with pickled onion rings, watercress and chips ticks all the right boxes. For dessert, try the 'gorgeous' bread-and-butter pudding – 'crisply caramelised on top, moist and creamy underneath'. Besides great beers, ciders and perry, there is an appealing selection of mostly European wines starting at £17.
Chef/s: Steve Reynolds. **Open:** Wed to Sun L 12 to 2 (2.30 Sun), D 6.30 to 9 (8.30 Sun). **Closed:** Mon, Tue, 25 Dec, 1 Jan, 1 week Feb, first 2 weeks Nov. **Meals:** main courses £17 to £25. Sun L £22. **Details:** 70 seats. 20 seats outside. V menu. Bar. Parking.

■ Wigmore
★ NEW ENTRY ★
The Oak

Cooking score: 3
British | £30
Ford Street, Wigmore, HR6 9UJ
Tel no: (01568) 770424
theoakwigmore.com
🛏

On the crossroads in a well-preserved Herefordshire village stands the Oak, a country inn for our times. Its venerable shell is visible in the roughcast walls and antique fireplace implements, but the place has had an intelligent contemporary design job that includes a tiled dining area where hanging fronds of fairy lights, and faultlessly cheery service, illuminate the scene. Local suppliers buttress the menus, which are of impeccably timely, smartly presented modern dishes full of precision and inspiration. A generous bowl of smoked river Lugg trout and crayfish chowder, or gently spiced potted rabbit with sensational Agen prune purée, might be the preludes to delicately timed sea bass with puréed peas and watercress dressing, or a threeway of pork – tenderloin, crumbed rillettes and glorious homemade black pudding with beetroot purée and apple jus. Finish with baked lemon cheesecake, or a brûlée jazzed up with coffee and white chocolate, served with a chunk of honeycomb. Wines from £18.
Chef/s: Rory Bunting. **Open:** Sat and Sun L 12 to 3, Wed to Sun D 6.30 to 9 (6 Sat). **Closed:** Mon, Tue, 26 Dec. **Meals:** main courses £15 to £25. Sun L £15 (1 course) to £23. **Details:** 40 seats. 10 seats outside. Bar. Wheelchairs. Music. Parking.

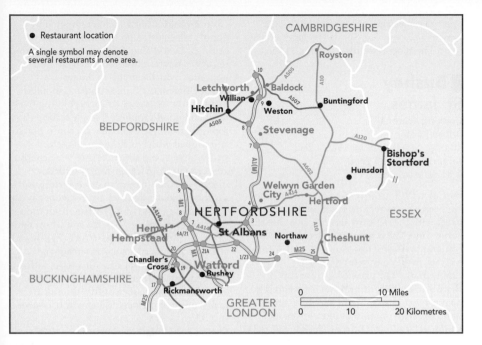

Restaurant location

A single symbol may denote several restaurants in one area.

CAMBRIDGESHIRE

Royston

Letchworth
Willian
Hitchin
Baldock
Weston
Buntingford

BEDFORDSHIRE

Stevenage

Bishop's Stortford

Hunsdon

Welwyn Garden City
Hertford

HERTFORDSHIRE

ESSEX

Hemel Hempstead
St Albans
Northaw
Cheshunt

Chandler's Cross
Watford
Bushey

BUCKINGHAMSHIRE

Rickmansworth

GREATER LONDON

0   10 Miles
0   10   20 Kilometres

▌Bishop's Stortford
Water Lane
Cooking score: 1
Modern British | £29
31 Water Lane, Bishop's Stortford, CM23 2JZ
Tel no: (01279) 211888
waterlane.co
£30

Hewn out of the Georgian Hawkes brewery building, Water Lane boasts a vaulted cellar bar and a spacious ground-floor restaurant and mezzanine level. Part of the Anglian Country Inns group (see Hermitage Rd, Hitchin), it specialises in market-driven menus of eclectic modern British food with obvious appeal. Sharing boards of nibbly things are perfect for piquing the appetite, which might then take in herb-crusted cod with wild mushrooms and mash in clam and spinach cream, or a chilli-chicken and chorizo burger with lime mayo. A sticky pudding flavoured with bourbon and cola, glooped in butterscotch sauce, is the way to go. House Duboeuf is £17.50.

Chef/s: Kumour Uddin. **Open:** all week 12 to 10 (10 to 4 Sun). **Meals:** main courses £10 to £24. Set L and D £13 (2 courses) to £16. **Details:** 80 seats. Bar. Wheelchairs. Music.

▌Buntingford

LOCAL GEM
Pearce's Farmshop and Café
Modern European | £28
Hamels Mead, Buntingford, SG9 9ND
Tel no: (01920) 821246
pearcesfarmshop.com
£30

Just off a lay-by on the A10 is a farm shop that is quite the foodie hot spot. Fill your boot with fruit and veg and artisan British cheeses, or pick your own raspberries and strawberries, but make sure you pop into the charming café with its rural aspect and wooden tables and chairs. Expect sandwiches, crispy duck salad, open game pie and whole plaice with tiger prawns and caponata. Sunday includes a classic roast. The short wine list starts at £14.95.

▮ Bushey
St James
Cooking score: 1
British | £35
30 High Street, Bushey, WD23 3HL
Tel no: (020) 8950 2480
stjamesrestaurant.co.uk

Hitting its 20th anniversary in 2017, St James has been a consistent presence on the high street with the same owner and same chef the entire time. The interior is smart and contemporary, but not too fancy, and Alfonso La Cava makes sure everything goes swimmingly. The kitchen's output covers British and broader European bases and is by no means stuck in the past; seared sea bream to start, say, with textures of cauliflower and lemon gel, followed by roast duck breast with a samosa filled with confit leg, or a blackened halibut with charred Little Gem. Set menus are a bonus. Wines start at £16.95.
Chef/s: Matt Cook. **Open:** all week L 12 to 2, Mon to Sat D 6.30 to 10. **Closed:** 25 and 26 Dec, bank hols. **Meals:** main courses £15 to £24. Set L £17 (2 courses) to £22. Set D £19 (2 courses) to £24. Sun L £21 (2 courses) to £26. **Details:** 100 seats. 20 seats outside. Bar. Wheelchairs. Music.

▮ Chandler's Cross
The Grove, Colette's
Cooking score: 5
Modern British | £65
Chandler's Cross, WD3 4TG
Tel no: (01923) 296010
thegrove.co.uk

Once 'one of the greatest political houses of the 19th century,' the Grove's smart urban conversion to a majestic hotel, spa and golf course is tailor-made for the gentrified affluence of Chandler's Cross. This is especially so of the dining room, the cosmopolitan air of which is tempered by double tablecloths and towering ornate ceilings. Everything here screams fine-dining luxury – but 'without too much faff and nonsense, which extends to the service.' Russell Bateman offers a compact, modern carte or five-course taster incorporating lively ideas and good supplies. A single scallop ('a top-spec example'), perhaps, on confit potato and topped with truffle mayo, apple and truffle slivers, and superb turbot – 'a generous amount cut from a large fish' – with 'an ingenious combination' of dried shrimp and scallop cooked down in a super-savoury syrup 'to resemble a kind of XO-paste', itself topped with super-crisp potato flakes and set on a pile of peas, pea purée and gem lettuce. Finish with an éclair filled with chocolate cream and banana ice cream topped with a crisp, toffee wafer and toasted peanuts. Canapés, bread, and the impressive slate of five cheeses, are really 'quite remarkable'. The wine list opens at £32.
Chef/s: Russell Bateman. **Open:** Sun L 12.30 to 2.30. Tue to Sat D only 6.30 to 9.30. **Closed:** Mon. **Meals:** Tue to Thur £59 (3 courses). Tasting menu £70. Fri and Sat £65 (3 courses). Tasting menu £85. Sun L £55. **Details:** 40 seats. 20 seats outside. Bar. Wheelchairs. Music. Parking. No children.

▮ Hitchin
Hermitage Rd
Cooking score: 2
Modern British | £28
20-21 Hermitage Road, Hitchin, SG5 1BT
Tel no: (01462) 433603
hermitagerd.co.uk
£30

The Nye family's Hermitage Rd is a clever operation designed to appeal to all-comers. The transition from a run-down ballroom/ nightclub to a striking dining pub with a popular, high-decibel bar shows what can be done with a little ingenuity and bags of expertise. With real ales on tap, a serious wine list and an open kitchen that's a hive of activity, attention to detail is shown where it matters – 'the atmosphere is fabulous, the food exceptional and service spot-on'. This is a huge first-floor operation and the menu works hard, structured and priced to allow one to dip in or take three courses, going from lunchtime sandwiches, char-grilled steaks and Sunday roasts to evening plates of sea bass with saffron, clam, pea and leek chowder, and Barbary duck breast with thyme potatoes, red cabbage, carrot and star anise purée and red wine jus. The spacious, light-filled surroundings fit the casual ethos very well. Wines from £17.50.

Chef/s: Will Ingarfill. **Open:** Mon to Fri L 12 to 2, D 6.30 to 10. Sat and Sun 12 to 10 (8 Sun). **Closed:** 25 Dec. **Meals:** main courses £12 to £25. **Details:** 150 seats. Bar. Wheelchairs. Music.

▮ Hunsdon

LOCAL GEM
Fox & Hounds
Modern British | £30
2 High Street, Hunsdon, SG12 8NH
Tel no: (01279) 043???
foxandhounds-hunsdon.co.uk

Chef-proprietor James Rix has worked in some canny kitchens over the years – Alastair Little to name but one – and with his wife, Bianca, has run this smart village pub since the mid-noughties. It's a proper pub with a garden and Adnams on tap, and a menu that goes from Cornish crab tacos to shepherd's pie. A Josper oven further beefs up its foodie credentials, turning out squid with piquillo peppers or spatchcocked French quail. Wines start at £17.

▮ Northaw
The Sun at Northaw
Cooking score: 2
British | £29
1 Judges Hill, Northaw, EN6 4NL
Tel no: (01707) 655507
thesunatnorthaw.co.uk
£5 OFF £30

A fashionably folksy vision of old Britannia, with echoes of farmers' markets and village hall get-togethers, this revamped 'free house

and dining rooms' is a cluttered hotchpotch of cookbooks, floral posies and odd-job furnishings with food maps on each table and boxes of produce deliberately laid out for all to see. Artisan ingredients from England's eastern counties show up strongly on a daily menu that might run from Hertfordshire wild rabbit and smoked bacon terrine with piccalilli or cured East Coast herrings with potatoes and dill crème fraîche, to thyme-roasted Norfolk chicken with Savoy cabbage and 'pigs in blankets', Blythburgh pork cutlets or smoked haddock fillet with colcannon, poached egg and grain-mustard sauce. Salads include some unexpected pairings, while fiercely patriotic desserts might feature a baked duck-egg custard tart with poached quince. Hand-pulled regional ales, farmhouse cheeses and around three dozen hand-picked wines (from £18 a bottle) complete the picture.

Chef/s: Oliver Smith. **Open:** Tue to Sun L 12 to 3 (4 Sun), Tue to Sat D 6 to 10. **Closed:** Mon. **Meals:** main courses £13 to £27. **Details:** 80 seats. 50 seats outside. Bar. Music. Parking.

▮ Rickmansworth

LOCAL GEM
Café in the Park
International | £15
The Aquadrome, Frogmoor Lane, Rickmansworth, WD3 1NB
Tel no: (01923) 711131
thecafeinthepark.com
£30

There's no doubt that this lovely café at the Aquadrome in Rickmansworth takes a dressed-down, casual approach to things. Honest intent and bold-as-brass food is the deal and the menu lays down an emphatic marker with the likes of cauliflower rice, za'atar chicken, pomegranate, macadamia and bacon crumb, Aberdeen Angus beef burgers in a brioche bun, and open sandwiches of, say, falafel, hummus and harissa. Breakfast ranges from French toast to the full Monty, there are 'gorgeous-looking homemade cakes', friendly pricing and 'smiling and happy' service.

St Albans

Bistro Paprika

Cooking score: 2
Modern European | £36
13 Catherine Street, St Albans, AL3 5BJ
Tel no: (01727) 568187
bistropaprika.co.uk

£5
OFF

Bistro Paprika may be a good ten-minute walk from the cathedral and slightly off the tourist track, but locals value the warmth of the welcome, the boho-chic dining room that is 'part French bistro, part old English tea room', and applaud the kitchen's efforts. The short, regularly changing menu delivers some ambitious cooking noted for unusual combinations and a feel for flavours and textures. A fine rabbit ballotine with carrot granita and tea mousse, followed by a sea bass fillet served with basil polenta, gazpacho, fennel and heirloom tomatoes ('fresh and summery'), and a generous plate of monkfish (three pieces) wrapped in pancetta, with smoked belly of pork (two pieces) and saffron potatoes, impressed at a test meal. Elaborately constructed desserts might feature a 'really, really delicious' white chocolate cheesecake with carrot jelly and orange sorbet. Wines offer serious global drinking, from £18.
Chef/s: Kyle Prunty. **Open:** Tue to Sat L 12 to 2.30, D 6 to 9 (9.30 Fri and Sat). **Closed:** Sun, Mon, 2 weeks Aug. **Meals:** main courses £18 to £23. **Details:** 24 seats. Music. Children over 12 yrs only.

Lussmanns

Cooking score: 1
Modern European | £28
Waxhouse Gate, off High Street, St Albans, AL3 4EW
Tel no: (01727) 851941
lussmanns.com

£5   £30
OFF

Andrei Lussmann's gang of three independently minded brasseries is doing Hertfordshire proud, although most plaudits go to this original branch hard by St Albans Cathedral. Billed as a 'Fish & Grill', Lussmann's has always taken consummate care with sourcing and provenance, which helps to make its 'reliable' all-day offer even more appealing. From Sussex free-range pork rillettes or Wobbly Bottom goats' cheese arancini to North African-spiced organic lamb salad or line-caught haddock and chips, everything on the 'well-balanced' menu sings of sustainability. Beers and wines (from £16.95) are also in keeping with the restaurant's ethos.
Chef/s: Nick McGeown. **Open:** all week 12 to 9.30 (10.30 Fri and Sat, 9 Sun). **Closed:** 25 and 26 Dec. **Meals:** main courses £13 to £24. Set L and early D £13 (2 courses) to £15. **Details:** 105 seats. Wheelchairs. Music.

Thompson St Albans

Cooking score: 5
Modern British | £45
2 Hatfield Road, St Albans, AL1 3RP
Tel no: (01727) 730777
thompsonstalbans.co.uk

Phil Thompson has been cooking at this weatherboarded cottage conversion for nigh on three years, so there's no longer any need to mention its former incarnation (Darcy's) in the restaurant name. Instead, St Albans itself now gets top billing, reminding everyone that Thompson's is, first and foremost, a community-minded neighbourhood destination. 'Ladies that lunch' packages, Sunday roasts, kids' menus and special fund-raising events reinforce the venue's local cred, while the chic brasserie-style interior is dressed up with stripped floors, floral artwork and pastel walls. Thompson's approach is all about giving acutely judged modern ideas a populist edge, with clever, modish themes and pin-sharp presentation as standard: roast loin of Lincolnshire rabbit with beer-pickled Roscoff onions, crisp bacon and anise jus; line-caught brill with coastal herbs, pear, mushroom ketchup and tarragon cream; 40-day sirloin of Dedham Vale beef with roast and pickled parsnip, Madeira-braised snails and black garlic. To finish, desserts such as rose-poached rhubarb with custard mousse and pistachio granola are equally on-trend. Seventeen wines by the glass open a kindly priced wine list with bottles from £22.

Chef/s: Phil Thompson. **Open:** Wed to Sun L 12 to 2 (3 Sun), Tue to Sat D 6 to 9 (9.30 Fri and Sat). **Closed:** Mon. **Meals:** main courses £23 to £27. Set L £19 (2 courses) to £23. Set D £21 (2 courses) to £25. Sun L £25 (2 courses) to £30. **Details:** 90 seats. 18 seats outside. Bar. Wheelchairs. Music.

LOCAL GEM

The Foragers

Modern British | £24

The Verulam Arms, 41 Lower Dagnall Street, St Albans, AL3 4QE

Tel no: (01727) 836004

the-foragers.com

£30

As its name suggests, this backstreet pub by St Albans Cathedral specialises in wild food, gleaned and foraged from the local countryside – plus additional maritime pickings from the coast. Check out the borscht with alexander-stem sauerkraut, slow-roast 'hogbelly' with pickled crab apples or the sweet woodruff cheesecake for afters. 'Verulam' venison burgers are apparently made to a Roman recipe, while the Highland 'seaside' broth is dressed with sea purslane and seaweed. Wild pickings also invigorate the Forager's home-brewed micro beers, cocktails and liqueurs. Wines from £16.95.

■ Weston

LOCAL GEM

The Cricketers

Modern British | £21

Damask Green Road, Weston, SG4 7DA

Tel no: (01462) 790273

thecricketersweston.co.uk

£30

Anglian Country Inns (aka the Nye family) are the brains behind this much extended and refurbished village pub. It still maintains that cosy pub feel – drinkers are warmly

welcomed with a lovely open fire in the bar area – but it is the wood-fired pizzas that are a major attraction, backed up by hearty dishes made with good ingredients. Pub classics predominate, along the lines of fish and chips, burgers, steaks, pies, generous lunchtime sandwiches and well-reported Sunday lunches. It's all very good value. Wines from £17.50.

■ Willian

The Fox

Cooking score: 2
Modern British | £30

Willian, SG6 2AE

Tel no: (01462) 480233

foxatwillian.co.uk

The Nye family of the White Horse, Brancaster Staithe (see entry, Norfolk) has set itself up as a champion of regional produce, and put its money where its mouth is at this classily refurbished village hostelry, which dates from the 18th century. It remains a local boozer with regularly changing real ales but trades as a serious eatery, too. Pub classics are outshone by an upbeat menu that touts anything from half a dozen tempura oysters with sweet chilli sauce, gin-cured sea trout and cucumber tartare with roasted lemon and tonic purée and a crispy poached egg, and braised lamb shoulder with truffle and champ potato cake. Readers have also endorsed old favourites such as deep-fried squid and cod goujons with roasted garlic aïoli, and a beef and pork burger with grilled Cheddar, smoked chilli and pepper relish and hand-cut chips. Finish with chocolate crémeux with compressed pineapple and coconut sorbet. Wines from £17.50.

Chef/s: Sherwin Jacobs. **Open:** all week L 12 to 2 (3 Sun), Mon to Sat D 6.30 to 9.15. **Meals:** main courses £12 to £22. **Details:** 120 seats. 80 seats outside. Bar. Wheelchairs. Music. Parking.

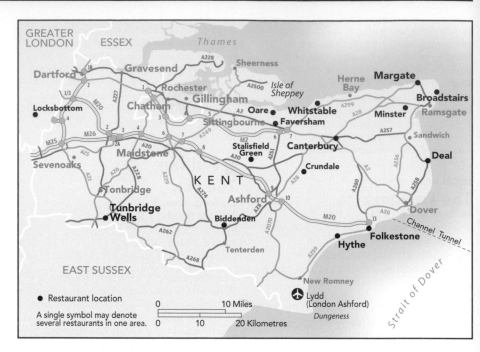

Biddenden
The West House

Cooking score: 5
Modern European | £45
28 High Street, Biddenden, TN27 8AH
Tel no: (01580) 291341
thewesthouserestaurant.co.uk

🍾

Drive slowly along the high street, or you may miss the West House, which has been fashioned from a pair of late-Tudor weavers' cottages. Inside feels appealingly snug, and the atmosphere balances the kind of warmth that makes everyone feel welcome with serious professional intent. In late 2015, Graham Garrett brought in Tony Parkin to work alongside him in the kitchen, and the creative fusion of modern European cooking and the produce of Kentish fields, farms and coasts is maintained to dynamic effect. First up might be a pairing of confit chicken wing with a cauliflower cheese croquette in silky velouté, or perhaps 'gravmax', a mackerel take on the cured salmon classic, served with charcoaled beetroot, blackberries and horseradish. Sika deer venison with smoked pear and puréed parsley roots is an outstanding main dish, with a dulce de leche custard tart and green apple sorbet the must-have dessert. A list of obscurities and minimal-intervention modern wines, also laced with classic offerings, is as classy a list as you'd expect to find in a wine village. Glasses start at £5.50, half-litre carafes at £13 and bottles at £18.
Chef/s: Graham Garrett and Tony Parkin. **Open:** Tue to Fri and Sun L 12 to 2 (2.30 Sun), Tue to Sat D 7 to 9 (9.30 Sat). **Closed:** Mon, 24 to 26 Dec, 1 Jan. **Meals:** set L £25 (3 courses). Set D £38 (2 courses) to £45. Tasting menu £60 (6 courses). **Details:** 35 seats. Music. Parking.

Average price 🍴

The average price denotes the price of a three-course meal without wine.

◼ Broadstairs

Albariño

Cooking score: 3
Tapas | £25
29 Albion Street, Broadstairs, CT10 1LX
Tel no: (01843) 600991
albarinorestaurant.co.uk
£5 OFF £30 ▼

The small dining room looks rather a plain Jane with its cramped tables, bar-counter seats and tiny open-to-view kitchen at the back, but it's the unpretentious setting for Steven and Stephanie Dray's mission to deliver a slice of Spain in an English seaside town. And they do a highly professional job, pleasing with a relaxed atmosphere, fresh, often local, ingredients and dependable kitchen. A simple, no-nonsense carte doesn't waste words, offering cured meat and cheeseboards, local crab on toast with pancetta and apple, potato and onion tortilla, ham and cheese croquettes, slow-cooked ox cheeks with liquorice, macaroni and Manchego cheese, and a pear, blue cheese and baby gem salad with walnuts. Everyone praises the chickpea and fennel chips, and deep-fried Catalan custard with spiced pear continues to make a great finish. Wines from Albariño open the concise, all-Spanish list (from £16) and there's a good selection of sherries.
Chef/s: Steven Dray. **Open:** Sat L 12 to 3, Mon to Sat D 6 to 10. **Closed:** Sun, 25 and 26 Dec, 1 Jan. **Meals:** tapas £5 to £9. **Details:** 26 seats. Bar. Wheelchairs. Music.

Wyatt & Jones

Cooking score: 2
British | £29
23-27 Harbour Street, Broadstairs, CT10 1EU
Tel no: (01843) 865126
wyattandjones.co.uk
£30 ▼

'Definitely the best in Broadstairs' is a view shared by the burgeoning flock of locals and seasiders who clamour for a table at this stepped, glass-fronted, all-day operation by York Gate arch. Opt for the lower dining area with its open kitchen and take in the vista of Viking Bay while you choose from the native goods on offer. Devotion to British produce and a deft hand in the kitchen result in imaginative and strongly seasonal dishes: try, perhaps, smoked duck with pickled rhubarb, celeriac purée and lamb's leaf, followed by sea trout in cep butter with leek, fennel, clams and parsley potatoes, or bouillabaisse. Blackberry cheesecake soufflé is worth the wait. A recent rejig has seen part of the restaurant transformed into a bar with seating, extensive gin selection and sharing boards for drop-ins. Do book for breakfast and weekend lunches – it gets rammed. Wines start at £18.
Chef/s: Jessica Leah and Craig Edgell. **Open:** Wed to Sun L 12 to 3 (5 Sun), Wed to Sat D 6.30 to 9 (10 Fri and Sat). **Closed:** Mon, Tue. **Meals:** main courses £13 to £21. Set L £15 (2 courses) to £19. **Details:** 60 seats. Bar. Music.

◼ Canterbury

The Goods Shed

Cooking score: 2
Modern British | £32
Station Road West, Canterbury, CT2 8AN
Tel no: (01227) 459153
thegoodsshed.co.uk

Occupying the upper level of a former Victorian railway shed (now home to a daily farmers' market), this delightfully casual restaurant has been a fixture on the Canterbury dining scene for more than a decade. Full use is made of the stalls selling fish, locally reared meats, fruit, vegetables and cheeses. It's a fruitful tie-in that regularly yields satisfying dishes, from potted shoulder of lamb with cauliflower purée and salsa verde, or asparagus custard with smoked eel and tarragon dressing, to guinea fowl with soft polenta, black pudding and sage. Fish lovers might prefer red mullet stew with fried bread and rouille, and monkfish with white beans, lobster sauce and mussels – in the words of one regular, this is 'plain cooking raised to remarkable heights by quality ingredients'. Elsewhere, reporters have praised leek and curd cheese terrine, the onion focaccia, a vanilla and goats' curd cheesecake with Cointreau orange, and the friendly service. Wines from £16.

Chef/s: Rafael Lopez. **Open:** Tue to Sun L 12 to 2.30 (3 Sat and Sun), Tue to Sat D 6 to 9.30. **Closed:** Mon, 25 to 27 Dec, 1 and 2 Jan. **Meals:** main courses £15 to £24. **Details:** 60 seats. Parking.

▌Crundale

**★ LOCAL RESTAURANT AWARD ★
REGIONAL WINNER**

The Compasses Inn

Cooking score: 3
Modern British | £28
Sole Street, Crundale, CT4 7ES
Tel no: (01227) 700300
thecompassescrundale.co.uk
£5 OFF £30

With its low ceiling, hop-garlanded beams, timbers, unclothed tables and winter fires, plus bags of atmosphere throughout, the centuries-old Compasses has everything you might expect to find in a rural pub. Its unpretentious approach is matched by Robert Taylor's 'tremendous enthusiasm and passion for food'. He sources some of the best regional produce in the area, making the most of the harvest by sending out dishes that are carefully crafted and full of flavour. Reporters have praised a host of things, from caramelised red onion tart with creamed onions and rocket pesto to loin of cod with crispy ox cheek, fondant potato, buttered spinach and horseradish cream, and roasted guinea fowl with salt-baked celeriac, sticky red cabbage and suet pudding. Desserts are 'awesome', especially a rich chocolate-mousse brownie with salted-caramel ice cream. A fairly priced wine list opens at £15 or there's beer from local brewers Shepherd Neame.

Chef/s: Robert Taylor. **Open:** Tue to Sun L 12 to 2.30 (3 Sat and Sun), Tue to Sat D 6 to 9. **Closed:** Mon. **Meals:** main courses £13 to £19. Set L £15 (2 courses) to £18. **Details:** 60 seats. Bar. Music. Parking.

Best of... East Kent

Our undercover inspectors open their Little Black Books

In a city full of chains **Micro Roastery**, Canterbury, is a tiny, independent, artisan coffee shop worth knowing about. Good home-baked cakes, too.

Coffee éclairs, strawberry mille feuille, lemon tarts – there's cake galore at the most delicious French patisserie, **La Salamandre** on Hythe High Street.

Find any excuse to pop into **The Black Dog**, a welcoming micropub in Whitstable with a good choice of real ciders and cask ales.

Hand-crafted sandwiches, especially rare roast-beef on white bread with horseradish, onion marmalade and loads of rocket, are a treat at Jonny Sandwich at the **Goods Shed** in Canterbury.

Everyone praises the chips but the very fresh fish is excellent, and great value at **Ossie's Best Fish and Chips** in Whitstable.

For thin-crust pizzas topped with seasonal, local ingredients it has to be **GB Pizza Co** on Marine Drive, Margate. Great views over the beach as well.

For a picnic on the beach, **Wheelers Oyster Bar** is the 'go to' place for quiches, tartlets (love the crab) as well as seafood platters or a selection of seafood. Find them on Whitstable High Street.

One foodie thing you must do is get a scoop or three of the best artisanal ice cream in east Kent at **Sundae Sundae**, Whitstable.

▌Deal
Victuals & Co.
Cooking score: 2
Modern British | £35
2-3 St George's Passage, Deal, CT14 6TA
Tel no: (01304) 374389
victualsandco.com

'A little gem of a restaurant down a small alley between the high street and the sea,' is how one reader describes Andy and Suzy Kirkwood's personally run local eatery. It's a model of tasteful domesticity and the food rings true, with sound local ingredients the building blocks for regularly changing menus. Yet in among the chicken and tarragon terrine with artichoke purée, Seasalter Marsh lamb chop with mash, peas and mint gravy, and local hake with spinach tagliatelle and white wine sauce, there might be a Thai coconut soup with white crabmeat and crayfish, and Malaysian beef and coconut curry with herbed rice and cauliflower pickle – the common denominator is a lively sense of flavours. Finish with raspberry soufflé or a pear and frangipane tart with pear and ginger sorbet. Reporters have found it costly by local standards, but the food satisfies and the service runs well. Wines from £17.50.
Chef/s: Suzy Kirkwood. **Open:** Sat and Sun L 12 to 2.30, Wed to Sun D 6 to 9 (5.30 Sat, 5.30 to 8.30 Sun). **Closed:** Mon, Tue, Jan. **Meals:** main courses £16 to £26. Set L £19 (2 courses) to £21. **Details:** 40 seats. 10 seats outside. Bar. Music. Children over 9 yrs only at D.

▌Faversham
Read's
Cooking score: 6
Modern British | £60
Macknade Manor, Canterbury Road, Faversham, ME13 8XE
Tel no: (01795) 535344
reads.com

Starting with the advantage of a fine Georgian manor house set in pleasant gardens and confident in its role of gently old-fashioned country-restaurant-with-rooms, 'Read's remains a beacon of quality'. Chef-owner David Pitchford's passion for good ingredients underpins the whole enterprise. Besides using local suppliers, he has established a kitchen garden, and his kitchen pays its dues to 'modern British' – slices of citrus-marinated Scottish salmon with pickled cucumbers and tangerine purée, for example – but there is also a strong comfort factor, as in a mature Montgomery's Cheddar cheese soufflé with smoked haddock in a cream sauce, considered 'sensational', and pink-roasted loin of Kentish lamb with slow-braised breast, described as 'well balanced and full flavoured'. British cheeses are highly rated and puddings might include a vanilla pannacotta with fresh raspberries and shortbread. The wine list is lovingly compiled, with page after page of quality names from around the world. But the Best Buys list shows real effort has been made to provide an excellent choice under £30, and half-bottles seem to go on for ever. Bottles from £24.
Chef/s: David Pitchford. **Open:** Tue to Sat L 12 to 2, D 7 to 9. **Closed:** Sun, Mon, 25 to 27 Dec, first week Jan, first 2 weeks Sept. **Meals:** set L £28. Set D £50 (2 courses) to £60. Tasting menu £65. **Details:** 50 seats. 30 seats outside. Bar. Wheelchairs. Parking.

▊ Folkestone
Rocksalt
Cooking score: 2
Seafood | £28
4-5 Fishmarket Road, Folkestone, CT19 6AA
Tel no: (01303) 212070
rocksaltfolkestone.co.uk

£5 OFF £30

If you're going to open a restaurant in Folkestone, 'you couldn't pick a better spot'. With the sun shining and boats bobbing, just a great plate of seafood and a chilled glass of wine is required to complete the scene. Fish is the main draw at this 'stunning' modern outfit, where huge windows capitalise on its harbour aspect, and localism looms large on the menu: seafood classics – perhaps potted shrimps (from nearby Dungeness), dressed crab or push-the-boat-out shellfish platter – feature alongside more refined offerings of pan-fried Rye Bay lemon sole with brown shrimps or creamed smoked coley 'thermidor' with a poached egg, following 'excellent' amuse-bouches. Accents from further afield can be timid – 'fiery 'njuda' in a hake dish was barely detectable on inspection – but impeccably cooked seafood is a given, as is top-rate produce. Kentish gypsy tart makes a fine finish. For lighter bites, head upstairs to the sea-facing bar. Wines from £16.50.
Chef/s: Simon Dyer. **Open:** all week L 12 to 3, Mon to Sat D 7 to 10.30. **Meals:** main courses £16 to £40. Set L £22 (2 courses, Mon to Fri) to £25. Sun L £30. **Details:** 84 seats. 44 seats outside. V menu. Bar.

▊ Hythe
LOCAL GEM
La Salamandre
French | £15
30 High Street, Hythe, CT21 5AT
Tel no: (01303) 239853

£30

France comes to Hythe in chef Alain Ronez's staunchly Gallic patisserie-café and it's a runaway success. Backed up by charming service, it's a useful place to stop for a good-value quick bite, with breakfast delivering egg and mushrooms on toasted sourdough, while light lunches run to delicate quiches, omelettes and pâté lorrain (a traditional pork and white wine pie). However, it's as an expert pâtissier that Ronez shines, and his display of beautifully worked pastries, tarts and viennoiseries draw the crowds (for eating in and taking away). Unlicensed: cash only.

▊ Locksbottom
Chapter One
Cooking score: 6
Modern European | £40
Farnborough Common, Locksbottom, BR6 8NF
Tel no: (01689) 854848
chaptersrestaurants.com

A faithful contributor to Kent's culinary reputation for many a year, this landmark restaurant is a relaxing, expansive venue, stylishly designed with white-clad tables, comfortable leather padded chairs and good division of space so you are not totally overwhelmed – this place can seat over 100. Long-standing chef Andrew McLeish's forward-thinking but generally restrained cooking displays obvious talent. Among starters there may be a skilfully straightforward dish of velouté of spring pea with a soft poached egg, though there's also a fondness for no-holds-barred flavours, seen in a dish of Josper-roast octopus with chorizo, chilli and garlic. Intense flavours show up in mains, too, in well-balanced combinations of, say, braised beef cheek with Perigord truffle potato purée and buttered hispi greens, and poached and roasted wood pigeon with orange-braised chicory, Savoy cabbage, pancetta and beurre noisette potato purée. Intricately wrought desserts could include a rhubarb custard tart with white wine jelly and rhubarb sorbet. Wines from £19.
Chef/s: Andrew McLeish. **Open:** all week L 12 to 2.30 (2.45 Sun), D 6.30 to 11 (9 Sun). **Closed:** 2 to 4 Jan. **Meals:** set L £20 and £30. Set D £40. **Details:** 100 seats. 16 seats outside. Bar. Wheelchairs. Music. Parking.

∎ Margate

GB Pizza Co.
Italian | £16
14a Marine Drive, Margate, CT9 1DH
Tel no: (01843) 297700
greatbritishpizzacompany.com

£30

This smart pizzeria, run by dough-loving duo Lisa Richards and Rachel Seed, has settled in nicely on Margate's seafront. Breathtaking sunsets and sweep of golden beach aside, locals flock to GB Pizza Co. for perfectly proportioned thin-crust pizzas topped with seasonal, local ingredients – try Kentish ham, portobello mushroom, tomato and mozzarella – baked in the wood-fired oven. 'Amazing' gluten-free bases get a shout-out from one reader, and locally made puds, help-yourself wine or local Kentish beers round things off nicely. Their latest Margate venture is Roost (see entry).

LOCAL GEM
Greedy Cow
British | £15
3 Market Place, Old Town, Margate, CT9 1ER
Tel no: (01843) 447557
thegreedycow.com

£30

The Hunts' compact all-day café in the heart of Margate's Old Town may be quite tightly laid out with steep stairs up to the first-floor dining room – there are tables on the pavement – but it is known for friendly service and good, reasonably priced food. Breakfast is a top deal, but come lunch and the headline act is 'the best burgers around' served with homemade coleslaw (but no chips). The pulled pork has impressed, too, as has the falafel flatbread and homemade vanilla-chocolate cheesecake. Italian red or white is £15.

LOCAL GEM
Hantverk & Found
Seafood | £26
18 King Street, Margate, CT9 1DA
Tel no: (01843) 280454
hantverk-found.co.uk

£30

Migrating from Hackney, London to 'Hackney-on-sea', chef Kate de Syllas set up shop in Margate's Old Town with her tiny seafood café and gallery in 2015, and locals have been quick to embrace it and spread the word. What the boat brings in dictates the choice scribbled on the blackboard-wall: typical dishes include local crispy squid with harissa yoghurt or pan-roasted cod with wild garlic polenta and kale, though prawns, smoked on site, should not be missed. Thirst-quenchers include local ales and natural wines from the refreshingly forward-thinking list.

LOCAL GEM
Roost
British | £15
19 Cliff Terrace, Margate, CT9 1RU
Tel no: (01843) 229708
roostmargate.com

£5 OFF   £30

Rotisserie chicken dominates the menu at this second Margate opening from Rachel Seed and Lisa Richards (GB Pizza, see entry). Ideal for a good-value feed with friends, Roost has all the ramshackle charm of its elder sibling, including the plate-glass North Sea views. The ethically sourced birds are teamed with chips, Asian-style slaw or Caesar salad and a choice of sauces, with macaroni and cheese, bone broth infused with seaweed and a rather good pecan pie filling any remaining gaps. Wines from the barrel are £3.75 a glass, £15 a bottle.

Minster

The Corner House
British | £30
42 Station Road, Minster, CT12 4BZ
Tel no: (01843) 823000
cornerhouserestaurants.co.uk

A slightly wonky 300-year-old building opposite the church is home to Matt Sworder's restaurant-with-rooms. There's period charm inside and out and a relaxed mood pervades. The kitchen team makes its own bread and ice cream, and seeks out some good local ingredients to ensure a sense of place. The uncomplicated roster runs to Kentish-style mussels (with leeks, chilli and Biddenden cider cream sauce) to start, or kedgeree maybe, followed by venison pudding with winter greens, or steak with triple-cooked chips. Wines from £16.50.

Oare
The Three Mariners
Cooking score: 2
Modern British | £28
2 Church Road, Oare, ME13 0QA
Tel no: (01795) 533633
thethreemarinersoare.co.uk
£30

Described as a true village local by many visitors, John O'Riordan's 18th-century pub is nothing fancy. In the bar the bare floorboards, beams, a roaring winter fire and Shepherd Neame ales keep up traditional appearances and in the pair of dining rooms the regularly changing menu is appealing and modern. While much is made of local sourcing of ingredients, inspiration for dishes comes from wider-spread European roots. Thus an early spring meal might feature London porter hot-smoked salmon with a light mustard crème fraîche mayo, and local skate with tomatoes, capers and brown butter or salt-cured duck confit with mashed potatoes. For dessert, homemade ice cream comes in for praise. The general consensus is that dishes are well presented, generous and feel like excellent value. Friendly and helpful service is a bonus, as is the back terrace overlooking Oare Creek, a natural suntrap in fine weather. The wine list opens at £14.85.
Chef/s: John O'Riordan. **Open:** all week L 12 to 2.30 (3 Sat and Sun), D 6.30 to 9 (9.30 Fri and Sat, 7 to 9 Sun). **Meals:** main courses £14 to £20. Set L £13 to £18. Set D £18 to £21. Sun L £18. **Details:** 65 seats. 34 seats outside. Bar. Music. Parking.

Stalisfield Green
The Plough Inn
Cooking score: 2
British | £29
Stalisfield Green, ME13 0HY
Tel no: (01795) 890256
stalisfieldgreen.co.uk
£30

Amid the chatter of contented patrons and the sound of Kent's finest craft ales being poured, Marianne and Richard Baker pull out all the stops to ensure you want to return to their 15th-century 'hall house'. The picturesque village green setting enforces country-pub credentials, and the cooking is superior. The please-all approach keeps punters with a weakness for burger, fish and chips or ploughman's happy (try the glorious Proper pie), while the kitchen flexes its muscles elsewhere on the menu. Daily-changing chalked-up 'specials' might feature Thornback ray, chilli, ginger, lemongrass and samphire broth with blackeye peas, confit duck leg or rope-grown mussels. The commitment to native, seasonal produce comes across loud and clear and doesn't wane at the sweet end of the meal, either. A winter warming of rhubarb with chestnut sponge pudding will have you pushing away your companions' eager spoons. Wines from £14.50.
Chef/s: Richard Baker. **Open:** Tue to Sun L 12 to 2 (2.30 Sat, 3.30 Sun), Tue to Sat D 6 to 9. **Closed:** Mon, 2 to 6 Jan. **Meals:** main courses £11 to £19. Set L £14 (2 courses) to £17. **Details:** 70 seats. 40 seats outside. Bar. Music. Parking.

■ Tunbridge Wells
Thackeray's
Cooking score: 5
Modern European | £55
85 London Road, Tunbridge Wells, TN1 1EA
Tel no: (01892) 511921
thackerays-restaurant.co.uk

Set in Tunbridge Wells' oldest house (circa 1660) and taking its name from Victorian novelist William Makepeace Thackeray, this is one of Kent's thoroughbred restaurants – a chic proposition that blends ancient floorboards and low ceilings with up-to-the-minute touches including lavish wallpapers, twinkling lamps and a soothing Japanese-style garden terrace. Richard Phillips steers the ship, but day-to-day cooking is in the capable hands of Shane Hughes – an exponent of elaborate contemporary cuisine who gives top-drawer ingredients the respect they deserve. A flash of fusion finds seared Scottish langoustines alongside a Japanese omelette, pak choi, spiced pine nut and banana crunch, while Anjou squab has foie gras, celeriac fondant and a saucisson 'sandwich' for company. Meat is also subjected to sympathetic treatment, from 55-day aged Hereford sirloin to roast best end of lamb and a spice-crusted sweetbread accompanied by an assiette of char-grilled and confit vegetables ('roots, tubers and squash'). After that, masterly desserts such as a frozen praline parfait with citrus sorbet conclude proceedings. Serious global wines start at £21.
Chef/s: Shane Hughes. **Open:** Tue to Sun L 12 to 2.30, Tue to Sat D 6.30 to 10.30. **Closed:** Mon.
Meals: set L £18 (2 courses) to £20. Set D £43 (2 courses) to £55. Sun L £35. Tasting menu £98 (10 courses). **Details:** 48 seats. 30 seats outside. V menu. Bar. Music.

Visit us online

To find out more about The Good Food Guide, please visit thegoodfoodguide.co.uk

■ Whitstable
JoJo's
Cooking score: 4
Tapas | £30
2 Herne Bay Road, Whitstable, CT5 2LQ
Tel no: (01227) 274591
jojosrestaurant.co.uk

Since opening over a decade ago and relocating from its original spot in town to its current light and airy seafront premises, JoJo's sunny disposition remains undiminished. Owners Nikki Billington and Paul Watson bill their perennially top-order tapas as 'meze with a Mediterranean influence', and turn out down-to-earth yet impeccably wrought plates of Kent's finest ingredients and sustainably sourced meat and fish, alongside produce from sunnier climes. Mixed meze 'sharing plates' from the single-page menu – presented on hefty wooden boards – feature hummus, tzatziki, carrot salad, cured meats, cheeses and homemade seasonal jelly, and tapas of the Greek variety dominates: perhaps calamari, or mutton and feta koftas. Alternatively, go for a 'special' from the daily-changing blackboard menu, then choose from a fine selection of cheeses to finish. Getting a table in warmer months can require a bit of forward planning, and be warned, it's a cash or cheque enterprise. The fairly priced, pithy wine list starts at £17.
Chef/s: Nikki Billington. **Open:** Thur to Sun L 12.30 to 2.30, Wed to Sat D 6.30 to 9. **Closed:** Mon, Tue. **Meals:** tapas £5 to £11. **Details:** 60 seats. Wheelchairs. Music.

The Sportsman
Cooking score: 6
Modern British | £39
Faversham Road, Seasalter, Whitstable, CT5 4BP
Tel no: (01227) 273370
thesportsmanseasalter.co.uk

In 2017, Steve Harris will celebrate 18 years at the stoves of this 'excellent pub on the Kent coast', and his commitment to local and seasonal produce prepared with sensitivity remains undimmed. Mr Harris's cooking is at the gentler end of the modern British spectrum and depends on long-established connections with a trusted food network. The à la carte is complemented by a daily tasting menu – four courses plus oysters 'and other little bits and bobs' – that produced for one autumn diner 'perfectly cooked partridge with the best bread sauce I have ever tasted'. Order the full tasting menu (in advance, on booking) and a 'copious complement of nibbles', among them airy pork scratching with apple and mustard purée, smoked herring, and pork in brik pastry with onion and shallot, will precede flawlessly executed dishes such as mushroom and celeriac tart, and the ever-popular slip sole in a seaweed butter. That spring meal also produced braised brill in a 'wonderful' smoked roe sauce, roast saddle of Kentish lamb with cauliflower, romanesco, celeriac and spring onion, and a 'faultless' raspberry soufflé with ripple ice cream. Elsewhere, there's been applause for the 'best oysters ever', homemade bread and home-churned butter, and a pre-dessert of a 'lovely' pear-and-ginger ice lolly. Informal service contributes to the laid-back feel and the remarkably friendly prices of the wine selection add to the pleasure; bottles from £16.95.

Chef/s: Stephen Harris and Dan Flavell. **Open:** Tue to Sun L 12 to 2 (12.30 to 2.30 Sun), Tue to Sat D 7 to 9. **Closed:** Mon, 25 and 26 Dec. **Meals:** main courses £20 to £25. Daily tasting menu £45 (5 courses), full tasting menu £65 (8 courses). **Details:** 50 seats. Music. Parking. No children at D.

Wheelers Oyster Bar
Cooking score: 4
Seafood | £36
8 High Street, Whitstable, CT5 1BQ
Tel no: (01227) 273311
wheelersoysterbar.com

'Consistently great' declares a devotee who has been frequenting this remarkable eatery for the past 15 years – although Wheelers has been peddling its oysters for a lot longer than that. Set up in 1856, its candyfloss-pink and blue frontage is now part of Whitstable's heritage,

while a proposed new dining area should help to ease the pressure of bagging a seat here. Wherever you hang your hat, a plate of Whitstable natives au naturel is a must – unless you prefer some 'rockys' cooked in Guinness tempura batter. Otherwise, the zesty global menu promises a carnival of vivid flavours from a ceviche of John Dory finished with grapefruit granita to a dramatic dish of turbot with all kinds of maritime embellishments including steamed prawn dumplings, sea vegetable 'bubble' and seaweed ash. Also, don't miss the show-stealing Kentish lobsters or creative desserts such as rhubarb 'three ways' (brûlée, fool and sorbet). Unlicensed, but you can BYO (no corkage); cash only.

Chef/s: Mark Stubbs. **Open:** Thur to Tue 1 to 7.30. **Closed:** Wed, 25 and 26 Dec, 1 Jan, 2 to 3 weeks Jan. **Meals:** main courses £20 to £32. **Details:** 16 seats. Wheelchairs.

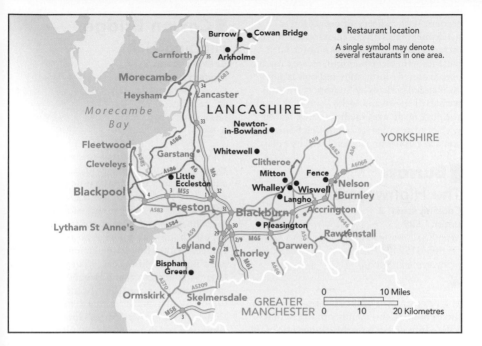

Arkholme
The Red Well

Cooking score: 2
Modern British | £29
Kirkby Lonsdale Road, Arkholme, LA6 1BQ
Tel no: (01524) 221240
redwellcountryinn.co.uk

With the Lune Valley Smokehouse and shop on site – plus a fully formed restaurant – this stone-built Lancashire country inn has come a long way since its days as a 17th-century courthouse and 20th-century disco venue. A wood-burning stove and comfy leather sofas ensure everyone is suitably relaxed, while the kitchen deals in gratifying modern pub food with plenty of North Country accents: Lancashire cheese appears in a twice-baked soufflé, while locally made black pudding is served with duck egg yolk, cauliflower and sage. Also look for muscular mains ranging from pig's cheeks with bourguignon garnish or duck accompanied by salt-baked celeriac,

blackberries and heritage potatoes to sea bass fillet with red onion, chorizo and gnocchi. To finish, don't miss the sticky toffee pudding with salted-caramel macaroon and banana ice cream. Local ales from the likes of Bowland and Tirril star at the bar, while quaffable wines start at £19.
Chef/s: Rob Talbot. **Open:** all week L 12 to 2, D 6 to 8.30 (8 Sun). **Meals:** main courses £13 to £19.
Details: 80 seats. 30 seats outside. Bar. Wheelchairs. Music. Parking.

Bispham Green

LOCAL GEM
The Eagle & Child

British | £25
Malt Kiln Lane, Bispham Green, L40 3SG
Tel no: (01257) 462297
eagleandchildbispham.co.uk

A whitewashed pub worth tracking down on the unlit country roads between Ormskirk and Chorley, the Eagle & Child is full of cosy corners, with a cheery air prevailing at mealtimes especially. Gold-standard pub fare includes the Ainscoughs' own home farm sausages with black pudding, creamy mash, beer-battered onion rings and onion gravy, bookended perhaps by Southport shrimps with garlic pesto and rocket, and sticky toffee pudding made with medjool dates, served with bonfire toffee ice cream. Ten house wines come at a uniform £15, or £5 a large glass.

▋ Burrow
The Highwayman

Cooking score: 2
British | £29
Main Road, Burrow, LA6 2RJ
Tel no: (01524) 273338
highwaymaninn.co.uk

£30

In a 'beautiful part of the country' bordering three counties, this member of the Ribble Valley Inns group is on the dapper side of the pub spectrum. The sturdy building's decorative finish is 'posh country', while the kitchen's output follows the company's founding father's philosophy – 'traditional, local, unpretentious northern grub'. Goosnargh duck livers are duly potted, Sandham's Martha's Choice Lancashire cheese finds its way into a soufflé, the North Sea offers up hake (served with mace butter sauce), and, if you just fancy a lunchtime sandwich, how about one filled with the fruits of the Port of Lancaster Smokehouse? Burgers, fish pie, haddock and chips and char-grilled British steaks are all populist numbers, while to finish, Emma's sticky toffee pudding was for one 'simply the best sticky toffee pudding I have eaten'. A terrace out back is a warm-weather treat. Drink draught ales or wines from £16.50.
Chef/s: Bruno Birkbeck. **Open:** all week 12 to 9 (9.30 Fri and Sat). **Meals:** main courses £11 to £23. Set L and D £14 (2 courses) to £16. **Details:** 110 seats. 45 seats outside. Bar. Wheelchairs. Music. Parking.

▋ Cowan Bridge
Hipping Hall

Cooking score: 5
Modern British | £55
Cowan Bridge, LA6 2JJ
Tel no: (01524) 271187
hippinghall.com

There's a wholesome, back-to-nature feel to Hipping Hall that begins with a list of almost entirely organic and biodynamic wines and extends to Oli Martin's cooking, which feels equally right-on, with plenty of foraged ingredients and heritage flavours. Don't expect a homespun interior, however; this is a genteel country house hotel from its oil paintings to its plush sofas, where dinner begins in the classical and elegant lounge before settling in the magnificent medieval dining room beneath a pitched, many-timbered ceiling. Mr Martin's food is 'well conceived and different,' but while menu descriptions are 'as brief as haiku', there are spins and flourishes on the plate: 'asparagus, egg yolk, whey' translated at inspection as shaved asparagus, confit egg yolk, whey jelly and milk curd. While proportions were a tad unbalanced (with the asparagus losing ground), a main of brill with shrimp butter, broccoli flowers and spring cabbage was a study in simplicity and harmony. Desserts are a major strength, with 'milk, honey, lavender' delivering salted honey parfait, lavender sorbet, honeycomb crisp and shortbread crumble, all sprinkled with sweet cicely leaves. The organic wines are a must, with plenty of lesser-known finds all divided by style and nicely annotated. Bottles start at £22.
Chef/s: Oli Martin. **Open:** Sat and Sun L 12 to 2, all week D 7 to 9. **Meals:** set D £55 (3 courses). Tasting menu £65. **Details:** 32 seats. Bar. Wheelchairs. Music. Parking. Children over 12 yrs only.

▌Fence
White Swan
Cooking score: 6
British | £32
300 Wheatley Lane Road, Fence, BB12 9QA
Tel no: (01282) 611773
whiteswanatfence.co.uk

'The atmosphere suggested a very loved local,' and indeed, village pubs don't come any more charming than this. Two real fires, gilt-framed paintings and high ceilings create a smart but homely feel and there's a warm welcome and plenty of chat. But the food is leagues ahead of your average pub offering. Chef Tom Parker has a high-end restaurant background and he knows how to use it – yet his food also sits comfortably within the pub setting. A lunchtime visit revealed a bargain set menu plus à la carte dishes of more complexity. A starter of lobster with intensely flavoured tomato water, watermelon, herbs and flowers was 'an absolute joy, the flavours fresh and vivid', and the bar stayed high for a generous dish of John Dory, fennel, plump rock oysters, caviar and a 'beautiful, foamy' lemon butter sauce. To finish, a gariguette strawberry trifle impressed with fruity ripeness and intensity. Drinks include a range of Timothy Taylor beers in immaculate condition and Kilner jars of homemade flavoured gins and rums (on display on the bar). Wine-wise, there is plenty of interest, with bottles starting at £17.
Chef/s: Tom Parker. **Open:** Tue to Sat L 12 to 2, D 5.30 to 8.30 (9 Fri and Sat). Sun 12 to 6.30. **Closed:** Mon. **Meals:** main courses £15 to £30. **Details:** 42 seats. 15 seats outside. Bar. Wheelchairs. Music. Parking.

▌Langho
Northcote
Cooking score: 6
Modern British | £60
Northcote Road, Langho, BB6 8BE
Tel no: (01254) 240555
northcote.com
£5 OFF 🍷 🛏

'It's one of those places where the kitchen wants you to eat good food and front-of-house want you to have a good time,' notes a reader who 'can't recall ever having a duff dish' at Nigel Haworth's Lancastrian grandee. For many, this is still the ultimate 'special occasion' restaurant, a paragon of bountiful generosity renowned for its unsurpassed attention to detail and highly personal way of doing things. Head chef Lisa Allen is now back from maternity leave, so all is right with the world – a view confirmed by a stuffed inbox of feedback: a starter of cod cheeks sitting on strips of ham hock and lardo with black pea hummus did the trick for one reporter with its 'knockout balance of flavours', while others save their drooling until dessert – perhaps chocolate and caramel tart offset by peanut ice cream and 'balls of poached pear'. Elsewhere, muscular North Country flavours meet big-city brio in the shape of seared wild turbot with pickled lemon, seaweed, smoked crème fraîche and 'chips' or Goosnargh duckling with smoked duck 'ham', pulled leg, spicy cabbage and blood orange. Co-owner Craig Bancroft's 'fantastic' wine list is an impeccably curated worldwide selection of matchless quality, with bottles from £25.
Chef/s: Nigel Haworth and Lisa Allen. **Open:** all week L 12 to 2, D 7 to 9.30 (6.30 to 10 Fri and Sat, 9 Sun). **Meals:** main courses £30 to £60. Set L £23 (2 courses) to £32. Set D £45 (2 courses) to £60. Sun L £42. Tasting menu £88 (8 courses). **Details:** 60 seats. 30 seats outside. V menu. Bar. Wheelchairs. Music. Parking.

▌Little Eccleston
The Cartford Inn
Cooking score: 2
Modern British | £26
Cartford Lane, Little Eccleston, PR3 0YP
Tel no: (01995) 670166
thecartfordinn.co.uk

🛏 £30

'It really is a lovely setting, rural Lancashire, by the river Wyre and with pleasant outside space and a new deli Taste of the Inn selling their greatest hits,' ran the notes of one visitor. With delightfully quirky décor, boutique bedrooms and 21st-century comforts, Julie and Patrick Beaume's lovingly refurbished and extended 17th-century coaching inn is 'a lovely change from the classic idea of a country inn.' Real ales and comforting pub classics (fish and chips, oxtail, beef and ale suet pudding) are two of its pubby attributes, but the menu also entices with boards of deli meats or Fleetwood seafood, and standouts (at inspection) of smoked mackerel, 'really firm and rich with a good level of smoke, and a little cocktail of cockles and samphire', and a 'very accomplished' chocolate délice with coffee, 'properly dark, an effective, grown-up pairing'. Service can be rather erratic at times. Wines from £15.50.
Chef/s: Patrick Beaume and Ian Manning. **Open:** Tue to Sat L 12 to 2, Mon to Sat D 5.30 to 9 (10 Fri and Sat). Sun 12 to 8.30. **Closed:** 25 Dec. **Meals:** main courses £11 to £22. **Details:** 90 seats. 20 seats outside. Wheelchairs. Music. Parking. No children in restaurant.

Please send us your feedback

To register your opinion about any restaurant listed in this guide, or a new restaurant that you wish to bring to our attention, please visit the web address at the bottom of the page. Your feedback informs the content of the book and will be used to compile next year's reviews.

▌Mitton
The Three Fishes
Cooking score: 2
British | £25
Mitton Road, Mitton, BB7 9PQ
Tel no: (01254) 826888
thethreefishes.com

£30

Something about the Three Fishes hits exactly the right spot, and year in, year out it remains one of the area's most popular pubs. The whitewashed stone inn is the flagship of Nigel Haworth's Ribble Valley Inns (chef-proprietor of nearby Northcote, see entry) and is noted for a general buzzy atmosphere, unstuffy modern décor and local ales for those with just a liquid appetite. But what sets this place apart is its uncompromising local and regional sourcing, and readers applaud the kitchen's efforts – it is comforting northern food with no pretensions. A starter of pheasant and ham hock terrine with homemade piccalilli has gone down well, but also look for warm Morecambe Bay shrimps, and baked cod with Lancashire cheese crumb, butternut squash and sage pearl barley risotto, as well as the famous Lancashire hotpot. Otherwise, investigate the regional cheeses, and desserts such as pear doughnuts with pine sugar and dippy custard. Wines from £16.50.
Chef/s: Ian Moss. **Open:** all week 12 to 9 (9.30 Fri and Sat). **Meals:** main courses £10 to £25. Set L and D £14 (2 courses, Mon to Thur) to £16. **Details:** 130 seats. 40 seats outside. Wheelchairs. Music. Parking.

▌Newton-in-Bowland
The Parkers Arms
Cooking score: 2
Modern British | £29
Hallgate Hill, Newton-in-Bowland, BB7 3DY
Tel no: (01200) 446236
parkersarms.co.uk

£5 OFF 🛏 £30

What is apparently the pub closest to the centre of the UK is also, surely, in one of its most tranquil settings. And here in the

Hodder Valley the conventions of pub food are turned on their heads. Yes, you can have a beef burger or fish and chips, but chef Stosi Madi's fancies run to more vibrant things: spiced cauliflower fritters with mint yoghurt dip, hand-raised salt marsh hogget and cockle pie, and much-praised lamb kofte. 'We are yet to have an average meal,' says one regular. In season, local game is a speciality, and pheasant might be spiced with cumin, glazed with pomegranate and grilled over charcoal. For pudding, co-owner Kathy Smith's Wet Nelly, fruited bread pudding served with pouring cream, vies for attention with the Portuguese custard tarts. Customers with allergies will find a capable kitchen ready and willing to offer gluten-free alternatives. Wines are from £18.

Chef/s: Stosi Madi. **Open:** Wed to Sat L 12 to 2.30 (12.30 to 4.30 Sat), D 6 to 8.30 (9 Sat). Sun 12 to 6. **Closed:** Mon, Tue. **Meals:** main courses £13 to £19. **Details:** 90 seats. 150 seats outside. Bar. Wheelchairs. Parking.

◼ Pleasington

LOCAL GEM

The Clog & Billycock

British | £25
Billinge End Road, Pleasington, BB2 6QB
Tel no: (01254) 201163
theclogandbillycock.com

£30

A pair of clogs and a billycock hat were the sartorial trademarks of a former landlord, before this Lancashire boozer was reinvented as part of Nigel Haworth's Ribble Valley Inns group. Expect stylish interiors, locally brewed ales galore and a thumping menu peppered with nostalgic flavours – from home-cured corned beef hash to rhubarb and custard trifle. In between, char-grilled steaks share the billing with shortcrust 'plate' pies, slow-cooked Cumbrian lamb shank and gussied-up Goosnargh duck breast with 'dripping' chips. Wines from £16.50.

◼ Whalley

Food by Breda Murphy

Cooking score: 2
Modern British | £33
Abbots Court, 41 Station Road, Whalley, BB7 9RH
Tel no: (01254) 823446
foodbybredamurphy.com

Regulars writing in to praise the well-oiled machine that is Breda Murphy's all-day café are unanimous in their enthusiasm for the consistency and attention to detail that always distinguish a visit here. It occupies the ground floor of a suburban house opposite Whalley railway station and offers food without airs and graces. The kitchen goes for down-home ingredients, serving lunches of Kirkham's cheese croquette with spinach and tomato salad, then breast of chicken with bordelaise beans, wilted kale, red wine and shallot sauce, and rounding off with something simple like seasonal fruit compote with almond scone crumble and vanilla bean ice cream. It's also a handy drop-in for breakfast (fried potato and cabbage cake, streaky bacon, fried duck egg and rapeseed hollandaise, say) and teas – there's a loaded display of cakes. There's also much praise for the friendly service and for occasional evening meals. Wines from £16.95.

Chef/s: Gareth Bevan. **Open:** Tue to Sat 10 to 6, occasional evenings 7 to 9.30. **Closed:** Sun, Mon, 24 Dec to 5 Jan. **Meals:** main courses £13 to £18. **Details:** 46 seats. 20 seats outside. Wheelchairs. Music. Parking.

◼ Whitewell

The Inn at Whitewell

Cooking score: 2
Modern British | £33
Forest of Bowland, Whitewell, BB7 3AT
Tel no: (01200) 448222
innatwhitewell.com

'What a location!' This striking inn, deep in the Forest of Bowland with hills rising all around, dates in part from the 1300s. The interior includes a series of traditional bars and lounges with rug-strewn flagstones and curios, while the restaurant is more formal with linen-clad tables, equestrian prints on the walls and Turner-esque views over a winding river to a distant, ragged skyline. While the bar majors in competent and satisfying pub classics, the restaurant takes the lead in the evening with a menu of, say, a generous bowl of mussels in a white wine and cream sauce, an equally 'generous and enjoyable' loin of halibut with crushed buttered potatoes, ratatouille, crispy pancetta, wilted spinach and a lemon butter sauce, then a rich sticky toffee pudding with a flawless vanilla custard. Wines are a strength: there's an in-house wine shop and the restaurant list is compiled with a mind for food pairings, offering an excellent selection by the glass, plus many pages of bottles divided by style, starting at £16.90.

Chef/s: Jamie Cadman. **Open:** all week L 12 to 2, D 7.30 to 9.30. **Meals:** main courses £16 to £26. **Details:** 150 seats. 40 seats outside. Bar. Parking.

▌Wiswell

★ TOP 50 ★

Freemasons at Wiswell
Cooking score: 7
Modern British | £45
8 Vicarage Fold, Wiswell, BB7 9DF
Tel no: (01254) 822218
freemasonswiswell.co.uk

Steven Smith's captivating village inn is now firmly established as a serious but relaxed dining destination and the promotion of Matt Smith from sous to head chef sees no slippage in quality. Matt is clearly comfortable with the sophisticated but gutsy slant of the cooking – these dishes may surprise with their gleeful fusion of local and international flavours ('always a twist on a classic'), but they'll also leave you feeling heartily well fed – note a velvety cauliflower soup, for instance, studded with florets and topped with an intense and airy Lancashire cheese fondue, or butter-poached lobster tail with crispy claw won ton,

gariguette strawberry, coastal herbs and a punchy black pepper sauce. This cooking never takes the humdrum route when there is something more interesting to offer: a classic baked vanilla rice pudding comes topped with saké baked apple on a vivid green apple jelly and a layer of fine pastry, with a cooling scoop of buttermilk ice cream for good measure. All this is done against a pristine but resolutely pubby backdrop, complete with rug-strewn flagstones and wood-burner (there is a more formal dining area upstairs). 'The staff are friendly, professional and pitch themselves perfectly. The bar is an added experience and the wine list is superb,' notes one reporter. The weighty list includes an interesting selection of fine and rare wines and plenty of attractive options by the glass. The waiting staff can be relied upon for sound recommendations – and bottles start from just £16.50.

Chef/s: Steven Smith and Matt Smith. **Open:** Wed to Sat L 12 to 2.30, D 5.30 to 9 (6 to 10 Sat). Sun 12 to 7. **Closed:** Mon, Tue, 2 to 16 Jan. **Meals:** main courses £18 to £35. Set L and early D £16 (2 courses) to £20. Sun L £25. Tasting menu £70. **Details:** 70 seats. 14 seats outside. V menu. Bar. Wheelchairs. Music.

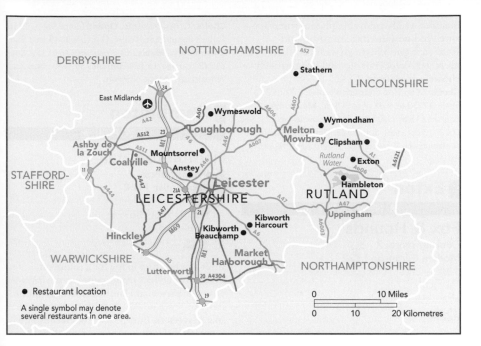

▮ Anstey

LOCAL GEM

Sapori
Italian | £27
40 Stadon Road, Anstey, LE7 7AY
Tel no: (0116) 2368900
sapori-restaurant.co.uk

£30

In a village on the outskirts of Leicester, Sapori continues to delight locals with its 'usual high standards'. Renouncing short-cuts, it's the epitome of a great family-run Italian, making pasta, bread and ice cream from scratch. Homemade linguine pasta with cream of prawns, julienne of vegetables and pan-fried prawns, 'cooked to order', garners high praise, as does a 'beautifully presented' Sorrento lemon posset with raspberry sorbet and brûlée meringue. The friendly staff get a special mention, too. Wines from £16.

▮ Clipsham

The Olive Branch
Cooking score: 2
Modern British | £35
Main Street, Clipsham, LE15 7SH
Tel no: (01780) 410355
theolivebranchpub.com

A 'peace offering' to Clipsham from a vandalising local squire back in 1890, the aptly named Olive Branch is still hugely popular – even if local competitors are now snapping at its heels. Handily placed for the A1, this stone-walled posh-rustic hostelry-with-rooms is a true champion of local and regional produce (note the food map on the back of each menu) and the kitchen covers a lot of ground from pub staples (fish and chips, sausage and mash) to more ambitious ideas. Starters sound 'really appealing', whipped goats' cheese with black olive tuile, garden beetroot and balsamic dressing, for example, or a pea pannacotta with duck prosciutto and garden salad. Mains include a 'really enjoyable' plate of rosemary-cured cod with heritage tomatoes and watercress gnocchi, to go with a cracking line-up of well-kept craft ales and imaginatively chosen wines (from £19).

Chef/s: Sean Hope. **Open:** all week L 12 to 2 (3 Sun), D 6.30 to 9.30 (7 to 9 Sun). **Meals:** main courses £15 to £28. Set L £18 (2 courses) to £21. Set D £30 (3 courses). Sun L £28. **Details:** 60 seats. 20 seats outside. V menu. Bar. Wheelchairs. Music. Parking.

▌Exton

★ NEW ENTRY ★

Fox & Hounds

Cooking score: 2
Modern European | £32
19 The Green, Exton, LE15 8AP
Tel no: (01572) 812403
afoxinexton.co.uk
£5 OFF 🍷

'The location is straight out of a Richard Curtis film – a bucolic spot overlooking the village green in a beautiful village – the pub itself a very handsome coaching inn dating from the 17th century. With its 'country hunting lodge meets gentleman's club' interior and its bang-up-to-date cooking, the Fox & Hounds fits the bill perfectly. One late spring visitor enjoyed 'beautifully cooked' scallops with 'creamy' roasted butternut, 'absolutely delicious' white cauliflower velouté, and Lincolnshire pork loin in a yoghurt, maple and rosemary marinade with apple purée, a woodland mushroom and tenderstem salad nicely complementing the meat, pork air ('essentially pork crackling popcorn') and a cider and wholegrain mustard jus. Sunday roasts are popular and elsewhere, fish and chips from the bar menu and lunchtime sandwiches (grilled cheese, steak) show respect for pub tradition. The wine list hits the spot, short on pretension and reasonably priced (from £18).

Chef/s: Omar Palazzolo. **Open:** Tue to Sun L 12 to 2.30 (3 Fri and Sat, 4 Sun), D 6 to 9.30 (5 to 8 Sun). **Closed:** Mon. **Meals:** main courses £16 to £22. Set L £19 (2 courses) to £24. **Details:** 30 seats. Bar. Wheelchairs. Music. Parking.

▌Hambleton

★ TOP 50 ★

Hambleton Hall

Cooking score: 7
Modern British | £68
Ketton Road, Hambleton, LE15 8TH
Tel no: (01572) 756991
hambleton.co.uk
£5 OFF 🍷 🛏

Built as a hunting lodge for a colourful bachelor who had made a mint in the brewery business, Victorian Hambleton stands on the shore of Rutland Water, the largest artificial lake in western Europe. Although the place is run with due country-house formality, the interior décor is less staid than most, with blaring primary colours in the lounges and light-touch elegance in the dining room. Aaron Patterson has been here since the early 1990s, and his enthusiasm and finesse burn as brightly as ever. A simpler approach recently is yielding dividends in terms of the lack of presentational distraction on the plate, allowing ingredients their star roles. The ballotine of foie gras with its own ice cream amid shards of orangey rhubarb is a signature starter that makes a bold opening impression, or there could be variations of squid under a crispy tapioca hat with blobs of minty pea purée. Textural balancing of elements produces ingenious main courses like a pale slab of Old Spot pork, its crackling puffed up like Quavers, on a verdant bed of chard and endive, or flawlessly timed fillet and sweetbread of veal with heritage carrots, the dish garnished with enough summer truffle to suggest it might be going out of fashion. Dessert could be chocolate ganache in a circlet of passion-fruit jelly with smashed peanuts and honeycomb. Only an overly tart kumquat soufflé with orange sorbet let down an

inspection dinner. Breads, on the other hand, are sensational, as is the drinking, which extends from Wines of the Moment across the vinous globe, with quality paramount and prices quickly stiffening from a base of £25.
Chef/s: Aaron Patterson. **Open:** all week L 12 to 2, D 6.45 to 9.30. **Meals:** set L £27 (2 courses) to £33. Set D £68. Tasting menu £80. Sun L £55 (3 courses). **Details:** 60 seats. V menu. Bar. Parking. Children over 5 yrs only.

■ Kibworth Beauchamp
The Lighthouse
Cooking score: 3
Seafood | £29
9 Station Street, Kibworth Beauchamp, LE8 0LN
Tel no: (0116) 2796260
lighthousekibworth.co.uk
£5 OFF £30

'Although we are far inland, in the heart of buzzing Kibworth, we bring a tantalising taste of the sea to south Leicestershire,' write Sarah and Lino Poli. That little Kibworth is abuzz is in no small measure owing to the Lighthouse itself, where the breezy interior is hung with seascapes in defiance of the absent waves. There are regular paella nights with tapas and sangria, and a Captain's Table *menu surprise* deal, while Spoonerists will relish the midweek Nibbles and Tipples nights. The traditional approach to fish brings forth shellfish-crammed bouillabaisse, mussels in leeks and cider, herb-crumbed halibut with shrimps and crab, monkfish on Spanish-style bean and chorizo stew, and jolly old fish and chips. Seafood refuseniks might look to griddled fillet steaks, or chicken in mustard sauce, and it all ends happily with sticky toffee pudding or vanilla pannacotta and winter fruit compote. A simple wine list begins at £17.50.
Chef/s: Lino Poli and Tom Wilde. **Open:** Tue to Sat D only 6 to 10. **Closed:** Sun, Mon, 25 and 26 Dec, 1 Jan, bank hols. **Meals:** main courses £7 to £22. Set D £15 (2 courses) to £18. **Details:** 60 seats. Music.

The Good Food Guide Scoring System

Score 1: Capable cooking with simple food combinations and clear flavours.

Score 2: Decent cooking, displaying good technical skills and interesting combinations and flavours.

Score 3: Good cooking, showing sound technical skills and using quality ingredients.

Score 4: Dedicated, focused approach to cooking; good classical skills and high-quality ingredients.

Score 5: Exact cooking techniques and a degree of ambition; showing balance and depth of flavour in dishes.

Score 6: Exemplary cooking skills, innovative ideas, impeccable ingredients and an element of excitement.

Score 7: High level of ambition and individuality, attention to the smallest detail, accurate and vibrant dishes.

Score 8: A kitchen cooking close to or at the top of its game. Highly individual with impressive artistry.

Score 9: Cooking that has reached a pinnacle of achievement, making it a hugely memorable experience.

Score 10: Just perfect dishes, showing faultless technique at every service; extremely rare and the highest accolade the Guide can give.

◼ Kibworth Harcourt

Boboli

Italian | £28

88 Main Street, Kibworth Harcourt, LE8 0NQ

Tel no: (0116) 2793303

bobolirestaurant.co.uk

£30

This all-day eatery certainly pulls in the crowds. It offers a lively, clattery ambience and reporters agree that all the basics are right: good-quality ingredients, freshly cooked food, sensible prices and impeccable service. On offer is a menu of the kind of Italian dishes everyone likes to eat, from spaghetti with mussels in white wine, garlic and tomato sauce and cannelloni with pork, beef and mushroom stuffing, to veal escalope with Parma ham and calf's liver and onions with griddled polenta. Wood-fired pizzas extend choice and there's tiramisu to finish. Italian wines from £15. Related to the Lighthouse in Kibworth Beauchamp (see entry).

◼ Mountsorrel

John's House

Cooking score: 4

British | £47

Stonehurst Farm, 139-141 Loughborough Road, Mountsorrel, LE12 7AR

Tel no: (01509) 415569

johnshouse.co.uk

£5 OFF

This 'little restaurant with lots of style' is in a 17th-century cottage on the edge of chef John Duffin's family farm – 'on arrival, park up next to the old farm machinery, vintage signs and outbuildings'. The rustic feel is continued inside, taking in a homely lounge with battered leather chairs, and upstairs, two interconnecting dining rooms – the larger the preferred space, say reporters. Mr Duffin is obviously ambitious and pulls off a really appealing menu – 'clearly head and shoulders above anything else we've eaten since moving up here'. The cooking draws comparisons to

London's The Dairy (see entry), especially with its fiercely seasonal farm-to-plate philosophy, seen in dishes such as heritage carrots with ox tongue, crème fraîche and mint, and Stonehurst hogget with charred onions and wood blewits. Poached fillet of Cornish halibut with caramelised cauliflower, charred cabbage and brown shrimps has an earthiness that echoes the surroundings, while for dessert, look no further than parsnip ice cream with liquorice, yoghurt and mint. Gentle pricing extends to the short, modern wine list, which opens at £24.

Chef/s: John Duffin. **Open:** Tue to Sat L 12 to 2, D 6.30 to 9. **Closed:** Sun, Mon, 24 Dec to 5 Jan, 2 weeks Aug. **Meals:** set L £24 (2 courses) to £28. Set D £42 (2 courses) to £47. Tasting menu £70 (8 courses). **Details:** 30 seats. Bar. Music. Parking.

◼ Stathern

Red Lion Inn

British | £33

2 Red Lion Street, Stathern, LE14 4HS

Tel no: (01949) 860868

theredlioninn.co.uk

Refurbished and given a new lease of life by new owners, this small village local in the Vale of Belvoir continues to strike a good balance between its restaurant and pub personalities. The menu delivers bang-on flavours and doesn't mess about with things too much. The reference point is classic pub repertoire, with dishes ranging from burgers, steaks and beer-battered fish and chips to double pork chop with creamy mash, cider sauce and mustard cream, and good old sticky toffee pudding. Wines from £17.50.

▌ Wymeswold

★ NEW ENTRY ★

The Hammer and Pincers

Cooking score: 2
Modern British | £35
5 East Road, Wymeswold, LE12 6ST
Tel no: (01509) 880735
hammerandpincers.co.uk

£5
OFF

Set in rolling Leicestershire countryside, the spiritual homeland of pork pies and Stilton cheese, the Hammer and Pincers is a likeable country pub that evangelises about Midlands produce (even providing a small leaflet on the topic for diners to study in the handsome beamed dining room). Start locally, with Stilton pannacotta with apple, walnut and grape salad. Mains are intricate affairs: spiced duck breast, confit leg, rose-poached quince and couscous wowed on our visit, as did a rich (and also presumably not quite so local) hake fillet and squid-ink linguine, with wild garlic, chilli and mussels. End with lemon posset and poached rhubarb. Wines from £16.
Chef/s: Daniel Jimminson. **Open:** Tue to Sun L 12 to 2 (4 Sun), Tue to Sat D 6 to 9. **Closed:** Mon, 24 and 25 Dec. **Meals:** main courses £15 to £25. Set L £19 (2 courses) to £23. Set D £25 (2 courses). Sun L £23 (2 courses). **Details:** 46 seats. 30 seats outside. Bar. Music. Parking.

▌ Wymondham

The Berkeley Arms

Cooking score: 3
Modern British | £31
59 Main Street, Wymondham, LE14 2AG
Tel no: (01572) 787587
theberkeleyarms.co.uk

The locals seem well aware what a gem they have on their doorstep, judging by the happy throng. It's a proper 16th-century stone-built village pub, run by a couple who have made their mark since taking over in 2010. The original bones of the building remain, while the decorative style could be described as rustic-country-chic. In the kitchen, Neil Hitchen and his team deliver a seasonal repertoire with regional produce and no little refinement (we're back to rustic-country-chic again). Start with some pan-seared scallops with celeriac purée and black pudding fritters, or a wobbly goats' cheese pannacotta served with Waldorf salad, before a hearty steak and ale casserole, classic fish and chips or red mullet with a pan-European medley of chorizo, pesto and balsamic. Among desserts, orange marmalade bread-and-butter pudding is home comfort writ large, or go for coffee crème brûlée with shortbread biscuits. Wines start at £18.50.
Chef/s: Neil Hitchen. **Open:** Tue to Sun L 12 to 1.45 (3 Sun), Tue to Sat D 6 to 9 (9.30 Fri and Sat). **Closed:** Mon, first 2 weeks Jan, 2 weeks summer, Tue after bank hols. **Meals:** main courses £13 to £25. Set L £15 (2 courses) to £19. Set D £19 (2 courses) to £23. Sun L £24 (3 courses). **Details:** 48 seats. 24 seats outside. Bar. Wheelchairs. Parking.

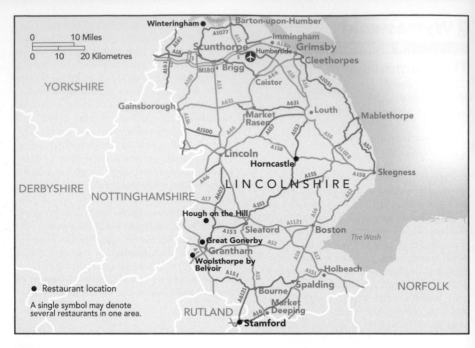

Great Gonerby

Harry's Place

Cooking score: 4
Modern French | £70
17 High Street, Great Gonerby, NG31 8JS
Tel no: (01476) 561780

The Hallams' endearingly domestic operation is fast approaching its fourth decade and remains a picture of unruffled consistency, not bad for an enterprise established at the sunset of the nouvelle cuisine era, when the tides of restaurant fashion were just starting their ceaseless raging. Up to a dozen people eat in their commodious red front room, from a menu that offers a pair of choices at each course. Harry's cooking style is still firmly fixed in French classicism, the carefully timed principal ingredients offset with alcohol-infused sauces and a plethora of accompanying veg. You may begin with king scallop, red pepper, shallot and lemon terrine in Sauternes jelly, before moving to Lincoln Red beef fillet with red onion and caper relish, horseradish

mayo and a herby reduction sauce of red wine and Armagnac. Dessert is as simple as can be, perhaps rhubarb ice cream in Cointreau syrup. A short wine list gets the job done, from £26 a bottle or £6.50 a glass.
Chef/s: Harry Hallam. Open: Tue to Sat L 12.30 to 2, D 7 to 8.30. Closed: Sun, Mon, Christmas, 2 weeks Aug, bank hols. Meals: main courses £40.
Details: 10 seats. Parking. Children over 5 yrs only.

Horncastle

Magpies

Cooking score: 5
Modern British | £49
73 East Street, Horncastle, LN9 6AA
Tel no: (01507) 527004
magpiesresturant.co.uk

A model of relaxed restraint, this low-key restaurant-with-rooms works to a brief of fixed-price menus and manages to generate fulsome praise from readers. 'Each course a delight', commented one visitor, who also appreciated that Magpies is a 'gem in Lincolnshire'. The Gilberts, chef Andrew and front-of-house Caroline, go about their business in a terrace of converted cottages, the low-ceilinged interior described as 'cosy with a relaxed atmosphere'. But there's nothing folksy about a menu that offers the likes of gravadlax with horseradish ice cream ('flavour combinations complemented each other beautifully'), guinea fowl and lobster terrine with goats' cheese fritters and home-dried grapes, or ribeye of Lincolnshire beef on a potato galette with a baby steak and kidney pudding, pan-fried calf's liver and foie gras. Desserts might bring a mini sticky toffee pudding with homemade cinder toffee sauce or a passion fruit soufflé. Wine is taken seriously, too: reasonable prices (from £16.90), reliable producers, plenty for the French purists, but with some good southern-hemisphere selections.

Chef/s: Andrew Gilbert. **Open:** Wed to Fri and Sun L 12 to 2, Wed to Sun D 7 to 9.30. **Closed:** Mon, Tue, 26 to 30 Dec, first week Jan. **Meals:** set L £16 (weekday) and £21 (2 courses) to £26. Set D £27 and £43 (2 courses) to £49. Sun L £21 (2 courses) to £26. **Details:** 34 seats. V menu. Wheelchairs. Music.

Hough on the Hill
The Brownlow Arms

Cooking score: 2
British | £40
Grantham Road, Hough on the Hill, NG32 2AZ
Tel no: (01400) 250234
thebrownlowarms.com

This 17th-century country inn tucked away in a tiny village a few miles north of Grantham continues to be a safe bet for a good meal in a pleasant, welcoming environment. Paul and Lorraine Willoughby have chalked up some 14 years of hospitality, offering a straightforward menu to an appreciative Lincolnshire crowd. Notable successes have been chicken liver parfait, and slow-braised ox tongue beautifully paired with celeriac rémoulade and piccalilli purée, while main courses have delivered specials of 'pot au poisson', a creamy

fish broth containing halibut, hake and plaice alongside shellfish such as prawns, scallops, mussels and little brown shrimps, 'together with an exceptionally tasty seafood mousse', as well as Barbary duck breast with spiced ginger-beer sauce, stir-fried julienne of vegetables and steamed basmati rice. Desserts might include vanilla and mascarpone cheesecake with poached local rhubarb and rhubarb sorbet. Wines from £16.95.

Chef/s: Ruaraidh Bealby. **Open:** Wed to Sun L 12 to 2 (2.30 Sun), Tue to Sat D 6 to 9 (9.30 Fri and Sat). **Closed:** Mon, 25 and 26 Dec, bank hols. **Meals:** main courses £16 to £28. Sun L £24. **Details:** 80 seats. 30 seats outside. Bar. Music. Parking. Children before 8pm only.

Stamford
No. 3 The Yard

Cooking score: 3
Modern European | £30
3 Ironmonger Street, Stamford, PE9 1PL
Tel no: (01780) 756080
no3theyard.co.uk

Described as 'a little oasis of calm, done out in old stone', this amicable bistro is hidden away just off Stamford's busy high street. Pass through a tiny blackened door to reach the old covered courtyard and modern conservatory dining room – a charming backdrop for 'simple cooking at its best'. Printed menus are supplemented by inviting daily specials, perhaps a buttery fillet of brill ('from a seriously big fish') served with well-timed Jersey Royals, new season's asparagus and 'pleasantly tart' hollandaise. Otherwise, begin with deeply flavoured 'truffle butter' chicken liver parfait before sampling confit duck with buttered Savoy cabbage, slow-roast pork belly with butternut squash and pearl barley risotto or a ribeye steak and chips with Café de Paris butter. For afters, cherry custard tart with some extra Kirsch-soaked cherries makes an enjoyable finish. Set lunches are terrific value, as is the modest wine list (from £14.95).

Chef/s: Tim Luff. **Open:** Tue to Sun L 11.30 to 2.30 (12 to 3 Sun), Tue to Sat D 6 to 9.30 (10 Fri and Sat). **Closed:** Mon, 26 Dec. **Meals:** main courses £15 to

£22. Set L £16 (2 courses) to £20. Set D £22 (3 courses). Sun L £16 (2 courses) to £20. **Details:** 70 seats. 16 seats outside. Bar. Wheelchairs. Music.

▌Winteringham
Winteringham Fields

Cooking score: 6
Modern British | £55
1 Silver Street, Winteringham, DN15 9ND
Tel no: (01724) 733096
winteringhamfields.co.uk

There's a lot happening at this renovated farmhouse out in the flatlands: long established as Lincolnshire's premier restaurant-with-rooms, Winteringham Fields is going back to its roots with a burgeoning kitchen garden and an increasing emphasis on provenance. That said, the interior still feels 'smart but chintzy', with drapes, chandeliers, grand paintings and widely spaced tables inviting special-occasion bookings. Colin McGurran's pursuit of seasonal clarity and flavour shows throughout his menus, which have yielded plenty of standout dishes: some have highlighted the mushroom tea with Parmesan foam and the salt-baked squab; others have applauded more intricate creations underpinned by restless creativity and a modish obsession with cooking temperatures. A 'clever and very pretty' spin on steak tartare with slivers of home-grown radish and garlic flowers nailed it for one diner, closely followed by a 'neat' plate of guinea fowl breast, 12-hour braised leg meat, onion purée and semi-dried blueberries. For dessert, the Brillat-Savarin cheesecake offset by a 'cutting' grappa sorbet and a rolled-up strip of poached pear is recommended. Service is chatty but professional, and the wine list is packed with serious bottles from £28.
Chef/s: Colin McGurran. **Open:** Tue to Sat L 12 to 2, D 7 to 9. **Closed:** Sun, Mon, 2 weeks Dec, 1 week Jan, 2 weeks Aug. **Meals:** set L £40 to £45 (4 courses). Set D £55. Tasting menu £75 (7 courses). **Details:** 65 seats. Bar. Wheelchairs. Music. Parking.

▌Woolsthorpe by Belvoir
Chequers Inn

Cooking score: 1
Modern British | £28
Main Street, Woolsthorpe by Belvoir,
NG32 1LU
Tel no: (01476) 870701
chequersinn.net

The 17th-century inn is ensconced in the Vale of Belvoir within sight of the castle, its old bakehouse, complete with original bread oven, the setting for both modern and classic pub cooking. If sausages and mash or cod and bacon fishcakes sound too trad, look to a starter of wood pigeon Wellington with celeriac rémoulade, perhaps followed by sea bream katsu curry and spicy rice. Hefty sandwiches should fortify the walkers, while desserts can be as light as marshmallow with pineapple carpaccio and lime sorbet, or as stonking as sticky toffee pudding and butterscotch. Well-chosen wines open at £16.50, or £4.50 a standard glass.
Chef/s: James Wallace. **Open:** all week L 12 to 2.30 (4 Sun), D 6 to 9.30 (8.30 Sun). **Meals:** main courses £11 to £20. Sun L £14 (2 courses). **Details:** 120 seats. 80 seats outside. Bar. Wheelchairs. Music. Parking.

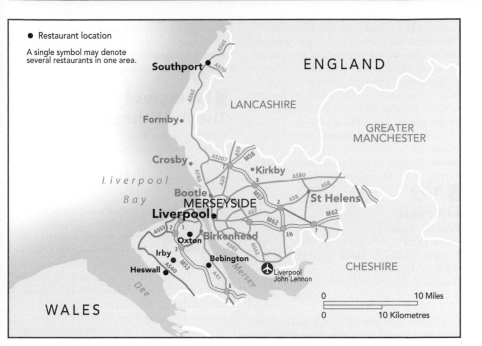

▌Bebington

LOCAL GEM
Claremont Farm Café
British | £20
Old Clatterbridge Road, Bebington,
CH63 4JB
Tel no: (0151) 3341133
claremontfarm.co.uk

£30

It's the down-to-earth cooking and the
seasonal British produce that have locals
competing for space at this easy-going café
housed in a bustling farm shop overlooking
the Wirral countryside. Generous breakfasts
('can't beat scrambled eggs and bacon with
fresh bread, toasted'), interesting salads, fresh
asparagus grown on the farm, fresh fish from
the coast, and chicken, leek and ham filo pie
have all struck a chord with reporters, as have
homemade cakes. Wines from £12.

▌Heswall

★ NEW ENTRY ★
Burnt Truffle
Cooking score: 3
Modern British | £30
104-106 Telegraph Road, Heswall, CH60 0AQ
Tel no: (0151) 3421111
burnttruffle.net

Gary Usher's crowdfunded second restaurant
kindles the bistro spirit on the Wirral. The
neutral dining space features the unclothed
tables, bare brick and flickering candles that
make neighbourhood restaurants so versatile.
With cooking strong and prices sensible
(especially at lunch), Burnt Truffle should
replicate the success of Hoole's Sticky Walnut.
Head chef Michael Wong knows a trend when
he sees one, so beef tartare comes with smoked
mayonnaise and a blanket of earthy puffed
wild rice. A plate of roasted cauliflower, every
veggie's new jam, is mined with pickled
onions and the spreading tentacles of crisp,
finger-like onion bhajis; as an exercise in

balance and contrast, it works. For afters, Paris-Brest with chocolate mousse, whipped cream, crunchy sugared banana *and* caramel ice cream has too many bells and whistles. As at the mother ship, both bread and chips, the latter with truffle and Parmesan, are the stuff of carby reveries. Wines are from £17.50.

Chef/s: Michael Wong. **Open:** all week L 12 to 2.30, D 6 to 9 (10 Fri and Sat). **Closed:** 25 to 27 Dec. **Meals:** main courses £14 to £23. Sun L £18. **Details:** 53 seats. 30 seats outside. Music. Parking.

∎ Irby
Da Piero
Cooking score: 3
Italian | £32
5-7 Mill Hill Road, Irby, CH61 4UB
Tel no: (0151) 6487373
dapiero.co.uk
£5
OFF

Chef-proprietor Piero Di Bella and his family recently returned from a food-hunting trip to their native Sicily, armed with supplies of 'Siccagno' tomatoes (grown with the tiniest amount of water) plus various ancient grains for use in their home-baked breads and pasta. As ever, recipes and ingredients from Italy's volcanic island form the backbone of the menu at this affectionately run neighbourhood restaurant, although Merseyside's markets also contribute to proceedings. As an opener, look no further than the sashimi-grade tuna tartare, the octopus salad or the swordfish carpaccio scattered with dill and pink peppercorns. To follow, the aforementioned pasta is a must – perhaps spaghettini with bottarga (grated mullet roe) or tagliatelle made from 'tumminia' grains with Trapani pesto. Robust rusticity is also the key to mains ranging from Sicilian-style marinated beef to grilled halibut fillet dressed with tomato vinaigrette, while assorted homemade ice creams dominate the desserts. Italian house wines start at £11.40 per 500ml carafe.

Chef/s: Piero Di Bella. **Open:** Tue to Sat D only 6 to 11. **Closed:** Sun, Mon, 25 and 26 Dec, 1 and 2 Jan, 2 weeks Aug. **Meals:** main courses £12 to £23. **Details:** 32 seats. V menu.

∎ Liverpool
The Art School
Cooking score: 5
Modern European | £69
1 Sugnall Street, Liverpool, L7 7DX
Tel no: (0151) 2308600
theartschoolrestaurant.co.uk

Sugnall Street isn't exactly out in the sticks – it's immediately behind the Liverpool Philharmonic Hall between the gastronomic entrepôt of Hope Street and the University quarter – but it can feel that way to first-timers. Be assured that it's worth the journey for Paul Askew's ambitious urban cooking, another plank of Liverpool's culinary renaissance. Under a skylight roof in the lantern room of what was once a home for destitute children, north-western food producers are showcased in dishes like lemon sole with Filey crab and a poached oyster parcelled in lettuce, all glammed up with Champagne sauce, and mains such as St Asaph lamb – pot-roast loin, braised shoulder and sautéed sweetbreads – with Puy lentils, charred aubergine and anchovies. There are vegetarian and vegan menus, too, as well as a six-course taster that proceeds from a glass of luxuriously rich Charles Heidsieck champers to a dessert platter taking in hibiscus pannacotta, Turkish Delight ice cream and chocolate-orange torte. Wines open at £22.

Chef/s: Paul Askew. **Open:** Tue to Sat L 12 to 2.30, D 5 to 10. **Closed:** Sun, Mon, 25 and 26 Dec, 1 week Jan. **Meals:** set L £24 (2 courses) to £29. Set D £69 (3 courses). Tasting menu £95. **Details:** 48 seats. V menu. Bar. Wheelchairs. Music. No children after 7.

Paul Askew
The Art School, Liverpool

What inspired you to become a chef?
I was lucky to travel a lot as a youngster as my father was a Merchant Navy sea captain. Memories of the first fish market in Dubai and the first spice market I saw remain with me to this day. I got to see a lot of good quality restaurants and what great hospitality looked like.

What is the vital ingredient for a successful kitchen?
Team work. There must be a common vision and a common mission; you can't work with prima donnas in the kitchen. You're only as good as your last plate of food.

If you could cook for anyone who would it be, and what would you cook for them?
My absolute food hero is Albert Roux, I'd cook him king scallops with morcilla, cauliflower purée and Granny Smith salad. I'd love to hear his opinion on the flavour combinations.

And finally...tell us something about yourself that will surprise your diners.
My twitter handle is 'chef porky askew'; there's a pedigree pig farm on the Wirral that has recently named its breeding boar – a Tamworth red – Porky Junior, so now I have a four-legged protégé who looks remarkably like me!

Delifonseca Dockside
Cooking score: 2
International | £25
Brunswick Quay, Liverpool, L3 4BN
Tel no: (0151) 2550808
delifonseca.co.uk
£5 OFF £30

Bring your bag-for-life and stock up on all sorts of goodies at this deli and eatery, but better still, grab a cosy booth and take a look at the blackboard menu where something like sautéed Cumbrian venison and salt-baked celeriac in a red wine jus might just get you to stick around. A global spread includes a frittata to get the day started, a po' boy sandwich (from ol' New Orleans) for lunch and platters of charcuterie designed for sharing. The blackboard offers up a proper pie filled with tender oxtail and cheek, or pan-roasted sea bass with tabbouleh and crispy squid, while Sunday roasts are a classic Brit affair. Apple and damson crumble competes with bitter chocolate tart among desserts. Drink world beers off an interesting list, or wines starting at £16.50. Its sister establishment, Fonseca's, is in the city centre (see entry).
Chef/s: Marc Lara. **Open:** all week 12 to 9 (5 Sun). **Closed:** 25 and 26 Dec, 1 Jan. **Meals:** main courses £11 to £19. Sun L £12. **Details:** 66 seats. 24 seats outside. Wheelchairs. Music. Parking.

Fonseca's
Cooking score: 1
Modern European | £25
12 Stanley Street, Liverpool, L1 6AF
Tel no: (0151) 2550808
delifonseca.co.uk
£5 OFF £30

'Always a great vibe,' thought one reporter of this restaurant and clubby basement bar in the heart of Liverpool. Reclaimed theatre seats give the bar a quirky feel while the upper floor channels vintage diner and urban brasserie in equal measure – think high-sided booths, statement lighting and blackboard menus. 'Friendly, knowledgeable and polite' staff will guide you through a menu brimming with international flavours: gin-and-beetroot-cured salmon with confit rhubarb and ricotta, then roasted duo of Goosnargh chicken with saffron rice, char-grilled piquillo peppers and fiery 'Mojo' sauce, and a salt caramel chocolate pot with a crispy tuile. Wines start at £15.95. **Chef/s:** Rikki Vidamour. **Open:** Tue to Thur L 12 to 2.30, D 5 to 9.30. Fri and Sat 12 to 10. **Closed:** Sun, Mon, 26 Dec to 30 Dec, bank hols. **Meals:** main courses £11 to £23. **Details:** 60 seats. Bar. Music.

The London Carriage Works

Cooking score: 2
Modern British | £39
Hope Street Hotel, 40 Hope Street, Liverpool, L1 9DA
Tel no: (0151) 7052222
thelondoncarriageworks.co.uk

It's rather a grand building for a former carriage works, built in 1866 in the then fashionable Italian palazzo style, with a great location next door to its sister hotel (Hope Street Hotel), close to the Everyman and Philharmonic Hall. The stripped-back interior is a suitably contemporary-looking spot for head chef David Critchley's modern and locally minded menus. Cumbrian air-dried ham might turn up in a first course with a simple salad of green veg, or go for ravioli filled with Brixham crab and Cheshire saffron (yes, Cheshire). Sea bass is caught by line in Liverpool Bay and served up with crab bisque and Southport shrimps, while desserts are a creative bunch too (rice pudding flavoured with peach and Cassis, for example, with walnut granola and a citrus madeleine). It's open all day for breakfast, afternoon tea, cocktails, the works, and service doesn't always keep up the pace. Wines start at £18.95. **Chef/s:** David Critchley. **Open:** all week L 11 to 3, D 5 to 10 (9 Sun). **Meals:** main courses £15 to £30. Set L and D £20 (2 courses) to £25. Sun L £20 (2 courses). **Details:** 60 seats. Bar. Wheelchairs. Music.

Lunya

Cooking score: 2
Spanish | £26
18-20 College Lane, Liverpool One, Liverpool, L1 3DS
Tel no: (0151) 7069770
lunya.co.uk
£5 OFF £30

Peter and Elaine Kinsella's cracking tapas restaurant has proved a great concept and they've expanded their horizons with a new place in Manchester (see entry). The original Lunya, in Liverpool's state-of-the art retail complex, continues to fly the flag for a vast array of Spanish – or more specifically Catalan – provisions. Encompassing part of the city's oldest warehouse, this rough-walled space is a mecca for shoppers, office workers and fans of all things Iberian. Fried Catalan breakfasts, kids' deals and suckling pig banquets top up an all-day offer that centres on a prodigious array of cured meats, jamóns, breads and artisan cheeses – over 40 at the last count. Alternatively, feast on tapas dishes with a Scouse twist – perhaps chorizo sausage rolls, cuttlefish à la plancha on black rice or lightly battered cauliflower and broccoli buñuelos with romesco sauce. A terrific 80-bin wine list covers just about every Spanish 'DO', with bottles from £17.95. **Chef/s:** Dave Upson. **Open:** all week 10 to 9 (9.30pm Wed and Thur, 10pm Fri and Sat, 8.30pm Sun). **Closed:** 25 Dec, 1 Jan. **Meals:** tapas £5 to £10. Set L £13 (2 courses). Tapas banquet £27. **Details:** 150 seats. 30 seats outside. V menu. Bar. Wheelchairs. Music.

Salt House Tapas

Cooking score: 3
Spanish | £20
1 Hanover Street, Liverpool, L1 3DW
Tel no: (0151) 7060092
salthousetapas.co.uk
£5 OFF £30

Top-notch execution and a generous hand with quality ingredients contribute to the ongoing popularity of this home-grown

Spanish joint not far from the river. It's set over two floors, with a new heated terrace outside and laid-back contemporary décor within. Tapas dishes extend through Spain to the whole Mediterranean basin, so there's roasted purple sprouting broccoli with harissa dressing, yoghurt and garlic croûtons alongside heavily loaded boards of jamón and, closer to home, seared fillet steak with bone-marrow toast, veal jus and confit shallots. Dessert might be buttermilk and cardamom pudding with Valencian orange marmalade. Strangers in need of a chat can take a seat at communal table 14, where all-comers are encouraged to break crusty bread with olive oil and PZ vinegar. There's a gin bar, with a handful of Spanish examples, and a neat selection of cava in addition to a predominantly Iberian wine list, from £15.95.
Chef/s: Martin Renshaw. **Open:** all week 12 to 10.30 (11 Fri and Sat). **Closed:** 25 Dec. **Meals:** tapas £5 to £8. Set L £12. **Details:** 90 seats. 30 seats outside. Wheelchairs. Music.

60 Hope Street
Cooking score: 2
Modern British | £45
60 Hope Street, Liverpool, L1 9BZ
Tel no: (0151) 7076060
60hopestreet.com

An independent family business in the heart of the Georgian quarter, 60 Hope Street occupies a stylish but relaxed town house with a wine bar downstairs (replete with banquettes and Chesterfields) and a light and airy upstairs dining room. The food brims with freshness and flavour, and is broadly European in style: you could start with braised pig's cheeks with artichoke, black pudding and crackling, then move on to a main course such as roast breast of Goosnargh duck with salt-baked, candied and golden beetroot, violet potatoes, smoked pear and blackberries. Dishes singled out for special praise include the 'delicious' pea soup and the beef faggots. Desserts are fun and imaginative, with recent examples including salted-caramel fondant with tonka bean ice cream and parsnip, and deep-fried jam

sandwich with Carnation milk ice cream. The substantial wine list includes some classy and lesser-known finds, and plenty by the glass. Bottles start at £19.95.
Chef/s: Gary Manning and Neil Devereux. **Open:** Mon to Sat L 12 to 2.30, D 5 to 10.30. Sun 12 to 6. **Meals:** main courses £22 to £32. Set L and D £20 (2 courses) to £25. Sun L £15. **Details:** 160 seats. 10 seats outside. Bar. Music.

Spire
Cooking score: 5
Modern European | £35
1 Church Road, Liverpool, L15 9EA
Tel no: (0151) 7345040
spirerestaurant.co.uk

The Locke brothers' neighbourhood spot a penny's throw from Penny Lane has made spectacular waves since opening eight years ago. Two levels connected by spiral stairs are kitted out with abstract and minimal artworks on exposed brick walls, with unclothed tables and friendly, capable service creating a mood of city cool. Matt's cooking manages a deft amalgam of demotic British and continental modes that always seems to produce satisfaction, whether it be for a bowl of truffled cauliflower soup, or the trio of salmon starters that offers hot-smoked, a crisply horseradished fishcake and a sensational cure in star anise and Liverpool gin. Main courses spin variations on familiar ideas, offering a vegetarian Wellington bursting with roast veg and mushrooms, or adding rarebit, black pudding and mash to flavourful Goosnargh chicken breast. Form an orderly queue for Malteser hot chocolate fondant with salt caramel ice cream, or look to something fruitier for raspberry pavlova cheesecake and matching sorbet. Wines start at £15.95.
Chef/s: Matt Locke. **Open:** Tue to Fri L 12 to 2, Mon to Sat D 5.30 to 9 (6 Mon, 9.30 Fri and Sat). **Closed:** Sun, first week Jan. **Meals:** main courses £14 to £22. Set L £12 (2 courses) to £16. Set D £16 (2 courses) to £19. **Details:** 70 seats. Music.

LOCAL GEM

Etsu

Japanese | £25
25 The Strand (off Brunswick Street),
Liverpool, L2 0XJ
Tel no: (0151) 2367530
etsu-restaurant.co.uk

£30

Within the starkly modern block that is Brunswick Plaza, David Abe's sleek and minimalist restaurant is a top spot for Japanese food with the ring of authenticity. Bento boxes are just the job at lunchtime, sea bass, say, with a teriyaki sauce, while sushi and sashimi continue to impress. Begin with niku gyoza (pork and veg) before grilled eel donburi or a bowl of udon noodles with prawn tempura. Warm or chilled saké and shochu compete with a short wine list starting at £12.95.

Oxton

★ TOP 10 ★

Fraiche

Cooking score: 8
Modern French | £85
11 Rose Mount, Oxton, CH43 5SG
Tel no: (0151) 6522914
restaurantfraiche.com

It's a suburban restaurant that opens four nights a week, serves eight people (12 for Sunday lunch) and where it's 'a bugger to get a reservation.' Persevere, though, for a meal at Fraiche is a highly memorable experience. In the dining room, Marc Wilkinson has created a special environment, with the lights and sights changing throughout the meal thanks to video projections on the two main walls – autumnal trees, fallen leaves and a stream on November visit – as a fitting backdrop to his 'stunning food, created with passion and flair with the finest attention to every detail.' He offers a fixed six-course tasting menu, but with the various nibbles, including two bread courses, a pre-dessert and petits fours, in total

you're getting on for twenty. Mr Wilkinson continues to push the boundaries of contemporary cooking while keeping in touch with his classical background and standout dishes this year have included an appetiser of apple soda – a shot glass with a little apple and apple jelly, topped with apple foam – and a starter described enigmatically as 'autumn tree': a sculpted tree branch with nasturtium leaves and seeded crisps shaped like leaves that you pick off and eat. Other showstoppers have included a disc of scallop tartare topped with a yuzu jelly, butternut squash purée with a horseradish crème fraîche, and a dish simply titled 'beetroot' comprising a purée, sweet yet earthy baby beets, a verjus dressing and slivers of smoked duck giving a hint of fatty savouriness. Fish comes in for special praise, for example a perfectly cooked fillet of wild sea bass served with softened fennel, spring onion and smoked yoghurt. Elsewhere, a late autumn dish has delivered bang on seasonality in the form of a perfectly pink venison loin with celeriac, chard and artfully crafted potato crisps shaped like leaves. And then comes dessert. At the beginning of the meal, you are asked if you want to end with salt or sugar. Salt will take you to goats' curd and cheeses from the extensive trolley, sugar might translate as a lemongrass pannacotta topped with a fruit purée, followed by 'an absolute knockout finale' of peanut ice cream and chocolate ganache topped with strips of an orange jelly. For a final bow there are Wilkinson's signature fizzy grapes. A 300-bin wine list, full of international delights, starts at a gentle £18.
Chef/s: Marc Wilkinson. **Open:** Sun L 12 to 1, Wed to Sat D 7 to 8.30. **Closed:** Mon, Tue. **Meals:** Set D £85 (6 courses). Sun L £45 (4 courses). **Details:** 8 seats. Children over 8 yrs only at D.

Symbols

🛏 Accommodation is available
£30 Three courses for less than £30
£5 OFF £5-off voucher scheme
🍾 Notable wine list

Southport
Bistro 21
Cooking score: 4
Modern European | £32
21 Stanley Street, Southport, PR9 0BS
Tel no: (01704) 501414
bistro21.co.uk

Tucked along a back-street behind Debenham's, hidden behind half-frosted windows, the pint-sized, white-tiled room feels light and refreshing. Tables are stiffly linened; staff are just the opposite, all smiles and bonhomie. As the name attests, the drill is modern European bistro food with plenty of Mediterranean sunshine, sometimes extending to the southern shore, as for glutinously braised Moroccan-style lamb shoulder with apricots, raisins, red pepper purée and herbed couscous. Sun-dried tomatoes and Parma ham contribute sweet and salty notes as toppings for fillets of sea bass, the skin separately crisped for a garnish, a snow of Jerusalem artichoke purée adding earthiness. Before that, there may be fat ham hock croquettes on creamed peas with asparagus and a poached egg, and finishings will have you torn between the likes of strawberry and mascarpone crème brûlée or chocolate and honeycomb torte with passion fruit sorbet. A small wine list does its job briskly, from £14.95.
Chef/s: Michael Glayzer. **Open:** Wed to Sat L 12 to 2, D 5.30 to 9.30. Sun 12 to 6. **Closed:** Mon, Tue. **Meals:** main courses £14 to £24. Set L £11. Set D £18. Sun L £13. Tasting menu £19. **Details:** 28 seats. V menu. Bar. Wheelchairs. Music.

Bistrot Vérité
Cooking score: 3
French | £28
7 Liverpool Road, Birkdale, Southport, PR8 4AR
Tel no: (01704) 564199
bistrotverite.co.uk
£30

'Epitomises all the good things a local restaurant should stand for,' declares one reader who reckons that Marc Vérité's big-hearted bourgeois food is 'comfortably the best in the area'. Set in the sedate surroundings of Birkdale village, this white-fronted, pine-floored bistro has an infectiously buzzy vibe, while Michaela Vérité and her exemplary front-of-house team welcome visitors as 'part of the family'. The kitchen has 'stayed true to its Gallic roots', although some reports suggest that the cooking has gone up a gear of late – witness goats' cheese bonbons with beetroot jam, roast duckling with blood oranges and pistachios or pigeon breasts 'cooked to pink perfection' in brik pastry. Marc Vérité is also known for his 'exceptional' seafood specialities (grilled wild turbot with warm potted Southport shrimps, for example), while plates of fish and chips with mushy peas keep the holidaymakers happy. Easy-drinking French wines start at £16.75 (£9.95 a carafe).
Chef/s: Marc Vérité. **Open:** Wed to Sat L 12 to 1.30, Tue to Sat D from 5.30. **Closed:** Sun, Mon, 1 week Feb, 1 week Aug. **Meals:** main courses £13 to £29. Set L £15 (2 courses) to £18. **Details:** 45 seats. 16 seats outside. Music.

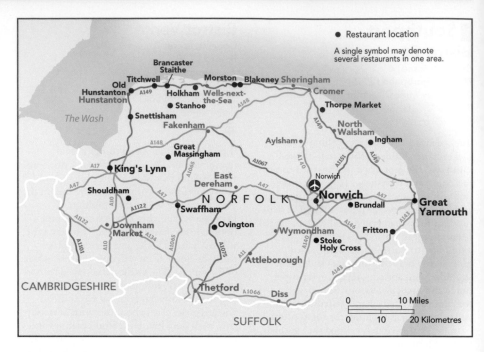

- Restaurant location

A single symbol may denote several restaurants in one area.

Brancaster Staithe
Titchwell
Morston Blakeney Sheringham
Old Hunstanton
Hunstanton
A149 Holkham Wells-next-the-Sea Cromer
Stanhoe
Snettisham
The Wash
Fakenham
Thorpe Market
North Walsham
Aylsham Ingham
A148
Great Massingham
A17 King's Lynn
A1067
East Dereham
NORFOLK
Norwich
Shouldham
A1122 Swaffham
Brundall
Great Yarmouth
Downham Market
Ovington
Wymondham
Fritton
Stoke Holy Cross
Attleborough
CAMBRIDGESHIRE
Thetford
A1066 Diss
SUFFOLK

0   10 Miles
0   10   20 Kilometres

▉ Blakeney
The Moorings
Cooking score: 2
Modern British | £33
High Street, Blakeney, NR25 7NA
Tel no: (01263) 740054
blakeney-moorings.co.uk

The sailing people, day-trippers, birdwatchers and seal-spotters who descend on Blakeney in their droves yearn for somewhere decent to eat, and the Moorings obliges with suitably crowd-friendly refreshments. Occupying a cluster of converted bait sheds close to the quay, Richard and Angela Long's affable restaurant keeps the daytime crowd satisfied with a café-style menu (sandwiches, soups, salads), before the laying of tablecloths and lighting of candles signal that it's time for dinner. Fish from the north Norfolk boats and other seasonal gleanings figure prominently as the kitchen shows its true mettle: bowls of mussel, smoked haddock and sweetcorn chowder go down well or you could start with

a plate of pan-fried pigeon breast with braised lentils and wilted spinach. Mains offer steaks and venison alongside, say, sea bass fillet with fennel, thyme and salsa verde, while Angela's desserts might include white chocolate and raspberry tart. Wines from £15.
Chef/s: Richard and Angela Long. **Open:** Tue to Sun L 10.30 to 4, Tue to Sat D 6 to 10. **Closed:** Mon, Dec, Jan. **Meals:** main courses £15 to £23. Sun L £18. **Details:** 55 seats.

▉ Brancaster Staithe
The White Horse
Cooking score: 2
Modern British | £32
Brancaster Staithe, PE31 8BY
Tel no: (01485) 210262
whitehorsebrancaster.co.uk

Feast on one of Norfolk's most seductive sea views (even better following a revamp of the conservatory – 'view even clearer through bigger panes') over a generous panful of lusciously plump mussels raked from the salt marsh behind this ever-popular pub. No need to deviate from classic moules marinière with such a perfect raw ingredient, though you may be tempted off-piste by the warming flavours of Moroccan ras-el-hanout or fresh Thai tom yum broth. Arguably more elegant is a starter of baked queen scallops, a vivid-green gremolata crunch hiding the scallops, curls of King's Lynn brown shrimp and buttery, garlicky spinach. Stay fishy with a delicate fillet of plaice with saffron gnocchi, the combination lifted by the tang of puttanesca, or look inland for a locally reared Red Poll steak or smoked pork tenderloin with butter beans. Enjoy the ever-changing coastal light as you finish with a sublime lemon tart with citrusy yuzu meringues and slivers of confit lime. Wine from £17.50.

Chef/s: Fran Hartshorne. **Open:** all week L 12 to 2, D 6.15 to 9. **Meals:** main courses £13 to £22. **Details:** 100 seats. 100 seats outside. Bar. Wheelchairs. Music. Parking.

LOCAL GEM

The Jolly Sailors
British | £23
Brancaster Staithe, PE31 8BJ
Tel no: (01485) 210314
jollysailorsbrancaster.co.uk
£30

The Nye family (of the nearby White Horse, see entry) has been custodians of this unassuming roadside pub for some seven years. Amid beams and stone floors you can sample Brancaster Brewery ales and a workmanlike version of honest pub food – say fish and chips or steak and ale pie. Smoked prawns, ribs, wings and brisket (added to a chilli con carne) come from the pub's own smokehouse, there are local mussels, wood-fired pizzas to eat in or takeaway, and the beer garden is popular in summer. House Georges Duboeuf is £17.50.

■ Brundall
The Lavender House
Cooking score: 4
Modern British | £45
39 The Street, Brundall, NR13 5AA
Tel no: (01603) 712215
thelavenderhouse.co.uk

Operating in a sensitively updated former pub, Richard Hughes' restaurant is a relaxing treat. Black beams and inglenook fireplaces provide the backdrop to some pretty nifty cooking starring Norfolk ingredients. Guests peruse the menu over canapés in an ante-room before being guided to the terracotta-floored restaurant. Choose between the tasting menu or a fixed-price list where meltingly rich pork belly might be given a South-East Asian slant with peanut sauce; or Cley smoked salmon could be paired with blobs of faintly flavoured crabmeat mayonnaise. Next, an undoubted highlight: beef served as pink tender steak and flavour-packed cheek with mash and tenderstem broccoli, though a succulent cod steak in a 'minestrone' of taut prawns, squid and borlotti beans comes a close second. Puddings maintain standards – especially a crunchy peanut-butter parfait with moist chocolate brownies – as do the unaffected, congenial staff. The concise, well-chosen wine list has prices starting at £23.

Chef/s: Richard Hughes. **Open:** Sun L 12 to 3, Thur to Sat D 6.30 to 9.30. **Closed:** Mon, Tue, Wed, 26 Dec to 9 Jan. **Meals:** set D £45 (6 courses). Tasting menu £60 (9 courses). Sun L £28. **Details:** 44 seats. Bar. Wheelchairs. Music. Parking.

Local Gem

Local Gems are the perfect neighbourhood venues, delivering good, freshly cooked food at great value for money.

▌Fritton

LOCAL GEM
The Fritton Arms
Modern British | £28
Church Lane, Fritton, NR31 9HA
Tel no: (01493) 484008
frittonarms.co.uk

🛏 £30

Sit back in shabby chic style at this comfortable pub on the banks of Fritton Lake, a pretty spot (with bags of outside space) on the Somerleyton Estate. The estate's herd of Welsh Black cattle provides much of the beef, but you may prefer slow-braised pork belly with crushed Jersey Royals or a pizza from the wood-fired oven. Lighter options include grilled sardines with a cockle, wild fennel and lemon butter or locally picked St George's mushrooms on toast. Finish with a raspberry pannacotta and fresh berries. Wines start at £16.50.

▌Great Massingham
The Dabbling Duck
Cooking score: 2
British | £28
11 Abbey Road, Great Massingham,
PE32 2HN
Tel no: (01485) 520827
thedabblingduck.co.uk

 🛏 £30

Sometimes, when you walk into a pub, you feel you're in a place that really does belong at the heart of a village. That's absolutely where this much-loved pub sits, drawing customers from immediate surroundings and further afield with its winning mix of charm (go in spring for the duckling extravaganza) and good food. Jason 'Mitch' Mitchell is at home turning game from nearby shoots into firmly flavoured food: rabbit rillettes, pheasant pastrami or game sausage roll will get a meal off to a tasty start. You'd do well to follow it with a fillet of roe deer served with confit shoulder and richly tasty potato gratin and wild mushrooms or braised ox cheek with

borlotti bean cassoulet. Not so hungry? Choose a delicate piece of poached plaice with salt cod croquette and pea purée. There's applause for the chef's white-wine-poached pear with frangipane, almond crunch ice cream and sherry vinegar caramel. Wine from £15.95.
Chef/s: Jason Mitchell. **Open:** Mon to Sat L 12 to 2.30, D 6.30 to 9 (6 to 9.30 Fri and Sat). Sun 12 to 8. **Meals:** main courses £12 to £20. **Details:** 70 seats. 50 seats outside. Bar. Wheelchairs. Music. Parking.

▌Great Yarmouth
Seafood Restaurant
Cooking score: 1
Seafood | £35
85 North Quay, Great Yarmouth, NR30 1JF
Tel no: (01493) 856009
theseafood.co.uk

£5 OFF

On a busy road near the quay, this long-standing fish specialist occupies a former Victorian pub. Inside, swirly carpets and dinky light fittings speak of 1950s guest houses. Likewise, the cooking is from another age: fish in rich sauces (turbot with copious amounts of herb butter, say); mixed salad topped with cress. Nevertheless, you'll also find a Mediterranean slant in dishes such as homemade taramasalata or spicy seafood soup packed with prawns and little scallops. Steaks provide the meaty alternative. Pricing might return you to the 21st century with a bump, but the besuited host exudes an ageless charm. Wine from £16.75.
Chef/s: Christopher Kikis. **Open:** Mon to Fri L 12 to 1.45, Mon to Sat D 6.30 to 10.30. **Closed:** Sun, 2 weeks Christmas, last 2 weeks May, bank hols. **Meals:** main courses £14 to £37. **Details:** 42 seats. Bar. Wheelchairs. Music. Children over 7 yrs only.

Average price 🍴

The average price denotes the price of a three-course meal without wine.

Holkham

★ NEW ENTRY ★

The Victoria Inn
Cooking score: 1
British | £35
Park Road, Holkham, NR23 1RG
Tel no: (01328) 711008
holkham.co.uk

Anyone working up an appetite on the magnificent north Norfolk coast is in luck: the Victoria Inn – or 'Vic' as it's affectionately known – is just a sandy shuffle away on the Holkham Estate. Comfortable dining areas have a predictable huntin' shootin' fishin' décor, and, while inconsistencies have been noted, the kitchen turns the best estate-sourced ingredients into tasty, attractive food: venison sausages with champ mash, game in season, rack of lamb with tender asparagus and sweet Chantenay carrots, for example. Offal gets its moment (sweetbreads with crispy tripe, or black pudding Scotch egg) reflecting a laudable commitment to reducing waste. Pear frangipane tart is a top pudding. Cellar doors open at £18.
Chef/s: Nik Hare. **Open:** all week L 12 to 2.30, D 6.30 to 9. **Meals:** main courses £13 to £30. **Details:** 70 seats. 80 seats outside. Bar. Parking.

Ingham
The Ingham Swan
Cooking score: 3
Modern European | £36
Sea Palling Road, Ingham, NR12 9AB
Tel no: (01692) 581099
theinghamswan.co.uk

Daniel Smith's ancient hostelry commands great loyalty. 'The food is exceptional –an innovative menu with seasonal produce that makes you want to try all that is on it,' says one fan. It's a beautifully renovated 14th-century inn – all beams, rough stone and exposed brickwork – and it's run with great warmth.

Daniel is in charge of the kitchen, his repertoire of confident modern cooking delivering the likes of sea bass with parsnip (purée and crisps), morteau sausage, hazelnut and chestnut crumb, and pork tenderloin with sea-salt-crackling pork belly and crispy pork cake, black pudding potato purée, shallot-braised Savoy cabbage and compressed apple and jus. To finish, a Madagascan vanilla mousse arrives with orange ice cream, or you could choose Norfolk poached rhubarb with vanilla pannacotta, ginger sponge and rhubarb sorbet. The attractively priced set deals are a popular choice and there are good reports of Sunday lunch. The concise and well-chosen wine list starts at £20.
Chef/s: Daniel Smith. **Open:** all week L 12 to 2 (3 Sun), D 6 to 9. **Closed:** 25 and 26 Dec. **Meals:** main courses £13 to £26. Set L £17 (2 courses) to £21. Set D £28 (3 courses). Sun L £28 (3 courses). Tasting menu £55. **Details:** 50 seats. 20 seats outside. Bar. Music. Parking.

King's Lynn
Market Bistro
Cooking score: 2
Modern British | £35
11 Saturday Market Place, King's Lynn, PE30 5DQ
Tel no: (01553) 771483
marketbistro.co.uk
£5 OFF

'Head and shoulders above local competition' is how one regular describes this neighbourhood restaurant in the charming heart of King's Lynn. The Goldings (he's in the kitchen, she's front-of-house) provide the 'complete package', with 'friendly, knowledgeable' service the perfect backdrop to the 'real skill' shown by the kitchen. A short menu – it's deemed 'beyond delicious' by one enthusiast – puts an abundance of locally and sustainably sourced ingredients through their paces. Try Richard's home-smoked salmon with a summery Cromer crab cannelloni and carrot slaw, or a smoked chicken and ham hock terrine with poached egg and salad leaves from the restaurant's nearby garden. Otherwise, enjoy the fresh-blood black pudding that accompanies a feast of rare-breed loin and belly pork with parsnips and pear; a lighter option might be herb-crusted line-caught pollack with tempura mussels. And do try the chocolate bavarois with salted caramel, white chocolate macaroon and a dash of orange. Wine from £17.

Chef/s: Richard Golding. **Open:** Wed to Sat L 12 to 2, Tue to Sat D 6 to 8.30 (9 Fri and Sat). **Closed:** Sun, Mon. **Meals:** main courses £11 to £24. **Details:** 35 seats. Wheelchairs.

LOCAL GEM

Marriott's Warehouse
Modern British | £24
South Quay, King's Lynn, PE30 5DT
Tel no: (01553) 818500
marriottswarehouse.co.uk

£5 OFF £30

A 16th-century warehouse given over to more hedonistic pursuits than mere storage these days – expect views over the revamped wharf and Great Ouse, old beams, local art and plenty of hustle and bustle. Open all day for breakfast and lunchtime sandwiches, the kitchen also turns out modern stuff like beetroot pannacotta with goats' cheese and pistachio salad, followed by chicken tagine or seafood crumble, plus the *de rigueur* burger in a brioche bun. Wines start at £14.50.

■ Letheringsett

READERS RECOMMEND

Back to the Garden
British
Fakenham Road, Letheringsett, NR25 7JJ
Tel no: (01263) 715996
back-to-the-garden.co.uk
'Freshly cooked, mainly organic food set in a lovely restored barn. Always busy and buzzing, with good vibes; it's a pleasure to eat in their restaurant.'

■ Morston
Morston Hall
Cooking score: 6
Modern British | £68
The Street, Morston, NR25 7AA
Tel no: (01263) 741041
morstonhall.com

Established she may be, but this gracious grande dame of the Norfolk dining scene excites and surprises in equal measure, such is the talent of Galton Blackiston and his team – a brigade recently bolstered by the arrival of head chef Greg Anderson. Regulars note a more modern style to the food, but the seven-course set menu remains a triumph of classic flavours and combinations, a journey of delights that might start with a cauliflower velouté, gentle silkiness lifted by a salty-crunchy scattering of deep-fried capers and the sweet surprise of sultanas. A Champagne sauce is a fittingly luxurious accompaniment to unforgettably delicious turbot, while meat might be 'sublime' Wagyu beef or the tenderest of guinea fowl, skin seared crisp, confit leg packed tastily into a translucent raviolo. Humble ingredients often star: beetroot segments, sweetly roasted and served with compressed cucumber, punchy horseradish cream and a swirl of dill oil, are fresh and colourful; elsewhere, foraged sea vegetables remind us that we're by the coast. At every course, top-notch ingredients, few of which have travelled far, shine unclouded by cheffy flimflam. A 'cherry' pre-dessert (a sphere of mousse encased in glossy red gel with an arcing chocolate 'stem') wows, while a whisper of gold leaf tops a flamboyant chocolate and hazelnut finale. A suitably magnificent wine cellar includes plenty of interest from £30.

Chef/s: Galton Blackiston and Greg Anderson. **Open:** Sun L 12 for 1 (1 sitting), all week D 7 for 8 (1 sitting). **Closed:** 3 days Christmas, Jan. **Meals:** set D £68 (7 courses). Sun L £37. **Details:** 50 seats. V menu. Wheelchairs. Parking.

Norwich

★ NEW ENTRY ★

Benedicts

Cooking score: 5
Modern British | £36
9 St Benedict's Street, Norwich, NR2 4PE
Tel no: (01603) 926080
restaurantbenedicts.com

Richard Bainbridge's first solo restaurant is ambitious, creative, even 'edgy', and all in the Norwich lanes. Bainbridge is ex-Morston Hall, with a profile boosted by TV appearances; he could have gone flashy, but the dining room is an understated space with a smart take on classic bistro décor. Only the service seems a little formal, with relaxation required. To start, Jerusalem artichoke with Norfolk Horn lamb, parsley sponge and truffle has its own measure of small screen fame, and delivers in the clever interplay of crisp lamb crackling and lightly confited egg yolk. Main courses might include North Sea cod with cracked wheat, kohlrabi, hazelnut and beer butter sauce, or roast quail with chutney-flavoured stuffing on a 'superb' pearl barley risotto loaded with Parmesan. To finish, swerve the overset slice of trifle in favour of, perhaps, peach Melba with custard, basil and puff pastry. A wider pool of suppliers would enhance the wine list, which opens at £23.
Chef/s: Richard Bainbridge. **Open:** Tue to Sat L 12 to 2, D 6 to 10. **Closed:** Sun, Mon, 25 Dec to 9 Jan, 1 week Apr, 2 weeks Aug. **Meals:** set L £16 (2 courses) to £20. Set D £29 (two courses) to £36. **Details:** 34 seats. Music.

Roger Hickman's

Cooking score: 5
Modern British | £45
79 Upper St Giles Street, Norwich, NR2 1AB
Tel no: (01603) 633522
rogerhickmansrestaurant.com
£5
OFF

Seven years on, Roger Hickman's elegant restaurant continues to enjoy faithful support. 'Real food cooked really, really well with just enough invention to be interesting,' confided one reporter, mightily impressed by the comfortable dining room hung with modern canvases. Hickman's concertedly seasonal menus don't overreach in ambition, with familiar ideas typically forming the backbone – witness the beautifully presented poached salmon with beetroot and horseradish, and roasted partridge with bacon, cabbage, celeriac and poached pear that was served at one winter lunch. Dinner could bring roe deer tartare with fennel and capers, and halibut with curried parsnip purée, cavolo nero and burnt butter crumb, while desserts draw plenty of enthusiasm, especially a ginger pannacotta with rhubarb, blood-orange sorbet and orange sponge cake, although a plate of quality cheeses is another way to round things off. Proceedings run at a gentle pace, overseen by attentive staff, and readers also applaud the well-chosen wine list, which starts at £26.
Chef/s: Roger Hickman. **Open:** Tue to Sat L 12 to 2.30, D 7 to 10.30. **Closed:** Sun, Mon, 26 Dec to early Jan. **Meals:** set L £20 (2 courses) to £25. Set D £36 (2 courses) to £45. Tasting menu £60. **Details:** 45 seats.

Shiki

Cooking score: 3
Japanese | £20
6 Tombland, Norwich, NR3 1HE
Tel no: (01603) 619262
shikirestaurant.co.uk
£30

'London quality and variety at Norwich prices,' was the verdict of one impressed visitor to this Japanese restaurant in the heart of Norwich. Housed in a pretty, all-brick town house and spread over three floors, it's fairly spartan inside – white walls, bare floorboards, wooden bench-style seating and low, matching tables – with a sushi bar in the entrance. The menu at lunchtime is 'a real bargain', providing a mix of soup, salad and sushi or cooked dishes – say donburi (rice bowls) or chicken teriyaki – as well as bento boxes with their mix of everything. However, it is the à la carte that throws up the real gems, with decent renditions of the cooked classics such as gyoza dumplings, tempura, pork tonkatsu and noodles (udon and soba). Then there's the sushi: as-fresh-as-they-come slices of salmon, raw prawn, lean tuna and hamachi, say, served either as sashimi or nigiri. There's an 'above average selection of saké' and wine starts at £18.

Chef/s: Chef Shun. **Open:** Mon to Sat L 12 to 2.30, D 6 to 10. **Closed:** Sun. **Meals:** main courses £6 to £12. Sushi set £10 to £15. Sashimi £9 to £13

■ Old Hunstanton
The Neptune
Cooking score: 4
Modern British | £55
85 Old Hunstanton Road, Old Hunstanton, PE36 6HZ
Tel no: (01485) 532122
theneptune.co.uk
£5 OFF

A sailboat in the window peeps out from the luxuriant cladding of climbing foliage, indicating that the briny and Hunstanton beach are not far away. Seized contraband was stored here in Victorian times, but all is above board and shipshape these days, with the highly experienced Team Mangeolles at the helm. Jacki oversees the wine side, while Kevin cooks a characteristically exuberant modern British menu that follows the East Anglian seasons. Norfolk quail with puréed butternut, endive and shallot and sultana dressing, or crab raviolo with pea purée and shaved fennel, provide bracing openers on a prix fixe that proceeds to halibut with mussels and gnocchi, or loin and braised shoulder of pork with leeks and Savoy, adorned with a cloud of Yukon Gold mash. To conclude, there's a panettone version of pain perdu, served with coffee ice cream, chocolate sauce and blueberries, or else a trio of cheeses with grape and almond chutney. Wines open at £20 (£6.30 a standard glass).

Chef/s: Kevin Mangeolles. **Open:** Sun L 12 to 1.30, Tue to Sun D 7 to 9. **Closed:** Mon, 26 Dec, 3 weeks Jan, 2 weeks Nov. **Meals:** set D £43 (2 courses) to

£56. Sun L £29 (2 courses) to £35. Tasting menu £72 (9 courses). **Details:** 22 seats. Bar. Music. Parking. Children over 10 yrs only.

■ Ovington
The Café at Brovey Lair
Cooking score: 6
Global/Seafood | £53
Carbrooke Road, Ovington, IP25 6SD
Tel no: (01953) 882706
broveylair.com
£5 OFF

Don't let the word 'café' put you off eating here, for Brovey Lair is one of the most enjoyable places to eat in Norfolk. It is also a serious restaurant, albeit one located in the open-plan kitchen-dining room of a private house – a surprisingly contemporary and professional set-up with front-row seats for all the teppan grill action in the kitchen – and the food easily surpasses that served in many restaurants with more formal pretensions. Mike Pemberton runs front-of-house with infectious enthusiasm; Tina Pemberton is the confident chef, her four-course, no-choice seafood menu delivering cohesive flavours garnered from the world larder. There has been praise for 'sensational' sesame-coated Chinese five-spice chilli scallops with a zingy lime, coriander, ginger and spring onion vinaigrette, while others have singled out portobello and oyster mushroom soup with miso and Japanese sea vegetables, the halibut tagine, and monkfish with squid-ink noodles. A dozen or so fish-friendly wines start at £22.50.

Chef/s: Tina Pemberton. **Open:** all week D only 7.30 to 11. **Closed:** 25 and 26 Dec, 1 Jan. **Meals:** set D £53 (4 courses). **Details:** 20 seats. 20 seats outside. V menu. Parking. No children.

Visit us online

To find out more about The Good Food Guide, please visit thegoodfoodguide.co.uk

▌Shouldham

King's Arms
Modern British | £24
28 The Green, Shouldham, PE33 0BY
Tel no: (01366) 347410
kingsarmsshouldham.co.uk

£30

How uplifting to see a pub saved to serve another pint thanks to the enterprising efforts of local residents. What's more, the now community-owned King's Arms is a tasty spot to eat: choose from a daily-changing menu that might offer a pulled pork burger with dill pickle, homemade falafels, or a homemade pie generously filled with steak and ale or chicken and leek and topped with the flakiest puff pastry. Bread-and-butter or sticky toffee puddings end a meal sweetly. Wine from £14.95.

▌Snettisham

The Rose & Crown
Modern British | £27
Old Church Road, Snettisham, PE31 7LX
Tel no: (01485) 541382
roseandcrownsnettisham.co.uk

£5 OFF   £30

From the roses entwined over its whitewashed walls to the hidden nooks, low beams, open fires and real ales, this is every inch the quintessential Norfolk hostelry. Built in the 14th century to house workers erecting the local church, it's still a vintage haunt – although the food strikes a more modern note. Expect anything from seared scallops with cauliflower and tonka bean purée to Taleggio-stuffed chicken breast with polenta and balsamic figs, alongside burgers, scampi and other pub classics. Wines from £17.50.

▌Stanhoe

★ LOCAL RESTAURANT AWARD ★
REGIONAL WINNER

The Duck Inn
Cooking score: 3
British | £30
Burnham Road, Stanhoe, PE31 8QD
Tel no: (01485) 518330
duckinn.co.uk

£5 OFF

This delightful pub, a peaceful step back from the coast road, is a little black book essential for locals and visitors to this part of Norfolk. Those in the know flock here for Ben Handley's Sunday lunch, choosing dry-aged beef sirloin, slow-roasted shoulder of pork or poach-roast chicken (with trimmings aplenty); at other times, they might pop in for a bowlful of Brancaster mussels, half a dozen Thornham oysters or a few Norfolk crab beignets. Continue perhaps with sea bass with brown shrimp and mussel butter, or wild mushroom risotto with truffle and pine nuts. The Duck is a convivial place, not only to linger over the inventive, impeccably presented plates that Ben and his brigade turn out consistently well from their tiny kitchen, but also to enjoy a pint and a bar bite, maybe crisp-crusted Scotch quails' eggs made with sausage meat and black pudding from legendary local butcher, Arthur Howell. However you've started your meal, a sublime pear tarte Tatin finishes it well. Wine from £15.50.
Chef/s: Ben Handley. **Open:** Mon to Sat L 12 to 2.30, D 6.30 to 9. Sun 12 to 9. **Closed:** 25 Dec. **Meals:** main courses £9 to £25. **Details:** 60 seats. 80 seats outside. Bar. Wheelchairs. Music. Parking.

■ Stoke Holy Cross
Stoke Mill
Cooking score: 4
Modern British | £34
Mill Road, Stoke Holy Cross, NR14 8PA
Tel no: (01508) 493337
stokemill.co.uk

Norfolk's world-famous mustard was created at Stoke's 'idyllic' watermill back in 1814, when Jeremiah Colman's workers began to grind the seeds for his pungent English condiment. Nowadays, this enchanting spot by the river Tas is home to an immensely likeable contemporary restaurant done out in shades of grey and white. Chef/co-owner Andy Rudd learned his craft with the chef David Adlard and is capable of delivering some 'truly first-class food' based on a bedrock of regional ingredients. Colman's esteemed tongue-tingler shows up in a dish of local beef with duck mousse, celeriac and beetroot, while the North Sea provides the raw materials for a seafood paella with halibut. Elsewhere, venison loin is served with a mini pie and boudin noir, before desserts usher in a millionaire chocolate bar with salted-caramel ice cream. Readers also praise the polite, professional staff who make eating here a 'really personal experience every time'. Decently priced wines from £20.
Chef/s: Andy Rudd. **Open:** Wed to Sun L 12 to 2 (2.30 Sun), Wed to Sat D 7 to 9 (9.30 Fri, 10 Sat). **Closed:** Mon, Tue, first week Jan. **Meals:** main courses £16 to £25. Set L £17 (2 courses) to £20. Set D £20 (2 courses) to £24. Sun L £25. Tasting menu £37 (5 courses) to £42 (7 courses). **Details:** 65 seats. V menu. Bar. Music. Parking.

The Wildebeest
Cooking score: 2
Modern British | £35
82-86 Norwich Road, Stoke Holy Cross, NR14 8QJ
Tel no: (01508) 492497
thewildebeest.co.uk

Under the same ownership as the Ingham Swan (see entry), the Wildebeest is a former country pub tweaked for the 21st century. Neutral colours, modern oak-slab tables, comfortable chocolate leather chairs and a partially open kitchen keep things 'traditional with a contemporary feel', while a menu of nicely turned-out popular staples – smooth chicken liver parfait with tomato chutney and celeriac rémoulade, ribeye with triple-cooked chips, red pepper purée, confit onion, garlic-baked field mushrooms and a Parmesan and wild rocket salad – keeps diners happy. As the kitchen uses a lot of local and regional produce expect, too, a trio of Cromer crab (white meat, crab cake, wild garlic claws) served with harissa aïoli and orange salad, and pot-roast Gressingham duck with golden beetroot, heritage carrots, tenderstem broccoli, saffron cocotte potato and red wine jus. As for dessert, consider double chocolate marquise with burnt white-chocolate mousse, orange ice cream and chocolate soil. Wine from £20.
Chef/s: Daniel Smith and Mark Elvin. **Open:** all week L 12 to 2 (3 Sun), D 6.30 to 9 (8 Sun). **Closed:** 25 Dec. **Meals:** main courses £16 to £26. Set L £17 (2 courses) to £22. Set D £23 (2 courses) to £28. Sun L £23. **Details:** 75 seats. 35 seats outside. Wheelchairs. Music. Parking.

Swaffham
Strattons Hotel
Cooking score: 2
Modern British | £30
4 Ash Close, Swaffham, PE37 7NH
Tel no: (01760) 723845
strattonshotel.com

Swaffham may be an unremarkable Brecks town, but the owners of this hotel, restaurant, café and deli have made it their mission to champion the region's food with as much vigour as they have their award-winning eco credentials. Make your way down a narrow town-centre lane to the boho Palladian villa (it's packed with the owners' unconventional, intriguing art finds) to linger over Julia Hetherton's unpretentious, taste-packed food, made using ethically, locally and where possible organically sourced ingredients. Baked celeriac with smoked trout from Pinneys of Orford and a caper salsa could be followed by slow-cooked Scotts Field rare breed pork belly with hasselback potatoes, or salmon and fennel en papillote with wilted summer greens. Julia is a dab hand at pastry, so make room for her jam doughnuts with sea salt praline ice cream and peanut brittle, or a warm chocolate and almond torte. The helpfully arranged wine list suggests bottles from £20.
Chef/s: Julia Hetherton. **Open:** Sun L 12 to 2.30, all week D 6.30 to 8.30 (9 Fri and Sat). **Closed:** 1 week Christmas. **Meals:** main courses £14 to £18. **Details:** 40 seats. 12 seats outside. Bar. Music. Parking.

Readers recommend

A 'readers recommend' review is a genuine quote from a report sent in by one of our readers. We intend to follow up these suggestions throughout the year to come.

Thornham
READERS RECOMMEND
Shuck's at the Yurt
International
Drove Orchards, Thornham, PE36 6LS
Tel no: (01485) 525889
shucksattheyurt.co.uk
'A yurt where amazing food is cooked out the back by two brilliant chefs! My fish stew was packed with flavour and had the most enormous langoustine on top and a hunk of soft brioche to soak up the juices. Can't wait to come back.'

Thorpe Market
The Gunton Arms
Cooking score: 3
British | £35
Cromer Road, Thorpe Market, NR11 8TZ
Tel no: (01263) 832010
theguntonarms.co.uk

Gird your loins for a visit to this extraordinary pub. Everything is on a massive, meaty scale: the open fire, with vast, prehistoric elk antlers above, is big, the portions are big, the flavours are big, the walls are packed with works by big-name artists from the art-dealer owner's collection. Choose Gunton Estate venison, transformed into sausage and mash or red deer curry with rice and naan, or watch as a serious rib of beef is cooked and properly rested in front of you. This being a real pub (there's a pool table and live TV sport), there are fish fingers with mushy peas and the likes of chicken and leek pie. Vegetarians might go for a fried duck egg with bubble and squeak, or beetroot and walnut hummus with goats' curd from their own menu. Norfolk treacle tart with clotted cream is as good as it sounds. Watch the wine bill: the list offers a £20 red or white, but doesn't really get going until £30.
Chef/s: Stuart Tattersall. **Open:** all week L 12 to 3, D 6 to 10 (9 Sun). **Closed:** 25 Dec. **Meals:** main courses £12 to £60. **Details:** 60 seats. 100 seats outside. V menu. Bar. Wheelchairs. Music. Parking.

▉ Titchwell
Titchwell Manor
Cooking score: 5
Modern European | £34
Titchwell, PE31 8BB
Tel no: (01485) 210221
titchwellmanor.com
£5 OFF 🚗

Self-taught chef Eric Snaith is as modest as his
coastal restaurant is unpretentious. But his
culinary ability and ambition dazzle,
demonstrating his thrilling agility with
flavours and contemporary style. Take time to
savour the imaginative, seven-course
Conversation Menu (with its paired flight of
wine, if you can), a journey that might start
with morsels of Brancaster crab, sitting
happily with salad cream (yes), translucent
curls of cucumber and salty caviar. A fillet of
North Sea plaice is bewitching in its
sweetness, texture, and comfortable
association with the youngest of broad beans
and just-wilted marsh vegetables, while meat
might be tenderly pink Norfolk lamb with
buttery, garlicky Jersey Royals. Eric enjoys
treading the line between sweet and savoury, a
balancing act that reaches its climax with a
nugget of panéed Lancashire Bomb cheese
served with salted honey ice cream. A dark
chocolate délice finishes the experience
decadently. The conventional menu is simpler
– think vigorous fish pie with cheesy mash
and King's Lynn brown shrimps, or barbecue
short ribs. The wine list opens with
Portuguese rosé for £18.
Chef/s: Eric Snaith. **Open:** all week L 12 to 5, D 6 to
9.30. **Meals:** main courses £10 to £28. Set L £15 (2
courses) to £20. Sun L £29 (3 courses). Tasting menu
£55 (5 courses) to £65. **Details:** 80 seats. 20 seats
outside. Bar. Wheelchairs. Music. Parking.

Eating out
with children 🍴

**Horizons are broadening for young
diners. As restaurants cotton on to
the idea that children might want to
eat what grown-ups are eating, the
sausage-and-chips formula is looking
decidedly passé.**

For decades, high-street chains have
been the go-to spots for families,
with the guarantee of child-pleasing
accoutrements overriding the quest for
a good meal. Fast forward to the present
day and many of our best destinations
are answering the call for better quality
offerings for young tums.

Of the many restaurants addressing this,
blazing a trail at the top-end is Marcus
Wareing at **Tredwell's**, with his 'Culinary
Kids Tasting Menu' for adventurous young
diners. Elsewhere, pubs, restaurants and
brasseries, such as **Lussmanns** (St Albans)
are offering children's menus of nutritious,
simple food – a fresh tomato sauce with
fish or a homemade pie with oven-baked
potato – as well as smaller portions from
the main menu.

For ethnic restaurants, however, children's
menus have always been a rarity, and
children readily eat what the grown-ups
eat. For a parent wanting their child to
try new foods, going out for dim sum, or
lunch at their local Indian, is a good bet.

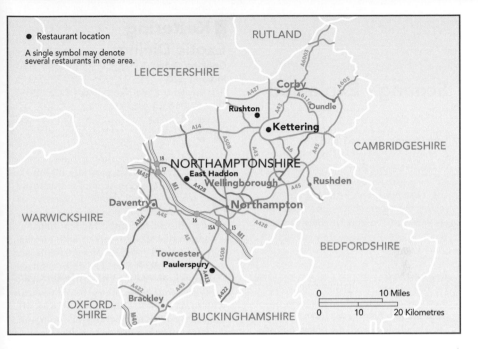

■ East Haddon
The Red Lion

Cooking score: 2
Modern British | £30
Main Street, East Haddon, NN6 8BU
Tel no: (01604) 770223
redlioneasthaddon.co.uk

£5 OFF

Secure within the confines of a well-preserved
village near Northampton, the Red Lion is a
smart country inn with an extensive dining
area and outdoor tables to soak up the summer
atmosphere in trimly maintained gardens.
Chloe Haycock cooks a menu that doesn't
stray too far beyond the boundaries of
country-pub food, ancient and modern.
Scotch eggs are back in fashion, seen here with
piccalilli mayonnaise, and a pulled pork fritter
with BBQ sauce won't lack for takers. Among
the beef and ale pie, beer-battered fish and
chips and chicken Caesars for main are lamb
shoulder with spiced couscous and mint
yoghurt, or cod poached with chorizo, while

veggies might head for a fragrant risotto of
asparagus, peas and mint, topped off with
crumbled Stilton. Doughnuts, brownies and
treacle tart are all present and correct on the
dessert list, or there's a crossover Arctic roll and
lemon meringue creation in mango coulis.
Wines start at £16.50.
Chef/s: Chloe Haycock. **Open:** Mon to Fri L 12 to
2.30, D 6 to 9. Sat and Sun 12 to 10 (8 Sun). **Closed:**
25 Dec. **Meals:** main courses £11 to £27.
Details: 104 seats. 50 seats outside. Bar.
Wheelchairs. Music. Parking.

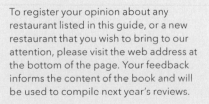

Please send us your feedback

To register your opinion about any
restaurant listed in this guide, or a new
restaurant that you wish to bring to our
attention, please visit the web address at
the bottom of the page. Your feedback
informs the content of the book and will
be used to compile next year's reviews.

Scoring – Explained

Local Gems, Scores 1 and 2

Scoring a 1 or a 2 in *The Good Food Guide*, or being awarded Local Gem status, is a huge achievement. We list the very best restaurants in the UK; for the reader, this means that these restaurants are well worth visiting if in the area – and you're extremely lucky if they are on your doorstep.

Scores 3 to 6

Further up the scale, scores 3 to 6 range from up-and-coming restaurants to places to watch; there will be real talent in the kitchen. These are the places that are well worth seeking out.

Scores 7 to 9

A score of 7 and above means entering the big league, with high expectations of the chef. In other words, these are destination restaurants, the places you'll long to talk about – if you're lucky enough to get a booking.

Score 10

This score is extremely rare, with chefs expected to achieve faultless technique at every service. In total, only eight restaurants have achieved 10 out of 10 for cooking since the scoring system was introduced in 1998.

See page 16 for an in-depth breakdown of *The Good Food Guide*'s scoring system.

▌Kettering
Exotic Dining
Cooking score: 3
Indian | £28
3-5 Newland Street, Kettering, NN16 8JH
Tel no: (01536) 411176
dineexotic.co.uk
£5 OFF £30

It's a bold claim, exotic dining, but few could argue that ostrich chaat, partridge hussaini and grilled ribeye camel steak with red wine jus aren't worthy of such a quixotic adjective. A first-floor dining room in the heart of the town is the setting for this modern Indian restaurant that aims to impress with unusual ingredients and 'exquisite presentation' – and you know what? It does. The décor is smart and contemporary, if a little corporate, while the (very long) menu mixes the old favourites with some eye-catching new stuff. Kick off with that ostrich number (hot and sour), or duck spring roll, move on to a classic lamb madras or the more exciting goat kali mirchi. Seafood options include lobster piri-piri and sea bass cooked in the clay oven and simmered in sweet chilli salsa, and steaks from Wagyu to elk offer a more European flavour. The short wine list starts at £12.95.
Chef/s: Mohammed Abadur and S. Mondol. **Open:** all week L 12 to 2.30, D 5.30 to 11 (12 Fri and Sat). **Meals:** main courses £6 to £25. **Details:** 85 seats. Wheelchairs. Music.

▌Paulerspury
The Vine House
Cooking score: 3
Modern British | £33
100 High Street, Paulerspury, NN12 7NA
Tel no: (01327) 811267
vinehousehotel.com
£5 OFF

Marcus and Julie Springett's 300-year-old rural restaurant-with-rooms celebrated its quarter century in 2016. After so many years, the dining room may feel slightly old-fashioned but, with an eye on fashion and a

nod to seasonal ingredients, Marcus Springett's cooking has moved with the times and he produces beautifully wrought dishes to please the locals. The quality is undeniably good, from excellent home-baked bread via air-dried Trealy Farm ham with roast garlic and walnut pesto to fillet of herb-cured skrei cod with spinach and grain-mustard tartare. Readers have praised saddle of venison with a heritage potato terrine and hen-of-the-woods mushroom purée, and aged beef with thick-cut duck fat chips and marrow-bone butter, while dessert might be blood-orange jelly with white chocolate, pistachio and vanilla shortbread. House wines in all three colours from Vin du Pays d'Oc are £18.50.
Chef/s: Marcus Springett. **Open:** Tue to Sat L 12 to 2, Mon to Sat D 6.30 to 9. **Closed:** Sun, first week Jan. **Meals:** set L and D £29 (2 courses) to £33. **Details:** 33 seats. Bar. Music. Parking. Children over 8 yrs only.

barbecued shoulder and sweetbreads, served with caponata, stem broccoli and Parmesan gnocchi, or cod on brandade with white beans, morteau sausage and gherkins. Finish with lemon meringue and basil moss, or a more familiar pear soufflé and marzipan sorbet. The classical wine list opens at £22.
Chef/s: Adrian Coulthard. **Open:** Sun L 12 to 2, all week D 7 to 9. **Meals:** set D £55. Sun L £30. **Details:** 40 seats. Bar. Wheelchairs. Music. Parking. Children over 10 yrs only at D.

▌Rushton
Rushton Hall, Tresham Restaurant
Cooking score: 3
Modern British | £55
Desborough Road, Rushton, NN14 1RR
Tel no: (01536) 713001
rushtonhall.com

£5 OFF 🍴

The Tresham family who built Rushton in the reign of Henry VI supplied a Speaker to the House of Commons, but drifted out of affection for Parliament sufficiently for one of their successors to be involved in the Gunpowder Plot. It's a virtual palace, built around a quadrangle, with a stately dining room panelled in oak at its heart. Adrian Coulthard blows away any historical cobwebs here with cooking of innovative intensity, mobilising all the latest tricks. Salmon ballotine is poached in a herb liquor at 50°C before being served with squid-ink sponge, yoghurt and keta as an opening gambit, following which there may be lamb anatomised into the forms of seared loin,

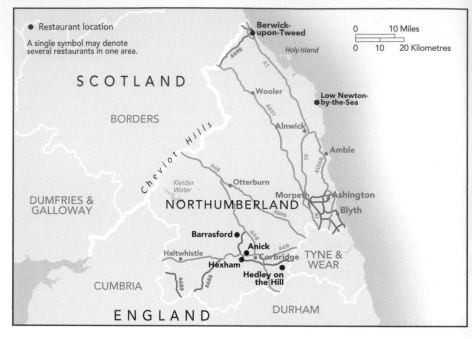

▌Anick

LOCAL GEM

The Rat Inn
British | £27
Anick, NE46 4LN
Tel no: (01434) 602814
theratinn.com

£5 OFF £30

Views of the Tyne Valley add to the allure of
this hilltop drovers' inn not far from Hexham,
although the Rat also has its full quota of
rustic trappings, among them real ales,
flagstone floors and a blazing fire. The food is
gaining impetus, too, following the arrival of
chef Kevin Maclean from the Three
Chimneys, Colbost (see entry): North
Country pub staples now sit alongside
upmarket dishes ranging from crispy ox
tongue with celeriac rémoulade and pickled
onions to pan-fried coley with squid, creamed
leeks and salsify. Wines from £15.95.

▌Barrasford

The Barrasford Arms
Cooking score: 2
Modern British | £25
Barrasford, NE48 4AA
Tel no: (01434) 681237
barrasfordarms.co.uk

£5 OFF £30

Deep in Northumberland's tourist and hiking
heartland, this substantial Victorian hostelry
promotes itself as a 'restaurant and country-
pub-with-rooms' – an inviting prospect for
the throngs who regularly meander
hereabouts. A roaring fire awaits in the bar,
while three dining rooms cater to those with
hunger pangs. You could call in for a
restorative lunch of lamb's liver and bacon
followed by treacle tart, or save yourself for
the evening when the kitchen flexes its
muscles with a repertoire of more ambitious-
sounding dishes – albeit with strong North
Country connections. To start there might be
'very local' potted rabbit with Chablis and

saffron-pickled vegetables, while mains could bring slow-cooked lamb shank niçoise or seared Shields monkfish with creamed leeks, tomato and sauté potatoes. As for dessert, a jazzed-up fruit crumble with apples, sultanas, rum, hazelnuts and polenta is about as good as it gets. Corney & Barrow house French is £14.95.

Chef/s: Tony Binks. **Open:** Tue to Sun L 12 to 2 (3 Sun), Tue to Sat D 6.30 to 9. **Closed:** Mon, 24 to 26 Dec, 1 Jan, bank hols. **Meals:** main courses £14 to £23. Set L £15 (2 courses) to £19. Sun L £17 (2 courses) to £20. **Details:** 65 seats. 25 seats outside. Bar. Wheelchairs. Music. Parking.

Berwick-upon-Tweed

LOCAL GEM
Audela
Modern British | £29
41-47 Bridge Street, Berwick-upon-Tweed, TD15 1ES
Tel no: (01289) 308827
audela.co.uk
£5 OFF £30

'This is a real gem in the culinary desert of north Northumberland. The menu is interesting and varied using seasonal and local ingredients,' sums up one visitor, catching the tone of this smart-casual café-cum-restaurant in the heart of Berwick. Open from breakfast through dinner, there are some very good things to eat, with praise for twice-baked Northumberland cheese soufflé, Berwick crab and smoked salmon risotto, and Borders wood pigeon with heritage pommes fondant, white turnip, confit garlic, green lentils and a thyme sauce. Wines from £15.95.

Local Gem
🍴

Local Gems are the perfect neighbourhood venues, delivering good, freshly cooked food at great value for money.

Hedley on the Hill
The Feathers Inn
Cooking score: 3
British | £24
Main Street, Hedley on the Hill, NE43 7SW
Tel no: (01661) 843607
thefeathers.net
£5 OFF £30

A venerable refuelling point on the old drovers' road between Hadrian's Wall and the Derwent Valley, this 200-year-old hilltop hostelry is now a village champion with a long list of attributes. The parish council meets here, the pub acts as a polling station and there's a thriving 'leek club' for gardeners, plus piano classes, star-gazing, beer festivals and more besides. Chef/landlord Rhian Cradock also serves thumpingly good food with an emphatic North Country accent and bags of local pride. His homemade black pudding with a poached duck egg and devilled gravy is a signature dish, but the repertoire also extends to whisky-laced Craster kipper pâté, braised ox cheek in Allendale stout, roe deer haggis and even roast North Sea turbot with mussels, kale, beer and bacon. To finish, what better than the burnt Northumbrian cream? Wines start at £15, although hand-pumped local ales are the sups of choice.

Chef/s: Rhian Cradock. **Open:** Thur to Sun L 12 to 2 (2.30 Sat, 4.30 Sun), Wed to Sat D 6 to 8.30. **Closed:** Mon, Tue, first 2 weeks Jan. **Meals:** main courses £10 to £16. **Details:** 40 seats. 12 seats outside. Parking.

Hexham
Bouchon Bistrot
Cooking score: 4
French | £29
4-6 Gilesgate, Hexham, NE46 3NJ
Tel no: (01434) 609943
bouchonbistrot.co.uk
£5 OFF £30

'France over two floors', Gregory Bureau's place is a real find in a pretty English market town. A 'proper French restaurant', it's at the smarter end of the bistro spectrum with a soothingly warm colour scheme and comfy chairs, and real fires for those chilly nights. The menu is classically appealing but not stuck in the past. Seared scallops with buttered samphire is straight-up and full of respect for the ingredients, the same goes for the plate of charcuterie and, rest assured, escargots de Bourgogne is present and correct (although one reader hankered for more garlic). Main courses such as crispy duck confit and a 'fine piece of halibut' with pommes Anna maintain the illusion that somehow the English Channel has been traversed. To finish, crème brûlée is traditional and true, chocolate fondant gets perked up with griottine cherries, and prune and Armagnac clafoutis is served with walnut ice cream. The mostly French wine list kicks off at £15.50.

Chef/s: Nicolas Kleist. **Open:** all week L 12 to 2 (3 Sun), Mon to Sat D 6 to 9 (9.30 Fri and Sat). **Closed:** 24 to 26 Dec, 1 Jan. **Meals:** main courses £12 to £20. Set L and D £15 (2 courses) to £16. Sun L £20. **Details:** 150 seats. Wheelchairs. Music. Parking.

■ Low Newton

LOCAL GEM

The Ship Inn

British | £25
Newton Square, Low Newton, NE66 3EL
Tel no: (01665) 576262
shipinnnewton.co.uk

£30

The North Sea is only 50 yards from the front door of the Ship Inn, its lawn sweeping down to meet the beach. The view is lovely, of course, but inside there is rustic charm, well-kept beer (they even brew their own) and a menu of unpretentious grub made from (mostly) local ingredients. Come rain or shine, tuck into whole mackerel with salsa verde, slow-cooked free-range pork belly with apple sauce and gravy, and locally caught crab with salad and crusty bread. Wines start at £16.45.

Waste watching

Taking the sustainable approach feeds creativity, producing ingenious solutions to the problem of waste, and inspiring new dishes and modern concepts.

Silo is designed 'with the bin in mind'. This zero-waste Brighton restaurant has an in-house compost machine and a rigorous approach to choosing produce.

At **Opus**, a stalwart of Birmingham's brasserie scene, sustainability is king. The kitchen is particularly hot on fish and seafood, insisting on sustainable wild-caught fish and suppliers who know good fishing-gear from bad.

Tasting menus have replaced à la carte options at the **Checkers**, a restaurant with rooms in the Welsh borders, allowing the kitchen to predict demand and cut down on unnecessary waste.

Seafood restaurants have a clear opportunity to source well and limit waste. Derek Marshall's **Gamba** takes fish stocks of both kinds seriously, as well as keeping an eye on its carbon footprint.

Food waste is a fact of life in many kitchens, but some chefs are determined to get it as close to zero as possible. And we salute the attempt.

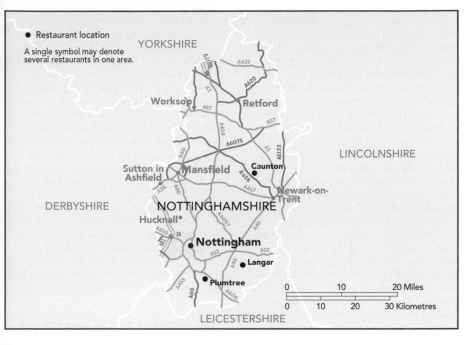

Map legend:
● Restaurant location

A single symbol may denote
several restaurants in one area.

YORKSHIRE

Worksop
Retford

LINCOLNSHIRE

Sutton in
Ashfield
Mansfield
Caunton

Newark-on-
Trent

DERBYSHIRE

NOTTINGHAMSHIRE

Hucknall

26

Nottingham

Langar

Plumtree

0   10   20 Miles
0   10   20   30 Kilometres

LEICESTERSHIRE

▉ Caunton
Caunton Beck
Cooking score: 2
Modern European | £25
Main Street, Caunton, NG23 6AB
Tel no: (01636) 636793
wigandmitre.com

£30

Just a few miles off the A1, this well-run all-
day watering hole and restaurant is in a
cracking location – a delightful village with
the bubbling Caunton Beck running through
– and serves its community well. Breakfast
provides a daily wake-up call and 'sets you up
for the day', nibbles, sandwiches and bar
snacks suit the grazing crowd, and the honest-
to-goodness menu with rustic flavours in its
blood satisfies the rest. Starters such as twice-
baked smoked haddock, leek and Wensleydale
cheese soufflé give way to braised ox cheek
bourguignon with horseradish mash, lamb's
liver with bacon and onion gravy or grilled
whole sea bass with mussels, baby capers and

garlic butter, and there's a good selection of
British cheeses if warm sticky toffee pudding
with butterscotch sauce doesn't appeal. To
drink, there are real ales or plenty of well-
priced gluggable wines by the bottle (from
£14.95), pichet or glass.
Chef/s: Ben Hughes. **Open:** all week 12 to 9.30.
Closed: 25 Dec. **Meals:** main courses £11 to £22.
Set L and D £15 (2 courses) to £18. **Details:** 100
seats. 45 seats outside. Bar. Wheelchairs. Parking.

▉ Langar
Langar Hall
Cooking score: 4
Modern British | £40
Church Lane, Langar, NG13 9HG
Tel no: (01949) 860559
langarhall.com

£5
OFF

Loved as much by prosperous weekenders as
by celebrating locals, this engaging country
house hotel is a tribute to proprietor Imogen
Skirving, who tragically died in a car accident

in Spain at the end of June 2016. She ran 'a very tight ship in the most relaxed way,' and we hope that this will continue. Langar Hall has always put on a visibly stylish and well-priced show for customers in search of food, with lunch served in the conservatory and dinner in the more formal dining room 'overlooked by two fine Greco-Roman statues and a graceful chandelier'. The kitchen doesn't try to reinvent the culinary wheel, though the carefully sourced, often local (and frequently home-grown) produce is precisely cooked – say chicken liver and foie gras parfait with fig compote and walnut and raisin toast, then poached guinea fowl breast and stuffed leg with confit potatoes, heritage carrots and Muscat sauce, and baked vanilla cheesecake with lemon jelly and sorbet. Generous hospitality abounds, and charmingly accommodating service makes everyone feel at home. Wines from £19.95.

Chef/s: Gary Booth and Ross Jeffery. **Open:** all week L 12 to 2, D 6 to 10. **Meals:** set L £18 (2 courses) to £23. Set D £25 (2 courses) to £30. Sun L £40. **Details:** 60 seats. 20 seats outside. Bar. Wheelchairs. Parking.

▌Nottingham

Hart's

Cooking score: 5
Modern British | £34
Standard Hill, Park Row, Nottingham, NG1 6GN
Tel no: (0115) 9881900
hartsnottingham.co.uk
£5 OFF 🍷 🛏

Tim and Stefa Hart's glossy contemporary hotel looks every inch the boutique deal, and recent refurbishment in the restaurant brings an invigorating colour scheme of rich throbbing blues and shimmering tawny to the scene. Slickly attentive staff keep things moving smoothly, while Daniel Burridge's voguish brasserie food feels entirely in keeping. Beetroot will ever find goats' cheese its best friend, as indeed here when a terrine of the root is offset by cheese beignets, which might be followed by an earthy main course of

roast pheasant with a warm salad of Puy lentils, spelt and quinoa, or perhaps herb-and Parmesan-crusted halibut with burnt celeriac in wild garlic and walnut dressing. Satisfaction radiates from an autumn report of notable Norfolk quail with fregola, macadamias, pomegranate and roast lemon, and then a 'triumphantly tasty' smoked haddock and prawn risotto. Lemon and hazelnut parfait with blackberries and yoghurt ends things on a lighter note. An intelligently composed wine list strays beyond the grapes variety comfort zone for Grüner Veltliner, Grillo, Monastrell and Negroamaro, but there are classics, too, with eloquent tasting notes and demonstrably fair prices starting at £21.50.

Chef/s: Daniel Burridge. **Open:** all week L 12 to 2.30, D 6 to 10.30. **Closed:** 1 Jan. **Meals:** main courses £17 to £25. Set L £19 (2 courses) to £24. Set D £22 (2 courses) to £28. Sun L £25. **Details:** 80 seats. Bar. Wheelchairs. Parking.

The Larder on Goosegate

Cooking score: 2
Modern British | £27
16-22 Goosegate, Hockley, Nottingham, NG1 1FE
Tel no: (0115) 9500111
thelarderongoosegate.co.uk
£5 OFF £30

A one-time chemist – local lad Jesse Boot's first shop – the Larder on Goosegate has become something of a Nottingham institution since it opened in the city's boho quarter in 2008. The first-floor dining room is stylishly understated and unshowy, the modern British food is robust and everybody seems to find it all delicious. Seasonality is close to the kitchen's heart. In winter, for example, dinner might start with game terrine and carrot marmalade, and continue with lemon sole, salsify, winter greens, olive and capers or braised ox cheek with celeriac and horseradish. The selection of steaks served with classic accompaniments also cut the mustard, the keenly priced lunch deal remains a popular option and for dessert there could be spiced new-season rhubarb tart with ginger

and cinnamon ice cream. Booze is taken seriously, too, with 10 bottled beers from the Notts area, and global wines from £15.95.
Chef/s: David Sneddon. **Open:** Fri to Sun L 12 to 2.30 (3.30 Sun), Tue to Sat D 5.30 to 10. **Closed:** Mon. **Meals:** main courses £12 to £22. Set L and D £13 (2 courses) to £16. Sun £13. **Details:** 67 seats. Music.

★ TOP 10 ★

Restaurant Sat Bains

Cooking score: 9
Modern British | £85
Lenton Lane, Nottingham, NG7 2SA
Tel no: (0115) 9866566
restaurantsatbains.com

Newcomers have been known to phone in lost. Once on the right track, the turn down a narrow lane in a rural pocket on the city's edge leads to an unassuming set of buildings that resemble a French auberge, where well-spaced, cloth-covered tables and a soothing, tranquil setting might lull some customers into thinking that this is an ordinary restaurant. But Restaurant Sat Bains is a one-off; Sat Bains himself, without doubt, one of the country's foremost chefs. He is also one of the best to work the taste spectrum – dishes on his seven- or ten-course tasting menus are colour-coded to highlight the dominant tastes. Singling out winning dishes is difficult. Highlights at inspection included a serving of meltingly tender lamb cheeks teamed with Jersey Royals and then juxtaposed sharply with a sublime tart/sweet mint jus. Scallop with crisp pork scratchings is a lesson in taste and texture; an umami-rich kombu purée, that seemed too intense on its own, supported the sweet scallop perfectly. Kohlrabi 'tagliatelle' with its foraged hedgerow pesto is a tantalising and inventive combination. A 'crossover' nugget of powerfully flavoured miso fudge, given heft by a dot of passion fruit gel, leads on to a mini-sphere of dark chocolate ganache and mousse, its richness offset by sea salt and the tang of yoghurt-olive oil ice cream. And in a winning finale, what appears to be a signature dessert: a tangle of strawberries, meringue, crème fraîche, fresh tarragon and rocket with just a hint of strawberry vinegar to cut the sweetness. It isn't easy matching wine to the myriad of flavours, so advice from the sommelier provides verbal notes to a wine list (from £34) that ticks the boxes for serious intent and quality. Although the dining room is not open for lunch, the seven-course menu is offered at the chef's table or kitchen bench at lunchtimes (minimum two people, maximum eight) where you get to see the kitchen action and be served by the chefs themselves.
Chef/s: Sat Bains and John Freeman. **Open:** Wed to Sat L 12 to 1.30, D 6.30 to 9 (6 to 9.45 Fri and Sat). **Closed:** Sun, Mon, Tue, 3 weeks Dec, 1 week Apr, 2 weeks Aug. **Meals:** tasting menu £85 (7 courses) to £95 (10 courses). **Details:** 40 seats. V menu. Bar. Music. Parking. Children over 8 yrs only.

LOCAL GEM

Delilah

Modern European | £20
12 Victoria Street, Nottingham, NG1 2EX
Tel no: (0115) 9484461
delilahfinefoods.co.uk

A fixture in central Nottingham for a dozen years, Delilah is an upmarket delicatessen, a chilled-out sort of place with an urban vibe – high ceilings, tall windows and a bar lined with counter-stools – and dining tables placed among the merchandise. The well-endowed larder drives the menu, via breakfasts of, say, rarebit with Alderton marmalade ham to platters of cheese and charcuterie, various salads and the likes of salt beef and morcilla hash, and confit duck leg. Good cakes, too. Wines from £12.95.

Average price

The average price denotes the price of a three course meal without wine.

▌Plumtree
Perkins
Cooking score: 2
Modern British | £35
Station House, Station Road, Plumtree,
NG12 5NA
Tel no: (0115) 9373695
perkinsrestaurant.co.uk

Not far from Nottingham, Perkins made its home in a disused Victorian railway station in the early 1980s. The location is enjoyed to the extent of setting outdoor tables on the old platform. In house hot and cold smokers are applied to duck breast and salmon alike, for memorable starters that come respectively with Jerusalem artichoke purée and a Scotch quail's egg, and pickled fennel and tiger prawn in ravigote dressing. Locally reared meats contribute class to mains such as beef fillet with truffled mash in red wine, while game from the Belvoir Estate might be venison haunch with potato and garlic terrine and smokehouse beetroot. The fixed-price menus are top value, and it's important not to miss finishers like lemon posset with candied orange, or authentic tarte Tatin with cinnamon ice cream. House selection wines come by the regular or large glass, half-litre carafe or bottle, the last from £17.50.
Chef/s: Sarah Newham. **Open:** all week L 12 to 2 (3 Sun), Mon to Sat D 6 to 10. **Closed:** 1 Jan.
Meals: main courses £15 to £23. Set L £14 (2 courses) to £17. Set D £17 (2 courses) to £19. Sun L £17 (2 courses) to £20. **Details:** 73 seats. 24 seats outside. Bar. Wheelchairs. Music. Parking.

The Good Food Guide Scoring System

Score 1: Capable cooking with simple food combinations and clear flavours.

Score 2: Decent cooking, displaying good technical skills and interesting combinations and flavours.

Score 3: Good cooking, showing sound technical skills and using quality ingredients.

Score 4: Dedicated, focused approach to cooking; good classical skills and high-quality ingredients.

Score 5: Exact cooking techniques and a degree of ambition; showing balance and depth of flavour in dishes.

Score 6: Exemplary cooking skills, innovative ideas, impeccable ingredients and an element of excitement.

Score 7: High level of ambition and individuality, attention to the smallest detail, accurate and vibrant dishes.

Score 8: A kitchen cooking close to or at the top of its game. Highly individual with impressive artistry.

Score 9: Cooking that has reached a pinnacle of achievement, making it a hugely memorable experience.

Score 10: Just perfect dishes, showing faultless technique at every service; extremely rare and the highest accolade the Guide can give.

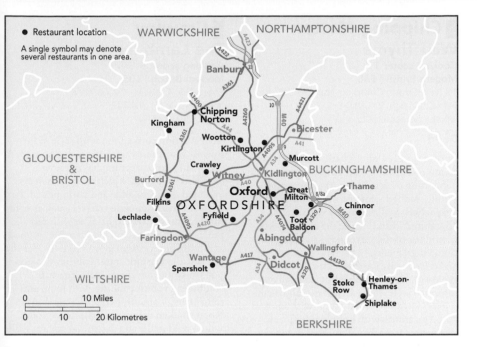

■ Chinnor
The Sir Charles Napier
Cooking score: 3
Modern British | £45
Sprigg's Alley, Chinnor, OX39 4BX
Tel no: (01494) 483011
sircharlesnapier.co.uk

Hidden away in a verdant Oxfordshire backwater, this is one of the Guide's more venerable establishments – celebrating 36 consecutive years in 2017. Part inn, part gentrified country restaurant, it is full of character with a comfortably well-worn bar, a couple of cottagey dining rooms mixing old polished tables and dining chairs with interesting art, and in fine weather the chance to overflow into the lovely sculpture-filled garden at the rear. The menu, by way of contrast, shows preference for a broadly contemporary way of doing things, relying on sound technique rather than culinary fireworks to impress: perhaps double-baked smoked haddock and Cheddar soufflé, crab

with avocado, lemon and excellent crab beignet, and lemon sole fillets with a fricassee of squid, tomato and Parmesan and bouillabaisse jus, highlights of a June test meal. The food is popular, though service at weekends can be somewhat erratic. Ten easy drinkers (from £19.50) set the ball rolling on a wine list that breathes class.
Chef/s: Anthony Skeats. **Open:** Tue to Sun L 12 to 2.30 (4 Sun), Tue to Sat D 6 to 9.30 (10 Sat). **Closed:** Mon, 25 to 27 Dec, 2 to 15 Jan. **Meals:** main courses £20 to £29. Set L Tue to Fri £18 (2 courses) to £26. Set D Tue to Fri £20 (2 courses) to £28. **Details:** 70 seats. 70 seats outside. Bar. Music. Parking. Children over 5 yrs only at D.

Symbols

🖛 Accommodation is available
£30 Three courses for less than £30
£5 OFF £5-off voucher scheme
🍶 Notable wine list

▌Chipping Norton
Wild Thyme
Cooking score: 3
Modern British | £38
10 New Street, Chipping Norton, OX7 5LJ
Tel no: (01608) 645060
wildthymerestaurant.co.uk

£5 OFF 🛏

Nick and Sally Pullen's little restaurant-with-rooms is charming, the shabby-chic interior combining original artwork, bare wood, artfully scuffed white furniture and sparkling chandeliers. It all fits nicely with smart Chipping Norton, while the menu makes gleeful use of the surrounding countryside's tiptop ingredients. Local wild duck with apple and celeriac salad and hazelnut dressing is typical of Nick's modern but classically informed style; indeed, in season the menu rejoices in game – wild rabbit with smoked bacon en croûte with bubble and squeak, trompettes and a Dijon mustard cream sauce being another appealing example. Further choices could include Cornish sea bass with steamed mussels, spaghetti nero, cavolo nero and sauce bouillabaisse, and attractive vegetarian options such as Jerusalem artichoke and spring onion risotto with Parmesan and extra-virgin olive oil. The great-value wine list kicks off at £15 and includes monthly wine recommendations to suit the menu.
Chef/s: Nick Pullen. **Open:** Tue to Sat L 12 to 2, D 7 to 9 (6.30 to 9.30 Fri and Sat). **Closed:** Sun, Mon. **Meals:** main courses £15 to £25. Set L £20 (2 courses) to £25. Set D £20 (2 courses) to £38. **Details:** 35 seats. 8 seats outside.

Symbols

🛏 Accommodation is available
£30 Three courses for less than £30
£5 OFF £5-off voucher scheme
🍷 Notable wine list

▌Crawley
The Lamb Inn
Cooking score: 5
Modern British | £35
Steep Hill, Crawley, OX29 9TW
Tel no: (01993) 708792
lambcrawley.co.uk

Matt Weedon cooks 'food with style' at this historic but smart Oxfordshire dining pub. A subtle shift since opening has put new emphasis on mains, which are impressively executed, but accessible and fairly priced. For more fireworks, look to starters (such as wild mushrooms on toasted brioche with cep purée, poached egg and black truffle, 'as good as mushrooms on toast gets') and puds. Service can lack the warmth and flexibility of a good pub welcome, but this is still a rare inn, combining robust cooking with focus and refinement – and its own pork scratchings. Roast chicken comes with copious girolles, wilted wild garlic and dry sherry cream, while beef fillet with braised short rib and roasted carrots is meat and veg at its finest. Finish with a 'barnstorming' dessert of chocolate, bay and banana, quenelles of mousse, ice and sorbet surrounding a chocolate fondant. Wine is from £16.50; seek out the bin ends for real interest.
Chef/s: Matt Weedon. **Open:** Wed to Sun L 12 to 2 (2.30 Fri and Sat, 12.30 to 2.30 Sun), Wed to Sun D 6.30 to 9 (9.30 Fri and Sat, 7 to 9 Sun). **Closed:** Mon, Tue. **Meals:** main courses £13 to £26. Sun L £28 (3 courses). **Details:** 40 seats. 50 seats outside. Bar. Music. Parking.

▌Filkins
The Five Alls
Cooking score: 4
Modern British | £30
Filkins, GL7 3JQ
Tel no: (01367) 860875
thefiveallsfilkins.co.uk

🛏

Sebastian and Lana Snow bring their experience to bear on the confident, classy food at this Gloucestershire hostelry, opened after their years in London and at the nearby Swan at Southrop. With its beamed bar, clattery floorboards, real ales and comfortable rug-strewn dining room with mismatched polished tables and soft lighting, the Five Alls is exactly what you might expect to find in a genuine country inn-with-rooms. There's a pleasing seasonal (and local) rhythm to a menu featuring warm salad of beetroot, blood orange, goats' cheese and hazelnuts, baked cod fillet with chorizo, mussels, broad beans, wild garlic and mash, and rhubarb crumble with stem ginger ice cream. And with upbeat pub classics such as steak and kidney pie or char-grilled ribeye steak with thrice-cooked truffled wedges and peppercorn sauce, the kitchen has judged nicely what local people want. The amiable service has the warmth required to get people coming back. Carefully chosen wines start at £17.95.

Chef/s: Sebastian Snow. **Open:** all week L 12 to 2.30 (3 Fri to Sun), Mon to Sat D 6 to 9.30 (10 Fri and Sat). **Closed:** 25 Dec. **Meals:** main courses £14 to £23. Set L and D £16 (2 courses) to £21. Sun L £22. **Details:** 90 seats. 50 seats outside. Bar. Music. Parking.

■ Fyfield
The White Hart
Cooking score: 3
Modern British | £34
Main Road, Fyfield, OX13 5LW
Tel no: (01865) 390585
whitehart-fyfield.com

Built in the reign of Henry VI as a chantry house, the White Hart passed into the ownership of St John's College, Oxford at the Dissolution. Ravaged by time and the tides of English history, it has been solicitously restored by the Chandlers to a state that befits its beamed magnificence, all minstrels' gallery and secret passages. Its various crannies provide spaces for private functions, and Mark Chandler's cooking pleases locals for its spot-on judgement: 'no style over substance here, just beautiful and delicious food served with minimum fuss but maximum grace'. A starter of black pudding and foie gras with

caramelised apple in scrumpy reduction indicates the unpretentious approach, and mains such as rack of Cotswold lamb with moussaka, smoked aubergine purée and harissa a willingness to look further afield. Sharing boards of fish, meze and antipasti are popular, as are puddings like date and rum sponge with caramelised banana. Wines are arranged by style, from £17.50.

Chef/s: Mark Chandler. **Open:** Tue to Sun L 12 to 2.30 (3 Sun), Tue to Sat D 6.45 to 9.15. **Closed:** Mon. **Meals:** main courses £12 to £25. Set L £17 (2 courses) to £20. Sun L £26 (2 courses) to £29. **Details:** 60 seats. 40 seats outside. Bar. Music. Parking.

■ Great Milton
★ TOP 50 ★
Le Manoir aux Quat'Saisons
Cooking score: 7
Modern French | £150
Church Road, Great Milton, OX44 7PD
Tel no: (01844) 278881
manoir.com

The mellow stone, the leaded windows, the two-acre kitchen garden, the English water garden, the open fires, oak panelling, sofa-strewn lounge and perfectly drilled service all add up to a place supremely comfortable with its reputation as the most famous country house hotel in the UK. For many years Raymond Blanc's Le Manoir has been seen as a major establishment by people who enjoy food and by people who don't. But things have come on apace in recent years and there is an impression that while Le Manoir's standards have not changed, others have surpassed it through the astonishing enthusiasm and dedication that has become more and more apparent in British cooking over the last decade. Technique is not always as skilful as it might be, given the impeccable materials, but the kitchen has produced some enjoyable dishes on its monthly changing seasonal menus. Reporters have applauded faultless risottos, one 'packed with flavour' of summer vegetables, tomato essence and chervil cream, another of wild mushrooms with winter truffle, and been reassured by excellent roast loin of venison with celeriac and truffle, a captivating pistachio soufflé ('the best I've had') served with a bitter cocoa sorbet and the tiptop cheese trolley. The wine list aims for the top and is priced accordingly, with entry level around £45.

Chef/s: Raymond Blanc. **Open:** all week L 11.45 to 1.45, D 6.45 to 8.45. **Meals:** main courses £52 to £54. Set L £82 (5 courses) to £127 (7 courses). Set D £138 (5 courses) to £159 (7 courses). **Details:** 80 seats. V menu. Bar. Wheelchairs. Parking.

∎ Henley-on-Thames
Shaun Dickens at the Boathouse
Cooking score: 4
British | £46
Station Road, Henley-on-Thames, RG9 1AZ
Tel no: (01491) 577937
shaundickens.co.uk

A 'real asset' to Henley in a lovely spot, Shaun Dickens' restaurant offers the kind of cooking that made one reader hope lunch would 'keep on going until bedtime'. The Thames-side location may have more appeal than the dining room, with its polystyrene ceiling tiles and rather bland décor, but service is 'charming' and the food outclasses the surroundings by several degrees. Intricate starters might include deep-fried leek with wild and black garlic purées, tarragon foam and smoked potato, or pig's cheek with white beans, brassica and sorrel, with the kitchen and serving staff happy to take account of younger guests and dietary limitations. To follow, cod is given robust accompaniments of bacon, chicken of the woods and red wine, and desserts are far from run-of-the-mill; try macadamia with chocolate brûlée, candied artichoke and crispy milk. Wine matches continue to be a real strength, from a list divided by style from £26.

Chef/s: Shaun Dickens. **Open:** Wed to Sun L 12 to 2.30, D 6.30 to 9.30. **Closed:** Mon, Tue, 25 Dec. **Meals:** main courses £20 to £26. Set L £26 (2 courses) to £30. **Details:** 48 seats. 26 seats outside. Bar. Wheelchairs. Music.

∎ Kingham
The Kingham Plough
Cooking score: 4
Modern British | £40
The Green, Kingham, OX7 6YD
Tel no: (01608) 658327
thekinghamplough.co.uk
£5 OFF ⟋

'Emily's cooking is consistently good and imaginative, and never pretentious. Miles is a welcoming host and the waiting staff are charming and efficient.' This is the Kingham Plough, a really quite skilful balancing act (with splendid bedrooms, too) that adds up to a great local dining pub pursuing smart technique and quality ingredients in an atmosphere of beams, exposed stone and mismatched furniture. Start with the excellent liver, bacon and onions – chicken liver parfait, bacon and brioche crumb, glazed red onion – or Jerusalem artichoke with confit egg yolk, pearl barley, roasted chestnuts, Pied Bleu mushrooms and truffle, considered the best dish of the evening by one diner. Lamb Wellington is as tender as it can be, but also look for breast and cock-a-leekie pudding of Adlington chicken or keep it traditional with hanger steak with bone-marrow butter, onion rings and triple-cooked chips. And it's hard to go wrong with chocolate brownie and hazelnut cream. Wines from £22.

Chef/s: Emily Watkins and Tom Waller. **Open:** all week L 12 to 2 (2.30 Sat, 3 Sun), Mon to Sat D 6.30 to 9. **Meals:** main courses £17 to £25. **Details:** 70 seats. Parking.

The Wild Rabbit

Cooking score: 3
Modern European | £44
Church Street, Kingham, OX7 6YA
Tel no: (01608) 658389
thewildrabbit.co.uk

Beautifully renovated by the people behind Daylesford Organics, enthusiasm for this 18th-century inn remains undimmed. It's the entire package that appeals, including a welcoming atmosphere and the chance of alfresco eating on fine days. The rustic feel – beams, stone, log-stuffed fireplace – is relaxed enough to cater for those who just want a drink in the bar, but with a stylish modern dining room where the open-to-view kitchen produces classy bistro dishes with a high comfort factor (the duck egg with truffle purée, slow-cooked bacon and crispy sourdough is a good call). A satisfying main course of sea bass offers accurately timed fish teamed with purple sprouting broccoli, roast chicken wing, brown shrimps and gentlemen's relish, or there could be Wootton Estate lamb with butternut squash, ras-el-hanout, black radish and strained yoghurt. And for dessert? The cheesecake with Braeburn apple, sorrel and caramelised honey should fit the bill. Wines from £17.50.
Chef/s: Tim Allen. **Open:** all week L 12 to 2.15 (2.45 Sat and Sun), D 7 to 9.15 (9.30 Fri and Sat, 9 Sun). **Meals:** main courses £20 to £24. **Details:** 50 seats. 50 seats outside. Bar. Wheelchairs. Music. Parking.

∎ Kirtlington

LOCAL GEM
The Oxford Arms
Modern British | £28
Troy Lane, Kirtlington, OX5 3HA
Tel no: (01869) 350208
oxford-arms.co.uk

The 19th-century stone-built village pub has kept pace with the times thanks to Bryn Jones, who has spent over a dozen years keeping the

Oxford Arms on the straight and narrow. It's a proper pub with Hook Norton ales at the pumps, log fires, patio garden and an unpretentious menu that fits the relaxed mood whether you're eating indoors or out. 'Posh' pâté with homemade chutney, Belgian endive and walnut salad pumped up with Roquefort, risotto of the day and a burger made from Blenheim Estate venison – it's all good. Wines start at £17.

∎ Lechlade

★ NEW ENTRY ★
The Plough
Cooking score: 3
British | £27
Lechlade, GL7 3HG
Tel no: (01367) 253543
theploughinnkelmscott.com

In a stunning location on the border between Gloucestershire and Oxfordshire, this pretty 17th-century pub-with-rooms is close to the Thames Path and Kelmscott Manor, once the summer home of the British Arts and Crafts Movement pioneer William Morris. Spruced up by Sebastian and Lana Snow, who also run the nearby Five Alls at Filkins (see entry), the Plough is small and cosy, just two rooms (one essentially the bar where there are stools for drinkers), with rugs on the flagstone floors, exposed stone walls dotted with modern artwork, distressed antique furniture, the smell of wood smoke and no background music. The bar menu deals in pub classics (sandwiches, burgers, fish and chips), while the carte delivers 'lovely, simple cooking' along the lines of scallops on a tangle of well-dressed leaves, warm pea purée and punchy mint vinaigrette, roast chump of new season lamb with summer bean compote coated with minty pesto and gravy, and a 'true to the cause' apple and cherry crumble. Wines from £18.
Chef/s: Matthew Read. **Open:** Tue to Sat L 12 to 2.30 (3 Sat), D 6 to 9.30 (10 Fri and Sat). Sun 12 to 7. **Closed:** Mon. **Meals:** main courses £12 to £23. **Details:** 40 seats. 40 seats outside. Bar. Parking.

▊ Murcott
The Nut Tree Inn
Cooking score: 5
Modern British | £43
Main Street, Murcott, OX5 2RE
Tel no: (01865) 331253
nuttreeinn.co.uk
£5
OFF

Over the past decade or so Imogen and Mike North have done a grand job in maintaining this whitewashed thatched pub overlooking the village pond. The beamed, exposed stone interior oozes character and it still operates as a traditional watering hole, but the real emphasis is on things culinary – as the substantial kitchen garden (and amuse-bouche, pre-dessert and petits fours) suggests. The menu reads well and there are some neatly considered ideas – from 'a fabulous coming-together of tastes and textures' in a pavé of own-smoked Loch Duart salmon with whipped horseradish cream, pickled cucumber and Avruga caviar, to an 'exceedingly well-executed' grilled fillet of line-caught Looe cod with wild garlic, chicory and white wine sauce. The kitchen can also play it straight and true, offering 'a faultless' grilled fillet of aged Charolais beef, while dessert might feature hot blood-orange soufflé with blood-orange sorbet, a real 'wow dish', according to one reporter. Wines from £16.
Chef/s: Michael and Mary North. **Open:** Wed to Sun L 12 to 2.30 (3 Sun), Wed to Sat D 7 to 9. **Closed:** Mon, Tue, 27 Dec for 2 weeks. **Meals:** main courses £17 to £35. Tasting menu £60 (8 courses). **Details:** 70 seats. 30 seats outside. Bar. Music. Parking.

Symbols

	Accommodation is available
£30	Three courses for less than £30
£5 OFF	£5-off voucher scheme
	Notable wine list

▊ Oxford
Branca
Cooking score: 1
Italian | £25
110-111 Walton Street, Oxford, OX2 6AJ
Tel no: (01865) 556111
branca.co.uk
£5 £30
OFF

Branca has been pleasing town and gown since the millennium with its mix of all-day opening, student-friendly prices and special deals. All congregate in the high-ceilinged dining room to get their fill of stone-baked pizzas, pastas, salads and risottos, plus a contingent of generous trattoria-style plates ranging from fillet of sea bream with saffron and chive risotto to slow-braised lamb shank with soft polenta and lemon gremolata. Steaks, Italian cheeses and puddings such as chocolate nemesis complete the package, while aperitivi cocktails support a snappy wine list (from £18). The garden terrace comes into its own when the weather is fine.
Chef/s: Jamie King. **Open:** Mon to Fri 12 to 10. Sat and Sun 10 to 10. **Meals:** main courses £10 to £23. Set L and D £14 (2 courses). **Details:** 90 seats. 60 seats outside. Bar. Wheelchairs. Music.

Cherwell Boathouse
Cooking score: 2
Modern British | £32
50 Bardwell Road, Oxford, OX2 6ST
Tel no: (01865) 552746
cherwellboathouse.co.uk
£5 ▐
OFF

With punts and swans floating by and the distant thwock of leather on willow, it's possible to believe that hardly anything has changed since Lewis Carroll lived in Oxford. The Victorian boathouse on the Cherwell bank is one of the city's best-loved institutions, making a seductive spot at any season for traditionally based cooking with some modern flourishes. Octopus carpaccio with tempura squid in lime and chilli vinaigrette won't have been available to

Carroll, certainly, but braised Middle White pork belly with cabbage, crackling and apple sauce does maintain a firm hand on tradition's tiller. Finish with sticky toffee pudding and clotted cream ice cream. Not the least glory of the place has always been the superbly broad-minded and comprehensive wine list, where the newest fashions – Galician Albariño, Ventoux rosé, blended Douro reds – rub shoulders with the old aristocracy of France, Italy and even Germany, whose Mosel Rieslings are a virtually forgotten delight. The opening price is £15.25.

Chef/s: Nick Welford. **Open:** all week L 12 to 2 (2.30 Sat and Sun), D 6 to 9.30. **Closed:** 24 to 30 Dec. **Meals:** main courses £16 to £25. Set L and D £22 (2 courses) to £28. **Details:** 65 seats. 45 seats outside. Bar. Wheelchairs. Music. Parking.

Gee's
Cooking score: 2
Modern European | £30
61 Banbury Road, Oxford, OX2 6PE
Tel no: (01865) 553540
gees-restaurant.co.uk

Gee's has been an Oxford landmark since the early 1980s. It's effectively a fully stocked conservatory with a restaurant at its heart and a weathervane perched on its pitched roof. It's always been a safe bet for visiting parents treating students, and its Mediterranean-influenced menus of small appetiser plates and main dishes has plenty to inspire. A pair who happened in for a lunch of parsnip soup and tapas (expect chorizo in red wine, red pepper arancini, meatballs), followed by an eight-ounce ribeye in béarnaise and a risotto milanese, emerged entirely glad of the experience. Interesting menu byways might see coppa and Gorgonzola piled on to a pizzetta, with guinea fowl from the wood-fired oven next, served with baby artichokes and aïoli. If you're able to resist the lure of dark chocolate fondant with PX ice cream, there could be triple-milk Tuscan Rocchetta cheese, served with membrillo. The short wine list opens with house Spanish at £20.95.

Chef/s: Russell Helley. **Open:** all week 12 to 10.30. **Meals:** main courses £14 to £24. Set L £14 (2 courses) to £17. **Details:** 84 seats. 28 seats outside. Bar. Wheelchairs. Music.

The Magdalen Arms
Cooking score: 2
Modern British | £28
243 Iffley Road, Oxford, OX4 1SJ
Tel no: (01865) 243159
magdalenarms.co.uk
£30

For all its somewhat lugubrious interior, this place is a bright spot on Oxford's dining scene, well worth a bus or cycle ride up the Iffley Road (don't drive, the parking is as legendary – in a bad way – as the homemade focaccia for sale on Saturdays is good-legendary). Dive into the compact, daily changing menu for food that smacks you round the chops so full is it with simply prepared, properly flavourful ingredients. A crab soup is elevated to garlicky deliciousness by little rouille-topped toasts; pickled cucumbers cut the richness of rabbit and pork rillettes. Follow with translucent, generously filled spinach and ricotta ravioli, alive with sage, butter and Parmesan, or a fat skate wing, pan-seared to perfection and needing nothing more than a lightly dressed salad and punchy aïoli – oh, and hot, salty, thick, golden chips. A cream-topped chocolate pot is a pudding to savour teaspoon by teaspoon; share it if you really have to. There are bottles from £18 but it's nice to see carafe-sized options, too.

Chef/s: Tony Abarno. **Open:** Tue to Sun L 12 to 2.30 (3 Sun), all week D 5.30 to 10 (6 Sat, 6 to 9 Sun). **Closed:** 24 to 26 Dec, bank hols. **Meals:** main courses £14 to £30. **Details:** 200 seats. 100 seats outside. Bar. Wheelchairs. Music.

Top Puds

Our inspectors are happy to sacrifice their waistlines for the good of the Guide. Here are some more top picks for the finest puds in the UK.

'Pudding at **Orwells, Oxfordshire** was a riff on caramel apples: a cylinder of chopped, braised apple encased in a wafer of pastry, itself wrapped in a thin layer of apple jelly. Also on the plate a salted-caramel and a milk ice cream – both impeccably light and smooth – dots of caramel, dried apple slices, a little biscuit crumb, and a whole, poached baby apple encased in brûlée-like caramel. Extraordinary.'

'The Swiss lemon-meringue tart at **Antidote, London** is an amazing dessert: quite creamy meringue, like île flottante, topping an intense, lemon curd-style confection, not too sweet, and just held together by a thin ring of sweet biscuit.'

'There is one dessert at **Hedone**, **London**, that is world class. It is ostensibly a vanilla mille feuille, but with every component tuned up to another level. I don't see how puff pastry could be better and I have never seen puff pastry like this. Between the three pastry pieces is a piped vanilla crème pat like custard silk. It's nothing, though, compared to the ice cream, which makes a mockery of all vanilla ice creams.'

My Sichuan

Cooking score: 3
Chinese | £25
The Old School, Gloucester Green, Oxford, OX1 2DA
Tel no: (01865) 236899
mysichuan.co.uk
£30

You say Sichuan, I say Szechuan, but whatever you do, don't call the whole thing off, for this joint in a converted Victorian schoolhouse serves up some bang-on food from the region. It's positively vast – some 260 souls at the last count – and makes the most of its Victorian features and proportions, with private function rooms if you need one. Set menu banquets are an easy option, but dig a little deeper into the menu and you can have beef and ox tripe in chilli sauce, or sea snails with green pepper sauce. Crab and sweetcorn soup is a classic choice, with preserved egg and cucumber soup among more exciting alternatives, and, if you're a fan of the chilli heat that's a feature of this cuisine, go for hot and spicy king prawns or another of the many fired-up options. Desserts such as tofu pudding in a rice wine soup catch the eye.
Chef/s: Jian Juzhou. **Open:** all week 12 to 11 (12 to 12 Fri and Sat). **Meals:** main courses £7 to £19. **Details:** 260 seats.

Oli's Thai

Cooking score: 3
Thai | £20
38 Magdalen Road, Oxford, OX4 1RB
Tel no: (01865) 790223
olisthai.com
£30

The further along the Cowley Road you venture, the less Oxford feels like Oxford, but the intrepid are rewarded, if they can get in, with the dynamic traditional Thai cooking of the Thurstons' rough-and-ready, but seethingly popular, venue. A few tables and a tiny counter area are supplemented by outdoor accommodation, and that's it. Book way ahead. The food is alive with the razor-

sharpness and electrifying sizzle of Thai seasonings, from salmon with pickled cucumber in sesame and chilli to veggie options such as tofu in yellow bean, ginger, chilli and gai lan. The green curries are hot and creamy, the duck panang made with delicious confit, and it's worth ordering a side of apple and cashew salad dressed in mint and chilli while you're about it. Finish with custard tart (no, really). Five table wines at £17 or £28 and a couple of fizzes provide liquid cheer, or drink Chang beer.
Chef/s: Ladd Thurston. **Open:** Tue to Sat L 12 to 2 (3 Tue), Wed to Sat D 5 to 9. **Closed:** Sun, Mon, 2 weeks Dec. **Meals:** main courses £9 to £15. **Details:** 20 seats. Wheelchairs. Music. Children over 7 yrs only at D.

★ NEW ENTRY ★

The Oxford Kitchen
Cooking score: 3
Modern British | £37
215 Banbury Road, Oxford, OX2 7HQ
Tel no. (01865) 511149
theoxfordkitchen.co.uk

An otherwise underserved district of Oxford benefits from the contemporary dining touch of Steve Quinn and Samantha Davies' ambitious high-flyer, an aubergine-fronted place with an interior of simple fixtures against bare-brick walls adorned with Warhol tribute art. John Footman cooks to the modern British template, deconstructing and reconstructing respectively for a bowl of spring minestrone with a cornucopia of accompanying veg, or an aspirant burger with bacon jam and Comté, served with triple-cooked chips. Along the way, the more eye-catching dishes might include confit duck liver with foie gras mousse in a white chocolate shell and dots of blood-orange gel, an intricate but well-balanced dish; sea trout poached in lemon oil that comes with textured courgettes; and a copious serving of lamb that takes in baba ganoush, roasted tomatoes, couscous, puréed aubergine and much, much more. Pick of the desserts is very light, chilled

rice pudding topped with pecan crumble and a sprig of lemon verbena. A compact wine list opens at £22.
Chef/s: John Footman. **Open:** Tue to Fri L 12 to 2.30, D 6 to 9.30. Sat 9 to 2.30, D 6 to 9.30. Sun 9 to 4. **Closed:** Mon, first 2 weeks Jan. **Meals:** main courses £16 to £28. Set L and D £18 (2 courses) to £23. **Details:** 80 seats. 10 seats outside. Wheelchairs. Music.

LOCAL GEM

Turl Street Kitchen
Modern British | £21
16-17 Turl Street, Oxford, OX1 3DH
Tel no: (01865) 264171
turlstreetkitchen.co.uk
£30

This well-supported bar-café-restaurant is a bright, split-level venue with stripped floorboards and artwork from local artists on the walls. The menu is driven by local produce and changes twice a day, say 'very tasty' pork goulash, chicken with lentils, bacon and aïoli or a vegetarian dish of wild mushroom and Jerusalem artichoke risotto with goats' cheese. All profits go straight to the Oxford Hub, a collection of charities based in this handsome Georgian town house. Wines from £16.50.

▌Shiplake

★ TOP 50 ★

★ RESTAURANT OF THE YEAR ★

Orwells
Cooking score: 7
Modern British | £46
Shiplake Row, Shiplake, RG9 4DP
Tel no: (01189) 403673
orwellsatshiplake.co.uk

The whitewashed Georgian inn looks modest enough, but Messrs Simpson and Trotman's village venue has gradually emerged from the pub chrysalis into one of the Home Counties' most strikingly individual enterprises. There may still be bare-brick walls and low black beams, but the service approach is full of refined assurance, and the cooking is on a mission to impress. Start with beautifully chiselled gurnard tartare, sashimi-fresh, offset with translucent rhubarb purée and ponzu gel. Fish is handled with respect and confidence throughout, as when a firm fillet of turbot appears on purple potato crush, scattered with diced spring onion tops in raisin and verjus butter, a dish that balances delicacy and concentration. Standout at inspection was a main course of beef rump with charred baby onions, samphire and sticky short rib, all anointed in crystal-clear beef consommé, every ingredient impeccable. Dessert might be a featherlight cylindrical apple pastry with salt caramel ice cream and a whole poached baby apple encased in brûlée caramel. Own-grown vegetables and honey from Orwell's own hives contribute to the overall feeling of class, and there is a wine list to beat the band, with glasses that run from Gascony to Oregon and Hawkes Bay, and reference growers in every region, including natural and biodynamic selections, all offered at prices that city-dwellers have long forgotten. Prices open at £22, or £3.80 a small glass.

Chef/s: Ryan Simpson and Liam Trotman. **Open:** Wed to Sun L 11.30 to 3, Wed to Sat D 6.30 to 9.30. **Closed:** Mon, Tue, first 2 weeks Jan, 1 week Jun, first 2 weeks Sept. **Meals:** main courses £22 to £30. Set L £15 (2 courses) to £19. Set D £20 (2 courses) to £25. Sun L £35. **Details:** 40 seats. 20 seats outside. Bar. Wheelchairs. Music. Parking.

▌Sparsholt
The Star Inn
Cooking score: 4
Modern British | £30
Watery Lane, Sparsholt, OX12 9PL
Tel no: (01235) 751873
thestarsparsholt.co.uk
£5 OFF ⌷

Sparsholt sits comfortably below the ancient Ridgeway track with its famous White Horse, a soothingly sylvan location for Caron Williams' red-brick Georgian inn and barn conversion. Views of the attractive gardens

contribute to the restful mood in the dining room, where Matt Williams offers dynamically modernised pub food on seasonally changing menus that come with suggested wine pairings for each dish. Start with dill-cured gravadlax, vibrantly dressed in orange and beetroot, as the intro to sturdy main dishes like roast lamb chump with crisp-fried sweetbreads on broad beans and wild garlic, or seared smoked sea trout with a fricassee of chorizo, peas and gem lettuce. Sides include tempting French fries in their skins with Parmesan and thyme oil, and to finish, there's white chocolate crème brûlée with rhubarb and liquorice marshmallow. Pub favourites such as fishcakes, sausages and mash, and rice pudding will satisfy simpler tastes. The short wine list has plenty by the glass from £3, bottles from £17.

Chef/s: Matt Williams. **Open:** Mon to Sat L 12 to 2.30, D 6.30 to 9 (9.30 Fri and Sat). Sun 12 to 8. **Meals:** main courses £17 to £30. **Details:** 60 seats. 40 seats outside. Bar. Wheelchairs. Music. Parking.

▌Stoke Row
LOCAL GEM
The Crooked Billet
Modern British | £30
Newlands Lane, Stoke Row, RG9 5PU
Tel no: (01491) 681048
thecrookedbillet.co.uk

Down a typically narrow English lane, The Crooked Billet dates from the 1640s, and rumour has it one landlord's daughter dated Dick Turpin. Today's landlord, chef Paul Clerehugh, has run the place since 1989, and his latest development is an on-site bakery supplying the pub and local schools. A proper pub with low beams and real fire, the kitchen turns out classy stuff like pan-seared pigeon with candied beets, roast halibut with salt cod brandade and broad beans, and 'builder's tea' brûlée. Wines start at £20.

▐ Toot Baldon
The Mole Inn
Cooking score: 2
Modern British | £32
Toot Baldon, OX44 9NG
Tel no: (01865) 340001
themoleinn.com

The inviting rusticity of the interior and gloriously landscaped garden would make this inn an asset to any village. Add the cooking of owner Gary Witchalls to the equation and Toot Baldon is the envy of many a community. There's a lack of pretension to the kitchen's output, so chicken and tiger prawn Thai red curry stands alongside linguine with slow-roast tomatoes and wild mushrooms, and breast of Aylesbury duck with goats' cheese mousseline potatoes and beetroot and orange jus on a menu that includes steaks dry-aged for 28 days and served with skinny chips. There's more of that Asian influence in a starter of shredded duck and pork belly, while lunchtime offers up fish and chips and gammon with a fried local hen's egg. For dessert, sticky date pudding and classic crème brûlée hit the spot. Wines start at £19.25.
Chef/s: Gary Witchalls. **Open:** all week L 12 to 2.30 (4 Sun), D 7 to 9.30 (6.30 Fri and Sat, 6 to 8.30 Sun). **Closed:** 25 and 26 Dec. **Meals:** main courses £15 to £19. Set L and D £18 (2 courses) to £24. Sun L £15. **Details:** 120 seats. 60 seats outside. Bar. Music. Parking.

▐ Wootton
The Killingworth Castle
Cooking score: 3
Modern British | £28
Glympton Road, Wootton, OX20 1EJ
Tel no: (01993) 811401
thekillingworthcastle.com
🛏 £30

Dating from the 17th century and with an interior that looks the rustic part with beams, bare boards, exposed stone and a big open fire, this hostelry is everyone's idea of a classic country pub. The place certainly has a good

buzz – the bar dispenses real ales (from the owners' Yubberton Brewing Company) and the keenly priced menus foreshadow the cooking's direct style, which acknowledges current trends as well as offering tried-and-true pub dishes. So whether you're in the mood for ham hock terrine, a burger, flat-iron steak with mushroom, garlic butter, roast tomato and chips or, perhaps, cured salmon with avocado, wasabi, yoghurt, watermelon and coriander, then sea bream with samphire, fennel, crushed potatoes and tomato sauce, you won't put the kitchen off its stroke. Treacle tart with mandarin ice cream makes a great finish. Wines from £19.50.
Chef/s: Dale Ventham. **Open:** all week L 12 to 2.30 (3.30 Sun), D 6 to 9 (9.30 Fri and Sat, 8.30 Sun). **Meals:** main courses £13 to £23. **Details:** 68 seats. 40 seats outside. Bar. Parking.

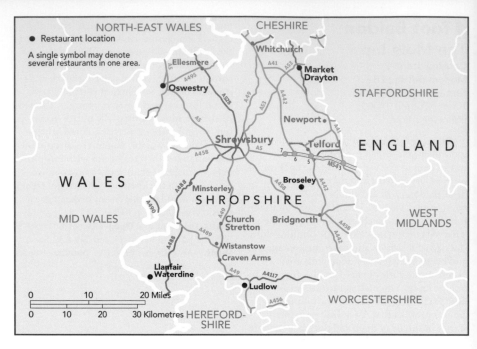

- ● Restaurant location

A single symbol may denote
several restaurants in one area.

NORTH-EAST WALES

CHESHIRE

Whitchurch

Ellesmere

Market
Drayton

Oswestry

STAFFORDSHIRE

Newport

Shrewsbury

Telford

E N G L A N D

WALES

Broseley

Minsterley

SHROPSHIRE

MID WALES

Church
Stretton

Bridgnorth

WEST
MIDLANDS

Wistanstow

Craven Arms

Llanfair
Waterdine

Ludlow

0   10   20 Miles
0   10   20   30 Kilometres

WORCESTERSHIRE

HEREFORD-
SHIRE

■ Broseley

LOCAL GEM
The King & Thai
Thai | £30
The Forester Arms, Avenue Road, Broseley,
TF12 5DL
Tel no: (01952) 882004
thekingandthai.co.uk

£5
OFF

Moving swiftly on from the punning name,
Suree Coates' Thai restaurant in a 200-year-
old roadside pub serves up that nation's cuisine
cooked with passion and precision. The décor
is smart, the mood cheerful and the excellent
ingredients help it stand out from the crowd.
The sharing platter is a good starting point –
pork balls with sweet dipping sauce, chicken
satay and so forth – and main courses run to
sweet-and-sour tiger prawns and classic red
and green curries. Wines start at £14.95.

■ Llanfair Waterdine
The Waterdine
Cooking score: 4
Modern British | £33
Llanfair Waterdine, LD7 1TU
Tel no: (01547) 528214
waterdine.com

Local resident Colonel John Hunt apparently
planned the triumphant ascent of Everest
from the lounge of this 16th-century thatched
long house. It's one of the more colourful
footnotes to a bucolic destination that has kept
its vintage looks, with thick stone walls,
leaded windows and an ancient inglenook
verifying the building's antiquity. Chef/
proprietor Ken Adams is steeped in the world
of classical haute cuisine, and it shows in
everything from the ramekins of Cornish crab
and smoked salmon served as a starter to the
mousseline potatoes that accompany a dish of
duck breast with bilberry sauce. Welsh Black
beef and mountain lamb put down a local

marker, although seasonal game is the kitchen's great strength – from butter-roasted partridge to Mortimer Forest roe deer with wild mushroom and celeriac hotpot. To conclude, desserts move confidently from apple biscotti crumble to lavender pannacotta with rhubarb compote. Wines from £20.

Chef/s: Ken Adams. **Open:** Sun L 12 to 1.30, Tue to Sat D 7 to 8.30. **Closed:** Mon, 24 to 26 Dec, 1 week early summer, 1 week autumn. **Meals:** set D £33. Sun L £23. **Details:** 14 seats. Parking.

◼ Ludlow
The Charlton Arms

Cooking score: 1
Modern British | £27
Ludford Bridge, Ludlow, SY8 1PJ
Tel no: (01584) 872813
thecharltonarms.co.uk

This ancient stone inn is in a lovely location overlooking the Teme river and Ludford bridge. A clean-lined and modern conversion has made a smart restaurant with views across the water – in the summer you can take advantage of the decked gardens. As for food, it does a good job across the spectrum, with twice-baked cheese soufflé with cheese sauce, braised ox cheek with watercress pomme purée, a hearty fisherman's pie and treacle tart with ginger ice cream coming in for praise.

Chef/s: Alex Marston. **Open:** all week L 12 to 3, D 6 to 9.30 (8.30 Sun). **Closed:** 25 Dec. **Meals:** main courses £11 to £19. **Details:** 69 seats. 92 seats outside. Bar. Wheelchairs. Music. Parking.

The Green Café

Cooking score: 1
Modern British | £17
Mill on the Green, Ludlow, SY8 1EG
Tel no: (01584) 879872
thegreencafe.co.uk

For its many fans, this idyllic café means 'lunch with friends by the weir on a sunny day'. It's distinguished by warm service as well as its

lovely setting in a community-owned converted mill. Outdoor seating almost doubles capacity in good weather, but its well-made soups (red onion and red wine, perhaps) keep things going year-round. Main courses might be roast squash with goats' cheese and curd, lentils, pine nuts and seeds, and afterwards there's pannacotta with blood orange and honey. Beers, ciders and perry are produced within 30 miles; wines from £19.

Chef/s: Clive Davis. **Open:** Tue to Sun L only 12 to 2.30. **Closed:** Mon, 24 to 26 Dec, 4 to 30 Jan. **Meals:** main courses £8 to £13. **Details:** 30 seats. 25 seats outside. Wheelchairs.

◼ Market Drayton
Goldstone Hall

Cooking score: 3
Modern British | £45
Goldstone Road, Market Drayton, TF9 2NA
Tel no: (01630) 661202
goldstonehall.com

A herbal walkway is one of the standout features of the magnificent kitchen garden that dominates the scene at Goldstone Hall – a family-owned country pile. Horticulture isn't simply about ornamentation here, it fuels the kitchen itself and provides Chris Weatherstone with seasonal pickings for his bright, vivid cooking. Eat in the oak-panelled dining room or the Victorian-style conservatory and terrace: either way, expect pretty dishes and emphatic flavours in the shape of, say, smoked eel parfait with celery and apple, beef fillet with red cabbage, oca, turnip and cavolo nero or an earthy extravaganza involving salt-baked celeriac, chanterelles, lentils and Swiss chard. Desserts such as a combination of pineapple, hazelnut, coconut and lemon verbena mix ingredients from near and far, while Shropshire cheeses bring it all back home. The food is matched by an impressive, highly personal wine list with a bias towards terroir and organic production; a dozen house selections start at £20 (£4.85 a glass).

Chef/s: Chris Weatherstone. **Open:** all week L 12 to 2.30, D 6.30 to 9.30 (8.30 Sun). **Closed:** 26 Dec. **Meals:** set L £27 (2 courses) to £32. Set D £45. Sun L £32. **Details:** 90 seats. 20 seats outside. Bar. Wheelchairs. Music. Parking.

▌Oswestry
Sebastians
Cooking score: 3
French | £45
45 Willow Street, Oswestry, SY11 1AQ
Tel no: (01691) 655444
sebastians-hotel.co.uk

The Fishers' restaurant-with-rooms, a 17th-century coaching inn, is all charm, from the sheltered courtyard to the oak-beamed dining room, where orange walls and a big fireplace assist the sense of comfort. Mark Fisher's monthly changing five-course menus take a French tack that's delicately poised between traditional and modern ways, starting with a soup such as Jerusalem artichoke, and then proceeding to scallop, fennel, tangerine and tarragon, or mushrooms in Roquefort cream. A sorbet pops up before the main business of sea bass with celeriac purée and smoked bacon in red wine, or lamb loin with ratatouille and pesto. Cheeses and chutney with a rarebit-topped croûton cater to those not seduced by sweetness, but if you are so seduced, expect banana sponge and chocolate ice cream, or lemon sablé with meringue and blackberry coulis. A French-led wine list opens at £19, and there's a useful selection of half-bottles from £12.
Chef/s: Mark Sebastian Fisher. **Open:** Tue to Sat D only 6.30 to 9.30. **Closed:** Sun, Mon, 25 to 26 Dec, 1 Jan, bank hols. **Meals:** set D £45 (5 courses). **Details:** 35 seats. 15 seats outside. Music. Parking.

www.signaturedish.co.uk

Suree Coates
The King & Thai, Broseley

What food could you not live without?
Thai food! Creating it is like a therapy with all the prepping, chopping and flavours and aromas that are released from the produce. Flaming and stirring a wok is also therapeutic, it releases frustrations as well as lots of good oils and natural goodness from the produce.

What's your favourite dish on your menu?
Beef massaman. Beautiful local Shropshire beef, slow cooked with fragrant herbs, spices and seasonal vegetables. Our customers love it – it's so colourful.

What is the vital ingredient for a successful kitchen?
Passion! It gets you through a long, hot and stressful service. Good organisation also helps – and a bit of laughter!

Do you have anything exciting coming up that you would like to share?
We are developing our Thai street food dishes into a daily menu option.

And finally...tell us something about yourself that will surprise your diners.
I've always been fascinated by architecture, I even studied it at school. But my belly kept telling me to cook and eat; I love food, so I guess my belly won!

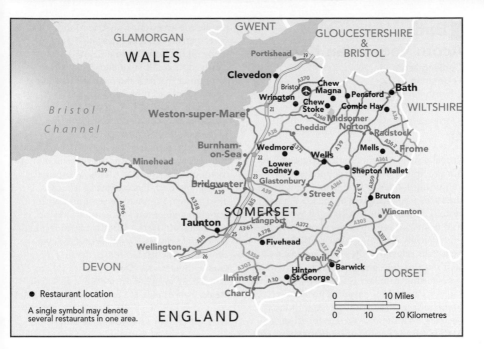

Restaurant location

A single symbol may denote several restaurants in one area.

ENGLAND

0   10 Miles

0   10   20 Kilometres

▊ Barwick
Little Barwick House

Cooking score: 5
Modern British | £50
Rexes Hollow Lane, Barwick, BA22 9TD
Tel no: (01935) 423902
littlebarwick.co.uk

Ten minutes should be all that's needed to transport you from the purgatorial A303 to the leafily enshrouded Little Barwick, a white-fronted Georgian country house peeping between trees in its three acres of gardens. The Fords have refurbed the place recently, but retained the same level of soothing boutique class, and views over the grounds – perhaps from an aperitif table on the terrace – come as standard. Father and son Tim and Olly make a formidable double act in the kitchen, cooking up-to-date English food that highlights thoroughbred ingredients with style. Start with crab-stuffed paupiette of lemon sole in chive butter, or a modern classic pairing of scallops with butternut purée, before setting about pinkly roasted squab pigeon with braised lentils, or the superb roe deer saddle with puréed beetroot, beautifully presented with baby vegetables and excellent reductions. A Comice pear mille-feuille with matching sorbet in honey and walnut sauce finishes things off majestically. Wines arranged by style search out the great and the good all over the show, with a huge choice by the glass from £4.75, plenty of halves, and bottles from £19.95.

Chef/s: Tim and Olly Ford. **Open:** Wed to Sat L 12 to 2, Tue to Sat D 7 to 9. **Closed:** Sun, Mon. **Meals:** set L £27 (2 courses) to £30. Set D £44 (2 courses) to £50. **Details:** 44 seats. 12 seats outside. Parking. Children over 5 yrs only.

Average price

The average price denotes the price of a three-course meal without wine.

▌Bath
Acorn Vegetarian Kitchen
Cooking score: 3
Vegetarian | £32
2 North Parade Passage, Bath, BA1 1NX
Tel no: (01225) 446059
acornvegetariankitchen.co.uk
£5
OFF

'It really surprised me', remarked one reader not previously versed in the merits of this veggie high-flyer in a building dating from the 1620s (the birthplace of the UK's postal system no less – the first stamp was actually sold from its doorstep). Spread over two floors of a typically charming piece of Bath real estate, the relaxed and friendly approach of the staff sets the tone, and this is a place where the 'fine-dining' moniker is freely attached to the kitchen's ambitious output. The fixed-price menu reflects an interest in contemporary cooking techniques as well as revealing a passion for the natural ingredients themselves. Frozen parsnip to start, or slivers of Chioggia beetroot with fermented cashew purée, before three types of winter squash (purée, fondant and pickle) with gnudi. Everything looks pretty on the plate, including salted chocolate tart with blood-orange sorbet. Wines start at £17.50.
Chef/s: Richard Buckley and Steven Yates. **Open:** all week L 12 to 3 (3.30 Sat), D 5.30 to 9.30. **Closed:** 25 and 26 Dec. **Meals:** set L £17 (2 courses) to £20. Set D £26 (2 courses) to £32. Sun L £18. **Details:** 32 seats. V menu. Music.

Allium
Cooking score: 4
Modern European | £38
Abbey Hotel, 1-3 North Parade, Bath, BA1 1LF
Tel no: (01225) 461603
abbeyhotelbath.co.uk
£5
OFF

Housed in a revamped Georgian town house that now functions as a privately run hotel and repository for the owners' eclectic art collection, Allium is in the business of producing accessible brasserie food for Bath. Chef-patron Chris Staines was once a big name on the London scene, noted for his clever ideas and love of pan-Asian riffs – something that still shows in dishes such as Portland white crabmeat with wasabi emulsion, white radish, grapefruit and avocado, or coconut-crusted stone bass fillet with cocoa beans, spring onions and soy-braised octopus. Staines also knows his local audience, which explains why the menu now includes sharing plates, salads, a bespoke burger and beer-battered haddock, plus desserts such as chocolate marquise with popcorn and lemon ice cream. It may be populist stuff, but the results are fine-tuned, classy and immensely satisfying. An ever-evolving wine list has bottles from £22.
Chef/s: Chris Staines. **Open:** all week L 12 to 3 (4 Sun), D 5.30 to 9 (9.45 Fri and Sat, 6 to 9 Sun). **Meals:** main courses £16 to £25. Set L and D £20 (2 courses) to £25. Sun L £28. **Details:** 68 seats. 48 seats outside. Bar. Wheelchairs. Music.

The Bath Priory
Cooking score: 4
Modern European | £80
Weston Road, Bath, BA1 2XT
Tel no: (01225) 331922
thebathpriory.co.uk

'There's no denying it's a wonderful spot, a lovely hotel in beautifully peaceful grounds,' noted one reporter of this handsome Victorian pile in a residential area a mile from Bath city centre. It may come across as country-house elegance personified with its generous, antique-filled interiors and opulent dining room with well-spaced tables, but it is surprisingly relaxed. Sam Moody's finely-tuned modern cooking sticks rigidly to the seasons and rarely looks beyond the West Country for materials – as seen in dishes such as seared scallops with girolle mushrooms, pickled radish, apple and hazelnuts, and pork cheek, belly and shoulder served with cheesy mash, spring onions and paprika jus. Desserts follow suit with spiced caramel-poached pineapple, Granny Smith, truffle and vanilla Chantilly. From the good-value lunchtime menu, a spring meal could deliver a 'well-handled' pressed terrine of confit chicken with truffled peas and broad beans, and 'delicately flavoured' Cornish lobster fricassee with saffron linguine, spring vegetable and lobster butter sauce. Wines start at £28.

Chef/s: Sam Moody. **Open:** all week L 12.30 to 2.30, D 6.30 to 9.30. **Meals:** Set L £25 (2 courses) to £30. Set D £62 (2 courses) to £80. Tasting menu £95 (7 courses). **Details:** 50 seats. Bar. Parking. Children over 12 yrs only.

Casanis

Cooking score: 3
French | £35
4 Saville Row, Bath, BA1 2QP
Tel no: (01225) 780055
casanis.co.uk

Laurent Couvreur cheffed his way along the Côte d'Azur before pitching up in Bath in 2007 to open this highly *sympathique* classic bistro in a listed Georgian townhouse. The décor is all old-school elegance, with a stone-walled courtyard for when the Côte d'Azur weather comes to western England, while the cuisine style is unreconstructed French demotic, and all the more popular for it. Skewered scallops come with croquettes of crab risotto, aniseed-boosted fennel purée, crispy leeks and crab and tarragon sauce for a starter with a lot to say for itself. At main, there may be a trio of lamb – rump, merguez and a minced lamb cake – with cumined bean ragoût, or St Mawes catch of the day. Finish with crème brûlée infused with orange wine, or with properly sticky Tatin served with chestnut and brandy ice cream. A pre-theatre menu is useful, and the handful of French wines starts at £19, or £5 a glass.

Chef/s: Laurent Couvreur. **Open:** Wed, Fri and Sat L 12 to 1.30, Tue to Sat D 6 to 10 (10.30 Fri and Sat). **Closed:** Sun, Mon, 25 and 26 Dec, 2 weeks Jan, 1 week Jul/Aug. **Meals:** main courses £14 to £28. Set L £18 (2 courses) to £23. Early D £20 (2 courses) to £25. **Details:** 50 seats. 14 seats outside. Music.

The Circus Restaurant

Cooking score: 3
Modern European | £29
34 Brock Street, Bath, BA1 2LN
Tel no: (01225) 466020
thecircuscafeandrestaurant.co.uk
£5 OFF £30

Occupying a fine Georgian building in the street that connects two architectural gems – The Circus and the Royal Crescent – this intimate restaurant continues to attract both locals and visitors. After nine years the compact family-run eatery has dropped the 'café' tag from its title to concentrate on the restaurant side – not having to break off to make cups of coffee for tourists has allowed chef-patron Alison Golden to focus on her Elizabeth David/Jane Grigson-inspired cooking, which concentrates on clear, simple flavours. In an elegant setting of muted colours and original fireplaces, guests can start with a comforting gratin of south Devon crab and leek, followed by loin of English rose veal, pan-fried with prosciutto, sage and globe artichoke hearts, white wine, wilted spinach and lemon aïoli. To finish, it has to be nutmeg crème brûlée with raisins soaked in Pedro Ximénez sherry. The European wine list starts at £17.70.

Chef/s: Alison Golden and Máté Andrasko. **Open:** Mon to Sat L 12 to 2.30, D 5.30 to 10.30. **Closed:** Sun, 23 Dec for 3 weeks. **Meals:** main courses £17 to £19. **Details:** 50 seats. 8 seats outside. Music. Children over 7 yrs only.

★ NEW ENTRY ★

Corkage

Cooking score: 1
Modern European | £18
132a Walcot Street, Bath, BA1 5BG
Tel no: (01225) 422577
corkagebath.com
£30

What started in early 2016 as a pop-up within a wine shop has quickly become a fully-fledged wine bar and one of the hottest new

openings in Bath – 'so busy you really have to book,' says our local spy. Run by Marty Grant and Richard Knighting, this cramped, convivial bar has a genuine buzz to it. With 50 wines served by the glass and minimal mark-ups on bottles, good drinking is guaranteed, accompanied by seasonal small plates delivered from a tiny open kitchen – perhaps toasted sourdough piled high with white crabmeat or pan-fried duck breast fragrant with Chinese five-spice and served with peas, broad beans, green beans and braised gem lettuce. Wines start at £16.50.
Chef/s: Richard Knighting. **Open:** variable, see website. **Meals:** main courses £5 to £9. **Details:** 30 seats. Wheelchairs. Music.

The Dower House
Cooking score: 3
Modern European | £65
Royal Crescent Hotel, 16 Royal Crescent, Bath, BA1 2LS
Tel no: (01225) 823333
royalcrescent.co.uk

The Royal Crescent Hotel, set in the centre of that sweeping Georgian landmark, has always been one of Bath's most elegant addresses. Muted tones and crisp linen make a relaxing setting in the dining room that looks out over the sheltered secret garden, and David Campbell matches the tone of the place with a menu of classically based cooking with a distinct modernist edge. A serving of rich duck liver with a cigar of parfait, alongside spiced plum and bitter chocolate, offers a satisfying array of flavours, while an ozone-fresh atmosphere pervades sea bream tartare and ceviche with smoked eel and roe. The menu follows on with local guinea fowl and asparagus with wild garlic in truffle butter, or an impeccable spring dish of new-season lamb and baked Jersey Royals with monk's beard, spring onions and Parmesan. Dessert could be a fragrant mélange of apple, honeycomb, cider granita and rosemary cream. An international

trove of wines begins at £28 and doesn't stop until the four-figure barrier has been breached.
Chef/s: David Campbell. **Open:** all week L 12.30 to 2, D 7 to 9 (9.30 Fri and Sat). **Meals:** main courses £27 to £30. Tasting menu £72 (6 courses). **Details:** 45 seats. 60 seats outside. Bar. Wheelchairs. Music. Parking.

Menu Gordon Jones
Cooking score: 5
Modern British | £55
2 Wellsway, Bath, BA2 3AQ
Tel no: (01225) 480871
menugordonjones.co.uk

Gordon Jones grew up on the Moray coast, but has gone native in the English West Country with an idiosyncratic, resoundingly popular approach. The drill is no-choice surprise tasters of five courses at lunch, six at dinner, and since we hardly like to spoil a surprise, the temptation is to leave it there. The attraction isn't hard to fathom: 'We love the intimate atmosphere and being able to watch Gordon Jones (and chat with him) and his team at work,' confides a reader. If you'd still like a clue, you wouldn't be far wrong if you were to expect, say, cauliflower mousse with black-pudding cakes in curry oil to start, building through the courses to loin, liver and kidney of rabbit with asparagus, Roscoff onion, braised rice and apricot purée. Lunch has taken in smoked eel with purple mash, golden raisins and maple syrup, while purple carrot cake could be the final flourish, served with blood-orange and yoghurt parfait and white chocolate and fennel cream. Wines begin at £24.
Chef/s: Gordon Jones. **Open:** Tue to Sat L 12.30 to 2, D 7 to 9. **Closed:** Sun, Mon, 2 weeks Jan. **Meals:** set L £45 (5 courses). Set D £55 (6 courses). **Details:** 22 seats. Music. Children over 12 yrs only.

The Olive Tree

Cooking score: 4
Modern British | £55
The Queensberry Hotel, 4-7 Russel Street,
Bath, BA1 2QF
Tel no: (01225) 447928
olivetreebath.co.uk

£5 OFF 🍷 🛏️

The Queensberry blends seamlessly with its neighbours, a row of Georgian townhouses in a gently rising terrace. Down below, extending across three rooms extensively refurbished in 2015, is the Olive Tree, all dark banquettes, framed cartoon prints and soothing light levels. Chris Cleghorn knows his constituency well, so that regulars celebrating a milestone birthday duly received 'a splendid evening of glorious and outstanding food', served by good-humoured staff to boot. The crab lasagne with its matching mousse and bisque, fragrant with basil and ginger, remains a signature starter, and the fixed-price menus might roll on with quail, charred sweetcorn purée and popcorn, and hake in red wine, on their way to veal loin with Roscoff onion, truffle and sage. A final flourish is saved for desserts such as hot chocolate fondant with pistachio ice cream, or rhubarb with vanilla yoghurt mousse. The wine list is an obvious labour of love, stylistically arranged so you can pick your way from 'full, ripe, rich and toasty' to 'black fruits full of body', equally good at foraging thriftily as it is at scaling the heights. Prices start at £24.
Chef/s: Chris Cleghorn. **Open:** Fri to Sun L 12.30 to 2, Tue to Sun D 7 to 10 (6.30 Fri and Sat). **Closed:** Mon, 1 week in: Jan, Jul, Aug, Nov. **Meals:** main courses £19 to £27. Set L £24 (2 courses) to £30. Tasting menu £60 (6 courses) to £75. **Details:** 55 seats. V menu. Bar. Music.

LOCAL GEM

Aió Sardinia

Sardinian | £30
7 Edgar Buildings, George Street, Bath,
BA1 2EE
Tel no: (01225) 443900
aiorestaurant.co.uk

£5 OFF

Sardinia comes to Georgian Bath in the shape of this jolly, warm-hearted eatery – complete with tables on the pavement and folksy trinkets dotted around the dining room. The food also has a really authentic edge, from 'carta da musica' bread and island charcuterie (including mutton prosciutto) to bruschetta spread with bottarga (salted mullet roe) and fregola pasta 'pearls' with monkfish, mussels and clams. Also check out the classic oven-baked kid layered with flatbread and cheese. Fascinating Sardinian wines from £19.

LOCAL GEM

King William

British | £30
36 Thomas Street, Bath, BA1 5NN
Tel no: (01225) 428096
kingwilliampub.com

Modest, with mismatched tables and looking a bit worn around the edges, this Georgian pub not far from the city centre reminded one visitor of the first wave of boho London foodie pubs (think Anchor & Hope, see entry). The short, robust menu is all about straightforward seasonal flavours, say curried parsnip soup, salt-beef brisket, slow-cooked pork belly with white beans, sage pesto, chicory and cider syrup, and rhubarb sponge pudding with stem ginger ice cream. The wine list opens at £17.50.

Yak Yeti Yak

Nepalese | £20

12 Pierrepont Street, Bath, BA1 1LA
Tel no: (01225) 442299
yakyetiyak.co.uk

£30

This family-run Nepalese restaurant occupies simple quarters in the converted basements of three Georgian townhouses. Windows and a courtyard garden throw light on the classic steamed pork dumplings, rice and dhal, and delicate vegetable dishes including fermented bamboo shoots braised with new potatoes, blackeye beans and cumin, as well as lamb or beef stir-fries with the house masala. It's all cooked to order — just let the kitchen know how hot you like it. Wine is from £15.50.

Bruton

Roth Bar & Grill

Cooking score: 3
Modern British | £28

Durslade Farm, Dropping Lane, Bruton, BA10 0NL
Tel no: (01749) 814700
rothbarandgrill.co.uk

£30

Channelling Shoreditch in a bucolic Somerset cowshed, this unlikely project combines homespun modern gastronomy (including rare-breed meats from the farm) with a cocktail bar and a gallery of contemporary art and word-class installations — plus occasional live events. Lime-washed walls, theatre lighting, Emin-style neons and various surreal eccentricities form the backdrop to honest cooking that makes admirable use of fresh local ingredients. Burgers, charcuterie and kitchen salads line up alongside steaks from the salt room, but the menu also covers everything from bream fingers with tartare sauce or ricotta fritters with beetroot and walnuts to homemade venison sausages with Savoy cabbage, or whole mackerel with gremolata. Brunch goes down well with 'nutri' juices or 'morning cocktails', and there's afternoon tea, too (with Prosecco, if you're in the mood). Drinks also include artisan ales from the Wild Beer Company just up the road, in addition to some decent wines from £24.

Chef/s: Steve Horrell. **Open:** Tue to Fri and Sun L 12 to 3 (Sun 3.30), Fri D 6 to 10. Sat 12 to 8. **Closed:** Mon, 25 and 26 Dec. **Meals:** main courses £12 to £24. **Details:** 70 seats. 70 seats outside. Bar. Wheelchairs. Music. Parking.

Chew Magna

The Pony & Trap

Cooking score: 6
Modern British | £35

Knowle Hill, Chew Magna, BS40 8TQ
Tel no: (01275) 332627
theponyandtrap.co.uk

Need we say that the Chew Valley seems an apt place to find some good eating? Tucked in between Bristol and Bath, and sourcing from the rolling countryside hereabouts, the Eggleton family's West Country pub strikes the perfect balance between community hostelry and aspirational dining spot. Josh is responsible for the latter, scrupulously crediting his suppliers on the reverse of the menu and drawing on a seemingly limitless fund of imaginative verve for dynamic, exciting dishes. Slow-poached salmon with mustard, peanuts and cucumber might kick off one of the daily-changing menus, before tenderloin, neck and Marmite-glazed cheek of pork turn up with turnip and smoked chestnut to follow on. Even the more trad-sounding offerings are presented with panache and style, perhaps rabbit and pistachio terrine with mushrooms à la grecque, or grilled brill with brown shrimps and celery. Given the pub environs, a finisher of sticky ale pudding and stout ice cream seems only fitting. There are some decent wines, too, from £16.50.

Chef/s: Josh Eggleton. **Open:** all week L 12 to 2 (3.30 Sun), D 7 to 9 (6 Fri and Sat). **Closed:** 25 Dec. **Meals:** main courses £18 to £27. Tasting menu £60 (8 courses). Sun L £30. **Details:** 65 seats. 20 seats outside. Bar. Music. Parking.

Chew Stoke

LOCAL GEM
Salt & Malt
British | £20
Wally Lane, Chew Stoke, BS40 8TF
Tel no: (01275) 333345
saltmalt.com

£30

The toasted teacakes and full English breakfasts still satisfy visitors who remember Salt & Malt as a lakeside tea room, but since being taken over by chef Josh Eggleton of the nearby Pony & Trap (see entry), seafood is the main hook. The nautical-themed décor and separate takeaway fish and chip shop add to the piscine vibe, as do dishes like grilled scallops, seaweed butter, leek and pancetta or baked fillet of hake, mustard and cockle sauce. Wines from £16.

Clevedon

LOCAL GEM
Murrays of Clevedon
Italian | £22
87-93 Hill Road, Clevedon, BS21 7PN
Tel no: (01275) 341555
murraysofclevedon.co.uk

£5 OFF £30

Going great guns since 1984, Murrays is set to expand into next door to create an enoteca-style wine bar. The current deli and caffè draws in the punters with its eye-catching displays of fresh fruit and veg, cheeses, cured meats and Italian wines, many of whom stick around for the excellent coffee, cakes, sandwiches and pizzas. There's more though, such as a starter of Cornish crab and fennel tart and main courses like ribollita or braised beef shin with wet polenta and salsa verde. Italian wines start at £14.50.

Combe Hay

The Wheatsheaf
Cooking score: 3
Modern British | £25
Combe Hay, BA2 7EG
Tel no: (01225) 833504
wheatsheafcombehay.com

£30

Locals and visitors who tire of Bath's Georgian splendours can take a trip out to this genteel whitewashed pub for a whiff of fresh Somerset air just 10 minutes' drive from the city – 'a hidden gem in a beautiful setting'. Squirrelled away in a verdant valley with terraced gardens and even a few beehives, its instantly appealing look is enhanced by interiors that blend original stone floors and log fires with distressed mirrors, rural photographs and high-backed wicker chairs. The kitchen adds a few modern flourishes to its 'consistently excellent' core repertoire, moving from cured local pheasant breast with pickled red cabbage and quince, via a risotto made with artichokes from the pub garden to loin of Wiltshire venison with celeriac dauphinoise and chestnut purée. After that, consider the array of British cheeses or go for something sweeter – perhaps dark chocolate fondant with marmalade ice cream or peach and cherry trifle dotted with toasted almonds. Wines start at £19.
Chef/s: Eddy Rains. **Open:** Tue to Sun L 12 to 2.30, Tue to Sat D 6.30 to 9. **Closed:** Mon, 25 and 26 Dec, 1 week Jan. **Meals:** main courses £17 to £25. Set L £16 (2 courses) to £20. Set D £18 (2 courses) to £23. Sun L £21. **Details:** 45 seats. 60 seats outside. V menu. Music. Parking.

▌Fivehead
The Langford

Cooking score: 6
Modern British | £38
Langford Fivehead, Lower Swell, Fivehead,
TA3 6PH
Tel no: (01460) 282020
langfordfivehead.co.uk

£5
OFF

'We're so lucky to have this restaurant in our village,' said one fortunate reader. Enclosed within ancient box and yew hedges, the Jacksons' 15th-century house on the edge of the Levels also boasts its own kitchen gardens and orchard extending over seven acres, giving strong indication that Olly Jackson is a chef with his roots in the local soil. It's a serene setting for what one visitor reckoned is cooking of 'imagination and flair, with flavours and textures superbly combined'. Fixed-price menus keep things concise at three choices per course, running to pan-seared scallop with home-smoked salmon, celeriac remoulade and watercress, or duck and pistachio terrine, to start, and then gurnard fillet with leeks, Jerusalems and cabbage, or breast and confit leg of duck with a prune croquette and curly kale. Nobody can feel neglected when there's chocolate délice and praline ice cream to finish, or a slate of West Country cheeses with walnut and sultana bread. The wine list pitches its camp in France and doesn't budge, starting at £22.
Chef/s: Olly Jackson. **Open:** Wed to Fri L 12.30 to 2, Tue to Sat D 7 to 11. **Closed:** Sun, Mon, 25 and 26 Dec, 2 weeks Jan, 1 week Jul and Aug. **Meals:** set L £28 (2 courses) to £33. Set D £38. **Details:** 20 seats. V menu. Music. Parking. Children over 8 yrs only.

Local Gem

Local Gems are the perfect neighbourhood venues, delivering good, freshly cooked food at great value for money.

▌Hinton St George
The Lord Poulett Arms

Cooking score: 2
Modern British | £29
High Street, Hinton St George, TA17 8SE
Tel no: (01460) 73149
lordpoulettarms.com

£30

An ever-so-English village ('one of the most beautiful in Somerset') creates just the right impression for visitors to this well-groomed 17th-century thatched inn. Garlanded beams, flagstones, bare boards and real fires reinforce the mood, and in keeping with the rustic-chic surrounds, the cooking is British, executed in a modern style, and tapping into a network of local producers. Among some cleverly honed ideas, say dressed wood pigeon and chicken terrine with salt-baked beets, black pudding crumb and cider gel, there are true Brit classics such as 'excellent fried fish and copious quantities of chips', beef burger in a brioche bun with Wookey Hole Cheddar cheese, and roast rump of grass-fed lamb with a lamb shoulder shepherd's pie. The West Country cheeses are hard to resist if you haven't been snared by the dark chocolate délice with burnt orange sorbet and praline crunch. Wines from £16.
Chef/s: Philip Verden. **Open:** all week L 12 to 2.30 (3 Sun), D 6.30 to 9.15. **Closed:** 25 and 26 Dec, 1 Jan. **Meals:** main courses £15 to £20. Set L and D £16 (2 courses) to £20. Sun L £23. **Details:** 60 seats. 40 seats outside. Bar. Music. Parking.

▌Lower Godney

LOCAL GEM
The Sheppey Inn

International | £27
Lower Godney, BA5 1RZ
Tel no: (01458) 831594
thesheppey.co.uk

£30

On the Levels, The Sheppey is a country pub that dances to its own tune – or that of the visiting musicians. There are no roses round this door; rather a pared-back interior, dotted with art and eccentric trinkets, and a terrace with lush, watery views. Food is excitedly international, featuring the house fish stew with rouille, monkfish burger in a squid-ink bun, and banana marshmallow wth gingerbread crumb and banana mousse. They make their own beer and cider, but wine is from £18.

Mells
Talbot Inn
Cooking score: 3
British | £27
Selwood Street, Mells, BA11 3PN
Tel no: (01373) 812254
talbotinn.com

The dashing stone-built late-Plantagenet inn has a high arch at the entrance for those of you arriving by carriage. Inside is a honeycomb of rooms and passageways, as well as eating options by the bushel. Outdoor tables, medieval-style feasting at long trestles for food grilled over open coals, and traditional pub dining are all encompassed, and Pravin Nayar is amply supplied by the Talbot kitchen garden. Pub classics like beer-battered fish and chips and Westcombe Cheddar ploughman's supplement the more upmarket offerings. A lamb and veal fritter in harissa yoghurt with capers and charred onions might fanfare main courses such as skrei cod with lemon and dill fregola and romanesco purée in crab bisque, or a local pork chop in anchovy and parsley butter with kale and mash. Tuck into West Country cheeses, or something like white chocolate cheesecake with quince sorbet and hazelnut granola, to round things off. The imaginatively compiled wine list opens at £17.50.
Chef/s: Pravin Nayar. **Open:** all week L 12 to 3, D 6 to 9.30. **Meals:** main courses £13 to £19. **Details:** 80 seats. 30 seats outside. Bar. Music. Parking.

Pensford
LOCAL GEM
The Pig
British | £32
Hunstrete House, Pensford, BS39 4NS
Tel no: (01761) 490490
thepighotel.com

'An amazing hotel with a good restaurant' sums up this outpost of the Pig country-house collection, located in the genteel Georgian surrounds of Hunstrete House. With its '25-mile menu' and starters 'literally picked this morning', it ticks all the eco boxes, fuelling its offer with trug-loads of produce from an ever-expanding kitchen garden. Expect spry seasonal flavours, from leek and Tamworth pancetta with poached egg and hollandaise to 'fall-apart' ox cheek with oak-smoked mash and flower sprouts. 'Wonderful' service and brilliantly eclectic wines from £17.50.

Shepton Mallet
LOCAL GEM
Blostin's
Anglo-French | £34
29-33 Waterloo Road, Shepton Mallet, BA4 5HH
Tel no: (01749) 343648
blostins.co.uk

'This small restaurant produces excellent and varied food,' noted one regular to this long-standing neighbourhood gem – it's been in the Reed family for over three decades. Nick Reed cooks in a gentle Anglo-French style: say goats' cheese, red onion and sun-dried tomato tart, fillet of hake with spinach and saffron sauce or fillet of beef baked in pastry with Madeira sauce, and iced ginger meringue parfait with cappuccino cream. The atmosphere is cosy and chatty, service is 'always excellent' and wines start at £16.50.

■ Taunton

Augustus

Cooking score: 5
Modern British | £30
3 The Courtyard, St James Street, Taunton,
TA1 1JR
Tel no: (01823) 324354
augustustaunton.co.uk

It's not clear exactly why this trim clean-lined bistro was named after gluttonous Augustus Gloop from *Charlie and The Chocolate Factory*, but there's no denying the venue's populist credentials, easy prices or damn fine cooking. Chef/co-proprietor Richard Guest made his name at the nearby Castle Hotel, and he brings oodles of experience to this latest venture – an appealing little spot in a tiny courtyard, complete with an all-weather terrace. The kitchen makes a virtue of modesty, turning out fine-tuned renditions of dishes that most people lock away as guilty pleasures – think raclette cheese bake with bacon jam or plates of ribeye steak piled high with pommes Anna, cauliflower cheese and crispy onions. However, if something niftier is required, Guest and his team can also muster up smart modern assemblages ranging from seared Brixham scallops with garlic and parsley purée to fillet of turbot with Jerusalem artichokes, fennel and button mushrooms. After that, choose some cheese 'from the block' or a self-styled lemon meringue pie 'of sorts'. Wines cover all eventualities, with equitable prices from £17.
Chef/s: Richard Guest. **Open:** Tue to Sat L 10 to 3, D 6 to 9.30. **Closed:** Sun, Mon, 2 weeks Christmas and New Year. **Meals:** main courses £11 to £22. **Details:** 28 seats. 16 seats outside.

Symbols

🛏 Accommodation is available
£30 Three courses for less than £30
£5 OFF £5-off voucher scheme
🍷 Notable wine list

Castle Bow Restaurant

Cooking score: 5
Modern British | £36
Castle Green, Taunton, TA1 1NF
Tel no: (01823) 328328
the-castle-hotel.com

🛏

The Chapman family's 65-year tenure at the Castle has been an important one, launching several chefs' careers and playing a part in revolutionising the way we eat now, by the simple expedient of tracking down first-rate ingredients and cooking them with skill and intelligence. Like many of his contemporaries, current chef Liam Finnegan doubtless takes such an approach for granted. For him seasonality is king and fresh flavours are evident at every turn, from Brixham crab with bisque, blood orange and sea herbs to just-cooked Lyme Bay turbot served with broccoli, pine nuts and split lemon jus or a well-reported dish of various treatments of Old Spot pork, served with apple, spring cabbage and watercress. For dessert, a lemon trifle with ginger and poppy seed makes a thoughtful endnote. Some feel that the Castle Bow's understated, square-shaped dining room makes rather a bland setting for what is some distinctly superior cooking, but there is praise for welcoming service and good wine advice (bottles from £20).
Chef/s: Liam Finnegan. **Open:** Wed to Sat D only 7 to 9.30. **Closed:** Sun, Mon, Tue, Jan. **Meals:** main courses £15 to £24. **Details:** 36 seats. Bar. Music. Parking.

The Willow Tree

Cooking score: 4
Modern British | £33
3 Tower Lane, Taunton, TA1 4AR
Tel no: (01823) 352835
thewillowtreerestaurant.com

'An always reliable restaurant,' is how one regular describes Darren Sherlock and Rita Rambellas's intimate venue – so much so that after some 15 years locals can't imagine life without it. Its well-heeled clientele are not short of choice for decent dining in Taunton, but the Willow Tree has won their loyalty – half the customers are regular enough to be known by name; those who are not are welcomed with equal politeness and ushered into the reassuringly unchanging, cottagey dining room. The menu is a seasonal affair featuring modern classics: salad of free-range poached egg with new-season English asparagus and a butter sauce (though the comfort factor of Montgomery's Cheddar soufflé with a celery, walnut and cream sauce is hard to ignore), followed by roast rump of lamb with oven-dried tomatoes, sautéed potatoes, aubergine, spring greens and smoked red pepper purée, with an excellent bread-and-butter pudding to finish. Wines from £19.95.

Chef/s: Darren Sherlock. **Open:** Tue, Wed, Fri and Sat D only 6.30 to 9. **Closed:** Sun, Mon, Thur, Jan, Aug. **Meals:** set D £28 (Tue and Wed), £33 (Fri and Sat). **Details:** 25 seats. 10 seats outside. Bar. Music.

Brazz
Modern British | £30
Castle Bow, Taunton, TA1 1NF
Tel no: (01823) 252000
brazz.co.uk

Behind the mellow old stone of the Castle Hotel is a light, modern bar-café-restaurant. It's fun, wonderfully relaxed and run with positive enthusiasm. The seasonally based cooking delivers the kind of easy-to-like brasserie dishes (ham hock terrine, pork chop with tarragon cream sauce) that are all the better for being plain speaking. Chicken supreme with Savoy cabbage, sprouts, bacon and mash, and beer-battered Brixham haddock with minted peas and tartare sauce have also found favour, as has a rhubarb and almond trifle. Wines from £19.

■ Waterrow
READERS RECOMMEND
The Rock Inn
Modern British
Waterrow, TA4 2AX
Tel no: (01984) 623293
rockinnwaterrow.co.uk
'Pub specials and an à la carte menu included the mouthwatering Arnold Bennett omelette and succulent, slow-cooked Angus beef. The pub was buzzing with happy diners in a friendly informal atmosphere – a great place to enjoy excellent food.'

■ Wedmore
The Swan
Cooking score: 2
Modern British | £27
Cheddar Road, Wedmore, BS28 4EQ
Tel no: (01934) 710337
theswanwedmore.com

Whatever the weather and whatever the season, there's always something to please locals and travellers alike at this revitalised village inn: the beer garden is at its best in summer, while the cosy but smartly attired interior is a draw when the wood-burner is blazing. Bare boards, quarry tiles, leather upholstery and acres of polished woodwork set the tone for a menu that takes its cues from the surrounding region. Steaks and burgers depend on supplies of Ruby Red beef, venison is turned into a slow-cooked ragoût (with spinach gnocchi, squash purée and salsa verde on the side), and Cornish fish dishes could range from gurnard ceviche with beetroot and rocket salad to pan-fried hake fillet with a Mediterranean combo of white beans, roasted cauliflower and cavolo nero. Meze-style platters are good for sharing, while creamy, calorific desserts might run to a Rocky Road sundae with toffee sauce. Wines from £17.

Chef/s: Rob Smart. **Open:** all week L 12 to 3, D 6 to 10. **Meals:** main courses £13 to £24. **Details:** 65 seats. 52 seats outside. Bar. Music. Parking.

■ Wells
Goodfellows
Cooking score: 4
Seafood | £36
5 Sadler Street, Wells, BA5 2RR
Tel no: (01749) 673866
goodfellowswells.co.uk
£5 OFF

Adam Fellows' well-established operation in the centre of Wells is 'open for breakfast or lunch as a café, as well as a venue for dinner – it seems to cope extremely well'. Although the décor is 'a little Spartan and quirky', it is clean and modern and makes a decent job out of getting the maximum from a pretty awkward space. Mr Fellows is known for fish, and a pair of winter diners found his five-course seafood tasting menu struck just the right note, with impressive quality of ingredients found in dishes such as 'quite delicious' tuna sashimi, served with cubes of umami-rich soy and ginger jelly and some creamy wasabi, hake with its skin 'cooked to a delicious crispness', and perfect seared scallops, which arrived with fondant potato, braised cabbage and carrot. This is cooking with no geographical boundaries: from spicy minced lamb with hummus and tortilla chips to a single-origin dark chocolate tart with cocoa nibs and mandarin sorbet, Fellows navigates the globe with confidence. A keenly priced European wine list opens at £18.
Chef/s: Adam Fellows. **Open:** Tue to Sat L 12 to 3.30, Wed to Sat D 6 to 9.30 (10 Fri and Sat). **Closed:** Sun, Mon, 25 to 27 Dec. **Meals:** main courses £12 to £24. Set L £21 (2 courses) to £25. Tasting menu £48. **Details:** 50 seats. 10 seats outside. Music.

■ Wrington
The Ethicurean
Cooking score: 3
British | £33
Barley Wood Walled Garden, Long Lane, Wrington, BS40 5SA
Tel no: (01934) 863713
theethicurean.com

Please leave any cynicism at home and bury any scepticism in a box in your back garden, for it is time to embrace the idealism and enthusiasm of Iain and Matthew Pennington. And anyway, it's pretty much impossible to resist. In a charmingly rustic and extended Victorian glasshouse, in an equally delightful restored walled garden, the brothers make full use of the garden alongside stuff foraged from hereabouts, or sourced from the region's top producers and growers, to produce 'deeply flavourful and sophisticated food'. Seasonality and sustainability is a given. Kick off with rabbit rillettes with anise-flavoured labneh and apple and cucumber pickle, before pork belly, which has cooked for 12 hours and is served with 'fermented and fresh slaw', or a veggie number such as charred and pickled red peppers with aubergine purée, haricot beans and courgette flower. 'The Full Feast' gives you five thrilling courses. They even make their own cider and vermouth. Wines start at £22.
Chef/s: Iain and Matthew Pennington. **Open:** Tues to Sun L 12 to 2 (2.30 Sat, 3.30 Sun), Tue to Sat D 7 to 9 (6.30 Fri and Sat). **Closed:** Mon, 24 to 26 Dec, 31 Dec to 2 Jan. **Meals:** main courses £16 to £22. 'The Full Feast' (Wed to Sat D) £41. **Details:** 60 seats. 40 seats outside. V menu. Wheelchairs. Music. Parking.

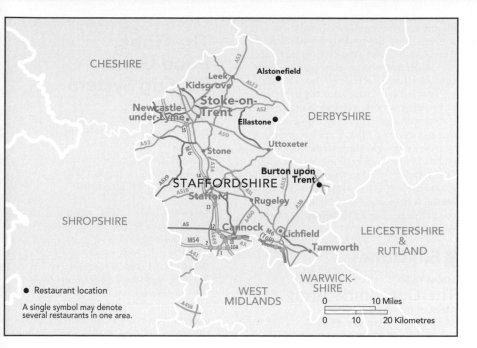

Restaurant location

A single symbol may denote
several restaurants in one area.

■ Alstonefield
The George
Cooking score: 2
Modern British | £35
Alstonefield, DE6 2FX
Tel no: (01335) 310205
thegeorgeatalstonefield.com

Behind the stone walls of this Peakland village
inn, locals, hikers and visiting diners can be
found happily ensconced. Standards are high
– 'from the very tasteful and warm décor, the
log fires, the dog- and people-friendly
atmosphere' – and the food is definitely the
highlight of any visit. The kitchen delivers
simple, robustly flavoured dishes that rely on
quality ingredients, including seasonal
vegetables grown in the pub's own garden.
Start with a splendid full English (roasted
breast of local estate game bird with fried
quail's egg and eggy bread) or twice-baked
organic Cheddar and thyme soufflé, followed
by red-wine-braised ox cheek with
horseradish mashed potato and bone marrow

or a pink breast of duck with a confit leg
croquette and fondant potato. There are some
pubby-sounding dishes, too, perhaps venison
sausage toad-in-the-hole, and lunch brings
fish and chips and Gloucester Old Spot
sausages. Wines from £18.
Chef/s: Scott Brown and Kelvin Guest. **Open:** all
week L 12 to 2.30, D 6.30 to 9 (8 Sun). **Closed:** 25
Dec. **Meals:** main courses £12 to £28. **Details:** 42
seats. 40 seats outside. Bar. Parking.

■ Burton upon Trent
99 Station Street
Cooking score: 1
Modern British | £26
99 Station Street, Burton upon Trent,
DE14 1BT
Tel no: (01283) 516859
99stationstreet.com
£30

Daniel Pilkington's pint-sized venue close to
the heart of the Burton brewing industry is a
sustained homage to locavore principles –

buying regionally produced, and therefore seasonal, food and cooking it with respect. There is more than a touch of pizazz to dishes such as smoked trout mousse packaged in smoked salmon, served with beetroot aïoli and pickled angel hair, followed by roast loin of Packington pork rolled in aromatic spices, served with sautéed kale, a crisp-fried quail's egg and an onion bhaji. To finish, get stuck into sticky orange cake with caramel ice cream and malted milkshake. Wines start at £13.95.
Chef/s: Daniel Pilkington. **Open:** Thur to Sun L 12 to 2, Wed to Sat D 6.30 to 9. **Closed:** Mon, Tue. **Meals:** main courses £13 to £22. Set L £14 (2 courses) to £15. Sun L £18. **Details:** 42 seats. Wheelchairs. Music.

▌Ellastone

LOCAL GEM
The Duncombe Arms
Modern British | £29
Main Road, Ellastone, DE6 2GZ
Tel no: (01335) 324275
duncombearms.co.uk

£5 OFF £30

'The food has never let us down – it's innovative without losing reference to traditional and local dishes,' runs one appraisal of this reinvigorated country pub. A gorgeous old building that's evolved with time, it offers plenty of real fires, exposed brickwork and original flooring alongside hearty food, including 'the never disappointing Duncombe burger' or Jerusalem artichoke risotto with roast salsify and hen-of-the-woods mushrooms. Toffee apple bread-and-butter pudding with vanilla ice cream gets a big thumbs-up. Wines from £17.50.

The Good Food Guide Scoring System

Score 1: Capable cooking with simple food combinations and clear flavours.

Score 2: Decent cooking, displaying good technical skills and interesting combinations and flavours.

Score 3: Good cooking, showing sound technical skills and using quality ingredients.

Score 4: Dedicated, focused approach to cooking; good classical skills and high-quality ingredients.

Score 5: Exact cooking techniques and a degree of ambition; showing balance and depth of flavour in dishes.

Score 6: Exemplary cooking skills, innovative ideas, impeccable ingredients and an element of excitement.

Score 7: High level of ambition and individuality, attention to the smallest detail, accurate and vibrant dishes.

Score 8: A kitchen cooking close to or at the top of its game. Highly individual with impressive artistry.

Score 9: Cooking that has reached a pinnacle of achievement, making it a hugely memorable experience.

Score 10: Just perfect dishes, showing faultless technique at every service; extremely rare and the highest accolade the Guide can give.

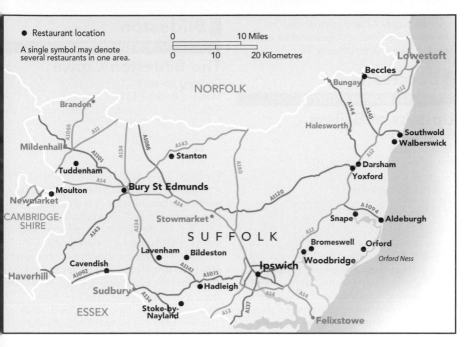

Map legend:
● Restaurant location
A single symbol may denote several restaurants in one area.

0 — 10 Miles
0 — 10 — 20 Kilometres

NORFOLK

Lowestoft
Beccles
Bungay
Brandon
Halesworth
Southwold
Walberswick
Mildenhall
Stanton
Darsham
Yoxford
Tuddenham
Moulton
Newmarket
Bury St Edmunds
CAMBRIDGE-SHIRE
Stowmarket
Snape
Aldeburgh
SUFFOLK
Bromeswell
Orford
Lavenham
Bildeston
Orford Ness
Cavendish
Woodbridge
Haverhill
Ipswich
Sudbury
Hadleigh
ESSEX
Stoke-by-Nayland
Felixstowe

◼ Aldeburgh

Regatta

Cooking score: 1
Modern British | £28
171-173 High Street, Aldeburgh, IP15 5AN
Tel no: (01728) 452011
regattaaldeburgh.com

£30

The cheery seafaring décor within alludes to the penchant for seafood among the kitchen team here at this long-running local favourite. Chef-proprietor Robert Mabey offers up meat options, too, such as crispy Gressingham duck leg with sweet garlic and carrot purée, but with the sea a stroll away and their own smoke-house on-site, it's the seafood that catches the eye. Oak-smoked salmon arrives with Thai cucumber salad, Mediterranean-style trimmings augment the fish soup, baked fillet of halibut is served with crayfish and basil sauce, and, to finish, toasted almonds and Amaretto flavour a pannacotta. Wines start at £17.

Chef/s: Robert Mabey and Sam Tecklenberg.
Open: all week L 12 to 2, D 6 to 10. **Closed:** 24 to 26 and 30 to 31 Dec, 1 Jan. **Meals:** main courses £12 to £22. Set L and early D £15 (2 courses) to £18.
Details: 90 seats.

LOCAL GEM

The Aldeburgh Market

Seafood | £20
170-172 High Street, Aldeburgh, IP15 5AQ
Tel no: (01728) 452520
thealdeburghmarket.co.uk

£5 OFF £30

'Lovely spot for a quick bite; well run; deli particularly good.' So ran the notes of one visitor who thought this combination fishmonger-deli-café could not be more appealing. Locals and in-the-know visitors squeeze into 'the slightly cramped room' for very fresh fish dishes, some with an Asian/oriental spin – so expect to find potted shrimps, fish soup and crab salad, as well as Singapore noodles with king prawns or South

Indian fish curry. There's praise, too, for excellent breakfasts, very good coffee and delicious cakes. Wines from £16.

Beccles

★ NEW ENTRY ★

Upstairs at Baileys

Cooking score: 2
Spanish | £35
2 Hungate, Beccles, NR34 9TL
Tel no: (01502) 710609
upstairsatbaileys.co.uk
£5 OFF

This spot in the charming heart of Beccles is a foodie treasure trove, a fragrant delicatessen topped with a restaurant that transports you to Spain at its gastronomic best. Go Friday or Saturday evening for the full 'exquisitely crafted' dining experience – think salmorejo, a cold tomato soup made glamorous by the addition of lobster, Ibérico ham and sweet melon, suquet de rap (a Catalan stew of monkfish, prawns, mussels and potatoes with garlicky rouille), or salted cod with San Marzano tomatoes, pistachio pesto and anchovies. Flavours punch above their weight on the steal of a set lunch menu too. Slivers of jewel-coloured beetroot with shiny stems of sprouting broccoli and delicate Cromer crab are a delicious prelude to richly-flavoured pulled pork wrapped in homemade black pudding. Shards of meringue, the freshest of berries and lightest of whipped cream make a perfect Eton mess. Portions can be on the small side for some, but the friendly service gets a resounding thumbs up. Wine from £12.90.
Chef/s: Mauro R. Prat. **Open:** Tue to Sat L 12 to 3, Fri and Sat D 7 to 10. **Closed:** Sun, Mon. **Meals:** main courses £16 to £20. Set L £15 (3 courses). **Details:** 38 seats. Music.

Bildeston

★ NEW ENTRY ★

The Bildeston Crown

Cooking score: 4
Modern British | £38
High Street, Bildeston, IP7 7EB
Tel no: (01449) 740510
thebildestoncrown.com
£5 OFF

Firing on all cylinders following Chris Lee's return to the stove, the Bildeston Crown is worth a culinary detour. The slimmed-down menu promises and delivers in equal measure, whether you choose salt cod nuggets and chips from the Classic menu, or decide on sophisticated Select dishes. Serious bar snacks (tandoori soft-shell crab with mango salsa, or giblet pie) are memorable appetisers, but save space to immerse yourself in Lee's expert understanding of ingredients that result in 'flawless' food that is 'surprising time after time', and above all very tasty. A magnificent Red Poll burger becomes a dish fit for royalty with the addition of foie gras, while Caesar salad is transformed by lobster, the sweetness of the shellfish balanced by a salty anchovy-bacon punch. A cannon of Nedging lamb is tender, rested and pink, the flavour enhanced by judicious slivers of radish and plump blackberries. Pastry chef Nick Henn brings an exquisite touch to an utterly delicious chocolate marquise, and palate-cleansingly flavourful lemon tart and sorbet. House wine is a steal at £17.50.
Chef/s: Chris Lee. **Open:** all week L 12 to 2.30, D 7 to 9.30 (9 Sun). **Meals:** main courses £16 to £21. Set L £15 (2 courses) to £20. **Details:** 80 seats. 30 seats outside. Bar. Wheelchairs. Music. Parking.

▋Brandeston

READERS RECOMMEND
The Queen
Modern British
The Street, Brandeston, IP13 7AD
Tel no: (01728) 685307
thequeenatbrandeston.co.uk
'The minimalist descriptions in its seasonal menus result in surprise when the dishes appear. Homemade bread, superb, well-cooked starters and mains are followed by attractive and delicious desserts. All of this and it's on my doorstep.'

▋Bromeswell
The Unruly Pig
Cooking score: 3
Modern British | £28
Orford Road, Bromeswell, IP12 2PU
Tel no: (01394) 460310
theunrulypig.co.uk
£5 OFF £30

Back on its trotters after a devastating fire just weeks after opening, the Unruly Pig is once again pulling in the foodie crowds of east Suffolk and beyond. Dave Wall brings restrained but assured flourishes to a glammed-up pub menu that nods to the earthy tastes of Italy. Deeply flavourful brisket and bone marrow on toast ('exceptional') is a hefty starter; salmon rillettes, the sweetness of the fish punctuated by vinegary caperberries, a lighter option. Inka-grilled ribeye steak, chicken breast with homemade wild mushroom agnolotti, or a magnificent brioche-bunned burger, make sound main courses, while vegetarians could choose leek and chanterelle risotto with poached egg from a dedicated menu. Enjoy the owner's art collection, some pieces as provocative as the pub's pig-head symbol, before tucking into an exquisite salted-caramel tart with Jersey milk purée or comforting rice pudding with blood orange. There's wine from a wallet-friendly £14.95 but a collection of 'dream' bottles can transport you to the stars.

Dave Wall
The Unruly Pig, Bromeswell

What food could you not live without?
Eggs. I have at least four for brekkie everyday and love them cooked in every way possible. On top of that they're a huge unsung hero in the kitchen, used in so many sauces, dressings and pastry recipes. Without them the restaurant repertoire would be slashed.

What's your favourite dish on your menu?
I love our 'braised rabbit ravioli with pancetta and porcini velouté'. It embodies everything I love in a dish – perfectly cooked elements brought together and presented simply with the main emphasis on flavour.

What is the most unusual preparation technique you use?
I have a unique technique for making liver parfait, but I couldn't possibly reveal the method!

At the end of a long day, what do you like to cook?
To be honest, at the end of a long, hard day the first thing I'll pull out of the fridge is a cold one! But if I am in the mood for eating, it's usually because I'm shattered, so a good gorge on carbs is always nice; leftover dauphinoise is deeply satisfying!

Chef/s: Dave Wall. **Open:** Mon to Sat L 12 to 3, D 6 to 9 (9.30 Fri, 5 to 9.30 Sat). Sun 12 to 8. **Meals:** main courses £14 to £24. Set L and D £15 (2 courses) to £18. Sun L £20. **Details:** 90 seats. 50 seats outside. V menu. Bar. Wheelchairs. Music. Parking.

▌Bury St Edmunds
Maison Bleue
Cooking score: 4
Modern French | £49
30-31 Churchgate Street, Bury St Edmunds, IP33 1RG
Tel no: (01284) 760623
maisonbleue.co.uk

This confident French restaurant wears its fine-dining credentials lightly. Cloths are white and crockery immaculate, but diners recognise the friendliness of the 'excellent, attentive staff', and agree that the kitchen has 'upped its game' since being taken over by Karine and Pascal Canevet. A hand-dived king scallop with scallop pannacotta and peppery mooli is deemed 'divine' by one diner, similar praise being poured on a plump langoustine tail and crab tortellini, the sweetness of the shellfish accurately balanced by a fennel and orange ice. Continue the fish theme if you will (the reputation of Maison Bleue is built on seafood), but a classic Aberdeen Angus beef fillet with celeriac and caramelised onion (or morels and leeks in spring) makes a superb main, as does pinkly perfect lamb rump with a whizz of carrot-cumin velouté and gently-pokey little turnips. The cheeseboard is 'to die for'; so too are puddings like crème fraîche tartlet, the pastry a masterclass in crisp butteriness, topped with a disc of rhubarb gel and all-zinging grapefruit sorbet. The wine list celebrates France, offering bottles from £17.95. **Chef/s:** Pascal Canevet. **Open:** Tue to Sat L 12 to 2, D 7 to 9 (9.30 Sat). **Closed:** Sun, Mon, 3 weeks Jan, 2 weeks summer. **Meals:** main courses £20 to £30. Set L £20 (2 courses) to £25. Set D £37 (3 courses). **Details:** 60 seats. Music.

1921 Angel Hill
Cooking score: 4
Modern British | £32
19-21 Angel Hill, Bury St Edmunds, IP33 1UZ
Tel no: (01284) 704870
nineteen-twentyone.co.uk

Don't underestimate this tasteful restaurant on its quiet town-centre street. Fans say it's more than just a good local; it's a destination restaurant in its own right. Menus garner praise for their enticing range and strong seasonal outlook, and there's applause, too, for Zack Deakins' good-value cooking. Flavours sing out loud in fashionable assemblies of crab with wasabi-pickled mooli, tempura squid and avocado or scallop with oxtail spring roll, beetroot and quince, and the roll call of dishes recommended by readers includes carpaccio of local venison, confit duck leg and liver terrine with plum jam, pickled walnuts and Maderia jelly, and locally shot hare (rack, loin and leg) with truffle dumplings, red wine salsify and parsley root. Lemon curd parfait with pistachio cake and Vietnamese yoghurt or dark chocolate fondant with caramelised banana and passion fruit jelly make a good finish. The set lunch is a bargain and the wine list starts at £19. **Chef/s:** Zack Deakins. **Open:** Mon to Sat L 12 to 2.15 (2.30 Sat), D 6 to 9.15 (9.30 Fri and Sat). **Closed:** Sun, 23 to 30 Dec. **Meals:** main courses £16 to £22. Set L £15 (2 courses) to £18. **Details:** 50 seats. Bar. Wheelchairs. Music.

Pea Porridge
Cooking score: 4
Modern British | £30
28-29 Cannon Street, Bury St Edmunds, IP33 1JR
Tel no: (01284) 700200
peaporridge.co.uk
🍾

For some of the most authentic food in these parts – and a 'truly professional' front-of-house – push open the door of this former bakery. This is a place where unloved cuts of meat and offal find their robust champion in chef-owner Justin Sharp: sautéed snails with bone marrow are elevated into a thing of true deliciousness by parsley, capers and garlic butter; curried duck hearts or sweetbreads are tenderly tasty; and slow-braised shoulder of mutton is a generously flavoured sharing dish. Justin's understanding of Middle Eastern and Spanish flavours shows in his take on the Turkish classic, imam bayaldi, and a cod fillet with crushed Jerusalem artichokes, pepper-bold chorizo, monk's beard and romesco. It's worth saving space for a 'heavenly' tarte Tatin or rice pudding cooked creamily long and slow in a charcoal-burning Bertha oven. A passion for natural and organic wines permeates a fascinating wine list – qvevri-fermented Tsolikauri from Georgian producer Pheasant's Tears, anyone? Conventional bottles from £17.95.

Chef/s: Justin Sharp. **Open:** Thur to Sat L 12 to 2, Tue to Sat D 6.30 to 9.30. **Closed:** Sun, Mon, 2 weeks Christmas, 2 weeks summer. **Meals:** main courses £13 to £22. Set L and D £15 (2 courses) to £19. **Details:** 46 seats. Wheelchairs. Music. Babies at L only.

LOCAL GEM
Ben's
Modern British | £30
43-45 Churchgate Street, Bury St Edmunds, IP33 1RG
Tel no: (01284) 762119
bensrestaurant.co.uk

Couple 'welcoming and obliging' staff with a menu that roots for local producers and a young owner who rears much of the pork and lamb on the menu, and 'what more could you wish for' from this popular neighbourhood restaurant? Cajun-spiced pigeon breast might precede a plate of Ben's bangers, made by a local butcher, or pulled pork suet pudding with Aspall cyder glaze. Desserts get mixed reports, but you could do worse than a rhubarb, ginger and pear crumble. As one visitor noted, it 'adds a welcome mid-market offer to the town.' Wines from £18.

■ Cavendish
The George
Cooking score: 1
British | £28
The Green, Cavendish, CO10 8BA
Tel no: (01787) 280248
thecavendishgeorge.co.uk
£5 OFF 🍴 £30

The George is a restaurant-with-rooms rather than a traditional boozer, but it's still 'a lively place', and they have a couple of handpumps serving up local ales. Situated overlooking the green of a village seemingly preserved in aspic, the 16th-century bones of the building add character inside and out. The kitchen aims to please with moules marinière, the house cheeseburger and ribeye steak with triple-cooked chips, but ventures into more ambitious territory with black bream with roasted fennel, salmon mousse and shellfish velouté, and a whizzo dessert of Yorkshire rhubarb with a hint of liquorice. Wines start at £16.85.

Chef/s: Lewis Bennet. **Open:** all week L 12 to 2 (3 Sun), Mon to Sat D 6 to 9.30. **Closed:** 24 to 26 and 31 Dec, 1 Jan. **Meals:** main courses £11 to £23. Set L and D £13 (2 courses) to £15. **Details:** 48 seats. 40 seats outside. Bar. Music.

■ Darsham
LOCAL GEM
Darsham Nurseries
Global | £18
Main Road (A12), Darsham, IP17 3PW
Tel no: (01728) 667022
darshamnurseries.co.uk
£30

Plot-to-plate is quite the thing – and in the hands of the Darsham Nurseries team, it becomes a very delicious thing indeed. Middle Eastern flavours lead the way, many of the small plates centring on ingredients from the potager outside. Try wilted radicchio, goats' curd and pistachio, or nuttily roasted cauliflower with herb yoghurt and pine nuts. Nuggets of syrupy pork belly are tastily partnered with spicy rhubarb, while a feta and honey cheesecake rounds things off sweetly. Wines from the short list start at £21.50.

▌Hadleigh
The Hadleigh Ram
Cooking score: 2
Modern British | £32
5 Market Place, Hadleigh, IP7 5DL
Tel no: (01473) 822880
thehadleighram.co.uk

The old inn – the oldest in the village they say – has an opened-up interior where a colour scheme straight off the contemporary palette combines with exposed beams and some pretty fabrics and wallpapers to create a series of engaging spaces. The extensive repertoire covers brunch (perhaps croque monsieur), a good-value daily set menu, classic Sunday lunches, and an imaginative carte available lunch and dinner. Start with braised collar of Suffolk pork partnered with Stornoway black pudding and the more unexpected almond sponge and hit of rhubarb and ginger; follow on with loin of Scottish monkfish and poached octopus with squid-ink linguine, 21-day aged steaks with classic sauces or haddock in an IPA beer batter. Creative combinations abound at dessert stage, where chocolate is matched with avocado in a marquise with avocado sorbet, chilli syrup and white chocolate sauce. Wines start at £18.

Chef/s: Oliver Macmillan. **Open:** all week L 12 to 2.30 (4 Sun), Mon to Sat D 6 to 9 (10 Fri and Sat). **Meals:** main courses £15 to £20. Set L and D £16 (2 courses) to £20. **Details:** 40 seats. 20 seats outside. V menu. Wheelchairs. Music.

▌Hasketon
READERS RECOMMEND
The Turks Head
International
Low Road, Hasketon, IP13 6JG
Tel no: (01394) 610343
theturksheadhasketon.co.uk
'Amazing food, friendly staff and very family-friendly. Not to mention amazing surroundings. The roast beef is utterly mouthwatering and is a pure joy to eat. We are lucky to have this new hidden gem.'

▌Ipswich
LOCAL GEM
The Brewery Tap
Modern British | £26
Cliff Road, Ipswich, IP3 0AT
Tel no: (01473) 225501
thebrewerytap.org
£30

Bear with the rumble of lorries heading for Ipswich Docks, because this unpromising quayside road takes you to a rather special urban idyll. This proper pub has been spared the Farrow & Ball brush, the focus being on the food (and beer) it serves to a mix of dock workers and those in the know. Here, meat is cured and pasta is homemade. Who says devilled Sutton Hoo chicken hearts, slow-cooked Dingley Dell pork belly, a sturdy game pie or silky mango crème brûlée should be the preserve of conventionally pretty hostelries? Wines from £15.50.

Lavenham
The Great House
Cooking score: 5
Modern French | £48
Market Place, Lavenham, CO10 9QZ
Tel no: (01787) 247431
greathouse.co.uk

Perhaps the comment of one guest who felt 'spoilt with food and kindness' best captures the generous spirit of this elegant restaurant, a place *bien dans sa peau* that in 30 years appears rarely to have put a foot wrong. 'Outstanding' baked Manx queen scallops make a fine starter, but you could choose foie gras with pear and the butteriest, pillowiest brioche. A tender piece of Blythburgh pork fillet gets a poke with hints of wasabi and mustard, while things stay ultra-classic for turbot with soft veal sweetbread, cauliflower mousseline, fragrant with truffle oil, and earthy porcini oil emulsion. If lemon tart is off the menu, choose a coffee and praline mille-feuille with caramelised hazelnuts for a masterclass in balancing taste and texture, or indulge in the extraordinary array of cheeses, mainly French. 'Precise, formal, but not at all intimidating' service is the norm. The heart of the strong wine list (bottles from £17.95) beats for France.

Chef/s: Régis Crépy. **Open:** Wed to Sun L 12 to 2.30, Tue to Sat D 7 to 9 (9.30 Fri and Sat). **Closed:** Mon, Jan, 2 weeks summer. **Meals:** main courses £22 to £30. Set L £20 (2 courses) to £25. Set D £32 (2 courses) to £37. Sun L £37. **Details:** 50 seats. 20 seats outside. Music.

Symbols

- Accommodation is available
- £30 Three courses for less than £30
- £5 OFF £5-off voucher scheme
- Notable wine list

Moulton
The Packhorse Inn
Cooking score: 3
Modern British | £34
Bridge Street, Moulton, CB8 8SP
Tel no: (01638) 751818
thepackhorseinn.com

'A truly excellent meal, one to remember' enthused one diner after a visit to this pub-restaurant. It pulls in a lively mix of horse-racing types (it's a clip-clop from Newmarket) and weekenders appreciative of Phil Skinner's magic touch at the stove. Portions are generous, flavours equally so: start with an 'exceptional' salmon and hen's egg fishcake, or truffly goats' cheese with pretty curls of beetroot and scoops of pear. Enjoy a handsome Red Poll burger or exemplary ribeye from the Packhorse Favourites list (both come with all the bits you'd expect) but find more refinement in a prettily plated, well-seasoned fillet of trout with vivid-green broccoli and sweetly braised onions. A 'unique and imaginative' banana pudding triggers applause from one diner, another swooning over a rich white chocolate crémeux with rhubarb sorbet, nuggets of honeycomb and a scattering of delicate violas. A £17.50 Chilean Sauvignon Blanc opens the wine list.

Chef/s: Phil Skinner. **Open:** all week L 12 to 2.30, D 7 to 9.30 (9 Sun). **Meals:** main courses £14 to £22. Set L £18 (2 courses) to £24. **Details:** 85 seats. 20 seats outside. Bar. Wheelchairs. Music. Parking.

Orford
The Crown & Castle
Cooking score: 3
British/Italian | £36
Market Hill, Orford, IP12 2LJ
Tel no: (01394) 450205
crownandcastle.co.uk

It may have been licked with paint, dressed in classy checks and splashed with funky, vibrant colour in the soft furnishings, but the familiar comfort and welcome at this favourite Orford inn remains intact. This is a place for no-nonsense, well-cooked British food – think sausages with onion gravy, fish and chips, or veal kidneys cooked pinkly, tenderly, and seasoned to perfection. A nod to Italy tempts with risotto, gnocchi with porcini mushrooms or a platter of 'cicchetti' that might include air-cured coppa, pecorino and sweet-pickled chillies. Plates, whatever their inspiration, are simple, but satisfyingly tasty, the whole served with a relaxed friendliness. Finish with a vanilla-flecked pannacotta – mercifully not sickly-sweet – that wobbles just so and sits happily alongside sweet-tart baked rhubarb. The opening salvo on the well-annotated wine list comes in at £20, and there is something for every taste by the glass.

Chef/s: Charlene Gavazzi and Ruth Watson. **Open:** all week L 12.15 to 2, D 6.30 to 9. **Meals:** main courses £18 to £27. **Details:** 50 seats. 40 seats outside. V menu. Bar. Wheelchairs. Children over 8 yrs only at D.

▌Snape
The Plough & Sail
Cooking score: 1
Modern British | £25
Snape, IP17 1SR
Tel no: (01728) 688413
theploughandsailsnape.com

£30

This spacious and 'very well-run' pub draws visitors aplenty, attracted by its lively, welcoming atmosphere – the owners know what they're doing and manage to cope with big numbers admirably well. Start perhaps with asparagus spears with just the right buttery bite, or homemade potted shrimps and sourdough melba toast. 'Magnificent' sea bass on squid-ink risotto could follow, or a steaming bowl of Thai noodle broth, packed with pokey, colourful flavour and topped with soft, just-cooked sea bream. A generous ribeye steak or chicken Kiev with celeriac rémoulade will please meatlovers. Pear frangipane tart and stem ginger ice cream finishes a meal nicely. Wines from £15.50.

Chef/s: Oliver Burnside. **Open:** all week L 12 to 2.30 (3 Sun), D 6 to 9. **Meals:** main courses £11 to £21. Set L and D £15 (2 courses) to £19. **Details:** 120 seats. 50 seats outside. Bar. Wheelchairs. Music. Parking.

▌Southwold
Sutherland House
Cooking score: 2
Modern British | £33
56 High Street, Southwold, IP18 6DN
Tel no: (01502) 724544
sutherlandhouse.co.uk

Southwold's high street – at times peacefully genteel, at others lively with holidaymakers – is not short of places to snack on fine pastries or linger over a pint of the local brew. But if you fancy a taste of Suffolk's finest coastal produce, prepared and presented with flair and served with genuine friendliness, you could do worse than choose this spot. Fish dominates with the likes of crispy whitebait, or tempura squid with saffron and chilli mayonnaise a good start to a meal that might proceed with a piece of halibut, its firm, meaty flesh kept juicy with flavour-packed bouillabaisse, or a tangle of linguine with a garlicky, lemony clatter of shellfish. Prefer meat? Homemade black pudding is a perfect foil to succulent slow-braised Blythburgh pork belly. The bread and butter pudding with marmalade ice cream is well-known in these parts, but you could happily finish with a rich chocolate ganache with blackberry compote and sorbet. Wines from £17.

Chef/s: Carl Slaymaker. **Open:** Tue to Sun L 12 to 2, D 6 to 9. **Closed:** Mon, 2 weeks Jan. **Meals:** main courses £12 to £24. **Details:** 40 seats. 40 seats outside. Bar. Wheelchairs. Music.

LOCAL GEM

Solebay Fish Co.

Seafood | £20

Shed 22e, Blackshore, Southwold, IP18 6ND

Tel no: (01502) 724241

solebayfishco.co.uk

£30

A black-weatherboard quayside shack, slate menus promising the freshest of fish landed from the boat a few steps away – really, what's not to like about this friendly smokehouse-fishmonger-restaurant? This place delivers in bucket-and-spadefuls, piling sharing platters high with crab, lobster, smoked fish, cockles, mussels and prawns. Mix and match to your own taste from what's available or indulge in a char-grilled whole lobster or pan-fried sea bass with the chunkiest chips. £16 buys you a bottle of wine from a short list.

■ Stanton

The Leaping Hare

Cooking score: 3

Modern British | £32

Wyken Hall, Stanton, IP31 2DW

Tel no: (01359) 250287

wykenvineyards.co.uk

£5 OFF

The first vines on the Wyken Estate were planted in 1988, on the site of a former Roman vineyard, so it's wholly appropriate that it is Wyken Bacchus winning awards in the 21st century. Wander through the vineyard and gardens, shop in the Country Store and settle into the restaurant in a lofty 400-year-old barn for some arresting tucker. It's a charming spot – very civilised, too – with a menu that makes excellent use of the farm estate and wider regional ingredients. Begin with Walsham pigeon breasts, which have been smoked over vine prunings, and arrive with celeriac rémoulade and walnuts, before moving on to roast Wyken lamb rack with boulangère potatoes and wild garlic soubise, or roast cod with winter vegetable chowder. Finish with a fashionable number such as

buttermilk pannacotta with poached rhubarb, honeycomb and pistachios. The estate's wines feature on the short list, with a Spanish red opening proceedings at £21.

Chef/s: Simon Woodrow. **Open:** all week L 12 to 2.30, Fri and Sat D 7 to 9. **Closed:** 25 Dec to 6 Jan. **Meals:** main courses £15 to £22. Set L £19 (2 courses) to £22. Set D £28 (Fri). **Details:** 40 seats. 20 seats outside. Bar. Wheelchairs. Parking.

■ Stoke by Nayland

The Angel Inn

Cooking score: 2

Modern British | £28

Polstead Street, Stoke by Nayland, CO6 4SA

Tel no: (01206) 263245

angelinnsuffolk.co.uk

£30

In deepest Constable country, this gloriously picturesque village actually features in the great man's work. The 16th-century Angel shows off its historic charms to good effect in its old beams, ancient bricks and roaring log fires. Part of a small local group with three addresses to its name, it is very much a dining destination thanks to chef Mark Allen's appealing, gently modern cooking. Admire the venerable beams in the double-height room open to the eaves and tuck into a playful first-course take on ham, egg and chips (ham hock terrine, crispy fried poached egg and sweet potato fries, plus a nifty piccalilli gel). Move on to Suffolk pork three ways, classic fish and chips, a burger or steak cooked on the BBQ grill or pan-fried hake with clam emulsion and girolles. Among desserts, lemon meringue Knickerbocker glory and Black Forest cheesecake are inventive mash-ups. Wines start at £18.

Chef/s: Mark Allen. **Open:** all week L 12 to 2.30, D 6 to 9.30. **Meals:** main courses £12 to £27. Set L £15 (2 courses) to £18. Sun L £22. **Details:** 85 seats. Bar. Music. Parking.

▌Tuddenham
Tuddenham Mill
Cooking score: 5
Modern British | £39
High Street, Tuddenham, IP28 6SQ
Tel no: (01638) 713552
tuddenhammill.co.uk
£5 OFF ⨾

With the millpond outside and the original waterwheel on show in the dining room, Tuddenham Mill is an instantly captivating, oh-so-pretty prospect – although much of the 18th-century building now goes about its business as a thoroughly modern boutique hotel. Contemporary touches such as bare black tables and downlights set the scene for Lee Bye's increasingly assured cooking, which shows his liking for zesty flavours, intricacy and the trappings of reinvented British cuisine – witness a plate of chicken liver parfait and pig's head croquette with beer-pickled onions, artichoke and punchy mushroom ketchup. Native ingredients of impeccable pedigree also wax strongly here, from rump and shoulder of Norfolk Horn lamb with Pink Fir Apple potato, white broccoli, almonds and honey porter to North Sea hake with Debenham cider, mussels, brown shrimps, chervil spätzle and lettuce. To finish, the croissant pudding is a favourite pick – perhaps embellished with salted toffee, Earl Grey ice cream and blackberries. Set lunches offer brilliant value and the broad selection of wines by the glass is much appreciated; bottles start at £18.95.
Chef/s: Lee Bye. **Open:** all week L 12 to 2.15, D 6.30 to 9.15. **Meals:** main courses £18 to £27. Set L £16 (2 courses) to £20. Set D £20. Sun L £20 (2 courses) to £25. **Details:** 50 seats. 40 seats outside. V menu. Bar. Music. Parking.

▌Walberswick
The Anchor
Cooking score: 3
Modern British | £30
The Street, Walberswick, IP18 6UA
Tel no: (01502) 722112
anchoratwalberswick.com
⨾

Southwold was nicknamed 'Hampstead-on-Sea' back in the day, and across the river in Walberswick, when the out-of-town weekenders and holiday crowds throng the vast lawned spaces outside the Anchor, you can believe the hype. Food and drink share the limelight at this revitalised Arts & Crafts hostelry: Sophie Dorber cooks, while husband Mark uses his nous as a beer guru to mastermind the liquid refreshments. The menu brings both strands together, offering matching brews for just about every dish: try brawn from Blythburgh-reared pigs with piccalilli and a bottle of Sierra Nevada Pale Ale, for example. Sophie is from the country-meets-city school of seasonal eclectic cookery, so expect strong flavours and generosity in the shape of mackerel escabèche, cod stew with Brancaster mussels or duck breast with sautéed potatoes, braised red cabbage and chorizo jus. Lemon meringue pie and banana fritters are typical family-friendly desserts. Wines from £15.95.
Chef/s: Sophie Dorber. **Open:** all week L 12 to 3, D 6 to 9 (10 Fri and Sat). **Closed:** 25 Dec. **Meals:** main courses £14 to £23. **Details:** 90 seats. 200 seats outside. Bar. Wheelchairs. Parking.

◼ Woodbridge
The Riverside
Cooking score: 1
Modern British | £30
Quay Street, Woodbridge, IP12 1BH
Tel no: (01394) 382174
theriverside.co.uk
£5
OFF

'I love to find good food in unexpected places,' notes a reporter who stumbled upon this enterprising glass-fronted venue close to Woodbridge Quay. Run as a cinema/bar/restaurant complex, it's a stylish-looking local asset where the kitchen does its best to champion seasonal East Anglian produce (Deben mussels and Dedham Vale beef, for example). The 'stylistically varied, please-all menu' also accommodates everything from queen scallops with chorizo and garlic butter to coconut-braised Sri Lankan chicken curry, and you can roll the credits with a luscious chocolate sundae. 'Fish and flick' deals attract the crowds, likewise tapas feasts before the matinee. Wines from £16.

Chef/s: Dan Jones. **Open:** all week L 12 to 3 (3.30 Sun), Mon to Sat D 6 to 9.30 (10 Fri and Sat). **Closed:** 25 and 26 Dec. **Meals:** main courses £12 to £20. **Details:** 45 seats. 35 seats outside. Bar. Wheelchairs. Music.

LOCAL GEM
The Table
International | £25
3 Quay Street, Woodbridge, IP12 1BX
Tel no: (01394) 382428
thetablewoodbridge.co.uk
£30

In summer, diners spill from the warren of rooms that make up this delightfully welcoming brasserie on to its sunny courtyard, but whatever the weather it's a perfect spot for coffee and cake, a light lunch, or more substantial evening meal. Part-Malaysian chef-owner Vernon Blackmore is known for his authentic curries (try a fresh king prawn Goan curry or nutty Thai beef massaman) but offers more conventional fare, too: ham hock terrine with red onion marmalade, confit duck leg, or grilled skate wing with lemon-caper butter are recommended.

◼ Yoxford
Main's
Cooking score: 1
European | £28
High Street, Yoxford, IP17 3EU
Tel no: (01728) 668882
mainsrestaurant.co.uk
£30

Don't be deceived by the demure frontage of this neighbourhood favourite: Main's compact, daily changing menu offers food you could happily eat day in, day out. What a creamy salt-cod brandade lacks in crunch, it makes up for in sublime salt-sweet taste; ditto a savoury broad bean baked custard with rich mornay sauce. A celeriac purée is appropriately delicate for a flaking piece of wild sea bass, flavours lifted by a dash of wild garlic oil, and while a generous trio of Crozier Blue-topped beetroot patties is short on looks, herbs, spices and seasoning are used deftly. A crème caramel needs a touch more wobble, but an affogato hits that bitter-sweet note bang on. Wines from £15.

Chef/s: Jason Vincent. **Open:** Thur to Sat D 7 to 10. **Closed:** Sun to Wed. **Meals:** main courses £12 to £25. **Details:** 40 seats.

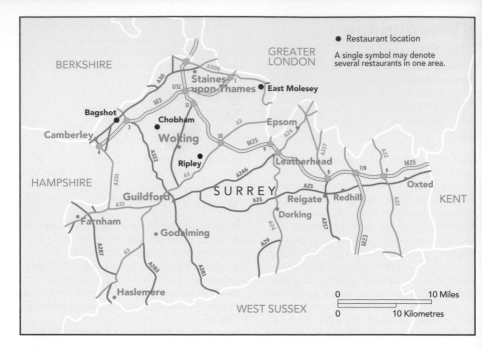

▌Bagshot

The Latymer

Cooking score: 6
Modern European | £80

Pennyhill Park Hotel, London Road, Bagshot,
GU19 5EU
Tel no: (01276) 486156
pennyhillpark.co.uk

🛏

The gargantuan estate at Bagshot is worth
arriving early for. Perambulating the gardens
is the best way to prepare for the special
occasion of eating here. With Michael
Wignall's departure for Gidleigh Park (see
entry, Chagford, Devon), Matt Worswick is
the latest incumbent. A sober room of dark-
wood panelling, plush fabrics and gentle
lighting is the arena for bold, pioneering food
full of technical precision and ingenuity. Whet
the appetite with a fluffy cloud of Wagyu beef
fat and onion ash, light as candyfloss, before
the tasting plates start coming. Crunchy pig's
trotter cromesquis with piccalilli gel and
smoked baba ganoush may be the harmonious
prelude to a tiny octopus satay, then red mullet
with baby squid and brown crab foam. The
principal meat could be Hertfordshire beef
with braised snails and wild garlic pesto, while
the gold-leafed chocolate délice with yoghurt
sorbet is the standout dessert. Wines open at an
unforgiving £49.

Chef/s: Matt Worswick. **Open:** Thur and Fri L 12 to
2, Wed to Sun D 7 to 9. **Closed:** Mon, Tue, first 2
weeks Jan. **Meals:** set L £47 (5 courses) to £80. Set
D £60 (7 courses) to £100. **Details:** 56 seats. V
menu. Bar. Wheelchairs. Parking. Children over 12
yrs only.

Symbols 🥄

🛏 Accommodation is available
£30 Three courses for less than £30
£5 OFF £5-off voucher scheme
🍷 Notable wine list

Chobham

Stovell's

Cooking score: 6
Modern European | £45
125 Windsor Road, Chobham, GU24 8QS
Tel no: (01276) 858000
stovells.com

£5
OFF

A rose-tinted picture of heritage solidity with its mullioned windows, gnarled beams and country comforts, this half-timbered 16th-century farmhouse is continuing on its upward path with Fernando Stovell firmly at the helm. The building may look folksy, but bold wallpaper and contemporary furnishings suggest that something very different is going on here: forget twee 'olde English' tea room treats, Stovell's menu bristles with vigorous modern ideas, cheffy touches and 'between-course action' (home-baked breads, individually garnished cheeses). Polish, refinement and fancy presentation are a given as Fernando fashions some rather challenging ideas from bang-on ingredients: how about a plate of warm aromatic foie gras with burnt grelot onions, toasted cobnuts, hay-tea dressing and pennywort, or 'grandma's remedy' (a dessert involving Chobham honey, lemon and eucalyptus)? There are also a few exotic specialities inspired by the chef's Mexican homeland (wood-fired guinea fowl with mole verde, tomatillo and pumpkin-seed couscous, for example), and he's not averse to the odd cheeky trick (note the deconstructed beef Wellington). Service is as polished as the cooking, and the wine list offers plenty of well-chosen bottles from £22.
Chef/s: Fernando Stovell. **Open:** Tue to Fri and Sun L 12 to 3.30 (4 Sun), Tue to Sat D 6 to 10. **Closed:** Mon, first week Jan. **Meals:** set L £18 (2 courses) to £23. Set D £37 (2 courses) to £45. **Details:** 74 seats. 20 seats outside. Bar. Music. Parking.

East Molesey

★ NEW ENTRY ★

Petriti's

Cooking score: 3
Modern European | £35
98 Walton Road, East Molesey, KT8 0DL
Tel no: (020) 8979 5577
petritisrestaurant.co.uk

Everyone mentions the wonderfully warm welcome, engagingly friendly service and happy vibes that pervade this modern restaurant, though one reporter was surprised to find a 'spot-on neighbourhood venture' in such a 'gastro-strapped area as East Molesey'. Pastel greys with comfortable modern chairs and colourful artwork create a sophisticated place to eat. Tom Petriti mans the stove, Nargisa Petriti is the smiling face out front, and you can expect skilful, creative and prettily presented modern European cooking. The appealing repertoire delivers fine ingredients with balanced combinations and generous portions and flavours: very fresh pan-fried plaice fillet beurre noisette with charred romanesco ('adding texture'), braised fennel, pickled carrot and sea rosemary, say, or slow-cooked Surrey lamb rump ('perfectly pink'), given heft by harissa-spiced couscous, carrot and cumin, artichoke and roasting jus, and five-spice oven-roast baby poussin with artichoke, broad beans and lemon thyme risotto. Raspberry soufflé with poppy seed custard, saffron and rosewater ice cream is a great way to finish. The wine list starts at £25.
Chef/s: Tom Petriti. **Open:** Tue to Sat L 12 to 3, D 6 to 10. Sun 12 to 8. **Closed:** Mon. **Meals:** main courses £10 to £19. Set L £10 (1 course). Tasting menu £49 (6 courses). **Details:** 68 seats. V menu.

▌Ripley
The Anchor
Cooking score: 3
Modern British | £30
High Street, Ripley, GU23 6AE
Tel no: (01483) 211866
ripleyanchor.co.uk

£5
OFF

The brick-built Anchor traces its roots back to the 16th century. It's been carefully remodelled in modern style with simple pub furniture inside, and an inviting little alfresco area with wicker armchairs for sunny Surrey days. A menu of bright, up-to-date pub cooking draws European influences into its British ambit, marrying roast cod and mussels with tagliatelle, capers and saffron oil, or adding balsamic shallots to roast duck breast and butternut purée. Prior to those, there are imaginative takes on pub stalwarts such as chicken Kiev and cep ketchup, or leek and potato soup with beery onions and truffle oil, and the inventive stops are pulled out for afters such as ginger rice pudding with rhubarb jam and toasted pistachios. If you're still working up an appetite, the menu of bar snacks – salmon burger in tartare, blue cheese puffs, black pudding Scotch egg – should do the trick. Wines start with a Chilean Sauvignon at £18.50.
Chef/s: Michael Wall-Palmer. **Open:** Tue to Sat L 12 to 2.30, D 6 to 9.30. Sun 12 to 8. **Closed:** Mon, 25 Dec. **Meals:** main courses £12 to £22. Set L £15 (2 courses) to £19. **Details:** 40 seats. 20 seats outside. Bar. Wheelchairs. Music. Parking. No children after 7.30pm.

Kim Woodward
Savoy Grill, London

What's your favourite dish on your menu?
I love to cook the signatures here, they're classics that define what we stand for. From the glazed omelette Arnold Bennett, to the beef Wellington trolley, the freshest Dover sole and wild sea bass en papillote, finishing with crêpe suzette flambéed table-side, or a Yorkshire rhubarb and custard mille-feuille.

How do you start developing a new recipe?
I'm very much a seasonal chef. A recipe is about perfecting the taste and marrying all the flavours. It could take two minutes or two weeks to perfect; trial and error is always the best way.

Who is the most interesting person you have cooked for?
Her Royal Majesty, The Queen, at the Chelsea Flower Show.

Which chef do you most admire at the moment?
Hélène Darroze - a powerful woman at the top of her game, always striving.

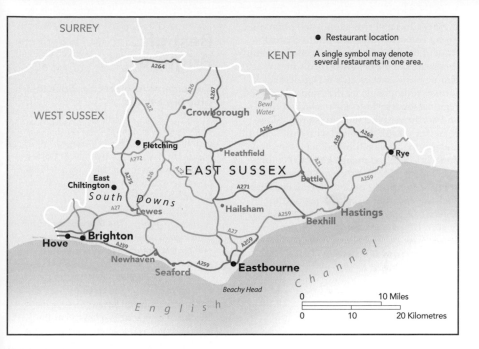

Brighton

Bincho Yakitori

Cooking score: 1
Japanese | £20
63 Preston Street, Brighton, BN1 2IIΕ
Tel no: (01273) 779021
binchoyakitori.com
£30

Based on a Japanese izakaya, at Bincho you can combine the fiery delights of food cooked over charcoal (yakitori) with the warming hit of saké in a spirited atmosphere with a trance music soundtrack (the latter not everyone's cup of ocha perhaps). Watch the grill action from a counter-stool or nearby table and await a panoply of sharing dishes such as super-tender pork belly, properly pink chicken livers, and Korean chicken wings, or daily specials like mackerel with pickled mooli and Wagyu chuck beef for the (relatively) big

spenders. It's good value and great fun. Drink Japanese beer, saké or something from the minimalist wine list; bottles start at £17.50. **Chef/s:** Tomo Ishii. **Open:** Tue to Sun D only 6 to 10 (5.30 to 10.30 Fri and Sat, 5.30 Sun). **Closed:** Mon, 2 weeks Dec, 16 Apr. **Meals:** main courses £4 to £12. **Details:** 32 seats.

The Chilli Pickle

Cooking score: 2
Indian | £26
17 Jubilee Street, Brighton, BN1 1GE
Tel no: (01273) 900383
thechillipickle.com
£30

Since 2008 Alun Sperring has been combining regional Indian flavours and Sussex ingredients to winning effect in dishes such as chilli methi keemar (minced South Downs lamb fired up with Punjabi spices), and even though it seats over 100, booking is advisable much of the time. The Chilli Pickle is 'busy busy'. The modern building opposite the city's Turner-Prize-nominated library is a glassy, colourful place that positively rocks most of the time. The service keeps pace amid the hustle and bustle. Properly distinctive chutneys and starters such as Nepalese duck momos (dumplings) set the standard, and the regional focus includes Goan chicken curry and northern-style tandoori platters. Slow-roast lamb shank flavoured with chilli, cumin and garam masala is finished in the fire, and dark chocolate and orange kulfi makes for a fusion finale. Thalis, dosas and railway trays are great lunchtime options. Drink craft beer, cocktails and wine from £19 per bottle.

Chef/s: Alun Sperring. **Open:** all week L 12 to 3, D 6 to 10.30 (10 Sun). **Closed:** 25 and 26 Dec. **Meals:** main courses £12 to £18. Early D £14. Set D £25 (2 courses) to £29. **Details:** 115 seats. 15 seats outside. Wheelchairs. Music.

Food For Friends

Cooking score: 1
Vegetarian | £22
17-18 Prince Albert Street, The Lanes, Brighton, BN1 1HF
Tel no: (01273) 202310
foodforfriends.com

£30

The food 'didn't just look good, it tasted good, and I strongly suspect did me good as well,' raved one, who professed an aversion to veggie fare until dining here. A stalwart of Brighton's dining scene, with a plum city-centre spot, it has been raising the bar for vegetarian food since 1981. The menu's three-course breakdown is blissfully 'concept' free: the fun is all in the eclectic offerings, which pluck ingredients from North Africa, Asia and beyond. Opt for Persian-spiced grilled aubergine, dried lime and tomato timbale or lunch on the popular sharing platter followed by classic sticky toffee pudding. Wines from £18.

Chef/s: Tomas Kowalski. **Open:** all week 12 to 10 (10.30 Fri and Sat). **Closed:** 25 Dec. **Meals:** main courses £11 to £13. Set L (2 courses) £18. Set L and D (3 courses) £24. Sun L £12. **Details:** 70 seats. 20 seats outside. Wheelchairs. Music.

Best of... Brighton

Our undercover inspectors open their Little Black Books

With one trillion coffee shops and counting, Brighton loves the bean. Ponder that while sat on a sack at **Coffee at 33** (Trafalgar Street), sipping a double espresso made from freshly ground Monmouth beans.

Gloriously grungy, **The Marwood** on Ship Street has a daily-changing blackboard of teas, a roster of cakes (fab carrot cake), and the coffee ain't half bad either.

For a pint, head to **The Evening Star**, a Brighton outpost of Sussex brewer, Dark Star. It's just off the main drag near the station, so remains hidden from passing tourists. Drink Dark Star's hophead or espresso (yes, it's a beer), or go off-piste for a guest ale.

Ten Green Bottles on Jubilee Street is a wine shop and wine bar with English fizz by the glass and plates of cheese and charcuterie to help prolong the fun. A large communal table rocks when the place is busy (metaphorically, not literally).

Okay, so it's nowhere near the seafront, but open since 1926, **Bardsley's** on Baker Street know what they're doing, and that's right and proper fish and chips. A blackboard lists specials...although the haddock and chips it keeps a calling.

The Chilli Pickle on Jubilee Street is an Indian restaurant with a great rep, go for the takeaway grand thali and tuck into a distinctively spiced chicken or Sussex mutton shoulder curry. They arrive with a host of pickles, chutneys and side dishes.

The Gingerman

Cooking score: 3
Modern European | £37
21a Norfolk Square, Brighton, BN1 2PD
Tel no: (01273) 326688
gingermanrestaurants.com

Trailblazer, game-changer – call it what you will, this pioneering eatery helped to kick-start Brighton as a bona fide foodie destination. Discreetly located on a side street near the seafront, Ben 'Gingerman' McKellar's flagship looks even more casual in its new skin (thanks to some tidy refurbishment in 2015), although nothing has changed at the stoves. On offer are some real bargains and a seemingly endless supply of smart cosmopolitan ideas: pulled pork shoulder with scratchings, honey jelly, mustard mayonnaise and pickled cauliflower is a typically confident, resourceful idea that chimes perfectly with Brighton's left-field leanings. The day's fish is always a good shout (perhaps Shoreham brill with smoked salmon, carrot purée, haricot beans and coconut velouté), likewise high-protein offerings such as a three-part assiette of beef with Savoy cabbage, seaweed and confit potato. As a finale, banana soufflé and pineapple tarte Tatin are testament to a highly skilled kitchen. Wines from £18.

Chef/s: Ben McKellar and Mark Charker. **Open:** Tue to Sun L 12.30 to 2, D 7 to 10. **Closed:** Mon. **Meals:** set L £17 (2 courses) to £20. Set D £32 (2 courses) to £37. Sun L £25. **Details:** 32 seats. Music.

The Jolly Poacher

Cooking score: 2
Modern European | £30
100 Ditchling Road, Brighton, BN1 4SG
Tel no: (01273) 683967
thejollypoacher.com

A corner pub that's more restaurant and bar than local boozer, the JP still serves up a fine pint of Harvey's Best alongside the cocktails and food-friendly wines. The fuss-free interior has a contemporary colour scheme, wooden tables and local artworks, and most

people come to eat. Anthony Burns' menu has evolved over the years into a more contemporary affair, where Thai crab fritters and chilli-salt squid sit alongside goose parfait with onion marmalade among first courses. Next up, crab and mango salsa is a vibrant partner to sea bream, quince aïoli and roast beets are complementary to roast pork belly, and veggies might go for baked aubergine with salsa verde. Finish with walnut, ginger and apricot pudding. The set menu is terrific value for two courses. A few outside tables give opportunities to catch some rays, but Ditchling Road isn't very far away. Wines start at £17.

Chef/s: Anthony Burns. **Open:** Wed to Sun L 12 to 2.30 (3 Sat, 4.30 Sun), Wed to Sat D 6 to 9.30 (10 Fri and Sat). **Closed:** Mon, Tue. **Meals:** main courses £15 to £23. Set L and D £14 (2 courses) to £20. Sun L £20 (2 courses). **Details:** 60 seats. 14 seats outside. Music.

The Restaurant at Drakes

Cooking score: 4
Modern European | £45
43-44 Marine Parade, Brighton, BN2 1PE
Tel no: (01273) 696934
therestaurantatdrakes.co.uk

Brighton at its boutique best, Drakes hotel has dashing Georgian good looks and stylish bedrooms. A cocktail bar gives views over the sea and pier, while the basement restaurant (or lower-ground floor, as it does have windows, just without a view) provides a polished dining experience with white linen and comfy banquettes. A new head chef, Andy Vitez, has stepped up from senior sous-chef to lead the line delivering refined contemporary menus. A first-course sea trout ceviche arrives with a crab beignet and dill and cucumber granita, while brill is served as a main course crusted with lemon ash and matched with cockles and sea vegetables. Classically minded pairings include rump of lamb with its sweetbreads, shallot purée and morels, and there's more derring-do in a dessert of violet soufflé with lemon curd ice cream and crystallised flowers. A tasting menu comes with optional wine flight. Wines start at £21.

Chef/s: Andy Vitez. **Open:** all week L 12.30 to 1.45, D 7 to 9.45. **Meals:** set L £20 (2 courses) to £25. Set D £33 (2 courses) to £45. Tasting menu £60. Sun L £25 (2 courses) to £30. **Details:** 50 seats. Bar. Music. Parking.

★ NEW ENTRY ★

Riddle & Finns

Cooking score: 1
Seafood | £35
138 King's Road Arches, Brighton, BN1 2FN
Tel no: (01273) 821218
riddleandfinns.co.uk
£5
OFF

Among the arches down on the meandering lower promenade, Riddle & Finns is just what you want on the seafront. Outside tables, a sea view (get a table at the front) and some pretty decent seafood make it 'a lovely place in which to have dinner'. Daily specials such as surf and turf of lobster and ribeye, or Dover sole, add up-to-the-minute support to a long carte that travels the globe — 'fantastic' fresh oysters, fruits de mer, wok-fried crab with 'sweet and addictive' Malaysian sauce, ceviche, sashimi or good old fish pie. The original branch can be found in the nearby Lanes. Wines start at £17.50.

Chef/s: David Roy. **Open:** all week 12 to 11. **Meals:** main courses £12 to £33. Set L £13 (2 courses) to £16. Sun L £40. **Details:** 48 seats. 50 seats outside. Music.

The Salt Room

Cooking score: 2
Modern British | £36
106 Kings Road, Brighton, BN1 2FN
Tel no: (01273) 929488
saltroom-restaurant.co.uk

Right on the seafront road near Brighton's newest landmark, the 173-metre i360 viewing tower, the Salt Room is physically attached to the Hilton Metropole hotel but is an independent business from the chap behind

the Coal Shed (see entry). The cool black façade, floor-to-ceiling windows and sea-facing terrace make a fine first impression, while the interior ticks the contemporary boxes with its exposed brickwork, retro light fittings and trendy cocktails. A seafood (and more) restaurant of such verve is just what the city needed, with the Josper charcoal grill turning out the day's catch alongside lobsters and ribeye steak — 'yes, bring on the surf and turf'. Starters such as roasted scallops with black garlic, bacon and puffed rice are on the refined side, but then again the day's selection of shellfish is hard to ignore. To finish, Taste of the Pier is a creative play on seaside favourites such as 99s and doughnuts. Wines start at £18.

Chef/s: Dave Mothersill. **Open:** all week L 12 to 4, D 6 to 10 (10.30 Fri and Sat). **Meals:** main courses £14 to £24. Set L and early D £15 (2 courses) to £18. **Details:** 84 seats. 55 seats outside. Bar.

★ NEW ENTRY ★

Semolina

Cooking score: 1
Modern European | £27
15 Baker Street, Brighton, BN1 4JN
Tel no: (01273) 697259
semolinabrighton.co.uk
£5
OFF £30

Semolina is simplicity itself — a proper bistro run by a keen couple with a passion for seasonal, regional ingredients. On a very unassuming road in a non-touristy part of the city, it's a real local asset, the unpretentious setting and cheerful service fitting the bistro bill, while the perfectly formed menu offers up some stylish contemporary grub. Everything is made in-house. 'Tender and delicious' cuttlefish stars in a first course with almond tarator, local cod is matched with a stonking black pudding made in Sussex, and loin of pork comes with an 'amazingly light' piece of crackling. Wines start at £17.

Chef/s: Orson Whitfield. **Open:** Wed to Sat L 12 to 3, D 6 to 10. Sun 12 to 6. **Closed:** Mon, Tue, 1 week Christmas, 2 weeks Jan, 2 weeks Aug. **Meals:** main courses £11 to £15. Set L £12 (2 courses) to £15. Sun L £9 to £14. **Details:** 28 seats. Music.

The Set

Cooking score: 2
Modern British | £31
Artist Residence, 33 Regency Square,
Brighton, BN1 2GG
Tel no: (01273) 324302
thesetrestaurant.com

Part of the new generation of chefs for whom fine dining is a dirty word, the guys at the Set have found an ideal home at the achingly cool Artist Residence hotel. Plenty of thought has gone into the seemingly down-home restaurant design: wood from the old West Pier adds to the recycled vibe, coffee sacks act as cushions, the crockery is proper pottery and there are ringside seats at the open kitchen. The choice is easy enough: go for one of three set menus (one of which is veggie), and don't ignore the excellent-value wine flight. Modern cooking techniques and a creative mindset see things kick off with a 'snack' such as chicken nugget with red cabbage ketchup before the four courses proper (cod and oxtail, say, and a pork number with black pudding), including an inventive sweet course that recalls the joys of cereal milk. Drink cracking cocktails or wines starting at £20.
Chef/s: Dan Kenny and Semone Bonner. **Open:** Tue to Sun L 12 to 3 (1 to 4 Sun), Tue to Sat D 6 to 10.
Closed: Mon, 25 and 26 Dec. **Meals:** set L and D £29 to £35. **Details:** 20 seats. V menu. Bar. Music. No children.

Silo

Cooking score: 3
Modern British | £28
39 Upper Gardner Street, Brighton, BN1 4AN
Tel no: (01273) 674259
silobrighton.com

£30

A lot of restaurants reference concern for environmental matters and make moves to do the right thing for the planet, but surely there is no more dedicated and effective outfit than Silo. The zero-waste philosophy includes the presence of a composter and the interior is kitted out with recycled materials. Douglas McMaster's café, bakery and restaurant is serious about the end product, too, with a menu built around high principles of animal welfare and sustainability. They're now open later five nights a week, with set menus offering 'Plant', 'Fish' or 'Meat' options, or go your own way from the main menu. Candy beetroot with pickled dulse (sea lettuce) and apple is a vibrant opener, or go for pheasant leg with fermented cabbage coleslaw, with cauliflower, green rye porridge and red onion an impressive veggie main. The drinks list is an inspiring read, including their own-brew ale and zesty non-alcoholic concoctions. Wines start at £21.
Chef/s: Douglas McMaster. **Open:** Mon to Sat 8.30am to 11pm (8.30 to 5 Mon). Sun 10 to 5.
Meals: main courses £12 to £16. Set D £31 (4 courses). **Details:** 55 seats. Wheelchairs. Music.

64 Degrees

Cooking score: 4
Modern British | £30
53 Meeting House Lane, Brighton, BN1 1HB
Tel no: (01273) 767914
64degrees.co.uk

Considered by some to be 'the best restaurant in Brighton', 64 Degrees affects a cool simplicity in everything, from its understated modern furniture – a long counter at the open kitchen provides half the seating – to a concise list of small plates, each described in around three words. While all these are designed for sharing, sizes range from a petite plate of roast parsnips with honey and a Parmesan foam, to a more substantial seared beef onglet with pressed and puréed swede and bone-marrow crumb. Chef-proprietor Michael Bremner's cooking conveys a passion for the very best ingredients, including wild or less obvious options: lemon sole with chamomile and fennel; Alexanders buds with hollandaise and lime; and pork belly with pineapple and chilli are springtime examples. To conclude, maybe coconut pannacotta with passion fruit and macadamia nuts. The 20 or so wines on offer are grouped under three-word-style descriptions. As with the ingredients, there are some interesting finds and bottles start at £20.

Chef/s: Michael Bremner and Samuel Lambert. **Open:** all week L 12 to 3, D 6 to 9.45. **Closed:** 25 Dec, 1 Jan. **Meals:** small plates £12 to £25. **Details:** 22 seats. Music.

Terre à Terre

Cooking score: 3
Vegetarian | £34
71 East Street, Brighton, BN1 1HQ
Tel no: (01273) 729051
terreaterre.co.uk

Defiantly quirky since 1993, Terre à Terre specialises in complex dishes described in punning terms and painstaking detail; the menu, says one reader, demands 'considerable study'. In surroundings that are well loved but dated, it might seem an unnecessary performance, but the effect is to give vegetarian and vegan dishes a sense of ceremony and status they can still lack elsewhere. Surrender to a snack of 'Bangkok broken balls' of coconut rice, peanuts and myriad Asian flavours, or a starter of haloumi-stuffed 'peeking buns', and the all-in approach to global flavours and textures starts to make sense. You don't get to Terre à Terre's age without a few classics, and the topped röstis (perhaps with mushroom juniper ragoût with walnut tarator, prune pickle and pine oil brassica leaves with salty blue cream cheese, cauliflower and turmeric lemon myrtle sauce) and house-made chocolate truffles are favourites. Wines are organic and vegetarian, from £18.95.

Chef/s: Matty Bowling. **Open:** all week 12 to 10.30 (11 Sat). **Closed:** 25 and 26 Dec. **Meals:** main courses £15 to £16. Set L and D £35 (3 courses). **Details:** 100 seats. 15 seats outside. V menu. Music.

Average price

The average price denotes the price of a three-course meal without wine.

Twenty Four St Georges

Cooking score: 3
Modern European | £37
24-25 St George's Road, Brighton, BN2 1ED
Tel no: (01273) 626060
24stgeorges.co.uk

'The essence of simple food pleasure,' according to chef-proprietor Jamie Everton-Jones, but don't go thinking simplicity plays any part in what arrives at your table. This is complex, ambitious modern cooking that mostly hits the mark, although there's 'too much action on the plate' for some. In a relatively formal atmosphere – for Brighton at least – professional service ensures it all goes swimmingly, while careful sourcing by the kitchen helps give each dish a solid foundation. A nicely balanced opener might be goats' cheese with walnut and fennel granola, plus some measured acidity from pickled apple and pear, followed by an optional sorbet (virgin mojito, say). Main course sees pan-roasted monkfish served up with textures of carrot and a hint of spice, and loin and braised shoulder of venison in the classic company of a rösti, wild mushrooms and port jus. Finish with the chef's take on Black Forest gâteau. Wines start at £19.

Chef/s: Jamie Everton-Jones and Alex Savage-Boudot. **Open:** Sat L 12.30 to 5, Tue to Sat D 5.30 to 9.30. **Closed:** Sun, Mon, 25 and 26 Dec, 1 Jan. **Meals:** main courses £13 to £24. Set D £22 (2 courses) to £25. Tasting menu £59. **Details:** 52 seats. Music. Children before 6.30pm only.

LOCAL GEM

The Coal Shed

British | £40
8 Boyces Street, Brighton, BN1 1AN
Tel no: (01273) 322998
coalshed-restaurant.co.uk

The proposition of dry-aged Scottish steaks and seafood cooked over charcoal has been a hit with the locals – 'the best steaks in Brighton,' some say – and resulted in a second outfit on the seafront (see entry for the Salt Room). At the end of a narrow twitten, the

Coal Shed's confident kitchen also offers up appealingly contemporary starters such as pigeon, salt-baked beetroot and blood orange, and a winsome dessert of lemon, Champagne and sherbet. Back to those steaks: pick a weight and cut (bone-in prime rib, say), add half a lobster for a surf and turf experience, and keep an eye on the cost. Wines start at £18.

Curry Leaf Cafe
Indian | £24
60 Ship Street, Brighton, BN1 1AE
Tel no: (01273) 207070
curryleafcafe.com
£30

The split-level dining room with its sunny colour scheme can generate quite a hubbub when it's busy, packing them in for South Indian street food – the feel-good food of the urban warrior. Guinea fowl chettinad, pork vindaloo, tandoori mackerel, veggie malpas curry – expect distinct spicing and stimulating preparations. Lunchtime thalis and dosas are a good bet, and to drink, craft ales and Indian-inspired versions of classic cocktails lead the way (Bloody Meera, anybody?). House wine is £17.

■ East Chiltington
The Jolly Sportsman
Cooking score: 2
Modern British | £30
Chapel Lane, East Chiltington, BN7 3BA
Tel no: (01273) 890400
thejollysportsman.com

Off the beaten track down a leafy dead-end lane, the Jolly Sportsman is a dining destination – and in this isolated location, it needs to be. It sells a nice drop, though, with local ales straight from the barrel and an intelligently put together wine list, with options by the carafe. The series of opened-up spaces include a wee bar with real fire and a main dining area with fashionably muted colours, wooden tables and local artworks.

The menu covers the ground from England, France and broader European territories, so a daily special might be cottage pie, while a more refined alternative could be crisp-skinned bream with chive gnocchi and bouillabaisse sauce. Punchy flavours brighten a spring salad of white anchovies with tapenade, asparagus and tomato confit, and desserts are a heavy bunch, including steamed marmalade pudding. On a summer's day the garden is positively bucolic. Wines start at £18.75.

Chef/s: Bruce Wass. **Open:** Tue to Sun L 12 to 2.30 (3.30 Sun), Tue to Sat D 6 to 9.30 (10 Fri, 9 Sat). **Closed:** Mon. **Meals:** main courses £15 to £18. Set L £15 (2 courses) to £18. **Details:** 80 seats. 60 seats outside. Bar. Wheelchairs. Parking.

■ Eastbourne
The Mirabelle
Cooking score: 5
Modern European | £45
The Grand Hotel, King Edward's Parade, Eastbourne, BN21 4EQ
Tel no: (01323) 412345
grandeastbourne.com
£5 OFF

The Grand is an enduring slice of old-world sophistication on the Eastbourne seafront, a hotel from an era when you expected an entrance that resembled that of an Athenian temple, with tiers of balconied rooms rising above it in dazzling meringue-white, from which you can glimpse Beachy Head. Formal dress is as de rigueur now as it was when the BBC used to broadcast light music from here on Sunday evenings. You may even fancy you hear the toll of a ghostly dinner gong. Gerald Röser's menus are thoughtfully amenable to those who aren't quite ready for modern British. There's crab and avocado, with perhaps guinea fowl, bacon and chestnuts in Madeira sauce to follow, and the midday meal is still called 'luncheon'. Then again, if you're all about daring innovation, get set for port-soaked dolcelatte with salt-baked beetroot dressed in honey and thyme, and a finale of deconstructed tiramisu, which comes as mascarpone and Amaretto mousse with sponge cake, espresso jelly and coffee foam. Wines are carefully annotated, strongest in the French heartlands, and with a good showing of rosés. Prices are not necessarily as intimidating as you might anticipate, if you start at £27.

Chef/s: Gerald Röser. **Open:** Tue to Sat L 12.30 to 2, D 7 to 10. **Closed:** Sun, Mon, first 2 weeks Jan. **Meals:** set L £20 (2 courses) to £24. Set D £35 (2 courses) to £40. Tasting menu £63 (7 courses). Sun L £30. **Details:** 50 seats. Bar. Wheelchairs. Music. Parking. Children over 12 yrs only.

▌Fletching
The Griffin Inn
Cooking score: 3
Modern British | £32
Fletching, TN22 3SS
Tel no: (01825) 722890
thegriffininn.co.uk
£5 OFF 🍷 🚃

Run by the Pullan family since 1979, this ancient listed building makes a heart-warming country-inn-with-rooms – big on atmosphere, with traditional bars, a smart restaurant, crackling fires in winter and a fine garden with far-reaching views to the South Downs for fair-weather alfresco dining. It's a delightful setting for some good cooking – the kitchen knows what is required and delivers in fine fashion. Basic materials are well sourced and well handled, offering sesame tempura monkfish with spicy red pepper jam and grilled lime as one way to start. Main dishes run a broadly based course from oak-smoked rump of Romney Marsh lamb with Parmesan mash, green beans, spinach and quince jus, to skate wing teamed with sautéed potatoes, beans, broccoli, mussels, samphire and caper butter. To finish, the selection of British cheeses is highly rated, or there's marmalade bread-and-butter pudding with orange caramel and white chocolate ice cream. One of the Griffin Inn's glories is a wine list compiled by a true

enthusiast, its tasting notes full of missionary zeal, the selections full of interest and character; bottles from £15.50.

Chef/s: Matthew Starkey. **Open:** all week L 12 to 2.30 (3 Sat and Sun), Mon to Sat D 7 to 9.30. **Closed:** 25 Dec. **Meals:** main courses £14 to £25. Sun L £25 (2 courses) to £30. **Details:** 70 seats. 60 seats outside. Bar. Wheelchairs. Parking.

▌Hove
The Ginger Pig
Cooking score: 3
Modern British | £32
3 Hove Street, Hove, BN3 2TR
Tel no: (01273) 736123
thegingerpigpub.com

It's knocking on for a dozen years now since Ben McKellar's corner pub entered the fray and the Ginger Pig was established as a foodie hot spot close to the seafront. It does attract drinkers to its front bar, but it's the dining area that, with its brasserie DNA, brings in the punters for its rather stylish brand of pan-European plates of food. A grilled octopus starter, with hot 'nduja sausage and grelot onions, is the real deal and does not lack refinement. Aloo tikki with coconut chutney shows a willingness to explore beyond European borders, while among main courses, hogget hotpot with Brussels sprout tops and anchovy butter is an updated version of the sort of hearty stuff you might hope to find in a pub. Whole lemon sole arrives with salt-baked kohlrabi and grapefruit dressing, and, to finish, roast pineapple, black sesame ice cream and miso caramel is a satisfying partnership. Wines start at £18.

Chef/s: Tom Wright. **Open:** all week L 12 to 2.30 (3 Fri and Sat, 4 Sun), D 6.30 to 10 (6 Sat, 6 to 9 Sun). **Closed:** 25 Dec. **Meals:** main courses £13 to £22. Set L and D £15 (2 courses) to £18. **Details:** 80 seats. 20 seats outside. Bar. Music.

The Little Fish Market

Cooking score: 5
Seafood | £50
10 Upper Market Street, Hove, BN3 1AS
Tel no: (01273) 722213
thelittlefishmarket.co.uk
£5
OFF

Duncan Ray is a singular chef inasmuch as he's prodigiously talented and works pretty much alone in the kitchen (don't begrudge him help with the washing-up). With just a solo chap out front – the universally admired Rob – and a no-choice, five-course (mostly seafood) menu, it's the sort of place where the table is yours all night and you 'just go with the flow – and what a flow'. Slip sole with seaweed butter reveals the cut of Duncan's jib – just a beautifully fresh fish served on the bone, lightly cooked and smothered in a lush green sauce, while another course such as 'deliciously aromatic' pork belly with fab cockles hints at the experience the chef has gained at some fancy addresses, including the Fat Duck. There's no sciencey stuff here, though, just clean, clear flavours, such as the silky gazpacho that comes with perfectly cooked mackerel, or the wild strawberry sorbet that outshines its accompanying mille-feuille. The dressed down space suits the relaxed mood here in Brighton and Hove. A short wine list kicks off at £23.
Chef/s: Duncan Ray. **Open:** Sat L 12 to 2, Tue to Sat D 7 to 9. **Closed:** Sun, Mon, 1 week Apr, 2 weeks Sept, 1 week Dec. **Meals:** set L £20 (2 courses) to £25. Tasting menu £50. **Details:** 22 seats. Music. Children over 12 yrs only.

◼ Rye

Landgate Bistro

Cooking score: 2
British | £30
5-6 Landgate, Rye, TN31 7LH
Tel no: (01797) 222829
landgatebistro.co.uk

The 14th-century Landgate was built to keep out French invaders, while the restaurant that bears its name occupies two knocked-through

Georgian cottages in a 'charmingly wonky' terrace across the way. The modest interior with simple blond tables dressed with flowers and candles is due for refurbishment as we write. The menu deals in seasonal local ingredients with the famous scallops and lamb among the star attractions. Modern touches run through a menu that is underpinned with classical good sense. Out of the sea hereabouts comes tender cuttlefish, served on a silky, pitch-black ink risotto, while contemporary fashion dictates that scallops pitch up with cauliflower prepared several ways. Main-course marsh lamb is a feast of cuts – the hotpot a 'rich, tender delight', the sweetbreads sadly over-seasoned – and 'gloriously translucent' roasted cod arrives with marsh vegetables including lightly battered alexanders and sea purslane. Wines start at £18.50.
Chef/s: Martin Peacock. **Open:** Sat and Sun L 12 to 2.15, Wed to Sat D 7 to 9 (6.30 to 9.15 Sat). **Closed:** Mon, Tue, 24 to 26 and 31 Dec. **Meals:** main courses £14 to £20. Set L £16 (2 courses) to £20. Set D £19 (2 courses) to £23. Sun L 16 (2 courses) to £20. **Details:** 32 seats. V menu. Bar. Music.

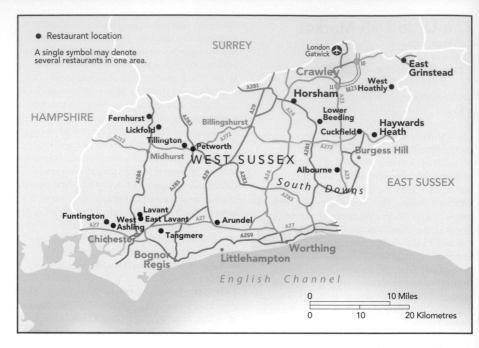

▋Albourne
The Ginger Fox
Cooking score: 3
Modern British | £35
Muddleswood Road, Albourne, BN6 9EA
Tel no: (01273) 857888
gingermanrestaurants.com

A folksy effigy of a fox on the prowl crowns the trim thatched roof of this rejigged Sussex hostelry – a country outpost of the Brighton-based Gingerman empire, complete with fetching views of the South Downs. The Ginger Fox is a family-friendly set-up, with a dedicated kids' play area and a full quota of well-considered rustic-chic trappings for the grown-ups. Gingerman supremo Ben McKellar and chef James Dearden have devised a rolling menu of complicated, multi-part dishes that fulfil their local remit while accumulating influences from far and wide – as in breast and liver of duck with port-infused turnips, salt-baked carrot purée, hazelnuts and pak choi. Elsewhere, fillet of Redland Farm

beef arrives with a BBQ short-rib croquette and duck-fat chips, while cod is paired with cured ham, brown crab, Puy lentil velouté and creamed Savoy cabbage. Desserts such as pistachio parfait with banana pannacotta also run with the intricate theme. Easy-drinking wines from £18.

Chef/s: James Dearden and Ben McKellar. **Open:** all week L 12 to 2 (3 Sat, 4 Sun), D 6 to 10 (6.30 Sat, 9 Sun). **Closed:** 25 Dec. **Meals:** main courses £15 to £23. Set L £15 (2 courses) to £18. **Details:** 66 seats. 84 seats outside. Bar. Music. Parking.

Please send us your feedback

To register your opinion about any restaurant listed in this guide, or a new restaurant that you wish to bring to our attention, please visit the web address at the bottom of the page. Your feedback informs the content of the book and will be used to compile next year's reviews.

Arundel

★ NEW ENTRY ★

The Parsons Table
Cooking score: 3
British | £32
2 & 8 Castle Mews, Tarrant Street, Arundel,
BN18 9DG
Tel no: (01903) 883477
theparsonstable.co.uk

In a town overflowing with old-world charm and a 'mahoosive' castle to call its own, the Parsons Table is a breath of fresh air with its contemporary finish of blond wood, white walls, trendy filament light bulbs and locally inspired Eric Ravilious prints. Chef-patron Lee Parsons' experience at the classical end of the dining spectrum (including a stint at Le Manoir aux Quat'Saisons) is evident in an output that features ace regional and seasonal ingredients. Wonderfully fat scallops arrive 'seared to perfection' with a sunny Sussex salsa verde, while a daily special might be chilled essence of Nutbourne tomatoes. Main-course saddle of rabbit (another special) comes with asparagus and a fennel purée that outshines the accompanying mustard cream, and catch of the day might be pan-seared sea trout with crab risotto. To finish, honey-roasted pears with streusel and Greek yoghurt ice cream is like a deconstructed crumble. Wines start at £17.50.
Chef/s: Lee Parsons. **Open:** Tue to Sun L 11.30 to 2.30 (3 Sat and Sun), Tue to Sat D 6 to 9.30. **Closed:** Mon. **Meals:** main courses £11 to £20. Tasting menu £65. **Details:** 35 seats.

The Town House
Cooking score: 3
Modern British | £30
65 High Street, Arundel, BN18 9AJ
Tel no: (01903) 883847
thetownhouse.co.uk
£5 OFF 🛏

It may inhabit a Grade II-listed Georgian town house within sight of Arundel's medieval castle, but the crowning glory of Lee and Kate Williams' elegant dining room is a fabulously intricate, carved walnut ceiling that originated in 16th-century Florence. It adds a certain frisson to eating here, although Lee's expertly rendered brasserie-style food is guaranteed to turn heads away from the Renaissance magnificence above. The kitchen may be grounded in the world of chateaubriand, seared foie gras and roast quail with wild mushrooms, but it also injects a few more contemporary ideas along the way – as in tempura crevettes with mango salsa and pickled ginger or pan-fried fillet of stone bass with langoustine and pea risotto. Home-smoked duck and locally sourced South Downs venison show the kitchen's commitment to quality, while pinpoint desserts might feature anything from banana fritters to pistachio parfait with lemon and vodka sorbet. Wines start at £18.
Chef/s: Lee Williams. **Open:** Tue to Sat L 12 to 2, D 7 to 9.30. **Closed:** Sun, Mon, 25 to 27 Dec, 1 to 3 Jan, 2 weeks Easter, 2 weeks Oct. **Meals:** set L £18 (2 courses) to £22. Set D £26 (2 courses) to £30. **Details:** 24 seats. Music.

Cuckfield

Ockenden Manor
Cooking score: 5
Modern French | £66
Ockenden Lane, Cuckfield, RH17 5LD
Tel no: (01444) 416111
hshotels.co.uk
£5 OFF 🛏

It's not the grandest Elizabethan house in southern England, but Ockenden Manor still creates an air of gentility and elegance with its sprouting chimneys and discreet location in nine acres of manicured grounds. Log fires and oak panelling add the necessary homeliness and intimacy, while long-serving chef Stephen Crane takes care of business in the smartly appointed restaurant. Since arriving in 2001, he has honed his approach, creating dishes defined by their restrained intricacy and refinement – consider a plate of hand-dived scallops with truffled potato purée, charred spring onion and crispy bacon or saddle and belly of lamb from the Goodwood Estate with a meatball, pesto pasta and provençale sauce. Home-smoked fish and game are something of a speciality, while fine-tuned desserts such as oat crème brûlée with blood orange, chocolate emulsion and whisky ice cream show off Crane's artistic and technical nous. A serious-minded globetrotting wine list opens with 13 house selections from £29 (£7 a glass).

Chef/s: Stephen Crane. **Open:** all week L 12 to 2, D 7 to 9 (6.30 Fri to Sun). **Meals:** set L £22 (2 courses) to £29. Set D £65. Sun L £37. **Details:** 96 seats. Bar. Wheelchairs. Parking.

■ East Grinstead
Gravetye Manor
Cooking score: 5
Modern British | £68
Vowels Lane, East Grinstead, RH19 4LJ
Tel no: (01342) 810567
gravetyemanor.co.uk

🍷 🛏

This alluring Elizabethan manor still works its magic, enchanting visitors with its richly panelled interiors and lovely gardens – the work of pioneering Victorian horticulturist William Robinson. George Blogg judiciously combines pickings from the raised beds and greenhouses with supplies of regional produce to create gently persuasive dishes with a proper sense of ambition, but also an allegiance to the calendar. Fish is always garlanded for the season, from a plate of flaked Dorset cock crab with sorrel, brown crab emulsion and Exmoor caviar to poached South Coast brill with cuttlefish-ink macaroni, celery hearts, salsify and gem lettuce. Meat and game are also strong suits, judging by the pine-smoked haunch of local venison or charred rump of English rose veal with sweetbread, Jerusalem artichoke, leeks and gremolata. To finish, Blogg's soufflés are a hit (try the rhubarb crumble version with clotted cream ice cream). The voluminous wine list promises gilt-edged vintages and glorious drinking opportunities at every turn, whether you're

after a frisky English sparkler, a rare Bordeaux or a vigorous young Australian. Bottles start at £32.

Chef/s: George Blogg. **Open:** all week L 12 to 2, D 6.30 to 9. **Meals:** set L £28 (2 courses) to £33. Set D £68. Sun L £48. **Details:** 50 seats. 20 seats outside. V menu. Bar. Wheelchairs. Parking. Children over 7 yrs only.

■ East Lavant
The Royal Oak Inn
Cooking score: 1
Modern British | £35
Pook Lane, East Lavant, PO18 0AX
Tel no: (01243) 527434
royaloakeastlavant.co.uk

£5 OFF 🛏

With its oak beams, real fire and local ales, this charming pub-cum-restaurant-with-rooms scores many hits for its cooking – its strength lying in the quality of the mainly local supplies. Alongside the more traditional pub staples of ham hock terrine and cod and chips there are plenty of modern British combinations: roast pigeon breast with Puy lentils and bacon; local venison with black pudding, red cabbage and fondant potatoes. If you've got room, finish off with an apple crumble or some ice cream from Jude's nearby dairy. The front-of-house team is genuinely warm and an above average wine list starts at £19 a bottle.

Chef/s: Fran Joyce. **Open:** all week L 12 to 2.30 (3 Fri, 4 Sat and Sun), D 6 to 9.30 (10 Fri and Sat). **Meals:** main courses £15 to £28. **Details:** 55 seats. 35 seats outside. Bar. Wheelchairs. Music. Parking.

Fernhurst
The Duke of Cumberland Arms
Cooking score: 4
Modern British | £35
Henley Hill, Fernhurst, GU27 3HQ
Tel no: (01428) 652280
dukeofcumberland.com

The English countryside hereabouts is pretty darn idyllic – lush green hills studded with trees, and all within the South Downs National Park. Soak up the view from the pretty tiered garden at this 16th-century country pub. A rustic bar with local ales on tap and a log fire to warm the cockles keeps the pub side of the bargain, while the dining-room extension is the setting for some rather inspiring modern British food. House-cured salmon, scallop ceviche, horseradish snow and cucumber jelly is not what you'd usually find at your average rural hostelry. Chef-patron Simon Goodman has his supply lines ticking along nicely, with a local flavour guaranteed, and there's undoubted refinement and precision in the execution of his menu. Expect well-judged stuff such as herb- and mustard-crusted neck and rack of lamb with dauphinois, pan-fried line-caught cod with a sauce made from local ale, and grass-fed sirloin steak with classic accoutrements. Lunchtime sourdough baguettes fuel walkers in style. Wines start at £16.50.
Chef/s: Simon Goodman. **Open:** all week L 12 to 2, Tue to Sat D 6 to 9. **Closed:** 26 Dec. **Meals:** main courses £15 to £30. **Details:** 65 seats. 150 seats outside. Bar. Wheelchairs. Music. Parking.

Funtington
Hallidays
Cooking score: 2
Modern British | £37
Watery Lane, Funtington, PO18 9LF
Tel no: (01243) 575331
hallidays.info
£5 OFF

The three thatched cottages of which Hallidays is composed were amalgamated into one in the 1950s, and Andy and Julia Stephenson have called it home since 1997. Hanging baskets and twittering birdsong make the place irresistible on a summer day, for those who fancy the run out from Chichester, and Andy's carefully conceived British dishes offer plenty of modern seasonal exuberance without pitching headlong into the unfathomable. A Selsey crab version of Scotch egg is neatly done, offset with shaved fennel and lemony mayonnaise, while chunky venison terrine is served with spiced blood orange and saladings. At main, there are properly aged sirloins with wood blewits and wild garlic leaves, or perhaps herb-crusted stone bass in saffron butter. Fixed-price lunches are a bargain, and covetable desserts include Seville orange buttermilk mousse with Yorkshire rhubarb and sugared almonds. Cheese might be Charlton, a Cheddar made on the nearby Goodwood Estate. Wines start at £19.50, or £12 the half-bottle carafe.
Chef/s: Andrew Stephenson. **Open:** Wed to Fri and Sun L 12 to 1.30, Wed to Sat D 7 to 9.30. **Closed:** Mon, Tue, 1 week Christmas, 1 week Mar, 2 weeks Aug. **Meals:** main courses £19 to £22. Set L £18 (2 courses) to £24. Set D £30 (2 courses) to £37. Sun L £24. **Details:** 26 seats. Bar. Wheelchairs. Parking.

▌Haywards Heath
Jeremy's
Cooking score: 4
Modern European | £36
Borde Hill Garden, Balcombe Road, Haywards Heath, RH16 1XP
Tel no: (01444) 441102
jeremysrestaurant.co.uk

The instantly captivating, verdant delights of Borde Hill Garden making eating alfresco at Jeremy's a must-do in summer, although the restaurant's refurbished interior also has a charm all its own. Bare tables now contribute to the fresh contemporary look, while the kitchen takes its cue from bounteous supplies of seasonal produce (some of it from the Victorian walled garden). Owner Jeremy Ashpool has handed over cheffing duties to Jimmy Gray, but creative, ingredients-led cooking is still the order of the day: grilled mackerel is enlivened with oyster, monk's beard, apple and fennel, Southdown lamb keeps earthy company with beetroot, pearl barley, turnips and sheep's cheese, while veggies might be swayed by a dish of tagliatelle with pied de mouton, Brie de Meaux and truffle oil. To conclude, don't miss desserts such as the chervil and vanilla ice lolly with raspberry and white chocolate. A snappy global wine list starts at £18.
Chef/s: Jimmy Gray. **Open:** Tue to Sun L 12.30 to 2.30, Tue to Sat D 7 to 10. **Closed:** Mon, first 2 weeks Jan. **Meals:** main courses £15 to £24. Set L and D £20 (2 courses) to £25. Sun L £28 (2 courses) to £35. **Details:** 55 seats. 40 seats outside. Bar. Wheelchairs. Music. Parking.

▌Horsham
Restaurant Tristan
Cooking score: 6
Modern British | £45
3 Stans Way, Horsham, RH12 1HU
Tel no: (01403) 255688
restauranttristan.co.uk

A fire did some serious damage to Restaurant Tristan in the early hours of Christmas Eve 2015, but Tristan and Candy Mason reopened just two months later – and the foodies of Sussex could breathe again. The fabric of the 16th-century building lends character to a space dressed in fashionable neutrality, with the first-floor dining room open to the rafters and furnished in a sleek Scandi style that is the modern British way. It's a confidently contemporary setting for pin-sharp cooking that is complex but never overwrought. Prepare for an opening salvo of foie gras three ways (pan-fried, parfait and ice cream), in a dish of balance and poise, with mango and honeycomb in support, before squab pigeon is served up with hits of pickled onion and cacao. Stone bass is delicately smoked and matched with textures of beetroot, and suckling pig delivers 'the best piece of pork belly I've even eaten' for one reader. Desserts are no less well judged, with the flavours of mint and orange sending a raspberry soufflé into orbit. Wines start at £24.
Chef/s: Tristan Mason. **Open:** Tue to Sat L 12 to 2.30, D 6.30 to 9.30. **Closed:** Sun, Mon. **Meals:** set L £25 (3 courses) to £30. Set D £30 (3 courses) to £45. Tasting Menu £65 (6 courses) to £80. **Details:** 42 seats. Bar. Wheelchairs. Music. Children over 10 yrs only.

◼ Lavant
The Earl of March

Cooking score: 3
Modern British | £35
Lavant Road, Lavant, PO18 0BQ
Tel no: (01243) 533993
theearlofmarch.com

£5 OFF

The Earl is a proper country pub with bucolic views over the Goodwood Estate, and it was here that William Blake wrote 'Jerusalem' back in the early 1800s. A table in the garden delivers the inspirational view. Dining is a major draw, which given the owner's culinary pedigree is no surprise at all – Giles Thompson was head chef at the Ritz and headed up London's Cordon Bleu cookery school. The restaurant area is adorned with images of sports cars and Spitfires, both associated with the local area, and makes a smart setting for the kitchen's classic and modern output. Begin with roast pumpkin and chestnut gnocchi, with burnt apple and goats' curd keeping fashionable company, before an egalitarian fish and chips done properly, whole lemon sole meunière, or duck breast finished with a glossy Madeira jus. To finish, sticky toffee pudding arrives with salted-caramel sauce. Wines start at £18.
Chef/s: Adam Hawden and Giles Thompson. **Open:** all week L 12 to 2.30 (3 Sat and Sun), D 5.30 to 9 (9.30 Fri and Sat, 6 Sun). **Meals:** main courses £16 to £22. Set L and D £22 (2 courses) to £25. **Details:** 70 seats. 50 seats outside. Bar. Wheelchairs. Music. Parking.

◼ Lickfold
The Lickfold Inn

Cooking score: 6
Modern British | £45
Highstead Lane, Lickfold, GU28 9EY
Tel no: (01789) 532535
thelickfoldinn.co.uk

Its Tudor credentials are visible for all to see. The original building dates from the 16th century and still functions as a pub on the ground floor – local real ales, roaring fire in the inglenook – but it's the state-of-the-art glassed-in kitchen adjacent to the bar that is the biggest single clue as to what is going down amid the pretty West Sussex countryside. You don't build a kitchen like that to serve sausage and mash. This is Tom Sellers' country gaff (he of Restaurant Story in London – see entry). Head up to the classy rustic first-floor restaurant to feel the full force of the cutting-edge repertoire showcased by head chef Graham Squire. Creative thinking and contemporary cooking techniques result in complex flavours and imaginative compositions, but not to the detriment of the high-quality ingredients. Foie gras parfait with new-season rhubarb shows acute sensitivity to the balance of flavours, hake keeps company with treacle bacon, salsify and wild mushrooms, and bitter chocolate and blood orange are a perfect match to finish. Wines start at £19.
Chef/s: Graham Squire. **Open:** Wed to Sun L 12 to 3 (5.30 Sun), Wed to Sat D 6 to 9 (9.30 Sat). **Closed:** Mon, Tue, first 2 weeks Jan. **Meals:** main courses £18 to £30. Set L £19 (2 courses) to £25. Sun L £28. **Details:** 40 seats. 20 seats outside. V menu. Bar. Music. Parking.

◼ Lower Beeding
The Crabtree

Cooking score: 2
Modern British | £30
Brighton Road, Lower Beeding, RH13 6PT
Tel no: (01403) 892666
crabtreesussex.co.uk

£5 OFF

Shored up by a good local reputation, this ancient roadside pub has few pretensions beyond providing pints of real ale in the bar, impeccably sourced food in the dining rooms (the oldest dating from the 16th century) and a lovely garden for when the weather co-operates. Simon May has taken over the kitchen since the last edition of the Guide and his food is a mix of traditional British (beer-battered haddock and chips) with modern European touches (fillet of gilt-head bream served with cavolo nero, potato and chive emulsion). That February meal opened with a very good mushroom soup and homemade bread, and roast pigeon, mushrooms and Roquefort risotto, and finished with chocolate brownie and coffee ice cream. There has been praise, too, for Sunday roasts, 'hugely tasty and wholly satisfying, one of the best I've had', for apple and pear crumble with salted caramel and clotted cream, and for friendly, informed service. Wines from £18.

Chef/s: Simon May. **Open:** all week L 12 to 3 (5 Sun), Mon to Sat D 6 to 9.30. **Closed:** 25 Dec. **Meals:** main courses £12 to £23. Set L Mon to Fri £15 (2 courses) to £18. **Details:** 70 seats. 150 seats outside. Bar. Wheelchairs. Music. Parking.

The Pass

Cooking score: 4
Modern British | £70
South Lodge Hotel, Brighton Road, Lower Beeding, RH13 6PS
Tel no: (01403) 891711
southlodgehotel.co.uk

A grandiose 19th-century mansion, originally home to a 'gentleman explorer', South Lodge serves up views over the Sussex countryside to the South Downs. Among a brace of dining options at this swanky hotel is the Pass, a restaurant that puts the diner in the kitchen, and, following the departure of Matt Gillan, it's the domain of Ian Swainson. The no-choice format remains the same – eight or ten courses at dinner – with diners seated at high stools or banquettes, with TV screens showing the pass if you're facing the wall. Not everyone gets a great view, but you do get to meet the chefs as they bring the food to your table. It's early days for the new man. 'What lies beneath' delivers 'a wonderfully sweet onion flavour', 'A potato with its head in the clouds' is gone in a few crunchy seconds, while 'Homage to the cow' was the star for one visitor – tender Jacob's Ladder beef with pickled and raw veg and a sauce that brings whey and curd back together in perfect harmony. Wines start at £27.

Chef/s: Ian Swainson. **Open:** Wed to Sun L 12 to 1.30 (12.30 Sun), D 7 to 8.30. **Closed:** Mon, Tue, 25 Dec, 2 weeks Jan. **Meals:** set L £30 (4 courses) to £60. Set D £70 (6 courses) to £90. **Details:** 28 seats. V menu. Bar. Parking. Children over 12 yrs only.

▌Petworth
The Leconfield

Cooking score: 4
Modern British | £45
New Street, Petworth, GU28 0AS
Tel no: (01798) 345111
theleconfield.co.uk

This large and listed corner house offers the complete package when it comes to the world of smart country town restaurants. Whether you're having a drink in the bar or taking advantage of alfresco tables in the courtyard, it all sets the scene for some exceptional seasonal cooking. Paul Welburn heads the kitchen and his network of suppliers is at the heart of the operation. Crispy pork croquettes ('crunchy outside, tender and flavoursome within') with sticks of green apple, a smoked emulsion and a 'sort of mimosa dressing on top', and 'very prettily presented' tender griddled asparagus with 'duck ham', confit duck egg yolk and chilled asparagus mousse made good openers at a test meal. After that, big seasonal flavours prevailed in roast cod, crusty and golden, served on a bed of white beans and mussels with a 'whipped and light' taramasalata. To finish, try the 'smooth and zingy' toasted lemon parfait, well matched by a Pimms and lemonade sorbet. Wines from £22.

Chef/s: Paul Welburn. **Open:** Wed to Sun L 12 to 3 (4 Sun), Tue to Sat D 6 to 9. **Closed:** Mon, 25 and 26 Dec. **Meals:** main courses £15 to £28. Set L £23 (2 courses) to £27. Set D £25 (2 courses) to £30. Sun L £25. Tasting menu £45. **Details:** 75 seats. 28 seats outside. Bar. Wheelchairs. Music.

Ian Swainson

The Pass, Lower Beeding

What inspired you to become a chef?

At school we were asked to find work experience in an area of interest to us. I mentioned cooking, and fortunately my mother had a friend that owned the East Anglia Hotel in Bournemouth. After my time there, I dedicated my studying in this direction, and that, combined with hard work, is why I am the chef I am today.

What's your favourite dish on your menu, and why?

A dish called 'in the eye of the beholder' consisting of whelks, shrimps, seaweed and oysters. The dish is dressed like an eye looking back at you, with a concept of the beauty of flavour being found in ingredients where we might not normally look to find them.

What food could you not live without?

Bread, I have tried to give it up and it was really not for me. You never realise just how many foods need bread to accompany them!

Which chef do you most admire at the moment?

I draw inspiration from a variety of sources and not just chefs. At the moment I'm really interested in a sculptor called Nancy Fouts as she managed to convey a really powerful image whilst only using a couple of objects.

▌Tangmere
Cassons
Cooking score: 3
Modern British | £39
Arundel Road, Tangmere, PO18 0DU
Tel no: (01243) 773294
cassonsrestaurant.co.uk

The sporty inducements of nearby 'Glorious Goodwood' help to stoke interest in this rather unprepossessing country restaurant, which is run with great enthusiasm and passion by Viv and 'Cass' Casson (she cooks, he attends to front-of-house). Set in a pair of 18th-century farm cottages a couple of miles from Chichester, the whole place feels eminently homely, although the kitchen looks to France for most of its culinary inspiration – albeit with more than a nod to native British ingredients. Fish from the South Coast might include seared scallops with lemon hollandaise, brown shrimps and cucumber, while fans of meat and game could choose, say, smoked duck breast with rémoulade, foie gras pâté and balsamic leaves followed by a mighty plate of suckling pig with beluga lentils, curly kale and cider reduction. To finish, lemon curd ice cream wrapped in clementine sorbet with chocolate aero sounds fun. Wines from £21.
Chef/s: Vivian Casson. **Open:** Wed to Sun L 12 to 1.30 (2 Sun), Tue to Sat D 7 to 9. **Closed:** Mon, Christmas to New Year. **Meals:** set L £17 (2 courses) to £20. Set D £31 (2 courses) to £39. Sun L £23 (2 courses) to £28. **Details:** 38 seats. 14 seats outside. Bar. Wheelchairs. Music. Parking.

▌Tillington
The Horse Guards Inn
Cooking score: 2
British | £30
Upperton Road, Tillington, GU28 9AF
Tel no: (01798) 342332
thehorseguardsinn.co.uk

Named after the Household Cavalry regiment whose men used to frequent the place in Victorian times (when it was already a couple of hundred years old), the Horse Guards looks the business these days. The period character lives on – chunky floorboards, real fires, low ceilings – while the interior dressing is 'eclectic country rustic-chic'. The garden is a real gem, too, with roaming hens and some quirky touches. The kitchen delivers a contemporary slate that might start with pheasant and pork rillettes with pickles and apple chutney, and potted brown shrimps. Next up, locally sourced Aberdeen Angus steaks, or stone bass with roasted fennel and celeriac and black olive salsa, while lunchtime options include a sandwich and classy burger. Buttermilk pudding with blood orange, medjool dates and Sussex honey is a richly satisfying conclusion. The service gets good notices, local real ales are on tap and the wine list kicks off at £17.25.

Chef/s: Mark Robinson. **Open:** all week L 12 to 2.30 (3 Sat, 3.30 Sun), D 6.30 to 9 (9.30 Fri and Sat). **Closed:** 25 and 26 Dec. **Meals:** main courses £10 to £22. **Details:** 50 seats. 40 seats outside. Music.

■ West Ashling
The Richmond Arms

Cooking score: 4
Modern British | £31
Mill Road, West Ashling, PO18 8EA
Tel no: (01243) 572046
therichmondarms.co.uk

£5 OFF

William and Emma Jack 'make the most amazing and passionate team' at this sprucely updated pub-with-rooms on the fringes of the South Downs National Park. The Richmond Arms not only is an 'incredibly popular' community hub and boozy watering hole, but it also offers some of the most skilful and free-spirited food in the area – a jaunty celebration of all things local and seasonal. Eat in the restaurant from a live-wire menu that channels London's globetrotting hipster trends – from trendy BLTs (bacon, lobster, toast) or homemade 'Spam' fritters with mustard maple syrup and white radish to sticky, slow-cooked beef brisket with winter slaw and dripping chips, home-shot hare

lasagne or Kashmiri-spiced BBQ pheasant with 'bubble and sikh'. Fish is from the Sussex day boats, while desserts might run to a Nutella brûlée with Amaretto crunch. Outside, a vintage Citroen van produces wood-fired tapas and pizzas most evenings. Wines from £15.95.

Chef/s: William Jack. **Open:** Wed to Sun L 12 to 2 (3 Sun), Wed to Sat D 6 to 9. **Closed:** Mon, Tue, 23 Dec to 13 Jan, 25 Mar to 5 Apr, 17 to 24 Jul, 28 Oct to 6 Nov. **Meals:** main courses £15 to £27. **Details:** 98 seats. 40 seats outside. Bar. Music. Parking.

■ West Hoathly
The Cat Inn

Cooking score: 2
Modern British | £29
North Lane, West Hoathly, RH19 4PP
Tel no: (01342) 810369
catinn.co.uk

£5 OFF £30

The English pub is under pressure with a couple of dozen closing each week, but the 16th-century Cat is no endangered species. That's partly as it is both a proper pub – full of locals, real ales, real fires, beams – and a pretty decent dining destination to boot. The two personas rub along together very well indeed and the setting opposite the pretty village church is a bonus. A sizeable dining area at the rear leads on to the terrace out back (no views, sadly). The kitchen offers up everything from lunchtime sandwiches, via classy versions of pub classics, to the more rarefied roasted stone bass with spätzle, brown shrimps and wild mushrooms. Localism is alive and well, with well-kept regional ales and artisan cheeses, and a wine list that includes some damn fine fizz from the South East. For dessert, vanilla pannacotta with spiced blackberries and verjus sorbet reveals a broader outlook. Wines start at £18.

Chef/s: Alex Jacquemin. **Open:** all week L 12 to 2 (2.30 Fri to Sun), Mon to Sat D 6 to 9 (Fri and Sat 9.30). **Closed:** 25 Dec. **Meals:** main courses £10 to £26. **Details:** 80 seats. 40 seats outside. Wheelchairs. Parking. Children over 7 yrs only.

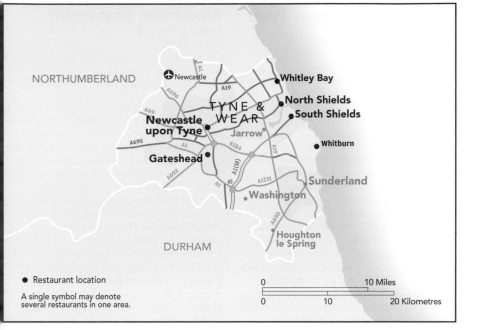

* Restaurant location

A single symbol may denote
several restaurants in one area.

■ Gateshead
Eslington Villa

Cooking score: 2
Modern British | £30
8 Station Road, Low Fell, Gateshead, NE9 6DR
Tel no: (0191) 4876017
eslingtonvilla.co.uk

£5 OFF ▭

A world away from the hustle of Newcastle
and Gateshead, this imposing Victorian villa is
secluded and tranquil, set in two acres of
grounds with splendid views across a bosky
valley. Within, the rather elegant conservatory
dining room overlooks well-manicured,
sloping gardens and is a fittingly serene setting
for cooking that continues to achieve
satisfying results thanks to skilful techniques
and well-sourced ingredients rather than
outlandish ideas. From the good-value set
dinner menu, crispy duck salad, egg noodles,
watercress, beansprouts and sesame oil is
'simple but tasty', a 'remarkably tender' main
course of Chinese slow-cooked beef shin is

served with spiced lentils and wilted pak choi,
its 'bitter crunch' countering the richness of a
dark, glossy sauce, while North Sea hake fillet
comes with Parmesan crust, dauphinois
potatoes and fine beans. Finish with almond
sponge, Lanchester cream, orange jelly and
ginger. Wines from £18, with around a dozen
under the £20 mark.
Chef/s: Jamie Walsh. **Open:** Mon to Sat L 12 to
2.30, D 5.30 to 10 (6.30 Sat). Sun 12 to 9.30. **Closed:**
25 and 26 Dec, 1 Jan. **Meals:** set L and early D £15
(2 courses) to £18. Set D £25 (2 courses) to £29. Sun
L £18 (2 courses) to £21. **Details:** 90 seats. 24 seats
outside. Bar. Wheelchairs. Music. Parking.

Symbols

▭ Accommodation is available
£30 Three courses for less than £30
£5 OFF £5-off voucher scheme
🍾 Notable wine list

▋Newcastle upon Tyne

Artisan

Cooking score: 3
Modern British | £30
The Biscuit Factory, Stoddart Street, Newcastle upon Tyne, NE2 1AN
Tel no: (0191) 2605411
artisannewcastle.com

£5 OFF

After its Victorian heyday, the former Tyne Biscuit Factory became a warehouse for everything from wallpaper and paint to carpets and kitchen furniture, and in 2001 the building was turned into the art space and restaurant it is today – diners can view the contemporary artwork through a glass wall that separates the restaurant from the ground-floor gallery. The tagline here is 'where food is art' and chef Andrew Wilkinson's precisely executed seasonal dishes live up to the billing. Caramelised king scallops, for example, might turn up in a winter menu paired with Jerusalem artichokes, crispy chicken wing and hazelnuts. To follow, a carefully cooked fillet of halibut could be teamed with caramelised fennel, orange and crab mayonnaise, perhaps finishing with vanilla crème brûlée with poached rhubarb and sorbet. A seven-course tasting menu is also available on the first Wednesday of every month. Wines from £16.50.
Chef/s: Andrew Wilkinson. **Open:** all week L 12 to 2.30 (4.30 Sun), Mon to Sat D 5.30 to 9.30. **Closed:** 24 to 26 Dec. **Meals:** main courses £15 to £24. Set L £15 (2 courses) to £20. Set D £20 (2 courses) to £24. Sun L £12 to £19. **Details:** 80 seats. 30 seats outside. Bar. Wheelchairs. Music. Parking.

Visit us online

To find out more about The Good Food Guide, please visit thegoodfoodguide.co.uk

Blackfriars Restaurant

Cooking score: 3
British | £35
Friars Street, Newcastle upon Tyne, NE1 4XN
Tel no: (0191) 2615945
blackfriarsrestaurant.co.uk

Dating from 1239, and originally the site of a 13th-century monastery, Blackfriars was built as the Dominicans' refectory – the current owners proudly lay claim to it being Britain's oldest eating house. It's hugely atmospheric, with its wooden tables and exposed stone walls, while the kitchen sticks to gutsy regional British cooking with good use of seasonal raw materials, along the lines of North Yorkshire wood pigeon with caramelised rhubarb and hazelnuts, and pan-fried Shetland scallops with cauliflower purée, black pudding fritter and crispy bacon. Elsewhere, Northumbrian ribeye steak is teamed with marrow butter, chips and peppercorn sauce, and pan haggerty (a Northumbrian potato, onion and cheese dish) is served with spring greens, poached hen's egg, sage and mustard cream. Desserts are a delight, too, whether sticky toffee pudding with salted-caramel sauce and banana ice cream or Yorkshire rhubarb crumble tart and rhubarb sorbet. The set menu is very good value. House wines from £19.
Chef/s: Christopher Wardale. **Open:** all week L 12 to 2.30 (4 Sun), Mon to Sat D 5.30 to 10. **Closed:** Bank hols. **Meals:** main courses £12 to £25. Set L and D £15 (2 courses) to £18. **Details:** 72 seats. 15 seats outside. Music.

The Broad Chare

Cooking score: 4
Modern British | £24
25 Broad Chare, Newcastle upon Tyne, NE1 3DQ
Tel no: (0191) 2112144
thebroadchare.co.uk

£30

A converted 18th-century warehouse close to the Quayside and the Tyne Bridge, the Broad Chare is part of local food hero Terry

Laybourne's empire. It's opposite the city's law courts and surrounded by lawyers' chambers, and it remains very much a pub downstairs with excellent local ales (they even serve old-school 'black and tan') and bar snacks (hand-raised pork pies; Lindisfarne oysters). Climb the stairs to the dining room – all stripped floors and leather banquettes – and the food is similarly no-frills, with a 'dish of the day' (perhaps braised oxtail on Tuesday or steak and kidney pudding on Thursday). But the kitchen keeps a close eye on the seasons and has a nose-to-tail philosophy, as can be seen in a robust and generous starter of lamb's offal on sourdough toast: sweetbreads, kidney, liver with young onions and a rich tarragon-flecked sauce. That summer meal also produced roast hake with broad beans and smoked bacon, and was followed by a wonderfully wobbly buttermilk cream with poached apricots. Wines from £17.10.
Chef/s: Dan Warren. **Open:** all week L 12 to 2.30 (5 Sun), Mon to Sat D 5.30 to 10. **Closed:** 25 and 26 Dec, 1 Jan. **Meals:** main courses £10 to £20. Sun L £13. **Details:** 46 seats. Bar. Music.

★ NEW ENTRY ★

Cook House
Cooking score: 2
Modern British | £12
20 Ouse Street, Newcastle upon Tyne, NE1 2PF
cookhouse.org
£30

Cook House is well worth a detour. Housed in two shipping containers and sandwiched between the back of Newcastle's Hotel du Vin and a carpet warehouse, close to the river in the Ouseburn Valley (and five minutes from the Quayside next to the Tyne), it started life as a supper club run by food blogger Anna Hedworth and has become one of Newcastle's most talked about local gems. In an open, domestic-sized kitchen Ms Hedworth prepares and cooks everything herself and even serves the food. It's open for breakfast and regular supper club evenings, with the lunch menu kicking in at midday when the daily-changing, six-item blackboard menu might offer roast ham with fennel, radish, mint coleslaw and sourdough, then roast chicken and lovage salad with aïoli and sourdough crumbs. Finish with a local cheese plate, lemon and rosemary posset or cherry and almond cake with a glass of homemade elderflower lemonade – there's no alcohol but you can BYO. Note: it's cash only.
Chef/s: Anna Hedworth. **Open:** Mon to Sat 8.30 to 3.30. **Closed:** Sun. **Meals:** main courses £6 to £8. **Details:** 20 seats. 8 seats outside.

House of Tides
Cooking score: 5
Modern British | £55
28-30 The Close, Newcastle upon Tyne, NE1 3RF
Tel no: (0191) 2303720
houseoftides.co.uk

When much-travelled Geordie chef Kenny Atkinson decided to return to Tyneside, he picked a peach of a site for his homecoming – a Grade I-listed 16th-century merchant's house on Newcastle's Quayside. Mullioned windows, girders and heavy flagstones are reminders of the past in the ground-floor bar, while upstairs rustic heritage meets contemporary chic in the dining room. A parade of innovative modern plates with unimpeachable seasonal credentials means all eyes are on the food, with mackerel, gooseberries, lemon and mustard or a humbler assemblage of Cumbrian hogget with broccoli, kohlrabi, onion and mint revealing a fascinating amalgam of flavours with bags of serious intent and just enough risk-taking to keep everyone on their toes. Top-notch home-baked breads and appetite-piquing snacks (Lindisfarne oyster dressed with cucumber, ginger and caviar, say) add kudos to the set-up, while desserts such as Yorkshire rhubarb with ginger, rosewater and rose ash also doff their cap to the North Country larder. Well-spread international wines start at £28.
Chef/s: Kenny Atkinson. **Open:** Tue to Sat L 12 to 1.30, D 6 to 10. **Closed:** Sun, Mon, 24 Dec to 10 Jan. **Meals:** set L £25 (2 courses) to £30. Set D £45 (2

courses) to £55. Tasting menu L £45, D £60 (6 courses). **Details:** 70 seats. V menu. Bar. Wheelchairs. Music. Parking. Babies at L only.

Jesmond Dene House

Cooking score: 4
Modern European | £40
Jesmond Dene Road, Newcastle upon Tyne, NE2 2EY
Tel no: (0191) 2123000
jesmonddenehouse.co.uk

A formidable Gothic Arts and Crafts mansion in one of Newcastle upon Tyne's swankier suburbs, this elegant contemporary hotel was once home to the industrialist who created nearby Jesmond Dene park. Diners can choose to eat in the peaceful former music room or in the lighter, less formal conservatory overlooking the immaculate grounds. Michael Penaluna keeps his cooking admirably simple, his confident dishes proudly showcasing top-drawer ingredients from named local suppliers. Starters might include smoked haddock, parsley risotto, tempura kale and pickled lemon, while mains take in the likes of confit pork belly with black pudding fritter, carrot, glazed shallot and pancetta. Portions are generous, but it is worth finding space for desserts such as dark chocolate sphere with salted caramel, peanuts and caramel ice cream. The wine list trawls the globe for interesting bottles and there are bargains to be had under £30 (including the house at £22), with around 20 by the glass or carafe.
Chef/s: Michael Penaluna. **Open:** all week 12 to 9.30. **Meals:** main courses £15 to £35. Set L and early D £19 (2 courses) to £21. Sun L £22 (2 courses) to £26. **Details:** 60 seats. 20 seats outside. Bar. Wheelchairs. Music. Parking.

Peace & Loaf

Cooking score: 4
Modern British | £36
217 Jesmond Road, Newcastle upon Tyne, NE2 1LA
Tel no: (0191) 2815222
peaceandloaf.co.uk
£5
OFF

With its punning name and fashionably ramshackle approach to design, Peace & Loaf certainly reflects the mood of our times. The location in an anonymous row of shops adds to the allure and 'it's not a dressy place but anything goes, which adds to the relaxed style,' while easy-going and affable service fits the bill. Chef-owner David Coulson was a finalist in *MasterChef: The Professionals* and brings his brand of innovative contemporary British food to an appreciative public. There's no lack of refinement on show, with a tasting menu for the big spenders and a great-value prix fixe early doors. Off the main menu, cured cod with bone marrow and braised lamb shoulder with turnip spaghetti and salsa verde arrive as contemporary-looking plates delivering clearly defined flavours. There's playfulness, too, with a 'cheeky Nando's-like' piri-piri guinea fowl ('absolutely fabulous'), or play it straight with stone bass with scampi dressing and seaweed risotto, and finish with 'boozy sorbet of the day'. Wines start at £17.95.
Chef/s: David Coulson. **Open:** all week L 12 to 2.30 (2 Sat, 3.30 Sun), Mon to Sat D 5.30 to 9.30. **Closed:** 25 and 26 Dec, 1 Jan. **Meals:** main courses £16 to £25. Set L £15 (2 courses) to £20. Set D £20 (2 courses) to £25. Sun L £15. Tasting menu £70 (10 courses). **Details:** 53 seats. Wheelchairs. Music.

21

Cooking score: 3
Modern British | £40
Trinity Gardens, Quayside, Newcastle upon
Tyne, NE1 2HH
Tel no: (0191) 2220755
21newcastle.co.uk

Eight years after Terry Laybourne moved his
flagship restaurant from Queen Street to this
larger site at the back of Newcastle's Crown
Courts, it's been given a makeover and new
identity. Now simply called 21, the stylish
dining room has a warmer, richer look but the
service is as polished as ever. The brasserie style
of the menu hasn't changed, either, and the
kitchen continues to send out carefully cooked
classics. Seared scallops with bacon, garlic
butter and cauliflower is a tried-and-tested
starter, as is a terrine of ham knuckle and foie
gras served with pease pudding, while main
courses could be something as simple and well
executed as a generous plate of monkfish
medallions with tenderstem broccoli and
romesco sauce, or slow-cooked shoulder of
beef in red wine, glazed onions and carrots. To
finish, an intensely flavoured banana soufflé
('un-improvably good') with 'an impressive
chocolate swirl running through' was
partnered by peanut-butter ice cream. A
thoughtful wine list starts at £18.90.
Chef/s: Chris Dobson. **Open:** Mon to Sat L 12 to
2.30, D 5.30 to 10.30. Sun 12 to 8. **Closed:** 25 and
26 Dec, 1 Jan, Easter Mon. **Meals:** main courses £16
to £30. Set L and D £19 (2 courses) to £22. Sun L £19
(2 courses) to £22. **Details:** 130 seats. Bar.
Wheelchairs. Music.

LOCAL GEM
Caffè Vivo
Italian | £30
29 Broad Chare, Newcastle upon Tyne,
NE1 3DQ
Tel no: (0191) 2321331
caffevivo.co.uk

Terry Laybourne's lively Italian eatery, based at
Live Theatre just off the Newcastle quayside, is
an infectious, buzzy place and there is good
eating to be had. There are three menus – à la
carte, menu of the day and a specials board –
and the cooking is confident, ranging from
borlotti bean soup with herb pesto, via a
traditional lasagne, to devilled spring chicken
with lemon, spinach and rosemary roast
potatoes. Honey-roast peaches with vanilla ice
cream has been a particular delight. The
(almost) all-Italian wine list (from £16) offers
plenty by the glass.

LOCAL GEM
Cal's Own
Italian | £24
1-2 Holly Avenue, Newcastle upon Tyne,
NE2 2AR
Tel no: (0191) 2815522
calsown.co.uk
£30

Since moving from their BYOB takeaway-
cum-restaurant in Heaton last year, brothers
Kerry and Cal Kitchin have seriously stepped
things up in their new pizza restaurant in the
heart of Jesmond. They've retained the
character and charm that first made them a hit,
but the new venue has an elegant design, a
purpose-built bar area and additional menu
items that give Cal's Own a much more
refined feel. Couple this with a hand-built
pizza oven imported from Naples and
Neapolitan-style pizza and you're in for a slice
of pizza heaven. Cal ensures all products are
the finest Italy has to offer; an equally
meticulous approach to his pizza dough, and a
thoughtful wine list, make this a truly
authentic experience. No bookings.

Please send us your feedback

To register your opinion about any
restaurant listed in this guide, or a new
restaurant that you wish to bring to our
attention, please visit the web address at
the bottom of the page. Your feedback
informs the content of the book and will
be used to compile next year's reviews.

∎ North Shields

Irvins Brasserie

Cooking score: 3
Modern British | £25
Union Road, The Fish Quay, North Shields,
NE30 1HJ
Tel no: (0191) 2963238
irvinsbrasserie.co.uk
£5 £30
OFF

With its broad stone arches, the building could almost have been a fire station, but the location says differently. It was once the fishing store for trawlers that put out on the North Sea. These days, it fulfils an equally vital purpose as an all-day brasserie, opening for breakfasts at a civilised 9am and chugging on through the day with simple menus of impeccably fresh, enlivening food, from snacks of smoked haddock Scotch eggs and vinaigretted clams to sophisticated indulgences such as fig frangipane tart with ginger ice cream. In between, there are fish options that do justice to the architectural heritage, such as roast halibut with brown shrimps and mash, or baked hake with lentils and chorizo, and comforting meats like calf's liver and bacon or roast rack of lamb. Capable staff keep things running smoothly, and there's a petite wine list starting at £17.50, on which most listings are available by the glass (from £4.50).
Chef/s: Graeme Cuthell. **Open:** Wed to Sun 9am to 10pm (7.30pm Sun). **Closed:** Mon, Tue. **Meals:** main courses £11 to £21. Set L and D £12 (2 courses) to £17. Sun L £21 (3 courses). **Details:** 70 seats. 8 seats outside. Bar. Wheelchairs. Music.

The Staith House

Cooking score: 2
Modern British | £28
57 Low Lights, Fish Quay, North Shields,
NE30 1JA
Tel no: (0191) 2708441
thestaithhouse.co.uk
£5 £30
OFF

'By far my favourite place to eat locally' gives notice that chef John Calton has settled into his role as proprietor of this abidingly popular modern pub overlooking North Shields' Fish Quay – although he isn't about to neglect his cooking duties. Bare tables, reclaimed wood and exposed brick walls, along with a few portholes and maritime knick-knacks, create a laid-back vibe, while the food shows just the right amount of ambition for such an understated local asset. The menu of retooled pub classics eschews pretension in favour of big, hearty flavours. Fish and chips, steaks or an excellent halibut with chip-shop curry sauce, black pudding and chunky chips are its stock-in-trade, but there's also crab soup with local crab mayo on toast, rump of lamb with braised spelt, Berkswell cheese, capers and fresh mint, and dark chocolate fondant with peanut-butter and Horlicks ice cream. Wines from £17.50.
Chef/s: John Calton and James Laffan. **Open:** all week L 12 to 3 (3.30 Sat, 4 Sun), Mon to Sat D 6 to 9 (9.30 Fri and Sat). **Closed:** 25 and 26 Dec, 1 and 2 Jan. **Meals:** main courses £11 to £25. **Details:** 45 seats. 16 seats outside. Wheelchairs. Music.

■ South Shields

LOCAL GEM

Colmans

Seafood | £15

182-186 Ocean Road, South Shields,
NE33 2JQ
Tel no: (0191) 4561202
colmansfishandchips.com

£30

In the same family since 1926, the current
generation of Colmans to run this fish and
chip shop have very sensibly kept all that made
it great in the first place while embracing
newfangled ideas like sustainability. The
service is super-friendly (note they don't take
bookings), the menu has a lot of choice,
including grilled Dover sole and lobster, Thai
fishcakes, and calamari with chilli sauce, while
the mainstay remains battered cod and
haddock. The chips are the business, and a
short wine list starts at £14.95.

■ Whitburn

LOCAL GEM

Latimer's

Seafood | £25

Shell Hill, Bents Road, Whitburn, SR6 7NT
Tel no: (0191) 5292200
latimers.com

£30

Independent fishmonger Robert Latimer
offers up no-frills seafood in this simple café
with a decked terrace serving up a view of the
beach. They don't take bookings, so rock up
and take a chance, and bring a bottle if you
want some booze (corkage is £3). Check the
blackboard to see what's on the Scandi-style
seafood platter (herring with pickled
beetroot, maybe), dive into a 'boat' of local
langoustines or go for something hot such as
Cullen skink. The crab sandwich is a winner.

■ Whitley Bay

LOCAL GEM

The Roxburgh

British | £20

4 Roxburgh House, Park Avenue, Whitley Bay,
NE26 1DQ
Tel no: (07794) 554020

£30

A super little café where décor is simple (bare
brick, polished wood tables) matched by a
menu of breakfast favourites, with bread,
sausages, black pudding, baked beans, ketchup
and hash browns all made in-house. A
straightforward bistro menu is served on
Saturday nights, when the likes of Arbroath
smokie and Cheddar soufflé, 12-hour-cooked
lamb with buttery mash and gravy (for two to
share), beef short rib and beet 'jam sandwich'
and white chocolate doughnuts have delighted
– and there's stellar roast beef on Sundays.
BYO helps keep prices in check.

Local Gem

Local Gems are the perfect
neighbourhood venues, delivering
good, freshly cooked food at great
value for money.

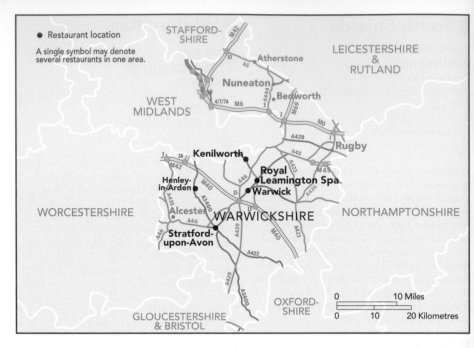

Henley-in-Arden
The Bluebell
Cooking score: 3
Modern British | £34
93 High Street, Henley-in-Arden, B95 5AT
Tel no: (01564) 793049
bluebellhenley.co.uk

This black-and-white free house has proper historic credentials in a town not short of an ancient building or two – 1513, they say. Local ales are stocked in the bar, where a plate of 'Warwickshire tapas' is up for grabs, or head through to the restaurant to get the measure of this kitchen's nifty modern British output. Midweek and Saturday during the day give the option of a 'classic' such as a Herefordshire beef burger or moules-frites, while the main carte turns out a starter of braised pig's cheek with lobster bisque, or another where Barkham Blue cheese finds its way into croquettes. Main-course halibut arrives with a cassoulet of butter beans and chorizo, and Gressingham chicken comes in the rather refined company of parsnip purée, charred baby leeks and smoked almonds. To finish, a sunny orange and mascarpone cheesecake is matched with milk ice cream and honeycomb. Wines start at £19.
Chef/s: Andrew Taylor. **Open:** Tue to Sun L 12 to 2.30 (3.30 Sun), Tue to Sat D 6 to 9.30. **Closed:** Mon. **Meals:** main courses £14 to £23. **Details:** 50 seats. 40 seats outside. Bar. Music. Parking. Children over 12 yrs only at D.

★ NEW ENTRY ★

Cheal's of Henley
Cooking score: 5
British | £50
64 High Street, Henley-in-Arden, B95 5BX
Tel no: (01564) 793856
chealsofhenley.co.uk

This prettily wonky old house is full of charming irregularities with rooms on varying levels, weathered beams and a layout that defies symmetry. The smart white tablecloths are a statement of intent, though –

this is a restaurant with ambition, chef Matt Cheal's first solo venture since departing Simpsons in Edgbaston (see entry). He creates dishes of real interest and complexity – note a beguiling opener of crispy duck egg yolk, Jerusalem artichoke risotto, goats' cheese and wild garlic, the egg spilling into the flowing, perfectly al dente risotto that impressed at inspection. There are times when the balance wavers: a main course of Cornish brill with squid, mussels, violet potatoes, samphire, rouille and saffron sauce included 'very salty' spinach, but delighted nonetheless. The supporting cast includes 'some of the best sourdough I've ever had' and a 'cauliflower cheese' amuse full of rich umami flavours. A chilled, dainty tarte Tatin paled slightly in contrast, but was bolstered by a magnificently light, boozy Calvados ice cream. Wines – many from France – start at £20 a bottle, and there are some keenly priced carafes.

Chef/s: Matt Cheal. **Open:** Wed to Sun L 12 to 2 (2.30 Sun), Wed to Sat D 7 to 9 (6.30 to 9.30 Fri and Sat). **Closed:** Mon, Tue, 25 to 27 Dec, 1 week Apr, 2 weeks Aug. **Meals:** set L £23 (2 courses) to £30. Set D £30 (2 courses) to £40. Sun L £40. **Details:** 40 seats. V menu. Music.

▉ Kenilworth
The Cross at Kenilworth
Cooking score: 6
Modern British | £50
16 New Street, Kenilworth, CV8 2EZ
Tel no: (01926) 853840
thecrosskenilworth.co.uk

'This is the future of fine dining,' thought one reporter of a meal at the 'remarkable' Cross, where pubby relaxation and high-end cooking run happily in tandem. You can order steak and chips or sophisticated modern European dishes from the same menu, and enjoy them amid a happy buzz and bustle with no whiff of starched formality. That said, the service is right on the money and while there is a proper bar, the main dining room (hall-like, with high ceilings, a grand fireplace and clubby banquettes) is a far cry from your regular pub. One triumphant meal opened

with crispy duck egg, celeriac, mushroom purée, English cured ham and truffle – a seamless run of flavours, from buttery yolk to darkly umami mushroom. A main course of ruby red venison fillet with haggis, crunchy-buttery potato terrine, lingonberries, vivid green kale and intense Laphroaig sauce was equally stunning, full of richly rounded flavours and textural contrasts, while a dessert of chai pannacotta with mango, coconut tuiles and coconut sorbet provided a floral, softly spiced spin on a classic dessert. This is cooking with a 'wow factor', washed down with a decent selection of beers or interesting wines from a France-weighted list, with many bottles under £30.

Chef/s: Adam Bennett. **Open:** all week L 12 to 2 (2.30 Sat, 4 Sun), Mon to Sat D 6.30 to 10 (6 Fri and Sat). **Closed:** 25 and 26 Dec, 1 Jan. **Meals:** main courses £24 to £30. Set L £25 (2 courses) to £30. Sun L £30. Tasting menu £65. **Details:** 74 seats. 20 seats outside. V menu. Bar. Wheelchairs. Music. Parking.

▉ Leamington Spa
Restaurant 23
Cooking score: 4
Modern British | £44
34 Hamilton Terrace, Leamington Spa, CV32 4LY
Tel no: (01926) 422422
restaurant23.co.uk
£5 OFF

The cream-coloured Georgian building does a resourceful job at encompassing everything that Leamington sophisticates might require in a dining venue. A private dining library, lounge and patio are only the half of it, with Morgan's, a stylish cocktail bar, and the main restaurant on hand to flesh out the deal. Peter Knibb lives up to the striking setting with vigorous renditions of modern British food, in which combinations of ingredients are never less than apposite. Beetroot and pickled cherries add sweet-and-sour notes to a starter of smoked squab and black pudding, while crab bisque is the medium for a positively old-school raviolo of Loch Duart salmon and crab. At main, multi-layering achieves convincing impact for dishes such as Middle White pork with barley, artichoke, morels and asparagus, or the fried brill that comes in a mussel ragoût with sea veg. Finish with lemon and poppy seed cake, bergamot curd and goats' milk sorbet. Wines open at £24.

Chef/s: Peter Knibb. **Open:** Tue to Sat L 12 to 2, D 6 to 9.45. **Closed:** Sun, Mon, 25 and 26 Dec, 2 weeks Jan, 2 weeks Aug. **Meals:** main courses £22 to £29. Set L £17 (2 courses) to £21. Tasting menu £55 (6 courses) to £70. **Details:** 70 seats. 35 seats outside. Bar. Music.

■ Stratford-upon-Avon
No. 9 Church St
Cooking score: 2
Modern British | £35
9 Church Street, Stratford-upon-Avon, CV37 6HB
Tel no: (01789) 415522
no9churchst.com

'There is real passion here and it shines through on the plate,' noted one visitor to this smart but relaxed little restaurant in the heart of Stratford-upon-Avon. It's a venerable building with the kitchen downstairs and the dining area upstairs, so expect a bit of a climb to your table. Framed menus from the UK's most iconic restaurants testify to some dedicated research, and the result is creative and ambitious cooking combining modern European recipes and great British ingredients. A quail Kiev served in watercress and wild garlic soup impressed with its 'textural contrasts and pinpoint seasoning', while 'beautifully fresh' stone bass fillet with crab arancini, baby spinach, fennel, tomato and saffron proved a sophisticated main. Desserts display equal care and complexity: witness glazed blood-orange cream with raspberry compote, warm madeleines and almond brittle. Wines from £15.50.

Chef/s: Wayne Thomson. **Open:** Tue to Sat L 12 to 2, D 5 to 9.30. **Closed:** Sun, Mon, 25 and 26 Dec, 1 week Nov, bank hols. **Meals:** main courses £14 to £22. Set L and early D £14 (2 courses) to £18. Tasting menu £40 (5 courses) to £60. **Details:** 40 seats. Bar. Music.

■ Warwick
Tailors
Cooking score: 3
Modern British | £40
22 Market Place, Warwick, CV34 4SL
Tel no: (01926) 410590
tailorsrestaurant.co.uk

Long-time cheffing buddies Dan Cavell and Mark Fry are determined to have some fun at their bijou restaurant wedged into Warwick's Market Square, and they continue to amuse, challenge and satisfy with their highly intricate, but mischievous cooking. How about a freewheeling 'breakfast' starter of cornflake doughnuts with ewe's milk cheese and crumble, onion purée, pickled onions, bacon jam and nasturtium leaves or the cheeky 'ham, mushroom and pine-apple' (gammon hock, pine-scented sponge, burnt apple purée and winter truffle)? Mains follow a slightly more orthodox path (loin and ragoût of Stowell Park venison with red cabbage, roasted celeriac, wholegrain mustard and onion jus, say), while desserts with names such as 'Rhubarb and Custard' (marinated rhubarb with vanilla custard and chocolate soil) take their cue from the sweet shop. Set lunches and early-evening deals are terrific value, and the wine list (from £18.95) also keeps its prices in check.

Chef/s: Dan Cavell and Mark Fry. **Open:** Tue to Sat L 12 to 1.30, D 6.30 to 8.45. **Closed:** Sun, Mon, 2 weeks Christmas. **Meals:** set L £18 (2 courses) to £23. Set D £30 (2 courses) to £40. Tasting menu £65 (6 courses). **Details:** 28 seats. V menu. Music. Children over 10 yrs only.

Please send us your feedback

To register your opinion about any restaurant listed in this guide, or a new restaurant that you wish to bring to our attention, please visit the web address at the bottom of the page. Your feedback informs the content of the book and will be used to compile next year's reviews.

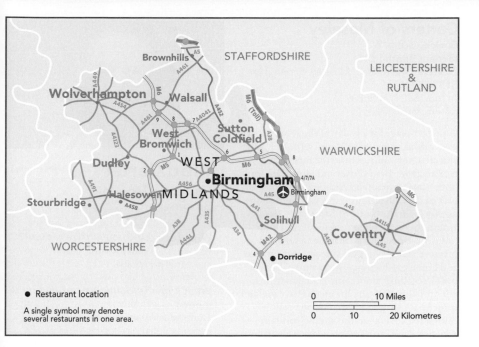

Birmingham

Adam's

Cooking score: 7
Modern British | £60
New Oxford House, 16 Waterloo Street,
Birmingham, B2 5UG
Tel no: (0121) 6433745
adamsrestaurant.co.uk
£5
OFF

Adam Stokes' new venue looks as though it means business with a bold glass frontage and a spacious restaurant that manages to feel simultaneously smart, formal and intimate. Mr Stokes' appeal is simple, direct and unfussy food that is easy to understand. High-quality materials are handled well, seen in the opening salvo of four delicious appetisers: beetroot meringue with goats' cheese; steak tartare with a mini egg yolk; crab on crispy chicken skin; and tempura prawns in a warm béarnaise sauce. Dishes often have a classic air about them, say veal sweetbread with cauliflower slivers, air-dried ham and tiny cubes of fantastic, well-flavoured homemade black pudding and a purée of golden raisins ('a perfect start'), and sea trout with apple, broad beans and oregano, revealing a chef who has tailored his food to the needs of customers rather than aiming to show off how clever he is. Reporters find desserts equally impressive – a delicate confection of fresh raspberries, raspberry sorbet, violet, milk and almond cream, for instance – and have heaped praise on the sourdough bread and smoked pork fat. The set-price lunch is a comparative bargain, service is 'superb, very well trained', and wines are a bright collection, a skilful blend of modern styles and traditional flavours providing an apt complement to the cuisine. Bottles from £23.

Chef/s: Adam Stokes. **Open:** Tue to Sat L 12 to 2, D 7 to 9.30. **Closed:** Sun, Mon, 2 weeks Dec to Jan, 2 weeks summer. **Meals:** set L £28 (2 courses) to £35. Set D £45 (2 courses) to £60. Tasting menu £85 (9 courses). **Details:** 46 seats. Bar. Wheelchairs. Music.

Carters of Moseley

Cooking score: 6
Modern British | £35
2c Wake Green Road, Moseley, Birmingham,
B13 9EZ
Tel no: (0121) 4498885
cartersofmoseley.co.uk

'A perfect place for any day of the week; not pretentious, just perfect.' A real sense of loyalty and affection radiates from the reports we receive about Brad Carter and Holly Jackson's understated restaurant. Although the location isn't exactly auspicious – in a parade of shops not far from the centre of Moseley – Brad's ambitious and refined cooking is noted for industriousness and dedication to seasonal produce and makes a big impact. Provenance and home production – including baking bread, foraging, preserving – makes this an enterprising place and his menus have yielded some seriously good stuff. For one couple dining in November, this meant 'brilliant appetisers', Orkney scallop with an 'intense' mushroom broth, monkfish, artichoke and smoked bacon fat, and 'one of the best partridge dishes we've ever had'. Standout dishes in February included skrei cod with green kale and whey butter, red deer with parsnips and black cardamom, and English apple tart with bay leaf ice cream. There's genuine front-of-house warmth, and the concise but interesting selection of wines opens at £24.
Chef/s: Brad Carter. **Open:** Tue to Sat L 12 to 1.45, D 6.30 to 9.30. **Closed:** Sun, Mon, first 2 weeks Jan, first 2 weeks Aug. **Meals:** set L £35 to £55 (5 courses). Set D £60 (5 courses) to £75 (7 courses). **Details:** 32 seats. V menu. Wheelchairs. Music. Parking. Children over 8 yrs only.

Brad Carter

Carters of Moseley,
Birmingham

What food could you not live without?
I couldn't live without eggs, they feature in most of my meals.

What's your favourite dish on your menu?
Our menus are very ingredient-led, so the dishes change a lot, I'm very keen on ancient rare breeds of meat like Manx lamb and Tamworth pork.

What is the most unusual preparation technique you use?
We sometimes blow-dry mushrooms! It's a great way of keeping them longer after washing.

Which chef do you most admire at the moment?
My sous chef! He has been with me from day one and keeps on giving and progressing daily. Behind every great chef lies an amazing sous chef…

And finally…tell us something about yourself that will surprise your diners.
I haven't missed a service in five years – and I plan to hit 25 years never having missed one too!

Edmunds

Cooking score: 3
French | £50
6 Brindleyplace, Birmingham, B1 2JB
Tel no: (0121) 6334944
edmundsrestaurant.co.uk

Unashamedly bearing the 'fine dining' moniker, Edmunds is a posh modern restaurant in the canalside Brindleyplace development, where classically inspired contemporary French cuisine is the order of the day. It's all 'very tasteful and monochrome' within, and the Franco-Brummie service suits the mood. Six- or eight-course tasting menus allow chef Didier Philipot to show his mettle, but the à la carte still feels 'special occasion' with its amuse-bouche (asparagus soup, say, flavoured with truffle oil), and a pre-dessert such as a lemon posset and raspberry number. Asparagus might appear again in a first course with whipped goats' cheese and lightly pickled beetroots, or go for Périgord duck liver with mango and raisin chutney. Sea bass arrives with freshwater shrimps and a bouillabaisse sauce poured at the table, and Welsh Black beef with girolles, parsnip purée and port jus. Finish with Cointreau and orange soufflé.
Chef/s: Didier Philipot. **Open:** Tue to Fri L 12 to 2, Tue to Sat D 5.30 to 10. **Closed:** Sun, Mon. **Meals:** £45 (2 courses) to £50 (3 courses). Set L and early D £25 (3 courses). Tasting menu £59 (6 courses) to £75. **Details:** 40 seats.

Lasan

Cooking score: 3
Indian | £40
3-4 Dakota Buildings, James Street, St Paul's Square, Birmingham, B3 1SD
Tel no: (0121) 2123664
lasan.co.uk
£5 OFF

From its plush interior to its inventive, artfully presented dishes, Lasan sings a different tune from your average Birmingham curry house. Set in a quiet area not far from the city centre and within walking distance of the cathedral, it delighted one visitor with 'delicate and subtle' spicing and 'possibly the best naan bread I have ever tasted'. After aperitifs in the 'large welcoming lounge', settle in to the split-level dining room for a meal that opens with an amuse-bouche and complimentary dainty poppadoms. The cooking makes a feature of top-drawer British ingredients, as in a starter of free-range Wiltshire Downlands lamb cutlet with a soft galouti patty, lightly pickled onion and green chutney, or a main course of Devon Creedy Carver duck, pan-roasted and served with spiced confit leg, South Indian cabbage poriyal, and traditional Hyderabadi peanut and sesame-seed gravy. To finish, try Bombay mess. The 'reasonably priced' wine list is helpfully annotated and divided by style. Bottles start at £19.
Chef/s: Aktar Islam. **Open:** Mon to Fri L 12 to 2, Mon to Sat D 6 to 10.30. Sun 12 to 9. **Closed:** 25 Dec. **Meals:** main courses £17 to £25. Set L and D £30 (2 courses) to £40. **Details:** 74 seats. Bar. Wheelchairs. Music. Children over 10 yrs only.

Opus

Cooking score: 2
Modern British | £37
54 Cornwall Street, Birmingham, B3 2DE
Tel no: (0121) 2002323
opusrestaurant.co.uk

'Opus remains extremely consistent,' summed up one regular to this contemporary brasserie in Birmingham's commercial quarter. Floor-to-ceiling windows, comfortable chairs and white-clothed tables, well-drilled service, a genuinely buzzy atmosphere and a kitchen that cooks with confidence have ensured that Opus continues to attract local custom after more than a decade. The modern British menu is built around what's best at the market that day, with an inspection meal displaying 'a degree of technical nous'. It opened with pink, juicy breast of squab pigeon accompanied by a full-flavoured stuffed leg and textures of red onion (including a marmalade and purée), went on to a 'delicate and precisely cooked' steamed fillet of wild turbot that was teamed with two fat, perfectly timed Brixham scallops and served with an intensely flavoured broccoli purée, layered potato cake and crab mayo. To finish, a deconstructed apple and ginger cake with baked baby apples and toffee sauce. Wines start at £19.95.

Chef/s: Ben Ternent. **Open:** Mon to Fri and Sun L 12 to 2.15 (3 Sun), Mon to Sat D 6 to 9.30. **Closed:** 24 Dec to 2 Jan, bank hols. **Meals:** main courses £13 to £26. Set L and D £14 (2 courses) to £16. Sun L £25. **Details:** 85 seats. Bar. Wheelchairs. Music.

Purnell's

Cooking score: 5
Modern British | £68
55 Cornwall Street, Birmingham, B3 2DH
Tel no: (0121) 2129799
purnellsrestaurant.com

£5 OFF

Although Birmingham's most celebrated home-grown chef Glynn Purnell now has two strings to his bow (see Purnell's Bistro), his flagship in the city's financial district looks to be on top form judging by recent reports citing everything from the 'glorious' five-course grazing lunch to the 'fabulous' seasonal tasting menu – 'simply the best meal we've had here'. A minor refurb in 2015 saw the inclusion of a new 'window slot' allowing views into the kitchen; otherwise, the overall package is much the same as before, namely dynamic contemporary cooking with a fondness for fascinating forays down memory lane. Purnell's monkfish masala tips its hat to Brum's balti houses, and there are retro 'cheese and pineapple' tacos to nibble, but the star turns sit nearer to the cutting edge: cured sea trout with watermelon, cucumber ketchup and apple jelly; poached duck egg yolk with cauliflower, black pudding, bacon and birch syrup; 'really rich but deliciously warm' chocolate tart with caramelised bananas, frozen yoghurt and salted caramel. Service is 'extremely professional', and the 'wine book' is filled with fine drinking from £25.

Chef/s: Glynn Purnell. **Open:** Tue to Fri L 12 to 1.30, Tue to Sat D 7 to 9 (Sat 6.30 to 9.30). **Closed:** Sun, Mon, 2 weeks Christmas, 1 week Easter, 2 weeks

Aug. **Meals:** set L £35 to £45 (5 courses). Tasting menu £68 (6 courses) to £88 (9 courses). **Details:** 45 seats. Bar. Music. Children over 10 yrs only.

Purnell's Bistro

Cooking score: 2
Modern British | £30
11 Newhall Street, Birmingham, B3 3NY
Tel no: (0121) 2001588
purnellsbistro-gingers.com

A friendly buzz of contentment radiates from the sleek, light-wood and leather-toned interior of Glynn Purnell's bistro, not far from New Street station. At the front, Ginger's Bar plays to the crowds with slouchy leather sofas, tapas-high tables, an enterprising cocktail list and bar snacks such as smoked bacon Scotch egg or a plate of hand-cut chips with roasted garlic mayo and ketchup. In the pair of dining rooms at the back there's a stylish informality that embraces the service as much as the food – a formula that attracts a full house. The food has a deep reassurance about it, thanks not least to breast of lamb croquette with split peas and mint, stone bass with roasted cauliflower, pearl barley and shrimps, and coconut parfait with pineapple sorbet and pineapple. Elsewhere, reporters have praised the home-baked focaccia, the Sunday roast beef and the friendliness of the staff. Wines from £17.75.

Chef/s: Glynn Purnell. **Open:** all week L 12 to 2 (3 Sat, 4 Sun), Mon to Sat D 6.30 to 9.30 (5 Sat). **Closed:** 25 to 31 Dec, 1 Jan. **Meals:** main courses £15 to £20. Set L and D £16 (2 courses) to £20. Sun L £20. **Details:** 70 seats. Bar. Wheelchairs. Music.

Please send us your feedback

To register your opinion about any restaurant listed in this guide, or a new restaurant that you wish to bring to our attention, please visit the web address at the bottom of the page. Your feedback informs the content of the book and will be used to compile next year's reviews.

★ TOP 50 ★

Simpsons

Cooking score: 7
Modern British | £55
20 Highfield Road, Edgbaston, Birmingham,
B15 3DU
Tel no: (0121) 4543434
simpsonsrestaurant.co.uk

Not every city restaurant is about exposed ducting and bare light bulbs. Simpsons occupies a strikingly handsome Grade II-listed mansion in Edgbaston. Since our last edition, an extension to the dining has seen a new spacious room opening out on to the manicured lawn and outdoor seating, with views into the huge kitchen on the opposite side. Blond woods and a skylight contribute to the lightness of tone. It all makes for a comfortable context in which to experience Luke Tipping's contemporary British stylings, which continue to scale new heights of sophistication and technical dazzle. Start perhaps with a tender cheek of pork teamed with smoked eel, roasted shallots in onion ash and a foaming cream sauce, or the DIY fun of a heritage tomato and lobster salad, which comes with a savoury tomato and coriander tea for swirling into and slurping from the emptied bowl. At main, brined turbot is a sensation, timed to flaking translucence with a roasted courgette flower, tiny shrimps and charred fennel, while the lamb dish that takes in roasted belly, a pink cutlet and sweetbread fritter with sheep's curd and a salad of radishes and beans is a harmonious spring display. If you think you know everything a soufflé can do, think again. Tipping's hazelnut version is a sizeable but graceful specimen, its mousse-like interior a little underdone but gorgeous, or there may be superb gold-leafed Brazilian Itakuja chocolate torte with mango sorbet and eye-watering passion fruit brûlée. An enterprising wine list sets off around the world with its grape-variety hat on, and there are many fine producers. Prices open at £26.

Chef/s: Luke Tipping. Open: all week L 12 to 2 (5 Sun), Mon to Sat D 7 to 9 (9.30 Fri and Sat). Closed: 25 and 26 Dec, bank hols. Meals: set L £45 (3 courses). Set D £55 (3 courses). Sun L £55. Tasting menu £85. Details: 80 seats. 20 seats outside. V menu. Wheelchairs. Parking.

Turners

Modern British
69 High Street, Harborne, Birmingham,
B17 9NS
Tel no: (0121) 4264440
turnersrestaurantbirmingham.co.uk

Numbered among a fistful of 'big' restaurants scattered across increasingly food-aware Brum, Richard Turner's modest gaff is secreted in the leafy suburban environs of Harborne – a 10-minute drive from the city centre. The modest shop frontage gives little away, but inside is a small 26-cover dining room known for its assured modern British cooking and score of 5 in the 2016 edition of this Guide. However, as we went to press, we learnt that Mr Turner is planning a complete overhaul of his restaurant and cooking style. When the restaurant reopens after its annual August (2016) holiday, the £90 tasting menu will no longer be offered, cast aside for a simpler, more affordable à la carte focusing on classic dishes and casual eating in a more relaxed environment; there are plans to extend opening times, too. Please check the restaurant's website for more details.

Chef/s: Richard Turner. Open: Fri and Sat L 12 to 2, Tue to Sat D 6 to 9.30. Closed: Sun, Mon. Details: 26 seats. Wheelchairs. Music. Children over 12 yrs only.

Symbols

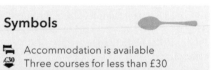

🍴 Accommodation is available
£30 Three courses for less than £30
£5 OFF £5-off voucher scheme
🍷 Notable wine list

Two Cats Kitchen

Cooking score: 2
Baltic-Russian | £44
27 Warstone Lane, Jewellery Quarter,
Birmingham, B18 6JQ
Tel no: (0121) 2120070
twocatskitchen.com

Beginning life as a transient pop-up, the feline duo has now made a more permanent home in a former gold forge in the Jewellery Quarter of the city. The focus is nouveau Baltic and Russian cuisine, drawing on the theoretically more restricted repertoire of chilly northern climes to produce tasting menus that are defiantly protean in their resourcefulness. Look at the opener of cured and smoked ox heart pastrami that comes with 29 accompanying ingredients, including linseed crackers, edible flowers and bundles of finely chopped herbs. Successive dishes offer squid ribbons and kohlrabi in dashi with pork crackles, and the signature lovage-oiled goats' cheese pelmeni. The main meat has been perfectly rendered pigeon in a nest of deep-fried potato with pine sprigs and grated summer truffle, while the finale could be a study in elderflower, its floral fragrance lighting up a cake, pannacotta, meringue, jelly and cream. A brief wine list opens at £20.
Chef/s: Nick Astley. **Open:** Sat L 12 to 1.45, Tue to Sat D 6 to 11. **Closed:** Sun, Mon, 20 Dec to 12 Jan, 1 to 17 Jul. **Meals:** tasting menu £44 (7 courses). **Details:** 24 seats. Music.

LOCAL GEM

Café Opus at Ikon

Modern British | £15
1 Oozells Square, Brindleyplace, Birmingham, B1 2HS
Tel no: (0121) 2483226
cafeopus.co.uk

£30

On the ground floor of a neo-Gothic former schoolhouse that is home to the Ikon contemporary art gallery (free entry), Café Opus is open all day for cakes, sandwiches, plates of British cheeses and daily specials that are led by what's looking good at the market. Slow-baked aubergine in rich tomato and Quorn ragoût saves the day for hungry vegetarians, while pescatarians might be drawn to Brixham fish pie. Set menus are great value, and the concise wine list kicks off at £18.

▌Dorridge

The Forest

new chef/no score
Modern European | £30
25 Station Approach, Dorridge, B93 8JA
Tel no: (01564) 772120
forest-hotel.com

£5 OFF

Gary and Tracey Perkins have been presiding over this former Victorian railway hotel (opposite Dorridge railway station) since 2001 and have kept the building in fine fettle. Since the last edition of the Guide, long-serving chef Dean Grub, and his replacement Tom Jackson, have both departed, with sous-chef Luke Haddow promoted too late for us to inspect. Judging by an early menu, the lively emphasis on brasserie-style food looks set to remain, in the form of scallops with creamed leeks and chorizo, and Warwickshire lamb rump with chickpea purée, lemon spinach and potato fondant, while desserts are likely to include frozen milk chocolate parfait with hazelnut ice cream and roasted hazelnuts. The wine list offers dependable drinking from £16.95.
Chef/s: Luke Haddow. **Open:** all week L 12 to 2.30 (3 Sun), Mon to Sat D 6.30 to 9.30. **Closed:** 25 Dec. **Meals:** main courses £11 to £20. Sun L £23. **Details:** 60 seats. 60 seats outside. Bar. Wheelchairs. Music. Parking.

Average price

The average price denotes the price of a three-course meal without wine.

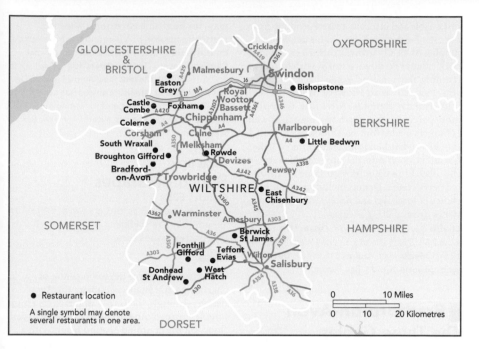

A single symbol may denote several restaurants in one area.

● Restaurant location

■ Berwick St James
The Boot Inn
Cooking score: 1
British | £25
High Street, Berwick St James, SP3 4TN
Tel no: (01722) 790243
thcboot.pub
£5 OFF £30

Giles and Cathy Dickinson's personally run village pub may be small but it is big on atmosphere (helped by a good local drinking trade) with simple décor, crackling winter fires and the option of a beer garden on fine days. Sturdily agreeable pub food includes a home-smoked platter ('seven different meats, a trout pâté, smoked prawn and cured salmon'), slow-roast duck leg with rosemary roast root vegetables and Madeira sauce, and a 'really good homemade heart-stopper' of date and toffee pudding with salted-caramel ice cream. Wines from £17.

Chef/s: Giles Dickinson. **Open:** Tue to Sun L 12 to 2.15 (2.30 Sun), Tue to Sat D 6.30 to 9.15 (9.30 Sat). **Closed:** Mon, 25 Dec, first 2 weeks Feb. **Meals:** main courses £12 to £18. **Details:** 33 seats. 30 seats outside. Music. Parking.

■ Bishopstone
Helen Browning at the Royal Oak
Cooking score: 3
British | £29
Cues Lane, Bishopstone, SN6 8PP
Tel no: (01793) 790481
helenbrowningorganics.co.uk
£5 OFF £30

'I received the warmest welcome I've ever received in a pub,' admitted one reader after a trip to this 'gloriously wacky place' – part boozer/part restaurant/part community hub/part green crusader. Co-owned by organic pioneer and Director of the Soil Association, Helen Browning OBE, it's a showcase for sustainable and ethically reared produce from her own Eastbrook Farm – plus generous supplies of locally grown stuff. Home-reared pork rillettes go down a storm with hunks of crumbly, 'flavoursome' home-baked bread, or you could start with a bowl of Moroccan-style mussels and chermoula. After that, there are more porcine pickings (chops, roasts), as well as burgers made from Eastbrook beef, pulled shoulder of lamb pie and beer-battered hake. For afters, don't miss the 'moist and lovely' chocolate brownie with vanilla ice cream and red berry coulis. Drinks include a splendid choice of local ales and noteworthy organic wines (from £20, £5 a glass).

Chef/s: David Crabtree-Logan. **Open:** Mon to Sat L 12 to 2.30 (3 Sat), D 6 to 8.30 (9.30 Wed to Sat). Sun 12 to 8. **Meals:** main courses £12 to £27. **Details:** 50 seats. 50 seats outside. Bar. Parking.

◼ Bradford-on-Avon
The Three Gables
Cooking score: 3
Modern British | £35
St Margaret's Street, Bradford-on-Avon, BA15 1DA
Tel no: (01225) 781666
thethreegables.com
£5 OFF 🍾

The Grade II-listed building has been on the high street for knocking on 400 years and has served time as a malt house, brewery and sweet shop. Within these historic old bones owner Vito Scaduto has created a refined restaurant with a dapper finish. The kitchen draws on high-quality West Country ingredients to deliver a menu that is modern British inasmuch as it draws on European classical traditions with a gently handled modernity. Thus ham hock and hare terrine keeps company with pickled figs and the yolk of a hen's egg, and Cornish mackerel gets the escabèche treatment. Main-course Cornish brill comes with a simple butter sauce, and poached guinea fowl with a top-notch Parmesan and rosemary risotto. For dessert, rhubarb crumble with rice pudding ice cream

plays on English heartstrings. Wine is a particular passion of Vito's and the list is strong on Italy and France; bottles start at £17.50.
Chef/s: Giacomo Carreca. **Open:** Tue to Sat L 12 to 2, D 6.30 to 9.30. **Closed:** Sun, Mon, 25 and 26 Dec, first 2 weeks Aug. **Meals:** main courses from £19 to £27. Set L £14 (2 courses) to £18. Tasting menu £45. **Details:** 55 seats. 30 seats outside. V menu. Bar. Wheelchairs. Music.

LOCAL GEM
Bunch of Grapes
French | £25
14 Silver Street, Bradford-on-Avon, BA15 1JY
Tel no: (01225) 938088
thebunchofgrapes.com
£5 OFF £30

On a rising street off the town centre of charming little Bradford, where the Avon babbles through, the Bunch of Grapes is a local hostelry turned modern bistro. Bare-boarded floors on the confined ground floor, with a restaurant room above, are the drill, and the cooking is all about simple satisfaction. Soy-marinated salmon with pea shoots, crispy duck salad with caramelised walnuts, and chocolate-orange mousse make for a well-weighted lunch, while in the evenings, there is pork belly with clams and dauphinois, or wood-roasted sea bream with apple and fennel salad, to conjure with. Snacking plates and pub standards broaden the repertoire, and wines don't let the name down, starting at £18.

◼ Broughton Gifford

LOCAL GEM
The Fox
British | £33
Broughton Gifford, SN12 8PN
Tel no: (01225) 782949
thefox-broughtongifford.co.uk
£5 OFF 🛏

A broad-fronted rustic inn, the Fox is a proper country beast. It has the authentic feel of a community resource, with local ales on tap and a smallholding where much of the produce is grown, and pigs and poultry are kept. Inside is cool from the whitewashed stone walls, but there are parasoled tables in a back garden for summer. A pleasing mix of pub classics and dishes out of the normal safety range produces piquillo peppers stuffed with salt cod, garnished with char-grilled squid, in red pepper cream sauce, and hefty servings of confit duck on braised peas with buttery mash, or bream fillet on baby veg. Finish with old-school chocolate mousse or a 'fully loaded' ice cream sundae. Wines starts at £18.50.

Castle Combe
The Manor House Hotel, Bybrook Restaurant
Cooking score: 6
Modern British | £66
Castle Combe, SN14 7HR
Tel no: (01249) 782206
manorhouse.co.uk

The original Manor House has stood since the 14th century, a lasting monument to the Barony of Combe, lording it discreetly over a heart-wrenchingly beautiful medieval village. Stone walls may not a prison make, but they make for an atmospheric dining room, and weathered old panels a lounge bar, such is the entrancing venerability of the place. Rob Potter took up the reins in autumn 2015, and there is fresh momentum to the cooking. Ingredients are painstakingly selected, presented in illuminating ways, and there is a refreshing willingness to mix tradition and modernity. A terrine of foie gras is classically done, accompanied by sweet wine jelly and raisin purée, while main courses might add ceps and a celeriac and pancetta fricassee to Cornish turbot, or furnish superb Middle White pork belly with finely diced apple, girolles and a sauce of organic cider. At dessert, electrically intense Amalfi lemon tart comes with raspberries in various guises, including a turbo-charged sorbet. Wines from a plutocratic list start at £25.

Chef/s: Robert Potter. Open: Sun L 12.30 to 2, all week D 6.30 to 9. Meals: set D £66 (3 courses). Sun L £35. Tasting menu £78. Details: 60 seats. Bar. Wheelchairs. Music. Parking. Children over 11 yrs only.

Colerne
Lucknam Park
Cooking score: 5
Modern British | £80
Colerne, SN14 8AZ
Tel no: (01225) 742777
lucknampark.co.uk

The 500 acres of Lucknam are well hidden among B-roads and arboreal borders, the experience beginning with the gliding open of automatic gates and a long approach beneath the trees. Its public rooms are huge and stately, watched over by oil portraits, and the principal dining room, the Park Restaurant (there's also a less formal Brasserie) has a bow window at one end, gigantic drapes and a ceiling fresco of puffs of cloud floating across the azure. Hywel Jones' long tenure at Lucknam has produced an undeniable smoothness to the culinary operation, with new techniques incorporated selectively. Shellfish are treated with respect, as in the brace of plump langoustines that come with quenelles of chilled potato mousse, a brown crab croquette, Exmoor caviar and gribiche, while seasonal meats such as Brecon lamb – seared loin and braised ham-wrapped shoulder, alongside verdant spring veg – are nonpareil. A pre-dessert of kalamansi sorbet in white chocolate might herald the arrival of the strawberry season, with gariguette berries, doughnuts, sorbet and jelly to accompany a pair of impeccable mini crème brûlées. The wine list is a very old-school array with no notes, just layers of quality drinking, with a few by the glass (from £7) tucked at the back. Bottles start at £25.

Chef/s: Hywel Jones. Open: Sun L 12.30 to 2.30, Tue to Sat D 6.30 to 10. Closed: Mon. Meals: set D £80. Sun L £39. Gourmet menu £110. Details: 64 seats. V menu. Wheelchairs. Parking.

Brits abroad... and at home

The impulse to expand has kept chefs and restaurateurs busy for the last couple of years, with some of our best talent launching either carbon copies or diffusion versions of their original restaurants. And they're not slowing down: there's plenty more to come, both abroad and closer to home.

Near: Adam Byatt has stayed very close to home in Clapham with his latest casual dining venture. The clue's in the name: **Upstairs**. Meanwhile, Ramsbottom's much-loved Levanter has produced pintxos bar **Baratxuri**, all bright tiles and enticing nibbles, just round the corner. Gary Usher, of **Sticky Walnut**, plans to open the crowdfunded **Hispi** down the motorway in south Manchester, and **D&D** London will also arrive in Manchester (they're already in Leeds) on the top floor of new tower No. 1 Spinningfields, once construction is completed.

And far: The UK's boldest restaurant export for some years is likely to be **Hawksmoor** New York, due to open in Tower 3 of the World Trade Center at the end of 2017. At the same time, the **Cinnamon Collection** is making plans to expand and **Australasia**, one of the late Tim Bacon's most admired Manchester projects, could make it to London or New York.

▌Devizes

READERS RECOMMEND

The Peppermill

Modern British
40 St John's Street, Devizes, SN10 1BL
Tel no: (01380) 710407
peppermilldevizes.co.uk

'A reliably good, popular local bistro, very welcome in the gastronomic desert around Devizes. Recently we have enjoyed asparagus salad with asparagus cream and a poached duck egg, and pan-fried chicken breast with a creamy leek and mushroom ragoût.'

▌Donhead St Andrew

The Forester

Cooking score: 2
Modern British | £30
Lower Street, Donhead St Andrew, SP7 9EE
Tel no: (01747) 828038
theforesterdonheadstandrew.co.uk

A late-medieval thatched inn buried deep among ribbon-thin country lanes, the Forester is a warren of low-ceilinged, darkly panelled rooms inside, entirely enveloping on a bitter winter evening. It's the kind of place that plays a conscientious part in its community, with regional meats and fresh produce proudly to the fore. Carpaccio of locally farmed beef fillet is of melting buttery tenderness, dressed with finely grated Parmesan, slivered radish and watercress, while mains run the rule over plenty of fine fish, such as crisp-skinned sea bass with a block of Anna potatoes and a fricassee of asparagus and girolles, or perhaps rose veal chop with cavolo nero, sage butter and chips. Pub classics include a tempting burger laden with smoked bacon and Cheddar, and desserts showcase lots of fruit, including roast figs with Marsala ice cream, or wine-poached pear and blue cheese tart. An inspired choice of wines includes a good range by the glass from £4.80, bottles from £19.

Chef/s: Andrew Kilburn. **Open:** Tue to Sun L 12 to 2, Tue to Sat D 6.30 to 9. **Closed:** Mon. **Meals:** main courses £14 to £22. Set L and D £19 (2 courses) to £23. Sun L £19. **Details:** 55 seats. 30 seats outside. Bar. Music. Parking.

East Chisenbury
The Red Lion

Cooking score: 5
Modern British | £40
East Chisenbury, SN9 6AQ
Tel no: (01980) 671124
redlionfreehouse.com

£5
OFF

In verdant countryside near Salisbury Plain, the Red Lion still performs its duty as a rural pub – wood-burning stove, local ales, bucolic beer garden and all. Guy Manning's oft-changing menu might at first seem to follow suit: there could be pea soup, burgers and belly pork. But the delight is in the detail. That velvety pea soup, the essence of springtime, comes with two crisp pig's head croquettes, spongy homemade sourdough and sublime, salty butter churned by Guy's father up the road. Charcuterie is another highlight: cured in-house from locally reared livestock. An inspection following the appointment of new head chef, Dave Watts, found everything ship-shape. Main-course crisp-topped turbot was paired with crunchy spears of wild asparagus; plump mussels, sliced fennel and a glutinous log of herb gnocchi provided further textural variation. Strawberry salad for dessert was similarly complex, enhanced by cubes of frangipane, crunchy almonds and jellied white balsamic. Innovative cocktails, knowledgeable service and ample by-the-glass choice on the diverting wine list (bottles from £20) complete this peach of a pub.
Chef/s: Guy Manning and Dave Watts. **Open:** all week L 12 to 2.30, D 6 to 9 (9.30 Fri and Sat, 8 Sun). **Meals:** main courses £13 to £33. Set L £18 (2 courses) to £24. **Details:** 50 seats. 20 seats outside. Bar. Music. Parking.

Easton Grey
★ TOP 50 ★
Whatley Manor, The Dining Room

Cooking score: 8
Modern French | £116
Easton Grey, SN16 0RB
Tel no: (01666) 822888
whatleymanor.com

Lavishly refurbished and rebranded as a country-chic hotel, this ivy-clad Wiltshire beau is now one of the UK's great escapes – an epicurean package complete with a spa, cinema and 12 acres of grounds divided into no fewer than 26 distinctive gardens. At Whatley's heart is the Dining Room, an immaculately appointed space done out in neutral tones with striped upholstery, polished floors and spruce bouquets emphasising the mood of measured decorum and civility. This is chef Martin Burge's domain and he stamps his mark on proceedings with three tasting menus that are designed to showcase his formidable talents. From the singularly fine canapés and four kinds of home-baked bread to the last spoonful of prune and orange soufflé, this is ambitious food, delivered with supreme confidence, precision and style. A scintillating starter involving a hand-dived scallop with lightly warmed smoked salmon, pickled cockles and a soupçon of walnut cream shows restraint and a delicate touch, but Burge knows all about bigger, more robust flavours, too – witness poached and roasted squab pigeon dressed with foie gras cream, pomme soufflé and Pedro Ximénez sauce. As dessert approaches there are even more wonders to behold, from an exotic pairing of banana pannacotta with passion fruit granité and lychee sorbet to an eye-popping chicory mousse layered with coffee and mascarpone cream – all decorated with gold leaf. An epically proportioned, regionally organised wine list promises quality and desirable sipping at every turn, opening with 10 house selections from £30 (£6.50 a glass).

Chef/s: Martin Burge. **Open:** Wed to Sun D only 7 to 10. **Closed:** Mon, Tue, 2 to 6 Jan. **Meals:** tasting menu £116 (7 courses). **Details:** 40 seats. V menu. Bar. Wheelchairs. Music. Parking. Children over 12 yrs only.

■ Fonthill Gifford
Beckford Arms
Cooking score: 3
Modern British | £32
Hindon Lane, Fonthill Gifford, SP3 6PX
Tel no: (01747) 870385
beckfordarms.com

Enveloped by the green acres of the Fonthill Estate, this 18th-century inn has a certain gentrified clout, and it doesn't lack for smart accoutrements – note the soothing colour schemes, inglenook fireplace, wood panelling and a traditional sitting room straight out of a lifestyle shoot. Enjoy a 'mug of soup' and a pint of Beckford Phoenix in the bar, or repair to the dining room for something more sustaining. 'Pub classics' such as burgers and beer-battered fish and chips show up on the menu, although most of the kitchen's efforts are channelled into more ambitious contemporary ideas – from char-grilled pigeon breast with Trealy Farm black pudding, bacon and artichoke purée to pan-fried skrei cod partnered by ricotta dumplings, kale and hollandaise sauce. Trout is smoked on the premises, while desserts such as salted-caramel and chocolate mousse with peanut brittle and roasted peanut ice cream add the final flourish. Wines from £17.50.
Chef/s: Nigel Everett. **Open:** all week L 12 to 3 , D 6 to 9.30 (9 Sun). **Closed:** 25 Dec. **Meals:** main courses £14 to £23. Set L and D £23 (2 courses) to £28. **Details:** 56 seats. 36 seats outside. Bar. Music. Parking.

Average price

The average price denotes the price of a three-course meal without wine.

■ Foxham
The Foxham Inn
Cooking score: 1
Modern British | £30
Foxham, SN15 4NQ
Tel no: (01249) 740665
thefoxhaminn.co.uk

It 'continues to delight' cheers one happy regular, not alone in his appreciation of this friendly pub's attention to detail. Careful use of local ingredients is apparent on a menu that combines adventurous dishes with pub favourites, and they're flexible and accommodating if informed of allergies or intolerances in advance. Marlborough mushrooms in a creamy garlic sauce could precede slow-cooked belly of West Country lamb or locally shot roe deer with beetroot, chorizo and spinach. A duck egg custard tart with raspberry sorbet or almond milk rice pudding with blackcurrant jam are comforting ways to end a meal. Wine from £16.75.
Chef/s: Neil Cooper. **Open:** Tue to Sun L 12 to 2 (2.30 Sat and Sun), Tue to Sat D 7 to 9.30. **Closed:** Mon, first 2 weeks Jan. **Meals:** main courses £13 to £22. Set L £20 (2 courses) to £25. Set D £25 (2 courses) to £30. Sun L £13. **Details:** 60 seats. 30 seats outside. Bar. Wheelchairs. Music. Parking.

■ Little Bedwyn
The Harrow at Little Bedwyn
Cooking score: 6
Modern British | £50
High Street, Little Bedwyn, SN8 3JP
Tel no: (01672) 870871
theharrowatlittlebedwyn.com

Despite its location in a secluded rural nook, Sue and Roger Jones' red-brick ex-pub is often full. Widespread acclaim both for Roger's seasonally astute modern cooking and his stupendous, 900-bin wine list attracts

gastronomic pilgrims from afar. While relaxing in the comfortable, understated interior, diners pick from three no-choice set meals. Sourcing is paramount, textures complementary, flavours punchy. The six-course tasting menu might commence with an amuse of borscht-like beetroot purée brilliantly matched with creamy blue Perl Las cheese. Asparagus and broad beans could follow, their vernal sweetness accentuated by precisely seared Orkney scallops and lobster meat. The springtime feel continues with turbot and beautifully resilient morels in an intense jus, before Kelmscott pork platter (five variations: from the lightest of black puddings to confit pork cheek). Puddings further raise the bar, introduced by a pre-dessert 'boiled egg and soldier': an exciting pastiche of the breakfast favourite involving a 'yolk' of passion fruit and mango purée. Sue Jones' quietly good-natured service, and expert wine matching from a congenial sommelier (bottles from £28), complete this first-class operation.
Chef/s: Roger Jones and John Brown. **Open:** Wed to Sat L 12 to 2, D 7 to 9. **Closed:** Sun, Mon, Tue, 25 Dec to second week Jan. **Meals:** set L £30 (3 courses). Set D £50 (6 courses). Tasting menu £75. **Details:** 34 seats. 24 seats outside. V menu. Music.

▌Rowde
The George & Dragon
Cooking score: 3
Modern British | £30
High Street, Rowde, SN10 2PN
Tel no: (01380) 723053
thegeorgeanddragonrowde.co.uk

Who would have thought that this ancient, plain white pub on the main road through Rowde village and 'a million miles from the sea' would have a culinary reputation built on great fresh fish delivered daily from Cornwall. But what a selection they have, chalked up on boards above the bar – maybe lemon or megrim sole, whole sea bream, Cornish crabs, even lobsters. Reporters have enjoyed the fish-sharing platter (scallops, deep-fried whiting, fish balls, whitebait and a whole lobster), beer-battered whiting and chips, and lobster thermidor; for those not in the mood for fish, there has been praise for meat dishes such as pork escalope with winter greens and sautéed potatoes, and ribeye with wild mushroom sauce and chips. Elsewhere, a starter of double-baked cheese soufflé with Parmesan cream and dessert of warm chocolate brownie with caramel ice cream both get high marks. The selection on the modest, global wine list starts at £17.50.
Chef/s: Christopher Day. **Open:** all week L 12 to 3 (4 Sat and Sun), Mon to Sat D 6.30 to 10 (11 Fri and Sat). **Closed:** 25 Dec. **Meals:** main courses £14 to £40. Set L and D £17 (2 courses) to £20. Sun L £20. **Details:** 40 seats. 36 seats outside. Bar. Wheelchairs. Parking.

▌South Wraxall
★ NEW ENTRY ★
The Longs Arms
Cooking score: 3
British | £28
South Wraxall, BA15 2SB
Tel no: (01225) 864450
thelongsarms.com
£30

Opposite the church and red telephone box in the pretty village of South Wraxall, this stone-built pub has been home to Rob and Liz Allcock since 2011. Not only is it very much the place for locals to put the world to rights over a pint of Wadworth 6X in the flagstoned bar, but it also attracts diners from afar. The village hasn't had a shop for years, so the Longs Arms fills that void by selling its own bread and smoked products at the bar, along with local milk and eggs from a neighbour. Rob runs the kitchen single-handedly and his robust British food combines classic with contemporary. A well-balanced smoked haddock Arnold Bennett might be followed by St Margaret's Farm free-range smoked pork loin, crackling, black pudding, truffle mash and Savoy cabbage. If you still have room, try Jersey buttermilk pudding, bee pollen and Yorkshire rhubarb. Wines from £16.

Chef/s: Rob Allcock. **Open:** Tue to Sun L 12 to 2.30 (3 Sun), Tue to Sat D 5.30 to 9.30. **Closed:** Mon, 3 weeks Jan. **Meals:** main courses £11 to £28. **Details:** 35 seats. 30 seats outside. Bar. Wheelchairs. Music. Parking.

▮ Teffont Evias
Howard's House Hotel

Cooking score: 3
Modern European | £45
Teffont Evias, SP3 5RJ
Tel no: (01722) 716392
howardshousehotel.co.uk

£5
OFF

'Delightful,' declared one couple after sampling the 'fine food' and pleasing accommodation provided by this dependable hotel. Built as a dower house in 1623, with lovely gardens, a burbling brook and trimmed topiary, it's now a spick-and-span family-run enterprise with Nick Wentworth confidently tending to the culinary side of things. Locally sourced meat and game are the undoubted stars, judging by recent reports: readers have singled out the Wiltshire lamb with chard, pea purée and mint jus, as well as the thinly sliced loin of roe deer (cooked pink) with dauphinois potato, tenderstem broccoli and blackberry compote. Seasonal specials such as herb-crusted salmon with sweet potato fondant and caramelised chicory are worth a punt, as is the British cheeseboard, and desserts have included a spot-on rhubarb soufflé with poached rhubarb and sorbet. A 'very useful' wine list opens with house selections from £18.

Chef/s: Nick Wentworth. **Open:** all week L 12 to 2, D 7 to 9. **Closed:** 23 to 27 Dec. **Meals:** set L and D £36 (2 courses) to £45. Sun L £33. **Details:** 25 seats. 25 seats outside. Music. Parking.

▮ West Hatch

LOCAL GEM
Pythouse Kitchen

British | £20
West Hatch, SP3 6PA
Tel no: (01747) 870444
pythouse-farm.co.uk

£30

'Wiltshire's answer to Petersham Nurseries, without the eye-watering prices,' quipped one visitor to this Victorian walled garden and nursery. The rustic café has won many friends with its honest, good-value dishes, from ploughman's (with Adams & Harlow chicken and ham pie, goats' cheese and apple and herb salad) via pan-fried shrimps with wild garlic and hazelnut pesto and a quinoa salad, to spiced beef meatballs served in a pitta with lime and coriander yoghurt, tomato salsa and herb salad. All-day coffee, tea and a luscious display of cakes are a bonus.

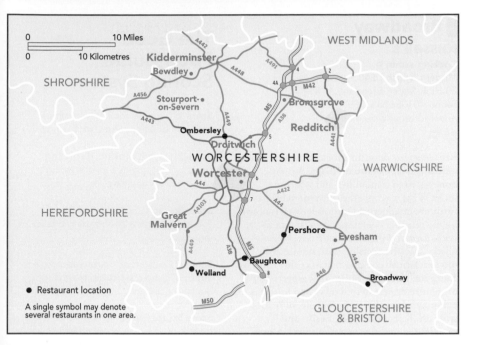

- Restaurant location

A single symbol may denote several restaurants in one area.

▮ Baughton

LOCAL GEM

★ LOCAL RESTAURANT AWARD ★ REGIONAL WINNER

The Jockey Inn
Modern British | £28
Pershore Road, Baughton, WR8 9DQ
Tel no: (01684) 592153
thejockeyinn.co.uk

£5 OFF £30

Still in fine fettle after an extensive refurb, Rebekah Seddon-Wickens' village pub attracts customers county-wide thanks to a 'very superior,' if extremely horsey, ambience. Its peaceful and secluded location, just off the A38, doesn't hurt either. Expect 'efficient, friendly' service, sharing boards of charcuterie or fish, pub staples along the lines of burgers, fish and chips, and good Sunday roasts, as well as straightforward dishes such as smoked mackerel rillettes with pickled cucumber, followed by herb-crusted lamb loin with Mediterranean vegetables and thyme pomme purée or a well-reported chicken Kiev. Pudding might be apricot-glazed bread-and-butter pudding or apple and pear crumble. Wines are from £14.95.

▮ Bransford

READERS RECOMMEND

The Bear and Ragged Staff
British
Station Road, Bransford, WR6 5JH
Tel no: (01886) 833399
bearatbransford.co.uk
'Their Sunday roast cannot be beaten, at least I've never met its match; they must have a secret recipe for their Oscar-winning English mustard.'

Average price

The average price denotes the price of a three-course meal without wine.

▋Broadway

Russell's

Cooking score: 4
Modern British | £40
20 High Street, Broadway, WR12 7DT
Tel no: (01386) 853555
russellsofbroadway.co.uk
£5 OFF 🚗

Broadway has done time for many years as the quintessential Cotswold village, with its honey-stoned tranquillity and winsome looks. What was once the showroom of master furniture designer Sir Gordon Russell is now a highly relaxing contemporary restaurant-with-rooms, with tables out front. Neil Clarke suits the occasion with resourceful modern British cooking that has some roots in European tradition, while other aspects go out on a limb. Expect to find quail and foie gras ballotine with celeriac rémoulade, or scallops and pork belly with apple, raisins and caramelised cauliflower among first-course offerings, presaging a seafood cornucopia of skate and dressed crab with brown shrimps and Parmesan gnocchi in mussel and caper butter. Spring brings on herb-crusted cannon of lamb, the breast pressed in black olives, with salsify, feta and smoked garlic purée, and the finale could be a simple duo of wine-poached pear and cinnamon pannacotta. An annotated wine list starts at £20.
Chef/s: Neil Clarke. **Open:** all week L 12 to 2.30, Mon to Sat D 6 to 9.30. **Closed:** Mon bank hols.
Meals: main courses £15 to £29. Set L and D £18 (2 courses) to £22. Sun L £25 (2 courses) to £29.
Details: 60 seats. 25 seats outside. Bar. Wheelchairs. Music. Parking.

The Good Food Guide Scoring System

Score 1: Capable cooking with simple food combinations and clear flavours.

Score 2: Decent cooking, displaying good technical skills and interesting combinations and flavours.

Score 3: Good cooking, showing sound technical skills and using quality ingredients.

Score 4: Dedicated, focused approach to cooking; good classical skills and high-quality ingredients.

Score 5: Exact cooking techniques and a degree of ambition; showing balance and depth of flavour in dishes.

Score 6: Exemplary cooking skills, innovative ideas, impeccable ingredients and an element of excitement.

Score 7: High level of ambition and individuality, attention to the smallest detail, accurate and vibrant dishes.

Score 8: A kitchen cooking close to or at the top of its game. Highly individual with impressive artistry.

Score 9: Cooking that has reached a pinnacle of achievement, making it a hugely memorable experience.

Score 10: Just perfect dishes, showing faultless technique at every service; extremely rare and the highest accolade the Guide can give.

▌Feckenham

READERS RECOMMEND

The Forest

Modern British

1 Droitwich Road, Feckenham, B96 6JE
Tel no: (01527) 894422
theforestatfeckenham.com

'A superb restaurant, providing great, reasonably priced food, amazing service and ambience. We have visited many times over the months and can honestly say the food and service have been to the highest standard every time.'

▌Great Malvern

READERS RECOMMEND

Terrace on the Hill

Modern British

Worcester Road, Great Malvern, WR14 4QW
Tel no: (01684) 438130

'We had the seven-course taster menu, served on Fridays and Saturdays. The food was fabulous – decorative, tasty, imaginative. We loved it and we'll go there again. Often.'

▌Ombersley

The Venture In

Cooking score: 4
Modern European | £41

Main Road, Ombersley, WR9 0EW
Tel no: (01905) 620552
theventurein.co.uk

From its external whitewash and beams to its internal wonky charm, The Venture In oozes the kind of personality that only comes with age. Throw in an inglenook fireplace, squashy sofas and a resident ghost and you've got the picture: this interior has evolved over time, and so has chef-proprietor Toby Fletcher's cooking, which strikes a winning balance between comfort and innovation. Time spent in Australia gave him a love for seafood, which manifests in dishes such as seared West Coast scallops with a tasting of cauliflower and curry spices. There's always a market fresh-fish

option, while other choices range from imaginative vegetarian dishes – maybe roast pumpkin timbale with sautéed seasonal mushrooms and a truffle scented emulsion – to a hearty seared fillet of beef with shallot Tatin, celeriac cream and sautéed, garlic-scented pied de mouton. An iced whiskey parfait with caramelised oats, tea soaked prunes, Earl Grey sorbet and shortbread is a good way to end. The substantial, well-annotated, international wine list opens at £18.

Chef/s: Toby Fletcher. **Open:** Tue to Sun L 12 to 2, Tue to Sat D 7 to 9. **Closed:** Mon, 1 week Christmas, 1 week Mar, 1 week Jun, 2 weeks Aug. **Meals:** set L £27 (2 courses) to £31. Set D £41. Sun L £31. **Details:** 28 seats. Music. Parking.

▌Pershore

Belle House

Cooking score: 3
Modern British | £35

5 Bridge Street, Pershore, WR10 1AJ
Tel no: (01386) 555055
belle-house.co.uk

The red-brick building on the high street of this market town on the river Avon was once a fire station, and its generous interior space has been intelligently converted into a modern brasserie with an airy feel. Combined with the restaurant arm of the business is a traiteur-deli that's well worth a look, but if you're determined on somebody else doing the cooking, let Steve Waites regale you with gently conceived modern British dishes brought off with flair. Roast partridge and beetroot in orzo pasta might set the ball rolling, ahead of herb-crusted cod in roast tomato sauce with hazelnut pesto, or braised and roasted free-range pork with endive tart, apple sauce and scratchings. Desserts bring technical inventiveness to creations like pear financier with almond gravel and milk ice cream, or simply add value to classic crème brûlée with a clutch of warm poached berries. Wines start at £19.50, or £4.75 a standard glass.

Chef/s: Steve Waites. **Open:** Tue to Sat L 12 to 2, D 7 to 9.30. **Closed:** Sun, Mon, 25 to 30 Dec, first 2 weeks Jan. **Meals:** set L £16 (2 courses) to £24. Set D £27 (2 courses) to £35. Tasting menu £45. **Details:** 78 seats. Bar. Wheelchairs. Music.

READERS RECOMMEND
The Angel
British
9 High Street, Pershore, WR10 1AF
Tel no: (01386) 552046
angelpershore.co.uk
'Service and food are brilliant. What sets it apart is the quality of the local produce with lamb, pork and bacon being produced on its very own smallholding. The more I visit the Angel the more I enjoy it.'

▌Welland
The Inn at Welland
Cooking score: 4
Modern British | £28
Hook Bank, Drake Street, Welland, WR13 6LN
Tel no: (01684) 592317
theinnatwelland.co.uk
£5 OFF £30

Over the last five years David and Gillian Pinchbeck have established this restored and updated rural hostelry as a successful food pub, full of warmth and honest intent. Stripped beams, stone floors and tasteful artwork create a mellow mood and, according to a pair of regulars, the entire experience is 'enormously enjoyable' with the cooking a beacon of quality defined by clear flavours. Among some fortifying cold-weather dishes, roast fillet of veal accompanied by lardons, mushrooms, purple sprouting broccoli, croquette potato and a really good jus has proved a winter hit. Fish is a strength, whether a well-reported starter of Dorset crab risotto or fillet of sea bream with artichoke, chorizo, straw potatoes and watercress pesto. To conclude, visitors have been impressed by marmalade bread-and-butter pudding with Seville orange and apricot compote, and

lemon meringue mousse with lemon curd and a blueberry sorbet. British cheeses and wines from £15 complete the picture.
Chef/s: Chris Exley. **Open:** Tue to Sun L 12 to 2.30, Tue to Sat D 6 to 9.30. **Closed:** Mon, bank hols. **Meals:** main courses £13 to £25. Sun L £22 (2 courses) to £26. **Details:** 60 seats. 40 seats outside. Wheelchairs. Music. Parking.

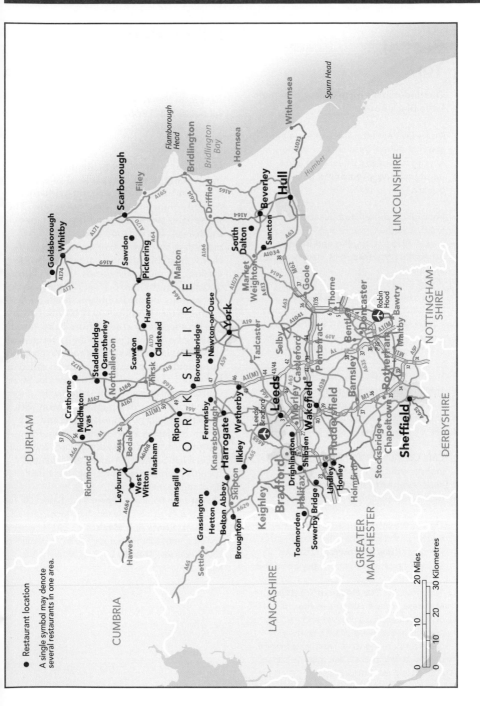

Best of... York

Our undercover inspectors open their Little Black Books

A silver tea pot, real leaves and a tiered stand of sandwiches, cakes and the famous *fat rascal* scones. It's the full monty at **Betty's Tearooms**, St Helen's Square.

For brunch, Bishy Road (Bishopthorpe Road) won the Great British High Street Award 2015 and the **Pig and Pastry** is a winner for eggs Benedict, bacon sarnies and more.

Have a pint at **The Golden Ball**, a community pub on Cromwell Road that runs open-mic nights, art exhibitions and a quiz. They sell local eggs, sourdough bread and well kept ales.

Healthy but not worthy, you can eat in at **Filmore & Union** or take out and take home. Chose from granola, bagels, juices and smoothies at Petergate, or at the train station.

Café Concerto is an informal, independent café just a short stroll from York Theatre Royal. No special pre-theatre offer but they open at 6pm.

The roast beef, horseradish, crème fraîche and crispy onion sandwich is the winner at **Brew & Brownie**, Museum Street. The brownies are pretty good too.

A must-visit is **The House of Trembling Madness**, a shop with thousands of bottled beers. You'd never know it, but upstairs is a wondrous 12th century candlelit drinking den. Their simple stew, platters and good ale are just the job after a long day shopping.

■ Beverley
Whites
Cooking score: 4
Modern British | £50
12a North Bar Without, Beverley, HU17 7AB
Tel no: (01482) 866121
whitesrestaurant.co.uk

Occupying a three-storey townhouse overlooking Beverley's medieval gate, John Robinson's tidy little restaurant-with-rooms certainly 'punches well above its weight'. The sparse bare-tabled surroundings don't give much away, but the food is startlingly innovative stuff, with two tasting menus to choose from (including a bargain midweek version). Home-baked breads, freshly churned butter and audaciously clever canapés open proceedings, before Robinson shows off his cutting-edge techniques, new Nordic riffs and excellent feel for texture – from hand-dived scallop ceviche with juniper dashi, fermented carrots, caviar and oyster leaf to skrei cod with miso emulsion or sous-vide venison rolled in burnt herbs with pork fat and brassicas. Sweet courses are also marvels of fashionable complexity – think Douglas fir cream with rhubarb 'five ways', granola, sorrel and tarragon. Here is a chef with 'passion, flair, imagination and a very good palate', concludes one reader. Service is 'timely, efficient and friendly', while wines promise dependable drinking from £18.50.
Chef/s: John Robinson. **Open:** Sat L 12 to 1.30, Tue to Sat D 6.45 to 8.30. **Closed:** Sun, Mon, 2 weeks Christmas, 1 week Aug. **Meals:** set L £23 (4 courses). Tasting menus £25 (4 courses, Tue to Thur only) to £50 (9 courses). **Details:** 22 seats. Wheelchairs. Music.

▌Bolton Abbey
The Burlington

new chef/no score
Modern British | £70
The Devonshire Arms, Bolton Abbey,
BD23 6AJ
Tel no: (01756) 710441
burlingtonrestaurant.co.uk

🍷 🛏

Built of the same grey stone as nearby Bolton Abbey, the Devonshire Arms has always been in the hospitality business. Acquired by the Duke of Devonshire in 1753, these days it accommodates a spa alongside its plush lounges and artworks from the Chatsworth Collection, with pride of place (gastronomically speaking) going to the Burlington – a softly lit dining room with a conservatory extension. However, we heard the news of head chef Adam Smith's departure just as we were about to go to press. The good news is that his replacement is Paul Evans, formerly senior sous chef at Lords of the Manor in Gloucestershire (see entry). Paul arrived too close to publication for us to see new menus, but he has experience in some excellent kitchens with stints at L'Enclume in the Lake District and the Waterside Inn at Bray (see entries) under his belt. What you can be sure of is the encyclopaedic global wine list, a legend of epic proportions, bulging with great names and treasured rarities – although intelligent pricing means you can pick up bottles from £22.
Chef/s: Paul Evans. **Open:** Tue to Sun D only 6.30 to 10. **Closed:** Mon. **Meals:** set D £70 (5 courses). Tasting menu £80 (8 courses). **Details:** 62 seats. Bar. Wheelchairs. Parking.

The Devonshire Brasserie

Cooking score: 3
Modern British | £35
The Devonshire Arms, Bolton Abbey,
BD23 6AJ
Tel no: (01756) 710710
devonshirebrasserie.co.uk

🛏

The unbuttoned dining option at this upmarket and greatly extended inn is a breezy brasserie charmingly at odds with the rest of the hotel's darkly classic public rooms: think whitewashed walls, funky jewel-coloured tub chairs and beautiful Dales views. Staff are 'smart and smiley' and the menu is equally accommodating, running from grills and the likes of sea bass with wild garlic mash, shellfish bisque and shepherds pie, to some attractive snacks and set-price lunch options. Local ingredients get a decent outing, as in an 'absolute joy' of a starter featuring Whitby crab cocktail with quail's egg and a crisp salt-and-pepper flatbread. Macaroni in a creamy sauce came with 'a handsome hum of truffle', topped with caramelised onions, pickled shallots and sprouting broccoli, while herb-fed chicken with mustard pommes purée, red wine jus and smoked pancetta showcased beautiful ingredients and accurate cooking. A classic sticky toffee pudding with a fudgy-rich sauce is a good way to finish. The ample wine list is nicely annotated and includes plenty for under £23.
Chef/s: Sean Pleasants. **Open:** all week L 12 to 2.30 (4 Sun), D 6 to 9.30 (9 Sun). **Meals:** main courses £16 to £25. **Details:** 70 seats. 40 seats outside. Bar. Parking.

■ Boroughbridge
The Dining Room
Cooking score: 2
Modern British | £35
20 St James Square, Boroughbridge,
YO51 9AR
Tel no: (01423) 326426
thediningroomonline.co.uk

£5
OFF

Safe, sound, reassuring, congenial – just some of the words that spring to mind when describing Chris and Lisa Astley's restaurant in a listed Georgian house overlooking Boroughbridge market square. Since 2000, they have honed their refined approach and personal take on hospitality, from pre-prandial drinks served in the upstairs lounge to the business of dining in their smart ground-floor oasis. Chris understands his customers and knows that they value polished familiarity above showboating – although he's not above throwing in the occasional surprise (confit duck dressed with pomegranate and granola, for example). Otherwise, he plays it straight, offering chicken liver and almond pâté with gherkins and chutney ahead of pork fillet with apple compote and grain-mustard sauce or char-grilled 'grand reserve' beef with blue cheese and Cognac sauce – all served with spinach and petits pois. To conclude, choose Yorkshire cheeses or baked chocolate mousse with Horlicks ice cream. Wines from £18.95.
Chef/s: Chris Astley. **Open:** Sun L 12 to 2, Tue to Sat D 6 to 9.15. **Closed:** Mon, 1 week Jan, 1 week Jul, 1 week Sept, bank hols. **Meals:** main courses £15 to £27. Early D (Tue to Fri) £16 (2 courses) to £20. Sun L £22 (2 courses). **Details:** 34 seats. 22 seats outside. Bar. Music.

Local Gem

Local Gems are the perfect neighbourhood venues, delivering good, freshly cooked food at great value for money.

■ Broughton
LOCAL GEM
The Bull
British | £25
Broughton, BD23 3AE
Tel no: (01756) 792065
thebullatbroughton.com

£30

The Yorkshire arm of Nigel Haworth's Ribble Valley Inns subscribes to the same group theme – stone floors, beams and plenty of local ingredients – and is known for 'proper hearty pub food'. The menu features steak and Hetton ale pie, Yorkshire venison steak and baked North Sea cod with parsley sauce, alongside fish pie, two thick slabs of cider-braised Waterford Farm pork belly with black pudding mashed potato, and 'very well judged' apple crumble with custard. Wines from £16.50.

■ Crathorne

★ NEW ENTRY ★
Crathorne Arms
Cooking score: 2
British | £30
Crathorne, TS15 0BA
Tel no: (01642) 961402
thecrathornearms.co.uk

Eugene McCoy, who made his name at the Cleveland Tontine, has brought his idiosyncratic style to another new venture, a whitewashed village pub south of Middlesbrough. Like the Tontine of old, it's hugger-mugger with lamps and parasols, rugs and sofas, country furniture, mismatched crockery and log fires, all making for a warm welcome, with a comforting menu of food you want to eat to match. Seafood pancake, duck in cherry sauce, venison loin, pork belly with crisp squid, shrimps and samphire and desserts of pistachio cake with figs and tonka bean rice pudding typify the fare, backed up by a lively wine list starting at £18. Real ales, music nights, 'ladies' lunches, bar meals, hot scones and tea and an early doors prix fixe menu appear to be a good way to keep a pub open and vibrant. It's good to see Mr McCoy back and on form.

Chef/s: David Henry. **Open:** Tue to Sun L 12 to 2.30 (3.30 Sun), Tue to Sat D 6 to 9.30. **Closed:** Mon, 25 Dec, 1 Jan. **Meals:** main courses £12 to £21. Set L and D £18 (2 courses) to £20. Sun L £23 (3 courses). **Details:** 70 seats. 30 seats outside. Bar. Wheelchairs. Music. Parking.

▋ Drighlington
Prashad

Cooking score: 2
Indian Vegetarian | £26
137 Whitehall Road, Drighlington, BD11 1AT
Tel no: (0113) 2852037
prashad.co.uk

There is colour and vibrancy on the plate and in the interior decoration of the Patel family's long-running Indian vegetarian restaurant. Some Gujarati designs on the walls, and a menu including the region's street snacks, reveals the focus is very much on India's most western state. A tasting menu takes a route across the Subcontinent to include a Keralan masala dosa and Punjabi capsicum curry. From the carte, kick off with khanda bhajia (deliciously crisp onion bhajis), or hathi chak vada (artichokes with root ginger and mint). Among main courses, mustard seeds and ajowan flavour aubergine and beans, while the thali includes three curries and all the bits and bobs. Finish with shrikhand or the more Western orange-infused chocolate ice cream with honeycomb. Spicing is well judged and the menu lists vegan, gluten-free and zero chilli options; wine starts at £14.95.

Chef/s: Minal Patel. **Open:** Sat and Sun L 12 to 5, Tue to Sun D 5 to 11. Tasting menu £34 (5 courses). **Closed:** Mon. **Meals:** main courses £11 to £18. **Details:** 80 seats. V menu. Wheelchairs. Music. Parking.

▋ Ferrensby
The General Tarleton

Cooking score: 4
Modern British | £30
Boroughbridge Road, Ferrensby, HG5 0PZ
Tel no: (01423) 340284
generaltarleton.co.uk

The GT may well have the beams, the real fires, the exposed stone walls and the inn moniker, but in its heart it's a restaurant-with-rooms, and its been on the foodie map hereabouts for 20 years. The spruce cocktail lounge with its cosseting formality sets the tone, while the kitchen offers up modern plates with a bit of Yorkshire soul. A starter of braised pig's cheek with black pudding Scotch egg may sound like something to bring in local trenchermen, but there's no lack of refinement. The signature 'little moneybags' of seafood sits alongside heritage beetroot salad with goats' curd, and main courses such as slow-braised confit shoulder of lamb with a Middle Eastern spin, or fish and chips made with Black Sheep beer batter. Local steaks are dry-aged in a Himalayan salt-brick chamber, and, among desserts, the taste of Yorkshire rhubarb is a seasonal treat. Wines start at £20.

Chef/s: John Topham and Marc Williams. **Open:** all week L 12 to 2, D 6 to 9 (9.15 Fri and Sat, 8.30 Sun). **Meals:** main courses £14 to £27. Set L and D £15 (2 courses) to £19. **Details:** 120 seats. 60 seats outside. Music. Parking.

▋ Goldsborough
The Fox & Hounds

Cooking score: 5
Modern European | £36
Goldsborough, YO21 3RX
Tel no: (01947) 893372

Big bold flavours and consistent quality are the hallmarks of Jason Davies' cooking in this former pub turned restaurant near Whitby. Once you've located it, tucked away down a country lane in the hamlet of Goldsborough, you'll be rewarded with a homely ambience and a short but decidedly sharp menu. Begin with grilled Scottish langoustines or partridge ravioli with sage butter or maybe crab bruschetta using their own sourdough. Mains invariably include superb dry-aged, rare-breed fillet steak with seared radicchio and a herb salsa. So close to the coast, fish is a strong suit with locally caught halibut, turbot and wild sea bass frequently on the menu, served perhaps with Puy lentils, kale and a rosemary and anchovy sauce. Dark chocolate truffle cake and their own ice creams are regular desserts along with a superior cheese plate. A quality wine list, opening at £20, has been selected by energetic front-of-house Sue Davies.

Chef/s: Jason Davies. **Open:** Wed to Sat D only 6.30 to 8. **Closed:** Sun, Mon, Tue, Christmas, bank hols. **Meals:** main courses £18 to £30. **Details:** 18 seats. Parking.

▮ Grassington
Grassington House
Cooking score: 3
Modern British | £35
5 The Square, Grassington, BD23 5AQ
Tel no: (01756) 752406
grassingtonhousehotel.co.uk

John and Sue Rudden are heading towards their tenth birthday as custodians of this elegantly refurbished Georgian residence in a desirable Dales village. Tourists and locals congregate in the bar, but the serious gastronomic business takes place in Grassington House's smartly appointed restaurant. 'Taster slates' are built for sharing, and the kitchen makes impressive use of Yorkshire meat and game for its seasonally attuned menus. Well-aged steaks come with all the requisite trimmings, local lamb appears with pickled red cabbage, crispy kale and potatoes cooked in lamb stock, and there's a stonking dish of herb-cured rare-breed 'côte de porc' served with a sage and onion fritter, apple, mustard, shallot and caper sauce. Fish is sustainable and line-caught where possible, while desserts usher in the likes of egg custard

tart with poached pear and elderflower ice cream. On Sundays, 14-hour slow-cooked rump of Pateley beef is the star attraction. Wines from £17.

Chef/s: John Rudden. **Open:** all week L 12 to 2.30 (4 Sat and Sun), D 6 to 9.30 (8.30 Sun). **Closed:** 25 Dec. **Meals:** main courses £13 to £26. **Details:** 56 seats. 32 seats outside. Bar. Wheelchairs. Music. Parking.

▮ Harome
The Pheasant Hotel
Cooking score: 4
Modern British | £40
Mill Street, Harome, YO62 5JG
Tel no: (01439) 771241
thepheasanthotel.com

Those who think of the Yorkshire countryside only as rugged in tooth and claw should get a load of Harome, and in particular the Pheasant Hotel, which has been pieced together cleverly from the old smithy and surrounding barns, with a courtyard of blooming fruit trees as a focus and the village millpond for company. Inside, a pale leafy colour scheme is the dining-room backdrop for double-covered, well-spaced tables, where Peter Neville's modern British cooking makes its appearance. Dishes familiar from classical tradition – rabbit and foie gras terrine with carrot and raisin salad – mix it with more surprising touches, as when venison loin arrives skewered on wood-liquorice with spiced parsley roots in venison tea, or sea bass and Shetland mussels join forces, with chestnut gnocchi in attendance. Beef fillet dry-aged in salt for two months takes meat maturation to a peak, and the homeliest of desserts, rice pudding with muscovado, damson jam and biscotti, is the main concluding draw. The wine list doesn't go in for voluble tasting notes, but sets up some broad style groups, and then lets you go happily foraging. Choices are sound, prices sane and there's plenty by the glass from £4 (bottles £20).

Chef/s: Peter Neville. **Open:** all week L 12 to 2 (2.30 Sun), D 6.30 to 9 (9.30 Sat). **Meals:** main courses £22 to £30. Set L £24 (2 courses) to £29. Set D £30 (2 courses) to £40. Sun L £34 (3 courses). **Details:** 70 seats. 30 seats outside. V menu. Bar. Wheelchairs. Music. Parking.

The Star Inn
Cooking score: 5
Modern British | £45
High Street, Harome, YO62 5JE
Tel no: (01439) 770397
thestaratharome.co.uk

'We liked the Star as soon as we walked in – folk propping up the bar, others getting stuck into good-looking plates of food.' Readers are back in love with Andrew Pern's gorgeous 14th-century thatched hostelry – especially as it's also a premier-league repository for top regional produce. Fish and game are seasonal trump cards, from fillet of North Sea turbot with poached Whitby langoustines, pickled cockles and a brandy glass of 'nigh-on perfect' gazpacho to pot-roast Rievaulx partridge with homemade morcilla, wilted cavolo nero and 'coffee bean' carrots. Fans have also endorsed the Yorkshire-reared lamb ('perfectly pink and moist') and the local asparagus (served as a summery bavarois surrounded by broad beans, peas and a quail's egg), while puds might feature a reinvented peach Melba or a cheesecake topped with poached 'goosegogs'. You can eat without booking in the bar (amid 'Mouseman' oak furniture and brass ornaments), reserve a table in one of the dining rooms or head out to the sheltered terrace – one menu is served throughout. The wine list is a rich and varied assortment of carefully chosen bottles, with prices from £19.50 (£5 a glass).
Chef/s: Andrew Pern and Steve Smith. **Open:** Tue to Sat L 11.30 to 2, Mon to Sat D 6.30 to 9.30. Sun 12 to 6. **Meals:** main courses £19 to £27. Set L and D £20 (2 courses) to £25. Sun L £17. Tasting menu £85 (7 courses). **Details:** 100 seats. 60 seats outside. V menu. Bar. Music. Parking.

■ Harrogate
Norse
Cooking score: 3
Scandinavian | £40
22 Oxford Street (at Baltzersen's), Harrogate, HG1 1PU
Tel no: (01423) 202363
norserestaurant.co.uk
£30

'Very hip for Harrogate', this Nordic-inspired restaurant is the night-time incarnation of Baltzersen's white-tiled café – although it inhabits a very different gastronomic universe. Four- or eight-course tasting menus are the deal, which the kitchen loads with esoteric ingredients that are bang in tune with the zeitgeist – puffed cod skin, sorrel oil, cocoa nib crumble – all eagerly demystified by the young staff. The kitchen's compass points to northerly climes, and past dishes have included the likes of yeast-roasted cauliflower with egg yolk, trompette mushrooms, wild garlic, capers and brown butter or striploin of veal with turnip, kohlrabi, broccoli and a sauce laced with oyster stout. Vegetarian and vegan versions of the menu are available (with 48 hours' notice), and desserts explore the voguish sweet/savoury possibilities of, say, caramelised white chocolate ganache with apple, green juniper sauce and sea buckthorn sorbet. An equally enlightened drinks list embraces house-infused 'snaps', obscure gins, craft beers and eclectic wines (from £19).
Chef/s: Simon Jewitt. **Open:** Tue to Sat D only 6 to 9. **Closed:** Sun, Mon, 25 and 26 Dec, 1 Jan. **Meals:** tasting menu £40 (4 courses) to £80 (8 courses). **Details:** 39 seats. V menu. Music.

Visit us online

To find out more about The Good Food Guide, please visit thegoodfoodguide.co.uk

Orchid

Cooking score: 2
Pan-Asian | £30
Studley Hotel, 28 Swan Road, Harrogate,
HG1 2SE
Tel no: (01423) 560425
orchidrestaurant.co.uk

£5 OFF 🛏

An unlikely location within Harrogate's Studley Hotel hasn't dimmed the popularity of this oriental-themed restaurant, which is now something of a local destination for devotees of pan-Asian food. Despite its Japanese wood screens, lacquered mango wood and cosy alcoves, the Orchid feels a tad Westernised, although the food is generally on target. Long-serving Kenneth Poon oversees a team of chefs from Thailand, China, Hong Kong and Malaysia, who rustle up all manner of confident, professional dishes ranging from aromatic lamb pancakes to plates of Singapore noodles. In between, the menu has eclectic appeal, whether your taste-buds are ready for steamed Peking dumplings, Taiwanese 'three cup' chicken, massaman curry or Calabasa prawns (a Filipino dish of king prawns with butternut squash, green beans and coconut milk). Express lunches are tailor-made for Harrogate's business crowd, while Sunday ushers in a family-friendly buffet. Look for aromatic wines on the modest list; bottles from £17.90

Chef/s: Kenneth Poon. **Open:** Mon to Fri and Sun L 12 to 2, all week D 6 to 10. **Closed:** 25 and 26 Dec. **Meals:** main courses £10 to £24. Set L £13 (2 courses) to £15. Set D £26. Sun L £17. **Details:** 70 seats. 24 seats outside. Bar. Music. Parking.

Symbols

🛏 Accommodation is available
£30 Three courses for less than £30
£5 OFF £5-off voucher scheme
🍶 Notable wine list

Sasso

Cooking score: 3
Italian | £30
8-10 Princes Square, Harrogate, HG1 1LX
Tel no: (01423) 508838
sassorestaurant.co.uk

£5 OFF

In a classic gabled terrace, Stefano Lancellotti's restaurant makes the very best of its lower-ground floor setting to create a soothingly sophisticated dining experience. An aubergine colour scheme and contemporary artworks from Tony Brummell Smith's Harrogate studio make for a special-occasion vibe, which is matched by genuinely charming and professional service. The chef hails from the northern region near Bologna, so pasta is a good bet (Parma ham and mortadella tortellini enriched with Parmesan and truffle fondue sauce, say), preceded perhaps by duck liver pâté with orange crème caramel topping. There is a tendency towards over-complication, but more often than not it adds to the sense of occasion. English duck breast arrives with glazed tangerine segments and rich Madeira jus, while foie gras upgrades a fillet of local beef, and, to finish, tiramisu is perked up with a sambuca sauce. The mostly regional Italian wine list starts at £13.95.

Chef/s: Stefano Lancellotti. **Open:** Mon to Sat L 12 to 2 (2.30 Sat), D 5.45 to 9.30 (10 Fri and Sat). **Closed:** Sun, 25 and 26 Dec, 1 Jan. **Meals:** main courses £15 to £23. Set L £10 (2 courses) to £14. Early D £10 (2 courses) to £19. Set D £25. **Details:** 110 seats. 24 seats outside. Music.

LOCAL GEM

Stuzzi

Italian | £25
46b Kings Road, Harrogate, HG1 5JW
Tel no: (01423) 705852

£30

In its first year of opening this lively deli-café earned itself many dining disciples. Building on its success, Stuzzi continues as a modest operation during the day and as a restaurant come evening. The cooking is simplicity itself, inspired by scrupulously sourced ingredients and by the owners' Italian travels. Stuzzi (small plates) of, say, homemade ravioli with spiced pork belly or beef and mortadella meatballs alternate with sharing platters of cheese or cured meats and lunchtime deli sandwiches. Italian wines are a well-considered selection from £16.

Hetton
The Angel Inn
Cooking score: 3
Modern British | £40
Hetton, BD23 6LT
Tel no: (01756) 730263
angelhetton.co.uk

The Angel is a real old country inn, an early pioneer of pub food and a Guide stalwart – celebrating 33 years of consecutive entries in 2017. The bar has lots of nooks and crannies and you can eat pretty well here, or wend your way through to the main restaurant where white linen, plenty of space between tables and comfortable upholstered chairs make for a cosy atmosphere. 'Fresh, fragrant' spring green risotto (peas, baby broad beans, asparagus, garden mint) or a hearty homemade black pudding, butter-bean and haricot stew might start proceedings followed, perhaps, by a special of garlic chicken saltimbocca served with a rösti drumstick, girolle and spinach fricassee, roasted beetroot and grelot onion or pan-seared cod fillet with bean and pancetta stew, beetroot and wild garlic creamed potatoes. Follow that with pear and chestnut cake with red wine pear and Earl Grey crème patisserie or an 'admirable' selection of local and British cheeses. An Old World-leaning wine list with some really lovely, great value drinking, starts at £17.25.
Chef/s: Bruce Elsworth. **Open:** Sun L 12 to 2.30, all week D 6.30 to 9 (6 to 9.30 Sat). **Meals:** main courses £18 to £30. Early D £18 (2 courses) to £26. Tasting menu £65. Sun L £29 (3 courses). **Details:** 100 seats. 40 seats outside. Bar. Wheelchairs. Parking.

Honley
Mustard & Punch
Cooking score: 3
British | £26
6 Westgate, Honley, HD9 6AA
Tel no: (01484) 662066
mustardandpunch.co.uk
£30

Richard Dunn has run this unassuming but sophisticated bistro in the heart of *Last of the Summer Wine* country for the best part of two decades and it's still a firm favourite with locals and tourists. In keeping with its history as a former village shop, Mustard & Punch retains a homespun feel, baking its own bread, churning its own ice cream and making pretty much everything else from scratch. Hand-dived king scallops with boudin noir, pork belly and shellfish bisque is a good way to start, perhaps followed by braised ox cheek (teamed with smoked garlic, creamed potatoes and roasted onions), or pan-fried sea trout (with leek, roasted broccoli, lemon risotto, watercress and walnut pesto). To finish, try chocolate délice with roasted almond, cherries and Chantilly cream, or the impressive board of British cheeses. The compact wine list opens at £18, with half a dozen available by the glass or half-bottle.
Chef/s: Richard Dunn and David Hampshaw. **Open:** Tue to Sat D only 5.30 to 9.30. **Closed:** Sun, Mon. **Meals:** set D £23 (2 courses) to £26. Tasting menu £30 (6 courses). **Details:** 64 seats. Bar. Wheelchairs. Music. Parking.

Hull
1884 Dock Street Kitchen
Cooking score: 2
Modern British | £45
Humber Dock Street, Hull, HU1 1TB
Tel no: (01482) 222260
1884dockstreetkitchen.co.uk

The imaginative repurposing of an old warehouse on the Marina has produced a reference address for Hull's cognoscenti. Tables dotted across an expansive space that looks as though it could be easily cleared for dances, and some up close to the kitchen hatchway, compete with chandeliers and panelling to create a mood of elegant relaxation. Unimpeachably modern British dishes have a say in the matter too. An egg yolk coddled at 62°C is the precise garnish for beef carpaccio, shallots, pickles, Berkswell cheese and truffled mayo, as a pump-primer for inventive main assemblages of lemon sole with girolles, ham and sprout petals, or venison Wellington with liquoriced parsnip, carrots and kale in juniper jus. Steak lovers are doubly spoiled with beef-dripping chips to go with prime cuts and a whole heap of accompaniments, and nor will desserters lack for stimulation, in the form of chocolate and violet ice cream or blackberry and ginger mille-feuille. An exhilarating wine list starts with over two dozen by the glass or carafe, and the choices radiate confidence, especially in Iberia, Australasia and – for the spendthrift – cru classé Bordeaux. Italian varietals, Fiano and Primitivo, are £18.

Chef/s: Laura Waller. **Open:** Tue to Sun L 12 to 2 (3 Sun), Mon to Sat D 6 to 9.30. **Closed:** 26 to 30 Dec, first week Jan. **Meals:** main courses £17 to £33. Set L £16 (2 courses) to £21. Set D £20 (2 courses) to £25. Sun L £25. **Details:** 100 seats. Wheelchairs. Music.

▊ Ilkley
The Box Tree
Cooking score: 6
Anglo-French | £65
35-37 Church Street, Ilkley, LS29 9DR
Tel no: (01943) 608484
theboxtree.co.uk

There have been changes at the top of this revered Ilkley restaurant since the last edition of the Guide, but the arrival of new head chef Mark Owens to work alongside executive chef Simon Gueller has caused barely a ripple in the enduringly smooth operation. Service remains impeccable. The interior, progressively pared down since the gaudy old

days, is classically elegant. The food by contrast is anything but. Ballotine of raw salmon wrapped in fresh herbs, a Gueller signature, remains exceptional, presented on this occasion alongside lobster cocktail garnished with caviar, finely sliced radish and served with rye crispbread. The best of ingredients are celebrated, whether it's squab pigeon with beetroot and orange; lemon sole with brown shrimps or new-season Wye Valley asparagus and soft-boiled quails' eggs in deep-fried crumbs. Granny Smith apple soufflé with Calvados sauce heads up a strong dessert menu. Wines start at a manageable £25 on an impressive list.

Chef/s: Simon Gueller and Mark Owens. **Open:** Fri to Sun L 12 to 2 (3 Sun), Wed to Sat D 7 to 9.30 (6.30 Sat). **Closed:** Mon, Tue, 26 to 30 Dec, first week Jan. **Meals:** set L £33. Set D £65. Sun L £38. Tasting menu £75 (6 courses). **Details:** 50 seats. Bar. Music. Children over 10 yrs only at D.

▊ Leeds
Brasserie Forty 4
Cooking score: 2
Modern European | £30
44 The Calls, Leeds, LS2 7EW
Tel no: (0113) 2343232
brasserie44.com

There are edgier venues in Leeds these days, but regulars never tire of Brasserie Forty 4 – one of the first on-trend eateries to arrive in the now-fashionable Calls complex. Occupying a former grain warehouse on the banks of the river Aire, this place still cuts quite a dash with its lacquered floors, mirrors, arched windows and waterside balcony – you can even arrive in style by booking their lunchtime chauffeur service. Fans from the early days are reassured by the comforting prospect of pork tenderloin wrapped in Parma ham with Madeira sauce followed by the famed chocolate fondue with marshmallows, while others might prefer braised oxtail with winter truffle and orzo pasta or lamb rump with pearl barley, roasted celeriac and redcurrant sauce, ahead of vanilla pannacotta and Champagne strawberries. Keen prices and generous set deals are much appreciated, as is the cosmopolitan wine list, with house selections from £18.50.

Chef/s: David Robson. **Open:** Tue to Sat L 12 to 2 (1 to 3 Sat), D 6 to 9.30 (5 to 10 Sat). **Closed:** Sun, Mon, 25 and 26 Dec, bank hols (exc Good Fri). **Meals:** main courses £13 to £19. Set L and D £20. **Details:** 85 seats. 18 seats outside. Bar. Wheelchairs. Children over 2 yrs only.

Crafthouse

Cooking score: 2
Modern European | £40
Level 5, Trinity Leeds, 70 Boar Lane, Leeds, LS1 6HW
Tel no: (0113) 8970444
crafthouse-restaurant.com

Trinity is a shopping centre with gustatory ambition – the food court is a best-in-class showcase of regularly changing street food. But for table service and low-lit glamour, jump in the lift to D&D London's Yorkshire outpost, which encloses customers in a glossy, well-appointed bubble with partial city views. Contemporary touches crowd delicate (readers, with some justification, say 'small') dishes such as chilled Parmesan royale with confit tomato, Tokyo turnip, pickled courgette, tempura Thai onions and burnt butter powder. Not all the elements make their presence felt, but the sum of the parts is generally successful, as in red mullet with bourride sauce and tiny Yukon Gold gnocchi. Puddings such as sticky toffee soufflé, flecked with salty chips of caramel, and a rhubarb 'sandwich' topped with folds of custardy cream, take things up a very noticeable notch, and the friands with coffee are 'excellent'. Wine is from £18.

Chef/s: Lee Murdoch. **Open:** Tue to Sat L 12 to 3, Mon to Sat D 5 to 10. Sun 12 to 10. **Closed:** 25 Dec. **Meals:** main courses £17 to £40. Set L and D £20 (2 courses) to £24. Tasting menu £65. **Details:** 144 seats. Bar. Wheelchairs. Music.

The Man Behind the Curtain

Cooking score: 6
Modern British | £75
68-78 Vicar Lane, (Top Floor, Flannels), Leeds, LS1 7JH
Tel no: (0113) 2432376
themanbehindthecurtain.co.uk

'The most interesting meal we have eaten in a long time,' is one fan's view of Michael O'Hare's top-floor eyrie that's been wowing critics and diners alike since he opened in 2014. In Leeds it takes some bravura to offer nothing but a £75 tasting menu (£115 with wine) with no actual menu – just see what comes – but that's O'Hare, an uncompromising chef with a rock star swagger: swept back hair, spray-on jeans, leather apron and silver cuban heels. He takes diners through numerous small courses that at one recent meal began with a mouthful of octopus served on a pretty silver spoon – presentation is half the story here – followed by raw marinated langoustine. Edible 'cellophane-wrapped' Wagyu beef and built through Mongolian lamb pancake came next, then glazed sweetbreads in a hot-and-sour dipping sauce and spider crab with tomato chilli and garlic alongside a fried quail's egg topped with raspberry vinegar and bilberry jelly. There's wit and whimsy in his Gothic 'fish and chips': white fish buried in black squid ink, 'chips' of black shredded potato and a whiff of salt and vinegar. Or a 'Big Bang' explosion of Iberian pork with edible broken egg-shell filled with smoked egg yolk, barbecued 'cinders' and a splatter of ajo blanco – one reader's 'dish of the year'. A finale of silver, spray-painted leaves of crumpled chocolate atop violet ice cream and chocolate mousse confirms that despite the wizardry, O'Hare's skills are never in doubt, the whole joyous fantasy ending with a teeny white chocolate and passion fruit cupcake eaten in one mouthful, case and all. Sommelier Charlotte Rasburn curates a well-considered wine flight and an impressive wine list with plenty by the glass, carafe or bottle, starting at £38.

Chef/s: Michael O'Hare. **Open:** Fri and Sat L 12.30 to 2, Tue to Sat D 6.30 to 8.30 (5 Sat). **Closed:** Sun, Mon. **Meals:** set L £45. Tasting menu £75. **Details:** 40 seats. Music.

★ NEW ENTRY ★

Ox Club

Cooking score: 3
Modern British | £26
Headrow House, The Headrow, Leeds,
LS1 6PU
Tel no: (07470) 359961
oxclub.co.uk
£5 OFF **£30**

Placing campfire cooking in a resolutely urban setting, the Ox Club forms part of the impressive regeneration of an old textile mill, now multi-use Headrow House. While candles glow in the cosy beer hall next door, the Ox's open kitchen centres on a wood-fired grill, with simple preparations offering a respectful nod to St John et al. A starter of melting pig's cheek with confit egg yolk and watercress purée might need more focus on both cooking and seasoning, but skate wing slicked with 'nduja butter is simply and alluringly charred, and flat-iron steak with béarnaise and salsa verde is bob-on for a tenner. Roast cauliflower with romesco sauce is an on-trend side with bite (though veggies should note that it's cooked alongside those steaks), and rosemary adds extra fragrance to a (very) wobbly lemon meringue pie. Wines are from £20, but don't overlook the beer.
Chef/s: Ben Davy. **Open:** Sat and Sun L 11 to 3.30, Tue to Sat D 5 to 10. **Closed:** Mon, 25 and 26 Dec. **Meals:** main courses £9 to £12. Early D £17 (2 courses) to £20. **Details:** 36 seats. Bar. Wheelchairs. Music.

Visit us online

To find out more about
The Good Food Guide, please
visit thegoodfoodguide.co.uk

The Reliance

Cooking score: 3
Modern British | £25
76-78 North Street, Leeds, LS2 7PN
Tel no: (0113) 2956060
the-reliance.co.uk
£30

'I really liked the informality that is the Reliance,' noted one visitor to the former cloth mill in the heart of Leeds city centre. It's a real foodie hub with appetising menus 'full of stuff you really want to eat'. Share a board of home-cured salamis – fennel or chilli and black pepper, or their own bresaola – or a selection of small plates, say purple sprouting broccoli with romesco and almonds, and seared hanger steak with beetroot and horseradish. Bigger plates bring hake with rapeseed oil mash and Sunstream tomatoes, and wood pigeon with homemade pancetta, shallots and red wine sauce. There's applause for 'the lovely sourdough bread' served with homemade tapenade, desserts of passion fruit crème brûlée and spotted dick with clove custard, and the shabby chic décor that makes the place such a popular after-work meeting place. There are some natural unfiltered offerings on the short wine list. House Italian is £15.50.
Chef/s: Tom Hunter. **Open:** Mon to Sat L 12 to 5, D 5.30 to 10 (10.30 Thur to Sat). Sun 11 to 8. **Closed:** 25 to 27 Dec, bank hols. **Meals:** main courses £11 to £15. Set D £19 (2 courses) to £24. **Details:** 125 seats. 8 seats outside. Bar. Music.

Salvo's

Cooking score: 2
Italian | £28
115 Otley Road, Headingley, Leeds, LS6 3PX
Tel no: (0113) 2755017
salvos.co.uk
£30

Opening the same year as Abba's 'Dancing Queen' hit the Number One spot, the Dammone family's restaurant is a Headingley institution. It's handy for the cricket or rugby, and its not entirely unheard of to find a student being fuelled up with pizza by Mum and Dad. The relaxed, contemporary vibe has lost none of its appeal over the years, with a menu that plays the populist card with triple salami pizza or another topped with seafood and roast peppers, and pasta options like the classic homemade lasagne. But then again, there's also tagliatelle with a rich lamb ragù and a spiced anchovy and pecorino crumb, and secondi along the lines of fillet of sea bass with shellfish velouté. Kick off with calamari or a platter of cured Italian meats. Drink Italian lager, local Hellfire pale ale or wines from the motherland opening at £16.95.

Chef/s: Gip Dammone and Jonathan Elvin. **Open:** Mon to Fri L 12 to 2, D 6 to 10 (5.30 Fri). Sat and Sun 12 to 10. **Closed:** 25 and 26 Dec, 1 Jan. **Meals:** main courses £13 to £25. Set L £12. Set D £15. Sun L £16. **Details:** 88 seats. 20 seats outside. Bar. Wheelchairs. Music.

★ NEW ENTRY ★

The Swine that Dines
Cooking score: 3
Modern British | £27
The Greedy Pig Kitchen, 58 North Street, Leeds, LS2 7PN
Tel no: (07477) 834227
£5 OFF £30

This spare and simple little BYO café with just 16 covers opens only three nights a week but is rapidly making a name for itself – by day it's The Greedy Pig caff. Stuart Myers (ex Harvey Nichols) and his wife Jo, front-of-house, offer eight small plates (try to share them all) at just £6 each, that may range from buttermilk-fried chicken wings with mashed sweetcorn and brown butter to ox heart with kohlrabi pickle or smoked ham hock with cockles, caper berries and sourdough. There are always three non-meat options on the menu and for one week a month it's totally vegetarian, with creative partnerships like sweet potato, burnt butter, nori and citrusy yuzu or a rissole of oyster mushrooms, quinoa and hazelnut with a hoppy-rich porter sauce. Desserts of peanut-butter cheesecake and passion fruit tart sustain the confidence that any of these dishes would

grace a high-end restaurant. This little piggy cooks with heart and soul, backed by skill and originality.

Chef/s: Stuart Myers. **Open:** Thur to Sat D only 6 to 9. **Closed:** Sun to Wed. **Meals:** small plates £6 to £7. Sharing plates £11. **Details:** 16 seats. Music.

★ NEW ENTRY ★

Tharavadu
Cooking score: 2
Indian | £35
7-8 Mill Hill, Leeds, LS1 5DQ
Tel no: (0113) 2440500
tharavadurestaurants.com

It claims to be the first authentic Kerala restaurant in Leeds, and Tharavadu (aka ancestral home) has gained a keen following for its South Indian cuisine. It's a large, simply decorated and busy restaurant close to Leeds railway station offering a lengthy menu with lots of the traditional dishes, from 'light as a feather' dosas enclosing spicy fillings to traditional fish dishes (very much part of the cuisine due to Kerala's long coastline and rivers), such as meen varanjathu, a whole sea bass boned and stuffed with rice, vegetables and shrimps, or a fragrant seafood curry. Meat and vegetables make a good show, too, as in chicken in a black pepper sauce or aubergines cooked in a paste of coriander, roasted onions, chillies and cashew nut sauce. Puddings are traditional, perhaps semiya payasam (vermicelli pudding with cardamom and saffron) or flavoured kulfis. The wine list (from £14.50) is arranged to help match choices to the spicy food.

Chef/s: Ajith Kumar. **Open:** Mon to Sat L 12 to 2, D 6 to 10 (5 to 10.30 Fri and Sat). **Closed:** Sun. **Meals:** main courses £9 to £16. **Details:** 80 seats. Bar. Music.

Average price

The average price denotes the price of a three-course meal without wine.

LOCAL GEM
Friends of Ham
Modern European | £26
4-8 New Station Street, Leeds, LS1 5DL
Tel no: (0113) 2420275
friendsofham.com

£5 OFF £30

Visitors to this smart little bar and charcuteria not only make friends with elite, artisan jamóns, but also get introduced to other marvels of the charcutier's craft – from lardo di colonnata to cecina (Spanish dry-cured beef) and Alejandro Magno chorizo. Sharing boards are the way to go, but the kitchen also serves up a few cooked tapas plates – perhaps griddled morcilla with paprika potatoes, Spanish honey and a fried egg. Drinks include a prodigious range of world beers, plus some handy wines from £17.50. A second branch is at 8 Wells Road, Ilkley, LS29 9JD.

LOCAL GEM
Zucco
Italian | £28
603 Meanwood Road, Leeds, LS6 4AY
Tel no: (0113) 2249679
zucco.co.uk

£30

'Very hands-on, personable owner, a surprisingly smart venue and incredibly popular local', is how one visitor described this neighbourhood eatery in a buzzy on-the-up suburb of Leeds. The venue's winning charms are backed by Michael Leggiero's regularly changing menu of small sharing plates, including fritto misto, veal belly with vegetable broth and chicken diavola with garlic potatoes. Pizzetta, salumi and pasta are offered, too, there's cannoli with ricotta for dessert, plus Italian wines from £15.50.

▌Leyburn
The Sandpiper Inn
Cooking score: 2
Modern British | £32
Market Place, Leyburn, DL8 5AT
Tel no: (01969) 622206
sandpiperinn.co.uk

'Everything about this handsome, 17th-century stone-built inn just off the market square screams traditional from the moment you walk in,' noted one visitor. Comfortable and soothing, with beams, open fires and real ales, it's matched by a courteous, old-school welcome and is just what you would hope to find in a Dales market town. For sure there's fish and chips and sausage and mash, but there's also black pudding and pork belly ('the best I've ever tasted'), a thoroughly modern pheasant risotto with a paper-thin Parmesan shard ('perfectly cooked rice, deep flavours'), red mullet with gnocchi, and a delicious roast cod with mussels. Desserts win favour year on year, with the likes of rice pudding and Victoria plum compote, and dark chocolate marquise with cappuccino sauce, frozen custard and toffee popcorn. Service 'is unflustered and efficient', while a good-value wine list starts at £16.
Chef/s: Jonathan Harrison. **Open:** Tue to Sun L 12 to 2.30, D 6 to 8.30 (9 Sat, 8 Sun). **Closed:** Mon, Tue (winter), 2 weeks Jan. **Meals:** main courses £12 to £19. **Details:** 40 seats. 26 seats outside. Bar. Music. Parking.

▌Lindley
Eric's
Cooking score: 3
Modern British | £36
73-75 Lidget Street, Lindley, HD3 3JP
Tel no: (01484) 646416
ericsrestaurant.co.uk

The Eric in question is Mr Eric Paxman, who has turned this address in an unassuming row of shops into quite the dining destination. Using the 'F' word without fear or favour,

Paxman's take on contemporary 'fine dining' is drawn from his experiences working in London under Marco Pierre White and in Australia with Bill Granger. The dining room has a modern rustic finish of exposed stone walls, local artwork and smart banquettes in a fashionably neutral colour, while the menu shows an appreciation of both classical thinking and current culinary ideas. Thus wood pigeon arrives with wild mushroom gnocchi and avocado purée, Asian flavours infuse cured salmon, and main-course rump of local lamb gets a hit of chilli and lime. Bolster Moor Farm provides the steaks served with triple-cooked chips, and rum and rhubarb trifle makes for a creative finale. An inspiring vegetarian menu and some nifty lunchtime open sandwiches add to its usefulness. Wines start at £17.50.
Chef/s: Eric Paxman, James Thompson and Paul Cookson. **Open:** Tue to Fri and Sun L 12 to 2 (4 Sun), Tue to Sat D 6 to 10 (5.30 Fri, 5 Sat). **Closed:** Mon. **Meals:** main courses £22 to £28. Set L £17 (2 courses) to £20. Set D £20 (2 courses) to £25. Sun L £20. **Details:** 80 seats. V menu. Bar. Music.

▌Masham
Samuel's at Swinton Park
Cooking score: 4
Modern British | £58
Swinton Park, Masham, HG4 4JH
Tel no: (01765) 680900
swintonpark.com

With diversions ranging from falconry to a cookery school, Swinton Park is the quintessential Yorkshire heritage package, and it certainly looks the part – all crenellated battlements, turrets and towers, with a 20,000-acre estate as an aristocratic backdrop. The Cunliffe-Lister family's ancestral pile since the 1880s, it also offers special-occasion dining in an opulent restaurant overlooking the grounds. Simon Crannage has moved up to executive chef, but the kitchen still takes its cue from the estate, the hotel's four-acre walled garden and a network of local producers when it comes to sourcing. Swinton

trout is paired with charred leek, artichoke, pear and dill, while confit Yorkshire duck could appear with salsify, apple, grape and liver parfait. There's Masham Fell lamb and local pork, too (fillet and cheek served with celeriac, wild mushrooms and Madeira sauce, for example), while rhubarb is a seasonal favourite when it comes to dessert. A weighty wine list starts at £22.
Chef/s: Simon Crannage. **Open:** Sat and Sun L 12.30 to 2, all week D 7 to 9.30. **Meals:** set L £22 (2 courses) to £26 (Sat only). Set D £58. Sun L £28. Tasting menu £70 (7 courses). **Details:** 60 seats. 20 seats outside. Bar. Wheelchairs. Music. Parking.

Vennell's
Cooking score: 4
Modern British | £35
7 Silver Street, Masham, HG4 4DX
Tel no: (01765) 689000
vennellsrestaurant.co.uk
£5 OFF

Jon and Laura Vennell are cruising confidently into their second decade at this well-liked neighbourhood restaurant, which brings a touch of glamour to the market town of Masham. Inside, it's all very chic, with sparkling gold mirrors, striking aubergine colour schemes and a cool bar upstairs. Jon's cooking is invariably on the money, mixing classic and contemporary themes with more than a dash of Yorkshire generosity – think home-smoked haddock and pea risotto with Parmesan followed by confit of local rare-breed pork with a chunky bean stew and mash. Native flavours also shine through in a twice-baked Harrogate Blue cheese soufflé and a trencherman ox cheek and mushroom suet pudding with braised shallots, turned carrots and rich juices, while tried-and-trusted desserts could yield anything from chocolate fondant to a thoroughly traditional sherry-soaked rhubarb trifle with vanilla custard and whipped cream. Themed evenings and special events such as a summertime lobster festival are also greatly appreciated by Vennell's loyal locals. A well-spread wine list starts at £19.50.

Chef/s: Jon Vennell. **Open:** Sun L 12 to 4, Wed to Sat D 7.30 to 11. **Closed:** Mon, Tue, first 2 weeks Jan, 1 week Easter, last week Aug. **Meals:** set D £29 (2 courses) to £35. Sun L £23 (2 courses) to £28. **Details:** 30 seats. Bar. Music.

▌Middleton Tyas
The Coach House
Cooking score: 3
Modern British | £37
Middleton Lodge, Kneeton Lane, Middleton Tyas, DL10 6NJ
Tel no: (01325) 377977
middletonlodge.co.uk

'The surroundings could not be nicer, understated but absolutely beautiful,' noted one visitor, as smitten by the extensive grounds as by this convivial restaurant housed in the stylishly converted coach house and stables of a fine 18th-century manor house – now a hotel. It's an industrious kitchen, headed by Gareth Rayner and offering à la carte, gluten-free, children's and set-price menus. Sunday lunch brings roast beef and Yorkshire pudding, but otherwise the forward-thinking kitchen produces much of interest, not least charred broccoli with Jerusalem artichoke, Ibérico bellota, hazelnuts and aged Parmesan or cured salmon with oyster mayonnaise, apple, compressed cucumber and sea rosemary, and pork belly with crispy rillettes, pommes Anna, pickled red cabbage and roast apple. Recommended puddings have included pistachio parfait with gariguette strawberries, honeycomb and white chocolate ice cream, and rhubarb and custard cheesecake with rhubarb sorbet. Wines from £20.
Chef/s: Gareth Rayner. **Open:** Wed to Sun L 12 to 2 (3.45 Sun), D 6 to 9 (7 to 9 Sun). **Closed:** Mon, Tue. **Meals:** main courses £17 to £26. Set L and D £20 (2 courses) to £25. **Details:** 100 seats. 30 seats outside. Bar. Wheelchairs. Music. Parking.

▌Newton-on-Ouse
The Dawnay Arms
Cooking score: 3
Modern British | £30
Moor Lane, Newton-on-Ouse, YO30 2BR
Tel no: (01347) 848345
thedawnayatnewton.co.uk

With moorings at the bottom of the garden, it's no wonder this elegantly appointed 18th-century hostelry is a favourite with folk who like pottering about on the river Ouse. Landlubbers also relish everything about the place, from the original flagstone floors, church pews and contemporary fashion touches to the sturdy, incisive food emanating from chef-proprietor Martel Smith's swanky eco kitchen. His homemade black pudding is hard to resist (especially if it's jazzed up with pineapple pickle), but locally sourced ingredients are also treated with plenty of verve – be it smoked haddock croquettes, a wild mushroom and spinach tartlet or roast duck breast with a little cottage pie, spiced red cabbage, parsnip purée and port sauce. Grass-fed Yorkshire steaks are shown the plancha grill, while desserts might promise anything from hot blood-orange soufflé with caramel sauce to duck egg custard tart with a compote of rhubarb (another local touchstone). House wine is £18.95.
Chef/s: Martel Smith. **Open:** Tue to Sat L 12 to 2.30, Tue to Sat D 6 to 9.30. Sun 12 to 6. **Closed:** Mon. **Meals:** main courses £15 to £27. Set L and D £14 (2 courses) to £17. Sun L £16 (2 courses) to £19. **Details:** 80 seats. 80 seats outside. Bar. Wheelchairs. Music. Parking.

■ Oldstead
The Black Swan
Cooking score: 6
Modern British | £85
Oldstead, YO61 4BL
Tel no: (01347) 868387
blackswanoldstead.co.uk

🍷 🛏

Comments like 'the lunch last Saturday was inventive (mostly using the flowers, herbs and other plants from their extensive garden)', are testament to the inspiration Tommy Banks derives from his two-plus-acre allotment. The 16th-century pub is now a well-run restaurant-with-rooms offering a menu that changes in line with the growing season. Dishes are taken way beyond the meat-and-two-veg approach, indeed vegetables have a starring role and, by using techniques such as preserving, clamping and fermenting, the aim is to bring a year-round seasonality to the menu. Flavour is everything in a dish of carrots poached in butter or delicate langoustine teamed with cauliflower and kale, while others have praised aged Galloway beef with smoked bone marrow, wild garlic and capers, and fallow deer with alliums and wood sorrel. Sour bread with sour butter is morcish, the three crossover lollipops (from savoury to sweet) are startlingly good – ditto the inventive rhubarb and rosemary cocktail served with dessert proper of rhubarb with rosemary-infused honey. An enticing global wine list opens at £24.
Chef/s: Tommy Banks. **Open:** Sun L 12 to 2, all week D 6 to 9. **Meals:** Sun L £38. Tasting menus £60 (5 courses) to £85. **Details:** 40 seats. V menu. Bar.

Symbols

🛏 Accommodation is available
£30 Three courses for less than £30
£5 OFF £5-off voucher scheme
🍷 Notable wine list

■ Osmotherley
Golden Lion
Cooking score: 2
Anglo-European | £29
6 West End, Osmotherley, DL6 3AA
Tel no: (01609) 883526
goldenlionosmotherley.co.uk

🛏 £30

On the western fringes of the North York Moors National Park, Osmotherley is a pretty village with this foursquare old pub at its heart (right opposite the market cross in fact). It looks rather like a domestic dwelling at first glance, but it's an 18th-century inn with plenty of period charm and a rustic, 'proper pub' interior. There are seven simply done-out bedrooms, too. The kitchen goes for an uncomplicated approach (the menu doesn't change much), but delivers well-executed stuff such as king prawns in garlic butter and duck liver parfait with apricot relish and brioche. Main courses can be as similarly populist (steak and kidney pudding), but might also offer up whole roast poussin flavoured with rosemary and garlic, or warm Roquefort cheesecake with poached pear chutney. Keep an eye out for the daily specials. Finish with hazelnut, chocolate and raspberry pavlova. Wines start at £16.95.
Chef/s: Christopher Wright. **Open:** Wed to Sun L 12 to 3, all week D 6 to 9. **Closed:** 25 Dec. **Meals:** main courses £10 to £21. **Details:** 68 seats. 16 seats outside. Wheelchairs. Music.

■ Otley

READERS RECOMMEND
The Cheerful Chilli
Vegetarian
East Chevin Road, Otley, LS21 3DD
Tel no: (01943) 466567
thecheerfulchilli.co.uk
'A lively and very informal vegetarian café, very child-friendly with a more traditional restaurant feel in the evening. This is not haute cuisine and it's about as un-posh as you can get, but the food is homemade and delicious.'

▌Pickering
The White Swan Inn
Cooking score: 3
British | £36
Market Place, Pickering, YO18 7AA
Tel no: (01751) 472288
white-swan.co.uk

This may be a 17th-century coaching inn with many period attributes but the family who have run the White Swan for the past 30 years or so haven't preserved it in aspic. There's a traditional bar, confirming this is a proper pub, but elsewhere the ancient stone flags and beams are mixed in with modern ideas and there are smart up-to-date bedrooms, too. In the kitchen there's an unwavering commitment to seasonality, provenance and local produce and they've judged to a nicety what people want from an ancient market town hostelry. Potted crab with celeriac rémoulade and rye toast typifies the straightforward style, while hard-to-fault mains have included Tamworth bacon chop with béarnaise sauce and Gressingham duck breast with cavolo nero, bubble and squeak rösti and celeriac and honey figs. End proceedings with traditional desserts such as treacle tart. The well-spread, carefully curated wine list starts at £18.
Chef/s: Darren Clemmit. **Open:** all week L 12 to 2, D 6.45 to 9. **Meals:** main courses £14 to £26.
Details: 48 seats. 16 seats outside. Bar. Wheelchairs. Parking. No children after 8pm in restaurant.

▌Ramsgill
The Yorke Arms
Cooking score: 6
Modern British | £65
Ramsgill, HG3 5RL
Tel no: (01423) 755243
yorke-arms.co.uk

£5
OFF

'My favourite restaurant'; 'one of our highlights of the year': readers clearly have a great deal of affection for Frances and Gerald Atkins' hideaway in the tranquil nether regions of Nidderdale. Occupying a singularly civilised 18th-century shooting lodge stuffed with antiques and home comforts, the Yorke Arms delivers courteous family hospitality and cracking breakfasts – although Frances Atkins' sophisticated lunch and dinner menus are the main attraction, with their promise of 'clear flavours and excellent presentation'. Much depends on prime North Country ingredients, be it a starter of Whitby crab, halibut and scallops fashionably embellished with smoked turnip, dill, vanilla and sea buckthorn or crusted saddle of moorland venison with oxtail, kidney and caramelised apple. Other ideas show flashes of real ingenuity, as the kitchen adds lemongrass and pine to a dish of sweetbreads and morels or dresses a three-part celebration of dry-aged pork with roguish extras including alexanders, freekeh and pineapple. Desserts also receive ecstatic reviews, especially an audacious creation involving blackcurrant, liquorice, lemon curd and marshmallow. Brilliantly executed canapés and petits fours add to overall pleasure, while prices on the well-spread international wine list start at £35.
Chef/s: Frances Atkins. **Open:** Tue to Sat L 12 to 2, D 7 to 9. **Closed:** Sun, Mon. **Meals:** main courses £25 to £35. Set L £45. Tasting menu £85 (8 courses). **Details:** 40 seats. 20 seats outside. Bar. Music. Parking.

▌Ripon
Lockwoods
Cooking score: 1
Modern British | £29
83 North Street, Ripon, HG4 1DP
Tel no: (01765) 607555
lockwoodsrestaurant.co.uk

£30

The mood is leisurely, prices are fair and the food aims for generous, all-round satisfaction at this all-purpose café-bar-restaurant close to the market square. There's no doubt Matthew Lockwood knows how to win friends – people love the way he strikes the right note between traditional and contemporary, and applaud the cooking from a burger through to Sunday lunch. Fine British ingredients star in everything from Whitby crab salad to roast Nidderdale chicken breast (with homemade tomato ketchup, buttered spinach and fries) or Yorkshire pig pork chop (with smoked bacon potato cake and Ampleforth apple brandy jus), all delivered by a band of affable staff. The daily brunch (10.30 to 12) is popular, too. Wines from £15.95.

Chef/s: Louie Miller. **Open:** Tue to Sat L 12 to 2.30, D 5 to 9.30 (10 Fri and Sat). Sun 10 to 3. **Closed:** Mon, 25 and 26 Dec. **Meals:** main courses £14 to £18. Early D £14 (2 courses) to £17. **Details:** 60 seats. V menu. Bar. Wheelchairs. Music.

Sancton
The Star at Sancton
Cooking score: 4
Modern British | £34
King Street, Sancton, YO43 4QP
Tel no: (01430) 827269
thestaratsancton.co.uk

Walkers about to tackle the Yorkshire Wolds Trail may wish to fortify themselves against the forthcoming rigours at the Star, which sits at its foot. It received its licence as long ago as 1710, so you're in good hands, and the remade interior features bare brick and cream walls hung with small prints and a smart dining room with French doors on to the patio. Ben Cox is justly proud of his supply lines, crediting many of them in the menu specifications, and the Star's own orchard and gardens play their part. Expect servings of big-hearted British cooking subjected to light modernisation in starters such as Yorkshire pudding with braised oxtail and caramelised onion in red wine jus, or kedgeree balls of smoked haddock served with curried greens, prior to cod in saffron cream with roast cauliflower, or local ribeye in béarnaise. Finish with poached pear and blackberry clafoutis and liquorice ice cream. An enterprising collection of stylistically listed wines comes at prices nobody could complain about, with interesting growers and good notes throughout. Prices start at £15.95, or £4.50 a standard glass.

Chef/s: Ben Cox. **Open:** Tue to Sun L 12 to 2 (3 Sun), D 6 to 9.30 (8 Sun). **Closed:** Mon. **Meals:** main courses £12 to £23. Set L £17 (2 courses) to £19. **Details:** 80 seats. 38 seats outside. Bar. Wheelchairs. Music. Parking.

Sawdon
The Anvil Inn
Cooking score: 2
Modern British | £30
Main Street, Sawdon, YO13 9DY
Tel no: (01723) 859896
theanvilinnsawdon.co.uk

Like so many country pubs turned restaurants, this erstwhile village forge still provides a bar where locals can get a drink, but the rest of the place, a cosy little labyrinth of rooms, is turned over to eating. At lunch a British-inspired menu aims to deliver a feel-good factor – a lovely thyme-roasted beetroot tartlet with local goats' cheese or hearty staples like Yorkshire ham and eggs (with chips, obvs) or homemade steak pie. Though on the edge of the North York Moors National Park, the kitchen likes to make full use of proximity to the coast with the likes of Whitby-landed skate wings ('fantastic, meaty') with burnt shrimp butter or, from the dinner menu, a generous portion of medallions of Scarborough woof with king prawns, chorizo and tomato risotto. To finish, expect anything from berry and sherry trifle to lemon rice pudding. It is best to book as the place is 'clearly popular'. Wines from £17.60.

Chef/s: Mark Wilson. **Open:** Sat and Sun L 12 to 2 (2.30 Sun), Wed to Sun D 6.30 to 9 (6 to 8 Sun). **Closed:** Mon, Tue, 25 and 26 Dec, 1 Jan. **Meals:** main courses £14 to £24. **Details:** 36 seats. 12 seats outside. Bar. Music. Parking.

Scarborough

Lanterna

Cooking score: 3
Italian | £37
33 Queen Street, Scarborough, YO11 1HQ
Tel no: (01723) 363616
lanterna-ristorante.co.uk

£5
OFF

Tucked away on a back street, Lanterna is as much a Scarborough institution as the nearby Stephen Joseph Theatre. The cooking moves gracefully with the times but where many modern Italian restaurants aim for lightness, chef-proprietor Giorgio Alessio's food seems more at home with a richer style: in a sauce of porcini mushrooms, tomatoes and creamy white wine for a penne alla montanara, for instance, or in a sensational venison ravioli, filled with rich meat, dressed with a powerful venison ragù and topped with shavings of Parmesan. Elsewhere, white truffles from Moncalvo make a seasonal appearance, shaved over beef carpaccio perhaps, or enhancing a dish of veal escalopes, and the quality of the fish is outstanding, with applause for a lightly cooked local fish stew and 'perfectly cooked' brill fillets in a white wine sauce. Desserts offer few surprises. Directly imported regional Italian wines start at £15.95.
Chef/s: Giorgio Alessio. **Open:** Mon to Sat D only 7 to 9.30. **Closed:** Sun, Mon (Nov to Apr), last 2 weeks Oct. **Meals:** main courses £15 to £45. **Details:** 30 seats. Music.

LOCAL GEM

Eat Me Café

Modern British | £14
2 Hanover Road, Scarborough, YO11 1LS
Tel no: (07445) 475328
eatmecafe.com

£5   £30
OFF

Martyn Hyde and Stephen Dinardo have created a 'welcoming' food-forward café that works brilliantly in its location near the Stephen Joseph Theatre. A varied menu covers breakfast, burgers, sandwiches and cakes but also reveals Martyn's interest in Asian food via 'tin plate' lunches of Thai green curry and ramen noodle bowls (for bibimbap and more, readers also recommend their Friday and Saturday lunch pop-up, Eat Me Social, down the street at No.7). Devotees universally find service 'lovely'. Unlicensed. Note: cash only.

Scawton

The Hare Inn

Cooking score: 5
Modern British | £30
Scawton, YO7 2HG
Tel no: (01845) 597769
thehare-inn.com

£5
OFF

'Unexpected', 'outstanding', 'commendable' and 'brave' are some readers' comments about this ancient country inn in a remote hamlet near Rievaulx Abbey. Brave in ditching the à la carte in favour of three variously priced tasting menus of four, six and eight courses, matched with full vegetarian and pescatarian menus on request. The four-course menu (£30) begins with a complex beef tartare featuring Dexter beef, caper jam, smoked oil, macadamia nuts, dried and grated bone marrow and crisp-fried leeks and continues through three more superb courses, including some impressive rare-breed pork, an optional cheese course, a surprise pre-dessert of mousse, cinder toffee, bee pollen and milk ice cream – before finishing with a flourish of rhubarb, blood orange, meringue and white chocolate presented with the trailing vapours of liquid nitrogen. There may be showmanship but none of it detracts from Paul Jackson's creative, innovative and accomplished cooking. Wines start at £20 with good-value wine flights to accompany each menu.
Chef/s: Paul Jackson. **Open:** Wed to Sun L 12 to 2 (4 Sun), Wed to Sat D 6 to 9. **Closed:** Mon, Tue, 3 weeks Jan, 1 week Jun, 1 week Nov. **Meals:** Set L and D £30 (4 courses) to £60. Sun L £30 (3 courses). **Details:** 22 seats. Bar. Music. Parking. Children at L only.

▍Sheffield
Rafters

Cooking score: 4
Modern British | £43
220 Oakbrook Road, Nether Green, Sheffield,
S11 7ED
Tel no: (0114) 2304819
raftersrestaurant.co.uk

£5 OFF 🍷

Keenly supported by readers, Rafters is a
Sheffield stalwart. It's positively thriving
under the joint ownership of chef Tom
Lawson and restaurant manager Alistair
Myers. If the aim is to cook with creativity and
precision, and serve with down-to-earth
confidence, they've nailed it. The room, above
a row of shops, has the lofty ceiling you might
expect. It's set up to feel special enough for an
occasion, and at £60 the tasting menu looks
good value against the three-course
alternative. To start, try quail breast and confit
leg with sweetcorn purée, peanuts and a five-
spice syrup, the flavours working together for
mutual enhancement. The main event might
be Yorkshire venison with sarladaise potatoes,
smoked beetroot purée and juniper sauce, and
for pudding there's an 'almost miraculously
wobbly' honey pannacotta with strawberries
and honeycomb. In common with the food,
the wine list feels like a labour of love,
from £17.

Chef/s: Thomas Lawson. **Open:** Sun L 12 to 2, Wed
to Sun D 7 to 8.30 (9 Fri and Sat, 8 Sun). **Closed:**
Mon, Tue, 25 to 27 Dec, 1 to 10 Jan, 1 week Aug.
Meals: set D £43. Sun L £28 (2 courses) to £34.
Tasting menu £60. **Details:** 38 seats. Music. Children
over 12 yrs only.

▍Shibden
Shibden Mill Inn

Cooking score: 3
Modern British | £30
Shibden Mill Fold, Shibden, HX3 7UL
Tel no: (01422) 365840
shibdenmillinn.com

🛏

'Goodness me, it does confuse SatNavs and
lacks signage,' noted one traveller after a
tortuous trip to this seriously out-of-the-way
pub/restaurant-with-rooms hidden in a lush
Yorkshire fold. Originally a spinning mill, it
now cuts quite a dash with its semi-secret
snugs, huge hearths and bare stone walls. The
décor 'fits nicely with the food' which 'spans
everyday and affordable alongside slightly
more ambitious', although you have to
negotiate a plethora of confusing menus.
Some ideas sound cluttered, but the results are
generally 'fresh and lively': juicy lamb rump
sits on a superb salad of peas, asparagus and
chives with crunchy barley, croûtons and tart
raspberries, while a massive slab of butter-
poached halibut arrives with brown shrimps, a
huge langoustine, sea plants and boulangère-
style potatoes layered with smoked trout. Also
expect the odd curiosity, from a fennel
cheesecake accompanying king scallops to a
'firm-but-silky' butternut squash pannacotta
served with strawberry sorbet. Wines start
at £17.55.

Chef/s: Darren Parkinson. **Open:** Mon to Sat L 12 to
2 (2.30 Fri and Sat), D 5.30 to 9 (9.30 Fri, 6 to 9.30
Sat). Sun 12 to 7.30. **Closed:** 25 and 26 Dec.
Meals: main courses £17 to £25. Set L and D £14 (2
courses) to £17. **Details:** 88 seats. 50 seats outside.
Bar. Music. Parking.

◾ South Dalton
The Pipe and Glass Inn
Cooking score: 5
Modern British | £38
West End, South Dalton, HU17 7PN
Tel no: (01430) 810246
pipeandglass.co.uk

The red-tiled, white-fronted inn dates from the 17th century, and has been extensively and carefully redeveloped by James and Kate Mackenzie since 2006. A painstakingly tended garden, including kitchen plots, is not the least of it. Sitting on the edge of the Dalton Estate, it benefits from exemplary local produce, which James transforms into carefully worked modern dishes that retain the fun element. A salad of crackling and sticky apple is the apposite partner to a little jar of potted pork, and there may be devils on horseback advancing up the menu from savoury to main-course accompaniment for guinea fowl with heritage potato and kale in sherry sauce. Otherwise, start with salmon cured in Two Chefs ale with a Lindisfarne oyster fritter, and follow on with lamb shoulder, served with a mutton and kidney faggot, butternut, redcurrants and barley. A finisher of millionaire chocolate pudding with salted burnt butter ice cream pushes every possible button. Plentiful wines by the glass from £4.50 lead the charge on a list of exciting reach, arranged with food-matching in mind. The French growers are particularly inspired, and prices are by no means silly. House wines from the Hérault are £17.50.
Chef/s: James Mackenzie. **Open:** Tue to Sun L 12 to 2 (4 Sun), Tue to Sat D 6 to 9.30. **Closed:** Mon (exc bank hols), 2 weeks Jan. **Meals:** main courses £12 to £29. **Details:** 100 seats. 60 seats outside. Bar. Wheelchairs. Music. Parking.

◾ Sowerby Bridge
Gimbals
Cooking score: 4
Modern British | £30
76 Wharf Street, Sowerby Bridge, HX6 2AF
Tel no: (01422) 839329
gimbals.co.uk
£5 OFF

'They just get better and better,' noted one reader who was seduced by Gimbals' idiosyncratic charms. Co-owner Janet Baker helped design the interiors (note the rococo mirrors and metallic sculptures), while Simon Baker's culinary endeavours are more than a match for the highly personal décor. Seasonal ingredients from Yorkshire's farms and countryside are the building blocks for some exuberant and invigorating dishes spanning everything from a hot tossed salad of pickled chanterelles, Jerusalem artichokes, candied walnuts and sourdough croûtons to cod steak with dried pea purée, crispy Parma ham and capers. Baker also has a penchant for aromatic Persian flavours (spiced chicken and pomegranate koftas with wild fennel, yoghurt and pomegranate 'jewels'), while desserts such as salted-caramel millionaire's shortbread and a burnt crème brûlée ice cream find their inspiration closer to home. The tasting menu is an absolute steal, 'glorious gins' are a hit in the upstairs lounge, and house wines start at £17.
Chef/s: Simon Baker. **Open:** Mon to Sat D only 6.30 to 9.15. **Closed:** Sun, 24 to 27 Dec. **Meals:** main courses £14 to £22. Set D £19 (2 courses) to £23. Tasting menu £25 (5 courses). **Details:** 55 seats. Music.

▋ Staddlebridge
The Cleveland Tontine
Cooking score: 2
French | £40
Staddlebridge, DL6 3JB
Tel no: (01609) 882671
theclevelandtontine.co.uk
£5 OFF 🛏

Handsome and comfortable, if a little tricky to find, the two-centuries-old Tontine has scrubbed up nicely under the stewardship of Charles Tompkins. The refurbishment is current enough to attract first-timers, makes the most of the listed ornate plasterwork ceiling and magnificent fireplace in the restaurant, with the conservatory now popular locally for afternoon tea. Paul Bussey heads the kitchen, delivering classy, fine-tuned food such as dressed Whitby crab with fennel and pickled apple salad, crab bisque ketchup, sea herbs and squid-ink cracker, or locally shot wood pigeon Rossini with a crisp confit of the leg and smooth liver parfait. Locally reared steaks are a main-course mainstay, but there's also North Sea cod and creel-caught langoustines served with roast baby red peppers, pak choi and langoustine broth, and locally caught Dover sole meunière. Dessert could be almond and Yorkshire rapeseed oil cake with poached William pears. Wines from £25.
Chef/s: Paul Bussey. **Open:** all week L 12 to 2.30, D 6.30 to 9 (9.30 Fri and Sat). **Meals:** main courses £15 to £33. Set D £20. Sun L £25. **Details:** 80 seats. Bar. Music. Parking.

Please send us your feedback

To register your opinion about any restaurant listed in this guide, or a new restaurant that you wish to bring to our attention, please visit the web address at the bottom of the page. Your feedback informs the content of the book and will be used to compile next year's reviews.

▋ Todmorden
Blackbird
Cooking score: 2
International | £20
23 Water Street, Todmorden, OL14 5AB
Tel no: (01706) 813038
blackbirdbar.co.uk
£5 OFF £30

'Such delicious food in a wonderful little shop on a back street in Todmorden.' Deep satisfaction emanates from readers dining at this laid-back tapas bar. Blackbird is one of those informal, friendly places with a cool urban feel that belies its market town location, and is making a name for itself with a mix of contemporary Spanish and Mediterranean-style small plates. The cooking is 'really creative and tasty', locally sourced and seasonal, and the menu is a mixed bag: sharing platters of vegetarian or fish meze, gambas pil pil, lamb kofta, sherry and paprika braised pig's cheeks with cauliflower purée, parsnip crisps and wilted kale, and a vegetarian timbale of black rice and black garlic served with a truffle aïoli and pea shoots. Honey and Calvados zabaglione with biscotti crumble is one way to finish. To drink, wines have been selected with gusto (from £16.50) and there are bottled craft beers and an extensive cocktail list, too.
Chef/s: Tim Holdroyd. **Open:** all week L 12 to 3, D 4 to 9. **Closed:** 25 and 26 Dec, 1 Jan. **Meals:** tapas £5 to £8. **Details:** 40 seats. Bar. Wheelchairs. Music.

★ NEW ENTRY ★
The White Rabbit
Cooking score: 3
Modern British | £31
1 White Hart Fold, Todmorden, OL14 7BD
Tel no: (01706) 817828
whiterabbittodmorden.com
£5 OFF 🍾

Since taking over this small, narrow former shop in the heart of Todmorden, David and Robyn Gledhill have scrubbed up old oak floors, painted and added mismatched furniture and lots of candles and flowers to create a 'fabulous little restaurant' where 'there is always a warm welcome'. David has done time in respected Yorkshire eateries and is creating something very special here, setting the scene with a Swaledale cheese 'custard' and potato popcorn amuse-bouche. Confit duck and brioche egg shows an 'impressive lightness of touch'; 'Seen and Unseen' pasta – paper-thin ravioli, one of them dissolved with almond milk sauce – reveals consummate skill and a welcome playfulness, but it was a rabbit roulade with candied beets and parsnip jus that stole the show at inspection. Desserts might include lemon parfait and a delightfully light coconut sponge. A brief but interesting wine list starts at £15.

Chef/s: David and Robyn Gledhill. **Open:** Wed to Sat L 12 to 3, D 5.30 to 9. **Closed:** Sun, Mon, Tue, 26 and 27 Dec, first week Aug. **Meals:** main courses £15 to £19. **Details:** 22 seats. Bar. Music.

∎ Wakefield

LOCAL GEM

Iris
Modern British | £29
12 Bull Ring, Wakefield, WF1 1HA
Tel no: (01924) 367683
iris-restaurant.com
£5 OFF £30

'British, seasonal, local', proclaim the signs in the front window of this affable neighbourhood eatery, and chef-owner Liam Duffy – alongside his 'lovely staff' – delivers on his promise. Plenty of generous regional accents are strewn across the regularly changing menus, from wild mushrooms on toast with salsa verde and a crispy duck egg to Round Green venison with smoked mash and roasted shallots. Yorkshire provides steaks and cheeses too, and there's a homespun flavour to puds such as parkin with treacle stout sauce. Wines from £15.95.

∎ West Witton
The Wensleydale Heifer
Cooking score: 3
Seafood | £35
Main Street, West Witton, DL8 4LS
Tel no: (01969) 622322
wensleydaleheifer.co.uk
£5 OFF

Bring your sense of humour with you to the Heifer. A honeycomb of snugs and corridors, whitewashed stone and black beams, it's chock-full of chintzy artworks, ice buckets and ephemera, a menu that looks like a Victorian playbill, saucy adult comic strips plastering the bathrooms, and a Guinness World Record for the largest portion of fish and chips ever served. David Moss cooks exuberantly and with blithe disregard for culinary orthodoxy, offering a Thai-style salad of battered squid with chilli-rubbed pork crackling, green beans, peanuts and papaya, before rolling on with 30-day grass-fed steaks amid a barrage of accompaniments, to which their irrefutable quality stands up robustly. A ribeye at one test meal was juicy, nicely fatted and accurately timed, with great chips and onion rings. Otherwise, look to herb-crusted hake on truffled risotto. Dessert promises 'A Taste of Paradise' – white chocolate and coconut choc ice, pannacotta, piña colada and a pineapple kebab. A varied and interesting wine list opens at £21.50.

Chef/s: David Moss. **Open:** all week L 12 to 2.30, D 6 to 9.30. **Meals:** main courses £17 to £40. Set L and D £20 (2 courses) to £24. Sun L £23. **Details:** 90 seats. 50 seats outside. Bar. Wheelchairs. Music. Parking.

Local Gem

Local Gems are the perfect neighbourhood venues, delivering good, freshly cooked food at great value for money.

Karen Turner Photography

Joshua Overington

Le Cochon Aveugle, York

What inspired you to become a chef?
I fell into it on a gap year to Australia where I found myself pot washing in a café in Bondi.

What would you be doing if you weren't a chef?
I always liked the idea of being a drummer in a band.

What's your favourite junk food?
Pizza, I could eat it every day! Especially well-made, thin-crust, Italian-style ones. But I never really say no to any pizza – anywhere, anytime!

What is the vital ingredient for a successful kitchen?
A loyal team. If you don't have your boys and girls supporting you, you're not going anywhere.

Which chef do you most admire at the moment?
James Cross at Lake Road Kitchen. When I ate there recently it blew my mind.

And finally...tell us something about yourself that will surprise your diners.
I have over 400 cookbooks at home! I have now been limited to a one-in, one-out policy!

▪ Wetherby

LOCAL GEM
Mango Vegetarian
Indian | £25
12-14 Bank Street, Wetherby, LS22 6NQ
Tel no: (01937) 585755
mangovegetarian.com

£30

Formed from two cottages hewn from local stone, Mango sports a sleek contemporary look and serves up Indian vegetarian food that covers the ground from Gujarat to the deep south of the country. Get going with kachori or paneer rolls, and note the menu indicates vegan and gluten-free options. Move on to main courses like aloo palak and aurro (smoked aubergines in a rich tomato sauce), or strike a single blow by going for one of the thalis. It's licensed, with bottles starting at £13.50.

▪ Whitby
Bridge Cottage Bistro
Cooking score: 2
Modern British | £28
On the bridge, Sandsend, Whitby, YO21 3SU
Tel no: (01947) 893438
bridgecottagebistro.com

£30

Next to the bridge across the beck that flows on to Sandsend beach, this isn't your typical seaside café, but it does function as such during the day, with cakes and bread made on the premises. Make time for lunch, though, or get a reservation for dinner (three nights a week), and tuck into a menu where East Coast seafood figures large, especially on Friday night's tasting menu. Kick off with potted North Sea shrimps, or go for a fashionable surf and turf option – pig's cheek with butter-poached lobster and asparagus. Scarborough woof is partnered with cockle and barley risotto, Whitby lobster arrives with chips and béarnaise, hay-baked new-season lamb is perked up with salsa verde: the influences are a Brit, French and Italian tripartite. To finish,

Eccles cake comes with Wensleydale ice cream. It all takes place in a simply stylish, gently contemporary space. Wines start at £17.
Chef/s: Alexander Perkins. **Open:** Tue to Sun L 12 to 2.30 (3 Sun), Thur to Sat D 10 to 9. **Closed:** Mon. **Meals:** main courses £12 to £26. **Details:** 26 seats. 30 seats outside. Bar. Wheelchairs. Music. Parking.

LOCAL GEM

Magpie Café
Seafood | £25
14 Pier Road, Whitby, YO21 3PU
Tel no: (01947) 602058
magpiecafe.co.uk
£5 OFF £30

Fish and chips: it's what you've come to Whitby for and this quaint old-fashioned whitewashed cottage with 'lovely' views to harbour and abbey is arguably the best place to get it – 'the queues on the steps outside are legendary'. What distinguishes the Magpie from a myriad of competing chippies is its range of fish, shellfish, fish pies, platters and specials in ever more convoluted and not always successful ways. Most revert to the mighty portions of crisply battered haddock (skin on) and cod (skin off) and fat-cut chips. Drink tea with proper tea leaves, Yorkshire bottled beers or wines from a standard list, from £15.95.

▌York
Le Cochon Aveugle
Cooking score: 4
French | £40
37 Walmgate, York, YO1 9TX
Tel no: (01904) 640222
lecochonaveugleyork.com

'Fantastic attention to detail' and 'unexpected but delicious combinations', are just two of many endorsements from readers who continue to enjoy this petite French restaurant with big ambitions – although it has now been extended upstairs, providing more seating for its loyal fans. Chef-patron Josh Overington offers two surprise menus of six-

or nine-courses that begin with superb sourdough bread and beurre noisette and progress through a series of complex dishes that might include white and green asparagus with an almond gazpacho, sourdough crumbs and lemon shavings, followed by Whitby crab pasta given a kick of orange zest. The dishes build with blow-torched mackerel, pickled melon and chilled melon soup, mussels cooked in Corsican beer are given a heady chestnut and truffle sauce, while pigeon breast is matched with a smoked aubergine purée. It's an exciting and challenging menu, although reporters were divided over chopped raw lamb with oyster emulsion and savoury sorbet – meat served 'bleu' is not to everyone's taste. There was no debate, however, over a paper-thin pastry tart with figs and wood sorrel, nor a tonka bean pannacotta with meringue. An exclusively French wine list starts at £18.50.
Chef/s: Joshua Overington. **Open:** Tue to Sat D only 6 to 9. **Closed:** Sun, Mon, 25 and 26 Dec, 3 weeks Jan, 1 week May, 1 week Sept. **Meals:** set D £40 (6 courses) to £60. **Details:** 28 seats. V menu. Bar. Music.

Le Langhe
Cooking score: 5
Italian | £32
The Old Coach House, Peasholme Green, York, YO1 7PW
Tel no: (01904) 622584
lelanghe.co.uk
★

Ottavio ('Otto') Bocca summons up and revitalises Italy's gastronomic heritage at this astonishing set-up named after Piedmont's Langhe hills (his home turf and birthplace of the Slow Food movement). At lunchtime, the place behaves like a neighbourhood deli-café serving a wondrous selection of artisan cheeses and salume (try the gold-standard culatello di zibello accompanied by homemade mostarda di frutti), although exquisitely silky hand-kneaded pasta is the kitchen's great strength, with sauces used to enhance rather than overwhelm. Casual meals are taken in the café and communal courtyard (weather permitting), but Le Langhe shows its true colours on Friday and Saturday evenings, when brilliant-value tasting menus and a more ambitious carte are served in the upstairs dining room. This is cooking on another level altogether – think seared tuna with Taggiasche olives and fennel salad, slow-cooked ox cheek in red wine or chicken breast with foie gras velouté and black truffles followed by hazelnut and marron glacé parfait. Obscure artisan beers such as Amarcord are worth a punt, although nothing can touch the stellar wine list – a staggeringly comprehensive oenophile tour of Italy's regions, with bottles from £15.

Chef/s: Ottavio Bocca. **Open:** Mon to Sat L 12 to 3, Fri and Sat D 6.45 to 11. **Closed:** Sun, 25 to 27 Dec, first 2 weeks Jan, bank hols. **Meals:** main courses £19 to £28. Tasting menu L £25 (4 courses), D £42 (8 courses). **Details:** 60 seats. 25 seats outside. Wheelchairs. Music.

Melton's

Cooking score: 5
Modern British | £32
7 Scarcroft Road, York, YO23 1ND
Tel no: (01904) 634341
meltonsrestaurant.co.uk

£5
OFF

An odds-on favourite for more than 25 years, Michael and Lucy Hjort's neighbourhood charmer is a local bolt-hole treasured by foodies as well as the punters who frequent York's nearby racecourse. Melton's charmingly familiar interiors have been freshened up of late, although the quaint murals depicting a bygone era remain – along with Lucy's well-tutored front-of-house team. Intelligently conceived, gently imaginative cooking at highly attractive prices is still the kitchen's USP, and Michael's food is dependent on painstaking local sourcing – note the Holme Farm venison served with kale, parsley root purée, roast pear and chocolate oil. Fish from the Yorkshire boats is the basis for a medley with mussels, warm cauliflower mousse and fennel, although scallops are hand-dived beauties from Kyle of Lochalsh. Alternatively, if you have a penchant for pork, try the 'whole hog' – a rare-breed bonanza involving belly, gammon and a ballotine with soured cabbage and boulangère potatoes. Melton's is also famed for its Yorkshire cheeses, or you can conclude in style with a take on Eton mess employing locally grown rhubarb. Michael and Lucy's personally chosen wine list is a highly impressive compendium kicking off at £18.

Chef/s: Michael Hjort and Calvin Miller. **Open:** Tue to Sat L 12 to 2, D 5.30 to 10. **Closed:** Sun, Mon, 2 weeks Christmas. **Meals:** main courses £17 to £25. Set L and early D £26 (2 courses) to £30. Tasting menu £40 (5 courses). **Details:** 42 seats. Music.

The Park

Cooking score: 3
British | £55
Marmadukes Town House Hotel, 4-5 St Peter's Grove, York, YO30 6AQ
Tel no: (01904) 540903
marmadukestownhousehotelyork.com

Now happily ensconced in this boutique hotel, Adam Jackson continues to impress with 'innovative' but 'uncontrived' modern British cooking: 'the food was beautiful to look at, and was packed with flavours that were traditional but with a surprising twist'. Served against the backdrop of a stylish Victorian hotel, Mr Jackson's cooking draws on a broad palette of international flavours, from crab with red curry to duck with sweet potato and game bolognese. In between might be game with white bread, pease and pickles, artichoke with mushroom, hazelnut and sorrel, and salmon gravadlax with beetroot. It all adds up to eight courses, with no choices and no complaints from diners: 'nothing could be criticised,' noted one who declared the bomber bread with Marmite butter 'out of this world'. For dessert, try rhubarb with white chocolate and tonka bean followed by a cheese course. 'Impeccable' service and interesting wine recommendations from a weighty list complete the picture. Bottles start at £25.

Chef/s: Adam Jackson. **Open:** Tue to Sat D only 7 to 9. **Closed:** Sun, Mon, 2 weeks Jan. **Meals:** set D £55 (8 courses). **Details:** 24 seats. Bar. Music. Parking.

The Star Inn the City

Cooking score: 2
British | £45
Lendal Engine House, Museum Street, York, YO1 7DR
Tel no: (01904) 619208
starinnthecity.co.uk

The city-slicker cousin of the renowned Star Inn in Harome (see entry). Where the country gaff has a mop of thatch and 14th-century bones, the York outpost occupies a bit of urban history in the form of an old engine house by the Museum Gardens on the banks of the river Ouse. It's a lovely spot – better still on the terrace – with an all-day menu that covers an awful lot of ground. 'Ceps in the city' may or may not raise a smile, but pan-fried wild mushrooms with truffle and tarragon cream and toasted English muffin is a heart-warming opener, or go for posh prawn cocktail. Beer-braised Yorkshire ox cheek with Blue Wensleydale dauphinois shows appreciation of the region's culinary heritage (properly gentrified), while pearl barley 'risotto' with Thorganby green peas and garden mint butter is a classy veggie option. Yorkshire rhubarb is a seasonal treat. Wines start at £21.
Chef/s: Matthew Hunter. **Open:** all week 12 to 9.30 (7.30 Sun). **Meals:** main courses £16 to £32. Set L and D £17 (2 courses) to £22. Sun L £16. **Details:** 100 seats. 50 seats outside. Music.

Walmgate Ale House

Cooking score: 2
British | £25
25 Walmgate, York, YO1 9TX
Tel no: (01904) 629222
walmgateale.co.uk
£30

No sooner, it seemed, had Michael Hjort transformed his Fossgate eatery from bistro to ale house with food, done out with skeins of

rope recalling its days as a ropery, than it was seriously damaged in the 2015 Boxing Day floods. Within three months it was back on track with decently priced, popular dishes like steak and chips, barley and mushroom risotto, coley with a crumb and olive crust and an excellent pea pancake with spiced cauliflower. Puddings might be sticky toffee, clementine sponge and custard, lemon posset or Yorkshire ices. Wines move steadily upwards from a Chilean rosé (£15) but this is an ale house with a dependable range of Yorkshire ales from York Brewery, Copper Dragon, Rudgate and Great Heck matched with substantial snacks of pork pie, sausage roll and pork scratchings. Good for set lunches, weekend brunches, Sunday roasts and themed specials.
Chef/s: Michael Hjort and Aaron Davey. **Open:** Tue to Sun 12 to 10.30 (10am Sat and Sun). **Closed:** Mon, 25, 26 and 31 Dec, 1 Jan. **Meals:** main courses £13 to £19. Set L and D £14 (2 courses) to £16. Sun L £14, Sun D £16. **Details:** 130 seats. Bar. Wheelchairs. Music.

LOCAL GEM

Mannion & Co.

British | £20
1 Blake Street, York, YO1 8QJ
Tel no: (01904) 631030
mannionandco.co.uk
£30

There are ample reasons to visit this busy little café beyond excellent coffee and handmade biscotti – deli boards, well-filled ciabatta sandwiches, mushrooms on toast and eggs Benedict. Blackboard mains feature the likes of pancetta, duck egg and sourdough toast. For sweetness there are fruit scones with jam and clotted cream, delicate cakes or enormous flouncy meringues served with berries and cream. Bag your own table, join the 'social table' or enjoy the hidden back garden. Italy and Spain star on the beer and wine list. Wines from £18.

SCOTLAND

Borders, Dumfries & Galloway,
Lothians (inc. Edinburgh),
Strathclyde (inc. Glasgow), Central, Fife,
Tayside, Grampian, Highlands & Islands

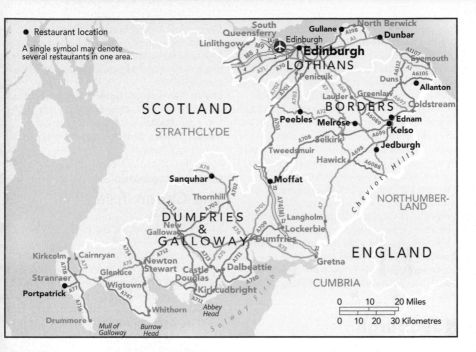

pannacotta with apricot compote, candied
fennel seeds and frozen blackberry yoghurt
makes a luscious finish, and the local and
Scottish cheeseboard is a winner, too. Service
is well judged and the short, global wine list
opens at £14.95.

Chef/s: Craig Rushden. **Open:** all week L 12 to 2, D
6 to 9. **Meals:** main courses £10 to £24. **Details:** 60
seats. 50 seats outside. Music.

■ Ednam
Edenwater House
Cooking score: 4
Modern British | £40
Ednam, TD5 7QL
Tel no: (01573) 224070
edenwaterhouse.co.uk

The Kellys' stone-built manse is hidden away
in the tiny village of Ednam in the
borderlands, not far from the racing at Kelso.
In a candlelit dining room run with
appreciable bonhomie, Jacqui Kelly offers a

■ Allanton
Allanton Inn
Cooking score: 2
Modern British | £26
Allanton, TD11 3JZ
Tel no: (01890) 818260
allantoninn.co.uk

The setting is a quiet Borders village of some
20 houses, its venerable inn a sturdy, pleasantly
updated stone hostelry that has not forsaken its
pub roots – so expect real ales in the hospitable
bar. On the food front, things have gone up
and down. If last year was no great vintage,
this year seems better. The cooking is a fine
compromise between local materials and a
style alert to the wider world. One wholly
satisfactory meal consisted of confit of pork
belly croquettes with red onion and thyme
marmalade and pumpkin-seed salad, then
breast of Gressingham duck with beetroot
dauphinois, roasted shallots and thyme- and
honey-infused jus. Delicate buttermilk

four-course table d'hôte dinner menu three nights a week. Proceedings often open with a characterful soup, perhaps chicken, avocado and lime, or east Asian-style hot-and-sour with prawns, before moving on to fish such as sea bass with pea purée in hazelnut and basil dressing, and a possible main course of herbed rack of lamb with ribboned root veg in sticky chicken jus. Occasionally, it's the other way round, when stuffed loin of rabbit and granola in tarragon jus might be followed by basil-crusted halibut in lemony beurre blanc. Flavours are clear as a bell throughout, with something like sponge-based vanilla bavarois topped with caramelised apple, served with pistachio cream, bringing up the rear. A varietally arranged wine list starts at £19.80. **Chef/s:** Jacqui Kelly. **Open:** Thur to Sat D only 6 to 10. **Closed:** Sun to Wed, Dec to Mar. **Meals:** set D £40 (4 courses). **Details:** 16 seats. Parking. Children over 12 yrs only.

▮ Jedburgh
The Caddy Mann
Cooking score: 2
Modern British | £25
Mounthooly, Jedburgh, TD8 6TJ
Tel no: (01835) 850787
caddymann.com
£30

It may be housed within three converted farm workers' cottages, but there's nothing remotely bucolic about this neighbourhood restaurant with its crimson cloths, napkins stuffed into wine glasses, prints and assorted auction-room knick-knacks. Chef/co-proprietor Ross Horrocks is happy to cook anything that's local, so expect a big bag of seasonal meat and game ranging from pheasant, chicken and snipe terrine, or chunks of roe deer braised in Burgundy, to slow-roast mutton with bubble and squeak or even a fricassee of grey squirrel. He's a fan of traditional suet puddings, too (try the pulled duck version), although his repertoire also extends to Thai crab cakes, free-range veal osso buco and blackened salmon fillet with fresh mango, coriander and red onion salsa.

Vegetarians have a choice of crêpes, wraps, tagines and suchlike, while desserts could span anything from steamed syrup sponge pudding to glazed lemon and passion fruit tart. Wines from £14.50.
Chef/s: Ross Horrocks. **Open:** Tue to Sun L 12 to 2, Fri and Sat D 7 to 12. **Closed:** Mon, 25 and 26 Dec, 1 to 3 Jan. **Meals:** main courses £13 to £20. **Details:** 50 seats. 20 seats outside. V menu. Wheelchairs. Parking.

READERS RECOMMEND

The Capon Tree
Modern British
61 The High Street, Jedburgh, TD8 6DQ
Tel no: (01835) 869596
'Main courses included venison three ways (Wellington, seared loin and mini cottage pie) and Dijon mustard-crusted local lamb chops with black pudding mash. I thought the lamb chops were exceptionally well cooked, with a super tasty, mild mustard crust.'

▮ Kelso
The Cobbles
Cooking score: 1
Modern British | £25
7 Bowmont Street, Kelso, TD5 7JH
Tel no: (01573) 223548
thecobbleskelso.co.uk
£30

Thoroughly rooted in the market town of Kelso – tucked away just off the main square – the Cobbles is an upbeat pub and restaurant where a jaunty, smiling welcome greets regulars and visitors, and the atmosphere is warm and inviting whatever the season. Ingredients are regional and top-notch, and sound cooking sees both bar meals and carte classics skilfully prepared. Steak, mushroom and Tempest pastry pie and fish and chips are favourites, but reporters have also praised pea and mint ravioli with garlic sauce, and mussels with bacon, garlic and white wine cream sauce. To drink there are Tempest ales or wine from £15.95.

Chef/s: Daniel Norcliffe. **Open:** Mon to Fri L 12 to
2.30, D 5.45 to 9. Sat and Sun 12 to 9 (8 Sun).
Closed: 25 and 26 Dec. **Meals:** main courses £10 to
£21. **Details:** 60 seats. 16 seats outside. Bar. Music.

Melrose
Burt's Hotel
Cooking score: 2
Modern British | £38
Market Square, Melrose, TD6 9PL
Tel no: (01896) 822285
burtshotel.co.uk

Burt's wears a traditional look, as befits a
Georgian inn, the smart white frontage lent
splashes of colour from window boxes. It's
been in the Henderson family since the year
decimal coinage was introduced (1971), and is
run with great care and attention to detail. The
cooking has moved with the times, and a
gently modern Scottish flavour now imbues
both bar and restaurant menus, the latter
dealing in the likes of lobster, scallop and
prawn terrine with avocado purée in sweet
pepper dressing and lemon oil, followed by
corn-fed guinea fowl with smoked bacon and
herb stuffing, with a sage and onion croquette
and dauphinois in chicken jus. Halibut comes
with the fashionable accoutrements of crispy
chicken skin, cauliflower purée and herbed
gnocchi, and proceedings come to a very
satisfying conclusion with rum-lashed crème
brûlée, garnished with a banoffee bonbon,
glazed banana, shortbread and rum and raisin
ice cream. A wine list arranged by grape
variety opens with four house selections
at £17.75.
Chef/s: Trevor Williams. **Open:** Sat and Sun L 12 to
2, all week D 7 to 9 (9.30 Fri and Sat). **Closed:** 3 Jan.
Meals: main courses £14 to £26. **Details:** 50 seats.
24 seats outside. Bar. Parking. Children over 8 yrs
only.

Peebles
Osso
Cooking score: 2
Modern British | £29
Innerleithen Road, Peebles, EH45 8BA
Tel no: (01721) 724477
ossorestaurant.com

£30

Chatty young staff in jeans and T-shirts keep
the mood upbeat while Osso goes through its
daytime café routine, accommodating a
cheery mixed bag of coach parties, office
workers, shoppers and mums with buggies.
The homemade black pudding is a star turn
(perhaps packed into a wholesome butty), but
the choice also runs to soups, brunch staples,
small plates and a few more substantial fillers
such as daube of beef with mash. Come
evening, Osso makes the seamless transition to
a classy little bistro, with soft candlelight
adding a subtle edge to more ambitious
culinary ideas based on regional produce –
think crispy pork with celeriac purée, pickled
pears and roasted hazelnuts or hake fillet with
cauliflower, stem broccoli, mussels and dulse
(seaweed) dressing. For afters, try the calorific
challenge of dark chocolate crémeux or keep it
light with rosewater pannacotta, pistachio,
honeycomb and pomegranate. Wines
from £17.25.
Chef/s: Ally McGrath and Stuart Smith. **Open:** all
week 10 to 4.30, Tue to Sat D 6 to 9. **Closed:** 25 Dec,
1 Jan. **Meals:** main courses £13 to £19. **Details:** 38
seats. 6 seats outside. Wheelchairs. Music.

▌Moffat
The Limetree
Cooking score: 4
Modern British | £29
Hartfell House, Hartfell Crescent, Moffat,
DG10 9AL
Tel no: (01683) 220153
hartfellhouse.co.uk
🛏️ £30

Enclosed within the Victorian Gothic Revival
pile of Hartfell House, the Limetree occupies
the old dining room, appropriately enough.
Its wood-grained doors and shutters, dating
from 1860, contribute to the singularity of the
ambience and, behind the scenes, Matt
Seddon toils alone to produce a modern
British repertoire that draws influences from
all over. The journey might begin with
Jamaican pepperpot and grilled bonito, before
hauling in some Spanish morcilla to go with
pork tenderloin, braised red cabbage and
apple, and then come home to sticky ginger
pudding, lemon custard and brown-bread ice
cream. A confirmed regular found no fault
with a winter dinner of brandade served with
a poached egg and tapenade crostini,
Cumbrian beef rump with celeriac dauphinois
and shallot sauce, and a finale of orange
frangipane tart with red gooseberries and
elderflower cream. A short wine list opens
with house wines, Languedoc Grenache Blanc
and Chilean Merlot, at £16.
Chef/s: Matt Seddon. **Open:** Tue to Sat D only 6.30
to 8.30. **Closed:** Sun, Mon, 24 to 30 Dec, 10 days
Jan, 10 days Oct. **Meals:** set D £24 (2 courses) to
£29. **Details:** 22 seats. Wheelchairs. Music. Parking.

▌Portpatrick
Knockinaam Lodge
Cooking score: 5
Modern British | £68
Portpatrick, DG9 9AD
Tel no: (01776) 810471
knockinaamlodge.com
£5 OFF 🍷 🛏️

The craggy cove nearby may be owned by the
hotel, but this is Scotland at its wildest – an
untamed wilderness of wooded glens, wind-
ravaged trees, rugged outcrops and rocky
shorelines. By contrast, Knockinaam is
serenity itself, coddled in 30 acres of grounds
with a Victorian hunting-lodge interior that
feels distinguished but homely – all squishy
armchairs, blazing fires and framed prints,
with gold-patterned wallpaper, plush carpets
and displays of gilt-trimmed crockery in the
sumptuous candlelit dining room. Chef Tony
Pierce works to a daily menu of quietly
assured, sophisticated dishes that bring a
French culinary sensibility to supplies of
seasonal Scottish produce. Dine in April, and
you might progress from grilled Drummore
lobster and smoked salmon dressed with
orange and chervil emulsion via a taster of
cauliflower and parsley soup to brioche-
crusted cannon of Galloway lamb served
alongside shallot purée, purple sprouting
broccoli and rosemary-scented jus. Dessert
might be chilled vanilla rice pudding with
poached fruits and an apple doughnut or you
could finish with some Anglo-French cheeses.
Owner David Ibbotson's lovingly accrued,
authoritative wine list is an endlessly
fascinating global compendium, with house
selections from £23.
Chef/s: Tony Pierce. **Open:** all week L 12 to 1.15, D
7 to 9. **Meals:** set L £40 (4 courses). Set D £68 (5
courses). Sun L £33 (4 courses). **Details:** 20 seats.
Bar. Music. Parking. Children over 12 yrs only at D.

■ Sanquhar
Blackaddie House Hotel

Cooking score: 4
Modern British | £55
Blackaddie Road, Sanquhar, DG4 6JJ
Tel no: (01659) 50270
blackaddiehotel.co.uk
£5 OFF 🚗

A 16th-century stone-built country house on the river Nith in Scotland's southwest, Blackaddie sits amid trim lawns and bracing country air. Inside is done in gentle pastels, the better to soothe the senses, a light minty green predominating in the dining room, which enjoys views of riparian tranquillity. Here, Ian McAndrew cooks in bold contemporary fashion, offering exquisitely presented dishes with colourful garnishes, the 'amazing freshness of the home-grown vegetables' being a particular high point for one reporter. That last might include beetroot and cucumber in pressed and sorbet forms, along with goats' cheese, as accompaniments to a starter of mi-cuit rainbow sea trout. After an intermediate such as fennel ice cream, it's on to a trio of pork (fillet, belly and pork and black pudding bonbons), imaginatively served with curried cauliflower and puréed butternut squash. Finale might be tremulous vanilla pannacotta with rhubarb jelly and sorbet and a pistachio tuile. Wines start at £22.50, or £5.75 a glass.
Chef/s: Ian McAndrew. **Open:** all week L 12.30 to 2, D 6.30 to 9. **Meals:** Set L £30 (2 courses) to £36. Set D £55 (4 courses). Gourmet menu £75. **Details:** 20 seats. Bar. Wheelchairs. Music. Parking.

Andrew Fairlie

Restaurant Andrew Fairlie, Gleneagles Hotel, Auchterarder

What inspired you to become a chef?
Tarragon. I worked part-time as a waiter while I was still at school and one weekend I was serving beef chasseur to a wedding party. On my way back to the kitchen I tasted the sauce and it literally stopped me in my tracks. I had never tasted fresh tarragon before and I immediately wanted to know how to make sauce chasseur and be a chef.

What's your favourite dish on your menu?
Roasted veal sweetbreads, wet polenta and girolles. I love all offal but there is something special about sweetbreads. I love the smell of the breads as they are cooking, basting them in plenty of foaming butter, watching the outside slowly caramelise, and adding a sprig of rosemary and some crushed garlic for the last two minutes of cooking. It's a dish that every time I plate it, I want to eat it.

What is the vital ingredient for a successful kitchen?
Good salt and a happy team.

What is your favourite restaurant?
For tasty casual eating I love Bocca di Lupo or Barrafina in London.

■ Dunbar
The Creel

Cooking score: 2
Modern British | £28
25 Lamer Street, Dunbar, EH42 1HJ
Tel no: (01368) 863279
creelrestaurant.co.uk

£5 OFF £30

An old stone building in the harbourside area, where Scotland's dwindling population of kittiwakes can be seen nesting every spring in the ruins of Dunbar Castle, the Creel has been Logan Thorburn's labour of love for a decade now. With incomparable supplies of fish and seafood on hand, and careful sourcing from local butchers, growers and smokeries, a menu of what is billed as 'modern rustic artisan' food is offered. Potted haugh – braised Angus beef shin set in its own jelly – served with piccalilli and Arran oaties sends out a strong opening message, or there may be grilled Islay scallops in a vinaigrette of Puy lentils and bacon. For mains, monkfish is parcelled in Parma ham, or hake served in its now customary Spanish livery, while meats include griddled pork loin and nutmegged mushrooms with potatoes crushed in olive oil. Few will balk at a double chocolate brownie with a dab of kumquat marmalade. House Italian is £16.95.
Chef/s: Logan Thorburn. **Open:** Thur to Sun L 12 to 2, Wed to Sat D 6.30 to 8.45. **Closed:** Mon, Tue.
Meals: set L £17 (2 courses) to £20. Set D £25 (2 courses) to £28. Sun L £20 (2 courses) to £25.
Details: 36 seats. Wheelchairs. Music.

Please send us your feedback

To register your opinion about any restaurant listed in this guide, or a new restaurant that you wish to bring to our attention, please visit the web address at the bottom of the page. Your feedback informs the content of the book and will be used to compile next year's reviews.

■ Edinburgh

★ NEW ENTRY ★
Aizle

Cooking score: 4
Modern British | £45
107-109 St Leonard's Street, Edinburgh, EH8 9QY
Tel no: (0131) 6629349
aizle.co.uk

Set at the edge of the city centre, Aizle may look spartan with its plain white walls, floorboards and hard wooden chairs, but it is inviting – 'a restaurant for those who eat out to eat'. A list of seasonal ingredients chalked up on a blackboard and seriously clued-up staff outline the bill of fare – a five-course, no-choice dinner – and it plays to a packed house. Outward simplicity with underlying sophistication defines the 'inventive, classy' cooking, seen in cured sea trout with roasted beetroot and horseradish cream under a sweet, beetroot juice wafer, in a tranche of accurately cooked halibut served on Arran Victory potatoes with a seaweed butter, a little 'caviar' and various sea herbs, and in a chunk of 40-day beef rump with braised cheek, cherry jam and crisps, purée and roasted parsnips. The 70-bin wine list ranges from £21.50 to £98 with pretty good representation throughout; there are some inventive cocktails, too.
Chef/s: Stuart Ralston. **Open:** Wed to Sun D only 6 to 9.30 (5 Fri and Sat, 10 Sun). **Closed:** Mon, Tue, 25 Dec to mid Jan, 2 weeks Jul. **Meals:** Set D £45.
Details: 35 seats. V menu. Wheelchairs. Music.

Angels with Bagpipes

Cooking score: 3
Modern European | £40
343 High Street, Royal Mile, Edinburgh, EH1 1PW
Tel no: (0131) 2201111
angelswithbagpipes.co.uk

A saunter along the Royal Mile will bring you to this distinctive venue in the heart of the Old Town. Look for that unforgettable name lit up in flowers on the façade. Inside, all is old-school elegance, with dining split over two floors, the upper room, Halo, illuminated by winged angel figures bearing candles. Fraser Smith cooks a versatile traditional and modern menu with various European touches overlaying the Scottish foundation. Start with scallops in Parma ham with puréed celeriac and miso caramel, or haggis with neeps and tatties, served with optional whisky of the month. For main, there could be salmon and cockles with fennel, haricots and watercress, or a regal serving of lamb – rump and shoulder – with goats' curd, aubergine, anchovies and almonds. Finish with a distinctly Lothian-style pannacotta, dressed with whisky, raspberries, toasted oats and shortbread. A dozen wines by the glass (from £6) kick off a well-chosen list, with bottles from £22.

Chef/s: Fraser Smith. **Open:** all week 12 to 9.45. **Closed:** 24 to 26 Dec. **Meals:** main courses £15 to £55. Set L £16 (2 courses) to £20. Set D £32 (2 courses) to £40. **Details:** 77 seats. 16 seats outside. Wheelchairs. Music.

★ NEW ENTRY ★

Brasserie Les Amis

Cooking score: 1
French | £25
83 Morrison Street, Edinburgh, EH3 8BU
Tel no: (0131) 2287517
brasserielesamis.co.uk

£30

It does multiple duty as a café, deli and bakery for Edinburgh's business district, but the brasserie element of Les Amis is 'smart and welcoming', and set menus a bargain. The kitchen claims a Scottish influence that doesn't, in the eating, alter the classic bistro food, although both nations' fondness for pastry is reflected well in an individual puff pastry tart of asparagus and blue cheese. Duck with chanterelles and Madeira sauce or bavette steak with a decent char have mains covered, while among the desserts, the îles flottantes hold promise. The wine list fits the set-up perfectly, from £16.

Open: Mon to Sat 7am to 11pm. **Closed:** Sun. **Meals:** set L £15 (2 courses) to £19. Set D £20 to £25

Cafe St Honoré

Cooking score: 4
French | £36
34 North West Thistle Street Lane, Edinburgh, EH2 1EA
Tel no: (0131) 2262211
cafesthonore.com

£5 OFF

The décor and the menu in Neil Forbes' tucked-away, New Town bistro may be rooted in the classic French tradition but in every other way this Parisian-inspired bistro is as Scottish as haggis and shortbread, an exuberant celebration of Scottish seasonal produce. The daily changing à la carte or the three-course classic may feature conventional standbys like beef stroganoff or confit duck leg but every dish comes with a local name-check from the Gartmorn free-range duck to Ronnie Eunson's organic native Shetland beef. The Parisian theme is manifest in the bentwood chairs, the black-and-white floor tiles, the dark wood and the starched white napery. The food, in three satisfying courses, might begin with pork rillettes and red onion jam followed by Perthshire venison stew, roots and buttered mash, finishing with crème brûlée and shortbread. A comprehensive and predominantly French wine list, opening at £18.50, also features Black Isle organic beer, Scottish gin, vodka and numerous single malts.

Chef/s: Neil Forbes. **Open:** all week L 12 to 2, D 5.15 to 10 (6 Sat and Sun). **Closed:** 24 to 26 Dec, 1 Jan. **Meals:** main courses £15 to £25. Set L £16 (2 courses) to £20. Set D £18 (2 courses) to £24. **Details:** 48 seats. Music.

Visit us online

To find out more about The Good Food Guide, please visit thegoodfoodguide.co.uk

Castle Terrace

Cooking score: 7
Modern French | £60
33-35 Castle Terrace, Edinburgh, EH1 2EL
Tel no: (0131) 2291222
castleterracerestaurant.com

The name gives a fair indication of where to find one of the capital's most innovative and exciting venues. Tucked into a restyled townhouse in the Georgian sweep below the Castle Mound, it feels convincingly special, informal but stylishly accoutred in mirrored walls with modern linear artworks depicting the immediate environs in stencilled outline against an azure ground. Service is excellent, the sommelier in particular a fount of imaginative suggestion and fun. The range of technique and work rate on display in Dominic Jack's modern Franco-Scottish cooking is breathtaking, as witness a poached Arbroath smokie that appears in its poaching cream set into a perfect ovoid, the yolk represented by mango purée. The balance of flavours is immaculate. Then contemplate a citrus-driven gurnard ceviche, served in circular array and topped with slivered radish, tiny mushrooms, sea herbs and sesame seeds, with a tart citrus sorbet. A gutsily classical approach to offal produces three perfectly pink breadcrumbed nuggets of veal kidney in mustard cream with braised celery, or there may be barbecued pork shoulder between two hemispheres of chicken fritter, garnished with a sheet of pickled turnip punctured to look like a slice of holey cheese, as well as tomato and lettuce, the best 'burger' you've ever eaten. For the final flourish, look to a chocolate cylinder that sits above orange mousse exuding little pockets of orange syrup, alongside a bracing orange sorbet perched on a chocolate biscuit. Wines are an authoritative French-led portfolio, with battalions of mature vintages, a clutch of Austrian stars and some seriously good Australians. Order with confidence. Glasses start at £6.50, bottles £22.50.

Chef/s: Dominic Jack. **Open:** Tue to Sat L 12 to 2, D 6.30 to 10. **Closed:** Sun, Mon, 2 weeks Dec to Jan, 1 week Mar, 1 week Jul and 1 week Oct. **Meals:** main courses £27 to £42. Set L £30. Tasting menu £75 (6 courses). **Details:** 70 seats. Bar. Wheelchairs. Music. Children over 5 yrs only.

Contini

Cooking score: 1
Italian | £35
103 George Street, Edinburgh, EH2 3ES
Tel no: (0131) 2251550
contini.com

£5 OFF

The pillars and decorative plasterwork of this former banking hall provide a grand George Street setting for what at first sight looks like a conventional Italian pasta/pizza/*secondi platti* menu. While it touches all the familiar bases, Contini is a sharp cut above the norm, whether it's in a generous serving of tender Scottish calamari fritti or a soothing spinach and ricotta ravioli dressed in butter and sage, or their own Contini sausages with cannellini beans and cavolo nero. Wines begin with a Sicilian Trapani at £19.95. Other branches at the Scottish National Gallery and Cannonball by the castle.

Chef/s: Carina Contini. **Open:** all week 7.30am to midnight (9am Sat and Sun, 10pm Sun). **Closed:** 25 and 26 Dec. **Meals:** main courses £5 to £30. Set L £15. **Details:** 80 seats. 30 seats outside. Bar. Wheelchairs. Music.

Field

Cooking score: 2
Modern British | £27
41 West Nicolson Street, Edinburgh, EH8 9DB
Tel no: (0131) 6677010
fieldrestaurant.co.uk

£30

Tables are set close together in this unobtrusive one-room restaurant, and the place is usually busy and noisy – 'it really is best to book'. A simple, to-the-point menu attracts a wide range of customers, the food noted for its strong seasonal bent and first-rate ingredients and for delivering bang-on flavours. It's all about vivid, modern combinations: crispy venison rissole with celeriac purée, pickled shimeji mushroom and cassis jus, say, or carrot and lemongrass soup. Sea bass might follow, teamed with purple potatoes, cavolo nero, nori-crusted mussels and fish velouté, while desserts confidently push the right buttons with the likes of 'absolutely gorgeous' dark chocolate and banana crémeux served with caramelised banana, roasted hazelnuts and banana ice cream. The set lunch menu is 'an absolute bargain', service is 'excellent' and reasonable prices extend to the short, global wine list, which opens at £17.

Chef/s: Georgia Cass. **Open:** Tue to Sun L 12 to 2, D 5.30 to 9. **Closed:** Mon, 25 and 25 Dec. **Meals:** main courses £11 to £26. Set L £13 (2 courses) to £16. **Details:** 22 seats. Music. Children over 5 yrs only.

★ NEW ENTRY ★

Field Grill House

Cooking score: 2
British | £33
1 Raeburn Place, Edinburgh, EH4 1HU
Tel no: (0131) 3329977
fieldgrillhouse.co.uk

A sibling to Field across town in Southside, Field Grill House opened in Stockbridge in September 2015. A similarly cool and unstuffy operation, the bold cooking is contemporary with good use of local raw materials. A choice of five steak cuts from Scottish Borders beef – all aged on the bone for at least 35 days and served with appropriate sauces and garnishes – is one way to go here, but at inspection grilled loin of lamb with a sweetbread croquette, wild garlic gnocchi, peas, broad beans, asparagus and lamb jus was a confident, full-flavoured dish. If you're in the mood for fish, there could be pan-fried scallops accompanied by black pudding, avocado and hazelnuts, ahead of roast hake with curried cauliflower, lemony avocado crème fraîche, mango salsa and prawn won ton. Banana crème brûlée with peanut-butter ice cream and hazelnut brownie is a great way to round things off. Wines start at £18.

Chef/s: Gordon Craig. **Open:** Tue to Sat L 12 to 2, D 6 to 9.30. Sun 12 to 8. **Closed:** Mon, 25 and 26 Dec. **Meals:** main courses £13 to £28. Set L £13 (2 courses) to £16. **Details:** 40 seats. Music. Children over 5 yrs only.

Fishers in Leith

Cooking score: 1
Seafood | £30
1 The Shore, Leith, Edinburgh, EH6 6QW
Tel no: (0131) 5545666
fishersrestaurantgroup.co.uk

Used as a signal tower during the Napoleonic Wars, this former pub overlooking Leith waterfront has been selling seafood since 1991. Long-standing favourites include Shetland mussels in white wine, cream and garlic, Anstruther-smoked salmon, and the 'order 24 hours in advance' hot shellfish platter. Elsewhere, there are whole sardines, capers and wild leeks, followed perhaps by pan-fried sea trout fillet with shrimps, watercress and Jersey Royals, or Aberdeen Angus steaks for those not in the mood for fish. Finish with a rich chocolate nemesis with salted bay caramel sauce and clotted cream ice cream. Wines from £16.50. Next door, the Shore is more of a pub (the live jazz in the evening is hugely popular), an atmospheric place with a bar and a separate dining room serving bream, salmon, razor clam, mussels and prawn consommé with peas, asparagus and crushed potatoes, as well as Borders pork shank with Asian-style pak choi and coriander rice.

Chef/s: Andrew Bird. **Open:** all week 12 to 10.30. **Closed:** 25 and 26 Dec, 1 and 2 Jan. **Meals:** main courses £11 to £30. Set L £14 (2 courses) to £17. **Details:** 45 seats. 20 seats outside. Bar. Music.

Average price

The average price denotes the price of a three-course meal without wine.

Galvin Brasserie de Luxe

Cooking score: 3
French | £39
Waldorf Astoria Edinburgh, The Caledonian, Princes Street, Edinburgh, EH1 2AB
Tel no: (0131) 2228988
galvinbrasseriedeluxe.com

This Edinburgh version of Jeff and Chris Galvin's Baker Street Bistrot de Luxe (see entry) is on a larger scale than the London original, but it's a perfect fit for a grand Victorian railway hotel like the Caledonian. With its wood panelling, powder-blue leather banquettes and central bar, it's an understated room, but this enables the polished service and confidently cooked French classics to grab the spotlight. From the carefully devised brasserie-style menu, a meal could start with hand-rolled pappardelle, braised Highland rabbit and aged pecorino. If you're not tempted by the 'from the grill' section with its Orkney scallops and Hereford steaks, a light main course of monkfish with spring greens, cauliflower and curried pinenut dressing might catch the eye. Finish with a towering and perfectly executed banana soufflé served with caramelised banana ice cream. A global wine list starts at £22, with a decent house selection by the glass and carafe.
Chef/s: Jamie Knox. **Open:** all week L 12 to 2.30 (12.30 to 3 Sun), D 6 to 10 (9.30 Sun). **Meals:** main courses £15 to £33. Set L and early D £16 (2 courses) to £19. Sun L £17. **Details:** 130 seats. Bar. Wheelchairs. Music. Parking.

The Gardener's Cottage

Cooking score: 2
British | £35
1 Royal Terrace Gardens, London Road, Edinburgh, EH7 5DX
Tel no: (0131) 5581221
thegardenerscottage.co

Even if it just sold souvenirs and ice cream, this converted Georgian cottage in Royal Terrace Gardens would have a whisper of magic about it. But the intervention of chef-owners Edward Murray and Dale Mailley in 2012 means it now offers something intriguing – an appealing, of-the-moment Scots-Scandi menu served at big tables set with linen napkins and antique cutlery. It's not perfect, but local readers love both casual lunches (based on sourdough, perhaps with potted pheasant or beetroot and walnut dip, and small plates such as leek and Keen's Cheddar quiche) and the evening set menu. Here you'll find the bigger ideas on a menu that's abuzz with fashionable notions, but intended to please: see burnt leek cone with sourdough and herb yoghurt; barbecue pheasant with smoked pumpkin purée, cavolo nero, pear, walnuts and spelt; apple with peanut, caramel and marshmallow ice cream. Service is 'lovely' and wine is from £22.
Chef/s: Dale Mailley and Edward Murray. **Open:** Thur to Mon L 12 to 2.30, D 5 to 9.30. **Closed:** Tue, Wed, 2 weeks Christmas. **Meals:** main courses £15 to £18 (L only). Tasting menu £35 (7 courses). **Details:** 30 seats. 12 seats outside. Music.

★ TOP 50 ★

The Kitchin

Cooking score: 7
Modern European | £75
78 Commercial Quay, Leith, Edinburgh, EH6 6LX
Tel no: (0131) 5551755
thekitchin.com

'The Kitchin represents modern high-end dining at its very best,' noted one well-travelled reporter after a visit to this refurbished former whisky warehouse on Leith's waterfront. 'Cloths and carpets' have never belonged here, although the dining room is unashamedly smart with polished floors, blue-painted pillars, puffy banquettes and heritage touches pointing up the theme. 'From nature to plate' is Tom Kitchin's mantra and he delivers on all counts – diners are even presented with a rolled-up food map indicating the provenance of most of the ingredients on the menu. Kitchin's way with seafood proves the point, suggesting that he's arguably the 'finest proponent of modern Scottish food in the UK': the lightest, sweetest spider-crabmeat presented in its shell with apple and carrot shards, herb flowers and a blob of sour cream; a 'show-stopping' whole scallop sealed in burnished pastry with the most delicate cream and chive sauce, a tranche of turbot, roasted until golden and sitting on stems of sea kale. Meat and game are also handled with awe-inspiring dexterity, from a complex selection of Highland hogget to a crispy sweetbread served with pressed Inverurie ox tongue, bone marrow and a 'silky smooth' Jerusalem artichoke purée. Such high-spec, high-impact dishes also conceal a huge amount of work invested behind the scenes – no more so than an intricate but 'deliciously refreshing' rendering of prickly sea buckthorn, which appears as a jelly layered into a 'striped' yoghurt pannacotta with a vivid-orange buckthorn consommé, apple sorbet and tiny meringues. The 'far from predictable' wine list is a stunning read, with modern names to the fore but prices in the upper regions: £35 is the bottom line, with glasses from £11.

Chef/s: Tom Kitchin. **Open:** Tue to Sat L 12.15 to 2.30, D 6.30 to 10. **Closed:** Sun, Mon, Christmas and New Year. **Meals:** main courses £29 to £45. Set L £30. Tasting menu £75 (8 courses). **Details:** 75 seats. 20 seats outside. Bar. Wheelchairs. Music. Parking. Children over 5 yrs only.

Number One

Cooking score: 6
Modern European | £75
The Balmoral, 1 Princes Street, Edinburgh, EH2 2EQ
Tel no: (0131) 5576727
roccofortehotels.com

Since it opened in 1902 next to Waverley station, the Balmoral has been a reliable landmark in the capital. Its clock tower, with courteous mendacity, shows the time three minutes later than it is, so you're less likely to miss your train. Then again, hang the train, and venture into Number One, the principal panelled dining space, where works from the Royal College of Art bestow class, and the contemporary cooking, under the aegis of Jeff Bland, exerts its own sophisticated allure, as when caviar-crowned smoked salmon arrives under a billowing dome of Scotch whisky smoke. Otherwise, expect to find cured foie gras in the company of hibiscus, apple and gingerbread, and then Inverurie hogget turning up euphoniously with mint yoghurt. A party whose experience was marred by service lapses nonetheless enjoyed the scallop and chicken wing starter combination, a veggie main of truffled cauliflower risotto, and the signature Brillat-Savarin cheesecake tricked out with poached rhubarb, blood orange and pistachios. The stupendous wine list opens with lashings of Champagne and heads for the stars in every region, with wine quotations chipping in along the route. With bottles starting at £35, glasses at £10, it doesn't come cheap, though.

Chef/s: Jeff Bland and Brian Grigor. **Open:** all week D only 6.30 to 10 (6 Fri to Sun). **Closed:** 2 weeks Jan. **Meals:** set D £70 (3 courses). Tasting menu £79 (7 courses) to £110. **Details:** 55 seats. Bar. Wheelchairs. Music.

Ondine

Cooking score: 4
Seafood | £55
2 George IV Bridge, Edinburgh, EH1 1AD
Tel no: (0131) 2261888
ondinerestaurant.co.uk
£5 OFF

Surveying the old town from its vantage on the George IV Bridge, seafood specialist Ondine participates in Edinburgh's culinary heritage by serving a dazzling array of oysters. Where once they were shucked for you amid the din of the streets, though, they are now regally stored on ice-stacks and you have the option of sitting up at a horseshoe-shaped counter to avail yourself. Striped upholstery and cheery portrait photographs make for an uplifting tone, which is further enhanced by the range of culinary tradition brought to bear on the finest and freshest. Salt-and-pepper squid tempura with Vietnamese-style dipping sauce might be the prelude to monkfish curry and raita, or classic lobster thermidor with skinny chips. The roll call of dishes that readers have enjoyed includes potted brown crab, sea bass ceviche, lemon sole and brown shrimp, and scallops with spicy sausages, and there's chocolate and caramel parfait to finish. Wines grouped by style start at £21.

Chef/s: Roy Brett. **Open:** Mon to Sat L 12 to 2.30, D 5.30 to 9.30. **Closed:** Sun, 24 to 26 Dec. **Meals:** main courses £15 to £35. Set L and D £22 (2 courses) to £26. **Details:** 75 seats. Bar. Wheelchairs. Music.

The Pompadour by Galvin

Cooking score: 6
French | £55
Waldorf Astoria Edinburgh, The Caledonian, Princes Street, Edinburgh, EH1 2AB
Tel no: (0131) 2228975
thepompadourbygalvin.com

Pompadour by Galvin, on the first floor of the Waldorf Astoria hotel, lives up to the regal reputation of its courtly Versailles namesake. Despite spectacular castle views, the genteel dining room may arguably overplay the pale and interesting card; however, the food soon adds colour. This is French cuisine rooted in classicism but fully embracing modernity, and chef Fraser Allan subtly reflects the Galvin philosophy through a Scottish lens. Dishes are deftly designed to maximise flavour combinations while introducing elements of smile-inducing surprise. Pastis-cured sea bream with brown shrimp and beurre noisette purée gains acidity from crisp, baked lemon yoghurt. A tortellini of globe artichoke packs flavour into the soft pasta pocket and then floats it in a barigoule nage, doubling the impact of this exotic thistle. Whether from the tasting menu, table d'hote or à la carte, each dish weaves a compelling story around its main ingredient. A Valrhona Ivoire and Manjari chocolate creation with bitter cherry sorbet offers the perfect balance of sweet and sharp to close. Classic formal service and extensive wine choices starting from £31 complete this elegant package.

Chef/s: Fraser Allan. **Open:** Fri L 12 to 2.30, Tue to Sat D 6.30 to 10 (6 Fri and Sat). **Closed:** Sun, Mon, 1 week Jan. **Meals:** main courses £26 to £37. Set L £29 (3 courses). Set D £29 (2 courses) to £35. Tasting menu £68. **Details:** 65 seats. V menu. Bar. Wheelchairs. Music. Parking.

Purslane

Cooking score: 2
Modern British | £30
33a St Stephen Street, Stockbridge, Edinburgh, EH3 5AH
Tel no: (0131) 2263500
purslanerestaurant.co.uk

£5 OFF

Accessed via stone steps leading to the basement in the type of grand Georgian building common in affluent Stockbridge, Purslane is run by Paul Gunning, who cut his culinary teeth at the Balmoral Hotel's Number One restaurant (see entry). An intimate (some say cramped) room with close-packed tables, reclaimed wood on the walls and a tiny bar in the corner, it's a surprisingly casual setting for the high ambition in the kitchen. Expect confident and classy cooking whether you choose from the two tasting menus or the à la carte. Seared scallops, 'perfectly timed', with crunchy celeriac, walnuts and apple purée made a perfect start at a test meal. An assiette of lamb (croquette of shoulder, nicely cooked rump and loin) followed, served with caramelised onions, asparagus, hasselback potatoes and all bound by a 'rich, dark sauce', with dessert of tea-marinated peaches, honey parfait, honey cake and peach sorbet 'well balanced and enjoyable'. A good-value global wine list kicks off at £17.

Chef/s: Paul Gunning. **Open:** Tue to Sun L 12 to 2, D 6 to 10. **Closed:** Mon, 25 Dec, 1 Jan. **Meals:** set L £15 (2 courses) to £18. Set D £26 (2 courses) to £30. Tasting menus £40 (5 courses) to £50. **Details:** 22 seats. Music. Children over 6 yrs only.

★ TOP 50 ★

Restaurant Martin Wishart

Cooking score: 7
Modern French | £75
54 The Shore, Leith, Edinburgh, EH6 6RA
Tel no: (0131) 5533557
martin-wishart.co.uk

Martin Wishart's flagship Edinburgh venue has played a focal part in the gastronomic scene of the redeveloped Port of Leith since 1999. It has enviable views over the Shore, with the art gallery nearby and the magnificence of the decommissioned royal yacht *Britannia* not far away. Inveigling itself among these cultural landmarks, Wishart's dining room is all gentle wood textures, coffee and cream hues, and classy service, a properly relaxing backdrop to the elevated cuisine, which takes a contemporary French approach to impeccable Scottish prime materials. That produces a successful marriage of langoustine and veal sweetbread roasted in buckwheat and thyme to start, served with braised endive in an Indian-spiced Sauternes sauce, or there may be unctuous sautéed foie gras, its traditional sweet accompaniments provided by apricot and carrot, supported by the aromatic note of cinnamon. At main, there may be another land-and-sea combination, this time in the form of pig's trotter to accompany a diaphanous fillet of turbot poached in red wine, served with baby leeks and new potatoes, or a sweet-sour array of red cabbage, beetroot, redcurrants and macadamias for Goosnargh duck, the roast breast partnered with Moroccan-style pastilla. Tasting menus cater for fish and shellfish aficionados, vegetarians or anything-goes enthusiasts, and desserts are composed of layers of bright, uplifting flavours – perhaps lemon bergamot crémeux with pink grapefruit meringue and yoghurt sorbet, or spiced Valrhona chocolate ganache with macerated pineapple and clementine juice. The wine list does its bit with commendable aplomb, strong in the French classics, but reliable elsewhere, too. Prices are well spread, opening at £24 for a minerally Picpoul de Pinet.
Chef/s: Martin Wishart. **Open:** Tue to Sat L 12 to 2, D 7 to 9 (6.30 to 9.30 Fri and Sat). **Closed:** Sun, Mon, 3 weeks Jan, 10 days Jul. **Meals:** set L £29. Set D £75. Tasting menu £80. **Details:** 50 seats. V menu. Wheelchairs. Music.

Rhubarb at Prestonfield

Cooking score: 4
Modern British | £55
Prestonfield House, Priestfield Road, Edinburgh, EH16 5UT
Tel no: (0131) 2251333
prestonfield.com

If you want an extravagant serving of showmanship then make for this 17th-century manor house beneath Arthur's Seat. Whether it's the black-kilted concierges, the blood-red wallpaper, the ancestral portraits or 'more cut velvet than Buckingham Palace', owner James Thomson has gone the whole hog, and then some. The candles – they are countless – create a rich, warm glow over the whole lavish, hyper-plush scene. Even the chairs have brass knobs on. The kitchen works hard to match the gilded surroundings and for the most part it succeeds – carpaccio of octopus and hand-dived scallops, for example, made for a light, fresh and original starter. Vermillion-red cured salmon with horseradish cream could be followed by a wintery dish of venison with deep-fried crisp haggis balls, red cabbage and a mini venison pic, while aged sirloin steak is the full retro monty: tomatoes, mushrooms, shallot rings and fat-cut chips. The comprehensive wine list starts reasonably at £24 for Picpoul and keeps climbing to £1,800 for premier cru claret.
Chef/s: John McMahon. **Open:** all week L 12 to 2 (12.30 to 3 Sun), D 6 to 10. **Meals:** main courses £18 to £35. Set L and D £35 (3 courses). **Details:** 120 seats. 40 seats outside. Wheelchairs. Music. Parking. No children after 7pm.

The Scran & Scallie

Cooking score: 2
Modern British | £31
1 Comely Bank Road, Edinburgh, EH4 1DT
Tel no: (0131) 3326281
scranandscallie.com

It's a rare pub that takes the care inherent in the Scran & Scallie operation, including in-house butchery and just-landed fish. But then, it's a rare pub that has such impressive lineage in co-owners Tom Kitchin and Dominic Jack. The classy, tactile blue-hued interior works all day long from newly introduced weekend breakfast to a nip after dinner, and if the 18th-century-inspired Scots menu-speak doesn't appeal, the no-fuss dishes it describes most probably will. 'Yer starters' include mussels, seaweed and garlic butter or smoked ox tongue on toast with turnip and walnut, while main courses – beef sausage and mash, steak au poivre and chips, duck leg confit and Puy lentils – occupy exactly the territory a good dining pub should. Puddings might be espresso pannacotta and hazelnut biscotti or sticky toffee 'puddin' with ice cream. The wine list has a more highbrow air than the menu, but opens at a reasonable £18.50.
Chef/s: Tom Kitchin, Dominic Jack and James Chapman. **Open:** Mon to Fri L 12 to 3, D 6 to 10. Sat and Sun 12 to 10. **Closed:** 25 Dec. **Meals:** main courses £10 to £21. Set L £15 (3 courses). Sun L £18. **Details:** 100 seats. Bar. Wheelchairs. Music.

Timberyard

Cooking score: 4
Modern British | £55
10 Lady Lawson Street, Edinburgh, EH3 9DS
Tel no: (0131) 2211222
timberyard.co

The big dining room at the Radford family's converted warehouse 'shouldn't work at all', says one reader – but it does. Through anonymous red doors is a space to 'relax, kick back and enjoy' the food of the north, both Scottish and Nordic in spirit. To start, there are little bites: crab with dill, fennel and rye or beetroot with smoked curd, garlic and

tarragon. Chef Ben Radford's careful approach is demonstrated in tasting menu fish dishes such as trout with artichoke, celery, knotroot and sea herbs or 'quite outstanding' halibut with smoked mussels, wild leek and crow garlic. At lunch, a large plate might carry pork with cauliflower, swede, cabbage, apple and kohlrabi, with a dessert of honey, woodruff, almond and milk. Drinks are a speciality, from soft brews of, say, lemon verbena (home-grown in the courtyard garden) and spinach to a wine list, starting at £23, crowded with interesting and often natural bottles.
Chef/s: Ben Radford. **Open:** Tue to Sat L 12 to 2, D 5.30 to 9.30. **Closed:** Sun, Mon, 24 to 26 Dec, 1 week Jan, 1 week Apr, 1 week Oct. **Meals:** main courses £14 to £25. Set L and D £55 (4 courses) to £75. **Details:** 72 seats. 24 seats outside. V menu. Wheelchairs. Music. Children over 12 yrs only at D.

21212

Cooking score: 5
Modern French | £55
3 Royal Terrace, Edinburgh, EH7 5AB
Tel no: (0131) 5231030
21212restaurant.co.uk

Damask walls veiled with gauze, 'loveseats' for two and sharp white linen are all part of the sumptuous set-dressing for Paul Kitching's theatrical and idiosyncratic restaurant in elegant Royal Terrace. Dinner here takes guests on a mystery tour via a whimsical menu that is more cryptic crossword than an explanation of what's to come. BBC is beef fillet and beef corned with vegetables crisp and vegetables cubed, prune purée, foam and a savoury tuile. Pork Pickle Ploughman's features slow-cooked pork with a side of celery, apple, tomato and cheese. An intricate 'amuse' layers pea purée, yoghurt and numerous vegetables topped with foam and a mushroom crisp. What to make of a palate cleanser of 'porridge milk' poured from a ceramic cow into a paper cup or fruit brûlée topped with a milk bottle sweetie. Playful or downright eccentric? Intricate, labour-intensive dishes of multiple ingredients, sous-vide protein, and foams and tuiles with a touch of humour are the hallmarks of Kitching's vision. Whether this translates into an exciting journey or an excessive jumble of flavours has divided some diners. His skill with vegetables is undoubted but there were disappointing technical hiccups in a tough lemon tart pastry and 'soapy' scallops. A plate of 15-plus small samples of cheese, each one confidently named and described by our waitress impressed, so too did the excellent sommelier. An excellent £48 bottle of Les Setilles white burgundy stood out in a list that rose dizzyingly from £38.

Chef/s: Paul Kitching. **Open:** Tue to Sat L 12 to 1.45, D 6.45 to 9.30. **Closed:** Sun, Mon. **Meals:** set L Tue to Fri £24 (2 courses) to £55 (5 courses), Sat £32 (3 courses) to £55. Set D Tue to Fri £65 (3 courses) to £79 (5 courses), Sat £79. **Details:** 38 seats.

Valvona & Crolla Caffè Bar

Cooking score: 3
Italian | £22
19 Elm Row, Edinburgh, EH7 4AA
Tel no: (0131) 5566066
valvonacrolla.co.uk
£5 OFF £30

The delicatessen and wine shop opened here in 1934, which makes the Caffè Bar a relative nipper by comparison, celebrating its 20th birthday in 2016. At the back of the shop, grab a table and tuck into Italian classics like bruschetta piled with caramelised red onions and Parma ham, polpettine meatballs in a rich ragù, or selections of regional cured meats. And that's just for starters – or antipasti, rather. Move on to pasta such as taglierini in a tomato sauce enriched with crab meat, a piatti principali (a rich lamb stew perhaps), or a pizza. Finish with a pistachio flavoured polenta cake. Pastries are made by hand in their bakery, the coffee meets exacting Italian standards, and, when it comes to wine, pick something from the shop and you'll only pay £10 corkage – and that's a great deal in any language. Wines start at £17.99.

Chef/s: Mary Contini and Pina Trano. **Open:** all week 8.30 to 6 (8 to 6.30 Fri and Sat, 10 to 5 Sun). **Closed:** 25 and 26 Dec, 1 and 2 Jan. **Meals:** main courses £11 to £17. Set L £19 (2 courses) to £22. **Details:** 66 seats. Wheelchairs. Music.

★ NEW ENTRY ★

The Wee Restaurant

Cooking score: 3
Modern European | £36
61 Frederick Street, Edinburgh, EH2 1LH
Tel no: (0131) 2257983
theweerestaurant.co.uk

After 10 years honing their offering in North Queensferry – The Wee Restaurant, see entry – Craig and Vikki Wood bring their ethos of simplicity and relaxed informality to Edinburgh's New Town. Dark décor and drapes promote cosy seclusion just yards away from the shopping bustle. A gentle culinary touch gives creative flourish to a roll call of Scotland's classic ingredients. The plump Shetland mussels house-style with bacon, basil, pine nuts and Parmesan cream are clearly a crowd-pleaser, while white onion and thyme soup with chive and truffle oil offers silky indulgence. Fish features heavily on the short menu and a crisply grilled sea bass pairs well with spiced crab and spring onion risotto, baby artichokes and micro fennel – a fragrant salsa verde bringing the dish neatly together. Desserts include the signature caramelised banana tarte Tatin cooked to order or lighter options such as a delicate vanilla pannacotta with bitter chocolate crumb. Wines start from £19.75

Chef/s: Craig Wood. **Open:** Tue to Fri and Sun L 12 to 2.30, D 6 to 9 (10 Fri). Sat 12 to 10. **Closed:** Mon, 25 and 26 Dec, 1 Jan. **Meals:** main courses £17 to £32. Set L and D £16 (2 courses) to £20. **Details:** 38 seats. Music.

Average price

The average price denotes the price of a three-course meal without wine.

LOCAL GEM

Tanjore
Indian | £18
6-8 Clerk Street, Edinburgh, EH8 9HX
Tel no: (0131) 4786518
tanjore.co.uk
£30

With its breezy café vibe and authentic menu of South Indian classics, Tanjore, named after a historic city in the southern state of Tamil Nadu, has dosas aplenty, including lamb masala and paneer cheese versions. Kick off with courgette bhaji or idli (steamed rice and lentil cakes), move on to a soft-shell crab curry, a cracking veggie number such as stuffed baby aubergines, or Hyderabadi biryani. It doesn't have a licence, so be sure to BYO.

■ Gullane

Chez Roux
new chef/no score
French | £40
Greywalls Hotel, Muirfield, Gullane, EH31 2EG
Tel no: (01620) 842144
greywalls.co.uk
£5 OFF

Greywalls Hotel offers refined Edwardian elegance on East Lothian's celebrated golf coast. Overlooking Muirfield's ninth green, its Chez Roux restaurant provides a genteel backdrop for classic French cuisine. But as we went to press we learned of the departure of chef Lee Lawrie, with his replacement yet to be announced. We are sure the cooking will continue to pay homage to Albert Roux's old-school approach with the focus on simplicity and flavour rather than any more contemporary Gallic flourishes – perhaps a signature pike quenelle (a delicate mousse in its rich savoury custard of shrimp and lobster), and a perfectly roast supreme of St Brides chicken with traditional spring accompaniments of peas, wilted lettuce and lardons. In the past, desserts have reflected Roux's personal grounding in patisserie, as

seen in a 'sublime' strawberry crumble soufflé with pistachio custard. A diverse wine list starts at a very reasonable £27.
Open: all week L 12 to 2.30, D 6.30 to 10.
Meals: main courses £17 to £29. Set L £30 (3 courses). Set D £32 (3 courses). Sun L £30.
Details: 60 seats. 20 seats outside. Wheelchairs. Music.

La Potinière
Cooking score: 6
Modern British | £38
34 Main Street, Gullane, EH31 2AA
Tel no: (01620) 843214
lapotiniere.co.uk

Gullane is a village of just a few thousand souls on the east coast some 30 minutes outside of Edinburgh. La Potinière is the antithesis of a city slicker, favouring a more homely and traditional approach to hospitality, which has proved to be a winning formula for Mary Runciman and Keith Marley, who run the place front and back with little or no assistance. Local and regional Scottish suppliers get a namecheck on the menu, and the couple grow some fruit, veg and herbs in their own garden. The menu offers just two options at each course, a sensible idea given the nature of the set-up, and flavours hit the mark. Choose one of two starters – tender supreme of partridge with spinach and wild mushroom sauce, say – before an 'intermediate' course such as Thai coconut soup with Thai fishcake. Main-course roast loin of Scotch lamb arrives with dauphinois, seasonal vegetables and lamb juices, while dessert could be an apple-fest (parfait, compote and coulis) with almond crumble and plum sorbet. Wines start at £17.
Chef/s: Mary Runciman and Keith Marley. **Open:** Wed to Sun L 12.30 to 1.30, Wed to Sat D 7 to 8.30.
Closed: Mon, Tue, 24 to 27 Dec, 1 and 2 Jan, bank hols. **Meals:** set L £20 (2 courses) to £25. Set D £38 (3 courses) to £43. **Details:** 24 seats. Wheelchairs. Parking.

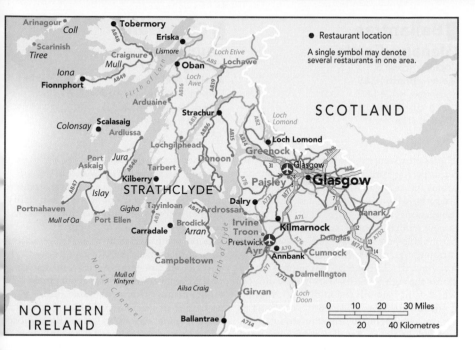

◼ Annbank
Enterkine House

Cooking score: 4
Modern European | £30
Enterkine Estate, Annbank, KA6 5AL
Tel no: (01292) 520580
enterkine.com

£5 OFF 🍴

The white-fronted house was built between
the wars, and only became a hotel in 2000, but
has taken to its most recent incarnation in
duck-to-water fashion. With its elegant
country-house décor, impeccable service and
views over the gardens and the sweeping river
Ayr, Browne's dining room is a relaxing place
to be, all the more so as it's the setting for Paul
Moffat's thoughtfully considered modern
Scottish cooking, which draws French and
Italian influences seamlessly into its ambit.
Classic foie gras parfait with cherries and
pistachios, served with brioche, is one way to
start, or there may be Arran Cheddar soufflé
with red pepper and Meaux mustard sauce, as
preludes to halibut gremolata with haricot
beans, artichoke and sun-dried tomato risotto,
or gloriously mature Scotch beef fillet, with
wild mushrooms and red cabbage. Finish with
hazelnut parfait and apple compote. A well-
annotated wine list has plenty by the glass
from £5.75, with bottles from £21.95.
Chef/s: Paul Moffat. **Open:** Tue to Sat L 12 to 2, Mon
to Sat D 6 to 10, all day Sun. **Closed:** first week Jan.
Meals: main courses £17 to £25. Set L £17 (2
courses) to £19. Set D £25 (2 courses) to £35. Sun L
£20. **Details:** 40 seats. 20 seats outside. Music.
Parking.

Please send us your feedback

To register your opinion about any
restaurant listed in this guide, or a new
restaurant that you wish to bring to our
attention, please visit the web address at
the bottom of the page. Your feedback
informs the content of the book and will
be used to compile next year's reviews.

▌Ballantrae
Glenapp Castle

Cooking score: 5
Modern British | £45
Ballantrae, KA26 0NZ
Tel no: (01465) 831212
glenappcastle.com

🛏

The lengthy security-gated drive sweeps up to the imposing castle with its impressive public rooms and amply upholstered furniture. Everything is on a grand scale, and while those international visitors, golfers and honeymooners already in residence at this luxury bolt-hole may have acclimatised to the surroundings, the newly arriving diner can feel somewhat Lilliputian. This impression carries through to the fixed six-course dinner where dainty morsels and miniature takes on modern Franco-British favourites continue the conceit of being in some sumptuous period dolls' house. A well-roasted supreme of quail with its confit leg is served on a rustic wild garlic and pearl barley salad, giving just a mouthful of moorland. A portion of duck breast, perfectly pink, continues the Gallic influence with its leg rillettes and caramelised shallots. Desserts might include a pillowy passion fruit soufflé. Homemade petits fours by the fire conclude the juxtaposition of French flavours in a Scottish château. A broad-based wine list starts at £34.
Chef/s: Tyron Ellul. **Open:** all week L 12.30 to 2, D 7 to 9.45. **Meals:** set L £40. Set D £45 (3 courses) to £65. Sun L £30. **Details:** 40 seats. Parking. Children over 5 yrs only at D.

▌Carradale
Dunvalanree

Cooking score: 2
Modern British | £28
Port Righ, Carradale, PA28 6SE
Tel no: (01583) 431226
dunvalanree.com

£5 OFF 🛏 £30

Reached via a tortuous road along the coast of Kintyre, Alan and Alyson Milstead's enchanting home from home is a wee treasure imbued with the spirit of Scottish hospitality and famed for its expansive clifftop views. As a cook, Alyson is an ardent supporter of regional producers, farmers and fishermen – a commitment that shines through as she reworks and fine-tunes her easy-to-manage seasonal repertoire. Succinct fixed-price dinner menus offer terrific value and a procession of clear, direct flavours, especially when it comes to seafood from the local boats – think pan-fried mackerel fillet with orange and olive salad or monkfish wrapped in seaweed and prosciutto with saffron and lemon sauce. Meat lovers might prefer Aberdeen Angus meatballs in spicy tomato sauce followed by collops of Argyll venison with poached brambles, while dessert could include a dish of home-grown rhubarb with rhubarb and ginger ice cream. Wines from a modest list start at £17.
Chef/s: Alyson Milstead. **Open:** all week D only 7.30 (1 sitting). **Closed:** Christmas. **Meals:** set D £28. **Details:** 20 seats. Music. Parking.

▌Dalry
Braidwoods

Cooking score: 5
Modern British | £46
Drumastle Mill Cottage, Dalry, KA24 4LN
Tel no: (01294) 833544
braidwoods.co.uk

Out in Ayrshire's Garnock Valley, Dalry feels reassuringly remote from urban bustle, although it isn't too much of a stretch from Glasgow. Keith and Nicola Braidwood's

---

Symbols

🛏 Accommodation is available
£30 Three courses for less than £30
£5 OFF £5-off voucher scheme
🍶 Notable wine list

whitewashed retreat on the edge of town is over 250 years old, and is consecrated to celebrating the pick of Scottish produce – lamb and venison, seasonal game and locally caught fish. Fixed-price menus change daily, but certain dishes have become stalwarts of the house: a starter of grilled Wester Ross scallops on leeks in Arran mustard butter, the shortcrusted Parmesan tart with red pepper coulis and watercress salad as an intermediate. Keith Braidwood avoids over elaboration and faddishness, the better to let principals have their say in main courses such as turbot in shellfish essence, or roe deer loin in wild mushroom sauce. Bringing up the rear might be Agen prune and Armagnac parfait in a sauce of caramelised orange. A seven-strong house selection from £23.95 opens the wine bidding.

Chef/s: Keith Braidwood. **Open:** Wed to Sun L 12 to 1.30 (Sun mid Sept to Apr only), Tue to Sat D 7 to 9. **Closed:** Mon, 25 Dec to 27 Jan, first 2 weeks Sept. **Meals:** set L £28 (2 courses) to £32. Set D £48 (3 courses) to £52. Sun L £32. **Details:** 24 seats. Parking. Children over 5 yrs only at L and 12 yrs only at D.

∎ Glasgow
Brian Maule at Chardon d'Or

Cooking score: 5
French | £48
176 West Regent Street, Glasgow, G2 4RL
Tel no: (0141) 2483801
brianmaule.com

After a recent refurbishment, the Victorian townhouse that houses Brian Maule's refined Franco-Scottish cooking has never looked smarter. Maule has a real feel for what Glasgow expects of ambitious dining, and ingredients are combined to both soothing and enlivening effect. A ragoût of morteau sausage with Jerusalem artichoke and green lentil bonbons is a comforting cold-weather start, or there may be seared peppered tuna with pickled mooli and preserved ginger for

something lighter. Prime proteins are handled with classical aplomb at main, perhaps fried hake with pak choi in saffron broth with an anchovy beignet, or irresistible fillet and confit of lamb with oyster mushrooms and roast salsify. Desserts are unapologetically *traditionnel*, as for tarte Tatin and ice cream, unmodified crème brûlée or warm chocolate fondant. Concise tasting notes on the wine list have a culinary air to them, and the selections inspire confidence throughout, especially in the classic French regions. Bottles start at £19.75, standard glasses £4.95.

Chef/s: Brian Maule. **Open:** Mon to Sat L 12 to 2.30, D 5 to 9.30 (10 Sat). **Closed:** Sun. **Meals:** main courses £27 to £29. Set L and early D £21 (2 courses) to £24. **Details:** 160 seats. V menu. Wheelchairs. Music. No children after 8pm.

Cail Bruich

Cooking score: 5
Modern British | £40
725 Great Western Road, Glasgow, G12 8QX
Tel no: (0141) 3346265
cailbruich.co.uk
£5 OFF

Sporting a dapper look of muted natural tones, a chef's table and a view into the kitchen at the back, Cail Bruich, just around the corner from the Botanic Gardens, makes for a polished dining destination. When it comes to reflecting our times, chef-patron Chris Charalambous' menu is as on the money as the décor, delivering some bright modern ideas based around diligently sourced Scottish ingredients. Mackerel is matched in a first course with tender pig's head, burnt apple and lovage, while among main courses Gartmorn Farm duck gets to shine on a plate with salt-baked turnips and blackcurrants. The market menu is outstanding value given the quality and creativity, and everything from the kitchen shows ambition, technical proficiency and respect for the produce. For dessert, rhubarb gets a workout with the help of ginger and blood orange. An interesting array of bottled beers adds lustre to the neatly put-together wine list; house wine is £20.

Chef/s: Chris Charalambous. **Open:** Wed to Sat L 12 to 2, Mon to Sat D 5.30 to 9.30. Sun 1 to 7. **Closed:** 25 and 26 Dec, 1 week Jan. **Meals:** main courses £16 to £24. Set L £16 (2 courses) to £21. Set D £19 (2 courses) to £25. Sun L £25. **Details:** 48 seats. Music. Children before 8pm only.

Crabshakk
Cooking score: 2
Seafood | £39
1114 Argyle Street, Glasgow, G3 8TD
Tel no: (0141) 3346127
crabshakk.com

This extremely convivial seafood restaurant in Finnieston is 'one of the most popular restaurants in the city', according to its many fans. Spread over two floors, Crabshakk makes clever use of its limited space, which extends to tightly packed, cramped tables and stool or bench seating – it becomes pleasantly boisterous during peak service. What draws the crowd is the superb quality of the fish and its simple presentation. Ordering classics is a good strategy: moules marinière or fish and chips never fail. But other highly rated dishes include grilled sardines, light tempura squid with soy and coriander dipping sauce, shellfish chowder, seared scallops with anchovies, and monkfish cheek scampi. There's rump steak and chips for those not in the mood for fish, and the flourless chocolate cake has been applauded. Wines from £20. A sister establishment, Table 11 oyster bar is nearby (at no 1132), providing a wraparound sherry and shellfish experience.
Chef/s: David Scott. **Open:** Tue to Sun 12 to 12. **Closed:** Mon. **Meals:** main courses £8 to £27. **Details:** 53 seats. 6 seats outside. Wheelchairs. Music.

★ NEW ENTRY ★

Eusebi Deli
Cooking score: 2
Italian | £25
152 Park Road, Glasgow, G4 9HB
Tel no: (0141) 6489999
eusebideli.com
£5 OFF £30

'Food, Family, Life & Passion' are the foundations upon which Giovanna Eusebi has distilled the core elements of traditional Italian neighbourhood dining. The family has pedigree, importing specialist ingredients from small artisan producers for over 40 years. Their vibrant new West End deli offers everything from a quick espresso, through take-home delicacies to a more lingering repast. Platters from the 'salumeria' paired with airy focaccia and honeycomb or wine jelly are a world away in flavour and texture from what often passes for cured meat elsewhere. Pasta is all homemade and the pizza dough mixes soy, wheat, rice and sourdough and proves for 72 hours, giving a light, flavoursome vehicle for classic toppings – no pineapple chunks here! A small selection of daily dishes might include a roasted duck panzanella with red chicory or fried Gorgonzola and date ravioli. The sweet-toothed can enjoy grandmotherly indulgence with luscious in-house cake and gelato selections. An all-Italian wine list starts at £16, or simply add corkage to any bottle from the deli.
Chef/s: Jamie Donald. **Open:** all week 7.30am to 10pm. **Closed:** 25 and 26 Dec, 1 and 2 Jan. **Meals:** main courses £9 to £18. **Details:** 60 seats. Wheelchairs. Music.

Gamba

Cooking score: 3
Seafood | £46
225a West George Street, Glasgow, G2 2ND
Tel no: (0141) 5720899
gamba.co.uk
£5 OFF

Derek Marshall's basement restaurant has been the go-to address for seafood lovers in the city since 1998 and continues to impress – 'could not fault it in any way,' enthused one fish fan. It's a basement with windows, so not at all gloomy, with flickering candles and informal, stylish décor. The pre-theatre menu is a nod to the trendy West End location, while the main menu offers everything from overt simplicity to an occasional Asian spin. A humble-sounding kipper spread comes in the company of a stimulating Thai jelly and crème fraîche, Cumbrae rock oysters arrive as nature intended, and non-seafood starters include smooth parfait of chicken livers and pistachio. Sustainable Scottish seafood lies at the heart of it all, with king scallops and monkfish cooked in paper, roast Shetland cod with star anise cream, and a classic lobster thermidor. Rosemary crème brûlée brings things to a close. Wines start at £21.
Chef/s: Derek Marshall. **Open:** Mon to Sat L 12 to 2.15, all week D 5 to 9.30 (9 Sun). **Closed:** 25 and 26 Dec, first week Jan. **Meals:** main courses £12 to £28. Set L and D £19 (2 courses) to £22. **Details:** 66 seats. Bar. Music.

★ NEW ENTRY ★

The Gannet

Cooking score: 4
Modern British | £32
1155 Argyle Street, Finnieston, Glasgow, G3 8TB
Tel no: (0141) 2042081
thegannetgla.com
£5 OFF

A formerly abandoned tenement building in the now ascendant Finnieston district, the Gannet is named after the bird with a proverbially indiscriminate appetite. The reality of Ivan Stein and Peter McKenna's cooking puts any such notion to flight: offering 'innovative and interesting combinations of flavour and taste all executed with great touch' in a combination of à la carte and small-plate dining. Meat dishes offer plenty of satisfaction in Borders hogget with Jerusalem artichoke, purple sprouting broccoli, mash and cumin sauce, or a diamond fillet of Scotch beef with dripping potatoes, spinach, salt-baked celeriac and shallots. Sometimes separate ingredients interact with each other, other times they stand aloof, but the quality of materials is palpable, perhaps in treacle-cured salmon with horseradish crème fraîche, Scrabster cod with Shetland mussels and wild leeks in squid ink, or homely desserts given the creative uptick, such as apple and brandy crumble tart with clove ice cream. Wines start at £19.50.
Chef/s: Ivan Stein and Peter McKenna. **Open:** Tue to Sat L 12 to 2.15, D 5 to 9.30. Sun 1 to 7.30. **Closed:** Mon. **Meals:** main courses £15 to £23. Sun L £30. **Details:** 50 seats. Bar. Wheelchairs. Music.

★ NEW ENTRY ★

111 by Nico

Cooking score: 2
Modern European | £20
111 Cleveden Road, Glasgow, G12 0JU
Tel no: (0141) 3340111
111bynico.co.uk
£30

Full tables and a bustling atmosphere midweek prove that even in a tired 1960s suburban shopping parade the combination of simple cooking coupled with a social conscience makes commercial and culinary sense. Italian-influenced dishes can show some inconsistencies but there are also real standouts. Traditional Scottish ham hough is updated with zingy fennel and green apple salad and a theatrical applewood smoke dome, and a perfectly seared stone bass is given an Indian twist with spiced cauliflower, coconut and sweet brown shrimp. Elsewhere, a starter of mackerel with an asparagus velouté, panko quail's egg and horseradish mousse is 'true to expectations', and duck breast is served beautifully pink with nicely caramelised skin and teamed with baby leek and 'dobs of a concentrated red wine gelée'. Desserts include a delicate deconstructed pear cheesecake with clever almond and lime accents. Wines from £17 a bottle.

Chef/s: Nico Simeone and Modou Diagme. **Open:** Tue to Fri L 12 to 2.30, Mon to Fri D 5 to 10. Sat and Sun 12 to 10 (9 Sun). **Meals:** set L and D £19 (2 courses) to £22. Tasting menu £30 (5 courses). **Details:** 44 seats.

Stravaigin
Cooking score: 1
Global | £35
28 Gibson Street, Glasgow, G12 8NX
Tel no: (0141) 3342665
stravaigin.co.uk

Spread over three floors in the city's West End, where vintage is modern and culture vultures roam, Stravaigin is suitably arty and egalitarian, with a team in the kitchen who take culinary inspiration from all over the world. Confit pheasant leg lasagne is a starter made in Europe (with a Scottish bird of course), while a main course of char-grilled rump steak with ajitsuke egg (marinated in a soy-based sauce) and nori purée looks to the Far East. Finish with custard tart with rhubarb sorbet and thyme and lime curd. Wines start at £19.50.

Chef/s: Kenny Mackay. **Open:** all week 11 to 11. **Closed:** 25 Dec, 1 Jan. **Meals:** main courses £15 to £26. **Details:** 120 seats. 10 seats outside. Bar. Wheelchairs. Music.

Ubiquitous Chip
Cooking score: 4
Modern British | £40
12 Ashton Lane, Glasgow, G12 8SJ
Tel no: (0141) 3345007
ubiquitouschip.co.uk

The Wee Bar at the Chip has to be one of the smallest drinking spaces in Scotland, but fortunately there are two others to take the overspill, not to mention a hugely attractive restaurant out in a glassed-over cobbled courtyard, a fixture of Glasgow's West End since 1971. One or two dishes from the old days survive – steak au poivre with duxelles and dauphinois is as reassuringly timeless as dawn breaking – but elsewhere things have moved on, to a world of seared scallops and cured pork loin with kohlrabi sauerkraut, apple and crackling, followed by sea bass with Jerusalem artichokes, roast broccoli and chestnut velouté. Combine cheese and dessert in a compendious plate of walnut cake, poached pear, port jelly and Gorgonzola ice cream, or close with vanilla rice pudding, white chocolate crumble and blood-orange gel. The kitchen's production makes a fitting complement to one of the country's greatest wine lists, a long-armed embrace of the great and the very good from the global vinescape. Burgundy and Bordeaux are classified into their superfine districts, but there are estimable German Rieslings, Gaja's monumental Piedmontese reds, curiosities from Armenia and Croatia, and some of South America's best. Prices open at £18.95.

Chef/s: Andrew Mitchell. **Open:** all week 12 to 11. **Closed:** 25 Dec, 1 Jan. **Meals:** main courses £16 to £35. Set L and early D £17 (2 courses) to £21. Sun L £21. **Details:** 100 seats. 20 seats outside. Bar. Wheelchairs. Music.

LOCAL GEM
The Finnieston
Seafood | £30
1125 Argyle Street, Finnieston, Glasgow,
G3 8ND
Tel no: (0141) 2222884
thefinniestonbar.com

Low ceilings and wooden snugs in a crooked building create an air of maritime boho appropriate to the seafood and cocktail-led menus. A core range of 'small plates' and regular fresh and battered fishes of the day are supplemented by a handful of specials. Oysters are served four ways – a baked version unashamedly Scottish with haggis crumb and whisky mist – but while the menu is compact, ingredients are fresh and simply handled, as in sweet, pearlescent hake, crisp on the outside and getting zing from a tangy sauce vierge. Stylish cocktail imbibers gain ascendancy over diners as the evening progresses, while wine drinkers will find the list opening at £18.

LOCAL GEM
Number 16
Modern British | £30
16 Byres Road, Glasgow, G11 5JY
Tel no: (0141) 3392544
number16.co.uk

£5
OFF

'It's a bit like a cabin on a ship – everything is designed to maximise space,' noted one visitor to this pint-sized mid-terrace restaurant. With space at a premium, expect a cosy atmosphere and a compact menu. Prime Scottish ingredients dictate the menu, say seared breast of partridge with poached pear, forced rhubarb, Jerusalem artichoke purée and brown butter or roast haunch of Perthshire venison with celeriac purée, potato gratin, salsify, parsley root and roast Brussels sprouts. Praline semifreddo popsicle with passion fruit gel, hazelnut sponge, cocoa soil and a Valrhona chocolate disc is a good way to finish. Wines from £17.95.

Best of... Glasgow

Our undercover inspectors open their Little Black Books

The friendly obsessives at **Artisan Roast**, Gibson Street, source, roast, grind and serve coffee purely for your pleasure. Enjoy in Chemex, Aeropress, V60 or just espresso-based brews.

Head to **WILLIAM** on Queen Margaret Drive for teas, banter, buns and brownies alongside other baking (and savoury) delights in a friendly neighbourhood café.

From breakfast baozi to bacon baps, you'll get a global brunch served with local warmth at **Stravaigin**, Gibson Street.

Fratelli Sarti, Bath Street is unashamedly Italian, offering a wide selection of unusual wines from trusted producers (and friends) for retail or to accompany your meal.

Don't let the fact that **Saramago Café Bar** (at the CCA) is all vegan scare you off; beetroot and lentil kofte with mint and cucumber yoghurt and seeds on homemade flatbread is just one of many healthy and tasty mouth-fillers.

Eat in with smart surroundings or enjoy a traditional takeaway with proper 'Chippie' chips at **Gandolfi Fish**, Albion Street. Haddock, cod, sea-bass or salmon (even that comfort food icon – fish-finger sandwich on white).

For pizza it has to be **Celino's**, Alexandra Parade. For over 30 years, East End regulars have sworn by the stone-baked thin-crusts at this family-run café/deli/restaurant.

Ox and Finch
International | £30
920 Sauchiehall Street, Glasgow, G3 7TF
Tel no: (0141) 3398627
oxandfinch.com

£5
OFF

Along with the contemporary design tropes of part-renovated and upcycled surfaces, Ox and Finch also subscribes to the current trend for small sharing dishes served in the order determined by the open kitchen. This creates conviviality and informality along with a brisk sense of pace. The menu embraces an eclectic mix of flavours and styles. Confit hogget with tahini, pomegranate and rose harissa is a rich fusion of sweet and earthy Middle Eastern flavours. An imaginative peanut butter, apple and sesame mille-feuille neatly sidesteps the risk of oversweetness. Wines from £17.

Porter & Rye
British | £40
1131 Argyle Street, Finnieston, Glasgow, G8 8ND
Tel no: (0141) 5721212
porterandrye.com

£5
OFF

In this bustling temple for modern carnivores, an obelisk-like display fridge brings dry-ageing to life. Small plates such as pig's head with burnt apple, ear scratchings and smoked bacon foam are starters or light mains but it's the Gaindykehead Farm beef that's the main attraction. Served by weight, it's a culinary tour of the butcher's slab – onglet, bavette, chateaubriand or porterhouse – simply prepared and served with sides and sauce. Foie gras and shaved truffle offer luxury 'customisation'. Imaginative desserts, wines and cocktails complement this protein-led proposition. Wines from £18.

▌Isle of Colonsay
The Colonsay
Modern British | £28
Scalasaig, Isle of Colonsay, PA61 7YT
Tel no: (01951) 200316
colonsayestate.co.uk

🛏 £30

Perched above the pier and harbour on a gorgeously remote island in the south Hebrides, the white-fronted Georgian hotel is in an idyllic spot. In the sparkling-white dining room, produce from the islands and the Argyll coast is the backbone of simple menus that trade in award-winning local oysters, home-cured gravadlax with garden leaves, seared halibut on creamed leeks, and slow-cooked pork belly with apple and black pudding mash. Lunch brings on soups and casseroles, and a steak and ale pie made with the island's beer. Finish with lemon drizzle cake and cream. Wines from £13.50.

▌Isle of Eriska
Isle of Eriska
Cooking score: 5
British | £55
Benderloch, Isle of Eriska, PA37 1SD
Tel no: (01631) 720371
eriska-hotel.co.uk

🍾 🛏

'It's not an easy trip unless you're staying, are happy to drive or can afford the helicopter arrival, but I'd definitely go back again – it's very good value and a relaxed though special feel', is a visitor's summary of this generously proportioned, late-Victorian, baronial-style house that's set on a 300-acre private island. Ross Stovold has left for pastures new, the kitchen now directed by Paul Leonard (from Restaurant Andrew Fairlie – see entry). Reports suggest a seamless transition, with the set, four-course dinner menu (24-hours notice for non-residents) continuing to be grounded in the abundance of regional materials, from Loch Creran salmon with Port

Appin mussels, garden leek and white turnip to leg of Perthshire hogget with braised shoulder, potatoes cooked in whey and roasted garlic or Peterhead-landed John Dory with Jerusalem artichoke, barbecued broccoli and capers. Presentation, right through to the 'stunner' of a cheese trolley, is impeccable. The wine list is an interesting mix of classics and more unusual choices, personalised recommendations and a good choice by glass and 375ml carafe. Given the quality of the venue and the wines there are a surprising number at very affordable prices (from £18). **Chef/s:** Paul Leonard. **Open:** all week D only 7.30 to 9. **Closed:** Jan. **Meals:** set D £55 (4 courses). **Details:** 50 seats. V menu. Bar. Wheelchairs. Parking.

∎ Isle of Mull
Café Fish
Cooking score: 3
Seafood | £30
The Pier, Main Street, Tobermory, Isle of Mull, PA75 6NU
Tel no: (01600) 301253
thecafefish.com

Right on the harbour of Mull's main town, occupying the first floor of the former CalMac ferry office, Café Fish is better placed than most to get the day's catch on the menu with minimal travel miles (more like travel yards). It has its own boat bringing in the shellfish. It's a simple sort of place with a cheery blue colour scheme and lots of natural wood, while a table on the terrace is a treat in warm weather. Kick off with whole langoustines, served warm with herby garlic butter, or some cracked crab claws. The 'Taste of Mull' is a whole lotta goodies in a bouillabaisse sauce (including halibut, scallops, mussels and more), and check out the blackboard to see what else is on. Non-seafood options are available – local ribeye steak – and desserts include a chocolate pot fuelled up with Tobermory malt whisky. Wines start at £18. Please note – it's closed in the winter.

Chef/s: Liz McGougan. **Open:** all week L 11 to 3, D 5.30 to 10. **Closed:** Nov to Mar. **Meals:** main courses £15 to £35. **Details:** 32 seats. 46 seats outside. Music. No children under 5 yrs at D.

Ninth Wave
Cooking score: 4
Modern British | £46
Bruach Mhor, Fionnphort, Isle of Mull, PA66 6BL
Tel no: (01681) 700757
ninthwaverestaurant.co.uk

A land of ethereal delights is to be found at the ninth wave, or so says Celtic myth, and the Lamonts make a fair job of recreating it here at their croft on the island moors. Most produce that makes its way to Carla's kitchen is home-grown in the gardens or orchard, or foraged from the Mull shores, together with premium Highland meat and west coast seafood. First up might be a sublime soup of garden peas and sweet seaweed, garnished with smoked haddock and a sea-lettuce tuile, before beef makes an appearance as intermediate, seared in oriental fashion with water chestnuts, greens and peppers, all fired up with wasabi. Return to the sea for a main course of wrasse seared in caper butter, dressed with salsa verde and a mussel stuffed courgette flower. Desserts come scented with meadowsweet, galangal and cardamom, and there are fine Scottish cheeses. Wines open with Chilean Sauvignon and Merlot at £16.30.

Chef/s: Carla Lamont. **Open:** Wed to Sun D only 7 to 11. **Closed:** Mon, Tue, Nov to Apr. **Meals:** set D £46 to £64 (5 courses). **Details:** 18 seats. Wheelchairs. Parking. Children over 12 yrs only.

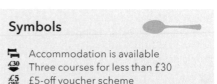

Symbols

🛏 Accommodation is available
£30 Three courses for less than £30
£5 £5-off voucher scheme
🍾 Notable wine list

■ Kilberry
The Kilberry Inn
Cooking score: 3
Modern British | £35
Kilberry Road, Kilberry, PA29 6YD
Tel no: (01880) 770223
kilberryinn.com
£5 OFF 🛏

Knapdale peninsula feels like another world as you slowly drive its 30-mile single-track coastline with spectacular views of Islay and Jura. Such isolation means you rarely just stumble across the jolly red tin roof of Kilberry Inn – its humble exterior undersells the warmly Scottish interior with its tasteful coastal vibe – and those who succeed feel special and are rewarded accordingly. It's that coast that delivers much of the concise daily menu prepared by Clare Johnson and her team: mussels in cider, thyme and pancetta ('some of the best I've eaten'); generous Loch Fyne queenies on the shell toasted with hazelnut and coriander butter that demand mopping with homemade fennel sourdough; a chunky Jura monkfish takes an eastern twist with spiced lentils, mint and yoghurt. Desserts such as treacle tart, lemon and mascarpone ice cream offer an elegant take on homely classics. Carefully selected wines start at £19.
Chef/s: Clare Johnson. **Open:** Fri to Sun L 12 to 2, Tue to Sun D from 6. **Closed:** Mon, 1 Jan to mid Mar. **Meals:** main courses £15 to £22. **Details:** 25 seats. 10 seats outside. Wheelchairs. Music. Parking.

■ Kilmarnock

LOCAL GEM
Titchfield's
British | £22
10 Titchfield Street, Kilmarnock, KA1 1PH
Tel no: (01563) 530100
titchfields.co.uk
£30

'A large-ish corner site in a run-down town-centre shopping area is not the most pre-possessing basic material to work with', but the dynamic team behind Titchfield's aren't prepared to let a drab external environment limit their ambition. A la carte and set menus supplemented by breakfasts, lunches and a daily tear-off 'specials flipchart' provide day-long opportunities to showcase seasonal ingredients and trusted suppliers. From clever comfort food such as a custardy sheep's cheese tart with kale pesto or home-salted cod hash to more complex workings of traditional cuts (lamb shank and caper croquettes or truffled beef flank polenta), this is what all town centres should offer.

■ Loch Lomond
Martin Wishart at Loch Lomond
Cooking score: 6
Modern French | £75
Cameron House on Loch Lomond, Loch Lomond, G83 8QZ
Tel no: (01389) 722504
martinwishartlochlomond.co.uk
🛏

Having planted his flag at the heart of Edinburgh's gastronomic scene (see entry), Martin Wishart decided to find himself a place in the country – by the bonnie, bonnie banks of Loch Lomond, to be precise. Set within the baronial confines of Cameron House Hotel, his Lowland outpost is a vision of elegance – an opulent backdrop for cooking of real authority. Tasting menus are normally the way to go: one reader was particularly enamoured of a 'very fine' courgette and basil velouté (not to mention a mouclade of Shetland mussels with curry and saffron), but there's much more to applaud. The kitchen is scrupulous about native ingredients, but gilds its efforts with liberal amounts of French polish: in a sublime pairing of Orkney scallops with beurre noisette and caramelised cauliflower or saddle of Borders roe deer with celeriac, black garlic and onion jus, while the Knockraich crème fraîche parfait with mango and passion fruit is rightly lauded as a signature dessert. Old World wines dominate the weighty list, with house selections from £28.

Chef/s: Graeme Cheevers. **Open:** Sat and Sun L 12 to 2, Wed to Sun D 6.30 to 9.30 (7 Sun). **Closed:** Mon, Tue, first 2 weeks Jan. **Meals:** set L £33. Set D £60 (2 courses) to £75. Sun L £33. Tasting menu £95 (8 courses). **Details:** 46 seats. V menu. Wheelchairs. Music. Parking.

Oban
Ee-Usk
Cooking score: 1
Seafood | £32
North Pier, Oban, PA34 5QD
Tel no: (01631) 565666
eeusk.com

Oban pitches as the 'seafood capital of Scotland', and Ee-Usk (Gaelic for fish) proclaims itself the 'seafood capital of Oban'. The MacLeod family's mission is to showcase the freshest fish, simply treated. Providing an exhaustive list of who fishes what and the specific waters in which they do so, this obsessive emphasis on local ingredients suggests their claim might be justified. The central pierhead location – all glass and steel and virtually on the water – provides a fitting backdrop for the platters of crustaceans and bivalves that take centre stage. A light touch in the kitchen might deliver shelled langoustines in tempura batter to demonstrate 'real scampi' or gild the pearlescent scallops with rustic chorizo. Blackboard specials, perhaps brill or John Dory, depend on the day-boats' catch. An indulgent dessert platter with zesty lemon cheesecake, chocolate shot, crème brûlée and meringue shows they care about the sweet as well as the savoury. Wines include a good range by the glass and bottles start at £16.50.
Chef/s: David Kariuki. **Open:** all week L 12 to 3, D 5.45 to 9.30. **Closed:** 25 and 26 Dec, 3 weeks Jan. **Meals:** main courses £14 to £24. Set L and D £15 (2 courses) to £18 (winter only). **Details:** 100 seats. 24 seats outside. Wheelchairs. Music. Children over 12 yrs only at D.

Strachur
★ NEW ENTRY ★
Inver
Cooking score: 6
British | £30
Strathlachlan, Strachur, PA27 8BU
Tel no: (01369) 860537
inverrestaurant.co.uk

Discovering Inver is like finding a pearl in a Loch Fyne oyster; rare, valuable and surprising yet nonetheless wholly natural. Since spring 2015, Pam Brunton and Rob Latimer's Scandi-Scottish approach has melded subtle design and innovation with tradition and heritage in swoon-worthy scenery. Isolated environments make you rely on your surrounding resources; here this is conscious choice not constraint. With the natural world and small independent producers as neighbours, they revel in testing culinary boundaries and mining forgotten ingredients and techniques. Dinner is a single fixed five-course event. Appetiser mouthfuls could include a seared chicken heart with emulsified fat and skirlie oatmeal. A deceptively simple broccoli, anchovy and garlic starter is an umami-laden showcase – pickling the stems carpaccio-style then offsetting with a punchy purée of leaf ash and squid ink before crowning with the tenderest florets. Rich mutton loin cooked sous-vide comes with a soured brose (broth) of slow-cooked shoulder and buckwheat with fermented turnip. Lighter lunches and all-day baking provide an accessible introduction to their bold ambition – don't miss the sourdough and home-churned butter. Compact but quirky wine choices from £17 a bottle.
Chef/s: Pam Brunton. **Open:** Wed to Sun L 12 to 2.30, D 6.30 to 8.30. **Closed:** Mon, Tue, Jan, Feb, 1 to 19 March. **Meals:** main courses £11 to £21. Set D £42. **Details:** 42 seats. Bar. Music. Parking.

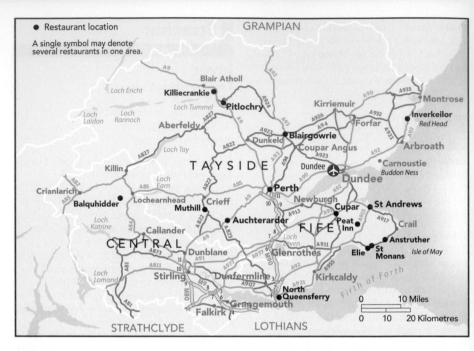

- ● Restaurant location

A single symbol may denote several restaurants in one area.

█ Balquhidder
Monachyle Mhor

Cooking score: 5
Modern British | £57
Balquhidder, FK19 8PQ
Tel no: (01877) 384622
mhor.net

The Lewises have farmed at Monachyle for over 30 years and food and hospitality are in the family psyche. Their remote restaurant and boutique hotel nestles snugly at the heart of the dramatic landscape in which they still rear, stalk, grow, bake or forage most of their own ingredients – ensuring the integrity of everything on the plate. This personal passion matched by solid technique allows them to pull off imaginative dishes that remain authentic to their local origins. A cauliflower pannacotta amuse-bouche presents the refined essence of this underrated brassica. Wild Glen Lethnot rabbit is succulent and elevated beyond the merely rustic by an elegant

smoked consommé, while their own Tamworth cross pork belly, paired with Gigha halibut and salsify purée and an aigre-douce of capers and sweet raisins offers an alternative insight into where land meets sea. The wine list offers interest to both traditionalists and explorers with bottles starting at £24.
Chef/s: Tom Lewis and Marysia Paszkowska. **Open:** all week L 12 to 1.45, D 7 to 8.45. **Meals:** Set L £24 (2 courses) to £30. Set D £57. Sun L £34. **Details:** 42 seats. 25 seats outside. V menu. Bar. Wheelchairs. Music. Parking.

Please send us your feedback

To register your opinion about any restaurant listed in this guide, or a new restaurant that you wish to bring to our attention, please visit the web address at the bottom of the page. Your feedback informs the content of the book and will be used to compile next year's reviews.

Tom Lewis

Monachyle Mhor, Balquhidder

What's your favourite dish on your menu, and why?
Our five-onion dish. The humble onion can be used in so many things, but is never fully appreciated.

How do you start developing a new recipe?
It's all about the seasonal changes and the smells - in the spring I'm desperate for something green to eat.

If you could cook for anyone who would it be, and what would you cook for them?
I'd cook a cave man a steak, just to show him how good we've got it.

What food could you not live without?
Colman's English mustard, because you can use it in so many different ways - it's a genius product!

At the end of a long day, what do you like to cook?
A bit of toast, a bit of pickle, cheese and cold meat if there's any left over.

Do you have anything exciting coming up that you would like to share?
Our mobile restaurant - it has 24 seats, panelled wood, white tablecloths and big windows. It's nice and warm and you can take it anywhere!

LOCAL GEM

Mhor 84

International | £28
Balquhidder, FK19 8NY
Tel no: (01877) 384646
mhor.net

The creative clan behind Monachyle Mhor (see entry) bring their culinary know-how to this informal restaurant-cum-bar-with-rooms. They serve non-stop from 8am to 9pm, attracting an eclectic mix of outdoorsy-types, destination foodies and passing motorists with their 'fresh air food for healthy appetites'. The good-value repertoire showcases local produce and bold approaches to old favourites. Daytime sees all-day breakfasts and snacks such as homemade sourdough tartines through to house-aged steaks and oysters, with teatime featuring gargantuan home-baking and retro mis-matched chinaware. Dinner service brings more complexity in dishes such as braised blade of beef with Balquhidder chanterelles and pickled walnuts. Queues for tables are not uncommon at weekends.

Anstruther
The Cellar

Cooking score: 6
Modern British | £48
East Green, Anstruther, KY10 3AA
Tel no: (01333) 310378
thecellaranstruther.co.uk

A 'cosy Scottish atmosphere' is one of the Cellar's most endearing (and enduring) qualities – not surprising since its rugged stone walls are ingrained with centuries of history. Secreted away in a hidden alley, the one-time smokery and cooperage enthrals visitors with its atmospheric candlelit interiors (the main beam is actually an old ship's mast), although dazzling food is the prime lure at this instantly captivating retreat. Local lad Billy Boyter is now into his third year as chef/proprietor and his 'innovative cuisine' is winning lots of friends with its true flavours and intelligent use of local raw materials. Fish and meat share the limelight on the compact fixed-price menu, but crystal-clear flavours are guaranteed, whether you opt for East Neuk crab with apple, juiced celeriac and hazelnut or local pork belly with oyster, kohlrabi and carrot. After that, a plate of Balblair lamb with sea kale and purple sprouting broccoli delivers plain-speaking satisfaction, while dessert could bring crowdie cheesecake pointed up with rhubarb and pistachio. 'Value for money' is never in doubt, right down to the list of knowledgeably chosen wines (from £20).
Chef/s: Billy Boyter. **Open:** Thur to Sun L 12.30 to 1.45, Wed to Sun D 6.30 to 9. **Closed:** Mon, Tue, 24 to 27 Dec, 1 to 20 Jan, 11 days May, 12 days Sept. **Meals:** set L £28. Set D £48. **Details:** 24 seats. Bar. Wheelchairs. Music.

Average price

The average price denotes the price of a three-course meal without wine.

Cupar
Ostlers Close

Cooking score: 5
Modern British | £42
25 Bonnygate, Cupar, KY15 4BU
Tel no: (01334) 655574
ostlersclose.co.uk

After more than 35 years at their intimate, cottagey restaurant, the Grahams' enthusiasm remains undimmed. Amanda's unfussy but professional approach ensures that diners are warmly welcomed and put instantly at ease, while in the kitchen, Jimmy continues to take advantage of the best that markets and local suppliers can come up with, supplementing with his own-grown fruits and vegetables and foraging trips. His commitment to seasonality is more than skin-deep, it constitutes the lifeblood of his handwritten menus, and the cooking is packed with flavour, and interest, from the mara seaweed hollandaise accompanying a winter starter of seared Isle of Mull scallops served in pastry, to the skirlie (Scottish oatmeal stuffing) that arrives with a gamekeeper's selection of roast game and red cabbage. It all comes to a suitably comforting conclusion with steamed marmalade sponge with cream custard and orange ice cream. There's good drinking to be had on the thoughtfully compiled wine list, with bottles from £20.
Chef/s: Jimmy Graham. **Open:** Tue to Sat D only 7 to 9.30. **Closed:** Sun, Mon, 25 to 27 Dec, 1 Jan. **Meals:** main courses £23 to £26. Set D £30 (Nov to May). **Details:** 26 seats. V menu.

Elie
Sangster's

Cooking score: 4
Modern British | £40
51 High Street, Elie, KY9 1BZ
Tel no: (01333) 331001
sangsters.co.uk

The white-fronted terraced premises feel distinctly homely inside, with their floral curtains, smartly attired tables and warm red carpet. Not for the Sangsters the hard-edged bare boards and unclothed tabletops of elsewhere. Bruce followed a corporate cheffing route to the promised land of Elie, but there is nothing anonymous about his traditionally based bistro cooking, which is full of heart and personality. A pea pannacotta with pickled mushrooms, pancetta and pesto makes all the right contemporary noises, while ham hock and foie gras terrine is sweetly, sharply dressed in pineapple and sultana relish. Fish is a strong suit, if you're up for seared turbot on shellfish risotto, or there are majestic meat dishes such as saddle of venison with truffled creamed celeriac in red wine, or duck breast with hazelnuts and fine beans, served with garlicky chips. Finish with strawberry parfait laced with Grand Marnier, or passion fruit posset and matching sorbet. Wines start at £21.50.

Chef/s: Bruce Sangster. **Open:** Sun L 12.30 to 1.30, Tue to Sat D 7 to 8.30. **Closed:** Mon, Jan, first week Nov. **Meals:** Set D £34 (2 courses) to £48. Sun L £29.50. **Details:** 28 seats. Children over 12 yrs only.

North Queensferry
The Wee Restaurant
Cooking score: 3
Modern European | £36
17 Main Street, North Queensferry, KY11 1JG
Tel no: (01383) 616263
theweerestaurant.co.uk

Sheltering under the Forth Rail Bridge, the Woods' single-storey, stone-clad restaurant is on the ample side of wee, but has a homely ambience nonetheless, its interior brickwork washed in white and yellow, the clothless tables simply set. Craig Wood cooks Scots bistro food with an overlay of French traditionalism, setting Shetland moules-frites in Parmesan cream (as starter or main) amid the likes of Gruyère-laced onion soup, and roast mallard with Puy lentils, Savoy cabbage and black pudding in red wine jus. There are no contemporary jolts here, just readily comprehensible populist dishes founded on fine regional produce, as when a papillote parcel disgorges sea bass, king prawns and

fennel, all fragrant with lime, coriander and chilli. Cheeses from Iain Mellis, or vanilla pannacotta with Champagne-poached fruits and toasted almonds, await at the finishing line. Wines from an intelligently annotated list start at £17.50, or £5.50 a glass.

Chef/s: Craig Wood. **Open:** Tue to Sun L 12 to 2, D 6.30 to 9. **Closed:** Mon, 25 Dec, 1 Jan. **Meals:** set L £18 (2 courses) to £22. Set D £27 (2 courses) to £36. **Details:** 40 seats. Music.

Peat Inn
★ TOP 50 ★
The Peat Inn
Cooking score: 8
Modern European | £56
Peat Inn, KY15 5LH
Tel no: (01334) 840206
thepeatinn.co.uk

The Peat Inn, tucked away in inland Fife, may not be at the heart of any action, but in gastronomic terms it's a carefully and sensitively run operation where front-of-house and kitchen work seamlessly together (perhaps unsurprising for a husband-and-wife team). Every little detail, from aperitifs and amuse-bouches by the fire through to the careful distribution of diners to one of three inter-linked dining rooms, is handled elegantly and with finesse. Extensive menu options (tasting, à la carte and table d'hôte) offered at both lunch and dinner allow the kitchen to push boundaries while still matching the aspirations and budgets of a varied clientele – indeed, flexibility to mix and match between menus demonstrates genuine customer focus and versatility. Geoffrey Smeddle's classically rooted cooking is clever and complex in design, often with multi-layered elements of flavour and texture, but his dishes are delivered in a way that doesn't ever feel contrived or overworked. In short this is complexity made to feel natural and effortless. A starter of poached and tempura calamari, smoked haddock and kohlrabi and artichoke crisps balances textures and flavours with a nod to both coast and farmland, and rich Gartmorn guinea fowl is complemented by a clove sauce, nutty salsify and spiced Puy lentils. An open ravioli of celeriac, cauliflower and smoked almonds with leek hearts, brassicas and horseradish shows vegetarians are well catered for, while among delicate and finely worked desserts, a hot mango and passion fruit soufflé proved an excellent ending to a superb and memorable meal. Service feels genuinely warm but unobtrusive, and the extensive wine list starts with a crisp Touraine at £26.

Chef/s: Geoffrey Smeddle. **Open:** Tue to Sat L 12.30 to 2, D 6.30 to 9. **Closed:** Sun, Mon, 25 to 27 Dec, first week Jan. **Meals:** main courses L £14 to £18, D £22 to £30. Set L £19. Set D £50. Tasting menu £70 (6 courses). **Details:** 50 seats. V menu. Bar. Wheelchairs. Music. Parking. Children at L only.

◼ St Andrews
The Seafood Restaurant
Cooking score: 2
Seafood | £50
The Scores, Bruce Embankment, St Andrews, KY16 9AB
Tel no: (01334) 479475
theseafoodrestaurant.com

A new head chef seems to be a seasonal occurrence at the Seafood Restaurant, where they chop and change with some regularity. The latest incumbent (as we go to press) is Chris Perret who has been promoted from sous-chef. Prime seafood continues to be the major draw, and Perret navigates the kitchen through its seasonal progress, making a decent fist of dishes such as smoked mackerel with artichoke, hollandaise and baby onion or scallop ceviche and chorizo jam served with smoked celeriac and apple. North Sea cod with a potato rösti, maple bacon mousse and charred sweetcorn could follow, with lemon curd, raspberry Italian meringue and caramelised puff pastry as a finale. With its refreshing modern design and impressive view – through floor-to-ceiling glass over the famous *Chariots of Fire* beach – you can see the appeal of such a unique setting. Wines from £20.

Chef/s: Chris Perret. **Open:** all week L 12 to 2.30 (12.30 to 3 Sun), Mon to Sat D 6 to 10. **Closed:** 25 and 26 Dec, 1 Jan. **Meals:** main courses £15 to £18. Set D £40 (2 courses) to £50. **Details:** 52 seats. 28 seats outside. Wheelchairs. Music. Parking.

◼ St Monans
Craig Millar at 16 West End
Cooking score: 4
Modern British | £45
16 West End, St Monans, KY10 2BX
Tel no: (01333) 730327
16westend.com

On a clear day, you can sit on the terrace outside Craig Millar's restaurant and gaze right across the Firth of Forth to Bass Rock – a reminder of the pulling power of a great location. And with St Monans harbour just a pebble's throw away, it's no surprise that super-fresh Scottish seafood is the shining star on the menu. But this is no touristy 'fish and chips' emporium: instead, Craig deploys the full gamut of cutting-edge techniques for a line-up of forceful contemporary dishes ranging from masala-spiced monkfish with curried lentils to turbot and scallops with asparagus, pink purslane and potato purée. Game might be represented by loin of venison with crosnes, charred corn and parsnip, while Craig's penchant for pannacottas could yield a savoury pea version with pickled mushrooms or a sweet classic served alongside cherry sorbet and lemon curd. An impressive international wine list opens with house recommendations from £26.

Chef/s: Craig Millar. **Open:** Wed to Sun L 12.30 to 2, Wed to Sat D 6.30 to 9. **Closed:** Mon, Tue, 25 and 26 Dec, 1 Jan, 2 weeks Jan. **Meals:** set L £22 (2 courses) to £26. Set D £45. Sun L £26. Tasting menu £60 (5 courses). **Details:** 40 seats. 20 seats outside. Bar. Wheelchairs. Parking. Children over 12 yrs only at D.

▮ Auchterarder

★ TOP 10 ★

Restaurant Andrew Fairlie

Cooking score: 8
Modern French | £95
Gleneagles Hotel, Auchterarder, PH3 1NF
Tel no: (01764) 694267
andrewfairlie.co.uk

Gleneagles' new owners are rolling out a
multi-million pound refurbishment, but it's
business as usual at Andrew Fairlie's celebrated
stand-alone restaurant, cocooned within the
heart of the world-famous hotel. The dining
room may be a windowless space, but it is lit
by fantastical chandeliers, with textured
brown/black walls and specially
commissioned artworks. Unimpeachable
ingredients are at the heart of Fairlie's culinary
endeavours, from the Gartmorn Farm duck
served with ceps or the signature home-
smoked lobster dressed with warm lime and
herb butter to the seasonal pickings from his
flourishing two-acre garden (some ten miles
away). At the stoves, he's a master technician,
eloquently schooled in the refined traditions
of French haute cuisine, but applying a
modern sensibility to dishes that always feel
newly minted. There's little in the way of
bluster or affectation, but every mouthful is a
thrill – from a foie gras bombe 'exploding in
the mouth' to slow-cooked Highland lamb
tasting like some ambrosial 'pulled' flesh.
However, the chef is at his most assured when
handling fish and game, be it an aristocratic
pairing of turbot fillet with 'marine mustard',
oyster and Champagne velouté or a
wholesome plate of roast roe deer sitting
centre stage with chou farci, red cabbage and
poivrade sauce. Readers recommend
'interjecting' a cheese course, while desserts
could include a 'stunning' super-rich hazelnut
and muscovado cake with poached pear and
caramel ice cream. High prices extend to the
heavyweight wine list, which starts at £35.

Chef/s: Andrew Fairlie and Stephen McLaughlin.
Open: Mon to Sat D only 6.30 to 10. **Closed:** Sun,
25 and 26 Dec, 3 weeks Jan. **Meals:** set D £95.
Tasting menu £125 (8 courses). **Details:** 52 seats. V
menu. Wheelchairs. Music. Parking. Children over
12 yrs only.

▮ Blairgowrie

Kinloch House Hotel

Cooking score: 5
Modern British | £53
Dunkeld Road, Blairgowrie, PH10 6SG
Tel no: (01250) 884237
kinlochhouse.com

Owned by the Allen family since 2002, this
ivy-clad Victorian stone mansion seems to
have everything your heritage-hungry tourist
could desire: 25 acres of bracing countryside
all its own, views of the Perthshire hills,
handsome baronial interiors, historic portraits
in oils, tartan fabrics, antiques galore and a
chef who knows his way around the native
larder. Steve MacCallum gives benchmark
ingredients a refined but gentle spin (roast
fillet and slow-cooked featherblade of beef
with fondant potato, truffled leeks and roasted
root vegetables, for example), but shows his
true mettle when applying a sympathetic hand
to seasonal game and fish – as in breast of
wood pigeon with green beans, artichoke and
a deep-fried truffled hen's egg or fillet of
Hebridean salmon with a smoked salmon
fishcake, sea spinach, asparagus, tomato and
lemon butter sauce. His desserts also display
fine technique and artistry, from a hot
chocolate fondant with milk ice cream to iced
rhubarb parfait with rhubarb and ginger
snaps. A substantial wine list gives prominence
to the vintage French classics, with bottles
from £26.50.
Chef/s: Steve MacCallum. **Open:** all week L 12 to 2,
D 7 to 8.30. **Closed:** 14 to 29 Dec. **Meals:** set L £20
(2 courses) to £26. Set D £53. Sun L £30. **Details:** 36
seats. Bar. Wheelchairs. Parking. Children over 7 yrs
only at D.

Little's

Cooking score: 2
Seafood | £35
4 Wellmeadow, Blairgowrie, PH10 6ND
Tel no: (01250) 875358
littlesrestaurant.co.uk

The jaunty blue 'fishbone' logo is a reminder that seafood is the main business at chef/proprietor Willie Little's 'pleasant and welcoming' restaurant in the centre of Blairgowrie. Fried fillet of Scrabster haddock and chips tops the bill, but there's much more to applaud, from a beautifully presented 'taster' of mussels, scallops, crab and salmon mousse to roast monkfish with cauliflower purée, smoked pork, pak choi and straw chips or grilled whole megrim sole with sautéed potatoes and vegetables ('one of the best fish dishes I've tasted'). Haggis and goats' cheese bonbons, steaks and curiously topped pizzas pander to other tastes (chorizo, black pudding, scallop and apple, anyone?), while desserts are a mixed bag of old faithfuls – 'absolutely delicious' warm rice pudding with stewed rhubarb, buttermilk pancakes with roast banana, apples with Calvados custard and so on. Agreeable pricing extends to the all-purpose international wine list, which starts at £18.95.
Chef/s: William Little. **Open:** Fri and Sat L 12 to 2.30, Tue to Sat D 4 to 9.30 (6 to 9.30 Fri and Sat). **Closed:** Sun, Mon, 25 Dec, 1 Jan, first 2 weeks Nov. **Meals:** main courses £17 to £24. Set L £20 (2 courses). **Details:** 48 seats. Wheelchairs. Music.

■ Glendevon

READERS RECOMMEND

Tormaukin

British
The Tormaukin Hotel, Glendevon, FK14 7JY
Tel no: (01259) 781252
tormaukinhotel.co.uk
'I had gravadlax of salmon with pickled lemons and vanilla aïoli followed by wild boar medallions with celeriac purée, red cabbage, crisp curly kale and a slice of pommes dauphinoise – very good.'

■ Inverkeilor

Gordon's

Cooking score: 5
Modern British | £57
Main Street, Inverkeilor, DD11 5RN
Tel no: (01241) 830364
gordonsrestaurant.co.uk

On the main street of a wee village close to the bracing North Sea is an unremarkable Georgian house, home to the Watsons' dapper restaurant-with-rooms since 1986. Over the last 30 years Gordon and Maria Watson, aided by son Garry who now leads the line at the stove, have lovingly upgraded the place to create a captivating address, where luxe boutique rooms and a contemporary dining room recall the natural colours and textures of the Scottish landscape. Service gets good notices – 'such a relaxed atmosphere' – and the kitchen delivers a sense of occasion even at lunch. Perthshire wood pigeon with Jerusalem artichoke ravioli and crispy truffled egg is a first course of distinction, followed by a velouté such as the 'vivid cep' version that wowed one reader. Next up, North Sea turbot with crispy chicken wings and curry vinaigrette, and, to finish, pistachio crème brûlée matched with bittersweet chocolate sorbet. The informative wine list kicks off at £19.95.
Chef/s: Gordon and Garry Watson. **Open:** Wed to Fri and Sun L 12.30 to 1.45, Tue to Sat D 7 to 9. **Closed:** Mon, Jan. **Meals:** set L £34. Set D £57. **Details:** 24 seats. Parking. Children over 12 yrs only.

Killiecrankie
The Killiecrankie

Cooking score: 2
Modern British | £42
Killiecrankie, PH16 5LG
Tel no: (01796) 473220
killiecrankiehotel.co.uk

Killiecrankie is a soothing and cosetting sort of place, which is partly down to its setting in four green acres, but also the manageable scale of the operation (just ten bedrooms) and its reassuringly traditional interior. The formal restaurant fits the bill, as does the cooking of Mark Easton – who celebrated 20 years here in 2016. Making use of the hotel's kitchen garden and with contemporary interventions carefully moderated, the kitchen turns out a warm salad of wood pigeon with Stornoway black pudding and petits pois, dressed with a raspberry vinaigrette. Follow on with Perthshire venison and grouse (fillet and breast respectively), with dauphinois, roasted beetroot and sloe gin jus, or a fish option such as roasted fillet of monkfish with roasted garlic mash. Among desserts, steamed sticky fig, walnut and stem ginger pudding is drizzled with Pedro Ximénez. Linger over a whisky in the bar. Wines start at £22.
Chef/s: Mark Easton. **Open:** all week D only 6.30 to 8.30. **Closed:** 3 Jan to mid Mar. **Meals:** set D £42 (4 courses). **Details:** 34 seats. V menu. Bar. Wheelchairs. Parking.

Muthill
Barley Bree

Cooking score: 3
Anglo-French | £42
6 Willoughby Street, Muthill, PH5 2AB
Tel no: (01764) 681451
barleybree.com

Gnarled beams, rough brick walls and painted panelling are reminders that Barley Bree was originally a village pub, although it now performs a very different function. Current owners Fabrice and Alison Bouteloup have brought a little *je ne sais quoi*, surprising visitors with their stylish contemporary approach ('rural chic') and resourcefulness – 'it is always a pleasure to dine there'. The bar has been moved out of the dining room (providing more covers), but the kitchen's culinary bias is unchanged: expect bold flavours with a strong European accent, as in pavé and pressé of Campbells Gold sirloin with charred shallot, Del Monico potato and Taleggio cheese. There's a fondness for Asian riffs, too (crispy sushi rice cake with hoisin sauce, mushroom won tons, pickled mooli and tempura cabbage, say), although desserts take diners back to Fabrice's roots – think a 'worth-waiting-for' tarte Tatin or a nifty take on clafoutis involving griottines and baby black figs. Prices on the strong French-led wine list start at £18.95.
Chef/s: Fabrice Bouteloup. **Open:** Wed to Sun L 12 to 2 (3 Sun), D 6.45 to 9 (6 Sun). **Closed:** Mon, Tue, 24 to 26 Dec. **Meals:** main courses £23 to £26. Set L £16 (2 courses) to £20. **Details:** 40 seats. 12 seats outside. V menu. Bar. Music. Parking.

Perth
Deans

Cooking score: 3
Modern British | £32
77-79 Kinnoull Street, Perth, PH3 1LU
Tel no: (01738) 643377
letseatperth.co.uk

Ensuring that a successful formula remains successful requires a great deal of hard work, so the continuing efforts of Willie and Margo Deans deserve applause. Here since 2005, their soft-toned, elegant restaurant is a thoroughly pleasant place, the introduction of a cocktail lounge has been well received, and Mr Deans' restrained contemporary menu offers some good cooking. A twice-baked cheese soufflé is lifted out of the ordinary by its accompaniment of Macsween's haggis, turnip mash and whisky cream. Main-course flavours are built into streamlined productions: a colour-coordinated dish of loin of Ochil venison on slow-cooked cassoulet comes with dauphinois potatoes, parsley and lemon gremolata, caraway carrot pudding, Madeira and garlic sauce, while fillet of lemon sole is partnered by seared king prawns, lemon-poached leeks, tomato-braised potatoes and lobster cream. Desserts include a well-reported iced apple terrine with a blueberry crumble, honeycomb candy and vanilla pod ice cream. Wines from £19.95.

Chef/s: Willie Deans. **Open:** Tue to Sat L 12 to 2.30, D 6 to 9 (9.30 Sat). **Closed:** Sun, Mon, 2 weeks Jan, 1 week Nov. **Meals:** main courses £14 to £26. Set L £13 (2 courses) to £18. Set D £19 (2 courses) to £23. **Details:** 60 seats. Wheelchairs. Music.

★ NEW ENTRY ★

North Port

Cooking score: 3
British | £30
8 North Port, Perth, PH1 5LU
Tel no: (01738) 580867
thenorthport.co.uk

It may be housed in a higgledy-piggledy, wood-panelled 18th-century building behind Perth's Concert Hall, but there's nothing old-fashioned about North Port. Andrew Moss and Karen Milne took over in 2014 after working at The Ubiquitous Chip in Glasgow (see entry) and they have breathed new life into what had been a bistro for the previous four decades. Using a network of local suppliers and foragers, raw materials are carefully sourced and sensitively handled. Excellent bread is served with homemade butters and leads on to precisely cooked Black Isle lamb sweetbreads with wild garlic dressing, St George's mushrooms and walnuts. Seasonal pickings also dominate the main courses, as in a fillet of Scrabster cod, potato terrine, roast shallot, Isle of Skye crab, wild leeks and crab sauce. An immaculate buttermilk custard, rhubarb, sorrel purée and rhubarb meringue is one way to finish. The compact wine list starts at £16.95.

Chef/s: Andrew Moss. **Open:** Tue to Sat L 12 to 2.30, D 5 to 10. **Closed:** Sun, Mon. **Meals:** main courses £13 to £21. Set L £12 (2 courses) to £15. Early D £15 (2 courses) to £18. **Details:** 35 seats.

▌Pitlochry

Sandemans

new chef/no score
Modern British | £65
Fonab Castle Hotel, Foss Road, Pitlochry, PH16 5ND
Tel no: (01796) 470140
fonabcastlehotel.com

Once owned by members of the Sandeman dynasty (of port and sherry fame), baronial Fonab Castle is now a fully functioning tourist and hospitality retreat with this namesake restaurant as its gastronomic zenith. A new chef arrived in summer 2016, but the food on offer in the sumptuous, dark-panelled dining room is much as before — namely a six-course tasting menu characterised by classic high-end cuisine and a fondness for Scottish ingredients. A typical opener could be a ham hock tian with celeriac rémoulade, apple, quail's egg and amontillado gel, while the centrepiece might see poached and roasted beef fillet in company with shoulder-blade beignet, chervil root purée, salsify and port reduction (Sandeman's, of course). To conclude, Valrhona chocolate fondant with salted-caramel ice cream fits the bill. Dishes are matched by specially selected wines from a high-class list that naturally features a raft of Sandeman's fortified tipples. Prices start with a Pinot Grigio 'Luna' 2014 at £26.95 (£6.95 a glass).

Chef/s: Grant MacNicol. **Open:** Tue to Sat D only 7 to 9. **Closed:** Sun, Mon. **Meals:** set D £65 (6 courses). **Details:** 26 seats. Bar. Wheelchairs. Music. Parking.

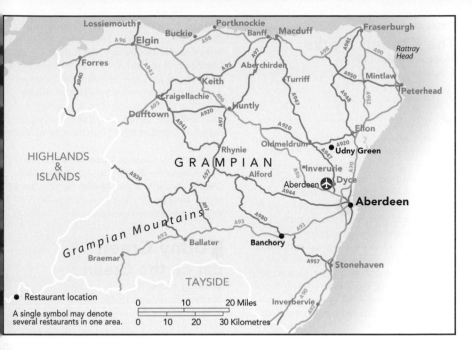

■ Aberdeen

Adelphi Kitchen

Cooking score: 3
Modern British | £30
28 Adelphi, Aberdeen, AB11 5BL
Tel no: (01224) 211414
theadelphikitchen.co.uk

Billing itself as a 'charcoal-cooked meat and seafood restaurant,' the Adelphi Kitchen is a relaxing cosy little cabin of a place, with plank walls and floors, muted tartan banquettes, low-hanging lights and an unobtrusive jazz soundtrack. Blackboard specials and seriously clued-up staff outline the bill of fare, which isn't as mainstream as that description might suggest. Open with king scallops and sugar-cured beef carpaccio with dripping breadcrumbs, pickled apple and lemongrass custard, and your attention is duly grabbed. The properly gnarled batter, Cajun-spiced and crisp as a new fiver, on an enormous piece of haddock fried in buttermilk is a triumph, and the accompaniments of whopping great chips sprinkled with powdered vinegar and home-made creamy mayo don't let it down. Otherwise, look to dry-aged steaks and luxed-up burgers piled with pickled cabbage, spicy onions, garlic dressing and chilli sauce, and come to a satisfied conclusion with lemon meringue pie kitted out with vodka'd raspberries and yoghurt sorbet. Castilian house blends are £19.50.

Chef/s: Chris Toner. **Open:** all week L 12 to 2.30 (5 Sun), Mon to Sat D 5 to 10. **Meals:** main courses £17 to £28. **Details:** 37 seats.

LOCAL GEM

The Kitchen Works

Modern British | £18

7 Summer Street, Aberdeen, AB10 1SB

Tel no: (01224) 632237

thekitchenworksaberdeen.co.uk

£30

Just off Union Street, opposite Gilcomston church, the thoroughly modern Kitchen Works is a great metropolitan pit-stop for daytime shoppers and a candlelit oasis for sociable nibbles come Friday and Saturday nights. Stripped-oak tables are lit by giant pendant spotlights, while smart grey woodwork and clean lines provide the backdrop to creamy coffees and irresistible home-baked breakfast goods – the light-as-air scones are not to be missed. Lunch brings simple sandwiches on rustic, organic breads, while the Evening Works menu offers on-trend small plates including cured cod with chickpea and anchovies, or warm golden beetroot, asparagus and pine kernels with lemon curd. To finish, try the ever-popular chocolate brownie. Wines from £22.

■ Banchory
Cow Shed Restaurant

Cooking score: 2

Modern British | £25

Raemoir Road, Banchory, AB31 5QB

Tel no: (01330) 820813

cowshedrestaurant.co.uk

£30

Now with an outside deck, full refurbishment and its very own fish and chip shop, this family-run business has proved itself adept at responding to the needs of its customers. It's an unapologetically modern building in timeless surrounds – views of the countryside, including the flat-topped moorland of the Hill of Fare, are uninterrupted. Those chip-shop chips make their way onto flavour-forward menus that show evident pride in the nation's suppliers and a fondness for feeding people. To start, there are Aberdeenshire sausages with crushed mustard potatoes and onion gravy, or lighter langoustine tails with butter, garlic and parsley. After that, Scotch beef features so heavily – steak and onion pie, burgers, sirloin cap with onion and mustard-seed marmalade – that you'd be foolish to ignore it. Pudding might be lemon tart with kiwi and lime sorbet, or try the homemade rapeseed oatcakes with Scottish cheeses. Wines from £18.

Chef/s: Graham Buchan. **Open:** all week L 12 to 2 (3 Sun), Wed to Sat D 6 to 7.30 (8.30 Fri and Sat). **Closed:** 25 Dec to 8 Jan. **Meals:** main courses £10 to £17. **Details:** 65 seats. 24 seats outside. Wheelchairs. Music. Parking.

■ Udny Green
Eat on the Green

Cooking score: 2

Modern European | £45

Udny Green, AB41 7RS

Tel no: (01651) 842337

eatonthegreen.co.uk

This stone-built former post office faces Udny's green and has a distinctly individual character. Tastefully decorated within, it's divided into a bar-lounge, unexpectedly formal dining room with well-spaced tables, and a private dining room. Mateusz Majer draws on home-grown and local produce from kitchen garden and polytunnel for a gentle style of modern cuisine that might begin with goats' cheese tart alongside beetroot and hazelnut salad in horseradish dressing, before going on to west coast sea bass with curried Shetland mussels and split pea dhal, or honey-glazed spiced duck leg with grilled plums, Vietnamese-style stir-fried veg and sweet potato purée. Puddings aim to tickle the fancy with white chocolate cheesecake, candied walnuts and blueberry yoghurt sorbet. The wine list gives an equitable shake of the stick to Old and New Worlds, starting at £23.50.

Chef/s: Mateusz Majer. **Open:** Wed to Fri and Sun L 12 to 2, Wed to Sun D 6 to 9 (5.30 Sat). **Closed:** Mon, Tue. **Meals:** main courses £27 to £33. **Details:** 80 seats. Bar. Music. Parking.

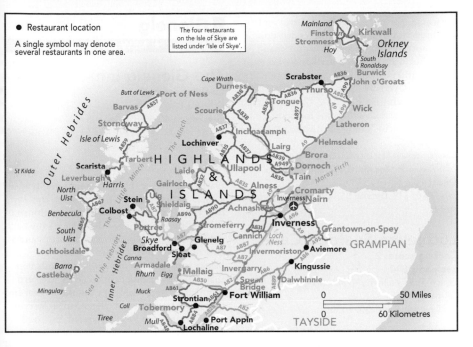

- Restaurant location

A single symbol may denote several restaurants in one area.

The four restaurants on the Isle of Skye are listed under 'Isle of Skye'.

Mainland
Finstown
Stromness
Hoy
South Ronaldsay
Kirkwall
Orkney Islands
Burwick
John o'Groats

Cape Wrath
Durness
Scrabster
Thurso
A836

Butt of Lewis
Port of Ness
A838
Tongue
A836
Wick
A99

Barvas
A857
Scourie
A838
A897
Latheron

Stornoway
The Minch
Inchnadamph
A827
Helmsdale

Isle of Lewis
A859
Lochinver
A835
A837
Lairg
A9
Brora

St Kilda
Scarista
Tarbert
Laide
HIGHLANDS
Ullapool
A835
A949
Dornoch
Moray Firth
A836
Tain

Leverburgh
Harris
Gairloch
A832
&
Alness
Cromarty

North Uist
Stein
A890
ISLANDS
Inverness
Nairn

Benbecula
Colbost
A896
Raasay
Achnasheen
A87

South Uist
Portree
Skye
Cannich
Loch Ness
Grantown-on-Spey
GRAMPIAN

Lochboisdale
Broadford
Glenelg
A87
Aviemore

Barra
Canna
Armadale
Sleat
Invergarry
Kingussie

Castlebay
Rhum
Eigg
Mallaig
A830
Spean
Bridge
Dalwhinnie

Mingulay
Muck
A861
Fort William
0   50 Miles

Coll
Strontian
A861
0   60 Kilometres

Tiree
Tobermory
Mull
Port Appin
Lochaline
TAYSIDE

Aviemore
Mountain Café
Cooking score: 1
British | £20
111 Grampian Road, Aviemore, PH22 1RH
Tel no: (01479) 812473
mountaincafe-aviemore.co.uk
£30

'Best food, best setting, best staff', the Mountain Café serves up homely, hearty stuff from early morning to the late afternoon, which you can 'scoff down while enjoying superb views of the Cairngorms'. Cakes and bread are baked on the premises, local art hangs on the walls, and everything from the all-day breakfast, focaccia doorstop sandwiches, lusty salads (a salmon number, say, with fennel and citrus sloe gin dressing), gluten-free chocolate berry roulade and venison burger are made with heartfelt enthusiasm and skill by Kiwi owner Kirsten Gilmour and her team. Wines from £15.

Chef/s: Kirsten Gilmour. **Open:** all week 8.30 to 5 (5.30 Sat and Sun). **Closed:** 25 and 26 Dec, 1 Jan. **Meals:** main courses from £5 to £12. **Details:** 50 seats. 12 seats outside. Music. Parking.

Fort William
Crannog
Cooking score: 1
Seafood | £34
Town Pier, Fort William, PH33 6DB
Tel no: (01397) 705589
crannog.net

The red-tin roof of this former bait shed on the edge of Loch Linnhe is a Fort William landmark that has been pleasing diners seven days a week for the last 26 years. The informal lochside restaurant has a wide-ranging menu that includes both meat and fish: Cullen skink, salmon pâté, hake, salmon and sole share a menu with cheese soufflé, ham and haggis croquettes, and lamb shoulder. Shellfish takes a star turn with mussels, oysters, Mallaig langoustines and crab claws or the whole shebang in a seafood platter for two. On inspection a smoked salmon salad was sadly short on salmon and heavy on salad leaves, but warm smoked mackerel with roast potatoes and poached leeks was exceptionally generous as were the Crannog fishcakes. The substantial wine list starts at £17.95, rising to £66 for Meursault with some interesting Scottish beers, including the distinctive Kelpie Seaweed ale. **Chef/s:** Stewart MacLachlan. **Open:** all week L 12 to 2.30, D 6 to 9. **Closed:** 25 and 26 Dec, 1 Jan. **Meals:** main courses £15 to £23. Set L £15 (2 courses) to £19. **Details:** 55 seats. Wheelchairs. Music.

Lochleven Seafood Café
Cooking score: 2
Seafood | £40
Onich, Fort William, PH33 6SA
Tel no: (01855) 821048
lochlevenseafoodcafe.co.uk

'We went here two years ago, and knew we had to come back again. Last time I ate grilled palourdes in garlic butter on the shell, followed by half a cold lobster – this time I had exactly the same as it was so perfect, and still is.' Reporters have written enthusiastically about this bright but very basic seafood restaurant next door to a shellfish dispatch centre. The kitchen doesn't overreach itself and 'knows what it is doing', sending out shellfish soup, Glencoe mussels cooked in cider, hot or cold shellfish platters or Loch Linnhe roasted langoustines with lemon and mayonnaise. Add bread and butter, a potato side dish or a mixed salad as you wish; non-fish options are ribeye steak or sweet potato, chickpea and spinach curry; and there are Scottish cheeses and citrus cheesecake with raspberry coulis for dessert. There's a great atmosphere with everyone eating with fingers and really enjoying themselves. Wines from £15.75. **Chef/s:** Marcel Videnka. **Open:** all week L 12 to 3, D 6 to 9. **Closed:** 31 Oct to 14 Mar. **Meals:** main courses £14 to £40. **Details:** 35 seats. 15 seats outside. Wheelchairs. Parking.

Glenelg
★ NEW ENTRY ★

The Glenelg Inn
Cooking score: 2
British | £25
Glenelg, IV40 8JR
Tel no: (01599) 522273
glenelg-inn.com
£30

Dark timbers line the walls, a sofa and lived-in armchairs are arranged around an eternal log fire. There's a touch of tartan in the cushions of this traditional old inn, otherwise it's the bar, pews and pine tables, candles in bottles and a cheerful little dining room. Beside the blackboard menu is a map that reminds you that you are in a quiet corner of the western Highlands overlooking the Sound of Sleat and two miles from the old Glenachulish ferry to Skye. Simple and locally sourced, the food matches the setting: smoked salmon with black onion seeds and herbs; wood pigeon and honey-roast figs, maybe wild mountain hare – the menu changes daily – with a mass of green olives and superbly roasted potatoes or bouillabaisse swimming with scallops, monkfish and langoustine. A lemon tart comes without adornment – it doesn't need it. A short and sensibly priced wine list, service by a friendly young team and regular music nights. **Chef/s:** Verity Hurding. **Open:** all week L 12.30 to 3.30, D 6.30 to 9.30. **Meals:** main meals £9 to £14. **Details:** 50 seats. Bar.

Please send us your feedback

To register your opinion about any restaurant listed in this guide, or a new restaurant that you wish to bring to our attention, please visit the web address at the bottom of the page. Your feedback informs the content of the book and will be used to compile next year's reviews.

Inverness

Chez Roux at Rocpool Reserve

Cooking score: 3
French | £35
Rocpool Reserve Hotel, 14 Culduthel Road,
Inverness, IV2 4AG
Tel no: (01463) 240089
rocpool.com

'A proper Roux restaurant,' notes one reporter of Albert Roux's glossy (and heavily Roux-branded) hotel dining room. If that brings to mind haute cuisine, think again. Roux claims 'good and honest country cooking', though we'd say it's rather more refined than that, evidenced by a delicately smoked duck breast salad with wild asparagus and a sesame and ginger dressing or well-judged pike quenelles with mushrooms and cream. Other pleasing dishes included plaice (on the bone) meunière with squid-ink linguine, capers and brown butter, and Parmesan-crusted rabbit stuffed with tarragon and pistachio and served with a Madeira jus. Overenthusiastic service — yes everything is fine, thank you — irritated a little, but was redeemed by an excellent coconut pannacotta with a sharp lime sorbet. A very good wine list — led by French and New World — has plenty at mid-range, rising to premier and grand crus, starting at £22.
Chef/s: Javier Santos. **Open:** all week L 12 to 2, D 7 to 10. **Meals:** main courses £16 to £24. Set L £30 (3 courses). Set D £32 (3 courses). **Details:** 50 seats. Bar. Parking.

Symbols

- Accommodation is available
- £30 Three courses for less than £30
- £5 OFF £5-off voucher scheme
- Notable wine list

Rocpool

Cooking score: 2
Modern European | £39
1 Ness Walk, Inverness, IV3 5NE
Tel no: (01463) 717274
rocpoolrestaurant.com

£5 OFF

Since 2002, Steven Devlin's glassed-in restaurant has seduced customers with its location, close to the river Ness and the castle beyond. Turn inwards and the long, narrow room, on a prime corner spot, is hung with abstract art and staffed by a charming team. If your instinct is to go for seafood you'll be rewarded with a 'terrific' main course of buttermilk and herb-spiced monkfish brochette with spinach and lentil dhal, cauliflower fritters and tzatziki, or a simple dish of linguine with grilled king prawns, queenie scallops and tomatoes. Elsewhere, combinations don't always convince, but beef carpaccio with fried artichokes, greens, shaved Manchego and gremolata is a good use of local meat. 'Pleasant' desserts might be chocolate caramel and hazelnut tart with zabaglione cream or hot baked lemon meringue pie, and there's cheese with handmade oatcakes, fruit and honey. Wines from a relatively short but well-annotated list start at £16.90.
Chef/s: Steven Devlin. **Open:** Mon to Sat L 12 to 2.30, D 5.45 to 10. **Closed:** Sun, 24 to 26 Dec, 1 to 3 Jan. **Meals:** main courses £18 to £26. Set L £16 (2 courses). Set D £18 (2 courses). **Details:** 55 seats. Wheelchairs. Music.

Isle of Harris

Scarista House

Cooking score: 2
Modern British | £44
Scarista, Isle of Harris, HS3 3HX
Tel no: (01859) 550238
scaristahouse.com

The location of this former manse above the spectacular Scarista beach with its white sand and turquoise sea is hard to beat and the well-established country house hotel remains a welcome retreat for dinner. They offer a straightforward four-course, no-choice menu making the most of hard-won local resources in this remote spot dominated by waves and weather. A convivial meal begins with drinks and canapés in the book-lined sitting room before moving on to dinner – less restaurant food, more superior home cooking – which may start with a satisfying spinach, cumin and coconut soup with a chicken and Lanark Blue cheese dumpling, followed by plain grilled turbot, sauce vierge, new potatoes and green beans, then tarte Tatin and cinnamon ice cream and/or a generous choice of excellent Scottish cheeses, before coffee and petits fours in the lounge. A predominantly French wine list starts at £20.

Chef/s: Tim and Patricia Martin. **Open:** all week D only 8 (1 sitting). **Closed:** Dec to Feb. **Meals:** Set D £34 (2 courses) to £52. **Details:** 20 seats. Wheelchairs. Parking. Children over 8 yrs only.

Isle of Skye

★ NEW ENTRY ★

Birlinn Restaurant

Cooking score: 3
British | £30
Hotel Eilean Iarmain, Isle Ornsay, Sleat, Isle of Skye, IV43 8QR
Tel no: (01471) 833332
eileaniarmain.co.uk

Eilean Iarmain and Birlinn are a small hotel and restaurant tucked away in an idyllic spot at the end of a single-track road overlooking the Isle Ornsay lighthouse, with long-distance views to the remote Knoydart peaks. The smart drawing room, wood-panelled dining room and conservatory all face the Sound of Sleat and offer a relaxed country-house vibe and a menu that maximises local produce at a fixed price for two or three courses. A spring dinner provided a gorgeous crab salad of white crabmeat, crème fraîche, lime juice and parsley, served with a sauce vierge and good sourdough. Excellent mains included salmon

with dauphinois potatoes and herb-crusted pork fillet with a cider jus, while an indulgent dessert brought together chocolate, praline crumbs and Amaretto custard. Next door, the casual Pràban bar sports its own Gaelic whiskies and a blackboard that tempts with the local catch of langoustines and squat lobster, as well as 'hearty dishes and things with chips. Great place all round.' A regulation wine list has glasses from £4.95.

Chef/s: Martin Nel. **Open:** all week D only 6.30 to 9. **Meals:** set D £25 (2 courses) to £30. **Details:** 35 seats. Bar.

Creelers of Skye

Cooking score: 2
French | £29
Lower Harrapool, Broadford, Isle of Skye, IV49 9AQ
Tel no: (01471) 822281
skye-seafood-restaurant.co.uk

£5 OFF £30

Gazing across Broadford Bay to the Sound of Sleat and the hills of Applecross, it's hard to imagine a better spot for a seafood-driven eatery. The simple café-style interior happily plays second fiddle to the views and to David Wilson's traditional French cooking, which places the emphasis on fresh, local produce, lack of fuss and value for money. Typical offerings include pan-browned, hand-dived scallops on saucisson d'Auvergne with a green bean velouté, and bouillabaisse stuffed with sea bass, monkfish, sea bream, red mullet, mussels and prawns. The French flavour is by no means restrictive, with Cajun-style haddock and fillet of Chardonnay-poached halibut with tagliatelle and a seafood and saffron velouté also making a showing. If you're not in the mood for fish, there are alternatives such as chicken gumbo or vegetable curry. To finish, try chocolate torte with Armagnac ganache and hot chocolate sauce. Wine from £17.50.

Chef/s: David Wilson and Ann Doyle. **Open:** Mon to Sat 12 to 9. **Closed:** Sun, Nov to Feb. **Meals:** main courses £15 to £31. **Details:** 30 seats. Wheelchairs. Music. Parking.

Kinloch Lodge

Cooking score: 5
Modern British | £70
Sleat, Isle of Skye, IV43 8QY
Tel no: (01471) 833214
kinloch-lodge.co.uk

'As refined and elegant as ever,' enthused one reader after spending a weekend at Kinloch Lodge – a stunning 17th-century hunting retreat overlooking the Sound of Sleat. The ancestral seat of the Macdonald clan for generations, this high-baronial pile is synonymous with hospitality grandee Lady Claire Macdonald OBE – although the kitchen is now headed up by Marcello Tully, who regularly delivers 'quite brilliant' food founded on ingredients from Scotland's seasonal larder. The highlight for one visitor was a plate of Black Isle lamb fillet with cashews, black olives, caramelised apples and pears, but fish is equally inviting – perhaps Scrabster hake fillet with fried seafood gnocchi, Drumfearn mussels and saffron cream sauce. Also look out for 'Marcello's special' – an extra diversion involving, say, a dinky portion of slow-roast Moray pork belly with apple gel and Madeira jus. Finally, there are Scottish and French cheeses, plus the day's dessert – vanilla crème fraiche pannacotta with orange and mint sorbet, for example. Kinloch's exhaustive and knowledgeably curated wine list delights connoisseurs and novices alike, with house selections by the glass offering easy access; bottles from £36.
Chef/s: Marcello Tully. **Open:** all week L 12 to 2, D 6 to 9. **Meals:** set L £35 (2 courses) to £38. Set D £70 (5 courses) to £80 (7 courses). **Details:** 45 seats. V menu. Bar. Wheelchairs. Music. Parking. Children at L and early D only.

Visit us online

To find out more about The Good Food Guide, please visit thegoodfoodguide.co.uk

Loch Bay

Cooking score: 4
Seafood | £38
1-2 Macleod Terrace, Stein, Isle of Skye, IV55 8GA
Tel no: (01470) 592235
lochbay-restaurant.co.uk

It's all change at this charming seafood restaurant, successfully run for 15 years by David and Alison Wilkinson until they sold in 2015 to Michael Smith, the former chef at the much garlanded Three Chimneys (see entry). The whitewashed cottage has been gently updated and so, equally sensitively, has the menu. Hare ragoût with neeps and ramsons and cannelloni of squash and crowdie are among the set menu choices, but the Skye seafood menu beckons with a nibble of deep-fried salt herring followed by fish soup pistou and wheaten scone; crab risotto with red mullet; scallop with hazelnut; finishing with a fine bouillabaisse of oyster, langoustine and lobster. It's simpler (and cheaper) than the Three Chimneys, but retains Smith's fine skills, attention to detail and commitment to the best Scottish traditions, never more than in a pudding of cloutie dumpling and whisky cream. The drinks list has Skye beers and wines starting at £19.
Chef/s: Michael Smith. **Open:** Wed to Sun L 12 to 1.30 (2.30 Sun), Tue to Sat D 6.15 to 9. **Closed:** Mon, Jan. **Meals:** main courses £21 to £25. Set D £38 (3 courses) to £55. **Details:** 22 seats. 8 seats outside. Music. Parking.

The Three Chimneys

Cooking score: 5
Modern British | £65
Colbost, Isle of Skye, IV55 8ZT
Tel no: (01470) 511258
threechimneys.co.uk

'Food to match the most breathtaking location' is the tribute of one who made the trek along four miles of single-track road to reach this former crofter's cottage that looks west across the sea to the Outer Hebrides.

Shirley and Eddie Spear have not destroyed the original feel of the place by importing luxury, though cosseting is the order of the day; in the main, most people swoon over the view, enjoy the cooking and clamour to return. The latterday reputation of the Three Chimneys has been founded on the fiercely seasonal cooking of Michael Smith. He has now been replaced by Scott Davies, but the menu sails on, built around Scotland's matchless produce, and there is plenty to admire. One spring lunch consisted of a superb pigeon breast served with a black pudding 'rubble' and textures of carrot, a beef tasting plate that included rump, oxtail and tongue, with a selection of onions 'including a quite perfect little tart', and an apple soufflé with 'pitch-perfect' rum and raisin ice cream. Praise, too, for bread and 'gorgeous' butter (heather-smoked and seaweed), the famous marmalade pudding with Drambuie custard, and an impressive wine list with a spread that's wide enough to cope with whatever the kitchen cooks. Bottles from £30.

Chef/s: Scott Davies. **Open:** all week L 12.15 to 1.45, D 6.30 to 9.30. **Closed:** 12 Dec to 14 Jan. **Meals:** Set L £38. Set D £65 (5 courses). Tasting menu £90 (8 courses). **Details:** 40 seats. Bar. Wheelchairs. Parking. Children over 5 yrs only at L, over 8 yrs at D.

∎ Kingussie
The Cross

Cooking score: 4
Modern British | £55
Ardbroilach Road, Kingussie, PH21 1LB
Tel no: (01540) 661166
thecross.co.uk

🍷 🛏

Close to town but secluded in woodland and beside a tumbling river, this former tweed mill in the heart of the Cairngorms National Park is owned and most professionally run by Derek and Celia Kitchingman, with chef David Skiggs presenting an accomplished menu that makes sound use of local produce. Canapés and drinks are served in the lounge, dinner in the spacious dining room where the rough stone walls of the old mill are now pristinely whitewashed and hung with original oils. A silky-smooth white onion soup with wild garlic is a substantial amuse-bouche, followed by an immaculately prepared and presented starter of red mullet, sliced rare tuna, aubergine purée and a crisp smoked haddock beignet. Mains offer fillet, belly and cheek of local pork, wild sea bass, well-judged halibut and a pleasing dish of lamb loin with a pearl barley risotto, artichokes and a lamb jus. Service is pleasant and correct, the wine list substantial and reasonably priced starting at £24 with many below £30.

Chef/s: David Skiggs. **Open:** All week L 12 to 2, D 7 to 8.30. **Closed:** 25 Dec, Jan. **Meals:** set L £25. Set D £55. Tasting menu £60 (6 courses). Sun L £25. **Details:** 26 seats. 12 seats outside. Wheelchairs. Parking.

∎ Lochaline

★ LOCAL RESTAURANT AWARD ★
REGIONAL WINNER

The Whitehouse

Cooking score: 5
Modern British | £40
Lochaline, PA80 5XT
Tel no: (01967) 421777
thewhitehouserestaurant.co.uk

At the end of the Ardnamurchan peninsula, about as remote as you get without leaving the mainland, but what a reward of exemplary Scottish cooking, which one visitor rightly described as 'local, fresh food, prepared unpretentiously and supremely well'. The expertise comes from Mike Burgoyne who was lured from some smart London addresses to this spot above the Sound of Mull by a lifestyle change and the abundance of regional, seasonal produce. It's a chef's dream and it shows in an 'I want everything' menu: Blackface lamb from the hill with ham powsowdie (aka hotchpotch), Ardshealach smoked salmon 'with backyard root rémoulade' and Scotch duck with 'granny's warm red cabbage'. His 'seawater poached Isle of Mull haddie, brown shrimp and saffron and caper butter' is sublime. Ditto Iona monkfish and scallops with baby leeks, fennel sprigs and Burgoyne's latest enthusiasm, 'miner's lettuce' or winter purslane. Sidekick Lee Myers makes the puddings: frozen Scottish raspberry bellini, a fruit-and-nut-filled 'North of the Border' tart, or a tasting plate of all things chocolate 'with a wee dram of 10-year-old Laphroaig'. This is what you dream of when you head for the Highlands. Wine from £18.95.

Chef/s: Mike Burgoyne. **Open:** Tue to Sat L 12 to 2.30, D 6 to 10. **Closed:** Sun, Mon, Nov to Easter. **Meals:** main courses £7 to £24. **Details:** 26 seats. 8 seats outside. Wheelchairs. Parking.

Lochinver
Albannach
Cooking score: 6
Modern British | £70
Baddidarroch, Lochinver, IV27 4LP
Tel no: (01571) 844407
thealbannach.co.uk

Sitting on the terrace as the sun goes down over the lowering peaks of Canisp and Suilven, you might resolve to have a go at scaling them tomorrow. They're quite accessible after all. Then again, it's hard to tear oneself away from Colin Craig and Lesley Crosfield's late-Georgian country house, so refined a pitch of enveloping hospitality have they achieved. Their cooking, presented in the format of a single-sitting dinner six nights a week, takes in what modern ideas are most conducive to highlighting the good things of moorland, croft and briny. Seared wood pigeon with Swiss chard and roast shallots in chocolate sauce might be followed by a vegetable soufflé, as transition to butter-poached turbot with wild asparagus, sea asters and black potato in red wine. Solid traditionalism brings on a finisher of caramelised pear tart with matching ice cream, after a serving of artisan cheeses and oatcakes. Wines start around £16.

Chef/s: Colin Craig and Lesley Crosfield. **Open:** Tue to Sun D only 7.30 (1 sitting). **Closed:** Mon, Mon to Wed (Nov to Dec), Jan to mid Feb. **Meals:** set D £70 (6 courses). **Details:** 20 seats. Parking. Children over 12 yrs only.

Port Appin
Airds Hotel
Cooking score: 3
Modern British | £55
Port Appin, PA38 4DF
Tel no: (01631) 730236
airds-hotel.com

A long-standing stalwart of the Guide, there's an old school decorum about this immaculate hotel in pretty Port Appin with its views to the Isle of Lismore. Drinks and canapés are served in one of the elegant drawing rooms and the three- or seven-course menu may well feature local lamb, roast monkfish tail, pork belly or lemon sole. The attractive dining room, flooded with evening light in late April, is policed by a well-drilled team while the kitchen presents involved dishes like a starter of white crab meat topped with a disc of sesame crisp and dainty towers of avocado and tomato concassé followed by lamb loin with wild garlic, gnocchi, goats' cheese and black olives. A carrot soufflé with sweet cicely ice cream impressed but the chocolate mousse cake with cherries was substantial enough to make the pre-dessert of lemon sponge and citrus sorbet redundant. The sizeable wine list starts at £24.

Chef/s: Chris Stanley. **Open:** all week L 12 to 2.30, D 7.15 to 9.15. **Closed:** first 2 weeks Dec. **Meals:** set L £19 (3 courses). Set D £55. **Details:** 32 seats. 12 seats outside. V menu. Bar. Wheelchairs. Music. Parking. Children over 9 yrs only at D.

Scrabster
The Captain's Galley
Cooking score: 3
Seafood | £41
The Harbour, Scrabster, KW14 7UJ
Tel no: (01847) 894999
captainsgalley.co.uk

Long before the days of domestic refrigeration, the Galley was an ice-house and salmon store, a Georgian stone building on the harbour restyled in the late 1990s by Jim and Mary Cowie as a destination seafood restaurant. Jim still heads to the Scrabster market each morning to haul in what looks irresistible for the day's menus, and in an ambience of roughcast stone walls and chunky bare tables, it all makes glorious sense. Grilled langoustines in lime chilli butter, or a daringly contemporary crab and daikon salad with jalapeño vinaigrette and beetroot ice cream, might provide the way into the daily main-course specials, which could be a nose-to-tail serving of monkfish (including the liver) with pak choi in carrot and ginger sauce, or opalescent pan-roasted sole in langoustine cream. Finish with winter fruit tart and blood-orange ice cream. House French is £16.75. The Cowies' second venture, an informal seafood bar, is just next door.
Chef/s: Jim Cowie. **Open:** Wed to Sun L 12 to 3, D 4.30 to 8.30. **Closed:** Mon, Tue, 25 and 26 Dec, 1 and 2 Jan. **Meals:** set L £12 (2 courses) to £25. Set D £41 (3 courses) to £54. Sun L £15. **Details:** 25 seats. 25 seats outside. Bar. Wheelchairs. Music. Parking.

coast vista is a good 'un'. The lodge was built in the 18th century and extended in the Victorian period and it remains on a human scale (some dozen bedrooms), with a brace of restaurants. The Driftwood Brasserie is a more informal alternative to the main restaurant ('especially good for lunch'), and they offer the same menu. The main dining room is a traditional, formal affair. Seafood daily specials might include grilled Tiree langoustines, or grilled mackerel fillets with Caesar-inspired salad and crispy whitebait, while the carte offers up wild mushroom and truffle risotto followed by roasted loin of Highland venison with classic accompaniments. To finish, a luxury chocolate brownie comes with yoghurt and cardamon ice cream. Wines start at £19.50.
Chef/s: Gary Phillips. **Open:** all week L 12 to 2 (3 Sun), D 6 to 9.30. **Closed:** Jan. **Meals:** main courses £19 to 24. Set L and D £31 (2 courses) to £39. Sun L £20. Tasting menu £65. **Details:** 40 seats. 14 seats outside. V menu. Bar. Music. Parking. Children over 5 yrs only in restaurant.

Strontian
Kilcamb Lodge
Cooking score: 4
Modern British | £55
Strontian, PH36 4HY
Tel no: (01967) 402257
kilcamblodge.co.uk
£5 OFF

Close to the pristine waters of Loch Sunart, surrounded by peaks and standing in 22 acres of its own private grounds, 'Kilcamb's west

WALES

Glamorgan, Gwent, Mid-Wales, North-
East Wales, North-West Wales, West Wales

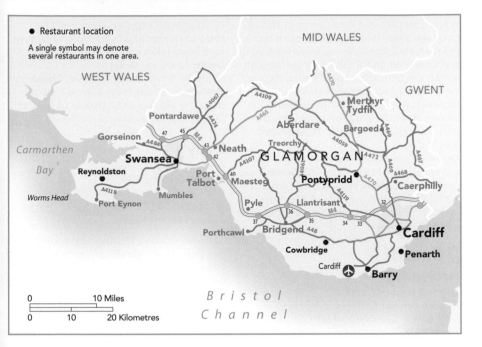

Restaurant location

A single symbol may denote several restaurants in one area.

MID WALES

WEST WALES

GWENT

Carmarthen Bay

Worms Head

GLAMORGAN

Bristol Channel

0   10 Miles
0   10   20 Kilometres

■ Bangor

Kyffin

Vegetarian

129 High Street, Bangor, LL57 1NT

Tel no: (01248) 355161

'Hands down the best café my partner and I have been to – we love the fact that everything is freshly grown and prepared, from the meze to their array of tarts and soups. Delicious, flavoursome and delightful.'

Readers recommend

A 'readers recommend' review is a genuine quote from a report sent in by one of our readers. We intend to follow up these suggestions throughout the year to come.

■ Barry
The Gallery

Cooking score: 4

Modern British | £29

2 Broad Street, Barry, CF62 7AA

Tel no: (01446) 735300

the-gallery-restaurant.co.uk

£5 OFF   £30

'This restaurant is amazing' is just one of many plaudits for chef-owner Barnaby Hibbert's relaxed but totally on-point bar-restaurant. The alluringly dark ground floor dispenses cocktails and Welsh beers in a stylishly stripped-back setting complete with exposed brickwork and wood-burner. Upstairs is lighter and swankier – a touch of damask here, a chandelier there, expensive-looking chunky wood furniture and an open kitchen. Mr Hibbert is in the process of raising his game, with additional chef Dmitri Baylis facilitating longer hours, tasting menus and express lunches. From the 'astonishing value' à la carte, typical options include 18-hour hare ragù with pappardelle pasta and Parmesan crisp, spruce-cured skate with lyonnaise potatoes, sweet braised fennel, lemon thyme, dried tomato and tomato oil, and Welsh honey parfait with nougat and homemade cinder toffee. Expect clear, harmonious flavours, top-drawer ingredients and modern twists on classic themes. A concise and great-value wine list includes options from Wales. House wines start at £16.

Chef/s: Barnaby Hibbert. **Open:** Fri to Sun L 12 to 2.30 (3 Sun), Wed to Sat D 6 to 9.30. **Closed:** Mon, Tue, 1 week Jan. **Meals:** set L £17 (2 courses) to £21. Set D £24 (2 courses) to £29. Sun L £16. Tasting menu £49 (7 courses). **Details:** 50 seats. 30 seats outside. Bar. Music.

▮ Cardiff
Arbennig
Cooking score: 4
Modern British | £29
6-10 Romilly Crescent, Cardiff, CF11 9NR
Tel no: (029) 2034 1264
arbennig.co.uk

£30

A fine day makes for a pleasant 10-minute saunter from the city centre into leafy Pontcanna to find the Cooks' centre of operations, a food emporium-cum-café and a wood-floored split-level restaurant with a sunny disposition. The name is Welsh for 'fresh', which neatly summarises both the quality of the raw materials John Cook works with, and the hallmark of his approach, with smartly presented dishes and classic combinations imaginatively reworked. An opening dish of braised squid with butter beans and salsa verde might lead to further Mediterranean explorations in the shape of lamb rump with haloumi, courgettes, olives and tomato, or there could be Cornish cod with the earthier accompaniments of roast garlic mash, woodland mushrooms and Tuscan greens, all topped off with a runny poached egg. A popular dessert recalls After Eights in its array of dark chocolate marquise,

mint ice cream and chocolate crisp. The compact international wine collection opens with house Chileans at £15.95.

Chef/s: John Cook. **Open:** Tue to Sun L 12 to 2.30 (4 Sun), Tue to Sat D 6 to 9.30 (10 Sat). **Closed:** Mon. **Meals:** main courses £12 to £24. Set L £13 (2 courses) to £16. Sun L £14. **Details:** 58 seats. 18 seats outside. Wheelchairs. Music. Parking.

Bully's
Cooking score: 2
Modern French | £35
5 Romilly Crescent, Cardiff, CF11 9NP
Tel no: (029) 2022 1905
bullysrestaurant.co.uk

The sense of a quart having been poured into a pint pot pervades Bully's, where free-standing tables are shoehorned next to cushioned banquette seating, and the walls are absolutely ram-jammed with prints, cartoons, old photographs and ornate mirrors. It's a thoroughly quirky setting for modern European dishes that mix French and Italian modes with influences from further afield, as in the seared scallops that come with curried bulgur wheat, cashews and lemon. Otherwise, look to start with wild mushroom tortellini in Madeira and peppercorn sauce, as a prelude to sea bream on potato risotto with brown shrimps and salsa verde, or Carmarthenshire pork belly and sauerkraut, turbo-charged with wholegrain-mustard mash and honey and bacon popcorn. Foie gras as a side dish is a first, and the sweet things encompass guava pannacotta with pineapple and toasted coconut, or dark chocolate torte with prune and Armagnac ice cream. French house wines at £15 lead off a decent list with helpful tasting notes.

Chef/s: Christie Matthews. **Open:** all week L 12 to 2 (3.30 Sun), Mon to Sat D 6.30 to 9 (10 Sat). **Closed:** 25, 26 and 31 Dec. **Meals:** main courses £15 to £26. Set L £12 (2 courses) to £16. Set D £15 (2 courses) to £20. Sun L £13. **Details:** 40 seats. Music.

Casanova

Cooking score: 1
Italian | £30
13 Quay Street, Cardiff, CF10 1EA
Tel no: (029) 2034 4044
casanovacardiff.com

Not far from the Principality (Millennium) Stadium, fiercely independent Casanova sparkles in a city centre dominated by chain restaurants. The interior is homely and unpretentious, blending simple bistro-style furnishings with the odd Venetian mask, and the welcome is warm and genuine. Venison and pork terrine with pickled cauliflower is a good way to begin, after that maybe fillet of hake, fresh from the market, with warm potato salad and bean purée, before rounding off with orange, almond and polenta cake. Wine from the proudly Italian list kicks off at £16.95.
Chef/s: Antonio Cersosimo. **Open:** Mon to Sat L 12 to 2.30, D 5.30 to 10. **Closed:** Sun, 25 and 26 Dec, bank hols. **Meals:** set L £15 (2 courses) to £20. Set D £25 (2 courses) to £30. **Details:** 36 seats. Music.

Chapel 1877

Cooking score: 2
Modern European | £34
Churchill Way, Cardiff, CF10 2WF
Tel no: (029) 2022 2020
chapel1877.com

£5 OFF

A Gothic-looking Methodist chapel, built in 1877, has been transformed into a striking backdrop for more sybaritic pursuits, with a ground-floor bar that generates quite a hubbub when it's busy, and a dining area on a mezzanine level that gives a view over the goings-on below. The open-to-view kitchen's broadly modern European output extends to matching seared scallops with spicy chorizo and white bean purée as a starter, and giving crispy Blythburgh pork belly and black pudding a French flavour with its accompanying celeriac rémoulade. Among main courses, Middlewood Farm venison stars in an earthy dish with wild mushrooms and

Welsh whiskey jus, while Anglesey sea bass comes with crab and sweetcorn fishcake and a punchy salsa. Welsh and Cornish steaks are cooked on the grill. To finish, ginger-beer syrup and marinated pineapple liven up sticky ginger pudding. The informative wine list kicks off at £19.
Chef/s: Ryan Mitchell. **Open:** all week L 12 to 2.30 (3 Fri and Sat, 5 Sun), Mon to Sat D 5.30 to 9.30 (10 Fri and Sat). **Closed:** 25 and 26 Dec, 1 Jan. **Meals:** main courses £12 to £29. Set L £13 (2 courses). Sun L £19 (3 courses). **Details:** 110 seats. 20 seats outside. Bar. Music.

Mint and Mustard

Cooking score: 2
Indian | £24
134 Whitchurch Road, Cardiff, CF14 3LZ
Tel no: (029) 2062 0333
mintandmustard.com

£30

The first of a quartet of restaurants in the region (South Wales and neighbouring Somerset), this one was the first and hits the 10-year mark in 2017. The contemporary space is filled with colourful images of India, and the cooking sits at the modern end of the Indian culinary spectrum, with the southern state of Kerala looming large. A prettily presented opener might be scallop thengapal – a hand-dived Scottish bivalve in a zesty lemon-flavoured coconut milk – or the more familiar Bombay chaat. Kashmiri lamb rogan josh is an old favourite done well, or go for Goan fish curry or pan-fried sea bass with curry-leaf-flavoured mash and a perky sauce of raw mango, ginger and coconut. The tandoor turns out Barbary duck, chicken, salmon and king prawns, while veggies might go for paneer masala. Tasting menus reflect the ambition in the kitchen. Wines start at £16.
Chef/s: Santhosh Nair. **Open:** all week L 12 to 2, D 5 to 11 (10.30 Sun). **Closed:** 25 and 26 Dec. **Meals:** main courses £8 to £24. Set L £15 (2 courses) to £20. Set D £25 (2 courses) to £35. Tasting menu £50. **Details:** 100 seats. Bar. Parking.

Purple Poppadom

Cooking score: 3

Indian | £30

Upper Floor, 185a Cowbridge Road East,
Cardiff, CF11 9AJ
Tel no: (029) 2022 0026
purplepoppadom.com

It's easy to miss in an uninspiring parade of shops, but head upstairs to the first floor and you'll find some rather refined Indian food on offer. The colour purple dominates the slick contemporary space, where chef-patron Anand George has won a solid fanbase over the last five years. A six-course tasting menu gives the opportunity to test the chef's mettle, with an optional flight of some well-chosen wines. Modern ideas combine with slick presentation, although it is the vivid Indian flavours that win the day. Kick off with 'nandu trio', which is three ways with crab, including crispy fried soft-shell dusted with curry spices and garlic. 'Tiffin sea bass' is somewhat of a signature dish, or go for Syrian Christian-style beef curry, or a classic Moghul slow-braised lamb shank cooked in the tandoor. Desserts are an East–West fusion such as 'chocomosa anand' (a crispy pastry filled with chocolate ganache). Wines start at £16.95.
Chef/s: Anand George. **Open:** Tue to Sat L 12 to 2, D 5.30 to 11. Sun 1 to 9. **Closed:** Mon, 25 and 26 Dec, 1 Jan. **Meals:** main courses £9 to £19. Set L £11 (2 courses). Tasting menu £45 (6 courses). **Details:** 70 seats. Bar. Music.

▮ Cowbridge

Bar 44

Cooking score: 2

Spanish | £20

44c High Street, Cowbridge, CF71 7AG
Tel no: (01446) 776488
bar44.co.uk

£5 OFF   £30

'Wonderful tapas – better than Barcelona.' It seems readers love this modern deli-cum-tapas bar. It's one of those special places that radiate warmth and its many fans consider it 'great for just a coffee or a lovely place to meet

friends for food and drink'. Unsuprisingly, top-drawer Ibérico charcuterie is a must-have, as well as myriad tapas treats at very gentle prices. Aside from breads, artisan cheeses and cured meats, look for plates of chipirones (baby squid), gambas à la plancha, lamb meatballs with red wine and tomato or cider-poached chorizo, as well as crispy aubergine with molasses and pomegranate. A glass of something from the fine selection of sherries makes an apt accompaniment or explore the enticing Spanish treasures on a well-annotated list. Bottles from £15.95. Note: branches at 15-23 Westgate Street Cardiff; tel: (029) 2009 0444; and 14 Windsor Road, Penarth; tel: (029) 2070 5497.
Chef/s: Felix Cadena. **Open:** all week 12 to 9 (12 to 5 Mon, 10 Fri and Sat). **Closed:** 25 Dec. **Meals:** tapas £4 to £8. Set L £10. **Details:** 55 seats. Music.

★ NEW ENTRY ★

Hare and Hounds

Cooking score: 1

British | £27

Maendy Road, Cowbridge, CF71 7LG
Tel no: (01446) 774892
hareandhoundsaberthin.com

£30

The dining room of this homely country pub is a fresh, whitewashed space where a wood-burner belts out warmth and the clatter from the open kitchen provides a merry backdrop. Throw in a healthy reverence for all things local, home-grown and wild, and there's much to love. Typical of the unfussy cooking is a game faggot with wild garlic purée, baked celeriac and wild mushrooms in a rich gravy, while a main of pan-fried hake with sprouting broccoli, cockles, brown shrimp and wild garlic showcased excellent ingredients treated with honesty. Occasionally, the flavours need fine-tuning – as in a dessert of buttermilk pannacotta, apple sorbet and 'overly bitter' honeycomb – but the authenticity of the cooking always shines through. An interesting selection of European wines kicks off at £13.95 a bottle.

Chef/s: Tom Watts-Jones. **Open:** Wed to Sun L 12 to 2.30 (3 Sun), Wed to Sat D 6 to 9 (9.30 Fri and Sat). **Closed:** Mon, Tue. **Meals:** main courses £10 to £20. Set L £17 (2 courses) to £20. **Details:** 40 seats. Bar. Wheelchairs. Music. Parking.

Oscars of Cowbridge

Cooking score: 1
International | £25
65 High Street, Cowbridge, CF71 7AF
Tel no: (01446) 771984
oscarsofcowbridge.com

£30

A cheery modern brasserie in the heart of Cowbridge, Oscars delivers colourful good looks and crowd-pleasing food, served from lunch right through to the evening. Dishes range from 'fantastic' burgers to luxuriant salads, and from lunchtime focaccias and wraps to hearty grills. A typical meal might encompass pear and Perl Las brioche with pickled shallots, Monmouthshire 28-day aged 10oz rump steak with plum tomatoes, crispy shallots and chips, and strawberry biscuit mess with rosewater whipped cream and candyfloss. An appealing selection of wines, all nicely annotated and divided by style, opens at £15.95.
Chef/s: Gareth Chivell. **Open:** Mon to Sat 12 to 9.30 (10 Sat). **Closed:** Sun, 25 and 26 Dec. **Meals:** main courses £10 to £27. **Details:** 50 seats. 25 seats outside. Wheelchairs. Music. Parking.

▌Penarth
The Fig Tree

Cooking score: 3
Modern British | £29
The Esplanade, Penarth, CF64 3AU
Tel no: (029) 2070 2512
thefigtreepenarth.co.uk

£30

You can gaze across the Bristol Channel to Somerset from this beautifully restored Victorian beach shelter, which has plenty of seating on the verandah and roof terrace for warmer days. The ever-changing views –

sometimes soft as watercolour, other times sharp and bright – are a joy, but there's a lot of beauty on the plate, too: chef-proprietor Mike Caplan-Hill has won many fans with his fresh, modern cooking built on mostly local ingredients. Duck hash with fried duck egg is a typical opener, followed perhaps by duo of Welsh lamb (braised and roast shoulder, and smoked breast) with dauphinois potatoes, greens and jus. Vegetarians are carefully considered, with the likes of leek and Perl Las blue cheese tart, and butternut squash, sage and pearl barley risotto. Local seafood also makes a good showing – maybe as Gower moules provençale. The well-annotated wine list includes a Welsh rosé and bottles start at £15.
Chef/s: Mike Caplan-Hill and Nathan Williams. **Open:** Tue to Sun L 12 to 3 (3.30 Sat, 4 Sun), Tue to Sat D 6 to 9. **Closed:** Mon, 25 and 26 Dec, 1 Jan. **Meals:** main courses £12 to £24. Set L £11 (2 courses) to £14. Sun L £20 (2 courses). **Details:** 54 seats. 28 seats outside. Wheelchairs. Music.

★ TOP 50 ★

Restaurant James Sommerin

Cooking score: 7
Modern British | £43
The Esplanade, Penarth, CF64 3AU
Tel no: (029) 2070 6559
jamessommerinrestaurant.co.uk

£5 OFF

'The best restaurant for hundreds of miles, and it's right on my doorstep,' enthuses a local reader who loves everything about this beautifully appointed restaurant-with-rooms overlooking Penarth's seafront. 'Kind and gracious' James Sommerin does his bit for the community hereabouts, participating in local events and organising kids' cookery classes as well as thrilling diners with his astonishing contemporary food. Designer features, combined with glorious views and a peek-a-boo letterbox window into the kitchen, provide the perfect backdrop to a procession of 'simply spectacular' dishes full of tantalising flavours and grace notes. Sommerin's cleverly embellished 'liquid' pea raviolo from the *Great British Menu* is still an outright winner ('delicious fun and great textures'), but his free-spirited culinary intelligence also conjures up exotica such as Gressingham duck with salt-baked swede, dates, chard and spices. Elsewhere, a penchant for classically executed local themes shows in everything from perfectly cooked cod with squid-ink, salty samphire and crab bisque to a multi-part dish of pork, including (among other things) a rich pig's head terrine, 'extremely moist' loin, crispy ears and an unctuous deep-fried nugget made from the trotters with wild garlic, parsnips and a pot of heady Calvados sauce. To finish, the treacle sponge with rosemary and olive oil ice cream is rated as one of the 'best desserts ever tasted'. James's wife Louise 'plays the role of a phenomenal host so naturally', and she's ably supported by a courteous but keen-as-mustard young team. A well-spread global wine list opens with house selections from £28 (£7 a glass).

Chef/s: James Sommerin. **Open:** Tue to Sun L 12 to 2.30, D 7 to 9.30. **Closed:** Mon. **Meals:** main courses £17 to £29. Tasting menu £60 (6 courses) to £80 (9 courses). **Details:** 60 seats. Wheelchairs. Music.

▉ Pontypridd
Bunch of Grapes

Cooking score: 4
Modern British | £29
Ynysangharad Road, Pontypridd, CF37 4DA
Tel no: (01443) 402934
bunchofgrapes.org.uk
£30

'I still hungrily recall the last meal I had there' is one of many endorsements for this 'lovely pub, serving local produce'. Run by Nick Otley (of the Otley Brewing Company), the Bunch of Grapes has all the rustic accoutrements you expect given its humble Victorian heritage, and the good sense to maintain proper space for drinkers. Lunchtime sandwiches, burgers and beer-battered fish and chips show it's willing to do the populist

thing (and do it well) but the menu extends to a brasserie-style repertoire, too, with the kitchen capable of delivering punchy flavours. There's a good degree of refinement in dishes such as assiette of lamb (devilled kidney, panko-crusted heart, black pudding-stuffed belly) and roasted whole south-coast lemon sole with sautéed leek, golden beetroot, lemon butter and pommes gaufrettes, while desserts include chestnut iced nougat with honey crumble and dark chocolate bonbons. A well-annotated wine list opens at £16.

Chef/s: Sebastien Vanoni. **Open:** all week L 12 to 2.30 (3 Fri and Sat, 3.30 Sun), Mon to Sat D 6.30 to 9 (9.30 Fri and Sat). **Meals:** main courses £13 to £18. Sun L £14 (2 courses). **Details:** 70 seats. 24 seats outside. Bar. Music. Parking.

▉ Reynoldston
Fairyhill

Cooking score: 4
Modern British | £50
Reynoldston, SA3 1BS
Tel no: (01792) 390139
fairyhill.net
▐ ◼

A vision of foursquare Georgian elegance in the Gower Peninsula, Fairyhill has cemented its reputation as a country retreat since launching in 1994. Surrounded by 24 acres of grounds and woodland, it's a smart prospect with a cluster of tasteful, classically styled dining rooms at the heart of things. The kitchen enlivens its repertoire with contemporary flavours and clever detailing, while peppering its menus with seasonal ingredients from the region: expect salt marsh lamb, Welsh beef and Pembrokeshire duck – perhaps served with char-grilled garden leeks, wild mushrooms, pear and Pedro Ximénez jus. Fish from Carmarthen Bay also receives precise treatment, as in pan-fried hake fillet with a Penclawdd cockle and caper fritter, caramelised onion fondue and crab bisque. To finish, splendid Welsh farmhouse cheeses might win the day over desserts such as coconut crème brûlée with dark chocolate sorbet. The serious-minded wine list has a

broad global reach, with classy labels, top producers and lesser-known names in the mix; house selections from £23.50 (£6 a glass).
Chef/s: Colin Lewis. **Open:** all week L 12 to 2 (3 Sun), D 6.30 to 9.30. **Closed:** first 3 weeks Jan. **Meals:** set L £20 (2 courses) to £25. Set D £39 (2 courses) to £50. Sun L £28. **Details:** 60 seats. 30 seats outside. V menu. Bar. Wheelchairs. Music. Parking. No children under 8 yrs at D.

▮ Swansea
Didier & Stephanie
Cooking score: 4
French | £30
56 St Helen's Road, Swansea, SA1 4BE
Tel no: (01792) 655603

It's remarkable that Didier Suvé and Stephanie Danvel's 20-cover restaurant has evolved into a paragon of French virtues without recourse to a website or PR bluster. Since arriving in 2000, the pair have stayed true to their task, serving impeccable bourgeois food in a setting that has lost none of its original allure – despite some luxurious new trappings (note the Art Deco-inspired lighting). What arrives on the plate is equally tasteful, a pitch-perfect homage to good things, from unbeatable home-baked rolls to a raft of desserts straight out of the annals of *cuisine ancienne*. Some might say it's deeply unfashionable, but there's no arguing when Didier's kitchen can deliver understated perfection in the shape of poached skate with Champagne sauce or roast rack of lamb with rosemary jus. The old skills aren't neglected either, be it a croustillant of boudin noir or chocolate and orange tart with crème anglaise. Wines (mostly French) start at £15.90.
Chef/s: Didier Suvé. **Open:** Tue to Sat L 12.30 to 2.30, D 7 to 10.30. **Closed:** Sun, Mon, 2 weeks Christmas and New Year. **Meals:** main courses £17 to £20. Set L £17 (2 courses) to £20. **Details:** 20 seats. Music.

Hanson at the Chelsea
Cooking score: 4
Modern European | £30
17 St Mary Street, Swansea, SA1 3LH
Tel no: (01792) 464068
hansonatthechelsea.co.uk
£5 OFF

Andrew Hanson's city-centre restaurant is to be found tucked down a side street, on the ground floor of a puce-fronted apartment building not far from the hurly-burly of Wind Street. Locally sourced seafood and meats such as 28-day aged beef fillet are among the obvious lures, and there's an appealing old-school bistro air to menus that take in ham hock and pistachio terrine with grain-mustard butter, served with toasted sourdough and Calvados-laced apple jam, and a salmon fishcake stuffed with melting Perl Wen cheese and tarragon, among starters. Move on to roast halibut in Eastern garb, alongside prawns seared in ginger and chilli, wilted pak choi and coriander, or else thyme-scented chicken breast with girolle risotto in Marsala velouté. Desserts have more than a hint of glam, when bread-and-butter pudding is made with brioche and ritzed up with honey and whisky. House Chilean is £13.95, or £3.75 a glass.
Chef/s: A Hanson, G Sillman, N Kirby and E Grove. **Open:** Mon to Sat L 12 to 2, D 7 to 9.30. **Closed:** Sun. **Meals:** main courses £14 to £24. Set L £15 (2 courses) to £19. Tasting menu £35 (6 courses). **Details:** 42 seats. Music.

Slice
Cooking score: 4
Modern British | £39
73-75 Eversley Road, Swansea, SA2 9DE
Tel no: (01792) 290929
sliceswansea.co.uk

Chris Harris and Adam Bannister's pint-sized, modestly decorated neighbourhood restaurant continues to raise the bar for dining in South Wales – and their success is reflected in the clamour for tables; it's best to book in advance as local spies report a six- to eight-week wait for a Saturday reservation. The charm lies not only on the plate but also in Chris and Adam's cheery presence; they alternate between kitchen and front-of-house, handling both with equal aplomb. The cooking is classy but not overly fussy, combining classical techniques and modern presentation. Veal tartare with crispy sweetbreads and onion textures is a typical opener, followed perhaps by pan-fried brill with langoustine, roast cauliflower, sprout flower and beurre blanc. To finish, try baked egg custard with rhubarb ripple ice cream and a ginger sablé. There's a keenly priced eight-course tasting menu for those who want to linger longer. The well-annotated wine list opens at £17.

Chef/s: Chris Harris and Adam Bannister. **Open:** Fri to Sun L 12 to 2, Wed to Sun D 6.30 to 9. **Closed:** Mon, Tue. **Meals:** set L £26 (2 courses) to £30. Set D £39. Tasting menu £52. **Details:** 16 seats. V menu. Music.

★ NEW ENTRY ★

TwoCann

Cooking score: 3
Modern British | £30
Unit 2, J Shed, Kings Road, Swansea, SA1 8PL
Tel no: (01792) 458000
cafetwocann.com

It's a fairly upmarket café by day – quite modern and swanky with lots of dark wood and clean-lined, modern furniture – offering decent-quality dishes including breakfast, steak sandwiches, omelettes and homemade cakes. The evening is more resolutely restauranty, with a modern British bistro menu cooked by a chef who 'clearly understands what works together'. A case in point is a 'stunning' curried cauliflower soup with honey and vanilla – 'an interesting twist, and brimming with flavour' – while a garlic-scented, crisp-skinned chicken breast arrives with artichoke purée, 'perfect' fondant potato and a 'wonderful, intense' enoki mushroom sauce. Other options include pub-style classics: maybe cod and chips; seafood pie with laverbread mash; or top-notch local sausages with mash and caramelised onion

gravy. To finish, try a chocolate tart with a gorgeously slick, rich filling, salted-caramel ice cream and 'perfectly bittersweet' honeycomb. A nicely annotated wine list opens at £18.50.

Chef/s: Kate Taylor. **Open:** all week L 12 to 2.30 (4 Sun), Wed to Sat D 6 to 9.30. **Closed:** 25 and 26 Dec. **Meals:** main courses £15 to £22. Set L £13 (2 courses) to £16. Set D £23 (2 courses) to £27. Sun £16. **Details:** 50 seats. 40 seats outside.

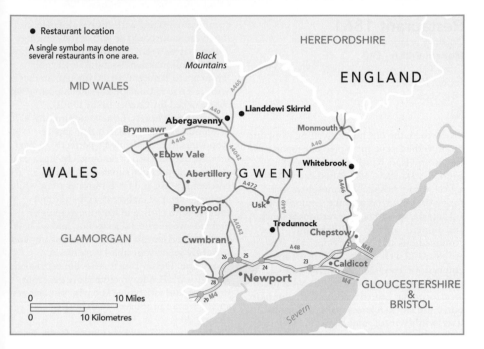

Restaurant location

A single symbol may denote several restaurants in one area.

HEREFORDSHIRE

Black Mountains

MID WALES

ENGLAND

Llanddewi Skirrid

Abergavenny

Brynmawr

Monmouth

Ebbw Vale

Whitebrook

WALES

Abertillery

GWENT

Pontypool

Usk

GLAMORGAN

Cwmbran

Tredunnock

Chepstow

Newport

Caldicot

GLOUCESTERSHIRE & BRISTOL

Severn

0   10 Miles

0   10 Kilometres

■ Abergavenny
The Hardwick
Cooking score: 3
Modern British | £35
Old Raglan Road, Abergavenny, NP7 9AA
Tel no: (01873) 854220
thehardwick.co.uk

The days when the Hardwick was a regular pub are now a distant memory. In Stephen Terry's hands it has grown into a large and convivial restaurant-with-rooms whose dining areas ramble through three rooms – all warmly rustic and deeply relaxing. Service is 'superb' and Terry's cooking remains gutsy and interesting, although some reporters have balked at the prices (and the fact that you have to pay for the very good sourdough served with butter and a nice fruity olive oil). A starter of cauliflower cream with Manchego, chorizo and quince is typical of the comforting but inventive style, but a main course of linguine with a dizzying list of ingredients including crab, brown shrimp and courgette tried at inspection 'was absurdly cluttered'. Terry has always had a flair for desserts, however, and a deconstructed baked vanilla cheesecake with gariguette strawberries delighted with its perfumed ripeness and 'perfect texture'. There's a substantial list of wines, all nicely annotated and including a list of Terry's personal favourites. Bottles start at £18.

Chef/s: Stephen Terry and Lee Evans. **Open:** all week L 12 to 3, D 6.30 to 10 (9.30 Sun). **Closed:** 25 and 26 Dec. **Meals:** main courses £14 to £30. Set L £20(2 courses) to £25. Set D £21 (2 courses) to £26. Sun L £22 (2 courses) to £28. **Details:** 100 seats. 25 seats outside. Bar. Wheelchairs. Music. Parking.

Symbols

🛏 Accommodation is available
£30 Three courses for less than £30
£5 off £5-off voucher scheme
🍷 Notable wine list

Restaurant 1861

Cooking score: 3
Modern British | £40
Cross Ash, Abergavenny, NP7 8PB
Tel no: (01873) 821297
18-61.co.uk
£5 OFF

'Well worth the one hour travelling from our home to the restaurant,' noted one reporter of Simon and Kate King's personally run country restaurant, while another added 'it has a welcoming, hospitable atmosphere that makes everyone feel at home'. Simon's menus – à la carte, set and tasting versions at lunch and dinner – are rich with appealing combinations and creative flourishes, flavours are clear and well defined and there's an emphasis on seasonal ingredients. Indeed, the use of raw materials is a strength, with much local sourcing. Seared scallops with pumpkin purée and chicken juices makes a glorious start, while winter game shows up well, in a dish of pheasant supreme, confit partridge and wild boar boudin, or as a fricassee of pheasant with grain mustard cream. To finish? A trio of chocolate hits the spot sweetly or try a zesty Seville orange marmalade crème brûlée. The reasonably priced wine list opens at £18.
Chef/s: Simon King. **Open:** Tue to Sun L 12 to 1.30, Tue to Sat D 7 to 8.30. **Closed:** Mon, 25 Dec to 10 Jan. **Meals:** main courses £21 to £25. Set L £22 (2 courses) to £25. Set D £35. Sun L £25. Tasting menu £60. **Details:** 35 seats. Music. Parking.

▇ Llanddewi Skirrid
The Walnut Tree

Cooking score: 5
Modern British | £45
Llanddewi Skirrid, NP7 8AW
Tel no: (01873) 852797
thewalnuttreeinn.com
🍷 🛏

Expect 'no-nonsense cooking' at Shaun Hill's welcoming country restaurant in the foothills of the Black Mountains. A cosy bar with a big fireplace opens on to a dining room that combines rusticity with simple elegance, and much the same could be said of the cooking. There may be a retro feel to some of the dishes, but Mr Hill makes old-school seem cool. 'Homage to Robert Carrier' pâté aux herbes with celeriac remoulade is a case in point (the chef worked for Carrier in the 1960s), exemplifying hearty, honest cooking that's often more complex than it first appears. Reporters have applauded 'a perfectly cooked bit of plaice on a bed of octopus, chickpeas and chilli', and 'excellent' squab pigeon with a chicken boudin and fresh summer peas, while a zingy starter of crabmeat, crab cake and mousse with chilli and lime mayonnaise, pickled sweetcorn and jalapeños, and sea bass with curried lentils, mash, onion chutney and sprightly green vegetables were hits at inspection. Desserts such as Seville marmalade sponge with Penderyn custard are generous, nostalgic and satisfying. The wine list favours small, artisan producers, with bottles from £20.
Chef/s: Shaun Hill and Roger Brook. **Open:** Tue to Sat L 12 to 2.30, D 6.30 to 9.30. **Closed:** Sun, Mon, 1 week Christmas. **Meals:** main courses £16 to £30. Set L £25 (2 courses) to £30. **Details:** 50 seats. 12 seats outside. Bar. Wheelchairs. Parking.

▇ Tredunnock
The Newbridge on Usk

Cooking score: 3
Modern British | £35
Tredunnock, NP15 1LY
Tel no: (01633) 451000
celtic-manor.com
🛏

As an adjunct to the Celtic Manor Resort, this one-time rural boozer has gone up in the world – think big standard lamps, leather easy chairs by the log-burner and assorted vintage trappings. On the menu, steaks and beer-battered fish and chips are about the only sops to pub tradition; otherwise, imaginative ideas and pretty plates abound. Slow-cooked Celtic Pride pork belly might be matched with smoked eel, Parma ham and salad cream, pan-roasted brill could keep company with curried

lentils, carrot and coconut, and there's a mighty 'celebration of chicken' to share. Local fish also turns up in various guises on generous 'market platters', while puds could include pear, caramel and lavender trifle. A sizeable global wine list opens with a dozen house selections from £18.50 (£4.25 a glass).
Chef/s: Adam Whittle. **Open:** all week L 12 to 2.30 (4 Sun), D 6.30 to 9.30. **Meals:** main courses £17 to £28. Set L £16 (2 courses) to £19. Sun L £25. **Details:** 70 seats. 20 seats outside. Bar. Music. Parking.

▋ Whitebrook

★ TOP 50 ★

The Whitebrook
Cooking score: 7
Modern British | £54
Whitebrook, NP25 4TX
Tel no: (01600) 860254
thewhitebrook.co.uk

£5 OFF

Chris Harrod's cooking shines out as a refreshing, original and, at times, brave take on native ingredients. It is resolutely British, totally rooted in our hedgerows and coastline, with a huge emphasis placed on foraged finds – 'it all feels fresh and new'. Those who remember this restaurant-with-rooms' previous incarnation (The Crown at Whitebrook) will find things turned around – the entrance has been moved and the interior is cooler and crisper than before, with a modest bar flowing into airy dining areas where wood floors and linen-clad tables channel a fresh, minimalist aesthetic. Canapés in the bar might include an onion sablé with nettle cream and a 'magnificent' wild garlic crisp topped with goats' curd and hedgerow pickings, and the rest of the meal falls in line, offering interesting techniques and wild ingredients that go way beyond the usual samphire and ramsons. An intense, peppery wild watercress and goats' curd cream preceded a starter of Wye Valley asparagus, maritime pine purée, hedgerow pickings and Tintern mead – a dish that trumpeted the beauty of fiddlehead fern,

pennywort and hogweed, and achieved textural contrast and depth of flavour solely with green vegetables. A generous piece of braised monkfish tail followed, served with a slick of nettle purée, rosebay willowherb, shaved courgette, little cylinders of Jersey Royals, and deep red seaweed, with apple and balsamic adding a spike of intensity. Harrod's masterful handling of native ingredients extends to desserts such as a frozen local honey cream with malt cake, lemon verbena and stout caramel. The charming waiting team can be relied upon for on-point wine recommendations from a substantial list that's nearly 50 per cent organic or biodynamic and includes an interesting selection of British wines. Bottles start at £23.
Chef/s: Chris Harrod. **Open:** Wed to Sun L 12 to 2, Tue to Sun D 7 to 9. **Closed:** Mon, first 2 weeks Jan. **Meals:** set L £29 (3 courses). Set D (3 courses) £54. Tasting Menu £67 (7 courses). **Details:** 30 seats. 16 seats outside. Bar. Music. Parking. Children over 12 yrs only at D

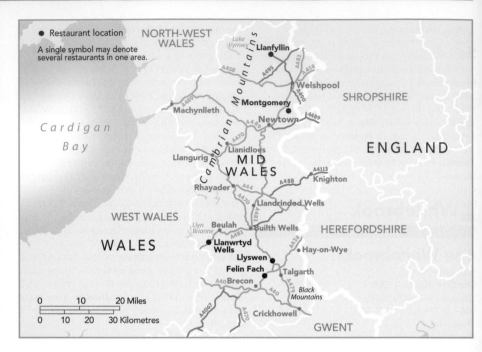

Felin Fach
The Felin Fach Griffin
Cooking score: 4
Modern British | £35
Felin Fach, LD3 0UB
Tel no: (01874) 620111
felinfachgriffin.co.uk
£5 ⌐

Edmund and Charles Inkin's stylish country
pub has inspired many imitators over the
years, but the Griffin still heads the pack in
these parts. It has that artfully rustic, rough-
around-the edges look you'd expect from an
upmarket dining pub: deep leather sofas,
blazing fires, an Aga here, a vintage table there
– it has been called 'impeccable'. Service is
smooth, and the cooking trumpets Welshness
while pulling in ideas from across the globe.
Among starters, dishes range from baba
ganoush with imam bayildi, goats' curd and a
buttermilk cracker, to warm cured salmon
with beetroot, liquorice and pomegranate,
while halibut with Welsh rarebit, mashed

potato and wild mushrooms is a typical main
course. Expect a bounty of home-grown and
Welsh ingredients, finishing with Welsh
cheeses. For dessert, there might be dark
chocolate mousse with coffee and
mascarpone. The wine list is a delight, packed
with personally sourced, interesting finds,
many available by the glass or carafe. Bottles
start at £20.
Chef/s: Ben Ogden. **Open:** all week L 12 to 2.30, D
6 to 9 (9.30 Fri and Sat). **Closed:** 25 Dec, 4 days
early Jan. **Meals:** main courses £17 to £21. Set L £18
(2 courses) to £22. Set D £23 (2 courses) to £29. Sun
L £26 (3 courses). **Details:** 60 seats. 30 seats
outside. Bar. Wheelchairs. Music. Parking.

Symbols

🥄

⌐ Accommodation is available
£30 Three courses for less than £30
£5 £5-off voucher scheme
OFF
🍾 Notable wine list

Llanfyllin
Seeds
Cooking score: 1
Modern British | £25
5 Penybryn Cottages, High Street, Llanfyllin,
SY22 5AP
Tel no: (01691) 648604
£30

There are only five tables at this engaging little
place on the high street, which means
everyone gets the full attention of the
charming Felicity Seager. The simple, rustic
appeal of the 16th-century property (slate
floor, copious beams) is matched by husband
Mark's homely and unpretentious menu. Pan-
seared tuna salad with sweet chilli dressing is
at the more contemporary end of the
repertoire, followed perhaps by fillet steak
with brandy and cream sauce, or roast rack of
lamb topped with a herby crust. Finish with
treacle tart. Supply lines are well established –
they've been here since 1991 – and wines start
at £14.75.
Chef/s: Mark Seager. **Open:** Thur to Sat L 11 to 2,
Wed to Sat D from 6.30. **Closed:** Mon, Tue, (Wed
winter), 24 and 25 Dec, 2 weeks Oct and Nov.
Meals: main courses £13 to £20. Set D £25 (2
courses) to £28. **Details:** 20 seats. 6 seats outside.

Llanwrtyd Wells
Carlton Riverside
Cooking score: 4
Modern British | £35
Irfon Crescent, Llanwrtyd Wells, LD5 4SP
Tel no: (01591) 610248
carltonriverside.com
£5 OFF

Mary Ann and Alan Gilchrist have sold their
homely riverside restaurant, but Alan is still
involved in the bookings. Chef Luke Roberts
previously worked under Mary Ann,
becoming her executive chef before taking the
helm – and anyone who loved her
wholesome, classically inspired style of
cooking will find the kitchen is in safe hands.
You can request the no-choice gourmet menu

in advance, which includes wine pairings, but
if you pop in for an evening meal you'll get the
à la carte. Either way, this is stonking good
food, making the most of native Welsh
ingredients and steering a course full of classic
combinations such as deep-fried poached egg
with bacon and leek cream via ribeye of Welsh
beef with all the trimmings to warm chocolate
fondant with vanilla ice cream. Standout
dishes in a test meal included creamy
mushroom and truffle fettuccine and a
'faultless' banana and honey soufflé with
sticky banana sauce. The substantial,
interesting wine list includes plenty of half-
bottles; full bottles start at £16.95.
Chef/s: Luke Roberts. **Open:** Mon to Sat D only 7 to
8.30. **Closed:** Sun, 21 to 30 Dec. **Meals:** main
courses £16 to £27. **Details:** 16 seats. Music.

Llyswen

★ TOP 50 ★

Llangoed Hall
Cooking score: 7
Modern British | £75
Llyswen, LD3 0YP
Tel no: (01874) 754525
llangoedhall.co.uk

In a particularly lovely spot in the Wye Valley,
Callum Milne's beautiful Edwardian country
house hotel is a welcome retreat from the
madding crowd. But beyond the open fires,
classic furnishings and impressive art
collection is something quite special.
'Incredibly talented' Nick Brodie heads up the
kitchen and a streak of culinary daring runs
through his full-strength tasting menus, with
plenty of attention-grabbing ideas – as in
scallops ceviche with caviar and English
wasabi, or foie gras, smoked eel and puffed
rice, and a winning combination of Wagyu
beef with black bean and mushroom – but the
focus is always on sound culinary principles,
backed up by well-sourced materials. There's
no denying the kitchen knows how to
impress, with all the incidentals just so, while
desserts dazzle, especially when a perfect

balance of sweetness and acidity is achieved in a brilliant juxtaposition of meringue, rhubarb, sorrel and pineapple. As for the wine list, it's a winner, well written, modern and wide-ranging, offering something for even the deepest pockets but with some excellent recommendations from £25.

Chef/s: Nick Brodie. **Open:** all week L 12 to 2, D 6.30 to 9. **Meals:** Sun L £35. Tasting menus £75 to £95. **Details:** 50 seats. 20 seats outside. V menu. Bar. Wheelchairs. Music. Parking.

▌Montgomery
The Checkers

Cooking score: 6
French | £55
Broad Street, Montgomery, SY15 6PN
Tel no: (01686) 669822
checkerswales.co.uk

🛏

To describe the Checkers as a former coaching inn doesn't quite convey the cottagey charm of the interior, which delivers rusticity teamed with a French elegance befitting the chef's Gallic origins. Fresh shades of duck egg and cream, a big wood-burner and exposed beams set a stylish yet homely scene. Chef Stéphane Borie arrived here via the Waterside Inn and Le Manoir (see entries), and classic French cooking is his *raison d'être*, yet his dishes don't feel backward-looking. Witness a 'superlatively good lunch' that took in ballotine of foie gras and 'fabulous pasta parcels' filled with crab as an accompaniment to scallops, while an evening visit began with 'some of the best breads I've had anywhere', featuring everything from olive fougasse to dense, sweet walnut and sultana bread. A cauliflower velouté of vivid intensity, teamed with curry cream and smoky toasted almonds, showcased an ability to tease the most out of even the simplest dishes, while monkfish wrapped in bacon and Roquefort with Puy lentils, syrupy red wine jus and spinach was rich yet balanced. A tangy passion fruit granita with a billowy lime and ginger foam was the perfect palate cleanser before roasted breast of corn-fed chicken with delicate boudin blanc,

ballotine of the leg and a Monbazillac sauce, while an airy white chocolate and caramel slice with 'stunning, crunchy hazelnut ice cream' ensured a triumphant finale. The lengthy wine list covers France admirably, but it also takes in lesser-known regions, including Wales. There's much for under £30, and bottles start at £18.

Chef/s: Stéphane Borie. **Open:** Tue to Sat D only 7.15 to 9. **Closed:** Sun, Mon, Jan. **Meals:** set D £55 (5 courses, Tue to Fri). Tasting menu £73 (8 courses). **Details:** 30 seats. Wheelchairs. Children over 8 yrs only.

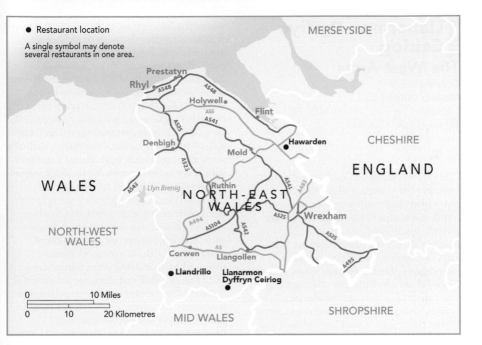

- ● Restaurant location

A single symbol may denote
several restaurants in one area.

▌Hawarden

The Glynne Arms

Cooking score: 3
British | £30
3 Glynne Way, Hawarden, CH5 3NS
Tel no: (01244) 569988
theglynnearms.co.uk

A foursquare 200-year-old coaching inn
owned by the people behind Pedlars online
emporium, it's hardly surprising that design
plays an important part at The Glynne Arms.
There's plenty to catch the eye within the
generous period spaces, including a stylish
restaurant with an open fire and banquette
seating. The kitchen can call on the Hawarden
Estate Farm, which is under the same
ownership as the pub, to provide the likes of
the steaks that are served up with traditional
accompaniments. Mussels come the short
distance from the Menai Strait and are cooked
marinière style, or start with the more outré
black pudding bonbons with quail's egg.
Rump of Welsh lamb arrives with a little vol-
au-vent filled with a rich lamb ragù, plus some
chard from the estate, spiced courgettes and a
red pepper sauce, while a fishy number might
be classic fish and chips made with Wrexham
lager batter. Finish with sticky toffee pudding.
Wines start at £16.

Chef/s: Adam Stanley. **Open:** all week 12 to 9 (8
Sun). **Meals:** main courses £12 to £25. Set L and D
£20 (2 courses) to £25. Sun L £11. **Details:** 94 seats.
65 seats outside. Bar. Music. Parking.

Please send us your feedback

To register your opinion about any
restaurant listed in this guide, or a new
restaurant that you wish to bring to our
attention, please visit the web address at
the bottom of the page. Your feedback
informs the content of the book and will
be used to compile next year's reviews.

Llanarmon Dyffryn Ceiriog
The West Arms
Cooking score: 1
Modern British | £30
Llanarmon Dyffryn Ceiriog, LL20 7LD
Tel no: (01691) 600665
thewestarms.co.uk
£5 OFF

'This is everything you could want from a country pub – blazing fires, friendly service, old-world charm and hearty, honest food,' noted one visitor to this rambling former drovers' inn in the foothills of the Berwyn Mountains. All the rustic tropes are here – farm implements and gleaming brass instruments of indeterminate usage, plus some beautiful antique furniture. The cooking is straight-talking: not only pubby pies, Whitby scampi, and gammon, egg and chips, but also lobster thermidor, a cracking haddock and mussel chowder and homely puds such as rhubarb crumble and custard. Wines from £17.95.
Chef/s: Grant Williams. **Open:** Mon to Sat L 12 to 2.30, D 6 to 9. Sun 12 to 9. **Meals:** main courses £16 to £27. Sun L £11 (1 course). **Details:** 80 seats. 30 seats outside. V menu. Bar. Wheelchairs. Music. Parking.

whose shades of green, high ceilings and many windows conjure the spirit of a Victorian garden room. Bryan Webb's cooking teams classical techniques with patriotic Welsh flourishes – pan-fried hake with a laverbread butter sauce, for example – and he knows when to keep things simple, relying on beautiful ingredients, pinpoint cooking and on-point flavour combinations to carry the dish. While it's true that some dishes, such as a vivid asparagus soup, have almost Zen-like simplicity, others – duck breast, duck faggot, confit potato, cider and apple sauce and creamed celeriac, for instance – reveal a deft hand with multiple elements, and this keen sense of balance carries through to desserts such as a 'rich, creamy and not too sweet' cherry soup with cinnamon ice cream followed by 'delectable' petits fours. Service is 'slick but not stiff' and the wine list provides helpful notes on everything from classics to less predictable finds. There's plenty by the glass or carafe, and bottles start at £24.
Chef/s: Bryan Webb. **Open:** Fri to Sun L 12.30 to 2 (2.30 Sun), Wed to Sun D 7 to 9. **Closed:** Mon, Tue, 3 weeks Jan. **Meals:** set L £27 (2 courses) to £34. Set D £50 (2 courses) to £60. Sun L £34. Tasting menu £75 (6 courses) to £90. **Details:** 40 seats. 8 seats outside. Bar. Wheelchairs. Parking.

Llandrillo
Tyddyn Llan
Cooking score: 6
Modern British | £60
Llandrillo, LL21 0ST
Tel no: (01490) 440264
tyddynllan.co.uk

A handsome grey-stone building in lush countryside, this was once the Duke of Westminster's shooting lodge, but has been in Bryan and Susan Webb's capable hands since 2002. It's a plush, timeless country house – a series of lounges, all traditionally styled with deep sofas and armchairs, with a dining room

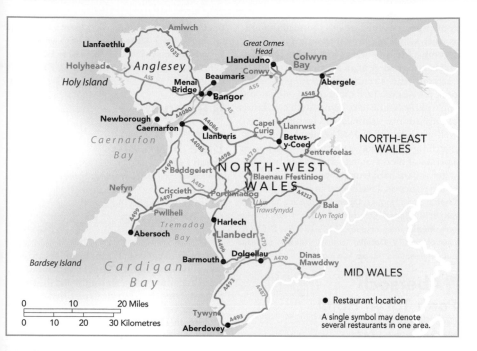

Llanfaethlu
Amlwch
A5025
Holyhead
Anglesey
Great Ormes Head
Llandudno
Colwyn Bay
A55
Beaumaris
Conwy
A55
Abergele
A548
Holy Island
Menai Bridge
Bangor
A5
Newborough
A4080
A5
Caernarfon
A4086
Capel Curig
Llanrwst
NORTH-EAST WALES
Caernarfon Bay
Llanberis
A4085
A498
A470
Betws-y-Coed
Pentrefoelas
A5
Beddgelert
A487
NORTH-WEST WALES
Blaenau Ffestiniog
Nefyn
Criccieth
A497
Porthmadog
A4212
Bala
A499
Pwllheli
Llyn Trawsfynydd
Llyn Tegid
Tremadog Bay
Harlech
Abersoch
Llanbedr
A494
Bardsey Island
Cardigan Bay
Barmouth
A496
A470
Dolgellau
A470
Dinas Mawddwy
MID WALES
A473
A487
Tywyn
A493
Aberdovey

0   10   20 Miles
0   10   20   30 Kilometres

● Restaurant location

A single symbol may denote several restaurants in one area.

■ Aberdovey

★ NEW ENTRY ★

Seabreeze

Cooking score: 1
British | £28
Bodfor Terrace, Aberdovey, LL35 0EA
Tel no: (01654) 767449
seabreeze-aberdovey.co.uk

There is a suitably breezy air to this little
restaurant on Aberdovey's seafront where
exposed wood and stonework and glimpses of
the sea set the stage for wholesome, generous
cooking. As the shelves of Welsh deli goods
suggest, local fare is championed, and fresh
fish is available to buy as well as to eat in. A
large bowl of smoked haddock chowder
featuring samphire, perky green peas and
grilled bacon, and Welsh lamb with
colcannon, salsify and thyme juice have been
applauded, as has sticky toffee pudding. Wines
start at £15.

Chef/s: Henry Benson. **Open:** all week L 12 to 2, D 6
to 9.30. **Closed:** 25 and 26 Dec, 2 weeks Jan.
Meals: main courses £12 to £25. **Details:** 40 seats. 8
seats outside. Music.

■ Abergele

The Kinmel Arms

Cooking score: 4
Modern British | £30
St George, Abergele, LL22 9BP
Tel no: (01745) 832207
thekinmelarms.co.uk

Co-proprietor Tim Watson isn't one for the
hiding of lights under bushels, but proudly
displays his own artworks throughout the pub
and dining space of the Kinmel, a Stuart-era
village inn in the midst of a wooded estate.
Pedigree North Wales produce is the mainstay
of Chad Hughes' kitchen, and even bar-food
stalwarts are more than perfunctory, when
Menai mussels in chive-strewn curry sauce
elicit gasps of pleasure from readers. More

contemporary notes are also sounded though, as when white and brown crabmeat is accompanied by watermelon, pickled mooli and lemongrass. A main course that reliably beats the band is venison loin with poached pear, port-braised red cabbage and celeriac and apple purée, while hake comes with two kinds of mushrooms – shiitake and trompette – as well as salsify and pickled grapes. Finish with matching soufflé and ice cream of pistachio, or a platter of blood-orange cheesecake, 'walnut whip' and orchard fruit pannacotta. Chilean house wines on a well-written list are £17.50. **Chef/s:** Chad Hughes. **Open:** Tue to Sat L 12 to 2, D 6 to 9.30. **Closed:** Sun, Mon, 25 Dec, 1 Jan, bank hols. **Meals:** main courses £14 to £26. Set D £15 (2 courses) to £19. **Details:** 76 seats. 32 seats outside. Bar. Wheelchairs. Music. Parking.

Abersoch
Porth Tocyn Hotel
Cooking score: 2
Modern British | £47
Bwlch Tocyn, Abersoch, LL53 7BU
Tel no: (01758) 713303
porthtocynhotel.co.uk

The view over modest, manicured grounds to the sea with Snowdonia beyond must surely be one of the best in North Wales. The hotel itself – whitewashed, rambling and homely – may feel stuck in a time warp, but it's well looked after with a warm welcome and plenty of places to lounge. A meal in the dining room (parquet floor, sea views, traditional styling) is in old-fashioned hotel-style but dishes are carefully done: cauliflower soup with grain mustard crème fraîche and herb oil; roast corn-fed chicken breast studded with black garlic over truffle mash with ginger-infused courgettes, baby carrots and red wine jus; and coconut cream with Malibu-infused fruits, Florentine biscuits and strawberry and mint coulis; all interspersed with canapés, a mid-course sorbet and petits fours. The wine list offers decent choice from £19.

Chef/s: Louise Fletcher-Brewer. **Open:** all week L 12 to 2.30, D 7 to 9. **Closed:** early Nov to week before Easter. **Meals:** set D £40 (2 courses) to £47. Sun L £26. **Details:** 50 seats. 40 seats outside. Parking. No children at D.

Bangor
LOCAL GEM
Blue Sky Café
British | £20
Ambassador Hall, 236 High Street, Bangor, LL57 1PA
Tel no: (01248) 355444
blueskybangor.co.uk

Originally a dance hall, this popular café is convivial and cosy, with big leather sofas, rustic furniture and a blazing wood-burner. Soup, sandwiches, burgers and filled ciabatta make up much of the menu, but you'll also find pig in a barm (crispy Asian-style rolled pork belly in an artisan roll with a soft-boiled egg and char siu sauce) and slow-cooked Welsh lamb with rosemary and garlic. The 'gloriously chunky, well-cooked' chips are a must, and desserts such as pistachio meringue with whipped cream are definitely worth a gander. A short wine list opens at £11.75.

Barmouth
Bistro Bermo
Cooking score: 2
Modern British | £30
6 Church Street, Barmouth, LL42 1EW
Tel no: (01341) 281284
bistrobarmouth.co.uk

Things are a little more upmarket than the humble bistro tag might suggest, with crisp table linen, folded napkins and candles adding a distinguished feel to the Ryders' appealing venue in a little harbour town. Paul Ryder cooks an extensive menu of classic and modern dishes, mixing Mediterranean modes with a solid seam of British domesticity. A simple serving of sautéed wild mushrooms

and caramelised onions on a big garlic croûton offers a world of earthy satisfaction to begin, while Conwy mussels appear in marinière guise. Following on, expect a meat-driven roll call of mains, from venison sirloin in Penderyn whisky and shallots to Welsh Black beef and lamb cuts. Welsh cheeses and chutney keep the dragon standard flying high, while desserts tend to the irresistible, with white chocolate and raspberry crème brûlée and hazelnut brittle among the possibilities. House wines are Chilean Sauvignon, Languedoc Merlot or Spanish rosado at £16.50 from a short but serviceable list.
Chef/s: Paul Ryder. **Open:** Tue to Sat D only 6 to 9. **Closed:** Sun, Mon. **Meals:** main courses £16 to £24. **Details:** 16 seats. Music.

◼ Beaumaris
The Loft
Cooking score: 5
Modern British | £49
The Bull – Beaumaris, Castle Street, Beaumaris, LL58 8AP
Tel no: (01248) 810329
bullsheadinn.co.uk

In a modernising move, the owners of Ye Olde Bull's Head Inn have rebranded the venue as simply The Bull – Beaumaris. That aside, little else has changed at this aristocratic centuries-old hostelry: the views of nearby Beaumaris Castle are as lordly as ever, a conservatory-style brasserie caters for daily needs, and the Loft is for serious dining. Occupying a dramatic space shoehorned into the eaves of the original building, its circular mirrors, arty partitions and skewed ceiling provide a striking backdrop for Hefin Roberts' culinary adventures. 'Delicious food, brilliantly cooked using local ingredients' is one verdict on a menu that is strewn with cutting-edge ideas: how about slow-cooked pork cheek with caramelised onion, burnt white chocolate and wild yeast beer? There's also no shortage of invention when it comes to, say, smoked loin of cod with cauliflower and potato 'sag aloo' and candied grapefruit, or a dessert of

caramelised Felin honey tart with chilled bee pollen, lemon and olive oil ice cream. France leads on the 'knowledgeably chosen' wine list, with bottles from £23.
Chef/s: Hefin Roberts. **Open:** Wed to Sat D only 7 to 9.30 (6.30 Fri and Sat). **Closed:** Sun, Mon, Tue, 25 and 26 Dec, 1 Jan. **Meals:** set D £49. **Details:** 45 seats. Bar. Children over 7 yrs only.

◼ Betws-y-Coed
LOCAL GEM
Bistro Betws-y-Coed
British | £27
Holyhead Road, Betws-y-Coed, LL24 0AY
Tel no: (01690) 710328
bistrobetws-y-coed.co.uk
£5 OFF £30

In the centre of a Welsh village well known for its photogenic appeal, Gerwyn Williams' bistro in a historic stone building is dedicated to the Conwy Valley's finest. He mostly takes a traditional approach to the cooking, although the tradition may be as much east Asian, say deep-fried pork belly on coconut rice with coriander dressing, as closer to home. For the latter, expect honey-marinated lamb cutlets with minted mash and a leek and laverbread sauce. Daily specials are chalked on the board, and dessert could be a citrus trio – warm orange cake, lemon posset and pink grapefruit sorbet. Wines from £14.50.

◼ Caernarfon
Blas
Cooking score: 1
Modern British | £31
23-25 Hole in the Wall Street, Caernarfon, LL55 1RF
Tel no: (01286) 677707
blascaernarfon.co.uk
£5 OFF

Built into Caernarfon Castle's wall, Blas is a charming find on a narrow lane in the oldest, prettiest part of town. The homely interior combines modern art and vintage touches, and segues comfortably between daytime café

and evening restaurant. Lunchtime options run from Welsh rarebit to crispy lamb breast with basil mayonnaise, feta, pomegranate and mint. In the evening the big guns come out, with the likes of Boksburg Blue cheese mousse, salt-baked celery, poached pear, brioche and thyme crumb, or seared pork loin with a mini braised pork and onion Wellington, fondant potato, creamy Savoy cabbage, carrot and swede, and butternut squash tarte Tatin with toffee apple, baked pecan nuts and ginger ice cream. There's also a competitively priced nine-course tasting menu. The bargain wine list includes plenty by the glass, with bottles from £15.95.
Chef/s: Daniel ap Geraint. **Open:** Tue to Sun L 12 to 3, Tue to Sat D 6 to 9. **Closed:** Mon, 25 and 26 Dec. **Meals:** main courses £14 to £21. Sun L £15 (2 courses) to £20. Tasting menu £45. **Details:** 40 seats. 16 seats outside. Wheelchairs. Music.

■ Dolgellau
Mawddach
Cooking score: 2
Modern British | £32
Llanelltyd, Dolgellau, LL40 2TA
Tel no: (01341) 421752
mawddach.com

Resourceful Welsh farmers Will and Ifan Dunn have added another string to their bow by converting one of their 17th-century barns into a restaurant and giving their home-reared lamb a starring role on the menu. Spread over two floors, Mawddach boasts dramatic views of Cader Idris from floor-to-ceiling windows, while slate floors emphasise the venue's Welsh identity. Ifan's cooking is more contemporary than you might expect from the location, with indigenous ingredients finding their way into an array of sparky Anglo-European dishes: free-range duck liver parfait is paired with gingerbread and pickles; slow-cooked pork belly arrives with greens, garlic and anchovy; roast hake sits on a butter-bean, chorizo and tomato stew. Aside from the aforementioned lamb, meat eaters might also fancy the dry-aged local sirloin steak with triple-cooked chips, while desserts could

feature milk chocolate cream with honeycomb and orange sauce. Wines include some Welsh sparklers, plus house selections from £15.75.
Chef/s: Ifan Dunn. **Open:** Thur to Sun L 12 to 2.30, Thur to Sat D 6.30 to 9. **Closed:** Mon, Tue, Wed, 26 Dec, 1 week Apr, 2 weeks Nov. **Meals:** main courses £16 to £23. Sun L £24. **Details:** 35 seats. 40 seats outside. Bar. Wheelchairs. Music. Parking. Children over 6 yrs only at D.

■ Harlech
Castle Cottage
Cooking score: 2
Modern British | £40
Y Llech, Harlech, LL46 2YL
Tel no: (01766) 780479
castlecottageharlech.co.uk

Glyn and Jacqueline Roberts took charge of these Grade II-listed premises back in 1989, putting Castle Cottage into the Guide's list of longest-serving restaurants. Occupying a pair of stone-built 16th-century cottages in the shadow of Harlech Castle, this place is all low beams and cosy congeniality, with Welsh oak tables and generous helpings of Welsh produce keeping the compass pointed in the right direction. Seasonal game always gets a good airing on Glyn's daily menus, be it breast of woodcock with grilled figs, Llyn bacon, croûtons and poppy seed dressing or a 'duet' of Coed-y-Brenin venison with port and chestnut sauce. Elsewhere, Menai mussels are given the marinière treatment, while mustard-crusted rack of local lamb sits alongside a mini Lancashire hotpot and buttered carrots. For afters, keep it sweet with rich, sticky date sponge or take the savoury route with Welsh rarebit and marinated anchovies. Wines from £16.50.
Chef/s: Glyn Roberts. **Open:** all week D only 7 to 9. **Closed:** 24 to 26 Dec, 3 weeks Nov. **Meals:** set D £35 (2 courses) to £40. Tasting menu £45 (5 courses). **Details:** 35 seats. Bar. Music. Parking.

Seek and ye shall find

There are brilliant restaurants in all sorts of unusual places, but it helps to know where to look. Here are some of our favourites:

Feeling agricultural? John Duffin went home to create his restaurant, **John's House**, on the family farm in Leicestershire, where precision food is served in a 17th century cottage that stands among outbuildings and farm machinery.

The market feels part of the restaurant and vice versa at laid-back Canterbury bistro the **Goods Shed**, which makes great use of local produce from the Goods Shed's stalls. Seasonality is always to the fore.

An Oxford institution that combines working Victorian boathouse with much-loved restaurant, the **Cherwell Boathouse** also has an extensive wine list marked up with considerable restraint. Have a punt.

Marram Grass Café, the Barrie brothers' campsite café, has evolved with them to become a destination for anyone seeking gutsy food and twinkly atmospherics on Anglesey.

▌Llanberis

LOCAL GEM
The Peak
International | £28
86 High Street, Llanberis, LL55 4SU
Tel no: (01286) 872777
peakrestaurant.co.uk

£5 OFF £30

'Small menu, fresh local produce' is the clarion call at this local eatery in the foothills of Snowdonia, and chef Angela Dwyer is true to her word. Expect a colourful international line-up running from Thai fishcakes or lavender-roasted peaches with Serrano ham and Manchego to pans of vegetable paella, rump of Welsh lamb with butternut squash and rosemary bake or polenta-crusted red snapper with ratatouille. Pies, steaks, Welsh cheeses and desserts such as chocolate brownie with Knickerbocker glory complete the picture. Wines from £14.95.

▌Llandudno
Jaya
Cooking score: 2
Indian | £25
36 Church Walks, Llandudno, LL30 2HN
Tel no: (01492) 818198
jayarestaurant.co.uk

£30

Located on the ground floor of a Llandudno town house B&B and opening only three evenings a week, nothing about Jaya fits the 'provincial curry house' template. However, the quality of the food on offer at Sunita Katoch's remarkable eatery is way above your usual chicken tikka masala. Glass-topped tables, striking artwork and other contemporary touches set the scene for a menu of emphatically spiced North Indian food with some noticeable Kenyan influences and recipes gleaned from Sunita's family back home. There are lamb 'tikki' burgers and achari prawns marinated in 'pickle spices' from the grill, or you could nibble on some fish pakoras with chilli jam, before sampling

Kenyan-style dhai chicken simmered in yoghurt, lamb masala or a mushroom and pea curry. To drink, try a mango mojito, Cobra beer or a spice-friendly wine (from £16.95 a bottle).

Chef/s: Sunita Katoch. **Open:** Thur to Sat D only 6 to 10. **Closed:** Sun to Wed, 19 Dec to 13 Jan. **Meals:** main courses £11 to £14. **Details:** 20 seats. Bar. Music. Parking.

■ Llanfaethlu
The Black Lion Inn
Cooking score: 1
Modern British | £28
Llanfaethlu, LL65 4NL
Tel no: (01407) 730718
blacklionanglesey.com
£5 OFF 🍴 £30

Leigh and Mari Faulkner presided over a serious refit when they moved into this once run-down village boozer: outside, the bracing views of Snowdonia are unchanged, but the pub's interior is now a telling mix of traditional and modern. The owners buy locally and have their own walled kitchen garden on a nearby estate, enabling them to offer a lively mix of pub staples and more intricate ideas – think beer-battered haddock goujons, rare-breed Longhorn steaks, pies and crumbles alongside beetroot and goats' cheese arancini or local lamb three ways (roast cutlet, shepherd's pie, braised shoulder). Interesting Rhyd Y Delyn cheeses, too. Wines from £16.10.

Chef/s: Wayne Roberts. **Open:** Thur to Sun L 12 to 2 (3 Sat), Wed to Sat D 6 to 8 (9 Fri and Sat). **Closed:** Mon, Tue, 10 days Jan. **Meals:** main courses £13 to £23. Sun L £18 (2 courses) to £23. **Details:** 75 seats. 20 seats outside. Wheelchairs. Music. Parking.

Visit us online

To find out more about The Good Food Guide, please visit thegoodfoodguide.co.uk

---

■ Menai Bridge

Sosban and the Old Butcher's
Cooking score: 6
Modern British | £50
Trinity House, 1 High Street, Menai Bridge, LL59 5EE
Tel no: (01248) 208131
sosbanandtheoldbutchers.com

Quite how a team of two manages to create the 'wondrous experience' that is Sosban may give you pause for thought, but there is no sign of strain in this homely, tranquil dining room or in the open kitchen where Stephen Stevens works with intensity and focus. His wife Bethan handles front-of-house with equal aplomb, providing a warm welcome and detailed descriptions of each dish in lieu of a menu. There are no choices here – just a perfectly executed sequence of eight courses drawn from sea and land, the ingredients second to none. A former butcher's shop decked out in heritage colours, it is characterful and warmly lit, with flickering candles on the simple wooden tables, but the informality of the setting doesn't prepare you for the high calibre of Stephen's cooking, which is 'on a par with much of what you'd find in swankier, more obviously high-end settings'. For all the serious intent of this cooking, there's more than a hint of fun too: witness a pair of radishes, harvested five minutes ago and still with their leaves attached, sitting in a pot of 'earth' made from rye and bacon crumble atop a rosemary cream; or a dessert of lemon ice cream lollies coated in intense dark chocolate and sprinklings of black olive. There's a penchant for bold and brilliant flavour combinations, as in a 'divine' main course of fresh salmon with carrots, baked fennel and a glorious, sticky liquorice syrup, all served under a smoke-filled cloche. Other standout dishes have included a rosy, tender chunk of lamb rump with asparagus, wild garlic purée, burnt onions and ricotta;

and rhubarb on a crumble of almond, wild rice and lemon thyme topped with a gold sugar sphere filled with 'beautiful' custard. Wines start at £19.50 a bottle.

Chef/s: Stephen Owen Stevens. **Open:** Sat L 12.30 to 1.30, Thur to Sat D 7 to 11. **Closed:** Sun to Wed, 23 Dec to mid Feb. **Meals:** set L £27 (3 courses). Tasting menu £50. **Details:** 16 seats. Children over 12 yrs only.

READERS RECOMMEND

Freckled Angel

Modern British

35 High Street, Menai Bridge, LL59 5EF
Tel no: (01248) 209952
freckled-angel-fine-catering.co.uk

'I had lamb neck fillet with smoked aubergine, deep-fried Perl Wen cheese and smoked mackerel pâté; my friend had mushroom fricassee and smoked salmon with quails' eggs and asparagus. Service was outstanding; the food excellent and all locally sourced.'

■ Newborough
The Marram Grass Café

Cooking score: 4

British | £27

White Lodge, Penlon, Newborough, LL61 6RS
Tel no: (01248) 440077
themarramgrass.com

£5 OFF £30 ▼

This delightfully quirky campsite restaurant 'somewhere between a Scout hut and ski lodge' has caused quite a stir since it opened, popping up in the national press and gaining quite a local following. At a recent midweek lunch it was bursting at the seams, so booking is advisable. The building has a cobbled-together, woody warmth, and there's a pretty, vine-strewn pagoda outside for warmer days, but for all its artless abandon, there is serious intent in the kitchen, with care put into everything from rustic breads with home-made dips to generous, hearty sides of dauphinois potatoes with fresh spinach leaves. A starter of baked oysters with home-reared pork, smoked pancetta and Welsh cheese

gratin piled on to creamy oyster-sauce-soaked sourdough is typical of the unpretentious style, while a main course of wild sea bass with carrot curry, sprouting broccoli, tea raisins, wild garlic aloo, herb dressing and sautéed potatoes delivered 'big flavours and beautiful ingredients'. To finish, try caramelised banana with cardamom purée and hazelnut cake, chocolate ice cream and a nutty crumble with cocoa nibs. Wines start at £29.

Chef/s: Ellis Barrie. **Open:** all week L 12 to 2.30, D 6 to 9. **Closed:** Mon and Tue (winter). **Meals:** main courses £14 to £17. **Details:** 40 seats. 40 seats outside. Bar. Music. Parking.

Readers recommend

A 'readers recommend' review is a genuine quote from a report sent in by one of our readers. We intend to follow up these suggestions throughout the year to come.

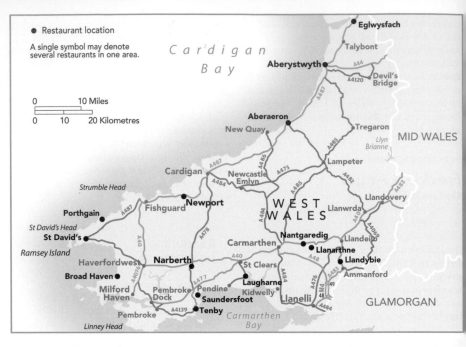

Cardigan Bay

MID WALES

WEST WALES

GLAMORGAN

- Restaurant location

A single symbol may denote several restaurants in one area.

0   10 Miles
0 10   20 Kilometres

Eglwysfach
Talybont
Aberystwyth
Devil's Bridge
Aberaeron
New Quay
Tregaron
Llyn Brianne
Lampeter
Cardigan
Newcastle Emlyn
Llandovery
Strumble Head
Porthgain
Fishguard
Newport
Llanwrda
Llandeilo
Nantgaredig
Llanarthne
Llandybie
Ammanford
Carmarthen
St David's Head
St David's
Ramsey Island
Haverfordwest
Narberth
St Clears
Broad Haven
Laugharne
Milford Haven
Pembroke Dock
Pendine
Kidwelly
Llanelli
Saundersfoot
Pembroke
Tenby
Linney Head
Carmarthen Bay

Aberaeron
Harbourmaster
Cooking score: 2
Modern British | £30
Pen Cei, Aberaeron, SA46 0BT
Tel no: (01545) 570755
harbour-master.com

This striking boutique hotel – once the harbourmaster's office and flour warehouse – occupies pole position on Aberaeron's harbourfront and is quite the poster boy for the Welsh tourist industry. The Harbourmaster has a classy little restaurant – all sea blue walls and seaside-inspired art – and a buzzy, atmospheric bar loved by the locals, where simpler, hearty food is served. Chef Ludo Dieumegard now has his feet firmly under a table groaning with top-notch Welsh ingredients: Cefn Gwyn wild duck breast with sour apple, feta and port syrup, and Brecon venison ravioli with thyme and hazelnut butter are among the starters, while

mains range from fillet of sea bass with prawn crust, barley, cockle and laverbread risotto with lemon purée, to sweet potato and squash curry with spinach, yoghurt and flatbread. The wine list offers a decent international selection of favourites, starting at £15.
Chef/s: Ludo Dieumegard. **Open:** all week L 12 to 2.30, D 6 to 9. **Closed:** 25 Dec. **Meals:** main courses £11 to £21. Set D £25 (2 courses) to £30. Sun L £19 (2 courses) to £25. **Details:** 100 seats. 15 seats outside. Bar. Wheelchairs. Music. Parking.

Aberystwyth
Ultracomida
Cooking score: 2
Spanish | £19
31 Pier Street, Aberystwyth, SY23 2LN
Tel no: (01970) 630686
ultracomida.co.uk
£30

Just a few yards away from the seafront is this surprisingly well-stocked Spanish delicatessen with a simple café at the back – which makes its case with large, round communal tables and likeable prices, and exudes honest authenticity. It's best to arrive early for lunch as no bookings are taken (you're safe in the evening), and tables fill rapidly with regular customers. From a selection of classic tapas, jamón Serrano, croquetas de queso, albondigas (meatballs), and Spanish black pudding with piquillo peppers and fried egg are often recommended, with special mention for the rabbit, pork and chorizo paella, and lentils cooked with Serrano ham and chorizo. To finish, there's a plate of Spanish cheeses with membrillo or tarta de Santiago, and it's hard not to linger in the delicatessen on the way out. Drink Spanish ciders and beers or choose from a selection of sherries and patriotic wines (bottles from £11.95). Another branch is at 7 High Street, Narberth; tel: (01834) 861491. **Chef/s:** Ian Davies. **Open:** Mon to Sat 10 to 9 (4.30 Mon). Sun L 12 to 3.30. **Closed:** 25 and 26 Dec, 1 Jan. **Meals:** tapas £4 to £7. **Details:** 32 seats. Wheelchairs. Music.

■ Broad Haven

LOCAL GEM
The Druidstone
Global | £32
Broad Haven, SA62 3NE
Tel no: (01437) 781221
druidstone.co.uk

High on the cliff above Druidston Haven's sandy beach, this country house hotel doesn't conform to stereotypes of the genre. Quirky, homely and inviting, there's an ecological ethos, animals are as welcome as young humans, and the food is rustic and unpretentious. Ceviche of monkfish with pickled cucumber is a starter full of modern spirit, but you might follow on with all the comfort and joy of lasagne al forno or best end of Welsh lamb with garlic and rosemary crust. Wines start at £14.50.

www.fionablack.com

Gareth Ward
Ynyshir, Eglwysfach

What inspired you to become a chef?
I was a bit of a tearaway at school and left not knowing what to do, except join the army or be a fireman. But my uncle Trevor said 'why don't you become a chef, as everyone needs to eat.' I went to the job centre and got a job in a pub, and just knew the kitchen was where I should be.

At the end of a long day, what do you like to cook?
Crumpets with Marmite and scrambled eggs, or Heinz tomato soup!

What food could you not live without?
Miso, maple and soy. These are the basis of almost every dish we cook in the restaurant.

What's your favourite dish on your menu?
I love every dish, as they only make the menu if we believe that they are incredible. But, if I had to pick some it would be tiramisu, 'not French onion' soup, or mackerel sweet and sour as they have been on my menus since day one and never change. In my eyes they are perfect.

Eglwysfach

★ TOP 50 ★

Ynyshir

Cooking score: 7
Modern British | £95
Eglwysfach, SY20 8TA
Tel no: (01654) 781209
ynyshirhall.co.uk
£5 OFF 🍷 🛏

It's a fitting tribute to hotelier Joan Reen, who died early in 2016, that the hotel she created remains as beautiful and luxurious as ever. A gracious whitewashed country house, Ynyshir Hall is now owned by John and Jenny Talbot, long-standing guests and previously shareholders in the hotel. They have preserved the things that make it special – not least the jewel-like turquoise restaurant where Gareth Ward cooks to an ever higher standard, his dishes nothing short of trailblazing in their use of unlikely flavour combinations that 'work so well you wonder why more people aren't putting these ingredients together'. Standout examples have included gently warmed sashimi mackerel with tart rhubarb ketchup, crunchy, punchy, acidic slivers of raw rhubarb and back fat shavings; a piece of fudge made with beef fat and topped with crackling; and a duck liver and tofu pâté paired with banana, miso and verjus. There's ample use of kitchen staff to finish dishes at the table, starting with the simple pouring of a dashi stock on to caramelised and pickled onions, tofu and crispy croûtons, to make an intensely sweet-savoury amuse-bouche, and progressing to much pouring, shaving and sprinkling in Ward's 'sensational' take on Caesar salad – comprising crunchy lettuce heart, lettuce purée and onion oil, topped with Parmesan-infused milk, a panko bacon anchovy crumb, grated Parmesan and shaved cured egg yolk. A spring meal included a four-stage beef dish paired with a 'stunning' confit onion cooked in beef fat, topped with onion jus and cubes of Wagyu fat; and a piece of seven-month aged Wagyu beef with seaweed, puffed rice and soy sauce. A quick-fire succession of 'original and exciting' desserts has included a white chocolate cream with salty, umami-packed black-bean syrup; a complex, distilled and deconstructed take on tiramisu; and then a final, fresh flourish in the form of goats' milk pannacotta with nettle oil, nettle granita, lime shavings, a nettle tuile and crunchy cereal. Staff are supremely efficient but also warm, charming and ready to chat – and they do a grand job recommending wines from a list that is weighty in both content and cost. You can spend north of £2,000 if you fancy, but there are also 'superb' house wines for £24 and plenty in between.
Chef/s: Gareth Ward. **Open:** Tue to Sat L 12 to 2, D 7 to 9. **Closed:** first 2 weeks Jan. **Meals:** set L £35 (5 courses). Set D £95 (15 courses). **Details:** 30 seats. Bar. Wheelchairs. Music. Parking. Children over 9 yrs only at D.

Laugharne
The Cors

Cooking score: 3
Modern British | £35
Newbridge Road, Laugharne, SA33 4SH
Tel no: (01994) 427219
thecors.co.uk
🛏

There's a true sense of dedication about Nick Priestland's highly original restaurant with rooms, although its location at the end of a winding lane, coupled with a lack of signage, made one visitor wonder if 'the owner doesn't want people to find it'. But once found, the Cors is 'perfectly attuned to the relaxed atmosphere of Laugharne', offering just the sort of hospitality that both travellers and locals appreciate. It's a very personal operation, with attentive service and good, modern British food served in the hugely atmospheric, candlelit dining room. The cooking is based on sound technique and 'clearly cooked with passion'. Highlights for reporters this year have been a mozzarella and tomato salad, smoked haddock brûlée, a generous grilled turbot with asparagus, glazed carrots and potato and onion slice, the selection of Welsh cheeses, and lemon tart.

Chef/s: Nick Priestland. **Open:** Thur to Sat D only 7 (1 sitting). **Closed:** Sun to Wed, first 2 weeks Nov. **Meals:** main courses £16 to £26. **Details:** 24 seats. 10 seats outside. Children over 12 yrs only.

▮ Llanarthne
Wright's Food Emporium
Cooking score: 3
Modern British | £20
Golden Grove Arms, Llanarthne, SA32 8JU
Tel no: (01558) 668929
wrightsfood.co.uk
£30

The Emporium is an Aladdin's Cave of gastronomic treasures: thoroughbred local meats, charcuterie, cheeses and organic fruit and vegetables jostle in happy profusion, and there's a wine corner, too, running on a refillable bottle basis. At the heart of it, should you have shopped until you dropped, is a daytime eatery (plus Friday and Saturday evenings), where seasonal, readily available ingredients find their way into European-influenced rustic dishes eaten amid shelves laden with cookbooks. Precisely rendered favourites like meatballs in tomato sauce, lamb moussaka or crab linguine are interspersed with more unusual offerings such as deep-fried aubergine in cumin with honey and labneh, baked mackerel with marinated beetroot, and a sustaining pie filled with squash and Teifi cheese. For those with less time, the sandwiches are all but irresistible (steak and Hafod Cheddar with caramelised onion), and the national pastime of cake is consecrated with lemon polenta and Ultra Chocolate examples. The short wine list starts at £15.50.
Chef/s: Maryann Wright and Phoebe Powell. **Open:** Mon to Sat 9 to 7 (11am Mon, 10pm Fri and Sat). Sun 11 to 5. **Closed:** Tue (low season), 25 and 26 Dec. **Meals:** main courses £10 to £14. **Details:** 80 seats. 20 seats outside. Wheelchairs. Music. Parking.

▮ Llandybie
Valans
Cooking score: 1
British | £24
29 High Street, Llandybie, SA18 3HX
Tel no: (01269) 851288
valans.co.uk
£30

'It's a little gem,' says one reporter of Dave and Remy Vale's modern village bistro, which has been feeding the locals well for over a decade. Classic techniques and great Welsh ingredients are the watchwords and a lack of fuss in the kitchen allows them to shine. Witness pearly-fresh hake, cooked so the skin crisps up, with buttered cabbage, green beans, tomato butter sauce and dauphinois potatoes. Elsewhere there's a simple dish of duck with homemade onion marmalade, Gower salt marsh lamb, and a comforting apricot bread-and-butter pudding with custard or honey cheesecake. Charming service, too. Wines start at £16.
Chef/s: Dave Vale. **Open:** Tue to Sun L 12 to 3, Tue to Sat D 7 to 11. **Closed:** Mon, 2 weeks Dec. **Meals:** main courses £16 to £24. Set L and D £13 (2 courses) to £17. Sun L £16 (2 courses) to £19. **Details:** 32 seats. Wheelchairs. Music.

▮ Nantgaredig
Y Polyn
Cooking score: 4
Modern British | £35
Capel Dewi, Nantgaredig, SA32 7LH
Tel no: (01267) 290000
ypolyn.co.uk

A former pub, and before that a tollhouse, Y Polyn has recently acquired a swish architect-designed extension leading to the upper floor. The kitchen keeps pace with the added capacity, Susan Manson at the stoves and husband Mark providing warm front-of-house hospitality. Homely and stylishly rustic, the interior suits a cooking style rooted in some of Europe's most delicious culinary traditions but also borrowing from places as diverse as the US, North Africa and Asia. The 'rich and savoury' fish soup with Gruyère, rouille and croûtons is a good way to start, perhaps followed by roast rump of Welsh lamb with potato and spinach lamb breast terrine and yoghurt harissa. To finish, try baked egg custard tart with raspberry ripple ice cream. It's essential to book ahead – Y Polyn is not only a 'solid locals' favourite' but also a destination restaurant in 'a part of Wales not noted for its gastronomy'. A substantial, interesting international wine list opens at £17.

Chef/s: Susan Manson. **Open:** Tue to Sun L 12 to 2 (2.30 Sat and Sun), Tue to Sat D 7 to 9 (6.30 to 9.30 Fri and Sat). **Closed:** Mon. **Meals:** main courses £15 to £19. Set L £14 (2 courses) to £17. Set D £29 (2 courses) to £35. Sun L £20 (2 courses) to £25. **Details:** 100 seats. Bar. Wheelchairs. Music. Parking.

▌Narberth
The Grove

Cooking score: 6
Modern British | £59
Molleston, Narberth, SA67 8BX
Tel no: (01834) 860915
thegrove-narberth.co.uk

🍷 🛏

The Grove is a polished neo-Gothic country house and its restaurant – classical, smart, with bucolic views – is developing into one of Wales' finest. Executive chef Allister Barsby hails from Gidleigh Park, where he was head chef under Michael Caines for three years – 'it shows'. Expect dazzling flavours at every course. Mr Barsby is a dab hand at intensifying everything from earthy cauliflower in a velvety velouté to the really 'massive, beautiful umami hit' in a mushroom risotto. An inspection meal took in a silken egg yolk ravioli on Jerusalem artichoke, the mellow flavours sharpened with punchy pickled mushrooms and the acid burst of pickled onion, while a faultless roasted turbot was teamed with asparagus, leek purée, meaty, salty brown shrimp, toasted almonds and pickled cucumber brunoise – all offset by the sharpness of wild garlic leaves. Equally sure-footed was a perfect pistachio soufflé with

pistachio ice cream popped in the middle and chocolate sauce creating a rich and bitter counterpoint to all the sweetness. A lengthy wine list, which mixes classics and rarer finds, is priced from £25.

Chef/s: Allister Barsby. **Open:** all week L 12 to 2.30, D 6 to 9. **Meals:** set L £29 (3 courses). Set D £59 (3 courses). Sun L £29 (3 courses). Tasting menu £89 (7 courses). **Details:** 55 seats. Bar. Wheelchairs. Music. Parking. No children under 12 yrs after 7pm.

▌Newport
Cnapan

Cooking score: 2
Modern British | £33
East Street, Newport, SA42 0SY
Tel no: (01239) 820575
cnapan.co.uk

£5 OFF 🛏

Opened in 1984 – and a Guide stalwart for nigh on three decades – Cnapan is testament to the unswerving dedication and commitment of long-time custodians Michael and Judith Cooper. Occupying a listed Georgian house in the historic heart of Newport, it looks and feels every inch the dutifully cared for home from home – from the infectiously hospitable atmosphere to the solid traditional furnishings (all Welsh dressers, comfy sofas and wood-burning stoves). The kitchen eschews anything too 'cheffy', instead focusing on seasonal ingredients cooked with a sure hand and a generous spirit. A bowl of spicy seafood chowder sets the tone, before marinated fillet of lamb with minted pea purée and salsa verde, honey-roast duck breast with sour cherry and port sauce or the day's fish from the market – all served with pots of splendid vegetables. To conclude, don't miss the Welsh cheeses or the sticky pear and cinnamon cake. Wines from £16.50.

Chef/s: Judith Cooper. **Open:** Wed to Sun D only 6.30 to 10. **Closed:** Mon, Tue, 21 Dec to 21 Mar. **Meals:** set D £27 (2 courses) to £33. **Details:** 36 seats. V menu. Bar. Wheelchairs. Music. Parking.

Allister Barsby

The Grove, Narberth

What food could you not live without?
Steak, there's something very satisfying about tucking into a piece of beef with a glass of red.

What's your favourite dish on your menu?
Cod with black garlic, brown shrimps, crosnes, rosemary and a lemon verbena-scented chicken jus. The umami flavour of the garlic works perfectly with the rosemary and lemon verbena. It's a light dish with loads of flavour!

What is the most unusual cooking technique you use?
I enjoy curing and smoking fish and meat, which we do on site here at The Grove.

What is the strangest request you have had from a diner?
I have cooked for a lady who was vegetarian but quite happy to order foie gras....

Which chef do you most admire at the moment?
Michael Caines - eight years working with him at Gidleigh Park defined me as a chef. Also leaving his executive chef role to purchase, renovate and open his own country-house hotel is inspiring.

▮ Porthgain
The Shed
Cooking score: 1
Seafood | £30
Porthgain, SA62 5BN
Tel no: (01348) 831518
theshedporthgain.co.uk

The stone building by the shore is a handy spot to fuel up before a trip out on the briny; there are tables outside to catch the sun. Although there is a carte of fancier stuff, like seared scallops with puréed cauliflower and crisp Parma, followed by sea bass en papillote with olives, herbs and lemon, it's the speciality fish and chip menu that's the heart of the operation. Expect monkfish tail or John Dory alongside the traditional cod and haddock, encased in crunchy beer batter and served with hand-cut chips and tartare. Grown-ups can then add whisky butterscotch to their banana splits with impunity. Wines go from £15.50.
Chef/s: Caroline Jones and Brian Mullins. **Open:** all week L 12 to 3, D 5.30 to 9 (Apr to Sep). **Closed:** Mon, Tue, Sun D (Oct to Mar). **Meals:** main courses £17 to £21. **Details:** 50 seats. 64 seats outside. Wheelchairs. Music. Parking.

▮ St David's
LOCAL GEM
Cwtch
Modern British | £32
22 High Street, St David's, SA62 6SD
Tel no: (01437) 720491
cwtchrestaurant.co.uk

£5
OFF

Since Jackie and John Hatton-Bell took over this long-established restaurant it's been pretty much business as usual — retaining the stripped-back charm and plenty of rustic edges of the previous owners. The kitchen continues to keep things simple and local, the cooking remains restrained and respectful of the raw materials. Leek and pea soup with crumbled Perl Las cheese, followed by rolled shoulder of Welsh lamb with 'Molly Parkin' parsnips, roast carrots and red wine jus are typical offerings. The wine list opens at £19.

∎ Saundersfoot
Coast
Cooking score: 4
Modern British | £45
Coppet Hall Beach, Saundersfoot, SA69 9AJ
Tel no: (01834) 810800
coastsaundersfoot.co.uk
£5
OFF

Opened in 2014 by the owners of the Grove at Narbeth (see entry), every table in this contemporary, glass-fronted, cedar-clad building provides panoramic views of Coppet Hall beach and Saundersfoot Bay, the seaside feel mirrored by sandy wood floors, white panelling and blue and beige fabrics. Chef Will Holland's relaxed, seasonal style reflects the family-friendly venue, where fish and seafood is as fresh as can be and kids get their own menu. Expertly char-grilled Milford Haven squid served with blood orange and a fennel salad lifted by the honey-aniseed flavours of 'spice of angels' (fennel pollen) makes a terrific opener, followed, perhaps, by pan-fried John Dory fillet teamed with curried cauliflower and spinach, coconut velouté, lime and coriander. There's char-grilled 28-day dry-aged Welsh beef sirloin for those in the mood for meat, and liquorice pannacotta with carrot cake, yoghurt and carrot ice cream among desserts. The west terrace catches the views and the sunset – a perfect spot for drinks and canapés. Wine from £19.
Chef/s: Will Holland. **Open:** all week L 12 to 2.30, D 6 to 9.30. **Closed:** Mon and Thur (winter), 25 and 26 Dec, 1 week Jan. **Meals:** main courses £15 to £26. Tasting menu £65 (6 courses). **Details:** 67 seats. 50 seats outside. V menu. Bar. Wheelchairs. Music. Parking.

∎ Tenby
★ NEW ENTRY ★
The Salt Cellar
Cooking score: 3
Modern British | £33
The Esplanade, Tenby, SA70 7DU
Tel no: (01834) 844005
thesaltcellartenby.com
£5 🚗
OFF

It's a shame this seaside restaurant is hidden away in the basement of the decidedly unglamorous Atlantic Hotel; not only is it criminal to forsake those views of Tenby's golden sands, but more people should know about the deft cooking of this young team. At lunchtime, unctuous soy-glazed pork comes in the springiest house-made brioche bun, with ginger-spiked Asian slaw and avocado. The evening menu gets more serious. Butter-roasted hake, cooked to perfection with firm flesh and crispy skin, features 'Pembrokeshire potatoes' a moreish combo of fondant and gratin. Ignore dessert at your peril: peanut butter parfait is a riff on a classic PB&J, served with caramelised banana purée and beautifully offset by booze-soaked griotte cherries. A fruity white from the Monnow Valley, and pale ale from the Tenby Brewing Co. maintain the local sourcing policy. Though the terrace opposite is a welcome antidote to the lacklustre dining room, you have to order, and pre-pay, at the bar.
Chef/s: Duncan Barham and Matthew Flowers. **Open:** all week L 12 to 2.30, D 6 to 9.30. **Closed:** 24 to 30 Dec. **Meals:** main courses £15 to £20. Sun L £20 to £25. **Details:** 45 seats. 20 seats outside. V menu. Bar. Wheelchairs. Music.

CHANNEL ISLANDS

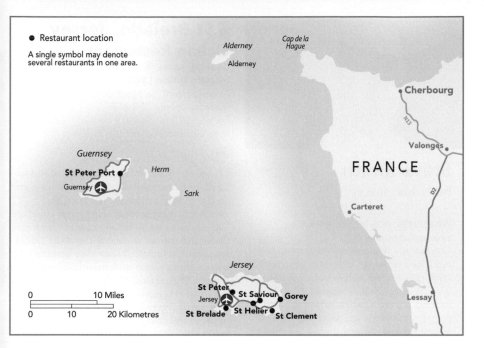

- ● Restaurant location

A single symbol may denote several restaurants in one area.

Alderney

Cap de la Hague

Alderney

● Cherbourg

N13

Valognes

Guernsey

Herm

St Peter Port ●

Guernsey ✈

Sark

FRANCE

D2

Carteret

Jersey

St Peter

Jersey ✈

St Saviour

Gorey

Lessay

St Brelade

St Helier

St Clement

| 0 | 10 Miles |
| 0 | 10 | 20 Kilometres |

▮ Gorey, Jersey

Sumas

Cooking score: 2

Modern British | £37

Gorey Hill, St Martin, Gorey, Jersey, JE3 6ET

Tel no: (01534) 853291

sumasrestaurant.com

£5
OFF

Sitting beneath Mont Orgueil castle, surveying the boat-crowded Gorey harbour on Jersey's eastern flank, Sumas has a lot going for it in the location stakes. A new terrace comes replete with Wimbledon-style retractable roof in case – perish the thought – it rains. Extensive menus deal in modern British food that acknowledges influences from neighbouring France, the Med and east Asia, taking in openers such as crab and clam risotto in lemongrass, coconut and coriander, or beef carpaccio dressed in white truffle oil with a yuzu-doused salad, and leading on to main dishes like venison loin with roast beetroot and dauphinois in blackberry jus.

Fish is an obvious strong point in the circumstances, with sea bass, turbot and John Dory turning up, the last with mussels and enoki mushrooms in saffron and rosemary cream, and simple desserts aim to seduce by means of raspberry mille-feuille or hot chocolate fondant with lemon thyme ice cream. Wines open at £18.

Chef/s: Patrice Bouffaut. **Open:** all week L 12 to 2.30 (12.30 to 3.30 Sun), Mon to Sat D 6 to 9.30. **Closed:** 21 Dec to 18 Jan. **Meals:** main courses £15 to £26. Set L and D £18 (2 courses) to £23. Sun L £25. **Details:** 34 seats. 20 seats outside. Bar. Wheelchairs. Music.

Symbols

- 🛏 Accommodation is available
- £30 Three courses for less than £30
- £5 OFF £5-off voucher scheme
- 🍷 Notable wine list

Steve Smith
Bohemia, Jersey

What is the vital ingredient for a successful kitchen?
Consistency. A successful kitchen must make sure that every diner receives the same quality meal. In terms of food, there is no shadow of doubt that salt is the most vital ingredient. It can be added to every recipe and it can turn a good dish into a fantastic dish. A bit of salt and a few drops of lemon juice can make the world of difference.

What's your favourite dish on your menu?
My favourite dish on our menu is our oyster dish 'Oyster – Cucumber – Fennel', purely because this dish takes advantage of local ingredients and modernises classic flavour combinations.

If you could cook for anyone, who would it be, and what would you cook for them?
I would cook for Russell Crowe or Michael Caine. I would cook them a good old-fashioned stonking Sunday roast!

Which chef do you most admire at the moment?
I admire any chef that has managed to sustain cooking at a high level; chefs such as the Roux brothers, Phil Howard, Pierre Koffmann, Marcus Wareing, Raymond Blanc and Daniel Clifford.

▌St Brelade, Jersey
Ocean Restaurant
Cooking score: 4
Modern British | £65
Atlantic Hotel, Le Mont de la Pulente, St Brelade, Jersey, JE3 8HE
Tel no: (01534) 744101
theatlantichotel.com

Overlooking beautiful St Ouen's Bay and its sandy beaches, with only the intervening golf course adding a more prosaic note, the Atlantic makes the most of the Jersey coastline. The interiors are all broad expanses, with pine floors and natural stone walls, and the Ocean restaurant, which looks out over its namesake, is a sparkling white-and-marine-blue place of light and relaxation. Mark Jordan matches the mood with creatively tooled contemporary dishes that aim to surprise. An opening risotto of squid and cauliflower is garnished with wafer-thin slices of scallop carpaccio, while a modern classic pairing of smoked eel and seared foie gras gains richness from celeriac purée and caramelised apple. Locally landed fish such as sole and turbot vie for main-course attention with squab pigeon with a brochette of its offals and truffled pearl barley, while desserts include coconut pannacotta in tropical fruit soup with passion fruit and mango sorbet. The French-led wine list opens at £24.
Chef/s: Mark Jordan. **Open:** all week L 12.30 to 2.30, D 6.30 to 10. **Closed:** 3 Jan to 2 Feb. **Meals:** set L £23 (2 courses) to £28. Set D £55 (3 courses). Sun L £33. Tasting menu £85. **Details:** 60 seats. V menu. Bar. Music. Parking.

Oyster Box

Cooking score: 3
Seafood | £30
Route de la Baie, St Brelade, Jersey, JE3 8EF
Tel no: (01534) 850888
oysterbox.co.uk

Views of the gorgeous expanse of St Brelade's Bay would make any restaurant easy to love, but the Jersey Pottery's brasserie dominates the beachside strip thanks to its breezy elegance, solid seafood cookery and blue-shaded terrace. Sustainable produce from the ocean by its door is treated with respect but not trepidation, with pink grapefruit revving up a generous seafood salad and Grouville oysters served with Worcestershire sauce, bacon, tomato and Gruyère as well as simply on ice. Specials showcase the work of local day boats and markets, as in delicately flaky plaice with crushed potatoes scented with dill and capers, and fresh-from-the-Med sauce vierge. Away from the sea, there's short rib and beetroot salad with truffled lentils, herb gnocchi or slow-roast spiced aubergine. Its popularity puts understandable pressure on window tables, and service can be rushed, but the clock stops when immaculate desserts, such as a crisp rhubarb and vanilla baked Alaska tartlet, arrive. Wine is from £18.75.
Chef/s: Tony Dorris. **Open:** Tue to Sun L 12 to 2.30 (3 Sun), Mon to Sat D 6 to 9 (9.30 Fri and Sat). **Closed:** 25 and 26 Dec, 1 Jan. **Meals:** main courses £13 to £36. Set L and D £26 (3 courses). **Details:** 100 seats. 60 seats outside. Bar. Wheelchairs.

Please send us your feedback

To register your opinion about any restaurant listed in this guide, or a new restaurant that you wish to bring to our attention, please visit the web address at the bottom of the page. Your feedback informs the content of the book and will be used to compile next year's reviews.

■ St Clement, Jersey

LOCAL GEM
Green Island Restaurant
Mediterranean | £35
Green Island, St Clement, Jersey, JE2 6LS
Tel no: (01534) 857787
greenisland.je

A beachside bolt-hole on the south coast of Jersey, Alan Winch's well-liked café/restaurant has good intentions and a big heart. It's known for its fresh fish and shellfish, say lobster thermidor, plump mussels in a cream sauce or fillet of brill with Parmesan polenta, char-grilled vegetables and asparagus with sauce vierge. But if you are in the mood for meat, there's rack of lamb with Jersey Royals or half a guinea fowl with fondant potato and mushroom duxelles. For dessert, baked Alaska is hard to resist. Wines from £16.75.

■ St Helier, Jersey
★ TOP 50 ★
Bohemia
Cooking score: 7
Modern European | £59
The Club Hotel & Spa, Green Street, St Helier, Jersey, JE2 4UH
Tel no: (01534) 880588
bohemiajersey.com
£5 OFF 🚗

Steve Smith's distinguished contemporary food remains a huge draw to the Club Hotel, tucked away not far from St Helier's main drag. The unshowy dining room and bar have been 'vastly improved' by gentle evolution, and the low-lit far reaches of the restaurant form a suavely relaxing backdrop for some serious cooking. There's humour and liveliness in dishes that dissolve the borders between tradition and modernity; an opener of grapefruit and tarragon salad has a sherbet top, and a potato dish pays homage to the island's most famous mini-tuber – spot the quail's egg rolled in mushroom powder. Plate-juggling is required to manage a crisp galette of spanking-fresh crab and mango, accompanied by an intense set custard of the brown meat overlaid with shellfish jelly. The rewards are ample, as with Anjou pigeon with hay-smoked confit leg, liver and pastrami on toast and multiple onion preparations. Two plates, a lidded pot, a jug and a finger-bowl later, the lasting impression is of superbly cooked pigeon breast and billows of rich liver mousse. Produce is first class; obscenely huge scallops showered with truffle, luscious smoked eel and turrets of Bordier seaweed butter. Puddings are often led by seasonal fruit, with rhubarb and Champagne turned into a velvety sphere with a flag of silver leaf. The wine list covers a lot of vineyard land, with mark-ups on the Channel Islands side of comfortable; glasses from £7, bottles £27.

Chef/s: Steve Smith. **Open:** Mon to Sat L 12 to 2.30, D 6.30 to 10. **Closed:** Sun, 25 and 26 Dec. **Meals:** set L £19 (2 courses) to £25. Set D £50 (2 courses) to £59. Tasting menu £75. **Details:** 66 seats. V menu. Bar. Wheelchairs. Music. Parking.

Ormer

Cooking score: 5
Modern European | £60
7-11 Don Street, St Helier, Jersey, JE2 4TQ
Tel no: (01534) 725100
ormerjersey.com

A sleek prospect for Jersey's business community, Shaun Rankin's high-profile brasserie makes an immediate impact thanks to designer Martin Brudnizki's smart, sophisticated interiors – think elegant panelled walls, soft blue banquettes and yellow leather chairs. Taking its name from one of the Channel Islands' more desirable seafood delicacies, Ormer is a showcase for Rankin's highly intricate cooking – a careful amalgam of British, European and Asian influences underpinned by supplies of Jersey produce. Fish is naturally a strong suit, from scallops with glazed chicken wings and sweetcorn to sea bass with roast baby fennel, marinated grapes, Pernod butter and star anise essence, but don't discount the eclectic meat and game specialities – venison, for example,

sits well with its sweet, spicy accompaniments of parsnip purée, quinoa, Medjool dates, ginger and smoked chocolate tortellini. A great deal of painstaking work also goes into desserts such as apple soufflé with apple compote, custard ice cream and olive oil shortbread. Alternatively, decamp to the classy bar if you're partial to incomparably fresh Royal Bay oysters and keenly priced cocktails. Serious international wines start at £22.

Chef/s: Shaun Rankin. **Open:** Mon to Sat L 12 to 2.30, D 6.30 to 10. **Closed:** Sun, 25 to 29 Dec, 1 to 3 Jan, bank hols. **Meals:** main courses £27 to £32. Set L £19 (2 courses) to £25. Tasting menu £75 (7 courses). **Details:** 50 seats. 22 seats outside. V menu. Bar. Music.

Tassili

Cooking score: 5
Modern European | £59
Grand Jersey Hotel, The Esplanade, St Helier, Jersey, JE2 3QA
Tel no: (01534) 722301
handpickedhotels.co.uk

Just as the Grand Jersey Hotel's no-frills exterior belies its status in St Helier, so Nicolas Valmagna's skilful cooking transcends a dark, plain room within earshot (and then some) of the function suite. Tassili's pleasures reveal themselves gradually. It's dinner only, and across the busy esplanade, St Aubin's Bay and Elizabeth Castle are bewitching in the fading light. Service combines serious intent with easy warmth. Valmagna has access to fine ingredients, and knows how to make them shine. Tasting menus cover land and sea, pescatarian and vegetarian options; looking over the bay, there's an obvious choice. Standout dishes celebrate what's here, close both to France and the water, with subtle modern flourishes – and rather a lot of foam. Crab salad is lightly creamy and draped with jellied stock, served with a hot crab croquette and dabs of yuzu gel just where they're needed. Turbot comes with a beautifully judged risotto, the bitter edge of saffron tempered by a dairy roundness and sea

vegetables that pop, salty and crisp, in the mouth. Langoustine is so satin-sweet against a punchy bisque and cool espuma that accompanying asparagus and morels are almost surplus to requirements. Pudding might be an assembly of strawberries, chocolate and tarragon, blowsy-looking in its glass bowl, which turns out to be seductively soft and fragrant. Knowledgeable wine service supports a quality list, from £18.50.
Chef/s: Nicolas Valmagna. **Open:** Tue to Sat D only 7 to 10. **Closed:** Sun, Mon, 25 and 26 Dec, first 2 weeks Jan. **Meals:** set D £59 (3 courses) to £67. **Details:** 24 seats. V menu. Bar. Wheelchairs. Music. Parking.

▌ St Peter Port, Guernsey
La Frégate
Cooking score: 4
Modern British | £40
Beauregard Lane, Les Cotils, St Peter Port, Guernsey, GY1 1UT
Tel no: (01481) 724624
lafregatehotel.com
£5 OFF

The frigate is grounded on a hill, snug within its own secluded gardens, overlooking the pretty harbour at St Peter Port, where cruise liners hover in the middle distance. A many-windowed dining room done in crisp white napery and nautical blue makes the most of the sea vistas, and Neil Maginnis brings 20 years of continuity to the kitchen. That allows him to offer an extensive choice that may take in local scallops with braised pork, pancetta and pea purée, or crab and sweetcorn risotto, as preludes to classic tournedos Rossini, five-spiced duck breast with roasted plums, and carefully seared brill fillet with mussels and leeks in beurre noisette. There are more straightforward steaks and fish for the consolidators, and a range of French-inspired desserts such as praline parfait in chocolate sauce, and apple tarte fine with vanilla ice cream and caramel syrup. Wines open with a house selection from £22, or £6.50 a glass.

Chef/s: Neil Maginnis. **Open:** all week L 12 to 1.30, D 7 to 9.30. **Meals:** main courses £20 to £26. Set L £18 (2 courses) to £24. Set D £29 (2 courses) to £37. **Details:** 70 seats. 20 seats outside. V menu. Music. Parking.

LOCAL GEM
Da Nello
Italian | £35
46 Lower Pollet, St Peter Port, Guernsey, GY1 1WF
Tel no: (01481) 721552
danello.gg
£5 OFF

Island ingredients play a leading role at this long-running Italian joint with a covered courtyard in a building dating from 1450. Chancre crab salad, lobster linguine or a tomato risotto topped with char-grilled brill, bass, scallops and prawns, the cooking is straight and true. Aberdeen Angus steaks come with classic sauces, and porcini mushrooms keep company with local scallops – and note the set lunch is a bargain. The mostly Italian wine list has some French bins; bottle prices start at £16.95.

▌ St Peter, Jersey
Mark Jordan at the Beach
Cooking score: 3
Modern British | £36
La Plage, La Route de la Haule, St Peter, Jersey, JE3 7YD
Tel no: (01534) 780180
markjordanatthebeach.com

This easy-going seafront venue sees Mark Jordan going casual, swapping his best bib and tucker for shorts and flip-flops. Better known as the chef behind the Ocean Restaurant at St Brelade's prestigious Atlantic Hotel (see entry), he set up this spin-off as a casual, affordable option for Jersey holidaymakers and locals alike. Done out with wicker chairs, seaside artwork and nautical trinkets, it delivers a please-all assortment of well-honed bistro-style dishes: Scotch eggs, burgers, fishcakes and battered cod appear right on cue, but they're joined by some more fanciful ideas from the pan-European repertoire – think hake fillet with confit shallots, sautéed wild mushrooms and caraway cabbage or five-spice duck breast with leg cannelloni, caramelised figs and vanilla jus. For a big blowout, tackle the 30-hour braised Harmony Farm short rib with horseradish pomme purée before rounding off with salted chocolate tart. Wines from £16.

Chef/s: Mark Jordan and Tamas Varsanyi. **Open:** all week L 12 to 2.30, D 6 to 9.30. **Closed:** Mon (winter), 7 to 22 Nov. **Meals:** main courses £15 to £35. Set L £20 (2 courses) to £25. Set D £28. Sun L £28. **Details:** 50 seats. 30 seats outside. Bar. Music. Parking.

■ St Saviour, Jersey
Longueville Manor
Cooking score: 5
Modern British | £60
Longueville Road, St Saviour, Jersey, JE2 7WF
Tel no: (01534) 725501
longuevillemanor.com

This lavishly decorated Norman house, cocooned in 15 acres of grounds, has been nourished by generations of the Lewis family, ably assisted by a brigade of faultlessly tutored staff who are reckoned to be 'the best on the island'. Longueville is 'so much more than a restaurant', although long-serving chef Andrew Baird also cares about the 'tiny details', matching the sumptuous all-enveloping surroundings with refined cooking of the best sort. His food is 'the stuff of dreams' – a geographically apposite amalgam of French and English traditions, buoyed up by the hotel's kitchen garden. A leisurely stroll through the menu might take you from butter-poached lobster with shumai and Asian broth or roast free-range quail with glazed grapes, fig, ginger, orange and quail's egg to a délice of sole with local shellfish or roast Gressingham duck breast with confit bonbon and plum-tomato jam. After that, passion fruit soufflé with raspberry ripple sorbet is worth the wait. An ever-expanding choice of stunning wines by the glass and half-bottle is good news for drinkers who want to explore the jaw-dropping breadth of Longueville's magisterial 400-bin list. House selections from £28.

Chef/s: Andrew Baird. **Open:** all week L 12 to 2, D 6 to 10. **Meals:** set L £25 (2 courses) to £30. Set D £53 (2 courses) to £60. Sun L £40. Tasting menu £80 (7 courses). **Details:** 90 seats. 35 seats outside. V menu. Bar. Music. Parking.

NORTHERN IRELAND

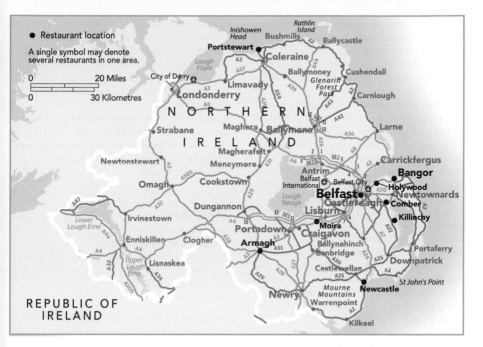

Restaurant location

A single symbol may denote several restaurants in one area.

▮ Armagh, Co Armagh
Uluru Bar & Grill

Cooking score: 2
Australian | £30
3-5 Market Street, Armagh, Co Armagh,
BT61 7BX
Tel no: (028) 3751 8051
ulurubistro.com

Owners Gavin Emerson and Dean Coppard met on Bondi Beach and when opening this bar and grill – or 'house of good spirit' as one reader describes it – they chose to name it after the sacred rock formation in the central Australian desert. The Aussie vibe runs deep, not least in the easy-going charm of the place, but also in the culinary output, where regional ingredients from this part of the world are given a global flavour. Starters take in Thai-style crispy chicken with Asian slaw and pan-seared pigeon breasts with wild mushroom risotto. Move on to a steak or burger cooked on the Josper grill, a stone-baked pizzette or daily specials such as goat curry or seafood pie.

Finish with a dark chocolate and rum tart. Weekend brunches and breakfast until noon increase its usefulness. Wines start at £14.95.
Chef/s: Dean Coppard. **Open:** all week 12 to 9 (10 Thur to Sun). **Closed:** 25 and 26 Dec, 1 Jan.
Meals: main courses £14 to £25. Early D £15 (2 courses) to £19. Sun L £16 (2 courses). **Details:** 155 seats. 16 seats outside. Bar. Wheelchairs. Music.

▮ Bangor, Co Down
The Boat House

Cooking score: 6
Modern European | £35
1a Seacliff Road, Bangor, Co Down, BT20 5HA
Tel no: (028) 9146 9253
theboathouseni.co.uk

The Victorian former harbourmaster's office and lifeboat station by the marina is illuminated in sea-blue at night to indicate its repurposing as a chic modern restaurant. Inside, the roughcast stone walls and tiled floor make a clean, simple backdrop for the Castel brothers' classy operation. Joery Castel's modernist commitments produce a diverting blend of European and Asian elements in dishes that don't stint on complexity of construction. That's easily seen in an opener that combines porridge oat biscuits with Kearny Blue cheese, carrots, white chocolate, macadamias and mizuna in blue cheese and macadamia cream. A steady nerve is held for mains such as sea trout with potato and almond cake, caper powder, parsley gel and potato sauce, or glazed pork belly with a Malaysian steamed bun, kumquat jelly and spiced coconut. And why stop there, when dessert might bring on maple syrup and buttermilk pannacotta with pecan churro and cider-laced apple compression? The well-written wine list starts at £18.50.

Chef/s: Joery Castel. **Open:** Wed to Sat L 12.30 to 2.30, D 5.30 to 10. Sun 1 to 9. **Closed:** Mon, Tue, 1 Jan. **Meals:** main courses £10 to £22. Set L £28 (2 courses) to £33. Set D £30 (2 courses) to £35. **Details:** 40 seats. 8 seats outside. Bar. Wheelchairs. Music. Parking.

■ Belfast, Co Antrim
Eipic
Cooking score: 4
Modern European | £40
28-40 Howard Street, Belfast, Co Antrim, BT1 6PF
Tel no: (028) 9033 1134
michaeldeane.co.uk
£5
OFF

Belfast restaurant supremo Michael Deane's latest venture could easily fall into the generic category of 'gastrodome' – a culinary multiplex involving the casual Love Fish and bullish Meat Locker as well as this aspirational contemporary brasserie. Ignore the limited opening times and the curious name (a rather laboured Irish pun on 'epic') and focus, instead, on the trend-conscious tasting menus dished up by chef Danni Barry and her team. After some intriguing amuse-style nibbles, the serious business might begin with a Nordic-inspired plate of wood blewits, duck egg yolk and mushroom ketchup; then, perhaps turbot with salt-baked celeriac and roasted bone-

marrow sauce followed by Mourne lamb with charred greens and black garlic; finally, diners are offered a single dessert (perhaps a pairing of poached rhubarb and sweet cheese with pink peppercorns) plus a choice of cheeses from the trolley. An extensive global wine list kicks off at £25.50.

Chef/s: Danni Barry. **Open:** Fri L 12 to 2.30, Wed to Sat D 5.30 to 9.30. **Closed:** Sun, Mon, Tue, 17 to 28 Dec, 1 Jan, Jul. **Meals:** Set D £60 (Sat). Tasting menu £40 to £60 (Wed to Fri). **Details:** 30 seats. Bar. Wheelchairs. Music.

Hadskis
Cooking score: 2
Modern European | £30
33 Donegall Street, Belfast, Co Antrim, BT1 2NB
Tel no: (028) 9032 5444
hadskis.co.uk

Found on a pedestrianised cobbled alleyway that's also home to the historic Duke of York pub ('a must-see in Belfast'), Hadskis is from the stable of acclaimed local chef/restaurateur Niall McKenna (see entry, James Street South). Named after the family who owned the iron foundry that once stood here, this eatery feels of the moment with its muted grey tones, cool bar, bare tables and kitchen counter-stools – an impression reinforced by the eclectic, brasserie-style food. The charcoal grill holds centre stage, but the menu covers a lot of ground, from a generous dish of Kilkeel scallops with cannellini beans and 'nduja ('great textures, a fiery kick of chilli') and 'delicious, crisp' gnudi with 'sweet, silky' peperonata, capers and basil to roast chicken with celery, crisp salsify and mushroom cream. There's an excellent-value one-course lunch, say flat iron, bone-marrow butter and chips, daily fish and charcuterie specials, and there are two-course 'meat feasts' on Wednesdays. Wines start at £17.

Chef/s: David Scott. **Open:** all week 12 to 9.30 (11am Sat and Sun, 10pm Thur to Sat). **Closed:** 25 and 26 Dec, 1 Jan, 16 and 17 Apr, 12 Jul. **Meals:** main courses £12 to £19. **Details:** 40 seats. 10 seats outside. Bar. Wheelchairs. Music.

Il Pirata

Cooking score: 3
Italian | £22
279-281 Upper Newtownards Road,
Ballyhackamore, Belfast, Co Antrim, BT4 3JF
Tel no: (028) 9067 3421
ilpiratabelfast.com
£5 OFF £30

White tiles, dangling light bulbs and a mishmash of chairs and tables give Il Pirata a street cred that is matched by a menu that delivers the populist flavours of Italy (via New York, maybe). Sharing is the best way to go, opening with cicchetti such as mushroom arancini or spiced pork and fennel slider, and pizzetta topped with the likes of Sicilian lamb, hazelnuts and truffled honey. There are big plates, too; scallop and prawn linguine, for example, or grilled chicken with chorizo and a roast pepper sauce. Sweet plates include the house tiramisu or a pannacotta flavoured with Amaretto. It's a chilled-out, lively sort of place where a spice pear Bellini or Italian sour might wet your whistle before delving into the global wine list. Wines start at £17.50.
Chef/s: Kyle Lockhart. **Open:** all week 12 to 10 (11 Fri and Sat, 9 Sun). **Closed:** 25 and 26 Dec.
Meals: main courses £11 to £15. Set L £8 (2 courses) to £10. Set D £15 (2 courses) to £18. **Details:** 80 seats. Bar. Wheelchairs. Music. Parking.

James Street South

Cooking score: 6
Modern European | £35
21 James Street South, Belfast, Co Antrim,
BT2 7GA
Tel no: (028) 9043 4310
jamesstreetsouth.co.uk

There's an enjoyable air of informality at Niall McKenna's ambitious city-centre venue. The Bar and Grill is for simpler food, but for the full modern Irish experience, the main dining room, with its slender white pillars, arches and flying-saucer light fittings, is the place. David Gillmore heads up an enthusiastic kitchen brigade that brings its energies to bear on thoroughbred regional produce. Hannan's

corned beef with Brussels sprouts, leeks and horseradish competes with the signature crab lasagne in brown crab and lemongrass bisque as openers to poached guinea fowl with celery, apple and mustard sauce, or a hefty serving of turbot on the bone, simply dressed in capers and parsley. A five-course tasting menu spans the range, from cured Glenarm salmon in passion fruit to baked Armagh apple with roasted nuts and Clandeboye yoghurt, or you might opt to finish petits fours-style with a plate of chocolate truffles and fruit jellies. Wines start at £18, or £5 a standard glass.
Chef/s: David Gillmore. **Open:** Tue to Sat L 12.30 to 2.30, Mon to Sat D 5.30 to 9.30. **Closed:** Sun, 25 and 26 Dec, 1 to 3 Jan, Easter Sun and Mon, 11 to 13 Jul.
Meals: main courses £16 to £24. Set L and D £16 (2 courses) to £19. **Details:** 65 seats. Wheelchairs. Music.

Mourne Seafood Bar

Cooking score: 3
Seafood | £35
34-36 Bank Street, Belfast, Co Antrim, BT1 1HL
Tel no: (028) 9024 8544
mourneseafood.com

The black frontage with its hanging baskets is the dignified outward face of a place that exists to celebrate the riches of the sea. Sourcing directly each day from the local ports of Annalong and Kilkeel, the kitchen wears its heart on its sleeve and its name in the foothills of the Mourne at Dundrum, where the original branch is located. Oysters sprinkled with mignonette pepper dressing, Tabasco and lemon is as fundamentalist as seafood gets, but they'll Japanese them for you with pickled ginger and shoyu if that's your bag. Elsewhere, expect laden bowls of chowder, piri-piri prawns with warm focaccia for sopping up the juices, and showpiece main courses like hake with roast garlic mash and a portobello mushroom in bacon and cider velouté, or spiced cod with curried slaw and crab fries. A 20-minute wait is rewarded with a whole fish – plaice or sea bass. House wines are £16.75 (£4.50 a glass).

Chef/s: Andy Rea. **Open:** Mon to Thur and Sun 12 to 9.30 (1 to 9 Sun). Fri and Sat L 12 to 4, D 5 to 10.30. **Meals:** main courses £9 to £23. **Details:** 80 seats. Bar. Wheelchairs.

★ NEW ENTRY ★

The Muddlers Club
Cooking score: 3
Modern European | £55
Warehouse Lane, Cathedral Quarter, Belfast, Co Antrim, BT1 2DX
Tel no: (028) 9031 3199
themuddlersclubbelfast.com
£5
OFF

The Cathedral Quarter of Belfast has got its hipster gear on these days, all warehouse conversions and cool graffiti. Take heart: what looks like a faintly insalubrious dark alley leads to the Muddlers, an industrial-chic bar-restaurant with filament light bulbs, brickwork, naked ducting and tattooed staff. Gareth McCaughey's food splashes in the currents of Euro-modernism, stuffing sage-buttered ravioli with ricotta, slicing gently charred lamb carpaccio-thin and piling it with mozzarella and inspired spiced tomatoes. At main, a monster fillet of halibut appears in spring veg array with a scattering of tinily diced pancetta, while the humble brigade of partners for duck – turnips, apple, black cabbage – are rather elevated by the enriching element of a foie gras jus. Dessert might be a populist assemblage of chocolate, caramel and espresso ice cream, or baked rice pudding with fragrant plum and lavender ice cream. A short but smart wine list offers nearly everything by the glass, from £4.75, with bottles from £17.
Chef/s: Gareth McCaughey. **Open:** Tue to Sat L 12 to 2.45, D 5.30 to 10. **Closed:** Sun, Mon, 24 to 26 Dec, Easter, 10 to 20 Jul. **Meals:** main courses £13 to £23. **Details:** 50 seats. Wheelchairs. Music. No children after 9pm.

OX
Cooking score: 6
Modern European | £35
1 Oxford Street, Belfast, Co Antrim, BT1 3LA
Tel no: (028) 9031 4121
oxbelfast.com
£5
OFF

A contemporary venue for a transformed city dining scene, Alain Kerloc'h and Stephen Toman's riverside restaurant overlooks the Lagan. Its light-filled space goes for the pared-down look, with whitewashed brick walls and unclothed small wood tables, and Toman offers short menus of modern Euro-food with the emphasis on seasonality. The quality of prime materials means that flavours stand out in three dimensions. If the name misleads you into expecting char-grilled steaks, be pleasantly surprised to find hay-baked celeriac with black trompettes and parsley to start, or scallops in lemongrass bisque. There is some beef for main, a regal serving of chateaubriand no less, along with ox tongue, chestnuts and cavolo nero, while fish may be pearly halibut teamed with mussels, salsify and sea lettuce. Technical wizardry adds lustre to desserts such as caramelised apple and treacle with figleaf ice cream, and the cheeses come garnished with fermented celeriac. An expertly chosen list has many good producers at keen prices, from £24.
Chef/s: Stephen Toman. **Open:** Tue to Sat L 12 to 2.30, D 6 to 9.30. **Closed:** Sun, Mon, 24 to 31 Dec, 1 week Easter, 2 weeks Jul. **Meals:** main courses £16 to £24. Set L £16 (2 courses) to £20. Tasting menu £45 (5 courses). **Details:** 40 seats. V menu. Bar. Wheelchairs. Music.

Shu

Cooking score: 4
Modern European | £32
253 Lisburn Road, Belfast, Co Antrim,
BT9 7EN
Tel no: (028) 9038 1655
shu-restaurant.com

£5 OFF 🍷

Set in a Victorian terrace on the Lisburn Road,
Shu has pretty much everything going for it
that we expect in a city dining venue: a
basement bar for cocktails, a ground-floor
restaurant offering modern European
brasserie dishes, done up in dark wood and
clubby brown leather, and a name from
Egyptian mythology. The place fairly buzzes
with a knowledgeable crowd who appreciate
the lively, confident cooking of Brian
McCann. His range of reference takes in
smoked haddock risotto with egg and
coriander, or buffalo mozzarella garnished
with Kalamata olives, pickled pumpkin and
chilli to kick off, followed perhaps by a gutsy
pairing of halibut and black pudding in
roasting juices and a forest floor's worth of
mushrooms. Beef sirloin is aged in the now
indispensable Himalayan salt chamber, and
desserts are designed to set taste-buds tingling
with white miso crème, green-tea crumbs and
kumquat marmalade. An expertly chosen list
of varietally arranged wines comes at
reasonable asking prices, opening at £17.50.
Chef/s: Brian McCann. **Open:** Mon to Sat L 12 to
2.30, D 5.30 to 9.30 (6 to 10 Sat). **Closed:** Sun, 24 to
26 Dec, 11 to 13 Jul. **Meals:** main courses £13 to
£27. Set L £13 (2 courses) to £19. Set D £23 (2
courses) to £28. **Details:** 80 seats. Bar. Music.
Parking.

Symbols

🛏 Accommodation is available
£30 Three courses for less than £30
£5 OFF £5-off voucher scheme
🍷 Notable wine list

The Ginger Bistro

Modern British | £35
7-8 Hope Street, Belfast, Co Antrim, BT12 5EE
Tel no: (028) 9024 4421
gingerbistro.com

Jolly conversation, keen prices and unfussy
décor are the hallmarks of Simon McCance's
Belfast bistro – a haven for fans of freestyle
food. Die-hards can order fish soup followed
by steak and chips, but the kitchen also dips its
toes in the global tub for some fancy eclectic
dishes ranging from twice-cooked duck with
wilted carrot salad and plum sauce to soy-
braised pork belly with sweet potato purée,
sautéed scallop, squid and chickpeas. After
that, perhaps try 'pears and cream' with
Champagne jelly. Wines from £17.50.

■ Comber, Co Down

Schoolhouse

Cooking score: 4
Modern British | £31
100 Ballydrain Road, Comber, Co Down,
BT23 6EA
Tel no: (028) 9754 1182
theoldschoolhouseinn.com

£5 OFF 🛏

Chef Will Brown did part of his learning away
from the family's schoolhouse turned B&B,
and lessons picked up in some of London's best
kitchens have produced a 'superb' restaurant. In
the school halls, all parquet flooring and
tactile art, Brown's clear-sighted pursuit of
quality takes form in dishes like Ballydugan
Estate pheasant cannelloni with chanterelles,
horseradish, almond and sea beet or a main
course of Mourne lamb with goats' curd,
onion and walnut. There's no snobbery here;
you can have a good-value five-course tasting
menu with matched wines, or equally
investigate the classic dishes including a
burger, fish and chips or Strangford Lough
fisherman's pie. It all involves liberal use of
produce from the restaurant's kitchen garden.
Dish descriptions can be coy, but puddings

like iced banana with peanut and malt ice cream tend to hit the sweet spot. Wines are from £18.

Chef/s: Will Brown. **Open:** Wed to Sun 12.30 to 9.30 (8 Sun). **Closed:** Mon, Tue. **Meals:** main courses £13 to £24. Set L and D £14 (2 courses) to £19. Sun L £25. **Details:** 60 seats. 20 seats outside. V menu. Bar. Wheelchairs. Music. Parking.

▌Holywood, Co Down

LOCAL GEM
The Bay Tree
Modern British | £20
118 High Street, Holywood, Co Down, BT18 9HW
Tel no: (028) 9042 1419
baytreeholywood.co.uk

£30

Things start bright and early at the easy-going Bay Tree with breakfast such as a full fry-up or something a little lighter. Next up, lunch is served, smoked fish chowder, say, with wheaten bread, and there are cakes to eat in or take away (the cinnamon scone has made a name for itself, apparently). Friday night dinner sees the ante upped with the kitchen turning out oxtail and Guinness soup, followed by spiced hake with Indian-style accompaniments. Wines start at £15.

▌Killinchy, Co Down
Balloo House
Cooking score: 2
Modern British | £27
1 Comber Road, Killinchy, Co Down, BT23 6PA
Tel no: (028) 9754 1210
balloohouse.com

£30

The 400-year-old white-fronted former farmhouse by Strangford Lough incorporates a straightforward ground-floor pub, with the option of aspirant dining at weekends in the first-floor restaurant. Live music nights mingle Irish and bluegrass in creative fusion, and Danny Millar strives for the same effect in the kitchen, where European and Asian elements mix it with traditional Irish and British modes. Lough mussels are immersed in Armagh cider with shallots and apple, while the whitebait is fried crisp in salt and chilli and served with Asian slaw and chipotle mayo. Among mains, chicken breasts are Thai-spiced, cod glazed in miso and partnered with tempura green beans and wasabi, and the locally reared beef is dry-aged for 28 days in a salt chamber before being béarnaised up and sent to your table. Dessert combinations of surpassing loveliness include peach sundae with berry ripple ice cream, honeycomb and a warm cinnamon doughnut. The well-written wine list begins with house Chileans at £16.45.

Chef/s: Danny Millar. **Open:** all week 12 to 9.30. **Closed:** 25 Dec. **Meals:** main courses £10 to £26. Set L and D £15 (2 courses) to £19. Sun L £23. **Details:** 90 seats. Bar. Wheelchairs. Music. Parking.

▌Moira, Co Armagh

★ LOCAL RESTAURANT OF THE YEAR ★
OVERALL WINNER

★ NEW ENTRY ★

Wine & Brine
Cooking score: 3
Modern British | £27
59 Main Street, Moira, Co Armagh, BT67 0LQ
Tel no: (028) 9261 0500
wineandbrine.co.uk

£5 OFF £30

Chris McGowan is a native Northern Irishman who returned home in 2015 after a good few years working for Richard Corrigan in London. The place that he and wife Davina have opened takes its place among the shops and pubs on Moira's high street as a relaxed town-centre venue offering regional produce, with on-trend preserving techniques – ageing, curing, pickling – a big feature. High Georgian ceilings and an open kitchen make the place feel airy and relaxed, but the next thing to catch your eye may well be the astonishingly restrained prices. There's certainly no stinting on quality, as witness a

pair of chorizo dumplings that have a creamy onion soup poured over them, with hits of fennel adding edge. That could presage a main of hefty ham knuckle with garlicky, truffly white bean purée, topped with avocado and capers in salsa verde, but a domed, thin-crusted pie of steak and mushroom covered in thyme with rich mushroom ketchup is also glorious. Generous desserts include a hazelnut ice cream version of affogato, or crème caramel adorned with brandy-drenched raisins. A concise wine list does its job from £18.
Chef/s: Chris McGowan. **Open:** Tue to Sat L 12 to 3, D 6 to 9.30 (10 Fri and Sat). Sun 12 to 6. **Closed:** Mon, 2 weeks Jan, 2 weeks Aug. **Meals:** main courses £11 to £28. Set L £11 (2 courses) to £14. Sun L £18 (2 courses) to £22. **Details:** 70 seats. 12 seats outside. V menu. Bar. Wheelchairs. Music.

▮ Newcastle, Co Down
Vanilla
Cooking score: 3
Modern British | £35
67 Main Street, Newcastle, Co Down, BT33 0AE
Tel no: (028) 4372 2268
vanillarestaurant.co.uk

Darren Ireland's family has cooking in its genes, and Vanilla represents his own contribution to an illustrious culinary lineage. Unmissable on Newcastle's high street, it's a breezily informal venue with banquette seating, tiled walls and globe light fixtures, where carefully worked modern Irish brasserie food incorporates touches of continental tradition and aromatic east Asian notes, too. A starter combines crispy pig's head and charred squid with celeriac and pickled apple, before a herb-crusted rump of Blackface lamb shows up in spectacular array, alongside some shredded shoulder meat, Parmesan gnocchi, caramelised onion purée, roast shallots, artichoke and broccoli. Pan-roasted salmon receives the Thai treatment with spiced rice and gremolata, all scented up with coriander, lemongrass, ginger and caramelised lime. Simple soup and sandwich lunches are a draw, while early-birders have a top-value menu to

go at. Divine decadence arrives at dessert stage in the form of lemon brûlée with peanut butter biscotti and ginger ice cream. Wines start at £17.50.
Chef/s: Alex Greene. **Open:** all week L 12 to 3.30, D 5 to 9.30 (5.30 Sat, 5 to 7 Sun). **Closed:** 25 Dec, 1 Jan. **Meals:** main courses £17 to £23. Set L and early D £16 (2 courses) to £20. **Details:** 40 seats. 8 seats outside. Wheelchairs. Music.

▮ Portstewart, Londonderry
Harry's Shack
Cooking score: 4
Seafood | £28
116 Strand Road, Portstewart, Londonderry, BT55 7PG
Tel no: (028) 7083 1783
£30

Right on the sandy beach, the roof of the Shack – a sturdy wooden, barn-like structure – has a covering of grass and sand to match the surrounding dunes. It's a visceral spot, which may well bring out your inner child, and whether you sit outside at a bench table or indoors at a chunky rustic one, the sea view is ready and waiting. Derek Creagh oversees the kitchen's output, as well as at Harry's Restaurant in Bridgend across the border in the Republic. The ideas are simple, the execution spot-on and tables hard to come by (be sure to book). Begin with hot-smoked salmon tart or some Asian-inspired honey and soy chicken wings, and if next you opt for fish and chips, expect a fine version with buttermilk batter. Main-course smoked cod comes with a spiced tomato and chorizo stew, and slow-cooked beef cheeks with mash and red wine sauce. Unlicensed, so BYO.
Chef/s: Derek Creagh. **Open:** All week summer 10.30 to 4, D 5 to 9. Call for winter openings. **Meals:** main courses £10 to £15. **Details:** 65 seats. 30 seats outside.

ATLAS MAPS

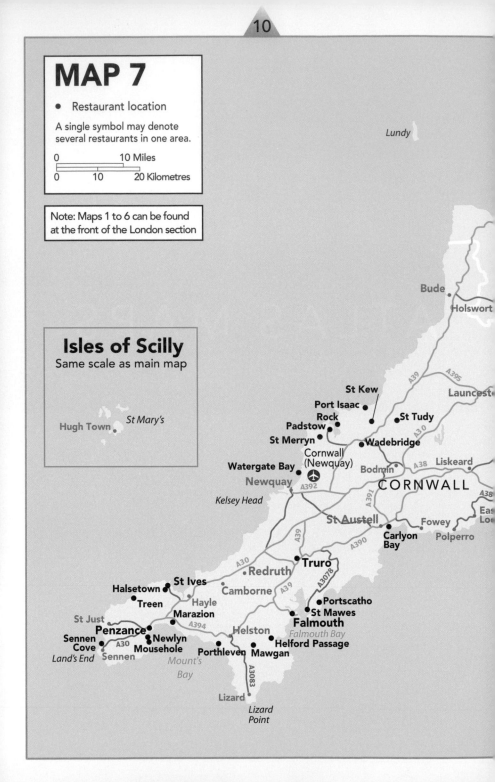

MAP 7

● Restaurant location

A single symbol may denote several restaurants in one area.

0   10 Miles

0   10   20 Kilometres

Note: Maps 1 to 6 can be found at the front of the London section

Isles of Scilly

Same scale as main map

Hugh Town   St Mary's

Lundy

Bude

Holswort

Launcest

St Kew

Port Isaac
Rock   St Tudy

Padstow

St Merryn   Wadebridge

Cornwall
(Newquay)

Watergate Bay   Bodmin   Liskeard

Newquay

CORNWALL

Kelsey Head

St Austell   Eas
Lo

Fowey

Carlyon
Bay   Polperro

Truro

Redruth

St Ives

Halsetown   Camborne

Portscatho

Treen   Hayle   St Mawes

Marazion   Falmouth

St Just

Penzance   Helston   Falmouth Bay

Sennen   Newlyn   Helford Passage

Cove   Mousehole   Porthleven   Mawgan

Land's End   Sennen

Mount's
Bay

Lizard

Lizard
Point

Bristol Channel

Weston-super-Mare

●Wrington 21

Cheddar

racombe

Lynton

Minehead

Burnham-
on-Sea ●

●Wedmore 22

A38

A371

●Lower
Godney

A39

A38

Bridgwater 23

Glastonbury

●aunton

A361

A39

Barnstaple

SOMERSET

A39

Street

Langport

●Instow

Knowstone ●

Wellington●

Taunton

A361

●Fivehead

25

Bideford ●

South
Molton

A361

26

M5

A38

A358

Great
Torrington ●

Kings
Nympton ●

Tiverton ●

27

Ilminster●

A303

Hinton
St George ●

A386

A388

Hatherleigh ●

Crediton

28

Clyst
Hydon ●

A373

Chard

A30

Crewkerne

A3072

A377

A3072

Exeter
●

Honiton ●

A358

Beaminster

D E V O N

Okehampton ●

Axminster ●

Bridport●

Drewsteignton ●

A30

Exeter

30

29

Topsham ●

Sidford ●

A3052

Seaton

Lyme
Regis

Lewdown ●

Chagford ●

31

Sidmouth

Lyme Bay

burley

A326

Dartmoor

A379

A376

Exmouth

●worthy

Tavistock ●

Bovey
Tracey

A380

Dawlish

90

Ashburton ●

A38

Teignmouth

Yelverton ●

Newton
Abbot

Shaldon ●

A388

Buckfastleigh ●

A385

Torquay ●

South
Brent ●

Totnes ●

Paignton

Sparkwell ●

Ivybridge

●Brixham

ash

Plymouth

A38

Dittisham ●

●brook

A379

Dartmouth

Kingsbridge

A381

A379

Bigbury-on-Sea ●

South
Pool

Salcombe ●

*Start
Point*

Channel
Islands
Not to same scale

Alderney

Alderney

Guernsey

St Peter Port ●
Guernsey

Herm

Sark

Jersey

St Peter ●

St Saviour ●

Jersey

●Gorey

St Brelade ●

●St Clement

St Helier

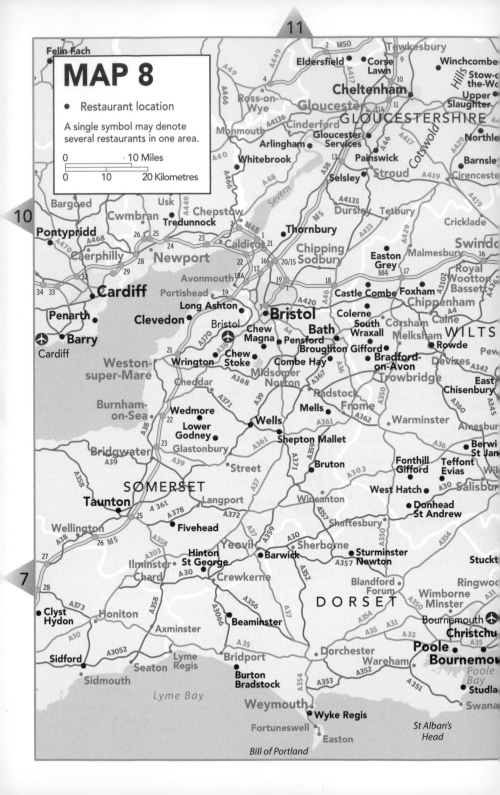

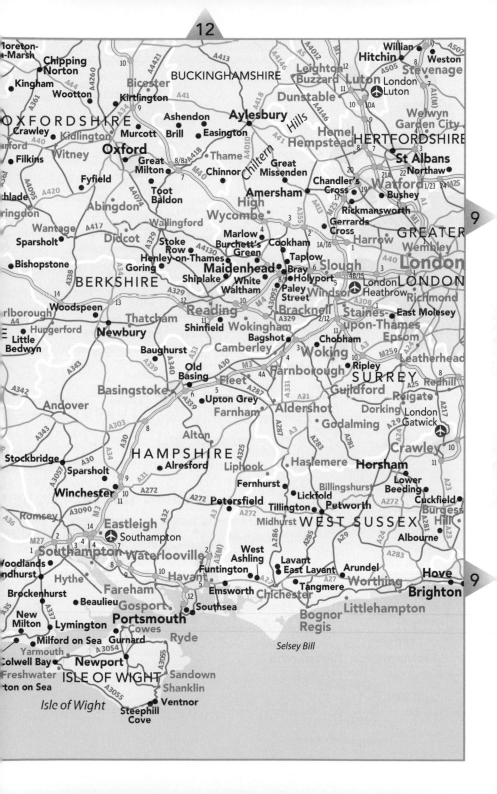

Moreton-in-Marsh
Chipping Norton
Kingham
Wootton
Kidlington
Crawley
Kidlington
Oxford
Filkins
Witney
Fyfield
Abingdon
Wantage
Sparsholt
Bishopstone
BERKSHIRE
Woodspeen
Hungerford
Little Bedwyn
Newbury
Baughurst
Old Basing
Basingstoke
Andover
Stockbridge
Sparsholt
Winchester
Romsey
Eastleigh
Southampton
Woodlands
Nursling
Hythe
Brockenhurst
Beaulieu
New Milton
Lymington
Milford on Sea
Yarmouth
Colwell Bay
Freshwater
Totton on Sea
Newport
ISLE OF WIGHT
Isle of Wight
Steephill Cove
Ventnor
Shanklin
Sandown
Ryde
Cowes
Gurnard

BUCKINGHAMSHIRE
Bicester
Kirtlington
Ashendon
Brill
Easington
Murcott
Great Milton
Thame
Chinnor
Toot Baldon
Wallingford
Stoke Row
Henley-on-Thames
Goring
Shiplake
White Waltham
Didcot
Marlow
Burchett's Green
Cookham
Taplow
Bray
Holyport
Paley Street
Bracknell
Reading
Shinfield
Wokingham
Bagshot
Camberley
Farnborough
Fleet
Upton Grey
Farnham
Alton
Alresford
LipHook
Fernhurst
HAMPSHIRE
Petersfield
Tillington
Midhurst
Waterlooville
Havant
Fareham
Gosport
Portsmouth
Southsea
Funtington
West Ashling
Emsworth
Chichester
Bognor Regis
Selsey Bill

Aylesbury
Chiltern Hills
Great Missenden
Amersham
High Wycombe
Maidenhead
Slough
Windsor
Staines-upon-Thames
Woking
Ripley
Guildford
Godalming
Haslemere
Billingshurst
Petworth
Lickfold
WEST SUSSEX
Lavant
East Lavant
Tangmere
Arundel
Worthing
Littlehampton

Leighton Buzzard
Dunstable
Hemel Hempstead
Chandler's Cross
Rickmansworth
Gerrards Cross
Harrow
GREATER
Wembley
London
LONDON
London Heathrow
Richmond
East Molesey
Epsom
Leatherhead
SURREY
Redhill
Reigate
Dorking
London Gatwick
Crawley
Horsham
Lower Beeding
Cuckfield
Burgess Hill
Albourne
Hove
Brighton

Willian
Hitchin
Weston
Stevenage
Luton
London Luton
Welwyn Garden City
HERTFORDSHIRE
St Albans
Northaw
Watford
Bushey

OXFORDSHIRE
Kingham
Crawley

Waterlooville
Chobham
Aldershot

9

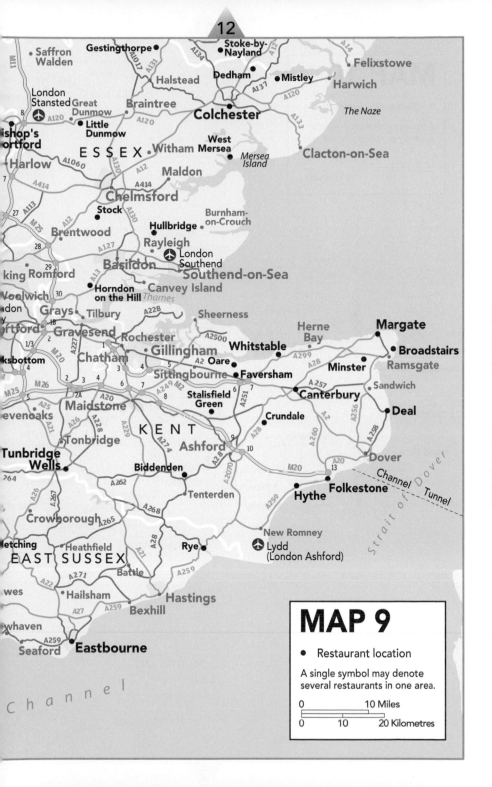

Saffron Walden
Gestingthorpe
Stoke-by-Nayland
Felixstowe
Halstead
Dedham
Mistley
Harwich
London Stansted
Great Dunmow
Braintree
Colchester
The Naze
Little Dunmow
ishop's ortford
ESSEX
Witham
West Mersea
Clacton-on-Sea
Mersea Island
Harlow
A1060
A414
A130
A12
Maldon
A414
Chelmsford
Stock
A130
Hullbridge
Burnham-on-Crouch
Brentwood
A127
Rayleigh
London Southend
Basildon
A13
Southend-on-Sea
king Romford
Horndon on the Hill
Canvey Island
Thames
Voolwich
Grays
Tilbury
A228
Sheerness
idon
Herne Bay
Margate
rtford
Gravesend
Rochester
A2500
Broadstairs
ksbottom
Chatham
Gillingham
Whitstable
A299
Minster
Ramsgate
A2
Oare
A28
M20
Sittingbourne
Faversham
A257
Sandwich
M26
Stalisfield Green
Canterbury
Deal
M25
Maidstone
A20
evenoaks
A26
A229
KENT
Crundale
A2
A256
Tonbridge
A274
Ashford
A28
A258
Tunbridge Wells
Biddenden
A2070
M20
Dover
264
A262
Tenterden
A299
Folkestone
Channel Tunnel
Crowborough
A265
Hythe
etching
Heathfield
A28
New Romney
Lydd (London Ashford)
EAST SUSSEX
Rye
Strait of Dover
Battle
A259
wes
Hailsham
Hastings
whaven
A27
A259
Bexhill
Seaford
A259
Eastbourne

Channel

MAP 9

- Restaurant location

A single symbol may denote several restaurants in one area.

| 0 | | 10 Miles |
| 0 | 10 | 20 Kilometres |

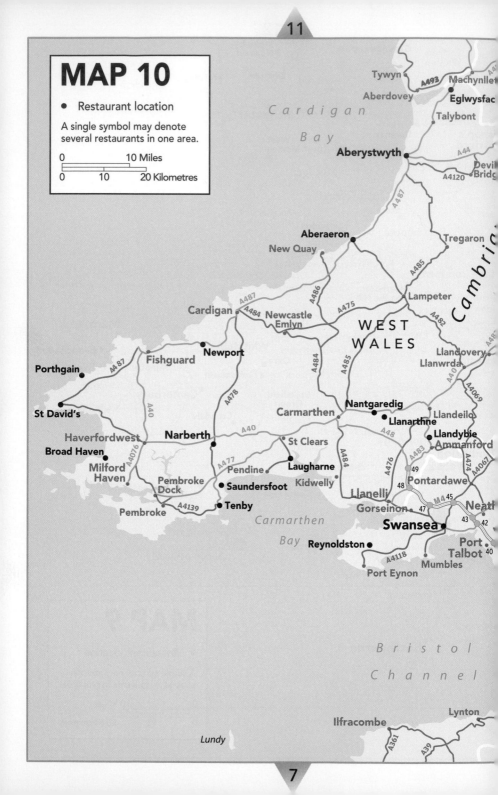

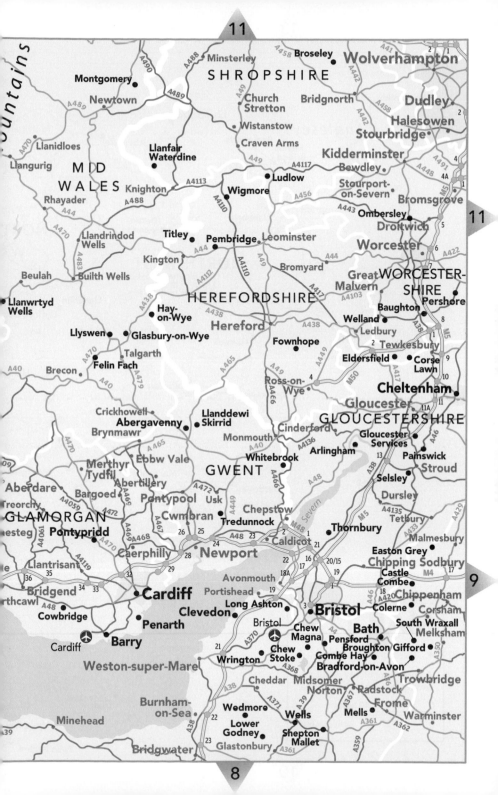

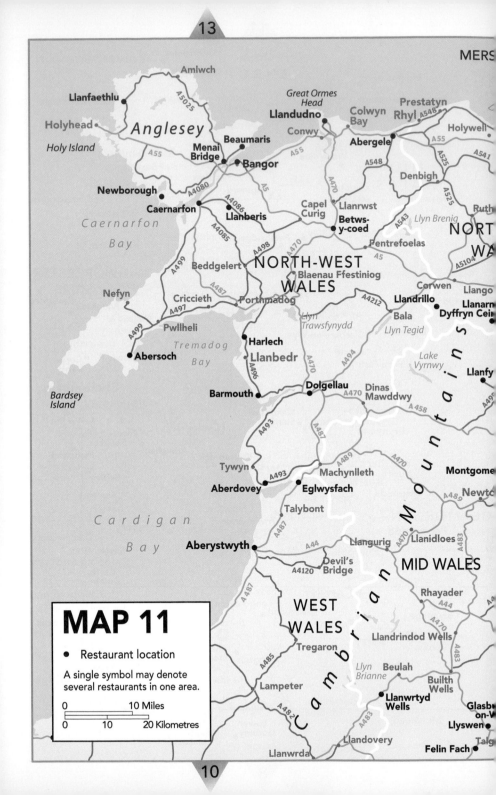

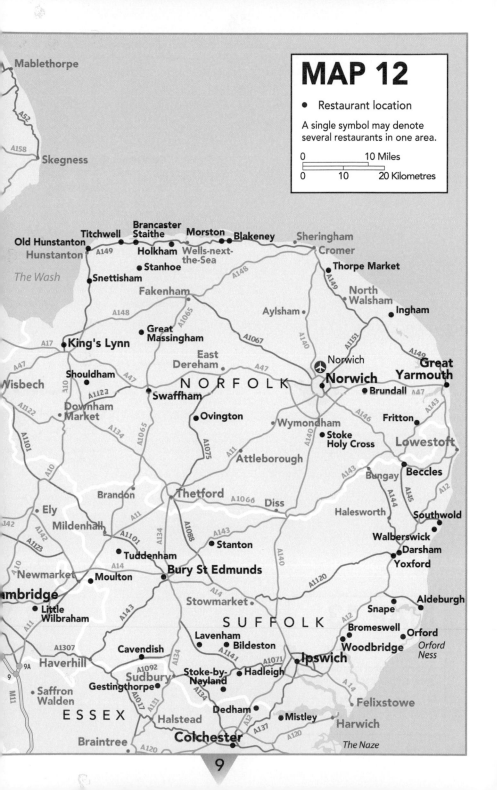

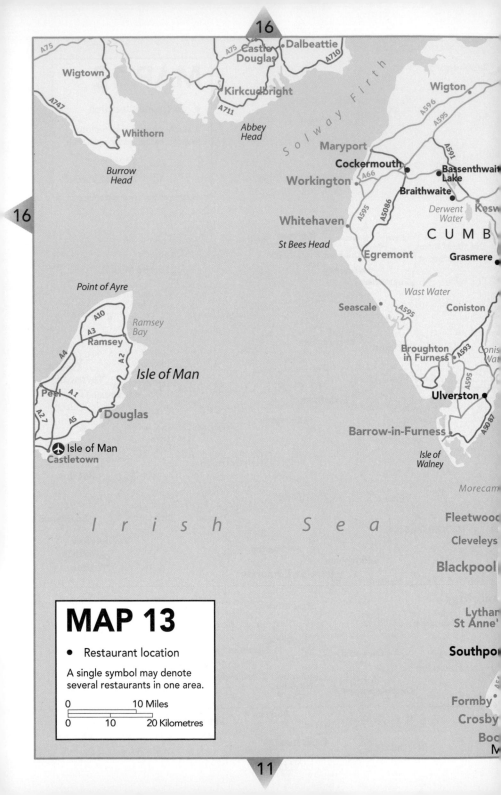

MAP 13

● Restaurant location

A single symbol may denote
several restaurants in one area.

0   10 Miles

0   10   20 Kilometres

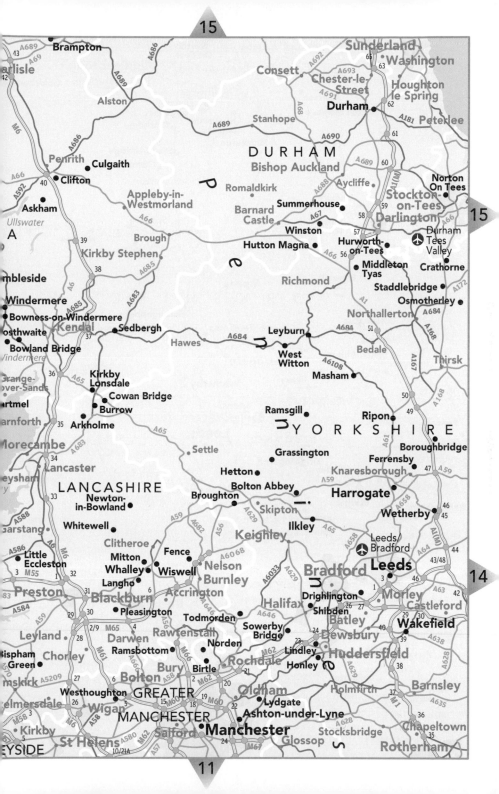

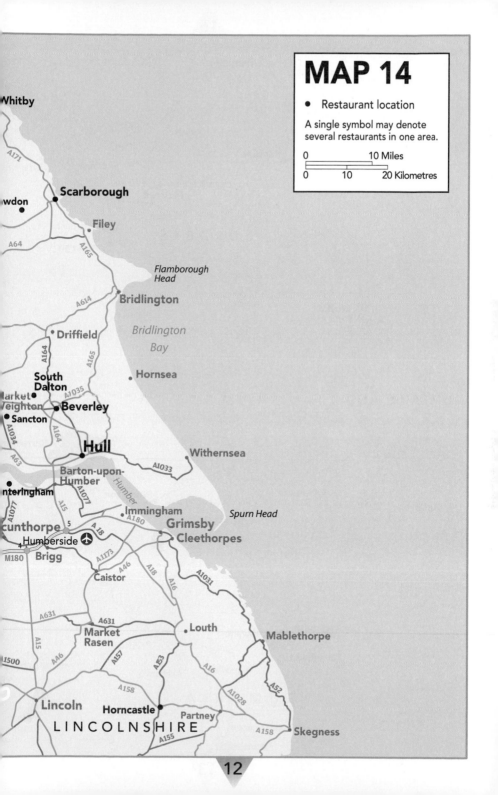

MAP 14

- Restaurant location

A single symbol may denote
several restaurants in one area.

0   10 Miles
0   10 20 Kilometres

Whitby

A171

wdon

Scarborough

Filey

A64

A165

Flamborough
Head

A614

Bridlington

Driffield

*Bridlington
Bay*

A164

A165

South
Dalton

Hornsea

A1035

Market
Weighton

Beverley

Sancton

A1034

A164

Hull

A63

Withernsea

A1033

Barton-upon-
Humber

Humber

nterIngham

A1077

A15

A1077

Immingham

A180

Spurn Head

cunthorpe 5

Grimsby

A18

Humberside ✈

Cleethorpes

4

M180 Brigg

A1173

Caistor

A46

A18

A16

A1031

A631

A631

Market
Rasen

Louth

Mablethorpe

A15

A46

A157

A153

A16

A52

A158

A1028

Lincoln

Horncastle

Partney

A158

Skegness

LINCOLNSHIRE

A155

12

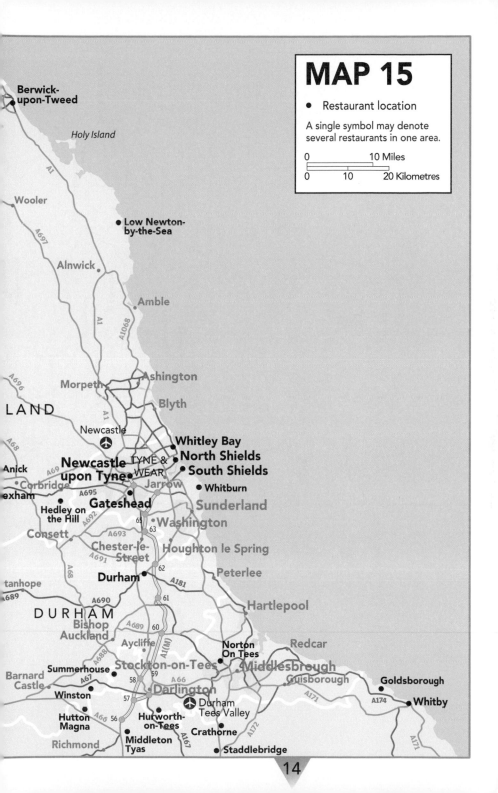

MAP 15

- Restaurant location

A single symbol may denote
several restaurants in one area.

0   10 Miles
0   10   20 Kilometres

Berwick-
upon-Tweed

Holy Island

Wooler

Low Newton-
by-the-Sea

Alnwick

Amble

A1068

A1

A697

A696

Morpeth

Ashington

LAND

Blyth

A1

Newcastle

Whitley Bay

North Shields

Newcastle
upon Tyne

TYNE &
WEAR

South Shields

Anick

A69

Jarrow

Whitburn

Corbridge

exham

A695

Gateshead

Hedley on
the Hill

A692

Sunderland

A68

Consett

65

63

Washington

A693

Chester-le-
Street

Houghton le Spring

A691

Durham

62

A181

Peterlee

tanhope

A690

61

Hartlepool

A689

DURHAM

Bishop
Auckland

A689

60

A68

Aycliffe

Norton
On Tees

Redcar

A688

Summerhouse

Stockton-on-Tees

Middlesbrough

Barnard
Castle

A67

58

59

A66

Guisborough

Goldsborough

Winston

57

Darlington

A171

A174

Whitby

Hutton
Magna

A66

56

Hurworth-
on-Tees

Durham
Tees Valley

Crathorne

A172

Richmond

Middleton
Tyas

A167

Staddlebridge

A171

14

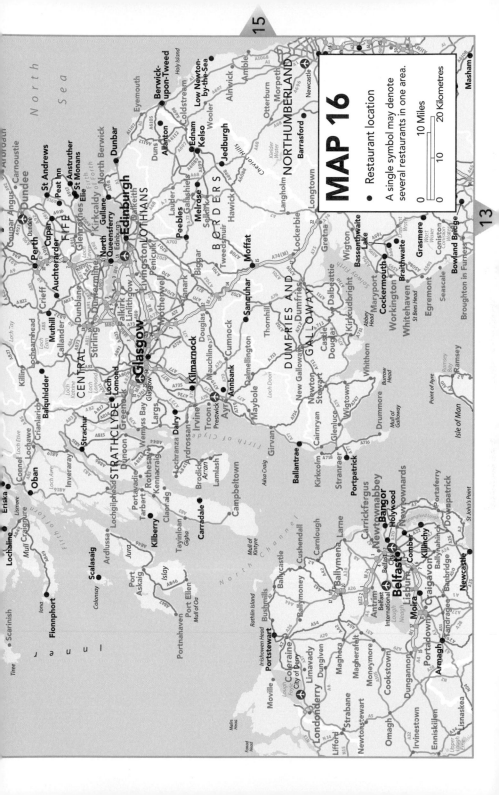

Note: The INDEX BY TOWN does not include London entries.

Join us at thegoodfoodguide.co.uk

Join us at thegoodfoodguide.co.uk

RESTAURANT | INDEX

Join us at thegoodfoodguide.co.uk

Thank you

This book couldn't have happened without a cast of thousands.
Our thanks are due to the following contributors,
among many others.

Sue Abela
Anthony Abrahams
Hannah Acking
Alasdair Adam
Judith Adam
Louise Adams
Margaret Adams
Nazneen Ahmad
Christine Ainsworth
  Smith
Caroline Aitchison
Sara Alali
Tim Aldridge
Lawrence
  Alexander
Philip Alexandrou
Emer Allan
Aisling Allardice
Chris Allen
Ian Allen
Roger Allen
Steph Allen
Kate Allison
Ben Ambridge
Donald Amer
Anthony Amos
Katie Amos
Jill Anderson
Yvonne Anderson
Julie Andrew
Victoria Andrews
Sebastian Anstey
Irene Archer
Melissa Ardern
Nikki Armes Read
Alison Armitage
Fiona Armstrong
Gill Armstrong
Hilary Armstrong
Richard Armstrong
Patrick Arnold
Sibel Arzulu
Phil Ascough
Janie Ash
Louise Ash
Amara Ashraf
Helen Ashton
Michael Ashwood
Helen Askew
Nadine Aspinwall
Catherine Astle
Kim Aston
Margaret Atherton
Paul Atkins

Elizabeth Atkinson
Suzi Attree
Frank Attwood
Terresa Aubrey
Holly Austen
Deborah Austin
Sharon
  Avard-Brown
Nigel Avey
Andrew Ayala
Bob Ayers
Suki Bahra
Anne Bailey
Jane Bailey
Samantha Bailey
Adrian Bain
Cameron Bain
Katie Bain
Christine
  Bainbridge
Jo Baines
Sarah Baines
Nicola Baker
Melvyn Bakewell
Denise Baldwin
Neil Baldwin
Jane Balinski
Mary Ballantine
Jan Ballard
Roger Bamber
Ashleigh Banks
Charlotte Banks
John Bannister
George Barber
Victoria Barden
Iain Barker
Richard Barker
Sharon Barker
Angela Barlow
Nina Barlow
Brad Barnes
David Barnes
Hannah Barnes
Steve Barnes
Sylvia Barnes
Graham Barnetson
Lorna Barnett
Franco Barnowski
Sian Barnsley
Rebecca Baron
Claire Barrett
Dean Barrett
Elizabeth Barrett
Deborah Barron

Lynda Barron
Chloe Bartle
Helen Barton
Robert Bass
Georgia Bateman
Gill Bates
Jackie Bates
Paul Bates
Thomas Bates
Jill Batson
Tim Battle
David Battrum
Lesley Beach
Stephen Beach
Kate Beacham
Robert Beaumont
Eileen Beaver
Peter Beddis
Quin Beech
Katie Belcher
Tracey Belcher
Amanda Bell
David Bell
Gayle Bell
Lord David Bell
Matt Bell
Steph Bell
John Belton
John Bence
David Benison
Ryan Bennett
Sheila Bennett
Suzy Bennett
Jackie Benny
Trevor Benson
Neil Berry
Tina Berry
Benjy Bethell
Vas Bevender
Robert Bewell
Rebecca Beynon
Dave Bielby
Liz Bignold
Tracey Binney
Thomas Binns
Diana Binstead
Victoria Birbeck
Chris Birch
Jen Bird
Daniel Bishop
Lucy Bishop
Val Bishopp
Mark Bixter
Robin Black

John Blackall
Mark Blackham
Caroline
  Blackmore
Vanessa Blackmore
Pat Blainey
Andrew Blair
Hannah Blake
Kevin Blake
Robert Blake
Sheryl Blanchard
Stephanie Bliss
Marina Blore
Martin Blore
Tim Boddington
Carol Bogle
Denise Bollans
Lexi Mai Bolt
Carol Bolton
Peter Bolton
Stephanie Bonnet
Alexis Boo
Darren Booth
Jill Booth
Peter Booth
Briony Bowers
Peter Bowers
Tara Bowers
Nicholas Bowlby
Romilly Bowlby
Will Bowlby
Rianna Bowles
Deena Bowman
Scott Bowman
Jacquie Boyce
Meriel Boyd
Glyn Brace
Lee Brace
Gill Bracey
Anthony Bradbury
Colin Bradford
Carla Bradley
Danny Bradley
Julian Bradley
Paul Bradley
Morrow Brady
Graham Bragg
David Braid
Jat Brainch
Jayne Bray
Simon Bray
Julie Breckon
Audrey Breese
Richard Brereton

Ilona Bricknell
Phil Briggs
Robert Brighton
Julian Britton
Mark Broadbent
Andrew Brodie
Sally Bromwich
Anthony Brooke
Tricia Brooking
Eric
  Brooks-Dowsett
Victoria Brotherson
Dawn Brough
Andrew Brown
Andy Brown
Angela Brown
Daniel Brown
Emily Brown
Jayne Brown
Lesley Brown
Penny Brown
Susan Brown
Suzanne Brown
Zoe Brown
Sue Browne
Tanya
  Bruce Lockhart
Jill Brumby
Jen Brush
Gail Bryson
Philip Bryson
Carol Buck
Joanne Buckley
Rachael Buckley
Stefan Buczacki
Malcolm Budd
Julia Bueno
Donna Buhagiar
Alex Bunning
Jayne Bunting
Stephen Burcham
Elaine Burke
Liam Burke
Susan Burley
Ally Burnett
James Burnham
Terence Burr
Timothy Burr
Peter Burrows
Richard Busby
Malcolm Bushell
Ken Butler
Sue Butler
Donna Butterfield

Sarah Butters
Bradley
  Butterworth
Jade Buttery
Sally Buttifant
Christopher Button
Nicky Button
Susan Byrne
Stephen Cabrera
Sara Caddel
Louise Cain
Janet Caines
Jenny Caley
Annette Callaghan
Anne Callan
Anthea Cameron
Archie Cameron
Donald Cameron
Flora Cameron
Jamie Cameron
Margaret Campbell
Sophie Campion
Robin Carey
Katie Carmichael
Ruth Carpenter
Katie Carr
Claire Carter
David Carter
Louise Carter
Molly Carter
Nicola Carter
Sue Carter
Philippa Cartmell
Matt Carver
Alina Casey
Brett Cash
Daryl Cashmore
Jane Cassell
James Casson
Vicky Caulfield
John Challis
Juliette
  Chamberlain
Liz Chamberlain
Christopher
  Chamberlin
Heidi Champion
Julie Chandler
Arun Chandran
Barbara Chapman
David Chapman
Gill Chapman
Laura Chapman
Sarah Chapman

Shirley Chapman
Mark Chard
Mark Charig
Janet Chase
Chelsey Cheadle
Gill Cheeseman
Sue Chesterman
Meryl Chetwood
Jose Cheung
Phil Cheung
Clare Chevassut
Angela Chidgey
Graham Chidgey
Sheila Child
Margaret Chilman
Lucy Chisholm
Hafiz Chittanoor
Pauline
  Christopher
Richard
  Christopher
Sally Church
Keith Churchill
Sue Churchill
Margaret Clancy
Jacqui Clark
Rachel Clark
Sarah Clark
Sophie Clark
Bernadette Clarke
Elaine Clarke
John Clarke
Lesley Clarke
Paul Clarke
Sheila Clarke
Paul Clay
Richard
  Claydon-Park
Robert Clayton
Sarah Clayton
Suzanne Clayton
Wendy Clegg
Charles
  Clifford-Turner
Diane Close
Richard Clothier
Si Clough
Susan Coar
Danielle Coates
Dave Cockerill
Gill Coe
Susan Coen
Ronald Coia
Di Coke
Stephen Cole
Sue Coleclough
Gemma Colk
Anne Collard
Steven Colley
Dianne Collier
Rosemary Collier
Stuart Collier
Kandy Collings
Keith Collings
Beverley Collins
Duncan Collins
Genna Collins
Patricia Collins
Roy Collins
John Patrick
  Connolly
Joanne Connor
Miriam Connor
Deirdre Conway
Jennifer Coogan

Joanne Cook
Michael Cook
Sheila Cook
Chris Cooke
Jane Cooke
Rebecca Cooke
Derek Cooknell
Abi Cooper
Ian Cooper
Kerry Cooper
Nicholas Cooper
Catherine Copley
Debbie Copper
Alistair Corbett
Tony Corbett
Claire Cordell
Natalie Corden
Anne Corrigan
Sally Cosgriff
Jennifer Coster
Lesley Costick
Anne Coulstock
Susan Coulthard
Frances Coupe
Paul Coupe
Jon Coupland
Jennifer Coward
Jim Cownie
Geoff Cowper
Anthony Cox
Fiona Crabtree
Joseph Craen
Wil Craig
Claire Craven
  Griffiths
Paul Crawley
Andy Creer
Paula Crewdson
Diane Critchard
David Critchley
Miriam Croasdale
Becky Crocker
Debbie Croft
Elaine Croft
David Crofts
Emily Cross
Eleanor Crossland
Chloe Crowe
Pauline Crowe
Anna Crowley
Morgan Crowley
Jamie Crowther
Paul Crowther
James Cullens
Frances Cummins
Paul Cunliffe
David Cunningham
Angharad
  Cunningham
  Jones
Cathy Curtis
Mark Curtis
Jenny Cuthbert
Stefan Dacyszyn
Russell Daems
Hannah Dakin
Vanessa Dale
Amber Dalton
Bethan Daniel
Sarah Daniels
Liz Dann
Paul Darby
Natalie Darnes
Ruth Darrah
Serena Davey

Erica Davidson
Izzi Davidson
Robert Davidson
Alan Davies
Claire Davies
Eddie Davies
Gomer Davies
Jane Davies
Kate Davies
Nigel Davies
Paul Davies
Rachael Davies
Sarahjane Davies
Tom Davies
Daska Davis
Helen Davis
Joceline Davis
Jules Davis
Natasha Davis
Sue Davis
Amy Dawes
Fiona Dawson
Elaine Day
Helen Day
Jean Day
Margaret Day
Peter Day
Maria Daza
Anne-Marie
  De Baudringhien
Sarah De Chair
Charles De Clerk
Claire De La Haye
Norman De Villiers
Cecelia Deacon
Kimberley Deamer
Richard Dean
Stuart Dean
Charles Dearlove
Jonathan Dearth
Caroline Debray
Nicholas Dee
Adam Deegan
Belinda Dennis
Jane Dennis
Ann Derizzio
Will Dexter
Vivienne Diazdavila
Helen Dickson
Laura Dickson
Rhiannon Dillon
Nick Dillow
Guy Dimond
Howard Dingwall
Natalie Dinh
Joan Dinning
Neda Djahansouzi
Owain Dobson
Martin Dodd
Christopher
  Dodson
Carole Doherty
Daniella Doherty
Stephen Dolphin
Wendy Dolton
Debbie Donnelly
Nicci Donnelly
Daphne Dooley
Gavin Douglas
Michael Doupe
Anthony Dove
Hamish Dow
Liz Doyle
Alan Drabble
Michael Drake

Emma Draper
Gill Draper
Alyssa Dreelan
Michelle Dubock
David Duckham
Raj Dudwall
Kate Duffell
Sally Duffell
Andrada Duinea
Kirstie Duke
Alistair Duncan
Benjamin Duncan
Lorraine Duncan
Paul Dunn
Bill Durrant
Angela Dyer
Judith Earnshaw
Clare Easterby
Duncan Ecclestone
Carole Edge
Kirsten Edginton
Laura Edirisinghe
Ann Edwards
Janet Edwards
Fidelis Egbudo
Nicola Eggleton
Matt Eld
Gary Elflett
Barbara Elliott
Christine Elliott
Louise Elliott
Debbie Ellis
Katie Ellis
Rachel Ellis
Philip David
  Ellwand
Rupert Ellwood
Darren Emery
Ashley Empson
Michael England
Anita Evans
Anna Marie Evans
Anne Evans
Cherise Evans
Graham Evans
Holly Evans
John Evans
Kathy Evans
Rachel Evans
Seb Fadian
Chris Faherty
Tom Fahey
Claire Fairbairn
Sandra Fairclough
Jacqueline Faller
Louise Fanshawe
Stephen Fanshawe
Sharon Farnell
Peter Farrell
Michael Farrington
Danielle Fear
Debbie Fell
Katie Felstead
Sonali Fenner
Katie Fenton
Sean Fenwick
Kay Ferguson
Carla Fernandez
Diane Ferraby
Geoff Field
Jason Field
Susan Field
Neville Filar
Nicky Fillmore
Ian Finch

Lynn Finch
Steve Finch
Tracy Finch
Adrian Finlay
Julie Finney
Claire Fisher
Jon Fisher
Tracey Fisher
Jenny Fishpool
Sam Fisk
Sophie Flanagan
Terence Flanagan
Charles Fletcher
John Fletcher
Lydia Fletcher
Victoria Fletcher
Sean Foley
Gordon Fong
Jennifer Ford
Rich Ford
Will Ford
Amanda Forie
Ian Forrest
Robert Forrester
Michael Forsdyke
Sean Forshaw
Mathew Forster
Roger Forward
Ann Foss
Sian Foster
Mike Foulis
Alison Fountain
Christopher Fowler
David Fowler
Amanda Fox
Daniel Fox
Jessica France
Kara Francis
Silvana Franco
Janet Franke
Brigette Frankgate
Iona Fraser
John Fraser
William Fraser
Leonie Frean
Rosie Freeland
Heath Freeman
Paul Frith
Heather Fuller
Sarah Fuller
Adam Furneaux
Jeremy Furtado
Andrew Gadsby
Jack Gaffney
Georgia Gallone
Tom Galvin
Anthony Gannon
Rosemary Gant
Dijon Gardiner
Tim Gardner
Carys Garner
Sam Garner
Anna Garratt
Shaun Garrett
Nikki Garrod
Nicholas
  Garthwaite
Cat Garvie
George Gascoigne
Aurelia Gavril
Jackie Gay
Aiste Gazdar
Pat Geddes
Hugo Gell
Ian Gell

Alan Gent
John Geoghegan
Peter Rodney
  George
Stephen Gerrard
Amanda Gibson
Lynda Gilbert
Cassandra Gilbey
Gemma Gilbey
Sarah Gilesharling
Rachel Gill
Siobhan Gill
Suzanne Gill
Stacey
  Gill Battersby
Olivia Gillard
James Gilson
Simon Girvan
Lauren Gissing
Emlyn
  Glanmor Harris
Tracy Gleeson
Margaret Glen
Karen Godiff
Carol Godsmark
Jane Golding
Stephanie
  Goldstone
Chris Goldthorp
Anand Gonsalves
Ben Goode
Nigel Gooding
Audrey Goodridge
Cate Goodwin
Michael Gordge
James Gore
Kay Gosbee
Roger Goshawk
Jennifer Gould
Catherine Grace
Barbara Graham
Rosalie Graham
David Grant
Lottie Grant
Becky Graveney
Karla Graves
Angela Gray
Peter Gray
Charles Greasley
Lawrence Greasley
Helen Greaves
Christopher Green
Jean Green
Margaret Green
Martin Green
Peter Green
Simon Green
Tony Green
Chris Greenfield
Harriet Greenham
Jo Greenslade
Samantha Greer
Conal Gregory
Gilbert Gregory
John Gregory
Anne Greig
Peter Grewar
Hayley Grice
Ben Griffin
Jill Griffin
Paul Griffin
Laura Griffith
Nikki Griffiths
Nicola Grimshaw
Alan Grimwade

Louise Grove
Claire Grumme
Stephen Grunshaw
John Guest
Tim Gulliver
Victoria Gulliver
Tracey Gutteridge
Alison Gutzu
Daphne Gwilliam
Chloe Hacking
Stephen Haddock
Emily Hadfield
Lyn Haemmerle
Richard Haes
Spencer Hagard
Pippa Haggart
Patrick Hagopian
Dean Haine
Catrin Hall
Fran Hall
Jake Hall
Keith Hall
Liam Hall
Sarah Hall
Valerie Hall
Daisy Hambro
Sarah Hamer
Andy Hamilton
Paula Hamilton
Caroline Hands
Brigid Hanlon
Kathy Hanretty
Stephanie Harbott
Penny Harcourt
Jayne
  Harding Wade
Chris Hardy
Ciaran Harkin
Robbie Harling
Melissa Harman
John Harper
Jo Harpur
Lyn Harris
Matthew Harris
Ross Harris
Stuart Harris
Cat Harrison
Grace Harrison
Kathryn Harrison
Phil Harriss
Harry Harrold
Chris Hart
Thomas Hart
Norah Hartless
John Hartley
Colin Hartwright
Robert Harvey
Arlene Haslett
Linda Haslett
Victoria Haspineall
Keith Haviland
Jon Hawkes
Leeann Hawkes
Sally Hawkesford
Jen Hawkins
Natalie Hayes
Christopher
  Haynes
Sarah Hayward
Stanley Haywood
Christine Heaffey
Nick Hedges
Kathy Hedworth
Paula Heenan
Olivia Heffernan

Annaleigh Heffron
Nicky Helliwell
Anne Helps
Jane Hemingway
Sarah Henderson
Elaine Hendrickson
Sandra Hendry
Rosemary
  Henneberry
Peter Hennessey
Judith Henshaw
Chris Hepworth
Barry Heron
Robert Heron
Michael Hession
Gad Heuman
Sarah Heward
Rob Hewitt
Howard Heywood
Leanne Hibbard
Marilyn Hickmore
Sue Hicks
Sheila Higgins
Sarka Hildon
Derek Hill
Frank Hill
Nicola Hill
Iris Hillery
Catherine Hilton
Michaela Hilton
Marie Hinckley
Jennie Hindle
Kevin Hird
Rod Hirsch
Volker Hirsch
Andrew Hjort
David Hoare
Shannon Hoben
Deborah Hodd
Margaret Hodge
Fiona Hodgson
Sue Hodkinson
Carole Holder
Jackie Holderness
  Laar
Jan Holdham
Michael
  Holdsworth
Susan Holdsworth
John Holland
Sarah Holland
Malcolm Holliday
John Holme
Joy Holmes
Katia Holmes
Paul Holmes
Martin Holsworth
Liane Holt
Hilary Honess
Chris Hood
Rachel Hood
Stuart Hood
Kevin Hopcroft
Valerie Hopgood
Pamela Hopkins
Paul Hopkins
Stephen Hopkins
Suzi Hopkins
Jonathan
  Hopkinson
Barrie Hopson
Jules Horne
Sarah Horrocks
Lis Horwich
Andrew Howe

Annabel Howell
Barrie Howell
Richard Howells
Tracey Howes
Susan Howstan
Lawrence Hoy
Gavin Hudson
David Hugh Smith
Elizabeth Hughes
Hayley Hughes
Katy Hughes
Lois Wyn Hughes
Teresa Humphreys
Charlotte Hunns
Denise Hunt
Paula Hunt
Sarah Hunt
Jimmy Hunter
Liz Hunter
Simon Huntley
Joanna
  Hurley Brown
Caroline Hurt
John Hutchings
Val Hutchinson
Rachel Hyde-Smith
Robert Ibbotson
Aurelia Idy
Peter Iesan
Roger Ife
Alan Iles
Rebecca Illes
Paul Ilott
Paul Ineson
Nikki Ireland
Stuart Isenberg
Molly Jackson
Rebecca Jackson
Simon Jackson
Fiona Jagger
Denise James
Louise James
Robert Jamieson
Andy Jardine
Alison Jarvis
Tom Jarvis
Angela Jefferson
Kat Jefferson
Ellise Jeffery
Emma Jeffery
Mary Jeffery
Michael Jelley
Angela Jenkins
Chris Jenkins
Tom Jenkins
Joanne Jennings
Keith Jennings
Sarah Jennion
Linda Jepson
Alan Jessop
Kenneth
  Jeyaretnam
Richard Johns
Tim Johns
Dawn Johnson
Lucy Johnson
Lyn Johnson
Maddy Johnson
R. Johnson
Rebecca Johnson
Roger Johnson
Rosamund
  Johnson
Margaret
  Johnstone

Alan Jones
Alvin Jones
Amanda Jones
Bonny Jones
Chris Jones
Colin Jones
Frances Jones
Ian Jones
Mary Jones
Olwen Jones
Penny Jones
Pippa Jones
Tina Jones
Tiff Jordan
David Joyce
Nikki Joyce
Barbara Joyner
Liam Judge
Nick Judge
Karen Juers Munby
Veronica Kane
Kavita Kapoor
Lesley Kay
Rachel Keaney
Alistair Keddie
Sophie Keegan
Lisa Keeling
Duncan Keenan
Ed Keith
James Keith
Neil Kellett
Gemma Kelly
Jenny Kelly
John Kelly
Leanne Kendrick
Andrew Kennedy
Miss Kennedy
Lisa Kent
Owen Kent
Judy Kenworthy
Richard Kenyon
Ruth Kerfoot
Michele Kershaw
Richard Kettles
Sheila Keynton
Nicholas Keyworth
Lorraine Khalaf
Nabeel Khalid
Patsy Khan
Ruby Khanna
Monica Kidd
Tom Kiely
Janetta Killin
Dave King
David King
Heney King
Kathleen King
Martin King
Paul King
Phil Kingsland
Ben Kinnaird
Tim Kirk
Mark Kirkbride
Seth Klinger
Josephine Knapp
Peter Knapp
Adrian Knight
Alastair Knight
Jane Knight
Jerry Knights
Robery Knowles
Rebecca Kocerhan
Eleni Kokkinos
Teresa Konopelska
Bahu Dipen Kotecha

Martha Krempel
Katrina Kutchinsky
David Laidlaw
Ian
  Laidlaw-Dickson
Barbara Laing
Eileen Laird
Claire Lambert
Michelle Lamburn
Adam Lampon
James Lancaster
Kathleen Lancaster
Jacqueline Lander
Julie Lane
Philip Lane
Susan Lang
Alison Langdon
Joanna Langfrey
Nikki Langley
Sarah Langstone
David Lanham
Carol Lasetzky
John Latham
Gillian Latimer
Elizabeth Laverack
Liz Lawrence
Mike Lawrence
Peter Lawrence
Hannah Lawson
Aimee Lax
Christopher
  Laybourn
Eileen Le Rossignol
Mark Leach
Del Leah
Josephine Leask
Belinda Lebrocq
Adrian Lee
Judy Lee
Petrushka Lee
Ryan Lee
Sue Lee
Thomas Lee
Laura Legg
Nicola Leghsmith
Ross Leighton
Rosi Leivas
Joy Lennick
Joanna Lennon
Gael Lenton
Zlatica Leskova
Claire Leslie
Matthew Lester
Richard Levy
David Lewis
Joanna Lewis
Margaret Lewis
Matthew Lewis
Stuart Lewis
Nell Leyshon
Ffion Liddell
Jarrod Light
Lydia Lim
Deborah Lindop
Roy Lindop
Helen Lindsay
Vera Lioveri
David Lister
Chris Liversedge
Sarah Liversedge
Alison Livesey
Lizzie Lloyd
Tom Lloyd
Patricia Lockwood
Adrian Lockyer

Robyn Loftus
Carl Loller
Angela London
Christopher Long
Sarah Long
Trisha Longley
Kevin Longree
Leslie Longstaff
Cliff Lonsdale
Angela Lort
Audrey Lovie
Lorna Lowe
Jenny Lucas
Ruth Lucas
Debbie Lunn
Iain Lyall
Sharon Lynch
Claire Lyon
Kurt Mabe
David Mabey
Jane Macaulay
Peter Macaulay
Lisa Macdonald
Susan Macdonald
Peter Mace
Sarah Macelvogue
Christine
  Macfarland
Rosie MacGregor
Francesca Machen
Leah Mackay
Peter Mackenzie-
  Williams
Hugh Mackintosh
  CBE
Eone MacLellan
Chloe MacLeod
Lucy MacLeod
Niall MacMahon
Alistair Macrow
Jan Macrow
Jan Madden
Sharon Maddocks
Ruth Maddox
Tara Madgwick
Alex Maguire
Emma Maguire
Joe Maguire
Christine
  Make Bion
Jennifer Malcolm
Fiona Malcomson
Pauline Maniere
Andrew Manning
Jenny Manning
Ian Mansfield
Tessa Mansfield
Sarah Mapplebeck
Joanna March
Rosanna Marini
Adrian Markley
Laurence Marks
Charles Markus
Gavin Markwick
Valerie Markwick
Wendy Marland
Phil Marler
Wendy Marrable
Philip Marsden
Gill Marshall
Lydia Marshall
Jo Marshallfraser
Clare Marsham
Julie Marsland
Stjohn Marston

Barbara Martin
Basil Martin
Graham Martin
Ian Martin
Izzie Martin
Josine Martin
Judi Martin
Kath Martin
Lesley Martin
Lily Martin
Natalie Martin
Nigel Martin
Stephen Martin
Valerie Martin
Dave Martinson
Michela Masci
Wendy Mason
Kieran Matharu
Simon Mathers
Roy Mathias
Paul Mathieu
Michele Matthews
Samantha Mattocks
Andrew Maund
Rebecca Mawson
Louise Mayhook
Jackie Mazzie
David McBrien
Gavin McBrode
Kamilah McCarthy
Lee McClure
Elaine McConaghy
Marie McConnell
Lucy McCormick
Kim McCrory
Sarah McDaid
Nigel McDonald
Zie McDonald
George McEwan
Jillian McEwan
Roseanne McEwan
Darren McGinley
James McGrann
Dee McGrath
Lucie McGrath
Fiona McGregor
Helen McGrigor
Amy McGuigan
Stuart McIntosh
Jacqui McKechnie
Ann McKegney
Sean McKegney
Thomas McKenzie
Linda McKeown
Laura McKoy
Richard McLachlan
Vicky Mclay
Nancy McLean
Michelle McLugash
Darren McMahon
Roy McNee
Terri Mcneillie
Matthew McNiff
Lisa McNulty
William McPhee
Milena McPheely
Cathy Mcshane
Valerie Meadows
Jen Meierhans
Galen Melling
Susan Melling
Charlotte Mellors
William Melton
Lisa Menzella
John Mercer

Wendy Mercer
Anna Merilainen
Judith Merriman
Anna Merton
Alison Middleton
Jennifer Middleton
Sandie Middleton
Thea Midgley
Mary Miers
Alicia Mikulak
Hughie Miles
Rachel Miles
Alexis
    Milford White
Clare Millar
Anthony Miller
Graeme Miller
Nick Miller
Sheila Miller
Maureen Milligan
Alexander Mills
Cheryl Mills
Jimmy Mills
Scott Mills
Beth Milner
Kat Milroy
Craig Mitchell
Gemma Mitchell
Leigh Mitchell
Tara Mitchell
Jane
    Mitchell Barnes
Alison Mitton
Roy Mollet
Siobhan Moloney
Alex Monahan
Jane Moody
Laura Moon
Jennifer Moore
John Moore
Julie Moore
Rowan Moore
Daren Mootoo
Terry Moran
Donna More
Darryl Morgan
Richard Morgan
Rose Morgan
Colin Morison
Derek Morley
Vivianne Morley
Alana Morris
Mara Morris
Matthew Morris
Olivia Morris
Felicity Morrison
Hazel Morrison
Terry Morrison
Joan Mortimer
Samantha
    Mortimer
Julie Moss
Lauren Moss
Stuart Motson
Laura Mott
Linda Moult
John Moy
Sarah Moylan
Michelle Mudd
Ray Mudie
Martin Muers
Stewart Muir
Clare Mulcahy
Mary Mundy
Vivien Mundy

John Munro
Kirstie Munro
Lee Munro
Simon Murgatroyd
Gill Murray
Jen Murray
Joanne Murray
Michael Murray
Bob Musk
Emily Musson
Stephanie Muzzall
Jan Nawrot
Sarah Neeson
David Nelson
Alexandra Newbert
Janice Newlove
Don Newman
Donna Newport
Jeffrey Ng
David Nicholls
Rachel Nicholls
Laura Nickoll
Bob Nicol
Kay Nicol
Adam Nicolson
Hamoudi Niff
E Nisbet
Julia Nish
Stephen Noble
Paul Norris
Bicky North
Frank North
Shirley North
Lesley Nsh
Martin Nutbeam
Nicholas Oakley
Felicite Ogerau
Sarah Okeefe
Priscilla Oldfield
Susan Oliver
Alexandra Olley
Amanda Oneill
Ronan Oneill
Michelle Orange
David Orman
Faye Ormes
Michael
    Orpen-Palmer
Rhisian Otley
Lyn Overton
Tara Overton
Sarah Owens
Martin Oxborrow
Claire Packer
Martin Packer
Grace Page
Malc Page
Stephen Page
Pauline Paine
Simon Paine
Desmond Palmer
Tish Palmer
Triona Palmer
Andrew Parffrey
Penny Park
Haley Parker
Hannah Parker
Kate Parker
Lornette Parker
Lee Parkin
Kate Parkington
Helen Parkinson
Jemimah Parnell
Anni Parr
Joanne Parsons

Laura Parsons
Nicola Parsons
Michael Partridge
Sue Pasternak
Shai Patel
Craig Paterson
Jean Paterson
Carol Patrick
Sarah Patteson
Alex Paul
Danielle Pauls
Marie Pauls
Jools Payne
Rosy Payne
Michelle Peach
Rachael Peacock
Carol Pearce
Carolyn Pearce
Carol Pearson
Graham
    Pemberton
Lauren Penman
Jordan Pennant
Linda Pennell
Thomas Peplinski
John Pepper
Tom Percy
Martin Perkins
Andy Perrin
Kate Perrott
Richard Perry
Paul Peschey
Anna Peter
Lesley Peters
Laurie Petrie
Andrea Phillips
Dave Phillips
Harriette Phillips
Pete Phillips
Sally Phillips
Robert Phillpott
Maria Piacentini
Maria Piccioni
Charlotte Pickup
David Pickup
Karen Pickup
Philippa Pickworth
Colin Pierce
Mark Pilgrim
Ben Pinches
Ben Pindar
Chris Pines
Alexandre
    Pinheiro-Torres
John Pinschof
Bev Pirie
Kundan Pitrola
Melissa Plimmer
Veronica Pointer
Tamara Pointon
Brian Pollard
Linda Pollard
Alina Pop
Mark Pope
David Porter
Malcolm Porter
Fiona Porter Smith
Tom Potter
Janette Povey
Glyn Powell
Mark Powell
Sharon Pratt
Julie Pressey
Gary Preston
Michael Prevost

Anna Price
Helen Price
Maurice Price
Nigel Price
Demelza Prince
Emma Pritchard
Hugh Proudman
Ruth Pryor Newton
John Purcell
Jane Purser
Victoria Pym
Philip Quaife
Lucie Quest
David Raad
Dan Radusin
Stuart Rae
Hazel Rafter
Jeremy Raqqett
Alan Rainford
Carol Ramsay
Simon Ramshaw
Simon Ramskill
T. A. Rankin
Ronald Rankine
Brian Ratcliffe
Peter Ratzer
Mick Rawlings
Trisha Rawlings
Ed Razzall
Gemma Read
Gilly Read
Russell Reading
Emma Reasbeck
Brenda Redfern
Charlotte Reed
Ellen Reed
Alex Rees
Trish Rees
Geniene Reese
Rose Reeves
Paul Reid
Barrie Reisseymour
Salem Retibi
Kate Retout
Claire Reuben
Carys Reynolds
Dave Reynolds
Eileen Rhodes
Sandra Rhodes
Ollie Rice
Angela Richards
Bryn Richards
Yvonne Richards
Fiona Richardson
Martyn Richardson
Michelle
    Richardson
Sharon Richman
Diane Rickard
Kim Ricketts
Peter Rickson
John Riddick
Kevin Riddoch
Carol Rider
David Rigden
Cassandra Rigg
Florence Riley
Martin Riley
Sarah Riley
Scarlett Riley
Elaine Rimmer
Bev Ritson
Luiven Rivas
Sanchez
Katie Rixson

Alexandra Roberts
Helen Roberts
Jane Roberts
Peter Roberts
Richard Roberts
Sheridan Roberts
Colleen Robertson
Adele Robinson
Annie Robinson
Joel Robinson
Mark Robinson
Ian Robinson
Lindsay Robson
Robert Robson
Nicola Rodley
Eilir Rogers
Meghan Rogers
Rebecca Rogers
Sarah Rogers
Stephen Rogers
Adrienne Rollason
Lew Rood
Oscar Rook
Jack Roster
Shaun Roster
Lisa Rouse
Mei Ling Routley
Lorraine Rowan
Alyson Rowden
Angela Rowe
Chris Rowe
Gary Rowe
Stephanie
    Rowlands
Tom Rowlay
Ed Rowley
Nathan Rowley
Marta Roxberg
Louise Rudd
Joanna Rushe
John Rushton
Susie Rushton
Claire Russell
Ed Russell
Keith Russell
Jean Ryan
Sue Ryan
Rachael Saint
Robin Sainty
Rachael Salt
Sarah Salvatori
Keith Salway
Lesley Sample
Jayne
    Samuel Walker
Rebecca Sanders
Thomas Sangster
Alex Saturley
Hannah Saunders
Jamie Saunders
Rob Saunders
Dorothee Savage
Oliver Savill
Huw Sayer
Matt Scanlon
Claire Scargill
Maddy Schiavone
Lee Schoolar
Rebecca Scoble
Wendy Scopes
Carolyn Scott
Gilly Scott
Iain Scott
Ian Scott
Katie Scott

Mike Scott
Peter Scott
Victoria Scott
William Scott
Sara Scott Tucker
Julie Screech
Pat Scully
Nicola Seagroatt
Andrew Seal
Jon Searl
Derek Seaward
Sheena Sebastian
Kaz Secker
Simone Segall
Linda Selway
Geoffrey Senior
Hanna Senior
Alice Sennett
Carol Sentz
Lesley Seperd
Paul Seton
Philip Shackley
Margaret Shade
Hugh Shanks
Annette Sharma
Jennifer Sharp
Richard Sharp
Simon Sharp
Judith Sharrock
Ross Sharrock
Dave Shaw
Jane Shaw
Linda Shaw
Patricia Shaw
Robert Shaw
Sally Shaw
Gill Shelton
Lucy Shelton
Kevin Shenton
Sarah Shepherd
Pat Shergold
David Sherwood
Mark Sherwood
Adam Shilling
Nicola Shingles
Arnold Shipp
Rachel
    Shoobridge
Gilbert Short
Mark Shutler
Selina Sibbald
Mick Sidaway
Jade Sidebotham
Suzanne Siebert
Peter Silva
Dianne Simcock
Helen Simmen
Byron Simmonds
Mike Simmons
Peter Simmons
David Simons
Sally Simpkins
Jane Simpson
Mandy Simpson
Josie Sinden
Adam Singer
Jo Sipi
Martin Siswick
Gerry Slade
Heather Slammon
Samir Smaili
David Smallwood
Dominic Smart
James Smethurst
Alex Smith

David Smith
Diane Smith
Emma Smith
Jes Smith
Kieran Smith
Maddie Smith
Morgan Smith
Oliver Smith
Sally Smith
Ronald Smith Galer
Lynda Snowden
Sherril Soliman
Paul Solomon
Hayley Soper
Barbara Sorkin
Lucinda Southall
John Southern
Virginia Speed
Claire Speer
John Speller
Joanne Spence
Lynda Spencer
Trish Spiers
Alice Spires
Lisa Spooner
Sue Spooner
Jules Spoors
Charlotte Spruce
Christian Spurrier
Pamela St Quinton
Francoise Stacey
Paul Stafford
Pamela Stanier
Derek Stark
Charlotte Startup
Ann Louise
    Stebbing
Lindsay Steele
Matthew Steele
Peter Steele
William Steele
Annabel Stemp
Martin Stenton
Hannah
    Stephenson
Julie Stephenson
Ian Stevens
Jane Stevens
Lloyd Stevens
Hugo Stevenson
Amanda Steward
David Steward
Anna Stewart
Calvin Stewart
Donald Stewart
Ian Stewart
Yvonne Stewart
Allen Stidwill
Iain Stirling
Stainsby
Michael Stobart
Julie Stott
Melissa Stout
Linda Strongitharm
Julian Strutt
Andrew Stuart
Luke Stuart Smith
Peter Stunell
Emma Sturgess
Des Styles
Jakub Stypulkowski
Ben Suermondt
Tamara Summer
Jo Summerbell
Stephen Summerlin

Rachel Summers
Janet Surbuts
Vicki Surgenor
Keith Sutcliffe
Jeannie Swales
Neil Swan
Robert Swinden
Adele Sykes
Sabrina Sykes
Seth Sykes
Laura Syvret
Su Tacey
Kalvin Tan
Yan Tan
Esther Tang
Daniel Tapper
Emily Tarren
Tom Tarver
Francis Taunton
Adrian Taylor
Andrew Taylor
Darren Taylor
Elena Taylor
Elizabeth Taylor
Fay Taylor
Hayley Taylor
Jean Taylor
Kate Taylor
Kathryn Taylor
Katrine Taylor
Mark Taylor
Pauline Taylor
Phil Taylor
Robin Taylor
Steven Taylor
Toni Taylor
Claire Teague
Sadie Teller
Tessa Tennant
Claire Thomas
Dawn Thomas
Huw Thomas
Kim Thomas
Laura Thomas
Robert Thomas
Suzie Thomas
Abigail
    Thomas Brown
Alice Thompson
Bryony Thompson
Emma Thompson
Ian Thompson
Lynn Thompson
Tina Thompson
John Thomson
Shael Thomson
John Thorne
Lara Jane Thorpe
Steve Thorpe
Bob Thurlow
Sue Thurlow
Barbara Thursten
Claire Thyne
Patricia Tibbitts
Marie Tierney
Alison Tilley
Christine Tilley
Vanessa Tilling
Anthony Timoney
Carly Tinkler
George Tinsley
Kath Tinsley
Ben Titcombe
Sophie Titcombe
Jay Titterington

Andy Todd
Sue Tolley
Carole Tomlinson
Denise Tomlinson
Michael Tomlinson
Dorothy Toth
Irene Totten
Esther Towers
Tracey Townsend
Hannah Tracey
Patrick Tracey
Steve Trayler
Phil Treacher
Lauren Treasure
Mags Trench
Richard Treuherz
Linda Truman
Anna Tsokur
Martha Tullberg
Lorraine Turnbull
Alan Turner
Gary Turner
Geoff Turner
Ken Turner
Melanie Turner
Michael Turner
Jill Turton
Katie Turton
Andrew Turvil
Kevin Twells
Victoria Twibell
Rachel Twomey
Andrew Tye
Robert Tyler
Jim Unsworth
Maria Unsworth
Christopher Upton
Jessica Upton
Patricia Urry
Jessica Valenghi
Billy
    Van Den Bergh
Emily Van Schaick
Keith Van Schaick
Oriane Van Vessem
Jonathan Varey
Jane Vass
Philip Vass
Julia Vegh
Jennifer Veitch
Vetrivel Velamail
Sid Verber
Hugh Vermont
Paul Veysey
Tony Villiers
Karen Vine
Lloyd Vitols
Joanna Voller
Darren
    Waddingham
Michael Wadkins
Laura Wager
Clair Waite
John Waite
Nick Waite
Carl Wake
Mark Wakerly
Paul Walden
David Walker
Jane Walker
Jonathan Walker
Keith Walker
Lyn Walker
Jen Wall
Michelle Wall

Richard Wall
Brenda Wallace
Janette Wallace
Andrew Walley
Russell Wallman
Elaine Walsh
Nicola Walter
Dawn Walton
Jill Walton
Stuart Walton
Brett Warburton
James Ward
Terry Ward-Hall
Duncan Wardle
Glen Wardle
Alexander Waring
Jocelyn Waring
Richard Warner
Anita Warren
Colin Warren
Matthew Warren
Sarah Warren
Jo Warwick
Caroline
    Waterhouse
Claire Waters
Lucy Watkins
Amanda Watson
Carole Watson
Tony Watt
Helen Watts
Rachael Watts
Sarah Watts
Pat Web
Jess Webb
Theresa Webb
Michelle Webber
Ruth Webber
Annie Weekes
Helen Weetch
Daniel Weinstein
Keith Wells
Paul Wells
Emma Welsh
Jo Weselby
Brenden West
Marie West
Jean Weston
Mathew Weston
Stacey Whatling
Rosemarie
    Whawell
Hayley White
Jenny White
Jessica White
Lesley White
Roger White
Barry Whitehouse
Christopher
    Whitehouse
Lisa Whitehouse
Alison Whiteley
John Scott
    Whiteley
Holly Whitmore
Anne Whittaker
John Whitworth
Anita Wickens
Marzee Wickens
Lynne Wiggins
Hannah Wilcox
Rosie Wild
Peter Wilde
John Wildman
Ann Wiliams

Dawn Wilkes
Chayda Wilkins
Harriette Wilkinson
Keely Wilkinson
Amanda Williams
Bleddyn Williams
Carol Williams
Claire Williams
Ian Williams
Mala Williams
Marilyn Williams
Mike Williams
Paul Williams
Pauline Williams
Phillip Williams
Rebecca Williams
Susan Williams
Victoria Williams
Jane Willis
Julian Willis
Amanda Wilson
David Wilson
Florence Wilson
Fran Wilson
Jack Wilson
Jane Wilson
Lisa Wilson
Michael Wilson
Ralph Wilson
Kate Wilton
Helen Winder
Jackie Wingrove
Nicholas Winpenny
Dominic Winter
Samuel
    Wisniewska
Sarah Withers
John Withington
Melanie Wold
Harry Wolfe Murray
Angela Wolfenden
Paul Woloszyn
Jenny Wong
Beverly Wood
Tom Wood
Paul Woodcock
Alison Woods
Malcolm Woods
Rebecca Woods
Sue Woodward
Anne Woodworth
Yolanda Woolf
Craig Woolmer
Rachel Woolner
Andrew Worby
Darren Worton
Amanda Wragg
Ally Wray
Karen Wright
Kelly Wright
Val Wright
Paul Wyman
James Wynes
David Yapp
Simon Yarwood
Robin Yeld
Julie Yeung
Alan Young
Bruce Young
Kayleigh Zab
Linda Zahri
Julie Zausmer
Daniel Zlupko
Mason Zoe
Susan Zwinkels

Longest serving

The Good Food Guide was founded in 1951. The following restaurants have appeared consistently since their first entry in the Guide.

The Connaught, London, 64 years

Gravetye Manor, West Sussex, 60 years

Porth Tocyn Hotel, Gwynedd, 60 years

Le Gavroche, London, 47 years

Ubiquitous Chip, Glasgow, 45 years

Plumber Manor, Dorset, 44 years

The Druidstone, Pembrokeshire, 44 years

The Waterside Inn, Berkshire, 44 years

Airds Hotel, Argyll & Bute, 41 years

Farlam Hall, Cumbria, 40 years

Corse Lawn House Hotel, Glos, 38 years

Hambleton Hall, Rutland, 38 years

Magpie Café, Whitby, North Yorkshire, 37 years

RSJ, London, 36 years

The Seafood Restaurant, Padstow, Cornwall, 36 years

The Sir Charles Napier, Oxfordshire, 36 years

Le Caprice, London, 35 years

Little Barwick House, Somerset, 35 years

Ostlers Close, Fife, 34 years

The Angel Inn, Hetton, 33 years

Brilliant, London, 32 years

Clarke's, London, 32 years

Le Manoir aux Quat'Saisons, Oxfordshire, 32 years

Blostin's, Somerset, 31 years

Read's, Kent, 31 years

The Castle at Taunton, Somerset, 31 years

The Three Chimneys, Isle of Skye, 31 years

Northcote, Lancashire, 30 years

The Old Vicarage, Ridgeway, 29 years

Cnapan, Pembrokeshire, 29 years

Kensington Place, London, 28 years

Le Champignon Sauvage, Glos, 28 years

Quince & Medlar, Cumbria, 28 years

Harry's Place, Lincolnshire, 27 years

Bibendum, London, 27 years

The Great House, Suffolk, 27 years

Ynyshir Hall, Powys, 27 years

Crannog, Fort William, 27 years

Eslington Villa, Tyne & Wear, 26 years

Melton's, York, 26 years

Castle Cottage, Harlech, 25 years

THE GOOD
FOOD GUIDE
2017
£5 VOUCHER

THE GOOD
FOOD GUIDE
2017
£5 VOUCHER

THE GOOD
FOOD GUIDE
2017
£5 VOUCHER

THE GOOD
FOOD GUIDE
2017
£5 VOUCHER

THE GOOD
FOOD GUIDE
2017
£5 VOUCHER

THE GOOD
FOOD GUIDE
2017
£5 VOUCHER

THE GOOD
FOOD GUIDE
2017
£5 VOUCHER

THE GOOD
FOOD GUIDE
2017
£5 VOUCHER

THE GOOD
FOOD GUIDE
2017
£5 VOUCHER

THE GOOD
FOOD GUIDE
2017
£5 VOUCHER

THE GOOD FOOD GUIDE
2017
Waitrose

TERMS & CONDITIONS

This voucher can only be used in participating restaurants, highlighted by the £5 OFF symbol. It is redeemable against a pre-booked meal for a minimum of two people, provided the customer highlights the intention to use the voucher at the time of booking. Only one voucher may be used per table booked. This voucher may not be used in conjunction with any other scheme.
Offer valid from 01/09/2016 to 01/09/2017.
For additional terms and conditions, see below.

TERMS & CONDITIONS

This voucher can only be used in participating restaurants, highlighted by the £5 OFF symbol. It is redeemable against a pre-booked meal for a minimum of two people, provided the customer highlights the intention to use the voucher at the time of booking. Only one voucher may be used per table booked. This voucher may not be used in conjunction with any other scheme.
Offer valid from 01/09/2016 to 01/09/2017.
For additional terms and conditions, see below.

TERMS & CONDITIONS

This voucher can only be used in participating restaurants, highlighted by the £5 OFF symbol. It is redeemable against a pre-booked meal for a minimum of two people, provided the customer highlights the intention to use the voucher at the time of booking. Only one voucher may be used per table booked. This voucher may not be used in conjunction with any other scheme.
Offer valid from 01/09/2016 to 01/09/2017.
For additional terms and conditions, see below.

TERMS & CONDITIONS

This voucher can only be used in participating restaurants, highlighted by the £5 OFF symbol. It is redeemable against a pre-booked meal for a minimum of two people, provided the customer highlights the intention to use the voucher at the time of booking. Only one voucher may be used per table booked. This voucher may not be used in conjunction with any other scheme.
Offer valid from 01/09/2016 to 01/09/2017.
For additional terms and conditions, see below.

TERMS & CONDITIONS

This voucher can only be used in participating restaurants, highlighted by the £5 OFF symbol. It is redeemable against a pre-booked meal for a minimum of two people, provided the customer highlights the intention to use the voucher at the time of booking. Only one voucher may be used per table booked. This voucher may not be used in conjunction with any other scheme.
Offer valid from 01/09/2016 to 01/09/2017.
For additional terms and conditions, see below.

TERMS & CONDITIONS

This voucher can only be used in participating restaurants, highlighted by the £5 OFF symbol. It is redeemable against a pre-booked meal for a minimum of two people, provided the customer highlights the intention to use the voucher at the time of booking. Only one voucher may be used per table booked. This voucher may not be used in conjunction with any other scheme.
Offer valid from 01/09/2016 to 01/09/2017.
For additional terms and conditions, see below.

TERMS & CONDITIONS

This voucher can only be used in participating restaurants, highlighted by the £5 OFF symbol. It is redeemable against a pre-booked meal for a minimum of two people, provided the customer highlights the intention to use the voucher at the time of booking. Only one voucher may be used per table booked. This voucher may not be used in conjunction with any other scheme.
Offer valid from 01/09/2016 to 01/09/2017.
For additional terms and conditions, see below.

TERMS & CONDITIONS

This voucher can only be used in participating restaurants, highlighted by the £5 OFF symbol. It is redeemable against a pre-booked meal for a minimum of two people, provided the customer highlights the intention to use the voucher at the time of booking. Only one voucher may be used per table booked. This voucher may not be used in conjunction with any other scheme.
Offer valid from 01/09/2016 to 01/09/2017.
For additional terms and conditions, see below.

TERMS & CONDITIONS

This voucher can only be used in participating restaurants, highlighted by the £5 OFF symbol. It is redeemable against a pre-booked meal for a minimum of two people, provided the customer highlights the intention to use the voucher at the time of booking. Only one voucher may be used per table booked. This voucher may not be used in conjunction with any other scheme.
Offer valid from 01/09/2016 to 01/09/2017.
For additional terms and conditions, see below.

TERMS & CONDITIONS

This voucher can only be used in participating restaurants, highlighted by the £5 OFF symbol. It is redeemable against a pre-booked meal for a minimum of two people, provided the customer highlights the intention to use the voucher at the time of booking. Only one voucher may be used per table booked. This voucher may not be used in conjunction with any other scheme.
Offer valid from 01/09/2016 to 01/09/2017.
For additional terms and conditions, see below.

Vouchers are valid from 01/09/2016 to 01/09/2017. Only one £5 voucher can be used per table booked (for a minimum of 2 people). No photocopies or any other kind of reproduction of vouchers will be accepted. Some participating establishments may exclude certain times, days or menus from the scheme so long as they a) advise customers of the restrictions at the time of booking and b) accept the vouchers at a minimum of 70% of sessions when the restaurant is open. Please note that the number of participating restaurants may vary from time to time.